THE VICTORIA HISTORY
OF THE
COUNTIES OF ENGLAND

—

A HISTORY OF
ESSEX

VOLUME VI

THE VICTORIA HISTORY
OF THE
COUNTIES OF ENGLAND

EDITED BY R. B. PUGH, D.LIT.

THE UNIVERSITY OF LONDON
INSTITUTE OF
HISTORICAL RESEARCH

Oxford University Press, Ely House, 37 Dover Street, London, W1X 4AH

GLASGOW   NEW YORK   TORONTO   MELBOURNE   WELLINGTON
CAPE TOWN   IBADAN   NAIROBI   DAR ES SALAAM   LUSAKA   ADDIS ABABA
DELHI   BOMBAY   CALCUTTA   MADRAS   KARACHI   LAHORE   DACCA
KUALA LUMPUR   SINGAPORE   HONG KONG   TOKYO

ISBN 0 19 722719 8

*Printed in Great Britain
at the University Press, Oxford
by Vivian Ridler
Printer to the University*

14 12

INSCRIBED TO THE

MEMORY OF HER LATE MAJESTY

QUEEN VICTORIA

WHO GRACIOUSLY GAVE THE TITLE TO

AND ACCEPTED THE DEDICATION

OF THIS HISTORY

VIEW of the RIVER LEA BRIDGE and STRATFORD VIADUCT as now constructing for the EASTERN COUNTIES RAILWAY COMPANY.

WEST HAM: RIVER LEA AND STRATFORD VIADUCT IN 1837
From the south-west

A HISTORY OF THE COUNTY OF

ESSEX

EDITED BY W. R. POWELL

VOLUME VI

PUBLISHED FOR

THE INSTITUTE OF HISTORICAL RESEARCH

BY

OXFORD UNIVERSITY PRESS

1973

Distributed by Oxford University Press until 1 January 1976
thereafter by Dawsons of Pall Mall

CONTENTS OF VOLUME SIX

LIST OF ILLUSTRATIONS

Thanks for the loan of illustrations, and for permission to reproduce them, are due to the British Museum, the Essex County Council, the Public Libraries of Newham and Waltham Forest, the Passmore Edwards Museum, Newham, Major Y. A. Burges, and Mr. J. McKeown. The coats of arms were drawn by Patricia Tattersfield.

LIST OF ILLUSTRATIONS

LIST OF MAPS AND PLANS

Unless otherwise stated all the maps and plans are based upon the Ordnance Survey, with the sanction of the Controller of H.M. Stationery Office, Crown Copyright reserved, and were drawn by K. J. Wass, of the Department of Geography, University College, London, from drafts by Hilda E. P. Grieve, B.E.M.

EDITORIAL NOTE

THIS volume of the *Victoria History of Essex* is the fifth to be published under the co-operative system described in the editorial note to Volume IV. The contributing Local Authorities have continued, and have substantially increased their grants, and the Essex Victoria County History Committee, formed mainly of representatives of those Authorities, has continued to survey the progress of the work under the chairmanship of Mr. William Addison. Mr. John O'Leary, Honorary Secretary of the Committee since its formation, retired in 1967. He was succeeded by Mr. Donald L. Forbes, who was already Honorary Treasurer, and who has since then held both offices. Mr. I. G. Sparkes, Honorary Assistant Secretary from 1967 to 1969, was succeeded by Mr. K. H. Sleat. The University of London expresses its thanks to these gentlemen and to the other officers and members of the Committee for their services, and to the participating Authorities (listed below) for their generous grants. During the compilation of the present volume the deputy editorship has been held by Miss Hilda E. P. Grieve, B.E.M. (1966–73). Mrs. Avril H. Powell (1959–70) and Mrs. Beryl A. Board (from 1969) have served as part-time editorial assistants.

The structure and aims of the *Victoria History* series as a whole are outlined in the *General Introduction* to the *History* (1970). As in Volumes IV and V the brief descriptions of the earlier parochial registers of each parish, commonly included in the topographical volumes of the *History*, have not been considered necessary because of the publication by the County Council of *Essex Parish Records, 1240–1894* (1950; revised edn. 1966).

The compilers have again received help from many persons, whose kindness is acknowledged in the text of the volume and in the lists of illustrations and of maps. Especial thanks are due to Major Y. A. Burges for arranging for the temporary deposit in the Essex Record Office of his estate documents relating to East Ham, and for other help, and to Mr. L. Johnson, for information on postal history. Valuable services, including proof-reading, were rendered by the staffs of the public libraries and museums at Newham and Waltham Forest, the public library at Redbridge, and the Essex Record Office. Proofs of parts of the volume were also read by Mr. G. Caunt, Mr. D. L. Forbes, Mr. W. G. S. Tonkin, and the late Mr. E. R. Gamester. The Department of the Environment has continued to allow the use of its unpublished lists of buildings of architectural or historical interest. A gift of £100 from Mr. Marc Fitch, towards the cost of drawing the maps, is also gratefully acknowledged.

LIST OF CLASSES OF DOCUMENTS
IN THE PUBLIC RECORD OFFICE
USED IN THIS VOLUME
WITH THEIR CLASS NUMBERS

Clerks of Assize
Assizes 35	Indictments	

Chancery
C 1	Proceedings, Early	
C 47	Miscellanea	
C 60	Fine Rolls	
C 66	Patent Rolls	
C 78	Decree Rolls	
	Inquisitions post mortem	
C 132	Series I, Henry III	
C 134		Edward II
C 135		Edward III
C 136		Richard II
C 137		Henry IV
C 138		Henry V
C 139		Henry VI
C 140		Edward IV and V
C 141		Richard III
C 142	Series II	
C 145	Miscellaneous Inquisitions	

Court of Common Pleas
	Feet of Fines	
C.P. 25 (1)	Series I	
C.P. 25 (2)	Series II	
C.P. 40	Plea Rolls	
C.P. 43	Recovery Rolls	

Duchy of Lancaster
D.L. 25	Deeds, Series L

Exchequer, Treasury of the Receipt
E 40	Ancient Deeds, Series A

Exchequer, King's Remembrancer
E 150	Inquisitions post mortem, Series II

E 179	Subsidy Rolls etc.
E 210	Ancient Deeds, Series D

Exchequer, Augmentation Office
E 315	Miscellaneous Books
E 318	Particulars for Grants of Crown Lands

Home Office
H.O. 67	Acreage Returns
	Various, Census
H.O. 107	Population Returns
H.O. 129	Ecclesiastical Returns

Justices Itinerant, Assize and Gaol Delivery Justices, etc.
J.I. 1	Eyre Rolls, Assize Rolls, etc.
J.I. 3	Gaol Delivery Rolls

Court of King's Bench (Crown Side)
K.B. 27	Coram Rege Rolls

Exchequer, Office of the Auditors of Land Revenue
L.R. 2	Miscellaneous Books

Special Collections
S.C. 2	Court Rolls
S.C. 6	Ministers' and Receivers' Accounts
S.C. 12	Rentals and Surveys

State Paper Office
S.P. 12	State Papers Domestic, Eliz. I

Court of Wards and Liveries
Wards 7	Inquisitions post mortem

LIST OF CLASSES OF DOCUMENTS
IN THE ESSEX RECORD OFFICE
USED IN THIS VOLUME
WITH THEIR CLASS NUMBERS

Court of Quarter Sessions

Q/AB	County Bridges
Q/AG	County Gaols
Q/CP	Clerk of the Peace: Precedents
Q/CR	Clerk of the Peace: Parliamentary Returns
Q/RDc	Inclosure Awards
Q/RHi	Highways: Diversion, Closure, Widening
Q/RLv	Alehouse Recognizances
Q/RPl	Land Tax Assessments
Q/RRp	Registers of Papists' Estates
Q/RRw	Registers of Nonconformist and Roman Catholic Meeting Places
Q/RSg	Deputations to Gamekeepers
Q/RTh	Hearth Tax Assessments
Q/RUm	Public Undertakings: Plans of Schemes
Q/SR	Quarter Sessions Rolls
Q/SB	Quarter Sessions Bundles
Q/SO	Sessions Order Books

Court of Petty Sessions

P/B	Becontree Division

County Council of Essex

C/M	Minutes
C/ME	Education Committee Minutes

Education Records

E/P	Schools Records: Plans
E/Z	Schools (Miscellaneous)

Deposited Records

D/AE	Court of Archdeacon of Essex
	Diocesan Records
D/CE	New Parishes, etc.
D/CF	Faculty Papers
D/CP	Deeds
D/CT	Tithe Apportionments and Maps
D/D	Estate and Family Archives (many sub-classes, D/DA to D/DZ)
D/F	Business Archives
D/P	Parish Records
D/SH	Court of Commissioners of Sewers: Havering
D/Z	Miscellaneous Archives

Transcripts

T/A	Originals in public repositories
T/B	Originals in private custody
T/G	Genealogical collections and pedigrees
T/M	Maps
T/P	Parish collections
T/Z	Miscellaneous

Some of the foregoing classes contain sub-classes which are denoted by additional letters, not shown here, but fully cited in footnotes in this volume. The group called 'Transcripts' includes all forms of copies or catalogues of documents of which the originals are elsewhere, or notes and extracts taken from them.

NOTE ON ABBREVIATIONS

Among abbreviations and short titles the following may need elucidation:

Arch.	*Archaeologia*
Arch. Jnl.	*The Archaeological Journal*
Chancellor, *Sep. Mons. Essex*	F. Chancellor, *The Ancient Sepulchral Monuments of Essex* (1890)
Ch. Bells Essex	C. Deedes and H. B. Walters, *The Church Bells of Essex* (1909)
Ch. Plate Essex	G. M. Benton, F. W. Galpin, and W. J. Pressey, *The Church Plate of Essex* (1926)
Davids, *Nonconformity in Essex*	T. W. Davids, *Annals of Evangelical Nonconformity in . . . Essex from the time of Wycliffe to the Restoration* (1863)
E.A.T.	*The Transactions of the Essex Archaeological Society*
E. Angl.	*The East Anglian*
E.H.L.	East Ham Library, Newham
E.J.	*The Essex Journal*
E. Nat.	*The Essex Naturalist*
E.R.	*The Essex Review*
E.R.O.	Essex Record Office
Feet of F. Essex	*Feet of Fines for Essex* (Essex Archaeological Society; issued in parts: vol. i, 1899–1910; vol. ii, 1913–28; vol. iii, 1929–49; vol. iv, 1964)
G.L.C.	Greater London Council Record Office
G.M.	*The Gentleman's Magazine*
Hist. Essex by Gent.	*A New and Complete History of Essex . . . by a Gentleman* (6 vols. 1769–72)
H.R.M.C.	Harold Road Methodist Church Records, in Stratford Reference Library, Newham
L.R.L.	Leyton Reference Library, Waltham Forest
Lysons, *London*	D. Lysons, *The Environs of London* (4 vols. 1795–6)
Morant, *Essex*	P. Morant, *The History and Antiquities of Essex* (2 vols. 1768)
Mudie-Smith, *Relig. Life Lond.*	R. Mudie-Smith, *The Religious Life of London* (1904)
Newcourt, *Repertorium*	R. Newcourt, *Repertorium Ecclesiasticum Parochiale Londinense* (2 vols. 1710)
Ogborne, *Essex*	E. Ogborne, *The History of Essex* (1814)
P.E.M.	Passmore Edwards Museum, Newham
Pevsner, *Essex*	W. Pevsner, *The Buildings of England, Essex* (2nd edn. 1965)
P.M.G.	Postmaster-General
P.N. Essex	P. H. Reaney, *The Place-Names of Essex* (English Place-Name Society, xii, 1935)
R.C.H.M., *Essex*	The Royal Commission on Historical Monuments (England), *An Inventory of the Historical Monuments in Essex* (4 vols. 1916–23)
Smith, *Eccl. Hist. Essex*	H. Smith, *The Ecclesiastical History of Essex under the Long Parliament and Commonwealth* [c. 1931]
Trans. E.F.C.	*The Transactions of the Essex Field Club*
V.H.M.	Vestry House Museum, Waltham Forest
W.A.M.	Westminster Abbey Muniments
W.A.S.	Walthamstow Antiquarian Society
W.H.L.	Stratford Reference Library, Newham (formerly West Ham)
W.R.	General Register Office, Worship Register
W.R.L.	Walthamstow Reference Library, Waltham Forest
Worship Reg.	General Register Office, Worship Register
Wright, *Essex*	T. Wright, *The History and Topography of the County of Essex* (2 vols. 1836)

THE HUNDRED OF BECONTREE

(*continued*)

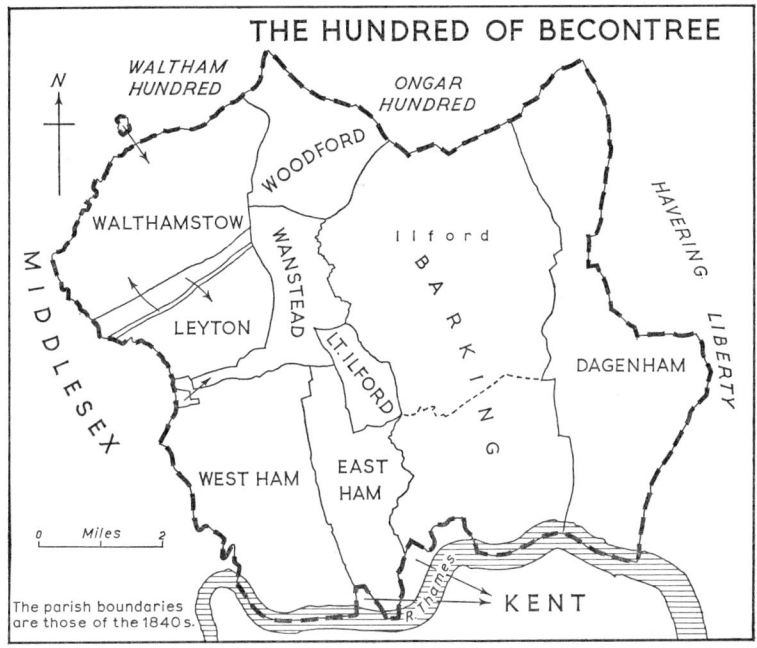

THE HUNDRED OF BECONTREE

The parish boundaries are those of the 1840s.

EAST HAM

The Origin of North Woolwich, p. 8. Manors and Other Estates, p. 8. Economic History, p. 14. Marshes and Sea Defences, p. 17. Forest, p. 18. Local Government, p. 18. Public Services, p. 23. Parliamentary Representation, p. 24. Churches, p. 25. Roman Catholicism, p. 31. Protestant Nonconformity, p. 32. Judaism, p. 38. Education, p. 38. Charities for the Poor, p. 42.

EAST HAM, about 7 miles east of London, is part of the London borough of Newham.[1] It is principally a dormitory suburb of small houses built between 1890 and 1910, with little industry except in the south, where are situated the Royal Docks and Beckton gasworks. The ancient parish extended from the Thames north for about 4 miles to Wanstead Flats. The eastern boundary, shared in the north with Little Ilford parish, followed White Post Lane (now High Street North) south to Jews Farm Lane (East Avenue). It then turned east to join Back river (a loop of the Roding), and marched with Barking parish down that river and across the marshes to the Thames.[2] The southern boundary followed the Thames for two short stretches, between which it curved inland, cutting off a small piece of Woolwich (Kent). Another piece of Woolwich, abutting on East Ham and Barking, lay farther east along Gallions Reach. The origin of these detached parts

of Woolwich is discussed below.[3] The western boundary marched with that of West Ham from the southern edge of Wanstead Flats, down Green Street to the Thames. The ancient parish, which was entirely rural until about 1850, had an area of 2,498 a.[4] It became an urban sanitary district in 1879, and this was enlarged in 1886 to 3,266 a. by the addition of Little Ilford parish.[5] Further boundary alterations took place in 1893 with Barking, in 1901 with Wanstead, and in 1907 with both Barking and Ilford.[6] The most important was that of 1901, by which 96 a. of Wanstead Flats were transferred to East Ham, thus extending the northern boundary of the urban district by about ½ mile. East Ham became a municipal borough in 1904 and a county borough in 1915. In 1961 its area was 3,324 a.[7] It became part of Newham in 1965. That year has been taken as the terminal point of the present article, though a little later information has been

[1] O.S. Map 2½″, sheets TQ 47, 48. See maps below, pp. 6, 48. Some preliminary work on this article was done by Mr. J. M. Montgomery.

[2] For this part of the boundary see *V.C.H. Essex*, v. 184.

[3] See p. 8.

[4] O.S. Map 6″, Essex, LXXIII (1863–73 edn.).

[5] *Census*, 1891.

[6] Ibid. 1901, 1911.

[7] Ibid. 1961. For E. Ham's civic arms, which were unofficial, see *E.R.* xxiv. 59–60.

included. This article also deals with the history of Little Ilford between 1886 and 1965; the earlier history of that parish is separately treated.[8]

The land rises from the Thames to a height of about 50 ft. on Wanstead Flats. Beside the Thames and the Roding are extensive alluvial marshes; elsewhere the soil is valley gravel. A former inlet of the Thames, called Ham creek, formed part of the boundary with West Ham.[9] Between 1656 and 1673 this seems to have been regularly used as a naval dockyard, subsidiary to the main yard at Woolwich.[10] It was occluded in the later 19th century during the industrial development of North Woolwich.[11] In the upland part of the parish there were a number of ponds and springs, of which the most notable was Miller's well, a medicinal spring situated at the point where the present Cheltenham Gardens joins Central Park Road.[12]

Roman remains, sufficiently numerous to prove a littoral settlement, have been found near St. Mary's church and at North Woolwich.[13] Until the later 12th century references to Ham ('low-lying pasture') do not distinguish between East and West Ham, and are therefore difficult to interpret precisely.[14] The Domesday evidence suggests that the main settlement then, as in Roman times, was in the south, and that the northern part of the parish was thickly wooded.[15] In 1086 the total recorded population of the two manors in East Ham was 72, indicating a substantial village. East Ham was not then greatly outranked in size by West Ham. It may have retained its relative position in the 12th century, when there was evidently much forest clearance in the parish, but between the 14th century and the 17th, while West Ham greatly increased in importance, East Ham seems to have stagnated or even declined. This was at least partly due to flooding in the later Middle Ages.

As late as 1670 there were only 79 houses in the parish.[16] The number increased to 94 in 1762 and to about 150 in 1796.[17] In 1801 the population was 1,165. It rose slowly to 2,264 in 1861.[18] Growth then became rapid, with industrial development on Thames-side, and suburban house-building advancing eastwards from West Ham. By 1891, having annexed Little Ilford, East Ham was a town of 32,713, and during the next 10 years it grew much faster than any other place of its size in England, to 96,018 in 1901. The peak population was reached about 1914, though the highest official figure, of 143,246, was recorded in 1921. Since the 1930s the population has decreased, partly as a result of war-time bombing, to 120,836 in 1951 and 105,682 in 1961. Since the Second World War many immigrants, mainly from the Commonwealth, India, and Pakistan, have settled in East Ham. In 1961 the resident population included 2,793 born outside the British Isles, or 2·6 per cent of the total.

Little is known of the later medieval pattern of settlement. The most important change in that period seems to have been the destruction by floods of the hamlet at North Woolwich.[19] The evidence for the existence of that hamlet includes the Domesday entry relating to Westminster Abbey's estate in East Ham (Hammarsh), and various later references, especially from 14th-century deeds.[20] Chapel field, mentioned in and after 1315, indicates the existence of a chapel then or earlier, and the foundations of that building were still visible in the 18th century.[21] Chapel field was in the larger or eastern detached part of Woolwich parish, just outside East Ham,[22] and it is clear that the hamlet lay across the boundary between the two parishes. One statement implies that this settlement was destroyed by a great flood in 1236[23] but the process may have been more gradual, possibly culminating in the floods of the late 14th and early 15th centuries. From about 1500 the flooded lands at North Woolwich were being reclaimed, but until the 19th century they seem to have been used only for grazing, and not for habitation.

Eighteenth-century maps show the parish before modern changes.[24] In the extreme south and south-east lay undeveloped marsh land. In the north the 'lower forest' (Wanstead Flats) ran down to the Romford–London road. The principal local road, then as now, ran south from the Romford Road past the parish church to the marshes. The name East Ham Street, recorded in 1443,[25] probably applied to the central part of this road. The northern end was known in the 18th century and later as White Post Lane, from a post standing at its junction with Romford Road. These two stretches of the road now form High Street North. The present High Street South was formerly called East Ham Manor Road. The most southerly section of this spinal road, between the parish church and North Woolwich, retains its old name of East Ham Manor Way. In the 18th and early 19th centuries, when there was a small ordnance store at North Woolwich, Manor Way appears to have been maintained by the army[26] but the tradition that stone shot was used in its repair was not substantiated in 1896, when the U.D.C.'s surveyor carried out a detailed examination of the road in connexion with its diversion and straightening.[27]

Along the spinal road, and especially at its junctions with other roads, were most of the houses in the parish. The hamlet of North End lay at the point where White Post Lane was joined by Plashet Lane

[8] See p. 163.
[9] Chapman and André, *Map of Essex*, 1777, sheet xxi.
[10] *Cal. S.P. Dom.* 1656–7, 456 and later refs. to: ibid. 1673, 67.
[11] Cf. O.S. Map 6″, Essex, LXXXI (1870–82 edn.); E. Ham U.D.C. Map, 1901. For Ham creek c. 1890 see plate f. p. 22.
[12] *Excursions in Essex* (1818), i. 183; A. Stokes, *E. Ham*, 123.
[13] *V.C.H. Essex*, iii. 137–8.
[14] *P.N. Essex*, 95.
[15] See p. 15.
[16] E.R.O., Q/RTh 5.
[17] Lysons, *London*, iv. 147.
[18] These and the following figures are from the *Census Reports*.

[19] For the floods see p. 17.
[20] *Cat. Anct. D.* vi. C 3285, 5756 etc. (see index s.v. Woolwich).
[21] Ibid. 4909, 4165; Morant, *Essex*, i. 39.
[22] E.R.O., D/SH 29.
[23] Lysons, *London*, iv. 558n.
[24] Chapman and André, *Map of Essex*, 1777, sheet xxi; cf. E.R.O., T/M 18 (dated 1764) and 21–5 (c. 1775) which show the centre and east of the parish; E.R.O., D/P 156/28 (1800), shows the whole parish; cf. O.S. Map 6″, Essex, LXXIII (1863–73 edn.).
[25] *Cal. Close* 1447–54, 350.
[26] A. P. Crouch, *Silvertown*, 55; W.A.M., Lease Bks. lxiv. 31b: lease of 1846 mentions a military road.
[27] E.H.L., E. Ham U.D.C. Mins. 19 Nov. 1896.

(now Plashet Grove) and Jews Farm Lane (now East Avenue). Jews Farm Lane probably acquired that name in the later 18th century.[28] In 1764 it was called Harrow Lane, from a public house. East Avenue commemorates Joseph East, first chairman of the U.D.C.[29] There was a cluster of houses at the junction of High Street and Wakefield Street, and another at South End, at the junction with White Horse Lane (now Rancliffe Road) and Vicarage Lane. Wakefield, from which the street was named, occurs in 1674.[30] There were also hamlets at Wall End, near the Barking boundary, and at Plashet, at the junction of Plashet Lane and Red Post Lane (now Katherine Road). Green Street, in the west of the parish, was the southern end of the present street of that name; the northern end was formerly Gipsy Lane. Wall End, Plashet, and Green Street are all mentioned in 1460–1.[31] The first probably refers to an early wall against Back river, and the second to forest clearance.[32] Gipsy Lane continued to be a resort of gipsies until the area was built over.[33] The southern continuation of Green Street, now Boundary Road, which formerly terminated in the marshes, was called Blind Lane. The road linking Green Street and Red Post Lane was also known as Blind Lane: this is now Plashet Grove and Grangewood Street. White Horse Lane, named from a public house, ran from South End to Green Street on the line of the present Rancliffe and Central Park Roads. In the south-eastern marshes were Gooseley Lane and Clapgate Lane. Those names, still used, are both found elsewhere in Essex.[34] The first, meaning 'goose pasture', no doubt refers to the wild fowl which frequented the marshes.[35] The second presumably comes from the swing gates preventing cattle from straying. The road from High Street to Wall End, now part of Barking Road, was formerly Watchhouse Lane or Wall End Lane.[36]

Before the 19th century East Ham's communications with the outside world depended mainly upon the Romford Road, which since 1721 had been maintained by the Middlesex and Essex turnpike trust.[37] There were also several lanes running west from Green Street to West Ham and Plaistow, but Barking, to the east, could be approached only by foot- or horse-bridges over Back river and the Roding.[38] About 1812 the Commercial Road turnpike trust built New Road (now Barking Road) from the East India Docks to Barking.[39] A toll-gate was set up at the junction with High Street.[40] New Road, which enabled traffic to by-pass Stratford, Ilford, and the centre of Barking, continued to serve as an

arterial road until the opening of the East Ham and Barking by-pass in 1928.[41]

Modern development has, in the main, preserved the lines of the old roads, though, as shown above, many of their names have been changed. Most of the changes took place between 1885 and 1905, and are recorded in the minutes of the local board and the U.D.C. They were usually dictated by a desire for clarity or refinement. Of the more important local roads of early origin only Katherine Road bears a completely new name, commemorating the daughter of Elizabeth Fry.[42]

Apart from the road pattern hardly anything remains in East Ham that is older than the 19th century, except the ancient parish church. Even before urban development began there appear to have been few surviving houses more than 150 years old, and none earlier than the 16th century. East Ham Hall, immediately north of the parish church, and the vicarage, about 500 yards farther north, were probably on medieval sites, but both were rebuilt in the earlier 19th century. The manor-house of East Ham Burnells had apparently been demolished before the early 17th century. The earliest secular building in the parish of which there is a detailed description was the mid-16th-century Green Street House, also known as Boleyn Castle, which survived until 1955.[43] Three other buildings were probably of 16th-century origin: the Harrow, High Street North,[44] the old Duke's Head, Barking Road,[45] and the old White Horse, on the west side of High Street South.[46] Of these the Harrow was converted into a private house in the 19th century, and later demolished, while the Duke's Head was rebuilt early in the present century. The White Horse, which had been rebuilt in the 18th century, was replaced in 1905 by a new building on the east side of the street; it was again rebuilt in 1965.[47] Plashet House, Plashet Lane, was mentioned in 1615, when Richard Glover, who had bought it from Robert Thomas, died leaving it to his son and namesake.[48] It later passed to the Bendish family, impropriators of East Ham rectory, who sold it in the middle of the 18th century to Charles Hitch.[49] From 1784 to 1829 it was the home of the Fry family, and it figures prominently in the reminiscences of Katharine Fry,[50] who also described its later history. It was demolished about 1883. A drawing made in 1806 shows a central block of two storeys with attics, apparently of the early 18th century.[51] There were two wings, said to have been added by Charles Hitch.[52]

Breame's alms-houses, High Street South, were erected about 1630, and rebuilt at the end of the

[28] Jews farm appears on Chapman and André, *Map of Essex*, 1777, sheet xxi. It was probably the home of the Jew recorded in E. Ham in 1766: Guildhall MS. 9558, f. 169.
[29] Stokes, *E. Ham*, 114.
[30] E.R.O., D/DPe M15, f. 30.
[31] E.R.O., D/DMs M3.
[32] For Plashet cf. p. 15.
[33] K. Fry and R. E. Cresswell, *Memoir of Eliz. Fry*, i. 170; E.H.L., E. Ham Loc. Bd. Mins. 9 Mar. 1880.
[34] *P.N. Essex*, 464, 82.
[35] Cf. E.R.O., Sage Coll. No. 860.
[36] E.R.O., T/M 18; K. Fry, *E. and W. Ham*, 277.
[37] Middlesex and Essex Highways Act, 8 Geo. I, c. 30; J. Mynde, *Map of Mdx. and Essex turnpike roads*, 1728.
[38] *V.C.H. Essex*, v. 187.
[39] E.R.O., Q/RUm 1/13; K. Fry, *E. and W. Ham*, 277.
[40] E.H.L., Photos. (Turnpikes).

[41] *E. Ham Municipal Diary*, 1928–9, p. 181.
[42] Katharine Fry, however, spelt her name thus.
[43] See p. 13.
[44] Stokes, *E. Ham*, 134 and pl. f.p. 118.
[45] E.H.L., Photos. (Public Houses).
[46] Ibid.; E.R.O., Sage Coll. No. 859; Stokes, *E. Ham*, pl. f. p. 48.
[47] O.S. Map 25″, Essex, LXXIII. 16 (1893–5); E.H.L. Photos. (Public Houses).
[48] C 142/350/69.
[49] The following account of the house is based on: Fry, *E. and W. Ham*, 174–5.
[50] *Katharine Fry's Bk.*, ed. J. Vansittart, 15, 67–8, 107–9, etc.
[51] Ibid., f. p. 64.
[52] E.H.L., Photos. (Houses), and sketch by Katharine Fry (1879).

18th century.[53] Rancliffe House, Rancliffe Road, was probably built early in the 18th century. It was a large square building of three storeys.[54] The house and grounds were bought in 1896 by the U.D.C., to make Central Park.[55] The house was demolished in 1908.[56] Oak Hall, High Street North, and Clock House Farm, High Street South, were other square brick houses of the same type and period. Burges House, Wakefield Street, was probably also contemporary with Rancliffe House. In the early 18th century it was the home of Ynyr Lloyd.[57] It was a two-storey brick building with a frontage of five bays.[58]

Lloyd, a wealthy business man working in London, was a type of resident already common in some Essex places near the city but previously rare here. Between 1750 and 1850 East Ham was attracting such men in increasing, though never large numbers, and this was naturally reflected in its buildings. Lloyd's nephew Ynyr Burges lived in an unnamed house in High Street South, which had been built about 1760 and which he enlarged in 1774.[59] Among other large houses probably dating from the later 18th century were The Limes and Wood House, both in High Street North; the latter was unusual in having a weather-boarded façade and may have been entirely of timber construction. At Potato (or Plashet) Hall, a house of the same period in Romford Road, the roof was surmounted by an octagonal lantern.[60] This seems to have been a favourite feature in the area, probably because of the view it could command of the river Thames and its shipping. The old Black Lion in High Street North and the White House in Plashet Grove were probably built in the early 19th century.[61] The Manor House at Manor Park[62] and Plashet Cottage in Katherine Road,[63] both associated with the Frys, were certainly of that period. East Ham House in St. Bartholomew's Road,[64] with its 'Greek' porch, dates from c. 1830, and the Green Man, at the junction of Plashet Grove and Katherine Road, is in the gabled Tudor style of the mid 19th century. Meanwhile East Ham was attracting cottagers of a new kind: Irish potato workers.[65] These men and their families were housed in short two-storey terraces: Irish Row in Romford Road, Bullyrag Row in Wakefield Street, Salt Box Row in High Street South, and others.[66] Of all the buildings mentioned in this paragraph only three survive: the Green Man, East Ham House, and the Manor House at Manor Park.

Some verses written about 1850 refer to East Ham's 'dead flats . . . Marshes full of water rats, onions and greens, black ditches and foul drains'.[67]

At that date, or a little earlier, the villagers still believed the parish to be haunted.[68] But it was beginning to lose its rural character. The first area to be thus affected was North Woolwich. In 1828 a philanthropist named Mills had tried to establish an industrial colony centred on a brickworks there.[69] This failed, but the opening of the North Woolwich railway (1847),[70] the Victoria Dock (1855),[71] and Henley's cable works (1859)[72] provided conditions more favourable to urban development. By the 1870s streets were being laid out on both sides of North Woolwich railway station,[73] and the transformation of the area was completed in 1880 by the opening of the Albert Dock. The houses built there during this period were crowded into long terraces, to accommodate the families of dock workers and sailors. The building of the King George V Dock (1912–21) necessitated the demolition of some of these houses. The area was heavily bombed during the Second World War, and since the war the East Ham section of North Woolwich has been largely redeveloped.

A mile north-east, still on the coastal fringe of the parish, the industrial village of Beckton grew up beside the great works of the Gas Light & Coke Co., opened in 1870. Here the workers lived in well-built company houses, which are still in use. Between Beckton and North Woolwich was the housing estate of New Beckton. The first part of this was built in 1881,[74] and its street names commemorate persons and places that had been in the news during the previous decade, including Plevna (Street) and Cyprus (Place). Cyprus, as the whole estate was called for many years, was a squalid development, a long-standing nuisance to the local board because of its lack of main drainage.[75] Contemporary with it was another small slum area north of Vicarage Lane, at Bonny Downs. This pleasant name, taken from a field originally called Burnels Downs,[76] was also applied to one of the streets of the estate, which disappeared from the map when Bonny Downs Road and adjacent streets were redeveloped after the Second World War.

In the central and northern areas of East Ham the opening of railway lines by the Eastern Counties and the London, Tilbury, and Southend companies[77] had by 1860 prepared the way for rapid suburban development, and this started about 1880, when houses began to go up on the eastern fringes of the parish.[78] The Boleyn estate, east of Green Street House, commemorated by its street names not only Anne Boleyn, whose legendary connexion with the house is discussed below,[79] but also most of the other wives of Henry VIII. The houses there were

[53] See p. 42.
[54] E.H.L., Photos. (Houses); Stokes, E. Ham, 146.
[55] See p. 23.
[56] E.H.L., E. Ham B.C. Mins. 14 Apr. 1908.
[57] See p. 14.
[58] E.H.L., Photos. (Houses).
[59] See p. 14.
[60] E.H.L., Photos. (Houses): cf. A. Stokes's Panoramic Map of E. Ham.
[61] Ibid. The White House had an earlier door-hood, perhaps brought from elsewhere.
[62] See p. 69.
[63] K. Fry and R. E. Cresswell, Memoir of Eliz. Fry, ii. 98.
[64] See p. 26.
[65] See p. 15.
[66] E.H.L., Photos. (Streets); A. Stokes's Panoramic Map of E. Ham.

[67] Stokes, E. Ham, 166.
[68] Ibid. 140.
[69] A. P. Crouch, Silvertown.
[70] See below.
[71] In West Ham.
[72] In Woolwich parish.
[73] O.S. Map 6″, Essex, LXXXI (1870–82 edn.).
[74] E.H.L., E. Ham Loc. Bd. Mins. 8 Mar., 14 June 1881.
[75] See p. 23.
[76] See p. 10.
[77] See below.
[78] The following details of housing estates are taken from E.H.L., E. Ham Loc. Bd. Mins., 1879 f. and U.D.C. Mins. 1895 f.
[79] See p. 12.

also of the slum type, erected by builders who were continually contravening the by-laws. The area is now (1966) being redeveloped. The Woodgrange estate, at Manor Park and Forest Gate, was much better, and included some larger detached houses as well as terraces. The Manor Park side of it, from Durham Road to Romford Road, was mostly completed about 1883, and the Forest Gate side, from Hampton Road to Romford Road (so far as this lay in East Ham) a few years later. The developer was A. Cameron Corbett, who later built much of Ilford.[80] He operated on a large scale, and kept down his prices while maintaining a good standard.

South of Woodgrange, at Plashet, development began in 1883 with the sale of the Plashet House estate (between St. Stephen's Road and Plashet Grove).[81] This estate, with adjoining parts of East and West Ham, became known as Upton Park. By 1890 building was in progress in the whole Plashet area from Green Street to High Street North, including the estates of Plashet Cottage (Grosvenor, Eversleigh, and Spencer Roads), Plashet Hall (Sherrard, Halley, Strone, and Monega Roads), and Wood House (between Woodhouse Grove and High Street North).

Shortly before 1890 the Burges family, who were the largest landowners in East Ham, began to develop their estate, comprising some 400 a., mainly in the centre and east of the parish, but including sections in the south near St. Mary's church and in Roman Road. These developments went on steadily until the First World War, and were completed after the war.[82] Among them was the area between High Street North and Burges Road, and that to the south of St. Bartholomew's church.

The new estates at Upton Park and Plashet, and those on the Burges lands, were nearly all the same: long terraces of small but well-built dwellings for clerks and skilled workers. Most of the other houses built in East Ham between 1890 and 1914 were of similar type. The most important exception was at Manor Park, where some poor building took place between 1895 and 1899 on the Little Ilford Manor farm estate, part of which, in Grantham, Alverstone, and Walton Roads, soon became slums, which are now (1966) being redeveloped.[83] Council housing, before 1914, was represented by some 200 dwellings in cottage terraces, in Savage Gardens, New Beckton, and Brooks Avenue, off High Street South.

The most notable public building erected during this period was the town hall, completed in 1903, which stands at the junction of Barking Road and High Street South. It was designed by Cheers & Smith[84] and is built of dark red brick, lavishly ornamented with buff terra-cotta in a variety of early Renaissance styles.[85] The two frontages are set back behind trees and the angle between them is emphasized by a tall clock-tower. Adjoining the town hall are other municipal buildings erected a little later in similar styles and materials. The

dominance of the clock-tower has been somewhat lessened since 1962 by the eight storeys of the new technical college on the opposite side of High Street South. The Methodist central hall, further east in Barking Road, formed part of the same group until its demolition in 1969. Other important churches built before 1914 are St. Michael's, Little Ilford (Romford Road) (1898–1906), St. Barnabas', Manor Park (Browning Road) (1900–9), and St. Bartholomew's, East Ham (Barking Road). St. Bartholomew's (1902–10) which replaced St. John's (High Street North) (1866, demolished 1925), was rebuilt in 1949–53 after war damage. East Ham's largest Anglican church, St. Stephen's, Upton Park (Green Street) (1887–94) was also bombed and was not rebuilt.

Between 1914 and 1939 there was little building. During the Second World War the borough suffered heavy bombing, especially in the south, and after the war the corporation undertook extensive redevelopment.[86] This includes Priory Court, Priory Road (1953), containing 96 flats in a multi-storey block, adjoining the old Boleyn estate,[87] and Durban Court, Katherine Road (1960), a 6-storey block with clinics on the ground floor and 30 flats above.[88] The largest scheme, completed in 1965, was the redevelopment of North Woolwich, providing 488 new dwellings.[89] This included the closure of the short roads linking Albert Road and Woodman Street; the building of small 'town squares' dominated by five-point blocks of 8-storey flats and closed by small blocks of flats and houses in Albert Walk; a local shopping precinct at the junction of Woodman Street and Pier Road; and the re-location of certain industries. The corporation also erected a number of new schools between 1945 and 1965. Plashet secondary school, Plashet Grove (1951), and the new technical college, High Street South (1962), both on confined sites, are multi-storey blocks of glass and concrete. The Langdon Crescent schools (1951–3), on the other hand, are low brick buildings, loosely grouped on an extensive site. A few churches have been erected since 1945, usually to replace older and larger ones, or those destroyed by bombing. Among them is the Wakefield Street Congregational church (1959).

The phenomenal growth of East Ham between 1880 and 1914 was made possible by a good transport system.[90] The first railway through the parish was the Eastern Counties line from London to Romford, opened in 1839, extended to Brentwood in 1840 and Colchester in 1843.[91] The nearest stations were originally at Stratford and Ilford, but Forest Gate station was opened by 1841, and Manor Park station in 1872.[92] The line was electrified in 1949.[93] A branch from Stratford to North Woolwich, with a ferry across to Woolwich, was opened in 1847, and extended to Beckton gasworks in 1874.[94] The next main line through the district was the London, Tilbury, and Southend, the first part of which, opened in 1854, ran from Forest Gate to

[80] V.C.H. Essex, v. 251.
[81] Fry, E. and W. Ham, 274.
[82] Inf. from Major Y. A. Burges. See also p. 14.
[83] See p. 21.
[84] Pevsner, Buildings of Essex, 166.
[85] See plate f. p. 15.
[86] See also p. 24.
[87] E.H.L., Pamph. E/EAS/301. 45: Priory Court, Official Opening.

[88] Ibid. Durban Court, Official Opening.
[89] Ibid. Redevelopment of N. Woolwich, Official Opening.
[90] For fuller details of some of the railways see p. 62.
[91] E. Carter, Hist. Geog. Brit. Rlys. 63.
[92] Railway Mag. x. 440; Stokes, E. Ham, 113.
[93] V.C.H. Essex, v. 72.
[94] Ibid. 23–4.

WEST HAM (NORTH) AND EAST HAM (NORTH), 1965
(INCLUDING THE FORMER PARISH OF LITTLE ILFORD)

See also separate maps of STRATFORD c.1930 and STRATFORD ABBEY PRECINCTS

- - - - Boundary of former parish of Little Ilford

— · — · — County and County Borough boundaries

Building estates with the date when development
began shown thus: *SHIRLEY HOUSE c.1890*

Ⓢ Site of earlier feature

WEST HAM (NORTH)
1. West Ham College of Technology
2. Sonables Ⓢ
3. Gift Lane Almshouses
4. Meggs's Almshouses
5. Metropolitan Academy of Music Ⓢ
6. Pawnbrokers' Almshouses Ⓢ
7. The Forest Gate Ⓢ

EAST HAM (NORTH)
8. Plashet House

Churches
+ Anglican
B Baptist
C Congregational
M Methodist
RC Roman Catholic

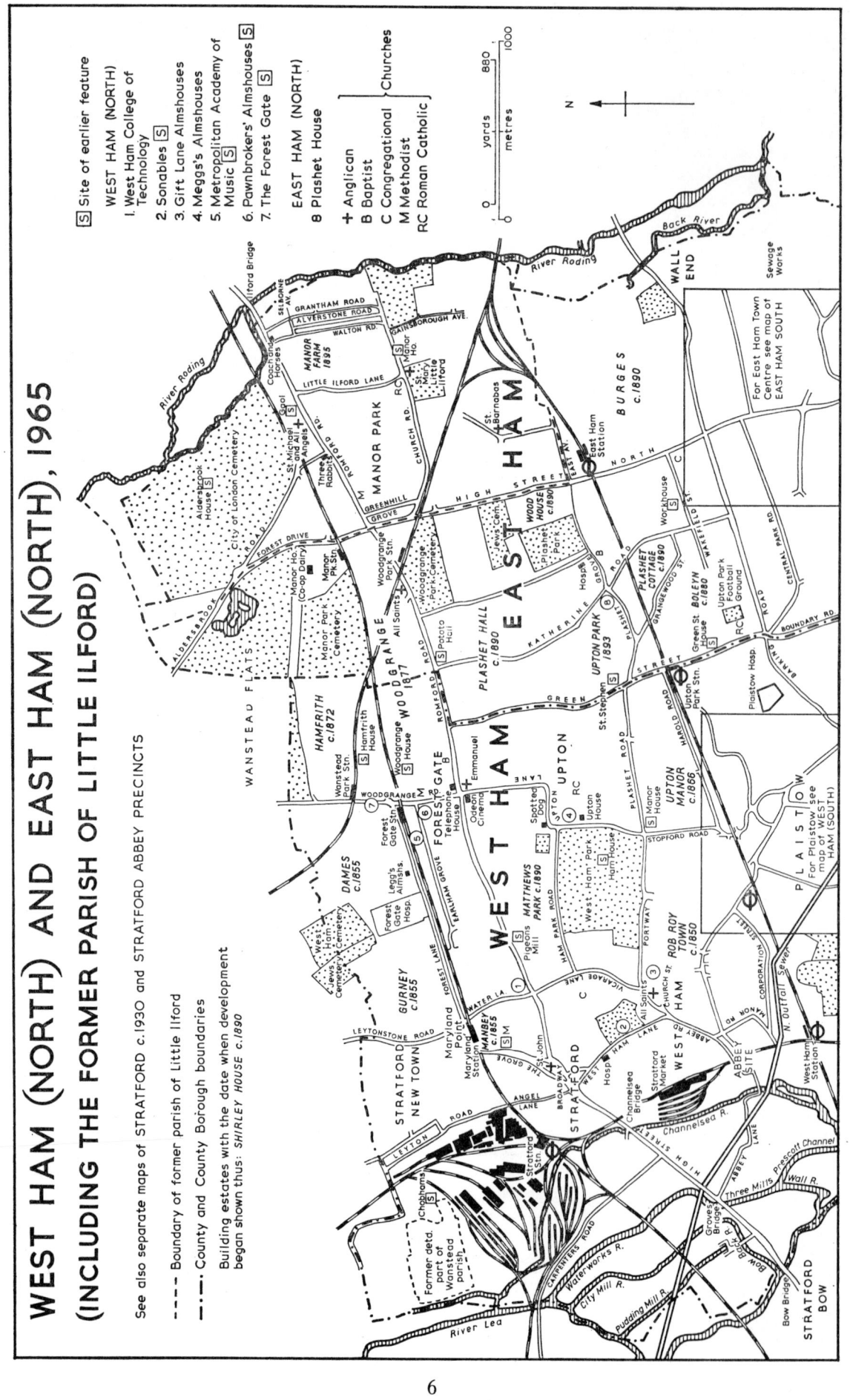

Tilbury, with a station at Barking. In 1858 the L.T.S. opened a cut-off between Bow and Barking, through the centre of East Ham, with a station at North End.[95] The Tottenham and Forest Gate railway, opened in 1894, included a short spur between East Ham station and a new station at Woodgrange Park.[96] In 1902 the District (underground) line was extended to East Ham; electrification of that line was completed as far as East Ham in 1905, and from East Ham to Barking in 1908.[97]

The North Metropolitan Tramways Co. opened services along Romford Road to Manor Park and along Barking Road to East Ham about 1884–7.[98] In 1901 the U.D.C. inaugurated an electric tramway system which by 1926 was providing services between Aldgate and Ilford, Aldgate and Barking, Wanstead Park to the docks, and East Ham town hall to Stratford via Plashet Grove.[99] In 1903 there were also horse bus services from East Ham to Poplar and to Blackwall.[1] About 1908 the London Road Car Co. began to run motor buses from East Ham to Swiss Cottage, and opened a garage at Upton Park. That company was soon absorbed by the London General Omnibus Co.[2] East Ham's buses and trams were all taken over by the London Passenger Transport Board in 1933.[3]

Letters were being collected and delivered twice daily at East Ham in 1692, and by 1794 there was a receiving house in the village.[4] When the London postal area was divided into districts in 1856 East Ham had a sub-post office in the eastern district.[5] From about 1873 this office was in a cottage on the corner of High Street North and Wakefield Street. The postmaster was James Stokes, father of Alfred Stokes, mayor and historian of East Ham, and the postman was Billy Twin, whose irreverent quick wit became legendary.[6] The post office has remained on the High Street site until the present day, though modern buildings have replaced the cottage. It became a branch office in 1917, when the E. 6 postal district, comprising East Ham, was formed.[7] A telegraph service was opened in 1895.[8] The National Telephone Co. opened an exchange at East Ham in 1907; it was taken over by the G.P.O. in 1912.[9] Between 1919 and 1927 subscribers were transferred to the Grangewood exchange, which became automatic in 1937.[10] The Clocktower exchange, which also serves East Ham, was opened in 1961.[11]

There was a post office at North Woolwich by 1863, and another at Cyprus Place, New Beckton, by 1886.[12] North Woolwich, with Victoria Dock, constitutes the E. 16 postal district formed in 1917.[13] It is served by the Albert Dock telephone exchange, opened by the National Telephone Co. in 1897.[14] The postal history of Manor Park (now the E. 12 district) is described below.[15]

Among notable persons connected with East Ham have been Sir Henry Holcroft of Green Street House, a zealous Parliamentarian during the Civil War, and his successor Sir Jacob Garrard, who had Royalist sympathies.[16] The most prominent figure in the 18th century was Ynyr Burges, who made a fortune in the service of the East India Company and used it to build up a large estate.[17] In the early 19th century Elizabeth Fry lived in the parish and helped to found one of its earliest schools.[18] Eminent vicars have included a non-juror, Richard Welton, and a scholar and journalist, Samuel Reynolds.[19] Outstanding among those who influenced the modern development of East Ham was Lord Bethell.[20]

East Ham's Volunteer detachments are mentioned elsewhere.[21] In the early 19th century prize-fighting was regularly carried on in the marshes of East Ham, just below the church, but it ceased in 1840, when the Metropolitan police took over the parish.[22] After the building of Beckton gasworks the Gas Light & Coke Co. provided facilities for sport, including football, cricket, and cycle-racing.[23] By 1897 there were at least 15 football clubs and about the same number of cricket clubs at East Ham.[24] Many of these were church clubs, and at that time most social activities in the town depended upon the churches. There were relatively few public houses, then or later.[25] Public halls, independent of churches, were even more scarce. Only two appear to have existed in the 1890s—East Ham public hall, Barking Road, and Manor Park recreation hall, Romford Road[26]—though the situation was later improved by the opening of the town hall, which contained two meeting halls. By 1901 there was a 'palace of varieties' in High Street North, near the corner of Harrow Road.[27] The East Ham Palace (later the Regal cinema) was built about 1906 farther north in the same road.[28] About 1910 cinemas began to appear: by 1915 there were ten in the borough.[29] In 1964 East Ham had a wide variety of local organizations, including over 60 youth clubs, but their

95 Ibid. 24, 188.
96 Ibid. 24.
97 Ibid. 26, 188.
98 E.H.L., E. Ham Loc. Bd. Mins. Jan. 1884, May 1885; *Kelly's Dir. Essex* 1890, p. 209.
99 Tramways Orders Confirmation (No. 2) Act, 1898, 61 and 62 Vict. c. 202 (local act); Tramways Orders Confirmation (No. 3) Act 1900, 63 and 64 Vict. c. 200 (local act); *E. Ham Municipal Diary*, 1925–6, p. 163; *V.C.H. Essex*, v. 28; for photographs of E. Ham tramcars see Museum of Transport, Clapham, and E.H.L. Photos.
1 *V.C.H. Essex*, v. 28.
2 *Kelly's Dir. Essex*, 1908, p. 246; E.H.L., *E. Ham B.C. Mins.* 24 Nov. 1908, and 12 Dec. 1911.
3 London Passenger Transport Act, 1933, 23 Geo. V, c. 14.
4 T. de Laune, *Present State of London* (1692); G. Brumell, *Local Posts of London*, 1640–1840, 75.
5 *Brit. Postal Guide*, 1856.
6 Ibid. 1873; O.S. Map 6″, Essex, LXXIII (1863–73 edn.); *Kelly's Dir. Essex*, 1878; Stokes, *E. Ham*, 129, 132; E.H.L., Photos. (G.P.O.).
7 *G.P.O. Guide*, 1917.

8 E.H.L., E. Ham U.D.C. Mins. 5 Feb. 1895.
9 *Nat. Telephone Jnl.* Oct. 1907, 135; *G.P.O. List of Telephone Exchanges*, 1913.
10 *G.P.O. List of Telephone Exchanges*, 1919, 1927, 1937.
11 Inf. from G.P.O.
12 *White's Dir. Essex*, 1863; *G.P.O. Guide*, 1886.
13 *G.P.O. Guide*, 1917.
14 *Nat. Telephone Jnl.* Oct. 1907, 135.
15 See p. 165.
16 See p. 13.
17 See p. 14.
18 See p. 39.
19 See p. 26.
20 See p. 20.
21 See p. 67.
22 Stokes, *E. Ham*, 137.
23 Ibid. 132; *V.C.H. Essex*, ii. 608.
24 E.H.L., *E. Ham U.D.C. Mins.*, 6 Apr., 5 Oct. 1897.
25 *V.C.H. Essex*, v. 58.
26 E. Ham U.D.C. Mins. 19 Mar., 18 June 1895.
27 E. Ham U.D.C. Map 1901.
28 *E. Ham B.C. Mins.* 14 Mar. 1905, 4 Sept. 1906.
29 *E. Ham B.C. Mins.* 8 Feb., 14 June 1910, 26 Oct. 1915.

number was not large in relation to the population.[30] Then, as earlier, many people evidently found recreation principally in their own homes. None can have done so with greater singleness of mind than Edmund Lusignea (d. 1961), who for 46 years spent his spare time embellishing the interior of his terrace house, 184 Byron Avenue, with marble floors, domed ceilings, recessed mirrors, classical columns, and statues in niches.[31]

THE ORIGIN OF NORTH WOOLWICH. The southern boundary of the ancient county of Essex followed the Thames everywhere except at two points, where it curved inland, leaving two pieces of the parish of Woolwich (Kent) on the north bank of the river, separated by a tongue of East Ham. Until the 19th century these detached parts of Woolwich were usually described as 'Woolwich in the parts of Essex' or something similar.[32] The term North Woolwich appears to have been applied first to the railway of that name, opened in 1847,[33] but soon came to be used for the whole coastal area on the north bank of the river opposite Woolwich.

Hasted, in his *History of Kent*, suggested that the detached parts of Woolwich originated through a connexion with Hamon *dapifer*, who in 1086 was sheriff of Kent and also held land at Woolwich and neighbouring places in that county.[34] He cited no evidence, apart from Domesday Book, to support his theory; but he was almost certainly right.

In 1846–7 the detached parts of Woolwich were stated to comprise a total of 402 a., out of 1,116 a. for the whole parish.[35] The smaller and more westerly part, containing 68 a., extended west for about half a mile from North Woolwich station. The larger detached part, of 334 a., had a Thames frontage of about 1½ mile, running west from Barking Creek, along Gallions Reach. The areas given in the first edition of the Ordnance Survey were slightly larger: 70 a. for the western detached part (No. 1) and 343 a. for the eastern (No. 2).[36]

There is little doubt that in 1086 Hamon *dapifer* held the whole of Woolwich including the detached parts. Woolwich is mentioned by that name only once in Domesday: Hamon held in demesne 63 a. 'which belong to (*pertinent in*) Woolwich'; and which before the Conquest had been held by William the Falconer.[37] *Pertinent in* is an appropriate phrase to describe a detached part, and the size of this tenement is remarkably similar to that of North Woolwich detached part No 1. Hamon also held, under Odo, Bishop of Bayeux, the manor of Eltham. This large manor undoubtedly included much of Woolwich,[38] probably including detached part No. 2.

Besides Woolwich and Eltham Hamon held several other manors in Kent, and many in Essex.[39] Most of his lands in Kent, and some at least of those in Essex, subsequently became part of the honor of Gloucester, which his granddaughter Maud, daughter of Robert Fitz Hamon brought in marriage to Robert, earl of Gloucester.[40] In 1242–3 ½ knight's fee in Eltham was held by William de Henlee of Margery de Rivers, and by her of the earl of Gloucester.[41] In 1339 rent at 'Woolwich in Essex' was held by John de Rivers of Tormarton (Glos.).[42]

At Woolwich, including the detached parts, Hamon was thus lord of the manor as well as sheriff. If, before his time, the detached parts had belonged to Essex, he would have had both a motive and an opportunity to add it to his own county of Kent. At this period the financial perquisites of a shrievalty were great, and some sheriffs made unscrupulous use of their opportunities.[43] Hamon's contemporary, Baldwin, sheriff of Devon, seems to have tampered with the boundary between Devon and Cornwall in his own interests.[44] What is known of Hamon's character strongly suggests that he was quite capable of doing the same. Domesday Book records several encroachments by him upon the lands of his Essex neighbours, including the king, and in one case his refusal to render a customary due.[45] His high-handedness as sheriff of Kent is implicit in his gift of the church of Dartford, which belonged to the king's manor there, to Rochester cathedral.[46] While absolute proof is lacking, it seems likely that the Woolwich boundaries, north of the Thames, were the result of a similar piece of aggression by this 11th-century baronial sheriff. The anomaly continued to exist until 1965, when North Woolwich was incorporated in the London borough of Newham.

MANORS AND OTHER ESTATES. The manorial history of East Ham is interwoven with that of West Ham. Ham is first mentioned in 958, when King Edgar granted to Ealdorman Athelstan of East Anglia 5 *mansae* there.[47] The bounds of the charter included the whole of East and West Ham. The subsequent descent of Athelstan's estate is not known. In 1086 there were three manors called Ham. One of them, comprising 2 hides held by Westminster Abbey, was undoubtedly in East Ham.[48] Another, held jointly by Robert Gernon and Ranulph Peverel, and comprising 8 hides and 30 a., was wholly or mainly in West Ham.[49] Before the Conquest it had been held by Alestan, a free man. Gernon alone also held a further 7 hides, which before the Conquest had belonged to Levred, a free man.[50] Three virgates which before 1066 had been

---

[30] *E. Ham Guide*, 1964; cf. Dagenham: *V.C.H. Essex*, v. 272.

[31] *Architects' Jnl.* 24 Dec. 1953; *Stratford Expr.* 11 Dec. 1953; *Newham Recorder* 14 Jan. 1965.

[32] Cf. *Cat. Anct. D.* vi. C 4754, C 5756.

[33] For this railway see p. 5.

[34] Hasted, *Kent*, i. 441.

[35] Tithe Redemption Com., Woolwich Tithe Award.

[36] O.S. Map 6″, Essex, LXXI (1870–82 edn.).

[37] *V.C.H. Kent*, iii. 251b; cf. D. Douglas, *Domesday Monachorum of Christ Ch. Canterbury*, 103.

[38] Lysons, *Lond.* iv. 559.

[39] Cf. *V.C.H. Kent*, iii. 251b; *V.C.H. Essex*, i. 500–3.

[40] I. J. Sanders, *English Baronies*, 6; *Bk. of Fees*, 654, 662–4, 668; *V.C.H. Essex*, iv. 151.

[41] *Bk. of Fees*, 668.

[42] Sanders, *English Baronies*, 5–6; *Wilts Inq. p.m. Edw. III* (Index Libr.), p. 136.

[43] Cf. Stenton, *Anglo-Saxon England*, 625.

[44] W. G. Hoskins and H. P. R. Finberg, *Devonshire Studies*, 19 f.

[45] *V.C.H. Essex*, i. 429, 559, 569.

[46] *Regesta Regum Anglo-Normannorum*, i, p. 111. The gift was subsequently confirmed by William II.

[47] C. Hart, *Early Charts. Essex: Saxon*, p. 14; *P.N. Essex*, 94.

[48] *V.C.H. Essex*, i. 444.

[49] Ibid. 515, 527.

[50] Ibid. 515.

held by Edwin, a free priest, had been subsequently added to the manor. Another 30 a. belonging to the manor were held in 1086 by a sokeman. The manor was all in demesne except for 40 a. held of Gernon by Ilger. This manor seems to have been mainly in East Ham. The fee of Robert Gernon thus included a considerable part of both East and West Ham. From it were derived the later manors of East Ham and East Ham Burnells and, in West Ham, the manors of West Ham, Covelee's, Woodgrange, Plaiz, West Ham Burnells, and East West Ham, part of Chobhams and possibly also of Bretts. From the fee of Ranulph Peverel were derived the manor of Sudbury and much of Bretts.

Robert Gernon was still living in 1118, but soon after that date his lands passed to William de Montfitchet.[51] In 1135 William founded the abbey of Stratford Langthorne, in West Ham, endowing it with land there, which became the nucleus of the manor of West Ham.[52] By 1189 his descendant, Richard de Montfitchet, had granted Woodgrange to the abbey.[53] The Montfitchets held the remainder of the fee until 1267. Parts of it were subinfeudated in or before the 12th century. Edmund the Chamberlain, who in 1166 held ⅕ knight's fee of Gilbert de Montfitchet,[54] had land in West Ham,[55] as later did his grandson Richard the Chamberlain.[56] Walter of Windsor held 1½ knight's fee of the Montfitchets in Wormingford, Great Maplestead, and Ham.[57] Between 1186 and 1189, when Windsor's lands were in the king's hands, the annual income from Ham was £2.[58] By 1189 Windsor, like his overlord, had given land in South Marsh to Stratford Abbey.[59] About 1200 Maud of Hesdin, daughter of Walter of Windsor,[60] granted the abbey, for 10s. a year, the land in South Marsh in Ham which Christine her mother gave her in dower.[61] Maud's descendant, Hugh of Hesdin, was still receiving this rent about 1242, when he died.[62] In 1203 Ginda, wife of William de Biskeley, quitclaimed to Stratford Abbey, for £6 13s. 4d., 40 a. land in Ham from her dower in the free tenement of Walter of Windsor, formerly her husband.[63]

Richard de Montfitchet, last of his family in the male line, died without issue in 1267. His heirs (subject to the life-interest in dower of his widow Joyce (d. 1274))[64] were the descendants of his three sisters, Margery de Bolbec, Aveline de Forz, Countess of Aumale, and Philippa de Plaiz.[65] Aveline de Forz, granddaughter of the countess, and Richard (d. 1269) son of Philippa de Plaiz, each received one-third of the inheritance. The remaining third was shared between the four granddaughters of Margery de Bolbec: Philippa de Lancaster, Margery Corbet

(d. 1303), Alice de Huntercombe (d. c. 1284), and Maud de la Val (d. 1281). Alice and Maud died without issue. After the deaths of their husbands, Walter de Huntercombe (1313) and Hugh de la Val (1302), their shares seem to have been divided between their sisters' heirs.[66] Aveline de Forz, who married Edmund, Earl of Lancaster, son of Henry III, was also childless, and when she died in 1274 her share was assigned to Philippa de Lancaster.[67]

The eventual result of this sequence of events was the division of the Montfitchet fee in East and West Ham into three unequal parts. The inheritance of Richard de Plaiz became the manor of Plaiz, while that of Margery Corbet became the manors of East and West Ham Burnells. The share of Philippa de Lancaster became the manor of *EAST HAM* or *EAST HAM HALL*. This lay mainly in the south of the parish; the manor-house adjoined the church to the north-east, and the lords of the manor originally held the advowson of East Ham. The name was first applied to the main part of Philippa's holding which passed to her on the death of Aveline de Forz. Philippa's lands were held in her right by her husband Roger de Lancaster until his death in 1291.[68] She herself died in 1294 holding East Ham manor in chief for ¼ knight's fee. It was then some 200 a. in area.[69] Her son and heir John de Lancaster inherited further properties in East Ham and West Ham after the deaths of Hugh de la Val and Walter de Huntercombe.

In 1306 John de Lancaster granted to Stratford Langthorne Abbey, in free alms, 2 a. land in East Ham, with the advowson.[70] This seems to have been the first step in a process, continuing until 1338, by which the abbey acquired the whole manor from Lancaster and his tenants. In May 1317 Lancaster granted the monks a further 40 a., and in 1319 he conveyed to them the reversion of the manor, after his death and that of Annora his wife.[71] Even before those grants, however, Stratford was holding the manor, for in April 1317 it was said to be on lease from the abbey to Terry of Almain.[72] In 1313 Thomas de Pernestede had granted the abbey a messuage and 100 a. land in East Ham, not held in chief,[73] and it is likely that he was a sub-tenant of John de Lancaster. In or before 1317–19 the abbey also acquired lands belonging to Walter of Yarmouth, at least some of which had been held of John de Lancaster.[74] Yarmouth's estate, comprising about 100 a. in West Ham and 50 a. in East Ham, can be traced back to 1248, when it was granted by Ralph Fitz Urse to John de Middleton and Maud his wife.[75] In 1278–9 Middleton conveyed it to Sir William de

51 I. J. Sanders, *English Baronies*, 83 gives the descent of Gernon's honor.
52 See p. 68.
53 See p. 73.
54 *Red Bk. Exch.* (Rolls Ser.), 351: the 1166 charter is mistakenly in the name of William de Montfitchet (d. bef. 1156).
55 *Feet of F. Essex*, i. 21.
56 *Bracton's Notebk.*, ed. Maitland, iii. 408.
57 *Red Bk. Exch.* 730, 733; Morant, *Essex*, ii. 231–2, 277; *Pipe R.* 1186 (P.R.S. xxxvi), 12.
58 *Pipe R.* 1186, 12; ibid. 1187 (P.R.S. xxxvii), 122; ibid. 1188 (P.R.S. xxxviii), 31; ibid. 1189 (Rec. Com.), 21.
59 *Cal. Chart. R. 1257–1300*, 312.
60 *Pipe R.* 1206 (P.R.S. N.S. xx), 41; *Red Bk. Exch.* 136, 139.
61 B.M. Harl. Ch. 51G. 41; *E. Angl.* N.S. vi. 345–6.

62 *Ex. e Rot. Fin.* (Rec. Com.), i. 97, 386; *Cal. Inq. p.m.* i, pp. 287–8.
63 *Feet of F. Essex*, i. 32.
64 *Cal. Close 1272–9*, 81–2, 86.
65 Sanders, *English Baronies*, 83–5; cf. *V.C.H. Essex*, iv. 227; *Cal. Inq. p.m.* ii, p. 235 (Maud de la Val).
66 See p. 10.
67 *Cal. Close 1272–9*, 244; *Cal. Inq. p.m.* ii, p. 508.
68 Sanders, *English Baronies*, 85.
69 *Cal. Inq. p.m.* iii, p. 106.
70 *Cal. Pat. 1301–7*, 482.
71 Ibid. 1313–17, 653; 1317–21, 318; *Feet of F. Essex* ii. 193.
72 *Cal. Pat. 1313–17*, 634.
73 Ibid. 39.
74 Ibid. 611; ibid. 1317–21, 317–18.
75 *Feet of F. Essex*, i. 173.

Monterville, in return for corrodies for himself, his son Thomas, and Thomas's wife.[76] Monterville conveyed it in 1285 to Walter of Windsor, who granted it in 1290 to Adam, son of William of Lincoln of Great Yarmouth.[77] Adam, who later used the surname of Yarmouth, was still alive in 1308,[78] but by 1314 had apparently been succeeded by Walter of Yarmouth.[79] The abbey seems to have acquired only Yarmouth's East Ham lands; his West Ham lands became part of the manor of Chobhams.

John de Lancaster died in 1334 and his wife Annora in 1338.[80] On her death the abbot assumed full control over the manor. He appears to have done so without due process in Chancery, and in 1373 one of his successors was fined £20 for that trespass.[81] In 1342–3 East Ham Hall was valued at 40 marks.[82] It was probably the ¼ knight's fee for which the abbot answered in 1346.[83] In 1343–4 the abbey also acquired from Peter de Chaumbre a tenement in East Ham worth £5.[84]

At its dissolution in 1538 the abbey was holding East Ham manor, farmed at £20 18s. 10d., and other lands in the parish, farmed at £35 10s. 2d.[85] In 1544 the king granted the manor with other lands to his servant Richard Breame.[86] In 1545 Breame was licensed to alienate certain marshlands in East Ham.[87] He died in 1546 holding East Ham manor, together with Stonehall in Ilford.[88] East Ham descended, like Stonehall, to his infant son Edward (d. 1558) and subsequently to Edward's brother Arthur.[89] Arthur Breame sold Stonehall, but retained East Ham, which appears to have descended at his death in 1602 to his son Giles[90] who made a conveyance of the manor in 1607.[91] Giles, who died in 1621, left most of his estate to be sold for the building and endowment of alms-houses in East Ham, naming as executor his kinsman Sir Giles Allington.[92] In 1632 Allington sold the manor to Sara, Lady Kempe, widow.[93] Lady Kempe appears to have suffered sequestration as a Papist recusant in 1643.[94] She was succeeded by (Sir) Thomas Draper (Bt.), her son by her first marriage, who was holding East Ham by 1650, and died in 1703.[95] Draper's daughter and heir Mary carried the manor in marriage to John Baber.[96] In 1764 Mary's son Thomas Draper Baber sold East Ham to John Henniker (d. 1803), who in 1781 succeeded to a baronetcy, and in 1800 became Baron Henniker in the Irish peerage.[97] The manor descended with the peerage until the middle of the 19th century. The East Ham Hall estate, as mapped in 1764, c. 1775, and 1829, comprised about 400 a.

in the centre and east of the parish.[98] In 1839, however, the Hennikers held only some 250 a. in East Ham,[99] and during the next 40 or 50 years this also seems to have been sold.[1]

East Ham Hall stood on what was probably an ancient site, but nothing is known of its early history. There is no evidence that it was ever more than a farm-house. It was rebuilt, probably in the earlier 19th century, as a small plain building of two storeys with a frontage of three bays. It was demolished in 1931 or 1932.[2]

The manor of *EAST AND WEST HAM*, or *HAWELOOWES*, or *BURNELLS FEE*, later called the manors of *EAST HAM BURNELLS AND WEST HAM BURNELLS*, originated at the end of the 13th century in the lands which came to Margery wife of Nicholas Corbet, as one of the heirs of Richard de Montfitchet (d. 1267).[3] These lands were widely scattered. In the 18th century the courts of these manors had jurisdiction over tenants in most parts of both parishes, and especially in Stratford, Plaistow, and the marshes (West Ham) and at Plashet and North End (East Ham). The manors had formerly included also Hamfrith in East and West Ham. The location of the original demesne is not known. Nicholas Corbet died in 1280, holding about 130 a., mainly marsh, in East and West Ham, in right of his wife.[4] Margery subsequently married Ralph fitz William of Greystoke (Cumb.).[5] In 1282–6 she and Ralph granted their lands in East and West Ham to Robert Burnell, bishop of Bath and Wells, from whose family these manors eventually took their name.[6] The bishop augmented his estate by other purchases. In 1287 he acquired all the lands in East and West Ham belonging to Sir Richard Battail,[7] whose family had been there since the reign of Richard I,[8] and in 1292 Gilbert le Jeuene granted 10½ a. in East Ham to the bishop.[9] Burnell also acquired the life interest of Hugh de la Val in the property in East and West Ham which he held by courtesy of England in right of his deceased wife Maud, sister of Margery Corbet.[10]

The bishop (d. 1292,) was succeeded by his nephew Philip Burnell, who wasted his estates.[11] When Philip died in 1294 his lands in East and West Ham, comprising 150 a. held in chief, 58 a. held of Giles de Plaiz, and 7 a. held of Stratford Abbey, were in the hands of a creditor, Adam de Creting.[12] Philip's heir was his infant son Edward, the wardship of whom was granted in 1295 to Hugolin de Wichio, subject to arrangements for discharging the

[76] *Cal. Close 1272–9*, 509, 562–3.
[77] *Feet of F. Essex*, ii. 41, 69.
[78] Ibid. 123.
[79] *Cal. Close 1313–18*, 207.
[80] *Cal. Inq. p.m.* vii, p. 419; ibid. viii, p. 105.
[81] *Cal. Fine R. 1369–77*, 128–9; *Cal. Pat. 1370–4*, 322.
[82] *Cal. Inq. Misc.* iii, p. 307.
[83] *Feud. Aids*, ii. 176.
[84] *Cal. Inq. Misc.* iii. p. 307.
[85] Dugdale, *Mon. Angl.* v. 588.
[86] *L. & P. Hen. VIII*, xix(1), pp. 373–4, 645.
[87] Ibid. 672; ibid. xx(1), pp. 129, 282.
[88] C 142/84/62.
[89] C 142/122/55; cf. *V.C.H. Essex*, v. 210.
[90] Lysons, *London*, iv. 139, 143–4; Morant, *Essex*, ii. 251.
[91] *E. Angl.* N.S. ix. 174.
[92] E. Ham Ch., Mon. to Giles Breame. For the alms-houses see below, p. 42.
[93] C.P. 25(2)/416 Mich. 8 Chas. I.
[94] B.M. Add. MS. 5505, f. 44a.
[95] *Complete Baronetage*, iii. 35; C.P. 43/272, m. 7.

[96] Lysons, *London*, iv. 139.
[97] Ibid. 139, 650; E.R.O., Q/RSg 3; C.P. 25(2)/1306 Hil. 5 Geo. III; *Complete Peerage* vi. 437.
[98] E.R.O., T/M 18 (1764); ibid. 21–5 (c. 1775); ibid. 10 (1829).
[99] E.R.O., D/CT 159.
[1] *Complete Peerage*, vi. 437; in 1883 Lord Henniker held no Essex estates.
[2] E.H.L., *E. Ham Reg. Parl. Electors*, Oct. 1931, Oct. 1932; ibid. Photos. (Houses).
[3] See p. 9.
[4] *Cal. Inq. p.m.* ii, p. 508.
[5] I. J. Sanders, *English Baronies*, 84.
[6] *Feet of F. Essex*, ii. 36, 50, 57; B.M., Lansd. Ch. 93.
[7] *Abbrev. Plac.* (Rec. Com.), 218.
[8] *Cur. Reg. R.* viii. 319; B.M., Cott. Ch. xxvii. 133.
[9] *Feet of F. Essex*, ii. 71.
[10] *Cal. Inq. p.m.* iv, p. 47.
[11] *D.N.B.* Robert Burnell.
[12] *Cal. Inq. p.m.* iii, p. 119; *Cal. Inq. Misc.* i, p. 468; *Cal. Close 1288–96*, 375.

debt on the estate.[13] In 1302, when Hugh de la Val died, Edward Burnell became entitled to the permanent possession of half his lands in East and West Ham, while legally bound to relinquish the other half, which he held only for Hugh's lifetime. In 1313 Burnell similarly became entitled to half the lands which Walter de Huntercombe had held for life in right of his deceased wife Alice, another sister of Margery Corbet.[14] Whether the de la Val and Huntercombe lands were partitioned exactly according to title is not certain. John de Lancaster, who should have inherited the other half shares in those lands, was evidently dissatisfied with the division, for in 1321 he brought an assize of mort d'ancestor against Edward Burnell's heir.[15] Burnell, who was summoned to Parliament as a baron in 1311–14, died in 1315, holding some 260 a. land and £21 rent in East and West Ham. The heir was his sister Maud, wife of John de Haudlo.[16]

In 1339–40, after several earlier family settlements, John and Maud de Haudlo entailed East and West Ham upon their second son Nicholas,[17] giving him priority in the succession, contrary to law, not only over his elder brother Edmund Haudlo, but also over John Lovel, Lord Lovel, Maud's son by a previous marriage.[18] In 1336 John de Haudlo granted a house and 50 a. land in East Ham to Stratford Abbey.[19] He died in 1346 and was duly succeeded by Nicholas, who assumed the surname of Burnell, by which he was summoned to Parliament as a baron.[20] Nicholas (d. 1383) was succeeded by his son Hugh Burnell, Lord Burnell (d. 1420), who in 1412 was holding Haweloowes (i.e. Haudlo's) manor in East and West Ham, worth £20 a year.[21] Hugh's son and heir Edward Burnell had been killed at Agincourt, leaving three daughters, of whom Margaret, wife of Sir Edmund Hungerford, succeeded to the manor, subject to the rights in dower of Edward's widow Elizabeth.[22] In 1460–1 Hungerford's manor of Burnell's Fee had among its free tenants Barking Abbey and the priory of Stratford Bow.[23] Sir Edmund died in 1484 and Margaret in 1486.[24] It was stated after her death that the manors of East Ham Burnells and West Ham Burnells had been given to them in fee by William Lovel, Lord Lovel, Burnell and Holand. Lovel (d. 1455) was a descendant of John Lovel, Lord Lovel, already mentioned,[25] and the reference shows that the settlement made by John and Maud de Haudlo in 1339–40 had not extinguished the Lovel rights to Maud's lands. The legality of that settlement had in fact been successfully challenged by the Lovels after the death of Lord Burnell in 1420. In the case of East and West

Ham Burnells they had evidently agreed to allow the Hungerfords to remain in possession, no doubt at a price.[26]

Thomas Hungerford, son of Margaret, succeeded her. About 1519 John Hungerford, then lord of the manor, began to clear some 60 a. of forest waste in Hamfrith wood, in the north-west of East Ham.[27] Shortly before 1548 Sir Anthony Hungerford, in return for payment by Sir William Sharyngton, conveyed this land to Henry VIII.[28] It was thus united with a smaller part of the same wood lying farther west, in the manor of West Ham, and subsequently descended along with that manor.[29] The remainder of East and West Ham Burnells remained in the Hungerford family until 1557, when Sir Roger Cholmley bought these manors from Anthony and John Hungerford.[30] Cholmley had already acquired the manors of East West Ham and Plaiz, both in West Ham. He had been chief justice of King's Bench in 1552–3 and was M.P. for Middlesex in 1554–9.[31] When he died in 1565 the manors were divided between his two daughters, Elizabeth, wife of Sir Leonard Beckwith and later of Christopher Kenn, and Frances, wife of Sir Thomas Russell.[32] The halves descended separately until the 18th century. In the later 16th and earlier 17th century, before and after the partition, there were various leases and sub-leases of the manors, some of which gave rise to litigation.[33]

Elizabeth Kenn (d. 1583) was succeeded by her son Roger Beckwith (d. 1586), whose heirs were his sister Frances, wife of (Sir) George Hervey, and his niece Frances, wife of Henry Slingsby, who was the daughter of another sister.[34] By a subsequent agreement Beckwith's lands in East and West Ham were assigned to the Herveys.[35] Sir George Hervey (d. 1605) bought Marks in Dagenham, and his wife's half of the Burnells manors descended along with Marks until 1718, when Carew Hervey alias Mildmay sold it to Henry Edwards of Little Waltham.[36] In 1720 Edwards sold it to John Gore,[37] who about the same time conveyed it to Sir John Blount, Bt., a director of the South Sea Company.[38] After the South Sea Bubble this property of Blount's, along with his Hamfrith lands,[39] was sold, probably to James Smyth of Upton, brother of Sir Robert Smyth, Bt. (d. 1745), owner of the other half of the Burnells manors. James Smyth, who was closely associated with his brother,[40] built up a large estate in Essex.[41] He died in 1741, leaving all of it, including his manors (so styled) of East and West Ham Burnells, to his nephew (Sir) Trafford Smyth (Bt.), son and heir of Sir Robert.[42] The halves of the

13 Cal. Pat. 1292–1301, 158.
14 B.M., Lansd. Ch. 93; Abbrev. Plac. (Rec. Com.), 303–4.
15 Cal. Close 1318–23, 308.
16 Cal. Inq. p.m. v, p. 390–1; Complete Peerage, ii. 434–5.
17 Cal. Pat. 1313–17, 612; 1330–4, 75; 1338–40, 302; Feet of F. Essex, iii. 21, 41, 56.
18 Cal. Fine R. 1337–47, 477.
19 Cal. Pat. 1334–8, 342–3; B.M., Add. Ch. 8049.
20 Complete Peerage, ii. 434–5.
21 Ibid.; Feud. Aids, vi. 435.
22 Complete Peerage, ii. 434–5; Cal. Pat. 1416–22, 374; Cal. Close 1419–22, 155; C 138/54/116.
23 E.R.O., D/DMs M3.
24 C 141/6/25; Cal. Inq. p.m. Hen. VII, iii, p. 362–3.
25 Complete Peerage, viii. 217.
26 Ancestor, viii. 167 f.
27 G.L.C., DL/C/207 f. 85.

28 Cal. Pat. 1547–8, 401–2.
29 See p. 68.
30 C.P. 40/1169 rot. 536.
31 D.N.B.
32 E.R.O., D/DHt T121/2; ibid. D/DMs T7/1–16.
33 Ibid. D/DMs T7/1–16 and E21/1–4; ibid. D/DM T43/2–4 and L4.
34 C 142/223/73.
35 E.R.O., D/DM L4.
36 V.C.H. Essex, v. 276; E.R.O., D/DMs T8.
37 C.P. 25(2)/1013 Hil. 6 Geo. I.
38 Morant, Essex, i. 17.
39 See p. 68.
40 e.g. acting as his manorial steward in West Ham: E.R.O., D/DPe M15–17.
41 Morant, Essex (Colchester), 138; ibid. i. 412, 430, 473 494.
42 E.R.O., D/DU 126/126.

manors thus seem to have been reunited, but about 1754 one half was sold to Stephen Comyn.[43] Comyn, and later his son of the same name, retained it until 1798, when both halves were bought by William Bentham.[44]

The half share of the manors which in 1565 came to Frances, Lady Russell, descended to her son (Sir) Thomas Russell.[45] It remained in the Russell family until 1649, when it was held by Sir William Russell, Bt.; in 1650 it was in the hands of Christopher and James Clitherow.[46] It seems to have been acquired about 1650 by (Sir) Robert Smyth, Bt. (d. 1669).[47] Sir Robert also bought the Rooke Hall, later called Ham House, estate in West Ham.[48] His son was holding half the Burnells manors by 1684.[49] This half descended with the baronetcy until 1798, when Sir Robert Smyth, Bt. (d. 1802), joined with Stephen Comyn in selling both halves to William Bentham.[50]

The Ham House estate had been sold separately from the manor, about 1761, and the property bought by Bentham comprised manorial rights without demesne.[51] He sold them in 1799 to William Holland, by whom they were conveyed in 1807 to Edward Holland.[52] In 1810 Edward sold them to Henry Hinde Pelly for £5,500.[53] No land was then mentioned: the value of the manors evidently lay in the income from the courts baron, quit-rents, and fines, which in 1780–98 had been producing about £250 a year.[54] Pelly's purchase was thus a substantial investment as well as a title of dignity. In 1780 he had inherited a large estate at Upton, in West Ham, and his service as captain of an East Indiaman had no doubt given him the means to increase this.[55] He died in 1818 and was succeeded in turn by his son (Sir) John H. Pelly (Bt.) (d. 1852), and his grandson Sir John H. Pelly, Bt. (d. 1856).[56] The manorial rights continued to descend in the Pelly family until the statutory abolition of copyhold tenures. The last manor courts were held as recently as 1925, although most of the copyholds had been enfranchised by the end of the 19th century.[57] The development of the Upton estate for building began in the 1850s.[58]

Although they were always under the same owner East Ham Burnells and West Ham Burnells were treated, at least from the 16th century, as having separate identities. The tenements coming under the jurisdiction of the manor court of East Ham Burnells were in the area lying between Green Street and the present High Street North. Those under the court of West Ham Burnells were mainly at Stratford and Plaistow, but also in several other parts of West Ham, including the marshes.[59]

An early-17th-century note on the customs of the manors of East and West Ham Burnells mentions partible inheritance, with choice for the youngest, an arrangement similar to the Kentish gavelkind.[60] Morant [1768] records another ancient custom, then still observed, by which the tenants of East Ham Burnells were obliged to 'treat and entertain' those of [East] West Ham, West Ham Burnells, and Plaiz. This duty was said to have been laid upon them as a punishment for failing to contribute towards a relief for the ransom of their lord when a prisoner in France.[61] This custom, of which no earlier evidence is known, was discontinued before 1796.[62]

The site of the manor-house of Burnells is not known. Morant states that it was 'near the London road' and implies that the house still existed,[63] but there is no doubt that it had disappeared by the early 17th century. Documents of 1653 and 1677 show that the site of the manor was then called Hawlers, in East Ham;[64] this is clearly identical with Hallers, which in 1623 was being let for pasture.[65] The name, which occurs again in 1718,[66] sounds like a corruption of Haweloowes. No later references to it have been found, but the site may have been in the field which in 1764 was called Burnels Downs, lying on the north side of Vicarage Lane.[67] The field was by then part of the manor of East Ham Hall. It was later called Bonny Downs.[68]

The estate called GREEN STREET or BOLEYN CASTLE appears to have been built up in the 16th century, all or most of it being copyhold of the manor of East Ham Burnells. It lay near the southern end of the street from which it took its name.

The estate may have been formed by Richard Breame (d. 1546), who was described in the probate of his will as 'of Green Street'.[69] His connexion with the house possibly inspired the tradition, of which there is no contemporary evidence, that Anne Boleyn lived at Green Street. Breame was a servant of Henry VIII from whom, in 1529–31, the king rented a house at Greenwich, nominally for the use of Anne's brother, Lord Rochford.[70] It was in 1531 that Henry VIII finally deserted Katharine of Aragon, and the legend connecting Anne with Green Street may have originated in a boast by Breame or his descendants that it was in his house that Henry courted his second queen.[71] In 1544 Breame bought from the king the manor of East Ham, but he may have been living at Green Street before that date.

It has been suggested that in the late 16th and early 17th centuries Green Street belonged to the Nevilles[72] whose monument is in St. Mary's church. In the

[43] Ibid. D/DPe M18; cf. Lysons, London, iv. 252.
[44] E.R.O., D/DHt E8; ibid. D/DPe M21–25; Wright, Essex, ii. 490.
[45] C 142/239/124; E.R.O., D/DMs T7/2, 10 and E 21/1–4.
[46] E.R.O., D/DPe M1.
[47] B.M., Add. Ro. 58414.
[48] See p. 72.
[49] G.E.C. Complete Baronetage, iv. 9–10; E.R.O., D/DC 41/163.
[50] E.R.O., D/DHt E8 (sale cat.); ibid. D/DPe M 2–5, 18, 21–5; ibid. D/DC 27/78; Wright, Essex, ii. 491.
[51] E.R.O., D/DHt E8.
[52] Lysons, London, (Suppl.) (1811), 348.
[53] E.R.O., D/DPe T1.
[54] E.R.O., D/DHt E8.
[55] K. Fry, East and West Ham, 228–30.
[56] Ibid.; Burke's Peerage &c., 1913 edn. p. 1522.

[57] E.R.O., D/DPe T1 and M15–27.
[58] K. Fry, East and West Ham, 230. For this estate see below, p. 73.
[59] E.R.O., D/DPe M52.
[60] Ibid. D/DMs M4.
[61] Morant, Essex, i. 15.
[62] Lysons, London, iv. 141.
[63] Morant, Essex, i. 14.
[64] E.R.O., D/DM T43/8 and 9.
[65] E.R.O., D/DMs E22.
[66] Ibid. D/DMs T8.
[67] E.R.O., T/M 18.
[68] Ibid. T/M 13.
[69] E.A.T. n.s. vi. 307; P.C.C. Wills, 1383–1558, i. 77.
[70] L. & P. Hen. VIII, v, p. 754.
[71] This is suggested by Mr. C. G. Parsloe: P.L.A. Monthly, May 1938, 523–4.
[72] Lysons, London, iv. 141.

1630s and 1640s the estate seems to have belonged to Sir Henry Holcroft (d. c. 1651) a Parliamentarian prominent in Essex during the Civil War, and later to his widow.[73] It was acquired about 1653 by Sir Jacob Garrard (Bt.), a London merchant of royalist sympathies who founded an apprenticing charity.[74] Green Street House descended with the baronetcy until the death in 1728 of Sir Nicholas Garrard. Cecilia, widow of Sir Nicholas, retained it until her death in 1753, when it passed to his grandnephew Sir Jacob Downing, Bt.[75] In 1755 Downing conveyed the estate, then comprising about 160 a., to James Barnard or Bernard.[76] Bernard (d. 1759) appears to have been succeeded by Mrs. Whiteside, who was probably his daughter.[77] The estate was partly broken up about this time.

In 1788–9 Maurice Bernard sold Green Street House and grounds, totalling 17 a., to William Morley.[78] Morley, a London corn merchant, lived there until his death in 1832.[79]

The house was subsequently bought by Mr. Lee, for his daughter Mrs. Morley, who was not related to the former owner.[80] In 1839 James Morley, presumably her husband, owned and occupied the house.[81] In 1863 the house and grounds, then comprising 30 a., were advertised for sale.[82] They do not appear to have changed hands then, but in 1869 they were bought from the Morleys by Cardinal Manning, for use as a Roman Catholic reformatory school.[83] After the reformatory was closed the southern part of the site was used for a Roman Catholic church and primary school. The house, after being used c. 1907–12 as a maternity home, was leased, with some adjoining land, to the West Ham United football club, which sub-let the house to the Boleyn Castle social club.[84] The social club occupied the house until the Second World War.[85] In 1955 the house, which had become very dilapidated, was demolished.[86]

Green Street House, a red-brick building, mostly of two storeys, was erected about the middle of the 16th century, possibly by Richard Breame.[87] It originally comprised a great hall at right angles to the street with a long range at its west end and a kitchen block at the east end, south of which was a staircase wing, with a three-storeyed tower east of that. At the north end of the west range, fronting Green Street, was an arched gateway.[88] In the late 17th century the upper parts of the hall, the west range, the kitchen, and staircase wing were partly rebuilt. In 1662 the house was taxed on 20 hearths; the figures for 1670 and 1674 were 16 and 18

respectively.[89] This suggests that alterations were then in progress, during the ownership of Sir Jacob and Sir Thomas Garrard. In the 18th century a wing was added east of the tower, and a later addition was made east of the kitchen. Inside the house there was panelling of the late 16th or early 17th century, and the main staircase was of the same period. In the garden, south of the west wing, was a detached tower which overlooked the street and was the best-known feature of the house. This was an octagonal building of red brick with crenellated parapet and stair-turret. It was built about the middle of the 16th century, and may originally have been balanced by another tower at the south-east corner of the garden. The upper part of the tower was rebuilt by William Morley about 1800.[90] Until the 18th century a room in the tower was hung with leather embossed with gold, but Morley's predecessor, Mrs. Whiteside, is said to have burnt these hangings and sold the gold.[91] The sale catalogue of 1863 lists all the rooms in the house and its outbuildings, and describes the gardens, which contained several fine cedars. When the Roman Catholics bought the house they demolished the gateway and erected a range of buildings along Green Street.[92]

The manor of *HAMMARSH* lay in the marshes of East Ham, adjoining the Thames. From the Conquest or earlier until the 19th century it belonged to Westminster Abbey. In 1086 the abbey's manor in Ham comprised 2 hides, worth £3.[93] When and how Westminster had acquired it is uncertain. Charters of Edward the Confessor and of King Edgar, purporting to confirm it to the abbey, are forgeries, though possibly embodying some authentic information.[94]

In the time of Abbot Gervase (c. 1137–56) the abbey confirmed to Alger the Clerk the land in Ham formerly held by his grandfather Puncelin, to hold for as long as he should serve faithfully, at an annual rent of £3.[95] There was probably a connexion between this estate and 'Algoresland' which occurs in 1338 as a field name in the Gallions Reach area of North Woolwich, adjoining East Ham.[96] John Flete, the 15th-century chronicler of Westminster, accuses Gervase of alienating abbey lands to his friends in perpetuity subject only to fee-farm rents, and cites the grant to Alger as an example.[97] In 1291 and 1381 the abbey's total income from East Ham was given as £3,[98] which was probably the rent paid by Alger's successors. This might be taken to mean that Alger had acquired all Westminster's land in the parish, but in fact the abbey did keep in hand

[73] E.R.O., D/DPe M15: Ct. Bk. of E. Ham Burnells, rental 1694 and list of beadles; *Visits. of Essex* (Harl. Soc.), 421; *E.R.* xxxiii. 149 f.; Morant, *Essex*, i. 15, names Sir Francis Holcroft as owner.
[74] *Complete Baronetage*, iii. 255; see below, p. 43.
[75] E.R.O., D/DPe M15, admission of Sir Nic. Garrard, 1690; D/DPe M18, ff. 309–11.
[76] E.R.O., D/DPe M18, f. 343.
[77] E.R.O., T/P 196 (King MSS.), Eccles. Essex, ii. 305; *New Display of Beauties of England* (1777), i. 57.
[78] E.R.O., D/DPe M52, no. 162; E.H.L., Deeds, E/EAS/333. 33.
[79] *G.M.* 1832(1), 372.
[80] Stokes, *E. Ham*, 126.
[81] E.R.O., D/CT 159.
[82] E.R.O., Sage Coll., *Sale Cats.* vol. 7/4.
[83] Stokes, *E. Ham*, 126; see below p. 42.
[84] *Kelly's Dir. Essex*, 1908, p. 550; 1910, p. 568; 1912, p. 606; E.R.O., T/P 57.

[85] E.R.O., T/P 57.
[86] E.H.L., Pamph. E/EAS/728.
[87] Unless otherwise stated this description is based on R.C.H.M., *Essex*, ii. 60; for illustrations see E.H.L., Photos. (Houses); K. Fry, *E. and W. Ham* 272, Stokes, *E. Ham*, f. p. 144; and plate below, f. p. 14.
[88] *Trans. E.F.C.* iv, p. cxlii.
[89] E.R.O. Q/RTh 1 and 5; E 179/246/22.
[90] *G.M. Libr. Eng. Top.* iv. 106–7.
[91] Ibid.
[92] *Trans. E.F.C.* iv, p. cxlii.
[93] *V.C.H. Essex*, i. 444.
[94] C. Hart, *Early Charts. Essex: Saxon*, pp. 30, 17.
[95] Westminster Abbey Domesday, f. 496b.
[96] *Cat. Anct. D.* vi, No. C. 5756.
[97] J. Flete, *Hist. Westminster Abbey*, ed. J. A. Robinson, 89.
[98] *Tax. Eccl.* (Rec. Com.), 25b; J. A. Robinson, *Gilbert Crispin, Abbot of Westminster*, 45.

a small estate there. In 1306 the abbot authorized payment of 55s. 'for one cask of wine with the carriage of our provisions sent to Ham'[99] which suggests that this land was being farmed in demesne. In 1530 the abbey's manor of 'Hammarsh juxta Barking' was leased to Thomas Chamberlayne of East Ham for 29 years at an annual rent of £4.[1] The absence of earlier references to an income from Hammarsh, apart from Alger's fee-farm rent, is not surprising. During the Middle Ages, when flooding was frequent, this small property, lying wholly in the marshes, may well have been a liability rather than an asset.

In 1556 Westminster's estate in East Ham, described as 'a cottage and a marsh' was on lease to Thomas Eaglesfield.[2] Between 1732 and 1841, for for which period a continuous series of leases is recorded, Hammarsh was still being let at £4 a year. Leases were usually renewed every 7 years, but the details of fines for renewal are not stated.[3] The last lessees were William Meredith and Edward Moss (1834, renewed in 1841). Their holding, incorrectly entered in the tithe award of 1839 under the name of 'Moss, William and Edward', comprised 50 a., lying in the tongue of East Ham which separated the two parts of North Woolwich.[4] In 1846 the abbey sold 34 a. of Hammarsh to the North Woolwich Railway Co. for £6,000.[5] The portion sold was bounded on the south by the Thames and on the north by the remainder of the manor. The remaining 16 a. were probably sold soon after.[6] Part of the land bought by the railway was later acquired by a company which in 1852–3 developed it as the Victoria Gardens.[7]

The *YNYR BURGES* estate was built up by Ynyr Burges, Paymaster of the East India Company, between 1762 and his death in 1792, at a total cost of £20,700.[8] He was succeeded by his daughter Margaret (d. 1838) wife of (Sir) John Smith-Burges (Bt.), a director of the East India Company. In 1799 the estate comprised 422 a., with a rent-roll of £1,217. Smith-Burges died in 1803 and in 1816 his widow married John Poulett, Earl Poulett (d. 1819). Lady Poulett, who was childless, was succeeded by John Ynyr Burges, grandson of her father's elder brother. In 1838 the estate, then about 410 a., produced an income of £1,549, but by 1840 this had been increased to £2,471. An estate map drawn in 1881, which includes details of recent and later changes, shows that most of the property lay near the present town centre. There were substantial blocks of land on both sides of East Ham Manor Road (now High Street South) and another to the north of Barking Road, with outliers at Beckton. One piece of land at Beckton had been sold in 1880.

John Ynyr Burges (d. 1889) was succeeded by his son Col. Ynyr Henry Burges. Col. Burges was largely responsible for developing the estate for building. He had started to do so, on his father's behalf, about 1887, and continued until his own death in 1908. The process involved buying land as well as selling. An estate map of 1892 shows he acquired in that year 98 a. adjoining the parish church in High Street South. This included the site of the ancient manor house of East Ham. With this exception the Burgeses do not appear to have acquired any important part of the manor of East Ham, whether land or manorial rights, in spite of statements to the contrary.[9] Col. Burges was succeeded by his grandson, (Major) Ynyr A. Burges, who completed the development of the estate during the 1920s.

Ynyr Burges (d. 1792) lived at East Ham for most of his life. As a boy he was adopted by his uncle, Ynyr Lloyd, deputy secretary of the East India Company, who had a house in Wakefield Street.[10] In 1764 Burges bought from George Higginson a newly built copyhold house, to which in 1774 he added a 30-foot wing on freehold land. The 1881 map shows that this house was behind the west side of High Street South, opposite Market Street, and that the copyhold part of it was enfranchised in 1854. A water-colour of 1788 shows an imposing mansion with a central block crowned by an octagonal lantern.[11] After 1792 the house was usually let, but by about 1840 it was unoccupied and dilapidated. A surveyor's report of 1853, in connexion with the enfranchisement, lists the mansion, and also the Clock House, and 'two tenements, a shop, orchard and sundry outbuildings, yard and land abutting on East Ham Street'. It is clear from this and other references that the mansion and the Clock House were not identical: the Clock House was probably the stable block. Both buildings seem to have been demolished soon after 1854.[12] The iron gates at the entrance to the drive from High Street South were left standing until the 1870s or later.[13] On the opposite side of the same street was Clock House farm, which also belonged to the Burgeses, and which survived until early in the 20th century. It was a square three-storey brick building of five bays, dating from the earlier 18th century.[14]

ECONOMIC HISTORY. Until the 19th century East Ham's main occupation was agriculture. In 1086 the manor of Ham held by Robert Gernon, and formerly by Levred, which probably comprised most of East Ham, contained 7 hides.[15] The arable land was being cultivated by 16 plough-teams—six more than in 1066. There was woodland for 700 swine,

[99] *Docs. Illustrating the Rule of Walter de Wenlock*, ed. B. Harvey (Camden 4th Ser. ii), 230.
[1] Westm. Abbey Lease Bk. ii, f. 263; cf. *Valor Eccl.* (Rec. Com.), i. 414; Dugdale, *Mon. Angl.* i. 328.
[2] *Cal Pat.* 1555–7, 353–4.
[3] Westm. Abbey Lease Bk. xxxiv, f. 559 and later Bks. to lxiii, f. 276 (full details in MS. index).
[4] E.R.O., D/CT 159.
[5] Westm. Abbey Lease Bk. lxiv, f. 331b.
[6] Inf. from Church Commissioners.
[7] Cf. Fry, *E. and W. Ham*, 4; Stokes, *E. Ham*, 103.
[8] Unless otherwise stated this account is based on the Family Papers of Major Y. A. Burges, Catsfield Manor (Suss.), on Major Burges's *Burgesaga* (copy in E.R.O., T/G 104), and on information supplied by him. The estate seems never to have had a name, other than that of its owner.

[9] e.g. by K. Fry, *East and West Ham*, 144.
[10] E. H. L., Photographs, Col. Y. H. Burges's Ho.
[11] See plate.
[12] The Clock House appears, as an empty building, in the rate book for 1850, but is not included in that for 1855: E.R.O., D/P 156/11/29–30. The mansion cannot be identified in either of these assessments, unless the name Clock House, in 1850, includes both buildings.
[13] A. Stokes, *E. Ham*, 122; cf. E.H.L., A. Stokes's Panoramic Map of E. Ham.
[14] E.H.L., Local Coll., Photographs, 1908; Stokes, *E. Ham*, 122.
[15] *V.C.H. Essex*, i. 515. Some of the figures relating to this manor are ambiguous. It has been assumed that the 'hundred' for sheep was the 'long hundred', or six score: cf. ibid. 369.

Green Street House about 1830: demolished 1955

Ynyr Burges's House in 1788: demolished about 1854

EAST HAM

EAST HAM: TOWN HALL, BUILT IN 1903

WALTHAMSTOW: TOWN HALL, BUILT IN 1941

and 50 a. of meadow. The livestock comprised 15 'beasts' (*animalia*), 34 swine, 200 sheep, 4 rounceys, and 3 hives of bees. The sheep, rounceys, and bees had all, apparently, been added since 1066, while the beasts and swine had increased from 8 and 20 respectively. Gernon's manor had been enlarged since the Conquest by the annexation of 3 virgates held by Edwin, a free priest. Edwin's estate had woodland for 10 swine and 9 a. meadow; there was half a plough-team there in 1086, compared with a whole team in 1066. At the Conquest Levred's manor had been worth £10. By the time that Gernon had acquired it the value had depreciated to £7, but under his control it had risen to £18 in 1086. The recorded population had also increased, from 56 (34 villeins, 3 bordars, 19 serfs), to 67 (38, 26, 3). Westminster Abbey's manor of Ham, which lay in the marshes, comprised 2 hides, with 1 plough-team and woodland for 8 swine; its value had increased, between 1066 and 1086, from £1 to £3, and its population from 3 bordars to 5.[16]

The most notable feature of East Ham's agrarian economy, as revealed by the above statistics, was the large area of woodland, reckoned to be sufficient for a total of 718 swine. This represents a ratio of 28·8 swine to each 100 a. of the parish area—one of the highest densities even in this well-wooded part of the county.[17] There is little doubt that in the 11th century the forest in East Ham extended well to the south of the main London road.[18] The Domesday figures relating to plough-teams on Gernon's manor show that there was a considerable area of arable in 1086 and that this had been greatly increased during the previous twenty years. The figures relating to livestock, population, and values provide further evidence that Gernon was farming the manor much more intensively than his Saxon predecessor. The figures relating to sheep are especially striking. In 1086, as later, these animals were probably pastured on the marshes beside the Thames and the Roding.

This intensive farming of the manor of East Ham probably continued for more than a century after 1086. This would account for the disappearance, by the later 13th century, of most of the Domesday woodland, and to references, in the 13th and 14th centuries, to 'worn out' land.[19] The small amount of documentary evidence which survives suggests that between the 14th century and the 19th the pattern of land use in East Ham remained more or less constant, with the northern half of the parish being tilled as arable,[20] and the coastal marshes used for grazing.[21] During the 14th and earlier 15th centuries there was serious flooding in the marshes, which must have greatly reduced the amount of profitable pasture, but land reclamation had started there by the earlier 16th century, and seems to have continued steadily thereafter.

It is doubtful whether open fields ever existed in the parish. A conveyance of 1244, relating to a virgate of land in East Ham (in this case 39 a.), describes it in detail as comprising 14 different portions, lying in 11 different *culturae*.[22] If the *cultura* here means a 'furlong' this would imply the existence of open fields, but it may here mean no more than 'field', since several of the *culturae* have names clearly suggesting inclosure: 'Heccroft', 'Littlehope', 'Morehope', and 'Newelond'. If open fields ever did exist, they were no doubt in the centre of the parish, between the forest and the marshes, and they must have been inclosed early.

Marshland commons, which are known to have existed in the neighbouring parish of Barking, and in Dagenham,[23] have not been found in East Ham, and it is quite certain that, from the 16th century if not earlier, all the marshlands there were owned in severalty. The absence of common rights probably facilitated the development of grazing for the London meat market. Butchers occur as tenants of land in East Ham level in various deeds of the 17th and 18th centuries.[24] John Combes, a grazier who reared cattle on the marshes there, was mentioned in 1648, when he suffered forfeiture as a royalist. He was also said to have sheep on the Woolwich marshes, and property in Westminster.[25] In addition to meat, the marshes furnished reeds and osiers, which were being cultivated at least as early as 1545 and as late as 1852.[26]

In the 18th century the farmers of East Ham began to grow potatoes and other garden produce on a commercial scale. By 1756 the potato and turnip crops were sufficiently important to be the subject of a special tithe agreement between the vestry and the vicar.[27] In 1794–5 about 450 a. were said to have been cropped with potatoes, and a further 120 a. with cabbages and other vegetables, representing in all over half the arable area of the parish.[28] Associated with the cultivation of potatoes was the immigration of Irish labourers, which was affecting East Ham by about 1800, if not earlier. It was reported in 1790 that a large body of men, who said they were Irish, had committed armed assaults in the parish.[29] They may have come from elsewhere, but there was certainly an Irish colony at East Ham in 1811, living in Irish Row on the main Stratford–Ilford road.[30] Near Irish Row was a farm previously called Plashet Hall, which during the earlier 19th century became known as Potato Hall.[31] An influx of Irish took place in 1816, and another in 1831.[32] In 1839 13 per cent of the occupiers of property in the parish had recognizably Irish names.[33] From 1845 to 1848 most of the East Ham potato crops were destroyed by disease,[34] but by that time the parish was becoming noted for its cabbages, which were taken up to the London markets

[16] Ibid. 444.
[17] Ibid. 375.
[18] For the forest see p. 95.
[19] *Cal. Inq. p.m.* ii. 508; ibid. v. 390–1.
[20] The later medieval evidence relating to arable land comes mainly from inquisitions *post mortem*, references to which are given under the manors of East Ham and East and West Ham Burnells.
[21] For the marshes see p. 17.
[22] *Feet of F. Essex*, i. 148.
[23] *V.C.H. Essex*, v. 215, 282.
[24] E.R.O., D/DB 400–32; ibid. D/DEl T367.
[25] *E.R.* xxi. 28.

[26] *L. & P. Hen. VIII*, xx(1), p. 672; B.M. Add. MS. 32450 B; cf. also *Feet of F. Essex*, iv. 291; *Cal. Pat.* 1554–5, 61; *Cal. S.P. Dom.* 1670, 128; E.R.O., D/CT 159.
[27] E.R.O., D/P 156/8/1 (20 Apr. 1756).
[28] Lysons, *London*, iv. 138: comparisons with later figures suggest that Lysons's estimates were far from precise.
[29] E.R.O., Q/SBb 338.
[30] K. Fry and R. E. Cresswell, *Memoir of Elizabeth Fry*, i. 167–9.
[31] Eastern Counties Rly. Map, 1853.
[32] E.R.O., D/P 156/8/3; ibid. Sage Coll. No. 860.
[33] E.R.O., D/CT 159.
[34] Stokes, *E. Ham*, 143.

in large quantities.[35] Onions also were an important local crop,[36] and were evidently grown for pickling, since Crosse & Blackwell had onion-sheds in Jews Farm Lane (now East Avenue) in 1880.[37] Watercress was still being grown in Little Ilford in 1894.[38]

In 1839 there were some 16 farms of more than 50 a. of which 5 were over 100 a.[39] Directories of 1848 and 1863 list under East Ham 18 and 16 farmers respectively; in each case 7 are stated to be also market-gardeners.[40] As late as 1886 there were still at least 9 farmers in the parish.[41] Most of these disappeared during the next decade as the land was cut up for building, though one or two small farms survived longer.[42] By 1905 there were only 122 a. arable and 93½ a. permanent grass in East Ham.[43]

There was a windmill on the manor of East Ham in 1268 and later.[44] It may have been on the site, about a mile north of East Ham creek, occupied in 1741 by a post mill.[45] That mill apparently survived until about 1870.[46]

Apart from agriculture, and the small crafts and trades common to all villages, few occupations have been noted in the parish before 1850. There is little evidence of maritime trades at East Ham itself, but some men from the parish are known to have practised such trades in neighbouring parishes. Between 1797 and 1827, for example, most of the East Ham parish apprentices were bound to Barking fishermen.[47] A ropemaker of Wall End, listed in 1848, no doubt did most of his business with the fishermen.[48] Gravel digging is occasionally mentioned in and after the 17th century.[49] A starchmaker occurs in 1604.[50] There was a silk-weaver at Wall End in 1826.[51] A pewterer (1616)[52] and a moneyer (1707),[53] both described as of East Ham, probably worked in London. Nine alehouses are listed in a return of 1670,[54] while a directory of 1848 mentions 6 inns and 4 beerhouses.[55]

The modern industrial development of East Ham started in the 1870s with the opening of Beckton gas works of the Gas Light & Coke Co., and its ancillary works making chemical by-products.[56] Beckton, enlarged several times, became one of the largest employers in south-west Essex, drawing thousands of workers from the whole surrounding district. East Ham was naturally affected by these developments. Part of the works lay in the parish, and so did the workers' houses built by the company, but the early influence of the works on the growth of East Ham was limited by poor communications between Beckton and the other parts of the parish. For many years after the opening of Beckton the

only public transport serving the works was the railway which connected at Canning Town with the North Woolwich line.[57] This made it much easier to travel from Canning Town, Plaistow, or Stratford, than from the central and northern districts of East Ham. Frequent workmen's trains also ensured that Beckton would be able to draw labour from those populous districts of West Ham. The National Union of Gas Workers, founded in 1889, set up its headquarters not in East Ham but in Canning Town.[58]

East Ham's other great modern industry is the docks, and here the links with West Ham are even more obvious, since the whole of the Royal Victoria Dock, opened in 1855, was in that parish. The Royal Albert Dock (1880) and the King George V Dock (1921) were mainly in East Ham, but, like Beckton, have always been more easily accessible from West Ham.[59]

The fact that both Beckton and the docks were able to draw much of their labour from West Ham is one reason why there was relatively little residential building at Beckton and North Woolwich. Another reason is that both those industries needed a great and increasing amount of land. Their demands not only reduced the areas of vacant land available for housing but sometimes, as in the case of the King George V Dock, necessitated the actual demolition of dwellings. At Beckton, no doubt, residential building was also discouraged by atmospheric pollution.

The extreme south of East Ham thus became, during the later 19th century, an industrial zone to which most of the workers travelled from elsewhere. Later developments have carried the process farther in the same direction. Other industries have been set up, including several closely associated with Beckton or the docks, for example G. J. Palmer & Sons, in East Ham Manor Way, who process clinker and coke, and R. H. Green & Silley Weir, ship repairers and marine engineers, of the Royal Albert Dock,[60] while bombing, during the Second World War, destroyed some of the dwellings, especially at North Woolwich.

Elsewhere modern industry has been on a much smaller scale. While East Ham was still a village, with plenty of space and few sanitary restrictions, it began to attract obnoxious trades. A factory in Romford Road making animal charcoal existed in 1861–3.[61] In 1879–81 there were several complaints concerning the nuisance caused by Charles Hart's horse slaughterer's (or horse-boiling) factory at the

[35] V.C.H. Essex, ii. 476; cf. K. Fry, E. and W. Ham, 16.
[36] Cf. W. C. Streatfeild's verses, c. 1850: Stokes, E. Ham, 166.
[37] E.H.L., E. Ham Loc. Bd. Mins. Mar. 1880; cf. Oct. 1886, where the sheds are again mentioned, but without the company's name. For a photograph of them see E.H.L., Photos. (Streets).
[38] Kelly's Dir. Essex, 1894, p. 219.
[39] E.R.O., D/CT 159.
[40] White's Dir. Essex, 1848 and 1863.
[41] Kelly's Dir. Essex, 1886.
[42] Ibid. 1908 lists, e.g. John Ivory, Wilson farm, Plashet Grove. Beddall's farm, Manor Way, still existed in 1964.
[43] Bd. of Agric., Rtns. of Acreages, 1905.
[44] Cal. Inq. p.m. i, p. 217–18; ibid. ii, p. 86; ibid. iii, p. 106; Reg. Baldock, 1304–13, 98–100.
[45] E.R.O., D/SH 8.
[46] Stokes, E. Ham, 122.

[47] E.R.O., D/P 156/14.
[48] White's Dir. Essex, 1848.
[49] Assizes 35/115/4 (1 Mar. 1675) and 35/117/2 (Winter 1676); E.R.O., Sage Coll. No. 860 (Irish gravel diggers in 1831).
[50] E.R.O., Q/SR 170/57.
[51] V.C.H. Essex, ii. 463.
[52] Cal. Middlesex Q.S. Recs. 1615–16, 213.
[53] Wills at Chelmsford, 1620–1720, 254.
[54] Assizes 35/111/3.
[55] White's Dir. Essex, 1848.
[56] V.C.H. Essex, v. 15.
[57] Ibid. 24, 25.
[58] Ibid. 61.
[59] For the docks see also p. 61.
[60] E. Ham Guide, 1964, pp. 57, 51.
[61] E.R.O., D/P 156/8/4; White's Dir. Essex, 1863, p. 640.

top of Red Post Lane.[62] This still existed in 1882 but was gone by 1886.[63] Its disappearance was evidently hastened by pressure from the newly-formed local board, which in 1883 also took action against an unlicensed slaughterhouse in Whitta Road, Manor Park.[64] In 1884 there were complaints about a fish-skin drying business at Plashet,[65] but there are no later references to factories of this kind:[66] no doubt they were driven away by the residential development of the district, which was, in fact, so rapid and complete that it left little room for factories of any kind. In the decade after 1900, when there was a good deal of local unemployment, the absence of industry came to be seen as a disadvantage, and in 1908 the influential East Ham ratepayers' association urged the borough council to advertise the borough as a suitable place for factories.[67] Since then the numbers of those employed within East Ham has increased considerably.[68] This has, of course, been partly due to the expansion of Beckton and the docks, but there has also been some industrial growth elsewhere in the town.

Shortage of space, as well as the need to preserve residential amenities, has meant that most of the factories outside the southern industrial region of East Ham have been relatively small. Products fall into five main groups: chemicals; engineering; timber; food and drink; clothing and footwear. Among the earliest chemical factories was that of Brisker & Co., who in 1878–82 were making matches, blacking, and blacklead at Upton Park.[69] This may have continued under different ownership, since there are various references to a match factory at Florence Road, Upton Park, between 1887 and 1906.[70] At Manor Park the manufacture of 'Gloy' and other adhesive pastes has been carried on since 1907 at the Eighth Avenue works by Associated Adhesives (formerly A. Wilme Collier & Co.).[71] Engineering, including metal work of various kinds, has been a local industry from about 1885. Many of the firms engaged in it have been short-lived, or are of recent foundation, but they include one, D. B. Foulger & Son, of Upton Park, which traces its origin to a blacksmith's shop opened about 1860.[72] There were several saw-mills in the parish between 1886 and the First World War.[73]

The first known reference to the processing of food or drink is the approval, in 1893, of building plans for a ginger-beer factory in Katherine Road.[74] The production of Mellin's Food for Infants was carried on for some years, about 1900–10, in a large factory in Redclyffe Road.[75] Robertson & Wood-cock, makers of 'Trebor' sweets, opened a factory in Shaftesbury Road in 1907; their present building was erected in 1937.[76] The manufacture of clothing, especially shirts, blouses, and corsets, has been carried on at East Ham at least since 1906, in a number of establishments.[77]

One other trade demands attention: that of monumental mason. East Ham has no fewer than five cemeteries, and the demand for masons' work had by 1886 led to the opening of six such firms at Manor Park. Those of Benjamin Clarke, Druitt, and Cosburn continued in business for at least 30 years.[78]

MARSHES AND SEA DEFENCES. The East Ham 'levels', as defined in and after the 16th century for the purposes of marshland drainage and flood control, comprised an area of over 1,500 acres. The greater part of this, about 1,000 a., lay in East Ham parish, between the church and the Thames, and along Back river.[79] A further 100 a. were in Little Ilford parish, beside the Roding. The remainder included the West marsh of Barking, which lay to the west of Barking creek, and the detached part of Woolwich to the north of the Thames.

Much of what has already been written concerning the marshes of Barking and of Dagenham, especially in relation to floods and their prevention, is applicable to East Ham.[80] During the Middle Ages nearly half the land in East Ham levels, and therefore the main responsibility for flood control, lay with the abbeys of Stratford and Barking. There, as in the Barking levels, flooding seems to have been especially severe in the 14th century. In 1309, when the monks of Stratford sought licence to appropriate the rectory of East Ham, they pleaded poverty resulting from flood-damage.[81] The floods of 1377, which devastated much of the east coast, probably affected East Ham as badly as they did Barking.[82] A record of 1386 mentions a 'breach towards Barking' in the marshes belonging to the abbot of Stratford and the abbess of Barking, who were accused of organizing illegal fishing within the breach.[83] Since Stratford Abbey had hardly any land in the Barking levels, the reference almost certainly relates to the East Ham levels. In 1421 Hugh, Lord Burnell (d. 1420) was said to have held 101 a. land in East and West Ham 'parcel of 145 a. marsh submerged under water'.[84] In 1500 'drowned marshes in the West marsh of Barking' were mentioned.[85] All these references, along with certain other features of the topography of the West marsh,[86] suggest that

62 E.H.L., E. Ham Loc. Bd. Mins. 10 June 1879, 9 Mar., 9 Nov., 1880, 8 Feb. 1881.
63 Kelly's Dir. Essex, 1882, p. 146; cf. ibid. 1886.
64 E. Ham Loc. Bd. Mins. Aug. 1883.
65 Ibid. May 1884.
66 As distinct from retail businesses such as fried-fish shops, which often caused complaints.
67 E.H.L., E. Ham B.C. Mins. 26 May 1908.
68 W. Ashworth, 'Types of social and Economic Development in Suburban Essex', London Aspects of Change, 84.
69 Kelly's Dir. Essex, 1878 and 1882.
70 E. Ham Loc. Bd. Mins. Nov. 1887; U.D.C. Mins. 18 June 1895, 5 Nov. 1902; Kelly's Dir. Essex, 1906, p. 552; E. Ham U.D.C. Map 1901.
71 E. Ham B.C. Mins. 10 June 1913, 13 Jan. 1914; Kelly's Dir. Essex 1922, p. 411 and 1926, p. 420; A. Wilme Collier, Jubilee Jnl. 1 Dec. 1948.
72 Kelly's Dir. Essex, 1890, p. 378–9 and later dirs.; E. Ham Guide, 1964, pp. 51–2.

73 Kelly's Dir. Essex, 1886, p. 157 and later dirs.
74 E. Ham Loc. Bd. Mins., Dec. 1893.
75 Kelly's Dir. Essex, 1906, p. 549; ibid. 1908, p. 555; E. Ham U.D.C. Map, 1901.
76 Kelly's Dir. Essex, 1908, p. 788; E. Ham Official Guide, 1964, pp. 54–5; Robertson & Woodcock, Trebor Golden Jubilee, 1957.
77 Kelly's Dir. Essex, 1906, pp. 252, 371, 379, 550–1 and later dirs.
78 Ibid. 1886, pp. 158, 185 and later dirs.
79 E.R.O., D/CT 159; D/SH 7, cf. D/SH 29.
80 V.C.H. Essex, v. 238, 285.
81 Reg. Baldock &c. (Cant. and York Soc.), 98–100.
82 H. Grieve, Great Tide, 12, cf. V.C.H. Essex, v. 238.
83 Cal. Plea and Memoranda Rolls of City of London 1381–1412, 116–17.
84 Cal. Pat. 1416–22, 374.
85 Cat. Anct. D. vi, C 5221.
86 Cf. V.C.H. Essex, v. 184.

during the 14th and 15th centuries the East Ham levels, and especially the south-eastern parts, were affected by serious and prolonged flooding.

A survey of 1563 shows East Ham under the jurisdiction of the commissioners of a court of sewers whose area extended from West Ham to Mucking.[87] The East Ham levels then comprised 1,579 a. Of this Ilford mead (122 a.) was in Little Ilford parish, adjoining the Roding. Farther south, beside Back river, were Sibley meads (17 a.), Dunns mead (6. a.), Butells marsh (13 a.), and Parley marsh (86½ a.). Adjoining Barking creek were Whitings marsh (191½ a.), Whitings marsh new grounds (20 a.), and Longs marsh (100 a.). Farther west, along the Thames, were Greens and Galleons marshes (180 a.), Woolwich marsh (180 a.), Wickland marsh (132 a.), New marsh (430 a.), Tonne marsh (28 a.), Old Tonne marsh (16 a.), and New Inned grounds (57 a.). Before the Dissolution Stratford Abbey had owned 399½ a. in those levels, Barking Abbey 352½ a., and the abbeys of St. Mary Graces (Lond.) and Westminster 100 a. and 40 a. respectively. The largest lay owner was the lord of the manor of East and West Ham Burnells, with 329 a.

This 1563 survey mentions specifically, as newly 'inned' (i.e. reclaimed), a total of 77 a. There is other evidence, also, that considerable progress was then being made in reclaiming the marshes. The 'New Inned marsh *alias* Green marsh' occurs in 1540:[88] this may have been one of the marshes in East and West Ham which had been reclaimed by William Hyccheman (or Hicheman), abbot of Stratford (*c.* 1499–1516) and Richard Gouge.[89] Even after the 16th century the process of reclamation was sometimes reversed, as in 1612–13, when 'divers dangerous breaches were made' in the East Ham and neighbouring levels,[90] but in the long run the area of marshland within the sea walls gradually increased. In 1741 the East Ham levels comprised 1,666 a.,[91] and by 1850 the area was 1,742 a.[92] Part of the increase may represent former 'upland' brought under the jurisdiction of the commissioners of sewers in order to promote better drainage, but part of it must have been reclaimed land.

In 1931 the East Ham levels, like those of Barking, came under the control of the Essex Rivers catchment board, which in 1952 was merged in the Essex river board. During the great flood of 1953 East Ham suffered hardly any damage.[93]

FOREST. The history of the forest is treated under West Ham.[94]

LOCAL GOVERNMENT. Very little evidence survives concerning the medieval local government of East Ham. In the 13th century the lord of the manor, Richard de Montfitchet, held the view of frankpledge, enforced the assize of bread and ale,

and set up gallows.[95] Robert Burnell, bishop of Bath and Wells, was holding view of frankpledge *c.* 1285.[96] On 30 June 1381, during the Peasants' Revolt, the king ordered the constables of East and West Ham to issue a proclamation requiring all the tenants of Stratford Abbey in their vills to perform the customary services due to their lords; any rebels were to be arrested.[97] This suggests that some East Ham men were among those who, about that time, sacked the abbey and burnt its charters.[98] No medieval court rolls relating to East Ham, even for periods after 1381, are known to survive. Court records of the 16th century and later contain only details of the courts baron.

Vestry minutes survive from 1736 to 1836 and later, together with a few other parish records.[99] At the beginning of this period vestry meetings usually opened at the parish church but were adjourned early in the proceedings to one or other of the public houses in the parish, where food and drink were bought out of the poor rates. Joseph Sims, vicar from 1756 to 1776, was evidently opposed to festive expenditure of this kind. He rarely attended the adjournments, and in 1758 he presided over a meeting at which it was resolved that in future no money should be spent at vestry on the parish account. This resolution was imperfectly kept. Payments for food and drink continued to be made occasionally, though they were usually smaller than before. In 1794 the vestry reaffirmed the resolution of 1758, and after that date such payments are rarely recorded. That they did not cease completely is shown by another resolution against them in 1806, and in 1818 it was 'ordered that £4 be allowed for each vestry for diet money'. The allowance for a vestry dinner was later raised to £5, but in 1821 was reduced to £2. In 1826 it was decided that the cost of the Easter vestry dinner for that year should be met out of the church rate, but in future out of the poor rate.

Between 1736 and 1755 attendances at vestry, so far as these are indicated by signatures in the minutes, were usually between 10 and 15. Between 1756 and 1836 they were usually between 5 and 10 except for the years 1785–95, when 10–14 was normal.[1] The decline after 1755 may initially have been due to Sims's attitude towards free drinks. Only one woman is recorded as attending vestry: Elizabeth Fry, who appeared in 1835 to dispute her rating assessment.

When present the vicar was chairman of the vestry. John Vade, vicar 1733–56, nearly always attended. Sims often did so up to 1767, but thereafter only twice. Francis Haultain, vicar 1776–1827, attended only two meetings, in 1778 and 1818. In the vicar's absence one of the churchwardens usually took the chair, or (from about 1800) the assistant curate, an overseer, or some other prominent vestryman. In 1818 the vestry formed a parish committee to advise the overseers and churchwardens. In 1825 it was resolved that this should meet weekly, and

[87] E.R.O., D/SH 7, cf. D/SH 29 (map of 1818).
[88] S.C. 6/964.
[89] *L. & P. Hen. VIII*, xix(1), pp. 373–4, 645.
[90] *Acts of P.C.* 1613–14, 13–14, 26.
[91] E.R.O., D/SH 8.
[92] Ibid. D/SH 3A.
[93] H. Grieve, *Great Tide*, 171, 255, 446.
[94] See p. 95.
[95] *Rot. Hundr.* (Rec. Com.), i. 152; cf. *V.C.H. Essex*, v. 182–3.
[96] J.I. 3/35B m. 13, i.e. in respect of Burnells manor.
[97] *Cal. Close* 1381–5, 74.
[98] *Cal. Pat.* 1381–5, 71–2.
[99] Unless otherwise stated the following account of parish government, up to 1878, is based on the Vestry Minutes: E.R.O., D/P 156/8/1–4. For some detailed extracts from these minutes see H. Denman, *Chronicles of East Ham*.
[1] From 1820 the vestry clerk included in the minutes a list of those attending: most, but not all of them, also signed the minute book.

that the members should be fined for non-attendance. A select vestry, with 20 members, was set up in 1827.

In 1742 the vestry resolved that those appointed to serve parish office should not themselves appoint deputies, and in the following year fixed a scale of fines for refusing to serve office. A list of those who had served, containing 37 names, was drawn up in 1746. Throughout the period covered by the minutes there were two churchwardens, two overseers, and two surveyors. One of the churchwardens was being appointed by the vicar at least as early as 1743, and the other by the vestry. This arrangement appears to have been followed in every year except 1828, when a new vicar, William Streatfeild, presided at a vestry which appointed both churchwardens on his nomination: this was never repeated. In 1813, for the first time, a salaried overseer was appointed; in 1817 his office was combined with that of salaried assistant surveyor, which dated from 1811. The dual office lasted at least until 1820.

One constable was nominated each year by the vestry, and from 1802 also a headborough, who was sometimes referred to as a constable. In 1806 the headborough was receiving a small salary. There were also a vestry clerk and a church clerk, both salaried. In 1743 the vestry appears to have obtained the services of a new clerk at a discount: Thomas Standbrook on his appointment undertook to pay £1 a year to a poor widow as long as he remained in office. A rate-collector was appointed in and after 1811. Some of these minor offices might be combined, especially those of vestry clerk and church clerk.

The vestry levied one rate for all parochial purposes. This sometimes included a small amount expressly stated to be for church purposes, but there was apparently no separate budgeting for expenses incurred by the surveyors and constable. In administering the income from the rates the overseers usually accounted for the regular items of expenditure, especially on poor relief, while the churchwardens dealt with casual items. In 1740 the rateable value of the parish was about £3,340; by 1800 it had risen to £4,500, and by 1819 to £6,200.

The parish was maintaining a poorhouse at least as early as 1738, when a building was rented for the purpose. The same house was still in use in 1749. The 'workhouse' is mentioned in 1783–4 and later. Between 1796 and 1803 the poor of the parish were apparently being farmed out to contractors named Hill and Woodcock. In 1804 the vestry leased a house at Wall End and converted it into a workhouse or poorhouse, both of which terms are used in the minutes. It appears to have been a small farm-house or a pair of cottages.[2] In 1813–15 about 25 paupers were accommodated there.[3] This Wall End building appears to have continued in use until about 1827, when the vestry bought land in Wakefield Street and borrowed £1,000 to build a workhouse there. The new house was used for the poor until the formation of the poor law union in 1836, when it became a church school.[4]

The parish also had a watch-house. In 1788 the vestry resolved to discover and prosecute the persons who had demolished this building a few days before. Whether they succeeded is not known. A new watch-house, 7 feet square, was built in 1805–6. This building, which was in High Street South, was demolished about 1850.[5]

In 1737–40 about 10 parish pensioners were receiving between 2s. and 3s. a week each. The number of pensioners in 1779–80, a year of unusual distress, rose to over 30, but during the 1780s it was usually under 20. Between 1791 and 1802 it fluctuated from 20 to 29. In 1813–15 there were about 40 regular adult pensioners and another 25 casual poor were relieved each year.[6] Altogether, in that three-year period, about 8 per cent of the population were receiving parish-relief in or out of the workhouse. In 1772 the vestry ordered the poor to wear badges, and in 1779 required them to attend church or forfeit their pensions.

Other methods of relief, besides pensions and the workhouse, included the payment of rent for cottages occupied by the poor, and the provision of medical care. A parish apothecary was employed throughout the period 1736–1836 at an annual stipend occasionally supplemented by allowances for extra work. In 1766 a newly-appointed apothecary was dismissed after he had refused to serve the poor with medicines unless they came to him. In 1818 the apothecary recorded 598 visits to pauper patients in this parish: the equivalent of one visit to every 2 inhabitants of East Ham. East Ham's apothecary nearly always held the same office under the vestry of the neighbouring parish of Barking.[7] Few details of parish apprenticeships have been noted, apart from a series of 17 running from 1797 to 1827, during which period the masters were mainly Barking fishermen.[8] A less common method of relief was used in 1792, when the vestry granted a poor man £5 to stock a shop.

During the Revolutionary and Napoleonic Wars the vestry met growing distress by special doles, fuel and food subsidies, and by the 'roundsmen' system. This last expedient was adopted in 1816 to cope with an influx of poor Irishmen.

Details of parish rates are recorded in the vestry minute books for most years from 1736 to 1802. At the beginning of this period the rateable value of the parish was about £3,340 and the rate poundage 1s. During the next 60 years the rateable value, periodically reassessed, rose steadily, reaching £4,700 by 1801. The poundage remained remarkably steady: as late as 1795 it was only 1s. 10d. Occasional higher rates, before that date, were necessary during and immediately after the Seven Years War and the American War of Independence. After 1795, again in wartime, the increase was rapid: in 1801 the poundage reached an unprecedented peak of 5s., producing £1,178, as compared with £167 produced by a 1s. rate in 1740. Poundage figures are not systematically recorded after 1802, but some indication of them is given by two sets of returns to Parliamentary inquiries, covering the

---

[2] Stokes, *E. Ham*, pl. f. p. 96.
[3] E.R.O., Q/CR 1/10.
[4] E.H.L., Photograph.
[5] E.R.O., Sage Coll., No. 860.
[6] E.R.O., Q/CR 1/10.

[7] Cf. Oxley, *Barking Vestry Mins.* 141–4: Sedgwick, Brooks, Cook, Bray, and Desormeaux also served East Ham.
[8] E.R.O., D/P 156/14.

years 1813–15 and 1816–21.[9] Between 1813 and 1821 the product of the rate fluctuated between £1,060 and £2,032, the highest figure being reached in 1819 and the lowest in 1821. Although the rise was steep after 1795, East Ham evidently suffered less distress than some neighbouring parishes. In 1815, for example, about 8 per cent of the population received poor-relief, compared with over 15 per cent at Barking and Wanstead and 12 per cent at West Ham.

East Ham became part of West Ham poor law union in 1836. In 1848 the vestry resolved to establish a local board of health, but this was not done. A 'local sanitary committee' apparently existed in 1853, when the vestry referred to it the question of improving roads and drainage. In 1878 East Ham was at last constituted a local government district, under a board which held its first meeting in 1879 and its last in 1894.[10] There were originally 9 members of the board, elected on a single roll for the whole parish; vacancies occurring between elections were filled by co-option. In 1886 the district was extended to include Little Ilford parish, which became a separate ward, returning three members to the local board.[11] In 1890 the district was divided into 4 wards, each with three members. The board's meetings were held in the parochial buildings, Wakefield Street, formerly the church schools, which were at first leased from the vicar, and in 1883 were bought by the board.

The chairman of the local board, throughout its existence, was Thomas Mathews, a farmer and landowner. The board appointed a full-time salaried surveyor, and a rate-collector paid on a 2½ per cent commission. Its other chief officers served part time: the clerk (a solicitor), the treasurer (a bank manager), and the medical officer of health.

In 1879 the urban development of East Ham had only just begun, and for more than 10 years after that date growth was not exceptional, at least by Metropolitan Essex standards. The local board thus had time to gain experience before the great expansion of the town took place in the 1890s. The scale of its activities, though small at first, steadily increased. In 1879 the general district rate of 3s. in £1 produced about £3,100; in 1894, at 2s. 4d., it produced £14,700.

The main burden of administration fell at first upon the board's surveyor, William H. Savage, who had to carry out public works, and also to inspect new private buildings to ensure that they conformed to the by-laws. His programme of public works can be divided into two periods. Between 1879 and 1886 he was concerned mainly with street levelling, paving, and drainage, especially at North Woolwich, where the improvement of a small slum area received immediate attention. Between 1886 and 1894 a system of main drainage was constructed, with outfall works on the Roding, the first public park was opened, at Plashet, a temporary fever hospital was built, and a part-time fire-brigade formed. The provision of works and services during this second period was stimulated by the absorption of Little Ilford, a parish where sanitary conditions were bad,

and where rapid development, around the railway lines, could be expected fairly soon.

The surveyor's duties of inspection and control of private building were in some respects more onerous, especially in his early years with the board, than those relating to public works. Between 1879 and 1884 he often had difficulty with builders who allowed new houses to be occupied before they had been connected to water mains or sewers. More serious, in the long run, was the poor construction of some of the buildings, especially those on the Boleyn Estate, and in the Kelly Road (now Market Street) area. In August 1880 Savage prosecuted five different builders for breaking by-laws, and he took, or threatened to take similar proceedings on several other occasions. He sometimes insisted on the demolition of new buildings, or parts of buildings, which were below the proper standard. Flagrant defiance was probably easier to handle than 'the ingenuity people display in evading or just coming within the requirements of the by-laws' on which he commented in September 1880. Occasionally he may have been too lenient. Several times he recommended the approval of plans which did not entirely comply with the by-laws, in order to avoid hardship to builders. In 1881 he appears to have approved without comment the building of a working-class estate, at Cyprus, equipped with pail-closets which soon became foul and were a problem to the local authority for the next 15 years. But on the whole Savage carried out his duties of inspection firmly and tactfully, in spite of occasional hostility from the builders, culminating two or three times in assaults on him or his assistants. Until 1884 he appears to have made all the inspections personally, but in November of that year the board authorized him to delegate them, if necessary, to a foreman and a bricklayer.

In 1895 the local board was succeeded by an urban district council of 15 members, representing 4 wards. This governed East Ham until 1904. It held its meetings at Plashet Lane board school until 1901, and then in the school board offices in Wakefield Street until 1903, when a new town hall was opened in Barking Road. Thomas Mathews, who had been chairman of the local board, did not seek election to the U.D.C., and from 1895 the chairman held office for one year only. In 1892 and 1893 Mathews's reappointment, previously unanimous, had been opposed by a minority of the board, including John H. (later Lord) Bethell, who had been elected in 1888 as the first 'Progressive' member. From the time of his election until his retirement from the council in 1907 Bethell constantly urged greater vigour and efficiency in local government. For most of that period he was also a member of the West Ham corporation, and his experience there must have helped him to foresee the problems that would face East Ham as it grew into a large town. No permanent party groupings are apparent from the minutes of the 1880s and 1890s, but it is clear that Bethell's influence grew steadily, and that he was at least partly successful in persuading his

---

[9] E.R.O., Q/CR 1/10 and 1/12.

[10] The following account of the local board's work and that of its successors the urban district council and the borough council, is based on: E.H.L., E. Ham Loc. Bd. Mins. 1879–94; U.D.C. Mins. 1895–1904; B.C. Mins.

1904–15; C.B.C. Mins. 1915–65; E. Ham Municipal Diary 1918–19 to 1965.

[11] Loc. Govt. Board's Provisional Orders Confirmation (No. 4) Act, 49 & 50 Vict. c. 61 (local act).

colleagues to spend much more than the absolute minimum on public works and services in order to anticipate future needs.[12] He was a surveyor, and at that stage of his career was actively employed in property development in East Ham. As is shown below, he was by no means the only councillor with such interests.

One of the first actions of the U.D.C. was to terminate the arrangement under which the rate-collector was paid on commission, and to substitute two salaried collectors. The Council appointed a full-time accountant and in 1902 promoted him to be full-time treasurer. A minority of the U.D.C. made several unsuccessful attempts to put the post of town clerk onto a full-time basis. In the case of the medical officer of health the U.D.C. resisted repeated pressure from the Local Government Board to substitute a full-time for a part-time appointment, giving way at last in 1904. The council's first librarian, appointed in 1896, was part-time; a full-time librarian was appointed in 1898, but he apparently did not have complete authority until 1901, when his part-time colleague resigned. The electrical engineer, appointed in 1899, served full-time from the first.

The life of the U.D.C. coincided with the district's most rapid growth, during which the population increased from about 45,000 to over 100,000. During that period the main sewers were extended to Cyprus, a full-time fire-brigade was formed, a permanent isolation hospital and the first council houses were built, important road improvements were effected, and electric tramways were opened. Additional powers for these and other purposes were acquired under the East Ham Improvement Acts of 1898 and 1903.[13] The council's new libraries cost the ratepayers relatively little, since their erection was met by Passmore Edwards and Carnegie, but the town hall and associated buildings were planned on a large scale, on a central site of 5 a., and cost over £80,000, a large sum for that time and place.[14] These new undertakings involved a great increase in spending, which outpaced even the rapidly rising rateable value of the town. In the first year of the U.D.C. (1895–6) its general district rate of 3s. 1d. in £1 produced about £22,000. In its last year (1904–5) the equivalent figures were 4s. and £87,000. In 1904 the council also became responsible for elementary education, a heavy expense which included the loan debt on many newly built schools. Education was met by the overseers' rate, which also covered the cost of poor-relief, and the police services for which the council was not responsible. The overseers' rate in 1904–5 amounted to 9s. 6d. in £1, so that the total poundage in that year was 13s. 6d. This was a high rate for the time,[15] and it was especially burdensome because many of the ratepayers were then young men of low income and with family responsibilities, who also had to meet the expense of travelling outside the district

to work. It was unfortunate, also, that the boom of the 1890s, which had largely created East Ham, was succeeded by a decade of economic stagnation.[16] The council's minutes, from 1902 onwards, often refer to distress caused by unemployment.

The U.D.C., like the local board, continued to inspect and control private building. During the 1890s East Ham was growing faster than any other town of its size in England.[17] The figures for the decade ending in 1901, upon which this statement is based, remarkable though they are, mask the fact that the town's rate of growth was far from uniform during that period, and reached its peak in 1896–9. In the years 1892–1901 inclusive the local board and U.D.C. approved the plans for 11,635 houses.[18] Of these no fewer than 6,613 were in the four years 1896–9, 5,404 in the three years 1897–9, and 2,252 in the one year 1898. The rate of growth was thus nearly twice as rapid in 1898 as it was over the whole decade. Much of the building during these peak years was concentrated in Little Ilford, where the Manor farm had come on to the market in 1895. In 1898 1,129 houses, accommodating about 6,000, were built in Little Ilford.[19]

The above figures give some indication of the amount of inspection and control which had to be carried out by the council's surveyor. His task during that period was complicated by the presence on the council of men who were themselves engaged in property development in the district. Between 1895 and 1904 at least 9 such councillors can be identified, several of whom held office as chairman of the works committee, to which the surveyor was responsible. In one case, in 1898, a member of the works committee submitted plans for a large-scale development in Little Ilford which were approved by that committee but were subsequently referred back to it for amendment after the surveyor had stated before the full council in committee that he considered the plans unsatisfactory. It is significant that this case related to Little Ilford, for it was there that local politics and geography combined with the exceptional pressure of building development to make the surveyor's task especially difficult and delicate.

The geography of Little Ilford was possibly the most important single factor affecting building development there during the 1890s. The area was bounded and intersected by main roads and railways. On its eastern side, where it sloped down to the Roding, it was subject to flooding. Development was therefore very likely to take the form of cheap houses for those who could not afford to live in pleasanter places. The duty of the council and its surveyor was to ensure that the rapid building of such houses did not create slums; in this they were not entirely successful.

The greatest difficulties arose from the development of the low-lying land by the river, especially in Southborough (later Grantham), Manor (later Alverstone), and Bessborough (later Walton) Roads,

---

[12] For Bethell's work at E. Ham see Stokes, *E. Ham*, 186 f.
[13] 61 & 62 Vict. c. 124 and 3 Edw. VII, c. 223 (local acts).
[14] For some financial details see E. Ham Improvement Acts, 1898, 61 & 62 Vict., c. 124 (local act) and 3 Edw. VII, c. 223 (local act); also Loc. Govt. Bd.'s Confirmation (No. 6) Act, 1908, 8 Edw. VII, c. 146 (local act). For the town hall see above, p. 5.
[15] Cf. figures for West Ham, in McDougall, *Fifty Years a Borough*, 97.

[16] Cf. R. C. K. Ensor, *England, 1870–1914*, 500–1.
[17] *V.C.H. Essex*, v. 5–6.
[18] These and the subsequent figures are taken from the returns recorded in the Minutes. The 1901 census, which covers a decade slightly different from the calendar years 1892–1901, gives the number of new houses as 11,220.
[19] *Little Ilford Parish Mag.* Feb. 1899. This is an official figure, which relates to houses completed and occupied.

and Manor (later Selborne) Avenue. Building had started at the northern end of the first three roads during the 1880s, on the Coach and Horses estate adjoining Romford Road,[20] but by far the greater part of these roads, and also Selborne Avenue, were built up in 1897–1900. The long terraces of small houses erected there presumably conformed to the local building by-laws, but at that period the by-laws apparently did not regulate the levels at which new houses were built: the power to regulate levels was eventually acquired by a clause in the East Ham Improvement Act of 1903. The council's surveyor realized that the new houses in the area between Walton Road and the river would be subject to flooding, and a number of the plans were amended, on his advice, to minimize this danger. But the inadequacy of such measures was shown in 1903, when the council had to hire boats for the use of flood victims there.[21] According to Alfred Stokes the council's policy of permitting building on this low-lying land was unsuccessfully opposed by J. H. Bethell, who urged that the land should all be acquired as a public park.[22] As early as 1899 the area was being mentioned in terms appropriate to slums,[23] and although the houses there are by no means the oldest in East Ham they are now (1966) being demolished as part of a redevelopment scheme.

None of the builders mainly responsible for developing the Grantham Road–Walton Road area in 1897–1900 was a member of the U.D.C. at that time so that direct pressure from within the council seems unlikely, but there were undoubtedly other pressures. Builders who submitted plans naturally complained if these were frequently rejected. There was also a peculiar local issue in this part of the district that probably made the U.D.C. reluctant to court further trouble there by acting firmly in controlling new building. Little Ilford had only recently joined East Ham. It had originally desired this union more than the larger parish, but in the 1890s a movement arose there in favour of secession.[24] In 1898 the county council ruled against separation, and the matter was clinched in the following year when the two parishes were united for poor-law assessment as well as sanitary purposes. But until 1898 secession was still a live issue.

Another kind of pressure upon the council and its officers at this time, and that most difficult to withstand, was the overwhelming pressure of work. Rejection of plans meant extra work for everyone concerned and this may have had as much bearing on the development of Little Ilford as political pressure or personal intrigue, for that development came at the peak of East Ham's phenomenal growth. In 1890 the surveyor was dealing with under 40 housing plans a month. In 1898, when most of the major developments in the east of Little Ilford were approved by the U.D.C., the average was 188 plans a month, and from April to July of that year it was 302.

These events placed a great strain upon the surveyor, Savage, and his small department, and in 1899 he resigned on appointment as agent to Col.

Ynyr Burges, one of the main property developers in East Ham. He left the council's service reluctantly, for he was proud of his achievements there, but with the comment that his salary had long been inadequate. His resignation was followed by that of his 'outdoor' assistant O. R. Anstead, who went into business as a contractor, became a member of the council in 1900, and was soon chairman of the works committee. Anstead's influence may well have been responsible for the firmer attitude of the council towards the development, in 1903–4, of the south-eastern part of Little Ilford, in and around Gainsborough Avenue, plans for which were repeatedly rejected, apparently because the proposed levels were too low.

The burden of increasing work also fell heavily upon the treasurer's department. The district auditor more than once criticized the financial methods of the U.D.C., and his report on the accounts for 1904 was such that the council set up a special committee of investigation. He had found serious irregularities, especially concerning a secret trust fund by which the council had, in effect, been speculating in the purchase of land at Manor Park. The investigating committee admitted irregularities but found that there had been no dishonesty. Some of the irregularities were probably due to overwork. In 1900 the four assistants in the treasurer's department were working between 16 and 19 hours a week unpaid overtime. The strain on the treasurer himself was no doubt even greater; the first full-time treasurer resigned in 1904, after unsuccessful attempts to secure a salary increase. His successor resigned in 1906, immediately after the investigating committee had reported.

In 1904 East Ham became a municipal borough with 18 councillors representing 6 wards, and 6 aldermen. The appointment, in 1905, of the first full-time medical officer of health left the town clerk as the only part-time chief officer. In 1906–8 there were further attempts to make the clerk's post full-time, but this did not happen until 1909, when C. E. Wilson, who had served since 1879, died: his son, who had for several years been acting as his deputy during illness, then succeeded him, full-time.

The borough council completed the buildings on the central town hall site with the technical college (1905), public health and education offices (1910), and indoor swimming bath (1912), and also built a new fire-station (1914). Additional borrowing powers for these purposes were confirmed in 1908.[25] Inspection and control of building was becoming a less serious problem: the number of new houses approved each month declined to about 60 in 1908, and to under 20 in 1913.

East Ham became a county borough in 1915, by a local Act promoted with the help of Sir John Bethell, then M.P., against strong opposition from the Local Government Board.[26] In 1919 the number of wards was increased to 10, represented by 30 councillors, and the number of aldermen was also increased to ten.[27] Between the two world wars

[20] Cf. Loc. Bd. Mins. Dec. 1887, Feb. 1893.
[21] *U.D.C. Mins.* 1 July 1903; E.H.L. Photos. (Floods): see plate.
[22] *E. Ham*, 188.
[23] *Little Ilford Parish Mag.* May 1899.
[24] Loc. Bd. Mins. 19 July 1892; *U.D.C. Mins.* 21 June 1898.

[25] L.G.B. Prov. Conf. (No. 6) Act 1908, 8 Edw. VII, c. 146 (local act).
[26] E. Ham Corporation Act, 1914, 4 Geo. V, c. 3 (local act); Stokes, *E. Ham*, 189–90.
[27] E. Ham Corporation Act, 1919, 9 & 10 Geo. V, c. 52 (local act).

EAST HAM: FLOODS IN SOUTHBOROUGH (LATER GRANTHAM) ROAD, MANOR PARK, IN 1903

WEST HAM: WILTON STREET AND HAM CREEK, SILVERTOWN, ABOUT 1890

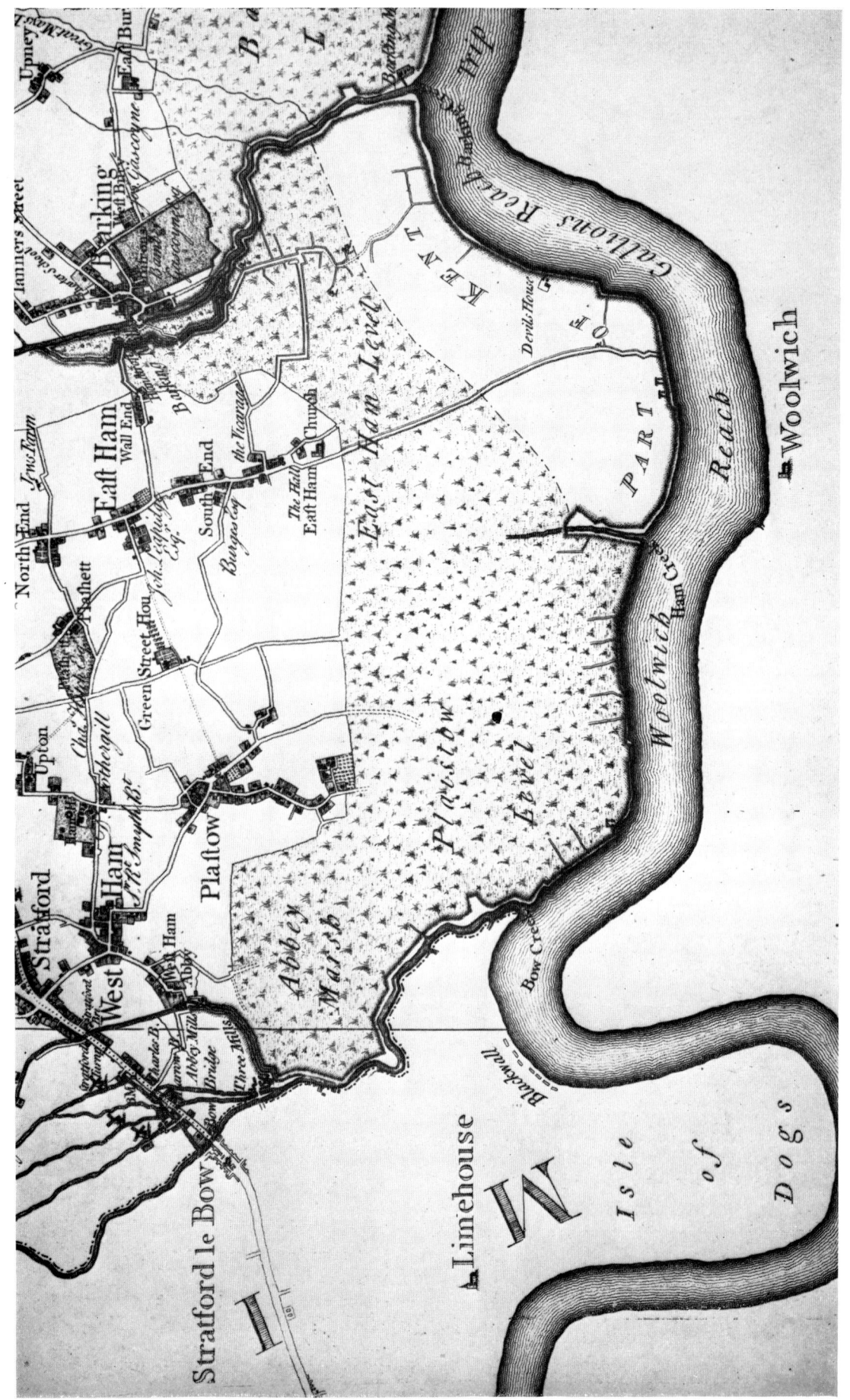

WEST HAM (SOUTH) AND EAST HAM (SOUTH) IN 1777

Scale c. 1·5 in. to 1 mile

the corporation extended the sewage works, the swimming baths, and the isolation hospital, opened several clinics and a tuberculosis sanatorium, and in 1939 built an annexe to the town hall.[28] The building of council houses, started by the U.D.C., was resumed on a larger scale. When the administration of public assistance was reorganized under the Local Government Act (1929) East Ham assumed responsibility for the children's homes of the former West Ham Union.

During the Second World War East Ham was praised for its efficient Civil Defence organization.[29] After the war the corporation's main task was house-building, at first to replace the many houses destroyed by bombing and later in connexion with slum clearance. Between 1946 and 1964 £13,800,000 were borrowed for that purpose, representing over 40 per cent of the total loans for all purposes administered by the corporation.[30] A local Act of 1957 gave the corporation additional powers relating to public health (including derelict buildings) and various other matters.[31] After the war, also, East Ham corporation, as the local education authority, built many new schools and a new technical college. Further details of its work will be found in the sections relating to Public Services and Education. In 1965 the county boroughs of East Ham and West Ham were united to form the London borough of Newham.

East Ham was included in the Metropolitan police district, formed in 1840,[32] but in spite of repeated requests by the local authority it was not until 1904 that a station was opened there.[33]

A separate commission of the peace was issued for East Ham in 1906. The court was headed by a stipendiary magistrate from 1906 to 1954, and subsequently by a part-time chairman.[34]

PUBLIC SERVICES. The development of gas, electricity, and water supplies, and of sewage disposal, have been outlined in a previous volume.[35] When the growth of East Ham began in the 1870s two gas companies already had powers of supply there: the West Ham Gas Co., to the north of Barking Road, and the Gas Light & Coke Co., to the south. Until the 1880s, however, there were considerable areas of the parish without gas mains; it was not until 1890 that the mains were extended to Wall End, and even in 1896 Rancliffe House, High Street South, still had no supply.[36]

East Ham U.D.C. began to supply electricity in 1901, and this was continued by the corporation until nationalization. Demand grew slowly, and as late as 1926 there were only 4,600 consumers, but by 1936 there were 29,200, representing virtually all the premises in the borough.[37]

Water was supplied to East Ham by the East London Waterworks Co., one of the predecessors of the Metropolitan water board, which began to extend its mains to the parish about 1869.[38] When the East Ham local board was formed in 1879 many houses in the parish were still served by contaminated wells. During the next three years the board and the water company acted vigorously to extend the supply. By 1882 mains had been laid in all the principal streets and a supply was available to every house in the district, but some landlords were reluctant to connect their houses to the mains and in 1887 about 2 per cent of the houses in the district were still served by pumps or wells.[39] In 1898, the year of East Ham's most rapid growth, there was a water shortage so severe that for three months the water company had to restrict supplies to four hours a day.[40]

There was no main drainage in East Ham in 1879.[41] The local board immediately sewered the part of North Woolwich within its district, and in 1880 concluded an agreement by which the sewage from there was fed into the system already maintained by the Woolwich local board. This arrangement continued until 1900, when the London county council took over the drainage of North Woolwich.[42] In 1885 the East Ham board planned a main drainage scheme for the central and northern parts of the district, but it was delayed by difficulties over the purchase of land for the outfall works, and the resignation of the consultant engineer. In 1887 a site near Barking creek was at last secured, and a new and much larger scheme was drawn up, which came into operation in 1891–2. The main sewers were extended in 1896 to Cyprus, where some 100 houses had previously had only pail closets, and about 1900 to the Beckton estate. Major extensions to the works were carried out in 1901–3. The sewage works were reconstructed in 1958–63.

East Ham showed greater foresight than the other inner suburbs of Metropolitan Essex in providing public parks and open spaces.[43] By 1889, when the local board first decided to buy land for a park, it was becoming accepted that the provision of these amenities was likely to promote local prosperity as well as health.[44] Plashet Park, opened in 1891, was bought from the Wood House estate. Part of the cost was provided by the City Parochial Trustees. In 1896 the U.D.C. bought Rancliffe House and grounds, which in the same year were opened as Central Park. Both Plashet Park and Central Park were enlarged by additional purchases, to 18 a. and 25 a. respectively, and the U.D.C., by arrangements

[28] E. Ham Official Guide, 1951 edn., 27, 28 (town hall annexe).
[29] E. D. Idle, War over West Ham, 66.
[30] E. Ham Municipal Diary, 1964–5, pp. 54–5; Loans under Housing Acts 1946–61.
[31] E. Ham Corporation Act, 1957, 5 & 6 Eliz. II, c. 37 (local act).
[32] V.C.H. Essex, v. 34.
[33] E. and W. Ham Year Bk. 1905, p. 49.
[34] E. Ham Municipal Diary, 1925–6 f.; E. Ham C.B.C. Mins. 1954–5, No. 320.
[35] V.C.H. Essex, v. 37–47, 75–81.
[36] E.H.L., E. Ham Loc. Bd. Mins. 12 Oct. 1880, Oct. 1882, Nov. 1883, Oct. 1886, Nov. 1890; U.D.C. Mins. 15 Sept. 1896.

[37] E. Ham Municipal Diary, 1936–7, p. 57.
[38] E.H.L., Pamphlets, E. Ham Civic Week Exhibition, 1949, p. 59.
[39] Loc. Bd. Mins. 1879–82, passim, Mar. 1887.
[40] U.D.C. Mins., M.o.H. Rep. for 1898.
[41] This paragraph is based on Loc. Bd. Mins., U.D.C. Mins., and B.C. Mins.
[42] Under the L.C.C. (General Powers) Act, 1897, 60 & 61 Vict. c. 252 (local act).
[43] Cf. V.C.H. Essex, v. 51. For a list of the public parks, with dates of opening, see E. Ham Municipal Diary, 1936–7, p. 54. Other details in this paragraph are taken mainly from Loc. Bd. Mins., U.D.C., and B.C. Mins.
[44] Loc. Bd. Mins., May 1889.

with the Epping Forest Commissioners, also acquired partial control over the 96 a. of Wanstead Flats transferred to East Ham in 1901. At North Woolwich the Royal Victoria Gardens, comprising 9 a., had originally been laid out in 1853 by a private company.[45] They acquired an unsavoury reputation, and in 1890 a fund was raised by public subscription, to which East Ham local board contributed, for their purchase, after which they were placed under the control of the London county council. Several other parks were provided by the urban district and borough councils, mostly before 1914, bringing the total area of public open spaces to over 200 a.[46]

An open air swimming pool was opened in Central Park in 1901.[47] It was closed in 1915–18 and in 1923 was converted into dressing rooms. In 1912 an indoor pool, with vapour and slipper baths, was opened on the town hall site. A smaller pool was added in 1932, and the other facilities were extended in 1919 and 1925.

In 1879 the local board arranged for the West Ham fire brigade to attend fires in East Ham, and in 1881 it accepted an offer by the Metropolitan board of works to provide a similar service at North Woolwich.[48] In 1893–4 the local board bought a second-hand manual fire-engine, fitted out a station behind its offices in Wakefield Street, and recruited a volunteer brigade. A full-time brigade was formed in 1897, and in the same year a horse-drawn steam fire-engine was bought. In 1914 a new fire station was built in High Street South, and in the following year was equipped with a motor fire-engine.

East Ham, like West Ham and Barking, made an early start with the building of council houses. In 1901 the U.D.C. built 132 dwellings in Savage Gardens, New Beckton, and in 1903 a further 80 in Brooks Avenue.[49] No more were built before 1914, but by 1939 the corporation had provided a total of 830 dwellings. During the Second World War some 27,000 houses, in fact most of those in the borough, were damaged by bombing. The corporation repaired these, and between 1945 and 1 March 1952 also built 934 temporary and 683 permanent houses. It then began to concentrate on slum-clearance. By March 1964 more than 2,600 permanent dwellings had been built within the borough since 1945, and a further 1,700 outside it, including the Ingrave estate near Brentwood.

During the 1880s and 1890s there were frequent outbreaks in East Ham of such serious infectious diseases as smallpox, typhoid, and diphtheria.[50] In 1885, for example, there were 253 cases of smallpox, with 37 deaths, and in 1894 there were 123 cases of smallpox, with 4 deaths, and 192 cases of diphtheria with 62 deaths. In 1893 the local board opened a temporary isolation hospital in an iron hut beside the sewage works. In 1902 this hospital, still in temporary buildings, was transferred to a new site in Roman Road. Permanent buildings were erected there in 1907 and 1909, and the hospital was reconstructed in 1931. In 1941 it was wrecked by bombing and after the war the site was used for new secondary schools.[51]

In 1902 a voluntary cottage hospital, named after Passmore Edwards, who had given £5,000 towards its cost, was opened in Shrewsbury Road; this became part of the much larger East Ham Memorial hospital, completed in 1929 on an adjoining site. The hospital was badly damaged by bombing in 1940, and was closed for two months at that time.[52] Mental patients were for many years accommodated in hospitals of the Essex county council, to which East Ham paid a fixed charge. When the county council terminated this arrangement, East Ham and the county borough of Southend-on-Sea built a joint mental hospital, opened in 1936, at Runwell.[53] East Ham corporation also opened a tuberculosis hospital at Harts, Woodford, in 1920.[54]

In 1930, when the West Ham poor-law union was dissolved, East Ham, as a county borough, took over public assistance within its own area, and it also agreed to take over the union's children's homes in Aldersbrook Road, together with several 'scattered' homes, and to maintain them on behalf of all the towns formerly in the union.[55] By 1964 the corporation's welfare service also included 10 homes for old people.[56]

The City of London cemetery, Little Ilford, comprising the greater part of the former Aldersbrook farm, was opened in 1857.[57] Manor Park cemetery (1875) and Woodgrange Park cemetery (1888) were formed by private companies.[58] There are also two Jews' cemeteries in East Ham.[59]

East Ham's public libraries, up to 1955, have been described in a previous volume.[60] It must be added in amendment that in 1927 East Ham, following the example of West Ham, decentralized its libraries, but that in 1934 a borough librarian was again appointed. Recent events include the closure of the libraries at the Gainsborough community centre (1960) and Roman Manor (1962). A mobile library service was introduced in 1962 and the joint arrangement with Woolwich and West Ham was then ended. In 1965 the book stock of East Ham libraries was 120,557.[61]

The municipal tramways are described above.[62]

PARLIAMENTARY REPRESENTATION. Under the Representation of the People Act (1918)

[45] E.R.O., D/P 156/8/4; Stokes, *E. Ham*, 22, 103.
[46] Stokes, *E. Ham*, 159; *E. Ham Official Guide*, 1964, p. 17.
[47] This paragraph is based on *E. Ham Municipal Diary*, 1934–5, p. 53; ibid. 1925–6, p. 158; inf. from Newham L. B.
[48] This paragraph is based on: Loc. Bd. Mins., *U.D.C. and B.C. Mins.*
[49] This paragraph is based on: *E. Ham Municipal Diary*, 1939–40, pp. 55–6; ibid. 1952–3, pp. 15–18; *E. Ham Official Guide*, 1951, p. 55; ibid. 1964, pp. 44–5.
[50] Paragraph based on: Loc. Bd. Mins., *U.D.C.* and *B.C. Mins.*; *E. Ham Municipal Diary*, 1923–4, pp. 175 f.; ibid. 1934–5, p. 44; Stokes, *E. Ham*, 258–61; *E. Ham Official Guide*, 1951, p. 36.
[51] *C.B.C. Mins.*, 1945–6, nos. 1387, 1753; for the bombing see E.H.L., Photos. (Second World War).

[52] E.H.L., File of Misc. Docs. on Second World War: TS. report on E. Ham Mem. Hosp.
[53] *E. Ham Municipal Diary*, 1936–7, p. 50; Stokes, *E. Ham*, 153–4.
[54] *E. Ham Municipal Diary*, 1935–6, p. 46.
[55] Ibid. 1933–4, p. 40.
[56] *E. Ham Official Guide*, 1964, p. 46.
[57] *E.R.* l. 166. For Aldersbrook see under Little Ilford.
[58] *Kelly's Dir. Essex*, 1890, p. 152; E. Ham Loc. Bd. Mins., May 1888.
[59] See p. 38.
[60] *V.C.H. Essex, Bibliography*, 329.
[61] Inf. from Borough Librarian, Newham L. B.
[62] See p. 7.

East Ham (previously in the Romford division) became a parliamentary borough with two divisions.[63] At the general election of 1918 two Liberals were returned, one of whom, representing East Ham (North) was Sir John (later Lord) Bethell, who had long been connected with the borough.[64] In 1922 one Conservative and one Labour member were elected. The latter, representing East Ham (South), was Alfred Barnes, who had been born at North Woolwich. He held the seat from 1922 to 1931 and again from 1935 to 1955. Except in 1931, when a Conservative captured it, East Ham (South) has been held by Labour at every general election up to and including that of 1966. East Ham (North) was, until 1945, a marginal constituency. In 1923 it was won by Miss Susan Lawrence, one of the first women Labour M.P.s. She was defeated in 1924 by a Conservative, but regained the seat at a by-election in 1926 and held it until 1931.[65] It was won in 1931 by the Conservative (Sir) John Mayhew, who held it in 1935. In 1945 it was regained for Labour, which has held it at every subsequent election, including that of 1966.

CHURCHES. In 1086 Robert Gernon's estate in (East) Ham included 3 virgates which in 1066 had belonged to Edwin, a free priest.[66] This suggests the existence of a church there before the Conquest, though the present building of St. Mary Magdalene is thought to be no earlier than the first half of the 12th century. In 1254 the advowson was held by Richard de Montfitchet (d. 1267), a successor of Gernon, and there was a vicarage as well as a rectory.[67] The advowson descended along with the manor of East Ham to John de Lancaster, who in 1306 was licensed by the Crown to grant it to Stratford Abbey.[68] In 1309, after the resignation of Richard de Luthteburgh, the last individual rector, the abbey obtained the bishop of London's licence to appropriate the rectory. At the same time a vicarage was formally ordained, of which the bishop became patron.[69] The advowson remained in the hands of the bishop until 1864, when it was conveyed to Brasenose College, Oxford, the present (1966) patron, as part of an exchange scheme involving several benefices.[70]

The rectory was retained by Stratford Abbey until the Dissolution. In 1544 it was granted, along with the manor of East Ham, to Richard Breame.[71] It descended with the manor to Breame's sons Edward (d. 1558) and Arthur (d. 1602). In 1587 Arthur Breame and his son Giles conveyed the rectory to Richard Stoneley.[72] When Stoneley died in 1600 he was said to have held the reversion of the rectory, which was then in the tenure of his son-in-law William Heigham (d. 1620).[73] The rectory descended to Heigham's son Sir Richard, whose son Francis was holding it in 1650.[74] It subsequently passed to Francis's daughter Mary, wife of Robert Bendish, to her son Heigham Bendish (d. 1723) and his son Heigham Bendish (d. 1746).[75] Frances (d. 1798), widow of the younger Heigham Bendish and later wife of Dr. Richard Wilkes (d. 1760), succeeded to a life-interest in the rectory. About 1765 she sold this to Charles Hitch (d. 1781), whose widow Elizabeth carried it in marriage to her second husband David Davies, who held it until 1798.[76] On Mrs. Wilkes's death the rectory reverted to her husband's family, who appear to have sold it soon after.[77] Thomas Lewis held it in 1799–1801, Peter Firmin in 1802, and Thomas Flockton in 1811; some or all of these may have been lessees.[78] Shortly before 1814 the rectory was bought by Robert Wilson. Thomas Wilson was the impropriator in 1839,[79] and the Revd. R. F. Wilson in 1863 and 1874.[80]

In 1254 the estimated value of the rectory was £27 13s. 4d. and that of the vicarage £5.[81] In 1291 the equivalent figures were £20 and £1 13s. 4d.[82] When the vicarage was ordained in 1309 its value was substantially improved: the vicar was to have the tithes of gardens and curtilages, and all other tithes except those of corn, of hay, and of the windmill. He was also to receive £3 6s. 8d. a year from the corn tithes.[83] In 1535 the total value of the vicarage was £14 3s. 8d.[84] In 1650 the rectory was valued at £70 and the vicarage at £65.[85] About that time the vicarage was temporarily augmented by a grant of £50 from the Committee for Plundered Ministers.[86]

By 1839, when the tithes were commuted, those of the vicar were worth £1,001 and those of the impropriator only £320.[87] Between the 13th century and the 19th the vicarage of East Ham had thus been transformed from one of the poorest in Essex to one of the richest. How this had happened is not completely clear, but there are hints. In 1519, when John Grenyng was cutting down trees and brushwood at Hamfrith, in the north-west of the parish, the vicar, John Waggot, exacted a tithe-rent charge from him, and two years later, when Grenyng resisted a similar imposition, Waggot took him to court.[88] In 1632 it was stated that the vicars had long been accustomed to take tithe-rents for 'herbage or feeding' from all tenants of pasture, including

[63] *E.R.* xxvii. 61. This section is based on *Whitaker's Almanack* for the relevant years, and on the M.P.s' biographies in *Who's Who*. E.H.L. Pamphlets include a number relating to Parliamentary elections.
[64] See p. 20.
[65] For her career see *D.N.B.* 1941–50.
[66] *V.C.H. Essex*, i. 515.
[67] *E.A.T.* n.s. xviii. 17.
[68] *Cal. Close* 1272–9, 244; *Cal. Pat.* 1301–07, 482.
[69] *Reg. Baldock* (Cant. and York Soc.), 98–100, 105–6.
[70] Newcourt, *Repertorium*, ii. 301–2; *Lond. Gaz.* 12 July 1864 (pp. 3487–8).
[71] *L. & P. Hen. VIII*, xix(1), pp. 373–4.
[72] C.P. 25(2)/133/1704.
[73] C 142/166/81; Morant, *Essex*, i. 15.
[74] H. Smith, *Eccl. Hist. Essex*, 249.
[75] Morant, *Essex*, i. 15–16.

[76] Ibid.; Lysons, *London*, iv. 146; E.R.O., D/P 156/8/1–3 (rate assessments); *D.N.B.*, Ric. Wilkes.
[77] E. Ogborne, *Essex*, 31, cf. Lysons, *London*, iv. 146 and *Suppl.* (1811), 349; E.R.O., D/P 156/8/3.
[78] For the sale of the year's great tithes in 1802, see E.R.O., Libr. File, E. Ham.
[79] E.R.O., D/CT 159.
[80] *White's Dir. Essex*, 1863, p. 639; E.R.O., D/AEM 1/6 (letter 16 Nov. 1874 from Revd. S. H. Reynolds).
[81] *E.A.T.* n.s. xviii. 17.
[82] *Tax. Eccl.* (Rec. Com.), 22, 24.
[83] *Reg. Baldock*, 105–6.
[84] *Valor Eccl.* (Rec. Com.), i. 435.
[85] H. Smith, *Eccl. Hist. Essex*, 249.
[86] Ibid. 209, 212, 214.
[87] E.R.O., D/CT 159.
[88] G.L.C., DL/C/207, ff. 85, 89–90. For 'herbage' see also Newcourt, *Repertorium*, ii. 610.

gardens and orchards. These rents varied from 18d. an acre in the marshes below the parish church to 4d. an acre in the extreme north of the parish. There was also a customary rate of 2d. from each parishioner for the Easter offerings.[89] These references show that the vicars were pressing their tithe claims vigorously. The payments for 'herbage' on pasture land were the equivalent of hay tithes, which as great tithes normally belonged to a rectory, and which in East Ham had been expressly excluded from the vicar's income by the ordination of 1309. At the end of the 18th century about half the parish was pasture (mainly marsh) and another quarter market-gardens.[90] The tithe award, while it does not reveal exactly how tithes were computed, shows that those of the impropriator came mainly from arable land and those of the vicar mainly from pasture. According to a later statement the vicar also took the tithe of market-gardens.[91]

The original vicarage house of East Ham was on the north side of Vicarage Lane.[92] In 1610 it had seven rooms.[93] It was said in 1683 to need underpinning and thatching.[94] By 1699 it was again in urgent need of repair.[95] During the 18th century there were periods when the vicars did not occupy the house. Sometimes this was because they lived outside East Ham, but at least two of them, Lewis Desbordes (1728–33) and John Vade (1733–56), although resident in the parish, found the vicarage unsatisfactory, and used other houses.[96] In 1832 the vicarage was rebuilt at a cost of £2,000.[97] It continued in use until about 1900 when East Ham House, adjoining the site of the new church of St. Bartholomew, was acquired as the vicarage.[98] In 1901 the old vicarage was converted for temporary use as the Vicarage Lane council school.[99] It was later demolished.[1] East Ham House served as the vicarage until 1962 when it was converted for other church purposes, and a new vicarage was built beside it.[2]

Nicholas Gouge, by his will proved 1528, left small sums of money to the brotherhoods of the Holy Trinity and of our Blessed Lady, both attached to East Ham church.[3] No other reference to these guilds is known.

Between the 16th century and the early 19th several vicars are known to have been non-resident, including Francis Haultain (1776–1827), who appears to have visited the parish rarely during his long incumbency.[4] The names of at least fifteen assistant curates have been noted between 1556 and

1817.[5] William Fairfax, instituted in 1626, was sequestrated in 1643.[6] He was later charged with having denied the sacrament to those not coming up to the rails, and with refusing to allow a lecturer to preach on Sunday afternoon 'except he might have £50 given him for the same'.[7] Subsequent ministers during the Civil War and Interregnum included Samuel Slater (1645), John Horne (1650), John Page (1653–5), John Watson (1655), and John Clarke (1656–59 or 60).[8] In 1660, shortly after the Restoration, Edward Rust was instituted as legitimate successor to Fairfax, who had died in 1655.[9] Richard Welton, instituted in 1710, was a non-juror; he was deprived of the living in 1716.[10] In 1711–13 he was employing as curate Robert Blakeway, who proved to be a zealous Whig. The bitter hostility which arose between them continued even after Blakeway had become rector of Little Ilford.[11]

William Streatfeild (1827–60) lived in the parish, as all his successors have done; and he died in the church while preaching. During his incumbency the church was restored, the vicarage rebuilt, and church extension was started by the foundation of the new parish of Emmanuel, Forest Gate, part of which was taken from East Ham.[12] Edward F. Boyle (1860–6) built the new chapel of St. John the Baptist, and John W. Knott (1866–9) was partly responsible for planning the church of St. John, North Woolwich.[13]

Samuel H. Reynolds (1869–93), was presented by Brasenose, his own college, when East Ham was still a village, and soon found himself facing the problems of a growing suburb. He was a scholar and journalist, with no previous parochial experience, and he found the work difficult.[14] Early in his incumbency he became involved in controversy concerning the place of the old church in the life of the parish. St. Mary's was far from the town centre and was poorly attended. In 1874 Reynolds was advocating its closure and demolition against strong opposition. For some years after this he was on bad terms with the people's churchwarden, John Dennison, and other parishioners, who accused him of neglecting St. Mary's.[15] In the 1880s Reynolds was partly responsible for the building of the new churches of All Saints, Forest Gate, and St. Stephen, Upton Park. In 1891 he commissioned an architect's report on St. Mary's, but with a view to restoration, and possibly even enlargement, rather than its demolition.[16] For many years after his retirement he was remembered with affection.[17]

---

[89] G.L.C., DL/C/232: Fairfax v. Wall, 3 Apr. 1632.
[90] Lysons, *London*, iv. 138.
[91] E.R.O., Sage Coll. no. 860.
[92] Chapman and André, *Map of Essex*, 1777, sheet xxi.
[93] Newcourt, *Repertorium*, ii. 301.
[94] E.R.O., D/AEV 12, f. 1a.
[95] Ibid. D/AEV 16, 24 May 1699.
[96] Guildhall MS. 9550.
[97] *White's Dir. Essex*, 1848, p. 230; E.R.O., D/AEM 2/6; *Rep. Com. Eccl. Rev.* H.C. 54, p. 648 (1835), xxii.
[98] *Kelly's Dir. Essex*, 1898; E.H.L., E. Ham U.D.C. Map, 1901.
[99] E.H.L., *E. Ham U.D.C. Mins.* 19 Feb. 1901.
[1] E.H.L., Photos. (Houses): it had two storeys and attics.
[2] Inf. from Revd. P. J. Langford.
[3] *E.A.T.* N.S. i. 177.
[4] E.R.O., D/AEV 1 f. 3v; ibid. 16, 24 May 1699; G.L.C., DL/C/253, f. 105r–113v; Guildhall MSS. 9550, 9558, 9560; E.R.O., D/AEM 2/3.

[5] B.M., Harl. Ch. 43 I. 14; E.R.O., D/AEV 4 ff. 1r, 27r, 61r, 87v, 100r, 178r; ibid. D/AEV 29; ibid. D/AEM 2/3; G.L.C. DL/C/253, f. 105r; Guildhall MS. 9550.
[6] *E.A.T.* N.S. xvii. 25; H. Smith, *Eccl. Hist. Essex*, 111, 123.
[7] Davids, *Nonconformity in Essex*, 233.
[8] H. Smith, *Eccl. Hist. Essex*, 193, 403 (cf. index); ibid. 161, 209, 212, 335, 351.
[9] Ibid. 351.
[10] Lysons, *London*, iv. 146; *D.N.B.*
[11] R. Blakeway, *Epitome of my Sufferings as delivered to a Lady in Pall Mall* [1716].
[12] Stokes, *E. Ham*, 236.
[13] Ibid.
[14] *E.R.* vi. 69–71; *D.N.B.* He was staff leader-writer on *The Times* 1873–96.
[15] E.R.O., D/AEM 1/6 and 1/2.
[16] J. T. Micklethwaite, *Report on the Parish Church of East Ham.*
[17] Stokes, *E. Ham*, 123, 207.

The ancient parish church of *ST. MARY MAG-DALENE* stands in a large churchyard near the south end of High Street South, and consists of nave, chancel, apse, west tower, and south and west porches.[18] The walls are mainly of coursed ragstone rubble containing some flint and Roman tile. The nave, chancel, and apse were built early in the 12th century, and have been relatively little altered. The tower probably dates from the early 13th century, but has been much restored.

In the nave the west and south doorways are both of the 12th century, and two windows of the same alterations of that period include two narrow low-side windows, now blocked, pierced through the eastern and western bays on the south wall of the chancel, and on the south wall of the apse a doorway, also blocked, a window, and a large double piscina. In the apse are the faint remains of 13th-century wall-paintings. Other paintings, since obliterated, have been seen in many parts of the church during the past century.[19]

The tower also was probably built in the 13th century, and may be even older. The absence of weathering in the masonry of the west door of the

EAST HAM, CHURCH OF ST. MARY MAGDALENE

period survive, one in the north wall and another in the south wall, where there is also part of the internal head of a third, now blocked. The north wall of the chancel has a similar window, below which internally is a 12th-century intersecting wall-arcade with chevron ornament. In the same wall is a small hatch with rounded head, probably the remains of an ankar-hold. There are also 12th-century vaulting shafts in the two eastern angles of the chancel. The wall arcade on the south wall of the chancel has been cut away except for part of one bay at each end. The east and north windows of the apse and the semi-circular arch dividing apse and chancel are of the 12th century, and some of the oak roof timbers may be of the same date. Externally the apse retains two flat pilaster buttresses.

In the 13th century a recess was cut in the south wall of the nave, next to the chancel, evidently for a nave altar, since it contains a small piscina. Other

nave suggests that it is not very much earlier than the tower which shields it. In the west wall of the tower at the second stage are two tall round-headed windows, much restored. The south-eastern stair-turret contains a small lancet window, reset, probably of the 13th century. The tower was undoubtedly in existence by 1380, when the existing bell was cast.

Early in the 16th century the tower was partly rebuilt: the bell-chamber has in each wall a window dating from that period. Other early-16th-century features include a few timbers in the south porch, the external archway of the ankar-hold, and possibly the doorway to the rood-loft stair.

Early in the 17th century the roofs were altered and ceiled, a wooden cornice was placed around the nave walls, and wooden panelling in the chancel. The panelling still existed in 1921 but has since disappeared, probably as a result of the bomb

[18] Unless otherwise stated this account of the church building is based on the following sources: R.C.H.M., *Essex*, ii. 58; J. T. Micklethwaite, *Report on Parish Church of E. Ham* (1891); J. B. Carlos, *E. Ham Parish Church* (1922, 2nd edn. 1928); P. M. Johnston, *St. Mary Mag-*

dalene's Church, E. Ham (1930); M. O. Hodson, *E. Ham Parish Church* (1937).
[19] *E.A.T.* i. 72–4; ii. 102–11; *E.R.* ix. 182–5; *Arch. Jnl.* xxiii. 63–5.

damage of 1941. It was possibly in the 17th century also that the large brick south window of the chancel was inserted and the chancel arch was removed. Apart from the addition of a double-decker pulpit and box-pews, and the loss of three of the bells (described below) there seem to have been few alterations to the church in the 18th century.[20]

In 1810 the vestry decided to build a west gallery to accommodate children.[21] This was eventually done in 1820.[22] In 1830 the south porch was converted into a vestry, and a new west porch of yellow brick was built, opening into the tower.[23] A board listing the subscribers to these alterations is on the ground stage of the tower. The contribution of the new vicar, Streatfeild, included a sum for stained glass, which probably means that the two 'Decorated' windows in the south wall of the nave were then inserted, replacing earlier ones. In 1845–8 a further restoration was carried out, the main feature of which was the repair of the tower, which had been so dilapidated that its complete rebuilding was considered.[24] In 1852 two new windows were inserted into the north wall of the nave 'to correspond with the new ones on the south side'.[25]

A restoration scheme planned in 1891 was completed in 1896.[26] The west gallery was removed at this time. In 1908 the south porch reverted to its proper use, an additional floor being built in the tower to accommodate the vestry.

The church was completely restored in 1931, under the architectural direction of Philip M. Johnston. The ceilings of the apse and chancel were removed, the rood-loft stair was opened out, and the tower repaired and stripped of its external plaster. Bombing in 1941 destroyed the chancel roof and did other damage. Repairs were done in the same year, and by 1945 a permanent restoration of the nave had also been completed, which included the removal of the ceiling. A fuller restoration was carried out in 1950.[27]

The church was again restored in 1965–6, when the stonework of the tower and apse was renewed, the timbers treated, and much internal plaster replaced. During this work the piscina of the nave altar was discovered.

The stained glass in the church was destroyed in 1941.[28] The oldest piece, said to have contained the arms of the Allingtons, who were related by marriage to the Breames of East Ham Hall, was in the north-west window of the nave. In one of the south windows of the nave was glass by Henri Gerente, inserted in 1854. The white marble font was given by Sir Richard Heigham, the impropriator, in 1639. The pedestal is an addition of about 1700 and the metal cover is a memorial to the Revd.

Samuel H. Reynolds (d. 1897). The plain oak pulpit and pews were installed during the 1890s to replace the 18th-century three-decker pulpit and box-pews.[29]

An organ was provided by the vicar in 1830.[30] Another, said to have come from St. John's church, Stratford, was acquired about 1850. This was originally a barrel organ, providing 45 tunes. It was fitted with a keyboard in 1882 and continued in use until 1897, when a small positive organ was purchased.[31] The present (1966) organ was installed in 1918, as a memorial to Vincent C. Boddington, a former curate.

There is one bell, cast about 1380.[32] In 1552 the tower contained four bells, and all appear to have survived until 1782, when three of them, which were cracked, were sent for recasting to Patrick & Osborn of London.[33] In 1784, before this work had been completed, the firm failed; the bells were never replaced, and the parish received only a token payment in compensation.[34] A new bell, by C. & G. Mears, was added in 1849.[35] This has disappeared since 1909.

The church plate includes a cup of 1563 with a paten-cover of 1574, and a cup and paten-cover of 1623, given by 'Lady Joan Boles'.[36]

In the apse is a fine wall-monument, with kneeling figures, to Edmund Neville, pretender to the barony of Latimer and the earldom of Westmorland, his wife Jane (1647), and their daughter Katherine (1613).[37] They are said to have lived at Green Street House. On the north wall of the chancel is a similar monument to Giles Breame (1621), lord of the manor of East Ham. A monument to William Heigham (1620) and Anne his wife (1612), flanked by standing cherubs, is on the south wall of the nave, having been removed from the apse in 1931. There are brasses on the floor of the chancel to Hester Neave (1610) and Elizabeth Heigham (1622), and on the wall of the apse is a brass recording the charity of Robert Rampston (1585). Among later monuments are tablets in the chancel to Heigham Bendish (1723) and his son of the same name (1746), impropriators, and Ynyr Burges (1792). William Stukeley (d. 1765), the antiquary, was buried in the churchyard without a monument. He is said to have chosen the site of his grave long before, when visiting East Ham.[38]

The parish of East Ham remained unchanged until 1852, when part of it, in the north-west, was assigned to the new parish of Emmanuel, Forest Gate.[39] In 1864 a small part of East Ham was similarly assigned to the new parish of St. Mark, Victoria Docks.[40] This East Ham portion of St. Mark's was in 1877 incorporated in the new parish of St. John,

[20] For the pulpit and pews in 1894, shortly before their removal, see E.R.O., Godman Coll., Pencil drawing.
[21] E.R.O., D/P 156/8/3.
[22] Ibid. 156/8/4.
[23] Ibid.
[24] Ibid.; cf. E.R.O., Sage Coll., No. 860.
[25] E.R.O., D/P 156/8/4.
[26] E.R. vi. 70.
[27] E. Ham Vestry, etc., Mins. 1941, 1945, 1950, 1951.
[28] E.H.L., TS. Account of St. Mary's Church by Miss W. L. Holman.
[29] A. P. Crouch, Silvertown and Neighbourhood, 18; cf. Micklethwaite's Report.
[30] Inscription in tower.
[31] Stokes, East Ham, 238–9.

[32] Ch. Bells Essex, 276.
[33] E.R.O., D/P 156/8/2: 1 July 1782.
[34] Ibid. 16 Nov. 1784; ibid. 156/8/3: 22 Sept. 1786.
[35] Ch. Bells Essex, 276.
[36] Ch. Plate Essex, 4. Possibly identical with Joan, wife of Sir George Bolles (Lord Mayor of London 1617–18): G.E.C. Complete Baronetage, ii. 47.
[37] For Neville (d. 1618) see D.N.B. For the monument see F. Chancellor, Anc. Sepul. Mons. Essex, 352.
[38] Lysons, London, iv. 147–8; Stukeley's coffin was accidentally dug up in 1886: A. P. Crouch, Silvertown, 21.
[39] See p. 120.
[40] See p. 120.

North Woolwich.[41] Within East Ham parish St. Mary's remained the only place of worship until 1866, when the chapel of ease of St. John the Baptist was built.

By 1903 there were 7 parish churches, 2 other large churches, and 5 mission halls, within the urban district.[42] In spite of this expansion East Ham then had a smaller proportion of Anglican worshippers than any other place in outer London except West Ham and Wealdstone (Mdx.).[43] In outer London as a whole the percentage of Anglican worshippers was about 46 and that of nonconformists 45, but at East Ham nonconformists were 63 per cent and Anglicans only 33.[44] An attempt is made elsewhere to explain why the nonconformists were then having more success than the Anglicans.[45] The slower initial progress of the Anglicans may have been partly due to the fact that in 1890, when rapid expansion of the town was beginning, both the vicar of East Ham (S. H. Reynolds) and the rector of Little Ilford (A. T. W. Shadwell) were old,[46] and lacking in experience of urban parishes. But their successors, J. H. Ware of East Ham (1893–1907) and P. M. Bayne of Little Ilford (1894–1913)[47] were energetic and able young men who came from east London curacies. The work of Ware and Bayne, by no means completed in 1903, included careful planning for the future development of the church in their districts. Equally important as a leader of church extension was E. N. Powell, vicar of St. Stephen's, Upton Park (1891–1908), which during his incumbency became the strongest Anglican church in East Ham.

Since 1903 Anglican development in the town seems to have been better sustained than that of the nonconformists. Between 1903 and 1939, while the nonconformists did little new building and closed several churches, the Anglicans went on steadily, completing churches already started and building new ones. Two new parishes were formed in the 1920s. Since 1939 four churches have been closed. The most important changes were precipitated by the war. St. Stephen's, St. Cuthbert's, and St. Michael's, Beckton, were wrecked by bombing and and were not rebuilt. St. Stephen's parish was subsequently merged with that of St. Edmund, Forest Gate, while St. Michael's mission district was reabsorbed into the mother parish of East Ham.

The church of *ST. JOHN THE BAPTIST*, High Street North, was built in 1866 as a chapel-of-ease of St. Mary's.[48] It was a cruciform building of flint with stone dressings in a late-13th-century style. Unlike St. Mary's it was in the centre of the village, and it soon became the main focus of parochial activity.[49] In 1902, when St. Bartholomew's was built, St. John's became a church hall. It was demolished in 1925.[50] The site is now (1966) occupied by the London Co-operative Society.

The church of *ST. BARTHOLOMEW*, Barking Road, was built in 1902 to replace St. John's: £1,000 towards the cost was a legacy from Thomas Mathews, formerly chairman of East Ham local board. It is a large aisled building of red brick, designed in the Gothic style by Micklethwaite & Somers Clarke.[51] The south aisle, added in 1910, is a memorial to J. H. Ware.[52] The church was gutted by bombing in 1941. In 1942 a wooden hut, known as 'St. Bartholomew-in-the-ruins', was erected within the shell, and was used for services for the rest of the war. It was burnt down in 1947 and services were subsequently held in the vestry until 1948, when St. John's institute was taken into use as a temporary church. The south aisle of St. Bartholomew's was restored in 1949, and the remainder of the church in 1953.[53] For most practical purposes St. Bartholomew's has been the parish church of East Ham ever since it was built, though St. Mary's has retained the title.

The church of *ST. MICHAEL AND ALL ANGELS*, Beckton Road, was opened in 1883 as a mission of St. Mary's.[54] It was destroyed by fire in 1887, but was immediately rebuilt.[55] About 1906 the original iron building was replaced by a permanent church on a new site, built mainly with funds supplied by the Gas Light & Coke Co.[56] A separate mission district was formed about 1922.[57] The church was bombed in 1941 and was not rebuilt.[58] In 1952 the mission district was dissolved, its area being re-united with the parish of St. Mary, East Ham.[59]

The mission church of *ST. MARK*, Ferndale Street, Cyprus, was built about 1890, in connexion with St. Michael's, Beckton.[60] An iron hall was added in 1911 at the expense of the Gas Light & Coke Co.[61] It was closed in 1952.[62] The building was derelict in 1966.

The church of *ST. ANDREW*, Roman Road, also a mission of St. Michael's, Beckton, was built in 1934 on a site given by J. Stokes & Sons. It was closed in 1952, and in 1957 it was sold for £450, which was given to the bishop's appeal for Essex churches and schools.[63]

Two other churches which started as missions of St. Mary's later became independent. The church of *ST. PAUL*, Burges Road, in the east of the town, was built in 1907, on land given by Col. Ynyr Burges. A new parish was formed in 1924, the

[41] *Lond. Gaz.* 13 Feb. 1877 (p. 682–3).
[42] Mudie-Smith, *Relig. Life Lond.*, 357, who omits St. Mark's, Cyprus.
[43] Ibid. 442.
[44] Ibid. 447, 357–9.
[45] See p. 32.
[46] For Reynolds see *D.N B.*; for Shadwell see *E.R.* iii. 8.
[47] For Ware see Stokes, E. Ham, 274; *E.R.* xvi. 43; for Bayne see Stokes, op. cit. 277–8; *Kelly's Dir. Essex,* 1890, p. 389.
[48] Stokes, *E. Ham*, 236, illus. f. p. 272.
[49] *Churches of Barking Deaneries* (1898), 20.
[50] Stokes, *E. Ham*, 236.
[51] Cf. Pevsner, *Essex*, 166.
[52] Inscriptions on church; *E.R.* x. 237.
[53] E. Ham Vestry, etc., Mins., 1941–9; *E. Ham Par. Mag.* Oct. and Nov. 1953.

[54] *Kelly's Dir. Essex*, 1886, p. 376; Stokes, E. Ham, 275.
[55] K. Fry, *E. & W. Ham*, 262; E.H.L., E. Ham Loc. Bd. Mins. Aug. 1887.
[56] Stokes, *E. Ham*, 275; E.H.L., *E. Ham B.C. Mins.* 19 Jan. 1906; *Stratford Express* 6 Oct. 1906.
[57] *Chelmsford Dioc. Year Bk.* 1926 s.v. Duckworth, Wm.
[58] Inf. from Revd. P. J. Langford; E.H.L., Photos. (Second World War).
[59] Inf. from Revd. H. F. Godwin.
[60] E.H.L., E. Ham Loc. Bd. Mins. Nov. 1889.
[61] E.H.L., *E. Ham B.C. Mins.* 26 Sept. 1911.
[62] Inf. from Revd. H. F. Godwin; cf. Char. Com. File G. 21.
[63] Stokes, *E. Ham*, 275; *Chelmsford Dioc. Chron.* June 1934, p. 88; Char. Com. File 138473; inf. from Revd. H. F. Godwin.

advowson of the vicarage being vested, in 1932, in the bishop of Chelmsford.[64] In 1933 a new church was erected beside the original building, which became the church hall.[65] The furnishings of the church were paid for by the diocesan Girls' Friendly Society.[66]

The church of *ST. GEORGE AND ST. ETHEL-BERT*, Burford Road, originated about 1912, when a site was bought on the Greatfield Estate with money provided by the bishop of St. Albans' fund and Sir John (later Lord) Bethell. By 1914 a temporary mission hall had been erected on the corner of Boston Road and Masterman Road.[67] It remained attached to St. Mary's until 1923, when a separate parish was formed.[68] The present church was erected in 1936–7, over half the cost being met from funds raised by the diocese of Hereford.[69] The advowson of the vicarage was in 1936 vested in the bishop of Chelmsford.[70]

About 1880 the development of the Woodgrange estate at Forest Gate was met by the erection of an iron mission church, within Emmanuel parish. In 1886 this was replaced by the permanent church of *ALL SAINTS*, Romford Road, Forest Gate, to which a new parish was assigned in the same year.[71] It is a cruciform building of flint in the Early English style, with crossing turret. The advowson of the vicarage was vested in the bishop of the diocese.[72]

Farther south at Forest Gate the Red Post Lane mission district, within All Saints parish, was formed in 1895, and a temporary church was erected.[73] In 1901 a new parish was established, and the church of *ST. EDMUND, KING AND MARTYR*, was opened in Halley Road. The advowson of the vicarage was vested in the bishop of the diocese.[74] The building was completed in 1932 by the addition of the clerestory.[75] This church has a ritualistic tradition going back to its early years.[76]

At Upton Park mission services were started in 1881, in a cottage in Crescent Road. A school-church was built in 1882, in 1887 a new parish was formed from parts of the parishes of East Ham, West Ham, and St. Mary's, Plaistow; the advowson of the vicarage was vested in the bishop of St. Albans. The first part of the church of *ST. STEPHEN*, Green Street, comprising nave and north and south aisles, was also opened in 1887. In 1891 the first vicar, W. G. Trousdale, was succeeded by E. N. Powell, who developed the work vigorously. The church was completed in 1894 by the addition of

chancel, north chapel, choir, south chancel aisle, and vestries, bringing the total accommodation to 1,150.[77] Some years later it was said to be the largest church in the diocese of St. Albans.[78] St. Stephen's, like the Upton Park Primitive Methodist church, conferred upon itself the distinction of being a memorial to Elizabeth Fry. It is said to have been built largely with money subscribed by evangelical churchmen: this statement comes from a Church Association tract of 1892, which attacks Powell for introducing ritualism.[79] The tract singles out St. Stephen's, from among all the churches of the diocese, as its principal target, and it is clear from other evidence also that the parish was then regarded as a mission field of especial importance. During Powell's incumbency over £20,000 were spent on purchasing sites and erecting mission churches. At one time he had 6 curates on his staff.[80] (Canon) Charles E. Butterfield, who joined Powell as a curate in 1901, succeeded him as vicar and remained at St. Stephen's until his death in 1951.[81]

St. Stephen's was renovated in 1938, but in 1940 it was wrecked by bombing. After the war the Diocesan Reorganization Committee decided that it should not be rebuilt, and in 1953, after some local opposition, the parish was united with that of St. Edmund, Forest Gate. The remains of St. Stephen's were demolished in 1954. A bell from it was placed in the church of St. Stephen, built in 1956 to serve the new housing estate built by East Ham at Ingrave, near Brentwood.[82]

The first of the three mission churches opened in connexion with St. Stephen's was that of St. Alban, for which a separate parish was later formed (see below). Second was the church of *ST. MICHAEL*, Rutland Road, which originated in 1895, with services held in Saxby Villas, Red Post Lane (now Katherine Road). An iron church was opened in Rutland Road in 1898. A permanent church was opened on an adjoining site in 1912. This building was the subject of a notable battle between its architect, E. Douglas Hoyland, and the borough council. The design, of terracotta blocks on a steel framework, was advanced for its time, and was at first rejected by the council, but Hoyland successfully appealed to the Local Government Board, which persuaded the council to alter its building by-laws to permit this type of construction in a public building.[83] After the bombing of St. Stephen's its congregation moved to St. Michael's, which on the amalgamation of the parishes was attached to

---

[64] Stokes, *E. Ham*, 275; *Lond. Gaz.* 22 Feb. 1924 (p. 1563); ibid. 14 June 1932 (pp. 3864–5).

[65] Inf. from Revd. G. F. Raggett; *Chelmsford Dioc. Chron.* July 1933, p. 102; Aug. 1933, p. 116.

[66] *Chel. Dioc. Chron.* Dec. 1935, p. 187.

[67] E. Ham Vestry, etc., Mins. 1912–14; O.S. Map 25″, Essex LXXXVI. 6 (1920 edn.).

[68] *Lond. Gaz.* 10 July 1923 (p. 4781).

[69] Foundation stone; *Chel. Dioc. Chron.* Feb. 1936, p. 23, May 1937, p. 73.

[70] *Lond. Gaz.* 6 Nov. 1936 (p. 7093).

[71] *Chs. Barking Deaneries*, 28; Stokes, *E. Ham*, 279; *Lond. Gaz.* 20 Aug. 1886 (p. 4075).

[72] E.R.O., D/CP 6/9.

[73] *Chs. Barking Deaneries*, 28; E.H.L., E. Ham U.D.C. Mins. 19 Nov. 1895; E.H.L. Pamphlets, 'Whistland' Bazaar Programme of St. Edmund's, 1903).

[74] E.R.O., D/CP 6/11.

[75] Stokes, *E. Ham*, 279; *Lond. Gaz.* 13 Dec. 1901 (p. 8828); *Chelmsford Dioc. Chron.* June 1932, p. 96.

[76] *R. Com. Eccl. Discip.* [Cd. 3069], p. 316, H.C. (1906) xxxiii; *St. Edmund Parish News*, Oct. 1965: list of services.

[77] *Chs. Barking Deaneries*, 73; Stokes, *E. Ham*, 275–6; *Lond. Gaz.* 3 Jan. 1888 (p. 4); E.H.L., Churches File, Papers relating to St. Stephen's.

[78] *Wilson and Whitworth's West Ham Almanac*, 1910, p. 84.

[79] E.H.L., Churches File: *Ritualism Rampant in the Diocese of St. Alban's.* These papers were discovered when the church was demolished in 1954.

[80] *Crockford's Cler. Dir.* 1895, p. 1674; for Powell see *Chel. Dioc. Chron.* May 1928, p. 76.

[81] *Chel. Dioc. Chron.* Mar. 1951, p. 23.

[82] E.H.L., Churches File: Papers re St. Stephen's; inf. from Revd. A. E. Cordell; *Essex Churchman*, Mar. 1955, Mar. 1956.

[83] *E.R.* xxii. 94; inf. from Revd. E. G. H. Turner; E.H.L., *E. Ham B.C. Mins.* 1910–11, nos. 1365, 1774: 1911–12, nos. 316, 439, 1151.

St. Edmund's, Forest Gate.[84] The third mission church founded by St. Stephen's was that of *ST. CUTHBERT*, Florence Road, opened in 1902.[85] It was bombed during the Second World War and was not rebuilt. The site was sold to the borough council after the war and was used for flats.[86]

The church of *ST. ALBAN*, Upton Park, was founded about 1889, when an iron building was opened in Boleyn Road.[87] A small brick church was opened in 1897 in Wakefield Street, on the corner of Friars Road.[88] A new parish was formed in 1903[89] and in the same year the nave and aisle of the present church were completed, on the opposite side of Wakefield Street; the chancel, Lady chapel, and vestries were added in 1934.[90] It is a brick building in the Early English style with an aisled and clere-storied nave and apsidal chancel. The church was damaged by bombing in 1940; repairs were completed in 1949. Miss Mary Dalloway, who came to Upton Park in 1900, at the request of the first vicar, remained there until her death in 1932, and was largely responsible for the church's growth. For many years she had charge of a small church settlement in Victoria Avenue, and it was on her initiative that a Church Army centre was opened, about 1914, in Hartley Avenue.

The history of the ancient parish church of St. Mary the Virgin, Little Ilford, is described in another section.[91] St. Mary's remained the only church in that parish until 1894 when a mission hall was opened in Romford Road (St. Michael and All Angels). Another hall (St. Barnabas) was opened in 1897 in Browning Road, and a third (St. Mary's mission) in 1899 in Southborough (now Grantham) Road.[92] St. Barnabas's became a separate parish in 1901. St. Michael's, and St. Mary's mission, remained attached to St. Mary the Virgin. Hugh Guy (rector 1913–18) was an ineffective successor to the vigorous Bayne.[93] E. Maughan Ettrick (1918–38) was a controversial figure who in 1921 was inhibited from duty for 12 months by the bishop (confirmed on appeal to the High Court), after various charges had been brought against him.[94] In 1928 St. Michael's was formed into a separate mission district, with a priest in charge under the direction of the bishop. This arrangement continued until 1939, when, after Ettrick's death, Little Ilford parish was re-united and re-arranged: St. Michael's became the parish church, with St. Mary's as a chapel of ease.[95]

The original church of *ST. MICHAEL AND ALL ANGELS*, Romford Road, was an iron building. In 1898 this was replaced by the nave and aisles of a permanent red-brick church, designed in the Perpendicular style by Charles Spooner, to which the chancel was added in 1906.[96]

St. Mary's mission, Grantham Road, was opened in 1899, in an iron room erected to serve a crowded district in which there were no other places of worship, and where the people were said to be in danger of drifting into 'heathenism of the worst kind'. A permanent mission church was dedicated ten years later.[97]

The church of *ST. BARNABAS*, Browning Road, originated in 1897, when an iron building was opened.[98] The first part of a permanent church was opened in 1900, and it was completed in 1906 and 1909. This was one of the first churches designed by (Sir) Ninian Comper. It is of red brick in perpendicular style. A separate parish was formed in 1901, the advowson of the vicarage being vested in the bishop of the diocese.[99] Since 1946 this church has been the setting for a liturgical experiment designed to enable the congregation to participate more actively in worship. Great emphasis has been placed on parish communion, and the altar has been brought into the nave.

In 1914 part of Little Ilford was transferred to the new parish of St. Gabriel, Aldersbrook, which is treated under Wanstead.

ROMAN CATHOLICISM. During the 1580s a secret Catholic printing press was operated for a short time at Green Street, East Ham, by the Jesuit missionary Robert Parsons, possibly assisted by members of the More family, one of whom, the wife of Thomas More, was presented for recusancy in 1582, along with another resident of the parish.[1] Lady Kempe, lady of the manor of East Ham, is included in a list, drawn up in 1643, of those whose lands were sequestrated by Parliament: she was said to be a Papist delinquent.[2] Another Roman Catholic landowner was Richard Langhorne (d. 1719).[3] A return of Essex papists drawn up in 1767 mentions under East Ham only the migrant Irish who visited the parish during the potato season, but in 1778 there were said to be 7 Roman Catholic families (presumably resident) in the parish.[4]

The Catholic industrial school, Manor Park, opened in 1868, contained the chapel of *ST. NICHOLAS*, Gladding Road, which was open to the public.[5] The church of St. Peter and St. Paul, Ilford, opened in 1899, included within its parish the northern part of East Ham.[6] The chapel of St. Nicholas was subsequently attached to Ilford until 1918, when it became the church of the

84 E.H.L., Churches File: Papers re St. Stephen's.
85 Stokes, *E. Ham*, 276–7.
86 Inf. from Revd. E. G. H. Turner.
87 Unless otherwise stated this account is based on: E. J. Chambers, *Hist. St. Alban's, Upton Park* (1953); for the Boleyn Rd. church see E.H.L., E. Ham Loc. Bd. Mins. June 1889.
88 Stokes, *E. Ham*, 276; E. Ham U.D.C. Map, 1901: this building still survives (1965) though no longer used for church purposes.
89 *Lond. Gaz.* 13 Oct. 1903 (p. 6222).
90 *Chelmsford Dioc. Chron.* Dec. 1934.
91 See p. 171.
92 Stokes, *E. Ham*, 278–9; *E.R.* vii. 4, 72; *Churches of Barking Deaneries*, 65.
93 W. J. Brown, *One Man's Life*, 25–30.
94 *The Times*, 4 Dec. 1920, 15 and 16 Apr. 1921.

95 *Chel. Dioc. Year Bks.* 1928–39; E.R.O., D/CP 9/14; inf. from the Rector of Little Ilford.
96 Pevsner, *Essex*, 166.
97 *Little Ilford Par. Mag.* May 1899; Stokes, *E. Ham*, 279.
98 *E.R.* vi. 131; *Hist. St. Barnabas, Little Ilford*; Stokes, *E. Ham*, 278–9; *Lond. Gaz.* 15 Mar. 1901 (p. 1846); E.H.L., *E. Ham B.C. Mins.* 12 June 1906, 26 Jan. 1909; *Essex Churchman*, Dec. 1962, Mar. 1964.
99 E.R.O., D/CP 9/12.
1 *Essex Recusant*, i. 68; E.R.O., Q/SR 79/100.
2 B.M., Add. MS. 5505, f. 44a.
3 J. Cosin, *Names of Roman Catholics . . . who refused to take the oaths . . . in 1715*, 30; J. O. Payne, *Records of English Catholics of 1715*, 16; E.R.O., Q/RRp 1/46.
4 *Essex Recusant*, i. 36; Guildhall, MS. 9558, f. 169.
5 *Kelly's Dir. Essex*, 1882.
6 Stokes, *E. Ham*, 288.

new parish of Manor Park.[7] The church of *ST. STEPHEN*, Church Road, was built in 1924 as a chapel to St. Nicholas. It was rebuilt in 1959 and then became the parish church, with St. Nicholas as its chapel.[8]

A Catholic chapel at Boleyn Castle, East Ham, was registered for public worship in 1901.[9] This was attached to St. Edward's industrial school, opened in 1870. In 1906, when St. Edward's was closed, services were transferred to the new Catholic elementary school in Castle Street, where they were held until the opening, in 1911, of the present church of *OUR LADY OF COMPASSION*, Green Street, adjoining the school, for the new parish of Upton Park.[10]

The eastern part of East Ham was served from Barking until 1926, when the church of *ST. MICHAEL*, also used as a day school, was built in Tilbury Road. A larger school was built in 1931 and the original building was then used only as the church. A new church was opened in 1959.[11]

The church of *OUR LADY AND ST. ED-WARD*, Silvertown, was opened in Bailey Street in 1887, and completed in 1892. The original building was in West Ham, though the adjoining school was in East Ham. In 1915, when the site of the church and school was taken over for the building of the King George V Dock, a temporary church was erected in Newland Street, East Ham. This was replaced by a permanent church in 1921.[12]

PROTESTANT NONCONFORMITY. There are occasional references to nonconformists in East Ham from the 17th century onwards, but no permanent congregation appears to have been formed before the 1870s. In 1615 a man and his wife were presented in the archdeacon's court for refusing to attend the parish church, and for holding a conventicle in their home; they were suspected of being Brownists.[13] In 1665 members of a conventicle meeting in the house of William Williams of East Ham, gentleman, were fined by the Stratford magistrates.[14] These dissenters came from London, Stepney, Barking, Dagenham, and Hornchurch, as well as East Ham. Most of them were craftsmen, with such occupations as bricklayer, wheelwright, weaver, tanner, and blacksmith. This was almost certainly a Quaker meeting, since several of its members can be identified as Friends, from presentments of the 1670s and 1680s.[15] There was said to be one Quaker family in the parish in 1766, and two were reported in 1790.[16] A dissenters' meeting-house appears to have existed in 1778, but had closed by 1790.[17] In 1802 and 1808 Baptist meetings were registered, in 1811 an Independent meeting,

and in 1823 two meetings whose denomination is not stated: all these were in private houses.[18]

No nonconformist meeting was returned for East Ham at the Parliamentary inquiry of 1829 or the religious census of 1851. Apart from the small mission hall in Greenhill Grove, Little Ilford,[19] the first permanent nonconformist churches seem to have been those of the Primitive Methodists at North Woolwich, the Wesleyans in Market Street (later in Barking Road), the Free Methodists at Manor Park, and the London City Mission in Plashet Lane (Grangewood Street), all of which were founded about 1870. By 1903 there were at least 37 nonconformist churches in the urban district, with Sunday congregations totalling 13,346.[20] At that time East Ham had a higher percentage [64] of nonconformists among its worshippers than any other place in outer London.[21] The reason for this was probably that the phenomenal growth of the town during the 1890s focused upon it the attention of all the denominations at a time when they were becoming well geared to Metropolitan church extension, through central agencies with special funds.

The high priority enjoyed by East Ham as a home mission field is shown, just after 1903, by the building of the Wesleyan central hall, one of the largest of its kind in England, at a cost of £26,000. The size of the congregations attracted to the hall before the First World War demonstrates the popularity of nonconformity in East Ham at that period, but this is also proved by the proliferation of small churches, using iron buildings or private houses. Little more than four walls and a roof was needed to start a church, and occasionally even less might suffice: in one case the archway between two houses was fitted up as a temporary Primitive Methodist chapel.

In hurrying to form new churches the denominations competed against each other, even when conditions favoured collaboration. This caused comment at the time. In 1894 the Primitive Methodist Richard Blair, one of East Ham's most successful evangelists, discussing free church activity at Manor Park, wrote: 'There has been a good deal of overlapping . . . it is a great pity that some of us are not in some other district needing us more.'[22] The pressure of competition led some congregations to erect buildings larger than they could afford, in the hope of future growth that did not materialize. Thus the Congregational church in High Street North, Manor Park, opened new buildings in 1904 with a debt of over £5,000, and by 1907 was facing ruin. This church was less than ½ mile from another of the same denomination and at least eight others of different denominations.

The preponderance of nonconformists over the Anglicans in 1903 was not achieved merely by more numerous buildings. The free church congregations,

---

[7] Stokes, *E. Ham*, 288; Worship Reg. 47359.
[8] Inf. from Canon V. Hurley.
[9] Worship Reg. 38556.
[10] Ibid. 41511, 44835; Stokes, *E. Ham*, 288; inf. from Revd. J. W. Hayes.
[11] Inf. from Revd. D. Petry.
[12] Inf. from Revd. J. Harding; *Kelly's Dir. Essex*, 1890, p. 313; Worship Reg. 30648, 34443, 46616, 48477; for the original site see E.H.L., East Ham U.D.C. Map, 1901; *Wilson and Whitworth's West Ham Almanack*, 1910, p. 98.
[13] Hale, *Precedents and Proceedings in Ecclesiastical Courts*, p. 238.
[14] E.R.O., Q/SR 405/11, 406/26 and 111.

[15] E.R.O., D/AEV 11, f. 3v; ibid. 4, ff. 1v–2r; *E.R.* lvii. 62, 63, 69. For an early Quaker meeting at 'Ham' see below, p. 131.
[16] Guildhall MS. 9558, f. 169.
[17] Ibid.
[18] G.R.O., Rtns. Noncf. Mtg. Hos. Cert. to Bps. Cts. before 1852, Nos. 562, 710, 871, 1337, 1366.
[19] See p. 173.
[20] R. Mudie-Smith, *Religious Life of London*, 357–9.
[21] Ibid. 359, cf. 444. In calculating this percentage 'other services' have been included in the nonconformist total.
[22] R. S. Blair, *Nailing Up the Old Barn (Chapel) door*, 68.

as computed by Mudie-Smith, were on average slightly the larger, and they also had three out of the four churches with total attendances for the day of over 1,000, and eight out of the fourteen with over 500.[23] The Wesleyans were the strongest body, followed by the Baptists, Congregationalists, Free Methodists, Primitive Methodists, and Presbyterians: these bodies between them had over 60 per cent of the nonconformist churches and 90 per cent of their worshippers. No exact attendance figures are available after 1903. Free church activity, as reflected in membership figures, seems to have been fairly well maintained until the 1930s, but since then has fallen greatly, especially in the larger churches. There has been little new building since 1903, and some churches have been closed. While the total number of nonconformist places of worship is not much lower than in 1903 the older bodies are much weaker, both in numbers of buildings and in membership. The Congregationalists, for example, who in 1900 had four churches and 807 members, in 1966 had three churches and 107 members.[24]

The following accounts of individual churches were compiled in 1965.

Baptists. New Beckton church, Beaconsfield Street, an iron building, was erected in 1888.[25]

Little Ilford Tabernacle, Sheringham Avenue, Manor Park, was founded in 1889, in White Post Lane (now High Street North).[26] In 1895 an iron building was erected in Salisbury Road. This was burnt down in 1897, but re-erected in the same year. In 1900 the congregation moved to Little Ilford Lane, still using an iron building. A permanent church was built in 1905. In 1957 a new hall, mainly for youth work, was added. This contains a large mural painting, completed in 1961, depicting 'Pilgrim's Progress'.

Manor Park Tabernacle, High Street North, was also founded in 1889.[27] It met first in a room in Carlyle Road, and later in the 'Gospel Shop', Romford Road (1890–93), and the former Congregational church in Greenhill Grove (1893–8). In 1898 an iron building was erected in High Street North, and in 1906 the present (1965) church was opened. The iron building was replaced in 1925 by a permanent Sunday school. For most of its history the church has had a settled minister.

Plashet Grove church, known at first as East Ham Tabernacle, originated about 1895 in services promoted by the London Baptist Association.[28] An iron building was erected on the corner of Katherine Road and Victoria Avenue, and was used until 1901, when the Plashet Grove church was completed. This is an aisled building of dark red brick, seating

1,000. In its early years it was one of the strongest nonconformist churches in East Ham, with a total attendance, on one Sunday in 1903, of 972.

Grantham gospel mission, Church Road, Manor Park, was founded in 1900 by F. Tite, a coal merchant, who erected an iron building in Southborough (now Grantham) Road.[29] In 1934 a new hall was built, on the corner of Church Road and Walton Road, and in 1959 a Sunday school was added. The honorary superintendents of the mission, all laymen, included Sydney P. Giller, who served from 1913 to 1946. From its early days the mission, though undenominational, had support from local Baptists, and in 1963 it joined the Baptist Union.

Bonny Downs church, Flanders Road,[30] originated in a Sunday school, held in the open air and later in a private house by Charles W. Howe, a young Baptist who had first visited the Bonny Downs district to distribute Spurgeon's tracts.[31] In 1908 he rented an empty shop on the corner of Bonny Downs Road (now Darwell Close) and Flanders Road, a free church was formed, and he became pastor. The present church was built in 1928. It joined the Baptist Union in 1946.

Strict Baptists. Hope church, Stafford Road, originally called Ebenezer, was founded in 1889 at Ferndale Road, Forest Gate, by two London ministers, F. C. Holden of Limehouse, and John Box of Soho.[32] In 1902 two rooms in Red Post Lane (now Katherine Road) were registered for worship, and these were used until 1906, when Hope was opened. A primary school hall was built in 1939, to which an upper storey with three classrooms was added in 1950.

Rehoboth church, High Street North, Manor Park, was built in 1907.[33] The congregation, which traced its origin back to 1830, had moved in 1905 from Rehoboth, Wellesley Street, Stepney (Lond.) to temporary rooms in Romford Road, Manor Park. The cost of the High Street church was met mainly by invested funds obtained by the sale, in 1874, of a previous building owned by the congregation. The move took place during the ministry (1895–1915) of Jabez Parnell. A new schoolroom was added in 1928. The present membership is 20.

Zion church, 764 Romford Road, Manor Park, was registered for worship in 1916.[34] It appears to have ceased by 1922.

Brethren. In 1903 a group of Brethren were meeting in the Recreation Hall, Romford Road (corner of Salisbury Road).[35] The Assembly Hall, Barking Road, was registered for worship from 1907 to 1940.[36] Milton Hall, Milton Avenue, was registered

[23] Mudie-Smith, *Relig. Life Lond.* 357–9.

[24] *Congr. Year Bk.* 1966.

[25] E.H.L., E. Ham Loc. Bd. Mins. Feb. 1888; Worship Reg. 27402.

[26] W. T. Whitley, *Baptists of London*, 237; inf. from Mr. N. A. Barwick; Worship Reg. 34090, 35110, 41060; E.H.L., *E. Ham U.D.C. Mins.* 5 Nov. 1895, 6 Apr., 18 May, 1 June, 1 Sept., 1897; E.H.L., E. Ham U.D.C. Map, 1901; *Kelly's Dir. Essex*, 1902. In its early years this church was called Manor Park Tabernacle, but it is distinct from the later church of that name.

[27] Following account from Mr. D. H. Nicholls.

[28] Whitley, *Baptists of London*, 245; E.H.L., E. Ham U.D.C. Mins. 15 June 1895, 9 June 1896; Worship Reg. 37610, 38401; Mudie-Smith, *Relig. Life Lond.* 357; foundation stone of church.

[29] *Grantham Gospel Mission* (1900–60); inf. from Mr. H. J. Payne.

[30] Account from Mrs. F. Dobson, ch. sec.

[31] An undenominational mission band had registered a meeting in Bonny Downs Road in 1903: G.R.O., Worship Reg. 39905.

[32] Whitley, *Baptists of London*, 237; Worship Reg. 39028, 42460; inf. from Mr. A. J. Rayner.

[33] *Looking Back: Rehoboth 1830–1930*; Whitley, *Baptists of London*, 159; inf. from Mr. F. E. Cornelius.

[34] Worship Reg. 46866; *Kelly's Dir. Essex*, 1917, cf. 1922.

[35] R. Mudie-Smith, *Religious Life of London*, 358; for the address of the Recreation Hall cf. *Kelly's Dir. Essex*, 1906.

[36] Worship Reg. 42840.

by Open Brethren from 1911 to 1953.[37] Gainsborough Hall, Gainsborough Avenue, was built about 1907. It was registered by 'Christians' in 1937, and in 1960 was re-registered by Brethren in a new building.[38]

Congregationalists. The village Congregational church, which existed in Greenhill Grove from the 1860s, has been treated under Little Ilford.[39] It was the predecessor of a larger, suburban church. E. T. Egg, well known for his church extension activities in south-west Essex, became temporary pastor at Greenhill Grove in 1886, remaining until 1890, when the congregation erected a lecture hall in Manor Park Road, and moved there.[40] H. D. Bull became the first settled minister in 1891. In 1895 a church was erected in Manor Park Road,[41] but it did not prosper: it was heavily mortgaged, its membership fell from 157 in 1899 to 90 in 1911, and it closed about 1914. This early decline may have been due in part to its back street position.

Plashet Park church, Chester Road, was founded in 1884, in a room in Crescent Road.[42] Meetings were subsequently held in the public hall, Green Street, from 1884 until 1887, when a two-storeyed building (later used for classrooms) was erected in Chester Road, during the temporary pastorate of E. T. Egg. An iron building was added in 1890, a permanent church in 1895, and an institute in 1914. In 1925 the iron hall was gutted by fire. Its site was sold to the borough council for a chest clinic, and in 1926 a new hall, fronting on Katherine Road, was opened. In 1941 the church was badly damaged by bombing. It was reconstructed and re-opened in 1952. For most of its history the church has had a settled minister. In its earlier years it was one of the stronger nonconformist churches in the district,[43] and it was still flourishing in the 1920s, with a membership of over 300, and a Sunday school of 600.[44] In 1965 the membership was about 60. The institute (1914) and hall (1926) were then on lease to the National Assistance Board.

Wakefield Street church originated in 1886, when S. W. Patmore opened a mission in the Holme Road Assembly Room.[45] In 1890 this work was taken over by the London Congregational Union, which erected an iron church in Stamford Road, with E. T. Egg as temporary pastor. In 1897 H. G. Brown became the first settled minister, and in 1901 a brick church, seating 800, was opened in Wakefield Street. In 1903 this was the strongest Congregational church in East Ham.[46] A Sunday school was built in 1911, when the church membership was 215.[47] In 1940 the church was destroyed by

bombing, and from 1941 to 1945 the congregation worshipped in East Avenue Presbyterian church.[48] The Sunday school, fronting on Myrtle Road, survived, and was later used for worship until 1957, when the church was rebuilt. By 1965 the active membership had fallen to about 20, but in that year the church was able to appoint the Revd. Phyllis Davies as minister.

Manor Park (formerly Little Ilford) church, High Street North, was formed in 1897, when an iron building was opened in Coleridge Avenue, with A. G. Prichard as minister.[49] In 1904 a new church, seating 750, with adjoining hall, was opened in High Street North on the corner of Strone Road. In building these premises the congregation incurred a debt of over £5,500, and by 1907, when Prichard was succeeded by George Packer (1907–12) they were 'diminished and ready to perish'.[50] Packer's energetic leadership, with financial help from the London Congregational Union and other benefactors, saved the church, though at the cost of the minister's health.[51] By 1911 there were 114 members and a Sunday school of 432. In 1966 the equivalent figures were 24 and 45.

Sibley Grove (Welsh Congregational) church was formed in 1901 by the King's Cross (Lond.) Congregational church.[52] In 1945 the iron building was sold to the London Welsh Methodist circuit.

Free Church of England and Reformed Episcopal Church. St. Saviour's church, Carlyle Road, was built in 1894–5, possibly to replace an iron church erected in the same road about two years before.[53] It was one of the two Reformed Episcopal churches said in 1894 to exist at Manor Park. Christ Church, Carlyle Road, registered in 1903, and given a new façade in the same year, was probably identical with St. Saviour's, or was its successor; it survived until 1905, when its premises were taken over by the Salvation Army.[54]

A Reformed Episcopal church next door to the Primitive Methodist church in Romford Road is mentioned in 1894; it was a 'split' from another, presumably that in Carlyle Road.[55] It may have been the forerunner of the next.

St. Stephen's church, Shrewsbury Road (corner of Strone Road), an iron building, was erected in 1897 and seems to have survived until 1909, when its premises were taken over by Spiritualists.[56]

Methodists. The three Methodist connexions which united in 1932 had a total of 11 churches in East Ham. These are listed under their pre-1932 groupings. Immediately after 1932 there was a

---

[37] Worship Reg. 44690.
[38] E.H.L., *E. Ham B.C. Mins.* 23 Apr., 1907; Worship Reg. 57589, 67791; personal observation.
[39] See p. 173.
[40] *Cong. Year Bks.* 1886–1915; *Kelly's Dir. Essex*, 1890; Worship Reg. 32150; E.H.L., E. Ham Loc. Bd. Mins. Oct., 1889; Char. Com. file 93591.
[41] Foundation stone of this building.
[42] *Cong. Year Bk.* 1890, p. 224; Plashet Cong. Ch., *Jubilee* (1934); *The New Entrance* (1952); *75th Anniversary* (1959); inf. from Mrs. A. R. Emery.
[43] Mudie-Smith, *Relig. Life Lond.* 357.
[44] *Cong. Year Bk.* 1925.
[45] Wakefield St. Cong. Ch., *Jubilee Handbks.* 1936; Stokes, *E. Ham*, 284.
[46] Mudie-Smith, *Relig. Life Lond.* 357.
[47] *Cong. Year Bk.* 1911.

[48] See p. 37.
[49] Worship Reg. 36105; *Cong. Year Bk.* 1898 f.; E.H.L., *E. Ham U.D.C. Mins.* 1 June, 20 July 1897.
[50] E.H.L., Churches File, Little Ilford Cong. Ch., *Bazaar Prog.* 9–11 Dec. 1909.
[51] *Cong. Year Bk.* 1914, p. 191 (obit. of Packer).
[52] Inf. from Revd. E. W. Blainey.
[53] E.H.L., E. Ham Loc. Bd. Mins. Sept. 1894, cf. Oct. 1892; Worship Reg. 34771; R. S. Blair, *Nailing Up*, 68.
[54] Worship Reg. 39782, cf. 41368; E.H.L., *E. Ham U.D.C. Mins.* 20 May, 17 June 1903; *East and West Ham Year Bk.* 1905, p. 83.
[55] Blair, op. cit. 68.
[56] Worship Reg. 36155, cf. 43925; E.H.L., E. Ham U.D.C. Mins. 16 Feb. 1897; *Kelly's Dir. Essex*, 1906, 1908; Mudie-Smith, *Relig. Life Lond.* 358.

strong movement towards local amalgamation, which was largely successful, though long resisted in at least one case. In 1965 the Methodist churches in the borough lay in three circuits: the London Mission (East Ham) (three churches), the Leytonstone and Forest Gate circuit (two), and the London Welsh circuit (one). In the following accounts the letters (W), (P), and (U) denote ex-Wesleyan, ex-Primitive, and ex-United Methodist churches.

East Ham (W) central hall, Barking Road, can trace its origin back to about 1870, when an iron church was erected in Kelly Road (now Market Street).[57] In 1880 a brick church was built in Barking Road. It was in the Barking circuit.[58] In 1904 the London Mission (East Ham) was formed with John E. Wakerley as superintendent. Services were started in the town hall, and plans made for a central hall on the site of the old church and on additional land bought for the purpose.[59] The central hall, seating over 2,000, was opened in 1906, at a cost of £26,000. It was designed by Gunton & Gunton in a 'Queen Anne' style of red brick with stone dressings, its most striking feature being a domed tower.[60] The church had great success in its early days.[61] In 1911 it was said to be crowded out, with the largest Sunday morning congregation in Methodism, while the Men's Brotherhood numbered nearly 3,000, and the Sunday school 1,700.[62] In 1967, when the membership of the hall was 337, social work, especially among old people, continued to be an important part of the church's activity.[63] The hall was demolished in 1969.

Upton Park (W) church, Green Street, was opened in 1882, in the Canning Town circuit.[64] A larger church was erected in 1893–4, the original building becoming the church hall. An extension was built in 1899–1900. In 1904 the membership was 261. The Upton Manor circuit was formed in 1907. Upton Park was transferred in 1926 to the Stratford circuit, and in 1930 to the Leytonstone and Forest Gate circuit, in which it has since remained. There were 68 members in 1962.[65]

Manor Park (W) church, Romford Road, originated in 1890, when Wesleyans from Forest Gate (Stratford circuit) first held services at Durham Cross, Manor Park.[66] Soon after, a site was acquired, and an iron building was erected in Romford Road, nearly opposite the United Methodist Free church in Herbert Road.[67] A large brick church was opened in 1900.[68] By 1903 the Wesleyan congregation was almost three times that of Herbert Road.[69] A school was added in 1907. Manor Park was included in the Leytonstone and Forest Gate circuit, formed in 1930.[70] In 1934 the Romford Road society amalgamated with that in Herbert Road. The Romford Road building continued in use for week-night activities until about 1937, when it was sold.[71]

Abbots Park (W) church, Arragon Road (Canning Town circuit), seems to have been erected in 1891–2 to serve the new Abbots Park housing estate.[72] It was closed in 1904, having no doubt become redundant with the opening of the services culminating in the building of the central hall.[73] The iron building was acquired by the Anglicans in 1905 and re-erected in Norman Road as a Sunday school for St. Mary's church.[74]

The growth of Primitive Methodism in East Ham was largely due to the remarkable efforts of one of their ministers, Richard S. Blair, who described his work in two books.[75] He was superintendent successively of the 8th London, 13th London (Canning Town), and Upton Park circuits. He worked at East Ham from about 1880 until his retirement in 1904.[76]

North Woolwich (P) church, Elizabeth (now Woodman) Street, originated about 1867.[77] Services were held in a cottage, then in a shop, and later in an archway between two houses, ingeniously fitted up by R. S. Blair, then superintendent of the 8th London circuit. In 1880 a brick church was built in Elizabeth Street (corner of Storey Street). From 1881 it was in the 13th London (Canning Town) circuit. The church was destroyed by bombing in the Second World War, and was not rebuilt.

High Street South (P) church originated in 1872, when A. G. Batten, a workman at Beckton Gas works, first held services in a house in Mountfield Road.[78] He maintained this work single-handed until 1877, when he invited the Primitive Methodists of the 8th London circuit to supply preachers. In 1880 R. S. Blair erected a temporary church in High Street South. A permanent brick building was opened in 1885. In 1881 the church was included in the 13th London (Canning Town) circuit. In 1895, when its membership was 57, it became part of the West Ham circuit.[79] It was transferred to the London Mission (East Ham) in 1945. A new youth hall was built in 1948, and in 1958 the church was renovated and new schoolrooms added. The present (1965) membership is 152.[80]

Beckton (P) church, Winsor Terrace, originated about 1875, in cottage services held by Mr. and Mrs. Fursey. Missioners from the Canning Town circuit later opened a Sunday school.[81] By 1901 the society was occupying its present building, which had been

[57] Stokes, E. Ham, 282–3.
[58] Wesleyan Chapel Ctee. Reps. 1880, 1881; Kelly's Dir. Lond. 1902, p. 3048.
[59] Mins. Wes. Conf. 1904; Grace Backus, E. Ham Meth. Mission, Central Hall, 1904–54.
[60] Meth. Recorder 5 Mar., 26 Oct., 2 Nov. 1905.
[61] Pevsner, Essex, 166.
[62] Meth. Recorder 9 Nov. 1911.
[63] Inf. from Revd. E. W. Tansley.
[64] Wes. Chapel Ctee. Reps. 1884, 1892–4, 1899, 1901; foundation stones; H.R.M.C., Mins. Q.M. Canning Town (later Upton Manor) circuit; Mins. Wes. Conf. 1930.
[65] Leytonstone and Forest Gate Circuit Plan, Apr.–June 1962.
[66] Meth. Recorder, 29 Oct. 1908; Worship Reg. 32281.
[67] Free Methodist, 6 Feb. 1890; E.H.L., E. Ham Loc. Bd. Mins. Feb. 1891.
[68] Worship Reg. 37554; Wes. Chap. Ctee. Reps. 1899, 1901.
[69] Mudie-Smith, Relig. Life Lond. 358.

[70] Mins. Wes. Conf. 1930.
[71] Manor Park Meth. Ch., Home Messenger, Aug. 1934 f.
[72] E.H.L., E. Ham Loc. Bd. Mins. Dec. 1891; E.H.L., E. Ham U.D.C. Survey Map, 1901.
[73] H.R.M.C., Mins. Q.M. Canning Town circuit, 1904; cf. Mudie-Smith, Relig. Life Lond. 358; Kelly's Dir. Lond. 1902, p. 3048; Char. Com. Files 85670 and G. 21.
[74] E.R.O., D/P 156/6/3.
[75] Reaching the Masses (1886) and Nailing Up the Old Barn (Chapel) Door (1894).
[76] E. and W. Ham Year Bk. 1905, p. 91, records his retirement.
[77] Blair, Reaching the Masses, 64–8; Nailing Up, 49; inf. from E. Ham Boro. Co.
[78] Blair, Nailing Up, 47–8; Stokes, E. Ham, 280.
[79] Mins. P.M. Conf. 1881 f.; H.R.M.C., W. Ham P.M. Circuit Steward's Bk. 1895–1918.
[80] Inf. from Revd. B. A. Morris.
[81] Blair, Reaching the Masses, 19–22.

erected by the Gas Light & Coke Co. as a school, and which now (1965) belongs to the North Thames Gas Board.[82] The church has been in the London Mission (East Ham) since 1940 or earlier.[83]

Elizabeth Fry Memorial (P) church, Plashet Grove, was R. S. Blair's most notable achievement in East Ham.[84] In 1884, while still superintendent of the Canning Town circuit, he started services at Upton Park, where building development was in progress on an estate formerly belonging to the Fry family. In 1886 he secured Conference's approval for an ambitious programme of evangelism, and in the same year the Upton Park circuit was formed, at first without members or officers except for Blair himself, as superintendent. He had already bought a site for a church and manse, in Plashet Grove. The manse, called Newgate Villa in allusion to Elizabeth Fry's prison work, was built in the same year, and was used for services until 1889, when the church with hall and schools beneath, designed by William Dartnall, was opened. Vestries and church parlour were added in 1891. By 1893 the Upton Park circuit returned 103 members and three preaching stations. After the Methodist union of 1932 the circuits in this area were reorganized and some churches were closed: among these was Elizabeth Fry Memorial, which was sold in 1934 to the Assemblies of God.[85]

Manor Park (P) church, Sixth Avenue, originated in 1885, when R. S. Blair bought a site on the corner with Romford Road.[86] Mission work was launched in 1886, and an iron building erected. Progress was slow at first, but in 1901 a permanent brick church was opened.[87] Sixth Avenue, originally in the Canning Town circuit, was in the Upton Park circuit from the 1890s until about 1934, when it was transferred to the Leytonstone and Forest Gate circuit as part of a scheme for uniting all three Methodist churches at Manor Park. Sixth Avenue was for long reluctant to accept amalgamation, but eventually did so in 1963, when its members joined those at Herbert Road.[88] Its buildings were sold to the Anglicans of Little Ilford parish.

Boleyn Road (P) hall was founded by J. C. Page, about 1886, as an undenominational mission for the poor district then called Morley's Corner.[89] In 1893 he sold it to the Primitive Methodists of the Upton Park circuit. They were still using it in 1907, but had apparently ceased to do so by 1923. The building later became the Latimer Hall chapel.[90]

Katherine Road (P) church was an iron building, erected in 1903. It still existed in 1912.[91]

The United Methodist churches of East Ham were all originally part of the Forest Gate circuit.

Those founded before 1907 belonged to the United Methodist Free Church.

Manor Park (U) church, Herbert Road, was founded about 1870, when Free Methodists from Field Road church, Forest Gate, held services in a disused beer shop in Greenhill Grove and later in a skittle alley.[92] In 1880 a building was erected in Herbert Road (corner of Romford Road), but this was soon overcrowded, and a larger church was built in 1891.[93] In 1934, after Methodist union, Herbert Road was joined by the members of the Romford Road (W) church, as a society of the Leytonstone and Forest Gate circuit, after which the Romford Road buildings were sold, and the proceeds used to build a new Sunday school and institute on the Herbert Road site.[94] Herbert Road was rebuilt in 1964 with funds raised by the sale of the Sixth Avenue (P) church.[95]

Tennyson Avenue (U) church originated about 1894, when the plans for a school-chapel were approved by the local board. It was extended in 1899–1900, and additions were made to the hall in 1909. In 1947 it was transferred from the Forest Gate circuit to the East Ham mission, and it was closed about 1948.[96]

Katherine Road (U) church was opened in 1907, as part of a scheme by which the old church in Bridge Road, Stratford (in West Ham), was closed and its activities were transferred to the expanding suburb of Forest Gate.[97] Katherine Road, which seated 1,150, was well filled in its first year. It developed a strong men's Brotherhood, and three of its members became Methodist ministers. It was damaged by bombing in 1941. In 1947, when the Forest Gate circuit was split up, Katherine Road went into the London Mission (East Ham). In 1957 it was closed and its members joined those of four other Methodist churches in the new building in Woodgrange Road (West Ham).[98] The Katherine Road church (corner of Sandringham Road) was demolished and the site covered with flats.

Sibley Road Welsh Methodist church was formed in 1945, when the London Welsh Methodist circuit took over the iron building previously used by the Welsh Congregationalists.[99] Some of those who then joined Sibley Road had previously been members of the Welsh Methodist church in Cumberland Road, Plaistow, West Ham.

Presbyterians. Trinity church, East Avenue, Manor Park, originated in the 1890s, when Alexander Thompson, a Scotsman who had previously worshipped at Plashet Park Congregational church, began to hold Presbyterian meetings at his house in

[82] Inf. from Revd. B. A. Morris; cf. Mudie-Smith, *Relig. Life Lond.* 358: 'Gas Works Hall'; for the school see p. 39.
[83] *Methodist Census*, 1940.
[84] Blair, *Nailing Up*, 56 f.
[85] *E. Ham Official Guide*, 1951–2 edn., p. 30; E. Barrett, *The Lamp Still Burns*, 58–9.
[86] Blair, *Nailing Up*, 68.
[87] Foundation stone.
[88] See below.
[89] Blair, *Nailing Up*, 97; Worship Reg. 29732; ibid. 42246 (canc. 1923); E.H.L., E. Ham. Loc. Bd. Mins. Aug. 1886.
[90] See below, p. 37.
[91] Mudie-Smith, *Relig. Life Lond.* 358; E.H.L., *E. Ham U.D.C. Mins.* 18 Nov. 1903; *Kelly's Dir. Essex*, 1908; *Stratford Express*, 30 Mar. 1912.

[92] G. Triggs, *Seventeen Years at the Police Courts*, 19.
[93] *Manor Park Meth. Ch.* 1891–1964.
[94] E.H.L., Churches File, Manor Park Meth. Ch., *Home Messenger*, Jan. 1934–Oct. 1937; ibid. *Souvenir Prog. Opening of New Sch. and Inst.* Sept. 1937.
[95] Inf. from Revd. J. H. Porter; E.H.L., Pictorial Coll., Photos of Manor Park Meth. Chs. (old and new), 1964. See plate below, f. p. 203.
[96] E.H.L., E. Ham Loc. Bd. Mins. Apr. and May 1894; *U.D.C. Mins* 18 July 1899, 4 Sept. 1900; *B.C. Mins.* 14 Dec. 1909; *Educ. Ctee. Mins.* 1947–9, p. 272; E. Barrett, *The Lamp Still Burns*, 50.
[97] Forest Gate Meth. Ch., *Fling Wide the Gates*, 5–6; H.R.M.C., *Forest Gate U.M. Circuit Plan*, 1911; Worship Reg. 42870; W. Mallinson, *Sketch of my Life*, 87, 91.
[98] See p. 134.
[99] Inf. from Revd. E. W. Blainey.

Victoria Avenue.[1] With help from the Presbytery of London North a site was bought in East Avenue, and in 1900 an iron church, given by Dr. J. A. Voelker, was erected there. There were early disagreements between the local congregation, which favoured a conventional organization, and the Presbytery, which advocated mission work of the 'central hall' type. These were settled by a compromise; in 1902 Thomas G. Murray became the first minister, in 1903 a permanent church was built, and in 1905 halls were added. By 1909 the membership was 424, and during the brilliant ministry of I. Gwessin Jenkins (1910–28) it rose to 600. Under Jenkins's successor there was a sharp decline, but the church revived after the coming in 1935 of W. Harding Jones. In 1941 the church was joined by the congregation of Trinity Presbyterian church, Maryland Point (West Ham),[2] from which it took over the name Trinity. From 1941 to 1945 it also accommodated the members of Wakefield Street Congregational church, whose own building had been bombed.

The Salvation Army. The Salvation Army started work in East Ham about 1900, when they took over the Holme Road Assembly Room, previously used by the Congregationalists.[3] They appear to have used it until about 1908, when they built the present (1965) hall in Wakefield Street.[4] Salvation Army missions were also held in Katherine Road, c. 1902–6, and in Crescent Road, from c. 1902.[5] The last of these moved in 1913 to Plashet Road, West Ham.

The Greenhill Grove hall, Manor Park, previously used by Congregationalists and Baptists, was first occupied by the Salvation Army about 1902. They registered it for worship from 1903 to 1910 and again from 1945 onwards.[6]

In 1905 the Salvation Army took over a hall in Carlyle Road, Manor Park, previously used as Christ Church Free Church of England, and registered it for worship from then until 1920.[7]

Spiritualists. Manor Park church, Shrewsbury Road (corner of Strone Road), was registered for worship in 1909, in a building previously used by the Free Church of England.[8] The present building was registered in 1940. This congregation was probably connected with an earlier one which in 1903 was meeting in the Temperance Hall, High Street, East Ham, and in 1904 bought the former Congregational church in Coleridge Avenue.[9]

Little Ilford Christian Spiritualist church, Third Avenue, was registered in 1925 and is still in use.[10] The congregation was already in existence by 1905,

and between then and 1925 was meeting in Church Road.[11]

The Silver Star Christian Spiritualist church was registered for worship in 1951 and is still in use; an earlier Spiritualist church on the same site was registered from 1932 to 1939.[12]

Other Churches and Missions. The London City Mission hall in Plashet Lane (later Grangewood Street) was founded about 1870.[13] Under the will of Thomas Mathews, proved in 1901, it received £250 in trust, for running expenses. The hall was sold in or shortly before 1937, in which year a Charity Commission scheme directed that the interest from the capital, £188 stock, should be used for the work of the London City Mission in East Ham and district.[14] At some time the London City Mission also had a branch at Wall End, in the old workhouse.[15]

Manor Park Gospel mission hall was registered for worship from 1886 to 1897.[16]

Plashet Gospel mission hall, Park Road, then newly erected, was registered for worship by Evangelical Christians in 1887, and recertified by them in 1924.[17] It was acquired by the borough council in 1959 under a compulsory purchase order, and was subsequently demolished as part of a redevelopment scheme.[18]

The All People's church, Plashet Lane, was registered for worship from 1892 to 1897.[19]

Woodman (formerly Elizabeth) Street mission hall, North Woolwich, is a brick building dating from the late 19th century. It lies near the old boundary between East Ham and Woolwich, and its early history may appear in records relating to Woolwich. It is probably identical with the Elizabeth Street gospel hall which existed in 1903.[20] It was registered for worship in 1952.[21]

Mizpah mission, King's Road, existed in 1903.[22]

Swinburne Gospel mission, Sheringham Avenue, Manor Park, was registered for worship from 1905 to 1913.[23]

Latimer Hall Martyrs' Memorial mission, Holme Road, was registered for worship from 1914 to 1935.[24] The building had previously been used by the Salvation Army and earlier by Congregationalists. Latimer Hall chapel, Boleyn Road, was registered in 1939 and was still in use in 1965.[25] That building had previously belonged to the Primitive Methodists.

Christadelphians were meeting from about 1914 in Essex Road, Manor Park, and later in Wakefield Street. In 1930 they registered Shrewsbury Road hall, which was still in use in 1965.[26]

[1] *Trinity Presbyterian Ch. Jubilee Handbk.* 1951.
[2] See p. 138.
[3] Mudie-Smith, *Relig. Life Lond.* 358; *Kelly's Dir. Essex,* 1906; *Kelly's Dir. Lond.,* 1902, p. 3043.
[4] Foundation stone.
[5] *Kelly's Dir. Essex,* 1902–8.
[6] Ibid. 1902; Worship Reg. 39092 (canc. 1910), 61202; Mudie-Smith, *Relig. Life Lond.* 358.
[7] Worship Reg. 41368 (canc. 1920); cf. *Kelly's Dir. Essex,* 1906–22; E.H.L., *E. Ham B.C. Mins.* 12 Dec. 1905.
[8] Worship Reg. 43925, 59229.
[9] Mudie-Smith, *Relig. Life Lond.* 359; E.H.L., *E. Ham U.D.C. Mins.* 2 Mar. 1904, and *B.C. Mins.* 31 Jan. 1905; E.H.L., Photos (Temperance Hall).
[10] Worship Reg. 50015.
[11] Ibid. 47332 (canc. 1925); *E. and W. Ham Year Bk.* 1905, p. 83.

[12] Worship Reg. 63151, 54059 (canc. 1939).
[13] Stokes, *E. Ham,* 284; Mudie-Smith, *Relig. Life Lond.* 359.
[14] Char. Com. File 75696.
[15] Stokes, *E. Ham,* 284.
[16] Worship Reg. 29309.
[17] Ibid. 30034; 49296; E.H.L., E. Ham Loc. Bd. Mins. Nov. 1886.
[18] Char. Com. File 144487.
[19] Worship Reg. 33208 (canc. 1897).
[20] Mudie-Smith, *Relig. Life Lond.* 251.
[21] Worship Reg. 63622.
[22] Mudie-Smith, op. cit. 359.
[23] Worship Reg. 40994 (canc. 1913).
[24] Ibid. 46034 (canc. 1935).
[25] Ibid. 59062.
[26] Ibid. 52395; *Kelly's Dir. Essex,* 1914–26.

Elim Tabernacle, Central Park Road, was registered in 1926, and was still in use in 1965.[27]

The Full Gospel Hall, Plashet Grove, previously the Elizabeth Fry Memorial (Primitive) Methodist church, was bought in 1934 by the Assemblies of God, which still occupies it. It was damaged by bombing in the Second World War.[28]

Priory Road hall was registered in 1951 by the Church of God Fellowship (Pentecostal),[29] and is still in use.

The Full Gospel Assembly room, Shaftesbury Road, Forest Gate, was registered in 1952,[30] and is still in use.

JUDAISM. East Ham, Manor Park, and Ilford District Synagogue, Carlyle Road, was consecrated in 1900 and became associated with the United Synagogue in 1902. It was rebuilt in 1927. In 1947 an adjoining building was bought for use as a youth centre.[31]

Upton Park District Synagogue, Tudor Road, originated about 1920, when temporary premises in Katherine Road were registered for worship.[32] The Tudor Road building was erected in 1923, and was extended in 1939. It has been affiliated to the United Synagogue since 1923.[33]

The Plashet cemetery, High Street North, was opened in 1896, and the East Ham cemetery, Lonsdale Avenue, in 1919. Both belong to the United Synagogue.[34]

EDUCATION. A school board was formed for East Ham in 1873. At that time the only school in the parish was a National school in Wakefield Street, founded about 1811. The board took over that school and maintained it in the same building until 1874, when a new board school was opened in High Street South. Between 1873 and 1900 the board opened 10 elementary schools (including one temporary school) and also took over a school at Beckton, previously maintained by the Gas Light & Coke Co. During the same period the Roman Catholics opened a school at Silvertown. A pupil teacher centre was opened by the board in 1898.

At Little Ilford a school board was formed in 1887. It immediately took over the National school there, and used its buildings temporarily while erecting a new school, opened in 1890, in Fourth Avenue. Between 1887 and 1900 the Little Ilford board built altogether three elementary schools.

In 1900 Little Ilford was merged in East Ham for educational purposes, under the control of an enlarged school board. Between 1900 and 1903 one temporary and three permanent board schools and one Roman Catholic school were opened, bringing the total of schools in the urban district to 20.

Under the Education Act (1902) East Ham urban district (from 1904 borough) council became a 'Part III' authority with responsibility for elementary education. In 1905 this arrangement almost broke down, when the council, in protest against the cost of education, passed a resolution refusing to administer the Act, and subsequently gave notice of dismissal to all its teachers. This action was reversed after the the government agreed to provide additional grants to necessitous areas.[35] Between 1903 and 1915 the council built four new elementary schools (two of which replaced temporary schools) and also a selective higher elementary school. The Beckton school was closed. In the same period one new Roman Catholic elementary school was opened.

Even before 1902 the urban district council was concerned with education through its technical instruction committee, formed by the local board in 1891, and as early as 1895 this committee, in association with the county council, was planning a technical college. The college, opened in 1905 at the joint expense of the county council and the borough council, was designed for use as a secondary day-school as well as an evening institute.

In 1915, when East Ham became a county borough, and so responsible for all education, there were thus 22 elementary schools (3 of them Roman Catholic), a higher elementary school, and a secondary school combined with a technical college. By that time the growth of the town was almost complete. There were some 20,000 children in its schools, most of which were large two- or three-storey buildings. Between the two world wars a programme of reorganization was carried out on lines like those proposed in the Hadow Report. East Ham actually started to do this before the publication of the Report. In 1921 one of its elementary schools was divided into separate senior and junior departments, and in 1924 two others. In 1927 all the schools in the south of the borough were reorganized, and in 1929 those in the north. At the same time most of the schools were renamed, usually by dropping such words as 'Street' from the original names. This reorganization took place mainly within the existing buildings, but the council built one new junior school (1923) and a new senior school (1932), and closed two of its oldest elementary schools. During the same period it also opened a second higher elementary, or selective central school, Sandringham (1921), and a school for mental defectives (1924), both in existing buildings, and built a new grammar school for girls (1932). Meanwhile the Roman Catholics had erected two new elementary schools (1917, 1926), the first of which replaced an older building.

During the Second World War several of the borough's schools were seriously damaged by bombing. By the end of the war, also, most of them were over 50 years old, and in 1946 the council drew up a development plan for the next 25 years, which included much new building. Between then and 1965 a new boys grammar school, 6 secondary (modern) schools, two primary schools, and a special school were built. Of the two pre-war central schools Sandringham became secondary (modern), while Wakefield was gradually run down, and closed in 1948. A large new technical college, on the site of the earliest board school, was opened in 1962.

27 Worship Reg. 50387.
28 Ibid. 55949; *E. Ham Official Guide* (1951–2), p. 30.
29 Worship Reg. 63063.   30 Ibid. 63601.
31 Inf. from Mr. J. Gilbey, United Synagogue, and Mr. L. Veronique.

32 Worship Reg. 47673.
33 Ibid. 48996; inf. from Mr. J. Gilbey, United Synagogue.
34 Inf. from Mr. J. Gilbey, United Synagogue.
35 Stokes, *E. Ham*, 244.

Plashet school, closed in 1940 as a result of bombing, was later reopened as an annexe of the technical college. East Ham academy of music was opened in 1963 in the former Wakefield buildings.

In the following chronological sections the account of each school is placed according to the date of its original foundation. Since there has been much rebuilding and reorganization the information in a section overlaps the date contained in the heading. The accounts do not attempt to give details of the temporary reorganization of schools during the Second World War, of which some details can be found in the minutes of the East Ham education committee.

Elementary schools founded before 1873. During the later 18th century the parish vestry occasionally paid for a pauper child to be put to school, probably to a master or mistress in the parish; in 1782 it was proposed that one of the alms-houses should be used as a parish school but there is no evidence that this was done.[36] A charity school existed in East Ham by 1807, when it had 25 pupils, but by 1818 it seems to have been closed.[37] In 1807 there was also a Church Sunday school; this was probably the school supported by the vestry, which in 1809 allowed the assistant curate £10 a year for attending it.[38] About 1811 Elizabeth Fry, who had recently come to live at Plashet House, opened a girls school in a building opposite the gates of her house. She was assisted by Harriet Howell, an organizer of Lancasterian schools, and by the assistant curate of East Ham. A boys department was probably added before 1828 when the 'schools' previously supported jointly by Elizabeth Fry and William Morley of Green Street House, were handed over to the vicar;[39] in the same year the vestry agreed to pay 3s. 6d. a week to a pauper from the workhouse whom the vicar had appointed schoolmaster.[40] By 1833 there were 86 children in the school, which was in union with the National Society; infants were taken at 18 months.[41] In 1837 the school was given accommodation in the former parish workhouse in Wakefield Street.[42] By 1846–7 attendance had risen to 110, under a master, two mistresses, and paid monitors. At that date the Church also supervised three dame schools in the parish, which together had 50 pupils.[43] In 1873 the school was taken over by the East Ham school board; it remained in the Wakefield Street buildings until 1874, when the board school in High Street was opened.[44]

Little Ilford National school, founded in 1865, is described elsewhere.[45]

Elementary schools founded between 1873 and 1903. All the schools in this section, unless otherwise stated, were opened by the East Ham school board.[46]

High Street board school was opened in 1874 with places for 520. It was later enlarged and by 1898 the average attendance was 1,110.[47] The senior and junior mixed departments were closed in 1933 and the infants department in 1935. The premises were subsequently used as an annexe to the technical college until 1962, when they were demolished to provide a site for the new technical college.

Beckton infants school was opened before 1882 by the Gas Light & Coke Co. In 1883 it was taken over by the school board, which reopened it for infants and for juniors under 10. In 1887 the juniors were transferred to the school at New Beckton. The infants school was closed in 1904. It was probably accommodated in the building in Winsor Terrace now (1965) used as the Methodist church.[48]

Shrewsbury Road board school was opened in 1887, was reorganized in 1915 for juniors and infants, and was closed in 1923. The building was later used as a special school.

Winsor junior mixed and infants school (East Ham Manor Way, New Beckton). New Beckton board school was opened in 1887. In 1924 it was renamed Winsor and reorganized into separate senior and junior departments.[49] In 1940 the building was destroyed by bombing. The school reopened in huts in 1944. It was reorganized for junior mixed and infants in 1945. In 1947 a single-storey temporary school was built; this was enlarged in 1954.

St. Mary and St. Edward Roman Catholic junior mixed and infants school (Kennard Street, North Woolwich). Silvertown R.C. school was built in 1889 and enlarged in 1895.[50] The original buildings, which were on the corner of Newland and Bailey Streets, were in 1915 acquired by the Port of London authority, as part of the scheme for the King George V Dock. The school then moved to Kennard Street, occupying temporary premises until 1917, when a new building was completed. It was reorganized for junior mixed and infants in 1945–7.

Avenue junior and infants schools (Fourth Avenue, Manor Park). Fourth Avenue school was opened in 1890 by Little Ilford school board as the successor to the former National school in Church Road. An infants department was added in 1892.[51] In 1929 the school was reorganized for junior boys, junior girls, and infants, and was given its present name. During the Second World War the infants school was destroyed by bombing. In 1947 it was reopened in a temporary building.

Plashet school (Plashet Lane, later Grangewood Street). Plashet Lane board school was opened in 1890. In 1927 it was reorganized for senior boys, junior boys, and infants. It was closed in 1940 because of war damage. The building was later repaired and used as a school of building in connexion with the technical college.

Salisbury junior mixed and infants schools (Romford Road, Manor Park). Manor Park board school was opened in 1893. In 1924 it was renamed Salisbury and reorganized into separate senior and junior

36 E.R.O., D/P 156/8/1–2.
37 E.R.O., D/AEM 2/4.
38 Ibid.; E.R.O., D/P 156/8/3.
39 K. Fry and E. Creswell, *Memoir of Eliz. Fry*, i. 166–7; ii. 42.
40 E.R.O., D/P 156/8/4.
41 *Educ. Enquiry Abstract*, H.C. 62, p. 299 (1835), xli.
42 *White's Dir. Essex*, 1848, p. 230; E.R.O., D/P 156/8/4.
43 *Nat. Soc. Enquiry into Church Schs.* 1846–7, pp. 8–9.
44 E.H.L., E. Ham Sch. Bd. Mins. 1873–4.
45 See p. 173.

46 Except where otherwise stated this and the following sections are based on the minutes of the East Ham school board and the East Ham education committee, all in East Ham library, on information from East Ham and Newham education committees and from the Ministry of Education.
47 Stokes, *E. Ham*, 243; *Kelly's Dir. Essex*, 1898.
48 See p. 35.
49 Stokes, *E. Ham*, 246.
50 *E. Ham Educ. Ctee. Mins.* 24 Nov. 1903.
51 E.H.L., Little Ilford Nat. Sch. Log Bks.; Little Ilford Sch. Bd. Mins. 1890–2.

departments.[52] An infants school was added in 1929. In 1945 Salisbury schools were reorganized for juniors and infants.

Storey Street junior mixed and infants school, North Woolwich. In 1878 the vicar of St. John's, North Woolwich, complained that his National school was suffering from East Ham school board's failure to enforce the compulsory attendance by-laws; he threatened to close the school and thus to force the board to build their own school at North Woolwich. In 1893, after the National school had, in fact, closed, it was leased by the board and re-opened under their management. That building, which adjoined St. John's church and was just outside East Ham, continued in use until 1915 when a new council school was built within the borough, in Storey Street. In 1945 the school was reorganized for juniors and infants.

Shaftesbury junior mixed school. Shaftesbury Road board school was opened in 1894. In 1904 it was badly damaged by fire and largely rebuilt. It was reorganized in 1929 for senior girls, junior girls, and infants, in 1945 for juniors and infants, and in 1951 for juniors only.

Sandringham infants school, Forest Gate. Sandringham Road board school was opened in 1896. In 1921 part of it became a central school. The remainder was reorganized for seniors and juniors in 1921, for juniors and infants in 1933, and for infants only in 1945.

Essex junior mixed and infants schools. Essex Road board school was opened in 1898 by Little Ilford school board.[53] It was reorganized in 1929 for senior boys, junior boys, and infants, and in 1945 for secondary (modern) girls and infants. In 1952, when the secondary school was transferred to the new Rectory Manor building, Essex was reorganized for junior mixed and infants.

Lathom junior mixed school. Lathom Road board school was opened in 1898. It was reorganized in 1932 for junior boys, junior girls, and infants, in 1945 for junior boys and junior girls only, in 1953 for junior mixed and infants, and in 1959 for juniors only.

Central Park junior mixed and infants schools. Central Park Road board school (see plate facing page 203) was opened in 1899. It was reorganized in 1927 for senior boys, junior boys, and infants and in 1945 for secondary (modern) boys and infants. In 1964 the secondary school was transferred to a new building in Roman Road.

Cornwell school (Walton Road, Manor Park) originated as the Bessborough Road board school built in 1900 by Little Ilford school board.[54] It was reorganized in 1929 for senior boys, senior girls, and infants, in 1945 for secondary boys and junior mixed, and in 1957 for secondary boys only. Jack Cornwell, who won the V.C. at the battle of Jutland, was a pupil at this school, which was renamed after him in 1929.

Vicarage junior and infants schools. Vicarage Lane board school was opened in 1901, in the old vicarage.[55] Permanent buildings were opened in 1911. The school was reorganized in 1927 for senior girls, junior girls, and infants, and in 1945 for

secondary (modern) girls, junior mixed, and infants. In 1951 the secondary school was transferred to the new Burges Manor building.

Kensington junior mixed school, Manor Park. Kensington Avenue board school was opened in 1901. It was reorganized in 1929 for senior girls, junior girls, and infants, in 1945 for junior mixed and infants, and in 1957 for junior mixed only.

St. Edward's Roman Catholic school (Castle Street) was opened as an elementary school in 1903 and was reorganized for junior mixed and infants in 1946. The buildings were destroyed by bombing during the Second World War; rebuilding was completed in 1954.

Napier junior mixed and infants schools. Napier Road board school was opened in 1902. It was reorganized in 1927 for senior boys, junior boys, and infants, in 1945 for secondary (modern) boys and infants, and in 1953 for junior mixed and infants, the secondary school being transferred to the new Thomas Lethaby building.

Hartley junior mixed and infants schools. Hartley Avenue board school was opened in 1903. It was reorganized in 1927 for senior girls, junior girls, and infants, in 1945 for junior boys, junior girls, and infants, and in 1964 for junior mixed and infants.

Elementary schools founded between 1903 and 1945. Monega junior mixed and infants schools. Monega Road council school was opened in 1905. It was reorganized in 1929 for senior boys, junior boys, and infants, in 1945 for secondary (modern) girls and infants, and in 1954 for junior mixed and infants, the secondary school being transferred to the new Plashet building.

St. Winefride's Roman Catholic school (Church Road, Manor Park) was opened in 1909 as an elementary school and was reorganized in 1945–7 for junior mixed and infants. It was enlarged in 1951.

Brampton junior mixed and infants school. Brampton Road council school was opened in 1915. It was reorganized in 1927 for senior girls, junior girls, and infants, in 1945 for secondary (modern) girls, junior mixed and infants, and in 1959 for junior mixed and infants only, the secondary school being transferred to the new Brampton Manor building.

Dersingham infants school. Dersingham Avenue council school was established in 1923 for junior mixed and infants. It was reorganized in 1945 for infants only. An extension was built in 1951.

St. Michael's Roman Catholic school (Tilbury Road) was established in 1926 for juniors and infants, in a small building also used as a church. A larger school was built in 1931, and the original building was then used solely as the church.[56] Seniors were admitted in 1934. During the Second World War the school was badly damaged by bombing and its pupils were temporarily accommodated at Napier school. They returned to Tilbury Road in 1946. The school was reorganized for junior mixed and infants in 1945–7.

Secondary and senior schools founded before 1945. East Ham technical college was opened by the county

[52] Stokes, *E. Ham*, 246.
[53] E.H.L., Little Ilford Sch. Bd. Mins. 26 May 1898.
[54] Ibid. 9 May 1900.
[55] E.H.L., *E. Ham U.D.C. Mins.* 19 Feb. 1901.
[56] Inf. from Revd. D. J. Petry.

council in 1905, in a building next to the town hall, in Barking Road. It provided accommodation for a mixed secondary (grammar) school and for evening technical classes. It was extended in 1909.[57] In 1932 East Ham grammar school for girls was opened in a new building in Plashet Grove. East Ham grammar school for boys remained in Barking Road until 1952, when it was transferred to a new building in Langdon Crescent.

Wakefield Street selective higher elementary school was opened in 1910, in buildings previously used as school board offices and pupil teacher centre.[58] It provided a course of about three years, up to the age of 15. By 1914 it was reporting successes in the Oxford junior local, civil service clerical, and Royal Society of Arts examinations. In 1921 it was renamed Wakefield central school. There were no further admissions to the school after 1945 and it was closed in 1948.

Sandringham central school, with the same status as Wakefield, was opened in 1921 in part of the buildings of Sandringham Road elementary school. It became a secondary (modern) school for boys in 1945.

Altmore (Avenue) school, opened for seniors in 1932, and reorganized for infants in 1945, was the only senior school built in East Ham between the two world wars. The other senior schools formed during that period used parts of existing elementary schools.[59] The first senior schools thus formed by reorganization were Sandringham (1921) and Winsor and Salisbury (both 1924). In 1927 Brampton, Central Park, Hartley, Napier, Plashet, and Vicarage were formed, and in 1929 Cornwell, Essex, Kensington, Monega, and Shaftesbury. Sandringham senior school (as distinct from the central school) ceased in 1933. Hartley, Kensington, Plashet, Salisbury, Shaftesbury, and Winsor senior schools, as well as Altmore, ceased during the Second World War, or immediately after. All the others, along with Sandringham (former central) school, became secondary (modern) in 1945. Between 1945 and 1965 all the secondary modern schools except Cornwell and Sandringham were given new buildings and new names, as described below.

Primary schools founded between 1945 and 1965. Altmore (Avenue) infants was formed in 1945 in a building previously used for seniors. St. Stephen's infants (Whitefield Road) was built in 1951, the former Shaftesbury infants being transferred to it. Roman Road junior mixed and infants was opened in 1949 in temporary buildings erected by the Ministry of Works.

Secondary schools founded between 1945 and 1965. All the schools in this section are secondary (modern). Burges Manor (girls, from Vicarage) was opened in 1951 and Thomas Lethaby (boys, from Napier) in 1953. They share a common site, in Langdon Crescent, with the boys grammar school. Plashet (girls, from Monega) was opened in 1951 opposite the girls grammar school, in Plashet Grove, and Rectory Manor (girls, from Essex), in 1957, in Browning Road. Brampton Manor (girls, from Brampton) (1959) and South East Ham (boys, from Central Park) (1964) are adjacent in Roman Road.

Special schools. In 1924 Shrewsbury school for mentally defective children was set up in the buildings of the former Shrewsbury Road elementary school. It continued until the Second World War. Lansbury school for educationally subnormal children was built in Park Avenue, adjoining the Sussex Road schools, in 1954.

East Ham Technical College. A boys night-school connected with the High Street board school was in existence in 1874.[60] In 1891 the East Ham Local board formed a technical instruction committee to organize evening classes in chemistry, mathematics, the use of tools, building, cookery, shorthand, and 'ambulance'.[61] In 1895 this committee appointed a full-time organizing secretary, and in the same year suggested the building of a technical institute.[62] It was eventually agreed that this institute should be built beside the new town hall, and that the Essex county council, which had from the first been associated with the committee, should share the cost of it.[63] As well as running its own evening classes the technical instruction committee provided scholarships for East Ham pupils attending secondary day-schools and evening classes outside the district,[64] and the technical college, opened in 1905 by the borough council and the county council, was designed for use as a secondary day-school as well as an evening college. This college, which stood beside the town hall in Barking Road, included carpenters' and plumbers' shops, a building department, and a clinical laboratory.[65] The first principal, W. H. Barker, had charge of both day and evening departments, and some of the teachers in the secondary school also taught evening classes. By 1932, when he retired, there were over 4,000 evening students.[66] The technical department continued to grow in and after the 1930s, developing day as well as evening classes. To facilitate this increasing activity two former elementary schools, High Street and Plashet, were taken over as annexes to the college, and the secondary school pupils were transferred to new buildings elsewhere. In 1962 a new technical college was built on the High Street school site. By 1967 this had some 10,000 students on its books.[67]

Academy of Music. East Ham Academy of Music, opened in 1963 in the buildings of the former Wakefield (Street) school, was by 1965 providing full-time courses for adults, and Saturday classes for 300 children, selected from 1,000 receiving music lessons in their own schools within the borough.[68]

Private schools and industrial schools. Thomasine Hockley, a Quaker, was in 1684 presented at the

[57] *Kelly's Dir. Essex*, 1922.
[58] Stokes, *E. Ham*, 245.
[59] See previous sections.
[60] E. Ham Sch. Bd. Mins. 12 Oct. 1874.
[61] E.H.L., E. Ham. Loc. Bd. Mins. 14 and 21 July 1891.
[62] Ibid. U.D.C. Mins. 2 July, 19 Nov. 1895.
[63] Ibid. 20 July 1897 and later.
[64] Ibid. 18 Sept. 1900.
[65] *E.R.* xiv. 184.
[66] Stokes, *E. Ham*, 243.
[67] Inf. from the Principal.
[68] Rose Grant, 'Saturday Musicians', *Guardian*, 24 Nov. 1965.

archdeacon's court for teaching school without a licence, and for failing to send the pupils to be catechized.[69] William Bull, a schoolmaster of East Ham, occurs in 1733.[70] In 1833 there were two private schools in the parish, containing a total of 43 children.[71] These were no doubt dame schools, like the three, with 50 pupils, which in 1846–7 were under Church supervision.[72] A few private schools are listed in directories and other sources from the 1880s, but they were mostly short-lived. Among the more pretentious of these was Woodgrange college, Romford Road, which existed in 1888–92, but had closed by 1899, when it was put up for sale.[73] Milton high school, Shrewsbury Road, existed for more than 20 years up to 1939.[74]

While East Ham was still a village three industrial schools were opened there. In 1851 St. George's-in-the-East (Lond.) poor-law union built a school in Green Street for its pauper children. It was closed in or shortly before 1927, and the building was later converted into the Carlton cinema.[75] St. Nicholas's Roman Catholic school, Gladding Road, Manor Park, was opened in 1868, in the Manor House, former home of the Fry family. In 1925 the school was closed, and the premises were sold to the London Co-operative Society.[76] St. Edward's Roman Catholic reformatory school was opened in 1870, at Green Street House (Boleyn Castle), Green Street. It was closed in 1906.[77]

CHARITIES FOR THE POOR.[78] By will dated 1618 Giles Breame (d. 1621) bequeathed £300 to build six alms-houses in East Ham for poor men, three from this parish and three from Bottisham (Cambs.). He also left land in East Ham for the maintenance of the alms-houses, but by a codicil of 1621 directed that his executor, Sir Giles Allington, should sell this along with the remainder of Breame's manor of East Ham, and should buy other land yielding £40 a year to provide the endowment. Allington built the houses, but before effecting the endowment he sold the manor to Lady Kempe, leaving £660 in her hands for that purpose. By 1638, following a Chancery decree, she had spent £800 on the purchase of a farm (later called Lake's farm) at Braintree, the rent from which became the endowment. The alms-house trustees were dissatisfied with this arrangement, mainly because Braintree was so far away, which made it difficult to collect the rent. Between 1640 and 1646 they made repeated attempts, unsuccessfully, to get the decree rescinded, and to secure the land in East Ham provided for by Breame's will, before his codicil.[79] In 1791–2, after the alms-houses had been damaged by a storm, substantial repairs were carried out, and they were further rebuilt in 1808.[80] They formed a plain brick terrace on the east side of East Ham Manor Road (now High Street South), each house comprising two rooms. In 1835 the three northern houses were occupied by East Ham alms-men, the three southern or Bottisham ones being let to the East Ham parish vestry to accommodate paupers. Bottisham was receiving £25, rather more than half the amount assigned for pensions. In 1873 the gross annual income from Lake's farm was £130, from which monthly payments of £1 10s. were made to each of three poor men at East Ham and three at Bottisham. A scheme of 1900 provided that Bottisham should receive £6 a year plus half the residue of the income from the charity. The other half was to be combined with the incomes from the East Ham charities of Hart, Heigham, Holt, Poulett, and Rampston, to be used for the alms-houses and for stipends of not more than three alms-men. The scheme placed Garrard's charity under the same trustees as the combined charities, but did not affect the terms of its application. In 1931 Lake's farm was sold for £630, which was invested.[81] By 1937 the alms-houses had so deteriorated that they were condemned, and in 1940 they were demolished.[82] The site was sold for £2,000, and this, with the other assets, was divided equally between East Ham and Bottisham. Under a scheme of 1946 the income from the combined charities was to be paid as pensions to poor men who had lived at East Ham for at least five years. A scheme of 1958 permitted these incomes to be used for various charitable purposes, in addition to pensions. In 1966 the endowments of the combined charities amounted to £4,041, producing an income of £166 in addition to Rampston's rent-charge. Four pensions, each of 10s. a week, were being paid.

Robert Rampston (d. 1585) left rent-charges for the poor of various Essex parishes.[83] That for East Ham was £1 a year, charged on Stone Hall in Little Canfield. In 1835 this was spent on quartern loaves at Christmas for the poorest inhabitants. The rent-charge was still being paid in 1966.

Sir John Hart, alderman of London, by will proved 1603, gave an annual rent-charge of £4 from his lands in East Ham for the relief of the poorest widows or householders. In 1835 it was used to provide bread. The rent-charge was redeemed in 1904 for £160 stock.

William Heigham, by will proved 1620, gave the rents of 2½ a. marshland in Barking for the poor. Twelve pennyworths of bread were to be provided each Sunday, and the remainder was to be spent on coal. By 1946 the charity consisted of £400 stock.

By a deed of 1641 Jane Neville, pretended countess of Westmoreland, gave to the vicar of East Ham an annual rent of £3, charged on land in West Ham, of which £1 was for a sermon, £1 10s. for the poor, and 10s. for maintaining her tomb. These sums were paid until 1834, when a new owner began to with-

[69] *E.R.* lvii. 63.
[70] Ibid. viii. 204.
[71] *Educ. Enquiry Abstract*, H.C. 62, p. 229 (1835), xli.
[72] *Nat. Soc. Enquiry into Church Schs.* 1846–7, pp. 8–9.
[73] E.H.L., E. Ham Loc. Bd. Mins. May 1888, Apr. 1892; *U.D.C. Mins.* 19 Sept. 1899.
[74] *Official Guide to E. Ham* [1939], adverts., p. 3.
[75] P.E.M., Pictorial Survey: East Ham; *White's Dir. Essex*, 1863, p. 639; *E. Ham Educ. Ctee. Mins.* Sept. 1927; E.H.L. Photos. (Schools).
[76] *Kelly's Dir. Essex*, 1882; P.E.M., Pictorial Survey: East Ham; inf. from the Crusade of Rescue. See also p. 312.
[77] *Lond. Gaz.* 8 Nov. 1870, 4774; inf. from the Crusade of Rescue.
[78] This section is based on notes by Mrs. F. Goodall. Unless otherwise stated the sources are: *Rep. Com. Char.* (*Essex*) H.C. 216, pp. 129–33 (1835), xxi (1); Char. Com. Files 212390 and G21; inf. from Town Clerk of Newham.
[79] *L.J.* vi. 333–5, 666; Hist. MSS. Com. *5th Rep.* App., 111, 114; ibid. *6th Rep.* App., 10, 110.
[80] E.R.O., D/P 156/8/3.
[81] Char. Com. File 76059.
[82] E.H.L., Photo Coll. (Almshouses).
[83] *Rep. Com. Char.* (*Essex*) H.C. 60, p. 157 (1833), xxviii.

hold the rent. The parish took legal proceedings against him, but these failed, apparently for want of trustees, and the charity was lost.[84]

Sir Jacob Garrard of Green Street House, by deed of 1653, gave a rent-charge of £3 to apprentice poor boys bound out by the parish. He did this as a thank-offering for his acquittal after being falsely accused of assisting the royalist rising of 1648.[85] A scheme of 1898 permitted the income to be spent either on apprenticeships or on exhibitions for higher education. In 1966 the assets of this charity included £1,476 capital, formed by accumulation of income and producing £67 a year in addition to the rent-charge. One payment of £10 was made towards the cost of a student's equipment.

Daniel Holt (d. 1833) bequeathed £20 in trust for bread.

Margaret, Countess Poulett (d. 1838) bequeathed £54 in trust for the poor.

James Freeman, by will proved 1909, left £487 stock in trust for the police court poor-box fund at East Ham. In 1964 the income was £12.[86]

Elizabeth Fleming, by will proved 1958, and Amelia Elston, by will proved 1961, left £2,800 and £200 respectively to the East Ham Hostels Residents' Comforts fund. A scheme of 1965 directed that the income from these two charities, which in that year totalled £173, should in future be used for Newham Hostels Residents' Comforts fund.[87]

WEST HAM

Growth, p. 44. Domestic Buildings, p. 50. Rivers, Bridges, Wharfs, and Docks, p. 57. Transport and Postal Services, p. 61. Worthies, p. 64. Entertainments, Sports, and Pastimes, p. 65. Manors and Other Estates, p. 68. Agriculture, p. 74. Industries, p. 76. Ancient Mills, p. 89. Markets and Fairs, p. 93. Marshes and Sea Defences, p. 94. Forest, p. 95. Local Government to 1836, p. 96. Local Government 1836–86, p. 99. Local Government 1886–1965, p. 103. Public Services, p. 108. Parliamentary Representation, p. 112. Stratford Abbey Precincts, p. 112. Churches, p. 114. Roman Catholicism, p. 123. Protestant Nonconformity, p. 124. Judaism, p. 140. Philanthropic Institutes, Settlements, and Hostels, p. 141. Education, p. 144. Charities, p. 157.

WEST HAM, about 5 miles east of the City of London, is part of the London borough of Newham.[1] It contains part of the royal docks, and a wide variety of industries, especially those concerned with engineering, chemicals, and food. The ancient parish extended from the Thames north for about 4 miles. The eastern boundary marched with East Ham from Wanstead Flats down Green Street to the Thames. The western boundary, which divided Essex from Middlesex, followed the river Lea for most of its length. Near the north-west corner of the parish, locally situated within West Ham, was a small detached part of Wanstead, recorded at least as early as the 16th century.[2] There was a small adjustment of the boundary with Wanstead in 1790, and of that with East Ham, near the Thames, in 1857.[3] In the 1860s the ancient parish of West Ham comprised 4,667 a.[4] In 1856 it was constituted a local government district, under a board of health, and in 1875 the detached part of Wanstead was merged in that district, increasing its area to 4,706 a.[5] West Ham became a municipal borough in 1886 and a county

WEST HAM COUNTY BOROUGH. *Per fesse gules and or, in a chief a ship under sail proper and two hammers in saltire of the second, in base three chevronels of the first, over all a pale ermine thereon a crosier erect also of the second.*

borough in 1889. It became part of Newham in 1965. In general that year has been taken as the terminal point of the present article.

The land rises from the Thames to a height of about 50 ft. on Wanstead Flats. Beside the Thames and the Lea are extensive alluvial marshes; elsewhere the soil is valley gravel. An inlet of the Thames, called Ham creek, formed part of the boundary with East Ham until it was occluded in the later 19th century.[6] More than half the land in the parish, in the south and west, lay below the level of ordinary spring tides. From early times those marshes were protected by embankments and drainage ditches.[7] During the past hundred years, in the course of building development, land levels have been raised in some parts of the low-lying areas by means of rubbish tipping,[8] while the open drainage ditches have been replaced by piped sewers.[9] The topography of that part of the parish was also much affected by the building, on the Thames, of the Royal Victoria Dock (1850–5) and the adjoining Royal Albert Dock (1875–80). The river Lea, as it enters the parish from the north-west, divides into several branches, of which the westernmost is the main channel of the Lea and the easternmost the Channelsea river. The channels pass under Stratford High Street and converge again at the Three Mills, below which the Lea, as Bow creek, flows down to the Thames. The ancient pattern of the channels was greatly altered by a flood relief scheme carried out in 1931–5.[10]

---

[84] Char. Com. Files 3213, 66390; E.R.O., D/P 156/8/4; E.R.O., Sage Coll. No. 860.

[85] *E.R.* xxi. 29–31.

[86] Char. Com. File 240105.   [87] Ibid. 245143.

[1] O.S. Map 2½", sheets TQ 38, 47, 48. See maps above and below, pp. 6, 48. Some preliminary work on this article was done by Mr. J. M. Montgomery.

[2] G.L.C., DL/C/212 (1574–5); and see p. 317 below.

[3] W.H.L., W. Ham Vestry Mins. 25 Feb. 1790; 5 Mar. 1857.

[4] O.S. Map 6", Essex, LXXIII (Surv. 1863–73). For a detailed perambulation see Vestry Mins. 5 May 1864.

[5] L.G.B. Prov. Ord. Conf. (Aberdare, etc.) Act, 1875, 38 & 39 Vict. c. 175 (local act); inf. from the Borough Engineer, Newham L.B.

[6] See p. 2.

[7] See p. 94.

[8] E. G. Howarth and M. Wilson, *West Ham*, 29.

[9] See p. 109.

[10] For the Rivers see p. 57.

THE GROWTH OF WEST HAM. Until the later 12th century references to Ham ('low-lying pasture') do not distinguish between East and West Ham, and cannot, therefore, be interpreted precisely.[11] In 1086 the manor of (West) Ham, with a recorded population of 130, was by contemporary standards a large village.[12] Until the 19th century West Ham remained largely rural, though more populous than its Essex neighbours. In 1327, 101 persons in the parish were assessed to the lay subsidy, the largest number in Becontree hundred except for Barking.[13] In 1381 there were 240 poll-tax payers in the parish,[14] and in the fiscal year 1523–4 238 paid the lay subsidy.[15] By 1670 West Ham contained some 415 houses,[16] but any estimate of the population at that date would have to take into account the Great Plague, which had killed 160 there between July 1665 and May 1666.[17] About 1740 the number of householders was estimated at 570.[18] In 1801 the population of West Ham was 6,485.[19] It rose steadily to 12,738 in 1841, and then began a phenomenal growth, which was especially rapid between 1871 and 1901, when over 204,000 were added. By 1911, with 289,030 inhabitants, West Ham was seventh in size among English county boroughs. The new population had all been crowded within the boundaries of the ancient parish. There was little room for further growth, and the population of 300,860 in 1921 proved to be the highest census figure. A slight decline after that was greatly accelerated by the Second World War, when heavy bombing destroyed many houses and forced large-scale evacuation. The population of the borough was 170,993 in 1951 and 157,367 in 1961. Since the Second World War many overseas immigrants, mainly from the Commonwealth, India, and Pakistan, have settled in West Ham. In 1961 the resident population included 5,383 born outside the British Isles, or 3·4 per cent of the total.

Little is known in detail of the pattern of settlement before the 16th century. The Domesday manor of (West) Ham, like those in neighbouring parishes to the east, lay on the gravel terraces above the marshes, with the forest immediately to the north.[20] Robert Gernon's section of it was possibly centred on West Ham village, about ½ m. east of the Channelsea river, where by the 12th century the parish church was in existence. Ranulph Peverel's section became known in the 12th century as Sudbury ('southern manor'). Sudbury, a lost name, was in the Plaistow area. In the 13th century part of it, with other lands, became the manor of Bretts, the manor-house of which was in Plaistow village. About ½ m. north and west of West Ham village was Stratford, often called Stratford Langthorne. The

'tall thorn' existed as a physical feature in 958, while Stratford, where the Roman road from London to Colchester crossed the river Lea, was first recorded as a place-name between 1066 and 1087.[21] The Roman crossing was probably at Old Ford at Bethnal Green (Mdx.),[22] and that route remained in use until early in the 12th century, when Maud (d. 1118), queen of Henry I, built Bow and Channelsea Bridges, linked by a causeway, to carry the main road over the Lea and the Channelsea, about a mile south-east of Old Ford.[23] Bow Bridge was the lowest bridge over the Lea, and remained so until the 19th century. Along the road, on each side of the bridge, grew up the villages of Stratford Bow (Mdx.) and Stratford Langthorne.[24] In 1135 William de Montfitchet, successor to Robert Gernon, founded the Cistercian abbey of Stratford Langthorne about ½ m. south of that road.[25] Among the abbey's earliest endowments was Woodgrange, an outlying farm on the edge of the forest, first mentioned in 1189.[26] Stratford became a rich and important house, often visited by royalty, especially in the 13th and 14th centuries,[27] and probably used as an administrative centre for south-west Essex.[28] It steadily enlarged its estates in West Ham, and by the 15th century controlled most of the parish. The abbey precincts, beside the Channelsea, included a few industrial buildings and private dwellings as well as the conventual buildings; but the Cistercian tradition of isolation was not without effect there, for Stratford Abbey, unlike those of Barking and Waltham Holy Cross, did not attract settlement outside its walls.

Two early 16th century rentals of the abbey's land provide much topographical information about West Ham.[29] The main settlements were in Church Street (West Ham village), Stratford, and Plaistow. Plaistow first appears in records in 1414.[30] Its name, and the shape of the old village, suggest settlement around a village green or place of 'play'. The rentals also contain a few references to Upton, in the east of the parish, but, though that name had been recorded as early as the 13th century,[31] there was no substantial settlement there. Stratford, Plaistow, and Upton are still well-known names, but one hamlet often mentioned in the rentals has left no trace on modern maps. That was Hook End, which lay about a mile south-east of Plaistow village, at the end of Greengate Street. There are occasional references to Hook End down to the 19th century, and as late as 1869 the north end of the present Tunmarsh Lane was known as Hook End Lane.[32]

Saxton's (1576) and Norden's (1594) maps both mark West Ham, Stratford Langthorne, and the bridges over the Lea. Norden also marks Woodgrange, and shows the Ilford–London road, joined

11 P.N. Essex, 95.
12 V.C.H. Essex, i. 515, 527.
13 E 179/107/13.   14 E 179/107/67.
15 E 179/108/50.
16 E.R.O., Q/RTh 5.
17 P.E.M., Transcript of W. Ham Par. Regs. (Burials).
18 K. Fry, Hist. East and West Ham, 219.
19 Census Reps. 1801 f.
20 For the manors see p. 68.
21 P.N. Essex, 96, 94.
22 V.C.H. Essex, iii. 24; E. Nat. xxxi. 208.
23 See p. 59.
24 These two Stratfords are often confused. For the attributes of Stratford (in W. Ham) see P. N. Essex, 96–7.
25 V.C.H. Essex, ii. 129 f. For the abbey site see below, p. 112.

26 See p. 73.
27 For royal visits: e.g. Cal. Pat. and Cal. Close, passim for Hen. III and later.
28 Courts held at Stratford, probably at the abbey, included: general eyre (e.g. Feet of F. Essex, i. 14, 38, 40); possessory assizes (Cal. Pat. 1225–32, 293–4, etc.); shire courts (Cal. Close 1234–7, 576, cf. Cal. Inq. p.m. ii. 235–6); inquisitions post mortem (Cal. Inq. p.m., iii. p. 143).
29 S.C. 12/15/20 (Sudbury manor, 1527); S.C. 6/962 (Stratford Abbey Lands, 1538).
30 P.N. Essex, 96.
31 Feet of F. Essex, i. 33.
32 W.H.L., W. Ham Manor Ct. Bks. 18 Apr. 1808, 18 Apr. 1811, 6 Sept. 1826, 9 Mar. 1830; J. G. B. Marshall, Map of W. Ham (1869).

at Stratford by the road leading north to Woodford and Dunmow. West Ham's minor roads do not appear on any surviving map before the 18th century.

From the 16th to the early 19th century West Ham was increasingly favoured as a place of residence or holiday resort by wealthy merchants and professional men working in London.[33] By the early 17th century the parish had been divided into wards: Church Street (including West Ham village), Stratford, Plaistow, and Upton; Upton ward was later merged in Church Street. In 1670 the houses of the parish were distributed among the wards as follows: 179 in Stratford, 103 in Church Street, 108 in Plaistow, and 25 in Upton.[34]

About 1700 there was a spurt of growth at Stratford. Defoe reported in 1722, no doubt with exaggeration, that it had more than doubled in size during the previous 20 or 30 years. He also stated that two new hamlets had grown up on the forest side of the village, namely Maryland Point, on the Woodford Road, and the Gravel Pits on the Ilford Road.[35] Maryland Point is shown on a map of 1696.[36] The first house there is said to have been built by a rich merchant who returned to England from Maryland.[37] Various attempts have been made to identify the merchant. The most likely candidate is Richard Lee (d. 1664), who emigrated to Virginia about 1640.[38] Among his estates was land on the Maryland side of the Potomac river, near a place known in 1676 as Maryland Point.[39] He returned to England in 1658, and in 1658-9 bought properties at Stratford Langthorne. In 1662 he had a house there with 9 hearths.[40] Whatever its origin, Maryland Point became a permanent place-name in West Ham. The Gravel Pits, the other new hamlet mentioned by Defoe, is not named on any map.[41] It was probably the settlement, north of Stratford Common (or Green), shown on later maps.

The growth of Stratford in the early 18th century emphasizes the importance of its position at the gateway to London. In the 17th century this had sometimes been literally true. A turnpike gate, at the Stratford end of Bow Bridge, was seized by the Royalists in 1648.[42] In 1681, at another time of national unrest, quarter sessions set up a turnpike in Stratford High Street, and another at the Abbey Mill in Abbey Lane, to prevent the escape of criminals from London.[43] The Abbey Mill gate was rebuilt by the county in 1698.[44] In the mid 18th century the parish vestry was employing a gatekeeper there.[45] By the later 19th century it had become a private

toll-gate, attached to the Abbey Mill.[46] Tolls were still being collected in 1933[47] but appear to have ceased soon after. The later history of the other turnpike set up in 1681 is not known, but that also may have become a toll-gate. In 1721 the main road through Stratford was taken over by the Middlesex and Essex turnpike trust, whose toll-gate in High Street was about 500 yd. west of Channelsea Bridge.[48] The trust, which survived until 1866, received composition payments from the landowners upon whom, as successors in title to Stratford Abbey, had fallen the obligation to maintain Queen Maud's bridges and causeway.[49]

The roads and settlements of the whole parish are shown, though not all are named, on Rocque's map (1744-6).[50] The roads of Plaistow ward also appear, without names, on John James's map (1742), which is part of a detailed survey including earlier information and later annotations up to the 1780s.[51] By 1744-6 development was already fairly continuous along the main road at Stratford from Charles (Channelsea) Bridge as far as the present Broadway and the Grove, with outlying hamlets near Bow Bridge, at Maryland Point, and on the north side of Stratford common. Stratford common (or green), about 6 a. in extent, was the site later used for West Ham's technical college.[52] It was inclosed by the West Ham manor court c. 1807-20 in a series of copyhold grants.[53] In the 18th century the name Stratford green was also used for the site now occupied by St. John's church, Stratford,[54] and it seems likely that those two sites were the eastern and western ends of what had once been a much larger green. Stratford green was also called Gallows green, probably from the gallows set up in the 13th century by Richard de Montfitchet.[55] It is thought to be the place where the Protestant martyrs were burnt in 1555-6.[56] Rocque also shows Forest Lane, Woodgrange Road, and Water Lane. West Ham village clustered round the church, with a few houses along Stratford (now West Ham) Lane to the north, and along Abbey Lane (now Abbey Road) which ran south-west to West Ham abbey. From the abbey a lane ran south through Abbey marsh. It was known as Marsh Lane until the later 19th century, when it became part of Manor Road. Ass House (now Vicarage) Lane and Church Street are named. In naming the former the cartographer may have been misled by a rustic informant: the form Jackass Lane, also recorded in the 18th century, seems more authentic.[57]

[33] See p. 64.
[34] E.R.O., Q/RTh 5. For the wards see below, p. 97.
[35] D. Defoe, *Tour through Great Britain*, ed. G. D. H. Cole, i. 5-6.
[36] J. Oliver, *Map of Essex* (1696).
[37] Morant, *Essex*, i. 18.
[38] W.H.L., File on Maryland Point. Much of the inf. on Ric. Lee comes from: Ludwell L. Montagu, 'Richard Lee the Emigrant', *Virginia Magazine of Hist. and Biog.* lxii (1954) I sqq., the writer of which does not, however, accept the identification of Lee with the merchant mentioned by Morant.
[39] *Speed's Map of Virginia and Maryland* (1676).
[40] E.R.O., Q/RTh 1.
[41] There are several references to gravel pits along the Ilford Road, e.g. in 1676-7: Assizes 35/117/2.
[42] *E.R.* xvii. 190-1.
[43] E.R.O., Q/CP 3, ff. 381, 392, 470.
[44] Ibid. 563.
[45] W.H.L., W. Ham Vestry Mins. 17 Oct. 1731, 8 Apr. 1740.

[46] W. Ham L.B. Mins. 25 Feb. 1879; *W. Ham C.B.C. Mins.* 30 May 1893. A post from this toll-gate is in P.E.M.
[47] *E.Nat.* xxiv. 143-4; W.H.L., Illus. Coll. (Toll-gates).
[48] Middlesex and Essex Highways Act, 8 Geo. I, c. 30; J. Mynde, *Map Mdx. and Essex turnpike roads* (1728); W.H.L., Map of Mill Meads and High Meads (1843); F. Sainsbury, *West Ham, Eight Hundred Years*, 20-1.
[49] See below p. 59.
[50] J. Rocque, *Surv. Lond.* (1744-6). The field boundaries on this map are largely fictitious, and there are some errors in the naming of roads. For Chapman and André's more accurate map see plates f. pp. 23 above and 53 below.
[51] E.R.O., D/DPe M55. Some of the names are mentioned in the text of the survey.
[52] E.R.O., T/M 175 (Map of W. Ham manor 1787).
[53] W.H.L., Register of Copyhold Tens., Manors of Poplar, Bromley, and W. Ham (c. 1805), ff. 182, 258; W. Ham Manor Ct. Bk. 12 Feb. 1835; Clayton Surv. of W. Ham (1821), Stratford N 50, 51.
[54] Guildhall MS. 9531/28 f. 399.
[55] See p. 96.   [56] See p. 116.   [57] See p. 128.

In the 1740s Plaistow village appears to have been the largest settlement in the parish. Its centre was roughly triangular, comprising the present High Street, North Street, and Richmond Street. There were also houses along Balaam Street to the south-west and Greengate Street to the south-east. High Street was known in the 16th century and later as Cordwainer Street, from the leather trade carried on there.[58] Balaam Street, first recorded in 1364–5,[59] took its name from the Balun family, who lived at Plaistow as early as 1183.[60] South of the village, in the 1740s, were several lanes running through the marshes towards the Thames. New Barn Street, the continuation of Balaam Street, was first recorded in 1527.[61] It took its name from New Barns farm, the ancient rectorial glebe of West Ham.[62] The present Butchers Road and Freemasons Road, which fork south from New Barn Street, are shown by both Rocque and James. Freemasons Road was then called Green Lane.[63] During the 19th century it was known for a time as Dirty Lane.[64] Butchers Road was formerly known as Butchers Hedge Lane.[65] West of it was a lane running down to Bow creek. In the earlier 19th century the whole of that was called Forty Acre Lane, but as a result of modern changes the name has been retained only for a short stretch of road.[66] Prince Regent Lane, which runs south from Greengate Street, was known in 1667 as Trinity Marsh Lane.[67]

Rocque and James also show Chargeable Lane and Star Lane, running west from Balaam Street and Forty Acre Lane respectively. Chargeable Lane led to a field called Shillingshaw, or Chargeables, the owner of which was bound to contribute to the maintenance of Chargeable Wall at Lea Mouth.[68] Star Lane led to Star field.[69] Running east from Plaistow village, above the marshes, were two roads named by Rocque: Brewers Lane and Pursey Lane. Brewers Lane was roughly equivalent to the part of Barking Road between the Abbey Arms and Green Street. Pursey (or Palsey, or Purles Hill) Lane was on the line of the present St. Mary's and Queen's Roads.[70] Running north from the village was the road to Upton, now Pelly Road and Upton Lane. Rocque also shows Portway, linking Upton with West Ham village, and the present Plashet Road, running from Upton to East Ham. Portway ('town way') is recorded from the 16th century,[71] Plashet Road was previously called Plashet Lane.[72] The junction of Upton Lane, Portway, and Plashet Lane was known, at least from the 16th century, as Upton Cross.[73] Around and to the north of the Cross were

several country houses, including Ham House in its park (now West Ham Park). Green Street, which formed part of the boundary with East Ham, was the southern end of the modern road of that name; the northern end was formerly Gipsy Lane.

In the later 18th century there was considerable further development, including some industry,[74] in the northern wards of the parish, but comparatively little in Plaistow ward. Between 1742 and c. 1780 the number of houses in Plaistow rose only from 152 to 159.[75] There are no corresponding figures for the other wards, but the trend can be seen from rateable values. In 1742 the rateable value of Plaistow was £3,800, compared with £3,700 for Stratford, and £3,500 for Church Street (including Upton).[76] In 1788–9 the values were: Stratford £7,500, Church Street £7,300, Plaistow £4,900, and in 1818–19: Stratford £12,600, Church Street £11,300, Plaistow £6,800.[77] These figures show the increasing influence of London upon the northern wards, and the relative isolation of Plaistow. Plaistow was at last provided with a main road, by-passing Stratford, about 1812, when the Commercial Road turnpike trust built New (now Barking) Road from the East India Docks, across the Plaistow marshes, to East Ham and Barking, with an iron bridge over the Lea by Bow creek,[78] and a toll-gate in Barking Road, near the bridge.[79] That road did not immediately influence local settlement,[80] but it eventually became the main thoroughfare and shopping centre of south West Ham. It was controlled by the Commercial Road trust until the trust expired in 1871.[81]

By the early 19th century West Ham was already a populous parish, and with the coming of the railways[82] it grew rapidly. Stratford became a junction on the Eastern Counties Railway (1839–40). In 1847 the E.C.R. transferred its main works, previously at Romford, to a site north-east of the junction. Beside the works the company built Hudson Town, named after its chairman, George Hudson 'the railway king'. It was stated in 1848 that 100 houses had already been completed there and that another 150 were being planned.[83] By 1855 Hudson Town extended east from Leyton Road to Leytonstone Road, and north from Windmill Lane to Maryland Road.[84] A little later it became known as Stratford New Town.[85] During the 1860s, as further building took place, that name was extended to include also the area between Maryland Road and the northern boundary of the parish.[86]

The growth of south West Ham also began in the 1840s. About 1843 the North Woolwich Land Co.

[58] See p. 77.
[59] *Cal. Inq. Misc.* 1348–77, 307.
[60] See p. 69.
[61] S.C. 12/15/20.
[62] See p. 115.
[63] E.R.O., D/DPe M55 (no. 35).
[64] O.S. Map 25″, London, XXXIX (surv. 1867).
[65] Ibid.
[66] Ibid.; W. Ham L.B. Mins. 28 Feb. 1882.
[67] E.R.O., D/DPe M55 (no. 109).
[68] E.R.O., D/DPe M55 (no. 181); E.R.O., D/SH 29.
[69] E.R.O., D/DPe M55 (no. 150).
[70] Fry, *E. and W. Ham*, 249; W.H.L., Cal. Rawsthorne Docs., (J.) Purles Hill seems the proper form of the name. St. Mary's Road was adopted in 1866: W. Ham L.B. Mins. 9 Oct. 1866.
[71] S.C. 6/962.
[72] O.S. Map 25″, London, XXI (surv. 1863).
[73] S.C. 6/962.

[74] See pp. 77–8.
[75] E.R.O., D/DPe M55: calculated from the lists of houses.
[76] These and the following rateable values are taken from: W.H.L., W. Ham Vestry Mins. and Overseers Accts.
[77] These values reflect monetary inflation as well as building development.
[78] E.R.O., Q/RUm 1/13; Fry, *E. and W. Ham*, 277.
[79] W.H.L., Illus. Coll. (Toll-gates). This gate was probably on the Middlesex side of the river.
[80] Cf. Curwen, *Old Plaistow*, 19.
[81] W. Ham L.B. Mins. 12 Apr. 1870, 25 Apr. 1871.
[82] See below, p. 62.
[83] *White's Dir. Essex* (1848), 239.
[84] A. L. Dickens, *Rep. to Gen. Bd. of Health on Sanitary Condition of W. Ham*, 1855 (map).
[85] *White's Dir. Essex* (1863), 614.
[86] J. G. B. Marshall, *Map of W. Ham* (1869).

bought and began to develop much of Plaistow marshes, between Barking Road and the Thames.[87] Prominent in that syndicate was George P. Bidder (1806–78), a civil engineer whose remarkable career had started in childhood as a 'calculating phenomenon.'[88] Bidder, more any other person, was the maker of modern West Ham. He was the projector of the Eastern Counties and Thames Junction Railway, opened in 1846–7, from Stratford to North Woolwich, with an intermediate station at Barking Road.[89] The line was intended mainly to carry coal from the Thames. Coal did indeed form a large part of the early traffic, but the line immediately gave rise also to manufacturing industries at Bow creek, including the shipyard of C. J. Mare & Co. (1846), later the Thames Ironworks and Shipbuilding Co.[90] Soon after the completion of the railway, work also started on the Victoria Dock, of which Bidder was the chief designer.

The workers in the new enterprises were housed in two townships near Barking Road station.[91] One of these was Canning Town, a name of unknown origin first applied to the small area north of Barking Road, between the Lea and the railway. In 1851 it comprised some 60 houses in Stephenson Street, Wharf Street, and Wharf Place.[92] The other township grew up south and east of Barking Road station, close to Mare's shipyard. In 1851 it was called Plaistow New Town, which contained about 80 houses, mostly in or near Victoria Dock Road.[93] By 1855 it had become known as Hallsville, apparently after the owner of some of the houses.[94] It then extended as far east as Rathbone Street and Roscoe Street (now Ruscoe Road).[95] In the course of the next 10 or 15 years the name Hallsville dropped out of use, except for a road, and the name Canning Town came to be used for the whole built-up area, south as well as north of Barking Road station.[96] The opening of the railway to North Woolwich was soon followed also by development along the Thames bank. About 1852 the rubber firm of S. W. Silver & Co. opened a factory near Ham creek, just inside the parish and thus founded Silvertown.[97] A few workers' houses were built beside the factory, but the development of the area was slow at first.

By the 1850s new building was going on in several other parts of the parish, mostly following the railways. In the north, at Forest Gate, development started about 1855, on the Gurney and Dames estates, west and north of the E.C.R. station.[98] In the centre new streets had been laid out north and south-west of Plaistow village by 1855,[99] and development there was stimulated by the opening, in 1858, of the London, Tilbury & Southend Railway's loop line to Barking, with a station at Plaistow Road. There was also new building immediately east of West Ham village. That area, which included Leabon Street, John Street, Plaistow Grove, and the north end of Plaistow Road, was known in 1855 as Rob Roy Town, a short-lived name of unknown origin.[1] At Stratford, by 1855, there had been development in two areas south of High Street. One was east of Stratford Bridge station, and included Chapel, Langthorne, and Paul Streets. The other was at Stratford Marsh, near the gasworks.[2] About then building was also starting on the Manbey estate, east of the Grove.[3]

Building continued steadily throughout the 1860s. The southern portion of the Upton 'Manor' estate, including Pelly Road, was being developed in 1866.[4] At the same time Canning Town was spreading eastwards. Among developments there were Hudson's estate, including Hudson's Road, and Ireland's estate, including Denmark Street.[5] Near those was Cherry Island, a small market-garden partly surrounded by marsh ditches.[6] There, about 1868, a speculator laid out Edwin, Bradley, and Thomas Streets, and built a number of squalid cottages which were a nuisance to the local board for many years.[7] Cherry Island was also a resort of gipsies, whose clean and orderly camp compared favourably with the cottages.[8] At Silvertown a small estate was built north of the railway about 1865, comprising Constance, Andrew, and Gray Streets.[9] At Stratford the Carpenters' Company of London began developing their estate about 1867.[10] It comprised 63 a. on the north side of High Street at Stratford marsh, which the company had owned since the 18th century. The Carpenters leased the land to builders who, during the next 20 years, erected factories, and some 600 workers' houses, in Carpenters Road and neighbouring streets.[11] South of High Street, in Sugar House Lane, the Reynolds estate was by 1862 being covered with factories.[12]

[87] *W. Ham C.B.C. Mins.* 22 Oct. 1909: Rep. by Borough Engineer on . . . Swing Bridge and Level Crossings, Silvertown.

[88] *D.N.B.* His son, G. P. Bidder Q.C. (1836–96) was an active partner in the North Woolwich Land Co. in 1884: W. Ham L.B. Mins. 25 Nov. 1884.

[89] *White's Dir. Essex* (1848), 239.

[90] See p. 79.

[91] For the early topography of these townships see: A. L. Dickens, *Rep. on W. Ham* (1855); E.R.O., D/CT 160 (tithe award, 1853); J. G. B. Marshall, *Map of W. Ham* (1869); H.O. 107/1768.

[92] H.O. 107/1768.

[93] Ibid. The census return mentions, among the street names of Plaistow New Town, only Durham Place, Victoria Terrace, Victoria Cottages, and Hume Row, North Woolwich Road. Hume Row was probably near the south end of the present Victoria Dock Road.

[94] A. L. Dickens, *Rep. on W. Ham* (1855), 50.

[95] Ibid. 50–1 and map.

[96] *Kelly's Dir. Essex* (1866); J. G. B. Marshall, *Map of W. Ham* (1869). Reaney (*P.N. Essex*, 97) stated that the name came from a firm of manufacturers, but no such firm is known.

[97] See p. 88.

[98] G. Howarth, and M. Wilson, *W. Ham*, 39; W.H.L., W. Ham L. B. Mins. 22 Mar. 1859; see also below, p. 74.

[99] Dickens, *Rep. on W. Ham* (1855) map.

[1] Ibid.; cf. O.S. Map 25", London, XXIX (surv. 1867).

[2] Ibid.

[3] E.R.O., *Sale Cat.* B 335 (Manbey Park, 1853); W. Ham L.B. Mins. 14 Feb. 1860.

[4] W. Ham L.B. Mins. 24 Apr. 1866. For this estate see below, p. 73.

[5] W. Ham L.B. Mins. 14 Mar. and 1 Apr. 1865; 22 Mar. 1870. Hudson's estate should not be confused with Hudson Town at Stratford.

[6] O.S. Map 25", London, XXIX (surv. 1867); Curwen, *Old Plaistow*, 54.

[7] W. Ham L.B. Mins. 28 July 1868, 26 Nov. 1878, 22 June 1880, 10 May 1881, 27 Jan. 1885.

[8] Ibid. 26 Nov. 1878: report by the board's medical officer.   [9] Ibid. 25 Mar. 1865.

[10] *Stratford Expr. W. Ham Jubilee Suppl.* 4 July 1936; W. Ham. L.B. Mins. 22 Dec. 1868; Howarth and Wilson, *W. Ham*, 33.

[11] For the Carpenters' institute and school see pp. 141, 154.

[12] W.H.L., Plan of Reynolds estate (1862).

WEST HAM (SOUTH) AND EAST HAM (SOUTH), 1965

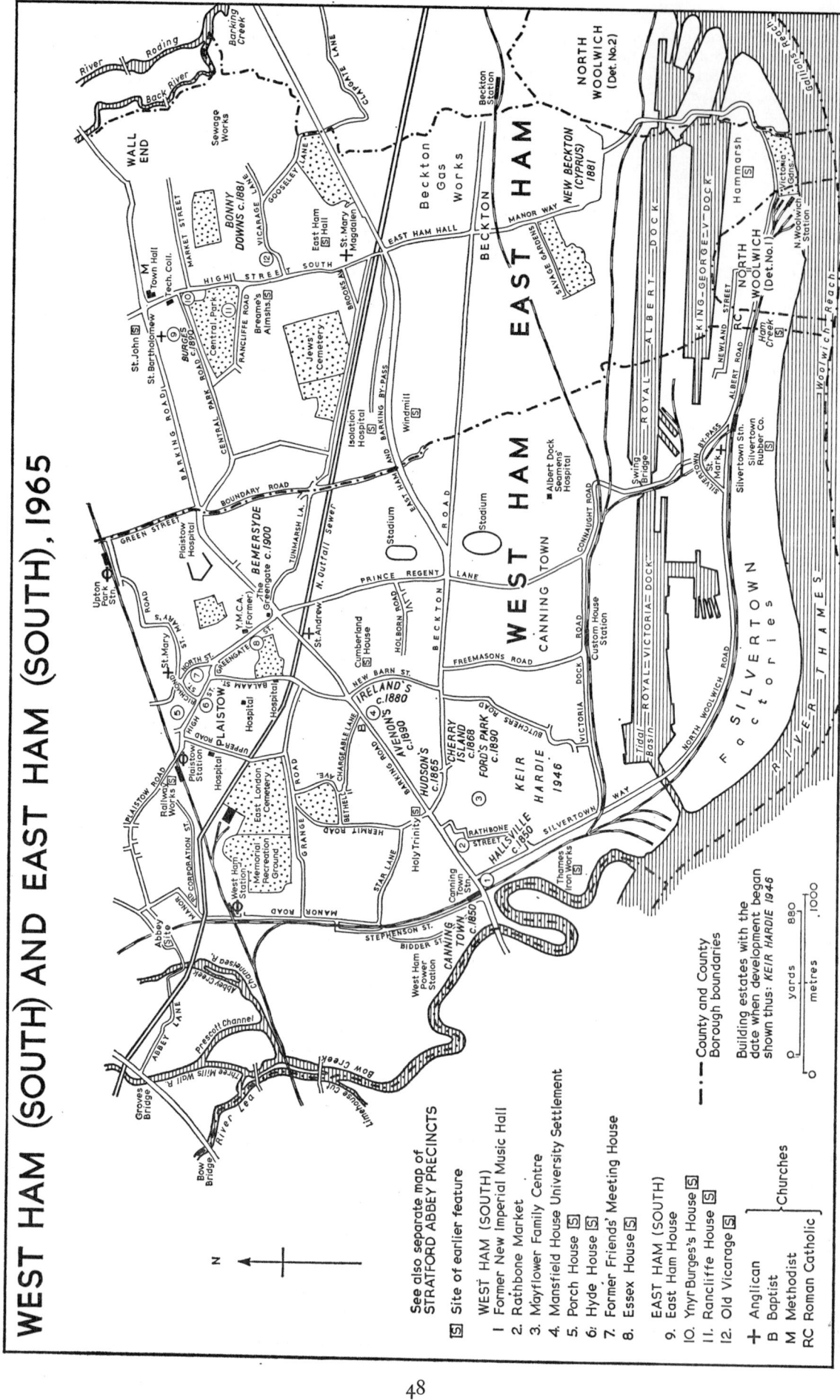

See also separate map of
STRATFORD ABBEY PRECINCTS

Ⓢ Site of earlier feature

WEST HAM (SOUTH)
1. Former New Imperial Music Hall
2. Rathbone Market
3. Mayflower Family Centre
4. Mansfield House University Settlement
5. Porch House Ⓢ
6. Hyde House Ⓢ
7. Former Friends' Meeting House
8. Essex House Ⓢ

EAST HAM (SOUTH)
9. East Ham House
10. Ynyr Burges's House Ⓢ
11. Rancliffe House Ⓢ
12. Old Vicarage Ⓢ

──── County and County
         Borough boundaries

Building estates with the
date when development began
shown thus: KEIR HARDIE 1946

✛ Anglican ⎫
B Baptist   ⎬ Churches
M Methodist ⎪
RC Roman Catholic ⎭

N

0 ────── yards ────── 880
0 ────── metres ────── 1000

After 1870 West Ham grew remarkably fast, and by the end of the century had become a great seaport and manufacturing town, with a northern fringe occupied by professional men and clerks working in London. Between 1871 and 1901 over 30,000 houses were built.[13] The peak building periods were about 1877–83 and 1897–1901.[14] In 1881–2 2,400 new plans were deposited with the local board, compared with 218 in 1870.[15] That was exceptional, but between 1886 and 1897 over 14,000 plans were deposited, and 13,000 buildings erected.[16] Most of the new building took place to the east of the older districts, but there was also a good deal of in-filling, especially in the areas west of old Plaistow, and north of Barking Road station.[17] Many of the new houses were on estates where building had started before 1870.[18] Among important new developments in the north were the Hamfrith (West Ham Hall) and Woodgrange estates, both at Forest Gate, east of Woodgrange Road. The Hamfrith estate, where development started about 1872, was bounded on the east by Manor Park cemetery, and included Godwin and Sebert Roads.[19] The Woodgrange estate, comprising 110 a. and extending into East Ham, lay between Romford Road and the railway,[20] Between 1877 and 1892 1,160 good quality houses were built there, mainly in Hampton, Osborne, Claremont, Balmoral, Windsor, and Romford Roads.[21] The development was started by Thomas Corbett, and continued by his son A. Cameron Corbett, later Lord Rowallan, whose work at Ilford has been described elsewhere.[22] The area south of Forest Gate was also growing fast. West Ham Park, dedicated to the public in 1874,[23] was an amenity likely to attract middle-class residents. The surrounding district was developed accordingly,[24] and the word 'park' was included in several of the local place-names. The area east of the park, previously occupied by country houses of wealthy Quakers,[25] was developed in the 1880s as the suburb of Upton Park.[26] The Matthews Park estate, comprising five roads north of the park, was developed in the 1890s.[27] The large Shirley House estate, built about the same time, lay in the angle between West Ham Lane and Romford Road.[28]

In the south of the borough, between 1871 and 1901, the building of houses followed industrial expansion, notably the completion of the Royal Albert Dock and the building of large new factories at Silvertown. West Ham was greatly affected also by the building of Beckton gasworks in East Ham, to which a railway, branching from the North Woolwich line, had been opened in 1874. During the 1880s there was much building in the Custom House district of Canning Town.[29] Developments in the 1890s included the Fords Park estate, which lay south of Beckton Road,[30] and the Avenon's charity estate, between Barking Road and Beckton Road.[31]

By 1901 most of the borough had been built up.[32] The development of the Bemersyde estate, occupying the triangle between Barking Road, Boundary Road, and Tunmarsh Lane, was completed about 1906.[33] The name Bemersyde was given to it by Henry Haig (1818–97), who acquired it about 1870. He was a distant descendant of an ancient Scottish family, the Haigs of Bemersyde (Roxburgh).[34] The estate was developed by his son Neil W. Haig (1868–1926). Its development coincided with the borough's first council houses, some 400 of which were built at Stratford, Plaistow, and Canning Town between 1899 and 1905.[35] By 1908 the only part of the borough which had still not been built upon was that east of Prince Regent Lane.[36] There was a little later building even there,[37] but some of that area still remains open.

Between 1918 and 1939 the borough council built about 1,200 more houses, under slum clearance and road improvement schemes. Some 600 more, built by the Ministry of Transport under the Silvertown Way scheme, were transferred to the council. There was little other building. During the Second World War some 14,000 houses, over a quarter of those in the borough, were destroyed. The damage was heaviest in the south, especially in Tidal Basin ward, which had contained some of the worst slums. Between 1945 and 1965 the borough council carried out redevelopment and slum clearance schemes in many areas, involving the building of over 9,500 dwellings, of which 8,000 were permanent. The main project was the Keir Hardie estate, north of the Royal Victoria Dock. Other large schemes were carried out at Bidder Street, Canning Town, Grange Road, Plaistow, Church Street, West Ham, Rokeby Street and Carpenters Road, Stratford, and at Stratford New Town.

Modern development has preserved the lines of most of West Ham's old roads, though, as shown above, some of the names have been changed. In the north of the borough the main thoroughfares

[13] V.C.H. Essex, v. 3, 5.
[14] Ibid.; W. Ham L.B. Mins. 1877–86; W. Ham B.C. (later C.B.C.) Works Ctee. Mins. 1886–90; W. Ham C.B.C. Mins. and Reps. 1890 f.
[15] W. Ham L.B. Mins. 10 Oct. 1882: Rep. of Surveyor.
[16] W. Ham C.B.C. Mins. Mar. 1897: Rep. of Borough Engineer.
[17] Works Ctee. Mins. 2 July 1889 (Grange Road); 4 Feb. 1890 (Star La.); C.B.C. Mins. 24 Oct. 1893 (Clarence Rd.).
[18] e.g. on the Gurney estate: E.R.O., D/DB E30 (Norwich and Clova Roads).
[19] See p. 69.
[20] This estate had been part of the manor of Woodgrange.
[21] 'Woodgrange Estate', Forest Gate Wkly. News, 9 Apr. 1897.
[22] V.C.H. Essex, v. 250–1.
[23] See p. 109.
[24] Cf. Howarth and Wilson, W. Ham, 43–4.
[25] See p. 53.
[26] W. Ham L.B. Mins. 28 Mar. 1882; W. Ham B.C. (later C.B.C.) Wks. Ctee. Mins. 4 Oct. 1887, 6 Feb. 1888, 2 Apr. 1889.

[27] Howarth and Wilson, W. Ham, 43; W. Ham C.B.C. Works Ctee. Mins. 7 Oct. 1890; C.B.C. Mins. 27 June 1893, 10 July 1894.
[28] W. Ham C.B.C. Works Ctee. Mins. 8 July 1890; C.B.C. Mins. 13 Dec. 1892.
[29] W. Ham L.B. Mins. 1881–6, passim; Howarth and Wilson, W. Ham, 57.
[30] W. Ham C.B.C. Mins. 12 July 1898.
[31] See p. 159.
[32] For descriptions of W. Ham about that time see: W. Besant, Shoreditch and the East End, 60–78; Howarth and Wilson, W. Ham, passim.
[33] Howarth and Wilson, W. Ham, 47–8; C.B.C. Mins. 5 Jan. 1904 (Kingsland, Olive, Patrick Roads); 7 Feb., 16 May 1905.
[34] Burke's Landed Gentry (1937 edn.) 1008–11; W.H.L., Bemersyde estate deeds c. 1898–1903; Kelly's Dir. Essex (1878 sqq.).
[35] See p. 110.
[36] Howarth and Wilson, W. Ham, map f. p. 32.
[37] e.g. C.B.C. Mins. 7 Feb. 1911 (Woodside Rd.); 7 Mar. and 4 Apr. 1911 (Connaught Garden estate).

are, in the main, the old roads widened and im-proved. In the south, however, some thoroughfares are entirely modern. The North Woolwich Land Co., when it began developing Plaistow Marshes in the 1840s, built North Woolwich Road from Can-ning Town to North Woolwich, parallel with the railway.[38] When the Victoria Dock was built shortly after, its entrance cut across that road and railway. The Eastern Counties Railway, which had acquired the North Woolwich branch, then built a new loop line to North Woolwich, skirting the north side of the dock and crossing its eastern tip by a swing bridge. A tunnel was later built under the dock for the loop. The old North Woolwich line, retained for goods traffic only, was carried over the dock entrance on a swing bridge only 23 ft. wide, which it shared, like a tram line, with the North Woolwich Road.[39] Along the north side of the dock, beside the railway, the North Woolwich Land Co. built Liliput Road, running from Victoria Dock Road, at Hoy Street, west to Custom House station. When the Albert Dock was built, Liliput Road was extended and linked with a new public road, Connaught Road, which ran parallel with the railway down to Silver-town station, passing between the two docks on the swing bridge. Traffic on both the upper and the lower roads to Silvertown was subject to long delays at the swing bridges and at several level crossings. Vehicles, though not pedestrians, were also obliged to pay tolls to the North Woolwich Land Co. About 1866 the local board took over the original part of Liliput Road, but the company retained control of North Woolwich Road, and of the Liliput Road extension when that was built. As Silvertown grew, the company came to draw a large income from tolls, while spending little on the repair of its roads. In 1884, under pressure from the local industrialists, the local board secured statutory powers to acquire North Woolwich Road and the Liliput Road ex-tension.[40] It completed the purchase in 1886, and immediately made up North Woolwich Road.[41] In 1887 Liliput Road was renamed as part of Victoria Dock Road.[42]

The difficulties caused by the level crossings and the swing bridges became increasingly serious until 1934, when Silvertown Way was completed.[43] That new road, linking Barking Road and North Woolwich Road, was carried over Victoria Dock Road, the North Woolwich railway, and the dock entrance by a viaduct and bridges. The scheme also included a new road bridge over the Lea at Canning Town, the widening of Barking Road at its west end, and a new road, Silvertown By-Pass (1935), carrying North Woolwich Road over the railway north of Silver-town station.

Beckton Road, linking Canning Town with the new gasworks at Beckton, was built about 1870.[44] The section of it east of Prince Regent Lane was a private road belonging to the Gas Light and Coke Co., which levied tolls there until 1931, when the road, so far as it lay in West Ham, was bought by the borough council.[45] The East Ham and Barking By-Pass, which diverges from Beckton Road at Prince Regent Lane, was opened in 1928 and given a second carriage-way in 1959.[46]

The need for a direct thoroughfare from the western side of Canning Town to Stratford was soon recognized, but has never been fully met. The local board discussed it as early as 1862, and in 1879 approved a scheme for a 50-ft. road running from Barking Road, opposite Rathbone Street, north to join Bridge Road.[47] That was not carried out, but a partial substitute was provided in 1889, when the Great Eastern Railway diverted and widened Manor Road during improvements to the North Woolwich branch line.[48]

In the north of the borough the most notable road works have been at High Street, Stratford, which during the past forty years has been altered almost beyond recognition. The High Street Im-provement Scheme, for which the borough council secured statutory powers in 1930, was closely linked with the River Lee Flood Relief Scheme.[49] It was delayed by the Second World War, but was com-pleted in 1964, providing a dual carriage-way from Station Street to Bow Bridge. Under a new scheme, completed in 1967, a flyover was built at Bow Bridge to carry east–west traffic.

Communications between Stratford and Plaistow have been improved by the construction of New Plaistow Road, completed in 1959, which links West Ham Lane and Plaistow Road, by-passing West Ham village.[50] That was part of a redevelopment scheme which also included the widening of Plaistow Road and High Street.

It is relevant to include the northern outfall sewer in an account of modern roads, because the flat-topped embankment which carries it is laid out as a public footpath. The sewer enters West Ham near Marshgate Lane, Stratford, and runs south-east, at a commanding height, to its outfall on the Thames by Barking creek. It was built by the Metropolitan board of works in 1868, to drain the northern half of London.[51]

The origins of many of West Ham's minor modern street names have been the subject of a special study.[52]

DOMESTIC BUILDINGS.[53] A survey of Plaistow ward carried out in 1742 lists 152 houses, of which

[38] For the early history of the North Woolwich and Victoria Dock Roads see: W.H.L., W. Ham L.B. Bill, Proc. in House of Commons Sel. Ctee. (1884); *Mins. W. Ham C.B.C.*, xxiii (1909), p. 1892.
[39] W.H.L., Illus. Coll., Box T (Photos. 1904). See below, p. 62.
[40] W. Ham L.B. Extension of Powers Act, 1884, 47 & 48 Vict. c. 61 (local act.).
[41] W. Ham L.B. Mins. 22 June, 27 July 1886.
[42] W. Ham B.C. Works Ctee. Mins. 16 Nov. 1887.
[43] For Silvertown Way see: D. McDougall, *Fifty Years a Borough: the story of W. Ham*, 177–82; *Engineering*, 21 Sept. 1934.
[44] O.S. Map 25″, London, XXXIX (1869 edn.); E.H.L., East Ham Par. Rate Bks. 1872.

[45] W. Ham L.B. Mins. 22 Apr. 1886; W. Besant, *Shore-ditch and the East End*, 65; *W. Ham C.B.C. Mins.*, xlv (1930–1), 459, 1557; inf. from Mrs. E. Taylor.
[46] *E. Ham Municipal Diary*, 1928–9, p. 181; *Stratford Expr.* 20 Feb. 1959.
[47] W. Ham. L.B. Mins. 25 Feb. 1862, 11 Nov. 1879.
[48] W. Ham C.B.C. Mins. Works Ctee. 5 June 1888, 21 May 1889.
[49] McDougall, *Fifty Years a Borough*, 188–90; F. Sainsbury, *W. Ham, Eight Hundred Years*, 21–2.
[50] Inf. from Newham L.B. Architect's Dept.
[51] See p. 109.
[52] W.H.L., Vert. File E/WES/929: 'Derivation of Street Names in West Ham in use in 1895.'
[53] This section was written in 1970.

119 appear from descriptions to have been timber-framed and 33 of brick.[54] Thirty-four are described as old, which probably means 16th century or earlier. At that date Plaistow had about 29 per cent of the houses in the parish.[55] The other wards, for which there are no corresponding surveys, may have had a higher proportion of new buildings, but even so it is likely that about 100 pre-17th-century houses still survived in 1742. By 1970 only one was known to survive.

The most notable group of medieval buildings in West Ham was associated with Stratford Abbey, which is described elsewhere.[56] New Barns farm, which lay east of New Barn Street, at the south end of Plaistow, was part of the rectorial glebe of West Ham.[57] The tithe barns from which it was named were mentioned in the 12th century, and one large medieval barn survived there, adjoining Cumberland House, until c. 1900. The original vicarage house of West Ham, at the south end of Vicarage Lane, still existed in 1853, but was later demolished.[58] Manor-houses may have existed during the Middle Ages at Bretts and Sudbury in Plaistow, at Chobhams in Stratford, and at Woodgrange, but nothing is known of them.[59] Christendom House at Plaistow was part of a small estate, probably in New Barn Street, which in the early 15th century belonged to Robert Christendom, draper of London.[60] In 1742 it was an old boarded house of three storeys; it was demolished in 1764.[61] Porch House, on the north side of High Street, Plaistow, is said to have been considered old even in the 16th century.[62] It was probably the large old boarded house which c. 1723 was given a brick front and two new wings.[63] From the 17th century to the 19th it belonged to the Rawstorne family. It was demolished in 1839. The site included the present Clegg Street. Sonables, or Senables, in West Ham Lane, Stratford, was a house belonging to the archdeacon of Essex *ex officio*. It has been traced from 1445 to 1708.[64] Nothing is known of its appearance or construction. The site, now part of the recreation ground, still belonged to the archdeacon in 1853.[65]

Among buildings probably dating from the 16th century was Hyde House, High Street, Plaistow, which was probably the mansion to which a tenement called The Hyde belonged in 1605.[66] A wall in the adjoining yard was dated 1559, and over a red brick gateway to the south were the date 1579 and

the inscription 'This is the gate of Everlasting Life'. The improbable tradition that the house was occupied after the Dissolution by the monks of Stratford is first recorded in the 18th century. In the later 17th century Hyde House was the seat of Sir Thomas Foot, lord mayor of London. In 1742 it was an old boarded house occupied by Aaron Hill (1685–1750), the dramatist and poet.[67] It was demolished shortly before 1811.[68] The gateway of 1579, which had latterly been built into the wall of a barn, was demolished in 1859.[69] The farm-house to which the barn then belonged was demolished at the same time. It had contained wall-paintings of biblical subjects.[70]

Essex House, Greengate Street, Plaistow, is said to have been a large white house with Tudor windows.[71] It was demolished in 1836, but part of the garden wall survived until 1905, and a wrought iron gateway still remains. After 1836 some of the materials from the house were used on the same site to build Essex Lodge, a cottage-style residence with gables and ornamental barge-boards, now occupied by the municipal parks department.[72] Features retained from the earlier house include an enriched shellhood of c. 1700 over the front door, and, internally, what appears to be an early-18th-century stone doorway adapted as a fire-place. Above the latter was the crest of the Willyams family, a ducal coronet surmounted by a falcon with folded wings.[73] This suggests that Essex House was the large old plastered house occupied in the mid 18th century by Thomas Willyams, and later by John Willyams, who left in 1768.[74]

The existence of several of West Ham's inns can be traced from the 16th century or earlier. The Cock at Stratford occurs in 1485.[75] The Blue Boar, High Street, Stratford, mentioned in 1538, was rebuilt in 1886, refronted c. 1936, and later demolished.[76] The Angel, Church Street, was formerly a timber-framed building of the 16th or early 17th century but was rebuilt in 1910.[77] The Spotted Dog, Upton Lane, is the only ancient building, apart from the parish church, which survives in West Ham. It is a timber-framed structure dating from the 16th century or earlier, but has been much restored. It consists of a central block, which may once have contained an open hall, flanked by two-storeyed and jettied cross-wings with weatherboarded gables. A large extension of yellow brick was built to the north

---

[54] E.R.O., D/DPe M55: calculated from the lists of houses. The total for timber-framed houses includes those with brick extensions or fronts.
[55] According to an estimate made c. 1740 there were about 570 householders in the parish: Fry, *E. and W. Ham*, 219.
[56] See p. 112.   [57] See p 115.
[58] See p. 115.
[59] See pp. 69–74.
[60] *Feet of F. Essex*, iv. 6; *Cal. Close 1441–7*, 146–7; Lysons, *London*, iv. 255.
[61] E.R.O., D/DPe M55, First N.
[62] Fry, *E. and W. Ham*, 248; Curwen, *Old Plaistow*, 10.
[63] E.R.O., D/DPe M55, Gothic F, cf. W.H.L., Cal. Rawstorne Docs., R.; Curwen, op. cit. 10 (illus.).
[64] *Cal. Close 1447–54*, 104–5 (conveyance by Zanobias Mulakyn, archdeacon 1435–61); *Cal. Pat. 1461–7*, 221; S.C. 6/962; E.R.O., D/DA T109.
[65] E.R.O., D/CT 160; cf. O.S. Map 25″, London, XX (surv 1867).
[66] Lysons, *London*, iv. 256; E.R.O., D/DPe M55, Italic Z and &. Fry, *E. and W. Ham*, 245–7, confuses the ownership with that of the adjoining house.

[67] *E.R.* xliii. 63, 67.
[68] Lysons, *London, Suppl.* (1811), 361.
[69] Curwen, *Old Plaistow*, 11.
[70] E.R.O., D/DPe M55, Italic Z probably refers to this house.
[71] Fry, *E. and W. Ham*, 250.
[72] Curwen, *Old Plaistow*, 3, 6, 7; W.H.L., Illus. Coll. (Houses), Photo of chimney-piece, Essex Lodge (1970).
[73] *Fairbairn's Crests*, ed. J. MacLaren, i, pl. 41, cf. ii. 509. This identification was made by Mrs. E. Taylor, Newham Libraries. The ducal coronet was also formerly depicted on the iron gateway outside Essex Lodge: Curwen, *Old Plaistow*, frontispiece.
[74] E.R.O., D/DPe M55, Small l. Cooper Willyams (1762–1816), son of John, is said to have been born at Plaistow House, which may have been the earlier name of Essex House: *D.N.B.*
[75] E.R.O., D/AER 1, f. 75v; S.C. 6/962.
[76] S.C. 6/962; W.H.L., W. Ham L.B. Mins. 23 Mar., 13 Apr. 1886; Illus. Coll. (Pub. Hos.).
[77] W.H.L., Illus. Coll. (Pub. Hos.); *W. Ham C.B.C. Mins.* 7 Dec. 1909; Bk. of Cuttings, 'Stratford and Bow', item dated 1910.

in the later 19th century. In 1968 the inn was thoroughly renovated and a smaller addition, partly weatherboarded, was built to the east.[78] In the later 19th century the Spotted Dog's tea-garden and cricket ground were well-known.[79] Among other early inns was the Swan, Stratford, first recorded in 1631.[80] Early in the present century the Swan, next to the town hall in High Street, was an 18th-century building of three storeys and attics, with a 19th-century frontage to the ground floor. It was rebuilt c. 1925.[81] The Bird in Hand, in the same street, existed in 1667 and survived until c. 1892.[82] The Unicorn, Church Street, is recorded from c. 1670 to 1908.[83]

By the 17th century West Ham's growth as a prosperous suburb of London could be seen in the high proportion of large houses. In 1670, for example, 30 per cent of the houses in the parish had 5 or more hearths, compared with only 17 per cent in Ongar hundred, a neighbouring rural area.[84] Within the parish, however, there were striking variations. Of the four wards Stratford contained 45 houses with 5 or more hearths (25 per cent of the total there), Plaistow 43 (40 per cent), Church Street 26 (25 per cent), and Upton 10 (40 per cent).

Rokeby House, Broadway, Stratford, is thought to have been built in the earlier 17th century.[85] The name, which has not been found before the 19th century, may be connected with the family of the Revd. H. R. Rokeby, who owned an estate at Stratford in 1853.[86] The earliest known occupants were the Clowes family, whose arms were carved in wood on a Jacobean chimneypiece in the house. William Clowes (1582–1648), of London and Stratford, compounded for his estates in 1646 as a royalist.[87] He had been surgeon to Charles I. In the 19th century Rokeby House became a school and later accommodated the offices of the parish vestry and the local board, and West Ham's first public library.[88] It was demolished in 1898.[89] Photographs taken then show a mainly 18th-century front of two storeys and attics, with 7 bays and two classical doorways, but the back of the building, with its irregular gabled roof-line, was considerably older; one gable with ornamental brickwork may well have dated from the earlier 17th century.[90]

At Plaistow Cumberland House, Elkington Road, off New Barn Street, must have been standing in the 17th century if not earlier. In 1742 it was a brick building of three storeys.[91] It was bought in 1787 by Henry, duke of Cumberland (d. 1790) and subsequently took his name. In 1902 it possessed a five-bay front of two storeys with a parapet swept up over a central attic window.[92] That front probably dated from the early 18th century, but the back of the house was probably older. Cumberland House was demolished shortly before 1936.[93]

After 1700 West Ham reached its hey-day as a residential area favoured by merchants and professional men occupying large detached houses. New houses were built and older ones were modernized. Although few of them survive the appearance of many has been recorded.[94] Several, including Upton House (rebuilt 1731)[95] contained early-18th-century panelling and fine staircases with slender twisted balusters. The evidence points to a boom in high-class building during the first 30 or 40 years of the century. Later development tended to include somewhat smaller middle-class houses as well as large residences in extensive grounds. In the late 18th and early 19th centuries terraced houses and pairs were built along the roads on comparatively narrow frontages, especially at Stratford. Such dwellings apparently filled the needs of professional and business men who did not keep their own carriages but were able to use the improving coach and bus services to London.

Between 1700 and 1840 Stratford, Plaistow, and Upton maintained their separate identities. At Stratford large houses were to be found at Maryland Point, The Grove, The Green, and along Romford Road. Stratford House, The Grove, 'a substantial mansion with a uniform front',[96] has been traced from the early 18th century. It was the seat of John Henniker (d. 1803), Lord Henniker, a large local landowner.[97] When the railway was built close by, the house ceased to be attractive as a gentleman's residence.[98] It appears to have been demolished late in the 19th century, when Great Eastern Road was built across its site.[99]

South of the Green, in Romford Road, was an 18th-century house of brown brick with a fine wrought-iron gateway.[1] For many years up to 1907 it was a private school.[2] It became Church House (diocesan offices, c. 1916–30) and was later used by the corporation.[3] During the Second World War it was bombed, and after the war it was demolished. North of the Green were several 18th- or early-19th-century houses which were also bombed.[4] One of them, later a Territorial Army centre called Artillery

[78] W.H.L., Illus. Coll. (Pub. Hos.) includes many views of the Spotted Dog.
[79] E. Walford, *Greater London*, i. (1894), 505; W. H.L., Illus. Coll. (Pub. Hos.), Poster showing inn and cricket ground. See plate.
[80] *E.A.T.* N.S. xiv. 149; *Cal. S.P. Dom.* 1637–8, 190–1; C 142/487/41; B.M. Add. MS. 37491, ff. 108, 114. See also E.R.O., T/A 12/2/11.
[81] W.H.L., Illus. Coll. (Pub. Hos.)
[82] *E.A.T.* N.S.xiv. 149; *E.R.* liv. 67; E.R.O., T/A 12/2/11; *Kelly's Dir. Stratford* (1891/2 cf. 1892/3).
[83] *E.A.T.* N.S. xiv. 153; E.R.O., T/A 12/2/11; *Kelly's Dir. Essex* (1908).
[84] E.R.O., Q/RTh 5, cf. *V.C.H. Essex*, iv. 306–8.
[85] *London*, 26 May 1898; W.H.L., Illus. Coll. (Houses).
[86] E.R.O., D/CT 160.
[87] *Cal. Ctee. for Compounding*, p. 1527.
[88] Fry, *E. and W. Ham*, 173; McDougall, *Fifty Years a Borough*, 145; and see p. 100 below.
[89] *W. Ham C.B.C. Mins.* 28 June 1898.
[90] W.H.L., Illus. Coll. (Houses).

[91] E.R.O., D/DPe M55, First C; Fry, *E. and W. Ham*, 252–3; Curwen, *Old Plaistow*, 16.
[92] *Fifty Years a Borough*, 59, cf. Curwen, *Old Plaistow*, f. pp. 16 and 17.
[93] *Fifty Years a Borough*, 59.
[94] W.H.L., Illus. Coll. (Houses).
[95] See p. 53.
[96] W.H.L., Press Cuttings, 'Stratford and Bow', Sale Notices, Stratford Ho. (1806).
[97] See pp. 10, 68.
[98] W.H.L., Press Cuttings, 'Stratford and Bow', Sale Notices, Stratford Ho. (1840).
[99] For the site cf.: Clayton's Surv. W. Ham (1821), Stratford K105; W.H.L., W. Ham Manor, Copyhold Tenements [c. 1805], no. 168; O.S. Maps 25", London XX (1867 edn.) and London VI (1916 edn.).
[1] W.H.L., Illus. Coll. (Houses), Church Ho.
[2] Stratford House school, see p. 157. It must be distinguished from Stratford House in The Grove.
[3] E.R.O., Pictorial Coll.; W.H.L., Illus. Coll. (Streets); *Chelmsford Dioc. Y.B.* (1916) sqq.
[4] W.H.L., Illus. Coll. (Streets).

THE SPOTTED DOG.

ESTABLISHED UPWARDS OF 250 YEARS & SITUATED IN ONE OF THE MOST PLEASANT PARTS OF ESSEX
GOOD ACCOMMODATION FOR CRICKET & OTHER FIELD SPORTS
A SPACIOUS DINING ROOM & BILLIARDS,
DINNERS & TEAS PROVIDED ON THE SHORTEST NOTICE FOR LARGE OR SMALL PARTIES,
WINES & SPIRITS OF THE BEST QUALITY.

TRAINS RUN FROM FENCHURCH S^T. TO PLAISTOW & FROM BISHOPSGATE S^T. TO STRATFORD BRIDGE,
FREQUENTLY THROUGHOUT THE DAY ACCESSIBLE FROM EITHER STATION, BY A TEN MINUTES WALK
WILLIAM VAUSE, PROPRIETOR.
UPTON.

WEST HAM: THE SPOTTED DOG ABOUT 1860

LEYTON: SKATING ON THE HOLLOW POND, LEYTONSTONE, ABOUT 1911

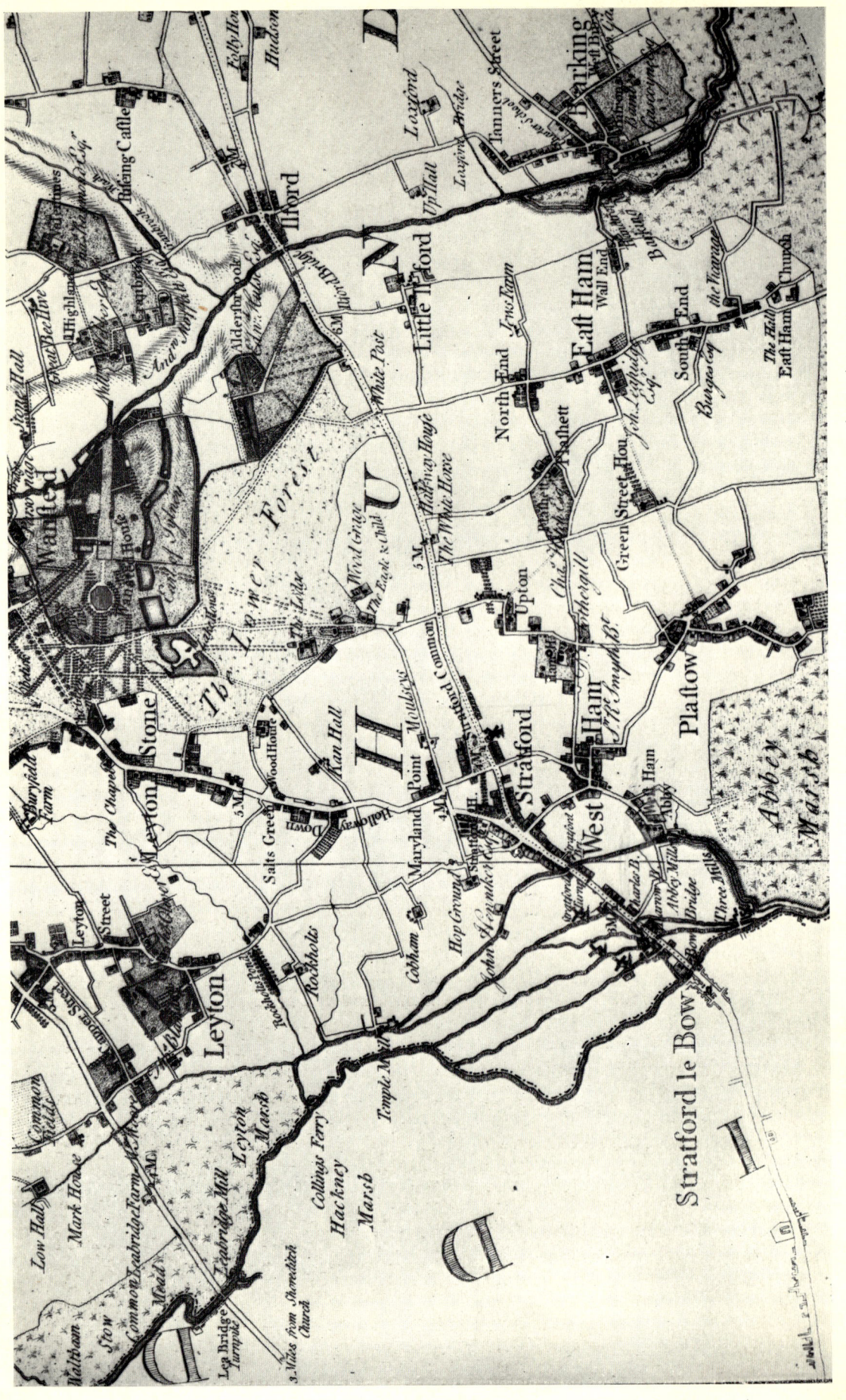

West Ham (north), East Ham (north), Little Ilford, Leyton, and Wanstead (south) in 1777

Scale c. 1·5 in. to 1 mile

House, had been built or rebuilt in Gothic style, probably *c.* 1840. Stratford Hall, on the corner of Romford and Carnarvon Roads, was an early-19th-century building, demolished in 1921.[5] A summer-house in the garden was thought to be older. Carnarvon Hall was at the north end of Carnarvon Road, on a site redeveloped *c.* 1868.[6] Near it, in Forest Lane, was Moulseys, which existed in 1777.[7] At that date there was also a cluster of buildings at Maryland Point.[8] The 18th-century gate piers of one of them survived until *c.* 1950.

The office of Arthur Webb Ltd., no. 30 Romford Road, Stratford, is an 18th-century weatherboarded building of 5 bays with a new roof. Angel Cottage, Windmill Lane, is a small double-fronted house dated 1826. Well-preserved and clad with creeper, it is a remarkable survival in an industrial area. The North West Ham Labour club (no. 62), Forest Lane and St. John's House (no. 2), Romford Road are substantial detached houses, of *c.* 1840, each with a classical portico. A few other houses in Broadway and High Street may date from the early 19th century, though altered by the insertion of shop-fronts.

At Plaistow development between 1700 and 1840 was mainly within the old village. In *c.* 1742–80 25 new houses were built and 13 old ones rebuilt.[9] The larger houses were typically of five bays and three storeys. Richmond House, Richmond Street, was an early-18th-century building with a segmental pediment and Corinthian pilasters to the front door.[10] John Curwen lived there in the 1860s.[11] The house was demolished in 1930.[12] Broadway (or Great) House, in Broadway, also built in the 18th century, belonged in the early 19th to the Martens, who were often visited by William Wilberforce.[13] It was demolished in 1882. In High Street one 18th-century house, no. 125, still survives. The front has recently been rebuilt.[14] At the north end of Balaam Street was an unnamed house occupied in 1754–66 by William Dodd.[15] In 1742 it was described as modern.[16] It was demolished in 1890 and replaced by the Laurels. Brunstock Cottage, no. 83 Balaam Street, still survived, greatly altered, in the 1930s, but was later demolished.[17] Edmund Burke lived there 1759–61. In 1742 it was apparently a boarded two-storey house.[18] Chesterton House, Balaam Street, had an early-19th-century front of seven bays, but an older interior.[19] Among its occupants

was Luke Howard.[20] It later became part of Plaistow maternity hospital,[21] but was demolished in 1960.[22] North of Plaistow village, on the site of the present Willow Grove and Valetta Grove, was the Willows, formerly Bedfords, a large house probably built in the early 19th century.[23] Its lodge, a single-storey gabled cottage of *c.* 1840, still stands in Willow Grove but slates have replaced the old thatched roof.[24]

Between 1700 and 1840, and indeed until after 1850, Upton remained an area of big houses in extensive grounds. In the earlier 19th century the residents included several leading Quakers, a closely-knit community linked by marriage with the Pelly family, West Ham's principal landowners.[25] Ham House, rebuilt in the 18th century, was the seat of Samuel Gurney (d. 1856).[26] The Cedars, adjoining Ham House in Portway, also belonged to him.[27] From 1829 to 1844 it was occupied by his sister Elizabeth Fry and her family, who in 1842 entertained Frederick William IV of Prussia there. The Cedars later became a Territorial Army centre. It had a yellow-brick front with a central pediment and classical porch and was said to have been constructed in the early 19th century from the barn and farm buildings of an earlier house. It was demolished in 1960.

Upton House, Upton Lane, was occupied in the early 19th century by another distinguished Quaker family, the Listers, including the future Lord Lister, who was born there. It had been rebuilt in 1731, possibly by Sir Philip Hall, as one of West Ham's finest houses.[28] It was a brick building of two storeys and attics. The entrance (west) front, of nine bays, was faced with stucco and altered in the 19th century. Most of the rooms had early-18th-century panelling, and there was a fine staircase with twisted balusters. In the kitchen there was a moulded beam of the 15th or 16th century, possibly brought from another building.[29] Adjoining the house to the north there was a smaller and longer building, possibly older.[30] This still existed in 1870, but must have been demolished soon after, probably during the 1880s, when Lancaster Road was built.[31] From 1893 to 1959 Upton House was St. Peter's vicarage.[32] It was demolished in 1968.

The Manor (or Four Manor) House, Upton Cross, demolished *c.* 1885, was the seat of the Pellys.[33] Herne House, Upton Lane, was built *c.* 1770 and

[5] Ibid. (Houses); C. Whitwell, 'Dictionary of W. Ham'.

[6] O.S. Map 25″, London, XX (1867 edn.); W. Ham L.B. Mins. 23 June 1868.

[7] Chapman and André, *Map of Essex*, 1777, sheet xxi.

[8] Ibid.

[9] E.R.O., D/DPe M55.

[10] Curwen, *Old Plaistow*, 20, 25, pls. f. pp. 4, 20; W.H.L., Illus. Coll. (Houses).

[11] Curwen, op. cit. 27; *White's Dir. Essex* (1863), 620.

[12] *Jeyes Sanitary Compounds Co.* (pamph.); *E.R.* xl. 22.

[13] Curwen, op. cit. 6, 8, 9.

[14] Cf. W.H.L., Illus. Coll. (Streets): Broadway (*recte* High St.), Water-colour 1926.

[15] Curwen, op. cit. 11–12. For Dodd see below, p. 116.

[16] E.R.O., D/DPe M55, Italic S.

[17] Curwen, op. cit. 14–15; Crouch, *Silvertown*, 42; Fry, *E. and W. Ham*, 252; P.E.M., P. Thompson, 'West Ham Gleanings'.

[18] E.R.O., D/DPe M55, First V.

[19] W.H.L., Illus. Coll. (Houses); Curwen, *Old Plaistow*, 13, pls. f. pp. 12, 13.

[20] See p. 82.

[21] See p. 111.

[22] Inf. from Newham Libraries.

[23] P.E.M., P. Thompson, 'West Ham Gleanings'; O.S. Map 25″, London, XXX (1863–7 edn.).

[24] Cf. Curwen, op. cit. 36.

[25] See *Katharine Fry's Bk.* ed. J. Vansittart, *passim*.

[26] See p. 72.

[27] Fry, *E. and W. Ham*, 237–9; W.H.L., Illus. Coll. (Houses); *Katharine Fry's Bk.*, f. p. 64.

[28] The date appeared above the porch. Hall certainly lived at Upton (Morant, *Essex*, i. x) but his connexion with this house has not been proved. The lands which he bought from the Buckeridges were mainly in the Manor Road and Vicarage Lane area: Fry, *E. and W. Ham*, 239; W.H.L., F. Dacre's Acct. of W. Ham Abbey Lands; Abbey Land Ratebooks.

[29] *E. Nat.* xxiv. 94–5, 136; W.H.L., Illus. Coll. (Houses).

[30] McDougall, *Fifty Years a Borough*, illus. p. 63.

[31] W.H.L., Illus. Coll. (Houses), Upton Ho., *Sale Cat.* 1870; Lancaster Rd. existed in 1890: *Kelly's Dir. Essex* (1890), Upton.

[32] *Chel. Dioc. Y.B.* (1959–60); *The Times*, 23 May 1966; see below p. 122. A baluster from Upton House is now (1972) in P.E.M.

[33] See p. 73.

demolished in 1896.[34] J. S. Curwen lived there c. 1882–90. The Red House, Upton Lane, has been traced from the 18th century, but was reconstructed in a florid style in the 1870s.[35] It is now St. Anthony's Catholic Club. Grove House, Upton Lane, was an 18th-century three-storey building.[36] It was for long the preparatory department of St. Angela's convent school, but was demolished in 1950.

At Forest Gate there were few buildings before the 19th century. Hamfrith House, which probably originated as a farm-house in the 18th century, was rebuilt c. 1800 as a gentleman's residence, later called West Ham Hall, in Sebert Road.[37] Forest House, Dames Road, was the home of the Dames family until the 1860s, and was probably demolished about then.[38] Between Forest House and Wanstead Flats were several other large houses, one of which, dating from c. 1840, survives as no. 91 Dames Road.

Little is known about the houses of the poor before 1840. A few timber-framed 16th-century cottages in Church Street, West Ham, survived until the 1930s or later.[39] Wenny's Cottages, Romford Road, Stratford, demolished 1907, formed a weatherboarded terrace probably dating from the 18th century.[40] Wilton's Yard, Angel Lane, Stratford, contained five wooden hovels built along the sides of the alley leading to an 18th-century detached house.[41] Such development, probably of the early 19th century, was also to be found in several other places in the Angel Lane and High Street areas of Stratford.[42] Wood's Yard, Dean's Court, and Channelsea Court, all off High Street, were slums singled out for reprobation in the Dickens report of 1855.[43] Opposite Channelsea Court was Rabbit Hutch Row, which was sometimes flooded by the Channelsea, and where the inhabitants used the stream both as a sewer and a source of drinking water. The houses had brick basements with one or two weatherboarded living rooms above. Among cottages at Plaistow were some occupied by the immigrant Irish potato workers, in Pinnocks Place, off North Street, and in Greengate Street.[44] Those also were mentioned in the Dickens report.[45]

A writer in c. 1740 stated that there were more than 60 public houses in West Ham.[46] In the later 18th century the number fell, no doubt as the result of stricter control by quarter sessions: 46 were licensed in 1769, 34 in 1795, and 32 in 1815.[47] In 1742 there were about 14 in Plaistow ward.[48] Among them were the Crown, later the Abbey Arms, Barking Road, the Black Lion and the Coach and Horses, both in High Street, and the Greyhound, Balaam Street.[49] The Abbey Arms was refronted c. 1820 and rebuilt in 1882.[50] The Black Lion, described in 1742 as an old plastered house, was largely rebuilt in 1875.[51] The Coach and Horses[52] appears also to have been rebuilt in the 19th century. The Greyhound, formerly the Greyhound and Hare, was rebuilt in 1773,[53] and the present building, though altered, may date from that time. The Greengate, Greengate Street, formerly the Gate, is recorded from 1776.[54] It was rebuilt in 1953–4.[55] The Prince Regent was built in 1811 on the river side at the northern end of the new ferry from Charlton (Kent).[56] When the North Woolwich railway was opened in 1847 the inn, no longer needed there, was demolished and rebuilt farther north in Prince Regent Lane.

At Stratford the Angel, the Cart and Horses, and the King of Prussia were listed in 1765.[57] The Angel, at the corner of Angel Lane and Broadway, was rebuilt c. 1870.[58] It is now a tailor's shop. About 1805 the Cart and Horses was in the Grove, adjoining Stratford House.[59] The building which it then occupied probably survived in 1970 as nos. 150 and 152 the Grove; parts of a staircase at no. 150 had slender twisted balusters of the early 18th century.[60] The sign of the Cart and Horses was removed after 1805 to the corner of Windmill Lane at Maryland Point, where a new building was erected c. 1880.[61] The King of Prussia, Broadway, probably commemorated Frederick the Great (king, 1740–86). It was renamed the King Edward VII in 1914.[62] The present building appears to date from the early 19th century.[63] Three other public houses of Stratford can be traced from 1776: the Pigeons, the Yorkshire Grey, and the Two Brewers.[64] The Pigeons (formerly Three Pigeons) Romford Road, was rebuilt c. 1898.[65] The Yorkshire Grey and the Two Brewers, both in High Street, were also rebuilt in the later 19th century.[66]

In West Ham village the King's Head, Church Street, recorded from 1765, was rebuilt in 1885.[67] The Adam and Eve, Abbey Road, was built amid the ruins of Stratford Abbey before 1732, when it

[34] Fry, E. and W. Ham, 242–3; Forest Gate Wkly. News 17 July 1896, 18 Aug. 1899.
[35] P.E.M., P. Thompson, 'West Ham Gleanings'.
[36] Inf. from Min. of Housing and L.G.; see below p. 154.
[37] See p. 69.
[38] O.S. Map 25″, London XIII (surv. 1863–7); Kelly's Dir. Essex (1866). For the development of the Dames estate see above, p. 47.
[39] McDougall, Fifty Years a Borough, 96; cf. W.H.L., Illus. Coll. (cardboard boxes).
[40] W.H.L., Illus. Coll. (Houses).
[41] Ibid. (Streets). See plate f. p. 117 below.
[42] O.S. Map 25″, London XX (surv. 1867).
[43] A. L. Dickens, Rep. to Gen. Bd. of Health on W. Ham, 42–8. For Channelsea Ct. see W.H.L., Illus. Coll. (Streets). For Wood's Yard see below p. 103.
[44] Curwen, Old Plaistow, 53, 6.
[45] A. L. Dickens, Rep. on W. Ham, 56.
[46] Fry, E. and W. Ham, 220.
[47] E.R.O., Q/RLv 24, 49, 69.
[48] E.R.O., D/DPe M55. The exact total is not certain because the record is obscure in one or two places.
[49] Ibid. First C, Gothic J, Italic V and L.
[50] Curwen, op. cit. 16.
[51] Curwen, op. cit. 42; W.H.L., Vert. File, Black Lion, Plaistow (pamph. N.D.); Illus. Coll. (Pub. Hos.).

[52] Curwen, op. cit. 6, 78.
[53] D/DPe M55, Italic L.
[54] E.R.O., Q/RLv 30; Curwen, op. cit. 38; Fifty Years a Borough, 58; W.H.L., Illus. Coll. (Pub. Hos.).
[55] Inf. from Charrington & Co.
[56] E.R.O., Q/RLv 64, cf. 65; Crouch, Silvertown, 55–6.
[57] E.R.O., Q/SBb 241.
[58] W.H.L., Illus. Coll. (Pub. Hos.). For deeds relating to the Angel see: E.R.O., T/A 12/2/11; W.H.L., Cal. Rawstorne Docs.
[59] W.H.L., W. Ham Manor, Copyhold Tenements [c. 1805], no. 167.
[60] For photographs of 150 and 152 The Grove see W.H.L., Illus. Coll. (Houses), Stratford House (with which 150 and 152 are sometimes identified).
[61] For deeds 1827 sqq. see E.R.O., T/A 12/2/11.
[62] Stratford Expr. 2 Oct. 1964.
[63] W.H.L., Illus. Coll. (Pub. Hos.).
[64] E.R.O., Q/RLv 30.
[65] E.R.O., D/Dch T52 and T/A 12/2/11; W.H.L., W. Ham C.B.C. Mins. 12 July 1898.
[66] For deeds of these houses: E.R.O., T/A 12/2/11.
[67] E.R.O., Q/SBb 241, Q/RLv 30, and T/A 12/2/11; W.H.L., W. Ham L.B. Mins. 11 Aug. 1885.

was 'a rendez-vous for fellows and wenches in the summer'.[68] It appears to have been enlarged in the mid 18th century and was rebuilt soon after 1900.[69] The Eagle and Child, Woodgrange Road, Forest Gate, existed, evidently as a house of some size, by 1744–6.[70] In the late 19th century, with pleasure grounds attached, it was a popular holiday resort.[71] It was rebuilt c. 1896.[72]

Between 1840 and 1914 over 40,000 houses were built in West Ham, mainly for letting to working-class tenants.[73] They were usually of two storeys in yellow or grey brick with slate roofs and contained 4–6 rooms. The simplest type, predominant c. 1840–60, was similar to the rural cottage of the period: a plain building, semi-detached or, more often, in a short terrace. A few examples survive: in Balaam Street, Plaistow (nos. 180–92);[74] Chant, Deason, and Union Streets, Stratford; Francis Street, Maryland (nos. 39–55); Odessa Road, Forest Gate (nos. 98 and 100, dated 1857); and Barking Road (nos. 588–606, formerly Augurs Cottages).[75] After 1860 such cottages, in long terraces, with front doors opening upon the pavement, and footscrapers in the walls beside them, were to be found mainly in the poorest areas, like William Street, Stratford (c. 1863, demolished 1969), Second Avenue (formerly Avenel Road) and Third Avenue (formerly Lennox Street), Plaistow (c. 1879), and Argyle and Garvary Roads, Canning Town (c. 1886).[76]

Terraces in a simple Georgian style, with the façades carried up to a cornice or coping, sometimes with billet-frieze ornament, were common throughout the town until c. 1880. Odessa Terrace (nos. 93–103), Odessa Road, Forest Gate (dated 1869) is in that style. Globe Crescent, (c. 1860), in Globe Road, Forest Gate, contains a rare example in West Ham of a curved terrace.[77] Another way of building on a curved frontage was to set the houses at an angle to the road in step formation. There is one such terrace, (c. 1860), in Chatsworth Road, Forest Gate, adjoining Globe Road, and another (c. 1870) in Stratford Road, Plaistow, where it forms a block of small shops called 'Market Place'.[78] Most houses built c. 1875–90 had ground-floor bay-windows. There are many dated examples, including Mabel Terrace, Cedars Road, Stratford (1876),[79] and Cornwall Terrace, Tunmarsh Lane, Plaistow (1889). From c. 1890 the bays were usually carried up to roof level as in Ness Terrace, Albert Road, Silvertown (1891), and Albion Terrace, Beckton Road, Canning Town (1898). After 1900 the bays were often square-sided,

with more pronounced gables, as in Crediton Road, Canning Town (c. 1903).[80] Houses with bays tended to fetch higher rents than those without,[81] and they predominated on most of the new estates built between 1880 and 1914. In spite of redevelopment they are still the commonest type in West Ham. Even in poor areas the windows were usually decorated with mass-produced stucco in the form of miniature columns with foliated capitals.

Some of the estates built in the later 19th century became slums. High land values and the great demand for cheap houses made good building unprofitable, especially in the south of the borough.[82] Most of the houses in that area were run up by speculative builders who had little capital or experience.[83] Here, as in other towns, this led not only to faulty workmanship and the use of poor materials[84] but to the wrong kind of houses. Many workers could not afford to rent a whole house, but until the 1890s very few flats were built in the borough. Consequently houses designed for a single family were often shared by two or more.[85] Conditions in West Ham, however, were much better than those in some older industrial areas.[86] A writer of c. 1900, in a book on the East End, could even state that 'poor people and dirty streets are the exception through West Ham'.[87]

The earliest council dwellings (1899–1905) were much better adapted to the needs of working-class tenants than those of the private builders. Most of them were two-storey 'double houses' with a flat on each floor. The flats varied in size from two to four rooms, with a wash-house to each flat. The original design was by Lewis Angell (borough surveyor 1867–99) who believed that such dwellings were 'healthier and more humanizing . . . especially for children', than large 'barrack-like' blocks of flats.[88] The largest estate, at Wise Road, Stratford (94 flats and 11 single houses) survives, along with others in Bethell Avenue, Plaistow, and in Eve and Corporation Streets, West Ham.[89]

Houses of more than six rooms formed only a small proportion of those built in the town after 1840.[90] The main group was at Forest Gate, in a belt extending from Romford Road north to the Great Eastern Railway, and from Carnarvon Road east to Balmoral Road. It included Hamfrith, Atherton, Norwich, Sprowston, and Clova Roads, and Earlham Grove, which were part of the Gurney estate (c. 1870–90),[91] and, farther east, most of the Woodgrange estate: Hampton,

[68] E. Nat. xxiv. 143. In 1968 the licensee said that the Adam and Eve was still 'a summer house'.

[69] W.H.L., Illus. Coll. (Pub. Hos.); Bk. of W. Ham (1923), 19. For deeds: E.R.O., T/A 12/2/11.

[70] J. Rocque, Surv. Lond. See also: Chapman and André, Map of Essex, 1777, sheet xxi; E.R.O., Q/RLv 30 and D/DA T129.

[71] E. Walford, Greater London, i. 505.

[72] W. Ham C.B.C. Mins. 22 Sept. 1896.

[73] V.C.H. Essex, v. 3, 5; Howarth and Wilson, W. Ham, 7 sqq.

[74] See plate f. p. 117.

[75] J. G. B. Marshall, Map of West Ham (1869).

[76] W. Ham L.B. Mins. 13 Jan. 1863; ibid. 24 June 1879; 28 Sept. 1886; B.C. Works Cttee. Mins. 28 Dec. 1886. Argyle and Garvary roads were awaiting redevelopment in 1970.

[77] O.S. Map 25" London, XX (surv. 1867); cf. Dickens, Rep. on W. Ham, map (1855).

[78] Stratford Road was being redeveloped in 1970, and

Globe and Chatsworth Roads were awaiting redevelopment.

[79] See plate f. p. 117.

[80] W. Ham C.B.C. Mins. 15 Sept. 1903.

[81] Howarth and Wilson, W. Ham, 44.

[82] Cf. V.C.H. Essex, v. 30–1.

[83] Howarth and Wilson, W. Ham, 9–19.

[84] Ibid. 55–6; Dickens, Rep. on W. Ham, 49.

[85] For slum conditions at Canning Town, c. 1895, see G. Gain, A Basinful of Revolution.

[86] Cf. 'Slum clearance and urban development', Architects' Jnl. 20 and 27 Sept. 1956.

[87] Sir W. Besant and others, Shoreditch and the East End, 77.

[88] London, 14 July 1898.

[89] W. Ham Mun. Yr. Bk. (1940), 188; Howarth and Wilson, W. Ham, 118–22.

[90] In 1961 the proportion was about 6 per cent.: Census (1961), Essex, 135.

[91] Cf. Howarth and Wilson, W. Ham, 41–3.

Osborne, Claremont, Windsor, and Richmond Roads, and the north side of Romford Road.[92] These houses, many of which survive, include detached, semi-detached, and terraced types. In Romford Road, where sites were no doubt more expensive, they are often three-storeyed. Some on the north side of that road had coach-houses in Atherton Mews and Sprowston Mews. One of the largest detached houses is Workington House, no. 328 Romford Road, built shortly before 1870.[93] It is a three-storey house of five bays with a Corinthian portico. John Curwen (d. 1880) lived there. The Woodgrange estate (1877–92) was much the largest middle-class development in West Ham.[94] It was laid out on the 'gridiron' plan common in the 19th century, but the plots are of good size, with gardens front and back. Most of the houses are double-fronted, some with glass-roofed verandahs.

Among other streets in north West Ham containing houses built for middle-class occupation are Westbury, Victoria (formerly Vale), and Palmerston Roads, at Upton, which were developed from c. 1860.[95] In Forest Lane, Forest Gate, are three pairs of semi-detached houses (nos. 122–7) built c. 1860. One pair still has the original porches, each supported by an iron column decorated with tracery. The columns resemble those supporting the canopy at the old (Windmill Lane) entrance to Stratford Railway station. At Plaistow only a few large houses were built between 1840 and 1914. No. 142 Balaam Street (c. 1850), is of three bays with three storeys and basement. In Chesterton and Howard's Roads are several pairs of large semi-detached houses of c. 1850–60.[96] The Laurels, Balaam Street (c. 1890)[97] is an imposing building of three storeys and basements, faced with ragstone. It was formerly the Freemasons' Club.[98] St. Andrew's Vicarage, St. Andrew's Road (1871), and St. Mary's Vicarage, Stopford Road (1897), are examples of the big houses sometimes built for professional men whose work required them to live among the poor.

The Pawnbrokers' alms-houses, Woodgrange Road, Forest Gate, were built in 1849 by the Pawnbrokers' Charitable Institution.[99] They accommodated 8 inmates, not necessarily from West Ham, who had qualified by subscription. The buildings formed an impressive group in 'Elizabethan' style. They were demolished in 1898. Legg's alms-houses, Odessa Road (1858–63), are small and plain, with gabled fronts.[1] Meggs's alms-houses, Upton Lane, were erected in 1893 by the rector and churchwardens of Whitechapel (Lond.), trustees of William Meggs's charity; the original buildings (1658) were in Whitechapel Road.[2] Among the few large shops have been J. R. Roberts (founded c. 1870) and Boardmans (1871), both drapers and furnishers in Broadway, Stratford.[3] Roberts was

demolished in 1957–62 to make way for the London Co-operative Society's new department store. Of the hundreds of small shops, in terraces or on street corners, few are notable, but in Water Lane, Stratford, is a single-storey butcher's shop (c. 1860, see plate facing page 203), with lively stucco ornament depicting bulls' heads over windows and doors, and an ironwork parapet.

After 1914 there was little private building. Of 1,200 municipal dwellings built in the 1920s and 1930s, mainly in connexion with slum-clearance, about half lay in the Manor Road area. They included over 400 flats in 4-storey blocks, in Memorial Avenue and neighbouring roads and in Star Lane.[4] Other council estates were built at Stratford, Plaistow, and Custom House. A further 600 houses, built by the Ministry of Transport in the Holborn Road area of Plaistow, to rehouse workers displaced by the Silvertown Way scheme, were taken over by the borough on their completion in 1931.[5] There and in all the council estates of the period much more use was made of red brick, which had superseded the standard yellow brick of the previous century.

After the Second World War West Ham council put in hand the huge building programme outlined elsewhere.[6] The main scheme was the Keir Hardie estate, comprising 230 a. north of the Royal Victoria Dock; it is one of the largest areas of comprehensive redevelopment in the country.[7] The earliest council building after the war followed a traditional 'garden city' pattern at a fairly low density. An example is the Bowman Avenue area, in the south-west corner of the Keir Hardie estate, where 70 per cent of the dwellings are houses and the remainder flats in low blocks.[8] In West Ham, as elsewhere, higher density housing became increasingly common after 1950. This is shown in the part of the Keir Hardie estate between Fife Road and Butchers Road, which contains 35 per cent houses, 36 per cent flats, and 29 per cent maisonettes, and incorporates experiments in plan, layout, and colours, intended to keep down costs and to suggest 'a living and bustling community'.[9] The trend towards even higher densities is obvious in the Claremont estate, east of Woodgrange Road, Forest Gate.[10] That scheme, completed about 1956, contains 76 per cent flats in an 11-storey tower or 'point' block, and 24 per cent maisonettes in 4-storey blocks. The schemes of the early 1960s include tower blocks of 15 storeys north of Fife Road, and of 22 storeys at The Green and Carpenters Road, both at Stratford.[11] In 1964 West Ham council decided to provide 1,000 dwellings in 200-ft. tower blocks erected on the Larsen-Nielsen industrialized system. The programme, continued by Newham council, suffered a setback in 1968, when part of Ronan Point, Clever Road, Canning Town, collapsed after a gas explosion.[12]

[92] See p. 49 and plate f. p. 117.
[93] *Kelly's Dir. Essex* (1866 sqq.); W.H.L., Illus. Coll. (Houses).
[94] *Forest Gate Wkly. News* 9 Apr. 1897.
[95] Howarth and Wilson, *W. Ham*, 44–5.
[96] Cf. O.S. Map 25", London, XXX (Surv. 1863–7).
[97] See p. 53.
[98] McDougall, *Fifty Years*, 60; *Bk. of W. Ham* (1923), 202; *W. Ham Official Guide* (1950), 92; (1963/4), 107.
[99] *Forest Gate Wkly. News* 18 Sept. 1896; 31 Mar. 1899; W.H.L., Illus. Coll. (Houses). [1] See p. 130.
[2] Inscription on Meggs's almshouses.

[3] *Kelly's Dir. Essex* (1878 sqq.); *E.R.* xxvii. 44; inf. from Newham Libraries.
[4] *W. Ham Municipal Y.B.* (1940).
[5] *W. Ham C.B.C. Mins.* xlv. 1010, 1022, 1095; xlvi. 1809.
[6] See pp. 49, 110.
[7] *W. Ham Official Guide* (1950), 25, 27. See below, plate f. p. 202.
[8] *Architects' Jnl.* 27 Sept. 1956, pp. 456–66.
[9] Ibid. [10] Ibid.
[11] Sainsbury, *Eight Hundred Years*, 58; Pevsner, *Essex*, 418.
[12] Min. of Housing, *Collapse of Flats at Ronan Point, Canning Town* (1968).

North of Beckton Road and in Kildare Road is a small but unusual estate designed for West Ham council by the Development Group of the Ministry of Housing and Local Government and completed in 1964.[13] Its 39 houses are of composite brick and timber construction and partly weatherboarded. They are of six types, some with movable internal partitions, grouped round a common open space of ½ a. They were built to Parker Morris standards after a social study designed to discover the needs of the kind of families for whom they were intended. In striking contrast to them is the landscape south of Beckton Road, where the skyline is increasingly dominated by tower blocks.

RIVERS, BRIDGES, WHARFS, AND DOCKS. *Rivers.* Much that has been written about the river Lea in relation to Waltham Holy Cross[14] is relevant also to West Ham. The old Lea, flowing south through Stratford, branches into several channels, collectively called the Stratford Back rivers. Before modern changes the course was as follows.[15] North of Temple Mills a stream, formerly known as the Temple Mills stream or the Shire stream and later as Waterworks river,[16] branched from the east bank. Channelsea river branched south-east from Waterworks river. Waterworks river rejoined the Lea north of Carpenters Road, Stratford. Below Carpenters Road three streams, branching from the east bank of the main river, flowed south, roughly parallel. From east to west these were Waterworks river, City Mill river, and Pudding Mill river. Those three, together with the main river to the west and the Channelsea to the east, all ran down to Stratford High Street, which crossed them by a series of bridges. North of High Street Waterworks river split into two branches, which rejoined south of the street as Three Mills Wall river, passing through Three Mills to Bow Creek. City Mills river also bifurcated north of High Street. One branch, called Bow Back river, flowed west to join the Lea at Bow Bridge. The other, joining Pudding Mill river, passed under High Street as Three Mills Back river, which joined Three Mills Wall river immediately north of Three Mills. Channelsea river ran into Bow creek (see plate facing page 79) south of Three Mills. All these streams were tidal.

At Stratford, as at Waltham Abbey, this complex pattern of channels has been associated with King Alfred,[17] who in 895 obstructed the river to strand the Danish fleet, but the evidence is inconclusive. The pattern seems to go back at least to the 11th century, when there was already a remarkable group of water-mills in West Ham.[18] Then, as later, the mills were probably on the branches rather than the main channel of the Lea. The branches were, in fact, mill streams, and probably originated as such.[19]

No major changes in the course of the river or its channels, affecting West Ham, seem to have occurred before the present century, though there were minor ones.[20] Some changes were the work of millers competing for water-power.[21] Others resulted from success or failure in the constant struggle against tidal flooding. In 1326 and later there are many references to a field called the Lake, which lay on the east bank of the Channelsea river just south of Channelsea Bridge.[22] Its name and position suggest that it had once been an actual lake, possibly caused by a breach in the river wall, but had been reclaimed. Before 1344 the abbot of Stratford and others obstructed and diverted the Lea to prevent flooding. The works, however, harmed shipping and had even caused the floods they were intended to cure, and their removal was ordered.[23] Under a general Act of 1351 similar commissions relating to the Lea, among other great rivers, were frequently issued in later years.[24]

From the 16th century various alterations were made to the course of the Lea to assist navigation. Those under an Act of 1571 seem not greatly to have affected West Ham.[25] Under an Act of 1767, however, Hackney Cut (1769) by-passed the old river between Lea Bridge and Old Ford, while Limehouse Cut ran south-west from Bromley, by-passing Bow creek.[26] Neither of the new cuts passed through West Ham, but they greatly improved the navigation immediately above and below the parish.

Since the 18th century the Lea, in West Ham, has also been directly affected by its use as one of the main sources of east London's water supply. The West Ham Waterworks Co., founded about 1745, established works at Saynes Mill, Stratford, on the stream which became known as Waterworks river.[27] The company later took over also St. Thomas's (or Pudding) Mill, on Pudding Mill river, and by 1849 its successor, the East London Waterworks Co., had a chain of reservoirs along the Lea on West Ham's north-western boundary.[28]

The greatest alteration to the channels of the Lea at Stratford was carried out in 1931–5 to improve drainage and navigation. Drainage was by then especially important. The Stratford Back rivers, linked with a network of open ditches, had for centuries drained the area north of High Street. In the later 19th century they had been polluted by domestic sewage from Leyton as well as West Ham

[13] Min. of Housing, *Family Houses at W. Ham* (1969).
[14] *V.C.H. Essex* v. 165–7.
[15] McDougall, *Fifty Years a Borough*, 183–5. Among many maps of the river are the following: S.P. 12/15/16 (c. 1560); W.H.L., Maps Coll., Mills at Bow (1676) (copy from Christ's Hosp. Docs.); E.R.O., D/DU 567/2 (1767); E.R.O., D/DYc 11/3 (1800); E.R.O., Q/RUm 1/7 (1804), 1/22 (1812) and 2/74 (1849).
[16] See p. 174.
[17] e.g. by K. Fry, *E. and W. Ham*, p. 7.
[18] See p. 89.
[19] As was stated by local jurors in 1303: B.M. Lansd. MS. 1 f. 19; K.B. 27/212 m. 95.
[20] e.g. W.H.L., Maps Coll., Map of Mills at Bow (1676) shows some channels not on later maps.
[21] R. Allison, 'The Changing Landscape of South-

West Essex, 1600–1850' (Lond. Ph.D. 1966), 156 n., 263–4.
[22] *Cat. Anct. D.* i, C 389, 743, 804, 1310, 1636, 7340; ii, C 2664, 2724; iii, C 3056, 3170; S.C. 12/15/20.
[23] *Pub. Works in Medieval Law* (Selden Soc.), i. 12.
[24] e.g. *Cal. Pat.* 1354–8, 234; ibid. 1358–61, 409; *Cal. Close* 1364–8, 48; *Cal. Inq. Misc.* 1348–77, 70–1.
[25] *V.C.H. Essex*, v. 166. But cf. E.R.O., T/P 48/2, f. 190: ref. to 'cutting of the shelf' near St. Thomas's mill in W. Ham.
[26] E.R.O., D/DU 567/2; Allison, op. cit. 167–9.
[27] See pp. 92, 108.
[28] E.R.O., Q/RUm 2/74 (map of Lea Navigation, 1849). Those reservoirs remained in use until early in the present century, when larger ones were built at Walthamstow and Chingford.

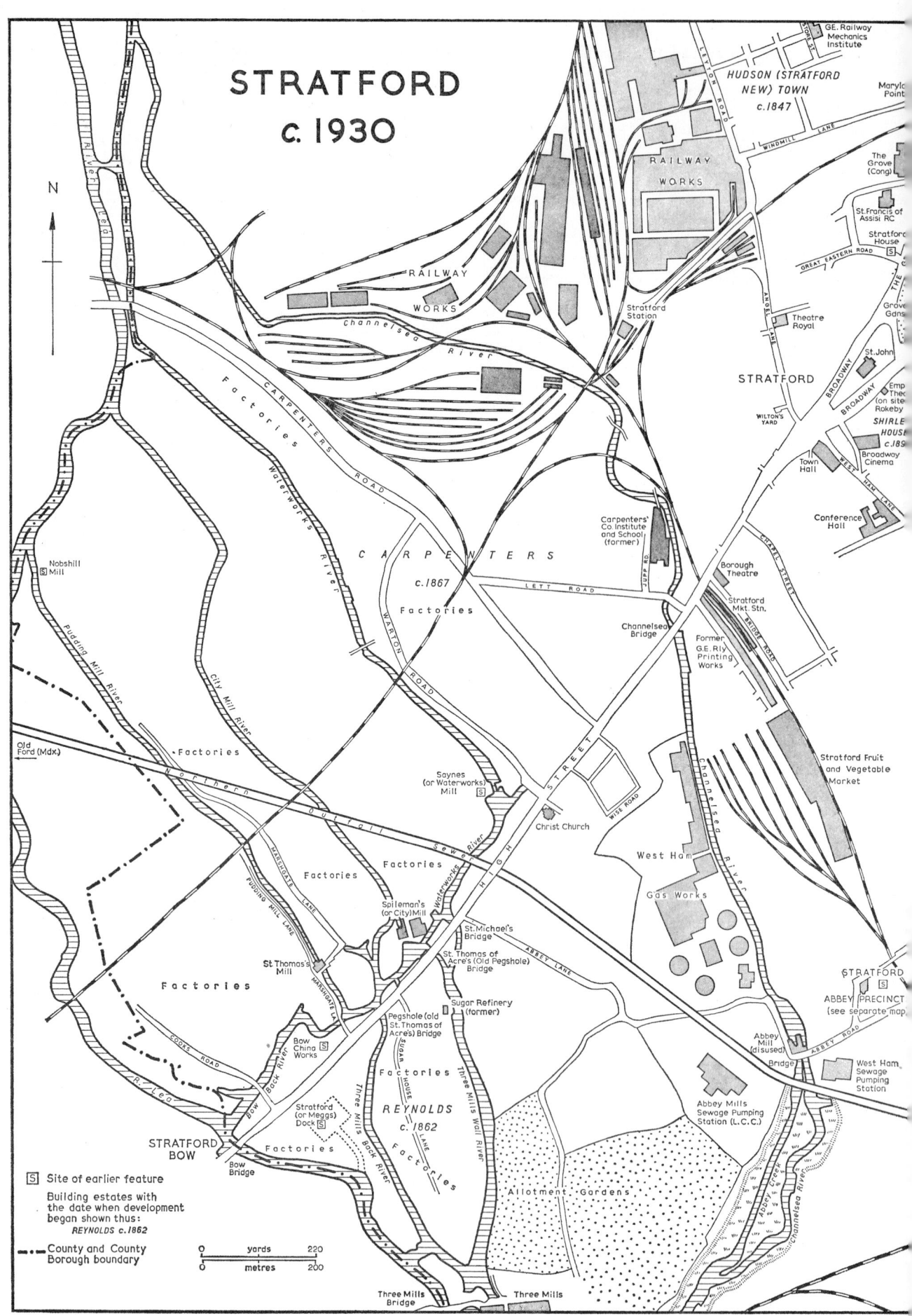

STRATFORD
c. 1930

N

HUDSON (STRATFORD NEW) TOWN c.1847

GE. Railway Mechanics Institute

Maryle Point

The Grove (Cong)

St.Francis of Assisi RC

Stratford House

STONE ROAD

WINDMILL LANE

RAILWAY WORKS

RAILWAY WORKS

River Lea Canal

Channelsea River

Stratford Station

Stratford Mkt. Stn.

Theatre Royal

STRATFORD

Grove Gdns

Emp Thea (on site Rokeby

SHIRLE HOUS c.189

Broadway Cinema

GREAT EASTERN ROAD

St.John

BROADWAY

WILTON'S YARD

Town Hall

Conference Hall

WEST HAM LANE

Carpenters' Co. Institute and School (former)

Borough Theatre

CARPENTERS

Factories Road

Waterworks River

c.1867

Factories

LETT ROAD

WARTON ROAD

Channelsea Bridge

Former G.E.Rly Printing Works

BRIDGE ROAD

ANGEL LANE

Nobshill Mill ⑤

Pudding Mill River

City Mill River

Old Ford (Mdx.)

Northern Outfall Sewer

Factories

Saynes (or Waterworks) Mill ⑤

Channelsea River

Stratford Fruit and Vegetable Market

HIGH STREET

WISE ROAD

Christ Church

West Ham

Gas Works

Factories

MARSHGATE LANE

Factories

Factories

Waterworks River

Spileman's (or City)Mill

St.Michael's Bridge

St.Thomas of Acre's (Old Pegshole) Bridge

ABBEY LANE

St Thomas's Mill

Sugar Refinery (former)

Pegshole (old St. Thomas of Acre's) Bridge

STRATFORD ABBEY PRECINCT (see separate map

Abbey Mill (disused)

Bridge

ABBEY ROAD

Factories

Bow China Works ⑤

SUGAR HOUSE LANE

Three Mills Back River

Three Mills Wall River

Abbey Creek

Channelsea River

West Ham Sewage Pumping Station

COOKS ROAD

River Lea

Bow Back River

REYNOLDS c.1862

Abbey Mills Sewage Pumping Station (L.C.C.)

STRATFORD BOW

Stratford (or Meggs) Dock ⑤

Factories

Factories

Bow Bridge

Allotment Gardens

⑤ Site of earlier feature

Building estates with the date when development began shown thus:
REYNOLDS c.1862

— — County and County Borough boundary

0 — 220
yards
0 — 200
metres

Three Mills Bridge

Three Mills

itself.[29] By 1931 all the foul sewers of the two boroughs were linked with the northern outfall sewer, but the Back rivers were still vital to storm drainage and they had become derelict and choked with rubbish. By an Act of 1930 the Lee conservancy board and West Ham borough council were empowered jointly to carry out a large-scale improvement scheme, involving the widening, dredging, and diversion of some streams, the filling-in of others, and the construction of new locks and bridges.[30] City Mill river was converted into a navigable stream 50 ft. wide. Waterworks river and Three Mills Wall river became a drainage stream 100 ft. wide, and the Prescott channel was constructed as a flood by-pass from Three Mills Wall river to Channelsea river. Three Mills Back river was occluded. There was another and minor alteration to the Stratford waterways in 1957–8, when Channelsea river was culverted between High Street and Lett Road.[31]

The course of the Thames, forming West Ham's southern boundary, appears to have changed little. East of Bow creek the only natural anchorage was Ham creek on the boundary with East Ham. In the later 17th century that was used as a naval dockyard, subsidiary to Woolwich. It was occluded in the later 19th century.[32]

Bridges. Before recent changes the main road from London crossed the Lea and its branches at Stratford by five bridges, all of ancient origin. The main river was spanned by Bow Bridge and Channelsea river by Channelsea Bridge. Between them were three smaller bridges: St. Michael's (or Harrow) Bridge and Pegshole Bridge spanning, respectively, the eastern and western arms of Waterworks river, and St. Thomas of Acre's Bridge, spanning Three Mills Back river. During the 19th century, as the result of confusion over the ownership of Pegshole and St. Thomas's bridges, the names of those two bridges were transposed. In 1933 St. Michael's, Pegshole, and St. Thomas's bridges were all replaced by the larger Groves Bridge, built in connexion with the flood relief scheme.

The original Bow and Channelsea bridges were built between 1100 and 1118 by Maud, Queen of Henry I.[33] Before her time the main road from London into Essex crossed the Lea by a dangerous ford at Old Ford, about ½ m. north of Stratford. Having built the bridges Maud bought the Abbey Mill and land in West Ham and gave them to Barking Abbey in trust for the maintenance of the bridges.[34] The bridges and their endowment were later taken over by Stratford Abbey (founded 1135). Stratford contracted for the repair of the bridges with a bridgemaster, who sought alms from travellers. William Prat (later Bridgewright), who succeeded his father as bridgemaster in the early 13th century, began levying tolls, but his toll-bar on Bow Bridge[35] was eventually broken down by Philip Basset[36] and the abbot of Waltham, and he then abandoned the bridges, probably about 1240. From then onwards responsibility for the two bridges was the subject of recurrent inquiry[37] until 1315, when Stratford Abbey formally accepted responsibility for them in return for £200 paid by Barking Abbey.[38] By 1366, however, Bow Bridge was again dilapidated and the government levied a pontage for its repair.[39] In 1465–6, after further litigation, Stratford Abbey's responsibility was confirmed.[40]

After the Dissolution there was again a long period of uncertainty concerning the repair of the two bridges, arising from the fragmentation of Stratford Abbey's lands.[41] In 1691 it was at last agreed that the bridges and the approaches to them were the responsibility of the landowners in West Ham whose lands were known to have belonged to Stratford Abbey.[42] Thenceforth the Abbey Landowners, organizing themselves as a corporation, levied rates on each member to maintain the bridges and the approaches to them.[43] When the Middlesex and Essex turnpike trust took over the main road through Stratford the Abbey Landowners made annual payments to the trust in respect of the road, but remained directly responsible for the bridges.

Bow and Channelsea bridges were widened in 1741.[44] By the early 19th century, however, they had become inadequate for the greatly increasing traffic, and in 1827 the Abbey Landowners secured an Act regulating their own functions and empowering them further to widen or to rebuild their bridges, in association with the local authorities and others.[45] That was followed by years of argument and litigation between the interested parties, terminated by agreement in 1834, when an Act provided that the Middlesex and Essex turnpike trust should manage all the five bridges, as well as the road, at Stratford.[46] The trust was to receive annual payments from the Abbey Landowners, and the owners of the three small bridges, towards the repair of the road. Bow Bridge was to be demolished and rebuilt on a larger scale. The Abbey Landowners would pay half the cost of its maintenance, and the other half would be shared equally by the counties of Essex and Middlesex. The cost of maintaining the other

[29] See p. 211.
[30] R. Lee (Flood Relief etc.) Act, 1930, 20 & 21 Geo. V, c. 192 (local act); McDougall, *Fifty Years*, 183–8; Newham C.B.C., R. Lee Flood Relief etc., Folders of Plans (1929–30); Official *Opening of River Improvement Works* (pamph. 1935).
[31] *W. Ham C.B.C. Mins.* lxxii. 394, 456; lxxiii. 511, 587.
[32] See p. 2. For the remains of Ham Creek at Wilton St., Silvertown, c. 1890, see plate f. p. 22.
[33] For the foundation and early history of the bridges see: C 145/62; *Abbrev. Plac.* (Rec. Com.), 316–17; K.B. 27/219, m. 72. For extracts from these sources see: *Arch.* xxvii, 77–95; Lysons, *Lond.* iii. 489–91. The accounts are not entirely consistent. What probably happened was as follows.
[34] Maud was at some time abbess of Barking: *V.C.H. Essex*, ii. 120.
[35] Then called Lock Bridge, from the lock on the toll-bar.
[36] Probably Sir Philip Basset (d. 1271): see *D.N.B.*

[37] e.g. *Cal. Close* 1247–51, 517; ibid. 1251–3, 335, 336; *Cal. Pat.* 1281–92, 397; ibid. 1292–1301, 375.
[38] *Cal. Close* 1313–18, 337.
[39] *Cal. Pat.* 1364–7, 257.
[40] Ogborne, *Essex*, 17.
[41] *Acts of P.C.* 1580–1, 108, 114, 129; E.R.O., Q/CP 2, ff. 51, 53; ibid. Q/CP 3, *passim*; ibid. Q/ABp 17 and 22; *Cal. S.P. Dom.* 1619–23, 486; *Acts of P.C.* 1621–3, 504–5; ibid. 1623–5, 52–4, 68–70; Fisher, *Forest of Essex*, 86; Fry, *E. and W. Ham*, 29–30.
[42] E.R.O., Q/ABp 17; Morant, *Essex*, i. 20.
[43] W.H.L., Abbey Landowners' Minutes and Rate Bks. 1715–1874.
[44] E.R.O., Q/ABp 17; *Archaeologia*, xxvii. 88; *E. Nat.* 144–5.
[45] Stratford Abbey Landowners Act, 1827, 7 & 8 Geo. IV, c. 108 (local act).
[46] Act for Rebuilding Bow Bridge, 4 & 5 Wm. IV, c. 106 (local act).

bridges would continue to be met by their owners, but the turnpike trust was empowered to widen or improve any bridge, and in that case the owner would be liable to repair only the parts of the bridge existing at the time of the Act, not the new ones.

The three smaller, intermediate bridges, which the Act of 1834 brought under the same management as Bow and Channelsea bridges, were already in existence in 1303, when it was stated that they had been built by the owners of the neighbouring mills, to span the gaps made when the millstreams were cut through Maud's causeway.[47] That account of their origin may not have been entirely correct, since, as suggested above, the mills were probably older than the causeway, but from the 14th century onwards the mill owners appear to have accepted responsibility for the bridges.[48] St. Thomas's Bridge was repaired by the owner of St. Thomas's Mill.[49] Pegshole and St. Michael's bridges both belonged to the City of London, as owners of Spileman's and Saynes mills.[50] Shortly before 1814 the London bridge house committee, on a tour of inspection, placed the City mark on St. Thomas's Bridge in mistake for Pegshole Bridge.[51] Since Pegshole Bridge was the smaller, and therefore cheaper to maintain, the owners of St. Thomas's Mill were content to accept it as their own. The error was never corrected, and was eventually rationalized: the old Pegshole Bridge became known as St. Thomas's Bridge and vice versa.[52]

Under the management of the Middlesex and Essex turnpike trust the new Bow Bridge was built in 1835–9.[53] The turnpike trust was dissolved in 1866, and in the following year the management of all five bridges and the approaches was vested in West Ham local board.[54] Under an Act of 1876 the Abbey Landowners discharged their liability for their two bridges and the approaches.[55] The annual composition payments by the owners of the three other bridges were not affected by the Act. As a result of the Local Government Act, 1888, the county borough of West Ham took over the north-eastern quarter of Bow Bridge in addition to the southern half, while the north-western quarter passed to London county council. In 1901–6 the bridge was again rebuilt, by the L.C.C. with financial contributions from West Ham C.B.C. and the Lee conservancy board.

The changes made in 1933 have already been mentioned. Groves Bridge, opened in that year, was named after Thomas Groves, mayor of West Ham and M.P. for the Stratford division of the borough. It was built on the site of St. Thomas's (old Pegshole) Bridge and also replaced St. Michael's and Pegshole (old St. Thomas's) bridges, the fabric of which was incorporated in the raised approaches to the new bridge.

By the 1930s the third Bow Bridge had already become inadequate. A new one was discussed, but not built.[56] In 1967, however, the Greater London council built a flyover to carry east–west traffic above the bridge.[57]

Queen Maud's Bow Bridge was one of the earliest medieval stone bridges in England and its name referred to its arched construction, then unusual.[58] Part of the original structure may still have survived down to 1835, but the bridge had been much restored.[59] Three arches were then visible, but a description published in 1814 states that about 30 years earlier, when an old public house on the Essex side of the bridge was demolished to widen the road, two other arches, filled up with brick, had been found in the cellar.[60] From this it was inferred that there were corresponding arches on the Middlesex side, so that the bridge had seven arches in all. Of the visible arches the two outermost, which were pointed, may have dated from the 15th century.[61] The centre arch, formerly pointed, had at some time been altered to a rounder profile giving greater clearance for barges. In 1741–3 the bridge was widened on both sides by the addition of angular pieces supported on the cutwaters of the piers. The arches of the additions were higher than the old arches and were circular.

The medieval Bow Bridge had upon it a chapel dedicated to St. Katherine and occupied by a hermit.[62] There are no references to the chapel after the 15th century, and nothing is known of its appearance or its exact location.

The second Bow Bridge, completed in 1839 to the design of James Walker and Alfred Burges, was a single-span structure with external stonework in granite.[63] It was replaced in 1906 by an iron bridge.[64]

Channelsea Bridge, alone of the five bridges in Stratford High Street, retains some ancient structure. It is a small single-span bridge of stone. A photograph of 1933, looking under the bridge from the north side, shows an outer arch, probably dating from the widening of 1741, and behind that an older, lower arch, thought to be medieval.[65] A similar widening was said in 1933 to be visible on the south side. Since 1957–8, when the Channelsea river was culverted between High Street and Lett Road,[66] the bridge has been visible only from the south, in Cam Road, and on that side the arch has been largely blocked with masonry.

St. Michael's Bridge was rebuilt in 1790, with a single stone arch.[67] Pegshole (old St. Thomas's) Bridge was a stone bridge, with two arches.[68] St. Thomas's (old Pegshole) Bridge was of brick.[69]

[47] B.M. Lansd. MS. 1 f. 19; K.B. 27/212 m. 95.
[48] Cal. Inq. Misc. 1348–77, pp. 70–1; E.R.O., T/P 48/1, ff. 159, 170; E.R.O., Q/ABp 17 and 22.
[49] See p. 90.
[50] See pp. 91–2.
[51] Ogborne, Essex, 18.
[52] Cf. E.R.O., Q/RUm 2/74 (map of Lee Navigation, 1849) and O.S. Map 25″, Lond. XXIX (1869 edn.).
[53] E.R.O., Q/ABp 22; Fry, E. and W. Ham, 32.
[54] W. Ham L.B. Ext. of Powers Act, 1867, 30 & 31 Vict. c. 56 (local act).
[55] W. Ham L.B. Act, 1876, 39 & 40 Vict. c. 220 (local act).
[56] McDougall, Fifty years a Borough, 45.
[57] Stratford Expr. 6 Oct. 1967, p. 17.
[58] P.N. Mdx. (E.P.N.S.), 134.

[59] For descriptions of the bridge see: E.R.O., Q/ABp 17 (James Walker's Rep. 1828); A. Burges, 'The Old Bridge at Stratford-le-Bow', Arch. xxvii. 77–95, with addition, Arch. xxix. 378–80. For pictures of the bridge see also: Ogborne, Essex, f. p. 16; W.H.L., Illus. Coll. (Bow Bridge).
[60] Ogborne, Essex, 17.
[61] E. Jervoise, Ancient Bridges of Mid and Eastern England, 142, suggests that Bow Bridge was rebuilt in the 15th cent.
[62] See p. 118.
[63] E.R.O., Q/ABp 22; Fry, E. and W. Ham, 32.
[64] W. Ham C.B.C. Mins. xxi. 239.
[65] E. Nat. xxiv. 144–5.
[66] W. Ham C.B.C. Mins. lxxii. 394, 456.
[67] E.R.O., Q/ABp 17; W.H.L., Illus. Coll. (Bridges).
[68] Ogborne, Essex, 18; W.H.L., Illus. Coll. (Bridges).
[69] Ogborne, Essex, 18.

Abbey Road Bridge over the Channelsea river occurs, as High Bridge, in the early 16th century.[70] Beside it was the Abbey Mill, and immediately east the gate of the abbey. It was rebuilt in 1967.[71] Thorn Bridge, also mentioned in the 16th century, was apparently identical with Three Mills Bridge over the Lea.[72]

The Iron Bridge, spanning the Lea at Barking Road, Canning Town, was built in 1810 by the Commercial Road turnpike trust, to the design of James Walker.[73] When that trust expired in 1871 the bridge became the joint responsibility of the counties of Essex and Middlesex.[74] It was described in 1872 as supported by five cast iron arches, three large and two small, with brick abutments.[75] The road platform comprised cast iron plates in an oak framework, over which was concrete and road metalling. It was unsafe for heavy industrial traffic.[76] In 1889 it was taken over by the London county council and the corporation of West Ham, which together built a new steel bridge, opened in 1896.[77] Under a scheme of 1935 this second bridge was replaced by a much larger one of steel a little farther north.[78]

Wharfs and Docks. West Ham's position at the mouth of the Lea, near London, favoured the growth of a small river port at Stratford. A wharf at West Ham, mentioned in the 15th century,[79] was probably one of a number serving the abbey and the mills at Stratford, and there is similar evidence in later centuries.[80] By 1821 there were specialized wharfs at Stratford for timber, chalk, stone, coal, and wheat, as well as some for general cargoes. They were situated on the Channelsea and the other branches of the Lea as well as on the main stream. The local mills and factories usually had their own wharfs.[81] By 1821 there also existed, at Stratford, West Ham's earliest proper dock, which appears to have been built a few years earlier.[82] It was then called Stratford Dock and later Meggs Dock.[83] It was about 80 yd. long and 50 yd. wide, lying south of High Street near Bow Bridge and approached from the Lea by a short channel. The dock may have been built by the Middlesex and Essex turnpike trust, which owned and occupied it in 1843 and 1854.[84] Its ownership subsequently passed to George W. Norman, a neighbouring landowner.[85] The later name of the dock may have been connected with John Meggs, who in 1866 was a ladder-maker in that area.[86] By

1896 the eastern half of the dock had been filled in and built over.[87] The western half, and the channel approach, still existed then, but those also had been filled in by 1920, when the whole site was occupied by factories.[88]

As long as West Ham remained largely rural the port of Stratford was adequate for its needs, and there is little early evidence of wharfs or docks in the south of the parish. Ham creek, mentioned above, was a small natural harbour, but does not appear to have been used as such after the 17th century.[89] The development of Canning Town and Silvertown, from the 1840s, transformed the situation. The new industries at Bow creek and Thames side came there primarily to take advantage of waterborne transport, based on their own wharfs. The shipyard of C. J. Mare & Co. (later the Thames Ironworks) had by 1848 been equipped with a quay 1,050 ft. long.[90] After the closure of the Thames Ironworks the site was bought by the Great Eastern railway, and in 1927 the London and North Eastern railway redeveloped it to receive cargo vessels.[91] Immediately south of Mare's works, in 1848, was a pier recently built by the Eastern Counties railway to import coal.[92] On Thames side the earliest wharfs were built to serve the factories at east and west Silvertown.[93]

The history of the royal group of docks has been treated elsewhere.[94] The Royal Victoria Dock, opened in 1855, was wholly in West Ham.[95] The Royal Albert Dock (1880) and the King George V Dock (1921) were built farther east, partly in West Ham, but mainly in East Ham. The royal docks are said to form the largest area of impounded water in the world. Their total area is over 1,000 a., including 230 a. water. There are 11 miles of quays, with berths for over 50 ocean-going vessels, and 140 miles of standard-gauge railway lines.[96]

TRANSPORT AND POSTAL SERVICES. Even before the coming of the railways Stratford was well served by public transport. In 1839 omnibuses and coaches ran to London four times an hour during the day, and coaches to and from Essex, Suffolk, and Norfolk passed through about once an hour.[97] Plaistow at that period was served by three coaches, each making three journeys a day.[98] During the 1830s steam coaches ran for varying periods on the

[70] L. & P. Hen. VIII, xiv (1), p. 162.
[71] Jnl. Industrial Arch. vi. 147–56.
[72] L. & P. Hen. VIII, xiv (1), pp. 162–3.
[73] E.R.O., Q/ABp 56, Bdle 2, Memo. 29 Mar. 1887 by Poplar Bd. of Works to Essex Quarter Sessions; Stratford Expr. 8 Aug. 1896.
[74] E.R.O., Q/ABp 55; Q/ABz 2/4.
[75] E.R.O., Q/ABp 3.
[76] E.R.O., Q/ABp 56.
[77] Stratford Expr. 8 Aug. 1896. For a picture of the second bridge see McDougall, Fifty Years, 168.
[78] McDougall, Fifty Years, 178.
[79] C 1/26/113.
[80] e.g. Select Pleas in Court of Admiralty (Selden Soc.), ii. 98; E.R.O., D/DLc T40; R. Allison, 'The Changing Landscape of South-West Essex, 1600–1850' (London Ph.D. 1966), 269, 415; E.R.O., D/DU 245/2 (map of 'West Ham Mill and Old Ford', 1810).
[81] R. Allison, op. cit. 415–16, quoting Clayton's Survey of W. Ham.
[82] Probably about 1812: Allison, op. cit. 416 n. 4.
[83] W.H.L., Clayton's Survey of W. Ham (1821) and map (1825); O.S. map 25", London, XXIX (1869 edn.).

[84] W.H.L. Havering and Dagenham Levels Sewers Presentments 1843, Mill Meads and High Meads, No. 140; Sewers Rate Bk. 1854, f. 128.
[85] Ibid. Sewers Presentments 1860.
[86] Kelly's Dir. Essex (1866).
[87] O.S. Map 6", London, VIII. NW. (1894–6 edn.).
[88] O.S. Map 6", Essex, LXXXVI (1920 edn.).
[89] See above, p. 59.
[90] White's Dir. Essex (1848), 240.
[91] Proc. Inst. Municipal and County Engineers, liv (1927–8), 1017.
[92] White's Dir. Essex (1848), 240.
[93] O.S. Map 25", London, XLVIII, XLIX (1869 edn.)
[94] V.C.H. Essex, v. 10–11. See also: McDougall, Fifty Years, 223–35; Howarth and Wilson, W. Ham, 185–254; London and St. Katharine Docks Act, 1864, 27 & 28 Vict. c. 178 (local act), which quotes the previous acts relating to the Victoria Dock.
[95] For the dock under construction see W.H.L., Illus. Coll. (Docks); after completion, see plate f. p. 78 below.
[96] Newham Official Guide (1969 edn.), 25.
[97] Pigot's Dir. Essex (1839).
[98] Curwen, Old Plaistow, 67.

road between Stratford and London, and on other local routes, but the experiment proved unprofitable, and was abandoned about 1840.[99]

The first railway through the parish was the Eastern Counties (later Great Eastern) line from London to Romford, opened in 1839, extended to Brentwood in 1840 and Colchester in 1843.[1] Stratford was one of the original stations,[2] and by 1841 there was also a small station at Forest Gate.[3] Maryland station was opened by 1874.[4] The line was electrified in 1949. The Northern and Eastern line was opened from Stratford to Broxbourne (Herts.) in 1840, extended to Hertford in 1843 and Cambridge in 1845. It was taken over by the Eastern Counties in 1844. The Eastern Counties branch from Stratford to Woodford and Loughton was opened in 1856 and extended to Epping and Ongar in 1865. The railway works at Stratford is described elsewhere.[5]

The North Woolwich branch originated in 1846, when the Eastern Counties and Thames Junction railway, originally intended for coal traffic only, was opened from Stratford via Stratford Bridge (later Stratford Market) station to Barking Road, Canning Town. In 1847 it was extended to North Woolwich and opened for passengers.[6] A pier was built opposite North Woolwich station from which there was a steam ferry to Woolwich. The North Woolwich branch was taken over by the Eastern Counties railway in 1847. When the Victoria Dock was built, its entrance cut across the line, and a new line was therefore built round the north side of the dock to Silvertown, where it rejoined the original line. The old line south of the dock, locally known as the Silvertown tramway, was retained to serve the local factories, and a swing bridge was built to carry it over the dock entrance.[7] On the new line Custom House station was opened in 1855 and Tidal Basin station in 1858. Silvertown station was opened in 1863. When the Royal Albert Dock was built in 1880 the railway was diverted through a tunnel under the cut between the two docks. The original high-level line, carried over the cut by another swing bridge, was retained as the property of the dock company, and later passed to the Port of London authority.

Several other lines were built to link with the North Woolwich branch. A line between Hackney Wick (Victoria Park) and Stratford was opened by the Eastern Counties railway in 1854, connecting the North Woolwich line with the North London railway. A service between Hackney Wick and Stratford Bridge was worked by the North London until 1866, and jointly by that company and the Great Eastern from 1866 to 1874. From 1874 the Great Eastern alone operated the service. The Victoria Park trains were extended to Canning Town in

1895. A branch from Custom House to Beckton was opened in 1874 by the Gas Light & Coke Co., which leased it to the Great Eastern; one from Custom House to Gallions, opened in 1880 by the dock company, was worked by the Great Eastern from 1896. Both were closed, after bombing, in 1940. The completion of the new lines in Middlesex made it possible, from 1880, to run trains from Palace Gates to Stratford and North Woolwich. The line between Palace Gates and Stratford was closed in 1963.[8]

The London, Tilbury & Southend railway was opened in 1854 from Forest Gate to Tilbury, and extended to Southend in 1856. A cut-off between Bow and Barking, with stations at Plaistow and East Ham, was completed in 1858. Additional stations were built at Upton Park in 1877 and West Ham (Manor Road) in 1901.[9] The line was electrified in 1961–2. The railway works at Plaistow is described elsewhere.[10]

The Tottenham & Forest Gate railway, opened in 1894, with a station at Wanstead Park, provided a new route from Barking to St. Pancras and Moorgate. The line, promoted jointly by the Midland railway and the London, Tilbury & Southend, was carried through the built-up area of Forest Gate on a long brick viaduct. It aroused considerable local opposition, which might have been more effective if West Ham council and Leyton local board had been able to agree upon a joint course of action in the matter.[11] In 1970 the line was worked by diesel electric trains.[12]

West Ham's first link with London's underground system was made in 1902, when the District line was extended from Whitechapel to join the London, Tilbury & Southend at Bow, and its trains began to work through to East Ham. The line was electrified to East Ham in 1905 and to Barking in 1908. The Central line extension was opened from Liverpool Street to Stratford in 1946, from Stratford to Leytonstone and Woodford in 1947, and to Hainault, Loughton, and Epping in 1948–9.

Many of the railway stations in West Ham were enlarged or rebuilt from time to time to deal with increasing traffic. Tidal Basin station, which had been damaged by bombing, was closed in 1943. Stratford Market station was closed in 1957. The railway works at Stratford and Plaistow have also been closed, but in 1967 an international freight-liner terminal was opened at Stratford station.

The North Metropolitan Tramways Co. opened a horse tramway from Aldgate to Leytonstone Road, via Broadway, Stratford, in 1870–1, and in 1886 extended it to Leytonstone, with another branch along Romford Road to Forest Gate and Manor Park.[13] In 1886 also the company opened a line from Canning Town along Barking Road to the Greengate,

[99] See p. 85.
[1] Unless otherwise stated the following account of the railways is based on: C. J. Allen, *The Great Eastern Rly.*; H. D. Welch, *London, Tilbury & Southend Rly.*; W.H.L., Vert. File E/WES/385, 'Railways in the London Borough of Newham' [Typescript]; *E.R.* lix. 57–61. See also *V.C.H. Essex*, v. 23–6, 72–3. For the viaduct at Stratford in 1837 see above, frontispiece.
[2] *Stratford Expr. W. Ham Jubilee Suppl.* 4 July 1936, p. 7. *Eastn. Co. Rly. Guide* (1838) has a picture of the original station.
[3] *Rly. Mag.* x. 440; *Forest Gate Wkly. News*, 24 July 1896, 18 Aug. 1899.
[4] *Kelly's Dir. Essex.* (1874).

[5] See p. 85.
[6] J. Morss, 'The Palace Gates to North Woolwich Line', *Rly. Mag.* Sept. 1962.
[7] See also p. 50.
[8] *Daily Telegraph*, 2 Jan. 1963.
[9] Sainsbury, *W. Ham, Eight Hundred Years*, 63.
[10] See p. 85.
[11] W.H.L., W. Ham C.B.C. Mins. Legal and Genl. Ctee., 27 Jan. and 12 July 1890.
[12] Inf. from Brit. Rlys. Eastern Region.
[13] For the tramways see: V. E. Burrows, *Tramways in Metropolitan Essex*; 'Rodinglea', *Tramways of East London*; *V.C.H. Essex*, v. 27–8.

Plaistow, with an extension to a depot in Tunmarsh Lane. In 1877 it experimented briefly, in Leytonstone Road, with a Merryweather steam tram locomotive. A further experiment, with a Beaumont compressed air locomotive, was made on the same line in 1881.[14] Battery-powered electric trams were used on regular services between Stratford and Manor Park in 1886–8, and on the Canning Town line in 1889–92, but they were not a success. In 1903–5 the West Ham corporation took over all the company's lines within the borough, extended and electrified them. As part of the process a new road, Tramway Avenue, was cut through from Stratford Broadway to West Ham Lane. In 1937–40 the trams were replaced by trolley buses, which remained in use until 1960.

The local horse bus services were not harmed, and in some cases were even stimulated by the coming of the railways. In the 1850s and 1860s buses ran every 10 minutes from Stratford to London, and there was also a service from Stratford station to Leyton and Walthamstow.[15] With the arrival of the tramways the horse buses declined, but motor bus services started in West Ham by 1906 and were rapidly extended.[16] In 1933 West Ham's trams and buses were taken over by the London Passenger Transport Board.[17]

A Thames ferry was established in 1811 between Charlton (Kent) and Plaistow Level (the present Silvertown), from which Prince Regent Lane was built across the marshes to Barking Road.[18] It survived until 1847, when the steam ferry was opened from North Woolwich.

Letters were being delivered and collected twice daily at Stratford and West Ham village in 1692, and once daily at Upton, Plaistow, and Green Street.[19] In 1794 there was a receiving and sorting office at Stratford, and a receiving house at Plaistow.[20] There were 4 post offices in the parish in 1848, and 9 by 1856.[21] When the London postal area was divided into districts in 1856, West Ham parish was included in the eastern district (Stratford and Canning Town sub-districts).[22] There were various changes in the sub-districts in the later 19th century. Of the numbered sub-districts formed in 1917 four lay wholly or mainly in West Ham: Stratford (E. 15), Plaistow (E. 13), Forest Gate (E. 7), and Victoria Docks and North Woolwich (E. 16).[23]

By 1829 Stratford had a main post office and two other offices.[24] In 1856 Stratford was constituted a sub-district.[25] The main office was in Broadway

c. 1848–80 and in Martin Street 1880–97; it became a branch office in 1880.[26] The present branch office, at no. 413 High Street, was opened in 1897.[27] Telegraph services were available at Stratford railway station by 1868 and at three of the post offices by 1870.[28] The National Telephone Co. opened an exchange at Stratford in 1896.[29] The area is now served by the Maryland exchange, opened in 1922.[30]

The Plaistow office, then in Balaam Street, was in 1856 included in the Stratford sub-district; the Plaistow sub-district was formed in 1872.[31] From 1857 until the Second World War the main office was in High Street.[32] The present branch office, so designated about 1949, is on the corner of Balaam Street and Barking Road.[33] Telegraph services were available by 1872.[34] The telephone had been extended to Plaistow by 1905.[35] The area is now served by the Grangewood, Clocktower, and Albert Dock exchanges.

Forest Gate was in Stratford sub-district from 1856 until 1880, when it became a separate sub-district.[36] Since the 1880s the main office has occupied various sites in Woodgrange Road.[37] It became a branch office in 1921.[38] The present branch was built in 1958 as part of Telephone House, Woodgrange Road, which is the headquarters of the eastern area of the London telecommunications region.[39] Telegraph services were available to the public at Forest Gate railway station by 1868, and at the post office by 1879.[40] The telephone was available by 1905.[41]

The Victoria Docks and North Woolwich sub-district (E. 16) is larger than its name suggests, since it includes most of Canning Town. In 1856 the Canning Town sub-district comprised offices at Canning Town, Victoria Docks, and North Woolwich.[42] In 1872 the Victoria Docks sub-district was formed, with a branch office at Tidal Basin, and an office at Canning Town, while North Woolwich became a separate sub-district.[43] The two sub-districts came together again in 1917. In the Victoria Docks sub-district a second branch office was opened in 1881 at the Royal Albert Dock.[44] The North Woolwich sub-district included Silvertown, where the first office was opened in 1878.[45] A branch office in Barking Road, Canning Town, was designated about 1949.[46] There were telegraph services at Canning Town by 1870.[47] The Albert Dock telephone exchange was opened by the National Telephone Co. in 1897.[48]

[14] Cf. W. Ham L.B. Mins. 8 Mar., 10 May, 25 Oct. 1881; Sainsbury, *Eight Hundred Years*, 64.
[15] *White's Dir. Essex* (1848), 247; (1863), 634; *Kelly's Dir. Essex* (1870).
[16] *Kelly's Dir. Essex* (1878, 1882, 1906); *V.C.H. Essex*, v. 27–8.
[17] London Passenger Transport Act, 1933, 23 Geo. V, c. 14.
[18] A. P. Crouch, *Silvertown*, 55–6. Prince Regent Lane followed part of the older Marsh Lane.
[19] T. de Laune, *Present State of London* (1692).
[20] G. Brumell, *Local Posts of London, 1680–1840*, 89.
[21] *White's Dir. Essex* (1848), 241; *Brit. Postal Guide* (1856).
[22] *Brit. Postal Guide* (1856).
[23] *Post Office Guide* (1917).
[24] Brumell, op. cit. 87.
[25] *Brit. Postal Guide* (1856).
[26] *White's Dir. Essex* (1848), 241; *Brit. Postal Guide* (1856 sqq.); *Post Office Guide* (1880 sqq.).
[27] *P.O. Guide* (1897).
[28] G.P.O. Rec. Off., Great Eastern Rly., *List of stations with telegraph* (1868); *Kelly's Dir. Essex* (1870).

[29] *Nat. Telephone Jnl.* Oct. 1907, 135.
[30] *Stratford Expr.* 8 Apr. 1922.
[31] *Brit. Post. Guide* (1856 sqq.).
[32] Ibid.; *P.O. Guide* (1880 sqq.); *London Post Offices and Streets* (1937, 1940).
[33] *London Post Offices and Streets* (1948, cf. 1950).
[34] *Brit. Post. Guide* (1872).
[35] *P.O. Guide* (1905).
[36] *Brit. Post Guide* (1856 sqq.).
[37] *P.O. Guide* (1880 sqq.).
[38] Ibid. (1921).
[39] Inf. from Mr. L. Johnson.
[40] G.E.R., *List of stations with telegraph* (1868); *Brit. Post Guide* (1879).
[41] *P.O. Guide* (1905).
[42] *Brit. Post. Guide* (1856).
[43] Ibid. (1872).   [44] *P.O. Guide* (1882).
[45] *Brit. Post. Guide* (1879).
[46] *London Post Offices* (1948, cf. 1950).
[47] *Kelly's Dir. Essex* (1870).
[48] *Nat. Telephone Jnl.* Oct. 1907, 135.

WORTHIES.[49] Richard de Montfitchet (d. 1267), lord of the principal manor in East Ham and West Ham, was one of the barons appointed to enforce Magna Carta.[50] Robert Fabyan (d. 1513), chronicler, acquired by marriage a small estate at Upton.[51] Margaret Pole (d. 1541), countess of Salisbury, executed by Henry VIII, held the manor of Bretts (1512–39), and appears to have been living within the precincts of Stratford Abbey shortly before 1537.[52] Gabriel Donne (d. 1558), monk of Stratford, took part in the treacherous arrest of William Tyndale at Louvain (Belgium) in 1535, and subsequently became abbot of Buckfastleigh, receiving other preferments after the Dissolution.[53]

Sir Thomas Lodge (d. 1584), merchant of London and formerly lord mayor, was living at West Ham in 1583,[54] and Sir Edward Coke, judge and law writer (1552–1634), at Upton in 1598.[55] Such residents became more numerous in the 17th century. Merchants included Sir Thomas Foot, Bt. (d. 1688), grocer and lord mayor, who lived at Hyde House, Plaistow,[56] and Sir Robert Smyth, Bt. (d. 1669), draper of London, who lived at Ham House, Upton, and was prominent in Essex local government during the Interregnum.[57] Sir John Wittewrong, Bt. (d. 1693), a London brewer of Flemish descent, lived at West Ham in the earlier 17th century.[58] William Clowes the elder (d. 1604), surgeon and writer, lived at Plaistow,[59] his son William Clowes the younger (1582–1648), surgeon to Charles I, at Rokeby House, Stratford.[60]

Edmund Burke (1729–97), statesman and writer, lived at Brunstock Cottage, Plaistow, c. 1759–61.[61] Among other 18th-century writers were George Edwards (1694–1773), naturalist,[62] and Aaron Hill (1685–1750), dramatist,[63] both of Plaistow. John Fothergill (1712–80), physician and botanist, owned Ham House.[64] Sir Richard Jebb, Bt. (1729–87), physician to George III, was born at Stratford.[65] Two notable industrialists working in the parish were Peter Lefebure (d. 1751), distiller at the Three Mills,[66] and Thomas Frye (1710–62), Bow china-maker at Stratford.[67] William Dodd (1729–77), executed for forgery, had been curate and parish lecturer.[68]

Since 1800, with the huge increase in population, West Ham has produced persons of distinction in many fields, but especially trade and industry, politics, philanthropy, and social service. Industrialists have included: Luke Howard (1772–1864), chemical manufacturer[69] and Walter Hancock (1799–1852), engineer and inventor,[70] both of Stratford; Charles Mare (1815–98), founder of the Thames Ironworks at Canning Town[71] and Arnold F. Hills (1857–1927), a later director of the same company;[72] George P. Bidder (1806–78), designer of the Victoria Dock;[73] and Sir Henry Tate, Bt. (1819–89), sugar refiner at Silvertown.[74] Among merchants was Sir John Pelly, Bt. (1777–1852), governor of the Hudson's Bay Company, who lived at the Manor House, Upton, and was one of the largest landowners in West Ham.[75] Sir William Mallinson, Bt. (1854–1936), timber merchant and philanthropist, lived in youth at Forest Gate, and always maintained a close connexion with the Field Road Methodist church there.[76] George G. Harrap (1867–1938), founder of the publishing firm of that name, was educated at West Ham Church school.[77]

Among politicians J. Keir Hardie (1856–1915), Charles F. G. Masterman (1874–1934), William J. (Will) Thorne (1857–1946), and John J. (Jack) Jones (1873–1941) all represented West Ham in Parliament.[78] The first two were better known outside the borough, but the last two were far more important within it, as trade union leaders and borough councillors.[79] John H. Bethell, later Lord Bethell (1861–1945), was a prominent borough councillor in West Ham, as in East Ham.[80]

Philanthropists included Elizabeth Fry (1780–1845), prison reformer, who lived at The Cedars, Portway,[81] her brother and neighbour Samuel Gurney, of Ham House,[82] and Sir Antonio Brady, of Maryland Point.[83] (Sir) Percy Alden (1865–1944) was warden of Mansfield House University settlement[84] and Sir Reginald Kennedy-Cox (d. 1966) of the Dockland settlements.[85] Thomas Given-Wilson (d. 1916), vicar of St. Mary's, Plaistow,[86] Robert Rowntree Clifford (d. 1943), superintendent of the West Ham Central (Baptist) mission,[87] and Father Andrew (1869–1946), of the Society of Divine

---

[49] See also: *V.C.H. Essex, Bibliography*, 222–3.
[50] *D.N.B.* See below, p. 68.
[51] *E.H.R.* iii. 318–21; *New Chrons. of Eng. and France, by Rbt. Fabyan*, ed. H. Ellis, pp. iii, xii.
[52] *D.N.B.* See below, p. 114.
[53] *D.N.B.*
[54] Ibid. He was father of Thomas Lodge (d. 1625), the writer.
[55] *Coll. Top. Gen.* vi. 117.
[56] *Misc. Gen. Her.* 5th ser. v. 51; *Complete Baronetage*, iii. 129. See above, p. 51.
[57] *Complete Baronetage*, iv. 9–10; *E.R.* xxxii. 12, 174; xxxiii. 149, 151; xxxiv. 175, 210; xlv. 101–4; H. Smith, *Eccl. Hist. Essex*, 340.
[58] *Complete Baronetage*, iii. 247; *Herald and Genealogist*, i. 169; *Misc. Gen. Her.* 4th ser. ii. 9–10.
[59] *D.N.B.*; McDougall, *Fifty Years a Borough*, 244.
[60] *D.N.B.* See above p. 52.
[61] J. S. Curwen, *Old Plaistow*, 14–15. See above, p. 53.
[62] *D.N.B.*; *E. Nat.* xiii. 343.
[63] *D.N.B.*; *E.R.* xliii. 61.
[64] *D.N.B.*; R. H. Fox, *Dr. John Fothergill and his friends*.
[65] *D.N.B.*; *Complete Baronetage*, v. 206.
[66] E. M. Gardner, *The Three Mills*, 7–8; E.R.O., T/P 48/3. See below, p. 93.
[67] *D.N.B.* See below, p. 77.
[68] *D.N.B.* See below, p. 116.

[69] *D.N.B.* See below, p. 82.
[70] *D.N.B.* See below, p. 85.
[71] G. C. Mackrow, *In Memoriam, C. J. Mare* (1898). See below, p. 85. There is a memorial bust to Mare in P.E.M.
[72] *D.N.B.*
[73] *D.N.B.* See below, p. 47.
[74] *D.N.B.* See below, p. 80.
[75] *D.N.B.* See below, p. 73.
[76] W. Mallinson, *Sketch of my life* (1935). See below, p. 137.
[77] *Who was Who* (1929–40).
[78] *D.N.B.* (Hardie; Masterman); *E.R.* lv. 99 (Thorne); W.H.L., Newscuttings, 1941–51, obit. 28 Nov. 1941 (Jones). See also below, p. 112.
[79] See p. 106.
[80] *E.R.* liv. 128. See below, p. 104.
[81] *D.N.B.*; *Katharine Fry's Bk.* ed. J. Vansittart; E.R.O., T/G 75 ('Family Book', compiled by Katharine Fry). See above, p. 53.
[82] *D.N.B.* See below, p. 72. For Gurney's memorial see plate f. p. 116 below.
[83] *Trans. E.F.C.* iii. 94.
[84] *Who was Who* (1941–50). See below, p. 142.
[85] *Who's Who* (1967), 30. See below, p. 142.
[86] *E.R.* xxvi. 30. See below, p. 119.
[87] See below, p. 126.

Compassion, Plaistow,[88] were religious leaders especially noted for social work.

Joseph Lister, Lord Lister (1827–1912), founder of antiseptic surgery, was born at Upton House.[89] Sir Patrick Manson (1844–1922), expert on tropical diseases, worked at the Albert Dock seamen's hospital, Custom House.[90] Dorothea Beale (1831–1906), principal of Cheltenham Ladies College, was educated at Stratford.[91] Thomas E. Cleworth (1854–1909), educational controversialist, attended and later taught at the West Ham Church school.[92] Edmund Curtis (1881–1943), historian,[93] was in 1896 working reluctantly in the rubber factory at Silvertown and expressing his melancholy in verses, some of which were published in the weekly journal *London*.[94] A fund was raised for his education, and by 1914 he was a regius professor at Trinity College, Dublin. Charles C. Winmill (1865–1945), architect,[95] was born at Plaistow and articled to J. T. Newman, architect to West Ham local board.[96]

Gerard Manley Hopkins (1844–89), poet,[97] and Anna Kingsford (1846–88), mystical writer,[98] were both born at Stratford.[99] John Curwen (1816–80), Congregational minister, musicologist and publisher, lived at Plaistow and later at Forest Gate.[1] George Glover (1854–1936), forger of archaeological remains, lived at West Ham.[2] Notable persons connected with the theatre and sport are mentioned elsewhere.[3]

ENTERTAINMENTS, SPORTS AND PASTIMES. West Ham's first permanent place of entertainment was Relf's, later the Royal Albert, music hall, Victoria Dock Road, Canning Town.[4] It was opened about 1875 by Charles Relf, who adapted the Town of Ayr public house for the purpose. He later rebuilt and enlarged the music hall and managed it until his retirement in 1906. In 1909 it was again rebuilt, partly with the materials of the Imperial theatre, Westminster, which had recently been demolished. The New Imperial, as it was then renamed, was burnt out in 1931, but was later rebuilt and became a cinema. It was renamed the Essoldo about 1958.[5] It became a bingo club in 1963 and was demolished about 1967.[6]

The Theatre Royal, Salway Road, Stratford, was built in 1884 by Charles Dillon (formerly Silver), an actor-manager.[7] There had been earlier attempts to establish a theatre at Stratford. A music hall, in Martin Street, existed in 1868.[8] In the early 1880s Dillon, his sister, and her husband Frederick Fredericks, had regularly visited Stratford with a mobile theatre, using a site in Oxford Road adjoining Angel Lane.[9] That may have been the theatre in Angel Lane, erected without a building licence in 1881, which the local board in 1882 ordered to be removed.[10] The Royal, designed by J. G. Buckle, was built on the site of a former wheelwright's shop, on the corner of Salway Road and Angel Lane. In 1886 Dillon sold it to Albert (brother of Frederick) Fredericks, who enlarged it in 1888 and again in 1891. The Fredericks family managed the theatre from 1888 to 1932. After the First World War it fell into financial difficulties, and from 1926 onwards it was often closed for long periods. In 1953, however, the Royal was taken over by Theatre Workshop, and became one of the best-known theatres in England. The East 15 Acting school, opened in 1961 in association with Theatre Workshop, met at Mansfield House, Canning Town, until 1966, when it was transferred to Loughton.[11] Theatre Workshop left Stratford in 1964 but returned in 1967.[12]

The Borough theatre, High Street, Stratford, was opened in 1896 by Albert Fredericks, owner of the Theatre Royal, to the design of Frank Matcham.[13] It was one of the largest theatres in Greater London, with seating for over 3,000. In its early years many well-known actors played there, including Beerbohm Tree, Sir Henry Irving, and Ellen Terry.[14] The Fredericks family managed the Borough until 1933, when it became the Rex cinema.[15] It became a bingo club in 1969.[16]

The Empire theatre of varieties, Broadway, Stratford, was opened by London District Empire Palaces (later Moss Empires) Ltd., in 1898, to the design of W. G. R. Sprague.[17] It was built on the site of Rokeby House.[18] It was wrecked by bombing during the Second World War, and was demolished in 1958.[19]

The Forest Gate public hall, Woodgrange Road, built about 1902, contained a theatre, known for many years as the Grand.[20] The Y.M.C.A., Greengate Street, Plaistow, built in 1921, included the Little Theatre, used for live productions as well as cinema shows.[21] A theatre at the Dockland

[88] See below, p. 143.
[89] *D.N.B.; E. Nat.* xxiv. 94–5.
[90] *D.N.B.* See below, p. 111.
[91] *D.N.B.*
[92] *D.N.B.*
[93] *D.N.B.*
[94] *London*, 4 and 11 June 1896.
[95] J. M. Winmill, *Charles Canning Winmill.*
[96] See also, below, p. 117.
[97] Newham Libraries, *Stratford in the 19th century . . . Gerard Manley Hopkins* [Exhibition booklet, 1969]; D. McChesney, *A Hopkins Commentary* (1968).
[98] *D.N.B.*
[99] For the literary associations of W. Ham see McDougall, *Fifty Years*, 244.
[1] *D.N.B.*
[2] *E. Nat.* xxvi. 193.
[3] See below.
[4] W.H.L., W. Ham L.B. Mins. 14 Sept. 1875; *East End News*, 8 Sept. 1908; W.H.L., Vert. File, E/WES/792, TS note on W. Ham theatres; *Daily Telegraph*, 25 Apr. 1923 (obit. of Chas. Relf.); Greater London Rec. Off. Deeds, Ac. 71.34.
[5] *W. Ham Official Guide* (1958/9); *Stratford Express* 19 Dec. 1958.

[6] *Stratford Express*, 27 Sept. 1963; W.H.L. Illus. Coll. (Theatres): Essoldo.
[7] O. Tapper, *The Other Stratford* (1962) provides a full history of the Theatre Royal.
[8] W. Ham L.B. Mins. 24 Nov. 1868.
[9] Tapper, op. cit. 3.
[10] W. Ham L.B. Mins. 24 Jan. 1882.
[11] W.H.L., Vert. File E/WES/792: *East 15 Acting School* [leaflet].
[12] *Stratford Expr.* 7 Aug. 1964; 3 Mar. 1967.
[13] Tapper, op. cit. 10; *Builder* 5 Oct. 1895; *London*, 20 Aug. 1896; W.H.L., Vert. File E/WES/792: Programmes of Borough Theatre, 1897–1904.
[14] *E.R.* lxi. 151.
[15] Tapper, op. cit. 19.
[16] *Strat. Expr.* 10 Jan. 1969.
[17] *Builder*, 22 Apr. 1899; *Strat. Expr.* 1 Apr. 1899; *Bk. of W. Ham* (1923), 271.
[18] See p. 52.
[19] W.H.L., Vert. File E/WES/792, TS Note on W. Ham Theatres.
[20] *W. Ham C.B.C. Mins.* 15 Apr., 16 Sept. 1902; 3 Oct. 1905; *Kelly's Dir. Essex* (1906–26).
[21] *Bk. of W. Ham*, 166; W.H.L., Vert. File, E/WES/792, Programmes of Plaistow Little Theatre, 14–28 Mar. 1932.

Settlement, Canning Town, was opened in 1926. The warden promised that Shakespeare would be played monthly or even fortnightly by the best companies at cinema prices.[22] The Passion plays produced at Plaistow by Father Andrew, S.D.C., are mentioned elsewhere.[23]

Cinema shows, 'the latest London craze', were advertised in 1897 by the Theatre Royal, which used them as supporting items between the acts of a play.[24] Occasional films were shown there again in 1907 and 1909, but never became a regular feature.[25] By then, however, cinemas were beginning to spring up throughout West Ham. The earliest ones used converted premises with serious fire hazards. The danger was demonstrated, in December 1908, at Gale's picture house (formerly Volckman's confectionery factory), High Street, Stratford, where a slight fire caused a stampede.[26] Three months later the borough council ordered five cinemas to close until they had been made safe.[27] By 1909, however, purpose-built cinemas were appearing: the Rathbone cinema, Rathbone Street, Canning Town, was one of the first.[28]

In 1917 there were at least 19 cinemas in the borough.[29] The number remained at about that level during the 1920s and 1930s,[30] but the total accommodation probably increased, since the new cinemas opened in that period included four very large ones. The New Imperial (former music hall) and the Rex (Borough theatre) have been mentioned above. The Broadway (later Gaumont), Tramway Avenue, Stratford, opened in 1927, claimed to be the largest in the country.[31] It was designed by George Coles for Philip and Sid Hyams. It was closed in 1960.[32] The Odeon, Romford Road, Forest Gate, was opened in 1937 by Odeon Theatres Ltd.[33]

During the Second World War several cinemas were bombed and by 1950 only seven remained open.[34] By 1969 only one, the Odeon, Forest Gate, was still a cinema, though several survived as bingo clubs.[35] Among cinemas, not previously mentioned, which survived for many years, were the Greengate, later the Rio, Barking Road, Plaistow (c. 1912–57),[36] the West Ham Lane Kinema, later the Century (c. 1922–63),[37] and the Queen's, Romford Road, Forest Gate (c. 1914–41).[38]

Music has played a remarkable part in the life of West Ham.[39] Much of this was due to the Curwen family. John Curwen (1816–80) established the Tonic Sol-Fa Press at Plaistow and the Tonic Sol-Fa college at Forest Gate.[40] In 1882 his son, John S. Curwen (1847–1916), founded the Stratford musical festival, which still survives.[41] Musical education in the borough was greatly stimulated also by the Forest Gate school, later the Metropolitan academy of music, founded by Harding Bonner in 1885.[42] The West Ham philharmonic society, founded in 1868, survived until 1877 or later.[43] Another society with the same name was founded by H. A. Donald in 1896 and ceased about 1912. In the late 19th and early 20th centuries there was also much musical activity in the churches and in several municipal schools. Some of the school choirs won prizes in international competitions. The borough council appointed a part-time official organist (later musical director), arranged concerts, plays, and recitals at the town hall, Stratford, and the public hall, Canning Town, and employed military bands to play in the public parks. Many musicians trained in West Ham achieved distinction elsewhere. Most of the town's musical activities were halted by the Second World War, and some, including the Metropolitan academy, came to a final end. In 1946 the council appointed a full-time music adviser and entertainments organizer.[44] That experiment ended in 1948, but after that the council supported cultural activities by providing accommodation for bodies like the public libraries Music Circle, and by subsidizing Theatre Workshop and amateur drama groups.[45]

Football, West Ham's main sport, was recorded as early as 1582, when a man was murdered during a game there.[46] West Ham United F.C. was formed as a professional club in 1900, but its origin has been traced back to three earlier amateur clubs, St. Luke's, Old Castle Swifts, and Thames Ironworks.[47] A. F. Hills, of the Thames Ironworks, was the principal founder of the professional club. West Ham entered the Football League in 1919, won the Football Association cup in 1964, and the European Cup Winners' cup in 1965.[48] Since 1904 the club's ground has been Upton Park, East Ham, formerly part of the grounds of Green Street House.[49] Clapton F.C., a leading amateur club founded in 1878, has played since 1888 in Upton Lane, on the ground previously attached to the Spotted Dog public house.[50] Several young players have gone

[22] *Daily Telegraph*, 17 Nov. 1926.
[23] See p. 143.
[24] O. Tapper, *The Other Stratford*, 12.
[25] Ibid. 14–15.
[26] *East End News*, 29 Dec. 1908; *W. Ham C.B.C. Mins* 5 Jan. 1909. For Volckman's see below, p. 80. Gale's cinema had opened in 1906.
[27] *W. Ham C.B.C. Mins*. 23 Mar. 1909.
[28] Ibid. 21 Sept. 1909; *Kelly's Dir. Essex* (1917 sqq.).
[29] *Kelly's Dir. Essex* (1917).
[30] *Bk. of W. Ham* (1923), 271; McDougall, *Fifty Years*, 244.
[31] *Daily Telegraph*, 19 and 20 Dec. 1927; *Builder*, 13 Jan. 1928.
[32] *Strat. Expr.* 25 Nov. 1960.
[33] W.H.L., Vert. File E/WES/791.4, Odeon Theatre opening; *Strat. Expr.* 6 Mar. 1937.
[34] *W. Ham Official Guide* (1950), 57.
[35] *Newham Official Guide* (1969), 115; *Strat. Expr.* 10 Jan. 1969.
[36] *Kelly's Dir. Essex* (1912); *W. Ham Official Guide* (1955/6), 72; *Strat. Expr.* 22 Jan. 1954 sqq. to 5 Apr. 1957.
[37] *Kelly's Dir. Essex* (1922); *W. Ham Official Guide* (1963/4), 84; *Strat. Expr.* 28 Dec. 1962.

[38] *Wilson and Whitworth's Strat. Alm.* (1914), 138; *Strat. Expr.* 18 cf. 25 Apr. 1941; inf. from Mrs. E. Taylor.
[39] Unless otherwise stated this paragraph is based on: McDougall, *Fifty Years*, 238 sqq.; *Bk. of W. Ham*, 106 sqq.
[40] See pp. 65, 87, 157.
[41] W.H.L. Pamphs., *Stratford Musical Festival, Silver Jubilee Prog.* (1907); *Newham Official Guide* (1969), 58.
[42] See p. 157.
[43] W.H.L., C. Whitwell, 'Dictionary of W. Ham', s.v. Philharmonic; W. Ham L.B. Mins. 5 Dec. 1871.
[44] *W. Ham C.B.C. Mins*. lxi (1946–7), 177.
[45] Ibid. lxiii (1947–8), 520, 775; inf. from Mr. F. Sainsbury; S. K. Ruck, *Municipal Entertainment and the Arts in Greater London* (1965), 65–6, 88, 135, 142, 160, 162; *W. Ham Official Guide* (1963/4), 60.
[46] Assizes 35/24/T/41.
[47] *Bk. of W. Ham*, 177; *Fifty Years*, 220.
[48] *W. Ham Official Guide* (1950), 55; *Newham Official Guide* (1967), 99.
[49] See p. 13.
[50] *Clapton F.C.: 75 Years of History*, ed. R. A. T. Ward (1953); *W. Ham Official Guide* (1963/4), 81.

from Clapton to West Ham United, and the professional club has also recruited many from the local schools. Early in the present century the West Ham schools football association was one of the strongest in the United Kingdom. Between 1907 and 1936 West Ham schools won the English shield three times and were runners-up four times, while individual boys won 36 international caps.[51] At a lower level football was being played in the 1920s by over 100 clubs in the borough.[52]

In the 18th and early 19th centuries prize fights were sometimes staged on the southern marshes of West Ham, despite opposition from magistrates and police.[53] Jem Mace (1831–1910), heavyweight champion of the world, lived at Stratford during his fighting career.[54] The Park council school produced three British schools boxing champions before 1936.[55]

The West Ham swimming club, founded in 1894, is said to be the oldest surviving in Essex.[56] Plaistow United swimming club, founded in 1920, soon became one of the best in the country and in 1936 supplied five members of the English Olympic water polo team.[57] E. H. Temme of Plaistow was the first person to swim the English Channel in both directions. There are several other swimming clubs in West Ham, including the Starfish, founded in 1948 for the south of the borough.[58]

In the mid 19th century cricket was played on the Spotted Dog pleasure ground, Upton Lane.[59] That may have been the ground used by the Cricket Company, a well-known club of the period.[60] The South Essex cricket club, said in 1923 to be one of the oldest in West Ham, was founded about 1888.[61]

Speedway (motor cycle) and greyhound racing are carried on at the West Ham stadium, Custom House, opened in 1928.[62] The stadium has been used occasionally for other sports, including stock car racing. A skittle ground, attached to a public house, was mentioned in 1764.[63] Several skittle alleys were built in the parish in the later 19th century.[64] Plans for a roller-skating rink, in Hamfrith Road, Stratford, were approved in 1876, and in 1909 there was a rink attached to the public hall, Woodgrange Road, Forest Gate.[65] The latter continued in use until after the Second World War.[66]

Among various forms of public or social service to which many West Ham residents devoted their leisure, especially before the First World War, was the promotion of temperance, thrift, or mutual aid

among a population living in conditions which made it difficult to cultivate such habits. Before the First World War there were some 75 temperance societies and 100 friendly societies in the borough.[67] The temperance societies, with their emphasis on total abstinence, were closely linked with the churches. Their strength was shown in 1897, when they successfully opposed the granting of a liquor licence to the new Borough theatre.[68] A few of the friendly societies were concerned with temperance as well as thrift, but most were not, and they usually met in public houses. Their total membership was low for a town of this size.[69] More important were the co-operative movement and the trade unions.[70]

Notable among cultural organisations has been the Essex Field club, founded in 1880, and based since 1900 on the Passmore Edwards museum, in Romford Road, Stratford.[71] The Canning Town Field club, later the Chip Chap club (1883–5), comprised five working men. It collected many prehistoric remains, which were eventually acquired by the Passmore Edwards museum.[72]

The Loyal United East Ham and West Ham Volunteers appear to have been formed in 1798.[73] In 1803, when the war with France was renewed, the West Ham Volunteer Infantry was formed, comprising two companies, commanded by Capt. (later Major) William Manbey, who had served with the earlier corps. It was demobilized in 1814. A separate East Ham corps, apparently formed after 1803, was demobilized in 1807.[74] When the volunteers were revived in the 1860s an artillery depot was opened at the Green, Stratford.[75] It closed c. 1960.[76] An infantry depot was opened about 1890 at the Cedars, Portway.[77] It survived in 1969.[78] In 1914 volunteer service became more than a pastime: during the First World War some 100,000 West Ham men served in the forces.[79]

The *Stratford Times*, West Ham's first paper, was founded in 1858.[80] It is said to have been closely identified, at least in its early days, with the Victoria Dock Co. The *Stratford Express*, following an independent line, was founded in 1866, absorbed the *Stratford Times*, and outpaced other rivals to become the leading local paper.[81] The *East and West Ham Gazette* (1888), which survived, as the *South Essex Mail*, until 1941, was a Liberal paper. The *West Ham Guardian* (c. 1888–1902) was Conservative.

[51] *Fifty Years*, 219.
[52] *Bk. of W. Ham* (1923), 177–84.
[53] E.R.O., Q/SBb 235; J. S. Curwen, *Old Plaistow*, 63.
[54] *Fifty Years*, 217; *D.N.B.* (Mace).
[55] *Fifty Years*, 217.
[56] *W. Ham Official Guide* (1963/4), 82; *Fifty Years*, 221.
[57] Ibid.
[58] *W. Ham Official Guide* (1963/4), 82; *Newham Official Guide* (1969), 75–6.
[59] W.H.L., Illus. Coll. (Pub. Hos.) Spotted Dog, display advert. c. 1860. See plate f. p. 52 above.
[60] *V.C.H. Essex*, ii. 599.
[61] *Bk. of W. Ham* (1923), 185.
[62] *W. Ham Official Guide* (1950), 56; *Newham Official Guide* (1967), 101–2; *Sunday Times* (colour mag.), 31 May 1964.
[63] E.R.O., Q/SBb 238.
[64] W. Ham L.B. Mins. 9 June 1868, 9 Mar. 1869; B.C. Works Ctee. Mins. 22 Nov. 1888.
[65] W. Ham L.B. Mins. 22 Aug. 1876; *C.B.C. Mins.* 6 July 1909.

[66] Inf. from Mr. F. Sainsbury.
[67] *Wilson and Whitworth's Stratford Almanack* (1914), 100 sqq.
[68] O. Tapper, *The Other Stratford*, 11–12.
[69] *V.C.H. Essex*, v. 60.
[70] Ibid. 60–1. See also p. 79 below.
[71] McDougall, *Fifty Years*, 142; *E. Nat.* xxii. 269 (history 1880–1929).
[72] *E. Nat.* xxi. 62–77.
[73] F. J. Wilkinson, *The West Ham Volunteers (1798–1814)* [Duplicated TS, 1961].
[74] Ibid.
[75] *Kelly's Dir. Essex* (1866), 191.
[76] *W. Ham Official Guide* (1960, cf. 1963–4).
[77] *Kelly's Dir. Essex* (1890, cf. 1886). In 1886 this had been a private house, occupied by Thos. Royle.
[78] *Newham Official Guide* (1969), 65, cf. *Kelly's Dir. Essex* (1908), 276, 563; *Bk. of W. Ham* (1923), 186.
[79] Sainsbury, *Eight Hundred Years*, 71.
[80] For journalism in W. Ham see: *Bk. of W. Ham* (1923), 213; *V.C.H. Essex*, Bibl. 39 sqq.
[81] See also p. 87.

MANORS AND OTHER ESTATES. In 1066 the manor of Ham, which comprised 8 hides and 30 a. and lay wholly or mainly in West Ham, was held by Alestan. In 1086 it was held jointly by Robert Gernon and Ranulph Peverel.[82] In 1135 Gernon's successor, William de Montfitchet, founded the abbey of Stratford Langthorne, granting to it all his lordship of Ham, which had been held by Ranulph the priest, 11 a. meadow and two mills there.[83] This endowment was the nucleus of the manor of *WEST HAM*, which was increased by later gifts to the abbey. Henry II, by a charter issued between 30 January 1164 and 21 October 1166, confirmed to the monks the grant of 40 *solidatae* of land in Ham made to them by his brother William (d. 1164).[84] About 1181 the same king confirmed to them the site of their abbey and the demesne of West Ham, as granted to them by William de Montfitchet and Gilbert his son, also land there given by Luke son of Martin, and the church of West Ham, given by Gilbert de Montfitchet.[85] A confirmation charter by Richard I in 1189[86] mentioned, among other donations to the abbey, Richard de Montfitchet's grange in the forest (Woodgrange)[87] and land in South marsh from the fee of Walter of Windsor.[88] During the 12th and earlier 13th centuries the abbey also acquired the manor of Sudbury, in West Ham, which in 1086 had constituted the greater part of Ranulph Peverel's share of Ham.[89] During the 14th century the abbey further acquired the manors of East Ham, East West Ham, and Plaiz,[90] all of which had formerly belonged to the Montfitchets.

In 1538, when the abbey was dissolved, its income from lands and rents in West Ham amounted to £316.[91] Of this £5 represented the farm of the manor of East West Ham, £4 that of Plaiz, and £5 the income from the rectory of West Ham. The farm of lands in West Ham and Stratford produced £223, a sum that presumably included the income from the demesne of the manors of West Ham and Woodgrange. The balance was made up mainly by assize rents. The manor of West Ham remained Crown property until the beginning of the 19th century. During the 15 years following the Dissolution many of the demesne lands were alienated.[92] Perhaps to compensate for this, the demesne of West Ham was augmented by the addition of Hamfrith wood, *c.* 100 a., of which a third had belonged to the manor of East Ham, and the remainder had been acquired by Henry VIII from Sir Anthony Hungerford, lord of East Ham Burnells.[93]

James I granted the manor of West Ham in 1610–11 to his elder son Henry, prince of Wales (d. 1612).[94]

On Henry's death it reverted to the king, who in 1617 granted it to Charles, prince of Wales (later Charles I), on a 99-year lease.[95] In 1629 Charles I assigned the manor for life to his queen, Henrietta Maria.[96] During the Interregnum the manor was seized by Parliament and sold to creditors of the government.[97] The manorial rights were apparently bought by Robert Smyth, who about the same time acquired half of West Ham Burnells and its associated manors: he was holding courts for the manor of West Ham from 1650 to 1659.[98] The demesne lands were sold to the sitting tenants, and some interest in the manor was also acquired by Humphrey Edwards (d. 1658) the regicide.[99] In 1660 the manor was restored to Henrietta Maria (d. 1669), and in 1672 it was granted by Charles II to his queen, Catherine of Braganza, for life.[1] On Catherine's death in 1705 George Booth assumed control of the manor under a 99-year lease running from that date.[2] In 1720 Booth made a grant which had the effect of splitting the manor into two parts.[3] He assigned Hamfrith farm (which had been made out of Hamfrith wood), together with most of the manorial rights in Stratford ward, to Sir John Blount, Bt., a director of the South Sea Company, for 69 years, starting in 1733. After the South Sea Bubble Blount's estates, with those of the other officials of the company, were sold. The Stratford and Hamfrith property was bought in 1734 by John Tylney, styled Viscount Castlemaine, later Earl Tylney.[4] It subsequently descended, until the end of the 18th century, with the neighbouring manor of Wanstead, being sometimes styled the manor of Stratford.[5]

The lease of the other part of the manor of West Ham was devised by Booth to Mrs. Hester Pinney, who was holding it in 1737.[6] She conveyed it to Azariah Pinney, who held in 1744.[7] In 1754 Pinney assigned the lease to Francis Smart, who conveyed it in 1764 to Mr. Brown. It was bought from Brown in the same year by John Henniker (later Lord Henniker), who seems to have retained the lease until its expiration.[8] Henniker was also lord of East Ham during that period.

Both parts of the manor remained Crown freehold until the end of the 18th century, but the demesne land and the manorial rights were then sold separately. As surveyed in 1787 the whole manor contained 290 a. demesne lands, and a further 54 a. commons, most of which formed part of Wanstead Flats.[9] The demesne lay mainly in small scattered parcels in the southern marshes, at Plaistow, Stratford, and near Bow Bridge. The only substantial tenement was Hamfrith farm, which comprised 128 a.,

[82] See p. 8.
[83] *V.C.H. Essex*, ii. 129*b*; Dugdale, *Mon. Angl.* v. 587.
[84] *Sir C. Hatton's Bk. of Seals*, ed. L. C. Loyd and D. M. Stenton, p. 282. See also Sudbury manor, below.
[85] Dugdale, *Mon. Angl.* v. 587–8; R. W. Eyton, *Itinerary of Henry II*, 244–6.
[86] *Cal. Chart. R.* 1257–1300, 311–13.
[87] See below, p. 73.
[88] For Windsor see p. 9.
[89] See below, p. 72.
[90] See pp. 9, 71, 72.
[91] Dugdale, *Mon. Angl.* v. 588.
[92] e.g. *L. & P. Hen. VIII*, xiv (1), p. 162; *Cal. Pat.* 1547–8, 410–11, 413, 339, 346; ibid. 1550–3, 150–1, 366, 368, 103, 106–7; ibid. 1553, 295, 297, 75–6, 226–7.
[93] *L. & P. Hen. VIII*, xix (1), pp. 373–4; G.L.C., DL/C/207 f. 85; *Cal. Pat.* 1547–8, 401–2; E.R.O., D/DQs 13. The name Hamfrith ('Ham Wood') goes back to the 13th cent.: *P.N. Essex*, 95.

[94] C 66/1879.
[95] E.R.O., D/DQs 13.
[96] Ibid.
[97] Lysons, *London*, iv. 251.
[98] B.M., Add. Ro. 58414.
[99] S. J. Madge, *Domesday of Crown Lands under Commonwealth*, 261, 371; *D.N.B.*, Humphrey Edwards.
[1] E.R.O., D/DQs 13.
[2] Ibid. This reversionary lease had been granted to Booth by William III in 1694, for services to the king: *Cal. S.P. Dom.* 1693, 74.
[3] E.R.O., D/DQs 13.
[4] Ibid. Tylney (d. 1784) was son and heir of the first Earl Tylney.
[5] E.R.O., Q/RSg 3; E.R.O., D/DQs 113/4.
[6] Lysons, *London*, iv. 251; E.R.O., Q/RSg 2.
[7] E.R.O., Q/RSg 3.
[8] Lysons, *London*, iv. 652; E.R.O., Q/RSg 3 and 4.
[9] E.R.O., T/M 175.

lying north of the London–Ilford road, on both sides of the boundary between East and West Ham. It was then occupied by John Greenhill. By 1799, when the occupiers were William, John, and Richard Greenhill, Hamfrith comprised 148 a.[10] In that year William Greenhill bought the freehold of the farm (without manorial rights) from the Crown for £8,642.[11] In 1824–8 he mortgaged the farm for a total of £9,000. He died in 1832, directing that Hamfrith should be held in trust for his wife for life, and should later be sold. The trustees sold it in 1851 to Samuel Gurney (d. 1856), owner of the neighbouring manor of Woodgrange and of Ham House, for £17,710. Hamfrith then comprised 131 a., bisected by the main line of the Eastern Counties Railway.

John Gurney, grandson of Samuel, sold most of Hamfrith in 1872 to the British Land Co., which in 1874 sold it to the Manor Park Cemetery Co. The eastern part was used for the cemetery. The remainder was gradually developed by the Cemetery Co. for building.[12] It was roughly the area bounded on the north by Godwin Road, west by Woodford Road, south by the railway line between Forest Gate and Manor Park, and east by Manor Park cemetery. Sebert Road, which had been built by 1878,[13] ran through the centre of the Hamfrith lands. The site of Hamfrith House was on the north side of that road between Avenue Road and Cranmer Road. A farm-house had existed at least since the early 18th century. In the 19th century it became a gentleman's residence, with ornamental gardens. From the 1860s it was known as West Ham Hall.[14] About 1890 it was acquired by the Tottenham and Forest Gate Railway Co., which was then building its line via Wanstead Park to Woodgrange Park. West Ham Hall was still standing in 1893, when the company put it up for sale with other surplus land.[15] The house was bought by the West Ham school board, which demolished it.[16] Shortly before its demolition it is revealed as a substantial brick building of three storeys and five bays, dating from the late 18th or the early 19th century.[17] It may well have been rebuilt by William Greenhill after he acquired the freehold of Hamfrith. In 1966 the site was a depot belonging to the education department of the London borough of Newham.

The manorial rights over the whole manor of West Ham were sold by the Crown in 1805 to James Humphreys and George Johnstone.[18] Johnstone's interest, secured by a mortgage, seems to have been that of a sleeping partner. He died in 1813, leaving it to his sister Sophia, who in 1814 married Francis Platamone, Count St. Antonio, later duke of Cannizzaro, a British subject of Sicilian birth.[19] No demesne lands are mentioned in the conveyances of 1805–14, and it is likely that the demesne, apart from Hamfrith, was sold off separately, and piecemeal. One field of 11 a. had been sold in 1804.[20] James Humphreys died in 1830, leaving his interest in the manor to his brother Edward, who in 1839 bought out the share of Sophia, duchess of Cannizzaro. Edward (d. 1856) was succeeded by his son Thomas Humphreys, subject to the life interest of Alice (d. 1863) wife of Edward. Thomas (d. 1885) was succeeded by his eldest son Charles J. C. Humphreys (d. 1914). Charles's heir was his brother Brig.-Gen. Gardiner Humphreys (d. 1942). It was stated in 1848 that the tenements on the manor of West Ham descended by custom of gavelkind.[21]

No ancient manor-house is known to have existed on the manor of West Ham, with the possible exception of the moated building called the Lodge, in the abbey precincts.[22] In 1848 Edward Humphreys, then lord, was said to have had, in East Ham, 'a large handsome mansion called the Manor House, which was lately sold . . . to the Eastern Counties Railway for £10,000, but which has since been sold for a much smaller sum to William Storrs Fry'.[23] This house, from which Manor Park took its name, had been in the E.C.R.'s possession in 1839, with Fry as tenant.[24] He died in 1844, but his family retained the Manor House until 1866, when it was sold to the Victoria Land Co.[25] Most of the grounds were built over, but the house itself became part of a Roman Catholic industrial school (1868–1925) and subsequently of the London Co-operative Society's milk depot.[26] It is a large 3-storey building of the early 19th century in Gladding Road, Manor Park. It seems to have been built between 1799 and 1838,[27] probably by James Humphreys soon after he bought the manorial rights.

The manor of *WEST HAM BURNELLS* was always associated with that of *EAST HAM BURNELLS*.[28] Some land in the manor was held by gavelkind.[29]

The manor of *BRETTS*, which was centred at Plaistow, but included tenements at Upton, Stratford, and elsewhere, seems to have been built up in the 13th century by the Bret family. Part of it was originally held of the honor of Peverel, and part of that of Montfitchet. In 1244 Hugh Wyschard enfeoffed Robert le Bret with 42 a. land in West Ham.[30] Another conveyance by Wyschard to Bret in 1257, of the same tenement, mentions as part of it 'that messuage . . . which was formerly of Hugh de Balun'.[31] Balun, after whose family Balaam Street is named, had held ¼ knight's fee in (West) Ham of the honor of Peverel in 1183.[32] In 1194–6 his land was in the king's hands, but he had recovered it by

[10] Ibid. 171.
[11] E.R.O., D/DQs 36. Unless otherwise stated the remainder of this paragraph is based on this source.
[12] E. G. Howarth and M. Wilson, *West Ham*, 39.
[13] *Kelly's Dir. Essex*, 1878, p. 114.
[14] *White's Dir. Essex*, 1863, p. 624; *Kelly's Dir. Essex*, 1870 f.
[15] E.R.O., Sale Cat. A 437.
[16] E.R.O., Pictorial Coll., Photograph of W. Ham Hall.
[17] Ibid.
[18] W.H.L., W. Ham Manor Deeds, on which, unless otherwise stated, the following paragraph is based.
[19] Cf. E.R.O., D/DFr T85.
[20] E.R.O., D/DC 27/61–2.
[21] *White's Dir. Essex*, 1848, p. 233.
[22] See p. 114.

[23] *White's Dir. Essex*, 1848, 230; in 1848 the house was let to Alexander Haldane, a barrister.
[24] E.R.O., D/CT 159.
[25] P.E.M., Pictorial Survey: note on photo. of Manor Ho.; E.R.O., D/P 156/11/29; *Katharine Fry's Bk.*, ed. J. Vansittart, 144–5.
[26] See p. 42.
[27] O.S. Map 1″ Essex (1805, surveyed 1799–1800); E.R.O., D/CT 159.
[28] See p. 10.
[29] W.H.L., W. Ham Burnells Manor Recs., Ct. Roll 23 Apr. 1617.
[30] *Feet of F. Essex*, i. 150.
[31] Ibid. 221.
[32] *Pipe R.* 1183 (P.R.S. xxxii), 24.

1199.[33] Robert le Bret had other tenements in West Ham. In 1239 Hugh Wyschard conveyed to him 24 a. land,[34] and in 1248 Richard de Kemeton and his wife conveyed to Bret possession of 60 a. land, of which 9 a. were granted back by Bret to Kemeton. Richard de Montfitchet put in his claim, presumably as overlord.[35]

Robert le Bret's estate seems to have descended until the middle of the 14th century in his family, various members of which occur in records.[36] Thomas le Bret, who in 1336 was holding lands in West Ham marsh,[37] was still alive in 1364, but died in or before 1367.[38] His widow Isabel, who later married Nicholas de Maryns, in 1368 released her dower in the estate to Thomas le Bret's heirs: his nephews John Aubrey and Thomas Hanampstede and niece Felice Pentrye.[39] In the same year Thomas Hanampstede and Felice Pentrye surrendered their shares of the estate to John Aubrey.[40] Aubrey, a London pepperer, appears to have used the estate as a security in his commercial transactions. He died in 1380 or 1381 leaving it to his widow Maud, who married secondly Sir Alan Buxhall (d. 1381) and thirdly John de Montagu, Earl of Salisbury.[41] Montagu, an opponent of Henry IV, was executed in 1400 and his lands were seized by the king. Those which he had held in right of his wife, comprising some 270 a. in East Ham, West Ham, and Barking, were restored to her in the same year.[42]

In 1412 'Birts' (i.e. Bretts) was held by William de Ferrers, Lord Ferrers de Groby, who had married, as his second wife, Margaret de Montagu, daughter of the above Earl of Salisbury and his wife Maud.[43] The manor apparently passed in the Ferrers family until the death in 1479 of John de Ferrers, subject to a reversionary interest held by the descendants of Maud de Montagu through her eldest son Thomas de Montagu, Earl of Salisbury. Maud herself died in or before 1424 and Thomas in 1428.[44] In 1429 the lands in East Ham, West Ham, and Stratford, formerly of John Aubrey, were settled upon Thomas's daughter and heir Alice, wife of Richard Nevill (d. 1460), Earl of Salisbury.[45] The reversion was later held by Isabel (d. 1476), Duchess of Clarence, daughter and coheir of Richard Nevill (d. 1471), Earl of Salisbury. After her death it passed by courtesy of England to her husband George, Duke of Clarence (d. 1478).[46]

When John de Ferrers died in 1479, the reversionary interest became effective, and Ferrers was thus succeeded by Clarence's son, Edward, Earl of Warwick, then an infant in the king's wardship.[47] During Warwick's minority Edward IV granted the custody of Bretts successively to Thomas Rede (1479), to Robert Nycholl and John Jenyns (1480), and to Robert Litton, John Clerk, and John Coton (1482).[48] Henry VII granted it in 1485 to Nicholas Harpesfeld, and in 1487 to his queen, Elizabeth.[49] On Warwick's execution in 1499 the manor was forfeited to the Crown.[50] In 1509 it was granted in jointure to Katharine of Aragon, queen of Henry VIII.[51] In 1512 it was granted to Warwick's sister, Margaret Pole, later Countess of Salisbury,[52] but on her attainder in 1539 again reverted to the Crown. In 1540 Bretts contained some 188 a. demesne, leased to 21 tenants, and 31 a. held by 10 copyholders, while the 17 free tenants of the manor held between them 66 a.[53] The demesne, which was widely scattered, included parcels in the marshes, near the Three Mills, and in Upton Lane, as well as at Plaistow. Some of the free and copyhold tenements lay in Balaam Street and in New Barn Street, Plaistow.

In 1540 Bretts was granted for life to (Sir) Peter Meautis or Mewtas and Joan (or Jane) his wife, who had previously acquired a large estate in West Ham at the dissolution of Stratford Abbey.[54] Lady Mewtas, who survived her husband, was still holding Bretts in 1567.[55] In 1576 Elizabeth I granted the manor to (Sir) Thomas Heneage, who conveyed it in 1583 to Roger Townsend.[56] Townsend conveyed it in the following year to Edward de Vere, Earl of Oxford, who died holding it in 1604.[57] In 1610 the earl's widow sold Bretts to Henry Wollaston.[58] Wollaston (d. 1619) left a son and heir of the same name.[59] About 1624 the manor was acquired by Sir William Courten, whose son William sold it in 1637 to Jacob Garrard.[60] It descended in the Garrard family until 1711, when Sir Francis Bickley, Bt., and his wife Alethia, coheir of another Jacob Garrard, sold it to Peter Courtney. Courtney (d. 1719) left Bretts to his sister Elizabeth, wife of William Beauchamp, from whom it descended to Joseph Beauchamp, the owner about 1814.[61] The manor was subsequently acquired by Henry Hinde Pelly (d. 1818), lord of East and West Ham Burnells, and was sold by his grandson for building about the middle of the 19th century.[62]

Bretts manor-house, depicted on an estate map of unknown date as a gatehouse called Bretts Bower, was on the site of the present St. Mary's church, Plaistow.[63] An earlier site is suggested by a reference,

[33] *Pipe R.* 1194 (P.R.S. N.S. v), 24; ibid. 1195 (P.R.S. N.S. vi), 52; *Chanc. R.* 1196 (P.R.S. N.S. vii), 210; *Pipe R.* 1199 (P.R.S. N.S. x), 105.
[34] *Feet of F. Essex*, i. 120.   [35] Ibid. 168.
[36] Ibid. 274; ibid. ii. 39, 61, 145; *Cal. Inq. Misc.* i. 498.
[37] *Cal. Pat.* 1338–40, 262–3.
[38] *Cal. Close* 1364–8, 92; ibid. 1369–74, 455.
[39] *Feet of F. Essex*, iii. 153, 154.
[40] *Cal. Close* 1364–8, 500; ibid. 1369–74, 456.
[41] Ibid. 1374–7, 82–3, 204; ibid. 1385–9, 634–5; *Complete Peerage*, xi. 392–3.
[42] *Cal. Fine R.* 1399–1405, 12–13; *Cal. Close* 1399–1402, 152–3.
[43] *Feud. Aids*, vi. 435; *Complete Peerage*, v. 354–7.
[44] *Complete Peerage*, xi. 392–3.
[45] *Cal. Close* 1429–35, 28.
[46] *Cal. Inq. p.m. Hen. VII*, iii. 374.
[47] C 140/67/46.
[48] *Cal. Fine R.* 1471–85, 186, 188, 224.
[49] Ibid. 1485–1509, 10; *Cal. Pat.* 1485–94, 293.

[50] *Cal. Inq. p. m. Hen. VII*, iii, p. 487.
[51] *L. & P. Hen. VIII*, i (1), p. 50.
[52] Ibid. iii (1), p. 153–4.
[53] Ibid. xv, p. 58.
[54] Ibid. p. 473; ibid. xiv (1), pp. 162–3.
[55] *Cal. Pat.* 1563–6, 251; ibid. 1566–9, 2.
[56] E.R.O., D/DHt T313/13; Morant, *Essex*, i. 17; C.P. 25(2)/132/1692.
[57] Morant *Essex*, i. 17–18.
[58] Ibid. 18; *Cal. S.P. Dom.* 1603–10, 617; *Lords Jnl.* ii. 610; Act for the sale of the manor of Bretts, 7 Jas. I, c. 9 (priv. act).
[59] Morant, *Essex*, i. 18.
[60] Lysons, *London*, iv. 253, on which, unless otherwise stated, the remainder of this paragraph is based. For maps of Bretts in 1624 and 1625 see E.R.O., D/DPe M55 and T/M 19.
[61] Ogborne, *Essex*, 25.
[62] Fry, *E. and W. Ham*, 52.
[63] Ibid. 52, 243–4.

in 1540, to a tenement, within the manor, called Oldbretts.[64] The house was last occupied by Sir Thomas Garrard, who left in 1683. It was demolished about 1696.[65]

The manor of *CHOBHAMS*, the name of which survives in Chobham Road, lay in the north-west corner of the parish. It was formed in 1329–31 by John de Preston, citizen and corder of London, who bought several tenements, of which the largest, comprising about 100 a., had belonged to Walter of Yarmouth.[66] In 1335 Preston sold the estate to John de Sutton of Wivenhoe, from whom it was bought in 1343 by Thomas de Chobham. Chobham, though he gave his name to the manor, held it only until 1356, when he sold it to Adam Fraunceys, a London merchant who also acquired Ruckholt in Leyton, and who recorded all the above details in his register.[67] Fraunceys's son, Sir Adam, died in 1417, holding Chobhams of Hugh Burnell, Lord Burnell, and the Abbot of Stratford, who were the lords of the larger manors of Burnells and West Ham.[68] Chobhams subsequently descended with Ruckholt until the end of the 16th century.[69] In 1597, shortly after selling Ruckholt, William Compton, Lord Compton, conveyed Chobhams to Richard Wiseman.[70] Wiseman, a London goldsmith, also held Battles Hall in Stapleford Abbots,[71] with which Chobhams descended until 1642, when Sir Richard Wiseman, younger son of the purchaser, conveyed it to Sir Thomas Hewett.[72] Hewett conveyed Chobhams in 1648 to Matthew and Thomas Young.[73] The manor remained in the Young family until 1705, when the executors of Thomas Young, recently deceased, sold it to John Hyett, distiller of London, subject to the discharge of mortgages raised by Young.[74] John Hyett (d. 1719) was succeeded by his grandson of the same name, whose daughter and heir, Elizabeth, married John Crewe.[75] Elizabeth and John, who were still holding the manor in 1777,[76] sold it about then to Allen, a calico printer, from whom it was bought in 1782 by Sir John Henniker, Bt., later Lord Henniker (d. 1803).[77] Chobhams descended to John Henniker-Major (d. 1821), the second Lord Henniker.[78] It was conveyed in 1824 to his nephew, Sir Frederick Henniker, Bt. (d. 1825).[79] Sir Frederick's brother and heir, Sir Augustus Henniker, Bt. (d. 1849), was holding it in 1845,[80] and the latter's son, Sir Brydges Henniker, Bt., in 1855.[81] In 1853 the estate comprised about 80 a.[82] Soon after this much of it was acquired by the Great Eastern Railway for the extension of their works and sidings.[83] The remainder seems to have

been built over a little later, as Henniker, Chobham, and Major Roads.[84] Chobhams house, which was at the west end of the present Chobham Road, still existed in the 1860s.[85] The Hennikers, during their ownership of Chobhams, lived at Stratford House, the Grove.[86]

The manor or estate of *COVELEE'S* comprised some 50 a. in the marshes, a pasture called the Hope, and 'Covelee's Wall', which formed part of the riverside defences against flooding, probably near the confluence of the Thames and the Lea. It was originally held in fee of the Montfitchets.[87] John de Covelee, who held it during the reign of Henry III, enfeoffed Robert le Ku with the Hope and the wall, and made similar grants of the remaining lands in small parcels to a number of tenants. Later, in or about 1248, he alienated his rights of lordship, consisting only of rents, which after further conveyances were acquired by the priory of Stratford Bow. In 1336–9 and again in 1351 the priory was involved in litigation with the tenants of the fee concerning their respective degrees of responsibility for the repair of 'Prioress Wall' (formerly Covelee's Wall).[88] Shortly before the Dissolution the priory's property in West Ham included 'one hope called Warwall, near the Four Mills',[89] which may have been identical with the Hope and the wall of John Covelee.

The manor of *EAST WEST HAM* was first mentioned by that name in 1538, as being among the former lands of Stratford Abbey, and was then at farm for £5.[90] Its earlier history is not certainly known, but East West Ham may have been part of the lands acquired by the abbey from John de Lancaster early in the 14th century.[91] In addition to the manor of East Ham John de Lancaster had inherited from his mother lands in East and West Ham representing her original share of the lands of Richard de Montfitchet, through her grandmother Margery de Bolbec. In 1346 the Abbot of Stratford was said to hold $\frac{1}{4}$ and $\frac{1}{8}$ of the knight's fee in East and West Ham formerly held by John de Lancaster and his partners.[92] It is possible that the smaller fraction represents the former Lancaster lands outside the manor of East Ham, and that this was identical with East West Ham.

In 1553 East West Ham and Plaiz were granted by the Crown to Sir Roger Cholmley.[93] Both subsequently descended along with East Ham Burnells and West Ham Burnells.[94] The demesne of East West Ham, which probably did not remain distinct after 1553, has not been identified. The tenements under the jurisdiction of the manor court were not,

[64] *L. & P. Hen. VIII*, xv, p. 58.
[65] E.R.O., D/DPe M 55 (item No. 282).
[66] Yarmouth's East Ham land was acquired by Stratford Abbey: see p. 9.
[67] Hatfield House, Cecil MSS. 291.
[68] C 138/29/53; cf. *Feet of F. Essex*, iii. 124.
[69] See p. 194.
[70] C.P. 43/57 ro. 29; *E. Angl.* N.S. v. 235.
[71] *V.C.H. Essex*, iv. 228.
[72] C.P. 25(2)/419 Eas. 18 Chas. I.
[73] Ibid. Mich. 24 Chas. I.
[74] E.R.O., D/DB T992/1 and 2.
[75] Lysons, *London*, iv. 652; cf. *V.C.H. Essex*, iv. 254.
[76] C.P. 25(2)/1308 Mich. 18 Geo. III.
[77] Lysons, *London*, iv. 652; *Complete Peerage*, vi. 437.
[78] Ogborne, *Essex*, 25.
[79] C.P. 25(2)/1530 Hil. 4 & 5 Geo. IV; *Burke's Peerage and Baronetage* (1913 edn.), pp. 1038–9.
[80] W.H.L., W. Ham Vestry Mins. 7 Aug. 1845.

[81] Char. Com., *W. Ham Char. Rep.* (1899), 93.
[82] E.R.O., D/CT 160.
[83] Fry, *E. and W. Ham*, 53.
[84] O.S. Map 25″, London (Surv. 1867) XX; W. Ham L.B. Mins. 27 Oct. 1868.
[85] Chapman and André, *Map of Essex*, 1777, sheet xxi; E.R.O., D/P 256/28/1–3; ibid. T/M 92; W. Ham L.B. Mins. 11 Sept. 1860; O.S. Map 25″, London (surv. 1867), XX.
[86] See p. 52.
[87] This paragraph is based on: *Cal. Pat.* 1338–40, 261–3; ibid. 1348–50, 116; *Public Works in Medieval Law*, ed. C. T. Flower, i. 58–60; *Feet of F. Essex*, i. 160, 164, 169.
[88] See p. 94.
[89] *Valor Eccl.* (Rec. Com.), i. 409.
[90] Dugdale, *Mon. Angl.* v. 588 *b*.
[91] See p. 9.
[92] *Feud. Aids*, ii. 176.
[93] *Cal. Pat.* 1553, 38–9.
[94] See p. 11.

as the manor's name suggests, concentrated in the east of the parish, but lay at Stratford, Plaistow, West Ham village, and in the marshes and elsewhere.[95]

The *HAM HOUSE* estate, now in public use as West Ham Park, appears to have originated as a small tenement called Grove House, or The Grove, later Rookes Hall. William Rooke, son of William, succeeded to a small estate in West Ham on his father's death in 1559.[96] He apparently enlarged it, and died in 1597 holding Grove House and 28 a. land at Upton, with other small properties in West Ham.[97] Grove House had previously been settled for life upon his wife Anne. Under William's will it reverted, after Anne's death, to his kinsman Robert, son of Samuel Rooke. Robert Rooke (d. 1630) was succeeded by his son Robert.[98] The estate is said to have been bought from the Rookes in 1666 by Sir Robert Smyth, Bt. (d. 1669).[99] It became the Smyths' family seat, and descended with their half of the manors of East and West Burnells until about 1760, when it was sold to Admiral Elliot. In 1762 it was bought by Dr. John Fothergill (d. 1780), who created there what was regarded by contemporaries as one of the finest botanical gardens in Europe. In 1786 or 1787 Ham House was acquired by James Sheppard (d. 1812), from whose executors it was bought by his son-in-law Samuel Gurney.[2] Sheppard's will refers to the house as 'Rookes Hall, since Ham House'. Gurney, who also acquired the manor of Woodgrange and Hamfrith farm,[3] died in 1856, and his son John later in the same year. In 1874 John's son John Gurney the younger sold the Ham House estate, then comprising 77 a., for use as a public park, to be controlled by the Corporation of the City of London.

Ham House mansion, demolished in 1872, was a large two-storey building with an 18th-century exterior. The half-H shaped plan suggests that it may have been of earlier origin.[4] Its site is marked by a cairn of stones in the park.

The manor of *PLAIZ* was the third part of the lands in East and West Ham inherited in 1268 by Richard de Montfitchet's nephew, Richard de Plaiz, from whose family the manor took its name.[5] Richard de Plaiz (d. 1269) was succeeded in turn by his sons Ralph (d. 1283) and Giles (d. 1302). Giles's son Richard (d. 1327) was succeeded by his own son Giles (d. 1334).[6] Richard de Plaiz, brother of the last Giles, was his heir, and the last of his family to hold the manor. In 1353 he granted all his lordship in East and West Ham to Stratford Abbey.[7] It was then said to comprise 10 a. wood, 12 a. heath at Hamfrith, and £8 3s. 4d. assize rents.

In 1538 Plaiz, then first mentioned under that name, was among the former possessions of Stratford Abbey, and was then farmed for £4.[8] It subsequently descended like the manor of East West Ham. No demesne lands can be distinguished after the Dissolution. The tenements under the jurisdiction of the manor court lay mainly at Plaistow, Upton, and in the marshes.[9]

After the Norman Conquest the king gave a manor in Ham, formerly held by Alestan and comprising 8 hides and 30 a., to Ranulph Peverel and Robert Gernon.[10] Most of Peverel's moiety became the manor of *SUDBURY* or *ABBEY PLACE*. Its exact location is not certain. The name Sudbury ('southern manor house') presumably described its position in relation to the other early manors in West Ham. In Trinity marsh, in the extreme south-east of the parish near Plaistow, there was a Sudbury field,[11] which suggests that the manorial demesne may have been in that area. Many of the free and customary tenements of the manor were at Plaistow, but there were others at Stratford and elsewhere in the parish.[12] The alternative name Abbey Place occurs only in a reference of 1545.[13] In 1086 Peverel's moiety of Ham was held in demesne. Between 1107 and 1130, after the death of William Peverel, Ranulph's successor, all the Peverel lands in the eastern counties escheated to the Crown: they were subsequently known as the honor of Peverel of London or Hatfield Peverel.[14] 'Hamam', which King Stephen granted in 1141 to Geoffrey de Mandeville, Earl of Essex (d. 1144), in fee and inheritance to the use of the earl's son Ernulf, may have been the Peverel fee in West Ham.[15] Ernulf de Mandeville was disinherited for supporting his father's revolt of 1143–4.[16] William de Longespée (d. 1164), brother of Henry II, gave land in (West) Ham, worth 40s. a year, to Stratford Abbey in free alms. The grant was confirmed by Henry II between 1164 and 1166,[17] and in 1189 by Richard I, whose charter refers to the land of Sudbury, which William his uncle and Adam de Falaise, his man, gave to the abbey.[18] That land was probably the ½ knight's fee of the honor of Peverel which the abbey was holding in 1190, and on which scutage was remitted by freedom of the king's charter.[19] The abbey held ½ fee in free alms in West Ham in 1346.[20]

The remainder of the Peverel fee in West Ham, except for the part that became Bretts, seems to have formed an estate that Richard I confirmed in 1190 to Isaac son of Josce the Rabbi, a prominent Jew. According to Richard's charter this land in (West) Ham had been granted to Isaac and his sons by Henry II.[21] It may have been temporarily in the

[95] E.R.O., D/DPe M55.
[96] C 142/144/130.
[97] C 142/273/74; C 142/272/4 and 6.
[98] C 142/464/16; Robt. Rooke's mon. in All Saints' ch., West Ham.
[99] K. Fry, *East and West Ham*, 230–7: unless otherwise stated the remainder of this paragraph is based on this source.
[1] Probably John Elliot (d. 1808): see *D.N.B.*
[2] Cf. E.R.O., Q/RPl 59 and 60; T/A 243.
[3] See pp. 69, 74.
[4] Fry, *E. and W. Ham*, illus. pp. 232, 234; W.H.L., Illus. Coll. (Houses). See plate f. p. 189 below.
[5] See p. 9.
[6] I. J. Sanders, *English Baronies*, 83; *Cal. Inq. p.m.* viii. 356.
[7] *Cal. Pat.* 1350–4, 476; *Cal. Close,* 1349–54, 601.

[8] Dugdale, *Mon. Angl.* v. 588b.
[9] E.R.O., D/DPe M55.
[10] *V.C.H. Essex,* i. 515, 527. See above, pp. 8, 68.
[11] S.C. 12/15/20; B.M. Add. Ro. 56384.
[12] S.C. 12/15/20.
[13] *L. & P. Hen. VIII,* xx (2), p. 450.
[14] I. J. Sanders, *English Baronies*, 121.
[15] J. H. Round, *Geoffrey de Mandeville*, 140–1.
[16] *D.N.B.*, Geof. de Mandeville.
[17] *Sir Christopher Hatton's Bk. of Seals*, ed. L. C. Loyd and D. M. Stenton, pp. 282–3.
[18] *Cal. Chart. R.* 1257–1300, 312.
[19] *Pipe R.* 1190 (P.R.S. n.s. i), 110; *Red Bk. Exch.* (Rolls Ser.), 732.
[20] *Feud. Aids,* ii. 176.
[21] J. Jacobs, *Jews of Angevin England*, 134–5, 137. For a later member of Isaac's family see below, p. 90.

king's hands during the anti-Semitic riots at the beginning of Richard's reign, for at Michaelmas 1189 Henry of Cornhill had rendered £7 16s. to the Exchequer from the farm of (West) Ham.[22] The land of (West) Ham, previously held by Josce the Jew, son of Isaac, was again in the king's hands at Michaelmas 1194, when its keeper rendered £15 as half a year's income.[23] In 1195, when the manor was being restocked, the income was only £12 6s. 10d.,[24] but in 1196 it rose to £25 2s. 8d.[25] This manor was probably identical with that of Sudbury in West Ham, worth £32 a year, granted by Richard I in 1198 to Leonard Succuhull' de Venez, along with land in Exning and Westhall (Suff.), for 1 knight's fee.[26] All those properties were confirmed to Leonard's son John de Venez by royal charter in January 1201.[27] In the same year John paid scutage on 1 knight's fee of the honor of Peverel of London.[28] In or before December 1201 he granted Sudbury to Stratford Abbey to hold at fee farm for £31 1s. a year. Venez was still liable for knight service, but if Sudbury reverted to the Crown the abbey was to hold it in chief, paying both the farm and the service due.[29] Venez continued to pay scutages on this fee at least until 1204,[30] but about that date the king disseised him of Sudbury and granted it to Peter de Préaux.[31] Préaux held it only until 1207, when the abbey agreed to pay the king £100 to have full seisin of Sudbury.[32] In 1211 the monks began to make a direct annual payment to the Exchequer of £31 1s. for the farm of the manor.[33] In later returns during the 13th century they were said to hold a knight's fee of the honor of Peverel by payment of this sum.[34]

The abbey retained Sudbury until the Dissolution. Its tenure in chief of the manor was briefly interrupted in 1230 when Henry III granted the honor of Peverel of London to Hubert de Burgh, Earl of Kent, to whom the abbot was ordered to render knight service and fee farm rent from his land in (West) Ham.[35] The earl was deprived of the honor in 1232.[36] Before 1230 the abbey had been ordered to pay portions of the annual fee farm of Sudbury direct to servants of the Crown,[37] and such grants were revived after 1232.[38] They tended to become hereditary, and eventually the abbey succeeded in buying up about two-thirds of the rent from the heirs of those to whom grants had been made. In 1309 £10 rent was thus acquired from Philip of Beauvais,[39] and in 1321 a further £10 from Richard le Rous.[40]

By the 16th century the manor of Sudbury seems to have been so closely linked with that of West Ham

that the distinction between them was far from clear.[41] A rental of Sudbury compiled in 1527 contains a long list of free and customary tenants whose rents totalled some £30.[42] Several of the customary tenements were then described as part of Gaysham's fee, which may link Sudbury with the manor of Gayshams in Ilford.[43] In 1538 the abbey's assize rents in 'West Ham and Stratford' were valued at £33.[44] Neither in 1527 nor in 1538 is there any specific reference to demesne lands of Sudbury. In 1545 the manor of 'Sudbury alias Abbey Place' was in the king's hands.[45] There are no later references to it. Presumably it was completely merged in that of West Ham.

Nothing is known about the manor-house of Sudbury.

The *UPTON 'MANOR'* estate extended from Upton Cross south to Plaistow village, and east to Green Street.[46] It belonged to Henry Hinde, from whom it descended in 1780 to his grandson Henry Hinde Pelly (d. 1818). In 1810 Pelly bought the manorial rights of East and West Ham Burnells, East West Ham, and Plaiz.[47] He was succeeded by his son (Sir) John Pelly (Bt.) (d. 1852), whose Upton estate comprised about 140 a. including a large house in a park of 40 a.[48] Soon after 1852 the property began to be developed for building as the Upton 'Manor' estate. The house, which stood at the south-east corner of Upton Cross, was a three-storey brick building, with two-storey wings, probably built or rebuilt in the 18th century. It was demolished about 1865. In the 19th century it was called the Manor House, or Four Manor House.[49] In 1875 the park was opened as a public tea-garden, called the Shrubberies, but by 1888 it had been laid out for building.

The manor of *WOODGRANGE* lay in the north of the parish, near Wanstead Flats. Its name and location suggest that it originated as an outlying farm in a forest clearing. It was part of the Montfitchet estate in East and West Ham, and may have formed part of the original endowment of Stratford Abbey by William de Montfitchet.[50] The first explicit reference to it was in 1189, when Richard I granted protection to the monks against interference with their grange next to 'le Frith' [Hamfrith] which was of the fee of Richard de Montfitchet.[51] Woodgrange, as part of West Ham manor, remained with the abbey until the Dissolution.

At the Dissolution Woodgrange, with a portion of tithes, was on lease to Morgan Phillips alias Wolfe, for 60 years from 1534.[52] Phillips, who later acquired Stratford Abbey's manor of Little Ilford and other

[22] *Pipe R.* 1189 (Rec. Com.), 10.
[23] Ibid. 1194 (P.R.S. N.S. v), 27.
[24] Ibid. 1195 (P.R.S. N.S. vi), 53.
[25] *Chanc. R.* 1196 (P.R.S. N.S. vii), 210.
[26] *Cart. Antiq.* (P.R.S. N.S. xvii), 78–9.
[27] Ibid.; *Pipe R.* 1201 (P.R.S. N.S. xiv), 173.
[28] *Pipe R.* 1201, 70.
[29] *Cart. Antiq.* 84, 78; *Rot. de Ob. et Fin.* (Rec. Com.), 182.
[30] *Pipe R.* 1204 (P.R.S. N.S. xviii), 36.
[31] *Rot. de Ob. et Fin.* 381.
[32] Ibid.; *Pipe R.* 1207 (P.R.S. N.S. xxii), 101.
[33] *Pipe R.* 1211 (P.R.S. N.S. xxviii), 114; ibid. 1212 (P.R.S. N.S. xxx), 52; ibid. 1214 (P.R.S. N.S. xxxv), 2.
[34] *Red Bk. Exch.* (Rolls Ser.), 740–1; *Bk. of Fees*, 1464.
[35] *Cal. Chart. R.* 1226–57, 108–9; *Cal. Pat.* 1225–32, 328–9; *Close R.* 1227–31, 424–5.
[36] *Complete Peerage*, vii. 138–9.
[37] *Rot. Litt. Claus.* (Rec. Com.), i. 196, 217, 348, 359, 413.

[38] *Cal. Pat.* 1232–47, 87.
[39] *Cal. Chart. R.* 1257–1300, 201; *Cal. Pat.* 1272–81, 172; ibid. 1307–13, 155.
[40] *Cal. Pat.* 1232–47, 330–1; ibid. 1317–21, 566–7.
[41] *E.A.T.* N.S. xiii. 64.
[42] S.C. 12/15/20.
[43] Cf. *V.C.H. Essex*, v. 204.
[44] Dugdale, *Mon. Angl.* v. 588.
[45] *L. & P. Hen. VIII*, xx (2), p. 450.
[46] Fry, *E. and W. Ham*, 228–30.
[47] See p. 12.
[48] E.R.O., D/CT 160.
[49] O.S. Map, 25″ (London), XXX (surv. 1863–7); *Brit. Columbia Hist. Quart.* xiii (1949), 23–32.
[50] See p. 68.
[51] *Cal. Chart. R.* 1257–1300, 312.
[52] S.C. 6/962. Unless otherwise stated this paragraph is based on Lysons, *London*, iv. 254.

local monastic property, died in 1552.[53] During the later 16th century Woodgrange passed through the hands of several lessees or sub-lessees. Depositions made in a tithe dispute in 1574–5 mention the following farmers of the manor: Nokes (about 1550), Ormesby (about 1563), Smith, who married Ormesby's widow and let the manor to William Chester (about 1564–74), and John Blackman (1574–5).[54] In 1579 Elizabeth I granted a reversionary lease of the manor to Robert Dudley, Earl of Leicester, to run for 70 years from 1595.[55] By 1605 the lease, then valued at £210 a year, belonged to George Carew, later Earl of Totness. Richard Wright held Woodgrange in 1608, presumably as a sub-tenant of Carew.[56] In 1627–8 the Earl bought the freehold of the manor from the Crown, subject to a reserved rent of £27.[57] After his death in 1629 and that of his widow in 1637[58] Woodgrange passed to his grandnephew Peter Apsley[59] who sold it in the same year to Charles Frankland. In 1649 Frankland sold the manor to (Sir) Thomas Cambell (Bt.), who already held Clay Hall in Ilford. Woodgrange subsequently descended with Clay Hall[60] until 1738, when Cambell Price sold it to John Pickering, merchant. Pickering left it, by his will dated 1754, to his niece Ann Machin, with remainder to her daughter Mary Machin, later the wife of John Peacock. Mary and John Peacock were holding the manor about 1796. It subsequently passed to John Pickering Peacock, who was the owner about 1814.[61]

After J. P. Peacock's time Woodgrange is said to have been divided among several owners.[62] A substantial part of it, however, called Woodgrange farm, was bought from Peacock's executors by Samuel Gurney of Ham House, the banker and philanthropist. Gurney was holding Woodgrange, comprising c. 200 a., in 1853.[63] In 1855 he sold part of the farm for making the West Ham and the Jews' cemeteries, and for building development which took place gradually in part of the area between those cemeteries and Woodford Road.[64]

The remainder of Woodgrange descended like Hamfrith farm[65] to Gurney's son and grandson. It was eventually acquired by Thomas Corbett, and was developed for building in 1877–92 as the Woodgrange estate: this was the area including the present Osborne, Claremont, Windsor, and Hampton Roads.

Woodgrange house is named on Norden's *Map of Essex* (1594), which shows that it was an important building. It is not known whether this was identical with the large house of the same name which still existed in the 1860s, and was approached by a drive running east from Woodgrange Road roughly on the line of Osborne Road.[66]

AGRICULTURE. In 1086 the manor of Ham, held jointly by Robert Gernon and Ranulph Peverel and

formerly by Alestan, contained 8 hides and 30 a.[67] It probably comprised most of West Ham. The arable land was being cultivated by 16 ploughs (4 on the demesne and 12 belonging to the tenants), compared with 13 in 1066 (5 demesne and 8 tenants'). There were 60 a. meadow, woodland for 100 swine, and 8 mills. Gernon's livestock comprised a rouncey, 9 beasts, 12 sheep, and 11 swine; when he received the manor there had been only a rouncey, a cow, 6 sheep, and 5 swine. Peverel's livestock had also increased during his tenure, from a rouncey, a cow, and 3 swine, to 2 rounceys, 2 colts, 2 cows with calves, 20 swine, and 60 sheep. The value of the manor, which had been £16 in 1066 and only £12 when Gernon and Peverel received it, had risen to £24 by 1086. The recorded population had increased from 51 in 1066 (32 villeins, 16 bordars, 3 serfs) to 130 in 1086 (48, 79, 3).

The most striking of the above figures are those relating to the mills, the value of the manor, and the population. West Ham had more mills in 1086 than any other place in Essex. In the Middle Ages these supplied a large local baking industry, and they remained an important feature of West Ham's economy down to the 19th century.[68] The increase in the value of the manor reflects the restocking that had taken place since the coming of Gernon and Peverel. The growth of population, however, was proportionately much larger than that of values, or ploughs, or stock. The arrival of 79 new families (63 bordars and 16 villeins) in a small community within 20 years was one of the 'obscure little revolutions in the Essex villages' noticed by Maitland.[69] The villeins had increased in the same proportion as the number of tenants' ploughs, and there may have been a connexion there, but the much greater increase in the number of bordars must have been related to a new economic activity not fully reflected in the other Domesday figures. The newcomers were probably engaged in some pioneering enterprise and it seems most likely that this was forest clearance. In the manor of (East) Ham, also held by Robert Gernon, there was a large woodland area in 1086, but most of it was cleared away during the next two centuries.[70] At (West) Ham there was comparatively little woodland left by 1086. How much there had been in 1066 is not stated, but forest clearance was no doubt part of the intensive farming practised by Gernon.[71] This may well have included the carving out of Woodgrange farm, which in the 12th century was given by his successors to Stratford Abbey.[72]

After the 11th century woodland did not figure largely in the economy of West Ham.[73] The northern fringe of the parish lay within the legal boundaries of the Forest of Essex, but as early as 1189 this comprised heath rather than woodland: in that year Richard I granted to Stratford Abbey protection against interference by foresters or others with the

[53] *V.C.H. Essex*, v. 209–10; and see Little Ilford, below, p. 166.
[54] G.L.C., DL/C/212.
[55] C 66/1178.
[56] B.M., Add. MS. 16273, p. 15.
[57] *Cal. S.P. Dom.* 1627–8, 581.
[58] *Complete Peerage*, xii (1), 798–801.
[59] Lysons, *London*, iv. 254, n. 44; cf. *D.N.B.* George Carew (1555–1629).
[60] *V.C.H. Essex*, v. 196; E.R.O., D/DB T1135–7; ibid. D/DXb 3; ibid. D/DC 23/408.
[61] Ogborne, *Essex*, 25; cf. C.P. 43/900 ro. 252.

[62] Fry, *East and West Ham*, 145, cf. 212: J. P. Peacock died in 1845.
[63] E.R.O., D/CT 160.
[64] E.R.O., D/DQs 36; Howarth and Wilson, *West Ham*, 39; *E.R.* xxxi 50–1.
[65] See p. 69.
[66] O.S. Map, 6″, Essex (surv. 1863–73), LXXIII
[67] *V.C.H. Essex*, i. 515, 527.
[68] See pp. 76, 89.
[69] *Domesday Bk. and Beyond*, 363.
[70] See p. 95.   [71] Cf. p. 15.
[72] See p. 73.   [73] For the Forest see p. 95.

pasture in the heath extending between the Frith (Hamfrith) and Walthamstow, in which heath he granted the abbey extensive sheep pastures.[74]

Much that is said about the medieval agriculture of East Ham applies to West Ham, since the manorial boundaries in several cases cut across those of the parishes.[75] Fourteenth-century references to 'worn out' land, relating to both parishes,[76] suggest that the intensive farming introduced by the Domesday lords had continued. West Ham, like East Ham, also suffered from flooding in the 14th and 15th centuries, but by the 16th century reclamation of the marshland was well under way.[77]

Open fields and meadows undoubtedly existed at some time in West Ham. The rental of Sudbury manor (1527) shows that most of the land there lay in small parcels, usually between $\frac{1}{2}$ a. and 2 a., which are otherwise difficult to explain.[78] Among the field names are the Hide, Half Hide, Hole (or Hoole) Hide, Bradymead, and Woodfields. Woodfields, which lay near Woodgrange,[79] was evidently a demesne field, for no fewer than 40 of the tenements of Sudbury were charged with rent in lieu of the service of reaping rye there. The rental also contains a number of references to 'dayworks', by then measures of land but originally measures of labour. Several of these were in Woodfields. Others were in the Hide, Ashen field, Downings field (near Green Street), Newerk Pightle, and the Hoopes in Newerk Knok. The rental also proves the earlier existence of 'leazes' or common pastures. One freeholder of the manor was charged with several separate rents for the right to pasture cows in Tunmanleys, Goodwyns (probably in West marsh),[80] and Sewalls. Several of the fields mentioned in the rental appear in earlier documents. Half Hide occurs in 1409–35.[81] Bradymead can be traced from 1202 when William of Stratford acknowledged the right of William Wrench to $\frac{1}{2}$ virgate of land in West Ham, from which Wrench granted to Stratford 6 a. (2 a. in Brademade, 3 a. in Sagodesmade, and 1 a. in Monemade).[82] In 1527 one free tenement in Wrenchefield comprised 6 a., while another of 2$\frac{1}{2}$ a., in the same field, was said to have belonged at one time to Richard Sagore. John James's 18th-century survey of Plaistow shows that Bradymead was in New marsh.[83] By then it had been cut up into a number of parcels, held in severalty, but showing in their shapes obvious traces of strips arranged in an open meadow. These field shapes were still preserved in 1867, immediately to the north of the Victoria Dock, between the present Prince Regent Lane and Freemasons Road.[84] James's

survey provides further evidence of common pasture. South of Tunmarsh Lane, in Trinity marsh, was a 33-acre field called Cow leaze,[85] while another of the same size, called Horse leaze, lay east of Prince Regent Lane opposite Bradymead.[86] All the above 'leazes' were at Plaistow, but there was at least one such field at Stratford: Oxleas in High mead (12 a.).[87]

Corn-growing must have been important in West Ham during the Middle Ages, to supply London and the retinues of visiting royalty and dignitaries.[88] In 1403 the king granted the bishop of Lincoln lodging for his household at Stratford during his visits to London.[89] Similar grants were made in 1408 to Sir Thomas Beaufort and in 1414 to the earl of Dorset,[90] while in 1414 also the bishop of Norwich was granted lodging for his horses at Plaistow and West Ham.[91] The few figures available[92] suggest that in and after the 13th century arable land predominated, at least in the upland areas of the parish. It is probable that until the floods of the late 14th century substantial parts of the marshes were under the plough. This may be inferred from a reference of 1421 to '101 a. arable land, parcel of 145 a. marsh submerged under water', belonging to Burnells manor,[93] from the field names Wheatfield (or Whitfield) and Wheatcrofte, both in Trinity marsh,[94] and from the ancient pattern of settlement at Plaistow.[95]

In the later Middle Ages cattle grazing and slaughtering, on a commercial scale, began to develop. The local meat trade, mainly with London, was established by the 14th century. In 1331 some London butchers complained to the City corporation that many butchers who had bought their freedom and were sworn of the franchise were renting houses at and near Stratford and were not taking their proper part in City affairs.[96] Later in the 14th century the Stratford trade was stimulated by royal ordinances that livestock destined for London butchers should not be brought into the City but should be slaughtered either at Stratford on one side or Knightsbridge (Mdx.) on the other, and no nearer.[97] Whether Stratford here means Stratford Langthorne or the adjoining Stratford Bow (Mdx.) is uncertain, but the purpose of the edicts, the banishment of an obnoxious London trade to the suburbs, is clear. By the 16th century there were many butchers with London connexions.[98] There was a slaughterhouse at Stratford Abbey just before the Dissolution.[99] It was stated in 1597 that much land in the parish was occupied by 'foreign' butchers and graziers.[1] Some of the then butchers were also cattle thieves.[2] Grazing continued to be important

[74] *Cal. Chart.* 1257–1300, 311–13. For this heath see also p. 199 below.
[75] See p. 14.
[76] *Cal. Inq. p.m.*, ii. 508; ibid. v. 390–1.
[77] For the Marshes and Sea Defences see p. 94.
[78] S.C. 12/15/20; cf. S.C. 6/962 (Stratford Abbey rental 1538).
[79] Cf. *Cal. Pat.* 1555–7, 443–4.
[80] Cf. Godynggs or Goodyngs Field, mentioned in the same rental and in S.C. 6/962.
[81] E.R.O., T/A 317.
[82] *Feet of F. Essex*, i. 27, cf. *Cur. Reg. R.* ii. 5.
[83] E.R.O., D/DPe M55 (items 104, 105, 107, 109).
[84] O.S. Map, 25″, London, XXXIX (surv. 1867).
[85] E.R.O., D/DPe M55 (items 202–5).
[86] Ibid. (item 62).
[87] *W. Ham Char. Rep.* (1899), 14.
[88] For royal visits see p. 44.
[89] *Cal. Pat.* 1401–5, 254.

[90] Ibid. 1405–8, 393; ibid. 1413–16, 231.
[91] Ibid. 1413–16, 244.
[92] e.g. in documents relating to Burnells and Bretts manors.
[93] *Cal. Pat.* 1416–22, 374.
[94] S.C. 12/15/20 m. 3 and 6d.; cf. E.R.O., D/DPe M55 (items 120–2, 160–1).
[95] See p. 44.
[96] H. T. Riley, *Memorials of London, 1276–1419*, 179–80.
[97] *Cal. Close* 1360–4, 248; ibid. 1377–81, 363–4; *Cal. Letter Bks. Lond.* (H.), 301.
[98] e.g. Assizes 35/2/3; Hist. MSS. Com. *10th Rep.*, pt. iv. 472; G.L.C., DL/C/211; *E.R.* lxvi. 72.
[99] S.C. 6/962.
[1] E.R.O., Q/SR 138/43.
[2] Assizes 35/53/H; ibid. 53A/T; cf. *Cal. S.P. Dom.* 1634–5, 422–3.

until the early 19th century.[3] It was said in 1734 that the largest ox ever bred in England had been fattened on Old Tunmarsh.[4] Henry, duke of Cumberland (1745–90), brother of George III, kept a racing stud at Cumberland House, Plaistow.[5] The prince of Wales, later George IV, is also said to have grazed his horses on Plaistow marshes.[6]

In 1796 West Ham was estimated to contain about 2,000 a. of arable and 2,500 a. of meadow and marshland.[7] Some 500 a. of arable were then being cropped with potatoes and 200 a. with turnips. According to the crop returns of 1801, thought 'tolerably accurate' by the vicar, only 1,026 a. were under cultivation, including 575 a. of potatoes, 272 a. of wheat, 87 a. of turnips, 67 a. of oats, and 25 a. of rye.[8] Potatoes had been grown commercially since the 1730s.[9] The labour for this was provided mainly by immigrant Irish, of whom there were about 50 in West Ham by 1767.[10] In the north, west, and central areas of the parish in 1800 the arable lay mainly north of Romford Road and to the east and west of Plaistow village. Most of the meadows adjoined the coastal marshes, but there were small patches at Plaistow and elsewhere. The market gardens, paddocks, and parks were mainly at Upton. There were also small patches of osiers beside the Channelsea river and the other branches of the Lea above the Three Mills.[11] Osiers had been cultivated in West Ham at least as early as 1539.[12]

In 1853 the parish contained some 1,100 a. of arable (including market-gardens), 2,600 a. of meadow and pasture, 8 a. of woodland, 62 a. of domestic gardens and orchards, and 82 a. of osiers and reeds.[13] By 1905 there remained only 127 a. of arable and 51 a. of permanent grass.[14] Most of that farm-land lay in the south of the borough, adjoining Prince Regent Lane.[15] The last market-garden at Plaistow is said to have closed in 1905,[16] and in the same year the closure of some watercress beds near Temple Mills, suspected of spreading cholera, was recommended.[17]

INDUSTRIES. West Ham was an industrial village long before it became a great manufacturing town. The marshes by the River Lea provided ample room for industry. The river was navigable and furnished power for a group of tidal mills which were already important in 1066, and during the next seven centuries served industries as diverse as calico-printing, paper-making, distilling, and gunpowder manufacture.[18] Until the 19th century most of the industries of the parish were in or near those western marshes.

During the Middle Ages the mills produced mainly flour, much of which was no doubt sold to local bakers, trading with London. From the 14th century the bakers of Stratford are often mentioned. Some, perhaps most, of these were at Stratford Bow (Mdx.), but others may have been at Stratford Langthorne.[19] This trade is said to have ceased about 1570.[20]

From the 13th century St. Thomas's and Spilemans mills, north of Stratford High Street, were used for fulling.[21] The cloth came steadily from London, despite a protest in 1298 that the City's rights were thereby infringed.[22] Both mills belonged to corporate bodies within the City, which probably helped them to resist pressure from other vested interests. How long fulling continued is not clear. Spilemans fulling mill is mentioned in 1738,[23] but there is no evidence that it had operated continuously since the 14th century.

In the 16th century other textile trades appear. Dyers occur at various dates from 1579 to 1751[24] and an embroiderer in 1582.[25] A silk-weaver of Stratford Langthorne, one of the earliest known in Essex, is mentioned in 1594,[26] and for much of the 17th century that trade seems to have flourished.[27] Paul Fox, a silk-weaver of Plaistow, was said in 1645 to have lived there for many years, making lace and ribbons.[28] In 1675 West Ham was affected by the widespread riots of silk-weavers against the use of the Dutch engine loom, recently introduced. On 11 August it was stated that militia had been sent to Stratford Bow, where the rioters numbered 2,000.[29] On the same day rioters broke into the house of Thomas Foster of West Ham and stole engine looms valued at £100.[30] Silk-weaving in West Ham seems then to have ended, for it is not mentioned later. An allied industry, the knitting of silk stockings, can be traced in 1668–86.[31]

Silk-weaving was succeeded by a rival industry, calico-printing. It has been suggested that the first calico-printer in England was William Sherwin of West Ham, who took out a 14-year patent in 1676,

[3] Cf. *E.R.* xxxvi. 186–90; R. Allison, 'The Changing Landscape of South-west Essex, 1600–1850' (London Ph.D. 1966), 305–9.
[4] Curwen, *Old Plaistow*, 69.
[5] Fry, *E. and W. Ham*, 252; E.R.O., D/DPe M55, Houses (first alphabet), C.
[6] Fry, ibid.
[7] Lysons, *London*, iv. 245.
[8] H.O. 67/16.
[9] E.R.O., T/A 114/1; *E.R.* xxxvi. 186–7; Curwen, *Old Plaistow*, 69.
[10] *Essex Recusant*, i. 35–6.
[11] T. Milne, *Plan of London and Westminster* (1800).
[12] *L. & P. Hen. VIII*, xiv (1), p. 162; cf. *Cal. Pat.* 1553–4, 122, 125, 127; E.R.O., Q/RUm 1/22.
[13] E.R.O., D/CT 160.
[14] Bd. of Agric., Rtns. of Acreages, 1905.
[15] E. G. Howarth and M. Wilson, *West Ham*, 51–2 and map f. p. 32.
[16] Curwen, *Old Plaistow*, 74.
[17] W. Ham C.B.C. Mins. 18 Oct. 1905.
[18] For the mills see p. 89.
[19] Lysons, *London*, ii. 492; *Munimenta Gildhallae Londoniensis*, (Rolls Ser.) i, pp. lxv, lxix; J. Stow, *Survey of London* (Everyman edn.), 141–2; H. T. Riley, *Memorials of London*, 71–2, 80, 121, 498; *Cal. Lett. Bks. Lond.* (H), 322 and (L), 308; *L. & P. Hen. VIII*, iii (1), p. 279–80, iv (1), p. 822, iv (2), p. 1228.
[20] Stow, *Survey of Lond.*, 142.
[21] *Cat. Anct. D.* i, A 480, 481; B.M. Lansd. MS. 1, f. 19; *Cal. Lett. Bks. Lond.* (G), 27.
[22] *Munimenta Gildhallae*, ii (1), 127; *Cal. Lett. Bks. Lond.* (C), pp. 51–2, (H), 37; *Cal. Plea and Memoranda Rolls, Lond.* 1323–64, 181; Riley, *Mems. Lond.* 401–4.
[23] E.R.O., T/P 48/1, f. 135: it was then untenanted.
[24] Assizes 35/21/7 and 35/97/H; *E.R.* l. 3–5; *Ipswich Jnl.* 16 Mar. 1751, p. 1.
[25] Assizes 35/24/T.
[26] *Cal. S.P. Dom.* 1591–4, 507.
[27] W.H.L., F. J. Wilkinson, 'Abstract of occupations of W. Ham residents from Essex Sessions Rolls, 1596–1699' (TS): 'silk weavers', and 'weavers'.
[28] *E.R.* xv. 203–6; *V.C.H. Essex*, ii. 462.
[29] *Cal. S.P. Dom.* 1675–6, 254–5.
[30] Assizes 35/116/2. For Foster see also: Assizes 35/112/3.
[31] *E.A.T.* n.s. xiv. 149, 153; Wilkinson, 'Occupations of W. Ham residents, 1590–1699': 'silk stocking weaver' and 'framework knotter'.

and then had a virtual monopoly.[32] In 1699 a calico-printer and two whitsters were said to have built sluices and dams in the Channelsea river.[33] Calico-printing soon became one of West Ham's main industries. In 1747 the 'calico grounds', of 81 a., formed a separate section of the marshes, lying between Stratford and the Abbey Mill.[34] Several of the early calico-printers were Frenchmen.[35] It cannot be assumed that these were all permanent immigrants. In the 1740s John Lefevre (or Lefebure) of West Ham was acting as the English agent of a textile-printer named Le Marcis, who apparently remained in France while carrying on a business on both sides of the Channel.[36] Richard Newman, calico-printer c. 1749–65,[37] was evidently employing Irish labourers in 1750, when he received an anonymous letter threatening him with death if he did not dismiss them 'as the English are starving for want of work'.[38] In 1796 there were two calico-printers, employing about 260 hands, and a third had just taken premises in Angel Lane.[39] By 1811 the number employed had risen to 360.[40] Soon after this the local calico-printers began to switch to silk-printing. By 1832 only one firm of calico-printers appears to have remained. This was D. & E. Burford, later E. Burford & Co., of Stratford, which carried on that business until about 1870 and continued as dyers for a little longer.[41] Silk-printing continued until about 1862, the last firm being John Tucker, of the Abbey Works, successor to R. and E. Littler.[42]

Tanners are occasionally mentioned in the 14th and 15th centuries.[43] In the early 16th century there was a tannery within the precincts of Stratford Abbey, but it apparently ceased shortly before 1534.[44] Richard Parker, who had been the tanner there, was also leasing property at Plaistow and elsewhere, and probably continued to ply his trade in West Ham after leaving the abbey. Several tanners occur in the later 16th and earlier 17th centuries,[45] including Thomas Staples (d. 1592).[46] At that period various other leather trades have been noticed. Thomas Parker, formerly a currier of West Ham, was living in 1558.[47] He was possibly a relative of Richard Parker the tanner. The trades of fell-monger, leather-dresser, saddler, bridle-maker, collar-maker, and whipseller all occur in the 17th

century.[48] Most important of all were the cord-wainers, from whom Cordwainer (now High) Street, Plaistow, was named.[49] Since that street is mentioned in 1527 the cordwainers must have been well established by then.[50] The leather trades were still well represented in the parish in 1848, when a directory lists 42 bootmakers and shoemakers, 2 curriers, and 4 saddlers.[51]

Gunpowder manufacture appears to have started in West Ham during the Spanish wars of Elizabeth I. Powder mills are mentioned in 1588 (at the Three Mills), 1597 (St. Thomas's mill), and 1615 (Spilemans mill).[52] They were probably the first in Essex, and were certainly among the earliest in England.[53] An unidentified gunpowder mill is mentioned in 1645.[54] No later reference to the industry has been found except in 1738, when a new lease of Spilemans mill prohibited gunpowder manufacture.[55]

The manufacture of Bow porcelain, the most notable of West Ham's earlier industries, has been described elsewhere.[56] Recent research has produced new evidence, especially concerning its early years.[57] The Bow porcelain works, one of the first in England, seems to have been established at Bow (Mdx.) in 1744 by George Arnold, alderman and haberdasher of London, Edward Heylyn of Bow, merchant, and Thomas Frye.[58] It was in production by the end of 1747. By 1749 it had moved across the Lea to High Street, Stratford. Arnold (1691–1751) probably provided the capital. Frye was the technical expert. By 1750 the factory was trading under his name, and he continued to direct it until his retirement in 1759. During that decade it produced its best pieces. Heylyn apparently left the business in its early days, but was again associated with Frye in 1757. After Frye's retirement the factory was carried on by Weatherby & Crowther, which had previously been handling the sales of Bow porcelain through their London warehouse. John Crowther, the last surviving partner, sold the factory in 1775 or 1776 to William Duesbury, who closed it and transferred the contents to his works at Derby. The Bow works stood on the north side of High Street, west of Marsh Gate Lane. Premises on the opposite side of the road were also used in connexion with the works.[59]

[32] P. C. Floud, 'The origins of English calico printing', *Jnl. of Soc. Dyers and Colourists*, May 1960, 275–80.

[33] Unless otherwise stated this paragraph is based on the following sources: W.H.L., Cal. Christ's Hosp. Docs. *re* Abbey Mill; W.H.L., F. Sainsbury, Notes on Textile Printing in W. Ham (TS); R. Allison, 'Changing Landscape of South-West Essex, 1600–1850' (Lond. Ph.D. 1966), pp. 270–3; *V.C.H. Essex*, ii. 404–8; *E.R.* xix. 112.

[34] W.H.L., Map of W. Ham Level, 1747.

[35] *Essex Recusant*, ii. 21; E.R.O., D/SH 1, f. 480.

[36] E.R.O., T/P 48/3, f. 343.

[37] W.H.L., W. Ham (Stratford) Manor Ct. R. 1749, f. 11*a*, 1765 ff. 22 and 22*a*.

[38] *Lond. Gaz.* 10–13 Nov., 13–17 Nov., 17–20 Nov. 1750.

[39] Lysons, *London*, iv. 272.

[40] Ibid. *Suppl.* (1811), 364.

[41] *Pigot's Dir. Essex* (1832); *Kelly's Dir. Essex* (1852–78).

[42] *V.C.H. Essex*, ii. 406–7; *E. Nat.* xii. 43–4.

[43] E. C. Furber, *Essex Sessions of the Peace*, 157; *Cal. Close* 1447–54, 490; ibid. 1454–61, 396; ibid. 1461–8, 188, 264, 462.

[44] S.C. 6/962; E.R.O., T/P 48/3, f. 21; K. Fry, *E. and W. Ham*, 119–20.

[45] *Cal. Pat.* 1566–9, 147; Wilkinson, 'Occupations of W. Ham residents, 1590–1699'.

[46] His monument is in the parish church, see p. 118.

[47] *Cal. Pat.* 1558–60, 134.

[48] Wilkinson, op. cit.

[49] Ibid.

[50] S.C. 12/15/20.

[51] *White's Dir. Essex* (1848), 245–7.

[52] Three Mills: E.R.O., T/P 48/1, f. 159, cf. 48/3, f. 100; St. Thomas's mill: ibid. 48/1, f. 165; Spilemans mill: ibid. 48/1 f. 174.

[53] Cf. W. H. Simmons, *Hist. Royal Gunpowder Factory at Waltham Abbey*, 1–11.

[54] E.R.O., T/P 48/1, f. 187.

[55] Ibid. f. 136.

[56] *V.C.H. Essex*, ii. 415–17; *V.C.H. Middlesex*, ii. 146–50.

[57] Unless otherwise stated this paragraph is based on the following, all by Hugh Tait: *Bow Porcelain, 1744–76* (British Museum, 1959); 'Some consequences of the Bow pottery special exhibition', *Apollo Mag.* Feb. 1960, 40–4, Apr. 1960, 93–8; 'The Bow factory under Alderman Arnold and Thomas Frye', *English Ceramic Circle Trans.* v (1963), 195–216. See also Elizabeth Adams, *Some links between porcelain factories of the 18th cent. and the N.W. of England* (Keele Univ. 1969).

[58] See also: G. A. R. Goyle, 'First porcelain making in America', *Chron. Early American Industries Assoc.* i, Nov. 1934–July 1935).

[59] E.R.O., D/DLo. T59.

Fragments of porcelain and kiln furniture have been excavated on both these sites.

Spirit-distilling on a large scale was begun *c.* 1730 by Peter Lefebure and his partners at the Three Mills and later at St. Thomas's mill. It continued at the Three Mills until 1941, and part of the premises was still occupied as a warehouse in 1969.[60]

Besides these larger industries there were many others before the end of the 18th century. In addition to the usual village craftsmen, there were in the 17th century brickmakers, glaziers, glovers, locksmiths, starchmakers, and lime-burners.[61] Lime became more important in the 18th century, when it was required by the local calico-printers,[62] and its production continued down to the 20th century.[63] Paper was being made at St. Thomas's mill in 1767[64] and at Spilemans in 1818.[65] In the 16th century there was a fishery on the Lea, and another at Ham creek.[66]

A pamphlet issued by the borough council *c.* 1910 was entitled *West Ham, the factory centre of the south of England*. That description was not unjustified. By then the town was fringed by a great industrial belt running from Temple Mills, down the Lea, and along the Thames to North Woolwich; and except for Bristol West Ham was the largest county borough south of Birmingham. A survey made in 1907 had stated that there were 130 'chief factories' in the borough.[67] The total number of factories was certainly much larger.[68] In 1910 there were at least 335 manufacturing, engineering, and constructional firms, among which the largest groups were those concerned with chemicals (102), engineering and metalwork (91), food, drink, and tobacco (37). Of these 228 were permanent firms, defined as those which are known to have completed, before or after 1910, a life of 20 years or more in West Ham. Many were probably small, but some, such as those at Silvertown engaged in shipbuilding, sugar-refining, flour-milling, and the production of sulphuric acid and rubber, were very large. The figures do not include firms concerned only with supplying raw materials, equipment, or machinery to other industries nor those providing only transport or storage, of which the largest concentration was at the Royal Victoria and Royal Albert Docks. The Great Eastern Railway Co. and the London, Tilbury and Southend Railway Co. both maintained engineering workshops in West Ham and have been included in the above total figure for engineering.

This remarkable industrial development had taken place mainly within the previous fifty years, but had been foreshadowed during the early 19th century. Its course and the main factors behind it have been outlined elsewhere.[69] West Ham's proximity to London was crucial in several ways, not least because of the constant tendency, stimulated by 19th-century legislation, for obnoxious industries to be driven from the City to the suburbs. Extensive waterways were also vital, for drainage and transport as well as water supply. Plenty of land was available, at first fairly cheap. The earliest 19th-century development was attracted by the absence of by-law restrictions, and even the local board (1856–86) exercised little control over industry. The borough council (from 1886) did not lack powers of control, but it applied them indulgently, no doubt because a stricter policy, besides affecting the rate income, might have aggravated the unemployment which was West Ham's worst problem. When the council set up its own electricity undertaking early in the present century it welcomed industrial consumers, and advertised widely to attract them to the borough. At least one of its publicity leaflets was also published in German. Between 1870 and 1914 Germans greatly influenced the growth of West Ham's industry, especially in chemicals. One important firm, Ohlendorff & Co., was controlled from Germany, while others, like Spencer Chapman & Messel, owed their development to immigrant German scientists or industrialists. Some German factory workers also settled in West Ham.[70] Scottish migrants played an important part in several industries, particularly sugar-refining and jute-spinning.

The history of West Ham's modern manufacturing industries can conveniently be divided into three periods, 1800–59, 1860–1919, and 1920–69. In 1800–59 34 permanent firms are known to have been established. Chemicals (8 firms) and engineering and metals (7) were the main groups. In the earlier part of that period development, still on a small scale, was mainly in the existing industrial area beside the Lea at Stratford Marsh. The chemical works of Howards & Sons, established at Plaistow in 1797, were transferred in 1805 to the old City Mills in High Street, Stratford, where they remained for over a century. During the 1820s and 1830s Walter Hancock was making steam carriages at Stratford and operating them on local routes. Later he turned to the manufacture of gutta percha. The building of the railway through Stratford (1839) with the North Woolwich branch (1847) prepared the way for more rapid development. The carriage works of the Eastern Counties Railway (1847) at Stratford and the Leathercloth Co.'s factory in Abbey Road (*c.* 1857) became two of the largest industries in the

[60] See p. 93.
[61] Wilkinson, 'Occupations of West Ham residents, 1590–1699'.
[62] R. Allison, 'Changing landscape of south-west Essex', 1600–1850, 272.
[63] *White's Dir. Essex* (1848), 243 (Thomas Meeson & Sons); *Kelly's Dir. Essex* (1866–1926) (Grays Chalk Quarries Ltd.).
[64] E.R.O., T/P 48/3.
[65] E.R.O., D/DB T782.
[66] *L. & P. Hen. VIII*, xiv (1), 162–3; C 142/173/37; C 142/84/75.
[67] Howarth and Wilson, *W. Ham*, 149.
[68] Unless otherwise stated this sub-section is based on the following sources: *Pigot's Dir. Essex* (1839); *White's Dir. Essex* (1848 and 1863); *Kelly's Dir. Essex* (1852–1926); *Kelly's Dir. Stratford* (1887–1905); *Kelly's Dir.*

Lond. (1927 f.); Howarth and Wilson, *W. Ham* (1908); *W. Ham, Factory Centre of the south of England* (*c.* 1910); *The Bk. of W. Ham* (1923 and 1924); *W. Ham, London's Industrial Centre* (1935/6); *Stratford Expr., W. Ham Jubilee Suppl.* (1936); *W. Ham Trade Index* (1948); *W. Ham Chamber of Commerce List of Members* (1954/5 f.); Questionnaire sent to local firms by W. Ham Borough Libraries, 1959–61; *West Ham Official Guide* (1950–64); *Newham Official Guide* (1967, 1969); M. P. Addington, 'Stratford Marsh: a study of an industrial complex' (Brentwood Coll. Educ. thesis, 1969); *London Tel. Dir.* (1968/9). In the course of this work much help was received from Newham Borough Libraries, especially in analysing directories.
[69] *V.C.H. Essex*, v. 13–21.
[70] Howarth and Wilson, *W. Ham*, 143; and see below, p. 135.

Victoria Dock, Graving Dock about 1860

The Three Mills in 1840, from the west

WEST HAM

Bow Creek in 1854, looking south to Mare's (later Thames) Ironworks

Bow Creek in 1972, looking north

WEST HAM

north of the parish. The shipyard of C. J. Mare & Co. (later the Thames Ironworks, Shipbuilding, and Engineering Co.), opened in 1846, brought industry to Canning Town. Farther south, on the Thames, the factory of S. W. Silver & Co., rubber manufacturers (1852), was followed by that of Odams Chemical Manure Co. (1855). The opening of the Victoria Dock (1855), though primarily of commercial importance, also stimulated the local growth of marine engineering and the manufacture of marine paints and glues.

During 1860–1919 at least 290 permanent manufacturing firms were formed, of which the main groups were chemicals (100 firms), engineering and metals (60), food, drink and tobacco (33), textiles, leather and clothing (23), timber, furniture, etc. (21), and bricks, pottery, cement, glass, etc. (20).[71] Between 1860 and 1899 the pace of development was remarkably even, with about 50 permanent new firms in each decade. From 1900 it was slower, partly because of economic depression and partly because there was little room left for further expansion. The totals for the whole of the 60-year period, together with those, given above, for 1910, show the pre-eminence of the chemical, engineering, and food groups, and also the importance and the variety of other industries, but there are other significant aspects of the industrial pattern which the totals cannot reveal. The Thames Ironworks shipyard, after many ups and downs, closed in 1912. Jute-spinning, brought to Stratford in 1865, ceased in 1904. In both these cases large works were involved, the closure of which caused much hardship, but this was mitigated by the growth of other industries. The manufacture of coarse textiles, rubber, and clothing, the processing of food, timber-milling, and printing, all grew steadily. Some of the largest new factories were at Silvertown, where riverside sites made it possible to handle in bulk such materials as sugar, grain, and rubber. Clothing manufacture, often in small workshops, was to be found in areas, like Forest Gate and Upton, unsuitable for heavy industry. Printing was concentrated mainly at Plaistow and timber-milling at Stratford and Silvertown. Within the two main groups, chemicals and engineering, there was also much diversity. The most important chemical factories during this period were those, mostly at Stratford and Silvertown, producing sulphuric acid, paint, printing ink, matches, fertilizers, and soap. During the First World War TNT was made by one Silvertown firm until 1917, when there was a catastrophic explosion. Engineering was concerned chiefly with railways and steamships, but various other kinds of work were carried on, including chemical engineering.

During the period 1920–69 at least 87 permanent manufacturing firms were formed, of which the main groups were engineering and metals (30), chemicals (11), textiles, leather, and clothing (11), timber, furniture, etc. (11), and food, drink, and tobacco (9). These, of course, were in addition to many earlier firms still surviving. West Ham's factories, especially at Silvertown, were heavily bombed during the Second World War, but most survived, and 243 appear in an admittedly incomplete list of 1948. In 1968–9 there were at least 154 permanent firms, of which the main groups were engineering and metals (41), chemicals (38), textiles, leather, and clothing (17), food, drink, and tobacco (16), and timber, furniture, etc. (13). These figures, of course, ignore the differences of size between factories; an analysis by workers employed per industry would show rather different results. The 1961 census of industry[72] is not ideal for this purpose, since its figures are presented according to place of residence, and not place of employment, but it is worth quoting, because a substantial proportion of West Ham's residents also work there.[73] On a 10 per cent sample the numbers of residents working in the main industrial groups were as follows: engineering and metals 11,92(0); food, drink, and tobacco 9,97(0); chemicals 7,57(0); construction 5,95(0); textiles, leather, and clothing 2,95(0); paper, printing, and publishing 2,56(0). In the first group 4,07(0) were employed in marine engineering, while in the second 4,20(0) were sugar workers. During the past 50 years local firms have increasingly been taken over by large national or international (especially U.S.) groups. Those with interests in West Ham now include Unilever, Nestlé, Spillers, Rowntrees, Tube Investments, B.T.R. Industries, and the Corn Products Co.

It will be clear then, that in spite of its reduced population, West Ham continues to be a great industrial centre, concerned mainly with chemicals, engineering, and food. The principal factory areas are still Silvertown and Stratford Marsh. Recently, industry at Stratford Marsh, where in 1969 14 per cent of the industrial land was vacant or derelict, has somewhat declined.[74] It has been suggested that the factory sites there are too small and inconvenient for large firms, but too large and expensive for small ones.[75]

West Ham's transport industries, which are described elsewhere,[76] have been hardly less important in the economic life of the town than the factories. Between 1896 and 1906 the docks were employing an average of 3,102 dockers and 736 stevedores.[77] In 1961, on the 10 per cent sample, no fewer than 22,72(0) of the resident population of the borough were employed in transport and communication, the main groups being port and inland water transport 9,11(0), railways 5,51(0), sea transport 2,53(0), and road haulage 2,32(0). The most important recent event in transport has been the opening, in 1967, of the Stratford freightliner terminal.

The history of local trade unionism and that of the early co-operative movement was outlined elsewhere.[78] West Ham was the birth-place of the National Union of Gas Workers and General Labourers (1889), of which W. J. Thorne was for many years the secretary. The Stratford Co-operative Society, founded in 1861, grew steadily,

---

[71] These groups were based on the Standard Industrial Classification, with the following modifications: 'engineering and metals' includes Standard Industrial groups V to IX; 'textile, leather and clothing' includes Standard Industrial groups X to XII; cf. *Census, 1961, Eng. & Wales, Occupation, Industry, Socio-Economic Groups (Essex)*.

[72] *Census, 1961, Occ. Ind. &c. (Essex)*, Table 3.
[73] Cf. *V.C.H. Essex*, v. 68.
[74] M. P. Addington, 'Stratford Marsh', f. 38.
[75] Ibid. 42.
[76] See pp. 61–3.
[77] Howarth and Wilson, *W. Ham*, 228.
[78] *V.C.H. Essex*, v. 60–1.

absorbing four other societies by 1898. In 1920 it joined with the Edmonton society to form the London Co-operative Society, with 124,000 members.[79] The L.C.S. subsequently took over a number of other societies, and by 1969 had a membership of over a million and annual sales of £38 million. Its central premises at Maryland Street, Stratford, were badly bombed in 1941. In 1954 the society bought J. R. Roberts Stores, Stratford Broadway, and between 1957 and 1962 built a new department store on that site. The society's headquarters are still in Maryland Street, where a new office block was completed in 1959.

There follow details of some 180 firms, past or present, which were founded after 1800 and which have been engaged in manufacture, engineering, or construction. Most of them are included because of their size or long life, but some for other reasons. They are grouped according to the Standard Industrial Classification.[80] Unless otherwise stated those mentioned were still operating in West Ham in 1969, when this survey was completed.

FOOD, DRINK, AND TOBACCO.[81] *Corn-milling*, West Ham's oldest industry, declined during the 19th century as the ancient mills were demolished or converted to other uses,[82] but early in the present century three very large mills were built at Victoria Dock. These were the first in the port of London designed to take imported grain direct from the ships.[83] The Co-operative Wholesale Society's mill was completed in 1901 on a 5 a. site which allowed room also for a food sundries factory (1904).[84] The Premier Mill was opened in 1904 by Joseph Rank Ltd., which is now part of Ranks Hovis McDougall Ltd.[85] Millennium Mill, built by W. Vernon & Sons in 1905, was destroyed in 1917 by the Silvertown explosion, but was rebuilt. Vernon & Sons was later taken over by Spillers Ltd.[86]

Sugar-refining,[87] which became one of West Ham's major industries, was being carried on at Stratford by 1843 in premises belonging to Elizabeth Reynolds and occupied by Charles Saunders.[88] This was no doubt the refinery in High Street occupied in 1851 by a German immigrant.[89] His workers, most of whom resided at the refinery, included several other Germans. In 1852 the refinery was apparently controlled by Law Bros.[90] By 1853 it was owned and occupied by William Corrie as devisee of the late Charles Reynolds.[91] This refinery, which evidently gave its name to Sugar House Lane, was set back on the south side of High Street immediately west of Three Mills river. No later reference has been found to sugar-refining there, but the original refinery, a tall gaunt building, with many windows, still survived in 1969.

The later sugar refineries have been at Silvertown. About 1862 the Greenock firm of Duncan, Bell & Scott built Clyde Wharf refinery.[92] James Duncan (1834–1905), the senior partner, took charge of this and eventually became the sole owner. It was for many years a large and profitable business.[93] It was closed in 1886, when Duncan was forced into bankruptcy by foreign competition. By 1890 it had been taken over by David Martineau & Sons, but in 1893 it was badly damaged by fire.[94] This appears to have been the end of sugar-refining at Clyde Wharf.[95]

The firm of Henry Tate & Sons came to Silvertown in 1877, and that of Abram Lyle & Sons in 1881.[96] Tate, at Thames Wharf, was best known for cube sugar, and Lyle, at Plaistow Wharf, for golden syrup. The two firms amalgamated in 1921 to form Tate & Lyle, one of the world's largest sugar-refiners.[97] Under a reorganization scheme of 1968 refining was concentrated at Thames Wharf and Plaistow Wharf was used only for packaging and making golden syrup.[98]

The earliest *manufacturing confectioner* in West Ham was Volckman & Sons, of High Street, Stratford, which was in business from 1839 or earlier until about 1890.[99] James Keiller & Sons, maker of marmalade and other confectionery, came to Silvertown from Scotland about 1880 and built a large factory at Tay Wharf. This firm was taken over in 1920 by Crosse and Blackwell and is now a subsidiary of the Nestlé Co.[1] Streimer's Nougat Ltd., of Victoria Street, Stratford, was founded about 1898 by Morris Streimer (1857–1935), a Jewish immigrant from Austria. The original factory was in High Street and Ward Road.[2] Loosé Ltd., cocoa and chocolate manufacturer, had a factory in Marshgate Lane, Stratford, c. 1898–1937.[3] Whitefields Ltd., chocolate manufacturer, was founded shortly before 1923, when the old tramway depot in Tunmarsh Lane, Plaistow, was converted into a factory; it is now a subsidiary of Rowntree & Co.[4] Caramel, used

[79] The rest of this paragraph is based on: L.C.S., *Twenty Years After* (1940); *L.C.S. Reps.* (1947–69); inf. from L.C.S.
[80] Cf. *Census, 1961, Eng. & Wales, occup., Ind., Socio-Econ. Groups (Essex)*.
[81] Standard Industrial Classification, Group III.
[82] See pp. 89 sqq.
[83] Howarth and Wilson, *W. Ham*, 210.
[84] *Stratford Expr. W. Ham Jubilee Suppl.* (1936).
[85] Ibid. p. 16; *Who Owns Whom* (1969).
[86] *Stratford Expr. Jubilee Suppl.* (1936); *Bk. of W. Ham* (1923), 221.
[87] Mr. F. Lewis, who is preparing a book on 'Essex and Sugar', has kindly helped in the compilation of the following account of West Ham's sugar industry.
[88] W.H.L., Havering and Dagenham Level, Sewers Presentment, 1843.
[89] H.O. 107/1768. The refiner's name is given in the return as 'Cord Càmpé', possibly a garbled version of 'Kurt Kempe'.
[90] *Kelly's Dir. Essex* (1852).
[91] E.R.O., D/CT 160.
[92] For this refinery see: *Kelly's Dir. Essex* (1862–86); N. Deerr, *Hist. Sugar*, 460; *International Sugar Jnl.* vii (1905), 563 (obit. of Jas. Duncan).

[93] In 1868–74 Duncan also had a sugar-beet factory at Lavenham (Suff.): C. L. Anderson, 'Lavenham Receivers', *Tate & Lyle Times*, Sept./Oct. 1964.
[94] *Kelly's Dir. Essex* (1890); *Stratford Expr.* 17 June 1893.
[95] Inf. from Mr. P. Martineau.
[96] *V.C.H. Essex*, ii. 496.
[97] O. Lyle, *The Plaistow Story* (1960) deals with the history of Abram Lyle & Sons and that of Tate & Lyle.
[98] Inf. from Mr. F. Lewis.
[99] *Pigot's Dir. Essex* (1839); *Kelly's Dir. Essex* (1852–90); W. G. Crory, *East London Industries*, 207; W.H.L., C. Whitwell, 'Dictionary of W. Ham'. Volckman's factory was later a cinema: see above, p. 66.
[1] *Kelly's Dir. Essex* (1882–1926); *Bk. of W. Ham*, 230; *Stratford Express, W. Ham Jubilee Suppl.* (1936); *Who Owns Whom* (1969).
[2] *Kelly's Dir. Stratford* (1898 f.); *Kelly's Dir. Essex* (1906–26); C. Whitwell, 'Dictionary of W. Ham'.
[3] *Kelly's Dir. Stratford* (1898/9); *Kelly's Dir. Essex* (1926); *Kelly's Dir. Lond.* (1937, 1938).
[4] *Bk. of W. Ham*, 223; *W. Ham Official Guide* (1955/6); *W. Ham Chamber of Commerce List of Members* (1959); *Who Owns Whom* (1969).

both in confectionery and in brewing, has been made by several West Ham firms, including Everest & Co. of Northern Road, Plaistow (1887–1961), and W. Ambrose & Co. (1895–1961),[5] both of which were taken over by Brown & Polson, now itself a subsidiary of an American firm, the Corn Products Co.[6]

The refining of *edible oils* has been carried on principally by Loders & Nucoline Ltd., of Cairn Mills, Silvertown.[7] This firm originated in 1887, when Petty & Co. began refining coconut oil at Cairn Mills under the management of F. H. Loder, son of F. W. Loder, one of the directors of the company. In 1890, when Petty & Co. went into liquidation, the two Loders opened a factory at Limehouse (Lond.), making coconut oil stearine. In 1898 Loder & Son amalgamated with Nucoline Ltd. to form Loders & Nucoline, and soon after moved back to Cairn Mills. The factory was burnt down in 1909, but was rebuilt and extended; by 1936 it covered 8 a. It was taken over in 1919 by the African & Eastern Trade Corporation, which itself merged with Unilever Ltd. in 1929. In 1940 Cairn Mills was again destroyed, this time by bombing, but refining started again within six weeks. After the war the factory was rebuilt.

Several firms have been engaged in the processing of *meat foods* such as sausages and pies, including the Excel Co. of Carpenters Road, Stratford, which existed by 1917. It was later taken over by Henry Telfer Ltd.[8] Among other human foods processed in West Ham have been *pickles*, at the C.W.S. factory at Silvertown.[9]

The manufacture of *animal foods* forms part of the work of Loders & Nucoline. Among other firms in that industry has been C. & A. Gould Ltd., High Street, Stratford (1885–c. 1965). Gould's mill was enlarged in 1932, with storage for 1,000 tons of grain. It was demolished in 1969.[10] British Feeding Meals & Milk Products came to Carpenters Road, Stratford, about 1929.[11] During the Second World War it was the pioneer in converting domestic refuse into animal food.[12] It is now a subsidiary of Spillers Ltd., operating in Carpenters Road as Seemeel Ltd.[13] Smithfield Animal Products Trading Co. built a factory in Marshgate Lane in 1920.[14] It is now part of the Smithfield & Zwanenberg Group Ltd.[15]

The leading firm of *brewers* was Savill Bros., whose Stratford brewery, Maryland Road, existed

from at least 1862 until *c.* 1926.[16] Several other brewers have had premises in West Ham, but some of these were probably warehouses only. A few firms of *distillers* were established in the later 19th century, but none lasted long, or rivalled in size J. & W. Nicholson, of the Three Mills. A distillery in West Ham Lane appears to have passed through several hands between 1848 and 1898 and was probably not continuously open.[17] *Mineral waters* were being made by two Stratford firms in 1862[18] and later by several others, including A. Wells, Stratford Road (*c.* 1878–1941), Thomas Curno, Southern Road, Plaistow (*c.* 1890–1961), Thomas (later Anne) Simpson, of Barking Road, Canning Town (*c.* 1890–1945), and Tullet, Tomlin & Co., Maryland Square, Stratford (from *c.* 1908).[19]

Gill Bros., *tobacco* manufacturer, has been in Barking Road, Canning Town since about 1906.[20] J. Wix & Son, maker of 'Kensitas' cigarettes, has had a factory in Livingstone Road, Stratford, since about 1962; it is a subsidiary of the American Tobacco Co.[21]

CHEMICALS.[22] The manufacture of *coke* for use by the Eastern Counties Railway was being carried on in 1848 at the railway's depot on Bow creek.[23] It was a large industry, which in 1851 was employing at least 34 local workers,[24] but was apparently short-lived.[25]

The refining of *mineral oils and tar* has been carried on by over 20 firms at different periods. In Marshgate Lane, Stratford, J. P. Murphy (*c.* 1818–63)[26] and Smith Bros. & Co. (*c.* 1866–1967)[27] distilled tar and turpentine. Another Stratford tar-distiller was Thomas Crow (*c.* 1862–1917), of Crows Road.[28] At Prince Regents Wharf, Silvertown, Burt, Boulton & Haywood was founded in 1856 by H. P. Burt.[29] Its original business, importing railway sleepers, was later extended to the distilling of tar, creosote, and disinfectants. It remained at Prince Regents Wharf for over a century, operating during its last years there through subsidiaries, Printar Industries and the Silvertown Tarmacadam Co. In 1969 the works of Printar Industries were closed, and those of the Silvertown Tarmacadam Co. were sold to Tarmac Roadstone Holdings.[30] Gulf Oil (Great Britain) Ltd., Minoco Wharf, Silvertown, originated in 1896 when the Mineral Oils Corporation (abbreviated as Minoco) was formed by Charles Hunting and others to distill and refine lubricants from Russian

[5] Inf. from Everest & Co. (1959) and Ambrose & Co. (1960), and from Mr. A. Kaye.
[6] *Kelly's Dir. Lond.* (1961, 1962); *Who Owns Whom* (1969).
[7] 'The Story of a Paradox', *Unilever House Mag.* Oct./Nov. 1951, p. 20; *Stratford Expr. Jubilee Suppl.* (1936).
[8] *Kelly's Dir. Essex* (1917–26); inf. from Excel Meat Co.
[9] *W. Ham the Factory Centre* (*c.* 1910).
[10] *C. & A. Gould Ltd. 1856–1956*; *Kelly's Dir. Lond.* (1956 f.); W.H.L., Illus. Coll. (Industries): photos 1969.
[11] *British Feeding Meals Mfg. Co. Ltd.* (1929) [Pamphlet].
[12] *W. Ham Official Guide* (1950–56); *Nature*, cxlvi, (1940) 47; W.H.L., Notes for 'Target Area W. Ham'.
[13] *Who Owns Whom* (1969).
[14] *Bk. of W. Ham*, 222.
[15] *Who Owns Whom* (1969).
[16] *Kelly's Dir. Essex* (1862–1922); *Bk. of W. Ham* (1923); W.H.L., W. Ham L.B. Mins. 28 June 1870; E.R.O., *Sale Cat.* A256 (1926).
[17] *White's Dir. Essex* (1848); *Kelly's Dir. Essex* (1852, 1878–86); *Kelly's Dir. Stratford &c.* (1898–9).
[18] *Kelly's Dir. Essex* (1862).

[19] Ibid. (1879–1926); *Kelly's Dir. Lond.* (1927–62).
[20] *Kelly's Dir. Essex* (1906 f.).
[21] *Kelly's Dir. Lond.* (1962 f.); *Who Owns Whom* (1969).
[22] Standard Industrial Classification Group IV.
[23] *White's Dir. Essex* (1848), 240; cf. *Eastern Co. Rly. Map* (1853).
[24] H.O. 107/1768.
[25] Coke Oven Cottages, which existed in 1853, are said to have been on the site of the later Thames Ironworks. See p. 136.
[26] R. Allison, 'Changing Landscape of S.W. Essex, 1600–1850', 277 (Crane & Murphy, 1818); *Pigot's Dir. Essex* (1839); *White's Dir. Essex* (1848, 1863).
[27] *Kelly's Dir. Essex* (1866 f.); *Kelly's Dir. Lond.* (1967, 1968).
[28] W. Ham L.B. Mins. 14 Oct. 1862; *Kelly's Dir. Essex* (1866 f.).
[29] W. G. Crory, *East London Industries*, 25–31; *Stratford Express, Jubilee Suppl.* (1936); *Kelly's Dir. Lond.* (1958).
[30] Inf. from Silvertown Tarmacadam Co.; *Kelly's Dir. Lond.* (1959 f.).

crude oil imported by a parent company, the Northern Petroleum Tank Steamship Co. of Newcastle upon Tyne.[31] The corporation built a jetty, wharf, and works on a 13 a. site at Silvertown. In 1901–2 Minoco was reconstituted as Silvertown Lubricants Ltd., and grew into a profitable business supplying railways and other large users throughout the British Empire and in South America. In 1929 Silvertown Lubricants was acquired by the Gulf Oil Corporation, and in 1950 its name was changed to Gulf Oil (Great Britain) Ltd. The Silvertown works now concentrate on oil blending, and are no longer concerned with distilling or refining.

Sulphuric acid is one of West Ham's main chemical industries.[32] The Crown Sulphur Works, Marshgate Lane, Stratford, existed for about 40 years, run by T. D. Scott & Co. (*c.* 1866–86) and later by Johnson & Hooper (*c.* 1890–1906).[33] The West Ham Chemical Works, Canning Road (off Abbey Lane), was apparently founded by James Childs, who made vitriol there (*c.* 1866–82); he was succeeded by W. C. Bacon & Co. (*c.* 1866–1917).[34] Near the last in Canning Road was the vitriol works of Thomas Bell & Co. (*c.* 1870–82), which was taken over before 1886 by F. W. Berk & Co.[35] Spencer Chapman & Messel (1872–*c.* 1964), of North Woolwich Road, Silvertown, was founded as Squires & Chapman.[36] Rudolf Messel (managing director 1878–1916) was an immigrant German chemist who invented new methods of producing sulphuric acid. Some of the local fertilizer manufacturers, notably the Anglo-Continental Guano Works Ltd., made sulphuric acid for their own use in producing superphosphates.

The manufacture of *pharmaceutical, technical, and toilet preparations* in West Ham goes back to 1797, when William Allen and Luke Howard opened a factory at Plaistow. In 1805 the partnership was dissolved and Howard moved to City Mills, Stratford, where he established the firm, later known as Howards & Sons, which remained there until its removal to Ilford was completed in 1914.[37] The Stirling Chemical Works, Canning Road, was founded in 1866 by Dunn, Squires & Co., later Dunn & Co.[38] Thomas Tyler & Co. leased the works from Dunn & Co. in 1891 and bought the freehold in 1900. In the 1930s Thomas Tyler & Co. became closely associated with the Albright & Wilson chemical group and in 1942 was taken over by them. A. Boake, Roberts & Co., manufacturer of perfumery and flavour chemicals, Carpenters Road, Stratford, originated about 1870.[39] In 1960

this firm also was taken over by Albright & Wilson and in 1966 was merged with others in the group to form Bush, Boake, Allen Ltd.[40] Jeyes Sanitary Compounds Co., Richmond Street, Plaistow, was formed in 1885, to manufacture the disinfectant fluid patented by John Jeyes in 1879.[41] Yardley of London Ltd., manufacturers of perfumes and cosmetics, built a factory in Carpenters Road in 1903.[42] An extension, in High Street, was built in 1937. Yardley, which is now a subsidiary of the British American Tobacco Co., moved most of its Stratford business to Basildon in 1966.[43] Brunner Mond & Co. built a caustic soda factory at Crescent Wharf, Silvertown, in 1893–5.[44] It was temporarily closed in 1912, made TNT during the First World War,[45] and resumed soda production in 1918. Brunner Mond became part of Imperial Chemical Industries in 1927, and by 1936 the Silvertown works was producing various kinds of chemicals. I.C.I. left Silvertown about 1961.[46]

Explosives and matches were among the earlier modern industries of the parish. There was a Congreve rocket factory at West Ham Abbey *c.* 1821–66.[47] Bell & Black, manufacturer of wax vestas, camphorated gas, and patent wire fuses, established a factory in High Street, Stratford, in 1839, and remained until about 1882.[48] There were several other match manufacturers during the later 19th and earlier 20th centuries, but none seems to have remained long except Benjamin Daniels (*c.* 1886–1905),[49] of Martin Street, and G. M. Judd & Bros. (*c.* 1908–27), Carpenters Road, both of Stratford.[50] During the First World War, under government pressure, Brunner Mond & Co.'s factory at Silvertown went over to the production of TNT, using a vacuum process invented by F. A. Freeth, chief scientist of the company. 'It worked,' wrote Freeth, many years later, 'but was manifestly very dangerous. At the end of every month we used to write to Silvertown to say that their plant would go up sooner or later, but were told that it was worth the risk.'[51] On 19 January 1917 the factory did blow up, causing 450 casualties, including 69 deaths, in the neighbourhood, and widespread damage to buildings.[52]

One of the largest groups of West Ham's industries includes *paint, varnish, dye, and printing ink.* Paint or varnish has been made by some 50 firms at different periods, mainly at Stratford. Jenson & Nicholson, of Carpenters Road, maker of 'Robbialac' paints, came to West Ham from London in

---

[31] *Inst. Petroleum Review*, Mar. 1967, p. 88; inf. from Gulf Oil (Great Britain) Ltd.; *Bk. of W. Ham* (1923), 224.
[32] Paragraph based on: W. A. Parks and E. A. Rudge, 'London's Chemical Industry: I. Sulphuric Acid in E. and W. Ham', *Chemical Age*, 6 Apr. 1946.
[33] *Kelly's Dir. Essex* (1866–1906).
[34] Ibid. (1866–1917).
[35] Ibid. (1870 f.).
[36] W. Ham L.B. Mins. 26 May 1874; *Kelly's Dir. Lond.* (1964, cf. 1965).
[37] *V.C.H. Essex*, ii. 494–5 and v. 255; Howards & Sons, *Howards: 1797–1947*; Autobiog. Memoir of *Joseph Jewell, 1763–1846*, ed. A. W. Slater (Camden 4th ser. i), 113. Some early records of Howards & Sons have recently been deposited in the Middlesex Record Office: *History Today*, Mar. 1970, 221.
[38] Parks and Rudge, 'London's Chemical Industry: I. Sulphuric Acid in E. and W. Ham', *Chem. Age*, 6 Apr. 1946; R. E. Threlfall, *One Hundred Years of Phosphorus Making* (1951), 327–41.
[39] *Stratford Expr. Jubilee Suppl.* (1936).

[40] Inf. from Bush, Boake, Allen Ltd.
[41] *Stratford Expr. Jubilee Suppl.* (1936).
[42] Ibid.; E. W. Thomas, *House of Yardley, 1770–1953*.
[43] *Kelly's Dir. Lond.* (1966, cf. 1967); *Who Owns Whom* (1969).
[44] J. I. Watts, *First Fifty Years of Brunner Mond*, 55–6, 71, 99; *Stratford Expr. Jubilee Suppl.* (1936).
[45] Described in the following sub-section.
[46] *Kelly's Dir. Lond.* (1961, cf. 1962).
[47] W.H.L., Clayton's Surv. W. Ham (1821); *Pigot's Dir. Essex* (1839); *White's Dir. Essex* (1848, 1863); *Kelly's Dir. Essex* (1866).
[48] *White's Dir. Essex* (1848, 1863); *Kelly's Dir. Essex* (1862–82).
[49] *Kelly's Dir. Essex* (1886 f.); *Kelly's Dir. Stratford* (1905).
[50] *Kelly's Dir. Essex*, (1908 f.); *Kelly's Dir. Lond.* (1927, cf. 1928).
[51] *New Scientist*, 30 July 1964.
[52] W.H.L., Silvertown Explosion: File of Cuttings &c.

1871.[53] The factory was badly damaged by bombing in the Second World War but was rebuilt. In the 1960s this firm became part of the Berger, Jenson & Nicholson group.[54] Pinchin, Johnson & Co., paint and varnish manufacturer, was established at Channelsea Road, Stratford, about 1905, and moved to North Woolwich Road, Canning Town, about 1920.[55] It has absorbed two other West Ham firms, Ingham Clark & Co. and R. Gay & Co. The first, which came to West Ham about 1882, established a large varnish factory in Abbey Lane, which ceased to produce c. 1930.[56] R. Gay & Co., paint manufacturer, Abbey Road, was in business by 1900.[57] A. T. Morse Sons & Co., paint, varnish, and distemper manufacturer, was established at Stratford about 1890, with works first in Ward Road and later in High Street and Chapel Street. It moved to Upper Road, Plaistow, about 1920, and to Hammersmith (Lond.) in 1958.[58] C. W. Schmidt (F. A. Glaeser) Ltd., varnish and japan manufacturer, Carpenters Road (c. 1886–1912), was succeeded there by the London Varnish and Enamel Co., now a subsidiary of Berger, Jenson & Nicholson.[59] Among varnish manufacturers at Canning Town have been Charles Turner & Sons, North Woolwich Road (from c. 1878), and Andrew G. Soutter, Liverpool Road (from c. 1906).[60] Soutter is now a subsidiary of Craig-Hubbuck Ltd.[61] Several firms have specialized in the manufacture of paints designed to prevent the fouling of steam boilers or ships' bottoms, including Suter, Hartmann & Rahtjen's Composition Co., Royal Albert Docks (c. 1882–1912)[62] and Charles G. Poupard, Romford Road, Forest Gate (c. 1886–1935).[63] The first dye manufacturer in the town seems to have been Harry Hodson & Co., Sugar House Lane, Stratford (c. 1862–1939).[64]

The production of printing ink was no doubt stimulated by the considerable growth of printing itself in West Ham.[65] Most of the printing ink firms have been at Stratford, especially in Sugar House Lane. Dane & Co. (founded 1853), Blackwell & Co. (at Stratford from 1871), and Johnstone & Cumbers Ltd. (from c. 1878) are all in Sugar House Lane; Blackwell & Co. is now a subsidiary of Johnstone & Cumbers.[66] B. Winstone & Sons, also of Sugar House Lane, opened a factory in 1875, enlarged it in 1935, and left West Ham about 1956.[67] Usher-

Walker Ltd. opened a factory in Sugar House Lane about 1892, which was bombed in 1940, and rebuilt in Marshgate Lane in 1948–54.[68] The Usher-Walker group also includes Slater & Palmer Ltd., Marshgate Lane, founded about 1882.[69] Coates Bros. & Co. had a factory in Canning Road from 1883 to 1937.[70] The only important ink firm in south West Ham is the Empire Printing Ink Co., Boyce Way, Plaistow, which in 1920 took over the business of Mason & Mason (founded c. 1866), of Mason Street and Anne Street, and which is now a subsidiary of Ault & Wiborg Ltd.[71]

Tallow, soap, glues, and fertilizers form a group based on the processing of animal or vegetable oils. John Wilton was making candles in Stratford Broadway, and later in Carpenters Road, c. 1839–96.[72] James Palmer, of Warton Road (c. 1876–1939), made candles and later also soap.[73] Cockman Bros. & Co., Barbers Road, Stratford, tallow melter, has been in business since 1905 or earlier.[74] Edward Cook & Co., maker of soap, tallow, and fertilizers, settled in High Street, Stratford, in 1859.[75] In 1936 it was taken over by T. H. Harris & Sons, which had been in Marshgate Lane since 1873 and in 1929 had become a subsidiary of Unilever Ltd.[76] T. H. Harris & Sons left West Ham about 1952.[77] The Royal Primrose Soap Works, Knights Road, Silvertown, was opened in 1880 by John Knight Ltd., previously at Wapping (Lond.).[78] In 1959 this well-known firm had over 1,200 employees, making soap, tallow, glue, fertilizers, vegetable adhesives, and dripping; it also is now a subsidiary of Unilever Ltd.[79] The earliest firm specializing in fertilizers was Odams Chemical Manure Co., North Woolwich Road, Silvertown.[80] This was established in 1855 by James Odams, originally to make manure from liquid blood. Odams ensured a supply of raw material by opening a slaughterhouse, adjoining his factory, for cattle imported through the Victoria Docks. His firm was taken over in 1920 by the neighbouring Anglo-Continental Guano Works Ltd. Anglo-Continental, originally Ohlendorff & Co., had been founded in 1873, and remained a German company until the First World War, when it was reconstituted under British control.[81] It was taken over in 1937 by Fisons Ltd. and closed in 1946. Fertilizers were closely linked with sulphuric acid. From the

[53] Jenson & Nicholson, *Story of an English Firm* (1948); H. Kimber, *Wilfred Nicholson (1821–1921)*.

[54] Cf. *Financial Times*, 14 Nov. 1969.

[55] *Kelly's Dir. Stratford* (1905); *Kelly's Dir. Essex* (1906 f.); *W. Ham the Factory Centre* (c. 1910).

[56] *Stratford Expr. Jubilee Suppl.* (1936); *Kelly's Dir. Essex* (1882 f.).

[57] *Kelly's Dir. Stratford* (1900); *Kelly's Dir. Essex* (1906 f.).

[58] *Kelly's Dir. Essex* (1890 f.); inf. from A. T. Morse Sons & Co.

[59] *Kelly's Dir. Essex* (1886 f.); M. P. Addington, 'Stratford Marsh' (1969); *Who Owns Whom* (1969).

[60] *Kelly's Dir. Essex* (1878 f.). In 1960 A. G. Soutter & Co. claimed to have come to West Ham about 1868, but had no records to prove it.

[61] *Who Owns Whom* (1969).

[62] *Kelly's Dir. Essex* (1882 f.).

[63] Ibid. (1886 f.); *Kelly's Dir. Lond.* (1935, cf. 1936).

[64] *Kelly's Dir. Essex* (1862 f.); *Kelly's Dir. Lond.* (1939, cf. 1940).

[65] For this industry see: A. H. Soane, 'Printing ink and W. Ham', *British Ink-Maker*, May 1963, pp. 156–9.

[66] Inf. from Dane & Co.; *Stratford Expr. Jubilee Suppl.* (1936); *Kelly's Dir. Essex* (1862 f.); *Who Owns Whom* (1969).

[67] *Stratford Expr. Jubilee Suppl.* (1936); *Kelly's Dir. Lond.* (1956, cf. 1957).

[68] Inf. from Usher-Walker Ltd.

[69] Ibid.; *Kelly's Dir. Essex* (1882 f.).

[70] Coates Bros. & Co., *Seventy Five Years* (1952).

[71] Inf. from Empire Printing Ink Co.; *Kelly's Dir. Essex* (1866 f.); *Who Owns Whom* (1969).

[72] *Pigot's Dir. Essex* (1839); *Kelly's Dir. Essex* (1852 f.); *Kelly's Dir. Stratford* (1895/6).

[73] W. G. Crory, *E. Lond. Inds.* (1876), 186; *Kelly's Dir. Essex* (1878–1926); *Kelly's Dir. Lond.* (1939, cf. 1940).

[74] *Kelly's Dir. Stratford* (1905); *Kelly's Dir. Essex* (1906 f.).

[75] *Soap: its history and connection with the House of Cook's, London* (pamph.); *Kelly's Dir. Essex* (1862 f.).

[76] *Stratford Expr. Jubilee Suppl.* (1936).

[77] *Kelly's Dir. Lond.* (1952, cf. 1953).

[78] *Stratford Expr. Jubilee Suppl.* (1936); *Bk. of W. Ham*, 229; *Kelly's Dir. Essex* (1882 f.).

[79] Inf. from Jn. Knight Ltd.; *Who Owns Whom* (1969).

[80] W. A. Parks and E. A. Rudge, 'London's Chemical Industry: II. Fertilizers in W. Ham', *Chemical Age*, 10 Aug. 1946.

[81] W.H.L., Pamphs., 'Outline Hist. Anglo-Continental Guano Wks. Ltd.' [TS, N.D.].

1880s Anglo-Continental were making their own sulphuric acid for use in superphosphates. Gibbs, Bell & Co., of Victoria Docks, appears to have started as a vitriol manufacturer about 1862 and to have extended the business to fertilizers by 1866.[82] It was probably the predecessor of James Gibbs & Co., later Gibbs Fertilizers Ltd., which apparently ceased *c.* 1939.[83] Frederick Hempleman's manure works, Abbey Lane, later Crows Road, established by 1866, appears to have been slower to abandon the old blood-boiling processes. As F. S. Hempleman & Co. his firm survived until about 1912.[84] J. T. Hunt & Son, now Hunt's Animal Products, moved to High Street, Stratford, in 1868, to escape from the by-law restrictions at Lambeth.[85] Hunt's products have included superphosphate, bone meal, and also, from *c.* 1883, animal charcoal.[86] Harrison, Barber & Co., manure and glue manufacturer, appears to have started at Forest Gate *c.* 1886, but has been in Sugar House Lane, Stratford, since 1890; it is now part of the Smithfield Zwanenberg Group Ltd.[87] Alfred Jeffery & Co., makers of marine glues, came to Marshgate Lane, Stratford, in 1879.[88]

ENGINEERING AND METALS.[89] Firms engaged in engineering and metal-working in West Ham have ranged from huge concerns like the Thames Ironworks to railway-arch workshops containing one man and a lathe. Small workshops have been much more common than large ones. Among firms in *metal manufacture* was Morewood & Rogers, later E. Morewood & Co., tinplate worker, Bridge Road, Stratford (*c.* 1862–74), which was succeeded by Shimwell & Co. (*c.* 1878–1928).[90] George Cohen & Sons, steel manufacturer, Bidder Street, Canning Town, came to West Ham in 1881; it is now part of the George Cohen 600 Group Ltd.[91] Wilmer Lea Foundries Ltd., iron-founder, High Street, Stratford, originated as Ashton & Green, which from *c.* 1820 was making cast-iron accessories for the building trade and which was recorded at Stratford from 1874.[92] Ashton & Green became Wilmer & Sons about 1900. It was sold to a new directorate in 1939, took over the neighbouring Lea Foundry (Bow) Ltd. in 1942, was renamed Wilmer Lea Foundries in 1945, and left West Ham about 1962.[93] Boiler makers have included A. W. Robertson & Co., Victoria Dock Road, Canning Town (*c.* 1878–1917),[94] and

Towler & Son, Sugar House Lane, Stratford. Towler & Son came to West Ham about 1896, occupying premises at Plaistow until works were built at Stratford in 1909.[95] The present factory, acquired in 1926, was badly damaged by bombing in 1940–1, but was repaired.[96] G. Pidduck & Co., sheet metal worker and thermal insulation contractor, Shirley Street, Canning Town, was established in 1877.[97] The Globe Foundry Ltd., engineer and iron-founder, Chatsworth Road, and the V.W. Co., sheet metal worker, Victoria Street, have been at Stratford since *c.* 1910 and *c.* 1922 respectively.[98] William Biggs & Sons, working cutler, traded in Stratford Broadway and later in the Grove (*c.* 1839–1943).[99] Among wire workers were Henry Aiano & Son (founded *c.* 1878) and G. & F. Dupree (*c.* 1882–1926), both of High Street, Stratford.[1] Aiano's business was taken over about 1927 by Robert Crampton as the Stratford Wire Works; it was later moved to Frederick Street, where it still continues under R. and A. Crampton.[2] Directories of 1905–26 list several tin box manufacturers. Venesta Ltd., now Aluminium Foils Ltd., North Woolwich Road, Silvertown, is described below.[3]

West Ham's *engineering* firms have varied greatly in speciality as well as size. E. J. Davis & Co., general engineers, Great Eastern Road, Stratford, was founded in 1901 and remained until *c.* 1955.[4] Two constructional engineers of long standing have been the Whitford Armstrong Structural Co., Wharf Road, Stratford (*c.* 1910–67), and Cearns Concrete Co., Carpenters Road (from *c.* 1917).[5] Woodward Bros., electrical engineer, Sugar House Lane, has been in West Ham since *c.* 1902, at various addresses.[6] Troup, Curtis & Co., electrical and general engineer, Victoria Dock Road, was established in 1897.[7] This was one of the first firms to specialize in electrical equipment aboard ships. Among firms making machinery or machine tools have been the Holbrook Machine Tool Co., Martin Street (*c.* 1862–1960),[8] and S. H. Johnson & Co., chemical engineer, Carpenters Road (founded 1876), now a subsidiary of Johnson-Progress Ltd.[9] Makers of precision instruments have included W. & T. Avery, scale makers, High Street, Stratford (from *c.* 1910).[10] William Goodacre & Sons, manufacturer of mechanical grabs, Butchers Road, Canning Town, and Young & Marten, Romford Road, Stratford,

[82] *Kelly's Dir. Essex* (1862, 1866).
[83] Ibid. (1870–1926); *Kelly's Dir. Lond.* (1939, cf. 1940).
[84] *Kelly's Dir. Essex* (1866–1912).
[85] Parks and Rudge, 'Fertilizers in W. Ham', *Chemical Age*, 10 Aug. 1946.
[86] Cf. W. Ham L.B. Mins. 27 Feb. 1883: licence to produce animal charcoal.
[87] *Kelly's Dir. Essex* (1886 f.); *Bk. of W. Ham*, 231; *W. Ham Trade Index* (1948); M. P. Addington, 'Stratford Marsh' (1969); *Who Owns Whom* (1969).
[88] Inf. from A. Jeffery & Co.; *Kelly's Dir. Essex* (1882 f.).
[89] Standard Industrial Classification Groups V–IX.
[90] *Kelly's Dir. Essex* (1862–1926); *Kelly's Dir. Lond.* (1928, cf. 1930).
[91] Inf. from George Cohen & Sons.
[92] Inf. from Wilmer Lea Foundries (1959); *Kelly's Dir. Essex* (1874 f.); A. Hess, *Some British Industries* (1956), 299; *Kelly's Dir. Lond.* (1962, cf. 1963).
[93] Wilmer Lea is now a subsidiary of Chas. Karen & Sons (Holdings) Ltd.: *Who Owns Whom* (1969).
[94] *Kelly's Dir. Essex* (1878–1917).
[95] *Stratford Expr. Jubilee Suppl.* (1936); inf. from Towler & Son.
[96] W.H.L., Unpub. Coll. for 'Target Area W. Ham, 1939–45'.

[97] *Kelly's Dir. Essex* (1882 f.); *Newham Official Guide* (1969), 120.
[98] *Kelly's Dir. Essex* (1910–26).
[99] *Pigot's Dir. Essex* (1839); *Kelly's Dir. Essex* (1852–1926); *Kelly's Dir. Lond.* (1943, cf. 1944).
[1] *Kelly's Dir. Essex* (1878–1926).
[2] *Kelly's Dir. Lond.* (1927 f.); inf. from Stratford Wire Works.
[3] See p. 87.
[4] *Kelly's Dir. Essex* (1906); *W. Ham Official Guide* (1955), 89.
[5] *Kelly's Dir. Essex* (1910–26); *W. Ham Elec. Bull.* Apr. 1910; *W. Ham, London's Industrial Centre* (1935/6), 69; *Kelly's Dir. Lond.* (1967, cf. 1968).
[6] *Kelly's Dir. Stratford* (1902/3, 1905); *Kelly's Dir. Essex* (1906–26); *W. Ham Trade Index* (1948).
[7] *Newham Official Guide* (1969), 142.
[8] *Kelly's Dir. Essex* (1862–1926); *Kelly's Dir. Lond.* (1960–5). Holbrook is now a subsidiary of Alfred Herbert Ltd.: *Who Owns Whom* (1969).
[9] *Stratford Expr. Jubilee Suppl.* (1936); *Newham Official Guide* (1967), 111; *Kelly's Dir. Essex* (1878 f.); *Who Owns Whom* (1969).
[10] *Kelly's Dir. Essex* (1910–26); M. P. Addington, 'Stratford Marsh' (1969).

formerly manufacturer of fire-grates, are treated elsewhere.[11]

Shipbuilding and marine engineering have been important in West Ham's industrial growth. The history of the Thames Ironworks, Shipbuilding, and Engineering Co., Victoria Dock Road, Canning Town, has been outlined elsewhere.[12] This firm, which originated in 1846 as C. J. Mare & Co., survived until 1912.[13] Throughout its life, and especially in its early years, it was one of the largest local employers. It built many warships, including the battleship *Thunderer* (1911). Another shipyard, that of Campbell, Johnstone & Co., was opened at Silvertown in the early 1860s, but closed about ten years later.[14] The leading marine engineer in West Ham is R. & H. Green & Silley Weir Ltd., formed in 1910 by the union of two firms.[15] R. & H. Green, shipbuilder at Blackwall (Lond.), had a branch at Canning Town in 1882, and in 1906 one at the Victoria Dock.[16] Silley Weir, which first occurs under that name in 1908, had acquired the Albert Dock Engine Works (dating from *c.* 1890) and later A. W. Robertson & Co., Victoria Docks, engineer and boiler maker (from *c.* 1878).[17] After the First World War R. & H. Green & Silley Weir expanded rapidly, in West Ham and elsewhere.[18] It is now a subsidiary of the Peninsular and Oriental Steam Navigation Co.[19]

The building of *road vehicles* has never been one of the main industries. Few wheelwrights or coach-builders are known to have survived for more than ten years. An exception was Stephen Gowar & Co., coachbuilder, the Broadway, Stratford, which survived from 1839 or earlier until 1886, when it was taken over by Bonallack & Sons, an old London firm.[20] Bonallack & Sons later built a factory in Nursery Lane, Forest Gate, to make motor vehicle bodies, and opened showrooms in Romford Road. The factory was transferred to Basildon in 1953. Bonallack is now a subsidiary of James Booth Aluminium Ltd.[21] The building of steam carriages was carried on by Walter Hancock in High Street, Stratford, *c.* 1824–40.[22] He was opposed by the owners of horse-drawn coaches and turnpike authorities, and could not secure adequate financial backing.[23] Several bicycle-makers are listed in directories of the 1890s and later. The Constrictor Tyre Co., Nursery Lane, Forest Gate, which was founded about 1906, makes cycle tyres and accessories.[24]

Railway engineering started in the 1840s. The Eastern Counties Railway had a small repair depot at Stratford by 1839[25] and in 1847 the main works were transferred there from Romford.[26] By 1848 the works already employed about 1,000. During the next sixty years the works was greatly enlarged: by 1906 it covered 78 a. and employed over 6,000. Locomotives and rolling stock were manufactured as well as repaired. James Holden (d. 1925) was in charge of the works during its most notable period, as locomotive superintendent of the Great Eastern Railway, 1885–1907. During his time new wagon shops were built at Temple Mills,[27] a chemical laboratory was opened, and the company's printing works was provided with a new building in Burford Road.[28] The Stratford railway works was closed in 1963.[29] A much smaller works was built in Plaistow Road by the London, Tilbury & Southend Railway soon after 1875; it was closed about 1934.[30]

TEXTILES AND CLOTHING.[31] In 1851 there were about 300 *textile* workers in West Ham.[32] Most of them were engaged in silk- or calico-printing, older industries, already described, which were soon to disappear. The new industries which began to replace them in the 1860s were mostly concerned with coarse textiles. William Ritchie & Son, jute-spinners, built a factory in Carpenters Road, Stratford, in 1864.[33] By 1876 this was employing about 1,000, mainly women. It closed in 1904.[34] The firm later turned to making jute sacks and bags, and cotton goods for industrial purposes, first in Carpenters Road and then at Caxton Street North, Canning Town. The Canning Town factory was bombed during the Second World War but was rebuilt after the war. William Goodacre & Sons, manufacturer of coconut matting, opened a factory in Abbey Lane in 1863, from which it had moved, by 1890, to Ceylon Mills, Russell Road (later in Butchers Road), Canning Town.[35] Early in the present century Goodacre also built up an engineering business, specializing in making and repairing mechanical grabs. Soon after the Second World War matting manufacture ceased at Ceylon Mills but the grab department continues. In 1964 William Goodacre & Sons was taken over by Beautility Ltd.[36] S. Lomas & Co., tarpaulin manufacturer, High Street, Stratford, first occurs in West Ham about 1870, under Thomas Lomas.[37] It has occupied

[11] See pp. 85, 87.
[12] *V.C.H. Essex*, ii. 470, 499; v. 15–16. See also: *Thames Ironworks Gazette*, i–xiii (1895–1906); W.H.L., Illus. Coll. (Industries): views of the works and of ships built there; Dagenham Pub. Lib., *London River Exhibition Cat.* (1960), nos. 198, 201, 203, 231–3; 'The Thames Ironworks', *W. Ham Elec. Bull.* Apr. 1911; E.R.O., T/M 287 (plan of works); *Cat. East London Trades, Industries, and Arts Exhibition* (1896), 32–7.
[13] For an early view of Mare's Works see plate f. p. 79.
[14] A. P. Crouch, *Silvertown*, 80–1; Howarth and Wilson, *W. Ham*, 142; *Kelly's Dir. Essex* (1867, 1870).
[15] *Stratford Expr. Jubilee Suppl.* (1936); W.H.L., Unpub. Coll. for 'Target Area W. Ham, 1939–45'.
[16] *Kelly's Dir. Essex* (1882, 1906).
[17] Ibid. (1878–1908).
[18] Inf. from R. & H. Green and Silley Weir.
[19] *Who Owns Whom* (1969).
[20] *Pigot's Dir. Essex* (1839); *Kelly's Dir. Essex* (1852–86).
[21] *Stratford Expr. Jubilee Suppl.* (1936); *Newham Official Guide* (1969), 123; *Who Owns Whom* (1969).
[22] W. Fletcher, *Hist. Steam Locomotion on the Common Roads* (1891), 109–19; *E.R.* lvi. 80–2; *D.N.B.*: Hancock, Wal.

[23] He later made gutta percha: see p. 88.
[24] Inf. from Constrictor Tyre Co.
[25] R. Allison, 'Changing Landscape of south-west Essex, 1600–1850', 238.
[26] Paragraph based on: *Stratford Expr. Jubilee Suppl.* (1936); Howarth and Wilson, *W. Ham*, 161; *White's Dir. Essex* (1848); *G.E.R. Mag.* xv. 123.
[27] In Leyton: see p. 203.
[28] *G.E.R. Mag.* i. 110.
[29] *Stratford Expr.* 6 Dec. 1963, p. 10.
[30] H. D. Welch, *London, Tilbury & Southend Rly.* 10–11; *Kelly's Dir. Lond.* (1934, cf. 1935). Running sheds, south of Plaistow station, remained in use until *c.* 1960: inf. from British Rlys.
[31] Standard Industrial Classification Groups X and XII.
[32] W.H.L., Index to 1851 Census Rtns.
[33] W. G. Crory, *E. London Inds.* (1876), 1–7; inf. from William Ritchie & Son (Textiles) Ltd.
[34] Cf. Howarth & Wilson, *W. Ham*, 33.
[35] *Stratford Expr. Jubilee Suppl.* (1936); *Kelly's Dir. Essex* (1878 f.); *W. Ham Official Guide* (1950, 1953).
[36] Inf. from William Goodacre & Sons.
[37] *Kelly's Dir. Essex* (1870 f.); inf. from S. Lomas & Co. (Tarpaulins) Ltd.; *Newham Official Guide* (1969).

successively various premises in or near High Street. It is now a subsidiary of Thomas Thomson Sons (Barrhead) Ltd.[38] John Alderson & Sons, rope and twine manufacturer, had a factory in Marshgate Lane by 1870 and perhaps by 1861.[39] It remained until about 1934.[40] John Slater, Son, & Slater, silk-weaver, had a factory in Queens Road, Plaistow, from about 1882; it was taken over in 1887 by Bailey, Fox & Co., which remained until about 1943.[41]

The *clothing* industry was critically examined in 1904, when 1,475 persons, including 1,355 women, were employed in workshops, and about 1,100 others, all women, as home workers.[42] It was fostered by the poverty of many casual male workers who needed the earnings of their wives and daughters to supplement their own. Many of the clothing factories stood in or near residential areas, such as Forest Gate and Upton. About 70 have been recorded at different periods, but most were small and short-lived. H. Wheeler & Co., maker of industrial overalls, founded in 1884 at Maud Road, Plaistow, later moved to London Road.[43] McIntyre, Hogg, Marsh & Co., maker of 'Radiac' shirts, collars, and pyjamas, opened a factory at Selsdon Road, Upton Park, in 1904.[44] About 1961 this firm was taken over by English Sewing Cotton (now English Calico) Ltd., which in 1964 merged McIntyre, Hogg, Marsh & Co. with another of its subsidiaries, Tootal Ltd., and closed the Selsdon Road factory.[45] E. Rosenthal & Son, maker of men's clothing, Romford Road, Forest Gate, was established in 1918.[46]

BUILDING MATERIALS, ABRASIVES, AND GLASS.[47] With so much building going on in and near West Ham in the later 19th century it is not surprising that one group of local industries was concerned with bricks, stone, cement, and similar *building materials*. In these industries it is sometimes hard to judge from the sources available whether a particular firm was manufacturing in West Ham or merely had a storage depot there. John Meeson & Co., lime-burner and cement manufacturer, High Street, Stratford, appears to have been founded before 1839 by Thomas Meeson.[48] John Meeson, who became head of the firm from about 1860, was a prominent member of West Ham local board. The Meesons were also in business at Grays Thurrock, and about 1866 the firm appears to have been reconstituted as Grays Chalk Quarries Ltd., which con-

tinued until about 1929.[49] William Lee & Son, later Lee & Eastwood, lime-burner and cement manu-facturer, Stratford wharf, High Street, existed *c.* 1852–1906.[50] W. H. Lascelles, of Sugar House Lane, is listed (1878–1908) as a concrete building manu-facturer.[51] Among several firms making paving materials have been the French Asphalte Co., Sugar House Lane (*c.* 1878–1930),[52] and the Lawford Asphalte Co., High Street, Stratford, which came to West Ham in 1913.[53] Many stone-masons occur in directories. Much of their business was no doubt the supply of monuments to the local cemeteries. The firm which survived longest was probably Theodore Druitt & Co., High Street, Stratford (*c.* 1862–1926).[54] A new and unusual business was being car-ried on in 1969 by John Rogers in Barking Road, Plaistow. This was the manufacture from fibreglass of period reproduction ornament and decoration for public houses, including panelling, fire-places, brick-work, armour, and complete façades. Much of this was exported to the United States.[55]

Emery cloth and other *abrasives* were being made in High Street, Stratford, by Barsham, Lonsdale & Co., later W. J. Barsham & Co., from about 1839.[56] W. J. Barsham was probably identical with the man of that name (d. 1862) who was clerk to the local board.[57] In 1862, or shortly before, the firm passed under new management as the Stratford Emery and Glass Cloth Co., later Charles Poupard & Son. It apparently ceased or moved soon after 1870.[58] Mann & Benford, later T. E. Mann & Co., manufacturers of emery cloth and glass cloth, Kelland Road, Plaistow, is recorded from 1878.[59] In 1928 it was taken over by the Universal Milling Co., abrasives manufacturers. The factory was transferred in 1953 to Bidder Street, Canning Town.[60]

The manufacture of *glass*, a small but highly skilled industry, was in 1904 employing 123 men and boys in West Ham.[61] The first glassworks in the parish had been opened at Silvertown in 1851 but soon failed.[62] In the 1890s two glassworks were opened at Canning Town, and one at Stratford. Of these three two had a long life. The City Glass Bottle Co., St. John's Road, Canning Town, is re-corded from 1890 to 1953; its factory was demolished in 1955.[63] Robinson, King & Co. have been in Marshgate Lane at least since 1898.[64] In 1916 it took over the British Challenge Glazing Co., and the Marshgate Lane site was later enlarged to accom-modate both firms.[65] Their factories were badly

[38] *Who Owns Whom* (1969).
[39] *Kelly's Dir. Essex* (1870 f.); W. Ham L.B. Mins. 12 Feb. 1861: fire at a coconut fibre factory, Marshgate La.
[40] *Kelly's Dir. Lond.* (1934, cf. 1935).
[41] *V.C.H. Essex*, ii. 468–9; *Kelly's Dir. Essex* (1882 f.); *Kelly's Dir. Lond.* (1943, cf. 1944).
[42] Howarth and Wilson, *West Ham* (1908), 255–302, Table XVIII.
[43] *Stratford Expr. Jubilee Suppl.* (1936); *Kelly's Dir. Essex* (1886 f.).
[44] Inf. from McIntyre, Hogg, Marsh & Co.; *Outfitter*, 15 July 1944.
[45] Inf. from Tootal Ltd.
[46] Inf. from E. Rosenthal & Sons.
[47] Standard Industrial Classification, Group XIII.
[48] *Pigot's Dir. Essex* (1839); *White's Dir. Essex* (1848, 1863); W.H.L., Index to 1851 Census Rtns.
[49] *Kelly's Dir. Essex* (1866 f.); *Kelly's Dir. Lond.* (1928, cf. 1930).
[50] *Kelly's Dir. Essex* (1852 f.).

[51] Ibid. (1878 f.).
[52] Ibid.; *Kelly's Dir. Lond.* (1930, cf. 1933).
[53] Inf. from Lawford Asphalte Co.
[54] *Kelly's Dir. Essex* (1862 f.).
[55] *Sunday Times* (Business News), 31 Aug. 1969, 'Beetle Proof Beams for Plastic Pubs'.
[56] *Pigot's Dir. Essex* (1839); *White's Dir. Essex* (1848); *Kelly's Dir. Essex* (1852, 1855).
[57] W. Ham L.B. Mins. 19 Aug. 1856, 8 July 1862.
[58] *Kelly's Dir. Essex* (1862–78).
[59] Ibid. (1878 f.). The Universal Milling Co. states that its West Ham Branch was founded in 1863, and operated at Kelland Road from 1872.
[60] Inf. from Universal Milling Co.
[61] Howarth & Wilson, *W. Ham*, Table XVIII.
[62] A. P. Crouch, *Silvertown*, 63.
[63] *Kelly's Dir. Essex* (1890 f.); *Kelly's Dir. Lond.* (1953, cf. 1954); W.H.L., Illus. Coll. (Industries).
[64] *Kelly's Dir. Stratford* (1898 f.)
[65] *W. Ham Official Guide* (1950), 106.

damaged by bombing during the Second World War but were rebuilt. They are now subsidiaries of Pillar Holdings Ltd.[66]

TIMBER AND FURNITURE.[67] Among West Ham's *timber merchants* Charles Deason & Son, High Street, Stratford, has had the longest history. It claims to have been founded early in the 19th century and has certainly been in High Street since 1851.[68] Scrutton & Campbell, Barking Road, Canning Town, is said to have existed in 1865. William W. Howard, who joined the firm in that year, became its owner in 1876. He was later joined by his brothers and the firm became W. W. Howard Bros. & Co.[69] The Saw Mills Co., Cooks Road, Stratford, is said to have been founded in 1854.[70] It appears to have been brought to Stratford about 1869, by Joseph Wilmott, and it operated until 1964, when its premises were taken over by W. I. Brine & Sons (Furniture Veneers) Ltd., as lessees of the Saw Mills Co.[71] J. Gliksten & Son, one of the largest timber merchants in Britain, is sometimes listed among Stratford firms, but the main part of its premises in Carpenters Road is just outside West Ham.[72]

Several firms have made *barrels* or *packing cases*. John Burton, Stratford Broadway (*c.* 1839–70), and Thomas Bush, Plaistow Road, West Ham (*c.* 1882–1922), were coopers.[73] The Albert Cooperage Ltd., Albert Square, Stratford, was founded about 1918 by S. A. Fisher; it now makes steel drums.[74] Venesta Ltd., maker of packing cases, plywood, and metal foil, came to North Woolwich Road, Silvertown, in 1910. Its factory was wrecked in the Silvertown explosion (1917), but was rebuilt, and by 1936 was employing 1,300.[75] It later concentrated on metal foils, and in 1960 Venesta sold it to Tube Investments and the Reynolds Metal Co., under which it now operates as Aluminium Foils Ltd.[76] Lawrence & Bathe & Co., shopfitter, and export case and joinery manufacturer, Shirley Street, Canning Town, was established in 1879.[77]

Among those making *furniture* or *joinery* have been John Meggs, ladder maker, High Street, Stratford (1862–6), whose business appears to have descended in his family until about 1926.[78] Mrs. M. E. Bates, Victoria Dock Road, Canning Town, was listed as a bed and bedstead dealer (1882–6) but later (1890–1917) as a bedding manufacturer.[79] William Matthews, High Street (1863–86), and Samuel Robinson, Leytonstone Road (1878–1917), both at Stratford, made window blinds.[80] Young & Marten, Romford Road, Stratford, builders' merch-

ant and manufacturer of joinery and leaded-light windows, was founded in 1872 by William Young, who was later joined by H. H. Marten.[81] The firm once had an engineering department, notable for its manufacture of the 'Hue' fire-grate, but this no longer exists.

PAPER AND PRINTING.[82] The manufacture of *paper* was apparently being carried on at Spilemans mills, Stratford, in 1818,[83] and by Warren & Simpson also at Stratford, in 1852.[84] A few paper-stainers, and several firms making paper bags and wall-paper, occur in directories, but none survived long. In the manufacture of business stationery Lamson Paragon Ltd., Fords Park Road, Canning Town, has been outstanding.[85] This firm originated in 1886, when the Paragon Check Book Co. was formed to manufacture in England the Paragon check book invented in Canada by J. R. Carter. In 1889 the Paragon Check Book Co. amalgamated with the Lamson Store Service Co. to form Lamson Paragon. The firm, previously in London, built its Canning Town factory, which has been several times enlarged, in 1893. The company has also built factories elsewhere in England and overseas.

Printing, mainly at Plaistow, has been among West Ham's more important smaller industries. Some 30 printers occur in directories at different periods and over half survived for at least twenty years. W. H. Thodey & Son, Balaam Street (*c.* 1839–90), appear to have combined printing with other activities.[86] George Harmer (1808–92) is said to have opened a printing office in 1848.[87] This was at first in Upton Lane, but by 1862 in West Ham Lane.[88] It was continued by the founder's son until 1911. The Curwen Press, North Street, Plaistow, originated in 1862, when John Curwen started printing music with the tonic-sol-fa notation. It became a large music and general printing business specializing in high-quality work.[89] Wilson & Whitworth Ltd., High Street, Stratford, originated in 1866, when Alfred Harvey began to publish the *Stratford Express* newspaper in the Broadway.[90] It was printed at Romford. Soon after 1870 the business was bought by two employees of Harvey, F. Wilson and J. C. Whitworth, who transferred the printing to William Street, Stratford, and later, about 1875, built larger works behind the office in the Broadway. The present works in High Street was opened in 1966.[91] The Whitwell Press was founded in 1901 by the Society of the Divine Compassion.[92] It was originally housed in two shops in

[66] *Who Owns Whom* (1969).
[67] Standard Industrial Classification, Group XIV.
[68] W.H.L., Index to 1851 Census Rtns.; inf. from Chas. Deason & Son; *Kelly's Dir. Essex* (1866 f.); *Bk. of W. Ham* (App., 1924), 16.
[69] R. Watson, *The House of Howard* (1952).
[70] Inf. from Saw Mills Co.
[71] W.H.L., W. Ham L.B. Mins. 27 Apr. 1869; *Kelly's Dir. Essex* (1870); inf. from Saw Mills Co.
[72] For Gliksten see M. P. Addington, 'Stratford Marsh', chap. iii.
[73] *Pigot's Dir. Essex* (1839); *Kelly's Dir. Essex* (1852–1922).
[74] Inf. from Albert Cooperage Ltd.
[75] *W. Ham Elec. Bull.* Apr. 1910; *Stratford Expr. Jubilee Suppl.* (1936).
[76] Inf. from Aluminium Foils Ltd.
[77] Inf. from Lawrence & Bathe & Co.
[78] *Kelly's Dir. Essex* (1862–1926); *Kelly's Dir. Lond.* (1926, cf. 1927).
[79] *Kelly's Dir. Essex* (1882–1917).
[80] Ibid. (1866–1917); *White's Dir. Essex* (1863).
[81] E. M. Edwards, *Progress: Young & Marten Ltd.* (1925); *Stratford Expr. Jubilee Suppl.* (1936); *Bk. of W. Ham* (1923); inf. from Young & Marten.
[82] Standard Industrial Classification, Group XV.
[83] E.R.O., D/DB T782.
[84] *Kelly's Dir. Essex* (1852).
[85] *Paragon Way, Golden Jubilee No.* (pt. 1, 1936).
[86] *Pigot's Dir. Essex* (1839); *Kelly's Dir. Essex* (1866–90).
[87] E. F. Fennemore, *Sketches of the Harmer family*.
[88] Ibid.; *Kelly's Dir. Essex* (1852–1910).
[89] Inf. from Curwen Press Ltd.; Holbrook Jackson, *The Printing of Books*, ch. vi; Oliver Simon, *Printer and Playground*.
[90] *Stratford Expr. W. Ham Jubilee Suppl.* (1936); *Bk. of W. Ham* (1923), 213–15.
[91] *Stratford Expr.* 28 Oct. 1966.
[92] *Life and Letters of Fr. Andrew, S.D.C.* (ed. K. E. Burne), 39. For the S.D.C. see below, p. 143.

Balaam Street, but in 1910 was moved to a larger building in the garden of the society's premises in the same street.[93] It was concerned mainly with religious printing and government contracts. In 1919 the Whitwell Press was closed, but two of the staff, William Ramsey and Benjamin Buckey, bought the machinery and established the Plaistow Press in Plaistow Road.[94] The Plaistow Press also took over much of the work of the Whitwell Press. About 1928 it moved to a new building on the opposite side of Plaistow Road. When that was compulsorily purchased by the borough council in 1955 the firm built new works in New Plaistow Road. Among other long-established printers are W. S. Caines Ltd., Balaam Street (founded in 1876), now a subsidiary of Turret Press (Holdings) Ltd., Godbold & Sons, Barking Road (c. 1898), and Helliar & Sons (1900).[95]

RUBBER, LEATHERCLOTH, ETC.[96] West Ham was an early centre of *rubber* manufacture. The Gutta Percha Co., High Street, Stratford, was established in 1846 by Charles and Walter Hancock in association with Henry Bewley.[97] The Hancocks were brothers of Thomas Hancock (1786–1865), the pioneer of rubber.[98] Bewley, with financial backing from Samuel Gurney the banker, soon gained control of the company, and developed a second and larger factory in Wharf Road, City Road (Lond.). In 1850 he dismissed the Hancocks, who then founded a rival firm, the West Ham Gutta Percha Co., probably in Abbey Road, West Ham, on the site of the old parish workhouse, where it continued until about the end of 1856.[99] The original Gutta Percha Co. had left Stratford by 1862.[1] At that period gutta percha was used mainly in the manufacture of submarine cables.

S. W. Silver & Co. originated in the 18th century as colonial and army agents, clothiers, and outfitters.[2] Stephen Winckworth Silver (d. 1855), who greatly expanded the firm, is said to have opened a waterproof clothing factory at Greenwich (Kent). About 1852 he moved this to the north bank of the Thames in West Ham; by 1859 that area was known as Silvertown. He was succeeded by his sons Stephen William Silver and Col. H. A. Silver. S. William Silver (d. 1905) was closely associated with Charles Hancock, and in 1862 they took out a joint patent for making waterproofing and insulating materials. In 1864 the Silvers promoted a new public company, called the India Rubber, Gutta Percha, and Telegraph Works Co., to take over the Silvertown factory. In the same year they took over Charles Hancock's West Ham Gutta Percha Co., then at Smithfield.[3] From 1866 to 1901 the company was

effectively directed by Matthew Gray. During that period it specialized mainly in making and laying submarine cables, but from the 1880s it also made other electrical products. It supplied electrical plants to many towns, at home and abroad. From the 1890s the production of bicycle and later motor tyres became increasingly important. By 1923 the works covered 17 a. and employed more than 4,000.[4] The company also had factories at Burton-on-Trent and Persan (Seine et Oise, France), and depots in many towns in Britain and abroad. About 1927 it fell into financial difficulties, which continued until 1933, when a controlling interest was acquired by the British Goodrich Rubber Co. (later the British Tyre and Rubber Co.), an associate of the B. F. Goodrich Co. of Akron (Ohio). Between 1935 and 1938 the Silvertown buildings were reconstructed on a smaller scale, part of the site being sold to Tate & Lyle. The factory was bombed in 1940–1 but had been rebuilt by 1962. In 1955 the firm was re-named the Silvertown Rubber Co., and became a wholly owned subsidiary of the British Tyre and Rubber Co. The parent company, now called BTR Industries, was completely reorganized during the 1960s and its Silvertown site was sold for redevelopment as the Thameside Industrial Estate. The company stopped making rubber at the site, but retained on lease a small factory on the estate for making plastics and gutta percha.

The Greengate & Irwell Rubber Co., Stephenson Street, Canning Town, originated in the 1880s.[5] In 1882–6 the Irwell (later Salford and Irwell) India Rubber and Gutta Percha Works Ltd. had premises at the Royal Albert Dock. In or before 1904 it merged with the Eastern Rubber Co., Tidal Basin, first listed in directories in 1886, to form the Irwell and Eastern Rubber Co. It is not known how far these firms made rather than sold rubber before 1914, but in that year the Irwell & Eastern Rubber Co. built a factory in Stephenson Street. In 1921 Irwell & Eastern merged with I. Frankenberg & Sons of Salford (Lancs.) to form the Greengate & Irwell Rubber Co. The firm lost its Canning Town works by bombing in the Second World War and afterwards retained only a small depot there. Greengate & Irwell is now part of a large and diverse industrial group, Slater, Walker Securities Ltd.

About 1857 the Leathercloth Co. acquired the sole rights of making *leathercloth*, patented in 1849 by J. R. & C. P. Crockett of Newark (N.J.). The company built a large factory in Abbey Road on a site previously occupied by the gutta percha works and originally by the parish workhouse.[6] An exten-

[93] *The Plaistow Press* (1959).   [94] Ibid.
[95] *Kelly's Dir. Essex* (1882 f.); *Who Owns Whom* (1969); *Kelly's Dir. Stratford* (1898/9); inf. from Helliar & Sons and Mr. L. Farley.
[96] Standard Industrial Classification, Group XVI.
[97] This paragraph is based on: W. C. Hancock, 'Charles Hancock, artist and inventor', *Chemistry and Industry*, 30 Sept. 1950, p. 675; Telegraph Construction and Maintenance Co., *The Telcon Story* (1950); *White's Dir. Essex* (1848), 241; *Kelly's Dir. Essex* (1855–62).
[98] For Walter Hancock's steam carriages see p. 85.
[99] A. L. Dickens, *Rep. on W. Ham* (1855), map; W.H.L., W. Ham L.B. Mins. 30 Dec. 1856. And see below: Leathercloth.
[1] *Kelly's Dir. Essex* (1862). In 1864 it amalgamated with Glass, Elliott & Co., as the Telegraph Construction and Maintenance Co.
[2] This paragraph is based on information kindly supplied by BTR Industries Ltd., through Mr. A. G.

Brown, Secretary, The Silvertown Rubber Co. Ltd. 1933–64. See also W.H.L., Papers, Plans and Photographs of Silvertown Rubber Co.
[3] The original name of the new company was Silver's India Rubber Works and Telegraph Cable Co., but this was used only for a short time.
[4] *Bk. of W. Ham* (1923), 225–6.
[5] Paragraph based on: *Kelly's Dir. Essex* (1882 f.); *Stratford Expr. Jubilee Suppl.* (1936); inf. from Greengate & Irwell Rubber Co.; *Who Owns Whom* (1969).
[6] Paragraph based on: *Haydn's Dictionary of Dates* (1898 edn.), 647; *Stratford Expr. Jubilee Suppl.* (1936); Fry, *E. & W. Ham*, 137; inf. from Jas. Williamson & Sons Ltd.; W.H.L., C. Whitwell, 'Dictionary of W. Ham'. The Leathercloth factory was certainly in operation by 1858: W. Ham L.B. Mins. 12 Oct. 1858. It may have incorporated part of the former workhouse building; inf. from Mr. F. Sainsbury.

sion, housing a cotton-mill, was added in 1866. Shortly before 1936, when there were 500 workers, the factory also began to make rubber cloth. In 1955 the firm was taken over by James Williamson & Son of Lancaster, which closed the Abbey Road works in 1961.[7]

Among other products in this group have been *asbestos*, *baskets*, and *brushes*. Dick's Asbestos and Insulating Co., North Woolwich Road, Silvertown, came to West Ham about 1906; it was at first in Trinity Street and later in Stephenson Street, Canning Town.[8] It is now a subsidiary of Thomas W. Ward Ltd.[9] William Gadsby, maker of baskets and sieves (c. 1874–1917), was in Windmill Lane, and later in Leytonstone Road, Stratford.[10] Augustus Smith, brush and mat manufacturer, Marshgate Lane, is recorded from 1862 to 1898.[11]

CONSTRUCTION.[12] It was stated in 1907 that hundreds of small builders had taken part in the development of the borough, chiefly in its southern districts, but that few of them had attained a sound financial position.[13] Later research confirms the latter conclusion, for few builders have long survived. James (later William J.) Rivett was a builder and undertaker in Chapel Street, and later in High Street, Stratford, from 1839 to 1878, but after 1878 was only an undertaker.[14] Members of the Curtis family, of the Broadway, Plaistow, through several generations (c. 1839–1904) were concerned with land development, as builders, and later as brickmakers, architects, surveyors, and estate agents.[15] Robert Leabon Curtis, mayor of West Ham 1889, built up a large estate agency and also bought the manor of Vange Hall, near Southend-on-Sea, part of which he exploited as brickfields with a depot at Stratford. John Dyer, builder, of Forest Gate, listed in 1852, appears to have been the predecessor of Henry Dyer & Sons, Woodgrange Road, builder and undertaker until the 1890s, after which it was an undertaker only.[16] Alfred Reed (c. 1852–98), High Street, later Burford Road, and John Chaffins (c. 1866–1902), Bridge Road, were both builders at Stratford.[17] Arthur Webb Ltd., builder and shopfitter, Romford Road (founded 1885), and J. T. Luton & Son, Forest Lane, Stratford (1897), commercial and industrial builder, both survive.[18] A. E. Symes Ltd., building and civil engineering contractor, High Street, Stratford, founded 1892, has grown from a small local firm into a large company active throughout the Home Counties and the Midlands. Its original premises in Carpenters Road were bombed during the Second World War and the present ones were built in 1956.[19] J. & R. Rooff Ltd., Barking Road, Plaistow, had been a maintenance builder at Poplar (Lond.) until about 1902; the business moved to Plaistow under J. H. Rooff, who greatly expanded and diversified it.[20]

ANCIENT MILLS. In 1086 there were 8 mills on the manor of (West) Ham owned jointly by Robert Gernon and Ranulph Peverel; there had been 9 in 1066.[21] All of them must have been water-mills on the Lea or its branches, and they probably included at least some of the mills identified below. One other mill, though entered in Domesday Book under Leyton, appears to have been in West Ham. In 1086 this was held by Ralph Baynard as a tenant of Westminster Abbey.[22] It was probably the mill at Stratford which the abbey claimed to have been given by Aelfnoth of London, nephew of Swein.[23] There are references to that abbey's mill at Stratford up to 1400,[24] but by 1535 Westminster held only pasture land there.[25] The location of the mill is unknown. Presumably it was on the Lea near West Ham's boundary with Leyton.

From the Middle Ages onwards water-mills can be identified on five sites in West Ham. Three were at Stratford, north of the causeway (High Street) between Bow Bridge and Channelsea Bridge: Fotes, later St. Thomas's (or Pudding) Mill, Spilemans (or City) Mill, and Saynes (or Waterworks) Mill. Farther south were Wiggen, later Honeredes or the Abbey Mill, on Channelsea river, and the Three Mills, which before modern alterations to the waterways stood at the confluence of Three Mills Back river, Three Mills Wall river, Channelsea river, and the main channel of the Lea.[26] Down stream from the Three Mills, on the west bank of the Lea, were the Four Mills of Bromley (Mdx.). All these mills were originally tidal, and for most of their history they continued to depend on water-power, for which they were inevitably in competition. In the Middle Ages they must have been employed mainly in grinding flour for the bakers of Stratford.[27] This was a flourishing trade, and from an early date each mill comprised a pair or a group rather than a single one. In the 13th and 14th centuries there are references to fulling mills on two of the sites. In the late 16th and early 17th centuries several mills were manufacturing gunpowder, an industry then new in England.[28] There are also references to oil-mills in West Ham at that period.[29] At the same time the struggle for water-power became fiercer, causing violent disputes.[30] The mills at Stratford were the most

[7] *Kelly's Dir. Lond.* (1961, cf. 1962); W.H.L., *Sale Cat.* 9 May 1961. P.E.M., Photos. of Leathercloth works before demolition.

[8] *Kelly's Dir. Essex* (1906 f.); *W. Ham Factory Centre* (c. 1910); *W. Ham, London's Industrial Centre* (1935/6).

[9] *Who Owns Whom* (1969).

[10] *Kelly's Dir. Essex* (1874 f.).

[11] Ibid. (1862–90); *Kelly's Dir. Stratford* (1898/9).

[12] Standard Industrial Classification, Group XVII. For structural engineers see above, p. 84.

[13] Howarth and Wilson, *W. Ham*, 12.

[14] *Pigot's Dir. Essex* (1839); *White's Dir. Essex* (1848); *Kelly's Dir. Essex* (1852 f.); *Kelly's Dir. Stratford &c.* (1895/6–1903/4).

[15] Ibid.

[16] *Kelly's Dir. Essex* (1852 f.); *Kelly's Dir. Stratford* 1887/8 f.).

[17] Ibid.

[18] Inf. from A. Webb Ltd. and J. T. Luton & Son.

[19] Inf. from A. E. Symes Ltd.

[20] Inf. from J. & R. Rooff Ltd.; *Newham Official Guide* (1969), 133.

[21] *V.C.H. Essex*, i. 515.   [22] Ibid. 444.

[23] J. A. Robinson, *Gilbert Crispin, Abbot of Westminster*, 128; H. W. C. Davis, *Regesta Regum Anglo-Normannorum*, i. 49; C. Hart, *Early Charters of Essex*, No. 81.

[24] Robinson, *Gilbert Crispin*, 41, 45, 46, 52.

[25] *Valor Eccl.* (Rec. Com.), i. 416.

[26] All these mills are shown on a sketch map of 1676: W.H.L., Maps Coll., Map of Mills 'at Bow' (copy, from Christ's Hosp. Docs., Abbey Mills, W. Ham).

[27] See p. 76.   [28] See p. 77.

[29] E.R.O., T/P 48/3, f. 106; ibid. 48/1, f. 95. These mills have not been identified.

[30] E. M. Gardner, *The Three Mills* (S.P.A.B. Wind and Watermill Section, 1957), 4; E.R.O., T/P 48/1, ff. 159, 167, 174, 181.

vulnerable, since they were the farthest up stream, and in 1711 the millers of Saynes and Spilemans were in desperate straights because the Bromley millers had penned up the tidal water.[31] During the 18th century the situation was somewhat eased by the introduction, at the Three Mills and St. Thomas's Mills, of distilling, which did not need so much water-power, and by the additional use of windmills on or near all the ancient sites. By that period there was also a windmill near the Pigeons public house in Romford Road. Since the early 19th century all West Ham's ancient mills have been demolished except the Three Mills.

The earliest mill in West Ham recorded by name was Wiggen Mill (possibly meaning 'Wicga's Mill'[32]), later called Honeredes or the Abbey Mill, lying on the Channelsea river within the precincts of Stratford Abbey. This was a water-mill, which was bought by Maud (d. 1118), queen of Henry I, and given by her to Barking Abbey as part of an endowment for Bow and Channelsea bridges.[33] It was later bought from Barking by Stratford Abbey, which retained it until the Dissolution. In 1538 the Abbey Mill comprised two water-mills under one roof.[34] In 1539 the mill was granted in reversion to (Sir) Peter Meautis or Mewtas.[35] It descended in the Meautis family until 1633, when it was sold, along with other parts of the abbey site, to (Sir) John Nulls.[36]

In 1662 Lady (Mary) Nulls, widow of Sir John, and their eldest son Peter Nulls, sold the Abbey Mill to William Curtis of Mile End (Mdx.) for £7,127.[37] Curtis, by his will proved in 1670, devised the mill to his brother John in trust for certain family purposes,[38] in accordance with which it was sold in 1672 to John Phillips of London.[39] By his will dated 1674 Phillips devised half the mill to Christ's Hospital (Lond.) and half to his wife Bridget for life, with reversion to the hospital. Christ's Hospital, which was in full possession of the mill by 1682, habitually let it on long leases.[40] The lessees often sub-let. The hospital sold the freehold of the mill in 1914 to West Ham borough council.[41] In 1881 the mill had been let to William and James Hunt, whose family remained tenants until about 1936.[42] It had apparently ceased to operate by 1929.[43] Throughout its history it seems to have been concerned mainly with corn-milling, but in 1703 it was producing oil from rape and linseed; by 1735 it included a smithy.[44]

The Abbey Mill stood on a small island in the Channelsea river.[45] It was rebuilt in 1768 at a cost of £7,676.[46] An engraving of 1783 shows a large group of buildings dominated by a smock windmill.[47] In 1819 the water-mill stood on the east of the site, the windmill on the west, and an engine house behind the windmill.[48] The mill was burnt down in 1861 or 1862.[49] It was rebuilt in 1863–4,[50] as a tall brick structure.[51] During the Second World War it was again burnt down, and most of the ruins were removed in 1967, when Abbey Road was straightened and a new bridge built.[52]

Fotes Mill, later called St. Thomas's Mill or Pudding Mill, was at the junction of Marshgate Lane and Pudding Mill Lane. It seems to have been the mill at Stratford which, about 1200, Richard son of Ranulph, and Hawise his wife conveyed in fee to Thomas Loc and his wife Sabina.[53] By a later charter, probably about 1245, Sabina of Benfleet, widow of John Faucilun, granted to her son William Faucilun an annual rent of 9s. 6d. which she had been receiving from the hospital of St. Thomas of Acre (Lond.) for a fulling mill at Stratford.[54] It appears from this charter that the mill was acquired by the hospital on lease from the Locs or their successors the Fauciluns. In 1244 Isaac, son of Josce the Rabbi (le prestre), a Jew, had an interest in the rent from the mill.[55] William, son of John Faucilun, granted 6s. 8d. rent from the fulling mill called 'Fotesmelne' in West Ham to Katherine, widow of Robert Faucilun.[56] This grant was probably made soon after that made by Sabina of Benfleet. A little later, apparently in the 1250s, John son of Robert Faucilun granted to the priory of Holy Trinity, Aldgate (Lond.), the whole rent of 9s. 6d. issuing from the mill at Stratford held by St. Thomas of Acre.[57] The hospital later fell behind with this rent, but in 1285 it undertook to clear off the arrears and to pay promptly in future.[58] In 1291 the hospital had an income of £6 16s. 4d. from rent and a mill (or mills) in West Ham.[59] In 1304 it held a fulling mill and the site of another mill, both north of the chalk causeway at Stratford.[60] This lost mill seems to have been the one formerly belonging to the Fauciluns, for in 1306 the hospital made an agreement with Holy Trinity concerning 9s. 6d. rent previously payable from the mill at Stratford, now destroyed.[61] The lost mill seems to have been rebuilt by 1315, when the hospital had two corn water-mills at Strat-

[31] E.R.O., T/P 48/1, ff. 52, 67, 72.
[32] P.N. Essex, 97.
[33] Abbrev. Plac. (Rec. Com.), 316; K.B. 27/219, m. 72. For these bridges see above, p. 59.
[34] S.C. 6/962.
[35] L. & P. Hen. VIII, xiv (1), p. 162.
[36] See also p. 113.
[37] E.R.O., T/P 48/3, f. 126; W.H.L., Calendar of Christ's Hospital Docs. relating to Abbey Mills, f. 33.
[38] E.R.O., T/P 48/3, f. 168.   [39] Ibid. f. 135.
[40] W.H.L., Cal. Christ's Hosp. Docs. re Abbey Mill. These documents have recently been deposited in the Guildhall Library, London (Archives Dept.).
[41] W.H.L., W. Ham C.B.C. Rate Bk. 1914, District 7, No. 2762.
[42] W.H.L., W. Ham Level Sewers' Rate Bk. 1881; Kelly's Dir. Lond. (1936, cf. 1937).
[43] It was described in 1929 as disused: W.H.L., W. Ham C.B.C. Rate Bks. (Special Properties, section IV), 1929.
[44] W.H.L., Cal. Docs. Abbey Mill, ff. 19, 21.
[45] W.H.L., Illus. Coll. (Mills), Plans of Abbey Mill, 1682 and 1819 (copies from Christ's Hosp. Docs.).
[46] W.H.L., Cal. Docs. Abbey Mill, f. 13.

[47] E.R.O., Pictorial Coll.
[48] W.H.L., Maps Coll. (copy from Christ's Hosp. Docs.).
[49] W.H.L., W. Ham Abbey Lands Rate Bks. 1861, 1862.
[50] Ibid. 1863, 1864.
[51] W.H.L., Illus. Coll. (Mills); McDougall, Fifty Years a Borough, 48.
[52] Jnl. of Industrial Arch. vi. 147–56. The remains were surveyed by Mr. A. C. Thomas and Mr. D. Smith before the road works were carried out.
[53] Cat. Anct. D. i. A. 808. The charter is undated, but Richard and Hawise occur elsewhere, e.g. Feet of F. Essex, i. 10.
[54] Cat. Anct. D. i. A. 481. For Sabina and John Faucilun and their relatives cf. Feet of F. Essex, i. 108, 149.
[55] Plea R. Exch. of Jews (Jewish Hist. Soc. 1905), i. 65, 80. For an earlier member of Isaac's family see above p. 72.   [56] Cat. Anct. D. i. A. 480.
[57] Ibid. A. 735. John de Toting was prior of Holy Trinity between 1250 and 1261: V.C.H. London, i. 474.
[58] Feet of F. Essex, ii. 46.
[59] Tax Eccl. (Rec. Com.), 25.
[60] B.M. Lansd. MS. 1, f. 19.
[61] Cat. Anct. D. i. A. 522.

ford.[62] The second mill was probably that given to the hospital in free alms by John Richeman, at an unknown date.[63] It was stated in the 15th century that since the reign of Henry III the hospital had had two water-mills at Stratford called St. Thomas's Mills.[64]

St. Thomas of Acre was dissolved in 1538, and in 1544 the king leased St. Thomas's Mills to his servant Gerard Harman or Harmond.[65] The mills had lately been occupied by Stefan von Haschenperg, an engineer in the king's service who had fallen out of favour.[66] In 1547 Harman's lease was converted into a tenure in fee.[67] He died in 1559 leaving Susan Harman his daughter and heir,[68] who seems to have carried the property in marriage to Nicholas Sturley or Strelley. Sturley and his wife Susan were holding the mills in 1573, and conveyed them in 1589 to Thomas and Christopher Gardiner.[69] 'The Gunpowder Mill, late Mr. Sturley's', was mentioned in 1597.[70] The Gardiners retained the mills at least until 1646, when Thomas Gardiner, possibly son of the above Christopher Gardiner, sought permission to compound, as a Royalist delinquent, for estates including a water-mill in West Ham.[71] The mills appear to have passed subsequently to Christopher Mercer, whose daughter Anne married John Swale. In 1668 Anne and John sold to Sir Thomas Chambers a water-mill, once 'two mills under one roof', called St. Thomas's Mills.[72]

It was stated in 1796 that St. Thomas's Mills had previously belonged to the Grenville family, of whom the marquess of Buckingham had sold them a few years earlier to Mr. Jones.[73] How long the Grenvilles had held the freehold is not known, but for much of the 18th century the mills were in any case controlled by lessees. Peter Lefevre (d. 1751), who bought the Three Mills in 1727, had acquired the lease of St. Thomas's Mills by 1734, when he expanded his distillery.[74] After Lefevre's death, his widow conveyed the remainder of the lease to his nephew John Lefevre and Daniel Bisson, who in 1752 sub-let St. Thomas's Mills, for the remaining 20 years of the lease, to John Grace.[75] St. Thomas's Mills then comprised a water corn-mill, a malt mill-house, and a windmill. In 1764 Grace sold the lease to his sons, and they sold it in 1767 to Thomas Gardner. Gardner immediately sub-let the premises to three other persons, one of whom opened a paper-mill, apparently in St. Thomas's water-mill.[76]

In 1811 St. Thomas's Mill was the property of 'Messrs. Jones and Morley', who were probably identical with Henry Jones and Robert Morley, mentioned together in 1801.[77] Richard Morley (or Mawley) was the owner in 1834.[78] The mill was later acquired by the Eastern Counties Railway, which offered it for sale in 1838.[79] The East London Waterworks Co. were the owners by 1853.[80] In 1875 the Waterworks Co. sold the mill to Du Barry & Co., which had been the lessee since 1864.[81] Du Barry & Co., originally a flour miller, was later a manufacturer of patent food.[82] It operated at St. Thomas's Mill until about 1925.[83] In 1926 Du Barry sold the mill to William Abbott, a builder.[84] About 1934 it was demolished as part of the River Lee Flood Relief Scheme.[85]

St. Thomas's windmill, mentioned in the lease of 1752, was possibly that shown on 18th-century maps, on the east bank of Pudding Mill river, about ¼ m. north of High Street.[86] An engraving (1837) of the new Stratford viaduct of the Eastern Counties Railway shows what was probably the same mill, immediately south of the railway.[87] It was a post-mill then in good condition. It seems to have disappeared soon after. In 1813 and 1838 there was a second windmill attached to St. Thomas's Mill.[88] It was possibly on the same site as the water-mill.

Saynes Mill, on Waterworks river, and Spilemans Mill, on City Mill river, were closely connected for most of their history. From the 13th century both were part of the endowment of London Bridge, administered by the wardens of the bridge house of St. Thomas, and later by the bridge house committee of the City corporation.[89] They were sometimes known, together, as the City Mills, but from the later 18th century that name was used only for the former Spilemans Mill.

The original forms of its name suggest that Saynes Mill means 'the lord's mill',[90] and early in the 13th century it was held of Richard de Montfitchet, lord of a large manor in East and West Ham, by Walter de Covelee. Covelee granted his right in the mill to St. Thomas, probably before 1221,[91] and about the same time Montfitchet made a similar grant, subject to an annual rent of 32s.[92] The wardens

[62] E.R.O., T/P 48/2, f. 132.

[63] *Cal. Pat.* 1340–3, 12; Dugdale, *Mon. Angl.* vi (2), 647.

[64] E.R.O., T/P 48/1, f. 284.

[65] *L. & P. Hen. VIII*, xix (1), p. 638; *Cal. Pat.* 1547–8, 163.

[66] *Archaeologia*, xci (1945), 149, 152.

[67] *Cal. Pat.* 1547–8, 163.

[68] C 142/125/41.

[69] C.P. 25(2)/129/1652; ibid. 132/1694; ibid. 143/1715; E.R.O., T/P 48/1, f. 159.

[70] E.R.O., T/P 48/1, f. 165.

[71] Ibid. 48/2, f. 97; cf. *Cal. Ctee. for Compounding* (2), 1431. For the Gardiner family cf. *Visitations of Essex*, 402.

[72] E.R.O., T/P 48/2, f. 193; ibid. 48/3, f. 132.

[73] Lysons, *London*, iv. 256. For George Nugent-Temple-Grenville, Marquess of Buckingham (1753–1813) see *D.N.B.*

[74] E.R.O., T/P 48/3, f. 307. For deeds relating to this business see Hampshire Rec. Off., Mildmay Docs., Essex T191.

[75] E.R.O., T/P48/3, f. 355.

[76] Ibid. ff. 355–87.

[77] Lysons, *London, Suppl.* (1811), 361; E.R.O., Q/ABp 22. A lease of the mill was put up for sale in 1813: W.H.L., Newscuttings, 'Stratford and Bow'.

[78] Act to provide for the rebuilding of Bow Bridge, 4 & 5 Wm. IV, c. 89, (local act).

[79] W.H.L., Newscuttings, 'Stratford and Bow'.

[80] E.R.O., D/CT 160; cf. W.H.L., W. Ham Level Sewers Rate Bk. 1854–70.

[81] Newham L.B.C., Deeds of St. Thomas's Mill.

[82] *Kelly's Dir. Essex* (1878, cf. 1886).

[83] *Kelly's Dir. Lond.* (1925, cf. 1926).

[84] Newham L.B.C., Deeds of St. Thomas's Mill.

[85] Ibid.; W.H.L., Mins. Joint Ctee. under R. Lee (Flood Relief &c.) Act (1930), 21 Feb. 1934.

[86] J. Rocque, *Surv. Lond.* (1744–6); Chapman and André, *Map of Essex*, 1777, sheet xxi.

[87] E.R.O., Pictorial Coll.; and in W.H.L., Illus. Coll. (Map Chest). See frontispiece.

[88] W.H.L., Newscuttings, 'Stratford and Bow'.

[89] For the Bridge House and Chapel see *V.C.H. Lond.* i. 572–3. They were distinct from the hospital of St. Thomas of Acre, mentioned above.

[90] Especially the form 'Seignemillne': E.R.O., T/P 48/1, f. 25.

[91] E.R.O., T/P 48/1, f. 29. The widow of Walter de Covelee occurs in 1221: *Feet of F. Essex*, i. 59.

[92] E.R.O., T/P 48/1 f. 30. For Montfitchet see above, p. 9.

of the bridge later granted the mill to Henry Schileman or Skileman, who was to pay annually 26s. 8d. to them, and 32s. to the lord.[93] Schileman's son Edmund granted the mill to Richard Renger or Rengery of London, to hold of the wardens of the bridge for 60s. a year.[94] The above conveyances, none of which is dated, must all have been made before 1232.[95] Renger later granted the mill back to St. Thomas in free alms.[96] In 1248, apparently after Richard Renger's death, his son John made a further conveyance of the mill to the bridge house.[97] Saynes Mill is mentioned, as a water-mill, in 1304,[98] and again in 1354, when it and Spilemans Mill were leased to Nicholas atte Wyke of Stratford.[99]

In the 17th and 18th centuries the City corporation usually let Saynes Mill on long leases.[1] Here, as elsewhere, the lessees sometimes sub-let. In 1615 the property comprised a water-mill and 38 a. land.[2] For many years (c. 1628–76) the mill was occupied by members of the Slipper family, and was sometimes called Slippers Mill.[3] In 1652, after recent rebuilding, there were two water-mills.[4] The West Ham Waterworks Co., founded about 1745, proposed, in its original articles of agreement, to set up works on land to be rented from John Cox of West Ham.[5] Cox was then the lessee of Saynes Mill, and by 1762, if not before, the Waterworks company had bought the residue of his lease, which included about 30 a. land as well as the mill itself.[6] It was stated in 1775 that the company had rebuilt the corn-mill and had installed a pumping engine on the east side of the premises.[7] The West Ham Waterworks Co., and its successor, the East London Waterworks Co., retained the mill until 1883.[8] In the 19th century Saynes Mill was known as the Waterworks Mill. In 1873–81 it was occupied by factories.[9] It had disappeared by 1893–4.[10]

In 1720 Saynes Mill included a windmill as well as a water-mill.[11] In 1744–6 and 1777 there was a windmill east of Waterworks river, about ¼ m. north of High Street.[12] Drawings of it made in 1849 show a derelict postmill.[13]

Spilemans Mill was held about the middle of the 13th century by John Spileman and Roger son of Roger of London. John, son and heir of Roger son of Roger, granted the site of the mill to Walter Everard, draper of London.[14] Everard sold it to Lawrence Stede of Stratford, who granted it to the wardens of London Bridge at 1d. rent.[15] These conveyances all appear to have been made before 1298–9, when Richard of St. Albans and Margaret his wife quitclaimed her dower in the mill.[16] She had previously been the wife of Lawrence le Redere, who was probably identical with Lawrence Stede. Spilemans Mill was mentioned, as a fulling mill, in 1304 and 1354.[17]

In the 17th and 18th centuries the City corporation was letting Spilemans Mill, with 5 a. land, on long leases.[18] In 1600 it comprised two water-mills under one roof.[19] In 1615 one of these was called the Gunpowder Mill.[20] In 1640 a new lessee undertook to build a new corn-mill in place of one recently removed.[21] In 1738 Spilemans comprised a corn-mill, fulling mill, limekiln, mill-house, old boarded house, warehouse, and five cottages.[22] The main buildings were ruinous; the corn-mill had been out of action for eight or nine years and the fulling mill was untenanted. Captain John Rochester, whose lease was renewed in 1739, undertook to rebuild the premises, and in 1742 he claimed to have spent nearly £4,000 in doing so.[23] He appears to have rebuilt the fulling mill as a corn-mill.[24] The lease of 1739 stipulated that Rochester was not to use the mills as gunpowder-mills. Early in the 19th century Spilemans, now called City Mills, was occupied by several tenants. Part of the premises was leased in 1805 by Howard & Allen, manufacturing chemists.[25] In 1818 other parts of the mill were being used for corn-grinding, and for calendering, presumably of paper.[26] Howard & Allen, later Howards & Sons, remained at the City Mills until 1914, and appears gradually to have taken over on lease the whole of the ancient site of Spilemans, and also much of the adjoining land to the east which previously belonged to Saynes Mill.[27] After 1914 the City of London, which had retained the freehold, let the premises in separate lots to a number of small manufacturers.[28] In 1932–3 the City Mills were demolished under the River Lee Flood Relief Scheme.[29]

The Three Mills, belonging to Stratford Abbey, may well have been among the oldest in West Ham, but nothing is known of their history before 1528, when they were on lease from the sacrist of the abbey.[30] In 1539 they were granted to (Sir) Peter

[93] E.R.O., T/P 48/1 f. 25.
[94] Ibid. f. 19.
[95] Ibid. f. 22.
[96] Ibid. ff. 23, 24.
[97] Feet of F. Essex, i. 172.
[98] B.M., Lansd. MS. 1, f. 19.
[99] Cal. Letter Bks. City of Lond., Bk. G, 27.
[1] E.R.O., T/P 48/1, ff. 48–51.
[2] Ibid. f. 48.
[3] Ibid. ff. 180, 182, 208; W.H.L., Maps Coll., Map of Mills 'at Bow', 1676 (copy from Christ's Hosp. Docs. Abbey Mill).
[4] E.R.O., T/P 48/1, ff. 49–51.
[5] E.R.O., D/DU 621.
[6] E.R.O., T/P 48/1, f. 147.
[7] Ibid. f. 151.
[8] F. Bolton, London Water Supply (1888 edn.), 73 sqq.; W.H.L., J. Clayton, Surv. of W. Ham (1821), Stratford H17; W.H.L., Com. of Sewers, Map of Mill Meads and High Meads, 1843.
[9] W.H.L., W. Ham Level Sewers Rate Bks. 1873, 1874, 1881. The East London Waterworks Co. was then stated to be the owner, but may have been sub-letting.
[10] O.S. Map 6", London, VIII. NW. (revised 1893–4).
[11] E.R.O., T/P 48/3, ff. 229, 237.
[12] J. Rocque, Survey of London (1744–6); Chapman and André, Map of Essex 1777, sheet xxi; W.H.L., Sewers Map of Mill Meads and High Meads, 1843.
[13] W.H.L., Illus. Coll. (Mills), Pencil drawing and water-colours, both by J. G. Waller (1849).
[14] E.R.O., T/P 48/1, f. 32. For Roger son of Roger cf. Feet of F. Essex, i. 232, 243, 238.
[15] E.R.O., T/P 48/1, f. 34.
[16] Ibid. 28.
[17] B.M. Lansd. MS. 1, f. 19; Cal. Letter Bks. City of Lond. Bk. G, 27.
[18] E.R.O., T/P 48/1, ff. 38, 52, 94, 100–6, 132–40, 231; 48/2, ff. 115, 192, 194.
[19] E.R.O., T/P 48/2, f. 192.
[20] Ibid. 48/1, f. 174 (23 Mar. 1615, cf. 30 Nov. 1616).
[21] Ibid. 48/1, f. 100.
[22] Ibid. ff. 132–6.
[23] Ibid. f. 138.
[24] Ibid. f. 231.
[25] Howards & Sons Ltd., Howards: 1797–1947.
[26] E.R.O., D/DB T782; cf. T/P 48/1 f. 194; W.H.L., Clayton, Surv. W. Ham (1821), Stratford G 56–64.
[27] E.R.O., D/CT 160; W.H.L., W. Ham Level Sewers Rate Bks., 1873, 1874, 1881; W. Ham C.B.C. Rate Bk. 1899.
[28] Kelly's Dir. Lond. (1922–30).
[29] W.H.L., Mins. of Jt. Ctee. under R. Lee (Flood Relief &c.) Act, (1930), 27 July 1932, 26 Apr. 1933.
[30] E.R.O., T/P 48/3, f. 24.

Meautis,[31] and they subsequently descended along with the Abbey Mill until 1670. In the later 16th century the Three Mills actually comprised two water-mills.[32] In 1588 one of these was a corn-mill and the other a gunpowder-mill.[33] William Curtis, by his will proved in 1670, devised the Three Mills to his daughter Anne, later wife of Sir Peter Anstey.[34] She left no issue, and the property passed in succession to Peter and Katherine, Sir Peter's children by a later marriage. Katherine married Allen Bathurst (d. 1775), Lord (later Earl) Bathurst, and in 1727 they sold the mills to Peter Lefevre (or Lefebure), who in partnership with others built up a large distilling business there.[35] The later history of the Three Mills was fully described in print in 1957.[36] The mills were then owned and occupied by J. & W. Nicholson, gin distillers, who had bought them in 1872, but distilling had ceased in 1941. In 1966 the mill was sold to the Greater London council, which leased part of the premises to Three Mills Bonded Warehouses Ltd., a company partly owned by J. & W. Nicholson.[37] The oldest surviving buildings are the House Mill (1776) and the Clock Mill (1817), in both of which some of the old water-powered machinery still remains.[38] A windmill, south of the main buildings, was first mentioned in 1734, and survived until about 1840. Other buildings were destroyed by fires in 1908 and 1920, and by bombing during the Second World War.

The Pigeons Mill, Stratford Green, was a smock windmill south of Romford Road, near the Pigeons public house.[39] There was apparently a pair of mills there in 1744–6, but only one in 1777.[40] By 1860 the Pigeons Mill was derelict and the ownership unknown. It appears to have been demolished by the local board late in that year.[41] This mill may be identical with the Oten Mill, mentioned in 1602.[42]

Nobshill Mill was a windmill on Pudding Mill river, a few yards from the main channel of the river Lea. It existed in 1867, but had disappeared by 1894.[43]

MARKETS AND FAIRS. In 1253 the king granted Richard de Montfitchet a Tuesday market at West Ham and an annual fair there on 19–22 July.[44] These had been discontinued by 1796, probably long before.[45] About 1806–9 there was a popular attempt to establish a pleasure fair at Plaistow.[46] This was held on Whit Monday opposite the Greengate Inn, and attracted large crowds from outside the parish. In 1809 Robert Marten, one of the founders of the

North Street Congregational church, took the lead in suppressing it. He and his associates posted bills declaring the fair illegal and called in constables to stop it. There was some disorder, which led to charges of conspiracy and riot. The defendants were acquitted, but this seems to have been the end of the fair.

The present retail markets in West Ham all originated spontaneously in the 19th century.[47] From 1858, or earlier hucksters were congregating in Stratford Broadway and High Street.[48] In 1879 the local board and the police removed all the stalls from those streets, but the traders later returned there. About that time there was also a cattle market on the south side of the Broadway, and an annual pleasure fair is said to have been held in the same place.[49] By the 1880s street trading was becoming established at Canning Town, in Victoria Dock Road and North Woolwich Road, which until 1886 were privately owned.[50] The borough council, when it took over those roads, wished to get rid of the market stalls, but the police would not agree to wholesale eviction, there or elsewhere, and the council therefore began to evolve a policy of containment. In 1891 it published regulations for street trading, and these were amended in 1895 to harmonize with those of the police in relation to obstruction. This policy rested partly on bluff, as the town clerk virtually admitted in 1910, when he commented that the matter 'bristles with (legal) difficulties'. But it seems to have been generally accepted, although it was not until 1925 that the council obtained statutory powers to license street traders.[51]

The increase of traffic during the early 20th century strengthened the council's hand in imposing regulations. When the borough's tramways were being extended and electrified, the council succeeded in moving the street traders out of the roads where they were likely to cause dangerous obstructions. This was the origin of the Queen's Road market, set up by traders who had migrated from Green Street shortly before 1904. About the same time some of those from Victoria Dock Road moved to the quieter Rathbone Street.[52] By 1911 the Queen's Road and Rathbone Street markets were well-established, and they seem to have grown in importance in the following years. The Victoria Dock Road market was closed in 1920.[53] In 1963, during the council's redevelopment of the area, the Rathbone market, retaining that name, was transferred to a specially designed pedestrian

[31] L. & P. Hen. VIII, xiv (1), 162–3.
[32] E.R.O., T/P 48/3, ff. 92, 95.
[33] Ibid. 48/1, f. 159.
[34] E.R.O., T/P 48/3, f. 163.
[35] Ibid. ff. 213, 221. For Lefevre see also below, p. 267.
[36] E. M. Gardner, The Three Mills (S.P.A.B. Wind and Watermill Section, 1957). For the Three Mills in the 19th cent. see plate f. p. 78 above.
[37] Inf. from J. & W. Nicholson & Co.
[38] For these and the other buildings see: Gardner, The Three Mills; R. Wailes, Tide Mills (S.P.A.B. Wind and Watermill Section, c. 1956); D. Smith, in East London Papers, xii, 104–8; W.H.L., Illus. Coll. (Mills).
[39] W.H.L., Illus. Coll. (Public Houses): mid-19th-c. photo.
[40] J. Rocque, Surv. Lond. (1744–6); Chapman and André, Map of Essex 1777, sheet xxi.
[41] W.H.L., W. Ham L.B. Mins. 12 June, 28 Aug., 9 Oct. 1860.
[42] E.R.O., T/P 48/3, f. 108.
[43] O.S. Map 25", London, XX. (surv. 1867); ibid. 6", London, VIII. N.W. (rev. 1893–4).

[44] Cal. Chart. R. 1226–57, 433.
[45] Lysons, London, iv. 246; cf. Ogborne, Essex, 15.
[46] Proceedings . . . against John Cochran . . . and others for a conspiracy and riot (1810), summarized by J. S. Curwen, Old Plaistow, 38–42.
[47] For a useful summary see W.H.L., W. Ham C.B.C. Mins. 1910, pp. 974–9, 'Rep. by Town Clerk on Obstructions on Highways'.
[48] W.H.L., W. Ham L.B. Mins. 23 Feb., 21 Dec. 1858, 11 Jan. 1859, 11 Oct. 1864, 14 Dec. 1869, 10 July and 13 Nov. 1877.
[49] Stratford Express, W. Ham Jubilee Suppl. 4 July 1936, p. 8, cf. illus. p. 4.
[50] Ibid. 22 June, 1 Aug. 1886; B.C. Mins. 21 Dec. 1886.
[51] W. Ham Corp. Act, 1925, 15 & 16 Geo. V, c. 120 (local act).
[52] W. Ham C.B.C. Mins. 1904, pp. 1406, 1804.
[53] Ibid. 1919–20, p. 447; 1920, pp. 1014, 1051, 1161, 1229F.

precinct for 60 shops and 160 stalls, on the south side of Barking Road.[54] The redevelopment of the Queen's Road market, on a similar scale, was undertaken by the council in association with Samuel Properties Ltd. This was still in progress in 1969.[55] In providing premises for these two markets the council has put into effect a plan that was mooted as early as 1911.[56]

At Stratford street trading seems to have continued throughout the present century in the Broadway, High Street, and Angel Lane. In 1969 Angel Lane was awaiting redevelopment, which had caused the market there to decline.[57]

Stratford market, Burford Road, is a wholesale fruit and vegetable market established in 1879 by the Great Eastern Railway Co.[58] In its early years it was the subject of a legal battle between the railway company and the lessee of Spitalfields market, who claimed that his vested interest, under royal charter, had been infringed.[59] In 1955 the redevelopment of the market was announced, but the plan was later dropped, partly because of road access difficulties.[60] In 1968 British Railways was offering to sell the market to its tenants there.[61]

MARSHES AND SEA DEFENCES. The West Ham 'level', as defined in 1563, comprised an area of 1,747 a.[62] At the Dissolution more than half the land in that level had belonged to Stratford Abbey, which thus had the main responsibility for land drainage and sea defences.[63] In the 14th and 15th centuries West Ham occasionally suffered from floods, though these were probably less severe than at East Ham.[64] Flood prevention was sometimes hampered by the complexities of feudal tenure, which could make it difficult to assign responsibility to small landowners. This is shown by a case of 1336–9 concerning the maintenance of a river wall called 'Prioress wall', formerly 'Covelee's wall' which probably lay near the confluence of the Thames and the Lea.[65] In 1563 West Ham was under the jurisdiction of a court of sewers whose area extended from Mucking to Bow Bridge.[66] West Ham level was then divided into six marshes. Trinity marsh (348 a.) adjoined East Ham. West of it was New marsh (523 a.), then Middle marsh (293 a.). Hendon Hope and Laywick comprised 40 a. near the mouth of the Lea. North of it lay West marsh (381 a.) beyond which were Stratford Meads (112 a.), running up to Bow Bridge. There was also a 'new inned' marsh called Blackwall and Basing, comprising 50 a. This must have been in effect an addition to Trinity marsh, where Blackwall and Basing sluice is shown on later maps. The total length of river wall protecting West Ham in 1563 was about 5½ miles. Before the Dissolution Stratford Abbey had owned 885 a. in that level. There were no outstanding lay owners.

The 'new inned' marsh already mentioned, with other evidence,[67] shows that by the early 16th century considerable progress was being made in reclaiming the marshes. This seems to have continued at least up to the 19th century. The process was sometimes reversed, as in 1612–13, when floods caused a serious breach in West marsh.[68] But in the long run the area of marshland within West Ham level increased considerably, to 2,249 a. in the 1740s[69] and to at least 2,369 a. in 1850.[70] Only part of this increase, however, can be attributed to reclamation. Much of it undoubtedly represented former 'upland' brought under the jurisdiction of the commissioners of sewers in order to improve drainage. The largest such area was High Meads, which lay beside the Lea north of Bow Bridge, and was brought under the court of sewers by 1601.[71] In 1747 this comprised 382 a.[72]

In the middle of the 19th century the commissioners of sewers were suddenly faced by new problems arising from the building of the Victoria Dock, and industrial and housing development at Stratford, Canning Town, and Hallsville. The open drainage ditches, which had served agricultural needs well enough, were now flooded and polluted with domestic sewage, and their ancient outfalls were partly destroyed by the dock. In 1854 the commissioners obtained statutory powers to carry out a new main drainage scheme, but this was badly drafted, and was abandoned in 1856 when the West Ham local board was formed.[73] The commissioners of sewers were, however, empowered to appoint three members of the local board. In 1863 the local board tried to end that power, and also to secure the revocation of the commissioners' Act of 1854, but without success,[74] and the commissioners retained their jurisdiction in West Ham until 1890, when it was transferred to the borough council.[75]

In relation to drainage the commissioners' responsibilities in West Ham had been declining for many years before 1890. The local board steadily extended its main sewers and in the 1880s also laid a number of storm sewers to relieve surface flooding. The commissioners' open ditches were gradually filled in or piped, though a few still survived into the 1890s, flowing foul through the slums of Silvertown and Canning Town.[76]

[54] *Municipal Jnl.* 9 Aug. 1963.
[55] *Stratford Express*, 25 July 1969.
[56] *W. Ham C.B.C. Mins.* 1909, p. 1905; 1910, pp. 970–9, 1107, 1267; 1911, pp. 2087, 2098.
[57] Personal observation; cf. *Stratford Express*, 22 Nov. 1963.
[58] 'The new . . . market at Stratford', *Builder*, xxxvii (1879), 1032; *Kelly's Dir. Essex* (1882); *G.E.R. Mag.* i (1911), 239; W.H.L., Illus. Coll. (Stratford Market); W. J. Passingham, *London's Markets*, 121 sqq.
[59] *Stratford Express*, 19 Nov. 1887 (Letter by 'W.W.').
[60] Ibid. 25 Nov. 1955, 28 Sept. 1956.
[61] Ibid. 16 and 23 Aug. 1968.
[62] E.R.O., D/SH 7.
[63] Ibid. For medieval flood-control cf. *V.C.H. Essex* v. 238, 235.
[64] See p.17 . For a possible earlier breach at Stratford, see p. 57.

[65] *Cal. Pat.* 1338–40, 261–3, See also *Public Works in Medieval Law*, ed. C. T. Flower, i. 58–60.
[66] E.R.O., D/SH 7, cf. D/SH 29 (map).
[67] See p. 18.
[68] *Acts of P.C. 1613–14*, 13–14, 26.
[69] W.H.L., Maps of Marshes in W. Ham Level, 1742–7.
[70] E.R.O., D/SH 3A: this survey is not quite complete for High Meads and Mill Meads. See also: W.H.L., Maps of Marshes in W. Ham Level, 1843–55.
[71] E.R.O., D/SH 26, f. 39.
[72] W.H.L., Maps of Marshes in W. Ham Level, 1742–7.
[73] See p. 100.
[74] Loc. Govt. Suppl. Act, 1863 (No. 2), 26 & 27 Vict. c. 64.
[75] W. Ham Corporation (Improvements) Act, 1888, 51 & 52 Vict. c. 179 (local act).
[76] W.H.L. Illus. Coll. (Sewers); W. Ham L.B. Mins. *passim*; W. Ham C.B.C. Mins. 1891–94 *passim*.

In the maintenance of flood defences, however, the commissioners' responsibilities had been greatly increased by the urban development of West Ham. More than half the borough lay below the level of ordinary spring tides, and three-fifths of it below the level reached by exceptionally high ones.[77] The lowest parts of the town were also the most densely populated. Silvertown, lying in a hollow between the Thames and the docks, was especially vulnerable. If the worst combination of tide and weather occurred there was danger of a terrible disaster, as the local board's surveyor pointed out in 1875, urging that the river walls should be strengthened.[78]

By 1928 there were some 20 miles of river embankments protecting the borough.[79] The council remained the sole catchment authority within its own area until 1930, when land drainage throughout the country was reorganized on a broader basis.[80] After 1930 the borough council continued to be the catchment authority for the area between the Thames and the north side of the docks, but the rest of the borough was divided between the Lee conservancy board (which took most of it) and the river Roding catchment board.[81] In 1952 the latter board was merged in the Essex river board.[82]

The fears of disaster expressed by the surveyor in 1875 have not been fulfilled, but West Ham suffered in the floods of 1897, and in those of 1928, when about 2,700 houses were affected at Stratford, Canning Town, and Silvertown.[83] The 1953 floods affected about 1,130 houses in Canning Town and Silvertown, including the new Keir Hardie estate.[84]

FOREST.[85] The southern boundary of the Forest of Essex, as defined by the perambulation of 1225, was the main road from Bow Bridge by Stratford to Romford, so that those parts of East and West Ham parishes to the north of the road lay within the forest.[86] In 1228 Henry III withdrew his agreement to the boundaries of 1225,[87] and a mid-13th-century document shows that the forest then included the whole of both parishes.[88] Edward I, after a perambulation of 1301, restored the 1225 boundaries, and from that time onward the main Romford Road continued to be the forest boundary.[89] Both parishes were in the forest bailiwick of Becontree during the Middle Ages, and were subsequently in Leyton 'walk'.[90]

The Domesday figures suggest that there was much woodland in East Ham and relatively little in West Ham,[91] but the manors to which those figures relate probably cut across the parish boundaries, as later defined, so that an exact comparison between the parishes is impossible. What seems likely, however, is that in East Ham the woodland extended south at least as far as Plashet (a Norman-French name denoting a type of forest inclosure),[92] while in West Ham it lay mainly to the north of the Romford Road. Most of the woodland, in both parishes, disappeared during the Middle Ages. As early as 1189 Stratford Abbey had a grange (Woodgrange) north of the main road, and extensive sheep pastures on the heath between the Frith (Hamfrith) and Walthamstow,[93] which indicates forest clearance in that area. Between the 12th century and the 16th there are occasional references to woodland in the two parishes, but none of these relates to large areas. In 1302 the only woodland mentioned on the manor of Plaiz was 6 a., wholly assarted.[94] When that manor was conveyed to Stratford Abbey in 1353 it included 10 a. wood and 12 a. heath in West Hamfrith and East Ham.[95] In 1315 the manor of Burnells contained 40 a. wood.[96]

By the 16th century the only substantial area of woodland in the two parishes was Hamfrith Wood, which straddled East Ham's north-west boundary with West Ham. That survived until about 1700 when it was cleared away to make a farm.[97] At the end of the 18th century the only uninclosed land within the forest in the two parishes was a few pieces on the southern fringes of Wanstead Flats.[98] They all lay within the manor of West Ham and were affected by the disafforestation and inclosure of most of that manor between 1805, when the Crown sold the manorial rights, and about 1856. One of the first of them to be inclosed was the only piece of forest remaining in East Ham. This was the tongue of Wanstead Flats extending down to the Romford Road, which became the Manor House estate.[99] About 1856 three pieces totalling 13 a., on the West Ham side of Wanstead Flats, were inclosed, leaving only 4 a. of open forest in West Ham.[1] Under the Epping Forest Act of 1878, however, those 13 a. were again thrown open, so that a total of 17 a. in the borough were preserved as part of the forest.[2] At the time of the Act none of the uninclosed or recently inclosed forest lay in East Ham, but a boundary alteration in 1901 brought 96 a. of Wanstead Flats into that district.[3]

Because of the relatively early inclosure of so much of the forest in East and West Ham there is little evidence concerning the customary forest rights of the inhabitants of those parishes. One unusual and important privilege, granted by Richard I to Stratford Abbey in 1189, was that of pasture for 960 sheep. This continued to be claimed by the monks throughout the Middle Ages, and subsequently, down to the 17th century, by their successors as lords of the manor of Woodgrange.[4] In

---

[77] W. L. Jenkins, 'Sewerage of W. Ham', *Proc. Inst. Municipal and County Engineers*, liv (1928), 994–7.
[78] L.B. Mins. 23 Nov. 1875.
[79] W. L. Jenkins, op. cit. 994.
[80] H. Grieve, *The Great Tide*, 53–5.
[81] D. McDougall, *Fifty Years a Borough*, 17.
[82] Grieve, *Great Tide*, 64.
[83] Ibid. 45, 53.
[84] Ibid. 171–2, 441–6, 448, 585, 721, 732, 744, 746.
[85] This section also covers East Ham.
[86] W. R. Fisher, *Forest of Essex*, 21 f.
[87] Ibid. 25–6.   [88] *E.R.* xlvi. 115–16.
[89] Fisher, *Forest*, 394–5, cf. 401–3.
[90] Ibid. 137; *E.R.* xiv, map f. p. 193.
[91] *V.C.H. Essex*, i. 515.
[92] *P.N. Essex*, 95.

[93] *Cal. Chart. R.* 1257–1300, 311–13.
[94] *Cal. Inq. p.m.* iv, pp. 79–80.
[95] *Cal. Pat.* 1350–4, 476.
[96] *Cal. Inq. p.m.* v, pp. 390–1.
[97] E.R.O., D/DQs 13: it was described as a wood in 1694, but in 1720 as a farm. A licence to fell the wood had been granted in 1680: E.R.O., D/DCv 1, f. 16v.
[98] Chapman and André, *Map of Essex*, 1777, sheet xxi.
[99] See p. 69.
[1] *Final Rep. Epping For. Com.* H.C. 187, p. 113 (1877) xxvi; *Sewers v. Glasse and others* (1871), Bill of Complaint, 18; those 13 a. were still uninclosed in 1853: E.R.O., D/DCw P26.
[2] *Epping Forest Arbitration Map*, 1882.
[3] See p. 1.
[4] Fisher, *Forest*, 291.

1253 the abbot of Stratford was granted free warren in his demesne lands in West Ham, within the forest,[5] and in 1489 it was stated that he was entitled to fee deer.[6] In the 16th and 17th centuries there were occasional disputes as to whether the inhabitants of East and West Ham were entitled to pasture within their own manors only, or whether they might exercise this common right on the forest wastes of other manors, in particular those of Ruckholt (in Leyton) and Wanstead.[7] This was a complex question of crucial importance in relation to the whole forest. According to one view forest right of common was by nature manorial; according to another it was rooted in forest law, and might be exercised throughout the forest irrespective of manorial boundaries. The sale of the Crown's forestal rights in the manor of West Ham, and the subsequent judgement relating to that manor[8] seemed to settle the matter in favour of the manorial view. It followed from that judgement that since forest common right was manorial it could be taken away under custom of the manor by inclosures. These events in West Ham undoubtedly accelerated inclosures throughout the forest during the next 60 years, and it was not until 1871 that the process was halted simultaneously by the legal action of the City of London and by that of the government in setting up the Epping Forest Commission.

The reeve of each forest parish customarily branded with the parish mark all the cattle belonging to those entitled to forest pasture. The original mark for West Ham is not known.[9] East Ham is not known to have had its own mark, or to have been separately represented at the forest courts.[10] No doubt it shared West Ham's mark, as Little Ilford shared that of Wanstead. From about 1808 West Ham ceased to send representatives to the forest court, and the lord of the manor appointed his own reeve, with power to mark, with the letters 'MWH', the cattle of persons having common right there.[11] Cattle pastured on Wanstead Flats were prevented from straying upon the main road by the Forest Gate from which the district has taken its name. This gate is mentioned, as Woodgrange Gate, in 1639.[12] It stood on the corner of Forest Street and Woodgrange Road, until its removal in 1883. Beside it was a hut occupied by the gatekeeper.[13] It is sometimes described as a toll-gate, but that is probably incorrect.

In the 14th century, and again in the 17th, forest courts were sometimes held at Stratford.[14] In 1617 the king granted to the lord warden of the forest the right to build and maintain a gaol at Stratford.[15] The gaol was in use in 1621, 1665, and 1682-8.[16] How long it continued to serve its original purpose is not known. In 1709 the buildings were granted with the wardenship of the forest to Sir Richard Child, and they subsequently descended as part of the Wanstead House estate.[17] In 1815 they were being used as shops, houses, and a chapel.[18] A survey of 1825 shows that they were on the island site at Stratford Green.[19] They were still standing in 1827[20] and presumably survived until 1834, when St. John's church was built on that site.

The erection of the forest prison was probably an expression of the lord warden's determination to assert the ancient prerogatives of his office. Among these was cheminage.[21] In 1630 the jury at the court of justice seat (the highest forest court) challenged the legality of the toll, then, they alleged, being levied at Stratford by the forest officers.[22] Cheminage was among the rights claimed by the lord warden in 1634.[23] Stratford, where the Epping and Romford roads to London converged, was the obvious place to levy toll, and the new prison, at that road junction, may well have incorporated a toll-house.

LOCAL GOVERNMENT TO 1836. In the mid 13th century Richard de Montfitchet (d. 1267) was holding view of frankpledge and enforcing the assize of bread and ale on his manor in East and West Ham.[24] He also set up gallows, probably at Gallows (later Stratford) Green.[25] In 1285 the abbot of Stratford was claiming the view of frankpledge and the assize of bread and ale on his manor of West Ham.[26]

Only one medieval court roll has survived for the manor of West Ham, that for 1463-75.[27] Courts were then meeting three or four times a year, the most important being in Whit week when the view of frankpledge was held and a constable and two aleconners appointed. Apart from a fragment of 1518[28] the next rolls for the manor are for 1581[29] and 1585-7,[30] when the court was appointing a constable, a headborough, and two aleconners. In 1650-9, during the temporary lordship of Robert Smyth, it was appointing three headboroughs and three aleconners, one of each for Plaistow, Church Street, and Stratford wards.[31] It also appointed four constables: in 1650 two of these were for Stratford ward and the others for Church Street and Plaistow, but from 1651 those three wards had one each, the fourth constable being for Upton ward. The

[5] *Cal. Chart.* 1226-57, 433.
[6] Fisher, *Forest*, 200.
[7] Ibid. 287, 290.
[8] Ibid. 334, 337. The judgement was given in the case of *Boulcott* v. *Winmill* (1807).
[9] Fisher, *Forest*, 299. It may have contained the letter 'S', since the previous letters of the alphabet are known to have been allotted to other parishes.
[10] Ibid. 177-9.
[11] Ibid. 179. From the 16th century E. Ham's small forest area was part of the manor of W. Ham.
[12] *Cal. S.P. Dom.* 1639, 498.
[13] Fry, *E. and W. Ham*, 228; *E.R.* xxx. 227, cf. xxxi. 51-2; W. Ham L.B. Mins. 26 Feb. 1867, 13 Sept., 13 Dec. 1881, 8 Aug. 1882, 27 Feb. 1883.
[14] Fisher, *Forest*, 35-7, 81-94; *Cal. S.P. Dom.* 1623-5, 591.
[15] E.R.O., D/DCw T1 (cf. Z2).
[16] *Acts of P.C.* 1621-3, 48; E 32/323; E.R.O., D/DCu 1.

[17] E.R.O., D/DCw T1 and 2.
[18] E.R.O., D/DCy P2B.
[19] E.R.O., D/P 256/28/1 (survey, 1825) and T/M 92 (map, 1821).
[20] E.R.O., D/DU 503/4.
[21] Fisher, *Forest*, 139.
[22] Ibid. 140 n.
[23] Ibid. 128.
[24] *Rot. Hund.* (Rec. Com.), i. 152; cf. *V.C.H. Essex*, v. 182.
[25] E.R.O., T/M 175.
[26] *Plac. de Quo Warr.* (Rec. Com.), 235.
[27] S.C. 2/172/18. Since this account was written other court rolls have been recorded, ranging from 1399 to 1739: *Exch. Land Rev. Class List*, i (1970) (List and Index Soc. liii), 90-1.
[28] S.C. 2/172/17.
[29] B.M. Add. Ro. 56383.
[30] Ibid. 56384 and S.C. 2/172/41.
[31] B.M. Add. Ro. 58414; E.R.O., D/DK M101 and 137A.

division of West Ham into wards was also used in the parochial administration, as shown below. The fact that the court of West Ham manor was appointing the Upton constable suggests that by 1651 Robert Smyth was also exercising jurisdiction over West Ham Burnells and its associated manors.[32]

In the 18th century, after the manor of West Ham had been temporarily divided, separate courts baron were held for its Stratford section, for which rolls survive for 1736–1802.[33] It is not known whether courts were held during that period for the other part of the manor. In 1805, when the whole manor was bought from the Crown by George Johnstone and James Humphreys, the full jurisdiction of its courts, both leet and baron, was revived. This aroused opposition from the parish vestry, which in April 1806 passed a long resolution of protest. The vestry was especially alarmed by the possible extension of credit 'calculated to involve and distress the labouring poor and likely to end in an increase in the poor-rate'. This presumably means that the court baron was proposing to revive its jurisdiction over small debts. The vestry was also annoyed because the court was claiming, as copyhold, Newman's alms-houses, which the vestry held to be freehold.[34] In both these matters the vestry's opposition seems to have been successful. Court books for the manor of West Ham survive from 1808 to 1922.[35] Courts leet were held only until 1819. For Stratford ward they appointed a constable and two headboroughs, and for each of the other two wards a constable and one headborough. Various other officials were appointed for all or part of the period 1808–17: bailiff, water bailiff, marsh bailiff, two pinders, a forest reeve. Formal courts baron continued until 1841, after which the books record only copyhold conveyances.

In 1587 the homage at the manor court said that a cage and a pillory should be set up at Stratford Street.[36] By 1732 stocks, whipping-post, and pillory were being maintained by the parish vestry, presumably because the court leet had lapsed.[37] In 1808–13 the manor court rebuilt two cattle pounds, in Stratford Broadway and in Barking Road, Plaistow.

For West Ham Burnells the earliest surviving court rolls are for 1603–24[38] and for 1627–8 (drafts).[39] During that period the court leet was appointing a constable for Upton ward. From 1649 to 1925 there is a continuous series of court rolls and books for this manor, including, for some periods, the associated manors of East Ham Burnells, East West Ham, and Plaiz.[40] A court leet was held for West Ham Burnells in 1681; with this exception the series records only courts baron.

Surviving parish records[41] include vestry minutes from 1646 to 1869, churchwardens' accounts for

1643–1710[42] and 1788–1803, and overseers' accounts for 1749–62 and 1787–1819. Vestry meetings appear to have been held in the vestry room or, when more accommodation was needed,[43] in the church. About 1740 they were often adjourned to public houses. The number signing the minutes was usually between 10 and 20, but at important meetings it sometimes rose to over 100, and there is evidence that signatures do not always indicate total attendance. Elections, particularly of lecturers, attracted the largest attendances.

There is no evidence that any vicar attended vestry meetings until 1672. Before then those who signed the minutes first, presumably as chairman, were prominent laymen like (Sir) Robert Smyth (Bt.) (1649 and later), Sir Jacob Garrard (1663), and Sir William Humble (1670 and later). In 1663–71 there are occasional references to the steward of the vestry, probably its convener. Richard Hollingsworth (vicar 1671–82) and Joshua Stanley (1682–90) usually attended and sometimes signed first. John Smith (1690–1708) usually attended and always signed first. In his absence one of the churchwardens usually signed first. From that time the vicar seems always to have taken the chair when present. When he was away it might be taken by the assistant curate, a churchwarden, or another vestryman.

From the 1640s the vestry appointed annually a committee to audit the accounts of the parish officers. In 1731 that committee was merged with the workhouse trustees, a body appointed for the first time in 1729. The joint committee, which included the vicar, churchwardens, overseers, and about 20 others, was re-appointed annually until 1819. It was powerful, taking an active part in the administration of the parish and controlling the parish officers. From 1769 its orders of poor-relief were shown as a separate section in the overseers' accounts. Other committees were sometimes formed for special purposes like the re-assessment of rates. In 1819 the parish set up a select vestry.[44] A committee of by-ways, appointed in 1823 to carry out an investigation, was made permanent in 1824 and was re-appointed at least until 1829.

By the early 17th century West Ham was divided into wards. There were originally four, Stratford, Plaistow, Church Street, and Upton, but by the 1640s Upton was for most purposes merged with Church Street and there are no references to it as a separate ward after 1661. From the 1640s until 1836 Stratford, Plaistow, and Church Street each had one churchwarden and one overseer. The wardens were all appointed by the vestry: there is no evidence, during this period, that any of them was appointed by the vicar. One of the three was by the 1670s being designated the 'head' warden, and from 1700 the

[32] See below.
[33] W.H.L., W. Ham Manor Recs.
[34] W.H.L., W. Ham Vestry Mins. 2 Oct. 1806, 24 Apr. 1810.
[35] W.H.L., W. Ham Manor Recs.
[36] S.C. 2/172/41.
[37] W.H.L., W. Ham Vestry Mins., 26 Feb. 1731/2, 22 Aug. 1732.
[38] W.H.L., W. Ham Burnells Manor Recs. (TS. Abstract by E. J. Erith.)
[39] E.R.O., D/DMs M6 and 7.
[40] E.R.O., D/DPe M1–41.
[41] List in *Essex Parish Records* (2nd. edn.), 126–7. Since that list was compiled a vestry minute bk. for 1723–39 has been found. The parish records, upon which the following

account is based, are all in W.H.L. unless otherwise stated. Some statistics from the vestry minutes and overseers' accounts were kindly tabulated by Dr. H. E. Priestley. Use has also been made of three unpublished theses, the first two of which are in W.H.L.: C. J. Atkins, 'Poor Law Administration in the Parish of W. Ham, 1660–1834' (Brentwood Coll. Educ. 1964); Patricia I. Morris, 'A Study of the Poor in W. Ham, 1735–1835' (Westminster Coll. Oxford, 1965); Ellen A. Strachan, 'The Administration of the Poor Laws in West Ham, 1725–1834' (Diploma in Local History, Univ. Lond. 1965).
[42] E.R.O., D/P 256/5.
[43] e.g. in Apr. 1772.
[44] The Select Vestry Mins., 1819–35, are in W.H.L.

'accountant' warden. Each of the three wards had two surveyors of highways until about 1720, when the number was reduced to one. From 1820, when West Ham manor court leet ceased to function, until 1840, the vestry nominated constables and headboroughs, for appointment by the magistrates. A vestry clerk, receiving a small honorarium, was being employed by 1663, the office remaining in the same family until 1736.[45] From 1730 to 1745 or later there was a parish treasurer, whose office was revived in 1819–36.

The vestry appointed various paid subordinate officials. The parish sexton, first mentioned in 1657, was primarily a church officer, but during the later 17th century appears also to have supervised newcomers to the parish in relation to the settlement laws. Newcomers subsequently became one of the responsibilities of the beadles, to whom there are references from 1701. There were usually two and sometimes three beadles, who acted as general assistants to the churchwardens and overseers. The 'upper' beadle was often designated as an 'extraordinary overseer', and between 1754 and 1777 was also workhouse master. The beadles were well paid and wore splendid uniforms. Vacancies were keenly contested. In 1781, for example, there were four candidates for the post of upper beadle, whose appointment was decided by a public poll in which over 200 votes were cast. The successful candidate served until 1795 and was then granted a retirement pension. The surveyors of highways were supported in 1767–84 and 1806–11 by three assistants, one for each ward. No assistant surveyors are recorded in the minutes from 1785 to 1805. From 1812 there was a single assistant surveyor for the whole parish, but in 1826 James Clarke, who then held the post, was dismissed for embezzlement, and no successor was appointed. Among other minor officials were three engineers (from 1795), who looked after the parish fire-engines.

The select vestry, formed in 1819, appointed an assistant overseer at £150 a year with £50 for the use of a room in his house. From 1827 to 1833 it was employing a second assistant.

Information concerning rating is incomplete and sometimes obscure until the later 18th century. The churchwardens' accounts for 1643–1710 relate to the parish charities and poor-relief as well as the church. During the first half of that period income and expenditure seem to have been carefully recorded, except in 1660, when a churchwarden was robbed and murdered before his books had been made up. The accounting system, however, was crude. Receipts from any source might be used for any parochial purpose, no proper distinction being made between income from charities, poor-rates, and church-rates. In 1674–5, for example, the church-rates of Plaistow and Church Street wards were spent entirely on poor-relief. From 1679 there are usually separate overseers' accounts, one for each ward, with another account for charities and the church. But for many years after that there were cross-payments from one account to another, and as late as 1737 the vestry found it necessary to order

that in future the church-rate should be made separate from the poor-rate and that nothing should be paid for the church out of the poor-rate. The rateable value of the parish increased from £10,500 in 1742 to £30,600 in 1818, but the poor-rate rose much more rapidly.[46] The main reason for the slower increase in the rateable value was that cottages occupied by the poor were altogether exempt from rates, whether payable by owners or by occupiers. By 1818 there were over 700 such houses in the parish. In 1804 a committee of the vestry urged that their owners should be forced to pay rates, if necessary by the promotion of a local Act of Parliament, but the owners defeated this move by packing the vestry with their cottage tenants, and it was not until 1820 that cottages were rated.[47]

Except for Newman's and Harris's alms-houses[48] and possibly one or two poorhouses,[49] there was no parish accommodation for the poor until 1725, when the vestry built a workhouse in Abbey Lane on a site given by Sir Gregory Page, Bt.[50] The house was enlarged in 1760 and on several later occasions, bringing the total accommodation by 1836 to about 280. In 1786–8 part of it had to be rebuilt after a fire. Between 1812 and 1818 the annual average number of inmates rose from 101 to 189. Later figures show great variation, by year and season, the highest, 283, being recorded in the winter of 1829–30. The house appears to have been well managed. Separate sick rooms were built in 1760 and children's rooms in 1819. Serious efforts were made to set the poor to work. In 1778 they were being taught to wind silk, and in 1819 a variety of textile and other trades was being carried on. In the 1820s and 1830s sack-making was especially profitable, producing an income of £500 in a good year. After 1836 the workhouse was let to various tenants until about 1866, when it was sold, its site being incorporated into a leathercloth factory.[51]

Until 1725 poor-relief consisted mainly of pensions or doles. In 1653–4 there were some 40 pensioners and in 1678–9 about 50. In 1686, before this became a legal requirement, the vestry ordered parish paupers to wear badges. When the workhouse was built the vestry decided to stop paying pensions, but in fact these, along with other forms of outdoor relief such as rent aid, medical care, boarding out, gifts of food, fuel, clothing, and the tools of trade, continued to account for a large proportion of the poor-rate up to 1836. The apprenticeship of pauper children was under the direct supervision of the workhouse and auditors' committee. Between 1755 and 1788 some 44 apprentices were bound, mostly to weavers, silk-weavers, or peruke-makers in London and east Middlesex. The vestry seems on the whole to have treated its poor with humanity. In 1788, for example, it prosecuted a master for ill-treating a parish apprentice, and in 1817 it erected a shelter outside the workhouse for those awaiting relief. In the early 19th century, when its policy was clearly influenced by the presence in the parish of prominent Quakers like the Gurneys and Frys, it even behaved kindly towards those for whom it had no legal obligation. Thus in 1823 the select vestry

[45] Cf. Fry, E. and W. Ham, 221–2.
[46] See below.
[47] Vestry Mins. 26 Sept. 1804, cf. 18 Feb. 1819, 10 Feb. 1820, 4 Apr. 1820.
[48] See pp. 158–9.

[49] E.R.O., D/P 256/5.
[50] Cf. W. Ham Char. Rep. (1899), 85; Fry, E. and W. Ham, 136 (map).
[51] Vestry Mins. 11 Oct. 1866; Fry, E. and W. Ham, 137. See above, p. 88.

reported that several travellers taken ill in the parish had recently expressed gratitude for care received from the parish officers.

A manuscript written about 1740 by an anonymous farmer, and entitled 'Some general observations on . . . West Ham',[52] described the parish as one of the poorest within seven miles of London. It stated that out of *c.* 570 houses in West Ham more than 200 were inhabited by those too poor to pay rates. It complained bitterly of the burden of the rates upon the shopkeepers and farmers and of recent extravagance and mismanagement by the parish vestry. The writer was probably Thomas Prat, a local magistrate who between 1735 and 1745 battled against the vestry, in and out of court, to keep down the rates and to prevent their mis-application. His campaign was apparently sparked off by the vestry's decision to exempt the vicar from rates. When it was over the parish received, apparently from quarter sessions, a set of instructions 'whereof for the future they may avoid such differences and inconveniences . . .'.[53] This urged more businesslike methods of parish government, including the careful keeping of accounts and minutes, greater care in levying rates, and the limitation of expenditure at vestry meetings adjourned to public houses.

Prat's reforming campaign was timely. In the 17th century, when West Ham was still small, casual methods of administration did little harm, but by the mid-18th century it had a rapidly growing population including many poor, and greater efficiency was needed. Prat, who left the parish in 1750, seems to have achieved his main object. Between 1736 and 1765 the rate poundage remained steady at about 1s. 6d. It then began to rise, but after some higher fluctuations it was no more than 3s. 1d. in 1795. In 1815 it was 5s. and during the next three years rose to 8s. This caused the vestry to appoint an investigating committee, whose report was printed early in 1819. The committee stated that the poor rate had risen from £5,080 in 1811 to £12,110 in 1818. The increase was due partly to the approach of the London docks and the other new industries, but above all to the influx of poor Irish, who worked elsewhere in the summer, returned to West Ham for the potato harvest, and remained there, unemployed, throughout the winter. Unlike English vagrants the Irish were not then normally subject to the settlement laws, so that it was difficult to remove them, though the vestry sometimes paid their fares back to Ireland. That anomaly was dealt with by an Act of 1819,[54] and from that year all Irish who became chargeable were removed from the parish. By then, however, many of them had acquired a settlement: in the winter of 1829–30 the Irish and their descendants formed a quarter of those applying for relief in West Ham. The report of 1819 comments on various other aspects of parish government, including the desirability of rating the owners of cottages, and the conduct of the work-house. On its recommendation the vestry appointed a committee of guardians of the poor, anticipating

the provisions of the Second Sturges Bourne Bill, then before Parliament. That committee was transformed into a select vestry later in the same year, when the Bill became law. After 1819 distress declined and from 1821 to 1836 the poor-rate poundage was kept down to about 4s. In 1836 the parish became part of the West Ham poor law union.

By the end of the 18th century, when the population had risen to over 5,000, the vestry had to deal with problems of policing as well as poverty. In 1786 it became concerned over 'night invaders', and ordered its officers to visit eating houses and lodging houses and arrest all suspicious persons. The parish then had three watch-houses, one in each ward. These may all have originated in 1662, when the vestry was planning them. The Stratford watch-house was certainly built about 1662. It was rebuilt in 1750–3, when the turnpike road was widened, and again in 1781. The Church Street watch-house was repaired in 1743 and rebuilt in 1778. A new watch-house, presumably for that ward, was built beside the workhouse in 1799, when the vestry resolved to employ an armed watchman to serve there from Michaelmas to Lady Day. The Plaistow watch-house was rebuilt in 1775 on a new site. In the early 19th century official action was reinforced by a West Ham society for the prosecution of felons.[55] In 1840 West Ham became part of the Metropolitan police district.

LOCAL GOVERNMENT 1836–86.[56] West Ham in 1836 was little more than a group of large villages. During the next fifty years it became an industrial town with a population of over 150,000, but the evolution of its local government lagged behind its physical growth. At the start of that period the only local authority within the parish was still the open vestry with its associated select vestry. In 1836 the open vestry set up a highway board of 10 members, enlarged to 12 in 1839, and to 20 in 1840, when, in addition to its responsibility for the roads, the board was given control of the parish fire-engines. The members were elected annually in the vestry meeting. Apart from the matters thus delegated to the highway board, the vestry now had no important civil powers, since poor-relief had become the responsibility of the guardians.

The vestry was reluctant to accept its diminished status. It continued to elect the select vestry until 1846, although that body seems to have done little after 1836. Also in face of opposition from the guardians it continued to appoint a salaried vestry clerk until 1845. It then abolished the post, resolving to appoint instead an additional assistant overseer, whose duties were to include those of vestry clerk. This was not merely a change of title. The vestry was displeased with the former clerk, George Dacre, who was said to have caused 'litigation and ill-feeling' in the parish, and it resolved that the new assistant overseer should not, like Dacre, be a lawyer. The new officer was appointed for the first

[52] Fry, *E. and W. Ham*, 219–27.
[53] Loose leaf at end of Vestry Min. Bk. for 1740–9.
[54] Poor Law Act, 1819, 59 Geo. III, c. 12.
[55] W.H.L., W. Ham. Soc. for Prosec. of Felons, Min. Bk. 1817–40.
[56] Unless otherwise stated this section is based on the following sources: W.H.L., W. Ham Vestry Mins. 1836–69; W. Ham Highway Bd. Mins. 1850–57 and Accounts, 1854–6; W. Ham L.B. Mins. 1856–86; A. L. Dickens, *Rep. to Gen. Bd. of Health on the Sanitary Condition of W. Ham*, 1855; W. Ham L.B., *Short Hist. Sketch of the development of W. Ham under the Local Board*, 1886.

time in 1847, when Robert Anderson of Rokeby House, Stratford Broadway, won a contested election. He began to provide parochial offices at Rokeby House, and the vestry later leased part of the house for that purpose.

When Dacre was ousted he began to stir up trouble for the vestry. In 1846 he noticed a technical illegality in the publication of the rates and successfully appealed against them. In 1853, when the vestry resolved to provide street lighting for the parish, he was among those who opposed the scheme and caused it to be restricted to Plaistow ward. He then played a prominent part in an attempt to deal with drainage problems.

By this time the inadequacy of West Ham's local government was obvious. Uncontrolled development was creating slums at Canning Town and Stratford. The population was approaching 20,000, but the only public drainage was the agricultural system of open ditches maintained by the Havering and Dagenham commissioners of sewers in the low-lying parts of the parish. These ditches were being increasingly fouled by domestic and industrial refuse, which also polluted the river Lea. The water supply was poor. Many of the streets were unpaved, unlighted, and unswept. In the seven years 1848–54 epidemic diseases, including cholera, accounted for more than a third of all deaths in the parish. Fire-fighting arrangements had become farcical.[57] The future development of the town was likely to be rapid. In recent years a number of offensive trades had moved into the parish to escape control under the Metropolitan Building Act, 1844,[58] and the great Victoria Dock was nearing completion.

In November 1853 Dacre convened a small meeting of ratepayers to discuss a main drainage scheme for the parish proposed by the commissioners of sewers. The scheme was referred to the vestry, which in the following month resolved to support it, though some of the members urged further consideration. A Bill empowering the commissioners to carry out the scheme was enacted in July 1854.[59] Though the commissioners have the credit of being the first body to take action in a serious situation, their scheme was inadequate. The new sewers would serve only a small part of the then inhabited area of the parish. The commissioners had no powers to extend them beyond the areas described in the Act, nor to compel persons to drain their premises into the main sewers. One of the main sewers was to be an open ditch or 'cut' running alongside the Victoria Dock to the Thames at Gallions Reach. This had originally been planned to replace the old land drains destroyed in making the dock. The dock company, which had undertaken to provide the cut, did not consider itself bound to complete it as far as Gallions Reach until it had cut off the existing surface outfalls in that direction, and opposed the use of the cut for house drainage.

The commissioners' Act ignored the other problems of public health, especially the control of new building. Even before the Act passed the vestry had realized the weaknesses of the scheme and had also become alarmed at its probable cost. In May 1854 Samuel Riles, a prominent vestryman and poor-law guardian, carried a motion condemning the Bill. It was then too late to stop it, but he continued to attack the scheme, and organized a petition of ratepayers to the General Board of Health, calling for a public enquiry into sanitary conditions. The enquiry was held in 1855 by Alfred Dickens, superintending inspector of the General Board, and brother of the novelist.[60] His report provided ample evidence of the dangers to public health. He recommended that the commissioners of sewers should abandon their main drainage scheme, and that a local board of health should be formed for the parish.

The West Ham local board was duly constituted in 1856, with 12 elected members (four for each of the three ancient wards) and 3 appointed by the commissioners of sewers.[61] In 1863 the number of elected members was increased to 18, the 3 appointed members continuing as before.[62] The board's meetings were held at Rokeby House until 1869, when a new town hall was opened in Stratford Broadway. This was designed by Lewis Angell, the board's surveyor, and John Giles, in an ornate renaissance style, dominated by a square tower with domed roof and tall cupola. It was enlarged in 1885.

The board's first chairman was Samuel Riles (1856–63), followed by John Meeson (1863–75), cement manufacturer, and George Rivett (1875–86), builder and undertaker. Meeson, who served on the board throughout its existence, was always prominent. The original members included five who had been on the parish highway board in its later years. Among the members appointed in 1856 by the commissioners of sewers were the vicar of West Ham (A. J. Ram), and Capt. R. W. Pelly, R.N., a fellow of Trinity House whose family owned much of the parish. Both served until 1869, and had considerable influence. But with these and two or three other exceptions the members of the board seem to have been tradesmen of narrow experience and outlook. A few were corrupt, as in 1872, when one was imprisoned and another resigned after the discovery of election malpractices. Others used their position as a stepping stone to an office of profit under the board, as in 1875, when two members resigned to contest the vacant post of rate-collector, one of them being successful. No regular groups or parties can be identified among the members. This was not a source of strength, for the board's meetings were sometimes quarrelsome, and its policies often capricious, irresolute, or short-sighted.

The board appointed a full-time surveyor, and a part-time clerk (a solicitor), medical officer, and honorary treasurer (a banker). The first surveyor was dismissed in 1859 for accepting bribes from private builders. The second, J. G. B. Marshall (1859–67), was dismissed after a disagreement about his terms of employment, in which the board was at fault, since it kept altering them arbitrarily. Marshall went into private practice and later became himself a member of the board. The board's third and last surveyor was Lewis Angell whose eventual

57 See p. 109.
58 7 & 8 Vict. c. 84.
59 Havering and Dagenham Com. of Sewers Act, 17 & 18 Vict. c. 89 (local and personal act); cf. E.R.O., D/SH 5.
60 A description of Canning Town, written by Henry Morley, appeared in Charles Dickens's magazine *Household Words*, 12 Sept. 1857: cf. Curwen, *Old Plaistow*, 73.
61 Public Health Suppl. Act, 1856, 19 & 20 Vict. c. 26.
62 Vestry Mins. 23 Feb. 1863; Loc. Govt. Suppl. Act, 1863 (No. 2), 26 & 27 Vict. c. 64.

dismissal, after a dispute with the borough council, is described below.[63] The board's first clerk died in 1862; it was found that he had been embezzling public funds. The third clerk, F. E. Hilleary, appointed in 1874, came from an old-established family firm of solicitors at Stratford. He served the board and the borough council with distinction until 1913. With an impressive mien, and holding many other part-time posts in the district, he was nicknamed 'the West Ham Pooh-Bah'.[64] The board was served in succession by two medical officers. In 1859 the West Ham Parochial Association suggested that this post should be abolished as unnecessary. The board took no action then, but a similar proposal in 1863 resulted in the reduction of the medical officer's salary.

The board's treasurer was no more than its bank manager, acting *ex officio*. There was no separate financial department. Responsibility for accounting was ill-defined but was mainly in the hands of the clerk. During the lifetime of the board several frauds were committed by its officers. That of 1862, by the clerk himself, has already been mentioned. In 1875 the assistant clerk and one of the rate-collectors were found to have conspired to commit much more serious fraud. Both fled abroad to escape prosecution. Another rate-collector, dismissed for embezzlement in 1884, was later imprisoned. At his trial the jury, recommending mercy, suggested that the laxity of the board's accounting methods had tempted him, and in general it is likely that the failings of the board's officers were due as much to the defects in the administrative system as to their personal weaknesses.

The administration was always under strain. The staff was very small by modern standards and was not expanded in proportion to the town's growth. Between 1856 and 1886 the rateable value increased from £80,000 to £652,000, but it was not until 1885 that the number of rate-collectors was raised from three to four. In 1878 the surveyor, asking the board to augment his staff, stated that it was no larger than it had been ten years earlier, and that his salary had also remained the same; during that decade the population of West Ham had doubled, to about 100,000.

The failure to employ staff in sufficient numbers, and to pay them adequately, which was not unique to West Ham, sprang from the board's chronic financial weakness, which hampered all its activities. During its early years the board had great difficulty in raising loans for public works, and it was also involved in a long and costly lawsuit concerning the rate assessment of the Victoria Dock Co., one of the largest ratepayers. Owing to the poverty of the town the poor-rates, and later also the school-rates, were very high, and the board, in making its own precept, always had to beware of pressing the ratepayers too hard.

On taking office the local board was vested with the powers specified in the Public Health Act, 1848, under which it had been formed. It immediately superseded the parish highway board, but had to wait until the passing of the Local Government Act,

1858, before it could supersede the Plaistow lighting inspectors or assume responsibility for the parish fire-engines. Even after 1858 its freedom of action was limited by the powers of many other public bodies. The parish was under the jurisdiction of Essex quarter sessions, the Metropolitan police, and West Ham poor law union. Elementary education, from 1871, was provided by West Ham school board. The Middlesex and Essex highway trust controlled the main road through Stratford, and the Commercial Road trust that through Canning Town. The Havering and Dagenham commissioners of sewers remained responsible for surface drainage, and although they did not try to carry out the drainage scheme as provided in their Act of 1854, that Act remained in force in spite of an attempt in 1863 to revoke it.[65] The Thames conservancy board and the river Lee trust (later Lee conservancy board) controlled the watercourses on the southern and western boundaries of the parish. The Metropolitan board of works, formed in 1855, built its great northern outfall sewer through West Ham, with a pumping station at Abbey Mills. The City of London, as the Port of London sanitary authority, created in 1872, was responsible for health and sanitation in the docks. Gas, water, and transport were provided by commercial companies, including the West Ham Gas Co., the East London Waterworks Co., and the Great Eastern Railway Co., all of which had works in the parish. The local board had to reckon with several other large firms, notably the Victoria Dock Co. and the Thames Ironworks Co., which were important as ratepayers and employers of labour, and many smaller ones, especially those concerned with building development or with offensive trades. Most of these bodies or groups came into conflict with the board at some time.

The local board's most urgent problems in 1856 were sewage disposal, street improvement and maintenance, and control of the town's development. The board's initial plans for the first were based on assurances from the Metropolitan board of works that West Ham would soon be able to make use of the northern outfall sewer then being planned as part of the metropolitan main drainage scheme. The local board failed to insist that these assurances be given statutory force in the Metropolitan Board of Works Act, 1858,[66] and the M.B.W. subsequently refused to permit access to the northern outfall sewer. Thus West Ham's temporary sewage system, completed in 1861 for a population of about 30,000, had to be expanded during the next forty years to serve nine times that number. The outfall works at Bow creek polluted both the Lea and the Thames, and under Acts of 1868 and 1870 the respective conservancy boards secured powers to force West Ham to purify its effluent.[67] Thus threatened, the local board unsuccessfully sought an alternative site for the works, first at Manor Park, and later at Barking. The second of these attempts failed, in 1872, when the Local Government Board, no doubt influenced by the protests from Barking, refused loan sanction. The L.G.B. considered that West Ham's sewage could be adequately treated at the

[63] See p. 105.
[64] W.H.L., C. Whitwell, 'Dictionary of West Ham', s.v. Hilleary, F. E. For his portrait see D. McDougall, *Fifty Years a Borough*, 31.
[65] Loc. Govt. Suppl. Act, 1863 (No. 2).

[66] 21 & 22 Vict. c. 104.
[67] Lee Conservancy Act, 1868, 31 & 32 Vict. c. 154 (local act); Thames Navigation Act, 1870, 33 & 34 Vict. c. 149 (local act).

existing works, but its opinion did not bind the river boards, which insisted on a high standard of purification. The refusal of loan sanction wrung from the local board a bewildered protest: West Ham had been placed 'in a position of great difficulty from which it does not see how to extricate itself'.[68]

After 1872 the local board tried to improve the works at Bow creek, and experimented with various methods of treatment, but the river boards remained dissatisfied. Nor was disposal the only sewage problem. Dangers to health lay in the foul open ditches, many of which were still controlled by the sewer commissioners. In its early years the board often complained to the commissioners or private owners about these ditches, usually producing only counter-protests against the inadequacy of the board's own scheme. By its local Act of 1867[69] the board obtained certain powers to cause offensive drains to be cleansed or covered, but these did not enable it to supersede the sewer commissioners, and although the board subsequently filled in many of the open ditches some still remained in 1886.

Other sewage difficulties arose from the fact that West Ham's rapid growth was totally unplanned. The board lacked powers to prevent building in places where no public sewers were available, and was therefore obliged to permit temporary cesspools in many cases. Silvertown was a special problem. That area, which began to develop during the 1850s, was cut off from the rest of West Ham by the docks. It was not included in the board's original drainage scheme, and in 1868 the local factory owners and estate developers sponsored a private Bill embodying a scheme for Silvertown and North Woolwich. This was eventually dropped after the local board had agreed to extend a main sewer to Silvertown. Further development, especially the building of the Royal Albert Dock, soon rendered that sewer inadequate, and in the 1880s, again under pressure from public opinion, the board put in hand a scheme for the whole of that area, with a separate outfall works at Ham creek. Those works, like the larger ones at Bow creek, would have been unnecessary if the board had obtained access to the Metropolitan sewer, and on one occasion it may have missed a chance of doing so, at least in part. In 1871 the Metropolitan board of works invited West Ham to discuss a joint scheme for North Woolwich, but the local board refused, saying that its own drainage system was complete.[70]

In addition to the problems caused by West Ham's own sewage were some caused by that of other parishes. For many years sewage from Leyton polluted a ditch discharging into the Channelsea river, in West Ham. That issue, involving several lawsuits, does not seem to have been settled until 1881. West Ham also suffered annoyance from the sewage of Wanstead, but this came mainly from the small detached part of Wanstead near Temple Mills, and the matter was resolved by a boundary change.[71]

Apart from drainage the local board's most urgent task in 1856 was street improvement and maintenance. The Dickens report had commented that the number of streets not under the management of the highway authorities was 'almost peculiar to this parish'.[72] Many of these streets, especially at Hallsville and Canning Town, were muddy tracks, deeply rutted and strewn with rubbish. The initial paving of private streets was the responsibility of their owners. This was difficult to enforce, and the board's powers in the matter were uncertain until the Local Government Act, 1858, enabled it to improve private streets, to levy special rates from their owners, and to raise loans on the security of those rates. For years the board had to devote much time and effort to private improvement works, in addition to the routine maintenance of public roads. When the highway trusts were wound up the board also became responsible for the main road through Stratford (in 1866) and that through Canning Town (in 1871). In taking over the Stratford road from the Middlesex and Essex trust the board found itself involved in complicated negotiations with the owners of the bridges over the Lea and its branches.[73] Even more important was the board's purchase, from the North Woolwich Land Co., of Victoria Dock Road and North Woolwich Road, leading to Silvertown and the docks. These had been laid out by the company before the board's time, but had been badly maintained and were subject to heavy tolls which caused great annoyance as Silvertown grew. In 1882 local industrialists forced a public enquiry, as a result of which the board secured powers of compulsory purchase under its Act of 1884[74] and took over the roads in 1886. During the 1880s the board also obtained statutory powers to buy land for widening main streets.[75]

One of the main reasons for the formation of the board had been the need to control the town's development. In 1855 West Ham already had considerable slums, including some recently built. In the Randall Street area of Canning Town 'the houses . . . though comparatively new, are all to pieces . . . the footings of the foundations for some of the house walls are actually on the surface'. In North Woolwich Road cellars were being built in the excavation of old ditches; yards were constantly under water in the winter and some even in summer; many single houses had been divided into two without additional sanitation.[76] Smallpox had lingered in that area for more than seven months and there had also been cholera. These conditions had been made possible by the absence of building controls in the parish before 1856. The local board prevented a repetition of the worst evils of the previous generation, but it cannot be said to have done, or tried to do, much more. Builders were often able to evade or defy the by-laws, or to persuade the board to take a narrow view of its duty. In July 1864, for example, the board's surveyor refused to certify a public house already built in Barking Road, because

[68] L.B. Mins. 4 July 1872, cf. 9 and 13 July 1872.
[69] L.B. for W. Ham, Extension of Powers Act, 1867, 30 & 31 Vict. c. 56 (local act).
[70] L.B. Mins. 28 Nov. 1871.
[71] L.G.B. Prov. Order Conf. (Aberdare &c.) Act, 1875, 38 & 39 Vict. c. 175 (local act).
[72] A. L. Dickens, *Rep. W. Ham*, 59.
[73] L.B. for W. Ham Extension of Powers Act, 1867;

W. Ham L.B. Act, 1876, 39 & 40 Vict. c. 220 (local act).
[74] W. Ham L.B. Extension of Powers Act, 1884, 47 & 48 Vict. c. 61 (local act).
[75] L.G.B. Prov. Order Conf. (Eastbourne &c.) Act, 1880, 43 & 44 Vict. c. 132 (local act); W. Ham L.B. Extension of Powers Act, 1881, 44 & 45 Vict. c. 81 (local act).
[76] *Rep. W. Ham*, 49.

he was dissatisfied with the drainage. The board, however, agreed to issue the certificate because the house was occupied by its owners 'and therefore in case the drainage be inadequate he will personally be the sufferer'. In 1865, reversing its own previous decision, it permitted the construction of cellars in North Woolwich Road, in spite of flood dangers. In considering applications to build in the southern marshes of the parish the board was certainly in a difficult position. The area was unsuitable for small houses at high densities, but its proximity to the docks and factories created a strong demand for them there. It was unfortunate also that the area was one of those most affected by West Ham's first period of rapid growth, about 1877–83, when the surveyor's department was overwhelmed with work. In 1870 only 218 plans for new buildings had been deposited with the board. The annual total rose to over 1,600 in 1878–9, over 2,000 in 1880–1, and 2,400 in 1881–2, when the board at last began to get the measure of the problem. In 1882 it obtained statutory powers to make new building by-laws and to appoint more building inspectors, whose salaries were to be met by charging inspection fees to builders.[77] Even later, however, there is evidence that its system of inspection was inadequate.

In controlling industrial development the board was a little more effective. From its earliest days the board often took action to check offensive trades, sometimes compelling them to close down completely, and restricting them, on the whole, to the western and southern fringes of the district. It was helped by public opinion, which readily protested against the dirt and stench from such factories, and probably also by the fact that many of the factories were small and easy to coerce. Nuisances introduced by public bodies were harder to deal with. The problem of Leyton's sewage has already been mentioned. A more serious threat to public health was the establishment of two smallpox hospitals on adjoining sites at Plaistow, by the Poplar board of works, and West Ham union.[78]

In view of the local board's uncertain handling of urgent tasks it is not surprising that it was often ineffective in dealing with those less pressing. It never attempted any systematic slum clearance, though it occasionally took emergency action when buildings were in danger of collapse, as in 1871, at Wood's Yard, High Street, Stratford. Wood's Yard, a court containing ten wooden houses, had been one of the worst areas described in the Dickens report of 1855.[79] The board provided no public baths, libraries, or parks. It did, indeed, make one attempt, in 1868–9, to buy Upton Park, but there was opposition from the West Ham ratepayers' association, and the scheme was rejected by a public poll. The board took no further action, and it was left to voluntary effort, helped by the Corporation of London, to secure the park for public use. The board's fire brigade was for many years sadly

inefficient. Refuse collection, performed by contract, was never satisfactory. Gas street lighting, also by contract, was apparently adequate, except in private streets, where the board was hampered by lack of legal powers.

The board was not responsible for policing or for water supply, but it exerted some influence on both. The squalor in which many of West Ham's inhabitants lived occasionally led to disorder, and to complaints, in which the board joined, against the inadequacy of the police. The outbreaks which attracted most attention were those occurring in main roads. In 1864 there were allegations of obstruction by crowds of roughs in Barking Road. There were frequent complaints, as in 1877, of disorder around the market stalls in Stratford Broadway. In 1880 there was an outburst of violence in Romford Road, Forest Gate, where windows were broken and gate-piers overturned. This was especially alarming, since it struck at a middle-class area, and in the following year the board secured the appointment of a stipendiary magistrate for West Ham, and planned a new court house, which was completed in 1885 as part of the town hall extension.

Problems of water supply are described elsewhere,[80] but it must be observed here that the local board's failure to co-operate with the water company in 1886, though not without reason, delayed the introduction of a constant supply in West Ham.

West Ham was incorporated as a municipal borough in 1886. The local board, in a farewell report, boasted of its thrifty administration. Between 1874 and 1886 the rate poundage had been reduced steadily, from 4s. 2d. to 2s., and the outstanding loan debt, amounting in 1886 to only a quarter of the rateable value, was exceptionally low. Those who came after saw the matter differently. Will Thorne, who joined the borough council in 1891 and served on it for over fifty years, blamed the board for 'calculated neglect and lack of foresight' and especially for failing to buy land for public purposes when it was relatively cheap.[81] The burden of this neglect fell heavily upon the board's successor, the borough corporation. The borough treasurer, commenting on this in 1901, noted especially that between 1871 and 1878 the board raised no capital loans at all.[82] The local board's neglect also appears in West Ham's mortality figures.[83] In 1876 the death-rate was 15·4 per 1,000, compared with 20·9 for the whole of England and Wales. By 1885 it had risen to 22·0 (England and Wales 19·2).

LOCAL GOVERNMENT 1886–1965.[84] The municipal borough of West Ham, formed in 1886, was divided into four wards, with a council comprising 36 councillors and 12 aldermen. It became a county borough in 1889 under the Local Government Act, 1888. The number of wards was increased to 12 in

[77] W. Ham L.B. Extension of Powers Act, 1882, 45 & 46 Vict. c. 37 (local act).
[78] See below, p. 110.
[79] *Rep. W. Ham*, 42.
[80] See p. 108.
[81] D. McDougall, *Fifty Years a Borough*, 21.
[82] Quoted by E. G. Howarth and M. Wilson, *W. Ham*, 309–10.
[83] W. Ham C.B.C., *Pub. Health Dept. Rep. for 1937*,

pp. 78–9: (crude death-rate figures 1876f.) The board was not, of course, entirely responsible for the increasing mortality, which was associated with a rapidly rising population.
[84] Unless otherwise stated this section is based on the following sources: W.H.L., W. Ham B.C. Mins. 1886–9; C.B.C. Mins. 1889–1965; W. Ham Municipal Year Bks. 1912–65; D. McDougall, *Fifty Years a Borough*. For public services see also below, p. 108.

1899, and to 16 in 1922, when the council was also enlarged to 48 councillors and 16 aldermen.[85]

The history of local government in the borough falls into three periods: 1886–1919, 1919–40, and 1940–65. In the first period the town continued to grow rapidly, reaching a population of about 300,000. Between 1886 and 1904 the borough council rapidly built up its services, but progress then became slower, partly because of an economic depression, and partly because the sensational success of the Socialists and their allies at the municipal elections of 1898 had provoked a reaction against their policies. The Labour group lost control in 1900. It did not completely regain it until 1919, but after that never lost it. During the second period, after 1919, the council made considerable advances in slum clearance and municipal housing, built Silvertown Way, and carried out a major scheme to widen Stratford High Street and improve the river Lea. But it was hampered by the poverty of the town, which made poor-relief a heavy charge on the rates, and led to a dispute, during the 1920s, between the West Ham poor law union and the Ministry of Health. The borough council, though not directly involved in that dispute, was inevitably affected by it, since the borough was by far the largest and the poorest place in the union, and in 1930, when public assistance was reorganized, took over many of the union's functions and debts. The third period started in September 1940 with heavy air attacks. By those and later bombing over a quarter of the houses in West Ham were destroyed. This made possible, after the war, large-scale slum-clearance and redevelopment, especially in the south of the borough.

Of the 21 retiring members of the local board 11 were elected to the borough council in 1886 and 2 others later. Seven of those 13 left the council within six years and only 3 remained after 1898. From the first the council thus had a very different membership from the board.

Of the chief officers taken over by the borough council from the local board in 1886 only the engineer, Lewis Angell, was serving full-time. His department included his nephew John Morley, and John Angell, probably his son. When Lewis Angell was dismissed in 1899, as described below, John Angell left also, but Morley succeeded his uncle, and served until 1924. The town clerk, Frederic E. Hilleary, remained a part-time officer until his retirement in 1913. In his later years there was criticism of his pluralism, and his successor, H. W. Greaves (1913–15) was appointed on a full-time basis. Greaves was succeeded by George E. Hilleary (1915–29) son of Frederic and previously for many years deputy clerk. The post of medical officer of health was made full-time in 1898. In 1889 the council appointed for the first time a borough accountant, heading its financial department, and in 1897 he became borough

treasurer. The first borough electrical engineer was appointed in 1896 and the first tramways manager in 1903. The first borough librarian (1891–1905) had no immediate successor, because the council adopted his suggestion that the post should be abolished on his retirement in order to save money. The public libraries, thus decentralized, were indeed then very short of money owing to the penny rate restriction. In 1894 West Ham was granted a separate quarter sessions, with a recorder, Edward Morten (1894–1929).

In most respects the quality of the borough's staff improved between 1888 and 1919, but there were a few cases of corruption. In 1899 all the senior staff of the stables department were forced to resign after irregularities had been revealed. The case of the clerk to the education committee (1903) is mentioned elsewhere.[86] In 1905 the clerk to the borough justices, also accused of fraud, fled abroad to escape prosecution.

The borough council soon proved itself far more vigorous and effective than the local board.[87] Among the original councillors were several Progressives, notably J. H. (later Lord) Bethell, who were soon joined by others, and by some Socialists, led by W. J. (Will) Thorne.[88] The Progressives and Socialists did not at first dominate the council, but they had a strong influence on its policies, partly based on the vigorous support of Mansfield House university settlement, whose warden, (Sir) Percy Alden, was a councillor from 1892 to 1901. In 1888 the council secured the transfer to itself of the remaining jurisdiction, within the borough, of the commissioners of sewers.[89] It also obtained powers to widen several main streets and to issue loan stock.[90] A new public hall, opened in 1894, was built at Canning Town. The West Ham Corporation Act, 1893, provided at last for the town's sewage to be admitted to the northern outfall sewer.[91] The necessary scheme was carried out in 1897–1901. By 1898 the council had also built two public libraries and a technical institute, had started building mental and smallpox hospitals, opened two recreation grounds, put in hand an electricity and tramway undertaking, and was planning public baths, council houses, and an isolation hospital.[92]

In 1897 the Socialists and some of the Progressives on the council formed a Labour group with a policy including, among other things, trade union wages for council employees, labour clauses in council contracts, the provision of council houses, and the establishment of a works department. At the election of 1898 this group, with 29 seats, won control. Their victory, then unique in English local government,[93] was attributed to good publicity, trade union support, and the hostility caused by the previous council's attitude during a recent dispute in the engineering industry. The new council proceeded vigorously with the schemes for the baths,

[85] W. Ham Corporation Act, 1921, 11 & 12 Geo. V, c. 112 (local act). [86] See p. 144.

[87] For local politics at this period see: H. Legge, 'Socialism in West Ham', Econ. Review ix. 489–502; 'Municipal Socialism' (leaflet reprinted from The Times, 16 Sept. 1902); J. J. Terrett, Municipal Socialism in West Ham (1902); The Labour Party and the W. Ham Borough Council (Civic Union Pamph., 1911).

[88] Thorne was originally sponsored by the Social Democratic Federation: Stratford Express, W. Ham Jubilee Suppl. 4 July 1936, p. 3.

[89] W. Ham Corporation (Improvements) Act, 1888, 51 & 52. Vict. c. 179 (local act).

[90] Ibid.; and W. Ham Corporation (Loans) Act, 1880, 51 & 52 Vict. c. 142 (local act).

[91] 56 & 57 Vict. c. 204 (local act).

[92] W. Ham Corporation Act, 1898, 61 & 62 Vict. c. 259 (local act) provided additional powers for these purposes.

[93] Cf. J. Redlich and F. W. Hirst, Local Govt. in England (1903 edn.), i. 275 n.

council houses, hospitals, the electricity undertaking, tramways, and sewage disposal already started or planned.[94] Its most controversial measure was to set up an independent works department, which brought it into collision with the aged borough engineer, Lewis Angell, who had held office for 32 years.[95] He had already fought one successful battle against an independent works department. That had been set up in 1894, but its manager proved ineffective, and in 1896 Angell forced his resignation and annexed his department.[96] In 1899, when the Labour council decided to re-establish the works department, Angell bitterly resisted the proposal and was dismissed. The works department, under a new manager, was given the task of building, by direct labour, the new isolation hospital at Plaistow.

Other controversies in which the council was involved in 1898-9 concerned the enforcement of trade union membership among council employees, labour clauses in council contracts, the *Freethinker* magazine, and the parochial charities. The *Freethinker* had been admitted to the borough library at Stratford before the Labour group won control of the council. It was at first kept under the counter but was later openly displayed. Early in 1899 there was a storm of protest against it, led by the churches, in which the 'godless' council was urged to exclude the magazine from the public libraries. After several acrimonious debates the *Freethinker* was relegated to its previous place under the counter.

The *Freethinker* issue became the rallying-cry of those who in 1899 formed the Municipal Alliance against the Socialists in the borough.[97] The Alliance received strong support from the churches, especially the middle-class free churches. Its leaders included such prominent nonconformists as Montague Edwards and Clement Boardman. At the 1899 municipal elections one Alliance candidate published a message from a Wesleyan superintendent mentioning the *Freethinker* and urging 'ministers, Sunday school teachers and parents who are interested in the purity of any young people to vote against any Socialist'.[98] This attitude helps to explain the local Socialists' dislike of the churches, then and later.[99] For the churches the *Freethinker* was only one of several local issues in which they found themselves opposed by the Socialists. Perhaps the most substantial was the struggle for control of the parochial charities, which is described elsewhere.[1] The antagonism between the churches and the Socialists was never absolute, but the Church Socialist League, which had a branch at Plaistow in 1911-16, found few supporters.[2] The Municipal Alliance worked through a number of ratepayers' associations, each embracing two or three wards. Some of these associations already existed, notably

the Forest Gate Ratepayers' Association, founded in 1883.[3] Others were promoted by the Alliance after 1899. At the municipal elections of 1899 the Alliance won nine out of the twelve wards into which the borough had for the first time been divided[4] and reduced the Labour majority to one.[5] In 1900 the Alliance won further seats and gained control of the council.[6] It had successfully exploited the fear of Socialism and the sense of outrage felt by many at the idea of working-class government.[7] These feelings, aroused by the Labour group's brief triumph, were echoed far beyond West Ham: the group is said to have been criticized in America, Australia, France, and Germany. The attacks continued even after the group had lost control. In 1902 *The Times*, in a series on 'Municipal Socialism'[8] published a hostile article on West Ham. This was answered by J. J. Terrett, a former Socialist councillor, in a pamphlet appraising West Ham's problems, especially the legacy of neglect left by the local board. *The Times'* article had urged that West Ham should restrict its services and amenities because it was a working-class town. Terrett showed that much of the heaviest expenditure had been necessitated by poverty and disease. In the heat of this controversy it was not remarked by either side that the Labour council of 1898-1900 had in fact initiated very little. All the public works with which it was particularly associated had been launched or planned before the 1898 elections. The works department was in another category, but even that had its precedent in West Ham before 1898. Friendly critics suggested that the Labour council tried to do too much, too soon,[9] but even this mild stricture is hardly supported by the facts. Between 1895-6 and 1900-1 the council's rates rose by only 8d., of which 3d. was accounted for by new undertakings that came upon the rates for the first time before November 1898.[10]

What is surprising is not that the Labour council may have tried to do too much but that it did not try to do more, for action was badly needed, not only to remedy past neglect, but also to provide for the future. At that time it seemed possible that the population of the borough might rise as high as 430,000. By 1896 about four-fifths of the borough's area had been built up mainly with small houses at high densities. The rateable value of these houses was so low that on one recently-built estate each house was paying £2 18s. 6d. a year less in rates than its share of the costs of municipal services, including education. The borough accountant noted that 900 a. within the borough were still undeveloped, and estimated that it would be cheaper for the council to buy all this land for playgrounds than to have it covered with similar small houses for which services would have to be provided. These warnings appear

[94] Additional powers were obtained by the W. Ham Corporation Act, 1900, 63 & 64 Vict. c. 246 (local act).
[95] Cf. 'Thirty Years West Ham's Surveyor', *Forest Gate Wkly. News*, 26 Nov. 1897.
[96] Cf. 'W. Ham Works Department on trial', *London*, 20 Feb. 1896.
[97] W.H.L., W. Ham Cuttings, No. 1, f. 90 and No. 3, f. 20; *Bk. of W. Ham*, 197-201.
[98] *Stratford Express*, 28 Oct. 1899.
[99] Inf. from Revd. C. Marchant.
[1] See p. 158.
[2] W.H.L., Mins. Church Socialist League, London over the border group, 1911-16.

[3] W.H.L., *Forest Gate R.A. Ann. Reps.* 1899-1917 (with some gaps).
[4] Cf. W.H.L., W. Ham Cuttings No. 3, f. 16.
[5] Howarth and Wilson, *W. Ham*, 314.
[6] *Stratford Express*, 3 Nov. 1900.
[7] Cf. C.F.G. Masterman, *The Condition of England* (6th edn. 1911), 66-9. Masterman was M.P. for North West Ham, 1906-10.
[8] For municipal socialism see Redlich and Hirst, *Local Govt. in England* (1903 edn.), i. 266 f.
[9] e.g. *Stratford Express*, 3 Nov. 1900 (editorial); *The Labour Party and the W. Ham Borough Council* (1911).
[10] Howarth and Wilson, *W. Ham*, 315.

to have led to some changes in rating assessment, and probably stimulated the council to extend its small area of parks and to restrict building. But by 1908 a further 200 a. had been built over.[11]

The Municipal Alliance retained control until 1910. Between 1901 and 1904 the public works already started were completed. This left the works department underemployed, and in 1907 it was again absorbed by the engineer's department. In 1903 the council took over from the school board control of the borough's schools. Between 1901 and 1910 the only important scheme initiated by the council was the extension of the municipal tramways.[12]

In and after 1902 the council provided winter relief works to help the unemployed, and in 1905 formed a distress committee, which established a farm colony at South Ockendon. None of these measures had much effect on the serious problem of unemployment, owing largely to the high proportion of casual labourers, especially at the docks. This was an unhappy period for the Labour councillors, powerless after their short triumph. In July 1906 one of them, Benjamin Cunningham, seized a vacant plot of municipal land near St. Mary's Road, Plaistow, and established there his own farm colony of unemployed, called Triangle Camp.[13] The council brought a legal action for trespass against the 'land-grabbers' and evicted them early in August. In September Cunningham led another attempt to occupy the site, but this failed after a brief scuffle with police and council workmen, and he was subsequently imprisoned for several weeks for contempt of court. At the municipal elections in November he stood as an Independent Labour candidate, disowned by his own party, came bottom of the poll, and never regained his seat.

In 1910 the Municipal Alliance was defeated by the Labour group in coalition with a small new party of Progressives led by J. R. Hurry.[14] The coalition was helped to power by an Act passed earlier that year providing that only councillors should be eligible to vote for new aldermen.[15] It retained control until 1912, when the Municipal Alliance came back with a small majority.[16] In 1910–12 the Labour group, no doubt recalling 1899, tended to avoid controversy.[17]

During the First World War there was an electoral truce, with the Municipal Alliance controlling the council by two or three votes. This frustrated the Labour group's hopes of regaining power, but every year they made a fierce contest of the mayoral election, and in 1916 the Alliance at last agreed to the nomination of the first Labour mayor, Richard Mansfield, an old friend and colleague of Will Thorne.[18] Thorne himself was mayor in the following year. By that time he was the outstanding public figure in the borough, as an alderman, a trade union leader, and as the M.P. for South West Ham since 1906.

In 1919 the Labour group at last won absolute control of the council. It was helped, no doubt, by middle-class migration from West Ham and by the prestige of Thorne and other veteran Socialists in the borough, including J. J. (Jack) Jones, who in 1918 had been elected M.P. for the new Silvertown division. Between 1919 and 1939 the Labour party retained and increased their control. By 1938 they held 54 seats on the council, while the Ratepayers' Association, successor to the Municipal Alliance, had only 10 seats and had ceased to contest several wards.[19] Such a large majority bred political torpor. Between 1927 and 1937 the proportion of the electorate voting at municipal elections in West Ham was in every year smaller than in any of the other 9 great towns of Britain which were the subject of a special study.[20] An observer at the last council meeting before the 1937 elections noticed 'no enthusiasm, no recriminations, no praise, and no farewells . . . harmonious indifference'.[21]

The Labour council of 1919 was faced with problems in some ways even more difficult than those of 20 years earlier. The population was larger, there was growing overcrowding in the older parts of the borough, and redevelopment was urgently needed, both for slum clearance and to improve main roads. But West Ham was still a very poor borough, with many unemployed or underemployed.

In 1919 the relief of poverty was still the responsibility of the West Ham poor law union, which included the neighbouring districts as well as West Ham itself. Early in the century the union had been notorious for extravagance and corruption, which in 1906–7 led to the imprisonment of five guardians and four officers.[22] During the 1920s the guardians were again accused of extravagance. There was then no charge of corruption, but the memory of the events of 1906–7 may have influenced the central government in its dealings with them.

By 1926 the guardians were deeply in debt owing to their policy of relieving beyond their resources. Neville Chamberlain, then Minister of Health, suspended them from office and replaced them with a nominated board, under Sir Alfred Woodgate, which greatly reduced expenditure. In 1929, when public assistance became the responsibility of county and county borough councils, Chamberlain proposed to retain the nominated guardians to administer West and East Ham, the rest of the old union being placed under the county council.[23] Soon after this the Conservative government went out of office, and the plan was dropped. West Ham borough council took over responsibility for its own poor, and, by arrangement with the other local authorities, for administering some of the union's institutions outside West Ham. It also took over much of the union's debt, along with the bitterness

---

[11] Howarth and Wilson, *W. Ham*, 25, 321–3, 324–5.
[12] W. Ham Corp. Act, 1902, 2 Edw. VII, c. 166 (loc. act) gave powers to extend the tramways.
[13] W.H.L., Pamph., B. Cunningham, *The Landgrabbers at Plaistow* (1906); *Stratford Express*, 21 July to 3 Nov. 1906. The squatters received some support from French Socialists.
[14] *Stratford Express* 5 Nov. 1910.
[15] Municipal Corporations Amendment Act, 1910, 10 Edw. VII and 1 Geo. V, c. 19.
[16] *Stratford Express*, 9 Nov. 1912.
[17] Ibid. 26 Oct. 1912.

[18] For these mayoral elections see W.H.L., W. Ham Cuttings, No. 1, ff. 227–33; No. 2, ff. 74–7, 143, 155–8, 171–4, 177; No. 3, f. 217.
[19] W.H.L., News Cuttings, 28 Oct. and 4 Nov. 1938.
[20] G. M. Harris, *Municipal Self-Government in Britain* (1939), 263.
[21] W.H.L., News Cuttings, 30 Oct. 1937.
[22] Howarth and Wilson, *W. Ham*, 352–6; E.R.O., P/BZ 3.
[23] K. Feiling, *Life of Neville Chamberlain*, 139–42; W.H.L., W. Ham Cuttings, No. 3, ff. 124–35, 150–60, 171–4.

aroused by Chamberlain and his ministry.[24] In and after 1929 the borough was also affected by industrial de-rating, as the result of which the council lost £250,000 of its rate income. This sum was made up by a block grant from the government, but the grant was not adjusted to cover either the rise in rates or the expansion of industry which took place in West Ham between 1929 and 1939.[25]

In spite of these and other difficulties the council achieved a good deal during this period. It erected some 1,200 dwellings, mainly under slum clearance schemes, in which its record was second only to that of Bermondsey among the boroughs in Greater London.[26] Two major engineering works were undertaken. Silvertown Way, by a viaduct and bridge, carried a new arterial road from Canning Town to the docks over railways and the dock entrance. In the north of the borough a joint scheme was carried out for widening High Street from Bow Bridge to Stratford Broadway, and, with the Lee conservancy board, for the improvement and flood relief of the river and its branches. The public health department was greatly expanded and did pioneer work in several fields, with such success that from 1923 onwards the borough's death-rate was lower than the average for England and Wales.[27] Large indoor baths were built in Romford Road, open air baths at Canning Town, and a number of new schools.[28]

Between 1919 and 1940 there were many changes among the staff of the council, including some caused by the retirement of officers who had served since the borough's early days. In filling senior posts the council tended to prefer those already on its staff or having local connexions. G. E. Hilleary was succeeded as town clerk by C. E. Cranfield (1929–45), previously managing clerk of the firm of Hilleary's. In 1933 the libraries were again centralized, under a borough librarian, and in 1939 responsibility for education was transferred from the town clerk to a separate education officer.

On 7 and 8 September 1940 West Ham was attacked by German bombers aiming especially at the docks and the power station. Canning Town was badly hit, much of the area between North Woolwich Road and the Thames was destroyed, and Silvertown was, for a time, encircled by fire. There were further attacks throughout the following autumn and winter, the heaviest being in March 1941, and in 1944–5 the borough suffered severely from flying bombs and rockets.[29] The borough council, as the civil defence authority, had an exceptionally difficult task. West Ham was one of the most densely populated towns in Great Britain, and few suffered bomb-damage so severe in relation to their size. By 1945 over 27 per cent of the houses in the borough had been destroyed, and in the southern wards the proportion was much higher, rising to 85 per cent in Tidal Basin, and 49 per cent in Beckton Road. During the intensive raids of 1940–1 the local leadership sometimes faltered, as it did in other towns under battle stress,[30] but over the whole war the council's record was not unimpressive. The normal municipal services were adjusted to wartime conditions with little difficulty. The experienced public health department even acted as a pioneer in several schemes of national importance. The technical college continued to function, being for a time the only one in England still open. The library services were maintained and even extended. Some of the council's emergency services, like public shelters and rest centres, were at first judged to be less efficient, but others, like the removal and storage of furniture from bombed houses, were always well-organized. Deaths from bombing in the borough throughout the war totalled only 0·4 per cent of the pre-war population.[31]

Between 1939 and 1945 there was again an electoral truce. After the war the Labour party continued to increase its already large majority at the expense of the Ratepayers' Association, whose candidates from 1947 were styled Conservatives.[32] In 1954 the Conservatives lost their last remaining seat, and for the next six years the council consisted entirely of Labour members. In 1960 municipal politics were enlivened by the Liberals, who won three seats and began to subject the majority to searching attack, especially on education. By 1962 they had seven seats, but they lost two of these in the following year.[33] By 1945 West Ham had been greatly altered. Some 14,000 houses had been destroyed by bombing and 500 a. land cleared. The population, which had already begun to decline before 1939, was now less than it had been for 60 years. War damage made it possible to undertake large-scale redevelopment, especially in the south of the borough, and between 1945 and 1965 the council built over 9,500 dwellings, of which 8,000 were permanent.[34] Public buildings completed since 1945 include a new fire station, new municipal offices in the Grove, Stratford (1960), two libraries, a health centre, a junior training centre, and a youth centre, as well as several schools. This programme of public works raised the council's loan debts from £4,758,385 in 1945 to £31,515,478 in 1965. Housing accounted for about two-thirds of the debts outstanding in 1965.[35]

Under the London Government Act, 1963, West Ham became part of the London borough of Newham.[36]

[24] Cf. R. M. Titmuss, *Problems of Social Policy* (Hist. Second World War, U.K. Civil Series), 269–70.
[25] E. D. Idle, *War over W. Ham*, 37.
[26] Ibid. 21; *W. Ham Municipal Year Bk.*, 1940.
[27] *W. Ham C.B.C., Pub. Health Dept. Rep. for 1937*, pp. 78–9: crude death rate figures.
[28] The council promoted the following local acts during this period: W. Ham Corpn. Act, 1921, 11 & 12 Geo. V, c. 120; W. Ham Corpn. Act, 1925, 15 & 16 Geo. V, c. 112; Royal Victoria and other Docks Approaches (Improvement) Act, 1929, 19 & 20 Geo. V, c. 47; R. Lee (Flood Relief &c.) Act, 1930, 20 & 21 Geo. V, c. 192; W. Ham Corpn. Act, 1930, 20 & 21 Geo. V, c. 194; W. Ham Corpn. Act, 1931, 21 & 22 Geo. V, c. 60; W. Ham Corpn. Act, 1937, 1 Edw. VIII and 1 Geo. VI, c. 35.
[29] For W. Ham during the war see: T. H. O'Brien, *Civil Defence* (Hist. Second World War, U.K. Civil Series),

388, 414; E. D. Idle, *War over W. Ham* 49f.; R. M. Titmuss, *Problems of Social Policy*, 258–9, 269–70, 317; Sainsbury, *Eight Hundred Years*, 71f.
[30] Cf. Titmuss, op. cit. 258–9, 295, 317.
[31] For the estimated population in 1938 see *W. Ham Municipal Year Bk.* 1940.
[32] W.H.L., News Cuttings, 8 Nov. 1946, 7 Nov. 1947, 20 May 1949, 9 May 1950, 18 May 1951.
[33] Election returns: *Stratford Express*, 21 May 1954 and corresponding issues to 1964; D. Peschek and J. Brand, *Policies and Politics in Secondary Education*, (L.S.E. Greater London Papers, No. 11), 13–75.   [34] See p. 110.
[35] *W. Ham C.B.C. Abstract o Accounts*, 1964–5.
[36] Newham includes also the former county borough of East Ham, the former detached parts of Woolwich north of the Thames, and part of the former borough of Barking west of the Roding.

PUBLIC SERVICES. The development of gas, electricity, and water supplies, and of sewage disposal, have been outlined elsewhere.[37] Gas was brought to Stratford in the 1820s from the works of the Whitechapel Gas Co., to light the turnpike road. In the 1850s, after several changes of ownership, that undertaking was in the hands of the Commercial Gas Co., which was supplying some western areas of West Ham parish. The West Ham Gas Co., founded in 1846, was incorporated in 1856, when it took over all the Commercial Gas Co.'s mains in the parish except those in a small part of Canning Town.[38] The directors of the West Ham Gas Co. were local men, including several, like Capt. R. W. Pelly and John Meeson, who were also prominent on the local board, and on one occasion it was alleged that the company and the local board were 'hand in glove'.[39] The company was taken over in 1910 by the Gas Light and Coke Co.[40] Its works, at Stratford, were still open in 1965. In the south of the parish the North Woolwich Gas Co. had built works at Silvertown by 1855.[41] These were taken over in 1857 by the Victoria Dock Gas Co., which opened new works in 1864. The Victoria Dock Gas Co. was absorbed in 1871 by the Gas Light & Coke Co., which closed the works in 1909.[42]

The borough council in 1892 obtained powers to supply electricity throughout West Ham.[43] In 1895 it set up a small generator behind the public hall in Barking Road, Canning Town, which lighted the hall, the public library, and later also Mansfield House and a neighbouring shop.[44] This operated until 1898, when a power station was completed at Abbey Mills and a general supply started. The Abbey Mills station soon became inadequate and was replaced by a larger one, opened in 1904 at Canning Town on the site of the former municipal sewage works. West Ham's municipal tramways were electrified in the same year.[45] The new power station was extended several times between 1904 and 1914 and again in 1922. It was said in 1926 that West Ham had the largest municipal electricity undertaking in the London area and the eighth largest in the country.[46] In 1930 another generator was added, and new offices and showrooms were completed in Romford Road. Demand was stimulated by vigorous publicity, designed especially to attract new industries to the borough. Between 1930 and 1940 the number of consumers rose from 15,000 to 56,000 and units sold from 98 million to 156 million. During the Second World War the power

station and the offices were heavily bombed. The electricity undertaking passed in 1947 to the London electricity board, which in 1951 completed the first part of West Ham 'B' power station, planned before nationalization and adjoining the old station, now designated West Ham 'A'.

West Ham waterworks originated in or about 1745, when Resta Patching of Dorking (Surr.), mealman, and Thomas Byrd of Queen Street, Westminster, went into partnership for the purpose.[47] Byrd, who evidently provided most of the capital, was to be manager, and Patching the turncock or overseer. A steam engine was to be erected on land rented from John Cox of West Ham, from which water would be pumped to this and neighbouring parishes. In 1748, shortly after Resta Patching's death, his son Ezra, with Thomas Byrd and John Montgomerie, obtained statutory powers to extend the works and to protect them from malicious damage.[48] Among the properties acquired by the company for its works was Saynes Mill, the lease of which, from the corporation of London, was bought before 1762. In 1775, when this lease was renewed for 61 years, the company stated that it had spent nearly £70,000 on its undertaking.[49] In 1807 the West Ham waterworks were taken over by the London Dock Co., which in 1808 sold them to the newly-formed East London Waterworks Co.[50] West Ham was supplied by the East London Waterworks Co. until the formation of the Metropolitan water board in 1904.[51] After 1850, when the town was growing fast, there were frequent complaints about the inadequacy and impurity of the company's supply there.[52] Since West Ham lay outside the area governed by the Metropolis Water Acts of 1852 and 1871,[53] the water company was not obliged to maintain a constant supply. Nevertheless the company professed its desire to do so, provided that certain regulations were met.[54] Failing that, it turned on its mains only for short periods each day. In 1886 it sought statutory power to ensure a constant supply in West Ham, but this was opposed by the local board and was not enacted. The board's ostensible objections were technical and financial, but behind these lay a quarrel with the company caused by the recent discovery of eels in the company's mains at West Ham.[55] With the formation of the borough council relations improved, and in 1895 the company began to provide a constant supply throughout West Ham.[56]

[37] V.C.H. Essex v. 37–47; 75–81.
[38] W.H.L., W. Ham Gas Co. Reps. 1850–96; W. Ham Gas Co.'s Act, 1856, 19 & 20 Vict. c. 59 (local act).
[39] W.H.L., W. Ham L.B. Mins. 12 Dec. 1882.
[40] Gas Light & Coke Co.'s Act, 1909, 9 Edw. VII, c. 87 (local act).
[41] A. L. Dickens, Rep. Sanitary Condition W. Ham (1855), map.
[42] Victoria Dock Gas Act, 1857, 20 & 21 Vict. c. 127 (local act); E. G. Stewart, Hist. Index of Gas Works in area now served by N. Thames Gas Bd., 87.
[43] Electric Lighting Orders Conf. (No. 3) Act, 1892, 55 & 56 Vict. c. 38 (local act).
[44] Unless otherwise stated this paragraph is based on the following: W.H.L., 'New Generating Station, Canning Town', Elec. Rev. Apr. 1904; W.Ham Elec. Dept., Opening of Extension to Works, 1922; 'Electrical Supply in W. Ham', Electrics, East London Suppl. 1930; W. Ham 'B' Power Stn. Opening, 1951; 'W. Ham Report for 1945', Electrical Times, 17 Jan. 1946; Sainsbury, Eight Hundred Years, 16.
[45] For the tramways see p. 62.
[46] W.H.L., W. Ham Cuttings, No. 3, f. 120.

[47] E.R.O., D/DU 621/1–6 (W. Ham Waterworks 1745–9); A. R. J. Ramsey, 'Beginnings of W. Ham's Water Supply', E.R. lii. 76–82.
[48] Act for empowering George Montgomerie, Thos. Byrd, and Ezra Patching to complete an undertaking for furnishing . . . Stratford, West Ham . . . and other places with water, 21 Geo. II, c. 8.
[49] E.R.O., T/P 48/1. For Saynes Mill see above p. 91.
[50] Act to enable the London Dock Co. to purchase . . . waterworks in Stratford, West Ham [&c.], 47 Geo. III, Sess. 2, c. 5 (local act); Act to enable the proprietors of the East London Waterworks to purchase . . . other Waterworks, 48 Geo. III, c. 8 (local and personal act).
[51] Cf. V.C.H. Essex, v. 37–9.
[52] e.g. W. Ham L.B. Mins. 27 Oct. 1857, 13 June 1865, 28 Aug. 1866.
[53] 15 & 16 Vict. c. 84; 34 & 35 Vict. c. 113.
[54] A. L. Dickens, Rep. W. Ham, 24.
[55] For this dispute see W. Ham L.B. Mins. 13 Oct. 1885 to 26 Oct. 1886 passim.
[56] W.H.L., Vert. File, E. London Waterworks Co., Notice to Householders (1895).

Provision for sewage disposal was the main task facing the local board when it was formed in 1856.[57] The board appointed as consultant (Sir) Robert Rawlinson, chief engineering inspector to the General Board of Health.[58] The Metropolitan board of works was then planning a drainage scheme for London, and Rawlinson obtained assurances that the metropolitan northern outfall sewer, which was to traverse West Ham, would soon be available for use by that district. On that assumption the local board approved his plans for a sewage scheme with temporary outfall works at Bow creek, and this was completed in 1861. The metropolitan scheme came into operation in 1868, but the local board's subsequent attempts to obtain access to the northern outfall sewer were unsuccessful, and the board was forced to go on using its Bow creek works, and eventually also to provide separate works for Silvertown, completed in 1886. In 1893 the borough council at last obtained statutory powers to use the northern outfall sewer, but the necessary conversion works, including a new pumping station in Abbey Road, near the Metropolitan pumping station, were not completed until 1901. This long delay, during the period of West Ham's most rapid growth, created great difficulties for the local board and the borough council.[59]

The pumping station at Abbey Mills, built by the Metropolitan board of works and opened in 1868, was designed by Sir Joseph Bazalgette and E. Cooper, and laid out on a lavish scale, surrounded by lawns and trees. The main pump-house is cruciform in plan, with domed turrets and a central cupola 110 ft. high. The building was originally flanked by two tall chimneys, also surmounted by cupolas, but these were taken down during the Second World War to prevent their use as landmarks for enemy aircraft; electric power had been introduced in 1933. The interior of the pump-house has elaborate decorative features, including cast ironwork of Venetian Gothic design.[60] The West Ham sewage pumping station (1899) is in a more restrained classical style. In 1970 it still retained a beam engine of 1895 and an impressive chimney.[61]

The local board's unsuccessful attempt in 1868–9 to buy Upton Park (73 a.) for public use, has been mentioned elsewhere.[62] In 1872, after the demolition of Ham House, the project was revived by a private committee. John Gurney, owner of the park, agreed to sell it cheap, and funds were raised by subscription. The City of London, which had been one of the main subscribers, also undertook to maintain the park in future. West Ham Park, so re-named, was opened to the public in 1874.[63] The first municipal parks[64] were opened in 1894, at Plaistow (8 a.), and Beckton Road, Canning Town (22 a.), and in the

same year the borough council took over, as tenant, the 17 a. of Wanstead Flats lying within West Ham. Hermit Road park, Canning Town (10 a.), was bought for the town by J. H. (later Lord) Bethell in 1899, with the aid of private subscriptions.[65] West Ham Lane park originated in 1900, when the first part was bought; it was later enlarged to 10½ a. Several other parks and playing fields were provided by the borough council, including the Grove Gardens, Stratford, laid out in 1901 on a small piece of roadside waste which the local board had bought from the lord of the manor in 1884. In 1963 the council owned 97½ a. of public open spaces.[66]

The earliest public baths in the borough were privately owned.[67] In 1886 and for a few years after, there was a swimming bath in Manbey Park Road, Stratford, on the site later occupied by Boardman's furniture depository.[68] The Carpenters' Company institute, Jupp Road, Stratford, founded in 1886, also contained a swimming bath. Municipal swimming baths were opened at Plaistow in 1901 and at Silvertown in 1922. The Silvertown baths were badly damaged by bombing during the Second World War and were finally closed in 1948. The corporation was planning baths for Stratford as early as 1895, but this project lapsed, and in 1905, when the Carpenters' Company's school closed, the council leased the bath in Jupp Road, retaining it until 1934, when large municipal baths were built in Romford Road. In 1937 an open-air bath was built in Canning Town park, replacing a smaller pool built by private subscription about 30 years earlier.[69] Slipper baths were opened at Fen Street, Tidal Basin, in 1912, and at Plaistow Road, West Ham, in 1932. The Fen Street baths were bombed in the Second World War and were finally closed in 1944.

West Ham already had public fire-engines in 1785, when the parish vestry arranged a new contract for their annual maintenance.[70] In 1792 the vestry, which then had two engines, bought a third,[71] and from 1795 to 1840 it appointed each year three 'engineers' (engine keepers), one for each ward.[72] In 1841 the engines were placed under the parish highway board. In 1848 it was found that they could not legally be maintained out of the highway-rates, and the vestry therefore began to charge them against the church-rates, contracting for their maintenance with Edward Thorman, engineer of the West Ham gasworks.[73] After 1854, when compulsory church-rates ended,[74] the vestry defaulted on its payments to Thorman, who impounded the engines and would not permit their use. In 1856–7 the vestry formed a voluntary fire brigade, by subscription, recovered the engines, repaired them, and appointed a trained fireman.[75] This was a temporary arrangement, pending the Local Government Act,

[57] This paragraph is based on W. Ham L.B. Mins., B.C. Mins., and C.B.C. Mins.

[58] See D.N.B.   [59] See pp. 101–2.

[60] Pevsner, Essex, 374; Illus. Lond. News, 28 May 1864, pp. 512–13; 13 Apr. 1867, p. 380; 15 Aug. 1868, pp. 161–2; E. Lond. Papers, xii. 92, 96–7; Sunday Times (col. suppl.) 25 Feb. 1968.

[61] E. Lond. Papers, xii. 94.

[62] See p. 103.

[63] G. Pagenstecher, Story of W. Ham Park, summarized in D. McDougall, Fifty Years a Borough, 210–16.

[64] The rest of this paragraph is based on W. Ham C.B.C. Mins.

[65] Stratford Express, W. Ham Jubilee Suppl. 4 July 1936, p. 2.

[66] W. Ham Official Guide (1963–4).

[67] Paragraph based on: W. Ham C.B.C. Mins.; Mc-Dougall, Fifty Years a Borough, 112–15; Sainsbury, Eight Hundred Years, 69–70; W.H.L., Pamph. W. Ham Municipal Baths, Romford Rd. (1934); Howarth and Wilson, West Ham, 392–3.

[68] Kelly's Dir. Essex (1886, 1890, 1906).

[69] W.H.L., News Cuttings 1935–41: 4 Sept. 1937.

[70] W.H.L., W. Ham Vestry Mins. 15 Sept. 1785.

[71] Ibid. 3 Aug. 1792.

[72] Ibid. 7 Apr. 1795 and later.

[73] Ibid. 25 Apr. 1848. For Thorman see W.H.L., W. Ham Gas Co. Rep. 1891.

[74] Vestry Mins. 28 Sept., 3 Oct. 1854.

[75] Vestry Mins. 18 Dec. 1856, 27 Mar. 1857.

1858, under which the local board was able to take over the fire brigade.[76] The board bought a new engine, leased a building in West Ham Lane, Stratford, as a fire station, and built another station near the Abbey Arms at Plaistow. A new station for Stratford was built in 1869 as part of the town hall scheme. For many years the brigade was far from efficient. The firemen, mostly part-timers, were ill-trained and badly led. In 1877–8 the local board reorganized the brigade on a more professional basis, rebuilt the Stratford fire station, built a new station in Barking Road, Canning Town, to replace the one at Plaistow, and opened a third station in rented premises at Forest Gate. By 1902 there were three main fire stations, at Stratford, Barking Road, and Silvertown, and three sub-stations, at Forest Gate, Plaistow, and Custom House. A new station was built for Silvertown in 1914.[77] In 1931 a new station was built in Prince Regent Lane to replace the old one at Canning Town. The three sub-stations were subsequently closed. In 1964 a new station was opened in Romford Road, Stratford, replacing the one adjoining the town hall.[78] The first motor fire appliance was bought in 1909, but it was not until 1923 that the last horse-drawn steam fire-engine went out of service.

Between 1899 and 1905 the borough council built 401 municipal dwellings, in Bethell Avenue (Plaistow), Corporation Street and Eve Road (West Ham), Wise Road (Stratford), and Invicta and Rendel Roads (Custom House).[79] Most of these were flats in 'double' houses. In building them the council was concerned to raise the standard of workmen's houses rather than to meet any housing shortage.[80] From 1905 to 1908 there were often as many as 40 or 50 council dwellings unoccupied, but after that vacancies became fewer. Between 1918 and 1939 the council built a further 1,200 dwellings, mainly under slum clearance schemes.[81] A further 600 dwellings, built by the Ministry of Transport to rehouse those displaced by the building of Silvertown Way, were transferred to the council on completion. The heavy bombing of the Second World War created the need and the opportunity for large-scale redevelopment, especially in the south of the borough. Before the war ended the council had drawn up a preliminary scheme proposing that the borough should eventually be restricted to a population of about 165,000, living in 16 'neighbourhood units'.[82] Under a plan approved by the government in 1956 the council designated 21 areas of 'comprehensive development', totalling some 785 a. The first quinquennial review of the plan increased the total area involved to 843 a. Land subject to compulsory purchase orders was also designated, and by 1965 the council had acquired over 400 a., mainly for housing and planning. The plan provided for the development of some 500 a. for housing, the improvement of

market and shopping areas, sites for new schools, the provision of nearly 200 a. of open spaces, and the resiting of certain industries. Between 1945 and 1965 the council built over 9,500 dwellings, of which 8,000 were permanent. A further 1,600 were under construction in 1965.[83]

During the 19th century West Ham was subject to serious epidemics.[84] There were cholera outbreaks in 1838[85] and many later occasions at least up to 1905, one of the most serious being in 1866, when there were about 300 fatal cases. Typhoid was still occurring as late as 1901. Most serious of all was smallpox which caused epidemics in 1867 and 1871–2. In spite of these diseases West Ham's death-rate was still relatively low in 1876: 15·4 per thousand compared with the national average of 20·9. But after that the rate rose sharply, reaching 22·0 in 1885 when the national average was 19·2. One cause of the rise was the opening of three smallpox hospitals at Plaistow. That source of infection was eliminated in the 1890s, but though the borough's death-rate declined after 1900, it remained above the national average until 1918. From 1919, in spite of overcrowding and industrial air-pollution, West Ham's death rate was below the national average. Much of the improvement was due to the borough's comprehensive health services.[86]

In 1871 the West Ham poor-law union opened a smallpox hospital in Western Road, Plaistow.[87] Another smallpox hospital, opposite the first, was built in 1877 by the Poplar board of works, in spite of protests from the local board. During the following years there were frequent smallpox epidemics near these hospitals, and in 1884 the local board itself had to open a temporary smallpox hospital, leasing for the purpose a row of cottages in Pragell Street, near Western Road. By then it was becoming clear that these hospitals, in a rapidly growing area, were a danger. In 1890 the borough council suggested that all three should be closed, that the Union and Poplar hospitals should be converted into a municipal hospital for infectious diseases other than smallpox, and that the council should build a new smallpox hospital in a more isolated place outside the borough. This scheme was carried out gradually over the next twelve years. In the final stage (1899–1902) the sites of the Union and Poplar hospitals were combined and extended by the closure of the road between them. Most of the old hospital buildings were demolished and the new Plaistow fever hospital, with 120 beds, was built there. It was recognized in 1906 as a teaching hospital, and during the next 37 years over 3,000 students received fever training there. It suffered bomb damage during the Second World War. In 1947 part of it became an annexe of Queen Mary's hospital for the East End. Since 1948 it has been known simply as Plaistow hospital. Associated with Plaistow fever hospital

[76] For the rest of this paragraph see: L.B. Mins., B.C. Mins. and C.B.C. Mins.
[77] Municipal Jnl. 6 Nov. 1914.
[78] W.H.L., Vert. File, New Stratford Fire Station, 1964.
[79] Paragraph based on: C.B.C. Mins.; Municipal Year Bks.; Sainsbury, Eight Hundred Years, 58–9; W. Ham Official Guide (1960), 23–33; D. R. Childs and J. Whittle, 'Post-War Housing in West Ham', Architects Jnl. 27 Sept. 1956.
[80] London, 14 July 1898.
[81] For the Manor Road scheme see Proc. Inst. Municipal and County Engineers, liv (1927–8), p. 1006.

[82] P. Abercrombie, The Greater London Plan, 1944, 173–4.
[83] For redevelopment after 1945 see above, p. 56.
[84] Paragraph based on: L.B. Mins., B.C. Mins., C.B.C. Mins.; W. Ham Pub. Health Dept., Annual Reps. 1876 f.: mortality figures for 1876–1937 are summarized in the Rep. for 1937.
[85] W.H.L., W. Ham Vestry Mins. 29 Mar. 1838.
[86] See below.
[87] Paragraph based on: W.H.L. Pamph., Opening Plaistow Fever Hosp. Extension (1901); W. Ham Group (No. 9) Management Ctee. Annual Rep. (1948–9); W. Ham L.B. Mins., B.C. Mins., C.B.C. Mins.

was a children's hospital at Harold Wood, Hornchurch. This was opened in 1909 as the Grange convalescent home, with 40 children's beds. In 1930 it was enlarged to 116 beds. By 1935 it was providing temporary accommodation for chronic adult cases, to relieve the public assistance home at Leyton.[88] West Ham's new smallpox hospital was opened in 1899 at Rookery Farm, Dagenham. Though built and maintained by the borough council it served all the places in West Ham union.[89]

The borough council also built a mental hospital at Goodmayes, Ilford, in 1901,[90] and in 1932 opened a colony for mental defectives at Little Mollands Farm, South Ockendon.[91] For the treatment of tuberculosis the council in 1912 converted the Dagenham smallpox hospital into a sanatorium.[92] A children's tuberculosis sanatorium was opened at Langdon Hills in 1927.[93] In 1930 the council became responsible also for the main institutions of the dissolved West Ham union, including Whipps Cross hospital and the central home (later Langthorne hospital), both in Leyton,[94] and also Forest Gate hospital.

Forest Gate hospital, Forest Lane, had been an industrial school from 1854 to 1906, and in 1908 became a branch workhouse of Poplar union.[95] In 1911 it was bought by West Ham union which reopened it in 1913 as a workhouse infirmary. By 1930 it had 500 beds for maternity, mental, and chronic sick cases. An extension with 200 beds was added in 1931. The hospital suffered bomb damage in 1940. New maternity wards were built in 1950. The principal building still retains its mid-Victorian institutional appearance. It is a brick range, 15 bays long and three storeys high, with round-headed windows to the ground floor and the central bay raised to form a low tower.

Of West Ham's former voluntary hospitals the oldest is Queen Mary's hospital for the East End, West Ham Lane.[96] This originated in 1861 when William Elliot, a prominent local doctor, opened the West Ham, Stratford, and South Essex dispensary in a house in Romford Road lent by Mrs. Mary Curtis. Mrs. Curtis later gave a site in West Ham Lane, where a new dispensary was built in 1879.[97] In 1890 a 32-bed hospital, mainly for accident cases, was built beside the dispensary. A new hospital wing, with 28 beds, was given in 1895 by Passmore Edwards. The hospital was further extended in 1906–10, on the site previously occupied by West Ham high school. In 1911 it received a legacy of £20,000 from Joseph Withers. Queen Mary became patron in 1916 and the hospital then adopted its present name. In 1917 it was incorporated by royal charter, and in the same year Charles Lyle gave it £10,000, including the freehold of the adjoining Chant Square. By 1931 after several recent extensions there were 219 beds, but in 1940 the hospital was partly destroyed by bombing, and reduced, even after repairs, to 164 beds.

St. Mary's hospital for women and children, London and Upper Roads, Plaistow, originated in 1886, when the vicar of St. Mary's, Thomas Given-Wilson, established a welfare clinic and day nursery.[98] In 1889 part of the work was transferred to Howard's Road, as St. Mary's Nurses. In 1893 a new building was erected in London Road for the nursery with 6 hospital beds for children. The site was provided by Given-Wilson and the building by the Revd. Henry Blisset. In 1896–8 the hospital accommodation was enlarged to 38 beds. The present name was adopted in 1905 and in 1911 a new 66-bed hospital was built. In 1946 a new out-patient building was completed and the hospital beds were increased to 100.

Plaistow maternity hospital, Howard's Road, originated in 1889, when Katherine Twining, who had been working at the clinic in London Road, moved to Howard's Road and established there St. Mary's Nurses, to provide a district midwifery and nursing service.[99] The nurses' home was gradually extended, in 1904 a 12-bed maternity hospital was opened in adjoining houses, and in 1915 Chesterton House was bought for a maternity clinic. The hospital was rebuilt in 1923 and was further enlarged, to 60 beds, in 1929. Extensions to the nurses' home and a lecture hall (1936) helped to make this an outstanding centre for midwifery training. The work of the district nursing branch was taken over in 1940 by the East Ham District Nursing Association.

The Invalid and Crippled Children's hospital, Balaam Street, Plaistow, was founded by the London Medical Mission Association.[1] The mission hospital was taken over in 1893 by the Canning Town Women's Settlement as a hospital for women and children. In 1895 it was transferred to two houses in Barking Road, remaining there until 1905, when a new building was erected in Balaam Street. In 1923 the settlement conveyed it rent-free to the South West Ham Invalid and Crippled Children's Society, for use by children only. The hospital was extended in 1932–3. It was closed for most of the Second World War, but subsequently reopened.

The Albert Dock seamen's hospital, Alnwick Road, Custom House, was founded in 1890, when the original buildings were opened in Connaught Road by the Seamen's Hospital Society, which has maintained the hospital ever since.[2] The London School of Tropical Medicine was founded at this hospital in 1899 by Sir Patrick Manson, and remained there until 1924. The old dock-side buildings suffered from subsidence, and in 1937 a new hospital was built on the present site with help from the Port of London authority.

In 1948 all the hospitals in West Ham, except the seamen's hospital, came under the control of the West Ham group (No. 9) hospital management committee of the N.E. Metropolitan regional board.

[88] W.H.L., *Opg. Harold Wood Children's Hosp.* (1930); McDougall, *Fifty Years*, 112.

[89] *W. Ham C.B.C. Mins.*; W. Ham Corp. Act, 1898 61 & 62 Vict. c. 259 (local act).

[90] 'W. Ham's new Lunatic Asylum', *Municipal Jnl.* 9 Aug. 1901; W.H.L., Goodmayes Mental Hosp., *Opening of Extension*, 1934; McDougall, *Fifty Years*, 106.

[91] McDougall, *Fifty Years*, 106.

[92] W. Ham *C.B.C. Mins.* 1912–13, p. 273.

[93] *Municipal Jnl.* 11 Nov. 1927.

[94] See p. 214.

[95] Paragraph based on: E. R. Gamester, *Hist. Forest Gate Hosp.* (1954).

[96] Paragraph based on: J. Parsons, *Short Hist. Queen Mary's Hosp. for East End* (1962).

[97] Cf. W.H.L., Vert. File, *New Dispensary, Rep. and Plan* (1877).

[98] Paragraph based on: W. Ham Group Hosp. Management Ctee. *Ann. Rep.* (1948–9); Sainsbury, *Eight Hundred Years*, 54–5; McDougall, *Fifty Years*, 262–4; *Kelly's Dir. Essex* (1906).

[99] Ibid.   [1] Ibid.   [2] Ibid.

In the provision of welfare services of all kinds much pioneer work was done by voluntary bodies, especially the churches and settlements. These were followed up and developed by the borough council, which made prompt use of permissive power given by statute.[3] West Ham was one of the first education authorities to provide school meals (1906) and to establish a school medical service (1908). By 1918 the council was giving financial aid to seven voluntary maternity and child welfare centres. The first such municipal clinic was opened at Silvertown in 1920, and by 1936 there were five, of which three had been built for the purpose in 1930-1.[4] A new health centre built in West Ham Lane in 1962 provides many specialist services. In 1932 the council took over from a voluntary society responsibility for training the blind, and opened temporary workshops in West Ham Lane; permanent workshops were built in 1938. Training centres for the mentally subnormal were opened at Forest Gate in 1950 and at Plaistow in 1961. The John F. Kennedy junior training centre, Pitchford Street, Stratford, for handicapped children, was built in 1964. In 1965 the council was maintaining nine old people's hostels, all outside the borough except for Adelaide House, Meath Road, Stratford, which was built in 1954 with aid from the Lord Mayor's National Air Raid Distress fund.[5] There were also two reception homes for children together with six 'family group' homes. The council's special schools are described elsewhere.[6]

A burial board for West Ham was set up by the parish vestry in 1854, and in 1857 laid out the West Ham cemetery at Forest Gate.[7] In 1901 the board was dissolved and the cemetery was taken over by the borough council.[8] The East London cemetery at Plaistow was laid out by a private company in 1871.[9] The Jews' cemetery at Forest Gate is treated elsewhere.[10]

The history of the public libraries up to 1955 is described elsewhere.[11] It should be added in amendment that the hospital library service inaugurated in 1899 did not last long, and that it was not revived until about 1945. In 1959 a permanent building was erected in Woodgrange Road for the Forest Gate library and in 1961 the Silvertown library was transferred from the Tate institute to new premises in Constance Street. The total book stock of West Ham libraries was 222,000 in 1964.

PARLIAMENTARY REPRESENTATION.
Under the Redistribution of Seats Act, 1885, West Ham became a parliamentary borough with two divisions.[12] At the general election of that year each division returned a Liberal. West Ham (South) was won by Joseph Leicester, a trade unionist and temperance reformer. He was defeated in 1886 by a local Conservative, G. E. Banes, but in 1892 the seat was won by Keir Hardie as the first Independent Labour M.P. Banes regained it in 1895, held it in 1900, but lost it in 1906 to W. J. (Will) Thorne (Labour). Thorne's support rested on his long-standing membership of the borough council as well as his position as secretary of the trade union which he had founded to protect the interests of the Beckton gas workers. He retained the seat at the elections of 1910.

West Ham (North) was gained in 1886 by the Conservative barrister (Sir) Forrest Fulton, lost to a Liberal in 1892, but won by another Conservative in 1895 and 1900. C. F. G. Masterman regained the seat for the Liberals in 1906 and held it at both the elections in 1910, but in 1911 he was unseated on petition because of illegal acts by his agent. Another Liberal held the seat at the subsequent by-election.

The Representation of the People Act, 1918, divided the borough into four constituencies: Plaistow, Silvertown, Stratford, and Upton. At every subsequent election before 1950 the first two divisions were held by Labour. Will Thorne represented Plaistow until 1945, when he was succeeded by (Sir) Elwyn Jones. Silvertown was held from 1918 to 1940 by J. J. (Jack) Jones, a trade union colleague of Thorne, and also a veteran member of the borough council. The Stratford division returned a Conservative in 1918 but was gained by Labour in 1922 and never lost after that. Upton was won by the Conservatives in 1918, 1922, 1924, and 1931, and by Labour in 1923 and 1929. Labour regained it at a by-election in 1934 and held it in 1945.

Under the Representation of the People Act, 1948, West Ham was reduced to two divisions, north and south. Both of these were won by Labour at every subsequent election up to and including 1966.

STRATFORD ABBEY PRECINCTS.[13]
The abbey of Stratford Langthorne lay between the Channelsea river and Marsh Lane (Manor Road) on a site now occupied by factories, railways, and a sewage pumping station. None of its buildings remain *in situ*. The abbey precincts appear to have comprised about 20 a., moated to north, east, and south. They constituted a separate parish, with its own parish church, distinct from the abbey church. The abbey exercised peculiar jurisdiction within the precincts.[14]

When the abbey was dissolved in 1538 several of the buildings in the precincts were occupied by lay persons, mostly under leases granted during the past five years. In 1539 the abbey site and the

[3] For the welfare services see: *Fifty Years*, 100–135; *Eight Hundred Years*, 25–34, 50–2.

[4] W.H.L., Vert. File, *Opg. Welfare Centre, Plaistow* (1930); *Stone Layings Welfare Centres, Forest Gate* and *Canning Town* (1930).

[5] *W. Ham Official Guide* (1963–4); W.H.L., Pamph. *Opg. of Adelaide House* (1954).

[6] See p. 156.

[7] W. Ham Vestry Mins. 13 and 26 June 1854, 21, 25 and 26 June 1855; 25 June and 2 July, 1857; E.R.O., D/DQs 36.　　　　　[8] *C.B.C. Mins.* 4 Jan. 1901.

[9] L.B. Mins. 28 Mar. and 11 July 1871.

[10] See p. 141.

[11] *V.C.H. Essex, Bibliography* 329. The following additional information was provided by the Libraries Dept. of Newham L.B.

[12] This section is based on: *Fifty Years a Borough*, 270–6; F. Sainsbury, *West Ham*, 80–4; and M.P.'s biographies in *Who's Who*. See also: Sheila Jones, 'Parliamentary Representation in West Ham (South), 1874–1914' (Balls Park Coll. Educ. thesis, 1969).

[13] This is a summary of a longer and fully annotated account by the same writer in E.R.O., T/Z 101. The main primary sources for the topography of the precincts are: S.C. 6/962 (Minister's account of Stratford Abbey lands, 1539); W.H.L., Abbey Landowners' Min. Bks. 1715 sqq.; W.H.L., Jn. Noble, Map of W. Marsh, 1747; O.S. Map 25″, London, XXIX. (1869 edn.). See also: *E. Nat.* xxiv. 140–3; Fry, *E. and W. Ham*, 133–42. For the institutional history of the abbey see *V.C.H. Essex*, ii. 129 sqq.

[14] *Cal. Pat.* 1549–51, 171–2.

reversion of the other property in the precincts were granted to Sir Peter Meautis or Mewtas (d. 1562), later ambassador to France. During the next two centuries the ownership of the precincts came to be divided between several owners. By 1732 an alehouse, the Adam and Eve, had been built on part of the site. That, with the adjoining land to east and south, was bought in 1784 by Thomas Holbrook (d. 1811), a brewer, who dug up the abbey founda-

pipe and an ancient sewer, both running west to the Adam and Eve, suggest that the domestic offices of the abbey to which they were probably connected lay south of the road through the precincts, with the church south of them. Such an arrangement would have been consistent with local custom. In west Essex most of the monasteries of which the plans are known, including Stratford's neighbours at Waltham and Barking, had churches to the south

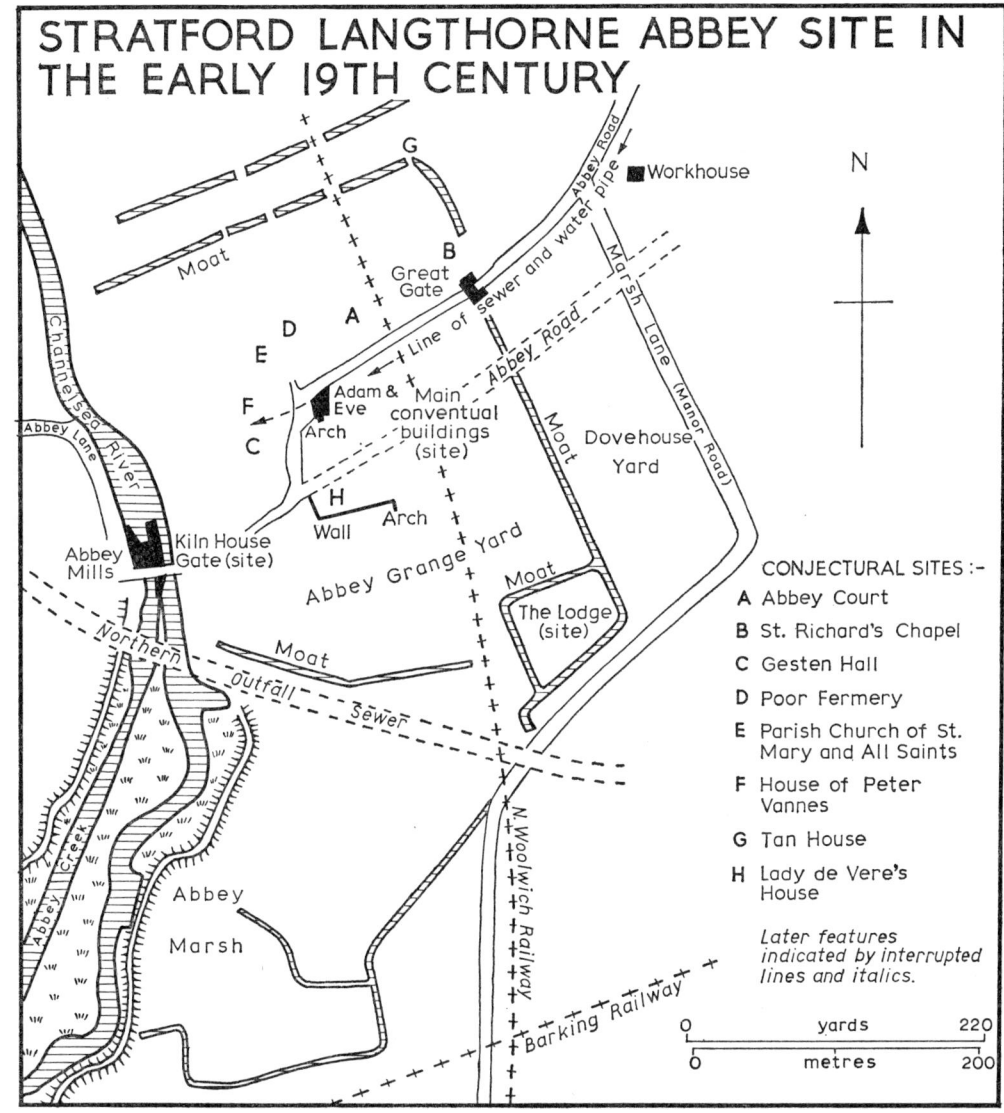

tions, used some of the stone for building and sold much of the rest.[15] In the 1840s the North Woolwich railway was built through the site, running north to south about 70 yd. east of the Adam and Eve. The site was again disturbed by railway works in the 1870s.

The topography of the precincts is not precisely known and the accompanying plan is partly conjectural. The main conventual buildings were probably demolished soon after the Dissolution. They were clearly in the immediate vicinity of the Adam and Eve. The existence of an ancient water-

of the other conventual buildings.[16] Such a layout is also consistent with the position of the abbey court at Stratford which lay on the north side of the precincts. Extensive building seems to have been going on at the abbey in the 13th century.[17] A great west window in the abbey church was mentioned in 1400 as newly built.[18] That work may have been connected with the patronage of Richard II, who came to the help of the abbey when it was in financial difficulties resulting from floods and other causes.[19] Leland's story that floods caused the temporary

[15] E. Nat. xxiv. 143; Lysons, London, iv. 249.
[16] R.C.H.M. Essex, i and ii (Little Leighs, Tilty, Hatfield Broad Oak, Waltham Abbey, Thoby, Barking, Ilford hospital) and V.C.H. Essex, v. 172. In West Essex only Latton and Little Dunmow priories had churches on the north side.

[17] E. Nat. xxiv. 141; Cal. Close 1237–42, 291; bid. 1264–8, 321.
[18] E.A.T. N.S. vi. 308.
[19] Cal. Pat. 1396–9, 143.

evacuation of the abbey probably relates to the same period.[20] When completed the conventual buildings probably occupied a frontage of about 180 yd. on the road through the precincts, and extended south for some 140 yd. Medieval masonry recorded from that area included a 13th-century arch which survived until *c.* 1870 in a wall at the Adam and Eve. Fragments of a two-light window of uncertain date, which are now (1971) in the long porch of All Saints church, West Ham, probably came from the conventual site. They were formerly built into a wall west of the Adam and Eve on the opposite side of the road. All Saints church also has an octagonal font bowl which may originally have come from the abbey. It was found on the site of the leathercloth factory just outside the precincts. Another probable relic of the abbey preserved in the church is a stone carved with five skulls. It was found *c.* 1874 in an ancient burial ground, during railway works near the Adam and Eve. Other sepulchral remains were found in the same area in the 18th and 19th centuries, including stone and lead coffins. It is usually assumed that these were all associated with the abbey, but the mention of urns in one report suggests an earlier period, and it may be significant that the site of the leathercloth factory was once called Barrow field.[21] Various other objects, since dispersed, have been found at the abbey, including an onyx seal depicting a griffin with the legend 'Nunc vobis gaudium et salutem'.[22]

Among the buildings in the precincts in 1539 was the Lodge, a moated house lying on the southern side near Marsh Lane. This may well have occupied the site of a manor-house even older than the abbey.[23] It apparently still existed in 1747, when it was called the Abbey House. Near the west end of the abbey church was a house occupied in 1538 by Lady de Vere and previously by the countess of Salisbury.[24] It was demolished immediately after the Dissolution. On the north side of the precincts was the parish church, dedicated to St. Mary and All Saints, and near it the 'pore fermery' and the 'gesten hall', both leased as private residences. In the same area were several other unnamed houses, one of which was on lease to Peter Vannes, dean of Salisbury. The gesten hall and Vannes's house appear to have survived until the early 19th century. The Abbey Mill, on the Channelsea river, is treated elsewhere.[25] Adjoining it were the bakehouse and kilnhouse. The slaughterhouse was in the grange yard, near the Lodge. A tannery, in the north-east corner of the precincts, went out of use shortly before the Dissolution.[26]

The main (eastern) entrance to the precincts was from Abbey Road through the Great Gate, which stood in the present Baker's Row, about 170 yd. from the Adam and Eve.[27] The gatehouse survived until about 1825. Its outer (eastern) side was of brick, apparently of the late 15th or early 16th century. The inner side was of timber with foliated spandrels. St. Richard's chapel, near the Great Gate, was probably identical with a chapel there mentioned in 1334.[28] It seems to have disappeared by 1576. The western entrance to the precincts was from Abbey Lane through the Kilnhouse Gate.

CHURCHES. During the Middle Ages the parish of All Saints included the whole of West Ham except the precincts of Stratford Abbey, which constituted a separate parish of about 24 a., with its own church of St. Mary and All Saints.[29] After the Dissolution St. Mary and All Saints was destroyed with the rest of the abbey. Its parish became in one sense extra-parochial; the landowners there did not pay tithes. But in other respects it seems to have been merged in the parish of All Saints.

The church of All Saints originated in the 12th century, if not earlier. William de Montfitchet, when he founded Stratford Abbey in 1135, endowed it with, *inter alia*, land in Ham that had belonged to Ranulph the priest.[30] This suggests the existence of a church, but the first explicit reference to one is in a charter of Henry II, probably issued between October 1181 and January 1182, confirming to the same abbey the church of West Ham, given by Gilbert de Montfitchet.[31] About the same time Gilbert Foliot (d. 1187), bishop of London, licensed this appropriation and ordained a vicarage.[32] The advowson of the vicarage was apparently not then given to the abbey, but descended with the Montfitchet estates at least until 1254, when Richard de Montfitchet (d. 1267) was listed as the patron.[33] The abbey did, however, acquire it by 1334, and held it until the Dissolution, since when it has been vested in the Crown.[34]

The rectory also remained with the abbey until the Dissolution. It was subject to an annual pension of £3 to Hatfield Peverel priory in lieu of tithes;[35] this, although not mentioned before the 16th century, may have dated from *c.* 1100, since the founders of the priory, the Peverels, were the lords of Sudbury in West Ham.[36] In 1537–8 the abbey was leasing the great tithes in two separate portions. Those of the area south of Portway were on lease along with New Barns (the rectorial glebe), while the remainder were on lease with the manor of Woodgrange.[37] After the Dissolution the rectory was permanently split up. The great tithes from some 2,480 a. were retained by the Crown and descended along with the manor of West Ham, though in the 18th century they were apparently leased, separately from that manor, to James Smyth of Upton.[38] They were held

---

[20] Cf. *V.C.H. Essex*, ii. 131.
[21] E.R.O., D/CT 160.
[22] Fry, *E. and W. Ham*, 133–4; 'A Layman', *W. Ham Ch.* 14.
[23] Fry, op. cit. 136.
[24] Probably Lady (Margaret) de Vere, mother of John de Vere (d. 1526), earl of Oxford. Margaret Pole, countess of Salisbury, was executed in 1541.
[25] See p. 90.
[26] See p. 77.
[27] The name Baker's Row appears to have originated in the 19th century.
[28] *Cal. Chart.* 1327–41, 306.
[29] For the Abbey and its parish see p. 112.

[30] Dugdale, *Mon. Angl.* v. 587.
[31] Ibid. 587–8; R. W. Eyton, *Itin. Hen. II*, 244.
[32] Newcourt, *Repertorium*, ii. 303; cf. confirmation by Baldwin, Abp. of Canterbury: Harl. Ch. 43 G. 26.
[33] *E.A.T.* N.S. xviii. 16.
[34] Newcourt, *Repertorium*, ii. 304; Fry, *E. and W. Ham*, 187; *Chel. Dioc. Year Bk.* 1966–7.
[35] *L. & P. Hen. VIII*, xiii (1), p. 142; ibid. xiv (2), p. 159; *Cal. Pat.* 1554–5, 142.
[36] *V.C.H. Essex*, ii. 105.
[37] S.C. 6/962.
[38] Morant, *Essex*, i. 22; Lysons, *London*, iv. 264; Ogborne, *Essex*, 22. For the Smyths see above p. 11.

in 1853 by Edward Humphreys[39] and in 1897 by John C. Humphreys.[40] A substantial part of the great tithes in the north of the parish descended with the manor of Woodgrange.[41] Some of these were eventually merged in Woodgrange: in 1853 216 a. comprising Woodgrange, and 32 a., previously belonging to that manor, were thus exempt from great tithes.[42] Other great tithes formerly annexed to Woodgrange must have been alienated by 1853. Some of them probably became attached to the Pelly's estate at Upton:[43] in 1853 Sir John H. Pelly was entitled to the great tithes from 173 a., of which all but 14 a. belonged to his family.[44] By 1853 there were, in addition to Woodgrange, some 1,850 a. land in the parish exempt from great tithes.[45] These included 590 a. of 'Abbey Rate' lands[46] and 109 a. belonging to the Coopers' Company.

The Coopers' land was the ancient rectorial glebe, formerly called New Barns, at Plaistow. When Gilbert Foliot ordained the vicarage, he excluded from it 'the house [curiam] where the barns are', which thus remained part of the rectory.[47] In 1541 Henry VIII leased New Barns for life to his servant Sir Thomas Spert and Spert's son Richard.[48] It was later leased to Henry Fanshawe (d. 1568) of Jenkins in Barking, and the lease apparently descended in his family until 1629, when the trustees of Sir Thomas Fanshawe (d. 1631) also bought the freehold.[49] In 1650 Thomas Fanshawe, son of Sir Thomas, was the proprietor of the 'parsonage impropriate called New Barns'.[50] As a delinquent he was then being forced to augment the vicarages of both West Ham and Leyton from the profits of this impropriation. His son, Sir Thomas Fanshawe, sold New Barns in 1702 to Thomas Owen and William Manlove, from whom it was bought in 1706 by the Coopers' Company with money left in trust by Henry Strode for the endowment of a school and alms-houses at Egham (Surr.).[51] New Barns remained a farm until about 1900 when the Strode Foundation started to develop it for building. The farm lay between New Barn Street and Prince Regent Lane, and an ancient barn, adjoining Cumberland House, survived until about 1900.[52]

In 1254 the estimated value of the rectory was £53 6s. 8d. and that of the vicarage £8[53] The equivalent figures in 1291 were £30 and £8 13s. 4d.[54] The ordination of the vicarage had provided that the vicar should pay 4 marks a year to the priory of Holy Trinity, Aldgate (Lond.) for two small fields evidently adjoining New Barns. This rent was still being paid in 1291, but no later reference to it has been found. In 1517, after a dispute between the vicar and Stratford Abbey, it was agreed that he should surrender his endowments in return for an annual pension of £39 13s. 8d.[55] After the Dissolution the Crown continued to pay this pension until 1638, when the vicar, Peter Blower, obtained a renewal of the original endowments in lieu of it.[56] In 1650 the vicar's glebe and tithes were valued at £60, and he was also receiving £20 in voluntary gifts from his parishioners and £20 augmentation from New Barns.[57] These improvements in the vicar's income were accompanied by an increase in his obligations. From 1644 or earlier until the early 19th century he seems to have been responsible for the maintenance of the chancel of the parish church.[58] In 1644 the churchwardens were paying him £2 for the chancel. This payment, later increased to £3 and then to £5, was kept up until 1682, when a disagreement between the vestry and a new vicar caused it to be discontinued. In 1853 the great tithes of Edward Humphreys were commuted for £164 and those of Sir John Pelly for £56.[59] The vicarial tithes were commuted for £794 together with 8s. an acre on market-gardens. A partial commutation of the small tithes had taken place long before. It was stated in 1853 that the owners of some 830 a. in the parish made ancient prescriptive payments in lieu of small tithes, and that the owners of other tithable lands paid the vicar 4d. an acre.[60] That rate of 4d. had apparently been unchanged for over a century.[61] The early-18th-century writer who first mentions this rate also states that the vicarial glebe had been augmented by bequests; in 1853 it comprised 32 a.[62]

In addition to the income from tithes and glebe the vicar was by the 18th century receiving a substantial income from offerings, fees, pew-rents, and charities.[63] Among the charities was that of Nicholas Avenon (d. 1599), which gradually increased in value up to the later 19th century, and was then transformed by building development into one of the main sources of parochial income:[64] by 1898 it was producing nearly £300 a year, and by 1964 about £2,000. A Chancery scheme of 1913 provided that most of the income should be used for curates' stipends.

The ancient vicarage house of West Ham was at the southern end of Vicarage Lane. That building of unknown appearance still survived in 1853, but by 1809 or earlier it was considered to be unfit for the vicar's use.[65] He and his successors appear to have used rented accommodation until about 1856, when The Farm, Portway, with 4 a. land, was bought for use as a vicarage.[66] That house was altered in 1879, when half the land was sold. In 1936 it was

[39] E.R.O., D/CT 160.
[40] Surrey R.O., S.C. 30/1/57 (Calendar in W.H.L.).
[41] Lysons, London, iv. 264; G.L.C., DL/C/212; E.R.O., D/DB T1135, 1137; ibid. D/DXb 3; Morant, Essex, i. 19–20.
[42] E.R.O., D/CT 160.
[43] See p. 12.
[44] E.R.O., D/CT 160.
[45] Ibid.
[46] See p. 59.
[47] Newcourt, Repertorium, ii. 303.
[48] L. & P. Hen. VIII, xvii, p. 692.
[49] Misc. Gen. Her. ii. 282, 292; Lysons, London, iv. 255–6; V.C.H. Essex, v. 200.
[50] H. Smith, Eccl. Hist. Essex, 248.
[51] Surrey R.O., S.C. 30/1/1–64 (Calendar in W.H.L.).
[52] K. Fry, E. and W. Ham, 253; W.H.L., Illus. Coll. (Houses); J. S. Curwen, Old Plaistow, 16–17.

[53] E.A.T. N.S. xviii. 16.
[54] Tax. Eccl. (Rec. Com.), 22.
[55] Newcourt, Repertorium, ii. 303–4.
[56] Lysons, London, iv. 264.
[57] H. Smith, Eccl. Hist. Essex, 248.
[58] E.R.O., D/P 256/5 passim; W.H.L., W. Ham Vestry Mins. 25 Mar. 1682, 12 Aug. 1735, 1 Jan. 1818.
[59] E.R.O., D/CT 160.
[60] Ibid.
[61] Fry, E. and W. Ham, 219, quoting MS. notes (not wholly reliable) by an anonymous farmer of W. Ham.
[62] Ibid.; E.R.O., D/CT 160.
[63] Fry, E. and W. Ham, 219. For the ecclesiastical charities see below p. 163.
[64] See p. 159.
[65] E.R.O., D/CT 160; Guildhall MS. 9560.
[66] A. W. W. Wallace, W. Ham Church, 9.

demolished, part of the site being used to develop Vicar's Close, at the south end of which a new vicarage was built.[67] The house in Portway was a large early-19th-century building, apparently on the site of an older and smaller one, to which had belonged a range of thatched out-buildings, also demolished in 1936.[68]

The architecture of All Saints church, described below, shows that by the 15th century it was of good size, fit for a populous parish near London. During the later Middle Ages there are occasional references to clergy assisting or deputizing for the vicars.[69] Robert Paynter (d. 1538), the last vicar presented by Stratford Abbey, showed by his will that his interests included theology, history, and music, and that he had been friendly with clergy and laymen in several of the neighbouring parishes.[70] Thomas Rose, presented in 1552, was a zealous Protestant whose inflammatory preaching, 20 years earlier, had provoked the theft and destruction of the rood at Dovercourt. He was ejected for marriage in 1554, but restored after the accession of Elizabeth I.[71] In 1555–6 18 Protestants were burnt at Stratford and Bow, including 13 who died in one fire. The memory of this never faded from local tradition and in 1879 it was commemorated by the erection, in St. John's churchyard, of a memorial to the martyrs.[72] Peter Blower (1638–44), whose re-endowment of the vicarage has already been mentioned, appears to have suffered sequestration in 1644 and to have died in the same year.[73] Of his five immediate successors the last, Thomas Walton (1656–60), was ejected at the Restoration.[74] William Marketman (1660–71) officiated for some months before being presented to the vicarage on the petition of the parishioners.[75] Richard Hollingsworth (1671–82) had been Marketman's curate for five years, and also secured the living on local recommendation.[76] These are the earliest occasions on which the parishioners can be shown to have influenced the appointment of vicars, but the tradition of popular choice probably went back to the early 17th century: at least one parish lecturer, William Holbrook (d. 1629), has been noticed before the Civil War.[77] A lecturer appointed in 1728[78] had several successors in the 18th century,[79] including William Dodd (1752–66) 'the macaroni parson', later executed for forgery.[80] According to some of his verses Dodd preached to a crowded congregation including several noblemen.[81] In 1766 there were two Sunday services, each with a sermon, also prayers on Wednesdays, Fridays, and Holy days.[82] In recent years the accommodation of the church had been increased by the erection of new galleries, a new organ had been installed, and a paid organist was being employed.[83] During the 18th century the vicars seem usually to have resided in the parish, though some also performed duties in London.[84] George Gregory (1804–8) is said to have obtained the living for political services.[85]

Hugh C. Jones (1809–45), also archdeacon of Essex, built West Ham's first two new churches, at Plaistow and Stratford. Canon Abel Ram (1845–68), Canon Thomas Scott (1868–91), and Canon Richard Pelly (1891–1916) each worked vigorously for church extension, in a period when West Ham's population increased by over 270,000.[86] Scott began the highly profitable development of the Avenon charity estate. Pelly continued this, and in 1912 also founded the West Ham Evangelical Trust, to promote the teaching of 'the Protestant and evangelical party in the Church of England' within this parish and that of St. Matthew, West Ham, and to provide an income for church building maintenance. The doctrinal object of the trust was clearly to combat the strong Roman Catholic and Anglo-Catholic movements in West Ham. Its practical scope was later widened to include poor-relief and prizes for school children. By 1964 its total income was £82.[87] In 1898 Pelly's staff comprised 3 curates, 2 lay readers, 2 women workers, and a parish nurse.[88] During the First World War Pelly's successor, Canon Guy Rogers, employed four women as curates for everything except the administration of the sacraments.[89]

The ancient parish church of *ALL SAINTS*, Church Street, consists of nave, chancel, north and south aisles, north and south chapels, west tower, south vestries, and two south porches.[90] The walls are mainly of ragstone and flint rubble, with white brick on the south and east, Reigate stone in the tower, and red brick in the north chapel. The church dates from the late 12th century, but was considerably altered in the 13th century, when it included a crossing and probably transepts, and again in the 15th century, when the crossing and transepts were demolished, the nave lengthened eastwards, and the present tower built. The north chapel was rebuilt about 1547. In 1803 the south aisle, south chapel, and east wall were refaced with yellow brick. During the 18th century north, south, and west galleries were added, but these were all removed in the later 19th century. The vestries were built in 1892–4.

A church existed on this site in the late 12th century: on each side of the nave there are three blocked clerestory windows of that period. In the

[67] Inf. from the Vicar.
[68] W.H.L., Illus. Coll. (Houses); ibid. Vert. File E/WES/728; Chapman and André, *Map of Essex*, 1777 sheet xxi.
[69] *E.A.T.* N.S. vi. 307–8; *Misc. Gen. Her.* 5th ser. vii. 9.
[70] *Misc. Gen. Her.* 5th Ser. vii. 19.
[71] Lysons, *London*, iv. 265; *Trans. R. Hist. S.* 4th ser. xxii. 150.
[72] Fry, *E. and W. Ham*, 159–61; W.H.L., Vert. File, E/WES/272. 6; W. J. Bolton, *A Martyrs' Memorial* (1875) and *Sketches of the Lives and Deaths of . . . Protestant Martyrs* (1878).
[73] *E.R.* xxxii. 178.
[74] Ibid. 178–9; H. Smith, *Eccl. Hist. Essex*, 193, 406–7.
[75] *Cal. S.P. Dom.* 1660–1, 235.
[76] Ibid. 1671, 563.
[77] B.M. Sloane MS. 271, f. 73; *E.A.T.* N.S. vi. 308.
[78] W.H.L., W. Ham Vestry Mins. 25 Jan. 1727/8.

[79] Ibid. 2 July 1730, 17 May 1748, 25 Aug. 1752, 11 Oct. 1770, 31 May 1787, 2 Mar. 1799.
[80] *D.N.B.*
[81] Fry, *E. and W. Ham*, 190.
[82] Guildhall MS. 9558, f. 170.
[83] Vestry Mins. 9 Feb. 1749; and see below.
[84] Guildhall MS. 9550; ibid. 9556, f. 63; *Gen.* N.S. vii. 155.
[85] *D.N.B.*
[86] Fry, *E. and W. Ham*, 192–3.
[87] Char. Com. File 226033.
[88] *Churches of Barking Deaneries* (1898), 3. For Pelly's early work see *Stratford Express*, Suppl. 10 Mar. 1894.
[89] *Essex Churchman*, May 1967.
[90] Unless otherwise stated this account of the building is based on: R.C.H.M., *Essex*, ii. 250; A. W. W. Wallace, *W. Ham church* (1934); E.R.O., T/P 196 (H. W. King MSS.), Eccl. Essex, iii, ff. 121–90; R. H. Clutterbuck, 'A wall painting . . . in West Ham church, with . . . notes on recent alterations . . . there', *E.A.T.* iv. 45–52.

Stratford Broadway in 1861, showing St. John's Church and the Gurney Memorial

All Saints Church, Alms-houses, and School in 1769

WEST HAM

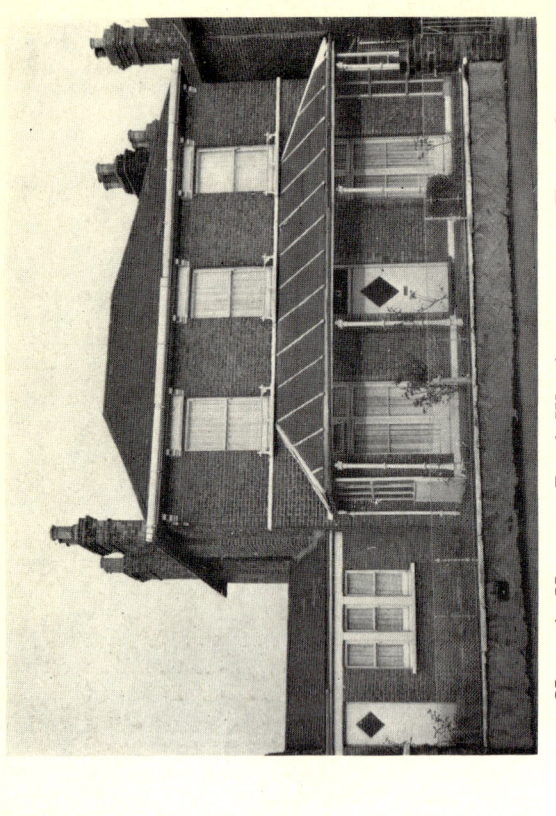

House in Hampton Road, Woodgrange estate, Forest Gate, built *c.* 1880

Mabel Terrace, Cedars Road, Stratford, built 1876

Wilton's Yard, Angel Lane, Stratford, in 1934

Houses in Balaam Street, Plaistow, built *c.* 1840

WEST HAM

mid 13th century the nave was largely rebuilt and given north and south arcades of five bays. The crossing which then existed appears to have been demolished about 1400, when the nave was extended eastwards by two bays, re-using material from the former transept arches; the chancel arch was rebuilt and the tall west tower, with south-eastern stair-turret, was added. In the mid 15th century a north chapel with an arcade dividing it from the chancel was built, and a little later a south chapel. The north aisle was probably rebuilt in the late 15th century, since several of its windows seem to be of that date. Wall-paintings, probably of the 15th century, were uncovered in the nave during 19th-century restorations, but were too imperfect for preservation. About 1547 the north chapel was rebuilt in dark red brick by the churchwardens, whose successors stated in 1548 that this had been done without the consent of the whole parish, and that funds for it had been raised by the sale of church property, including the communion plate and a house at Stratford.[91] This chapel, which externally is a fine example of Tudor brickwork, has a projecting rood-stair turret on the north side.

In 1707–8 over £500 was raised for church repairs and alterations,[92] which probably included the erection in 1710 of a west gallery,[93] where an organ was placed in 1731.[94] A south gallery, apparently replacing a smaller one, was added about 1727, and a similar north gallery in 1735.[95] In 1763 the vestry resolved to undertake further alterations including the rebuilding of the west gallery, and the insertion of two new dormer-windows, one above the north aisle, the other on the north side of the nave.[96] A drawing of the church from the south, made in 1769, shows a dormer-window in the nave.[97] A drawing from the north-east, made in 1794, shows three dormers in the north aisle and one in the nave.[98] Work done in 1788–90 included alterations to the pulpit, and the rebuilding of the churchyard walls in connexion with road widening.[99] A long south porch, in the form of a classical colonnade, which ran across the churchyard into Church Street, may have been built then: it certainly existed in 1799.[1] In 1800–3 substantial repairs were carried out at a total cost of nearly £3,000.[2] These included the refacing with yellow stock brick of the south aisle, the south chapel, and the east wall of the chancel, and probably also the insertion of the two dormers in the south aisle, shown in a drawing of 1808.[3] A sundial on the south wall of the south chapel is dated 1803.

In 1821–4 the north, south, and west galleries seem to have been again enlarged to meet the demand for sittings caused by the growth of the parish.[4] The third dormer in the north aisle was probably added at this time.[5] It was stated in 1827 that the church could seat only 1,400 out of an estimated population of 11,500.[6] During the 1830s the building of new district churches began to relieve this pressure. In 1847–9 All Saints was restored by George Dyson and (Sir) George Gilbert Scott.[7] The old box-seats were replaced by modern pews providing more free sittings. There were other alterations designed to lighten the church, probably including the replacement of the old dormers in the nave by the present small windows, comprising five triplets on each side, which were certainly in existence by 1861.[8] In 1865–9 the west gallery was removed, some new windows were inserted, and other repairs done.[9] This work was again directed by Scott, who also designed a new reredos. Alterations in 1879–80 probably included the removal of the north gallery.[10] In 1892 there was a further restoration, by C. C. Winmill.[11] The last remaining (south) gallery was removed, the south aisle was repaired, and new vestries were built at the south-west corner of the church. Some time in the 19th century the long south porch with its classical columns was replaced by the present structure in Jacobean style. In the 20th century there have been no important alterations, though much has been spent on maintenance. During recent years malicious damage has become a serious problem: between 1964 and 1968 this cost about £6,000 to repair.[12]

In 1804 Thomas Holbrook gave the royal arms to be placed at the east end of the church.[13] This is probably the arms, crudely and inaccurately re-painted, now (1968) above the chancel arch. There is another royal arms, of William IV, on the wall of the south aisle, beside the vestry door.

At the east end of the north aisle is a font dated 1707 with a plain octagonal bowl. A larger font, given by Lewis Angell in 1869, stands at the west end of the nave.[14] At the west end of the north aisle are the remains of a third font, possibly from Stratford Abbey.[15]

The original organ, placed in the west gallery in 1731, was replaced by a new one about 1821.[16] In 1865–6 this was removed to the north aisle, repaired and enlarged.[17] It was rebuilt in 1892 and again about 1924.[18]

In 1737 the six existing bells were recast by Samuel Knight as a peal of eight.[19] In 1752 Knight's successor, Robert Catlin, appears to have recast two of the bells and added two new ones. The present ten include four by Catlin, three by Knight, and

[91] *E.A.T.* n.s. xiii. 157–8.
[92] E.R.O., D/P 256/5, f. 484.
[93] Fry, *E. and W. Ham*, 179.
[94] Ibid.; W.H.L., W. Ham Vestry Mins. 21 Nov. 1731.
[95] Vestry Mins. 27 May, 10 June 1727, 19 July–18 Oct. 1735.
[96] Vestry Mins. 1 Mar., 5 Apr. 1763.
[97] E.R.O., Pictorial Coll. See plate f.p. 116.
[98] Guildhall Libr., Lysons, *London* (extra-illus.), iv, after p. 256.
[99] Vestry Mins. Jan.–Sept. 1791; W.H.L., W. Ham Churchwardens' Accs. 1788/9 and 1789/90.
[1] Guildhall Libr., Lysons, *London* (extra-illus.), iv, after p. 256.
[2] Ibid.
[3] W.H.L., Illus. Coll. (Churches).
[4] Vestry Mins. 24 Apr. 1821, 9 Apr. 1822, 31 Mar. 1824.
[5] Ibid. 1 Jan. 1818.

[6] Ibid. 25 Jan. 1827.
[7] Vestry Mins. 23 Sept. 1847, 13 Feb., 13 Sept. 1849; W.H.L., Plans of proposed alterations to W. Ham church, 1847–8 (G. Dyson and G. G. Scott, architects.)
[8] E.R.O., T/P 196 (King MSS.), Eccl. Essex., iii, f. 121.
[9] Vestry Mins. 9 Mar. 1865–1 Dec. 1869.
[10] W. Ham Ch., Ch. Ctee. Mins. 6 June, 5 Sept. 1879, 26 July 1880.
[11] Ibid. 29 Jan.–6 May 1892.
[12] Inf. from Vicar.
[13] Vestry Mins. 25 Apr. 1804.
[14] Ch. Ctee. Mins. 3 Nov. 1869.   [15] See p. 114.
[16] Vestry Mins. 24 Apr. 1821, 5 Apr. 1825.
[17] Ch. Ctee. Mins. 28 Jan., 30 Aug., 11 Dec. 1865, 21 Mar. 1866.
[18] *E.R.* ii. 202, iv. 143; McDougall, *Fifty Years a Borough*, 280; inscription on organ.
[19] Vestry Mins. 19 Feb., 3 Sept., 7 Nov. 1737.

one each by Thomas Mears (1795), C. & G. Mears (1846), and J. Warner & Sons (1852).[20]

The plate includes a cup and cover, a pair of patens, and a flagon, all of 1693.[21] A cup dated 1718 and four alms-dishes dated 1718 (one) and 1737 (three) appear to have been given in 1738 by Edward Flower.[22] A pewter alms-dish dated 1702 was given in 1959 by the West Ham Evangelical Trust in memory of Canon Pelly.[23]

The church contains many monuments.[24] Under the western arch of the north chapel is a late-15th-century altar-tomb with an indent of the figures of a man and two wives. On its sides are panels containing shields of arms, including those of the Brewers' Company, the Goldsmiths' Company, and possibly the Mercers' Company. On the south respond of the chancel arch is a brass to Thomas Staples (1592), tanner, and his four wives. In the south aisle is a tablet to Nicholas Avenon (1599), merchant tailor, formerly on an altar-tomb.[25] In the chancel is a wall monument, with kneeling figure, to John Faldo (1613) and a similar one to his brother Francis (1632). In the north chapel, behind the organ, is a monument to Robert Rooke (1630), captain of the trained band of this hundred, showing him in armour, with figures of his two wives and seven children. In the south chapel is the monument of William Fawcit (1631) depicting his wife and her second husband, William Toppesfield, as kneeling figures, with Fawcit himself reclining below.[26] In the north chapel, side by side, are two fine monuments with standing figures, one to Sir Thomas Foot, Bt. (1688), lord mayor of London,[27] the other to James Cooper (1743). A later lord mayor, Sir James Smyth (1706), is commemorated by a ponderous classical monument in the south chapel. Also in the south chapel is a monument with kneeling figures by Edward Stanton, to Amhurst Buckeridge (1710) and his brothers and sisters. There is an altar-tomb in the north chapel to Sir Philip Hall (1746) and his family. Among other monuments is one in the north aisle to John Finch (1748), lecturer of West Ham.

The church contains several fragments from Stratford Abbey, including the font mentioned above.[28]

The chapel of St. Katherine on Bow Bridge existed in 1344, when its custody was granted by the king to John de Ware, a hermit.[29] Another Stratford hermit occurs in 1370,[30] and there are occasional references to St. Katherine's chapel in the mid 15th century.[31] There may have been a link between the chapel and a leper hospital, which in 1315 lay in a meadow owned by the priory of Stratford Bow on Queen Maud's Causeway at Stratford.[32]

From the 16th century onwards All Saints church remained the only Anglican place of worship until

the building of St. Mary, Plaistow (1830), and St. John, Stratford (1834), both of which became parish churches in 1844. Two more new parishes were formed in 1852: Christ Church, Stratford Marsh, and Emmanuel, Forest Gate. By 1900 there were 17 parish churches and some 24 other churches within the borough. In 1903 the Anglican congregations in West Ham numbered about 17,600 a Sunday.[33] They comprised less than 32 per cent of the total worshippers, the lowest proportion in outer London except in one very small place.[34] They were, however, ahead of the other denominations in providing welfare services, both through the normal parochial organization, and through university and public school settlements,[35] and in the southern slums of the parish they had a higher proportion of the worshippers (39 per cent) than they did in the borough as a whole, in contrast to the nonconformists.[36] Their educational work is also notable. Church day-schools were built in 13 out of the 17 parishes created before 1900, though some closed after the formation of the school board.[37]

By 1910 there were 19 parish churches and some 28 others. After the First World War three more parishes were formed. During the Second World War most churches suffered bomb-damage, and all were affected by depopulation. This made a thorough reorganization inevitable. In 1961 the Church Commissioners confirmed a scheme (under the Reorganization Areas Measure, 1944) dealing with all except two of the parishes in the borough.[38] Five parishes ceased to exist and there were many smaller boundary changes. Two other parishes disappeared by amalgamation, in 1962 and 1966 respectively, thus reducing the total, in West Ham, to 15. The reorganization of the two Thames-side parishes, St. Barnabas and St. Mark, Victoria Docks, had not been completed by 1966. There were then only 14 parish churches and 8 other churches in the borough.

The following accounts of individual churches and missions are arranged by parishes, listed in the order of their formation. Scattered Sunday schools and temporary mission rooms are not usually included. Where it is stated that the advowson of a parish was vested in the bishop, this means the bishop of the diocese which then or later included West Ham. Details concerning the parish reorganization of 1961 are taken from the Church Commissioners' order, already mentioned.

In All Saints parish a large church hall, with ancillary rooms, was opened in Meeson Road in 1884.[39] A mission room was opened in Napier Road in 1889.[40] This may have been the predecessor of the mission church of *ST. JUDE*, Stephen's

[20] *Ch. Bells Essex*, 277–8.
[21] *Ch. Plate Essex*, 54–5.
[22] Ibid.; Vestry Mins. 8 July 1738; Fry, *E. and W. Ham*, 180. One of the almsdishes may have been re-cast from two older dishes.
[23] Inf. from Vicar.
[24] They have been fully described in print, with others now lost: R.C.H.M., *Essex*, ii. 251–2; Fry, *E. and W. Ham*, 201–14; Lysons, *London*, iv. 257–63. See also: J. Stow, *Survey of Lond.*, ed. J. Strype (1720), ii, App. 112–14; E.R.O., T/P 196 (King MSS.), Eccl. Essex., iii, ff. 121–90; W.H.L., Clutterbuck Coll.
[25] Lysons, *London*, iv. 261.
[26] Chancellor, *Sep. Mons. Essex*, 377.
[27] Ibid. 379.
[28] See p. 114.

[29] *Cal. Pat.* 1343–5, 352.
[30] *Reg. Sudbury* (Cant. and York Soc.), ii. 87.
[31] *Cal. Pat.* 1452–61, 220, 300.
[32] K.B. 27/219 m. 72: this is the only known reference to the hospital.
[33] Mudie Smith, *Relig. Life of London*, 352–6.
[34] Ibid. 444.
[35] See p. 141.
[36] Cf. p. 125.
[37] See also pp. 145–51.
[38] W.H.L., W. Ham Church Reorg. Scheme 1961, Order and Maps; cf. *Essex Churchman*, June 1961.
[39] *Chs. Barking Deaneries*, 3; Fry, *E. and W. Ham*, 193–4.
[40] W.H.L., E/WES/283: List of Docs. in Vestry, All Saints Ch.

Road, opened in 1898.[41] The Manor Road mission hall was opened about 1900.[42] A Charity Commission scheme of 1941 provided for it to be sold and the proceeds used for the maintenance of the remaining missions in the parish.[43] The Holbrook Road mission hall, also opened about 1900, was dilapidated and disused by 1957, when authority was obtained to sell it.[44] *ALL SAINTS* church for the deaf and dumb, East Road, though situated in All Saints parish, exists to serve all deaf and dumb people in east London, and has its own special organization. It originated in 1905, when the Royal Association in aid of the Deaf and Dumb bought a church previously used, it seems, by the West Ham Park Congregationalists, and reopened it as the Constance Fairbairn memorial church. It was rebuilt in 1959.[45] In 1961 most of the former parish of St. Thomas, West Ham, was again merged with that of All Saints.

The church of *ST. MARY*, Plaistow, St. Mary's Road, was built in 1830 as a chapel of ease to All Saints, on a site given by Sir John H. Pelly. It was a brick building designed by Thomas Curtis in a late Perpendicular style, with pinnacled turrets and a clock-tower.[46] West of it were added the National school (1831) and a hall for the men's guild (1836).[47] A separate parish was formed in 1844, the advowson of the vicarage being vested in the vicar of West Ham.[48] During the incumbency of W. B. Marsh (1842–84) the population of Plaistow was increasing rapidly, and much mission work was done, leading to the formation of the new parishes of St. Mark, Victoria Docks, The Holy Trinity, St. Andrew, and St. Gabriel, and the building of St. Peter's. Thomas Given-Wilson (vicar 1884–1914) was the outstanding figure in the history of the parish. He recruited a team of trained nurses to tend poor parishioners, opened two convalescent homes at Southend-on-Sea, founded a children's hospital, organized penny dinners, and sold second-hand clothes. By the 1890s the philanthropic work of St. Mary's was costing about £8,000 a year, which he raised by world-wide appeals.[49] His pamphlets describing poverty at Plaistow caused resentment among the more independent residents, partly because they were thought to have caused a decline in property values there.[50] He also rebuilt the parish church on a much larger scale, to seat 1,000. The new building, in the Early English style, was completed in 1894 to the design of Sir Arthur Blomfield. It is of yellow brick with grouped lancet windows and a tall double bellcote. During Given-Wilson's time St. Peter's church and

that of St. Matthias (opened 1887) were assigned their own parishes. The mission church of *ST. KATHERINE*, Chapman Road, was opened in 1891 in a building previously used as the infants department of St. Mary's day-schools; a permanent church was completed in 1894.[51] It was demolished in 1965 as part of a redevelopment scheme.[52] The mission church of *ST. THOMAS*, Northern Road, was built in 1898 and was demolished about 1950.[53] In 1912 Given-Wilson founded an institute named after him, independent of St. Mary's, and he retained control of it, after his retirement, until his death in 1916.[54] In 1935 the Given-Wilson institute was vested in a new committee with the vicar of St. Mary's as vice-chairman and secretary.[55] Its building was originally the Pelly Road United Free church, later the Upton Manor Congregational church.

The church of *ST. JOHN*, Stratford, The Broadway, was built in 1834 as a chapel of ease to All Saints, at Stratford (or Gallows) Green, on the island site at the junction of the Leytonstone and Romford Roads.[56] A separate parish was formed in 1844, the advowson of the vicarage being vested in the vicar of West Ham. St. John's, designed by Edward Blore in the Early English style, is of yellow brick with tall south-western tower and spire. The chancel was added in 1885 as a memorial to Sir Antonio Brady. The church was badly damaged by bombing in the Second World War but restored in 1951.[57] The martyrs' memorial (1879), in the churchyard, which is a polygonal Gothic structure designed by J. T. Newman, is thought to mark the site where the Protestants were burnt under Mary I.

Parts of St. John's parish were transferred to those of St. Paul (1865) and St. James (1881). A mission hall in connexion with St. John's was built in Chant Square in 1872 or soon after.[58] It continued in use until 1946. The mission church of *THE HOLY TRINITY*, Oxford Road, in connexion with Trinity College, Oxford, was founded in 1888, and finally closed in 1945 after bombing.[59] The iron mission church of *ST. STEPHEN*, Cedar Road, opened about 1883, was replaced in 1917 by a brick building.[60] This was closed in 1943 after bombing. The parishes of Christ Church and St. James were merged with that of St. John in 1961 and 1966 respectively. In 1961 St. John also acquired part of the former parish of St. Thomas.

CHRIST CHURCH, Stratford, High Street, was built in 1852 to serve Stratford Marsh.[61] A separate parish, taken from that of All Saints, was assigned in the same year.[62] Thomas Curtis contributed to

[41] Ibid.; *Chs. Barking Deaneries*, 3.
[42] *W. Ham C.B.C. Mins.* 24 July 1900; Mudie Smith, *Relig. Life Lond.* 352.
[43] Char. Com. File 122890.
[44] *W. Ham C.B.C. Mins.* 24 July 1900; Mudie Smith, *Relig. Life Lond.* 352; Char. Com. File 226033.
[45] *Wilson and Whitworth's W. Ham and Stratford Almanac*, 1914; *Essex Churchman*, Oct. 1959; and below, p. 131.
[46] J. S. Curwen, *Old Plaistow*, 30–1; *Stratford Express*, Suppl. 14 Apr. 1894.
[47] Foundation stones.
[48] *Lond. Gaz.* 20 Aug. 1844 (pp. 2902–4).
[49] W.H.L., pE/WES/283, *Out of the East End Fogs* (1890); *Chs. Barking Deaneries*, 7; *Stratford Express*, Suppl. 14 Apr. 1894.
[50] *Stratford Express*, 7 Mar. 1908; Curwen, *Old Plaistow*, p. vii.
[51] *Chs. Barking Deaneries*, 7; Char. Com., *W. Ham Char. Rep.* 1899, 129–30.

[52] Inf. from Vicar of Plaistow.
[53] *Chs. Barking Deaneries*, 7; inf. from Vicar of Plaistow.
[54] Inf. from Vicar of Plaistow; *Stratford Express*, 20 June 1914 and 20 Nov. 1916.
[55] *Chel. Dioc. Chron.* Oct. 1935, 153.
[56] See plate f. p. 116. Account based on: *Chs. Barking Deaneries*, 5; Pevsner, *Bdgs. of Essex*, 342; *Stratford Express*, Suppl. 9 June 1894; W.H.L., E/WES/029. 3, Scrapbook; *Lond. Gaz.* 20 Aug. 1844 (pp. 2902–4); inf. from Canon C. A. Fox.
[57] *Essex Churchman*, Jan. 1958.
[58] *W. Ham L.B. Mins.* 28 May 1872; *Kelly's Dir. Essex*, 1882.
[59] See also p. 141.
[60] *W. Ham L.B. Mins.* 8 May 1883; *Chel. Dioc. Chron.* June 1916, Feb. 1917.
[61] Account based on: H. Reseigh, *Christ Church, Stratford, 1852–1962*; *Chs. Barking Deaneries*, 11; inf. from Canon C. A. Fox.
[62] *Lond. Gaz.* 3 Dec. 1852 (pp. 3510–11).

the cost of the site and the building. Schools were erected first, and then the church, a stone building designed by John Johnson in 14th-century style with a north tower and spire.[63] In 1862 the vicarage was endowed and the advowson was vested in five trustees headed by the vicar of West Ham.[64] The advowson was acquired in 1888 by the Simeon Trust.[65] A mission was opened in Ward Road in 1882, and the church of *ST. AIDAN* was built there in 1895–9 to the design of Sir Banister Fletcher, the chancel being added in 1908.[66] St. Aidan's was closed in 1944 after bombing and was later demolished. There was another mission in Biggerstaff Road by 1906.[67] Christ Church parish was united with that of St. John in 1961.

The church of *EMMANUEL*, Forest Gate, Romford Road, was opened in 1852, and in the same year a separate parish was formed from parts of West Ham (All Saints) and East Ham, the advowson being vested alternately in the vicars of those two parishes.[68] The building, erected at the expense of the Revd. T. Cornthwaite, was designed by Sir Gilbert Scott in the Decorated style, using Kentish ragstone. By 1889 it had been slightly enlarged and in 1890 the north aisle was rebuilt on a larger scale in the Perpendicular style, forming a second nave with a new porch and choir vestry. The church suffered bomb damage during the Second World War, but was repaired. Parts of the parish were transferred to those of St. James (1881), St. Saviour (1884), All Saints, Forest Gate (in East Ham) (1886), and St. Mark (1894). About 1893 ritualism at Emmanuel caused some of its members, led by a churchwarden, to secede and form a Free Church of England in Earlham Grove.[69] In 1962 the parish of St. Peter was united with that of Emmanuel, the advowson being vested in the bishop.

The church of *ST. MARK*, Victoria Docks, North Woolwich Road, originated in 1857, when an iron building, also used as a school, was erected.[70] A permanent brick church was built in 1862, designed in an unorthodox Victorian Gothic style by S. S. Teulon. A separate parish was formed in 1864 from parts of St. Mary, Woolwich (Kent) and East Ham. It was provided that the first presentation to the vicarage was to be by Charles Capper, manager of the docks,[71] after which the bishop of London was to be the patron. In 1884 the advowson was transferred to the corporation of the City of London.[72] Henry Boyd, vicar 1862–75, built the church of St. John, North Woolwich (in Woolwich) (1872), to

which a parish was assigned in 1877, and planned that of St. Luke, Victoria Docks (1875). He was a pioneer of sanitary reform in the area.[73] The church of St. Matthew, Custom House, built in 1860, became a mission of St. Luke's. The church of St. Barnabas, opened in 1882, remained a mission of St. Mark's until 1926. St. Mark's survived the Second World War and now (1966) stands isolated amid the warehouses, roads, and railways of the reorganized dock area.

The church of *ST. PAUL*, Stratford, Maryland Road, originated about 1850 when a City Missionary opened a Sunday school at Stratford New Town, for which, in 1853, a building was erected in Queen Street by Samuel Gurney.[74] Although New Town was in St. John's parish, the vicar of St. John's, William Holloway, was half-hearted in his support of the mission, and in 1856 A. J. Ram, vicar of All Saints and patron of St. John's, obtained a site for a new church. Holloway resented this interference and a quarrel ensued, as the result of which Ram apparently took over the mission.[75] An iron hall, erected in 1859, was replaced in 1864 by the permanent church of St. Paul on the present site, built with help from Thomas Fowell Buxton and Raymond Pelly. A separate parish, taken out of St. John's, was assigned in 1865. The advowson of the vicarage was at first vested in trustees, including Buxton and Pelly, but by 1949 had been acquired by the Church Patronage Society.[76] The mission church of *ST. MARK*, Windmill Lane, originated in 1877, with services for factory girls held in a shop in Leytonstone Road. An iron hall was later erected, being replaced in 1891 by a permanent building.[77] St. Mark's was damaged by bombing during the Second World War, and after the war was sold to the Methodists.[78] Between 1891 and 1894 missions were also opened in the west of the parish, in Chandos Road and Leyton Road.[79] In 1945 St. Paul's was destroyed by a German rocket. A new church was consecrated in 1953.[80] In 1954 a bell of 1642 by Miles Graye, previously in the church of St. Giles, Colchester, was placed in the tower of St. Paul's, but it was found to be cracked and was subsequently removed.[81]

The church of *THE HOLY TRINITY*, Canning Town, Barking Road, originated in 1857 when the vicar of St. Mary's, Plaistow, and (Sir) Antonio Brady formed the Plaistow and Victoria Docks mission, to serve the rapidly-growing area previously called Hallsville.[82] In 1861 Brady built a new National school in Barking Road, which was used

[63] E.R.O., Pictorial Coll.
[64] *Lond. Gaz.* 22 July 1862 (pp. 3652–6); 8 Aug. 1862 (p. 3943).
[65] Inf. from Simeon's Trustees.
[66] Pevsner, *Bdgs. of Essex*, 374.
[67] *Kelly's Dir. Essex*, 1906; for a possible earlier reference see W. Ham L.B. Mins. 22 Feb. 1881.
[68] Account based on: *Lond. Gaz.* 3 Dec. 1852 (pp. 3510–11); *Chs. Barking Deaneries*, 9; W.H.L., *St. James's Bazaar Prog.* (1908); inf. from Revd. J. J. Wright.
[69] See p. 131.
[70] Account based on: *Chs. Barking Deaneries*, 13; *Lond. Gaz.* 5 Feb. 1864 (pp. 544–5).
[71] For Capper see *White's Dir. Essex* (1863), 619.
[72] Inf. from Corporation of London.
[73] *Chel. Dioc. Chron.* Apr. 1922, p. 57. He was Principal of Hertford College, Oxford, from 1877 until his death in 1922, at the age of 91.
[74] Account from: *Chs. Barking Deaneries*, 15; *Lond.*

Gaz. 12 Sept. 1865 (pp. 4399–400); *Essex Churchman*, Jan. 1965; W.H.L., R. H. Clutterbuck Coll., *Proposed New Church in Hudson Town* (pamph. 1856).
[75] Cf. *White's Dir. Essex* (1863), p. 616.
[76] Cf. *Lond. Gaz.* 11 Feb. 1879 (pp. 664–6); *Crockford* (1949–50).
[77] Foundation stone.
[78] See p. 134.
[79] *Chs. Barking Deaneries*, 15, cf. Mudie Smith, *Relig. Life Lond.* 352; *Kelly's Dir. Essex*, 1906.
[80] *Chel. Dioc. Chron.* Mar. 1952, p. 22; *Essex Churchman* Jan. 1953; *Architect and Building News*, 2 July 1953.
[81] W.H.L., Illus. Coll. (Churches) and C. Whitwell, 'Dictionary of W. Ham'; inf. from Vicar.
[82] Account from: *E.R.* vi. 68; J. W. Hayes, *Hist. Holy Trinity* (1925); *Chs. Barking Deaneries*, 17; *Lond. Gaz.* 6 Mar. 1868 (pp. 1512–13); W.H.L., E/WES/283, *St. Andrew's Mission, Plaistow* (1866); inf. from Revd. F. G. Steel.

also for worship until 1867, when the church was opened opposite on the Hermit Road corner.[83] A new parish, taken from those of St. Mary and All Saints, was formed in 1868. The advowson, originally vested in the bishop, was in 1886 transferred to the Lord Chancellor, so that the benefice could be augmented from the revenues of All Hallows, London Wall.[84] In 1894 the mission of *ST. ALBAN AND THE ENGLISH MARTYRS*, Cooper Street, was opened under the sponsorship of Malvern College. This grew into the dockland settlement, now the Mayflower family centre.[85] Its church was rebuilt in 1930 as that of *ST. GEORGE AND ST. HELENA*.[86] Another mission, opened in Woodstock Street by 1898, survived for some years.[87] Holy Trinity was badly damaged by bombing in 1941, re-opened in 1942 but finally closed in 1948. It was later sold to the borough council, which demolished it and built flats on the site. The parish was administered by the vicar of St. Matthias until 1961, when most of it was merged in his parish, smaller parts being transferred to those of St. Luke and St. Cedd.

The church of *ST. ANDREW*, Plaistow, Barking Road, originated in 1860, when a small mission (later that of St. Philip) was built in Whitwell Road in connexion with St. Mary's.[88] St. Andrew's itself was opened in 1870 on a site, given by the Revd. A. Kent, a few yards south of the northern outfall sewer embankment. The large stone building, designed by James Brooks, is in an Early English style with an apsidal chancel and large but uncompleted crossing tower; a spire, of which the fontcover may be a model, was part of the original plan. A separate parish was formed in 1871, the advowson of the vicarage being vested in the bishop.[89] Schools were added in 1873 and a parish hall in 1883. Under its first vicar George Godsell (retired 1898) St. Andrew's established a distinctive ceremonial tradition in the face of strong opposition from Bishop Claughton. During the Second World War St. Andrew's suffered heavy bomb damage. Extensive repairs were carried out after the war, and in 1957 the old school was rebuilt as a family centre.[90] The church of *ST. PHILIP*, Whitwell Road, remained in use as a mission after the building of St. Andrew's. In 1894 it was taken over by the Society of the Divine Compassion and became the centre of their settlement at Plaistow.[91] It was destroyed by bombing in 1941, but services continued in borrowed premises. In 1953 the S.D.C. was taken over by Anglican Franciscans, and in 1955 a new church of yellow brick with an Italian-style tower, dedicated to *ST. PHILIP AND ST. JAMES*, was opened.[92] The mission church of *ST. MARTIN*, Boundary Road, was built in 1894. For a period

between the two world wars it served a conventional district,[93] but it has since reverted to its original status.

The church of *ST. LUKE*, Victoria Docks, Boyd Road, planned by Henry Boyd, Vicar of St. Mark's, was consecrated in 1875, and in the same year a separate parish was formed from part of St. Mark's.[94] The advowson of the vicarage, originally vested in the bishop, was in 1886 transferred to the Lord Chancellor, so that the benefice might be augmented out of the revenues of All Hallows, London Wall.[95] The church is a lofty building in the Early English style, with an apsidal chancel and a flèche instead of a tower. The Boyd workmen's institute was built at the same time.[96] The church of St. Matthew, Custom House, previously a mission of St. Mark's, passed to St. Luke's, and remained in that parish until it became separate in 1920. The church of The Ascension (1887) remained a mission of St. Luke's until 1905. A Lascar mission, under an Indian curate, was opened in 1887; in 1898 this was one of three centres serving the docks. By 1890 there was also a mission in Ford Park Road,[97] probably the predecessor of the present (1966) St. Alban's mission, Butchers Road. St. Luke's was badly damaged by bombing in 1940. Services continued in a garage until the church hall was repaired.[98] Temporary repairs to the church were carried out in 1949, and permanent reconstruction was completed by 1960. Since the Second World War this part of West Ham has been redeveloped as the Keir Hardie estate, and in 1961 the parish was also augmented by parts of the parishes of The Holy Trinity, St. Gabriel, and St. Matthew, Custom House. In 1965 the Boyd institute was rebuilt as a youth centre.

The church of *ST. GABRIEL*, Canning Town, Wellington Street, originated about 1868. A map of that year shows an unnamed iron church between the river Lea and the railway, just north of Barking Road, in the position later occupied by St. Gabriel's.[99] A brick building was consecrated in 1876.[1] St. Gabriel's was at first a mission of West Ham, but in 1879 a separate parish was formed from parts of West Ham, St. Mary's, and St. Andrew's. The advowson of the vicarage, originally vested in the bishop, was in 1886 transferred to the Lord Chancellor, so that the benefice could be augmented from the revenues of All Hallows, London Wall.[2] In 1884 services were started in Hermit Road, where an iron church was erected in 1896. Another mission was started in Clifton Road, where the church of *ST. FAITH* was built in 1891–2. A third mission, in Grange Road, was opened in 1891. Of these only St. Faith's appears to have remained in use by the 1920s.[3] St. Gabriel's itself was damaged during the Second World War, and was demolished about

---

[83] For the school see p. 148.
[84] Inf. from Lord Chancellor's Eccl. Office.
[85] See p. 142.
[86] *Chel. Dioc. Chron.* May 1930, p. 80.
[87] Cf. *Kelly's Dir. Essex*, 1906, 1908.
[88] Account from: *Chs. Barking Deaneries*, 19; inf. from Revd. E. A. Shipman; Pevsner, *Bdgs. of Essex*, 288.
[89] *Lond. Gaz.* 7 Nov. 1871 (pp. 4507–8); *Rtns. New Parishes*, H.C. 413, p. 46 (1881), lxxii.
[90] *Essex Churchman*, Feb. 1957.
[91] See p. 143.
[92] *Life of Fr. Andrew, S.D.C.*, ed. K. E. Burne, 75–7; *Essex Churchman*, May 1955; W.H.L., Illus. Coll. (Churches), St. Philip's.
[93] *Chel. Dioc. Chron.* July 1929.

[94] Account from: *Chs. Barking Deaneries*, 21; *Chel. Dioc. Chron.* Apr. 1922, p. 57; *Lond. Gaz.* 29 Oct. 1875 (pp. 5100–2); *St. Luke's Year Bk.* 1966; inf. from Revd. L. R. Moore.
[95] Inf. from Lord Chancellor's Eccl. Office.
[96] *Building News*, 23 Apr. 1875.
[97] *Kelly's Dir. Essex*, 1890.
[98] *Essex Churchman*, Dec. 1959.
[99] E.R.O., D/AEM 2/12, cf. (for the date) 2/7.
[1] Account from: *Chs. Barking Deaneries*, 22; W.H.L., E/WES/283, List of Docs. in All Saints' Vestry (St. Gabriel's, 1878); *Lond. Gaz.* 22 Aug. 1879 (pp. 5115–16); K. Fry, *E. and W. Ham*, 193.
[2] Inf. from Lord Chancellor's Eccl. Office.
[3] *Kelly's Dir. Essex*, 1926.

1955. In 1961 part of the parish was merged in that of St. Matthias, the remainder going to St. Luke.

The church of *ST. JAMES*, Forest Gate, Forest Lane, originated about 1870, when an iron building was serving a conventional district.[4] A separate parish, taken from those of Emmanuel, St. John's, and All Saints, West Ham, was formed in 1881, the advowson of the vicarage being vested in the bishop. A permanent church was completed in 1882. The organ came from the church of St. Matthew, Friday Street (Lond.), and is said to have been built in the 18th century by George England. During the incumbency of G. W. Hanford (1895–1925) the church and schools were enlarged and parish halls were built. The church was demolished in 1964, after which its congregation met in the chapel of the Durning Hall community centre.[5] In 1966 the parish of St. James was united with that of St. John.

The church of *ST. SAVIOUR*, Forest Gate, Macdonald Road, originated in 1880, when an iron mission hall was opened in connexion with Emmanuel.[6] A large permanent church was opened in 1884, and a separate parish, taken from Emmanuel, was formed in the same year. The advowson, at first vested in trustees,[7] was conveyed in 1933 to the Church Pastoral Aid Society. The first vicar, Henderson Burnside, had been one of the first Anglican missionaries in Japan, and he worked vigorously at St. Saviour's in support of foreign missions. In 1903 St. Saviour's had a mission at '365, Railway Arches'.[8]

The church of *ST. THOMAS*, West Ham, Rokeby Street, was opened about 1878 as a mission of All Saints.[9] In 1889 the original iron building was replaced by one of brick, and in 1891 a new parish was formed from part of All Saints, the advowson of the vicarage being vested in the bishop. During the Second World War St. Thomas's was damaged by bombing and was closed. It was demolished in 1957 and in 1961 the parish ceased to exist, most of it being merged again with All Saints and a smaller part with St. John.

The church of *ST. MARK*, Forest Gate, Tylney Road, originated in 1886 as a mission of Emmanuel, to serve the area between Romford Road and Wanstead Flats.[10] Services were first held in a rented cow shed on the site of nos. 65–7 Tylney Road, and in 1888 an adjacent site was bought in Tylney and Lorne Roads. To avoid debt the church was built in three stages. Half the nave was consecrated in 1893, the other half, with the aisles, porch, and temporary chancel, in 1896. A permanent chancel was completed in 1898. The building is in the

Early English style, of red and yellow brick with stone facings; there is an eastern belfry. New vestries and a baptistery were added in 1925. A separate parish was formed in 1894 from parts of Emmanuel and All Saints, Forest Gate (in East Ham), the advowson of the vicarage being vested in the Church Patronage Society.[11]

The church of *ST. PETER*, Upton Cross, Upton Lane, originated as a mission in Pelly Road, in connexion with St. Mary, Plaistow. Services were held first in a barn, then in an iron church, licensed in 1877.[12] In 1885 the bishop of St. Albans' fund bought Upton House, Upton Lane, once the home of Lord Lister. The first part of St. Peter's church was built in the garden in 1893, Upton House itself becoming the vicarage and parish rooms. The church is a tall building of red and yellow brick in the Early English style with a chancel screen of open brick arches on black marble columns. A separate parish was formed in 1894, taken from All Saints (West Ham), St. Mary, Emmanuel, and St. Stephen, Upton Park (in East Ham). The advowson was vested in the bishop.[13] By 1906 there was a mission church in Gwendoline Avenue.[14] This was bombed during the Second World War and was not rebuilt.[15] In 1962 St. Peter's parish was united with Emmanuel.[16] The former vicarage was demolished in 1968.[17]

The church of *ST. MATTHEW*, West Ham, Vaughan Road, originated about 1891, when R. A. Pelly, vicar of All Saints, opened a mission to serve the area between Romford Road and West Ham Park.[18] A permanent building of flint and brick was completed in 1896, and a separate parish was formed in 1897. The first vicar, A. Armitage, provided an endowment of £140, a vicarage house, and an organ. The advowson was at first vested in trustees, but in 1933 was conveyed to the Church Pastoral Aid Society.[19] About 1900 St. Matthew's opened a mission in Vicarage Lane.[20] This was destroyed by bombing in the Second World War and the sale of the site was authorized in 1951.[21] St. Matthew's was included in the scheme for the West Ham Evangelical Trust, formed by Canon Pelly in 1912.[22]

The church of *THE ASCENSION*, Victoria Docks, Baxter Road, originated in 1887, when a mission hall was built by the vicar of St. Luke's.[23] This became the special charge of the Felsted School mission, which had previously been working at Bromley (Mdx.). Felsted provided a club room in 1892. A new church was built in 1903–7, to which a separate parish, taken from St. Luke's, was assigned in 1905; the advowson of the vicarage was vested in the bishop. A mission house for women workers was

---

[4] *Kelly's Dir. Essex*, 1870. Account from: W.H.L., pE/WES/283, *St. James's Carnival*, 1908; *Lond. Gaz.* 22 July 1881 (pp. 3593–5); *Chel. Dioc. Chron.* Aug. 1925, p. 125; inf. from Revd. J. S. Froud and Canon C. A. Fox.
[5] See p. 143.
[6] Account from: *Chs. Barking Deaneries*, 23; *Rtns. Parishes Divided*, H.C. 386, p. 21 (1890–1), lxi; inf. from Church Pastoral Aid Soc.
[7] E.R.O., D/CP 6/17.
[8] Mudie Smith, *Relig. Life Lond.* 352: i.e. under the viaduct of the Tottenham and Forest Gate Railway.
[9] Account from: W.H.L., E/WES/283, Docs. in All Saints Ch. (St. Thomas's, 1878); *Chs. Barking Deaneries*, 24; *Rtns. Parishes Divided*, H.C. 302, p. 14 (1897), lxvii (vi); *Stratford Express*, 18 Jan. 1957; *Essex Churchman*, June 1961.
[10] Account from: F. S. Sidall, *These Fifty Years* (1936); *Chs. Barking Deaneries*, 26–7.

[11] *Rtns. Parishes Divided*, H.C. 302, p. 5 (1897), lxvii (vi).
[12] *Chs. Barking Deaneries*, 29; *Kelly's Dir. Essex*, 1878; W. Ham L.B. Mins. 10 July 1877.
[13] *Rtns. Parishes Divided*, H.C. 302, p. 8 (1897), lxvii (vi).
[14] *Kelly's Dir. Essex*, 1906; cf. *W. Ham C.B.C. Mins.* 25 July 1905.
[15] Local inf.
[16] Inf. from the Vicar of Emmanuel.
[17] For its description see p. 53.
[18] Account from: *Chs. Barking Deaneries*, 31.
[19] *Crockford* (1902 f.); inf. from C.P.A.S.
[20] *W. Ham C.B.C. Mins.* 19 June 1900; Mudie Smith, *Relig. Life Lond.* 352.
[21] Char. Com. File G. 22 (West Ham).
[22] Char. Com. File 226033; and see above, p. 116.
[23] Account from: *Chel. Dioc. Chron.* Dec. 1917, p. 220; Apr. 1942, p. 46; Aug. 1946, p. 62; *Kelly's Dir. Essex*, 1908 foundation stones of the church; inf. from the Vicar.

opened in 1909 and still existed in 1966. During the Second World War, when the parish was depopulated by bombing, the clergy of The Ascension also had charge of the parish of Sandon, near Chelmsford, the vicar of which was then a prisoner of war in Japan. Felsted continues to give financial support. In 1961 most of the former parish of St. Matthew, Custom House, was merged with The Ascension.

The church of *ST. MATTHIAS*, Canning Town, Hermit Road, originated in 1887, when the vicar of St. Mary's, Plaistow, opened a mission in Garfield Road, with help from St. Matthias's church, Torquay (Devon).[24] This mission was merged in 1906 with that of *ST. CYPRIAN*, Beaconsfield Road, for which an iron church had been built in 1896.[25] In 1907 the church was built in Hermit Road, and a separate parish was formed from parts of St. Mary, St. Andrew, and St. Gabriel, the advowson of the vicarage being vested in the bishop.[26] In 1961 parts of the parishes of St. Gabriel and The Holy Trinity were merged with that of St. Matthias.

The church of *ST. MATTHEW*, Custom House, Victoria Docks, Ethel Road, was a small building erected in 1860 at the expense of the chairman of the Dock company, Charles Morrison.[27] It was a mission of St. Mark's and later of St. Luke's until 1920, when a separate parish was formed, the advowson of the vicarage being vested in the bishop. After the Second World War St. Matthew's was administered by the clergy of The Ascension. The church was closed in 1960, and in 1961 the parish was divided between those of The Ascension (which took most of it) and St. Luke. By 1966 St. Matthew's had been demolished in the course of redevelopment.

The church of *ST. BARNABAS*, West Silvertown, Eastwood Road, was built in 1882 as a mission of St. Mark's.[28] In the Silvertown explosion of 1917 the chancel was blown away and an iron hall destroyed.[29] Temporary buildings were used until 1926, when a new church was completed and a separate parish was formed, mainly from St. Mark's, with a small part from St. Luke's. The advowson of the vicarage was vested in the bishop.[30] In 1934 a 16th-century bell from the demolished church of Markshall was given to St. Barnabas.[31] After the Second World War the parish was administered by the vicar of St. John's, North Woolwich.[32]

The church of *ST. CEDD*, Canning Town, Beckton Road, was originally a mission of St. Andrew's.[33] A brick hall was built in 1903–4 on a site given by R. Foster. In 1905 a mission district was formed from parts of St. Andrew's and St. Luke's.[34] This became a separate parish in 1936, the advowson of the vicarage being vested in the bishop in 1938.[35] A new red-brick church, in Romanesque style, was opened in 1939 as a memorial to 'Tom' Varney, the first mission curate, whose nephew, John Varney became the first vicar.[36] In 1961 part of the parish of Holy Trinity was included in that of St. Cedd.

Voluntary settlements and community centres, most of which have had religious affiliation, are treated elsewhere.[37]

ROMAN CATHOLICISM. In 1903 the total attendance at Roman Catholic churches in West Ham was higher than that for any other borough in outer London.[38] The percentage of Roman Catholic worshippers was also far above the average for the area: 11·8 compared with 6·2 for the whole of outer London.[39] These high proportions were due mainly to Irish immigration, starting in the 18th century. A previous tradition of recusancy seems to have died out in the 17th century.

Margaret, widow of Sir John Throgmorton, incurred fines for non-attendance at church, and harboured a priest, James Young, during her residence at Upton from *c.* 1585 to 1591.[40] Some of her land was sequestered to pay the fines.[41] Several other West Ham recusants occur in records between 1577 and 1617.[42]

In 1706 there was said to be only one English papist, Mary Belchier, in West Ham, the other papists being the family and employees of a French calico-printer, Didier Richard.[43] By 1767 an influx of Irish labourers had raised the total to 53, and in 1780 it was 160.[44]

There are entries starting in 1770 in the baptismal and marriage register preserved at the Franciscan friary in Grove Crescent Road, and this is the traditional date for the foundation of the parish of Stratford, the first Roman Catholic parish in Essex.[45] About 1788 services were being held by Thomas Wright (d. 1799)[46] in a rented house at Plaistow. In 1789 he sought authority to rent a house in West Ham Lane, with two fields adjoining, which he registered for worship in 1791.[47] Wright was succeeded by John Jones (1799–1801) and John Singleton (1801–2).[48] Joseph Porter became chaplain in 1802, and in 1806 advertised for funds, pleading the extreme poverty of his congregation. He started a school, known first as Chapel House academy, then as Gaston Hall academy.[49] In 1810 this ran into

[24] *Chs. Barking Deaneries*, 7.
[25] *E.R.* vi. 4; *Stratford Express*, 27 Oct. 1906.
[26] *Crockford* (1908).
[27] Account from: *Chel. Dioc. Chron.* Mar. 1921, p. 36; ibid. Dec. 1941, p. 143; *Chs. Barking Deaneries*, 21; inf. from Revd. H. R. Cresswell.
[28] *Chs. Barking Deaneries*, 13; and see above, p. 120.
[29] *Stratford Express*, 21 Jan. 1917.
[30] *Chel. Dioc. Chron.* Dec. 1925, p. 189; Mar. 1926, pp. 39, 70; Aug. 1926, pp. 126, 133; Char. Com. File 104959.
[31] *Chel. Dioc. Chron.* July 1934, p. 111; cf. *Ch. Bells Essex*, 337.
[32] Inf. from the Vicar of St. John's, North Woolwich; *Essex Churchman*, May 1966; personal observation.
[33] Account based mainly on inf. from Vicar of St. Cedd.
[34] *Kelly's Dir. Essex*, 1906, 1908.
[35] E.R.O., D/CPc 290.
[36] *Chel. Dioc. Chron.* Sept. 1938, p. 135; Oct. 1938, p. 158; Jan. 1940, p. 5; July 1943, p. 56.

[37] See pp. 141 sqq.
[38] R. Mudie Smith, *Relig. Life Lond.* 444. The Rt. Revd. Brian Foley, Bishop of Lancaster, provided some of the information for this section.
[39] Ibid. 444, 447.
[40] *Essex Recusant*, ii. 4–5; Assizes 35/30/T, 15 July 1588, 27 July 1590; *Cal. S.P. Dom.* 1591–4, 257–8, 161–2.
[41] *Cath. Rec. Soc.* xviii. 114.
[42] *Essex Recusant*, i. 77, 108; ii. 117; *Cath. Rec. Soc.* xxii. 50; xviii. 114; E 377/24; Assizes 35/39 Trin. (Essex) 28 July 1617.   [43] Guildhall MS. 9800.
[44] *Essex Recusant*, iii. 93–100.
[45] B. Ward, *Dawn of Cath. Revival*, i. 42; inf. from Fr. C. Frost O.F.M.   [46] *Laity's Dir.* (1800).
[47] Westminster Archives, vol. xlii, no. 169; G.R.O., Rtns. of places of worship certified to . . . Qtr. Sessions, 19.
[48] *Cath. Rec. Soc.* xxvii. 10.
[49] *Essex Recusant*, i. 82; *Laity's Dir.* (1804, 1806, 1807, 1809); see below, p. 147.

debt, Porter absconded, and François-Joseph Chevrollais, a Frenchman who had taught at the school, took charge of the Stratford mission. Later in the same year the Catholics registered a chapel at Stratford Green.[50] This may have been the chapel occupying part of a dwelling-house (formerly the forest gaol) mentioned in a survey of the period; the congregation was said in 1813 to have been deprived of their place of worship 'by the death of a gentleman at whose house their chapel formerly was'.[51]

Chevrollais renewed the appeals for money, and in 1813 the church of *ST. VINCENT DE PAUL AND ST. PATRICK* was built on the south side of High Street, Stratford, between Channelsea Bridge and Harrow Bridge. As a precaution against rioters there were no windows on the High Street front.[52] The church also served the Roman Catholics in seven or eight neighbouring parishes; by 1820 the congregation was said to consist of over 1,200 labouring Irish.[53] Chevrollais opened a parish school for boys and girls. He continued to beg for money and to use his private fortune until his death in 1823.[54]

For the next thirty years the Stratford church and schools struggled against poverty, dilapidation, and the increasing population; the number of Easter communicants compared badly with those of other Essex congregations.[55] James McQuoin (d. 1870), who was appointed rector in 1856, found the High Street church inadequate and the schools closed. There had been no confirmations for 8 years. With great energy he set about raising money. He opened schools at Victoria Docks, and at Upton, where in 1862 he helped to establish St. Angela's Ursuline convent.[56] At last, in 1868, he was able to open the new church of *ST. VINCENT DE PAUL*, Grove Crescent Road, with a school-hall below. It is a red brick building with stone dressings in a simple Renaissance style, with a small spired bell turret at the west end. In 1873 the church was taken over by the Franciscan Friars Minor, and its dedication was changed to *ST. FRANCIS OF ASSISI*.[57] It was enlarged in 1931 and is still (1966) administered by the Franciscans, whose friary is in the Grove. The friars also served the chapel of *ST. PATRICK*, Lett Road, opened in 1897 and closed in 1945.[58]

Although Roman Catholic services had previously been held at the Ursuline convent, Upton Lane, it was not until 1884 that the Forest Gate parish, served by the Franciscans, was established, and the foundation stone of the church of *ST. ANTONY OF PADUA*, Khedive (later St. Antony's) Road, was laid. By 1891 the church, St. Bonaventure's school, and the friary buildings were completed to the design of Pugin & Pugin. They form an impressive group, all of yellow brick with lancet windows. The large church is in the Early English style.[59] By 1903, with Sunday congregations totalling over 2,600, St. Antony's was the strongest Roman Catholic church in Greater London.[60] According to Joseph McCabe, a former friar at St. Antony's, this success was the result of migration by 'the better middle-class Catholics from all parts of London' and 'nearly every priest in East London was exasperated against the friars for stealing his best parishioners'.[61] A convent of Franciscan minoresses in Clova Road, Forest Gate, removed to Maldon about 1957.[62]

James McQuoin started work in the Victoria Dock area in 1856. The iron chapel of *ST. MARGARET AND ALL SAINTS*, Barking Road, was opened in 1859, and Canning Town became an independent parish in 1870. The present building was consecrated in 1919.[63] The war memorial church of *OUR LADY OF SORROWS*, Wilberforce Street (later Killip Close), was built in 1925 as a chapel of ease to serve the Tidal Basin area. Within the same parish the Franciscan missionaries of Mary built a convent in Bethell Avenue in 1902 and added their chapel of the *SACRED HEART OF JESUS* in 1931. The convent, and St. Margaret's church, were damaged during the Second World War, when the congregation occupied premises in Chargeable Lane.[64] St. Margaret's was restored in 1951, and in 1966 the church of Our Lady of Sorrows was reconstructed as Bennett Hall for St. Margaret's Youth Club.[65]

The church of *ST. ANNE*, Throckmorton Road, Victoria Docks, with school attached, was opened in 1899. War damage was repaired in 1950–1 and a new presbytery built in 1953–4.[66]

The church of Our Lady and St. Edward, Silvertown, originally in West Ham but later rebuilt in East Ham, is treated under that place.

PROTESTANT NONCONFORMITY. There has been a continuous tradition of nonconformity in West Ham since the 17th century. The Friends were active there by 1656, and by 1671 had formed a meeting at Plaistow, which survived until the present century. During the 1670s and 1680s there are several references to dissenters,[67] including some Presbyterians (1672) who were the probable founders

[50] *Essex Recusant*, i. 82–6.
[51] E.R.O., D/DCy P23: the survey is dated 1815 but some of it was probably compiled a few years earlier, cf. E.R.O. D/P 256/28/1; *Laity's Dir.* (1813).
[52] *Laity's Dir.* (1813–16); E.R.O., D/P 256/28/3; *Brentwood Dioc. Year Bk.* (1953), 87 (illus.).
[53] *Laity's Dir.* (1816); *Ordo Recitandi Officii Divini* (1820).
[54] *Ordo* (1820, 1824, 1825). For the school see below, p. 147.
[55] Westminster Archives, B4 (L. & P. Bishop Griffiths, V. A.), pp. 35–6, 46.
[56] Westminster Archives, L. & P. Cdnl. Wiseman, (1856) Box W3/31–4, Nos. 115, 189 (1862–3), Box W3/35–8, Nos. 65, 127–8, 133, 146, 149a and b; for St. Angela's see: *Uptonian*, xxxix (1961–2); *Franciscan*, May 1962.
[57] F.S. of St. Francis's ch.; F. Sainsbury, *W. Ham*, 79; *Kelly's Dir. Essex* (1878).
[58] McDougall, *Fifty Years a Borough*, 284; *Cath. Dir.* (1943); inf. from Fr. C. Frost O.F.M.
[59] Pevsner, *Buildings of Essex*, 416.
[60] McDougall, *Fifty Years*, 284; F.S. of St. Antony's ch.; Mudie Smith, *Relig. Life Lond.* 355 and *passim*.
[61] J. McCabe, *Twelve Years in a Monastery*, 63.
[62] *Brentwood Dioc. Year Bk.* (1953); inf. from Fr. Andrew O.F.M.
[63] *St. Margaret and All Saints, Centenary*, 1959.
[64] Sainsbury, *W. Ham*, 79; McDougall, *Fifty Years*, 284–5; *Cath. Dir.* (1943).
[65] *Brentwood Dioc. Year Bk.* (1953); *St. Margaret's News*, 17 Apr. 1966.
[66] *Brentwood Dioc. Year Bk.* (1953); inf. from parish priest.
[67] *Cal. S.P. Dom.* 1670, 221; ibid. 1680–1, 422–3; Assizes 35/118/1, 35/124/2, 35/125/2; E.R.O., Q/SR 435/100; Hist. MSS. Com. *11th Rep. App.* VII, 16.

of Brickfields chapel, later Congregational, which still existed in 1967. No other permanent congregation was formed until about 1790, when an Independent meeting-house was opened at Plaistow, and a Methodist one at Stratford. By 1851 there were ten nonconformist churches in West Ham, belonging to the Baptists (two), Congregationalists (four), Friends, Wesleyan Methodists, Wesleyan Association, and Primitive Methodists.[68] By 1870 there were about 30, and in 1903, when the *Daily News* census was taken, the total was at least 90, with Sunday congregations totalling about 31,000.[69]

In 1903 the nonconformists comprised 56 per cent (compared with the Anglicans' 32 per cent) of the total worshippers, a figure well above the average for outer London, though lower than that for East Ham.[70] Many of them were meeting in small groups, but on the other hand they had 21 churches out of the 38 with total Sunday congregations of over 500, including five that were larger than any Anglican church. The Congregationalists, with 7,318 worshippers, were then the strongest of the free churches. As well as having had a long start over their rivals in West Ham they had benefited from the leadership of such able men as John Curwen. They were followed by the Baptists (5,351 worshippers), Wesleyans (4,305), Primitive Methodists (2,698), and United Free Methodists (1,954). Most of the smaller sects were also represented. The Peculiar People, a sect native to south Essex and north Kent, had two congregations.

A writer commenting on the *Daily News* census pointed out that a large proportion of West Ham's church-goers came from the middle-class areas of Upton and Forest Gate.[71] This was especially true of the nonconformists. Their numerical superiority was greatest there, and smallest in the slums of Canning Town, Silvertown, and Victoria Docks. None of the principal free churches had made much progress in those southern slums. The most successful were the Primitive Methodists, nearly half of whose adherents were there. While their success may have been partly due to the fact that their connexion was more working-class in character than most of the larger denominations, they owed it mainly to the efforts of one outstanding minister. Their success is notable in relation to their slender resources. Measured against the needs of the area it is less impressive. Between Barking Road and the Thames their congregations numbered only 1,300 (some of whom were no doubt 'twicers') out of a total population of about 80,000.[72] The total attendance at all the free churches in that area was some 6,600, compared with 6,000 for the Anglicans. Very few of the free churches in the slums of West Ham seem to have been providing the recreational and welfare facilities that were so badly needed there.[73] One important exception was the Congregational church in Barking Road, which was linked with the Mansfield House university settlement. Others were the non-sectarian Conference Hall, in West Ham

Lane, and the Baptist Tabernacle in Barking Road, where Robert Rowntree Clifford was minister.

After 1903 the number of nonconformist churches in the borough fell slowly, to about 70 in the 1930s. The decline in their congregations was probably more rapid. There are no comprehensive statistics, but such membership figures as are known usually fell steeply between the two world wars, except in places like the Barking Road Tabernacle where there was continuity of good leadership. This decline was greatest in the northern parts of the borough, from which most of the middle-class inhabitants had departed to suburbs farther east. The church remaining in that area tended to find itself with a reduced income, struggling to maintain large and ageing buildings still burdened with debts optimistically incurred at their erection in more prosperous times. All these causes of decay are illustrated in the later history of the Methodist church in Harold Road, Plaistow.

The Second World War hastened the process of decline, by bombing and by evacuation. After 1945 war damage compensation made it possible to rebuild some of the bombed churches, but many were not revived. Some wartime unions between congregations became permanent; other unions took place soon after the war. By 1966 there were only 41 free churches in West Ham—less than half the peak figure. Of the main denominations the Baptists had held their ground best, with 10 remaining, compared with 14 in 1903. The Congregationalists retained only 5 (15 in 1903) and the Methodists 5 (20 in 1903). The Methodists had suffered more severely from bombing than the others, which gave them opportunities for local reorganization and rebuilding, especially at Forest Gate and Canning Town, that were not altogether unwelcome.

The free church congregations in 1966 were much smaller than those at the beginning of the century. The Congregationalists, who had had 2,740 members in 1900, had then only 249.[74] Baptist numbers were 1,500 and 855 respectively. The Baptist Central mission, with 347 members in 1966, was then still one of the strongest churches in West Ham, though even this had greatly declined from its peak of over 1,000 in the 1930s.[75]

The following accounts of individual churches were, in most cases, completed in 1964–6. The dates in brackets after ministers' names show the period of their pastorates. Attendance statistics for 1903 are taken from the *Daily News* census.

Baptists.[76] There were Baptists in West Ham in 1676[77] but no permanent congregation was then formed. At the end of the 18th century Baptists helped to found the Plaistow Congregational church (Balaam Street), but the first churches of which they had undivided control were at Stratford.

The Ark chapel, Francis Street, Maryland Point, was registered for worship by Francis Bell in 1834.[78] It was still used by the Baptists in 1848, when it was

---

[68] H.O. 129/7/194.
[69] R. Mudie Smith, *Religious Life of London*, 352–6.
[70] Ibid. 356, cf. 444. In calculating this percentage 'other services' have been included in the nonconformist total.
[71] Ibid. 340.
[72] In 1901 the three southern wards of the borough had 79,637 inhabitants.

[73] For 'The Ideal Church for East London' see *Relig. Life Lond.* 43.
[74] *Cong. Year Bks.* 1900, 1966.
[75] *Bapt. Handbks.* 1900–67.
[76] In this sub-section figures of membership and the names and dates of ministers are taken, unless otherwise stated, from the annual *Baptist Handbook*.
[77] *Hist. MSS. Com. 11th Rep. App.* VII, 16.
[78] G.R.O., Rtns. Noncf. Mtg. Ho. before 1852, no. 1819.

said to have been built in 1832.[79] In 1851 it was taken over by the Primitive Methodists.[80]

The Central Baptist church, the Grove, Stratford, originated in 1852, when G. W. Fishbourne from Bow (Lond.) started services in Rokeby House.[81] In 1854 a site was bought on the corner of Manbey Grove, on which soon afterwards Stratford Grove, later called the Grove church, was built.[82] A Sunday school was opened in 1861.[83] James H. Banfield, minister 1875–95, was the founder of two charities for West Ham.[84] During the pastorate of W. H. Stevens (1895–1909) the church prospered, but membership fell rapidly under his successor.[85] In 1917, however, the Grove was joined by the members of the Stratford Tabernacle, with their minister W. P. Hicks, editor of the *Christian Herald*. The combined congregation, called the Central Baptist church, flourished for a few years, but has steadily declined since the 1920s. The building was damaged during the Second World War but was repaired.[86]

The Stratford Tabernacle, Carpenters Road, was probably founded about 1870 by Dr. Gratton Guiness, of Harley College, Bow Road (Lond.), and first met in rented premises in Barnby Street.[87] In 1877 the Tabernacle, seating over 800, was built in Carpenters Road, between High Street and Rosher Road.[88] During the ministry of G. Towner (1877–90) membership was over 200 and the Sunday school flourished.[89] After 1900 numbers fell, and in 1917 the congregation therefore joined that of the Grove. The Tabernacle was sold to the Y.M.C.A. It was destroyed during the Second World War.[90]

The West Ham Central mission, Barking Road, was founded in 1871. For some years before this Baptists had been trying to establish themselves in south West Ham. A group at Plaistow formed by J. E. Cracknell in 1858 lasted only until the following year.[91] Another, which in 1863–4 was meeting in Barking Road, Canning Town, later moved to Bow.[92] Also in 1863 W. Palmer came from Poplar (Lond.) and built Mount Zion chapel, Barking Road.[93] This remained his property, and after he died in 1867 the members moved to a barn in Anne Street.[94] Most of them soon transferred to Providence chapel, Shirley Street,[95] but a few carried on, and in 1871 Henry Lester and others leased Mount Zion and formed a new church,[96] from which sprang the West Ham Central mission.[97] Its membership rapidly increased, and in 1876 under R. H. Gillespie (1873–89) a new building, the Barking Road Tabernacle, was erected with the aid of £1,000 from James Duncan, a Silvertown sugar refiner and philanthropist. Mount Zion was sold, later became the

Labour Hall, and was destroyed in the Second World War. In 1887 a branch church, which still existed in 1966, was founded in Wythes Road, Silvertown.[98]

After Gillespie's departure the Tabernacle, burdened with debt, was almost forced to close, but Robert Rowntree Clifford, who became pastor in 1897, immediately revived and soon transformed it. By 1900 the debt had been cleared, 139 new members had been added, and there was a Sunday school of 500. In 1903 another branch church was opened in North Woolwich Road, West Silvertown; this was closed about 1939, and the site was later sold.[99] A third branch, in Prince Regent Lane, Custom House, became independent in 1915. Local unemployment after 1900 led Clifford to found the West Ham Baptist mission as a relief and welfare organization in conjunction with the Tabernacle. The mission, which issued its first report in 1905, gradually gained support from Baptists throughout the world. As early as 1907 larger church and mission buildings were being planned. These were completed in 1922 on a new site in Barking Road, at a total cost of £68,000. In 1926 the old Tabernacle was converted into a children's church. Several old people's homes and two country convalescent homes were also provided.

During this expansion of the West Ham Central mission, as it was now called, Clifford recruited a staff of full-time deaconesses, for whom Marnham House Settlement, Barking Road, was built in 1916, and of assistant ministers, including his brother, E. O. Clifford (1920–9). The membership of the mission rose during the 1930s to over 1,000. During the Second World War the basement of the children's church, equipped as an air-raid shelter, became the community centre in this heavily-bombed area. Most of the mission buildings were damaged in 1940–1 but were repaired. R. R. Clifford remained superintendent until his death in 1943, controlling its affairs with undivided authority. A trust deed of 1944 vested ownership and government in an undenominational church council and superintendent, with an executive committee. The new superintendent was Paul Clifford (1943–53), Robert's son and assistant. After the war the membership declined to 347 by 1966, but the mission was still active, and in touch with the social needs of the area. The main building (1922) is of red brick and stone in an elaborate Byzantine style with two domed towers. The old Tabernacle had by 1966 been taken over by a draper.

Woodgrange church, Romford Road, originated about 1880, with services in a hut lent by the builder of the Woodgrange estate.[1] In 1882 a church was built

[79] *White's Dir. Essex*, 1848.
[80] H.O. 129/7/194.
[81] Inf. from Mr. F. C. Thompson, based on Church Recs.; *Bapt. Manual*, 1854, 11, 40 gives the foundation date incorrectly as 1853.
[82] *Bapt. Manual*, 1855, 11; Church Deeds; Worship Reg. 8514.
[83] Inf. from Mr. F. C. Thompson.
[84] *Bapt. Handbks.*, 1875–95.
[85] W. T. Whitley, *Baptists of London*, 180; *Stratford Express*, 14 Nov. 1903; *Bapt. Handbks.* 1895–1913.
[86] Inf. from Mr. F. C. Thompson; Whitley, *Bapt. Lond.* 180, 222; *Bapt. Handbks.* 1917–67.
[87] Inf. from Mr. F. C. Thompson.
[88] Whitley, *Bapt. Lond.* 180, 222; *Bapt. Handbk.* 1889.
[89] Ibid.
[90] Inf. from Mr. F. C. Thompson.

[91] Whitley, *Bapt. Lond.* 185.
[92] Ibid. 194.
[93] Ibid.; Worship Reg. 17018; *Lond. Gaz.* 16 Jan. 1866 (p. 264).
[94] Whitley, *Bapt. Lond.* 194; P. R. Clifford, *Venture in Faith*, 18.
[95] See p. 128.
[96] Clifford, *Venture in Faith*, 19; Whitley, *Bapt. Lond.* 212.
[97] The following account, unless otherwise stated, is taken from Clifford, *Venture in Faith*.
[98] Whitley, *Bapt. Lond.* 236.
[99] Ibid. 251; Char. Com. File 126277.
[1] The following account, unless otherwise stated, is based on: inf. from Mr. S. P. Giller; Whitley, *Bapt. Lond.* 229; foundation stones.

and J. H. French became pastor. In 1899 the Richmond (later French Memorial) hall was built, with other rooms. In 1901 the church itself was enlarged and new classrooms built. By 1903 Woodgrange was easily the strongest Baptist church in West Ham, with Sunday congregations totalling 1,351. French, whose successful ministry continued until his retirement in 1917, was president of the London Baptist Association (1903) and also served on the West Ham school board and the board of guardians. The church has declined since his time, but in 1966, with a membership of 172, it remained one of the strongest free churches in Forest Gate. The buildings were damaged by bombing in the Second World War but were repaired.

Swanscombe Street church, meeting at the Temperance Hall, was formed about 1881 by James Brittain, previously minister of the Shirley Street Strict Baptist church. It was flourishing in 1883 but collapsed soon after when he left.[2]

Upton Cross church, Neville Road, appears to have originated about 1883, possibly through missionary work carried on by members of the Independent Methodist church in East Road,[3] which seems to have had some Baptist connexions. A hall was built in 1885 on the corner of Neville Road and Upton Lane. The church has had close connexions with the Central Baptist mission, especially between 1940 and 1950, but has usually been independent. In 1966 its membership was 33.

Stratford New Town church, Major Road, originated in 1885, when a large building was erected near the junction with Crownfield Road.[4] A lecture hall was added in 1900. In 1907 Major Road was joined by another group which had originated in 1892 in Chandos Road, as a mission of Cann Hall Baptist church, Leyton, and about 1894 had erected an iron building in Edith Road.[5] The pastor of Edith Road took over the united church, which then assumed its present name. The church was wrecked by bombing in 1941 and was later demolished. Worship continued in the lecture hall, which in 1953 was rebuilt, its lower floor being converted into a small church. In 1966 the membership was 41.

Custom House church, Prince Regent Lane, originated in 1906.[6] Meetings were held at first in a house in Jersey Road. In 1908 the members were joined by some from the Congregational mission in Prince Regent Lane, whose own building had been burnt down. An iron building was erected in 1911 on the corner of Jersey Road and Prince Regent Lane. This was at first a branch of the Central mission, but in 1915, after some friction, it became independent. From 1916 to 1923 its pulpit was supplied by students from Regent's Park College, who continued to help the church under later

pastors. In 1928 a new church was erected with funds left by Henry Lester, one of the founders of the Barking Road Tabernacle. It was wrecked by bombing in 1940 and reconstructed in 1950. In 1966 the membership was 32.

Strict Baptists. The West Ham Tabernacle, West Ham Lane,[7] originated in 1839, when members of Zoar, Whitechapel (Lond.), and the Ark, Francis Street, Maryland Point,[8] started preaching in the house of John Champness and under his leadership. In the same year a stable-loft was hired for services and symbolically named the Granary.[9] This leaked, and the congregation was disturbed by men swearing at the horses below. The Tabernacle was built in West Ham Lane in 1844. In 1847 it joined the London Strict Baptist Association, with which it had been informally linked from the first. It was enlarged in 1850, but in 1851 it had only a small membership.[10] Under William Bracher (1858–75) a gallery was added (1872), the Sunday school was revived (1873), and a new schoolroom opened (1882). G. Elven (1871–81) was paid no fixed salary, being supported by the profits of tea-meetings and anniversary gifts. James Clinch (1882–8) received £1 a week plus one annual collection. The Tabernacle flourished under Jabez Humphreys (1896–1901).[11] In 1902 the building was sold to the borough council for road-widening. In part payment the council gave another site in West Ham Lane, and the present Tabernacle was built there in 1903. Under H. J. Galley (1903–20) the congregation grew and the building debt was cleared. Membership reached a peak of 240 in 1926, and was fairly well maintained until 1939. In 1966 it was 78.

Enon chapel, Chapel Street, has sometimes been confused with the West Ham Lane Tabernacle, with which it may have had some connexion. It seems to have originated about 1840 in pioneer work led by Captain Whittle.[12] The chapel, built in 1842, was still in use in 1851, but closed by 1854, when Isabella Whittle sold it for use as the Stratford ragged school.[13]

Gurney Road church, Stratford, originated in 1870, when a small group led by James Mortar, a builder, met in a house in Forest Lane.[14] Soon after they moved to Chatsworth Road, using a room adjoining Mortar's house until 1882, when an iron church was erected in Gurney Road. A permanent church was built, probably by Mortar, in 1885. By 1889 the membership was 149, and it remained at about this level, with remarkable consistency, until 1939. A Sunday school, built in Buckingham Road in 1903, was used for services when the church was bombed during the Second World War. After the war the church was repaired. Its membership in 1966 was 85.

[2] Whitley, *Bapt. Lond.* 231; *Kelly's Dir. Essex,* 1882, 1886.

[3] Account based on inf. from Mr. A. H. Coleman; Whitley, *Bapt. Lond.* 634; foundation stones.

[4] Account based on: Whitley, *Bapt. Lond.* 233, 248; inf. from Mr. H. Chaplin; foundation stone.

[5] Wilkinson, *Leyton,* 31; W.H.L., W. Ham L.B. Mins. 9 Oct. 1894.

[6] Account from: D. A. Clarke, *Custom House Baptist Ch. 1915–65;* inf. from Mr. T. W. Payne.

[7] Account from: *Streams of Living Waters* (centenary hist. 1940); Whitley, *Bapt. Lond.* 165; *Bapt. Manuals,* 1845–62.

[8] See p. 125.

[9] G.R.O., Rtns. Noncf. Mtg. Ho. before 1852, no. 2030.

[10] H.O. 129/7/194.

[11] L. Lane, *The Uniform that Fitted* (1946) is Humphrey's biography.

[12] E.R.O., T/Z 8.

[13] *White's Dir. Essex,* 1848; H.O. 129/7/194; Char. Com., *W. Ham Char. Rep. 1899,* 111–12.

[14] Account from: Whitley, *Bapt. Lond.* 210; inf. from Mr. B. T. Leete and the Misses Mortar; foundation stones; *S. Essex Mail,* 25 Feb. 1903; Char. Com. File 229695; W.H.L., W. Ham L.B. Mins. 12 July 1870, 14 Mar. 1882.

Providence chapel, Shirley Street, Canning Town, was in existence by about 1870, when it was joined by some of those who had previously met at Mount Zion, Barking Road.[15] In 1878 it was taken over by a group which since 1876 had been meeting in the Temperance Hall, Wouldham Street.[16] James Brittain was minister in 1880, but by 1881 had left to form a church in Swanscombe Street.[17] The freehold of the Shirley Street site was bought in 1894, but about 1910 the membership, always small, was weakened by secession, and in 1917 the chapel was closed. It was sold in the following year, the proceeds being given to the Metropolitan Association of Strict Baptist churches, to which Providence had belonged.

Jireh chapel, Sebert Road, originated in 1888, when Mr. Allen began to hold meetings in a small building attached to Jireh Lodge, no. 133 Sebert Road.[18] In 1921 the present chapel was built at no. 244 Sebert Road with materials from one demolished at Woburn Sands (Beds.); the membership was then about 20. In 1965 Jireh had a membership of 2. Jireh Lodge was sold after 1921 and later used for a time by the Seventh Day Adventists. In 1965 it was occupied by a builder.

Brethren. The Bignold Hall, Bignold Road, Forest Gate, originated during the 1870s with services in an iron room.[19] In 1881, after summer tent meetings, a hall was built in Station Road on the corner with Bignold Road. In 1903 this was the largest Brethren's meeting in West Ham with total Sunday attendances of 430. During the Second World War part of the premises were bombed, and to replace them a new hall was opened in 1958, fronting Bignold Road. In 1965 the membership was about 50. There are references in 1906–8 to a Brethren's meeting room in Forest Lane, Forest Gate.[20] It is not known whether this was connected with the Bignold Hall.

There have been various other Brethren's meetings, mainly at Plaistow, none of which now survives. There was a chapel in Upper Road in 1878, and a mission room is mentioned, with no street name, in 1890.[21] A meeting in Lower Road (1903) still existed in the 1930s. There were also meetings in Plashet Road (1903–c. 1908), Beaumont Road (1903), and at the Hall, North Street (1903).[22] The last may have been identical with the Welcome mission hall, North Street, registered for worship in 1923.[23] The Children's Welcome mission hall, Pelly Road, was registered in 1916.[24]

The Catholic Apostolic Church.[25] Catholic Apostolic missionaries held meetings at the Artillery Hall,

Stratford, in 1868. They tried again in 1873, when Rokeby House, Stratford, was registered as their place of worship.[26] H. M. Prior, who had made the arrangements for the 1868 meetings, later seceded from the Catholic Apostolic church, and in 1875–7 gave lectures at Stratford, published as a book in 1880, attacking that church. In 1878 Catholic Apostolic meetings were held at the Workmen's hall, West Ham Lane, but again without permanent results.

Congregationalists.[27] Brickfields church, Welfare Road, Stratford, originally in Salway Place, off the Grove, is said to have been founded in 1662.[28] It is also suggested that its founder was an ejected vicar of West Ham.[29] Both claims are possible, since Thomas Walton, ejected in 1660, later taught school not far away, at Bethnal Green,[30] but there is no proof of them. The earliest certain evidence of a dissenters' meeting in West Ham is in 1672, when the houses of Benjamin Benton of Ham and James Day of Stratford were licensed for Presbyterian worship; Benton was also licensed to preach.[31] The church probably originated in one or both of these meetings. It is not known when the Salway Place meeting-house was opened. Apart from Benton the church's first known minister was Thomas Pakeman (1687–91), an old man who had suffered ejections elsewhere. He received no salary, and used his private income freely in the work of the church, even maintaining a school for poor children.[32] His successor, Joseph Bennet, a young man without private means, left before 1694, when he took Anglican orders.[33] Christopher Meidel is said to have been minister in 1696.[34] He may have been followed by John Gough, who was at Stratford by 1718 and remained until his death in 1729.[35] A document of his time describes the church, by implication, as 'Protestant, Presbyterian, or Independent'.[36] During the next 40 years it declined, and little is known except ministers' names.[37] It was revived by John Fleming and others who in 1773–4 reconstituted the church, as Independent, and appointed George Gold minister.[38] In 1775 the lease of the Salway Place meeting-house expired. With financial aid from Fleming the congregation therefore built a new chapel, opened in 1776, with a graveyard, on the present site at Brickfields, then open land off Jackass (now Vicarage) Lane.

Gold stayed until his death in 1810.[39] During his ministry the church was never strong: there were 33 members in 1776 and only 36 in 1810. By 1804, however, the debts incurred on the new building

[15] See p. 126.
[16] Account of Providence from: Whitley, *Bapt. Lond.* 219; *Kelly's Dir. Essex*, 1882 f.; Char. Com. File 96724.
[17] See p. 127.
[18] Account from Mr. D. T. Watts.
[19] Account from Mr. J. F. Hadley.
[20] *Kelly's Dir. Essex*, 1906, 1908.
[21] Ibid. 1878, 1890.
[22] Mudie Smith, *Relig. Life Lond.* 355; *Kelly's Dir. Essex*, 1906–26; inf. from Mr. F. Sainsbury.
[23] Worship Reg. 48985.
[24] Ibid. 46992.
[25] Account from: H. M. Prior, *My experience of the Catholic Apostolic Church.*
[26] Worship Reg. 21480.
[27] In this sub-section much statistical inf. is taken from *Cong. Year Bks.* 1846 f.
[28] Tablet, erected 1896, on N. wall of church; *Stratford Express*, 7 Nov. 1903.

[29] *E.R.* liii. 113.
[30] A. G. Matthews, *Calamy Revised*, 509.
[31] G. L. Turner, *Orig. Recs. Early Nonconformity*, 558, 533.
[32] A. Gordon, *Freedom after Ejection*, 39, 329; E. Calamy, *Noncf. Memorials*, ii. 457.
[33] Dr. Williams's Libr., Wilson MSS., E. Coll. f. 362 and A. Coll. ff. 53–8.
[34] *Trans. Cong. Hist. Soc.* v. 299.
[35] Dr. Williams's Libr., Wilson MSS., E. Coll. f. 362; ibid. Evans MSS. f. 39; *Trans. Bapt. Hist. Soc.* ii. 98–9.
[36] Will of John Hiett, whose legacy is described below.
[37] Dr. Williams's Libr., Wilson MSS., E. Coll. f. 362; *Trans. Cong. Hist. Soc.* i. 383, 388 and v. 216, 265.
[38] Following account based on: Ch. Min. Bks. 1773 f.; Ch. Trust Deeds; Sunday Sch. Min. Bk. 1895–1919 (which includes centenary rep. 1903); W.H.L., E/WES/ 285. 8 (TS. notes).
[39] Obituary in *Evang. Mag.* xviii. 161.

had been cleared. Gold was tough and determined as well as an effective evangelist. All these qualities were displayed in his encounter with a highwayman in Epping Forest.[40] Towards the end of his ministry the church opened a girls day-school and a Sunday school.[41]

Gold was succeeded by John Emblem (1810–40).[42] During Emblem's ministry the schools grew, and in 1816 a gallery was added to the church. Soon after this men from Brickfields founded the first Congregational church at Forest Gate. When the trust was renewed in 1836, a new constitution was drawn up for this society of 'Calvinistic Independents'. It provided, *inter alia*, that women were to have a voice in choosing the minister. Emblem's successor, Robert Ferguson (1841–9), was soon claiming a revival.[43] He was a man of some distinction[44] and may have felt himself too big for Brickfields, for he resigned after a dispute, possibly embittered by the political ferment of the times,[45] concerning his salary.

When Thomas Stallybrass (1850–82) succeeded Ferguson, the total Sunday congregations were averaging nearly 600, including children,[46] but by then, as West Ham grew less rural, Brickfields was beginning to lose its wealthier members, without gaining compensating recruits from among the new inhabitants, who at first settled some distance away, at Stratford, Forest Gate, and Plaistow. Brickfields's part in founding the Grove church at Stratford is described below. Another church which owed its foundation, at this period, at least partly to Brickfields, was that in Barking Road, Canning Town.

Tom Warren (1895–1902), who had previously been a lay agent at Shirley Street United Methodist church, was probably Brickfields's most effective pastor. He restored the church (1896), raised the membership from under 50 to its peak of about 180,[47] and built a new infants schoolroom (1897). He was also active in local government. When he left the membership soon fell back to its old level. In 1940 the church was badly damaged by bombing. Its members migrated to the Romford Road church, returning in 1943 to use the schoolroom behind Brickfields.[48] The main building was reopened, after repairs, in 1952. In 1966 there was a membership of 21.[49]

The chapel in Salway Place is shown on a map of 1744–6.[50] Brickfields is a plain, well-proportioned building not greatly altered since it was built in 1776. Until 1950 it was six feet higher than at present, the side walls containing round-headed windows above

and square-headed ones below. There was a fine 18th-century doorway to the front.[51] A rear gallery was erected in 1816. The reconstruction of 1896 included the addition of side galleries, approached from a foyer by a pair of pyramidal-topped towers, and the removal of the old box-pews.[52] In 1950–2 the roof was lowered, the side galleries removed, and the side windows reconstructed.[53] Since 1912 the graveyard has been maintained by the borough council, which in 1913 bought part of it for road widening.

Brickfields has received several endowments. John Hiett, distiller of London, by his will proved 1719, gave an annuity of £4 for the minister. Like Hiett's apprenticing charity this was not paid after 1839.[54] Anne Algehr, by will proved 1794, left £200, later converted into £262 stock, in trust for the minister.[55] Thomas W. Shipston, by will proved 1885, left £666 in trust for the maintenance of the church.[56]

Plaistow church, Balaam Street, originated in 1796 in a mission conducted by W. Newman, a Baptist minister from Bow (Lond.).[57] Regular meetings were held in private houses, and in the open air, until 1807, when a building was erected in North Street by a group of Independents and Baptists under Robert Marten, who was the leading layman until his death in 1839. A union church of the two denominations was constituted in 1812, with Henry Lacey (1812–24) as minister. 'Marten and his religious crew' encountered local opposition and even violence in the early days, but their numbers grew. John Curwen (1844–64) is best known as a music publisher, and advocate of the tonic sol-fa system, but his ministry was successful as well as his business.[58] A day-school was opened (1844) and in 1860 a new church was built in Balaam Street. The North Street church later became part of the Curwen Press premises, and still survived in 1970. In 1851 Curwen was also holding services in a house at Canning Town.[59] In retirement he helped to found the churches in the Grove and Romford Road. John Foster (1865–9) was the church's only Baptist minister. In 1869 part of the congregation—probably the Baptists—apparently seceded with him to form a church in Upper Road, Plaistow, which soon disappeared.[60] After this, Balaam Street seems to have had little or no Baptist connexions. Under Richard Partner (1888–1903) the membership increased rapidly as the area was built up, reaching 670 in 1902, by which time the church had been enlarged to accommodate 1,000. In 1887 a mission hall was built in Southern Road. After 1903 Balaam Street

[40] *E.R.* xxx. 242.
[41] Brickfields Sunday Sch. Min. Bk., 16 Mar. 1903. For the day school see below, p. 146.
[42] For his career see *Cong. Mag.* N.S. iv. 906; *Cong. Year Bk.* 1858, p. 199.
[43] *Cong. Mag.* N.S. v. 301.
[44] *Cong. Year Bk.* 1876, 331.
[45] Cf. the Wesleyan Reform movement of 1848–51, which affected the Stratford Wesleyan church, among many others.
[46] H.O. 129/7/194.
[47] *Stratford Express*, 25 Apr. and 20 June 1896; *Brickfields Ch. Pamph.* 1896.
[48] Inf. from church members.
[49] *Cong. Year Bk.* 1967.
[50] John Rocque, *Survey of London* (1st edn.).
[51] P.E.M., Pictorial Survey; D. McDougall, *Fifty Years a Borough*, 283.

[52] McDougall, op. cit. 283; *Stratford Express*, 20 June 1896; *Ch. Pamph.* 1896.
[53] Inf. from church members.
[54] Char. Com., *W. Ham Char. Rep.* (1899); see below, p. 162.
[55] *W. Ham Char. Rep.* (1899); Char. Com. File, G22 (W. Ham).
[56] Ibid.
[57] Account based on: J. Burton, *Origins and Progress Cong. Ch. Plaistow* (1857); *Record of a Century* (1907); J. S. Curwen, *Old Plaistow* (1905 edn.), 25 f.; Whitley, *Bapt. Lond.* 146; inf. from Mr. H. E. Kusel; S. A. Willis, *Plaistow Cong. Ch.* 1807–1957.
[58] J. S. Curwen, *Memorials of John Curwen*; D.N.B.
[59] H.O. 129/7/194.
[60] Worship Reg. 19432; Whitley, *Bapt. Lond.* 146, 208.

began to decline, though it remained fairly strong until 1939. During the Second World War the church was bombed, being finally abandoned in 1945 and later demolished. Meanwhile, in 1943, the members of Balaam Street and Southern Road united with Greengate as Plaistow Congregational church.

Forest Gate church, Sebert Road, originated about 1825, in services conducted by Jabez Legg, a trustee of Brickfields, in what was then a village.[61] In 1831 he and William Strange, another trustee, built a chapel at their own expense on the corner of Forest Lane and Woodgrange Road.[62] In 1856 a larger building was erected in Chapel (later Chapter) Street. Legg continued to assist the church until 1865.[63] Progress was slow until the time of William Skinner (1882–99), who doubled the membership in his first year, launched many new activities and, in 1884–8, built a new church, seating 1,100, in Sebert Road, on a new housing estate. The Chapter Street building was retained as a mission hall, and the original chapel in Forest Lane, which still existed, as a glass-works, in 1965, was sold. When Skinner retired the membership stood at 650, with Sunday schools of about 1,000. From this peak the church gradually declined. In 1928–30 the Chapter Street buildings were sold and Sebert Road was remodelled on a smaller scale. In 1966 the membership was 92. The founder of the Forest Gate church also established the Jabez Legg alms-houses, Odessa Road, Forest Lane.[64] He built three of the houses in 1858 and three more in 1863, for the accommodation of women formerly in domestic service. In 1939 the charity was amalgamated with the Edith Whittuck charity in Wimbledon (Lond.) as the Legg-Whittuck trust. The alms-women can come from any part of the country, but in practice most of them have local connexions.

The Canning Town church, Barking Road, originated in 1855, in services conducted at Plaistow Marsh by Thomas Perfect, who had been converted at Brickfields by Robert Ferguson.[65] Although lacking formal training, he served successfully as pastor until he retired in 1884. In 1860 a small chapel was built in Swanscombe Street. This was superseded in 1868 when a new building was erected in Barking Road, but remained in use as a mission hall. Another mission hall was maintained at North Woolwich from about 1879 to 1907. Under F. W. Newland (1884–94)[66] the Mansfield House university settlement became closely associated with the church, its boys' club being centred at the Swanscombe Street hall, which was rebuilt in 1891. The Canning Town church reached its peak membership of 261 in 1902. F. W. Piper (1905–9) devised a scheme to unite under his superintendency most of the Congregational churches in the area, as the South West Ham mission. Canning Town, Victoria Docks, and their missions came together in 1906, and were joined in 1909 by Greengate. The object of the mission was to ensure pastoral care for churches too poor to

support separate ministers, but the traditions of independence were too strong: Greengate left the union in 1914 and Victoria Docks in 1917. Canning Town continued to call itself the South West Ham mission until 1923. All its buildings were badly damaged in the Second World War. Swanscombe Street, wrecked in 1940, was later demolished. The Barking Road church, twice bombed, was derelict from 1941. Its dwindling congregation continued to meet elsewhere in various borrowed premises, under the leadership of Mrs. M. Angel, widow of a former minister. Through her efforts a smaller church, opened in 1949, was erected on the foundations of the old one. She died in 1959 and the church closed almost immediately.[67]

Stratford church, the Grove, originated in 1861, when the congregation of Brickfields started to plan a new church in the centre of Stratford, to replace their own.[68] Funds were raised and a site was bought in Grove Crescent Road, but in 1865 Brickfields withdrew from the scheme, thinking that the building committee was too ambitious. The committee continued under the leadership of William Settles, a City merchant living at Stork House, Ilford (now Romford) Road, and in 1866–7 built a church seating 1,600 with ancillary rooms beneath. It cost £11,500, most of which was lent by Settles, interest free. His creation was nicknamed 'Settles' Folly', but at first it flourished. James Knaggs, the first minister (1869–98), was a powerful figure, well-supported by prosperous local families like the Curwens and Boardmans. By the 1880s membership was about 600, with a Sunday school of 900, and new classrooms had been built. Missions were opened in Chapel Street (1885–1927) and Crownfield Road (1885–91), and help was given to new churches elsewhere. At this period the church was keenly interested in politics, displaying Liberal sympathies yet opposing the growing Socialism of the East End. In the 1890s the membership began to decline, though for many years it remained among the highest in West Ham. By 1941, however, it had become so small that the main building was abandoned, all activities being transferred to the classrooms behind, approached from the Grove. In 1966 the membership was only 21. 'Settles' Folly' had been sold in 1948, became a furniture factory, was gutted by fire in 1952, and later demolished. It has been called a 'big monstrosity' of white and yellow brick with columned portico, a 115-ft. spire, and 'debased classical' detail. Inside were two galleries, one above the other.[69]

The Victoria Docks church, Victoria Dock Road, was built in 1869 by James Duncan, the sugar-refiner.[70] It was at first a union church, embracing Congregationalists, Baptists, and a few Presbyterians, the last of whom soon set up on their own. The first minister, Josiah Foster (1871–99), was a Baptist. Duncan supported the church for many years. Later the London Congregational Union assumed

61 Account based on: C. E. Busby, *Hitherto, Henceforth* (1956). 62 *Cong. Year Bk.* 1857, p. 231.
63 For Legg see *E. Nat.* xx. 43–4.
64 Ibid.; inf. from Revd. C. E. Busby.
65 Account based on: *Cong. Year Bk.* 1893, 234 (obit. of Thomas Perfect); ibid. 1860 f.; inf. from Mr. T. W. Angel.
66 For his career see F. W. Newland, *Newland of Claremont and Canning Town.*
67 *Christian World*, 25 Jan. 1959; inf. from present (1966) owner of the building.

68 Account based on: Ch. Min. Bk. (to 1900); Trust Deeds; inf. from Mr. A. J. Birks; *Forest Gate Wkly. News*, 9 Apr. 1897, 30 Dec. 1898; *Cong. Year Bk.* 1909, p. 178 (obit. of Jas. Knaggs).
69 Pevsner, *Bdgs. of Essex* (1st edn.), 342; *Cong. Year Bk.* 1867, p. 347 and frontispiece.
70 Account based on: Whitley, *Bapt. Lond.* 212; *Cong. Year Bk.* 1903, p. 174 (obit. of Josiah Foster); inf. from Mr. W. J. Reeves.

responsibility for it. A mission was opened in West Silvertown in 1883; this was short-lived, but another, opened in Prince Regent Lane in 1885, continued until it was burnt down in 1908.[71] Foster published a magazine, *The Helping Hand*, which had a circulation of 3,000–4,000. From 1906 to 1917 Victoria Docks formed part of the South West Ham mission. In 1921 it was taken over by the Shaftesbury Society, which has maintained it since then as the Victoria Docks mission. An annexe was added in 1927. The main building was destroyed during the Second World War but subsequently rebuilt. The society publishes a small quarterly, *Dockland News*, and does much social work.

West Ham Park church, East Road, later Upton Manor church, Pelly Road, probably originated about 1879, when the West Ham Park Tabernacle was registered.[72] It was then said to be Independent Methodist, and there is also evidence of Baptist connexions.[73] Perhaps it was a union church like others in West Ham at that time. By 1890 it had become Congregational. In 1904 the congregation bought the former United Methodist Free church in Pelly Road, to which they moved as Upton Manor church, but this ceased by 1909. The East Road building was probably that taken over by the Anglicans as the Constance Fairbairn memorial church for the deaf and dumb, which is said to have belonged to the Strict Baptists and to have had a baptistery tank.[74] The Pelly Road building became the Given-Wilson institute, associated with St. Mary's, Plaistow.[75]

Romford Road church, Forest Gate, was founded by local Congregationalists under John Curwen.[76] The Norwich Hall was opened in 1880. The first minister, Robert Nobbs (1882–1900), built the main church (1885), opened a mission in Watson Street, Plaistow (c. 1890–1945), and increased the membership to over 300. A. Depledge Sykes (1900–4) was a follower of R. J. Campbell and caused dissension in the church. Early in the Second World War the main buildings were damaged and from 1941 meetings were held in the adjacent iron hall. Repairs, involving a complete internal reconstruction of the church, were completed in 1958.[77] In 1966 the membership was 22.

Greengate church, Barking Road, Plaistow, was founded in 1886 by George T. Allpress, a Primitive Methodist local preacher, who erected a small building in Samson Street and assembled a few working people.[78] These were mostly Methodists and followed Methodist procedures, but the church was completely independent, and in 1888 joined the

Essex Congregational Union. In 1892 an iron church was erected in Barking Road, Samson Street being retained as the Sunday school until the Second World War, when it was bombed. Missionary work at Ford's Park, Beckton Road, led to the formation of a new church there in 1894. Allpress left in 1896, though he later returned to the East End, where he worked until his death in 1949, becoming nationally prominent in the Congregational Church. From 1909 to 1914 the church, now called Greengate, belonged to the South West Ham mission. Its membership, which in 1902 was 108, was still as high as 97 in 1940, thanks partly to a revival under Frank Lenwood (1926–34)[79] during which the building was also renovated. In 1943 Greengate was joined by the members of Balaam Street, forming the united Plaistow church. Greengate was bombed in 1945, and was rebuilt in 1949–56. In 1966 it had 93 members.

Ford's Park church, Beckton Road, was founded in 1894 by G. T. Allpress of Greengate.[80] Services were held in a stable until 1904, when an iron building was erected. E. T. Egg, who helped to launch many new churches in the area, was temporary pastor from 1901 until his death in 1905. Although never strong the church continued steadily until it was bombed in 1940. The site was later sold.

Free Church of England and Reformed Episcopal Church. A Free Church of England, meeting at no. 13, Balaam Street, Plaistow, existed briefly in 1873.[81]

St. Alethia's Reformed Protestant church, Park Avenue, Stratford, was founded by Thomas Crow (d. 1886), a retired Baptist minister and temperance reformer who lived at Rokeby House.[82] A group of 'Rational Christians' registered a meeting at his house in 1875, and in 1882 moved to Park Avenue, where a permanent church was built in 1888.[83] His son continued to support the church after his death, and it survived until 1903 or later.

St. John's Reformed Episcopal church, Plashet Road, Upton, was built in 1889 by James (later Bishop) Renny, its first minister (1889–94); in 1912 it was taken over by the Moravians.[84]

Christ Church, Earlham Grove, was founded about 1893 by seceders from the established Anglican church of Emmanuel, Forest Gate, who disliked the ritualism of the vicar.[85] They were led by C. G. Poupard, a former churchwarden.[86] Christ Church still existed in 1903.[87]

Friends. A meeting at 'Ham' was in existence by 1656. It was short-lived, and probably fused with

[71] D. A. Clarke, *Custom House Baptist Church, 1915–65*.
[72] Account based on: Worship Reg. 24791, 33628, 40475; *Cong. Year Bk.* 1890 f.; ibid. 1912, p. 145; H.R.M.C., Harold Rd. Trust Mins. 22 Apr. 1904; see also W. Ham L.B. Mins. 11 Mar. 1879: new chapel, East Rd.
[73] See p. 127.
[74] *Essex Churchman*, Dec. 1959: this source may not be wholly accurate.
[75] See p. 119.
[76] Account based on: Ch. Min. Bks.; J. S. Curwen, *Mems. of Jn. Curwen*, 270; *Forest Gate Weekly News*, 30 Apr. 1897; inf. from Mr. H. J. Jones; *Cong. Year Bk.* 1883, p. 385.
[77] W.H.L., Illus. Coll., Churches, Noncf., Photo. Feb. 1958.
[78] Account based on: *Greengate Jubilee Souvenir Handbk.* (1936); inf. from Mr. H. E. Kusel; *Cong. Year Bk.* 1950,

p. 504 (obit. of G. T. Allpress); S. A. Willis, *Plaistow Cong. Ch. 1807–1957*.
[79] R. C. Wilson, *Frank Lenwood*.
[80] Account based on: inf. from London Cong. Union and Mr. H. E. Kusel; *Cong. Year Bk.* 1906, p. 210 (obit. of E. T. Egg).
[81] Worship Reg. 21320.
[82] Account based on: *London*, 26 May 1898; Worship Reg. 22572, 26208; *Kelly's Dir. Essex*, 1882, 1886; Mudie Smith, *Relig. Life Lond.* 354.
[83] W.H.L., Illus. Coll. (Bor. Engineer's photos.), St. Alethia's (1937) showing foundation stone dated 1888.
[84] Inf. from Revd. E. R. Brown, Upton Manor Moravian church; *E.R.* lxiii. 83.
[85] *E.R.* ii. 201; Worship Reg. 36388.
[86] W.H.L., Vertical File, E/WES/283, *Christ Church Earlham Grove* (appeal leaflet).
[87] Mudie Smith, *Relig. Life Lond.* 354.

one at Plaistow, of which there is evidence from 1671.[88] In 1677 the Plaistow meeting was being held at the house of Solomon Eccles (d. 1683), a well-known fanatic.[89] Solomon's wife Ann left the meeting the reversion, after his death, of two cottages and land in North Street, and in 1704 a meeting-house was built on that site. It was probably there that John Wesley preached on his visits to Plaistow in 1739.[90] Plaistow was part of the same monthly meeting as Barking.[91] In 1823 a larger meeting-house was built beside the old one at a cost of £1,700. Some of the most eminent Quakers of the early 19th century met there: the Frys, Gurneys, Listers, Howards, and Barclays.[92] John Bright was a frequent visitor.[93] In 1870 it was decided to transfer the meeting to Wanstead, to which area the richer members had already migrated. It had been intended to close the Plaistow meeting-house, but it was eventually agreed that meetings should continue in the 'small meeting-house' (possibly that built in 1704) adjoining the main building. In 1872 the remainder of the property was leased to the West Ham school board, which used the 1823 meeting-house as a schoolroom.[94] In 1879 the board bought the freehold of the whole property, but the Friends were granted a long lease of the small meeting-house[95] and continued to meet there until 1924.[96] The 1823 meeting-house, which in 1968 was the canteen of West Ham college of further education, was demolished in 1969. Its north end was originally the main front. Until 1879 it had a roof pediment and five windows, with an entrance portico supported on Doric columns which are said to have come from Wanstead House, demolished in 1823,[97] but which cannot be identified in any known picture or description of Wanstead House. When the school board bought the building it altered the front in order to build a new schoolroom, later a gymnasium abutting on it to the north.[98] The colonnade was dismantled and rebuilt as three sides of a square structure at the north end of the extension.[99] It was later boxed-in by the insertion of brickwork between the columns. The small meeting-house, which adjoined the 1823 building to the east, had by 1968 been replaced by a modern building, but the stone flagged approach to it from North Street, with its curved flanking wall, still survived. Oak panelling was preserved in the corridor outside the canteen of the college, and in the adjoining offices. The caretaker's cottage, north-east of the small meeting-house, also survived in 1968; it was a small brick building of the 18th or early 19th century with later additions.

The Barclay Hall, Green Street, was founded by the Bedford Institute Association in 1900, when an iron building was erected in memory of Joseph and Jane Barclay.[1] Within a year some 800 people were already connected with various religious, social, and educational activities of the centre, and another building had been added. In 1902 Barclay Hall became a full mission church, in 1904 the Sunday meeting was recognized under the Radcliff and Barking monthly meeting and in 1906 a permanent brick building was opened. The hall was bought by the borough council in 1948, and in 1949 was reopened as an adult education and social centre.

Latter-Day Saints (*Mormons*). In 1856 two societies of Latter-Day Saints registered premises in West Ham. One, at the Carpenters Arms, Church Street, cancelled its registration in 1866.[2] The other, at no. 5, Wharf Place, Canning Town, had ceased by 1897.[3] A meeting at the Assembly hall, Maryland Road, Stratford, was registered in 1868.[4] In 1903 the only Mormon congregation in the borough was using the Workmen's hall, West Ham Lane.[5]

Methodists. The three Methodist connexions which united in 1932 had a total of 18 or 19 churches in West Ham, most of them in decline. Amalgamations, already discussed before 1939, became inevitable as a result of bombing during the Second World War. The most notable new schemes have been the rebuilding of Woodgrange Road church to accommodate the remnants of five former societies at Forest Gate, and the building of a new church at Fife Road for three societies at Canning Town. In 1965 the five remaining churches in the borough lay in four circuits: the London mission (Poplar), London mission (Bow), London mission (Stratford New Town), and Leytonstone and Forest Gate. In the individual accounts below, ex-Wesleyan (W), ex-Primitive (P), and ex-United (U) churches are treated in that order, followed by the Conference hall, which became Methodist in 1934, and Fife Road.

John Wesley visited Plaistow in 1739 and preached at a meeting-house[6], presumably that of the Quakers, but there is no evidence that a Methodist society was formed in the parish until the end of the 18th century.

Stratford (W), successively in High Street, Chapel Street, and the Grove, was the first permanent Methodist church in West Ham. Wesley visited Stratford several times between 1783 and 1791, and there was a chapel there by 1790.[7] In the 1820s the Methodists were meeting in a building at the corner of Wood's Yard, High Street, between Chapel Street and Bridge Road. This was probably on the same

[88] Account based on: W. Crouch, *Posthuma Christiana* (1712), 19; W. Beck and T. F. Ball, *London Friends' Meetings*, 276; Friends House, Mins. Ratcliff and Barking M.M. 1821–89; *Friends Bk. of Meetings* (1924); *London Yearly Mtg. Reps.* (1925), p. 207.

[89] E.R.O., Q/SR 435/100; *D.N.B.*

[90] *J. Wesley's Jnl.* ed. N. Curnock, ii. 273–4, 278, 281.

[91] Cf. *V.C.H. Essex*, v. 232. See also W.H.L., D. Bambridge, 'Hist. of the Barking and Ratcliff Monthly Meeting' (Battersea Coll. Educ. 1969).

[92] Friends Ho., List of Members (1829); *D.N.B.*

[93] J. S. Curwen, *Old Plaistow*, 29.

[94] W.H.L., W. Ham Sch. Bd. Docs., North St. school.

[95] Ibid.

[96] Mudie Smith, *Relig. Life Lond.* 354; *Kelly's Dir. Essex*, 1906 f.; *Bk. of W. Ham* (1923), 158; Worship Reg. 5574 (registration of 1854, cancelled 1925).

[97] W.H.L., Illus. Coll. (Churches, Noncf.); Curwen, *Old Plaistow*, 28–9.

[98] W.H.L., Sch. Bd. Docs., Nth. St. sch.

[99] W.H.L., Illus. Coll. (Churches, Noncf.).

[1] Account based on: *The Friend*, 22 June 1900, p. 410; *Bedford Inst. Rep.* (1900), p. 67; (1901), p. 72; (1902), p. 86; (1904), p. 91; (1906), p. 9; W.H.L., *Reps. Sub. Ctees. to Educ. Ctee.* xlvi. 271; *Barclay Hall Adult Educ. Centre, Official Opening* (1949).

[2] Worship Reg. 7602.

[3] Ibid. 7466.

[4] Ibid. 19196.

[5] Mudie Smith, *Relig. Life Lond.* 356.

[6] *J. Wesley's Jnl.* ed. N. Curnock, ii. 273–4, 278, 281.

[7] Ibid. vi. 390, 396; vii. 50d, 125d, 134d, 221, 342d, 355d; viii. 120d; W. Myles, *Hist. Methodism* (1803), 327; Guildhall MS. 9558, f. 170.

site as the original chapel, though enlargement or rebuilding had taken place in 1811.[8] It was in the London, and later in the Spitalfields (or 3rd London) circuit.[9] In 1828 the society bought from Samuel Allen the former Unitarian chapel in Chapel Street. The Wood's Yard building was retained as a schoolroom until the lease expired in 1830. It was demolished for road widening in 1890.[10] The site was near no. 383, High Street, occupied in 1963 by the borough housing department.[11]

At Chapel Street the society added a schoolroom and a cottage completed by 1831. For the next 30 years it was constantly in debt, and it was further weakened by the Wesleyan Reform troubles of 1849–52, when it lost most of its members.[12] In 1851 the total Sunday congregations were only 80[13] and closure was contemplated. From 1851 to 1860 inclusive there were only 15 baptisms compared with 72 in 1841–50. During these years the church owed its survival mainly to George Biddle, a tailor, who supported it with service, as trust secretary, and with loans. It was included in the St. George's circuit, formed in 1863.[14] In the 1860s, with increasing population, the church revived and grew. From 1866 a mission was being held in the Workmen's hall, West Ham Lane, and about the same time a house meeting was started in Chandos Road.[15] In 1868 the Stratford circuit was formed under Alexander McAulay, a distinguished and influential minister. A much larger church was planned, and in 1870 Chapel Street was sold to the Primitive Methodists.

The new church was opened, on the east side of the Grove, in 1871, at a cost of £6,000. It seated 1,000 and was an imposing building with a pedimented classical front and a recessed portico. Schoolrooms were added in 1873. The Grove, at the head of the Stratford circuit, was for many years the leading Wesleyan church in West Ham and the mother of several others. About 1876 a mission was started at Abbey Lane, and in 1878 the Chandos Road mission was transferred to the Mechanics' institute, Store Street. The membership was 281 in 1887 and 413 in 1910. In 1891 the leaders supported the formation of a committee to sponsor candidates for local government elections.

After the First World War, and the constitution of Stratford New Town mission (the Mechanics' institute) as a separate church, the Grove declined. In 1919 it was renovated and re-named the Stratford Central hall,[16] with a membership of 262. It remained in the Stratford circuit, with Stratford New Town and Abbey Lane, as the Stratford mission. With the increasing local poverty social work became more important, and included a slate club, teas for the blind, and a weekly 'poor man's lawyer'. By this time, however, the cost of maintaining the

buildings was outrunning local resources, and in 1930, when its membership was 187, the Central hall sought inclusion in the London mission and an annual grant. It joined the existing Plaistow mission, which then became the London mission (West Ham). The Stratford circuit came to an end, its other churches joining the new Leytonstone and Forest Gate circuit. Financial difficulties continued, however, and the entry into the London mission (West Ham) of the previously undenominational Conference hall (1934),[17] situated near the Central hall and similar in character, probably split the decreasing membership, which in 1939 was 125. The Central hall was bombed in 1940, and the congregation was halved by evacuation. By then, if not before, the Abbey Lane mission had probably ceased. The London mission withdrew its grant, and in 1941 the remaining members joined Conference hall.[18] In 1953 the Central hall was demolished, and the site sold, the area being scheduled for offices. 'Portable' war damage compensation went towards the building of new churches at Princes Avenue, Southend-on-Sea, and Harold Hill, Romford. A foundation stone (1873) from the Grove has been incorporated in the Harold Hill church.

Ebenezer (W), Greengate Street, Plaistow, is said to have been built in 1825, but closed a few years later for non-payment of ground rent. Its members joined North Street Congregational church, where a gallery (presumably that of 1835) was built for them.[19] No more is known about Ebenezer, unless it originated in the society which registered a chapel in Greengate Street in 1818.[20]

Barking Road (W) originated in 1857, when Thomas Jacob, a Wesleyan from Cambridge, started services in Sabberton Street.[21] Services, Sunday school, and a day-school were later held in Hallsville Road. In 1862 a school-chapel, seating 250, was built on the north side of Barking Road, east of Canning Town railway station.[22] Owing mainly to the efforts of the superintendent minister, J. S. Workman, a larger building was opened in 1868,[23] heading a new Canning Town circuit, with a membership of 150. The society had previously belonged first to the Spitalfields, then to the Bow circuit. The old chapel continued in use as a day and Sunday school. The new one, with all its records, was destroyed by a fire of 1887 and rebuilt in the same year. Barking Road was transferred to the Seamen's Mission in 1907, when the Cory Institute was erected, costing £6,000, of which £2,000 was given by John Cory of Cardiff. Unemployment and movement of population after the closing of the Thames Ironworks weakened the church about this time, but it revived and flourished until the 1930s. It was

[8] E.R.O., D/P 256/28/3 and T/M 92 (Survey of W. Ham 1821); G.R.O., Rtns. Noncf. Mtg. Ho. before 1852, no. 778 (3 Apr. 1811). Unless otherwise stated this account of the Wesleyan churches in Wood's Yard, Chapel Street, and the Grove is based on the following sources in H.R.M.C. Coll.: *Stratford Circuit Bazaar Prog. 1883*, (annotated); Chapel Resolution Bk. 1826–70; Trust Accts. 1852–70 and Baptismal Reg. 1838–80; Grove Leaders' Mins. 1872–93, 1907–48; Grove Trustees Mins. 1872–99, 1916–53.
[9] L. Tyerman, *Life of J. Wesley*, iii. 223.
[10] W.H.L., *Stratford Circuit, Japanese Bazaar Programme*, 1906.
[11] Inf. from Mr. F. Sainsbury.
[12] *Meth. Recorder*, 23 Jan. 1913; and see below, p. 136.

[13] H.O. 129/7/194.
[14] Cf. *Hall's Circuits and Ministers*, 183.
[15] H.R.M.C.Coll., *Plan of Stratford Circuit*, 1870.
[16] Worship Reg. 47583.
[17] See p. 137.
[18] H.R.M.C.Coll., Lond. Miss. (W. Ham), Mins. Exec. Ctee. 14 Feb. 1941.
[19] J. S. Curwen, *Old Plaistow*, 29.
[20] G.R.O., Rtns. Noncf. Mtg. Ho. before 1852, no. 1103.
[21] The account of this church is taken mainly from: Meth. Arch. Dept., *Wesleyan Methodism in Canning Town 1868–1918*.
[22] *Wes. Chap. Ctee. Rtns.* 1863; Worship Reg. 15647.
[23] Meth. Arch. Dept., A. McAulay, *Stratford, London E.* (appeal pamphlet).

destroyed by bombing in September 1940, and a temporary building was erected on the site in 1948.[24] In 1957 it joined the London Mission (West Ham), with a membership of 50.[25] The temporary building was sold and in 1960 the congregation amalgamated with Custom House (P) and Shirley Street (U) in a new church at Fife Road, Canning Town.[26] War damage compensation from Barking Road helped to build a new church at Harold Wood, Hornchurch, in 1962.[27] In 1963 there was a petrol station on the Barking Road site.

High Street (W), Plaistow, originated about 1867, with meetings in North Street, and a chapel in Richmond Street was registered in 1870.[28] In 1876 the society built a hall at the corner of Swete Street and High Street. A church seating 900 was completed on the High Street front of the site in 1880 and a second hall in 1887.[29] In 1903 High Street was the second largest Methodist church in West Ham[30] and between 1904 and 1914 its membership increased from 303 to 408.[31] It was in the Canning Town circuit until 1907, when it headed the new Upton Manor circuit. This was divided again in 1926, High Street joining the London mission (Plaistow), which was merged in the London mission (West Ham) in 1930.[32] By 1940 the church membership was only 141, of whom 81 had been evacuated.[33] In 1941 the buildings were destroyed by bombing. Services were held at the Given-Wilson institute until 1942, when the congregation moved into the Harold Road (U) church.[34] Harold Road then became a refuge for the remnants of several bombed Methodist churches, and the repository of many of their records.[35] It was the High Street society, however, that finally assumed responsibility for the Harold Road buildings, and war damage compensation from High Street provided a new schoolroom at Harold Road in 1958.[36] In 1962 the society, with a membership of 57, was transferred to the London mission (Poplar). The High Street site was compulsorily acquired by the borough council in 1954 and was used for flats.[37]

Stratford New Town (W) originated about 1870 when members from Chapel Street started services in Chandos Road.[38] These were transferred in 1878 to the Mechanics' institute, Store Street.[39] As Stratford New Town mission this remained attached to the Grove until 1919, when it became a separate society, in the Stratford circuit. It was transferred to the Leytonstone and Forest Gate circuit in 1930.

Between 1918 and 1939 it was concerned mainly with youth work. Premises at the Anglican church of St. Mark, Windmill Lane, a mission of St. Paul's, Stratford, were borrowed for club meetings, and in 1939, when the institute became an A.R.P. post, Sunday services also were transferred to St. Mark's. After the Second World War the Methodists bought St. Mark's, then derelict as a result of bombing, restored it, and added club rooms. In 1955 it became a single station, the London Mission (Stratford New Town).[40]

North Woolwich (W), Albert Road, Silvertown, originated about 1870, with missions conducted by Wesleyans from Woolwich.[41] A brick church was opened on the north side of Albert Road in 1871. This building, near the docks and railway, was weakened by subsidence, and in 1914 it was demolished and replaced by an iron church. Membership rose from 28 in 1904 to 51 in 1911, but fell to 22 in 1916 and 12 in 1936. The church was closed for a time at the beginning of the Second World War and damaged by bombing in 1943. It was opened again in 1949 but finally closed in 1959, the site being sold.[42] The church was successively in the Canning Town and Upton Manor circuits, the London mission (Plaistow) and London mission (West Ham).

Woodgrange Road (W), Forest Gate, originated in 1878, when members of the Stratford circuit erected an iron building in this growing residential area. A permanent church was built in 1881–2 with the aid of funds from Sir Francis Lycett.[43] In 1903 this had the largest Protestant congregation in the borough. It remained strong even after the First World War. Under C. F. Ream (1919–25) services were crowded, debts cleared, and strong support given to overseas missions.[44] In 1930 Woodgrange was included in the Leytonstone and Forest Gate circuit.[45] Up to 1939 there was still a congregation of 800. In 1941 the church was bombed, and its members moved to the Field Road (U) church, where they were joined later that year by the remnant of Upton Lane (P). In 1956 a dual-purpose hall was opened on the Woodgrange site. The members of Katherine Road (U), East Ham, were incorporated at that time, followed by those from Clinton Road (P), whose premises were sold in 1959. The new Woodgrange church, designed by Paul Mauger, was opened in 1962, with the names of the five amalgamating societies on the foundation stone.

[24] Inf. from Mr. F. Murphy and Mr. F. Sainsbury.
[25] H.R.M.C.Coll., Lond. Miss. (W. Ham), Shorthand Draft Mins. Q.M. 26 Sept. 1957.
[26] See p. 137.
[27] Personal knowledge.
[28] *Meth. Recorder*, 7 Mar. 1907; Worship Reg. 19465.
[29] H.R.M.C.Coll., Grove Ch. Stratford, Letters *re* War Damage, 25 Nov. 1954; ibid. Upton Manor Circ. Trust Schedules 1908–25.
[30] Mudie Smith, *Relig. Life Lond.* 353–4.
[31] H.R.M.C.Coll., Canning Town and Upton Manor Circ. Mins. Quart. Mtgs. 30 Sept. 1904, 31 Mar. 1914.
[32] Ibid. 18 June 1907, 16 Mar. 1926; and see above.
[33] Ibid. High Street Ch. Trust Mins. 2 Apr. 1940.
[34] Ibid. High Street Ch. Collection Jnl. 1941–2.
[35] Ibid. High Street Ch. Letter *re* War Damage, 29 Apr. 1943.
[36] Ibid. Lond. Miss. (W. Ham), Mins. Q.M. 3 Mar. 1953; foundation stone of schoolroom.
[37] Inf. from Revd. J. Platten; H.R.M.C.Coll., High Street Ch. Letters *re* War Damage, 28 Jan. 1954–21 July 1955.

[38] H.R.M.C.Coll., *Plan of Stratford Circuit*, 1870. The following account is partly based on inf. from Mr. B Baddeley.
[39] H.R.M.C.Coll., Stratford Wes. Chapel Resolution Bk. 21 June 1866.
[40] H.R.M.C.Coll., Lond. Miss. (W. Ham.), Mins. Quarterly Mtg. 3 Mar. 1953, 13 Dec. 1954.
[41] Account based on: H.R.M.C.Coll., N. Woolwich Ch. Leaders' Mins. 1877–99 (include short history) and Trust Mins. 1879–1947; ibid. Canning Town, later Upton Manor Circ. Mins. Q.M. 1903–32 and Circ. Schedules 1925–44.
[42] Ibid. Lond. Miss. (W. Ham), Mins. Q.M. 1949, 1957 and Papers, 1960 *re* sale; inf. from Revd. E. Panton.
[43] Worship Reg. 24288; H.R.M.C.Coll., Stratford Wes. Ch. *Bazaar Prog.* 1883; E. Booth, *Fling Wide the Gates* (pamph. hist. 1962), on which following account is based.
[44] For Ream's obit. see *Mins. Wes. Conf.* 1926, p. 162.
[45] *Mins. Wes. Conf.* 1930.

Over the porch is the figure of an evangelist moulded in concrete by Peter Peri.

The German (W), Star Lane, Canning Town, originated about 1890. A London (German) circuit, established by the Wesleyan Conference in 1868, was headed after 1881 by the Peter Böhler church, Commercial Road (Lond.).[46] By 1881–2 German Methodists, possibly workers in the sugar-refineries, were seeking premises in Silvertown.[47] A Wesleyan hall registered in 1892 at 'Clover Road' (Clove Street?), Canning Town[48], may have been the first meeting-place of the Germans whose small church in Star Lane was opened in 1893.[49] In 1903 this had total Sunday congregations of 19. The Germans were still there in 1911[50] but left c. 1914. The building later served as Tyrell evangelical chapel and then as a branch of Canning Town Peculiar People's church.

Horeb Welsh (W) church, Cumberland Road, Plaistow, was opened in 1915 by a society founded at Poplar in 1880.[51] It was in the London (Welsh) circuit. Membership was under 50, and the church was sold in 1939. Some of the members joined the Welsh Methodist society which in 1945 took over Sibley Grove church, East Ham.

A Wesleyan church at 13–15 Tidal Basin Road, Canning Town, registered in 1926, had ceased by 1935.[52]

Primitive Methodism came to West Ham about 1850, but its growth was largely the work of Richard S. Blair, who as superintendent of the 8th London circuit (1874–81), the 13th London (Canning Town) circuit (1881–6), and the Upton Park circuit (1886–1904) built five new churches in West Ham.[53]

Ebenezer (P), Henniker Road, Stratford, probably originated about 1849. In 1851 a small society, which for two years had been 'driven from room to room' leased the Ark chapel, Francis Street, previously Baptist.[54] They still occupied the Ark in 1861.[55] This was no doubt the society which in 1863 built Ebenezer, on the corner of Henniker and Major Roads.[56] Additional buildings were erected in 1889.[57] In 1883 Ebenezer, previously in the 3rd London circuit, joined the new Stratford circuit, which it headed from 1894 to 1923.[58] In 1924 it was included in the new Leytonstone and Stratford circuit.[59] By 1940 it had been taken over by an undenominational Cripples Fellowship.[60] It was demolished in 1961 or 1962.[61]

Canning Town (P), Swanscombe Street, later Mary Street, originated in 1853 when members of

the 3rd London circuit started mission meetings.[62] A church was built in Swanscombe Street in 1858–9 and enlarged in 1861. It was included in the new 8th London circuit (1874) and in 1877, through the efforts of R. S. Blair and financial aid from James Duncan the sugar-refiner, a new church, seating over 1,000, was opened in Mary Street. The importance of open-air work was stressed by the erection of a permanent platform on land adjoining the church and by frequent street processions. In 1882 Blair and Duncan petitioned the brewster sessions against the granting of more indoor licences. Mary Street headed the new Canning Town circuit (1881)[63] and in 1903 had the largest Primitive Methodist congregation in West Ham. It was bombed about 1943 and was later demolished.[64]

Chapel Street (P), Stratford, originated about 1867 in cottage services.[65] In 1870 the former Wesleyan church in Chapel Street was bought for this working-class congregation, which advertised for funds to meet the price of £550.[66] It was at first in the 3rd London and later in the Stratford circuit.[67] The church still existed in 1903, but was put up for sale in 1906.[68]

Colne (formerly Charles) Street (P), Plaistow, originated about 1870 with services in Kelland Road.[69] In 1883 R. S. Blair and H. E. Lester built a small church in Charles Street. It was at first in the Canning Town circuit, later in the Custom House branch circuit, and in 1940, when the membership was 30, it entered the London Mission (West Ham).[70] It was later bombed, and the site was sold in 1960. War damage compensation helped to build a new church at Aveley.

West Ham Park (P), Stratford Road, originated in 1876, when open-air services were held in this growing district.[71] A school-chapel was built by R. S. Blair in 1877. Two houses were built next to the church in 1883, their rents providing an endowment. The church headed the West Ham circuit, formed in 1895. In 1896 a new church was erected. This, and the previous buildings, had been provided partly by borrowing, and West Ham Park was still in debt in 1940–1, when it was wrecked by bombing. Its assets were transferred to the London Mission (West Ham) in 1946, and by 1948 all the premises had been demolished. Portway junior school was built on the site. War damage compensation from Stratford Road helped to build a new church at Chingford Hatch.[72]

Custom House (P), Bridgeland (formerly Frederick) Road, originated in 1881, with open-air services

[46] Hall's Circs. and Ministers, 185; Meth. Rec. 31 Oct. 1907.
[47] H.R.M.C.Coll., N. Woolwich Wes. Ch. Trust Mins. 8 Dec. 1881, 26 Jan. 1882.
[48] Worship Reg. 33282.
[49] Meth. Rec. 31 Oct. 1907; W. Ham C.B.C. Mins. 11 July 1893.
[50] Wesleyan Rtns. Accomm. 1911.
[51] Account from Revd. E. W. Blainey.
[52] Worship Reg. 50116.
[53] See R. S. Blair, Reaching the Masses (1886) and Nailing up the Old Barn (chapel) Door (1894).
[54] H.O. 129/7/194; P.M. Mag. July 1851.
[55] Worship Reg. 12637.
[56] Foundation stone seen 1961.   [57] Ibid.
[58] P.M. Mins. Conf. 1870–1924.
[59] Gainsborough Bridge Meth. Ch. 1902–52.
[60] Worship Reg. 59253.
[61] Personal observation.
[62] Account (up to 1882) from: R. S. Blair, Reaching the Masses, 30 f. and Nailing up, 43 f.

[63] P.M. Mins. Conf. 1881.
[64] Inf. from Mrs. M. King; Worship Reg. 24039 (cert. of 1878, cancelled 1956).
[65] P.M. Mins. Conf. 1867.
[66] Prim. Meth. 1870, p. 187.
[67] P.M. Mins. Conf. 1867 f.
[68] Mudie Smith, Relig. Life Lond. 354; E.R.O., Sale Cat. A424.
[69] P.M. Mins. Conf. 1870; R. S. Blair, Reaching the Masses, 10? f. and Nailing up, 52.
[70] Wilson & Whitworth, W. Ham Almanac, 1892 f.; H.R.M.C. Coll., Lond. Miss. (W. Ham), Mins. Q.M. 11 June 1940; ibid. Mins. Exec. Ctee. 23 Jan. 1948; ibid. Colne St. Meth. Ch. Papers re Sale of Site, 1960.
[71] Account based on: Blair, Reaching the Masses, 49 f. and Nailing up, 45 f.; H.R.M.C. Coll., Stratford Rd. Trust Cash Bk. 1876–1929, Trust Accs. 1922–40, Trust Mins. 1932–53; ibid. W. Ham Circuit Steward's Accs. 1909; ibid. Lond. Miss. (W. Ham), Mins. Q.M. 4 Sept. 1946.
[72] For this church see V.C.H. Essex, v. 112.

led by R. S. Blair.[73] In 1882 a society was formed, meeting in Brindisi Terrace. An iron church was erected in Frederick Road in 1883. When this was burnt down in 1888 it was replaced by a small brick building. Frederick Road probably headed the Custom House branch circuit, formed in 1901.[74] During the Second World War it escaped serious damage, and in 1942 received the remnants of the Canning Town (P) and Shirley Street (U) churches.[75] It was then in the London Mission (Canning Town).[76] In 1960 Custom House united with the Shirley Street and Barking Road (W) societies to build a new church in Fife Road.[77] The Bridgeland Road building had been demolished by 1966.

Clinton (formerly Cobbold) Road (P), Forest Gate, was opened in 1882–3, probably as an offshoot of Ebenezer, Henniker Road.[78] It was in the Stratford circuit until 1924, the Leytonstone and Stratford circuit (1924–41), and the Leyton (P) circuit (1941–59).[79] In 1959 it united with four other societies in the new Woodgrange Road church. The Clinton Road building was sold to the Forest Gate Bible Students.

Upton Lane (P), Forest Gate, originated about 1889, in meetings led by R. S. Blair.[80] A church was erected in 1892 and placed under Blair's superintendence as the Forest Gate mission. It became the separate Forest Gate circuit in 1904.[81] By 1940 it was in the West Ham (P) circuit.[82] It was closed soon after, and its members joined Field Road (U), later moving with them to the new Woodgrange Road church.[83] In 1966 the Upton Lane building was a clothing factory.

Steele Road (P), West Ham (Canning Town circuit), was built in 1896, possibly as the successor to a mission which had existed in Marcus Street in 1893–6.[84] It had closed by 1922.[85]

United Methodism in West Ham goes back to a Wesleyan Association church opened near Bow Bridge in 1838. Whether this was a secession from the old Wesleyan church in Chapel Street, Stratford, is not known. There is no doubt, however, that Chapel Street was affected by the Reform troubles of 1849–52. The 3rd London circuit, to which it belonged, contained many Reformers, and when they seceded from it about 1850, they set up an exactly parallel organization. Peter McOwan, superintendent of the old Wesleyan circuit (1850–3), described the situation in a letter thus: '. . . we have the chief men of the [Reform] movement living within our borders. They . . . have resolved on an-

nihilating our circuit, their circuit they call the "Third London circuit" . . . they treat us . . . as if we had no existence . . . their success is great.'[86] Chapel Street just escaped annihilation, but the local Reformers were strong enough to set up their own society at Stratford and probably also a new one at Canning Town. At the union of 1857 these both became part of the United Methodist Free Church, and during the 1860s two other churches of that connexion were formed in West Ham. All four belonged to the 3rd London circuit, and later to the 5th London (Stratford) circuit, which after the union of 1907 became the Forest Gate circuit.[87]

The Wesleyan Association church, Stratford, the only one of this denomination known in Essex, was opened in 1838 on the south side of High Street, near Bow Bridge. Robert Eckett, a leading minister of the Association, preached at the opening services, and the society entered the London circuit.[88] In 1847 a new schoolroom was added, and in the following year the church seems to have been included in the new 2nd London circuit.[89] Its total Sunday congregations in 1851 were about 200.[90] In 1857 it was sold to the Unitarians.[91] Since that was the year of the national union between the Wesleyan Association and the Wesleyan Reformers to form the United Methodist Free Church it is likely that the Bow Bridge congregation joined the Bridge Road church.

Bridge Road (U), Stratford, was founded by Wesleyan Reformers seceding from Chapel Street. 'Stratford Broadway' appears in the joint plan of the 3rd and 8th London (Reform) circuits in 1852.[92] This was no doubt the society which in 1854 registered a church in Bridge Road.[93] A new building was erected there in 1860.[94] It was closed about 1907 as part of the scheme for building Katherine Road (U), East Ham.[95] The building was registered for worship in 1924 by an undenominational body, and in 1930 by the Elim Four Square Gospel Alliance.[96]

Shirley Street (U), Canning Town, was founded in 1853, when meetings were started, probably by Wesleyan Reformers, at Coke Oven Cottages, on the site of the later Thames Ironworks.[97] At least two of its early members, J. B. Day and J. Chipchase, had been delegates to the Reform meeting at Albion chapel, Moorgate (Lond.) in 1850.[98] A small church was built in Victoria Dock Road in 1860–1.[99] This was sold to the school board in 1873, when a new church and schoolroom were built in Shirley Street. Tom Warren, who was a successful lay agent at this church, left in 1895 to go as pastor to Brickfields

[73] R. S. Blair, *Reaching the Masses*, 98–9 and *Nailing up*, 51.
[74] *P.M. Mins. Conf.* 1901 f.
[75] Inf. Mrs. M. King.
[76] *Meth. Rtns. Accom.* 1940.
[77] H.R.M.C.Coll., Lond. Miss. (W. Ham), Shorthand Draft Mins. Q.M. 26 Sept. 1957.
[78] E. Booth, *Fling Wide the Gates*, 4–5; foundation stone; *Kelly's Dir. Essex*, 1882, p. 128.
[79] *Meth. Rtns. Accom.* 1940; *Gainsborough Bridge Meth. Ch. 1902–52*.
[80] Blair, *Nailing up*, 70–1; Booth, *Fling Wide the Gates*, 7.
[81] *P.M. Mins. Conf.* 1892 f.
[82] *Meth. Rtns. Accom.* 1940.
[83] Inf. from Mr. G. Attwell; Booth, *Fling Wide*, 7.
[84] Wilson & Whitworth, *West Ham Almanac*, 1893 f.; Worship Reg. 37055.
[85] *Kelly's Dir. Essex*, 1908, p. 257, cf. ibid. 1922, p. 276.
[86] J. McOwan, *Memoir of Revd. P. McOwan*, 218.
[87] *Wesleyan Reform, U.M.F.,* and *U.M. Mins. Conf.*

[88] *Wes. Assoc. Mag.* 1839; W.H.L., Sewers' Map of Millmeads and Highmeads in W. Ham Level, 1843, and Sewers' MS. presentments No. 145.
[89] *Wes. Assoc. Mag.* 1847, 1848.
[90] H.O. 129/7/194.
[91] See p. 139.
[92] *Meth. Arch. Dept.*, Circuit Plans.
[93] Worship Reg. 5432; for the site, at the north end of the road, see E.R.O., D/CT 160.
[94] *Meth. Free Ch. Mag.* 1860.
[95] H.R.M.C. Coll., Harold Road Ch., *Plans of Forest Gate circuit*, 1911; *Kelly's Dir. Essex*, 1906, pp. 505, 544; cf. ibid. 1908, pp. 511, 550. See above, p. 36.
[96] Worship Reg. 49252, 52292.
[97] Account based on: Album *penes* Mr. P. A. Payne; inf. from Mrs. M. King.
[98] Meth. Arch. Dept., Wes. Reform Tracts, *The Delegates Tested.*
[99] Cf. Worship Reg. 10088.

Congregational. Shirley Street was bombed in 1940, but continued in use until 1942, when the members moved to Canning Town (P). When that too was bombed a remnant went to Custom House (P). War damage compensation from Shirley Street helped to build the new church in Fife Road, Canning Town, in 1960. The Shirley Street site was sold to the borough council and by 1963 was occupied by houses.

Field Road (U), Forest Gate, originated about 1861, when Free Methodists from the 3rd London circuit started mission meetings.[1] In 1863 a school-chapel was built at the corner of Field Road and Essex Street, and the church, seating 500, was added in 1870. In 1880–2 the church was enlarged and a new hall was built at the corner of Essex Street and Norfolk Street. There were further extensions in 1907. Field Road became head of the Forest Gate circuit, for many years one of the leading United Methodist circuits. Among early converts there was Tom Elliott, who became a prominent evangelist, known as 'The Happy Shoemaker'.[2] The ministry of James Wright (1889–1902) was its most prosperous period. After the First World War it declined. Closure was averted by Sir William Mallinson, Bt. (1854–1936), the timber merchant, who had been associated with Field Road since its foundation. He settled £3,200 on the church and in 1930 re-seated the building at his own expense. Field Road was joined in 1941 by the members of Woodgrange Road (W), whose own church had been bombed, and a little later by those of Upton Lane (P). This united society met at Field Road until the opening of the new building at Woodgrange Road in 1956. The Field Road buildings were later demolished, and by 1962 flats had been built on the site.

Harold Road (U), Plaistow, originated in Free Methodist missions held about 1865.[3] A church was registered in 1868 in Pelly Road,[4] where a permanent building was erected in 1870–1.[5] By 1881 the membership was about 90, and there were several accessions of converts during the 1880s and 1890s. In 1903 a new church, seating 650, was opened in Harold Road. Pelly Road was sold to the West Ham Park Congregationalists, but for less than had been hoped, so that the new church remained in debt for twenty years. In 1907–8 mortgage interest consumed a third of its income; this burden was especially heavy since the congregation was by then almost entirely working-class.[6] In 1903 Harold Road was the largest Free Methodist society in West Ham and during the next 10 years membership was usually about 130, but after the war numbers fell continuously, to about 30 in 1939. Changes of minister were then very frequent, so that the decline was probably accelerated by lack of leadership. Closure was already

under consideration by 1938,[7] and by 1942 the church had almost ceased to function except for the Sunday school. This was the position when the bombed-out society from High Street (W) took over the premises.[8]

The West Ham Park Tabernacle, East Road, was registered as an Independent Methodist church in 1879.[9] Little is known about it, and it is unlikely to have belonged to one of the main branches of Methodism. Possibly it was the result of a secession from Pelly Road. It had Baptist links and the building was later used by the West Ham Park Congregationalists and then by All Saints church for the deaf and dumb.[10]

The Conference Hall, West Ham Lane, Stratford, which became Methodist in 1934, originated in 1884 when the American evangelists Moody and Sankey visited West Ham.[11] As a result of their mission about 300 men 'reclaimed from a life of drunkenness' formed the Mizpah band, which in the same year joined with the Young Men's Christian Association to build a hall seating 1,600 on a site given by Miss Eccles.[12] The hall was administered by a council of Anglicans and nonconformists. The leading member was Clement Boardman, a Congregationalist, who was treasurer until 1911, and whose sons continued his work. Activities included a Sunday school, a choir, a band, a library, and relief work. In 1903 the Sunday evening congregation at the hall was the largest at any church in West Ham. In 1890 the Mizpah band with their own hands built a cottage behind the hall. The Jubilee hall (1897) and Memorial hall (1912) were given by Boardman. Conference hall began to decline about 1923, partly because supporters were leaving the district, and in 1934 the hall was taken over by the Methodist London Mission (West Ham). In 1941 the main hall was destroyed by bombing. Work continued in the other buildings, and between 1962 and 1966 a small new church was built in Bryant Street behind the main hall site. Conference hall was transferred in 1962 to the London mission (Bow).

Fife Road church, Canning Town, was opened in 1960 in the London Mission (West Ham).[13] It replaced three older churches: Barking Road (W), Shirley Street (U), and Custom House (P), of which the first two had been bombed during the Second World War. The cost of Fife Road, which included a manse, was met partly by war damage compensation for Shirley Street. In 1962 the church was transferred to the London mission (Poplar).

Moravians. Upton Manor church, Plashet Road, previously Reformed Episcopal, was taken over by the Moravians in 1912.[14] In 1932, when it was

[1] Account based on: Sir W. Mallinson, *Story of My Life*, 17–19, 32–45, 112, 143–6; E. Booth, *Fling Wide the Gates*; inf. from Mr. G. Attwell.
[2] T. A. W. Martin, *A Brand Plucked from the Burning* [life of Elliott].
[3] *U.M.F.C. Mag.* 1865.
[4] Worship Reg. 18755.
[5] *Stratford Express*, 1 Oct. 1870. Remainder of account based on: H.R.M.C. Coll., Pelly Rd. and Harold Rd. Ch. Registers 1873–1940; Trust Mins. 1902–46; Leaders' Mins. 1909–24; Mins. Teachers' Mtgs. 1932–9 and 1942–51.
[6] W.H.L., *U.M. Church, Harold Rd., Xmas Bazaar, 1908*.

[7] H.R.M.C. Coll., Lond. Miss. (W. Ham), Mins. Q.M. 13 Dec. 1938.
[8] See p. 134.
[9] Worship Reg. 24791.
[10] See p. 131.
[11] Account based on: inf. from Revd. W. H. Ford; *Conference Hall* (pamph.), 1954; *Stratford Express*, 14 June 1884.
[12] For a photograph see W.H.L., Illus. Coll., Churches, Noncf.
[13] Account based on inf. from Revd. P. Beckwith, Revd. J. Platten, and Mr. F. Murphy.
[14] Account based on: *E.R.* lxiii. 83–6; inf. from Revd. E. R. Brown.

at the peak of its membership, the bicentenary of the Moravian missions was held at the town hall, Stratford. During the Second World War the church's iron schoolroom was destroyed by bombing.

Peculiar People (Union of Evangelical Churches). Canning Town Evangelical church, Cliff Street, originated about 1870 in meetings led by Daniel Tansley.[15] A church was built in 1873 and was affiliated to the Peculiar People. In 1897–8 a Plaistow man belonging to this sect, and probably to this church, was convicted of manslaughter after refusing, on religious grounds, to seek medical aid for his dying son.[16] In 1908 the local members of this sect were said to live especially in Fisher and Edward Streets, and to form exclusive work gangs at Beckton gasworks.[17] Additional buildings were erected before the First World War, and about 1925 the society also acquired the Tyrell chapel, Star Lane.[18] About 1959 the Cliff Street church was rebuilt.[19]

Silvertown church, Oriental Road, was built in 1893.[20] It was still open in the 1930s,[21] but by 1966 was a paper warehouse.

Holt Road mission hall was registered in 1910 by the 'Liberty Section' of the Peculiar People; it had ceased by 1956.[22]

Presbyterian Church of England. Trinity church, Leytonstone Road, Maryland Point, was founded in 1863 by Andrew Black, of the United Presbyterian Church, who became the first minister (1863–75).[23] A hall was built in 1864 and the church itself in 1870. It was a brick and stone building in the Gothic style, with a spired angle tower. After early difficulties Trinity flourished under Alexander Jeffrey (1888–1906), the building debt being cleared and communicants numbering over 400, including many seamen. The leading layman at this period was an engine-driver, Alexander Keir. From 1906 the church was declining, and in 1941 it was closed, the members joining East Avenue church, Manor Park, which then took the name Trinity.[24] The Leytonstone Road building, later used as a factory, was destroyed by fire in 1953. The church hall still survived, as a factory, in 1966.

Victoria Docks church, Hack Road, was built in 1872 by James Duncan, the sugar-refiner, to meet the needs of his Scottish workers.[25] It was bombed early in the Second World War, and not rebuilt.

Silvertown church, Tate Road, was built in 1882, also by local manufacturers, and it ended like Hack Road.[26]

Presbyterian Church of Wales (Calvinistic Methodists). Stratford church, Romford Road, originated in 1890, and the building was erected in 1894.[27] It was closed after bombing in 1940. Some of its former members later helped to build Moreia at Leytonstone.[28] The Romford Road building became a bedding factory.

Salvation Army. At Canning Town Salvation Army work started in 1872. A centre registered at Fox Street in 1875 moved to Bradley Street, Beckton Road, in 1910. It was closed in 1964 and later demolished for road widening.[29] A centre in Freemasons Road, opened 1909, moved to Coolfin Road in 1928. It was burnt down about 1940, but the Army retains the site for rebuilding.[30] Premises were also registered in Prince Regent Lane (1903–13), Woodstock Street (1922–32), and Ashburton Road (1925).[31]

At Plaistow work started in 1873, and a hall was registered in Upper Road in 1875. This was still in use in 1966.[32] There was a young people's hall in The Broadway, Plaistow, from 1903 to 1904.[33]

At Stratford a large hall was opened in Angel Lane in 1883.[34] In 1903 it had total Sunday congregations of 957, and it continued in strength and social importance through years of unemployment up to the 1930s. Membership was increased by a revival and faith-healing campaign in 1925. The hall was damaged during the Second World War. In 1965 it was closed under a redevelopment scheme, and the Stratford corps moved to the Goodwill community centre, Paul Street, built by the Army's centenary appeal fund. The soldiers' roll was then 32.

At Silvertown there was a centre in Parker Street from 1893; a hall built there in 1913 closed in 1961.[35] Premises were also registered in Oriental Road (1889) and Victoria Dock Road (1892).[36]

At Upton Park a centre (previously in Crescent Road, East Ham) was registered in 1913 in Plashet Road; it ceased by 1928.[37]

Spiritualists. Dames Road church, Forest Gate, registered in 1902, had ceased by 1913.[38]

Plaistow church, Cumberland Road, was formed by 1903.[39] Meetings were held above a shop in Braemar Road until 1932, when the present hall was built.

Stratford church, Idmiston Road, registered in 1904, still existed in 1965 as an iron building.[40]

Priory Christian Spiritualist church, 4, Palmerston Road, Forest Gate, registered in 1934, still existed in 1963.[41]

[15] Account based on inf. from Mr. B. J. Worm, Mr. H. Cousins, and Mrs. Williams.
[16] *Forest Gate Wkly. News*, 1 Oct. 1897; G. W. Foote, *Peculiar People: an Open Letter to Mr. Justice Wills* (1899).
[17] E. G. Howarth and M. Wilson, *West Ham* (1908), 51.
[18] See p. 140.   [19] Cf. Worship Reg. 67115.
[20] Foundation stone.
[21] *Bk. of W. Ham* (1923), 159; *Kelly's Dir. Essex*, 1926, p. 513; inf. from Mr. F. Sainsbury.
[22] Worship Reg. 44572.
[23] Account based on: *Jubilee Book of Trinity Ch.* (1913); W. Mackelvie; *Annals and Statistics of United Presbyt. Ch.* 502; *Christian Leader*, 12 Jan., 12 Mar. 1891; *Weekly Review*, 13 Mar. 1913; MS. in Presbyt. Hist. Soc. Libr.; inf. from Miss L. Kelley; personal knowledge.
[24] See p. 37.
[25] *Jnl. Presbyt. Hist. Soc.* vii. 80, 83, ix. 16.
[26] Ibid. ix. 16; *Bk. of W. Ham*, 153; Char. Com. File 141717.

[27] Account from Revd. M. Parry.
[28] See p. 302.
[29] Inf. from Lt. P. Sinclair and S.A. National H.Q.; Worship Reg. 22547, 44411.
[30] Worship Reg. 43604, 51369; inf. S.A. Nat. H.Q.
[31] Worship Reg. 39815, 48577, 49578.
[32] Ibid. 22546; inf. from Lt. P. Sinclair.
[33] Worship Reg. 39816.
[34] Ibid. 27045; following account based on the Corps Hist. Bk. and inf. from Capt. E. Cummings.
[35] Worship Reg. 33927; foundation stone; inf. from S.A. Nat. H.Q.
[36] Worship Reg. 31564, 33469.
[37] Ibid. 45675.
[38] Ibid. 39170.
[39] Mudie Smith, *Relig. Life Lond.* 356; inf. from Mr. E. Hayward.
[40] Worship Reg. 40794.
[41] Ibid. 54485; *W. Ham Guide*, 1963–4.

Two other Spiritualist congregations existed in 1903: at Wells Street, Stratford, and the Workmen's hall, West Ham Lane.[42] The latter was still meeting in 1914.[43]

Unitarians. Chapel Street church, Stratford, was registered in 1823 by Samuel Allen, who sold it in 1828 to the Wesleyans.[44]

Stratford church, West Ham Lane, does not appear to have been connected with the one in Chapel Street.[45] There was a Unitarian meeting at Stratford in 1810.[46] It was probably identical with the 'Christian Association' congregation formed about this time by Mr. Vidler, which is said to have met first at Bow Bridge and later at Bow (presumably in Middlesex). In 1857, under Thomas Rix (1857–79), a former Baptist, it bought the old Wesleyan Association chapel at Bow Bridge. A new church was built in West Ham Lane in 1869, to which a hall was added in 1885 and other rooms in 1910.[47] London Unitarians, including the Durning-Lawrence family, gave financial aid. From 1912 to 1933 the church was served by members of the order of Pioneer Preachers, founded by R. J. Campbell. In 1940, when it was bombed, the members found shelter in the Forest Gate church, but they later resumed services in the side buildings until about 1946, when the church was rebuilt.

Forest Gate church, Upton Lane, was formed in 1888 as an offshoot of Stratford; a hall was built in 1893.[48] It was intended to build the main church later, but this was never done. In 1901 an oak pulpit, preacher's desk, and other furnishings were bought from the factory of William Morris & Co.

Undenominational Missions. The Conference hall, West Ham Lane (1884), for long West Ham's largest undenominational church, became Methodist in 1934.[49]

The London City Mission had two centres at West Ham in 1903: North Street, Stratford, and Balaam Street, Plaistow.[50] The Stratford hall was probably the one in North Place, High Street, which still existed in 1926.[51] The Mission was still using the Balaam Street premises in 1930.[52] In 1914 it had 7 centres in the borough, including the two already mentioned, a German mission in Swanscombe Street, Canning Town, and the Louisa Ashburton Hall, Victoria Dock Road, founded in 1888.[53] The Ashburton Hall continued in use until 1937.[54] The Mission also registered premises in Fen Street, Tidal

Basin, in 1914, and in Nelson Street, Tidal Basin, in 1933.[55] Ridley Hall, Upton Lane, Forest Gate, registered as undenominational in 1894, and bombed in 1940, was rebuilt in 1951, and re-registered by the Mission.[56] The Goodwill mission, Ladysmith Road, Canning Town, registered in 1937, had been taken over by the London City Mission by 1960.[57] Varley Road hall, Custom House, known in 1922 as the Christian Community mission, was registered by the London City Mission in 1956.[58] The Mission also had premises in Naples Street, Stratford, in 1953.[59]

The Railway mission, Chobham Road, Stratford, was built in 1892. It received much early support from the Boardman family.[60] An evening congregation in 1903 numbered 624. The hall was bombed in 1940, but services continued in the remaining buildings. In 1965, when membership was about 40, rebuilding on another site was contemplated.

Other Churches and Missions. At Plaistow a non-sectarian group registered a meeting in George Street in 1862.[61] Bethany Full Salvation mission, Chesterton Terrace, first registered in 1935, was still active in 1966.[62]

At Stratford the Ark chapel, Francis Street, originally Baptist and later Primitive Methodist, apparently remained in use as a mission hall from 1864 until 1954 or later.[63] The Amity Hall, Amity Road, was used by the Disciples of Christ in 1903–21.[64] The Elim Four Square Gospel Alliance registered a hall in Bridge Road in 1930.[65] Highway Hall, Romford Road, was first registered in 1936 and still existed, as an Evangelical free church, in 1965.[66] The Cripples Fellowship mission, Henniker Road, was registered in 1940, in a building formerly used by the (Primitive) Methodists.[67] The Jehovah's Witnesses registered rooms above a shop in Stratford Broadway in 1945; in 1966 they still occupied them.[68] Non-sectarian Christians registered an iron church in Barnby Street (1878), a meeting at Stratford town hall (1892) and one in Bridge Road (1924).[69] Salway chapel, Great Eastern Road, first recorded in 1887, was known as Enterprise Hall (c. 1892–3), and as Tyne Hall (c. 1893–8).[70]

At Forest Gate the Church of God, Dames Road, originated about 1884, when a Christian Israelite began preaching on Wanstead Flats.[71] Among his converts was Robert Rosier, who by will, proved 1893, left to the Branch Society of Christian Israelites £338, two houses, and land in Dames Road.[72] A

[42] Mudie Smith, *Relig. Life Lond.* 356.
[43] *Wilson & Whitworth's West Ham and Stratford Almanack,* 1914.
[44] G.R.O., Rtns. Noncf. Mtg. Ho. before 1852, no. 1373; see above p. 133.
[45] Account based on: Stratford Unitarian Ch. *Calendar,* 1924; ibid. Letter from Mrs. T. Rix, 13 Nov. 1905; *Bk. of W. Ham,* 157; G. E. Evans, *Vestiges of Protestant Dissent,* 155–6; inf. from Revd. R. H. Barker.
[46] Guildhall MS. 9558 f. 169v.
[47] Foundation stones.
[48] Account from: G. E. Evans, *Protestant Dissent,* 145; inf. from Mr. T. E. Dalton and Mr. H. N. Panting.
[49] See p. 137.
[50] Mudie Smith, *Relig. Life Lond.* 356.
[51] *Kelly's Dir. Essex,* 1906, 1926.
[52] Worship Reg. 52412.
[53] *Wilson & Whitworth's West Ham and Stratford Almanack,* 1914.
[54] Worship Reg. 52561.
[55] Ibid. 46338, 46339, 54817.
[56] Ibid. 34211, 63145; plaque on building.
[57] Worship Reg. 57465; *W. Ham Guide,* 1960.
[58] *Kelly's Dir. Essex,* 1922; Worship Reg. 65525.
[59] *W. Ham Guide,* 1953.
[60] Account from Mr. D. A. Blake.
[61] Worship Reg. 15239.
[62] Ibid. 56072.
[63] Worship Reg. List 1954 (no. 16058); W. Ham L.B. Mins. 13 Nov. 1866; *Kelly's Dir. Essex,* 1906, 1912.
[64] Worship Reg. 44711; Mudie Smith, *Relig. Life Lond.* 355.
[65] Worship Reg. 52292.
[66] Ibid. 56457, 56473–4, 67815.
[67] Ibid. 59253.
[68] Ibid. 61258. For a mass baptism by this sect, in West Ham Baths in 1954, see W.H.L., Illus. Coll. (Meetings &c.).
[69] Worship Reg. 24035, 33508, 49252.
[70] *Kelly's Dir. Stratford* (1887–8 sqq.).
[71] Account from Mr. W. J. Legg.
[72] Char. Com. File 207309.

small building was erected on this land in 1894–5. It was damaged by bombing in 1940 and was unusable for a few months. Permanent repairs were completed in 1952. In 1959 the Society of Christian Israelites sought to affiliate the church, but it refused to accept their doctrines, and in 1962 adopted the name Church of God (Forest Gate). Also at Forest Gate was the Ethical church (or the Emerson Ethical Brotherhood) meeting at the Earlham Hall, Earlham Grove, c. 1902–22.[73] The Seventh-Day Adventists registered a church at no. 133, Sebert Road, in 1929.[74] The Forest Gate Bible Students in

Assemblies of God, and in 1966 was styled the Lighthouse Pentecostal church.[80] The Elim Four Square church, Bethell Avenue (1932), still survived in 1966.[81] The Pentecostal hall, Cranley Road, was registered in 1935.[82]

At Upton the Dock Labourers mission was registered in 1899.[83] A New Jerusalem (Swedenborgian) church, previously meeting in Cann Hall Road, Leyton,[84] moved to Woodford Road, Forest Gate, in 1900.[85] It appears to have moved again, to Plashet Road, by 1902.[86] The Plashet Road building was re-registered in 1949 by the Bible Pattern

WEST HAM, ROTHSCHILD MAUSOLEUM IN JEWS' CEMETERY

1959 bought the former (Primitive) Methodist church in Clinton Road.[75] The Kingsdown Christian mission, Tylney Road, was transferred to Forest Gate from Islington in 1960.[76] The Durning hall, Woodgrange Road, is described in another section.[77]

At Canning Town registrations include the Seamen's Bethel, Victoria Dock Road (1885), the Evangelical Tabernacle, Barking Road (1887), Emmanuel mission hall, Dartmouth Terrace (1904), and the New Barn Street gospel hall (1915).[78] Tyrell evangelical chapel, Star Lane, was opened c. 1916. It had previously been a German Methodist church, and its members included several former Methodists and one or two Germans. It was closed in 1924 and sold to the Peculiar People.[79] The Lighthouse mission, Victoria Dock Road (1921), was re-registered in Silvertown Way in 1949 by the

Fellowship as the Glad Tidings Tabernacle.[87] A non-sectarian body at Studley House, Upton Lane (1915), was still meeting in 1966.[88]

JUDAISM. The West Ham district synagogue originated in 1897, when Ephraim Samson, Symon Weber, and others organized services at Earlham Hall, Earlham Grove.[89] In 1899 a house was rented in Forest Lane and a reader appointed. The society bought no. 95, Earlham Grove, with land adjoining, and later no. 97, and in 1901 became associated with the United Synagogue. A permanent synagogue was built there in 1911. A communal hall and classrooms were added in 1928, when the synagogue acquired District status. A further extension on the north side took place in 1934. Bomb-damage received

[73] Kelly's Dir. Essex, 1906, 1922; Bk. of W. Ham (1923), 163.
[74] Worship Reg. 51947. Formerly Jireh Strict Baptist.
[75] See p. 136; local inf.
[76] Worship Reg. 67681.
[77] See p. 143.
[78] Worship Reg. 28897, 30408, 40799, 46400.
[79] Inf. from Mr. B. Sharman and Mr. F. Sainsbury.
[80] Worship Reg. 47993, 62185.
[81] Ibid. 53773.

[82] Ibid. 56198.
[83] Ibid. 37078.
[84] See p. 232.
[85] Leyton Express and Independent Almanack, 1900.
[86] Worship Reg. 39214.
[87] Ibid. 62506.
[88] Ibid. 46508.
[89] W. Ham Synagogue, Consecration and History, 1911; W. Ham Synagogue, Reconsecration, 1935; inf. from Mr. J. Gilbey (United Synagogue).

during the Second World War was repaired in 1948–9 and in 1958 the foundation stone of the West Ham Youth Synagogue was laid.

A Federated Synagogue was formed at Canning Town in 1901.[90] It was registered in 1908 as at no. 201, Barking Road, and in 1919 as at no. 269, where a new building was erected in 1923.[91]

Federated Synagogue meetings and classes were held in 1936–7 in Osborne Road and later in Claremont Road, Forest Gate.[92]

The Jews' cemetery, Forest Gate, originally comprising 5 a., was opened in 1858.[93] An ornate domed mausoleum, designed by Sir Matthew Digby Wyatt,[94] was erected there in 1866 for the burial of Evelina de Rothschild, whose husband, Ferdinand, was also buried there in 1898. The cemetery also contains the tomb of David Salomons (d. 1873), the first Jewish lord mayor of London. It had been extended to 11 a. by 1886; by 1965 it was a 'closed' cemetery.[95]

PHILANTHROPIC INSTITUTES, SETTLEMENTS, AND HOSTELS. There have been many philanthropic institutions in West Ham. In the town's early years voluntary efforts were directed mainly towards providing elementary schools.[96] After the formation of the school board (1871) other needs became more pressing. These included hospitals, clinics, and district nursing services.[97] Poverty and the lack of facilities for recreation and adult education were also urgent problems.

The churches of the different denominations have played a major role in meeting these needs. Christians also created some philanthropic institutions more or less independent of the local churches. These, often sponsored by a university or a public school, took various forms, of which the most important has been the slum 'settlement'. West Ham's most notable settlements have been Mansfield House and Dockland Settlement No. 1, later the Mayflower Family Centre. The Young Men's Christian Association also did good work in the borough, especially through its large club at Plaistow. Some of the larger local firms, for example the Thames Ironworks Co.,[98] provided recreational facilities for their workers. At least two, the Great Eastern Railway and Henry Tate & Sons, built their own institutes, while another was provided by the Carpenters' Company of London. At West Ham, as in other poor districts, the leaders in voluntary social work came mainly from outside the borough. Among them were Sir Percy Alden of Mansfield House and Sir Reginald Kennedy-Cox of the Dockland Settlement.

The institutions described below were of secular origin or, if Christian, were more or less independent of the local churches. Institutions closely identified with particular churches in the borough have usually been described in the sections relating to those churches. Alms-houses are also described elsewhere.

The Eastern Counties, later the Great Eastern Railway Mechanics' Institution, was opened in Angel Lane, Stratford, in 1851.[99] It held lectures, classes, and penny readings with success,[1] and opened a day-school. By 1864 it had 450 members and a library of 3,000 books.[2] In 1877 it moved to new buildings in Store Street, Stratford New Town. In 1881 the institution handed over its school[3] to the school board, and concentrated on adult classes, mainly in technical and vocational subjects. These were strongly supported by the railway company. The institution's most active period was c. 1900–14. It later declined, and was finally closed in 1946. The building was sold and demolished.

The Guild of St. Alban the Martyr, Balaam Street, was an Anglo-Catholic settlement which came to Plaistow from London in 1876, under the leadership of George Malim, a bank clerk.[4] The 'brethren' followed secular occupations, but in their spare time wore monastic dress and worked in connexion with St. Philip's church, a mission of St. Andrew's. They lived at St. Dunstan's, formerly Ivy House. They held radical views and in the general election of 1880 campaigned for the Liberals. This alienated many of their financial supporters, and after the election St. Andrew's severed its connexion with the guild. The settlement closed in 1882.

The Carpenters' Company institute, Jupp Road, Stratford, was built in 1886 to serve the Carpenters' estate.[5] It provided evening-classes in technical subjects, and included a gymnasium and indoor swimming-bath.[6] In 1891 it became a day-school, but evening-classes continued until the school was closed in 1905.[7]

The Tate institute, Albert Road, Silvertown, was built in 1887 by (Sir) Henry Tate (Bt.), for his sugar-workers.[8] In 1904 Sir William Tate, Bt., gave £1,500 to renovate the institute and in 1906 a further £1,200 to endow it. The institute was closed in 1933. The building was sold and later became a public library, but in 1961, when the library moved to new premises, the institute was leased by Tate & Lyle and reopened as a social centre.[9]

The Stratford Dockland settlement is the successor to the Trinity College (Oxford) mission and St. Helen's House women's settlement. Trinity College mission originated in 1887, when the Vicar of St. John's, Stratford, erected an iron church in

[90] Jewish Year Bk. 1954, 111.
[91] Worship Reg. 43143 and 47569.
[92] Ibid. 57038 and 57464.
[93] White's Dir. Essex, 1863; E. Walford, Old and New London, v. 573a [B.M. RR 2065a].
[94] N. Pevsner, Buildings of England (Essex), 382.
[95] Pers. obs. 14 July 1965 (A.H.P.); Kelly's Dir. Essex, 1886.
[96] See pp. 145–50.
[97] See p. 111.
[98] V.C.H. Essex, ii. 595.
[99] White's Dir. Essex (1863), 616.
[1] Essex Standard, 1852, 1855, 1858, passim.
[2] Ibid. 5 Feb. 1864. The institution's records, from 1859 to 1946, are in W.H.L. For the work of the institution see J. R. Soar, 'The historical development of tech-

nical . . . education in W. Ham' (London M.A. thesis, 1966), chap. iii.
[3] For the school see p. 149.
[4] J. S. Curwen, Old Plaistow (1905 edn.), 72–3; P.E.M., P. Thompson, 'W. Ham Gleanings': Some Religious Orders of modern times (MS. note); A Franciscan Revival, ed. A. C. Kelway, 15. For Malim see Kelly's Dir. Essex (1878 and 1882).
[5] Old Carpentarians, Story of the Carpenters' Co. Tech. Sch. and of the Old Carpentarians.
[6] Kelly's Dir. Essex (1890).
[7] Ibid. (1906). For the school see below, p. 154.
[8] W.H.L., J. Russell, 'Hist. Tate Institute, 1887–1933' (TS. 1951).
[9] Inf. from Mr. F. Sainsbury.

Tenby (later Oxford) Road.[10] This was burnt down, and was replaced by a brick church, dedicated to St. Philip, which was in existence by 1888,[11] when Trinity College took over the mission. The church was later re-dedicated to the Holy Trinity, and a hall was built beside it, with rooms for the missioner and visitors. A boys' club was built nearby in Great Eastern Road.[12] In 1898 no. 60 Romford Road was rented as a settlement house. E. G. Howarth, head of the settlement in 1905–9, directed a survey of West Ham's social and industrial problems.[13] The settlement later moved to Water Lane[14] and finally to rooms above the hall in Oxford Road. After the First World War the Tom Allen club was built in Grove Crescent Road to commemorate a former head of the settlement. In 1933 a conventional district was formed for the mission.[15] During the Second World War, however, the church and hall were wrecked by bombing and closed. They and the club in Great Eastern Road have since been demolished. The Tom Allen club survived and in 1943–4 was taken over by St. Helen's House women's settlement. St. Helen's House, Stratford, had been founded in 1896 in connexion with St. Margaret's House, Bethnal Green. From headquarters in the Grove it collaborated with the Trinity College mission.[16] In 1931 it moved to new buildings in Water Lane.[17] After the Second World War it was reconstituted as Dockland settlement No. 9.[18] In 1957 the Tom Allen club was rebuilt with help from Trinity College; a small chapel was added in 1958. In 1969 the club was the headquarters of this settlement, St. Helen's House being the warden's residence.

Mansfield House University settlement was founded in 1889 by students connected with Mansfield (Congregational) College, Oxford. The first warden was (Sir) Percy Alden (1891–1901).[19] Two shops in Barking Road, near the public hall, were taken as residences, and a hall was built behind them.[20] In 1897 a new residential block was built farther west, near Canning Town station, the original buildings becoming the men's club.[21] Fairbairn boys' club, founded in 1891, and named after the first principal of Mansfield,[22] moved in 1895 to the present site in Barking Road (nos. 310–16), occupying converted premises until 1900, when Fairbairn Hall was built there.[23] The settlement provided many welfare and educational services. In some

fields it was a pioneer, e.g. in its legal-aid scheme. Under Alden it was also very influential in local politics.[24] After the First World War the settlement declined and in 1923 had to sell the men's club premises.[25] (Sir) Ian Horobin, honorary warden 1923–61, brought about a revival. Fairbairn hall was extended in 1931[26] and in 1935 new residences were built behind it, replacing the old ones near the station.[27] A chapel was added in 1938.[28] By then the settlement had become undenominational. In 1968 the total membership of the Mansfield and Fairbairn clubs was about 900. Fairbairn hall includes a library, theatre, workshops, gymnasium, and canteen.[29]

The Canning Town women's settlement, Cumberland Road, was founded in 1892 by F. W. Newland, pastor of Canning Town Congregational church.[30] It has always been closely associated with Mansfield House settlement. Rebecca H. Cheetham, warden 1892–1922, was prominent in West Ham public life.[31] The settlement was originally at no. 461 Barking Road. In 1899 the Lees Hall, Barking Road, named after its donors, was opened as headquarters and offices. It was enlarged in 1913.[32] By 1910 there was also a settlement house in Cumberland Road. The settlement's early work included a small hospital[33] and an out-patients' clinic. Its activities were at first concerned mainly with women and children but gradually widened. Among them was a branch of the Metropolitan Association for Befriending Young Servants, which was primarily an employment agency. During the Second World War all the settlement's buildings were wrecked by bombing except the house in Cumberland Road, but the work continued. After the war the finances of the settlement deteriorated, and in 1968 it was taken over by the Aston Charities Trust. The Canning Town settlement, as it has since been named, was being rebuilt in 1969 on the Cumberland Road site, to provide flats for old people, with dining-rooms, club rooms, clinics, a theatre, and premises for the citizens' advice bureau.[34]

The Mayflower family centre, Cooper and Vincent Streets, Canning Town, originated as the Malvern College mission. In 1894 the college erected an iron church, dedicated to St. Alban and the English Martyrs, on a site in Cooper Street given by Peter Gellatly.[35] Other buildings were later added.[36] About 1905 (Sir) Reginald Kennedy-Cox, an Old Malvernian, joined the mission as a voluntary helper. In 1918

[10] Paragraph based on: *Trinity Coll. Mission, 21st Anniv. Commemoration* (1909); *Chel. Dioc. Chron.* Dec. 1941, p. 140; *Essex Churchman*, Jan. 1958; *Bk. of W. Ham*, 170–1; Dockland Settlements, *Ann. Reps.* 1947–64; inf. from Mrs. M. Wilkinson.

[11] *Wilson & Whitworth's Stratford &c. Almanack* (1888).

[12] *Kelly's Dir. Stratford* (1894/5).

[13] E. G. Howarth and M. Wilson, *West Ham* (1908).

[14] *Wilson & Whitworth's W. Ham and Stratford Almanack* (1914).

[15] E.R.O., D/CPc 256.

[16] Howarth and Wilson, *W. Ham*, 391.

[17] *Chel. Dioc. Chron.* Dec. 1930, June 1931.

[18] The numbering of the Dockland Settlements was discontinued in 1957.

[19] Mansfield House Univ. Sett. *Report on Some Specialized Activities* (c. 1951).

[20] *E.R.* i. 68–9; *Cong. Year Bk.* (1892), 208–10.

[21] *London*, 9 Dec. 1897; *Cong. Year Bk.* (1898), 160–1; W.H.L., *Mansfield House Rep.* 1908.

[22] Andrew M. Fairbairn (1838–1912), see *D.N.B.*; W.H.L., *Mansfield House Rep.* 1903, p. 18.

[23] *Mansfield Ho. Handbk.* (1936), 6.

[24] See p. 104.

[25] *Mansfield House Mag.* xxx (1923), *passim*.

[26] *Architect and Building News*, 13 Mar. 1931.

[27] Inf. from the Warden, Mansfield House.

[28] *Chel. Dioc. Chron.* Jan. 1939.

[29] Inf. from the Warden.

[30] Paragraph based on: *E.R.* i. 68–9 and ix. 39; Canning Town Women's Settlement, *Ann. Reps.* 1915, 1930, 1938, 1939, 1950–65 and *Magazine*, Sept./Oct. 1924, July 1925, July 1926, Mar./Apr. 1940, Mar. 1941, June 1942, Spring 1946.

[31] W.H.L., News Cuttings 20 and 26 Dec. 1939 (obits.).

[32] *Stratford Express*, 22 Mar. 1913.

[33] See p. 111.

[34] Inf. from Revd. J. Froud.

[35] Char. Com. File 102871: Copy of Letter from P. Bayne, Archdeacon of Southend, 22 Nov. 1923, describing origin of Malvern Coll. mission.

[36] Paragraph based on: *Fifty Years a Borough*, 264; Sir R. Kennedy-Cox, *Autobiography* (1931) and *Dockland Saga* (1955); B. Tinton, *My Twenty Five Years in Dockland* (1946).

he became the first lay warden of the mission, and began to build up the Dockland settlements and Malvern College clubs, formally constituted in 1923. Canning Town, called settlement No. 1, was the headquarters of an organization which by 1937 had six branches in the London area and others elsewhere. Kennedy-Cox subsidized the settlements from his own income, secured royal patronage, and raised large sums by appeals to private benefactors and charity dinners and balls.[37] At Canning Town new club rooms, gymnasium, dance hall, theatre, and swimming-bath were built in 1924–9. The settlement chapel was replaced in 1930 by a new one dedicated to St. George and St. Helena.[38] A new staff residence for men was added in 1931 and one for women in 1934. In 1937 Kennedy-Cox retired. During the Second World War most of the club activities ceased. In 1947 Kennedy-Cox returned for a few months to reorganize it. By 1957 it was again in difficulties.[39] It was saved by the Revd. David Sheppard, who reconstituted it as the Mayflower family centre, of which he became warden. He worked there from 1958 until he became suffragan bishop of Woolwich in 1969.[40] The centre, managed by an undenominational committee, provides facilities for people of all ages, but specializes in youth work and runs a nursery school. In addition to a small staff there are about 20 residents. The residential blocks, in 16th-century style, occupy two sides of a quadrangle. Connecting them at one end is the chapel, designed to imitate Lincoln's Inn hall. When the Mayflower centre was formed the headquarters of the Dockland settlements were transferred to Romford Road, Stratford.

The Society of St. Francis (Church of England), Balaam Street, is the successor of the Society of the Divine Compassion, founded in 1894 by Hon. J. G. Adderley (Superior 1894–7), H. R. Chappel, later Father Henry (Superior 1897–1906), and H. E. Hardy, later Father Andrew (Superior 1912–16 and 1924–35).[41] The S.D.C., which was monastic and Anglo-Catholic, became responsible for the mission church of St. Philip, Plaistow.[42] It was originally housed in Meredith Street but later moved to Balaam Street. In 1901 the society established printing and watchmaking shops at Plaistow.[43] For many years Father Andrew wrote and produced Nativity and Passion plays which won more than local recognition. In 1953 the society was dissolved. Its premises and work were taken over by Franciscans from Cerne Abbas (Dors.).[44]

The Church of England Missions to Seamen institute, Victoria Dock Road, Custom House, was in existence by about 1900.[45] In 1936 a large new institute was completed on and in front of the old site, and this became the headquarters of the Missions to Seamen.[46]

The Bancroft's boys' club, Prince Regent Lane, Canning Town, was founded in 1911. Until 1965 it was financed entirely by the old boys' association of Bancroft's school, Woodford. New premises were built in 1939 on the corner of Alnwick Road.[47]

The Young Men's Christian Association was active in West Ham by 1884, when it helped to build the Conference Hall, West Ham Lane.[48] In the present century its main centres have been at Forest Gate and Plaistow. It had a branch at Forest Gate by 1906[49] and in 1913 erected a hostel in Woodgrange Road.[50] That building was badly damaged by bombing during the Second World War and was finally closed in 1959.[51] Red Triangle club, Greengate Street, Plaistow, was opened in 1921 at a cost of about £100,000.[52] It included a theatre, swimming-bath, gymnasium, and sports ground, and was very successful until the Second World War. It was closed and sold in 1956. The proceeds of the sale of the Forest Gate and Plaistow premises were used to build a new Y.M.C.A. hostel at Walthamstow.[53]

Durning Hall Christian community centre, Earlham Grove and Woodgrange Road, Forest Gate, replaced an earlier Durning Hall, founded about 1885 at Limehouse (Lond.).[54] Premises in Woodgrange Road were registered for worship in 1953,[55] and in 1959 the main buildings of the centre were opened in Earlham Grove, containing a church, hall, offices, gymnasium, and chaplain's flat. A hostel, with shops below, was later completed on the Woodgrange Road frontage. Durning Hall, which is undenominational, is administered by the Aston charities trust, founded in 1930 by Miss Theodora Durning-Lawrence. It caters for all age-groups. The church of the Holy Carpenter, designed by Shingler and Risden Associates, has a fine altar wall of stained glass.

Anchor House, Barking Road, Canning Town, is a large residential club for seamen opened in 1962 by the Roman Catholic Apostleship of the Sea.[56] It stands on the site of Lees Hall (Canning Town Women's Settlement) and adjoining properties.

Among institutions narrower in scope is the John Barnes Memorial home for old people, Hamfrith Road.[57] About 1888 John Barnes of Stratford started private charitable work among old people. Friends joined him and in 1904 the John Barnes Philanthropic Society was constituted. About 1908 the society opened an old people's home in a house in Keogh Road.[58] It proved too small and by 1917[59] a larger one had been taken in Hamfrith Road. An

[37] Cf. Stratford Express, 9 Dec. 1938; Tatler, 10 May 1939.
[38] Chel. Dioc. Chron. May 1930.
[39] Dockland Settlements, Annual Reps. 1947–58.
[40] For the Mayflower Centre see: D. Sheppard, Parson's Pitch (1964); G. Burton, People matter more than things (1965); D. and J. Hewitt, George Burton, a study in contradictions (1969).
[41] Paragraph based on: A Franciscan Revival, ed. A. C. Kelway; Life and Letters of Fr. Andrew, S.D.C. ed. K. E. Burne; inf. from Fr. Alban, O.S.F.; Essex Churchman, Mar. 1962.
[42] See p. 121.
[43] Cf. Sainsbury, Eight Hundred Years, 27.
[44] For the Franciscans at Plaistow see Observer, 10 Feb. 1957.
[45] W. Besant, Shoreditch and the East End, 63; cf. Kelly's Dir. Essex (1910).
[46] Chel. Dioc. Chron. June 1936, p. 90.
[47] Inf. from Hon. Sec. Bancroft's boys' club.
[48] See p. 137.
[49] Kelly's Dir. Essex (1906).
[50] Bk. of W. Ham, 170.
[51] Inf. from Y.M.C.A. Metropolitan Union.
[52] Bk. of W. Ham, 166; Fifty Years, 266.
[53] Inf. from Y.M.C.A. Metropolitan Union.
[54] Paragraph based on: inf. from Revd. J. Froud; Durning Hall, Souvenir of Opening (1959).
[55] Worship Reg. 64129.
[56] Inf. from the chaplain, Anchor Ho.
[57] Paragraph based on: W.H.L., Pamphs., J. Niedermann, A silent but beautiful work (1904); Bk. of W. Ham, 164; Jn. Barnes Old Folks' Memorial Homes, Ann. Rep. (1948).
[58] Cf. Kelly's Dir. Essex (1908).
[59] Ibid. (1917).

adjoining property was later acquired, and in 1932 a new home was built on the site.

EDUCATION. West Ham's first parish school was opened in 1723. During the following years public elementary education was provided mainly by the churches until 1871, when a school board, one of the earliest in the country, was formed for the parish. The board's first report gave details of existing schools and assessed the deficiency of school places.[60] There were 27 schools, in 46 departments, of which the Church of England was responsible for 15, in 28 departments, the nonconformists for 7 (in 10), the Roman Catholics for 3 (in 5), the Great Eastern Railway for 1 (in 1), and the Ragged School Union for 1 (in 2). Among the Church schools was classed Sarah Bonnell's, a well-endowed charity school. All the other schools depended mainly on subscriptions and school-pence. For 20 years the churches had been making great efforts to educate West Ham's sharply rising population. Some Churchmen were still reluctant to admit that the task was beyond them. In 1870 the vicar of Christ Church, Stratford, had appealed to the public to vote against the formation of a school board.[61]

The board's report showed, however, that the public elementary schools had accommodation for only 8,183 children out of 14,512 between the ages of 3 and 13. There were places for a further 1,749 in private and dame schools. Allowing for these, for projected enlargements at some of the voluntary schools, and for children absent through illness or educated at home, the board put the deficiency at 3,100 places. This was clearly an underestimate, for many of the dame schools were admitted to be of a very low standard, some no more than nurseries. Nor does the report make any allowance for future population growth.

The school board, which was controlled by a Progressive majority until 1895, and by the Conservatives from 1895 to 1903, appointed as its full-time clerk Jeremiah Self, formerly headmaster of West Ham Church school, who served successfully until 1890. The board immediately planned to build three new schools, at Forest Gate, Canning Town, and Stratford. Meanwhile it opened several night-schools to provide elementary education for adolescents who had missed it.[62] In 1872–3 the board took over 4 of the voluntary schools and opened several other temporary day-schools, one of which became permanent. The first three new schools, Odessa Road, Hallsville, and High Street were completed in 1874. Others followed rapidly, since the 32 years of the board's existence coincided with the period of West Ham's most rapid growth, in which the school population rose to over 60,000. By 1903 the board had built 43 elementary schools, a school for the deaf, one for physical and mental defectives, one for truants, and two pupil-teacher centres.[63] Between 1871 and 1903 many of the voluntary schools were closed, including all those

belonging to the nonconformists. One new elementary school was, however, built by the Church of England and two by the Roman Catholics. A start was also made in providing public secondary education. The Sarah Bonnell school was refounded in new buildings (1876) as a high school for girls, and the Carpenters' Company opened a technical school for boys (1891).

Under the Education Act, 1902, West Ham, as a county borough, became responsible (1903) for all types of education. The clerk to the school board (Self's successor) became head of the new education department, but he died in the same year during inquiries which revealed that he had been embezzling public funds. The department was then placed under the town clerk, who controlled it until 1939, when a separate education officer was again appointed.

In 1903, in addition to the council schools, there were 7 Anglican, 6 Roman Catholic, and 1 undenominational elementary schools. Three more elementary schools, started by the school board, were completed in 1904, and before the First World War two others were built by the council and one by the Roman Catholics. In 1906 the two pupil-teacher centres were reopened as higher elementary (later called central) schools, and in the same year the council opened its first 'municipal secondary' school, at Stratford. Two Roman Catholic secondary schools, previously private, were recognized in 1904 as part of the public system, and for many years these, with the Bonnell school, provided most of the secondary school places in the borough. Higher education was provided by a technical institute (later college) opened by the council in 1898. From 1900 the institute was offering internal courses for the University of London's degrees in science and engineering, but most of its work was at a lower level. After the closure of the Carpenters' school (1905) the institute began to develop junior technical classes for those under 16, which overlapped those of the higher elementary schools.

In reorganizing the schools after 1903 the council became embroiled in a bitter struggle with the teachers over grading and salaries. This culminated in 1907, when the National Union of Teachers brought an unsuccessful suit against the council and some 150 of the borough's teachers were dismissed or resigned. The dispute was settled in September of that year.

In 1920 the education committee drew up a scheme concerned mainly with older children.[64] It proposed to open several temporary day-continuation institutes, pending the building of two new secondary schools and four central schools. Part-time attendance at the institutes was to be compulsory, and by 1926 the school-leaving age for all children in West Ham was to be raised to 15. Five institutes were opened in 1921, but compulsory attendance proved so unpopular that it was abandoned in the same year, two of the institutes being closed and the others continuing on a voluntary basis. By 1936 only one

[60] W.H.L., W. Ham Sch. Bd. Mins.; *Rep. on Educ. Requirements of W. Ham* (1871); W. Simms, 'An essay on the West Ham School Board . . . administration and other aspects'; 'An essay on the . . . history, politics and personalities of the W. Ham School Board'; 'The Voluntary Schools of W. Ham'; 'The Private Schools of W. Ham'; 'Secondary Education in W. Ham'.

[61] W.H.L., Handbill, Dec. 1870.
[62] W.H.L., W. Ham Sch. Bd. Mins. 1871–5.
[63] For these and later schools see W.H.L., W. Simms, 'The Architectural History of the schools in W. Ham' (illustrated TS.).
[64] *W. Ham Educ. Scheme* (1920).

remained.[65] A new council secondary school, at Plaistow, in the south of the borough, was opened in 1926. None of the other secondary or central schools proposed in the 1920 scheme was built, but this need was partly met by the steady expansion, between 1918 and 1939, of the junior departments of the technical college. The school-leaving age was not raised during that period.

The reorganization of the elementary schools, on the lines of the Hadow report, began in 1929.[66] This involved building a junior and two senior schools and new premises for the two existing central schools. Complete reorganization proved difficult, owing to the geographical isolation of some of the schools, but the main part of the programme was carried out in 1930–4, and by 1939 only 16 all-age (including voluntary) schools remained.[67] During the reorganization a few junior schools were given new names identical with those of associated senior schools, but in most cases they had reverted to their original names by 1939. Between 1918 and 1939 three more special schools (one a replacement) and 2 nursery schools were also built.

During the Second World War the elementary schools of the borough reverted to all-age type, in order to reduce travelling. Wartime bombing destroyed several schools, but the devastation which it caused, especially in the south, provided an opportunity for the educational planners, since it caused a great movement of population out of the borough, and at the same time facilitated the redevelopment of large areas, thus providing building sites that would otherwise have been difficult to find. After the war the reorganization of the elementary schools was completed. In anticipation of the post-war increase in the birth-rate priority was given to new primary schools: between 1945 and 1954 eight were built or rebuilt, of which six (including two voluntary) were in the south of the borough. Another voluntary primary school was rebuilt in 1964. Since 1945 all the primary schools have been mixed. Under a development plan of 1947 secondary education was provided in three 'streams', grammar, technical, and modern.[68] The old municipal secondary schools and the Sarah Bonnell school continued as grammar schools. Three new technical schools were formed by the separation of the junior departments of the technical college, the day-continuation institute being closed. The selective side of the new plan was completed by the two Roman Catholic schools, which became multilateral. Between 1945 and 1958 one of the grammar schools and two of the technical schools were provided with completely new buildings, while most of the other selective schools were substantially improved. No secondary modern schools were built or rebuilt in that period. The priority given to the selective schools was partly due to the intention that they should provide an unusually high proportion of places, 30 per cent for boys and 25 per cent for girls,

but this level was not reached, and many of those who did in fact gain selective places left before completing the initial five-year course.

In 1959 the education committee drew up a new plan, under which the secondary modern schools were to be gradually replaced by larger non-selective high schools and selective education was to be provided in two central high schools. The latter proposal had not been carried out by 1965, and the former only in part. By 1965 two high schools had been formed, one at Stratford, by the fusion of a grammar (formerly technical) and an adjacent secondary modern school, the other at Forest Gate, by the enlargement of a secondary modern school. These high schools have one selective class in each entry.

Other developments since 1945 have been the designation of the technical college as a college of technology and the opening of a college of further education. Two adult education centres, an outdoor activities centre (at Maldon), and two more nursery schools have also been opened, while improvements in public health have made it possible to close two special (open air) schools. In 1949 most of the schools in the borough were renamed, usually by dropping such words as 'Street' from the original names.

In the following chronological sections the account of each school is placed according to the date of its original foundation. Since there has been much rebuilding and reorganization the information in a section may overlap the dates in the heading. All changes of school names are described except the temporary ones of the 1930s.

Elementary schools founded before 1871. West Ham (All Saints) Church primary school, Portway,[69] was founded in 1723 as a parish charity school, supported by subscriptions, collections in the church, and £4 a year given under the will of Mary Battailhey, proved 1702, for teaching the poor children of Stratford and Plaistow to read.[70] The school appears to have been held at first in the church, but in 1731 a proper building was erected on the east side of the churchyard, and at the same time the management was vested in a body of regular subscribers. In 1752 a second building, for a 'school of industry' was added to the north of the original one.[71] The new building, sometimes called the 'workhouse',[72] had ceased to be used for its intended purpose by 1769, when most of it was handed over to the founding trustees of Sarah Bonnell's girls school.[73] For the next century the Church school and Bonnell's school were closely associated. The Church school originally comprised 10 boys. Girls were first admitted in 1725, and by 1769 there were 30 of each sex. It was stated in 1769 that 311 boys and 202 girls had attended the school since its foundation, including those still there. The children had been provided with clothing since 1725.

By 1812 the Church school had received endowments of some £3,000, and its total annual income

[65] For these institutes see: E. J. Morton, 'The Day Continuation Institutes of West Ham' (Manchester Univ. M.Ed. thesis, 1968).
[66] W. Ham Elem. Educ. Scheme (1929).
[67] Cf. W. Ham Educ. Ctee. Reps. 1944–5, p. 80.
[68] For an independent survey of West Ham's secondary education, 1945–63, see D. Peschek and J. Brand, *Policies and Politics in Secondary Education* (L.S.E. Greater London Papers, No. 11), 13–75.
[69] Unless otherwise stated this paragraph is based on:

W.H.L., W. Ham Char. Schs. Treasurer's Accs. 1723–1832; Char. Com., *W. Ham Char. Rep.* (1899), 86.
[70] *W. Ham Char. Rep.* (1899), 19, 50.
[71] Lysons, *London*, iv. 269. For both buildings see above, plate f.p. 116.
[72] There is no evidence that it was ever used for adult paupers.
[73] Lysons, *London*, iv. 269; W.H.L., W. Ham Vestry Mins. 27 June 1769, 23 Aug. 1770.

from these and from subscriptions was £260.[74] In 1812–13 it was enlarged, and by 1818 it had 120 boys and 60 girls.[75] In 1826–30 a new boys school was built to the east of the existing premises, with aid from the National Society, and the old Church school was leased to Bonnell's school, which became responsible for educating all the girls of the parish.[76] District schools were opened for Plaistow in 1830 and for Stratford in 1835: these remained in union with the original school until 1848, when they became separate, each of the three being given a share of the educational endowments of the parish. By 1846–7 there were 126 boys in All Saints school, under a trained master.[77] The first government grant was made in 1849.[78] By 1851 average attendance had risen to 145, but many of the pupils were factory boys who stayed only three months.[79] Meanwhile the Church school trustees had become dissatisfied with the arrangement made with Bonnell's school in 1828, and in 1851 opened an additional department, for girls and infants.[80]

In 1861 a new boys school was built about 200 yards farther east, at a total cost of over £3,000, about a third of which came from selling most of the remaining endowments.[81] In 1863, by a joint scheme, Bonnell's school was demolished and replaced by a range of buildings comprising a northern schoolroom for Bonnell's and a southern schoolroom for the Church girls, with two houses for teachers between them. The Church infants took over the former boys school of 1826. The boys school of 1861 was known at first as the Pelly Memorial, in tribute to Sir John Pelly, Bt. (d. 1852), but it was also known at that period as the Model school because of its high reputation. The headmaster (1846–71) was Jeremiah Self, later secretary to the West Ham school board. By 1871 attendance was 330, with a further 130 in the girls department and 190 infants.[82] In 1876, when Bonnell's school moved to West Ham Lane, the Church girls took over all the 1863 buildings. In 1934 the school was reorganized for mixed juniors and infants. It was granted Aided status in 1950 and Controlled status in 1956. In 1964 it was completely rebuilt.[83]

Bonnell's charity school was founded by the will of Sarah Bonnell, proved 1766.[84] She left £500 in trust to build and maintain a school for poor girls of the parish, which was to have the reversion of a further £3,500 after the death of her brother James Bonnell. James contested the will, and in 1769, after a Chancery suit, an agreement was reached between him and the trustees. The north end of the Church school, on the east side of the churchyard, was to be handed over by the parish for use as a school for 40 poor girls born in West Ham or adjacent places.[85] The parish gave up its claim to the £500, but was to

have the reversion to the remaining £3,500 after Bonnell's death. The schoolmistress, when appointed, was to receive £20 a year and £5 for coal and candles. A master was to receive £15 a year for teaching writing and accounts, and £5 for stationery. Clothing for the girls was to be provided at a cost of £100 a year. By 1772 the schoolroom had been partitioned off and fitted up by means of a loan.[86] James Bonnell died in 1774[87] and the school was opened in 1778.[88] In 1814 a new schoolroom was built to the north of the existing one. A Chancery scheme of 1820 empowered the trustees to admit 60 girls, or more if funds permitted, and to increase the master's and mistress's salaries and the payments for clothing. In 1826–30, as described above, Bonnell's took over all the old Church school, with responsibility for educating all the girls of the parish. In 1834 there were 140 pupils, of whom 80 were being clothed by the charity. In 1856 the schoolroom of 1814 was rebuilt, but in 1863 this and the original school were demolished as part of the joint scheme, already described, under which adjacent new buildings were erected for Bonnell's and the Church girls. Under a scheme of 1873, drawn up by the Endowed Schools Commissioners, Bonnell's became the West Ham high school for girls, reopening in new buildings in West Ham Lane in 1876.[89]

West Ham and Stratford British schools appear to have originated in 1802, when a girls charity school was opened in connexion with Brickfields Independent chapel.[90] A schoolroom was built beside the chapel in 1806–8. There were 20 girls in 1807.[91] In 1846 a ladies committee of leading dissenters was formed to manage the school, as the West Ham and Stratford girls British school, on a wider nonsectarian basis, and in 1847 a trained mistress was appointed. The school was then renting the Sunday schoolroom at Brickfields, but in 1851 new buildings for girls and infants were erected in Bridge Road, Stratford, with the aid of a government grant[92] and a contribution from Samuel Gurney. In 1871 there were 170 girls and 143 infants on the roll.[93] In 1889 the school was taken over by the school board, which moved it in 1890 to temporary quarters at the Workmen's hall, West Ham Lane, pending demolition of the old buildings, and the opening in 1892 of the new Bridge Road three-department school.[94]

Associated with the girls British school was one for boys, built in 1836 in Little North (now Station) Street, Stratford. Samuel Gurney was an original trustee. In 1846 there were 160 boys, paying 1d. or 2d. a week 'in very good tone and discipline' but 'not exhibiting much intelligence . . . under a master of the old style'.[95] In 1873 the school was taken over by the school board, which retained it until 1889,

74 W.H.L., Copy of Mins. Ch. Sch. Trustees, 1812–33.
75 Ibid.; *Rtns. Educ. Poor*, H.C. 224, p. 257 (1819) ix(1).
76 Mins. Ch. Sch. Trustees, 1812–33.
77 *Nat. Soc. Enquiry into Ch. Schs.* 1846–7.
78 *Mins. Educ. Ctee. of Council*, [1215], p. clxxxiv, H.C. (1850), xliii.
79 Ibid. [1479], p. 309 (1852), xxxix.
80 W.H.L., Copy of Mins. Ch. Sch. Trustees, 1839–51.
81 Ibid. 1851–63; *W. Ham Char. Rep.* (1899), 88, 91.
82 *Rep. Educ. W. Ham* (1871), 10, 11.
83 Inf. from Newham L.B. Educ. Ctee.
84 *W. Ham Char. Rep.* (1899) 2, 76, describes the history of this school. See also: W.H.L., Vertical Files E/WES/370 and 373; Rep. re Bonnell's Sch. Bdgs. (1899).

85 W.H.L., W. Ham Vestry Mins. 27 June 1769, cf. 23 Aug. 1770.
86 Ibid. 23 Aug. 1770, 21 Aug. 1772.
87 Lysons, *London*, iv. 212.
88 W.H.L., Bonnell's Sch. Trustees' Mins. 1777–98.
89 For its later history see p. 154.
90 For the girls British school see: *W. Ham Char. Rep.* (1899), 92, 94, 95, 99–105; W.H.L., Girls Brit. Sch. Min. Bk. 1846–62 and Log Bk. 1863–89.
91 E.R.O., D/AEM 2/4.
92 *Mins. Educ. Ctee. of Council*, [1787], p. 92, H.C. (1854), li.   93 *Rep. Educ. W. Ham* (1871), 10.
94 W.H.L., W. Ham Sch. Bd. Mins. 1889–92.
95 *Mins. Educ. Ctee. of Council*, [998], pp. 284, 310, H.C. (1847–8), l.

when the site was sold to the Great Eastern Railway. The boys moved to the Workmen's hall until the new Bridge Road school was ready.[96]

Both the British schools had endowments. Between 1815 and 1838 the girls charity school acquired a total of £440, of which £140 was spent in 1841–4. From 1849 the income from the remaining £300 was used exclusively for Brickfields Sunday school. Samuel Gurney, by his will proved 1856, gave £5,000 in trust for the British schools, to provide incomes of £50 for the girls and £100 for the boys.[97] When the school board took over the boys school the charity trustees agreed to pay the income of £100 to the board, and this arrangement was regularized by a Charity Commission scheme of 1878, under which the income might be spent in any of the board's schools, for various purposes stipulated, including prizes, exhibitions for promising pupils, special equipment, and payments to teachers for advanced tuition. In 1889, by agreement with the charity trustees, the girls school income of £50 was also assigned to the school board, to be used in the same way. By a scheme of 1899, however, the whole income of £150 was restricted to the provision of scholarships for higher education, tenable only by former pupils of the Bridge Road board school.[98]

St. Francis's Roman Catholic primary school, Park Avenue, Stratford, originated about 1816, when François-Joseph Chevrollais, the parish priest, opened a school in High Street, adjoining his church of St. Vincent de Paul and St. Patrick.[99] Two earlier priests had conducted schools in West Ham, but these were apparently private and short-lived.[1] The attendance at the parish school was 139 in 1819.[2] About 1870 part of the school was transferred to Grove Crescent Road, adjoining the new church of St. Vincent (later St. Francis), and another part to premises at the west end of Forest Lane. In 1871 the total attendance was 285.[3] St. Vincent's school was receiving a government grant from 1871, and Forest Lane from 1874.[4] Soon after this the two schools were combined at Grove Crescent Road.[5] In 1884 an additional infant school, St. Patrick's, was opened in the old High Street buildings.[6] By 1890 St. Vincent's (now St. Francis's) had again been divided, the girls and infants moving to Park Avenue and the boys remaining at Grove Crescent Road.[7] The boys moved to Park Avenue in or about 1900.[8] The school has remained at Park Avenue, in buildings progressively modernized. It

was reorganized for mixed juniors and infants in 1945 and was granted Aided status in 1949.[9] St. Patrick's infant school, which moved to Lett Road in 1896, was closed in 1940 and its pupils were transferred to St. Francis's school.[10]

Plaistow Lancasterian (British) school seems to have been founded about 1820, meeting in a large room in the Porch House, Cordwainer (now High) Street.[11] In 1830 it was taken over by the Anglicans, and merged in St. Mary's National school.

Forest Gate British school was probably founded about 1830 by Jabez Legg, in connexion with the Congregational church.[12] In 1871 it was situated on the northern corner of Forest Lane and Woodgrange Road, the position occupied by the original Congregational church.[13] The attendance was then 65. In 1872 it was taken over by the school board which retained it until Odessa Road school was opened in 1874.[14]

St. Mary's National school, Plaistow, originated in 1830, when the trustees of All Saints Church school took over Plaistow Lancasterian school.[15] A new school was built in 1831, to the west of St. Mary's church, funds being supplied by the National Society and by John Oliver, from whom the school was known at first as Oliver's.[16] In 1835 50 boys attended.[17] The school was enlarged in 1836, with the aid of a government grant, and by 1838 there were 62 girls as well as 47 boys.[18] In 1848 St. Mary's school received £936 as its share of the educational endowments of West Ham.[19] A further endowment of £300 was received under the will of Edith Clark, proved in 1860.[20] The school was further enlarged in 1871 and 1877, and attendance rose to 332 in 1881.[21] In 1895 the boys department was closed to reduce overcrowding.[22] The remainder of the school was closed in 1903 and its endowments, worth £34 a year, were assigned to St. Mary's church.[23] The school buildings still existed in 1970. The original school of 1831, designed by G. R. French, was a single-storeyed yellow-brick building with a 'Tudor' doorway at its gable end. Above the door was a carved tablet inscribed 'Oliver's National School' with arms and date.[24] The school connected with St. Peter's, Upton Cross, then a mission of St. Mary's, is described below.[25]

St. John's National school, Stratford, was opened in 1835 in a building also used as a Sunday school.[26] In 1836 a permanent school, for 526 children, was built in Great North (now Station) Street, on land previously occupied by a brewery, with the aid of

[96] W. Ham Sch. Bd. Mins. 1873, 1889–92.
[97] W. Ham Char. Rep. (1899), 99–105.
[98] W. Ham Sch. Bd. Mins. 1899.
[99] Essex Recusant, ii. 38–43.
[1] Westminster Archives, vol. xvii, Letters and Papers of Bp. Talbott, Letter of Thomas Wright (1789); E.R.O. Q/RRw 3 and Q/SBb 406; Laity's Dir. 1807.
[2] Rtns. Educ. Poor, H.C. 224, p. 257 (1819), ix(1).
[3] Rep. Educ. W. Ham (1871), 11, and map; Kelly's Dir. Essex (1870), pp. 106, 204.
[4] Rep. Educ. Ctee. of Council, [C.601], p. 259 H.C.(1872), xxii; Rtn. Elem. Schs. H.C. 133, pp. 60–1 (1875), lix.
[5] Kelly's Dir. Essex (1878); W.H.L., W. Ham Sch. Bd. Map, 1883.
[6] W. Ham Sch. Bd. Mins. 1884 and Map 1889.
[7] Kelly's Dir. Essex (1890).
[8] W.H.L., W. Ham C.B.C., Architect's Rep. on Non-Provided Schs. (1903).
[9] Inf. from Newham Educ. Ctee.
[10] W.H.L., W. Ham Sch. Bd. Mins. 1897; W. Ham Educ. Ctee., Devt. Plan, 1947.
[11] Fry, E. and W. Ham, 248; W.H.L., Clayton, Survey of W. Ham, 1821: school shown in High St.
[12] E.R. xxx. 227; xxxi. 52; E. Nat. xx. 43–4; White's Dir. Essex (1863), p. 625; Kelly's Dir. Essex (1870).
[13] Rep. Educ. W. Ham (1871), 11.
[14] W. Ham Sch. Bd. Mins. 1872–4.
[15] W.H.L., Mins. Ch. Sch. Trustees, 1812–33.
[16] W. Ham Char. Rep. (1899), 105; White's Dir. Essex (1848), p. 237.
[17] Educ. Enquiry Abs. H.C. 62, p. 277 (1835), xli.
[18] Mins. Educ. Ctee. of Council, [1215], p. clxxxv, H.C. (1850) xliii; Nat. Soc. Rep. 1838.
[19] W. Ham Char. Rep. (1899), 105.
[20] Ibid. 107, 110.
[21] W. Ham Sch. Bd. Mins. 1871, 1877, 1881; plaques on buildings.
[22] W. Ham Sch. Bd. Mins. 1895.
[23] Ibid. 1903.
[24] W.H.L., Illus. Coll. (Schools).
[25] See p. 150.
[26] E.R.O., D/AEM 1/1: Leaflet.

a government grant.[27] The choice of site was unfortunate. Stratford railway junction and repair works were soon built close by and noise from the trains made teaching difficult.[28] In 1848 the school received £735 as its share of the educational endowments of West Ham.[29] In 1851 it received a further £182, later used to improve the buildings, under the will of Mary Goldthorp.[30] In spite of this it was much in debt at this period, and closure was being considered.[31] In 1872, however, new buildings, with accommodation for 831, were erected in Chant Square.[32] The boys department was closed in 1894.[33] The school was reorganized in 1938 for mixed juniors and infants.[34] It was closed in 1947.[35]

Plaistow Public school was opened in 1844 by John Curwen, minister of the North Street (later in Balaam Street) Congregational church.[36] For a few months it was restricted to infants, meeting in the Sunday school. Then that building was enlarged and older children admitted, under a trained master, Alfred Brown. The school soon established a good reputation. For 27 years the managers allowed Brown to run it with a free hand, no government grants being sought. The children, mainly from the families of tradesmen or the upper working class, often learnt French and Latin. In 1866 new buildings were erected in Balaam Street, entirely by public subscription. These were described in 1871 as among the best in the parish, with accommodation for 425 (average attendance 237).[37] In 1872 the trustees leased them to the school board as a gesture in the cause of non-sectarian education. New classrooms were added in 1874 by the trustees, and in 1876 by the school board. A separate girls department was formed in 1874, Alfred Brown remaining in charge of the boys until his death in 1886. In 1897 the pupils were transferred to a new board school in the same street, the old buildings reverting to the Congregational church.

Holy Trinity National school, Canning Town, originated in 1848, when the vicar of Plaistow opened a class in a shed in Hallsville Road.[38] When the Victoria Dock was being built, attendance increased rapidly to over 200, some of whom were taught in an adjoining cottage. In 1857 the school was less crowded, but it was dilapidated and squalid: in wet weather the mistress had to teach under an umbrella.[39] The school received its first government

grant in 1858, as the Victoria Docks National.[40] By 1860 its name had been changed to Hallsville National.[41] Meanwhile the Plaistow and Victoria Docks mission had been formed to build schools and churches, and in 1861 this opened a new school in Barking Road, opposite the site where Holy Trinity church was later built.[42] The government made one of the largest building grants in the parish.[43] In 1871 the total attendance was 520.[44] The infants were then in Wouldham Street, but later in the same year a new building was erected for them on part of the girls' playground.[45] The boys and girls departments were closed in 1936–7 and the infants in 1940.[46]

Christ Church National school, Stratford, was built in 1850 in Union Street, adjoining the site chosen for the church. The government made a building grant.[47] By 1860 the boys department had reached a high standard.[48] The school was taken over by the school board in 1882 and closed in 1885 when the new Carpenters Road school was completed.[49] Christ Church also had a small school in rented buildings in Channelsea Road, opened by 1858.[50] It was closed in 1874 and the site was bought by the school board to build a new school.[51]

Chapel Street Ragged school is said to have been founded in 1851.[52] In 1855 a local committee, in association with the Ragged School Union, bought the former Enon chapel and established the school there.[53] Attendance was then 100.[54] Under the will of William H. Dean, proved 1871, the school was to receive the interest from certain residuary funds, and also the reversion of much larger funds after the death of various annuitants. If the school closed before reversion occurred the money then payable was to pass to some other charity, not necessarily in West Ham. In 1899 it was stated that income from the residuary funds had amounted to only £6 in the previous year, but that the reversion was estimated to be worth a capital sum of £3,827. This expectation from Dean's Gift made it seem important, from a local point of view, that the school should not close, and prolonged its life, in spite of a restricted site and unsuitable buildings. Situated in a very poor area, and without sectarian support, it lived precariously. A government grant was being received from 1881,[55] but by 1898 the school was £700 in debt, and in that year a further £500 was borrowed

[27] Essex Standard, 5 May 1836; Mins. Educ. Ctee. of Council, [1215], p. clxxv, H.C. (1850), xliii.
[28] Mins. Educ. Ctee. of Council, [2681], p. 57, H.C. (1890) liv.
[29] W. Ham Char. Rep. (1899), 97–8.
[30] Ibid. 99.
[31] Essex Standard, 18 July, 1 and 8 Aug. 1851.
[32] W. Ham Char. Rep. (1899), 98; Kelly's Dir. Essex (1886); W. Ham C.B.C., Architect's Rep. on Non-Provided Schs. (1903).
[33] W. Ham Sch. Bd. Mins. 1894.
[34] W.H.L., W. Ham C.B.C. Mins. lii(A), 890.
[35] W.H.L., W. Ham Educ. Ctee., Devt. Plan (1947), p. 25.
[36] For its history see: R. Partner and J. S. Curwen, In Memoriam Alfred Brown of Plaistow (1818–86); W. Ham Char. Rep. (1899), 116–18; J. S. Curwen, Memorials of John Curwen, 68, 165.
[37] Rep. Educ. W. Ham (1871) 11, and map.
[38] For the early history of the school see: W.H.L., Magazine Cutting, 'Pursuit of knowledge under difficulties, or a National school in the suburbs of London' [c. 1858].
[39] Household Words 12 Sept. 1857, p. 243.
[40] Rep. Educ. Ctee. of Council, [2510], p. 560, H.C. (1859–Sess. 1), xxi(1).

[41] Ibid. [2828], p. 571, H.C. (1861), xlix.
[42] W. Ham Char. Rep. (1899), 115–16. And see above, p. 120.
[43] Rep. Educ. Ctee. of Council, [3171], p. 401, H.C. (1863), xlvii.
[44] Rep. Educ. W. Ham (1871), 10.
[45] W. Ham Char. Rep. (1899), 116.
[46] W. Ham Educ. Ctee. Reps. 1935–6 and 1936–7; W. Ham Educ. Devt. Plan (1947).
[47] Mins. Educ. Ctee. of Council, [1215], p. lx, H.C. (1850), xliii.
[48] Rep. Educ. Ctee. of Council, [2681], p. 59, H.C. (1860), liv.
[49] W. Ham Sch. Bd. Mins., 1882, 1885.
[50] Essex Standard, 19 Mar. 1858; Rep. Educ. W. Ham (1871), 11.
[51] W. Ham Sch. Bd. Mins. 1874.
[52] Essex Standard, 12 Dec. 1866, reports its 15th anniversary.
[53] W. Ham Char. Rep. (1899), 108–15, describes the history of this school and Dean's Gift.
[54] Essex Standard, 12 Oct. 1855.
[55] Rep. Educ. Ctee. of Council, [C. 3312–I], p. 637, H.C. (1882), xxiii.

to enlarge the buildings. In 1899 the average attendance was 136. After 1902 the school was recognized by the government only on a temporary basis. In 1905 the income from Dean's Gift was £73, the whole of which was required to meet interest and repayment charges on debt.[56] By then all the surviving annuitants were old, so that the final reversion of the charity probably took place soon after 1905. The school closed in 1927, and by a scheme of 1932 its remaining assets, of £3,200, were invested as Dean's Gift, the income from which was to be used to help needy pupils in West Ham.[57]

Emmanuel (later St. Saviour's) National school, Forest Gate, was built in 1853 on a site, given by Samuel Gurney,[58] at the corner of Woodgrange Road and Forest Street. Government building grants were received in 1854, 1861, and 1867.[59] In 1871 the average attendance was 141.[60] In 1884 the school was handed over to the vicar of the new parish of St. Saviour. With the building of board schools at Forest Gate the maintenance of St. Saviour's school grew more difficult and it was closed in 1894.

The Public school, Victoria Dock Road, Canning Town, was established about 1853, in connexion with the Plaistow Congregational church (North Street, later in Balaam Street), and met in the Victoria Dock public rooms, built for this and other purposes.[61] It was sometimes described as a British school.[62] In 1871 it had an attendance of only 34 and received no government grant.[63] It was taken over in 1872 by the school board, which later bought the site, demolished the buildings, and there erected the new Hallsville school (1874).

St. Paul's National school, Stratford, was opened soon after 1850, probably in the mission schoolroom in Queen Street erected by Samuel Gurney.[64] The first government grant was received in 1855.[65] In 1869 a new building was erected in Maryland Road.[66] By 1871 attendance had risen to 501, including the infants, who were using the Queen Street building.[67] The school was badly damaged by bombing during the Second World War and was closed in 1945.[68]

The Eastern Counties (later Great Eastern) Railway school was in existence by 1856, when it first received a government grant.[69] It was associated with and housed in the railway mechanics' institution, at first in Angel Lane and later in Store Street.[70] By 1863 average attendance had risen to 200. The

school was intended primarily for railwaymen's sons, but other boys were admitted at higher fees, and in 1868 there were about 50 of these, paying 9d. to 1s. a week 'rather than lose the benefits of this well-taught school'. In the 1870s, with increasing competition from the board schools, the railway school ran into financial difficulties. In 1881 it was handed over to the school board, which in 1882 transferred the boys to the new school in Colegrave Road.[71]

St. Luke's Church primary school, Ruscoe Road, Victoria Docks, originated in 1857, when an iron church, the precursor of St. Mark's, was erected at Tidal Basin.[72] This was also a school which received a government grant from 1862.[73] After 1868 it was restricted to infants, the average attendance in 1871 being 77.[74] It was closed about 1882.[75] A second school for St. Mark's district was opened in 1862, at St. Matthew's church, Custom House. From 1864 this was restricted to boys.[76] The average attendance was 205 in 1871.[77] The school was reorganized in 1872 for girls and infants.[78] Accommodation was inadequate, and in 1880, after the government had directed that the school should be restricted to infants, the managers leased it to the school board, which maintained it until 1882 when Regents Lane board school was opened.[79] Meanwhile the efforts of Henry Boyd, vicar of St. Mark's, had led to the building of permanent schools, for this western part of his parish, in Nelson Street. The infants department was opened there in 1866, and the girls in 1868; in each case the initial intake came from the Tidal Basin school.[80] In 1872 the boys from Custom House were also transferred to Nelson Street.[81] In 1875 the Nelson Street, Tidal Basin, and Custom House schools were all transferred to the new parish of St. Luke. Nelson Street, from 1882 St. Luke's only school, was a good one, in spite of the difficulties arising from a poor and shifting population. In 1933 St. Luke's was reorganized for junior boys, junior girls, and infants.[82] It was badly damaged during the Second World War.[83] After the war its site was incorporated in the new Keir Hardie housing estate and a new primary school, opened in 1949, was built in Ruscoe Road.[84] The school was granted Aided status in 1949.[85]

St. Mark's National school, Silvertown, existed by 1860, when it received its first government grant.[86] About 1871 new buildings were erected by the vicar, Henry Boyd, between Constance Street and

[56] W.H.L., W. Ham C.B.C., *Rep. by Town Clerk on School Charities* (1905).
[57] *W. Ham Educ. Ctee. Rep.* 1932.
[58] *W. Ham Char. Rep.* (1899), 108–10, describes the history of this school.
[59] *Mins. Educ. Ctee. of Council*, [1926], p. 165, H.C. (1854–5), xlii; *Rep. Educ. Ctee. of Council* [3007], p. 511, H.C. (1862) xlii; ibid. [4051], p. 635, H.C. (1867–8), xxv.
[60] *Rep. Educ. W. Ham* (1871), 10.
[61] *W. Ham Char. Rep.* (1899), 107–8, describes its history.
[62] *White's Dir. Essex* (1863), p. 625; *Kelly's Dir. Essex* (1870).
[63] *Rep. Educ. W. Ham*, (1871), 11.
[64] See p. 120.
[65] *Mins. Educ. Ctee. of Council*, [2058], p. 86, H.C. (1856), xlvii.
[66] *Rep. Educ. Ctee. of Council*, [C. 165], p. 569 (1870), xxii.
[67] *Rep. Educ. W. Ham* (1871), 10, and map.
[68] *W. Ham Educ. Devt. Plan* (1947), p. 25.
[69] *Mins. Educ. Ctee. of Council*, [2237], p. 96, H.C. (1857), xxxiii.

[70] For the mechanics' institution see p. 141. For the history of the school see W.H.L., Mech. Inst. Sch. Log Bk.
[71] W. Ham Sch. Bd. Mins. 1881–2.
[72] *Churches of Barking Deaneries*, 13.
[73] *Rep. Educ. Ctee. of Council*, [3171], p. 401, H.C. (1863), xlvii.
[74] *Rep. Educ. W. Ham* (1871), 10.
[75] St. Luke's Sch., Admission Regs.
[76] St. Luke's Sch., Boys Sch. Log Bk.
[77] *Rep. Educ. W. Ham* (1871), 10.
[78] St. Luke's Sch., Custom Ho. Sch. Log Bk.
[79] Ibid.; W. Ham Sch. Bd. Mins. 1880–2.
[80] *Rep. Educ. Ctee. of Council*, [4051], p. 637, H.C. (1867–8), xxv; ibid. [4139], p. 529, H.C. (1868–9), xx.
[81] St. Luke's Sch., Boys Sch. Log Bk.
[82] *W. Ham Educ. Scheme* (1932); inf. from Newham Educ. Ctee.
[83] *W. Ham Educ. Ctee. Reps.* 1944–5, p. 80.
[84] Tablet on St. Luke's Sch.
[85] Inf. from Newham Educ. Ctee.
[86] *Rep. Educ. Ctee. of Council*, [2828], p. 572, H.C. (1861), xlix.

Drew Road.[87] The school was enlarged in 1882–3, to provide places for 470,[88] but in 1892 the boys and girls departments were closed, and by 1897 only 84 infants attended.[89] The school had closed by 1901.[90]

St. Margaret and All Saints' Roman Catholic school, Barking Road, Canning Town, was opened about 1860, when a building grant was made by the Poor Schools Committee.[91] The first government grant was made in 1871.[92] Attendance rose from 150 in 1871 to 300 in 1881,[93] and in 1883 new buildings were erected for 500.[94] A further enlargement, completing three storeys, was carried out in 1896.[95] In 1940 the school was wrecked by bombing and was closed.[96]

St. Ursula's Roman Catholic school was founded in 1862 by the Ursuline nuns of St. Angela's convent, Upton Lane. Classes were held in cottages at Sun Row, Green Street, until 1863, when stables adjoining the convent were converted into a school for 30 girls and infants.[97] By 1893, after several enlargements, attendance had risen to 229.[98] In 1903 St. Ursula's was amalgamated with St. Antony's school in the new buildings in Lancaster Road.

Plaistow Free school existed by 1866.[99] In 1871 it was a mixed school with an attendance of 125, meeting in the Temperance hall, North Street.[1] It appears to have closed soon after. This school, like the hall, was probably supported by nonconformists.

The Wesleyan school, Barking Road, Canning Town, was opened in 1868, and received its first government grant in 1869.[2] In 1871 the attendance was 190.[3] Fees were above those usual in West Ham, ranging from 3d. to 9d. a week in 1875.[4] The school was closed in 1894.[5]

Maryland Point school, Francis Street, supported by the London City Mission, existed by 1869.[6] In 1871, when the attendance was 87, it received its first government grant.[7] It was taken over by the school board in 1875 and closed in 1886.[8]

St. Andrew's National school, Plaistow, originated about 1870, as a temporary school in Webb Street, attached to St. Philip's mission, Whitwell Road.

The first government grant was received in 1871.[9] In 1873 a permanent school was built beside the church in St. Andrew's Road.[10] This was enlarged in 1883 to provide a new department for the infants, who had remained in Webb Street.[11] The school was reorganized in 1930 for mixed juniors and seniors.[12] It was closed in 1936.[13]

St. Gabriel's National school, Bidder Street, Canning Town, existed by 1871, receiving its first government grant in that year.[14] In 1875 it was transferred to the school board, which closed it in 1877, when the new Bidder Street school was completed.[15]

St. Peter's mission National school, Pelly Road, Upton, probably originated about 1870. In 1871 there were two church schools in this area.[16] Upton Cross school, with an attendance of 65, was east of West Ham vicarage. The Barn school, attendance 50, was near it to the south-west on or near the same site as the later St. Peter's school. No doubt the barn was that used for the mission services preceding the building of St. Peter's mission, Upton Cross.[17] St. Peter's school received its first government grant in 1879.[18] In 1884 a new infants department was opened in Chapman Road.[19] The school was closed about 1892.[20] Throughout its existence it had been controlled by the vicar of St. Mary's, Plaistow, since St. Peter's did not become a separate parish until 1894. The Pelly Road site was used for St. Mary's new vicarage, and the Chapman Road building became St. Katherine's mission.

Elementary schools founded between 1871 and 1903.[21] North Street board school, Plaistow, was opened in 1872. The board leased from the Quakers their larger meeting-house, a classroom, and a dwelling-house.[22] By 1873 attendance was 200. In 1878–9 the board bought the whole premises freehold, enlarged them to accommodate 436, and established the school as permanent.[23] Further extensions were made in 1882 and 1890, raising accommodation to 1,139 in 1897. It was a difficult school: in 1888, 60 per cent of the children were said to come from very poor families. The opening of new board schools at

[87] *Rep. Educ. Ctee. of Council*, [C. 406], p. 94, H.C. (1871), xxii; ibid. [C. 601], p. 259, H.C. (1872), xxii.
[88] *Kelly's Dir. Essex* (1890).
[89] W. Ham Sch. Bd. Mins. 1892, 1897.
[90] *Bd. of Educ. List of Schs.* [Cd. 1277], p. 67, H.C. (1902), lxxix.
[91] *Rep. R.C. Poor Schs. Ctee.* 1860; cf. W. Ham L.B. Mins. 28 Feb. 1860.
[92] *Mins. Educ. Ctee. of Council*, [C. 601], p. 257, H.C. (1872), xxii.
[93] *Rep. Educ. W. Ham* (1871), 11; W.H.L., Sch. Bd. Mins., 1881.
[94] W.H.L., W. Ham C.B.C., *Architect's Rep. on Non-Provided Schs.* (1903).
[95] Ibid.
[96] *W. Ham Educ. Devt. Plan* (1947), p. 25.
[97] St. Angela's Convent Annals.
[98] *Rep. Educ. Ctee. of Council*, [C. 7089–I], p. 716, H.C. (1893–4), xxvi; cf. ibid. [C. 2342–I], p. 889, H.C. (1878–9), xxiii; ibid. [C. 5123–I], p. 521, H.C. (1887), xxviii.
[99] *Kelly's Dir. Essex* (1866).
[1] *Rep. Educ. W. Ham* (1871), 11. For the hall see J. S. Curwen, *Old Plaistow*, 42, 53.
[2] *Wesleyan Methodist Educ. Ctee. Rep.* 1868; *Rep. Educ. Ctee. of Council*, [C. 165], p. 567, H.C. (1870), xxii.
[3] *Rep. Educ. W. Ham* (1871), 10.
[4] *Rtn. Elem. Schs.*, H.C. 133, pp. 58–9 (1875), lix.
[5] *Wesleyan Educ. Ctee. Rep.*, 1894.
[6] *Stratford Express*, 20 Nov. 1869 (Letter from A. B. Martin).
[7] *Rep. Educ. Ctee. of Council*, [C. 601], p. 259, H.C. (1872), xxii; *Rep. Educ. W. Ham* (1871), 11.
[8] W. Ham Sch. Bd. Mins. 1875–86.
[9] *Rep. Educ. Ctee. of Council*, [C. 601], p. 259, H.C. (1872), xxii.
[10] Ibid. [C. 1019–I], p. 324, H.C. (1874), xviii.
[11] Ibid. [C. 2948–I], p. 578, H.C. (1881), xxxii; ibid. [C. 3706–I], p. 654, H.C. (1883), xxv; *Kelly's Dir. Essex* (1890).
[12] *W. Ham Educ. Reps.* 1929–30, p. 103, cf. 1930–1, p. 96; inf. from Newham Educ. Ctee.
[13] Bd. of Educ., *Pub. Elem. Schs. in England*, 1936, pp. 116–18.
[14] *Rep. Educ. W. Ham* (1871), 11, and map; *Rep. Educ. Ctee. of Council*, [C. 601], p. 257, H.C. (1872), xxii.
[15] W. Ham Sch. Bd. Mins. 1875–7.
[16] *Rep. Educ. W. Ham* (1871), 11 and map.
[17] See p. 122.
[18] *Rep. Educ. Ctee. of Council*, [C. 2562–I], p. 592, H.C. (1880), xxii.
[19] *W. Ham Char. Rep.* (1899), 129–30.
[20] Ibid.; *Rep. Educ. Ctee. of Council*, [C. 7089–I], p. 714, H.C. (1893–4), xxvi.
[21] All the information in this section, unless otherwise stated, comes from the Minutes and Reports of the W. Ham Sch. Bd. and the *Minutes* and *Reports* of the W. Ham Educ. Ctee.
[22] For these Quaker buildings see p. 132.
[23] W.H.L., W. Ham Sch. Bd., Specifications for Alterations to North Street schools, 1879.

Plaistow in 1888 and 1894 depressed the school still more. The severity of its discipline attracted the attention of the board and the magistrates. It was reorganized in 1927 for mixed juniors and infants and in 1930 for infants only. It was closed in 1933. The buildings have since been used in turn by the Lister day-continuation institute, the West Ham technical school, and the West Ham college of further education.

Odessa primary school, Forest Gate. Odessa Road board school was opened in 1874 with places for 703. The school was enlarged in 1880 and 1889, and in 1899 it was reconstructed internally, raising the accommodation to 1,312. Owing to its isolated position it was not until 1945 that it was reorganized, for mixed juniors and infants.

Hallsville board school, Canning Town, with places for 639, was opened in 1874 on the site of the Public school, Victoria Dock Road. From the first it was overcrowded. In 1882–3 a new girls department was added on the Burnham Street frontage, and further extensions in 1892 raised the capacity to 903. The school was handicapped by the poverty of its pupils and the noise from traffic. It was closed in 1933 and later demolished as part of the Silvertown Way improvement scheme.

High Street board school, Stratford, was opened in 1874 on a restricted site near the northern outfall sewer. In 1881 there were places for 526. The boys department was closed in 1896 and the rest of the school in 1899. The buildings were used for other municipal purposes until they were demolished in 1937.

St. James's Church primary school, St. James's Road, Forest Gate. St. James's National school was built in 1874 by William Bolton, vicar of St. John's, Stratford, in competition with Odessa Road board school. It was transferred to St. James's parish when that became separate in 1881. It provided 395 places, increased by 1903 to 458. It was reorganized for mixed juniors and infants in 1945.

Channelsea Road board school was opened in 1875 on the site of the former school belonging to Christ Church, Stratford. After enlargement in 1877–9 it provided places for 434. In its early years it was a 'penny school', and later it included 'half-time' pupils who worked in the local jute-mills. A dining room was provided in 1889. Attendance declined after the First World War and the school was closed in 1924. The buildings, after temporary use as a junior instruction centre, were demolished in 1938.

Canning Town board school, Bidder Street, was opened in 1877 for 750 pupils. The playground was enlarged in 1891. The school served a poor district and suffered from frequent staff changes. It was reorganized in 1932 for mixed juniors and infants and by 1939 for infants only. It was closed in 1945 and later demolished, the site being incorporated in the electricity generating station.

South Hallsville board school, Agate Street, Tidal Basin, was opened in 1878 for 800. It was in a poor neighbourhood, and the early head teachers were appointed on condition that they resided there. Enlargements were made in 1884, 1887, and 1894–5, raising accommodation to 1,266. In 1929 a new mixed junior school was built to the east of the old school and in 1931 a new infants school to the west. These new buildings included medical rooms and shower-baths. In 1932 the 1878 buildings were replaced by a senior school. During the Second World War the Hallsville schools, as they were by then more shortly known, were all badly damaged. After the war the area was redeveloped, Agate Street disappearing in the process, and in 1948 the new Hallsville primary school, Radland Road, was built on the site.

Clarkson Street board school, Tidal Basin, was opened in 1879 for 621 boys and infants. It was enlarged in 1881 and again in 1883, when a girls department was opened. By 1902, after further enlargement and some reconstruction, there were places for 1,107. The school was reorganized in 1938 for junior boys and infants, and in 1945 for mixed juniors and infants. It was demolished in 1955.

Maryland primary school, Maryland Square, Stratford. Maryland Point board school was opened in 1879. Extra classrooms were added in 1883 and 1885, completing a quadrangular plan. In 1894 the site was extended eastwards, raising the accommodation from 912 to 1,354. During its early years the school had a high reputation, and it was used as an extra-mural centre for pupil-teachers until 1894, when the full-time pupil-teacher centres were opened. It was reorganized for junior girls and infants in 1937, and for mixed juniors and infants in 1945.

Abbey board school, Abbey Road, was opened in 1881 with places for 900. A wing was added in 1885, and by 1893, after further extensions, there was accommodation for 1,660. The school was reorganized in 1934 for junior boys, junior girls, and infants. It was closed in 1938. The buildings were demolished in 1946 and the site used for housing.

Grange infant school, Canning Town. Grange Road board school was opened in 1881 as a long single-storey building for 900. A school cookery room, the first in West Ham, was opened there in 1884, with funds provided by J. S. Curwen. A new infants department (1887) and later extensions raised the accommodation by 1902 to 1,332. The school was damaged by bombing in 1918 and again during the Second World War. It was reorganized in 1932 for junior boys, junior girls, and infants, and in 1945 for infants only.

Silvertown board school, Oriental Road, was opened for infants in 1881, boys and girls departments being added in 1892. It was damaged in the Silvertown explosion of 1917. By 1922 there were places for 962. In 1933 the school was reorganized for senior girls, junior girls, and infants. It was bombed and closed in 1940, the buildings being later used as a borough store.

Colegrave primary school, Stratford. Colegrave Road board school, opened in 1882 with places for 1,054, was one of the first of the three-storey buildings which became standard for the larger schools in West Ham during the next two decades. Infants were accommodated on the ground floor, girls on the first floor, and boys on the second. The barrack-like buildings were relieved only by 'Dutch' or 'Queen Anne' ornament on the top floor and gables. Owing to its isolated position it was not until 1945 that Colegrave Road school was reorganized for mixed juniors and infants.

Regent Lane board school, Custom House, was opened for boys and girls in 1882. An infants department (1884) and later extensions raised the accommodation to 1,059 by 1922. The school was reorganized in 1933 for junior boys, junior girls, and infants. It was bombed during the Second World War and was demolished in 1943. The new Regent primary school was built on the site in 1949.

The Grove primary school, Stratford. Salway Place board school was opened in 1882, with places for 903. It was reorganized in 1932 for mixed juniors and infants and in 1949 was renamed The Grove.

Carpenters primary school, Stratford. Carpenters Road board school was opened in 1885, with places for 1,244. In 1886 the Carpenters' Company provided cookery facilities there for schools in the north of the borough. A laundry was built in 1893 and a second storey added for cookery in 1899. Owing to its isolated position it was not until 1945 that it was reorganized, for mixed juniors and infants.

Custom House board school, Freemasons Road, was opened in 1885 with 967 places. It was badly damaged in the Silvertown explosion of 1917. In 1930 it was reorganized for junior boys, junior girls, and infants. It was closed in 1945 after bombing. A new Custom House infants school was opened on the site in 1954.

Ravenscroft primary school, Canning Town. Denmark Street board school was opened in 1885 for 1,272 and was extended in 1892. It was reorganized in 1933 for junior boys, junior girls, and infants, and for mixed juniors and infants in 1945. In 1949 it was renamed Ravenscroft.

Godwin primary school, Forest Gate. Godwin Road board school was opened in 1885 for 1,247 and by 1902 had places for 1,340. It was reorganized in 1945 for mixed juniors and infants.

Upton Cross primary school, Plashet Road. Upton Cross board school was opened in 1885 with places for 1,200. Some of its early pupils came from East Ham. It was reorganized in 1930 for junior boys, junior girls, and infants, and in 1945 for mixed juniors and infants.

West Silvertown board school, Boxley Street, was opened in 1885 with one mixed department for 250, two rooms being added for infants in 1887. In 1889 it became a three-department school, and further extensions in 1894 and 1910 provided a total of about 1,200 places. In 1888 Duncan Knight established a library and cookery prizes, and in 1897 endowed scholarships for further education or apprenticeship for boys at the school. The school was wrecked by the Silvertown explosion of 1917, but was repaired and modernized in the same year. It remained an all-age school until 1945, when it was reorganized for mixed juniors and infants. It was closed in 1962.

Beckton Road board school, Canning Town, was opened in 1888 with places for 1,542. By 1939, after several reorganizations, it was restricted to junior girls and infants. It was badly bombed during the Second World War, and was later demolished, the site being used for the new Hardie primary school (1952).

Curwen primary school, Plaistow. Stock Street board school was opened in 1888, as a three-storey building for 1,316. A school furniture store was added in 1891 and a drill hall in 1900. The school

was reorganized in 1930 for junior boys, junior girls, and infants, and in 1945 for mixed juniors and infants. It was renamed Curwen in 1949.

St. Antony's Roman Catholic primary school, Lancaster Road, Upton. In 1888 the Franciscans, who had recently settled at Upton, opened a boys school in Khedive (later St. Antony's) Road, in a building previously used as a mission church.[24] It received a government grant from 1890.[25] In 1903 new buildings, with 1,074 places, were built in Lancaster Road, St. Antony's being joined there by the girls from St. Ursula's school. The school was reorganized in 1945 for mixed juniors and infants. It was granted Aided status in 1949.

The Park primary school, Eleanor Road. West Ham Park board school was opened in 1889, as a three-storey building. In 1897 there were places for 1,366. The school was reorganized in 1934 for junior boys, junior girls, and infants, and in 1945 for mixed juniors and infants. Its present shorter name has been used since the 1930s.

Elmhurst primary school, Upton. Elmhurst Road board school, Upton, was opened in 1891 for 1,361. It was reorganized in 1930 for junior boys, junior girls, and infants, and in 1945 for mixed juniors and infants.

Bridge Road board school, Stratford, built to replace the British schools, was opened in 1892 with places for 1,370. It had a roof playground and other features new to West Ham. About 1938 it was reorganized for mixed juniors and infants. It was renamed Bridge school in 1949 and was closed in 1962.

Ashburton mixed secondary modern school, Freemasons Road, Custom House, originated as Russell Road board school, opened in 1893 with places for 1,568. Part of this was used as a pupil-teacher centre from 1894 until 1896, when a permanent centre, later a higher elementary school, was opened on the adjoining site. By 1939 Russell Road elementary school had been reorganized for junior boys, junior girls, and infants. In 1932, when the higher elementary school moved to Queens Road, its buildings were reopened as Ashburton senior boys school, but they were badly damaged during the Second World War, and in 1945 those that remained were combined with the buildings of the Russell Road elementary school to form Ashburton mixed secondary modern school.

Greengate primary school, Plaistow. Cave Road board school, opened in 1894 for 1,570, was the first school in the borough built without schoolrooms but with widened central corridors for assembly and drill. It was reorganized in 1930 for junior boys and junior girls, and in 1945 for mixed juniors and infants. In 1949 it was renamed Greengate.

Hermit Road board school, Canning Town, was opened in 1894, for 1,570. It was reorganized in 1935 for junior boys, junior girls, and infants, and in 1938 the junior boys department was closed. During the Second World War it was bombed and closed, the site being later used for housing.

Upton Lane board school was opened in 1894 for 1,367. It was reorganized in 1930 for senior boys, senior girls, and infants, the senior boys department

[24] *Rtn. non-Provided Schs.*, H.C. 178, p. 511 (1906), lxxxvii; W.H.L., W. Ham Educ. Ctee. *Architect's Rep.* 1903.

[25] *Rep. Educ. Ctee. of Council*, [C. 6438–I], p. 591, H.C. (1890–1), xxvii.

being closed in 1937. It was destroyed by bombing during the Second World War, and the site was later used for the new Stratford grammar school (1959).

Drew primary school, Silvertown. Drew Road board school was opened in 1895 and in 1902 had places for 1,215. It was near the docks, and in 1921 subsidence of the site necessitated extensive repairs. The school was reorganized in 1933 for boys and infants and in 1945 for mixed juniors and infants.

Manor primary school. Manor Road board school was opened in 1895 for 1,514. It was reorganized in 1934 for senior boys and senior girls, the infants department closing in 1935. During the Second World War it was used by the fire service and suffered bomb damage. In 1947 it was reopened for mixed juniors and infants.

Star primary school, Canning Town. Star Lane board school was opened in 1895 for 1,556. It was reorganized in 1937 for junior boys, junior girls, and infants, and in 1945 for mixed juniors and infants.

Three Mills primary school, Abbey Lane. Three Mills board school was opened in 1895 as the successor to High Street school, with places for 1,576. Craft and dining blocks were added in 1937. In 1945 the school was reorganized as a primary school with senior and junior departments. The senior department, which did not become a secondary modern school until 1953, was closed in 1965.

St. Joachim's Roman Catholic primary school, attached to St. Anne's church, Throckmorton Road, Victoria Docks, was opened about 1895. Its original building was enlarged in 1900. In 1903 there were places for 452. Temporary buildings were added in 1928. The school was reorganized in 1945 for mixed juniors and infants. It was granted Aided status in 1949.

Credon primary school, Plaistow. Credon Road board school was opened in 1896 for 1,576. It was reorganized in 1930 for senior boys, senior girls, and infants, was bombed and closed in 1940, and reopened in 1945 for mixed juniors and infants.

Holbrook secondary modern school. Holbrook Road board school was opened in 1896 for 1,560. In 1934, after alterations, it was reorganized for senior boys, senior girls, and infants, and in 1945 it became a mixed secondary modern school.

Forest Gate high school, Forest Street, originated as Whitehall Place board school, which was opened in 1896 and in 1902 had places for 1,411. It was reorganized in 1926 for mixed seniors and mixed juniors, and in 1945 as Forest Gate mixed secondary modern school. In 1965 it was transferred to new buildings as Forest Gate high school after the site had been redeveloped. During the 1920s and 1930s the Shakespeare day-continuation institute used part of the school.

Burke mixed secondary modern school, Plaistow, originated as Balaam Street board school, opened in 1897 for 1,556, as successor to the old Balaam Street school. On each floor it had a large central hall flanked by classrooms, to facilitate direct control by the head teachers. In 1930 it was reorganized for senior boys, senior girls, and infants, and renamed after Edmund Burke the statesman, who lived in Balaam Street for a short time. It became a mixed secondary modern school in 1945.

Frederick Road board school, Canning Town, was opened in 1897 for 1,572, on a site which included a deaf and dumb centre. It was reorganized in 1934 for senior boys, senior girls, and infants. It was bombed and closed in 1941, the buildings being later demolished.

Water Lane board school, Stratford, was opened in 1897 for 1,478, on a large site which also included a deaf and dumb centre, a pupil-teacher centre, and school board offices. It was reorganized in 1937 for senior girls, junior boys, and infants, and in 1945 as a secondary modern school with boys and girls in separate departments, renamed Stratford Green school in 1949. Stratford Green boys school was transferred in 1958 to the Tennyson Road buildings vacated by Stratford grammar school, and was closed in 1965. Stratford Green girls school remained in Water Lane and in 1961 amalgamated with the adjoining Deanery grammar school to form Deanery high school.

New City primary school, Plaistow. New City Road board school was opened in 1897 with places for 1,560. It took some years to fill, and was not divided into three separate departments until 1904. Its isolation prevented reorganization until 1945, when it became a junior mixed and infants school.

Harold secondary modern school, Upton. Harold Road board school was opened in 1901 for 1,552. It was reorganized in 1930 for senior boys, senior girls, and infants, the girls department closing in 1937. In 1945 it became a mixed secondary modern school.

Elementary schools founded between 1903 and 1945.[26] Faraday secondary school, Canning Town. Holborn Road council school, planned by the school board, was opened in 1904 for 1,600. The building was of the standard three-storey type, but hipped roofs and dormer-windows were substituted for the usual gables. It was reorganized in 1933 for senior boys, senior girls, and infants, and in 1945 as a mixed secondary modern school. From 1949 it was called Faraday, a name which had been used in the 1920s for the day-continuation institute occupying part of the Holborn Road premises.

Napier primary school. Napier Road council school, planned by the school board, was opened in 1904 for 1,500. It was reorganized in 1934 for junior boys, junior girls, and infants, and in 1945 for mixed juniors and infants.

Shipman secondary modern school, Canning Town. Shipman Road council school, planned by the school board, was opened in 1904 for 1,308. It was reorganized in 1933 for senior boys, senior girls, and infants, in 1945 for mixed juniors and infants, and in 1948 as a mixed secondary modern school.

Hilda Road council school, Canning Town, planned by the school board, was opened in 1906 for 1,000. It was built of steel and concrete and electrically lighted. It was reorganized in 1937 for junior boys and in 1945 for mixed juniors and infants. It was closed in 1963.

St. Helen's Roman Catholic primary school, Falcon Street, Canning Town, was opened as an elementary school in 1908, in connexion with the convent in Bethell Avenue, with places for 507. It

---

[26] The information in this and the following sections, unless otherwise stated, comes from the *Minutes* and *Reports* of the W. Ham Educ. Ctee., and inf. from Newham Educ. Ctee.

was reorganized for mixed juniors and infants in 1945, was granted Aided status in 1947, and was rebuilt in 1952.

Gainsborough primary school, Canning Town. Gainsborough Road council school was opened in 1912 for 1,500, in two separate blocks, comprising a senior school, and a junior school with craft centre above. Shower baths were provided. In 1937 the school was reorganized for senior boys, senior girls, and infants, and a new block with work rooms and gymnasium added. It became a junior mixed and infants school in 1945.

Rosetta primary school, Custom House. Rosetta Road council school was opened in 1919 for 1,500 on an open site which allowed a single-storey quadrangular arrangement. It was reorganized in 1930 for senior boys, senior girls, and infants and in 1945 for mixed juniors and infants.

South Hallsville council junior and infants schools, Canning Town, were built in 1929 and 1931 respectively, adjoining the old school in Agate Street. The history of all the schools on that site has been described above.[27]

Tollgate primary school, Barclay Road, Plaistow, was opened by the council in 1933 for 1,200 junior boys and junior girls. It was reorganized in 1945 for mixed juniors and infants.

Secondary and senior schools founded before 1945. Sarah Bonnell grammar school for girls, St. George's Road, Upton. The earlier history of this school, founded in the 18th century, has been described above.[28] In 1876 it was reopened as West Ham high school for girls in new buildings in West Ham Lane. That site was sold to West Ham hospital in 1905, and a new school was built in the Grove. In 1922 there were 280 girls on the roll. The school was destroyed by bombing during the Second World War and the pupils were accommodated in other schools until 1944, when they were rehoused in the buildings in St. George's Road previously occupied by the Grove central school. After the war the school was renamed the Sarah Bonnell grammar school.

St. Angela's Ursuline convent Roman Catholic multilateral school for girls, St. George's Road, Upton.[29] The Ursuline nuns, originally at Grove House, Upton Lane, admitted boarding pupils from 1862. The first wing of their convent, built in 1871–2, provided a hall, dormitories, and classrooms. There were then 40 girls. Day pupils were first admitted in 1879. By 1902 St. Angela's high school had been recognized by the Board of Education as a public secondary school, and the borough council, through its technical instruction committee, was providing junior scholarships tenable there.[30] A preparatory department, in Grove House, was opened in 1903. In 1904 there were 248 pupils, including 70 over 16 years.[31] By 1921 numbers had risen to 474. Under the Education Act, 1944, the school became a

multilateral secondary school. Between 1948 and 1955 Grove House was demolished and a new wing was built on the site.[32] The school was granted Aided status in 1946.

St. Bonaventure's Roman Catholic multilateral school for boys, St. Antony's Road, Upton, was opened in 1875 by the Franciscans of Stratford as a private school.[33] From 1890 or earlier it was called St. Bonaventure's grammar school.[34] It was recognized by the Board of Education as a secondary school in 1904. There were then 154 pupils, including 28 in the preparatory department, but only 3 were over 16 years.[35] In 1908 the school altered its name to the West Ham grammar school. Under the Education Act, 1944, it was reorganized as a multilateral secondary school for boys and reverted to the name St. Bonaventure's. It was granted Aided status in 1947. In addition to the original school a new range of buildings was built after the Second World War on the Boleyn Road frontage.

The Carpenters' Company technical school, Jupp Road, Stratford, was opened by that company in 1891 in buildings used also as an evening institute. It had a swimming bath and a gymnasium, which were also used by the local board schools. It was recognized by the Board of Education as a secondary school and for a short time the borough council's junior scholars were sent there. But it was inconveniently sited, near the Channelsea river, and the accommodation, though varied, was not well planned. The number of pupils averaged 250, of whom only 12 per cent stayed to 15 years. The fortunes of the school were affected by the opening of the municipal technical institute and the building of the municipal secondary school. The borough council's plans for the expansion of municipal secondary education were fiercely opposed by the headmaster of the Carpenters' school, as likely to damage the existing secondary schools, especially his own.[36] Eventually the Carpenters' Company offered to hand over the school to the council, but the offer was not accepted, and the company therefore closed the school in 1905. An Old Carpentarians' Association still existed in 1964, when it produced a short history of the school.[37]

All the following schools, in this sub-section, were built by the borough council.

Stratford grammar school, Upton Lane, originated in 1906, when West Ham municipal central secondary (mixed) school was opened in Whalebone Lane and Tennyson Road, in buildings for 680, planned by the school board as a higher elementary school.[38] The initial intake of 369 included the pupil-teachers from two centres opened by the school board in 1894 and given permanent buildings in Russell Road (1896) and Water Lane (1897). The last preparatory pupil-teachers were selected in 1909, and from 1912 bursaries were granted to intending teachers who followed a full secondary course. This bursary scheme ended in 1936. The

[27] See p. 151. [28] See p. 146.
[29] This paragraph is based on: St. Angela's Convent Annals; *Uptonian*, xxxix (1961–2); *Reps. Catholic Educ. Ctee.*
[30] *W. Ham C.B.C. Mins.* 15 Sept. 1902.
[31] W.H.L., W. Ham C.B.C., *Principal Briscoe's Rep. to Educ. Ctee. on Secondary Educ. in W. Ham, 1904*, App. B.
[32] *W. Ham Educ. Ctee. Reps.* 1953–4 and 1954–5; inf. from the Headmistress, St. Angela's school.
[33] Inf. from Father H. Docherty, O.F.M.

[34] *Kelly's Dir. Essex*, 1890.
[35] *Principal Briscoe's Rep.* 1904, App. B.
[36] W.H.L., W. Ham C.B.C., *Suggestions on W. Ham Education by the Principal of the Carpenters' Co. school* (1904); *Carpenters' Co. Correspondence re Whalebone Lane school* (1904).
[37] *Story of the Carpenters' Company's technical school (1891–1905) and of the Old Carpentarians.*
[38] This paragraph is partly based on reports to Governors and school magazines.

school was enlarged in 1914, c. 1920, and 1931. Between the two world wars, when attendance was about 600, its reputation was very high. The word 'central' was dropped from its name in 1925. The school was partly destroyed by bombing in 1941, after which some temporary huts were added. It was renamed Stratford grammar school in 1945, and in 1958 it was transferred to new buildings on the site of the former Upton Lane school.

Russell Road higher elementary (mixed) school was opened in 1906 in the buildings previously used by the pupil-teacher centre for the south of the borough. There was at first accommodation for only 190, but in 1920 the school was extended. In 1932 it was transferred to new buildings in Queens Road, Plaistow, and renamed the Russell central school. It was closed in 1940, the remaining pupils being transferred to the Grove central school.

Water Lane higher elementary (mixed) school, accommodating 295, was opened in 1906 in the buildings previously used by the northern pupil-teacher centre.[39] In 1932 it was transferred to new buildings in St. George's Road, Upton, and renamed the Grove central school. There was no intake after 1940 and the school closed in 1944.

Plaistow grammar school, Prince Regent Lane. Plaistow municipal secondary (mixed) school was opened in 1926 to serve the south of the borough. It was built in two parts, the first, for 250 pupils forming the northern quadrangle, the second, completed in 1930, forming the southern, with a further 350 places. After the Second World War it was renamed Plaistow grammar school.

Pretoria boys and girls secondary modern schools. Pretoria Road school, Canning Town, was built in 1932 for senior boys and senior girls. In 1945 it became a pair of secondary modern schools.

South Hallsville senior school, Tidal Basin, was built in 1932 on the site of the former Agate Street elementary school. It was originally for boys and girls in separate departments, but in 1938–9 was reorganized for boys only. In 1940 it was bombed and closed.

Ashburton senior school, Custom House, was opened in 1932 in the buildings previously used by the Russell Road higher elementary school. It was originally mixed, but by 1938 was restricted to boys. Much of it was destroyed by bombing during the Second World War, after which the remaining buildings were combined with those of Russell Road elementary school to form a secondary modern school.[40]

Deanery senior (mixed) school, Stratford, was opened in 1933 in the buildings previously used by Water Lane higher elementary school. It was bombed and closed in 1941, and later demolished.

The other senior schools formed in West Ham between the two world wars used parts of existing elementary schools.[41] Whitehall Place senior school was thus formed by reorganization in 1926. Upton Lane, Credon Road, Balaam Street, Harold Road, and Rosetta Road were formed in 1930. Silvertown, Shipman Road, and Holborn Road were formed in 1933, Clarkson Street, Manor Road, Holbrook Road, and Frederick Road in 1934, and Water Lane and Gainsborough Road in 1937. Clarkson Street senior school ceased in 1937. Upton Lane, Credon Road,

Rosetta Road, Silvertown, Manor Road, Frederick Road, and Gainsborough Road, ceased during the Second World War, or immediately after. All the others became secondary modern in 1945.

Before 1945 education in technical, commercial, and domestic subjects, for pupils of about 13–16 years, was provided mainly by the municipal technical college and the day-continuation institutes, to some extent in competition. The college, opened in 1898, and described more fully below, opened junior classes in trades (1912), engineering (1913), art (1914), and commerce (1929). In 1928 the college bought four houses in Water Lane and the Grove to accommodate these classes, and in 1936 it opened a trade school for girls in Water Lane (Deanery Road). When the trade school was bombed in the Second World War its work continued in part of the buildings of the former Grove central school in St. George's Road. In 1943 a school of building was opened in the former Russell central school, Queens Road.

In January 1921 West Ham introduced compulsory attendance at five day-continuation institutes, called Newton (in the Conference Hall, West Ham Lane), Raleigh (Fairbairn Hall, Canning Town), Shakespeare (Barclay Hall, Green Street), Faraday (Holborn Road school), and Livingstone (Balaam Street Congregational schoolroom). Compulsion was abandoned later in the same year and the Newton and Raleigh institutes were then closed. The Shakespeare institute, which later moved to Whitehall Place school, was closed in 1936. Faraday moved to Balaam Street Congregational schoolroom in 1931 and was closed in 1933. Livingstone was transferred in 1927 to North Street school and in 1933 was renamed Lister. After the Second World War it was absorbed into the North West Ham (later called the Lister) technical school.

Primary schools founded between 1945 and 1965. The following were built by the borough council. Hallsville school, Radland Road, Tidal Basin, was opened in 1948 on the site of the former South Hallsville elementary schools. Regent school, Prince Regent Lane, Custom House (1949), was built on the site of the former Regent Lane elementary school. Earlham school, Earlham Grove, Forest Gate, and Portway school, Park Road, were opened in 1951. Hardie school, Edwin Street, Canning Town (1952), was built on the site of the former Beckton Road elementary school, and Custom House school, Freemasons Road (1954), on that of the former Custom House elementary school. All the above were for mixed juniors and infants except Custom House, which was for infants only. Three voluntary schools were rebuilt: St. Luke's Church (1949), St. Helen's Roman Catholic (1952), and West Ham Church (1964). Other primary schools were formed by reorganizing all-age schools or senior schools.

Secondary schools founded between 1945 and 1965. The Education Act, 1944, made it possible to convert the junior departments of the technical college into separate technical schools. The girls trade school was rebuilt (1949) as the West Ham technical school for girls on the Water Lane (Deanery Road) site. This was renamed Deanery grammar school in

[39] The entrance was in Manbey St.   [40] See above, p. 152.   [41] See previous sections.

155

1959, and in 1961 amalgamated with Stratford Green girls secondary modern school to form Deanery high school. The school of building and the junior engineering department were combined to form the South West Ham technical school for boys in new buildings (1952) in Barking Road. The commerce and art departments became the North West Ham technical school. This was housed for a time in the old North Street schools, before moving, in 1952, to the Queens Road buildings of the former Russell school. In 1956 it was renamed Lister technical school.

Two existing schools were rebuilt during this period: Stratford grammar school (1958) and Forest Gate secondary modern school (1965), which became a high school. Other secondary modern schools were formed by the reorganization of all-age schools or junior schools.

Special and Nursery schools. Fyfield truant school, for boys, at Fyfield, near Chipping Ongar, was opened by the school board in 1885, and became a truant and industrial school in 1907. In 1925 it was converted into an open air school for delicate children.[42] It was closed in 1956.

In 1893 the school board opened two temporary centres for deaf and dumb children, one in the Workmen's hall, Stratford, the other in the Boyd institute, Victoria Docks. In 1894 the Stratford centre was transferred to St. John's school and a second class added at the Boyd institute. A permanent centre for the south of the borough, accommodating 44, was opened in 1897 in Frederick Road, Canning Town. By 1908 there were 31 on the roll, of whom 7 came from outside West Ham. A permanent centre for the north, with 36 places, was opened in Water Lane, Stratford, in 1900. These two centres were closed in 1938, when a new one, for 80 children, was opened by the council in Tunmarsh Lane, Plaistow: in 1949 this was renamed West Ham school for the deaf.

A class for defective children was opened at the Abbey board school in 1896, and in 1903 a permanent school for 120 mental and physical defectives was opened in Grange Road, Plaistow. This was subsequently extended, and by 1925 the attendance was 185. A craft block was added in 1937. The school was damaged during the Second World War and was later reconstructed. In 1949 it was renamed Elizabeth Fry school. In 1954 it was restricted to physically handicapped children.

A second school for mental and physical defectives was opened by the borough council in 1920, in Knox Road, Forest Gate. In 1925 the attendance was 193. In 1949 the school was renamed the Gurney school. In 1954 it was restricted to educationally subnormal children. The Knox Road school was designed for open air teaching, and in 1925 the Crosby Road open air school was opened on the same site, with places for 60 delicate girls. In 1932 it was extended to provide also for 30 boys. The school was closed in 1946, after which all delicate children were sent to Fyfield until that school closed.

In 1930 the borough council opened two nursery schools, Edith Kerrison (Sophia Road, Custom House) and Rebecca Cheetham (Marcus Street). Others were opened in Osborne Road, Forest Gate (1949), and Station Street, Stratford (1950). In 1964 the last was transferred to new buildings in Henniker Road, and renamed Ronald Openshaw.

West Ham College of Technology and West Ham College of Further Education. Technical classes were held for many years at the Great Eastern Railway mechanics' institution (founded in 1851) and at the Carpenters' Company institute (founded in 1886).[43] In 1890 the county borough council set up a technical instruction committee, and soon after began to give financial aid to university extension science classes held at Stratford, Canning Town, and Forest Gate. These classes drew large audiences, including many serious students: in 1892 chemistry lectures at Stratford were attended by about 1,000, of whom 100 were doing written work.[44] Meanwhile the council was accumulating its share of the government's 'whisky money', which since 1890 had been available for purposes of technical education. This was used to build a technical institute at the Green, Stratford, opened in 1898 with departments of science, engineering, art, and a women's department.[45] The institute was badly damaged by fire in 1899 but reopened in 1900. At first the institute offered many apprenticeship classes, but as early as 1900 it was also providing courses in science and engineering recognized by the University of London for internal degrees.[46] Shortly before the First World War junior technical classes were started. In 1921 the institute was renamed the municipal college. An extension, housing the women's work of the college, and the girls trade school, was built in Water Lane in 1936, and in 1938 the adjoining house was acquired as a science annexe. Both these buildings were destroyed by bombing in 1940. After the Second World War the college concentrated on advanced work in science and technology. The junior, trade, and commercial classes were transferred to separate technical schools or to the college of further education. The West Ham college of technology (thus renamed in 1952) was in 1956 designated by the government for development as a regional college. A new science wing was added in 1953–4, and in 1963 an extension was opened at the Green. In 1959–60 there were 158 students on full-time courses and 'sandwich' courses at university level, of whom 58 per cent came from overseas. By 1964–5 there were 1,003 (48 per cent from overseas).

The buildings of the institute, together with those of the adjoining central library (1898) and the Passmore Edwards museum (1900) form one of the most striking architectural groups in West Ham.[47] They were all designed by J. G. S. Gibson and S. B. Russell and executed in bright red brick, lavishly adorned with sculpture and stone dressings. Various Renaissance features were introduced in the unorthodox manner typical of the turn of the century. The symmetrical entrance front of the institute,

[42] *V.C.H. Essex*, iv. 57.
[43] See p. 141.
[44] W.H.L., W. Ham C.B.C. *Reps. of Ctees.* 29 Nov. 1892.
[45] For the institute, later college, see *W. Ham Municipal College and Central Library, 1898–1948*; D. McDougall,

Fifty Years a Borough, 140; W. Ham Coll. of Technology, *Information Booklet*, 1964; J. R. Soar, 'The historical development of technical and vocational education [in] West Ham since 1850' (London M.A. thesis, 1966).
[46] *W. Ham C.B.C. Mins. and Reps.* 19 Mar. 1900.
[47] For the museum, see p. 67.

facing Romford Road, is the most disciplined façade. It is divided horizontally at first-floor level by a deep carved frieze above which is a 9-bay colonnade framing the clerestory windows of the great hall. The steep roof is crowned by elaborate twin lanterns. Lower flanking wings link up with the museum to the east and with the library, which lies to the north, facing Water Lane.[48]

West Ham college of further education was opened in 1961 in the old North Street school buildings. It took over from the college of technology the department of commerce and all school-level and intermediate work.

Private schools. In 1627 Edward Lawford was licensed to teach a grammar school at West Ham.[49] Thomas Pakeman, minister of Stratford Presbyterian meeting (1687–91), provided a school for poor children and paid the teacher's salary.[50] William Dodd, curate and lecturer of West Ham (1752–66), conducted a private school for boys at Plaistow.[51] About 1800 there was a boys school at Essex House, North Street, Plaistow.[52] Stratford House school, founded about 1820 by John Freeman, was later for many years in Romford Road, being continued by his son and grandsons until 1907.[53] A directory of 1839 lists 27 private schools in the parish, of which 12 took boarders.[54] The school board report of 1871 revealed the existence of no fewer than 121 private schools, with an average attendance of 14.[55] Most of them, as the report emphasises, were dame schools or nurseries providing little education. Such schools must have disappeared as the board schools were built, but there continued to be a demand for middle-class private schools, especially at Stratford and Forest Gate. Some 38 schools were listed in a directory of 1886.[56] Among them was the Stratford school of art, Leytonstone Road, under Mrs. Harriet Taylor. This had existed since 1878 or earlier,[57] and apparently continued until about 1890.[58] In 1896, when an attempt was made to reopen it, the school was said to have been carried on in connexion with the government's science and art department.[59] Two of the schools listed in 1886 still survived in 1926: Miss Edgington's, in Manbey Park Road, Stratford, and Miss Ingold's, later called Claremont college in Claremont Road, Forest Gate.[60] In 1904 there were 13 private schools in the borough classed as secondary.[61] These included Forest Gate collegiate school for girls, Romford Road, founded in 1874, Forest Gate high school for boys, founded about 1894 in Claremont Road, later in Woodgrange Road and finally in Earlham Grove, and the associated Forest Gate high school for girls. Forest Gate collegiate school was later taken over by Clark's

college: in 1918 this was one of 11 private schools in the borough recognized by the Board of Education.[62] By 1939 hardly any private schools survived.

The Metropolitan Academy of Music. This academy originated in 1885, when Harding Bonner, an associate of J. S. Curwen at the Tonic Sol-Fa college, Earlham Grove, Forest Gate, started private classes there.[63] The college, founded in 1879, moved to London in 1890, and Bonner then leased the Earlham Grove premises as the Forest Gate school of music. In 1897, at his suggestion, the owners erected the Earlham Hall in front of the original buildings. By 1904 there were 1,000 pupils, and in 1906 the school was renamed the Metropolitan academy of music. Harding Bonner (d. 1906) was succeeded by his son Frank, who greatly expanded the academy. In 1916 it had 12 branches in Essex and London and, with a membership of about 2,300, claimed to be the largest musical institution in Great Britain. There was further expansion after the First World War, when attendance rose to 5,000 in 1920 and 5,600 in 1921. The academy continued to flourish until the 1930s but closed during the Second World War.

Forest Gate Industrial School.[64] In 1854 the Whitechapel poor-law union built an industrial school in Forest Lane, at a cost, including the site, of £42,000. In 1869 the Whitechapel union joined with those of Hackney and Poplar to form the Forest Gate school district, which took over the school. Hackney union withdrew from the district board in 1877 and Whitechapel union in 1897. In 1890 twenty-six boys died in a fire at the school. This disaster caused similar institutions to review fire precautions and stimulated interest in 'scattered homes' instead of 'barrack' schools. Poplar union continued to maintain the school until 1906, when the children were transferred to a new school at Hutton. The buildings were subsequently converted into Forest Gate hospital.[65]

CHARITIES.[66] Charitable bequests entrusted to the vicar and churchwardens of West Ham, for the use of the parishioners in general, were being divided equally between the three wards (Church Street, Plaistow, and Stratford) as early as the 16th century. In each ward the churchwarden kept what was known as the donation account, and each churchwarden in turn acted also as accountant to the whole parish. Bequests for the use of specific wards were paid into their donation accounts.

A Chancery order of 1848 apportioned the income of the charities then existing, except those of Sarah

[48] See *V.C.H. Essex, Bibliography,* f. p. 310.
[49] G.L.C., DL/C/343 f. 11.
[50] See p. 128.
[51] K. Fry, *E. and W. Ham,* 190.
[52] Ibid.
[53] E.R.O., Pictorial Coll., Stratford Ho. Sch.; W.H.L., W. Ham Cuttings, no. 1, f. 74.
[54] *Pigot's Dir. Essex* (1839).
[55] *Rep. Educ. W. Ham* (1871).
[56] *Kelly's Dir. Essex* (1886).
[57] Ibid. (1878); W. Ham L.B. Mins. 8 Jan. 1878.
[58] *Kelly's Dir. Essex* (1890).
[59] *W. Ham C.B.C. Mins.* 28 July 1896.
[60] Ibid. 1926; W.H.L., Vert. File, E/WES/373: *Prospectus of Claremont college, c. 1925.*
[61] *Principal Briscoe's Rep. 1904,* App. B.

[62] *W. Ham Educ. Scheme under 1918 Educ. Act,* App. 2.
[63] Account based on: W.H.L., Vert. File, 780, TS. Notes and printed *Prospectuses* and *Programmes*; Metrop. Acad. of Music, *Jubilee Souvenir,* 1934; *Forest Gate Weekly News,* 1 Oct. 1897; *Stratford Express,* 17 June 1922.
[64] E. R. Gamester, *Hist. Forest Gate Hospital.*
[65] See p. 111.
[66] Unless otherwise stated this section is based on the following sources: *Rep. Com. Char.* (Essex), H.C. 216, pp. 133–56 (1835) xxi (1); Charity Commission, *West Ham Charities, Assistant Commissioner's Report* (1899) [photocopy in W.H.L.]: this report, printed but not published, contains full historical accounts of all the charities up to that date; Records of the W.Ham United Non-Ecclesiastical Charities.

Bonnell, between the three ecclesiastical districts, each of which was also to share the right to nominate to vacancies in Newman's and Harris's alms-houses. A Charity Commission scheme of 1870 provided that the Alms-house Charities and the Distributive Charities for the poor should be administered by a central charity board consisting of the Vicar of All Saints', the churchwardens, and the parish overseers. In each of the eleven ecclesiastical districts the vicar and churchwardens were to apportion the district's share of the Distributive Charities and to appoint, in turn, to vacancies in Newman's alms-houses. In 1897 a controversy arose concerning the administration of the charities. By then West Ham had become a large county borough, and a strong section of public opinion was urging that the charities should no longer be controlled by the Church. An order of the Local Government Board on 19 March 1897 transferred the power of appointing the overseers from the vestry to the borough council. The council, exercising its powers under the Local Government Act, 1894, thereupon increased the number of overseers from three to seven (including the mayor *ex officio*), thus giving them potential control over the central charity board, though not of the district boards. Churchmen, under the determined leadership of the Vicar of All Saints', Canon Pelly, then pressed the Charity Commission to draw up a new scheme which would enable them to retain control. This was strongly opposed by the council, which in 1898–9 was controlled by the Socialists and their allies. A public inquiry was held in 1899 by an assistant commissioner who reported in favour of 'more popular and less ecclesiastical' control.

Under the resulting scheme (1903) a new board of trustees was set up, consisting of the vicar of All Saints', the mayor, 12 representatives appointed by the borough council, and 6 co-optative members. This board was to administer the United Non-Ecclesiastical Charities, i.e. all the Alms-house and Distributive Charities controlled by the old central charity board except Avenon's charity, together with three other charities that had been independent of the old board. The new board was to use the income of the Alms-house Charities for the purposes of those charities. The income from the Distributive Charities (except the ecclesiastical portions) was to be shared between the 12 wards of the borough, in each of which there was to be a local committee responsible for distributing the money. The Ecclesiastical Charities, drawing their income from the ecclesiastical portions of the Distributive Charities, were separated from the Non-Ecclesiastical Charities and placed under the control of the vicar and churchwardens of All Saints'.

A scheme of 1966 placed the United Non-Ecclesiastical Charities under the control of a board of trustees comprising the mayor of Newham, the vicar of All Saints', 14 members nominated by the Newham borough council, and 6 co-optative members. The ward committees were abolished.

In addition to the United Non-Ecclesiastical Charities there are various other charities for the poor or for the churches. These are all treated in the present section. Educational charities are described in the section on Education. Those connected with nonconformist churches are treated in the section on Protestant Nonconformity.

THE UNITED NON-ECCLESIASTICAL CHARITIES.[67] *Alms-house Charities.* In 1512 there was an alms-house in Church Street maintained by John Scott of Stratford, who gave instructions relating to it in his will of that year (proved in 1525).[68] Nothing further is known about Scott's alms-house. It must have been very near the later alms-houses of Newman and Harris, but there is no evidence that it was connected with either of those foundations.

In 1636 John Newman conveyed two copyhold cottages to the churchwardens of West Ham for the use of the parish poor. These provided seven alms-rooms without endowment. The site, which was declared freehold about 1810 after a dispute between the vestry and the West Ham manor court, lay east of the churchyard.[69]

James Cooper (d. 1743) left £200 for the rebuilding of the alms-houses, and this work was apparently completed between 1745 and 1748.[70] The new houses comprised a two-storey terrace of ten tenements, accommodating 20 alms-women. In 1899 the condition of the alms-houses was said to be unsatisfactory, but they were still in use in 1938.[71] A scheme of that year provided for the amalgamation of Newman's with Harris's alms-houses; the buildings of both were to be demolished and replaced by a block of 26 new alms-houses in Gift Lane. These were built in 1939–40.

The scheme of 1870 stipulated that the alms-women were to be over 60 years old or infirm, and to have been resident in the parish for at least two years. A scheme of 1913 permitted the trustees to employ a nurse to look after the alms-women, and to accommodate her in one of the alms-rooms.

For over a century after their foundation Newman's alms-houses appear to have been maintained entirely by the vestry, but from the middle of the 18th century they received a succession of endowments, mainly for the alms-women's stipends, which were providing a total income of £188 by 1898. In that year the alms-houses also received £20 from the Distributive Charities. The scheme of 1903 did not permit such payments, but that of 1913 gave the trustees power to spend up to £130 from the Distributive Charities on the alms-houses. Subsequent schemes increased the limit, and under the latest (1966) the trustees have discretion to use for the alms-houses whatever proportion of their total income they think necessary. In 1966 the total income from endowments of the United Non-Ecclesiastical Charities was £1,766, of which £140 was spent on eleemosynary grants and the remainder mainly on the maintenance of the alms-houses, the nurse's wages and Christmas gifts to the alms-women.

James Cooper (d. 1743)[72] left £600 stock in trust for various charitable purposes in the parish, includ-

[67] Char. Com. File 207309 now combines all the files relating jointly or severally to the United Non-Ecclesiastical Charities.   [68] *E.R.* lxii (Jan.), 48.
[69] W.H.L., W. Ham Vestry Mins. 24 Apr. 1810.
[70] Ibid. 19 Mar. 1745, cf. 13 Sept. 1748. Shown on plate f.p. 116 above.

[71] For pictures, 1933 and 1940, see W.H.L., Illus. Coll., Alms-houses. Two plaques from the old building, recording the gifts of Cooper (1745) and Gouge (1755) are in P.E.M.
[72] For the date see Lysons, *London*, iv. 257.

ing gifts of coal for the inmates of Newman's alms-houses. In 1834 £7 10s. was being spent on coal, one sack being given to each alms-woman and the remainder to the poor of Plaistow. Thomasin Gouge, by will dated 1754, left the residue of her estate for the relief of Newman's alms-women. In 1834 £1,300 stock yielded an income of £39, which was distributed to the alms-women half-yearly. John Snelgrave, by will proved 1810, left £700 stock, in addition to another bequest, for a yearly distribution to the alms-women. In 1834 the income was £21. Samuel Jones Vachell, by will dated 1831, gave £200 for the poor, from which in 1834 the income of £8 was being distributed among the alms-women. Isabella Wilson, by will proved 1834, gave £1,000 for the relief of 30 poor women attending the parish church. The Chancery order of 1848 apportioned the income among the three ecclesiastical districts of West Ham, but for some time before 1870 it was being used for Newman's alms-houses. Joseph Watts, by will proved 1836, gave £500 in trust for the alms-women. Elizabeth Hoyte and Mary Goldthorp by deed of 1844 gave £2,300 on reversion to augment the income of the alms-women, the gift becoming effective in 1851. By her will proved 1851 Mary Goldthorp left the reversion to a further £437 for the same purpose: this was received in 1875. All these charities were included in the scheme of 1870 and formed the Alms-house Charities, the charities of Cooper, Snelgrave, Vachell, and Wilson being numbered also among the Distributive Charities. Emily Cleypole, by will proved 1877, gave £100 for the benefit of Newman's alms-women, and this gift was included among the Alms-house Charities in the scheme of 1903. Under that scheme Wilson's charity ceased to be one of the Distributive Charities and Vachell's charity ceased to be one of the Alms-house Charities.

Roger Harris, by will dated 1633, devised two copyhold cottages in Little (later Gift) Lane for the use of the poor. In 1834 these were being maintained by the parish as poorhouses. They were rebuilt by subscription in 1853, as a single house with six living rooms,[73] the balance of the subscription, £39, being invested as an endowment for the alms-houses. In 1899 the upkeep of the buildings was being met by the vicar, mainly from parochial funds. There were six alms-women, usually from All Saints' parish, each receiving 2s. 6d. a week from the guardians of West Ham union, and gifts of bread and cash out of All Saints' share of the Distributive Charities. Harris's alms-houses were excluded from the schemes of 1870 and 1903, and remained under the control of the vicar and churchwardens of All Saints' until a scheme of 1932 placed them under the trustees of the United Non-Ecclesiastical Charities. From 1932 the conditions of admission to Harris's alms-houses were the same as for Newman's alms-houses, except that Harris's alms-women were expected to have a pension or other assured means.

Distributive Charities. Nicholas Avenon (d. 1599),[74] merchant tailor of London, conveyed to 12 trustees, by a deed of 1580, 6 a. marsh called Withering's mead. After his death the income from this land was to provide 24 poor persons with a penny loaf each every Sunday, any residue going towards an annual sermon to be preached in the parish church. The trustees, all laymen, were empowered to renew the trust as required, but by 1834 it had long lapsed and the charity was controlled by the vicar. The land, at Middle marsh, in Plaistow, was then let for £21, and the penny loaves were being distributed usually among the inmates of the alms-houses. Avenon's charity was included, as a Distributive Charity, in the scheme of 1870. It was later doubted whether the residue of the charity, as well as the £5 4s. applicable to bread, was governed by the scheme, but in 1879 the Charity Commissioners ruled that it was and that the central charity board should govern the whole charity. Up to that time the income from Withering's mead had remained at £21, but in 1880 the board sold one acre for £1,500, most of which was used, between 1881 and 1897, to develop the remaining land for building. When completed the estate, in Avenon's Road, Hayday Road, Ingal Road, and Denmark Street, comprised the sites for about 140 houses, let on building leases. By 1898 the gross income of the charity was £298; the profits, after deducting the £5 4s. for bread, were used by the vicar of All Saints' for church purposes.

During the 1890s and later the fact that the Church's share of the charity had so greatly increased caused great local resentment.[75] Thomas Scott, who as vicar of All Saints' from 1868 to 1891 had started to develop the land, is said to have wished to make over to the poor part of the increased income, but to have been prevented from doing this by Disraeli and later Prime Ministers, who would not permit any alienation of rights attached to this Crown living. The controversy concerning Avenon's charity caused it to be omitted from the scheme of 1903, pending further consideration. This created uncertainty about its management. The scheme of 1870, though in other respects superseded by that of 1903, presumably still applied in this case, so that Avenon's trustees continued to be the vicar and churchwardens of All Saints' and the parish overseers. The borough council's right to nominate the overseers, acquired by Local Government Board order in 1897, was reaffirmed in the West Ham Corporation Act (1900), but for some years after 1903 the overseers seem to have been unaware that they were still trustees of Avenon's charity and its control was left to the vicar and churchwardens. In 1909, however, the overseers were asked to sign a legal document relating to the charity, and thus realized that they were still entitled to share in its management. This precipitated a fight for the control of the charity between the Church and the borough council, in which the earlier controversy regarding its application was revived and became the main issue. The struggle was embittered by the fact that the clerk to the Avenon trustees was A. B. Banes, who had fought a previous battle with the council over his claim to compensation for losing the office of vestry clerk.[76] The

---

[73] For pictures, 1926 and 1940, see W.H.L., Illus. Coll. Alms-houses.

[74] Lysons, *London*, iv. 261, gives his date of death.

[75] Char. Com. File 31558; E. Willmore, *Nicholas Avenon's Charity and What Became of it* (1915).

[76] *C.B.C. Mins and Ctee. Reps.* 7 July 1911; cf. ibid. 1901–3, *passim*, for Banes's compensation.

overseers pressed for a new scheme which would enable part of the increased income to be used for non-ecclesiastical purposes. The vicar, Canon R. A. Pelly (1891–1916), was firmly opposed to surrendering any of the income, and he obtained the support of his bishop and the archbishop of Canterbury.

Avenon's endowment by then provided almost half the money required to pay the parochial staff of All Saints', whose duties included a great deal of charitable work. Pelly opposed a new scheme also because its publication would 'awake all the Socialist part of the place to opposition and cause infinite trouble and disturbance'. The matter was eventually referred to Chancery, which in 1912 ruled, in principle, that the increased income of Avenon's charity could only be used for Church purposes. A Chancery scheme of 1913 provided that the vicar was to receive £10 10s. a year for a sermon and that the balance of the income (after payment of the £5 4s. for bread) was to be used for curates' stipends. The trustees of the charity were in future to be the vicar, churchwardens, and two members appointed by the bishop. If and when the income of the charity exceeded £450 they were to apply for a new scheme. This did not become necessary until the 1960s, when the leases of the houses on Avenon's estate began to expire, enabling the trustees to sell the properties and invest the proceeds. By 1964 the income was about £2,000, and it was estimated that by 1975 it would rise to £5,000. A Charity Commission scheme of 1965 cancelled the provision of 1913 relating to the £450 limit. The payment of £5 4s. to the United Non-Ecclesiastical Charities was still being made in 1966.

John Shipman, by will dated 1583, left £6 a year for the poor of the parish. It was settled in 1608, after disputes, that the payment should take the form of two rent-charges, of £3 6s. 8d. and £1 4s. The larger rent-charge lapsed in 1861; the smaller was redeemed in 1896 for £48 stock.

Thomas Spaight of Stratford, yeoman, and Henry Store, woodmonger of London, by a deed of 1584, gave 3 a. marshland, let for £4 a year on a lease to run until A.D. 2112, for the relief of the poor. In 1916 the charity's interest in the land was sold for £300 stock.

Robert Rampston (d. 1585) left a rent of £2 for the poor, charged on Stone Hall in Little Canfield. This was still being received in 1966.

Margaret, Lady Throgmorton, of Upton,[77] by will proved 1591, left a rent-charge of £2 to be distributed quarterly to poor widows. This was redeemed in 1896 for £80 stock.

Thomas Staples, by will proved 1592, left a rent-charge of £1 for the poor. It was redeemed in 1878 for £30 stock.

William Rooke of Upton,[78] by will dated 1596, left a rent-charge of £5 for bread for the poor. In 1966 it was being paid by the City corporation as owners of West Ham Park.

Oliver Skinner, by will dated 1609, left a rent-charge of £2 for the relief of 40 poor persons. Half of this was redeemed for £40 stock in 1894 and the remainder for the same amount in 1924.

Peter Blower in 1616 settled in trust 1 a. land in New marsh, the profits to be distributed to 30 poor persons (8 in Plaistow, 3 in Upton, 12 in Church

Street, 7 in Stratford). The charity was omitted from the scheme of 1870, but included in that of 1903. In 1899, the land, in Prince Regent's Lane, Plaistow, was let for £5 a year to the borough council as a rubbish shoot. It was sold in 1928 for £1,500, which was invested.

Mary Gwilliam in 1633 gave for the poor a rent-charge of 30s. In 1834 it was distributed to two poor widows from each ward. In 1877 it was redeemed for £60 stock.

Roger Harris, founder of Harris's alms-houses, by his will dated 1633, gave a rent-charge of 52s. for coal for poor men or widows. This was included among the Distributive Charities under the scheme of 1870, along with the balance of £39 from the subscription for rebuilding the alms-houses, although the alms-houses themselves remained outside the scheme. The rent-charge was redeemed in 1893 for £104 stock.

Sir Richard Fenn, alderman of London, by will dated 1635, left the rents of two houses to buy bread for the poor. In 1834 the property comprised a terrace of 6 houses, let for a total of £10 a year. In 1865 the site was let on a building lease for 60 years at £80 a year. In 1926–7 it was sold for £5,500, which was invested.

Anne, Lady Middleton, by will dated 1645, left a rent-charge of £5 a year: £3 for apprenticing a boy, £1 for the poor of Plaistow ward, and 10s. each for those of Stratford and Church Street wards. The apprenticeship payments lapsed between 1848 and 1870. The whole rent-charge, however, continued to be received until 1930, when it was redeemed for £200 stock.

William Tudor of Stratford, merchant tailor of London, by will proved 1653, left a rent-charge of £5 for the poor of Stratford, to be distributed half in money and half in bread. Peter Ward, by will proved 1668, left £60 in trust for the poor, and this was used to buy 5 a. of the land liable for Tudor's rent-charge. The land, which in 1834 was let for £22, was sold in 1854 to the Victoria Dock Co. for £1,000, which was invested.

Sir Jacob Garrard,[79] by a deed of 1653, conveyed in trust land called Oxleas in High mead, West Ham, beside the river Lea, then let at £22 a year, from which £9 was to be paid for apprenticing a boy from each of the three wards of West Ham. Other charges, amounting to £7 12s., were payable for church purposes in West Ham and for charities in two other parishes. Any residue was to be distributed between 50 poor persons in West Ham. In 1830 Oxleas, about 12 a., was leased for 99 years at £70 a year. It was sold in 1927 for £14,000, which was invested.

Elizabeth Toppesfield, by will proved 1660, gave a rent-charge of 50s., of which £2 was to provide six poor wives or widows with waistcoats, in which they were to attend a yearly sermon paid for by the other 10s. The rent-charge was redeemed in 1888 for £100 stock. She also gave £30 to buy coal for selling to the poor at cost price, but the loss and trouble incurred in this scheme resulted in the remaining £20 being used, in 1819, to build a pump for the poor of Plaistow.

Clement Pragell of Stepney (Mdx.), by will dated 1680, gave a rent-charge of £5 for the poor. This

---

[77] See p. 123.   [78] See p. 72.   [79] For Garrard's charity see also p. 43.

was still being received in 1966 from the owners of land at Plaistow which included Pragell Street.

Nathaniel Peckover, by will proved 1686, left a rent-charge of £2 to be divided between 20 poor widows of Stratford. This was redeemed in 1905 for £80 stock.

Sir Thomas Foot, by will proved 1689, left an annuity of £42 of which £8 was for the poor of Plaistow. In 1720 this was transferred to South Sea Co. stock and lost most of its value, no dividends being received for many years. A reinvestment was made in 1783 from which in 1830 the parish was receiving £1 10s. a year. In 1893 £56 stock was specifically assigned to this charity.

Sir William Humble (d. 1687)[80] left £60 to buy land, the rent from which was to provide weekly doles of bread. In 1706 1 a. was bought in New marsh. This produced a rent, in 1834, of £4. In 1869 the Gas Light and Coke Co. took the land by compulsory purchase to make Beckton Road, at a price of £450, which was invested.

Daniel Ingoll (d. 1691)[81] left a rent of £10, charged on his land in Leadenhall Street, London, to buy coal for the poor. In 1772 the owner of the land conveyed it to the vicar and churchwardens of West Ham in recompense for 35 years' arrears, and between 1776 and 1879 the rent from it increased from £10 to £120. In 1891 it was let on an 80-year building lease at a rent of £105. In 1878 £97 stock was bought with money paid by the owners of adjoining properties in compensation for interference with light and air. The land was compulsorily purchased by the City corporation in 1913, and the proceeds invested in £4,731 stock.

Mary Battailhey (or Sherley), by will proved 1702, gave a rent of £10 charged on a house and land at Plaistow. Of this £1 was for bread for the poor of Plaistow, and £2 10s. for 'widows' groats', to be paid to eight poor widows of Plaistow and eight of Church Street ward; the rest was for ecclesiastical and educational purposes, which were excluded from the scheme of 1870. The rent-charge was redeemed in 1925 for £400 stock, of which £140 was allotted to the United Ecclesiastical Charities.

Samuel Sheppard, by his will dated 1733, gave £50 for coal and £200 for the sick poor.

The legacy of James Cooper (d. 1743), part of which was for Newman's alms-houses, was also to provide doles of 5s. for 30 poor householders of Plaistow on Midsummer Day and £1 2s. 6d. and 15s. for bread on New Year's Day for the poor of Plaistow and Church Street respectively.

Sarah Bonnell, by deed of 1754, gave £200 stock in trust to provide each year lengths of cloth at 10s. each for five poor widows, 10s. 6d. for education, and the residue for coal for the poor. All the beneficiaries were to belong to Church Street ward. In 1834 the interest of £6 was spent as directed, but in 1868 7s. 6d. was given to the alms-women and the vicar spent the residue on port wine for the sick.

Peter Bigot, by deed of 1771, gave a rent of £10, charged on a house and land in Upton Lane, for shoes, stockings, and 1s. each for six poor women in Plaistow and six in Stratford ward, the residue to be spent in the same way in Church Street ward. In 1966 the rent-charge was being paid by Barclay's bank, Forest Gate.

Jeremiah Atkinson, stationer of London, by will dated 1777, left the reversion of £300 for coal for the poor of Plaistow. This became effective some time between 1814[82] and 1834. The restriction to Plaistow lapsed under the scheme of 1870.

Margaretta Hodshon of Wandsworth (Surr.), by will proved 1779, left £200 for apprenticing one poor boy each year. The income continued to be used for this purpose until 1870, after which it was applied to the general purposes of the Distributive Charities.

Before 1791 William Winn gave £10, Penelope Colchester £20, and other parishioners £20. These sums were together invested in stock, and the interest, £1 15s. in 1834, was distributed in doles.

John Snelgrave, a benefactor of Newman's alms-houses, by will proved 1810, also left £200 for coal, bread, or clothing for the poor. In 1834 the income of £5 15s. was spent on blankets for 20 persons.

The charities of Samuel Jones Vachell and Isabella Wilson have been mentioned above under the Alms-house Charities.

The scheme of 1870 included, along with the above-mentioned charities, four others founded in the 17th century which had in fact lapsed before 1870. None of these was included in the scheme of 1903. Richard Pragell, by will dated 1617, gave for the use of the poor a rent-charge of £2. Richard Hale of Stepney, by will proved 1628, gave for the poor of Plaistow ward a rent-charge of £2. In each case the land charged was eventually acquired by the Victoria Dock Co., which made no payment of Pragell's rent after 1854 or of Hale's after 1860. William Fawcit, by will proved 1631, left a rent of £2 10s. charged on a house at Upton, to provide 10s. for a Gunpowder Plot sermon on 5 November and £2 for bread for the poor attending the sermon. This was regularly paid until 1851, after which the owner of the land withheld payment. William Davis, by will dated 1679, gave a rent-charge of £4 on reversion to buy waistcoats for 12 poor women each year. This rent, from land at Plaistow, also lapsed in the 1850s. In most of these cases attempts were made to prevent the loss of the charities, but with such small sums involved the trustees could not afford much litigation. The great changes that were taking place in the topography of West Ham at that time sometimes made it difficult to identify exactly the land upon which a rent was charged, and the defaulting landowners exploited these difficulties.

Rebecca Robinson, by her will proved 1866, left £90 stock to maintain her family's tombstone, the residue being for bread or coal for the poor. The charity was not included in the scheme of 1870, but from 1881 its trustees (the vicar and churchwardens) remitted the income to the central charity board, and it was included in the scheme of 1903 as one of the Distributive Charities, the tombstone bequest being invalid.

OTHER CHARITIES FOR THE POOR. The following charities are not included among the United Non-Ecclesiastical Charities, in most cases because they were not in operation when the scheme of 1870 was being prepared. Many of them are restricted to particular ecclesiastical parishes.

[80] Cf. Lysons, *London*, iv. 267.   [81] Ibid. 260.   [82] Ogborne, *Hist. Essex*, 27.

John Hiett, distiller of London, by will proved 1719, gave a rent of £5, charged on Chobhams farm, for apprenticing each year the son of a poor Protestant dissenter, preferably from Stratford. In 1834 this was paid to the minister of Brickfields Congregational church, who used it as directed. It was not paid after 1839 and efforts to recover it in 1855-7 failed.

George Dacre, by deed of 1855, conveyed to the vicar and churchwardens of All Saints', West Ham, land and houses in Church Street, then leased at an annual ground rent of £7 10s.[83] At the expiration of the lease in 1910 the houses were to be used as alms-houses, the rents meanwhile being saved. By 1910 the accumulated rents amounted to about £750. The houses were not used as alms-houses after 1910, but continued to be let, the income from rents and investments being used, under a scheme of 1911, to pay pensions to poor married couples, preferably aged, who were constant communicants of All Saints' church and had lived in West Ham for at least two years. In 1922 the property was sold for £630. In 1964, when the income of the charity was £86, four pensioners each received £1 a month and an almoner £5 for the year.

Edith Clark, by will proved 1860, gave £300 in trust to provide bread and coal at Christmas for the poor of the parish of St. Mary, Plaistow. In 1966 the income of £4 15s. 8d. was used to provide fuel for old people at Christmas.[84]

The Mary Curtis maternity charity was founded in 1872, when Mary Curtis, widow, gave £6,666 stock in trust to provide help at or after confinement to respectable poor married women living within a radius of 1 mile from St. John's church, Stratford. Six 'distributors' were appointed with power to grant letters of recommendation to objects of the charity. They included Mrs. Curtis herself and, ex officio, the vicars of West Ham and St. John's, Stratford. For many years the charity was administered by St. Helen's House women's settlement. A scheme of 1968 provided that after St. John's area had been served the charity could help any married woman living in the London Borough of Newham, before, during, or after confinement. In that year the income was £251, part of which was spent on the provision of gifts of food or clothing, usually costing about £5 in each case.[85]

The birthday gift of Thomas Wiseman Shipston was founded under his will, proved 1885, by which he gave £1,050 in trust to provide Christmas gifts for 30 poor aged inhabitants of West Ham. In 1966 each of the 30 pensioners received 16s. 3d.[86]

George Canning Edwards, by will proved 1902, left £100 to maintain the graves of his parents and his sister, the residue of the income to be used for the poor of the parish of St. John, Stratford. The provision concerning the graves was invalid. In 1964 the income of £2 13s. 8d. was distributed to 5 persons.[87] Edwards also left £100 to maintain his

own grave, the residue for the poor of the parish of Emmanuel, Forest Gate. In 1926 it was stated that in then recent years the income had been used for the general maintenance of Emmanuel church, and the Charity Commission reminded the vicar that it should be used only for the benefit of the poor. In 1966 the income of £2 13s. 8d. was distributed to the sick and needy.[88]

The Sir Henry Tate Memorial investment was founded in 1902 by his widow, who gave £3,330 stock to pay the salary of a nurse employed by the Silvertown and North Woolwich district nursing association. The association was dissolved in 1955, and a scheme of 1958 provided that the charity should be applied to the sick poor of Silvertown and North Woolwich by trustees appointed by the boroughs of East Ham, West Ham, and Woolwich. In 1966 £73 was spent on gifts in kind to 20 persons.[89]

The Richard Peck gift of coals was founded by Mrs. Dorothy Peck, who by will proved 1905 gave £105 for coal for the aged poor of the parish of St. John, Stratford. In 1964 £2 12s. was spent on coal for 5 persons.[90]

John Oliver Surtees, by will proved 1907, left £135, subject to a life interest which expired in 1914, for the sick and poor of the parish of St. Mary, Plaistow. In 1964 the income of £3 17s. 10d. was distributed in cash as directed.[91] Surtees also left £135 on the same terms for the parish of St. Mark, Victoria Docks. In 1964 the income of £5 1s. 8d. was spent on Christmas gifts for the aged poor.[92]

Miss Wetherall's trust was founded by deed of 1908 to provide coal at Christmas for poor members of St. Mary's church, Plaistow. In 1945 the income was £2 6s. 2d. from an endowment of £79.[93]

Joseph Withers, by will proved 1911, gave £1,000 in trust for the aged inmates of the West Ham union workhouse. In 1964 3s. 6d. was given to each of 160 old people in homes maintained by West Ham borough council.[94] Withers also gave £2,000 in trust for the aged poor of All Saints' parish and the same amount for those of the parish of St. John, Stratford.[95] In 1966 the income of the All Saints' charity was spent mainly on gifts of £1 each to 22 persons in June and again in December, and on an honorarium to an almoner. That of the St. John's charity was dispensed bi-monthly to about 10 old persons.[96]

Harriet Townsend, by will proved 1913, left £2,000, subject to a life interest which expired in 1924, for the poor of the parish of St. Mary, Plaistow. The vicar and churchwardens invested the capital. In 1964 the income of £89 was spent on a Christmas party for 120 aged poor and in other charitable ways.[97]

Thomas Geere, by will proved 1914, gave £114 10s. in trust to provide treats for inmates of Harris's alms-houses who were members of the Church of England. In 1964 £3 8s. was distributed in kind by the vicar of All Saints' among the Anglican inmates of the combined alms-houses.[98]

83 Char. Com. File 247079.
84 Ibid. 68802; 207309; inf. from the Vicar of Plaistow.
85 Inf. from the Secretary, Mary Curtis Charity; Char. Com. File 235036.
86 Ibid. 207774; inf. from Town Clerk of Newham.
87 Char. Com. File 240257.
88 Ibid. 208783; inf. from Vicar of Emmanuel.
89 Ibid. 212350; inf. from Town Clerk of Newham.
90 Char. Com. File 240256.
91 Ibid. 245754.

92 Ibid. 239928.
93 Ibid. 68802 and 87532. No other information appears to be available.
94 Char. Com. File 209034; inf. from Town Clerk of Newham.
95 Ibid.
96 Inf. from Mr. M. J. Kindred and the Vicar of St. John's.
97 Char. Com. File 245752.
98 Char. Com. File 247077.

James Hawkey Banfield, by will proved 1916, gave £100 in trust to the mayor as a Christmas fund for the poor. In 1966 the income of £3 6s. 2d. was shared among three persons.[99] Banfield also left his residuary estate in trust to provide holidays for members of the 'lower middle class or upper lower class . . . who often have to keep up appearances on very small means'. Free church ministers were to have first consideration and the borough of West Ham was to have a 'liberal first claim'. In 1964 the investments of the holiday fund stood at over £11,000, and the income was £594. Grants totalling £312 were made to 30 applicants.[1]

Elizabeth Bowerbank, by will proved 1916, left £650 in trust to supply food and coal to the aged poor of the parish of St. Mary, Plaistow. In 1964 £21 was spent on coal.[2]

St. Cuthbert's home was founded in 1944 by Mrs. G. E. de Fontaine, who bought a house in St. Vincent's Road, Westcliff-on-Sea, to provide holiday accommodation for the aged poor of West Ham. Funds were raised by public subscription to equip and endow the home, which was opened in 1947. After Mrs. de Fontaine's death in 1948, and a subsequent Chancery action for the enforcement of the charitable trust, a scheme of 1951 directed that the property should be administered by the borough council.[3]

Jabez Legg's alms-houses at Forest Gate, which are not restricted to West Ham, are described elsewhere.[4]

CHURCH OF ENGLAND CHARITIES. *The Ecclesiastical Charities.* The following charities were included among the Distributive Charities under the scheme of 1870. The scheme of 1903 formed them into a separate group called the Ecclesiastical Charities, to be administered by the vicar and churchwardens of All Saints'.

Sir Jacob Garrard's charity, founded by deed of 1653, included an annual payment to the vicar of £1 for a sermon on the Sunday following 9 January, together with 6s. 8d. for the curate, 3s. 4d. for the clerk, and 2s. for the sexton. Elizabeth Toppesfield's charity, under her will proved 1660, included 10s. for an annual sermon in her memory. Clement Pragell's charity, under his will dated 1680, included a rent-charge of £1 for the repair of his family's tomb in the churchyard. The legacy of James Cooper (d. 1743) included annual payments of 15s. to the vicar for a sermon and 3s. 9d. each to the clerk and the sexton. The scheme of 1903 provided that the trustees of the Ecclesiastical Charities should receive £41 5s. in trust as their share of the endowment of Cooper's charity, together with annual payments from the trustees of the United Non-Ecclesiastical Charities of £1 12s. for Garrard's charity, 10s. for Toppesfield's, and £1 for Pragell's.

Battailhey's Charity. The charity of Mary Battailhey, under her will proved 1702, included annual payments of £1 10s. to the vicar for a sermon on Good Friday and £1 for the repair of the vault in which she and her servant were to be buried. These and the payments for educational purposes were not included in the scheme of 1870, though the eleemosynary gifts under the charity were. In 1899, however, the whole income was being received by the central charity board, and was treated as part of the income of the Distributive Charities. Mary Battailhey's vault could no longer be identified. The payments for ecclesiastical and educational purposes were subsequently resumed. When Battailhey's rent-charge was redeemed in 1925 the Ecclesiastical Charities received £100 as their share of the endowment, in respect of the sermon and vault.[5]

Other Church Charities. Mary Ann Tickell Scott, by will proved 1922, gave to the vicar of St. John's, Stratford, £400 in trust for the maintenance of the church fabric.[6]

Col. Thomas Vernon, by will proved 1919, left £1,000 to the vicar of All Saints' for the poor of the parish. After a lawsuit the legacy was received in 1925 and the interest used to rent a house (no. 134 Portway) for parish women workers. In 1932 the house was bought for £615, the balance of the capital providing an endowment. In 1960 the house was sold for £2,150, which was invested for the ultimate purpose of providing a flat for a woman worker in one of the church halls. In 1964 the investments amounted to £2,217. The income was £141, of which £121 was spent during the year.[7]

CLOCK CHARITY. Samuel Gurney, by will proved 1856, gave £800 for the maintenance and winding of clocks on places of public worship, including one to be put up on Forest Gate Congregational church. In 1961 the income of £20 was paid to the borough treasurer.[8]

LITTLE ILFORD

THE ancient parish of Little Ilford, about 6 miles north-east of London, forms part of the London borough of Newham.[1] The area is now usually called Manor Park, a name first used in the 19th century for the suburban settlement near Manor Park railway station. Little Ilford was bounded east by the river Roding which divided it from Great Ilford, in Barking parish.[2] Its southern and western boundaries marched with East Ham and its northern boundary with Wanstead. The section of the parish north of the main road to Ilford and Romford, which formed the manor of Aldersbrook, appears to have been transferred from Wanstead to Little Ilford early in the 16th century.[3] Even after that Little Ilford was the smallest parish in Becontree hundred, with an area in the 19th century of 768 a.[4] Until about 1850

[99] Ibid. 208349; inf. from the Mayor of Newham.
[1] Char. Com. File 227349. Some preliminary work on this article was done by Dr. Cyril Hart and Miss Audrey Taylor.
[2] Ibid. 245755.
[3] Ibid. 127534; inf. from Town Clerk of Newham.
[4] See p. 130.
[5] Char. Com. File 209034.

[6] Ibid.
[8] Ibid. 105140 and G22.
[1] O.S. Map 2½″, sheet TQ 48. See map above, p. 6.
[2] *V.C.H. Essex*, v. 184 sqq.
[3] See below, pp. 167, 318.
[4] O.S. Map 6″, Essex LXXXIII (1863–73 edn.).
[7] Ibid. 247078.

it was thinly populated. Growth then began, slow at first but becoming more rapid in the 1880s. In 1886 the parish was merged in the sanitary district of East Ham, and it subsequently formed part of East Ham urban district, municipal borough, and county borough. The present account describes the history of Little Ilford up to 1886, while its later history is treated under East Ham. A few exceptions to this arrangement are made clear by means of cross-references.

The land is about 25 ft. above sea level in the west of the parish, and slightly lower in the east, by the Roding. The soil is mainly valley gravel. The name Ilford ('ford through the river Hile' [Roding]),[5] seems originally to have been applied to the area west of the river, but during the 13th century that area began to be called Little Ilford, to distinguish it from the growing settlement of Great Ilford, east of the river. After the 13th century Little Ilford is usually so styled, while references to Ilford, without an adjective, usually mean Great Ilford.

In an earlier volume the Roding and its bridges have already been described in relation to Great Ilford, and most of that account is relevant also to Little Ilford.[6] Little Ilford was like Great Ilford, also, in being partly within the Forest of Essex.[7] But in other respects the two places were very different. Great Ilford, a village on the main road from London to Colchester, grew steadily from the Middle Ages up to the 19th century. Little Ilford was traversed by the same road, but its centre of population, which lay ½ mile south of that road, by the church, seems to have grown little from the 11th century to the nineteenth. In 1086 the recorded population of Little Ilford manor was 10.[8] This probably did not include the area north of the main road,[9] but that area, which lay within the forest, and later formed the manor of Aldersbrook, is unlikely to have had many inhabitants then. In 1650 it was stated that the parish contained only 6 or 7 families south of the main road, and 4 to the north of it.[10] The total number of houses was listed as 14 in 1662 and 18 in 1670.[11] In 1801 there were 15.[12]

A map of 1777[13] shows the parish before modern changes. The hamlet of Little Ilford comprised the parish church, the Manor farm, and a few cottages. There was one building (the Three Rabbits) in the main road, north of which lay Aldersbrook House with its park and home farm. Aldersbrook was pulled down about 1786 and the park became farm-land, but this seems to have had little effect on the growth of the parish. Between 1801 and 1831 the population was about 100.[14] An increase to 189 in 1841 was due to the building of a gaol within the parish,[15] and it was not until after 1851 that the normal population began to grow substantially. The new development

started in the west of the parish. During the 1850s and 1860s a number of houses were built on the east side of White Post Lane (now High Street North) and in Greenhill Grove,[16] on a small estate previously belonging to the Greenhill family.[17] About 1870 building began on the East Ham side of the parish boundary, immediately north of Romford Road, at Manor Park, which took its name from the Manor House estate formerly owned by the Fry family.[18] By 1891 the population of Little Ilford was 3,969.[19] Building had by then advanced east along Romford Road and neighbouring streets at least as far as Third Avenue.[20] As elsewhere this development was largely dependent on the railways, but Manor Park was peculiar in that very little building was possible to the north of the railway. In 1854 Aldersbrook farm had been acquired by the city of London as a cemetery. The city subsequently took the lead in preventing the inclosure of Epping Forest, thus ensuring that Wanstead Flats, adjoining their cemetery to the west, should remain as a public open space.[21] Meanwhile another cemetery had been laid out, by a private company, on the East Ham side of Manor Park, south of Wanstead Flats.[22] There was thus great pressure on the limited building land available to the south of the railway: this may account for the speed with which that part of Little Ilford was developed in the 1890s, and for the poor quality of some of the new housing.[23]

The only pre-19th-century building remaining is the former parish church of St. Mary, Church Road.[24] Greenhill Grove contains a number of yellow-brick cottages dating from the 1850s and 1860s, and the original lodge and chapels of the city of London cemetery are of the same period, but most of the buildings in Little Ilford were erected between 1890 and 1910. Among the few larger buildings which existed before the 19th century but have been demolished were the manor-houses of Little Ilford and Aldersbrook, and the rectory.[25] The Three Rabbits and the Coach and Horses public houses, Romford Road, which dated from the 18th century or earlier, have been replaced by modern buildings of the same name.[26] Little Ilford house of correction (or county gaol) was built in 1829–31 by Essex quarter sessions.[27] In 1860 it was reorganized for prisoners on remand or serving short sentences.[28] It was closed in 1878 and demolished soon after.[29] Its site, now partly covered by houses and shops, was on the north side of Romford Road, between Worcester and Gloucester Roads.

In the 18th century the road system of Little Ilford was very simple.[30] Romford Road, running through the centre of the parish, was the ancient

---

[5] *P.N. Essex* (E.P.N.S.), 97–8.
[6] *V.C.H. Essex*, v. 184–7.
[7] See below, p. 168.
[8] *V.C.H. Essex*, i. 559a.
[9] See below, p. 168.
[10] H. Smith, *Eccl. Hist. Essex*, 251.
[11] E.R.O., Q/RTh 1 and 5.
[12] *Census*, 1801.   [13] See plate f. p. 53.
[14] *Census*, 1801–31.   [15] See below.
[16] Little Ilford Ch., Vestry Mins. 1857 *f.*; O.S. Map 6″, Essex LXXXIII (1863–73 edn.).
[17] Cf. E.R.O., D/P 175/8 (22 Apr. 1824); E.R.O., D/CT 191: 'Nine Acres' owned by Widow Greenhill.
[18] P.E.M., Pictorial Survey, East Ham: Manor Park Manor House.

[19] *Census*, 1891.
[20] *Kelly's Dir. Essex*, 1890.
[21] See below, p. 169.
[22] See p. 24.   [23] See p. 5.
[24] See p. 172.
[25] See pp. 166–7, 171.
[26] Stokes, *E. Ham*, f. pp. 64 and 22; for the Three Rabbits see below p. 169. The Coach and Horses was demolished in 1970 and is to be rebuilt.
[27] *E.R.* l. 163; E.R.O., Q/AGb 8.
[28] E.R.O., Q/AGp 17; ibid. Q/SO 43 (3 July 1860).
[29] E.R.O., Q/SO 50 (9 Apr., 2 July 1878, 1 July 1879); *E.R.* l. 163.
[30] See plate f.p. 53; cf. O.S. Map 6″, Essex LXXXIII (1863–73 edn.).

main road from London to Romford and Colchester. It is shown on early maps of Essex[31] and was probably of Roman origin.[32] It continued to be the main road until 1925, when Eastern Avenue was opened farther north. From 1721 it was controlled by the Middlesex and Essex turnpike trust.[33] A toll-gate stood immediately west of Ilford Bridge. A toll-house which was on the north side of the road, near Ilford Bridge, survived until about 1900 or later as the Little Wonder coffee house.[34] Running south from the main road was Little Ilford Lane,[35] leading to the church, where it joined Little Ilford Road (now Church Road). Little Ilford Road ran west to join White Post Lane. It went east only as far as the present Dersingham Avenue: at that end it served only the manor-house. White Post Lane (now High Street North), running from Romford Road south to East Ham, is described under that parish.[36] North of Romford Road there were tracks across Wanstead Flats roughly on the lines of the present Aldersbrook Road and Forest Drive.[37]

The ancient road system described in the previous paragraph survived almost unchanged until the 1880s, but before that time Little Ilford was intersected by railways: the Eastern Counties (later Great Eastern) line from London to Romford (1839) and beyond, the London, Tilbury and Southend line from Forest Gate to Barking (1854), and its cut-off from Bow to Barking (1858).[38] In 1872, after a petition from the inhabitants of Little Ilford, the G.E.R. opened Manor Park station. This was rebuilt in 1893–4.[39] A tramway from Stratford and Forest Gate to White Post Lane was completed in 1887.[40]

By 1861 there was a sub-post office at Little Ilford, receiving letters through Great Ilford, then in the London postal district.[41] In 1867 Great Ilford and its dependencies were transferred to the eastern counties district,[42] but in 1883 it was decided to form a new sub-district of Manor Park within the London postal district. In 1917 this became the E. 12 district.[43] A telegraph office was established at Manor Park in 1886.[44] Manor Park is served by the Ilford telephone exchange, opened by the National Telephone Co. in 1900.[45]

Eminent residents of Little Ilford include Sir John Heron (d. 1521), Henry Herbert, earl of Pembroke (d. 1601), John Lethieullier (d. 1737) and his son Smart (d. 1760), all of whom were lords of Aldersbrook.[46] Among rectors Thomas Newton (d. 1607) and Arthur T. W. Shadwell (d. 1893) achieved distinction.[47]

MANORS. The manor of *LITTLE ILFORD*, also known from the 17th century as *BERENGERS*,[48] comprised that part of the parish lying to the south of the ancient road to London. In 1066 it was held by two freemen as a manor and as 3 hides less 30 a.[49] In 1086 it was held by Jocelin the Lorimer, who had taken 24 a. from the manor of Barking.[50] In 1210–12 Halnoth de Sifrewast, who had succeeded William de Sifrewast at Purley (Berks.) before 1186[51] held Ilford in chief for one knight's fee.[52] By 1217 Halnoth had been succeeded by his son William,[53] who in 1226–8 was engaged in litigation with Barking Abbey concerning suit at the hundred court.[54] Statements made in this case seem to imply that William's family had held land at Ilford since the reign of Henry II, but the only member of the family who was named was his father's sister Isabel, widow of a certain Alan, who was holding land there (evidently not Little Ilford manor) in dower between 1170 and 1181. In 1233 William de Sifrewast granted 20 a. land in Ilford to Robert of Ilford for life.[55] In 1238–9 William was challenged by Roger de Quercu, in right of his wife Agnes, who claimed the manor as great-granddaughter of 'Joceamus', said to have been the tenant under Henry I.[56] Joceamus sounds like Jocelin the Lorimer, the Domesday tenant, who may well have survived into the reign of Henry I. The dispute was settled in 1240, when Roger and Agnes surrendered their claim.[57] William de Sifrewast was dead by 1244, leaving as his heir his son Nicholas, then a minor.[58] At his death he still held lands in Essex, but his Ilford estate seems to have passed soon after into the hands of William de la Pole. In 1254 Pole was patron of the church of Little Ilford, an appurtenance of the manor,[59] and in 1259 he granted the advowson and one carucate of land in Ilford, together with the tenement that Robert of Ilford once held there, to the abbey of Stratford Langthorne, to hold by rent of 45s. a year and service of $\frac{1}{4}$ knight's fee.[60] In 1291 the abbey's temporal estate at Ilford was valued at £11 12s. 1$\frac{1}{2}$d. a year.[61]

In 1538, when Stratford Abbey was surrendered to the Crown,[62] its estate in Little Ilford and the adjoining parish of Barking comprised the manors of Little Ilford, Rayhouse, and Berengers. Rayhouse, which was at Great Ilford,[63] and Berengers,[64] which was in Barking town, were both free tenements held of the manor of Barking. An account for the year 1537–8 shows that Little Ilford and Rayhouse were then farmed out for £17 10s. 8d. a year.[65]

[31] e.g. J. Norden, *Map of Essex*, 1594.
[32] *V.C.H. Essex*, iii. 24–5.
[33] Ibid. v. 186.
[34] P.E.M., Pictorial Survey, East Ham.
[35] Stokes, *E. Ham*, plate f.p. 44.
[36] See p. 2.
[37] For footpaths in that part of the parish see *E.R.* l. 167.
[38] For fuller details of these lines see p. 5.
[39] Stokes, *E. Ham*, 113 and plate f. p. 112. The station was on the Little Ilford–East Ham boundary.
[40] *Kelly's Dir. Essex*, 1890.
[41] *Brit. Post. Guide*, 1861.
[42] P.M.G. Mins. 1867, vol. 61, 4448.
[43] Ibid. 1883, vol. 251, 7488; *G.P.O. Guide*, 1917.
[44] P.M.G. Mins. 1886, vol. 306, 2815.
[45] *Nat. Telephone Jnl.* Oct. 1917, 135.
[46] See p. 166.
[47] See pp. 171–2.
[48] For the medieval manor of Berengers see below, p. 168.
[49] *V.C.H. Essex*, i. 559a.

[50] Ibid. 559a, 448b. For Barking manor see ibid. v. 190.
[51] *V.C.H. Berks.* iii. 420.
[52] *Red. Bk. Exch.* (Rolls Ser.), ii. 499.
[53] *Rot. Litt. Claus.* (Rec. Com.), i. 347; *Bracton's Notebook*, ed. Maitland, ii. 469.
[54] *Rot. Litt. Claus.* ii. 148, 156; J.I. 1/229 m. 5.
[55] *Feet of F. Essex*, i. 92.
[56] K.B. 26/120 m. 13d.
[57] *Feet of F. Essex*, i. 124.
[58] *Excerpta e Rot. Fin.* (Rec. Com.), i. 428; ii. 252; *V.C.H. Berks.* iv. 3, 74.
[59] *E.A.T.* N.S. xviii. 17.
[60] *Feet of F. Essex*, i. 232.
[61] *Tax. Eccl.* (Rec. Com.), 25.
[62] *V.C.H. Essex*, ii. 132.
[63] See ibid. v. 209.
[64] See below.
[65] *V.C.H. Essex*, ii. 132–3; S.C. 6/ Hen. VIII/962 m. 23.

In 1542 the Crown granted the manors of Little Ilford, Rayhouse, and Berengers, and the advowson of Little Ilford, to Morgan Phillips, *alias* Wolfe, king's goldsmith.[66] The three manors passed from Morgan Phillips (d. 1552) to his son Julian Morgan *alias* Wolfe (d. 1556).[67] Henry Morgan, son of Julian, succeeded to Little Ilford and Berengers, and was still holding them in 1583.[68] Rayhouse had been detached from the rest of the estate by 1570 or earlier.[69] Soon after 1583 Little Ilford and Berengers passed to Edward Onley, son of Julian Morgan's widow Jane by her second husband, Thomas Onley, and in 1596 Edward sold the two manors to Hugh, John, and Nicholas Hare.[70] In 1605 the estate was bought from the Hares by Bernard Hyde, salter of London.[71] Hyde was apparently living at Little Ilford in 1614–18,[72] but he and his descendants seem to have resided mainly in Mincing Lane, St. Dunstan's in the East (Lond.), or at Boar Place, Chiddingstone (Kent).[73] On his death in 1631 he was succeeded by his son Bernard (d. 1656) and he by his son Sir Bernard (d. 1674).[74] Another Sir Bernard was apparently holding the estate in 1683,[75] but by 1687 it had passed to Humphrey Hyde who in 1701 sold it to Henry Wight,[76] already the owner of Gayshams, in Great Ilford.[77] By the end of the 17th century the original distinction between Little Ilford and Berengers had been forgotten and the two names were being used indifferently to describe the whole property.

Little Ilford and Berengers descended along with Gayshams until 1873, when the estate of John Hibbit Wight (d. 1867) was advertised for sale by Chancery order,[78] and subsequently broken up. The Hibbit Wight family had been the largest landowners in Little Ilford. They do not appear to have lived in the parish, though for some years, about 1810–25, William Hibbit lived near by at West Ham.[79] In 1838 their lands in the parish comprised 363 a., of which 253 a. (Manor farm and Bolts farm) were let to Henry Hunsdon, who had been there since 1827.[80] The Hunsdons remained tenants until the 1860s.[81] In 1873 Manor farm (250 a.) was occupied by James Tyler, on a 21-year lease granted in 1868.[82] After the sale of 1873 Charles Bartholomew, of Ealing (Mdx., later Lond.), became principal landowner in the parish.[83] In 1890–4 he was running Manor farm through a bailiff.[84] He died

early in 1895, and the development of the 'Manor House Estate' for building began in the following year.[85]

Little Ilford Manor House, later Manor House farm, which stood near the present junction of Dersingham Avenue and Church Road,[86] had been demolished by 1901.[87] It was a modest building having a symmetrical front of five bays and a large octagonal lantern or look-out surmounting the roof.[88] Those features appear to have dated from the 18th century, but a central two-storeyed porch had an inner doorway surmounted by a four-centred arch.[89] Irregular structures at the rear also suggest that the house was of 16th- or early-17th-century origin.[90]

The manor of *ALDERSBROOK* occupied the part of Little Ilford parish lying to the north of the ancient highway to London; it was therefore wholly within the bounds of the forest of Essex.[91] The name derives from *ealdan hile*, the western of the two branches of the Roding at this point, which formed part of the bounds of *Hamme* in A.D. 958.[92] This branch was called the Old river about 1570[93] and Aldersbrook in 1815–16.[94]

Aldersbrook first appears as a separate manor in the early 16th century. Sir John Heron (d. 1521) left it to his wife Margaret for life, with reversion to his son Giles, then a minor.[95] Sir John, who was treasurer of the Chamber to Henry VII and Henry VIII, had been at Aldersbrook at least as early as 1517, when his son Thomas died there.[96] In 1523 the wardship of Giles Heron was granted by the Crown to Sir Thomas More.[97] Giles, who later married his guardian's daughter Cecily, was executed in 1540 for his continued loyalty to More.[98] In 1532, shortly before More resigned his office of lord chancellor, Giles sold to the Crown 'a great messuage called Nakedhall Hawe or Alderbroke', in the parish of Wanstead.[99] Another reference to the same transaction describes the property as the manor of Aldersbrook, in the parishes of Little Ilford and Wanstead.[1] In 1535 the Crown granted to Anthony Knevett, gentleman usher of the Privy Chamber, and Maud his wife, in survivorship, the manor of Aldersbrook, a tenement called Draginsford, adjoining Aldersbrook, Naked Hall Grove, and Millfield, which belonged to Draginsford, and other lands in Little Ilford and Wanstead.[2] Maud Knevett was dead by 1544, when the Crown sold the manor to

66 E.R.O., D/DVu 1.
67 E 150/325/3; C 142/111/39.
68 C.P. 43/5 Eas. 26 Eliz. ro. 55.
69 *V.C.H. Essex*, v. 209.
70 Lysons, *London*, iv. 151; cf. *Cal. Pat* 1558–60, 175.
71 Lysons, *London*, iv. 151; C.P. 25(2)/292 Mich. 3 Jas. I; E.R.O., Sage Coll. Nos. 337–41 (Hyde pedigree, etc.).
72 Lysons, *London*, iv. 153; *Acts of P.C.* 1618–19, 134.
73 E.R.O., Sage Coll., Nos. 337–41.
74 Ibid. Nos. 337–41; Stow, *Survey of London*, ed. J. Strype, Bk. ii. 46.
75 *E.A.T.* N.S. xix. 264.
76 C.P. 25(2)/777 Eas. 3 Jas. II; Lysons, *London*, iv. 151.
77 For Gayshams see *V.C.H. Essex*, v. 204–5.
78 Ibid.   79 See p. 170.
80 E.R.O., D/CT 191; E.R.O., Q/RPl 100.
81 *White's Dir. Essex*, 1863, p. 635.
82 E.R.O., Sage Coll., *Sale Cats.* vii. 3.
83 *Kelly's Dir. Essex*, 1878, 1894.
84 Ibid. 1890, 1894.
85 E.H.L., E. Ham U.D.C. Mins. 5 Mar. 1895, 2 Nov. 1896, 5 Feb. 1897.

86 O.S. Map 6″, Essex LXXIII (1893–4 edn.), cf. TQ 48 N.W. (1951 edn.).
87 E.H.L., E. Ham U.D.C. Map, 1901.
88 E. Stokes, *East Ham*, plate f.p. 32; E.R.O., Sage Coll. no. 395. See plate below, f.p. 307.
89 National Monuments Record, Pencil sketch (1895).
90 *E.A.T.* N.S. ix. 409.
91 W. R. Fisher, *Forest of Essex*, 178.
92 *Cart. Sax.* ed. Birch, no. 1037; cf. *P. N. Essex*, ii. 94.
93 E.R.O., D/DQs 17.
94 E.R.O., Map of manors of Wanstead, Aldersbrook &c., 1815–16.
95 *Misc. Gen. Her.* N.S. i (1874), 50; for his date of death see C 142/40/113; Margaret was dead by 1532: *Misc. Gen. Her.* N.S. i (1874), 66.
96 Little Ilford ch., brass to Thos. Heron, 1517.
97 *L. & P. Hen. VIII*, iii (2), p. 1223.
98 *Correspondence of Sir Thos. More*, ed. E. F. Rogers, 97; *L.J.* i. 134b, 162a.
99 *L. & P. Hen. VIII*, v, p. 385.
1 Ibid. p. 508.
2 Ibid. ix, p. 165.

Katherine Addington, widow, and her son Thomas, the king's skinner, who had acquired Knevett's interest in the estate.[3] The Crown reserved from the grant lands formerly belonging to Giles Heron, lying in Wanstead Park and lately inclosed.

From the details given above it is clear that in the early 16th century Aldersbrook manor extended into Wanstead, and it may be suggested that until that time Aldersbrook was appurtenant to the manor of Wanstead. The reference of 1532 shows that an alternative name for Aldersbrook was Naked Hall Hawe. That name, which also occurs as Naked Hall Grove, in 1535, was clearly identical with Naget Hall, which in 1383 was held of Barking Abbey by John Huntercombe, lord of Wanstead.[4] It seems likely that Aldersbrook descended along with Wanstead until after that manor came into the possession of the Crown about 1499,[5] and was subsequently granted to Sir John Heron, who is known to have received other Crown lands in south-west Essex.[6] The boundary disputes between the lords of Aldersbrook and Wanstead, in the 17th and early 18th centuries, probably reflect the ancient connexion of the two manors,[7] and in a different connexion it was stated, in 1650, that part of Little Ilford, lying north of the main road, had formerly been in Wanstead parish.[8]

In 1554 the manor of Aldersbrook was purchased from Thomas Addington by John Traves, scissor merchant of London.[9] Traves died in 1570 having settled the manor on his wife Elizabeth for life with remainder to his son John.[10] It was later said that at about this time 'one Gabriel, a brewer' lived at the manor-house.[11] In 1578 John Traves the younger, also a scissor merchant, granted Aldersbrook to Henry Herbert, earl of Pembroke, who lived there for a short time.[12] In 1580 Pembroke granted the manor in fee to Nicholas Fuller of Grays Inn (Mdx.) and Sara his wife.[13] Fuller sold it in 1585 to Robert Dudley, earl of Leicester, who already owned the manor of Wanstead.[14] Leicester (d. 1588) devised Aldersbrook to his bastard son Robert Dudley.[15] In 1595 Dudley sold it to Edward Bellingham.[16] Henry Bellingham, no doubt a relative of Edward, was living at the manor-house between 1594 and 1613.[17] Edward was succeeded before 1613 by his son Sir Edward, who died in 1637 leaving as his heir his father's sister Cecily, wife of Thomas West.[18] The Wests do not appear to have lived at Aldersbrook.

In 1655 Henry West, of Woodmancote, in West Bourne (Suss.) sold the manor to Henry Osbaldeston.[19] Henry (d. 1669)[20] was succeeded by his son Francis Osbaldeston who in 1677 also inherited his uncle's estate in Great Ilford.[21] Both Henry and Francis appear to have lived at Aldersbrook.[22] Francis died in 1678,[23] having settled all his estates on his daughter Mary with the provision that when she reached the age of 16 they should be sold to provide a portion for her.[24] Aldersbrook subsequently descended with Loxford, in Great Ilford, until 1786.[25] In 1693, when John Lethieullier bought the estate, Aldersbrook house was tenanted by Nathaniel Long, and Aldersbrook Warren by Andrew White.[26] Lethieullier (d. 1737) and his son Smart (d. 1760) both lived at Aldersbrook, and so also did Smart's niece Mary, and her husband Edward Hulse from the time of their marriage in 1769.[27]

In 1786 Aldersbrook was sold by Mary and Edward Hulse to Sir James Long, Bt., and was thus again merged in the manor of Wanstead.[28] In 1815 Aldersbrook consisted of a farm of 269 a., with manorial rights over 41 a. of Epping Forest and over 38 a. held by other proprietors.[29] It continued to descend with Wanstead until 1854, when William Pole-Tylney-Long-Wellesley, earl of Mornington, sold most of Aldersbrook (though not the manorial rights) to the city of London.[30] The land became a cemetery and is still used as such. The ownership of it gave the corporation of London a *locus standi* in the dispute concerning the preservation of Epping Forest.[31] A small part of Aldersbrook, not included in the sale of 1854, continued as a farm, under the same name, until the end of the 19th century when it was developed for building.[32]

Nothing is known concerning the medieval manor-house. From the early 16th century Aldersbrook was evidently a building of size and dignity, described in 1532 as a 'great messuage', and marked on Norden's map of Essex (1594).[33] Its importance is also shown by the fact that such owners as Sir John Heron and the earl of Pembroke lived there, but part of it may have been demolished before 1670, when it had only 12 hearths.[34] An early-18th-century map depicts it in elevation as an L-shaped building, with two storeys and gables.[35] A later map, of 1748, shows the ground-plan only.[36] Smart Lethieullier, a keen antiquary and collector, frequently entertained eminent scholars.[37] Richard Pococke, who visited Aldersbrook in 1750, noted that Lethieullier had

[3] E.R.O., Sage Coll., Hist. Barking &c., ii. 528–32; E 318/5; *L. & P. Hen. VIII*, xix (1), p. 284.
[4] *Cal. Close*, 1381–5, 321.
[5] See p. 323.
[6] See p. 254.
[7] E.R.O., D/DQs 17; *E.R.* xxxv. 216–20.
[8] H. Smith, *Eccl. Hist. Essex*, 247.
[9] *Cal. Pat.* 1555, 339.
[10] C 142/153/43.
[11] E.R.O., D/DQs 17.
[12] C.P. 25(2)/130/1670; E.R.O., D/DQs 17.
[13] E.R.O., D/DSa 83.
[14] C.P. 25(2)/133/1098.
[15] Lysons, *London*, iv. 152; *Complete Peerage*, vii. 551.
[16] C.P. 25(2)/136/1736.
[17] J. Norden, *Description of Essex*, 29; E.R.O., D/DQs 17.
[18] C 142/481/62; E.R.O., D/DQs 17.
[19] E.R.O., Sage Coll., Hist. Barking &c., ii. 538.
[20] Morant, *Essex*, i. 27.
[21] *V.C.H. Essex*, v. 206.
[22] E.R.O., Q/RTh 1 and 5; Little Ilford Ch., Reg. Baptisms.

[23] Mon. in Little Ilford Ch.
[24] *Commons' Jnls.* x. 767a.
[25] Cf. *V.C.H. Essex*, v. 206.
[26] E.R.O., Sage Coll., Hist. Barking &c., ii. 540.
[27] E.R.O., D/DCw T7; *Hist. Essex by Gent.* iv. 296–7; C. H. I. Chown, 'The Lethieullier family of Aldersbrook House', *E.R.* xxxv. 203f; xxxvi. 1f.
[28] E.R.O., D/DCw T7.
[29] *E.R.* l. 121–2.
[30] Ibid. 166.
[31] Fisher, *Forest of Essex*, 360; C. H. I. Chown, 'Aldersbrook Farm and the Preservation of Epping Forest', *E.R.* l. 20, 118, 163, gives additional information concerning the later history of this manor, the farm and its tenants.
[32] *E.R.* l. 168, 174.
[33] J. Norden, *Description of Essex*, 1594.
[34] E.R.O., Q/RTh 5.
[35] E.R.O., Map of Aldersbrook c. 1725.
[36] Ibid. 1748.
[37] *E.R.* xxxvi. 2, 7.

'made a very pretty improvement' there, and that his wife had 'made a beautiful hermitage in a wood, with lawn, water, a mount, parterre etc. . . .'. He also described Lethieullier's fossil collection and some of the books in his library.[38] When Sir James Long bought the estate in 1786 he immediately demolished the house.[39] Its site is on the east side of the cemetery opposite the catacombs.[40] Lysons's statement that a farm-house was built on the site[41] is incorrect. There was already a farm-house near the manor-house to the west, and this remained in use until 1854, when it was demolished to make way for the cemetery.[42] A new farm-house, erected about 1863 in Aldersbrook Road (Wanstead) to serve the remaining portion of Aldersbrook farm, was on the site of the Aldersbrook Garage[43] where some of its garden walls and out-buildings still survive.

The manor of *BERENGERS* was originally a free tenement held of the manor of Barking, and situated in the south of Barking town. It took its name from the family of Roger Berenger who was holding land in Barking in 1266.[44] In 1456 Stratford Langthorne Abbey held a garden beside Townedowne in Barking, formerly of Roger Berenger, a barn by Berengers garden, and a tenement in Hythe (now Heath) Street.[45] At the Dissolution Stratford Abbey was holding a tenement in Heath Street, with a grange, a tenement with a garden adjoining and a lane called Berengers, and a garden beside Turnedowne.[46] Turnedowne, which was clearly identical with the Townedowne of 1456, is shown south of the present Axe Street, on a map of 1653.[47] Berengers Lane may have been the alley running south from the west end of Axe Street, shown in the same map. In 1609[48] Turnedowne was stated to be east of Berengers garden. The tenements described thus evidently lay on the south side of Heath Street, but their exact location and extent is not known. Before the Dissolution they presumably constituted the demesne of the manor of Berengers; there also belonged to the manor assize rents valued in 1538–9 at £3 17s. 3d.[49]

In 1542 the Crown granted the manor of Berengers, along with those of Little Ilford and Rayhouse, which had also belonged to Stratford Abbey, to Morgan Phillips, *alias* Wolfe.[50] From that date Berengers and Little Ilford descended together, and eventually became completely merged.[51] The grant of 1542 probably did not include the former demesne tenements of Berengers, and there seems to be no evidence that subsequent owners of Little Ilford and Berengers held land in Barking town. In 1609 Berengers garden, abutting east on Turnedowne, was held by Thomas Moore, and two previous owners are mentioned, neither of whom is known to have held Berengers manor.[52]

ECONOMIC HISTORY. In 1086 the manor of (Little) Ilford was said to comprise 3 hides less 30 acres; it is not clear whether this included the 24 a. which its lord, Jocelin the Lorimer, had taken from the manor of Barking.[53] There was woodland for 20 swine and 20 a. meadow. In 1066 the arable land had been worked by 4½ plough-teams, but by 1086 there were only 2 teams. On the other hand, a mill and a fishery had been added between the two dates. They were no doubt on the river Roding on the eastern side of the manor, where also must have been the 20 a. meadow.

There is little doubt that this manor, with much arable and little woodland, lay south of the ancient highway to London, and did not include the forest area to the north of the road. This is borne out by the later history of the manor, which, down to the 19th century, comprised roughly the southern half of the parish. That part of Little Ilford continued as farm land until the later 19th century. Land use figures given in conveyances of the manor, from the 17th century onwards, suggest that arable farming was important, possibly predominant, and that was certainly the case in 1839, when the Wight estate, comprising 363 a., included about 230 a. arable.[54] The southern part of the parish also included a small area of marshland meadow along the Roding, which as 'Little Ilford Level' was controlled by the Havering commissioners of sewers.[55]

The northern half of the parish, which later formed the manor of Aldersbrook, was in 1086 almost certainly part of the thickly wooded manor of Wanstead, and included the saltpan mentioned there.[56] It was within the Forest of Essex, the boundary of which, as perambulated in 1225, 1301, and 1641, followed the London road.[57] During the Middle Ages it formed part of the forest bailiwick of Becontree;[58] from the 16th century it was in Leyton 'walk', sometimes called Wanstead, or Wanstead and Leyton 'walk'.[59] By the early 16th century, when Aldersbrook emerged as a separate manor, forest clearance was virtually complete in that part of the parish: in 1536 Aldersbrook was stated to contain 140 a. arable out of a total area of 216 a., and only 6 a. woodland remained.[60] In the 17th and early 18th centuries there was a recurrent dispute between the lords of Aldersbrook and Wanstead concerning the boundaries of their manors, and in particular their respective rights over the forest wastes of Wanstead Flats.[61] Aldersbrook claimed rights over some 300 a. waste, but was eventually restricted to about 40 a. From the 16th century onwards part of the wastes adjoining Aldersbrook was being used as a warren. The earl of Pembroke, when he lived there about 1580, kept at least 1,000 couple of rabbits.[62] In 1660 the tenant of the home farm (sometimes called

[38] *Travels through England of Dr. Richard Pococke*, ed. J. J. Cartwright (Camd. Soc. 2nd ser. xlii) i. 80.
[39] Lysons, *London*, iv. 152.
[40] Marked as 'Old House Lawn' on the tithe map: E.R.O., D/CT 191.
[41] Lysons, op. cit. 152.
[42] *E.R.* l. 168, cf. 24–5 (map). For a drawing of it, by J. Cawthorn, 1842, see P.E.M., Pictorial Coll.
[43] *E.R.* l. 168.
[44] *Feet of F. Essex*, i. 263.
[45] *Trans. Barking Arch. Soc.* 1937, p. 12 (assize rents owed to Barking Abbey).
[46] S.C. 6/964 [entries 844, 845, and 71 in D.P.L. photostat].
[47] *V.C.H. Essex*, v, plate f.p. 235.
[48] See below.
[49] S.C. 6/Hen. VIII/962 m. 23.
[50] E.R.O., D/DVu 1. [51] See above.
[52] L.R. 2/214 [entry 43 in D.P.L. photostat].
[53] *V.C.H. Essex*, i. 559a, 448b.
[54] E.R.O., D/CT 191.
[55] See p. 18.
[56] *V.C.H. Essex*, i. 438a; and see above p. 166, below p. 327.
[57] Fisher, *Forest of Essex*, maps f.pp. 21, 29, 50.
[58] Ibid. 137, 379.
[59] Ibid. 384; *E.R.* xiv, map f.p. 193.
[60] *Feet of F. Essex*, iv. 203.
[61] E.R.O., D/DQs 17; *E.R.* xxxv. 216–20.
[62] *E.R.* l. 20.

Warren House) was convicted at the forest court for encroaching into the wastes to extend his rabbit burrows.[63] In 1740, soon after Smart Lethieullier succeeded to Aldersbrook, he destroyed the warren, and obtained licence from the Crown to inclose the land for agriculture.[64] Much of the estate then consisted of park-land attached to Aldersbrook House,[65] but after Sir James Long's purchase of Aldersbrook, and the demolition of the house, most of it became farm-land. In 1816 Aldersbrook farm comprised 269 a., of which about half was arable.[66]

From the 17th century onwards, if not earlier, Little Ilford had hardly any inhabitants, except the lord of Aldersbrook and the tenant of the home farm, dwelling within the forest bounds.[67] This probably explains why little information has survived concerning forest rights exercised by parishioners. After 1803 Little Ilford ceased to be represented at the forest courts, and there appears to be no evidence that it possessed any separate cattle-mark, such as were used elsewhere.[68] In the 19th century beasts from Aldersbrook were being marked by the reeve of Wanstead.[69] Nevertheless, Little Ilford remained in part a forest parish, and was in fact one of the storm centres of the Epping Forest controversy in the later 19th century. In 1851–2 the owners of the Wanstead Park estate inclosed 34 a. of forest waste on Wanstead Flats; about 9 a. of this lay within the manor of Aldersbrook.[70] Opposition to this action, by Richard Plaxton, occupier of Cann Hall, in Wanstead, and other persons concerned to preserve the forest, was unsuccessful, and between 1852 and 1869 many other inclosures were made on Wanstead Flats.[71] These were all in Wanstead manor, but in 1871 the owners of Wanstead Park inclosed 20 a. in the south-eastern corner of the flats, which formed the last remaining piece of waste within Aldersbrook manor.[72] This brought a powerful protagonist to the defence of the forest: the corporation of the City of London.[73]

The City had bought most of Aldersbrook farm (though not the manorial rights) in 1854, and had made a cemetery there. During the 1860s it had begun to interest itself in the preservation of common rights in the forest, and in 1871 it took legal action, first against the lord of Wanstead and then more generally, against inclosers throughout the forest. The Epping Forest Commission was established in the same year, but the City pressed on with its action in order to prevent further inclosures, and gained a favourable verdict in 1874. This was reinforced by the findings of the commission, largely embodied in the Act of 1878, by which the forest was preserved as a public open space and placed under the control of the City of London as conservators. The Act provided, inter alia, that all inclosures made since 1851, except those built upon, should be thrown back into the forest. This included the inclosures made at Aldersbrook in 1852 and 1871. In 1882 the Wanstead Park trustees bought back the 34 a. of the 1852 inclosure, together with several other pieces of land, in part exchange, with the City, for 183 a. comprising the lakes and woodlands of the park.

The preservation of Wanstead Flats as an open space was of great benefit to the inhabitants of Little Ilford, now increasing in number, but it made little difference to land use within the parish. Much more important in that respect was the making of the City of London cemetery. In 1839 the parish contained some 450 a. arable and 200 a. meadow or pasture, divided among four farms and a few small-holdings.[74] When the cemetery was formed fifteen years later about a third of the farm-land in the parish was taken out of cultivation.

It was stated in 1796 that about 120 a. in Little Ilford were usually cropped with potatoes,[75] but in the 19th century this parish (unlike some neighbouring ones) does not seem to have been particularly noted as a market-gardening area. In 1839 there was a little osier-growing along the Roding.[76]

At the end of the 18th century a great cattle market was held on Wanstead Flats every year during March and April, and much of the business relating to it was transacted at the Three Rabbits public house, which stood on the north side of the main road at Little Ilford.[77] That house, which figures in Thomas Hood's novel Tylney Hall (1834), was still frequented by graziers and cattle dealers in 1876, though the market had long ceased.[78]

It was stated in 1613 that there were remains of a brick-kiln or clamps near Aldersbrook House, but no brick-making was then being carried on.[79] A field called Brick Clamps is shown on a map of 1816, lying between the Aldersbrook stream and Aldersbrook Lane.[80]

Until the later 19th century most of the small population of the parish was engaged in agriculture.[81] From the 1850s, however, other occupations began to appear. The opening of the City of London cemetery provided work for monumental stonemasons, of which there were at least three by 1863.[82] By 1870 Manor Park was growing into a small town, with a variety of tradesmen.[83]

PARISH GOVERNMENT AND POOR RELIEF. A vestry minute book for Little Ilford survives for the period 1751–1857.[84]

Until 1777 it was common to hold 4 or 5 vestry meetings a year. In the next half-century the usual practice seems to have been to hold only one or two such meetings a year. After 1815 the frequency of

[63] Ibid. 22.
[64] Ibid. 23; E.R.O., D/DSa 101.
[65] E.R.O., Map of Aldersbrook, 1748; cf. Chapman and André, Map of Essex, 1777, sheet xxi.
[66] E.R. l. 121–2.
[67] Ibid. 22; Fisher, Forest of Essex, 178.
[68] Fisher, Forest, 299.
[69] E.R. l. 172.
[70] Ibid. 164, cf. map 24–5.
[71] Fisher, Forest, 356.
[72] E.R. l. 170.
[73] For the following paragraph see ibid. 170–5; Fisher, Forest, 360–72.

[74] E.R.O., D/CT 191. Two of the farms, Manor and Bolts, were then occupied by one tenant.
[75] Lysons, London, iv. 150. For a potato-dealer in 1767 see Essex Recusant, iii. 94.
[76] E.R.O., D/CT 191.
[77] Lysons, London, iv. 157; E.R. l. 26–7; li. 171–2, 219.
[78] J. Thorne, Environs London, i. 377.
[79] E.R.O., D/DQs 17.
[80] E.R. l. 25.   [81] Census, 1801 f.
[82] White's Dir. Essex, 1863, cf. Kelly's Dir. Essex, 1870.
[83] Kelly's Dir. Essex, 1870.
[84] E.R.O., D/P 175/8. The following information is derived from this book unless otherwise stated.

meetings tended to increase again, to 3, 4, and occasionally 5 or 6 a year.

In the 18th century the rectors attended the vestry regularly. The only exception was John Chamberlayne (rector 1764–87), who attended only once during the last ten years of his incumbency. His absence may have been responsible for the infrequency of meetings during those years. T. L. Cooke (rector 1803–47) rarely attended, but his curate nearly always did so.

Considering the small population of the parish the attendance at vestry, as indicated by signatures, was good. For most of the period 1751–1834 meetings were usually attended by at least 3 or 4 persons. Only between 1779 and 1785 was the attendance less than that. Between 1815 and 1825 it was often 5, 6, or more. In July 1824, when a record number of 10 persons were present, there were still fewer than 20 families in the parish.

The lords of the manor of Little Ilford, who did not live in the parish in the later 18th century, never attended meetings before 1815. In 1815 William Hibbit, who was joint lord of the manor, and was then living in West Ham,[85] began to attend the vestry, and from 1818 to 1826 he rarely missed a meeting. In this period also he sometimes held parish office and in 1824, as surveyor of highways, he was involved in a lawsuit with a parishioner named Greenhill, who held land in White Post Lane (now High Street North). Hibbit, supported by the vestry, won his case but bore part of the costs himself. He does not appear to have attended any vestry meeting after 1826 though he was occasionally nominated for office until 1832. The lords of Aldersbrook sometimes attended meetings in the later 18th century. Smart Lethieullier attended regularly in 1751–2 and occasionally afterwards until his death in 1760. Edward Hulse, owner and occupier of Aldersbrook from 1769, attended vestry meetings regularly from 1772 until 1786, when he sold the manor. Another regular attendant, from 1755 to 1776, was George Parker, occupier of Aldersbrook farm and steward of the Lethieullier estate, who served several terms as churchwarden, and also as surveyor. Samuel Winmill, who occupied the farm in the early 19th century, was rarely out of office in the years between 1811 and 1836. In that period he was usually either churchwarden or overseer and once he served as constable.

The records for the later 18th century do not furnish an exact list of parish officers, but there were evidently some unusual customs in regard to their appointment. Until 1768 the offices of churchwarden and overseer were held by one person, who usually served for at least two years. After 1768 it became the practice, for over ten years, to appoint two persons, one of whom served in the first half of the period as churchwarden and overseer and afterwards simply as churchwarden, while the other served as overseer. For some years after the appointment of a separate overseer, however, the churchwarden continued to have the main responsibility for poor-relief. It was the churchwarden whom the vestry directed to take action in individual cases of pauperism and it was to him that poor-rates were granted. During the 1780s the parish reverted for a short time to its earlier practice of combining the two offices in one person. From 1789, or possibly a little earlier, two persons were again appointed, and the practice was now for both to serve as churchwardens and as overseers. From 1794 the distinction between the two offices became more marked and it was no longer taken for granted that the two persons serving as churchwardens should also serve as overseers. At this time one churchwarden was being nominated by the parishioners, the other by the rector. From 1802 the offices were always held by different persons and in this period the overseers were responsible for the poor-rates and all matters relating to poor-relief, the churchwarden confining himself to the needs of the church. There were then one churchwarden and two overseers, all of whom served for several successive years. From 1823, if not before, a paid overseer was appointed. There was one parish constable and one surveyor. In the 19th century the constable served sometimes for one, sometimes for two or more years. A parish clerk is occasionally mentioned. In 1804 his salary, which for the past 40 years had been £4, was raised to £6.

Until 1780 separate rates were levied for church purposes and for poor-relief. After that date the church was usually maintained out of the poor-rates, church-rates being levied only to meet exceptionally heavy expenditure. A separate highway rate was occasionally levied, as in 1803 and 1804. There is no evidence of a separate constable's rate.

Officers' accounts were carefully scrutinized by the vestry, although in the early part of the period they did not always submit them annually. Until about 1780 the vestry examined the case of every pauper and if necessary met specially to do so; the parish officers evidently took no independent action. After that time, when vestry meetings became less frequent, individual cases were rarely recorded in the minutes.

Poor-relief took the form of weekly doles, rent allowances, poorhouse accommodation, medical care, or apprenticeship. Between 1752 and 1769 five pauper children were apprenticed. They were evidently not bound to masters in the parish, though details are incomplete. In 1763 the churchwarden was to 'apply to a fisherman at Barking' to take one boy, and in 1769 it was resolved that another should be apprenticed to a blacksmith at Stratford.

About 1760 the vestry acquired two poorhouses by taking them over after the previous tenants had got into arrears with their rent. These houses were still being leased in 1776.[86] Little Ilford never had its own workhouse. On one occasion, in 1764, an attempt was made to place a pauper in a workhouse outside the parish, but this was an exceptional measure and never became a common practice even at a later date. In 1803 there were 8 persons on permanent relief, 5 of them being old or permanently disabled, but none of the 8 was in a workhouse. In each of the years 1813–15 there were 8–10 persons on permanent relief, none of them in a workhouse.[87]

For most years between 1750 and 1834 it is impossible to state exactly the cost of relief, owing to deficiencies in the records. At the beginning of the period a considerable proportion of the inhabitants were receiving relief in some form but in

[85] E. Ogborne, *Hist. Essex*, 36; cf. *Essex County Poll Bk.* 1810.

[86] *Rep. Sel. Ctees. on Poor Laws, 1775–7 and 1787*, H.C. Ser. 1, vol. ix, p. 347.   [87] E.R.O., Q/CR 1/10.

this parish, unlike many others, the rates seem to have remained steady right up to the end of the 18th century. The only years when expenditure did rise appreciably were 1756–7, 1759–60, and 1783–5. There are precise, or nearly precise, figures of costs for only six years of the second half of the 18th century. In 1750–2 the cost of relief was probably about £50 a year. In 1776 it was £52.[88] In 1783–5 the average annual cost was £89.[89] In 1803 it was £51. After 1804 there does seem to have been an increase.[90] In the five years ending in 1817 relief costs averaged £70. In the four years ending in 1821 the average was £88.[91]

Little Ilford was included in the West Ham poor law union, formed in 1836. In 1886 the parish was placed, for sanitary purposes, under the control of the East Ham local board.[92] Since 1840 Little Ilford has been part of the Metropolitan police district.[93]

CHURCH. This section deals only with the ancient church of St. Mary, Little Ilford. The modern churches of St. Michael, St. Barnabas, and St. Mary's mission are treated under East Ham.

The surviving architectural features of St. Mary's church show that it was built at least as early as the 12th century. In 1650, when parochial reorganization was being considered, it was suggested that this small parish should be divided between its neighbours, Wanstead and Great Ilford, and that Little Ilford church should be taken down and re-erected at Barkingside.[94] This was not done, however, and St. Mary's continued to be the parish church of Little Ilford until 1938, when it became a chapel of ease to St. Michael's, Romford Road.[95]

The advowson of the rectory descended with the manor of Little Ilford until 1873, when it was put up for sale as part of the Wight estate.[96] Then, or soon after, it was bought for Hertford College, Oxford, the present patrons.[97] On a number of occasions, from the 16th century to the 19th, the presentation was granted away for one or more terms.[98] Theophilus Leigh Cooke, rector 1803–47, appears to have obtained the living under an agreement between his family and the patrons.[99]

Although the advowson was held from the 13th century onwards by Stratford Abbey the church was never appropriated. In 1470 the abbey, pleading poverty, sought the pope's permission to appro-

priate, but this was evidently refused.[1] The rectory was valued at £3 in 1254 but at only £1 10s. in 1291.[2] In 1535 the net value was £11 13s. 8d.[3] In 1650 the gross value was £55,[4] in the early 18th century it was £110,[5] and in the three years 1829–31 the average was £450.[6] Tithes, which were valued at £37 in 1650, were commuted in 1839 for £328, which included £18 for tithes of the glebe.[7] Sir John Heron (d. 1521), of Aldersbrook, left a rent-charge of £3 6s. 8d. payable by the Fishmongers' Company to the rector of Little Ilford. This was redeemed in 1887 for £111 stock, which was used to augment the benefice.[8]

Until the later 19th century, when most of it was built over, there were 40 a. glebe, lying mainly in the centre and south of the parish.[9] In 1610 the parsonage house comprised eleven rooms in two storeys.[10] This house was on a moated site in Little Ilford Marsh.[11] Robert Blakeway, when he became rector in 1714, found it so dilapidated, and considered the site so unhealthy, that in 1720 he built a new three-storey rectory on higher ground immediately west of the church, with some financial help from others.[12] The controversy between Blakeway and his parishioners which preceded the building of the new house is described below. This house, which appears to have been altered in the early 19th century,[13] was demolished in 1963, when a new rectory was built on an adjoining site nearer Church Road. Part of the old rectory garden was sold for building.[14]

The most eminent rector of Little Ilford was probably Thomas Newton (1542–1607), poet and physician, who held the living from 1583 until his death.[15] He was evidently unpopular with the Puritans, who in 1585 included him in a list of non-preaching clergy, and described him as a 'grand drunkard'.[16] His successor, John Morse (1607–15), was probably identical with the man of that name who occurs, in 1639–46, as the Puritan minister of Romford.[17] Daniel Cawdrey, rector from 1617 to about 1625, also had Puritan leanings, for in 1662 he was ejected from Great Billing (Northants.) for nonconformity.[18] Morse or Cawdrey may well have been responsible for placing the communion table in the centre of the chancel, with benches around it, an arrangement noted at Little Ilford in 1638 during the visitation of the archdeacon, who ordered that the table should be cut shorter, placed against the east wall, and railed.[19] Richard Reekes, rector from

[88] E.R.O., Q/CR 1/1.
[89] Ibid.
[90] E.R.O., Q/CR 1/10 and 1/12.
[91] E.R.O., Q/CR 1/12.
[92] Stokes, *East Ham*, 113.
[93] *Lond. Gaz.* 13 Oct. 1840, p. 2250
[94] H. Smith, *Eccl. Hist. Essex*, 247, 251.
[95] Inf. from Rector. For the modern churches at Little Ilford see p. 31.
[96] E.R.O., *Sale Cat.* Little Ilford, 1873.
[97] *Kelly's Dir. Essex*, 1878; inf. from Principal, Hertford Coll.
[98] Newcourt, *Repertorium*, ii. 346; Guildhall MS. 9558, .193.
[99] E.R.O., D/AEM 2/3; Guildhall MS. 9558, f. 193.
[1] *Cal. Pap. Lett.* 1458–71, 729.
[2] *E.A.T.* N.S. xviii. 17; *Tax. Eccl.* (Rec. Com.), 24.
[3] *Valor Eccl.* (Rec. Com.), i. 435.
[4] H. Smith, *Eccl. Hist. Essex*, 249.
[5] Guildhall MSS. 9550 and 9556, f. 60.
[6] *Rep. Eccl. Rev. Com.* H.C. 54, p. 652 (1835), xxii.
[7] H. Smith, *Eccl. Hist. Essex*, 249; E.R.O., D/CT 191.

[8] Lysons, *London*, iv. 155; Char. Com. File 66857.
[9] E.R.O., D/CT 191 (tithe award, 1839). Earlier surveys give slightly different totals: cf. Newcourt, *Repertorium*, ii. 345; H. Smith, *Eccl. Hist. Essex*, 249; E.R.O., Maps, Little Ilford, 1737 and 1775.
[10] Newcourt, *Repertorium*, ii. 345.
[11] R. Blakeway, *Epitome of my sufferings as delivered to a Lady in Pall Mall* [1716], 3. In 1563 there belonged to the parsonage of Little Ilford 5 a. and a marsh wall in Little Ilford Marsh: E.R.O., D/SH 7.
[12] *E.R.* xxxviii. 69–70; E.R.O., D/AEV 19: entry for 1719 shows that the new rectory had not yet been built.
[13] E.H.L. Photos. (Churches).
[14] Inf. from Rector, who has photographs of the old house.
[15] *D.N.B.*; Lysons, *London*, iv. 155; Newcourt, *Repertorium*, ii. 346.
[16] Davids, *Nonconformity in Essex*, 96.
[17] H. Smith, *Eccl. Hist. Essex*, 38, 49, 50, 193, 200.
[18] A. G. Matthews, *Calamy Revised*, 106.
[19] E.R.O., D/AEV 7.

about 1625 to 1635,[20] was in 1630 involved in a dispute with the lord of the manor.[21] The church-warden, John Lord, who gave evidence in the case, and had himself quarrelled with Reekes, stated that the rector had recently been absent without making proper provision for serving the cure. When a baptism was necessary Lord, so he said, had to send for a minister to officiate, 'sometimes Motley, who says he is curate to Reekes, and sometimes another'. Humphrey Richards, rector 1639–55, was described in 1650 as an able, preaching minister.[22] He appears to have held the living until his death. His successor was Henry Osbaldeston, whose Puritanism was well attested in 1655[23] but who conformed in 1662, and retained the rectory until his death in 1669.

Robert Blakeway (rector 1714–36) had previously been for a short time curate to the non-juring vicar of East Ham, Richard Welton. Early in his incumbency he was involved in disputes with successive churchwardens, John Lethieullier (of Aldersbrook) and John Nurse, and with the patron of the living, Sarah Wight.[24] The main issue was the rebuilding of the rectory, already mentioned, but the under-lying cause of enmity was political. Blakeway was a Whig while they were Tories. According to one statement there was also a private feud resulting from Blakeway's unwelcome and unsuccessful court-ship of Lethieullier's daughter,[25] and these events at Little Ilford must also be regarded as the sequel to Blakeway's quarrels with Welton at East Ham. Feelings ran high in the parish during the Jacobite rebellion of 1715, and continued to do so for some years.

After 1720, when the new rectory was built, most 18th-century rectors seem to have been resident except John Chamberlayne (rector 1764–87) who was absent from 1777 to 1787.[26] During Chamberlayne's absence two curates were successively employed.[27] Theophilus Cooke, rector 1803–47, who was a pluralist living in Oxfordshire, depended on curates for most of his long incumbency.[28] His successors have all been resident. Arthur T. W. Shadwell (1879–93) was a distinguished oarsman.[29]

The church of *ST. MARY THE VIRGIN*, Church Road, consists of nave and chancel, north chapel (now the vestry), south porch, and west bell-turret.[30] The walls of the nave, and the lower parts of the chancel, are of flint rubble, faced with plaster or cement. Those of the chapel, porch, and the upper parts of the chancel are of 18th-century brick. The roofs are of slate.

The nave and the chancel were probably built early in the 12th century. In the north wall of the nave, now opening into the vestry, are a window and a doorway, both of that period. The south wall has a window and a doorway matching those in the north wall except that the window has been widened.

There is another widened 12th-century window in the west wall, above the gallery.

Until the 18th century there seem to have been no major alterations to the church except for the addition of a bell-turret and south porch. A painting of the church from the south-east, made in 1720, includes those features, and also shows two round-headed windows, probably of the 12th century, but no longer existing, in the south walls of the nave and chancel, and four others in the east wall of the chancel.[31]

About 1724, the year in which the wife of John Lethieullier died as the result of a carriage accident,[32] the Lethieulliers of Aldersbrook obtained a faculty to erect a family vault with a private chapel above it.[33] Work does not seem to have started for some years, probably not until after the death of John Lethieullier in 1737.[34] The chapel, which has been used as a vestry at least since 1848,[35] is a simple structure of reddish-brown brick with a coved cornice and two circular windows. Internally the whole of its north wall is occupied by a handsome classical memorial to members of the Lethieullier family. The chapel is separated from the nave by an iron gate and contains other Lethieullier monuments and a fire-place. In its east window is 15th-century stained glass depicting the arms of France and England flanked by a Tudor rose and a red rose, both crowned. Around the outer edge are 16th- and 17th-century fragments depicting shields and figures, including a heron. This glass was probably removed from the nave or chancel; some of it may have been connected with Sir John Heron of Aldersbrook. In 1801 part of it was in the west window of the chapel.[36]

The building of the chapel seems to have been accompanied by the rebuilding of the chancel, porch, and possibly the bell-turret, the alteration of the nave, and the insertion of the west gallery. The upper part of the chancel is built of the same reddish-brown brick as the chapel, having a high dentil cornice and a pedimented east gable. The windows are of wood with gothic lights and semi-circular or segmental heads; there are two similar windows in the nave. The west gallery is supported on square-shafted Tuscan pilasters. On the gallery front are the royal arms of one of the 18th-century Hanoverian kings, probably George II. During the Second World War the church was damaged by bombing. It was reopened, after repairs, in 1951.[37]

The organ, which in 1892 was removed from the gallery to the south wall of the chancel, and rebuilt, was replaced in the gallery in 1938.[38] Part of the earlier barrel organ is now in the vestry. On the north wall of the nave is a board recording James Hayes's charity.[39]

In 1552 the church had two small bells.[40] There was none in 1683,[41] but there are references to one

[20] Little Ilford Ch., Parish Registers. He is omitted from Newcourt's list.
[21] G.L.C., DL/C/232 and 233: case of Hyde v. Reekes.
[22] H. Smith, *Eccl. Hist. Essex*, 249.
[23] Ibid. 333.
[24] For this paragraph see: R. Blakeway, *Epitome of my sufferings delivered to a Lady in Pall Mall* [1716]; E.R.O., D/AEV 9.
[25] G.L.C., DL/C/153, f. 107.
[26] See p. 170.
[27] Guildhall MS. 9553.
[28] E.R.O., D/AEV 29; Guildhall MS. 9560.
[29] *E.R.* iii. 8.

[30] R.C.H.M. *Essex*, ii. 156.
[31] Copy of this painting, in vestry of St. Mary's.
[32] Inscription on monument in chapel.
[33] Lysons, *London*, iv. 154.
[34] *E.R.* xxxv. 215.
[35] *White's Dir. Essex*, 1848, p. 225.
[36] Printed description in vestry.
[37] Inf. from Rector.
[38] Ibid.; Inscription on gallery; Little Ilford Ch. Vestry Mins., 23 Apr. 1892.
[39] See below, p. 173.
[40] *Ch. Bells Essex*, 305.
[41] *E.A.T.* N.S. xix. 264.

bell in 1768 and 1814.[42] The present bell is dated 1861.[43] The church plate includes a silver cup and paten of 1890. What happened to the older plate is not known.[44]

On the north wall of the nave are a brass to Thomas (d. 1517), son of Sir John Heron of Aldersbrook depicting a schoolboy with inkhorn and pencase, and another to William (d. 1614) and Anne (d. 1630), children of Bernard Hyde, lord of the manor of Little Ilford.[45] The Heron brass was formerly on the floor of the chancel, and that of Hyde on the floor of the nave.[46] On the north wall of the chancel are a coloured marble monument, with kneeling figures, to William Waldegrave (d. 1610) and his wife Elizabeth (d. 1589), and a tablet to Francis Osbaldeston (d. 1678) of Aldersbrook and his two infant sons. On the east wall is a tablet to William S. Fry (d. 1844), of the Manor House, his two eldest daughters and his son.[47] The principal monument in the chapel takes the form of a marble colonnade of three bays with Tuscan columns and a central pediment. The central bay contains a sarcophagus of coloured marble commemorating John Lethieullier (d. 1737) and his wife (d. 1724). In the flanking bays two urns carry inscriptions to their son Smart (d. 1760) and his wife Margaret (d. 1753). On the south wall of the chapel is a tablet to Charles Lethieullier (d. 1759).

PROTESTANT NONCONFORMITY. It was stated in 1810 that Little Ilford contained one family of Quakers and three of other dissenters,[48] but no nonconformist congregation appears to have been formed until about 1860, when Little Ilford chapel, Greenhill Grove, was registered by a non-sectarian body, possibly of Brethren.[49] This is probably the small building on the west of Greenhill Grove now (1965) used by the Salvation Army, adjoining which is a row of houses inscribed 'Chapel Place, 1864'. About 1865 this chapel appears to have been taken over by Congregationalists, who remained there until 1890, when they moved to a new church in Manor Park Road, East Ham, called Manor Park Congregational church.[50] The Greenhill Grove chapel was subsequently used by Baptists before being taken over by the Salvation Army.[51] In and after the 1880s, as Manor Park expanded, many nonconformist churches were built. These are described under East Ham.[52]

EDUCATION. There was an Anglican Sunday school at Little Ilford from 1820, and in 1830 a

visitor reported seeing the parish clerk 'or some such dignitary' conducting a school in the church, but it was not until 1865 that a National day-school was built on glebe land in Church Road with the aid of grants from the government and the National Society.[53] The average attendance at the National school increased from 53 in 1867 to 149 in 1882. In 1883 two new classrooms were built and the school was divided into separate departments for boys, girls, and infants.[54] Places for 400 were thus provided, but by 1886 average attendance had reached 300, and in 1887 a school board was formed.[55] The school was immediately taken over by the board, which in 1890 transferred the boys and girls to new buildings in Fourth Avenue. The infants, who from 1887 to 1890 were in temporary accommodation elsewhere, then moved back to the Church Road buildings and remained there until 1892, when a new infants department was completed on the Fourth Avenue site.[56] The National school buildings were reopened as a temporary board school in 1895 and continued in use until 1901. They were subsequently used for church purposes.[57] In 1951 they were sold to the East Ham borough council, which shortly afterwards demolished them and built flats on the site, now called Leamington Close.[58]

There was a nonconformist school in Little Ilford in 1865.[59] Nothing further is known about it; possibly it was connected with the chapel in Greenhill Grove.[60]

Schools built since 1887 are described under East Ham.[61]

CHARITIES FOR THE POOR. By a deed of 1630 Bernard Hyde, lord of the manor of Little Ilford, provided that the Salters' Company of London should pay £1 a year to the churchwardens, to be given to four poor persons of the parish.[62] In 1835 the money was being used to give a bag of coal to every poor family at Christmas, any deficiency being made up by private contributions.[63] By 1894, however, it was used to give four poor people 5s. each. In 1961 it was being administered with Hayes's charity.[64]

James Hayes (d. 1821) left £1,000 stock in trust for the poor of the parish. In 1835 £30 a year was being distributed in sums ranging from 10s. to £2 10s.[65] In 1961 the income of £18 15s. was distributed, along with that from Hyde's charity, in £1 and 10s. portions.[66]

Elizabeth Bayne, by declaration of trust of 1960, gave £350 stock in memory of her husband Oswald

[42] Morant, *Essex*, i. 28; Ogborne, *Essex*, 33.
[43] *Ch. Bells Essex*, 305.
[44] *Ch. Plate Essex*, 7; cf. *E.A.T.* n.s. ii. 241.
[45] *E.A.T.* n.s. viii. 264; *Antiquary*, xxxix. 237.
[46] Lysons, *London*, iv. 153.
[47] For the Manor House see p. 69.
[48] Guildhall MS. 9558 f. 193.
[49] Gen. Reg. Off., Worship Reg. 9552, 10 Sept. 1860.
[50] *Cong. Year Bk.* 1866, p. 303; ibid. 1867 f. (lists of churches); *Kelly's Dir. Essex*, 1890.
[51] See pp. 33, 37.   [52] See pp. 33 sqq.
[53] *Nat. Soc. Reps.* 1820 f.; *G.M. Libr. Eng. Topog.* iv. 182–3; *Nat. Soc. Inquiry into Church Schs. 1846–7*; inf. from Nat. Soc.
[54] *Rep. Educ. Ctee. of Council, 1867*, [4051], p. 636, H.C. (1867–8), xxv; inf. from Nat. Soc.; E.H.L., Log Books, Little Ilford National schools.

[55] *Kelly's Dir. Essex*, 1886; E.H.L., Mins. Lt. Ilford Sch. Bd.
[56] Inf. from Min. of Educ.; E.H.L., Log Books, Lt. Ilford Nat. schs.; Mins. Lt. Ilford Sch. Bd.
[57] E.H.L., Mins. Lt. Ilford Sch. Bd.; *Lt. Ilford Par. Mag.* Mar. 1914.
[58] Inf. from Revd. R. J. Webb, Rector; for a picture of the school in 1952 see E.H.L. Photos. (Schools).
[59] Inf. from Nat. Soc.
[60] See above.   [61] See pp. 39 sqq.
[62] *Rep. Char. Com.* H.C. 312, p. 104–5 (1820), v.
[63] *Rep. Char. Com.* H.C. 216, p. 156 (1835), xxi(1).
[64] Char. Com. File 66857 and Lt. Ilford Accts. File.
[65] *Rep. Char. Com.* (1835), p. 156; inscription in St. Mary's church, in Little Ilford; E.R.O., D/P 175/8 (Mch. 1821).
[66] Char. Com. Lt. Ilford Accts. File.

Bayne, the proceeds to be used for charitable work by the church in Little Ilford parish, particularly for the assistance of students at university or training college. In 1961 £2 each was given to two students at King's College, London, and one at University College Hospital, London.[67]

All the above charities are administered by the rector and churchwardens of Little Ilford.

LEYTON

Manors and Other Estates, p. 184. Economic History, p. 197. Marshes, p. 203. Forest, p. 204. Local Government and Poor-Relief to 1836, p. 205. Local Government after 1836, p. 208. Public Services, p. 211. Parliamentary Representation, p. 214. Churches, p. 214. Roman Catholicism, p. 223. Protestant Nonconformity, p. 223. Judaism, p. 233. Education, p. 233. Charities for the Poor, p. 239.

LEYTON, the 'tun' on the river Lea, lies about 5 miles north-east of London between the river and Epping Forest. It is part of the London borough of Waltham Forest.[1] It is mainly a dormitory suburb of small houses built between 1870 and 1910, interspersed with modern block and tower housing. Industry is dispersed, apart from the Temple Mills railway complex in the south-west and a concentration of factories in the north-west. The ancient parish was known as Low Leyton, because part of it lay low by the Lea. In 1868, at the request of the vestry, the directors of the Great Eastern Railway agreed to rename Low Leyton station

LEYTON MUNICIPAL BOROUGH. *Or, three chevronels gules, on a chief gules a lion passant, or.*

'Leyton'.[2] The civil parish remained Low Leyton until 1921, when the prefix was dropped.[3] The parish was about 2 miles long from north to south. Its northern boundary, shared with Walthamstow, ran straight for 3 miles from forest to river, by Forest Rise to Whipps Cross, along Chestnut Walk (now part of Lea Bridge Road), then on the line of the modern Boundary Road to Mark House, and on to the river near Mount Wharf.[4] A suggestion that this long straight boundary may coincide with the line of a former Roman road[5] has not been confirmed by archaeological evidence. The east boundary marched southward with Wanstead, skirting the Eagle Pond and Bushwood in Wanstead, to Tinkers Lane (Harrow Road). The Wanstead ditch formed the southern boundary with Wanstead and West Ham. The west boundary followed the old course of the river Lea as it existed before the Lea Navigation by-

passed it in 1767,[6] from Mount Wharf southward to the fork in the river, where the boundary continued to Temple Mills along the Temple Mills or Lead Mill stream. This was known in 1602 as the Shire stream,[7] and after 1835 as the Waterworks river; it ran alongside Quartermile Lane, but was filled in in 1952. A small piece of Hackney lies on the east side of the river just above Lea Bridge.

The ancient parish comprised 2,271 a. Its northernmost part, of 588 a., was separated from the rest by the Walthamstow Slip. This 3-mile corridor belonging to Walthamstow parish varied in width from about 50 to 100 yards[8] and contained 98 a. Its origin is uncertain, though various traditions exist.[9] It ran from the Eagle Pond, behind Forest House, across King's End (Leyton Green), south of Capworth Street, through the grounds of Leyton House, to the river just below the Horse and Groom. On maps of 1699 and later[10] it is shown cutting across fields straight from mark to mark, usually regardless of natural boundaries. It is not known whether the Slip became detached from Leyton or the northern portion of Leyton from Walthamstow, leaving this narrow remnant on the south. But as the Slip was part of Walthamstow Tony manor,[11] the attachment of its tithes to Walthamstow parish probably dates from the early 12th century, when Walthamstow manor, church, and tithes were held by Ralph de Tony and his wife Alice.[12] The Slip's boundary marks were often disputed or, as in 1723, deliberately altered.[13] In 1858 Leyton challenged Walthamstow's attempt to establish its course through the most valuable part of the waterworks company's filter beds.[14] In 1873 the newly-constituted Leyton urban sanitary district included the Slip, which was also amalgamated with Leyton civil parish in 1878.[15] The Wanstead Slip (about

[67] Char. Com. File 208793.
[1] O.S. Map 2½″, sheet TQ 38; 6″ (1952 edn.) sheet TQ 38 N.E.; *P.N. Essex* (E.P.N.S.), 102. See map below, p. 180.
[2] L.R.L., L47 MS. Vestry Mins. 28 Nov. 1867, 16 Jan. 1868.
[3] *Census*, 1911, 1921.
[4] E.R.O., D/CT 221; O.S. Map 6″, Essex, LXXIII (1873–82 edn.), LXV (1868–76 edn.).
[5] *E.A.T.* N.S. xvii. 234.
[6] *V.C.H. Essex*, v. 22–3; Act for improving navigation of River Lea, 7 Geo. III, c. 51.
[7] E.R.O., D/DU 194/23.
[8] *Hist. Essex by Gent.* iv. 240; L.R.L., L47 MS. Ves. Mins. 1811–34 (1831 perambulation). For the Slip see map below, p. 242.
[9] G. Roebuck, *Story of Walthamstow*, 21–2; E.R.O., T/P 75; E. Clarke, *Walthamstow, past, present and future*, 13.

[10] E.R.O., T/M 252 (1699), D/DQs 31 (c. 1760), T/M 53 (1820), D/P 160/28 (1822), Q/RUm 1/65 (1838), D/CT 221 (1843), D/CT 382 (1843).
[11] E.R.O., T/M 252, 53; *John Coe's map of Walthamstow, 1822* (Walthamstow Ant. Soc., N.S. v, va); cf. L.R.L., L66. 2 Prints, Photographs of the manor boundary stones at the Eagle Pond.
[12] See pp. 253, 285.
[13] J. Kennedy, *Hist. Leyton*, 148, 383; E.R.O., T/P 75; L.R.L., L47 MS. Ves. Mins. 1781–1811 (1781); S. J. Barns, *Walthamstow Vestry Mins. . . . 1710–1740* (Walthamstow Ant. Soc. xiii), 20–1; *Walthamstow Matters*, iv, 4–9.
[14] L.R.L., L47 MS. Ves. Mins. 1834–74 (1858).
[15] *Census*, 1891 (table 14). Amalgamation with the ecclesiastical parish did not take place until 1885: Kennedy, *Leyton*, 412; E.R.O., D/CPc 64.

207 a.) was added to the district in 1875, but constituted a separate civil parish (Cann Hall) in 1894.[16] Minor boundary adjustments with Wanstead followed in 1887 and 1900. Leyton became a municipal borough in 1926. In 1961 its area was 2,595 a.[17] It became part of Waltham Forest in 1965, the year taken for most purposes as the terminal point of this article.

Leyton rises from the marshland of the Lea valley to over 100 ft. at Whipps Cross and the High Stone on the edge of the forest.[18] Between the alluvial marshes and the forest are terraces of valley gravel overlying brickearth.[19] Three principal watercourses run through the parish. The Wanstead ditch, also known as the river Holt, entered the parish from Walthamstow on the extreme north-east, crossed into Wanstead above the High Stone, reappeared in Leyspring flowing south to Tinkers Lane, and then south-west by Sauls Green to Holloway Down and west to Temple Mills.[20] Once an open sewer[21] it is now culverted. The Phillebrook or Fillebrook, 'Phepes Broke' in 1537,[22] entered Leyton from Walthamstow west of Whipps Cross, flowing south and south-west to join the Dagenham brook west of Ruckholts. In 1868 it was still open,[23] but by 1904 it was piped from James Lane to the sewage works in Auckland Road; the last open stretch from West End Avenue to James Lane was closed in soon after.[24] The valley eroded by the Phillebrook[25] is recognizable in Leyton High Road beside the Coronation Gardens, where once there was a ford. The Dagenham brook, flowing from Higham Hill in Walthamstow, divided marsh and upland.[26] North of Marsh Lane it was joined by a tributary, the Shortlands sewer, also flowing from Walthamstow, but farther to the west.[27] This formed the boundary between the inclosed marsh and lammas lands and is now incorporated in the flood relief channel flowing direct to the Lea. Since the occlusion of the Waterworks river the brook, too, has been diverted to the Lea. The Lea was apparently still tidal as far as Lockbridge in the 16th century.[28]

Palaeolithic implements and fossil bones found along the gravel terraces show that early man lived and hunted in Leyton.[29] There was a Roman cemetery south of Blind Lane, and massive foundations of some Roman building, with quantities of Roman brick, were discovered in the grounds of Leyton Grange.[30] The High Stone, near the eastern boundary of the parish at the junction of the roads from Woodford and Woodford Bridge, is a restored 18th-century obelisk set up on an earlier stump, but is traditionally described as a Roman milestone. It may occupy the site of one, if the Roman road from Dunmow to Chigwell continued to London, crossing the Lea by stone causeways discovered in Leyton between Temple Mills and Marsh Lane.[31] Tradition also explains that Leytonstone is the part of Leyton which was near the High Stone.[32]

In 1086 the recorded population was 43.[33] The medieval population remained small. In 1523–4 only 49 persons, including 18 labourers and 10 servants, were assessed to the subsidy.[34] In 1670 there were 83 houses in the parish, 23 of them in Leytonstone.[35] By 1778 there were said to be over 300.[36] In 1801 the population numbered 2,519.[37] Apart from an increase between 1841 and 1851 caused by the erection of the Union workhouse, there was no unusual growth until the 1860s, when the population doubled, from 4,794 in 1861 to 10,394 in 1871. By 1881 it had risen to 23,016 in the civil parish, and to 27,068 in the new sanitary urban district, which included the Walthamstow and Wanstead Slips. Between 1881 and 1891 the population of the district rose by 133·3 per cent, to 63,056, a larger proportionate increase than that of any other English town with over 50,000 inhabitants.[38] Rapid growth continued to 1911, when the figure was 124,735, reaching its peak in the next few years. In 1921 128,430 was recorded. Since 1931 (128,313) the population has declined, to 105,978 in 1951 and 93,959 in 1961.

The Domesday evidence suggests that settlement in 1086 was mainly in the centre and south of Leyton, with the densest woodland in the north-east.[39] Creation of the Haliwell priory estate in 1201 probably fostered settlement further east at 'Ladune' (Hollywell, later Holloway Down), while by the early 14th century a hamlet existed at 'Leyton atte Stone'.[40] In the later Middle Ages, as woodland was cleared in the north-east of the parish, settlement developed at Knotts Green and Diggons Cross, both mentioned in 1537.[41] Knotts Green probably originally comprised the waste between Leyton High Road and its right fork to the forest (Leyton Green Road). Diggons Cross was probably near the junction of Shernhall Street (Walthamstow) and the highway to the forest, for in 1454 Degonesbraches (Diggon's 'clearings') abutted north on this highway, by Leyton bridge.[42]

[16] Census, 1881; V.C.H. Essex, v. 5, n. 11. See also below, p. 326.
[17] Census, 1961.
[18] Chapman and André, Map of Essex, 1777, sheets xvi, xxi.
[19] V.C.H. Essex, i. 16, 261; F. W. Wilkinson, Hist. Leyton, 4.
[20] E.R.O., D/DCw P47, D/DCy P3 ff. 101, 115, 154, D/DCy P3A, D/CT 221, 384, T/M 128; F. Temple, 'Ancient lanes of the Borough', Leyton Express and Independent, 29 Dec. 1950. See also below, p. 318.
[21] L.R.L., L47 MS. Local Bd. Mins. 1877–81. See also below, p. 211.
[22] S.C. 6/962. 'Phillebrook' is the more usual form until the late 19th century. The form 'Fillebrook' was adopted by the Wallwood Farm estate development of that name in the 1870s and perpetuated in 'Fillebrook Road'.
[23] E.R.O. D/CE 79.
[24] Leyton and District Times, 28 Oct. 1904.
[25] A 6″ relief map of the Walthamstow district drawn at 5-ft. intervals shows this valley clearly (L.R.L., L69 Plan, Jones and Montgomery).
[26] E.R.O., D/SH 2 (1748), D/SH 29; Chapman and André, Map of Essex, 1777, sheets xvi, xxi. See also below, p. 203.
[27] E.R.O., D/SH 3A f. 336.
[28] S.P. 12/15 No. 16.
[29] E.Nat. xiii. 84; W. H. Weston, Story of Leyton and Leytonstone, 3, 5, 10; Trans. E.F.C. iii. 111.
[30] V.C.H. Essex, iii. 23, 155.
[31] Ibid. 25, 28, 155; Weston, Leyton, 16; Leyton Off. Guide (c. 1952), 22 (illus.). The 'obelisk' is shown on a turnpike map of 1728 (E.R.O., T/M 128).
[32] P.N. Essex (E.P.N.S.), 102.
[33] V.C.H. Essex, i. 444, 497, 515, 536, 546.
[34] E 179/108/150.   [35] E.R.O., Q/RTh 5.
[36] Guildhall MS. 9558, f. 218.
[37] These and the following figures are from the Census Reports.
[38] V.C.H. Essex, v. 6.
[39] Ibid. i. 444, 497, 515, 536, 546.
[40] Cal. Inq. Misc. iii, p. 307.
[41] S.C. 6/962. See also below, pp. 187, 192.
[42] Cal. Close, 1452–61, 353.

By the 18th century, when the parish is first shown on detailed maps,[43] Wallwood and Whitings Grove were cleared, and the pattern of the parish, much as it remained until the mid 19th century, was complete. On the west lay undeveloped marshland, and on the extreme north-east Leyton heath and the forest, the haunt of highwaymen.[44] Two principal roads, now Leyton High Road and Leytonstone High Road, ran approximately north and south through the parish. Along these lay the two main settlements, Low Leyton to the west and Leytonstone to the east. In Low Leyton, about a quarter of a mile west of the high road, stood the parish church with the manor house of Leyton Grange beside it. The high road, with local roads branching off it, was a continuation southward of Hoe Street (Walthamstow), by Knotts Green and Ruckholts to Angel Lane, Stratford. By the 18th century most of Knotts Green was inclosed, forming the triangle bounded today by the High Road, Lea Bridge Road, and Leyton Green Road. But its north-east corner was still waste, and Knights Green (now Leyton Green) at its southern apex was probably also a remnant of the original green. Low Leyton village lay mainly along Leyton Street, as the high road was usually known from Lea Bridge Road to Moyers Lane; the most crowded stretch, between Lea Bridge Road and Knights Green, was sometimes called Gossups Green.[45] Frog Row, an island of cottages, narrowed the high road at its junction with Forest (later James) Lane. Farther south a group of houses, later called Blue Row, clustered opposite the vicarage and a large triangle of waste where the road branched west to the church (Church Road). The neighbourhood south of Blue Row, where the road forded the Phillebrook, was usually known as Phillebrook. Several lanes led eastwards off the high road. Wide Street, mentioned in 1537,[46] later also called Wild Street, ran along the north side of Knotts Green, then continued as the Broad Lane (later Chestnut Walk) to Whipps Cross: both are now part of Lea Bridge Road. The Broad Lane existed in 1454 and is named in 1649.[47] It was described as 'the walk with trees' in 1726, and the chestnuts, planted before 1814 and cut down in the 1930s, are commemorated by the Chestnut Tree public house.[48] A lane (Leyton Green Road) linked Knights Green with Chestnut Walk. Forest (or James) Lane led from Frog Row to Buryfield (mentioned about 1484)[49] and Forest House. About 1968 it was partly renamed Fletcher Lane, commemorating Mary Fletcher. Moyers or Wallwood Lane, previously

known as Masters Lane[50] (now Hainault Road), led to Wallwood and the nearby locality called Geylewere, first mentioned in 1449 and repeated in various forms up to 1867.[51] The name may have originated as a gallows site. Westward from Knotts Green Butterfield Lane (Welstret in 1537 and 1645, but sometimes also called Wide or Wild Street, and now part of Lea Bridge Road)[52] led to Markhouse Lane, which was the way from Higham Hill, Walthamstow, to Leyton church and high road. From this junction Hemstall Lane, mentioned in 1601 and described in 1630 as a chase lane, continued westward to Hemstall or Hemstead Green, where a bridge crossed the Dagenham brook.[53] Vestiges of the green remained in 1777 on either side of the new Lea Bridge Road, which crossed it, and inclosures from it can be traced on the tithe map.[54] Hughes farm, sometimes called Hemstall Green farm,[55] lay south of the lane. From Markhouse Lane Church Lane (now Road) led south and east to the high road. Capworth (earlier Capport) Street linked Church Lane and Knights Green; another form, Copper Street, may suggest some association with Copping Down which lay south of it. South of Phillebrook two roads led off the high road to Temple Mills, one through Ruckholts, the other, Temple Mills Lane, on the parish boundary.

Leytonstone High Road, on the east side of the parish, was part of the main highway from Epping to London. It left the forest at the Green Man inn (mentioned in 1668) and ran southward to Sauls (later Harrow) Green, Holloway Down, and Stratford. From the Green Man Phipps Cross Lane (Whipps Cross Road), mentioned in 1492,[56] linked Leytonstone with Whipps Cross. Behind the Green Man was an unsavoury group of hovels called The Crib[57] and south of it Back Lane (Browning Road) led east from the high road to the forest. The houses of Leytonstone hamlet straggled southward from the Green Man. On the west side of the high road a chapel of ease to the parish church was in existence from the middle of the 18th century. More houses fringed Sauls Green farther south and clustered at the junction with Hollewell Lane. From upper Leytonstone a road (Church Lane and Grove Green Road) twisted south-west across the parish to Grove Green, then on to Ruckholt and Temple Mills.[58] Knaves Lane (Cathall Road) linked Sauls Green and Grove Green. 'Sales' Green is mentioned in 1577[59] and Grove Green in 1571.[60] Hollewell or Blind Lane (later Union, now Langthorne Road) linked Holloway Down and Leyton High Road. Tinkers

[43] John Rocque, *Survey of London, 1746* (1748 edn.), sheet iv; Chapman and André, *Map of Essex, 1777,* sheets xvi, xxi. Maps of 1721 (Kennedy, *Leyton,* f.p. 18, original in L.R.L.), and 1728 (E.R.O., D/DCy P3A) show the south and east of the parish; the centre is shown on maps of *c.* 1739 and 1777 (E.R.O., T/M 403, 173). Roads are shown on maps of 1728 and *c.* 1760 (E.R.O., T/M 128, D/DQs 31) and features near the Walthamstow boundary on maps of 1739, 1742–3 (E.R.O., T/M 167, 168).

[44] e.g. 1757, when the postboy was robbed of the Norwich mail by a highwayman at the High Stone (E.R.O., T/P 110/45).

[45] The site of the present King William IV, which can be traced through the Leyton manor court books, was described in 1709 as 'on Gossups Green alias Low Leighton Street': E.R.O., D/DU 101/1A (1709).

[46] S.C. 6/962.

[47] *Cal. Close,* 1454–61, p. 353; E.R.O., Q/SR 341/27.

[48] E.R.O., D/DU 417/8, T/M 53; F. Temple, 'Busy Lea

Bridge was once a lonely road', *Leytonstone Expr. and Independent,* 19 Apr. 1957.

[49] *E.A.T.* ii. 192.

[50] S.C. 6/962.

[51] *Cal. Close,* 1447–54, p. 165; S.C. 6/962; E.R.O., D/DLc T28 (1562), D/DU 101/1 (1719), 101/4 (1867).

[52] S.C. 6/962; E.R.O., T/A 12/2/8 (1645), D/DAc 153, D/DU 101/1A (1708).

[53] L.R.L., Deeds (Barns 16); E.R.O., D/DW E25, pp. 1966–7, 2009; D/SH 1 f. 503, 2 f. 209.

[54] E.R.O., D/DU 101/1 (1759, 1767); D/CT 221 (nos. 415, 484, 490); L.R.L., L47 MS. Vestry Mins. 1752–81 (1768).

[55] L.R.L., L55.6 MS. Rate Bks. 1651–1704 (at end reversed, survey of charities), and 1783–1807 (1799).

[56] E.R.O., D/DBq T1/1.

[57] Cf. Kennedy, *Leyton,* 397.

[58] Rocque in error names this Wallwood Lane.

[59] L.R.L., Deeds (B.R.A. 685).

[60] E.R.O., D/DCw M39.

Lane (or Withies, from the osiers bordering the Wanstead ditch)[61] led east from Sauls Green to Woodhouse and the lower forest (now Wanstead Flats); it is now known as Harrow Road. Further north a short road (Davies Lane) also led from the high road to the lower forest.

Leytonstone High Road, as a link in the London–Epping route, was by 1594 more important than Leyton High Road.[62] In the 17th century the inhabitants were presented at quarter sessions on several occasions for not repairing it.[63] In 1721 it was taken over by the Middlesex and Essex turnpike trust, which maintained it until 1866.[64] Both high roads carried market carts and waggons.[65] The road through Leytonstone also carried long-distance coach traffic[66] and in 1686 there were 17 beds for guests and stabling for 57 horses there.[67]

Foot and horse traffic crossed the Lea to Hackney, by Lockbridge and the adjoining ford to Clapton, and by Temple Mills to Homerton and Hackney Wick. Lockbridge is mentioned in 1486–7.[68] It was reported in 1551 that it was broken down, and that Lord Wentworth, lord of the manor of Hackney, ought to repair it sufficiently for foot traffic.[69] It was listed by Norden in 1594 among the most useful bridges in Middlesex,[70] but collapsed finally between 1612 and 1630, and was replaced by the ferry later known as Hackney or Jeremy's ferry.[71] The ford was still called Lockbridge in 1646.[72] Before Lockbridge collapsed a wooden causeway comprising 12 footbridges led from Blackbridge, which crossed the Shortlands sewer west of Hemstall Green, over the marsh to Lockbridge. In the 16th century this causeway was built or repaired by George Monoux (d. 1544), and repaired by Lady Laxton, probably about 1580, when it was reported in ruins. They did this 'of charity', having no lands in Leyton themselves.[73] When the bridges were again dangerously decayed in 1611–13 the county disclaimed responsibility for them, and by 1694 only the ruins remained; these were still visible in the 19th century.[74] Jeremy's ferry, and a second smaller one, called Smith's ferry, a little to the north, are shown on maps of 1747–8.[75] As both, with the adjoining land, belonged to the lord of the manor of Hackney,[76] Lockbridge

and the ferries are probably the origin of the portion of Hackney which lies on the east side of the river above Lea Bridge to this day. The maps show two tracks to Jeremy's ferry. One, Water Lane, led south from Marsh Street, Walthamstow, joined on the way by another lane from Low Hall. Water Lane crossed Walthamstow Marsh, which lay partly in Leyton parish; vestiges of it remained in the 19th century.[77] From Leyton a track led north-west from the bottom of Marsh Lane across Leyton Marsh. No way to the ferry is shown from Hemstall Green. Perhaps the risk of drowning, combined with the extortionate charges of the ferryman, had diverted to Stratford the passengers from other parishes and counties who used to travel that way.[78] Under the Lea Bridge Turnpike Act, 1757, the old route by Hemstall Green and Blackbridge was restored, to link Clapton with the Middlesex and Essex turnpike road at the Eagle pond. Jeremy's ferry was closed and the near-by ford destroyed. Lea Bridge was built, with a road across the marsh by Hemstall Green to Markhouse Lane; and Butterfield Lane and Broad Lane were widened.[79] In 1802 Leyton and Hackney settled their boundaries in relation to Lea Bridge, the land and buildings just above the bridge on the Leyton side remaining in Hackney, but the centre of the river forming the boundary from the upper side of the bridge southwards, leaving the Horse and Groom to Leyton.[80] The bridge was replaced in 1821 by an iron one.[81] On cessation of the turnpike trusts in 1871 the Essex half of the bridge was adopted by the county.[82]

There was a less important crossing to Hackney at Temple Mills where a 'common open way for horses' existed in the 1690s.[83] The bridge over the mill-stream was maintained by the occupants of the mills.[84] In the present century better communications between South Hackney and Leyton became necessary.[85] In 1908 the Leyton U.D.C. and Essex county council completed a broad road from Ruckholt Road railway bridge to the Waterworks river, and in 1912 the London county council completed a bridge over the river to meet it.[86] This bridge, which was vested in the two authorities, became part of the scheme, first recommended in 1915, for an Eastern

---

[61] F. Temple, 'Ancient lanes of the borough', *Leytonstone Expr. and Ind.*, 29 Dec. 1950.
[62] John Norden, *Map of Essex*, 1594.
[63] e.g. 1604, 1614, 1663, 1666 (E.R.O., Q/SR 166/142, Q/SBa 1/16, Q/SR 206/54–5, 395/14, 408/21).
[64] Middlesex and Essex Highways Act, 8 Geo. I, c. 30; E.R.O., T/M 128; *V.C.H. Essex*, v. 32; L.R.L., L47 MS. Vestry Mins. 1834–74 (1865, 1869).
[65] E.R.O., Q/SR 408/21; Act for amending road from Whitechapel . . ., 43 Geo. III, c. 66 (local act); L.R.L., L47 MS. Vestry Mins. 1834–74 (1865), L53.4 MS. Local Bd. Highways and Lighting Cttee. Mins., 1874.
[66] Act for repairing the road . . . to Woodford, 10 Geo. II, c. 36.   [67] *E.R.* liii. 11.
[68] G. S. Fry, *Walthamstow Wills, 1335–1559* (Walthamstow Ant. Soc. ix), 9, 10.
[69] Corpn. of Lond. R. O., River Lea: Proceedings in Star Chamber, etc. f. 169.
[70] J. Norden, *Essex*, xiv.
[71] E.R.O., Q/SR 198/138; W. R. Fisher, *Forest of Essex*, 85, 403; F. Temple, 'Busy Lea Bridge was once a lonely road', *Leytonstone Expr. and Independent*, 19 Apr. 1957; Kennedy, *Leyton*, 128, 265.
[72] L.R.L., L72. 2 Pamphlet, F. Temple's extracts from Westminster Abbey Muniments (W.A.M. 3323).
[73] E.R.O., Q/SR 74/33, 196/116–18, 197/145, 198/138, T/P 75; G. F. Bosworth, *George Monoux* (W.A.S. iii), 5.
[74] Assizes 35/54/T/29; E.R.O., T/P 75; Bosworth,

George Monoux, 5; W. Houghton, *Walthamstow: its highways and byways*, 4.
[75] Rocque, *Survey of Lond.*, 1748 edn.; L.R.L., L69 Plan, Leyton level sewers map, 1747.
[76] Lea Bridge turnpike Act, 30 Geo. II, c. 59; Tables on Sewers map, 1747 (L.R.L., L69 Plan).
[77] E.R.O., D/SH 29, T/M 53, D/CT 382; O.S. Map 6″, Essex, LXXIII (1873–82 edn.); John Warburton, *Map of Essex*, 1726; Emmanuel Bowen, *Map of Essex*, 1749. Cf. E.R.O., Q/SR 204/39.
[78] Fisher, *Forest*, 85; J. C. Jeaffreson, *Mdx. County Records*, i. 155; E.R.O., Q/SR 197/145, 198/138; Kennedy, *Leyton*, 128, 133; W. Robinson, *Hist. Hackney*, 60; Bosworth, *George Monoux*, 6.
[79] Lea Bridge Turnpike Act, 30 Geo. II, c. 59; Houghton, *Walthamstow: its highways and byways*, 4.
[80] L.R.L., L47 MS. Vestry Mins. 1781–1811 (1802).
[81] Walthamstow Vestry House Mus., P22/2/1 (Mins. Lea Bridge turnpike trustees, 1807–21).
[82] Annual Turnpike Acts Continuance Act, 1871, 34 & 35 Vict., c. 115; E.R.O., Q/SO 47, f. 193, 48, f. 32, Q/ABz 3.
[83] Assizes 35/138/2/11; E.R.O., D/SH 1, f. 45.
[84] E.R.O., D/SH 3, f. 237.
[85] L.R.L., L47 Pamphlet, *Address by U.D.C. Chairman*, 1909.
[86] *Leyton U.D.C. Eng. and Survs. Rep.* 1908; L.R.L., L47 Pamphlet, *Address by U.D.C. Chairman*, 1912.

Avenue leading out of London through Leyton.[87] The bridge was demolished soon after 1952, when the Waterworks river was filled in and replaced by a roadway.[88] Plans still existed, however, in 1965 to build an Eastern Avenue extension through Leyton linking Eastway (Hackney) and Ruckholt Road with Cambridge Park.[89]

Leyton Bridge, mentioned in 1454, crossed the Phillebrook in Broad Lane. It is not mentioned after 1698.[90] Marks Bridge crossed the Dagenham brook west of Mark House.[91]

Road development after 1850 took place within the framework of the ancient road system. The only important new thoroughfare was Francis Road, leading from Leyton High Road to Grove Green Road.[92] By the 1960s the existing main roads in Leyton were carrying heavy through traffic north-eastwards from London. Improved road junctions had been constructed at Whipps Cross, the Green Man, and Ruckholt Road, but congestion was often severe in the built-up shopping streets, particularly in Leytonstone High Road.

No very ancient building survives in Leyton, and there are no structural remains of the medieval parish church. Moyer House and Cross House, both in Leyton village, may have been medieval but were pulled down early in the 19th century. There was a pre-Dissolution Ruckholt Hall, but in the late 16th century it was replaced by a new one, which was demolished in its turn in the 18th century. The vicarage standing in 1537 was in ruins by 1650. The grange or manor house of Leyton which existed in the 1470s had probably disappeared by the late 1640s. Knotts, and the house at Diggons Cross in 1537,[93] were both replaced in the 18th century or earlier. Godsalves, occupied about 1547 by Sir John Godsalf,[94] was a large quadrangular building surrounded by a high wall and moat. By the 18th century it was derelict, its materials robbed to build other houses. One of these was probably the Bowling Green mentioned in 1658. This occupied part of the site before it was inherited about 1756 by Edward Rowe Mores the antiquary and printer who built on it the house in Church Road now known as Etloe House.[95] Leyton's oldest surviving building, the present Essex Hall, is structurally of the 16th century.[96] The first Forest House, built between 1537 and 1579, stood little more than 100 years. A Rose inn in Leytonstone is mentioned in 1585.[97]

No secular building which is known to date from the 17th century has survived in Leyton. Among buildings erected in the later part of the century were a new vicarage, the alms-houses next to the church, and a new Forest House. Lea Hall in Capworth Street, built in 1626, was occupied by Sir Richard Hopkins (d. 1735) and by the Quaker Joseph Hunton, who was hanged for forgery in 1828. It later became a girls school and was a branch of the county lunatic asylum in 1894 shortly before it was pulled down.[98] Drawings of the garden front suggest that it had been rebuilt or remodelled in the 18th century.[99] Ive Farm, south of Etloe House, was a two-storeyed brick house, probably built late in the 17th century. It survived, much altered, but retaining its original staircase, to the 1940s.[1] The Ferry House inn mentioned in 1702 and described as ancient in 1757 probably dated from the collapse of Lockbridge in the earlier 17th century. Later known as the Horse and Groom it was demolished in the 1850s when the waterworks filter beds were built.[2] Other inns named in the 17th century were the Harrow (1651), Green Man (1668), and Robin Hood (1670), all in Leytonstone. The Robin Hood became the Red Lion by 1766. The Three Blackbirds, Leyton, existed by 1705.[3] All these have been rebuilt, together with the Bell and the Lion and Key, both mentioned in the 18th century.[4] The house in Leytonstone High Road called Andrews[5] became known as Royal Lodge after 1821, when it ceased to be occupied as a school. It was burned down in 1878, rebuilt, and converted into the Rex cinema about 1928. The original Assembly House in Whipps Cross Road, in which London merchants were said to have transacted their business during the plague of 1665, was demolished about 1840 and replaced by a tall red-brick building.[6]

After the Restoration Leyton became increasingly a 'pretty retiring place from London' for wealthy merchants, bankers, and professional men.[7] They built fine houses or rebuilt existing ones, and established large households, including the 'blackamoor' servants whose births and burials are entered in the parish registers from 1667 to 1778.[8] In 1670 of the 83 houses in the parish 19 had 8 or more hearths.[9] By 1766 some 50 to 60 gentlemen's families were said to be living in the parish.[10] They included men of intellect and taste, such as the printers William

[87] V.C.H. Essex, v. 29; Lee Conservancy Catchment Bd. Act, 1938, 1 & 2 Geo. VI, c. 41.
[88] See p. 203. A photograph taken in 1952 shows the bridge still standing where the river had been: L.R.L., L53.5 Print.
[89] County of Essex Development Plan, 1952: Rep. of Survey, Pt. II, Met. Essex, pp. 79, 81; Leyton Housing Cttee. Yesterday, today and tomorrow, 1964/5.
[90] Cal. Close, 1454–61, 353; L.R.L., Deeds (Lee 5); E.R.O., Q/SR 341/27, D/DB T792/1.
[91] L.R.L., L69 Plan Leyton level (1747).
[92] O.S. Map 6" (1959 edn.) TQ 38 N.E.
[93] See pp. 188, 192.
[94] Kennedy, Leyton, 340; Shaw, Knights of England, ii, 59; E.R.O., D/DK T50.
[95] Kennedy, Leyton, 271, 340, 356–7; D.N.B.; V.C.H. Essex, ii. 471. See also below.
[96] See p. 190.
[97] E.R.O., Q/SR 95/58.
[98] Kennedy, Leyton, 332; E.A.T., 3rd ser. i. 164; E.R.O., D/DWv T80.
[99] L.R.L., L72.2. Print.
[1] R.C.H.M. Essex, ii. 168; F. Temple, 'Story of modern

street names', Leytonstone Express and Independent, 8 June 1951.
[2] Kennedy, Leyton, 131; Lea Bridge Turnpike Act, 30 Geo. II, c. 59; F. Temple, 'Busy Lea Bridge was once a lonely road', Leytonstone Express and Independent, 19 Apr. 1957.
[3] Kennedy, Leyton, 132, 264, 283; E.A.T. n.s. xiv. 6.
[4] E.R.O., D/DU 101/1 (1729, 1737, 1753); Kennedy, Leyton, 283.
[5] M. L. Savell, 'Echoes of old Leyton', Nos. 16, 17, 'Royal Lodge', Walthamstow Guardian, 2 and 9 July, 1965.
[6] Temple, 'More about the old roads and lanes', Leytonstone Express and Independent, 19 Jan. 1951. The Assembly House is named on Rocque's Survey of London (1746). For the school at the Assembly House, see below, p. 238.
[7] Morant, Essex, i. 25; E.R.O. T/P 168; Kennedy, Leyton, passim.
[8] Kennedy, Leyton, 116–19, 135, 314.
[9] E.R.O., Q/RTh. 5
[10] Guildhall MS. 9558, f. 218.

Bowyer the elder (d. 1737) and his son, William (d. 1777), and David Lewis (d. 1760) the poet, and friend of Alexander Pope.[11]

Most of the large residences were situated on the higher ground in the centre and north of the parish with a particular concentration in Low Leyton village. They stood, often in extensive grounds, at Knotts Green and in High Road, Church Lane, and Capworth Street. At least eight houses in this area were connected at one time with substantial estates, including the manor of Leyton, and are therefore described in another section;[12] of these buildings only Essex Hall and Grove House were still standing in 1970. The only other surviving house of any size is Etloe House in Church Road, which was built c. 1760. At the rear of its three-storeyed central block are sash windows and two full-height bays of the original date. The house was evidently enlarged by the addition of two flanking wings in the early or mid 19th century, perhaps as late as 1856 when Cardinal Wiseman moved there; at the same time the front was remodelled in a Tudor style with mullioned windows, embattled parapets, and a porch with Gothic arches. Two turrets with crocketed finials may have been part of the original house which, in 1796, was known as Etloe Place and described as 'whimsical'.[13] Also in Church Road was Leyton House, which disappeared c. 1910. It was built about 1706 by David Gansel and the elaborate layout of its grounds is shown on Rocque's map. It was a three-storeyed red-brick building with a front of seven bays and a scrolled pediment to the central doorway. The front faced a walled forecourt with entrance gates on the east and two flanking stable blocks. The site is now occupied by the London Electric Wire Works.[14] Other demolished houses in the area which were largely of 18th-century date were Suffolk House in Capworth Street, and Chingford Hall, Salway House, and Leyton Park (formerly Phillebrook House), all in High Road. In Leyton Green Road were the White House, demolished before the Second World War, and Cedar Lawn, which survived into the 1960s.[15] No. 669 High Road, a smaller village house, was still standing in 1970; built in the later 18th century it has three ogee-headed 'Gothick' windows to the first floor and a pedimented doorcase between Victorian bay-windows.

Forest House and Wallwood House stood at the edge of the forest on or near the sites of more ancient buildings. Both belonged to large estates and are described elsewhere.[16] In the 18th century the scenic attractions of the forest led to the building of new residences in this part of the parish. In the extreme north-east corner was the house, later known as Forest Edge or Buxton House, in which Isaac Buxton died in 1782; it had probably been built by his father-in-law, Thomas Fowell. Sir Edward North Buxton lived there in 1840–7. It was demolished shortly before 1939 and blocks of flats have been built on the former garden.[17] Near by, in a road now called The Forest, two smaller houses of 18th century origin, Marryats Lodge and Gwydir Lodge, are still standing, together with two early 19th-century terrace houses. On the south side of Whipps Cross Road, also overlooking forest land, a row of about twelve middle-class dwellings was built in 1767.[18] It was known as Assembly Row from the Assembly House at one end of it, and later as Forest Place. Six of the houses (nos. 133, 135, 139, 143, 153, and 155 Whipps Cross Road) survived in an altered form in 1968. They were originally two- and three-storeyed structures of brown brick, some terraced and some detached. They had mansard roofs, dormers, sash windows, pedimented doorways and, in a few cases, two-storeyed projecting bays.

Leytonstone contained fewer large residences than Leyton. One of the earliest was The Pastures in Davies Lane, the larger of Mary Bosanquet's two houses. It was built by Daniel van Mildert about 1686–7 but was remodelled and refaced in the 18th century. It contained staircases of both dates. After bombing in the Second World War it stood derelict until its demolition in the 1960s. The Pastures youth centre now occupies the site.[19] Park House, in Leytonstone High Road, was used as a branch library from 1908 until it was pulled down in 1934. It was a square three-storeyed building of the early 18th century with rusticated quoins, a modillion eaves-cornice, and a hipped roof. The central doorway had an open segmental pediment with the arms of Parry-Segar in the tympanum.[20] The elevation to Granleigh Road, which had been given a veranda and a balcony in the earlier 19th century, became the principal entrance front after the railway was constructed near by. Among other 18th-century houses which have now vanished were Dyers Hall, built on a small estate devised to the Dyers Company in 1739 for charitable purposes,[21] and Leyspring House, burnt down about 1870.[22] Norlington House was in High Road and Bushwood House stood by the pond near the Green Man. At the north end of High Road, however, a few buildings have survived from the former hamlet. Leytonstone House, now part of a mental hospital, was built c. 1800 and was the home of Thomas Fowell Buxton in 1857. The three-storeyed central block of five bays, which has a modillion cornice and a Doric portico, is flanked by two-storeyed wings;

[11] D.N.B.; Kennedy, Leyton, 341–3.
[12] See pp. 184 sqq.
[13] Lysons, London, iv. 226; Kennedy, Leyton, 335, 357; Pevsner, Essex, 2nd edn., 268. For Cardinal Wiseman at Etloe House, and St. Pelagia's Home, see below, p. 223.
[14] Kennedy, Leyton, 39, 271, 331–2; L.R.L., L55.6 MS. Rate Bk. 1704–33; Hist. Essex by Gent. iv. 240 (pl.); E.R. liii. 69. For its occupation as St. Agnes's Orphanage, see below, p. 236.
[15] In Leyton Reference Library there is a comprehensive collection of illustrations of houses which no longer exist, with notes on them, and including dated photographs, sometimes taken shortly before demolition.
[16] See pp. 189, 196.
[17] Kennedy, Leyton, 300–1; E.R. liv. 113, lviii, 109;

E.R.O., T/G 88 (TS), Letters of Catherine, Lady Buxton, 1814–1911, i, 49, 80.
[18] Temple, 'More about old roads and lanes', Leytonstone Expr. and Ind. 19 Jan. 1951.
[19] E.R.O., D/DU 322/1–10; L.R.L., L55.6 MS. Rate Colln. Bk. 1651–1704; Pevsner, Essex, 2nd edn., 269; Essex Churchman, Aug. 1966. For the Good Shepherd Home at the Pastures, see below, p. 238.
[20] R.C.H.M. Essex, ii. 168; V.C.H. Essex, Bibliog. 330.
[21] The charity was to support almshouses built in Bethnal Green for the widows of liverymen: Temple, 'Story of modern street names', Leytonstone Expr. and Ind. 7 July 1951; Lysons, London, ii. 36; Guildhall MS. 8185.
[22] Temple, 'Story of modern street names', Leytonstone Expr. and Ind. 7 July 1951.

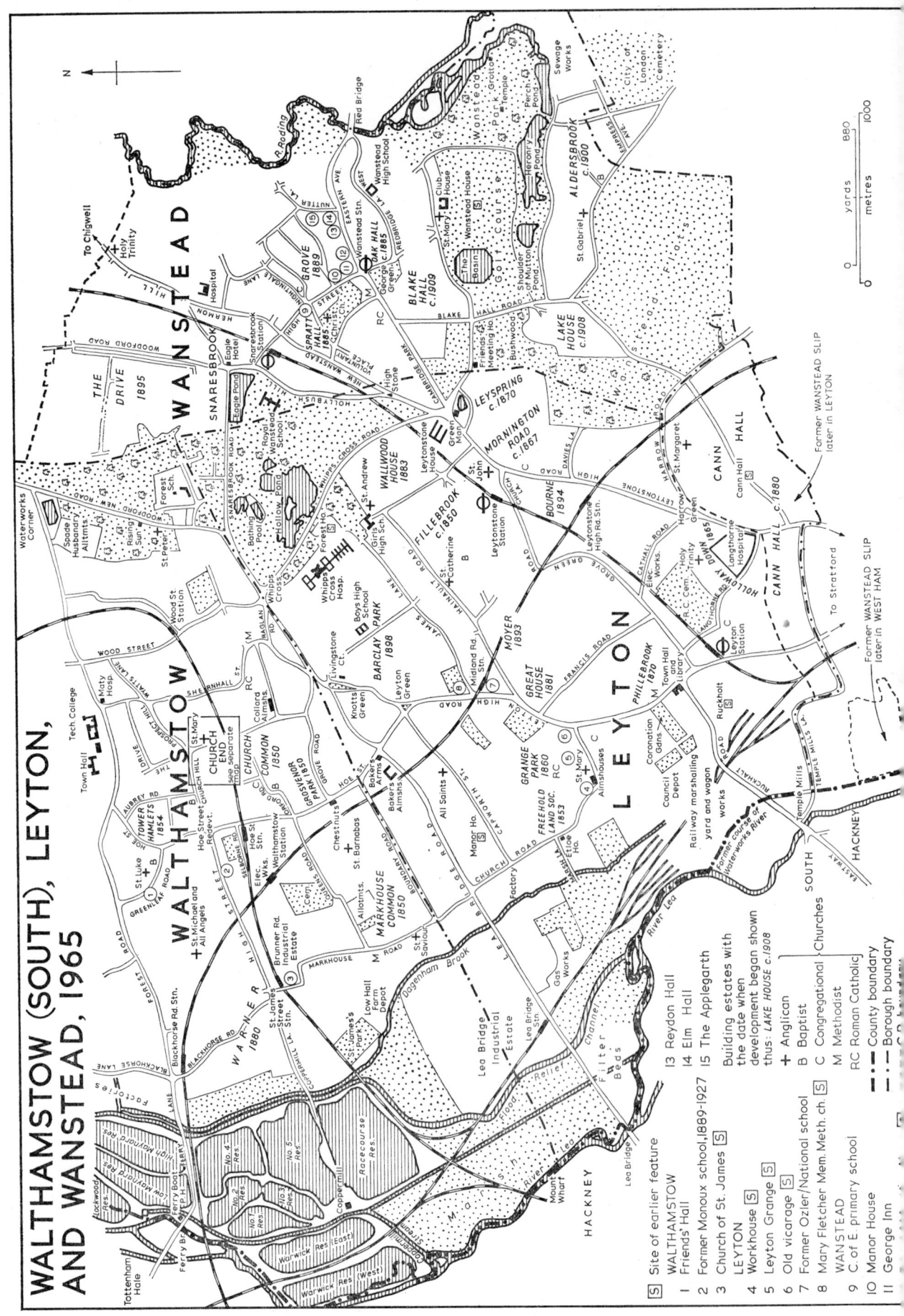

WALTHAMSTOW (SOUTH), LEYTON, AND WANSTEAD, 1965

S Site of earlier feature
WALTHAMSTOW
1 Friends' Hall
2 Former Monoux school,1889-1927 S
3 Church of St. James S
LEYTON
4 Workhouse S
5 Leyton Grange S
6 Old vicarage S
7 Former Ozier/National school S
8 Mary Fletcher Mem. Meth. ch. S
9 C. of E. primary school
WANSTEAD
10 Manor House
11 George Inn

13 Reydon Hall
14 Elm Hall
15 The Applegarth

Building estates with
the date when
development began shown
thus: LAKE HOUSE c.1908

+ Anglican
B Baptist
C Congregational ⎫ Churches
M Methodist
RC Roman Catholic
━ ━ County boundary
━ ・ ━ Borough boundary

like so many Georgian houses in the area, it has full-height bay-windows at the rear.[23] To the south a smaller and much altered house of *c.* 1700 stands at right angles to the road. Farther south again were the grounds of Sycamore House, an 18th-century building with later extensions; it was demolished in 1958[24] when the Presbyterian Church of Wales was built on the site. On the opposite side of High Road, behind the Green Man, several irregular groups of early-19th-century cottages have survived in Browning Road. Facing High Road was a terrace of three red-brick 18th-century houses with shops built over their front gardens. One, in which Sir Morell Mackenzie was born in 1837, is still standing. Farther south a later and more imposing three-storeyed terrace also has its frontage concealed by modern shops. It consists of three houses, each of five bays, with ground floors of rusticated stucco and central Doric porches.

A few surviving buildings in the parish date from the period immediately before its rapid mid-19th-century development, including St. John's church, Leytonstone (1833). A typical smaller residence, standing in its own garden, is Gainsborough Lodge in Leytonstone High Road. There are also small houses and cottages in Church Road, Leyton, and near the north-east end of Lea Bridge Road (formerly Chestnut Walk). The main front of the massive West Ham Union workhouse (now Langthorne hospital), built in 1840,[25] has stone dressings and is surmounted by a balustraded parapet with twin classical urns. In Lea Bridge Road the London Master Bakers' benevolent institution stands round three sides of a court, the fourth side open to the street and bounded by railings with wrought iron gates. It was designed in an elaborate Italianate style by T. E. Knightley and built in stages between 1857 and 1866.[26] The two-storeyed ranges are of grey brick with stone dressings and contain 52 alms-houses, known as 'villas'. Architectural features include two square turrets at the angles between the ranges, small low-pitched gables, and rows of projecting porches.

Leyton and Leytonstone remained rural until the mid 19th century.[27] Then came the opening of railways to London with stations at Lea Bridge (1840), Low Leyton and Leytonstone (1856), followed by the provision of other forms of cheap and speedy transport. This coincided with the expansion of opportunities for employment in offices, in industry, and in public undertakings, particularly railways, in London and in neighbouring districts,

such as West Ham. The effect was to transform two villages by the end of the 19th century into a suburban dormitory for clerks and workmen mostly employed outside the area.[28] In contrast, however, to the spread of building over most of the parish, the forest land in the extreme north-east remained largely untouched. Its survival was ensured by the Epping Forest Act of 1878 by which over 200 acres in Leyton were preserved for public use.[29] This area, with its established trees, ponds, glades, and open spaces, provided ample opportunities for outdoor recreation.

Development began in the district nearest to Lea Bridge station, and included Park Place in Church Road, and an estate laid out by the Freehold Land Society comprising Park, Grange, Shaftesbury, and Carlisle Roads, on which all plots were sold by 1853, and houses built and occupied by 1857.[30] In 1860 the Grange Park estate was sold to the British Land Co.[31] comprising roughly the rest of the district bounded by Park, Church, Vicarage, and Thornhill Roads. By 1867 Holloway Down was being laid out and the better-class district between Mornington Road and Leytonstone High Road.[32] Some of the early Holloway Down development, near the union workhouse and West Ham boundary, was of low standard, soon overcrowded, and insanitary;[33] the worst was demolished by the borough council in the 1960s. In the 1870s building was in progress on the Fillebrook (Wallwood farm) estate, bounded by Hainault, Fairlop, Colworth, and Fillebrook Roads, and on the Leyspring estate; also, farther south, on the Leyton Park and Phillebrook farm estates, north of the railway line, and in the Cann Hall district, which was almost entirely built over by 1895. The Cowley (Ruckholt manor) estate was sold off piecemeal from the late 1860s, including land in Grove Green Lane and 31 a. between Leyton railway station and Stratford sold in 1878–81.[34] Building accelerated on established schemes in the 1880s, and spread as the Great House estate, with 50 a. between Francis Road and Norlington Road, and the Leyton Manor estate (Palamos, Malta, and Waterloo Roads), came on the market. Development of the Wallwood Park estate, bounded by Colworth Road, Forest Glade, and the railway line, slow in the 1880s was completed in the next decade. In the 1890s most of the remaining estates were sold, including Dyers Hall, Lea Hall,[35] The Poplars, Moyer, and the Bourne nursery ground. In 1898 the Barclay Park sale made available another 100 a. Among the last developments, in the early

[23] *Gent. Mag.* cxli. 237; Pevsner, *Essex*, 2nd edn., 269; *E.R.* lviii. 109, 121. See also below, p. 238.

[24] Pevsner, *Essex*, 2nd edn., 269.

[25] W. H. Weston, *Leyton and Leytonstone*, 181; *White's Dir. Essex* (1848). The date is inscribed on the chapel. See also plate f.p. 203.

[26] Pevsner, *Essex*, 2nd edn., 269; *White's Dir. Essex* (1863); *Baker and Confectioner*, 20 May 1955; *Lond. Master Bakers' Ben. Instn. Ann. Rep.* 1961 (illus.); tablets on buildings.

[27] G. A. Cooke, *Top. and statistical desc. of Essex* (*c.* 1810), 123; *White's Dir. Essex* (1848).

[28] Wilkinson, *Leyton*, 36, 72; E. Gunn, *Great House*, 9–11; R. Mudie-Smith, *Relig. Life Lond.* 339–41; W. Ashworth, 'Types of social and econ. devt. in suburban Essex', *London aspects of change*, ch. III, 65, 75–6; *V.C.H. Essex*, v. 12, 19, 25; *New Survey of London . . .*, iii, *Social conditions* (1) Eastern Area, 398.

[29] See p. 205.

[30] O.S. Map 6″, Essex, LXXIII (1873–82 edn.); E.R.O., D/DB T836; L.R.L., L47 MS. Ves. Mins. 1834–74 (esp. 1868–9); D/SH 29; L.R.L., L55.3 MS. Highway Board Mins., 1856–61.

[31] Unless otherwise stated details of the progress of development are based on the following: Manors and other estates section on pp. 184 sqq.; L.R.L., L47 MS. Leyton Vestry Mins. 1834–74 and Local Board Mins. 1877–94, and L53.4 MS. Local Bd. Highways and Lighting Cttee. Mins. 1873–83; *Leyton Local Bd.* and *U.D.C. Highways Cttee. Reps.*; *Leyton Eng. and Survs. Reps.* 1895–1914.

[32] E.R.O., T/M 402, D/DCy T19; *E.Nat.* xxvii. 48; L.R.L., Deeds (BRA 219.1C, 1870).

[33] *V.C.H. Essex*, v. 48; *New survey of Lond. life and labour*, iii, *Survey of social conditions* (1) Eastern area, 397.

[34] E.R.O., D/DCy T19, 23, 28; D/DCy E45 f. 362, E46 f. 347.

[35] E.R.O., D/DB T1158.

1900s, were the Forest Lodge[36] and Etloe House estates, the Warner estate west of Markhouse Road, and the site of the Great House itself (1905). In 1912 only 250 a. of undeveloped building land remained, mainly represented by the Barclay Park estate and Fraser's Lea Bridge nursery ground. These remained undeveloped until the 1920s.[37]

Beyond the fringe of all this speculative development a bungalow town of 69 shacks, with wells and earth closets, and a wooden mission church, sprang up in the 1880s at Lea Bridge Gardens, west of Lea Bridge station.[38] The occupants reared ducks and grew vegetables. These buildings were demolished in the 1930s and the site is now mainly industrial.

By 1903 little remained apart from the forest to recall 'leafy Leyton's' former character, though the district council tried to restore it by mobilizing the unemployed to plant thousands of trees in the new streets in 1909–11.[39] Only the council's recreation grounds, and the Drapers Ground, a disused brick-field laid out in 1894 as a playing field for their school by the Drapers Company, relieved the prevailing monotony of brick.[40]

Once speculative development had begun, Leyton ceased to attract wealthy residents in search of rural seclusion. As a result there are no Victorian or Edwardian mansions in the area. The new houses were mainly yellow-brick two-storey terraces and villas, ranged in rows, their bow-windows and doorways freely ornamented with mass-produced cement foliage and tracery. The elaboration of the Red Lion inn and shops, designed by W. D. Church in 1890,[41] exemplifies on a larger scale the ornate features popular with the terrace builders. Retail shops, which became increasingly necessary for the growing population, were almost entirely confined to the main thoroughfares, long stretches of which were built up as shopping streets in the later 19th century. The new frontages were of two or three storeys with shops on the ground floor and living accommodation for their owners above. Later, as demand grew, residential terraces were brought into use, shops being built over their small front gardens. Public buildings dating from this period include the first town hall (1882), of yellow brick, with a corner clock-tower, now a library, and the present town hall (1896), designed by J. Johnson. This vivid red-brick building, with Portland stone bands and dressings, was said to be in the 'English Renaissance' style.[42] Whipps Cross hospital, then the Union infirmary, was completed in 1903. The Carnegie Library in Lea Bridge Road (1906), and girls high school in Colworth Road (1911) were designed by W. Jacques. The most striking churches built at this time were All Saints, Capworth Street (1864), the

Mary Fletcher Memorial Methodist church (1877), St. Andrew's, Forest Glade (1887), Gainsborough Bridge Primitive Methodist church (1902), and St. George's Presbyterian church (1893), Hainault Road.

During the First World War about 1,300 houses were damaged by bombing during airship raids in 1915–16.[43] Though there was little building between the two wars, notable new buildings included Leyton high school for boys in Essex Road (1929), Connaught Road school (1932), the High Road baths (1934), Emmanuel church (1934–5), and the Christian Science church (1937). During the Second World War hardly a house in Leyton escaped damage.[44] After 1945 municipal redevelopment began on vacant and cleared sites.[45] First schemes provided houses and bungalows of conventional design, such as those in the Borthwick Road and Ellingham Road area, or three- and four-storey blocks of flats such as Beaumont House (1947), Mills Court (1950), and Thornhill Gardens (1955). Villiers Close (1957) represented a new approach, grouping varied blocks in one development. The eleven-storey Slade Tower, completed in 1961 as part of the Leyton Grange development, was the first outcome of the council's new decision to build upward at higher population densities. The Slade Tower was followed by others, which now dominate the surrounding streets to a height of up to 17 storeys. The Beaumont Road development, under construction in 1965, comprised 444 dwellings in mixed blocks, including bungalows, grouped around the multi-storey All Saints Tower.

Public buildings completed after 1945 include the Harrow Green branch library, George Tomlinson primary school, and Ruckholt Manor school. The only modern church of note is the Welsh Presbyterian church in Leytonstone High Road.

In 1693 the parish was subsidizing a local stage coach.[46] In 1707 a stage coach service linked Leyton and Walthamstow.[47] By the late 18th century several coaches a day passed through the parish.[48] In 1839 five coaches ran daily to London from Leyton, and the Wanstead, Epping, Harlow, and Clare coaches stopped at Leytonstone.[49] The Northern and Eastern railway line from Stratford to Broxbourne opened in 1840 with a station at Lea Bridge,[50] and the Eastern Counties (later Great Eastern) branch line from Stratford to Loughton with stations at Leyton and Leytonstone in 1856.[51] The Midland railway's Tottenham and Forest Gate branch, crossing the parish from north-west to south-east, with stations in Leyton and Leytonstone was opened in 1894.[52] In 1947 the line from Stratford through Leytonstone to Woodford was electrified, as an extension of the Central London line.[53]

[36] E.R.O., *Sale Cat.* A641.
[37] Cf. ibid. A578.
[38] *Kelly's Dir. Essex* (1886); *Ann. Rep. of M.O.* 1893; L.R.L., L66. 1 Prints, Newspaper description, with illus. *c*. 1908, and photographs. See also below, p. 225, and plate f.p. 251.
[39] Gunn, *Great House*, 11; L.R.L., L47 Pamphlets, *Leyton U.D.C. Chairmen's addresses*, 1909–11.
[40] Wilkinson, *Leyton*, 72; *Ann. Rep. of M.O.* 1894; *Leyton Off. Guide* (1929), 35; (1934), 35.
[41] *Building News*, 30 Oct. 1891. For the Red Lion see below, plate f.p. 325.
[42] Wilkinson, *Leyton*, 59–60.
[43] Weston, *Leyton*, 215; *Leyton U.D.C. Mins.* 1915–16, p. 177, 1918–19, p. 311.
[44] *Essex C.C. Rep. of A.R.P. Cttee.* 1939–45, 27.

[45] Leyton B.C. Housing Cttee. 1964–5, *Yesterday, today and tomorrow: housing in Leyton.*
[46] L.R.L., L47 MS. Vestry Mins. 1686–1723.
[47] E.R.O., Q/SR 530/34.
[48] E.R.O., T/P 110/45; L.R.L., L35 Pamphlet, Leytonstone Academy advt. 1785.
[49] *Pigot's Dir. Essex* (1839); Wilkinson, *Leyton*, 20. Cf. L.R.L., L36 Print, Drawing by T. Moxon of Leyton daily coach, *c*. 1848.
[50] E.R.O., D/DCy T26; E. Carter, *Hist. Geog. of Railways*, 64; *V.C.H. Essex*, v. 23.
[51] Wilkinson, *Leyton*, 36; *V.C.H. Essex*, v. 24; *White's Dir. Essex* (1863), 641, 644.
[52] Wilkinson, *Leyton*, 71; *V.C.H. Essex*, v. 24; A. P. Wire, *Leyton*, 7–8.
[53] *V.C.H. Essex*, v. 72.

The North Metropolitan Tramways Co. in 1874 built tramcar construction works in Union Road, connected with the company's system at Stratford by a short length of horse tramway in Leytonstone High Road.[54] This was extended to the Green Man in 1878. The company used this route to experiment, in 1877 with the Merryweather steam tram, in 1881 with a car driven by the Beaumont compressed air engine, and in 1882 with an electric tram run on a battery.[55]

The Lea Bridge, Leyton and Walthamstow Tramways, incorporated in 1881, opened a single-line horse tram service along Lea Bridge Road in 1883.[56] Though the promoters failed in 1885, the undertaking was bought in 1888 by a new Lea Bridge, Leyton and Walthamstow Tramways Co., incorporated in 1889, and empowered to operate also down Leyton High Road to the railway station. By 1890 trams were operating from Lea Bridge to the Rising Sun in Woodford New Road, and from the Bakers Arms to the Great Eastern railway station.[57] Under powers obtained in 1898 and amplified in 1904[58] the district council in 1905 took over the Lea Bridge company's undertaking, and in 1906 the portion in the district of the North Metropolitan company's, though not their tramcar works. The council's whole system was electrified in 1906–7.[59] In 1910 the council made joint arrangements with the L.C.C. and other authorities for through tram services, and from 1921 to 1933 their tramways were operated by the L.C.C.[60]

A horse bus service between Walthamstow and Stratford via Leyton High Road was introduced in 1889.[61] It was replaced in 1905 by a motor bus service, run from 1906 by the Great Eastern London Motor Omnibus Co. The company built a bus garage at Leyton Green in 1906, when a new service was started from the Bakers Arms to Oxford Circus via Lea Bridge Road. The London General Omnibus Co., which had also established motor bus routes between London and the Bakers Arms by 1908, took over the Great Eastern in 1911, and

rebuilt and enlarged the Leyton Green depot in 1912.[62] In 1933 the buses and trams were taken over by the London Passenger Transport board.[63] Conversion of the tramways to trolley bus working was completed in 1939.[64] Since 1952 omnibuses have replaced trolley buses.[65]

In 1692 letters were collected and delivered at Low Leyton once daily by the London Penny Post's footpost.[66] By 1794 there was a receiving house with three daily deliveries, also a sorting office.[67] The Munn family, grocers in Leyton Street, were receivers continuously from before 1832 until about 1878.[68] In 1856 Leyton became a sub-office in the north eastern district, later merged with the eastern district.[69] The sub-office at Leyton Green in 1863 was known as the 'higher office'.[70] The sorting office at no. 713 High Road was established c. 1893;[71] in 1917 Leyton became the E.10 London delivery district.[72] As the number of sub-offices increased, to 11 by 1926, the Leyton Green office continued to be termed the 'higher office',[73] but there was no branch office until 1934 when the present one was built in Lea Bridge Road.[74] A telegraph service was available by 1870.[75] The National Telephone Co. extended their system to Leyton in 1892[76] and had opened an exchange by 1906.[77] The district is now served by the Leytonstone exchange.

In Leytonstone letters were collected and delivered in 1692 once daily.[78] There was a receiving house by 1794.[79] In 1856 Leytonstone was assigned to the north eastern (later eastern) district.[80] There was still only one sub-office in 1870, but another had opened at Harrow Green by 1874.[81] About 1912 a branch office was opened at no. 801 High Road; this remained the urban district's only branch office until 1934.[82] Soon after 1964 it was replaced by an office at no. 783 High Road.[83] Since about 1939 there has also been a branch office in Cathall Road, Harrow Green.[84] A sorting office, established in Church Lane in 1883,[85] moved to its present site in Fillebrook Road about 1912.[86] In 1917 Leytonstone became the E.11 delivery area.[87] Telegraph

[54] V. E. Burrows, 'Leyton Council Tramways', *Tramway Review*, historical supplement to *Modern Tramcar*, ii (1953), Nos. 10 and 11. Unless otherwise stated the account of tramways is based on this article.
[55] Cf. L.R.L., L47 MS. Local Bd. Mins. 3 Oct., 5 Dec. 1881.
[56] *V.C.H. Essex*, v. 27; Lea Bridge, Leyton and Walthamstow Tramways Act 1881: 44 & 45 Vict. c. 170 (local act); L. A. Thomson, *By bus, tram and coach* (W.A.S., N.S. xi), 5.
[57] *V.C.H. Essex*, v. 27; Wilkinson, *Leyton*, 64; L.R.L., L47 MS. Local Bd. Mins. 1886, 1888; Lea Bridge, Leyton and Walthamstow Tramways Act, 1889: 52 & 53 Vict. c. 158 (local act); Thomson, *By bus, tram and coach*, 6–7.
[58] Leyton U.D.C. Acts, 1898, 61 & 62 Vict. c. 175 (local act) and 1904, 4 Edw. VII, c. 240 (local act).
[59] *V.C.H. Essex*, v. 28; *Leyton U.D.C. Year Bk.* 1919–20; *Kelly's Dir. Essex* (1906); Leyton U.D.C. *Eng. and Survs. Rep.* 1907.
[60] L.R.L., L47 Pamphlet, *U.D.C. Chairman's address*, 1910, 1911; *V.C.H. Essex*, v. 28; Campfield, *Leyton*, 10; Leyton B.C. *Charter Day, 1926: souvenir programme*, 33; L.R.L., L47 Pamphlet. *Year Bk.* 1932–3.
[61] See p. 251.
[62] *V.C.H. Essex*, v. 28–9; L.R.L., L47 Pamphlet, *U.D.C. Chairman's address*, 1909, 1912; Thomson, *By bus, tram and coach*, 22–4, 36–7.
[63] London Passenger Transport Act, 1933, 23 & 24 Geo. V, c. 14.
[64] Burrows, *Tramway Review*, ii, no. 11, p. 44; *V.C.H Essex*, v. 73.

[65] *Leyton Off. Guide* (c. 1952), 51.
[66] T. de Laune, *Present State of London* (1692).
[67] G. Brumell, *Local Posts of London, 1640–1840*, 81.
[68] *Pigot's Dir. Essex* (1832); *White's Dir. Essex*, (1848, 1863); *Kelly's Dir. Essex* (1870–82).
[69] *British Postal Guide* (1856).
[70] *White's Dir. Essex* (1863); *Kelly's Dir. Essex* (1866).
[71] *Kelly's Dir. Walthamstow, Leyton and Leytonstone* (1893).
[72] *Post Office Guide* (1917).
[73] *Kelly's Dir. Essex* (1866–1926).
[74] Wilkinson, *Leyton*, 71; *Leyton Off. Guide* (1922), 18, (1934), 33.
[75] *Kelly's Dir. Essex* (1870).
[76] L.R.L., L47 MS. Local Bd. Mins. 1892; *Kelly's Dir. Walthamstow, Leyton and Leytonstone* (1893).
[77] *Kelly's Dir. Essex* (1906).
[78] T. de Laune, *Present State of London* (1692).
[79] Brumell, *Local Posts of Lond.* 81
[80] *Brit. Postal Guide* (1856).
[81] *Kelly's Dir. Essex* (1870, 1874).
[82] Wilkinson, *Leyton*, 71; *Kelly's Dir. Essex* (1878, 1910, 1912); *Leyton Off. Guide* (1922), 18.
[83] *G.P.O. London Post Offices and Streets*, 1964; *G.P.O. Tel. Dir. London Postal Area* (1967).
[84] *Leyton Off. Guide* (c. 1952); inf. from Miss M. E. Savell.
[85] *Kelly's Dir. Essex* (1890); L.R.L., L28 Prints, Photograph, c. 1905, showing dated tablet. Other photographs (L66.2 Prints) show the building, opposite Station Parade, at later dates; it was demolished by 1950.
[86] *Kelly's Dir. Essex* (1910, 1912).
[87] *Post Office Guide* (1917).

facilities were available by 1870.[88] The National Telephone Co. opened the Leytonstone exchange in 1908;[89] it was taken over by the G.P.O. in 1912.[90]

Leyton has been the birthplace or home of many notable persons. Some are mentioned in the sections which follow; others are listed in another volume.[91] Lady Margaret Bryan, governess to the children of Henry VIII, died at Leyton.[92] Thomas Lodge, (d. 1625) a leading physician, lived there[93] and Sir Morrell Mackenzie (d. 1892), the throat specialist, was born at Leytonstone, where his father, Stephen, practised as a surgeon.[94] The poet and dramatist John Drinkwater (d. 1937) was born in Leytonstone.[95] Among the more unusual of Leyton's worthies was John Henry Pepper (d. 1900), the illusionist, exhibitor of 'Pepper's Ghost'. Thomas Bowdler (d. 1856), Shakespeare's expurgator, was curate at Leyton in 1803. William Cotton Oswell (grandson of Joseph Cotton), accompanied Livingstone in his search for the Great Lake, and was with him in 1851 when the Zambesi was sighted.

In the 19th century the Lea was popular for boating, fishing, and bathing; several rowing clubs existed by 1880.[96] The *Eastern Mercury*, founded in 1887, paid special attention to sport, including football, cricket, cycling, and lacrosse.[97] Organized football was introduced in 1859, when the Forest Association football club was formed, playing its first games in Leytonstone on the forest adjoining Wanstead orphanage asylum. Among amateur clubs Leyton football club dates from 1868 and Leytonstone F.C. from 1886. The professional club, Clapton Orient, founded in 1881, moved to Leyton to the Brisbane Road stadium in 1936–7, and became known as Leyton Orient.[98] The Essex county cricket club in 1886 bought a permanent ground in Leyton High Road, where they played until it was sold in 1933. It is still a sports ground. Leyton cricket club, in existence by 1895, was by 1906 one of the strongest in Essex and a nursery for the county team.[99] In 1906–7 there were 20 cricket and football clubs in Leyton and in 1931 15 cricket clubs, over 20 football clubs, and a number of tennis, netball, swimming, athletics, cycling, motor-

ing, and gymnastics clubs.[1] Since 1905 the Hollow pond, deepened by the unemployed, has been used for sailing model yachts, boating, and skating.[2]

In 1806 a Women's Union society was meeting at the Red Lion.[3] By 1897 many societies existed, including masonic lodges, literary, camera, choral, orchestral, and phrenological societies.[4] They met in public houses, church halls, or schools, and, from 1896, in municipal halls,[5] of which there were six in 1965.[6] In 1955 there were over 50 societies in the district.[7] Three picture palaces were built in 1910–11.[8] One of Leytonstone's cinemas in 1917 was also a skating rink.[9] By 1932 there were eight cinemas; one of these, the Rex, in Leytonstone High Road, was converted to a bowling alley about 1962.[10] A Leyton Eisteddfod was organized by the public library committee from 1924 to 1939.[11] In 1947 Leyton took the lead among London boroughs pressing for more extensive permissive powers for local authorities in the entertainment field; these, as a result, became incorporated in the Local Government Act, 1948.[12]

MANORS AND OTHER ESTATES. Domesday Book describes six separate estates in Leyton. Ralph Baynard held of Westminster Abbey an estate worth 40s. comprising one hide held by Tosti before the Conquest, 20 a. of meadow, and a mill.[13] It was probably the estate 'near Walthamstow' which the abbey claimed to have been given by Aelfnoth of London, nephew of Swein.[14] This Baynard holding appears to have broken up. The mill remained among the abbey's possessions at least until the 14th century, but was considered to be in West Ham.[15] Another parcel, described from the 13th century as 15 a. of meadow, descended as part of another Baynard estate, the manor of Tothill, later Bloomsbury (Mdx.); this was held by the London Charterhouse from 1375 to the Dissolution.[16] This parcel, called Leyton Made,[17] lay in Walthamstow Marsh[18] north of the present Lea Bridge Road. Part of Baynard's manor may have become the estate in Leyton and Walthamstow held

---

[88] *Kelly's Dir. Essex* (1870).
[89] *Nat. Telephone Jnl.* 1908, p. 229.
[90] *G.P.O. List of Telephone Exchanges*, 1913.
[91] *V.C.H. Essex, Bibliography*, 246.
[92] Kennedy, *Leyton*, 343.
[93] *D.N.B.*; *E.R.* xxxiv. 36. There are biographies in *D.N.B.* of all the persons mentioned below.
[94] *E.R.* i. 144, l. 231.
[95] *E.R.* xliii. 123, xlvi. 121, xlvii. 42.
[96] *V.C.H. Essex*, ii. 590, v. 62.
[97] Wilkinson, *Leyton*, 71.
[98] *V.C.H. Essex*, ii. 612–13; 'Leyton Orient', *Football Association News*, July 1965; *Leytonstone F.C. Diamond Jubilee Handbook, 1886–7 to 1946–7*, p. 6; *Leyton F.C. Handbook*, 1951–2, pp. 11–16; 'Centenary of Leyton F.C.', *F.A. News*, Sept. 1968, 50–2; *Leyton Off. Guide* (1937), 14, (c. 1962), 8, 16.
[99] *E.R.* i. 31, xlii. 201; *V.C.H. Essex*, ii. 600, 605–8, v. 63, 88; *Leyton Off. Guide* (1934), 33.
[1] *Leyton U.D.C. Eng. and Survs. Rep.*, 1906–7; *Rotary Club of Leyton: Community Service Guide*, 1931.
[2] A. P. Wire, *Leyton*, 27–8; *Rep. R. Com. Poor Laws and Relief, 1909* [Cd. 4795], pp. 321–2, H.C. (1909), xliv. For skating on the Hollow pond see plate f.p. 52.
[3] L.R.L., L47 MS. Vestry Mins. 1781–1811.
[4] Wilkinson, *Leyton*, 71.
[5] R. Overton, *Hist. Leyton Literary Club* (1917); *Leyton, Leytonstone and District Scottish Association: Jubilee booklet 1903–52*.

[6] S. K. Ruck, *Municipal entertainment and the arts in Greater London* (1965), p. 166.
[7] *Leyton Pub. Libraries: List of Societies 1955*.
[8] A. P. Wire, *Leyton*, 28; L.R.L., L47 Pamphlet, *Leyton U.D.C. Chairman's address*, 1910–11.
[9] *Kelly's Dir. Essex* (1917).
[10] *V.C.H. Essex*, v. 88; *Leyton Off. Guide* (1949), 12, (c. 1962), 8.
[11] Leyton B.C. *Charter Day: souvenir programme, 1926*, p. 34; *Leyton and Leytonstone Eisteddfod Cttee.: Syllabus, 1924–39*; *Leyton Community Service Guide*, 79.
[12] *Leyton Off. Guide* (c. 1962), 21; S. K. Ruck, *Municipal entertainment . . . in Greater London*, 24; Local Govt. Act, 1948, 11 & 12 Geo. VI, c. 26, s. 132.
[13] *V.C.H. Essex*, i. 444.
[14] *Cal. Chart. R. 1327–41*, 333. A charter of 1066 which attributed to Atsere the swarthy the original gift to Westminster Abbey of land in Leyton (Lygetun) is spurious: C. Hart, *Early Charters of Essex*, No. 68; P. H. Sawyer, *Anglo-Saxon Charters*, pp. 310–11. See above, p. 89.
[15] See p. 89.
[16] E. Jeffries Davis, 'The University site, Bloomsbury', *Lond. Top. Record*, xvii (1936), 19 f.; *Feet of F. Essex*, i. 153, ii. 19, iii. 52; *Cal. Inq. p.m.* ix, pp. 15, 295; *Cal. Close, 1346–9*, pp. 434–5; *Cal. Pat. 1374–7*, pp. 125, 381; *V.C.H. Middlesex*, i. 169.
[17] *Cal. Inq. p.m.* ix, p. 295.
[18] *L. & P. Hen. VIII*, xix (2), p. 318.

in the 15th century by the Knott family,[19] for that estate was warranted against Westminster Abbey when it was sold in 1452.[20]

Hugh de Montfort held in demesne 3 hides and 30 a. which Alsi held as a manor before 1066,[21] including one hide once held by a sokeman of the manor of Havering.[22] This holding appears to have passed to the priory of Holy Trinity, Aldgate, about 1121, and subsequently formed the manor of Cann Hall, Wanstead.[23]

Robert Gernon held in demesne half a hide worth 5s. which a freeman had held in 1066.[24] This probably was later merged in the manor of Leyton (see below).

Peter de Valognes held in demesne a manor and 3 hides worth 40s.[25] The descent of this estate is traced below under Ruckholt manor.

The greatest part of the parish belonged in 1086 to Robert, son of Corbutio, whose two holdings, comprising 7¼ hides, descended together as the manor of *LEYTON*. The manor lay in the centre and north-east of the parish, stretching from the Lea marshes to the forest. The Phillebrook formed much of its southern boundary, and Walthamstow and the Leyton lands of Mark Hall the northern. Before 1066 four sokemen held 4 hides in Leyton of the manor of Havering.[26] Three of these hides were held in 1086 by Robert, son of Corbutio, who also held in demesne a manor and 4¼ hides which Harold held before 1066.[27] The manor probably remained in the Corbutio family until about 1200, when Ralph de Arderne confirmed a grant to the abbey of Stratford by Richard son of Walter Corbutio (Corpechun) of the church of St. Mary of Leyton and the wood of Leyton.[28] In 1237 or 1238 Richard, son and heir of Geoffrey, son of Richard Corbutio (Corbicun), acknowledged the right of Hugh, abbot of Stratford, to 2 hides in Leyton, which he had of the gift of Richard Corbutio, his grandfather; the abbot used to render 8 marks yearly, but henceforth was to hold in free alms.[29] In 1253 Henry III granted free warren to the abbot and convent of Stratford for their demesne lands in Leyton, with licence to inclose, assart, till, and empark their grove of 'Corpech' in Leyton.[30] By the late 12th century Stratford Abbey's estate in the parish may also have included the half-hide held in 1086 by Robert Gernon,[31] for Robert's fief, which escheated to the Crown, was granted by Henry I to William de Montfitchet,[32] the founder of

Stratford Abbey, whose son Gilbert was also a benefactor.[33] Among the possessions of the abbey taxed in 1291 Leyton was assessed at £23 3s. 6½d., excluding the rectory and advowson.[34] The abbot of Stratford held ½ a knight's fee in Leyton in 1303 and 1346.[35] By that time a fourth holding had been added to the estate.

In 1267 Godfrey de Liston died holding land in Leyton of Sir Hugh de Neville.[36] He was succeeded by his son and heir, John (d. 1303), who was in turn succeeded by his son, Sir John de Liston (d. 1332).[37] Before the latter's death part of his property in Leyton passed into the hands of Edmund Basset and Roger Samekyn, who had licence in 1331 to alienate to the abbey a messuage and 126 a. of land of the clear yearly value of 38s. 7d.[38] Stratford also acquired in 1329 or 1330 from Sir John de Liston a plot in Leytonstone called 'Jonesthyng of Liston', worth £10 yearly.[39] Alfred de Vere, earl of Oxford, appears to have been the abbot's tenant in 1401, but the manor had apparently reverted to demesne by 1428.[40] At the Dissolution much of the demesne land was shared by nine tenants, among them Morgan Wolfe, the remainder, with the manor-house and buildings, rectory and tithes, being leased to Thomas Campion.[41]

Stratford Abbey was surrendered to the King in 1538.[42] Thomas, Lord Wriothesley, Lord Chancellor, was granted the manor and rectory of Leyton for life in 1544, and in 1545 was granted the reversion in fee with licence to alienate to Sir Ralph Warren.[43] In 1546 Warren was granted the reversion of the rents which had been reserved in the grants to Wriothesley.[44] Sir Ralph, who had been lord mayor of London in 1536–7 and 1544, died in 1553,[45] devising the manor and advowson of Leyton for life to his wife Joan, daughter of John Lake of London. She married Sir Thomas White in 1558 and died in 1572,[46] being succeeded by her son Richard Warren. When Richard died in 1587 he held the manor of Leyton in chief for $\frac{1}{40}$ knight's fee, the yearly value being estimated at £20. His heir was his nephew, Oliver Cromwell, son and heir of his sister, Joan, wife of Sir Henry Williams *alias* Cromwell.[47] In 1599 Oliver Cromwell first leased the manor for 20 years to Edward Ryder, a London haberdasher, then later in the same year was licensed to alienate it to Ryder. In this lease and at other times later the manor was called *LEYTON GRANGE*.[48] Edward Ryder died in 1609. He left

[19] See p. 192.
[20] *Cal. Close*, 1447–54, 333; *Feet of F. Essex*, iv. 45.
[21] *V.C.H. Essex*, i. 497.
[22] Ibid. 430.
[23] See p. 326.
[24] *V.C.H. Essex*, i. 515.
[25] Ibid. 536.   [26] Ibid. 430.
[27] Ibid. 546.
[28] E.R.O., T/P 195/1 (no. 5): Holman's MS. history of Leyton, quoting MS. *penes* Peter Le Neve; the confirmation was witnessed by Hubert, Abp. Cant. (1193–1205). For the wood of Leyton, see Wallwood, below, p. 195.
[29] *Feet of F. Essex*, i. 119.
[30] *Cal. Chart. R.* 1226–57, 433; *V.C.H. Essex*, ii. 130.
[31] *V.C.H. Essex*, i. 515.
[32] Ibid. 347, iv. 227; *Complete Peerage*, x. 351.
[33] *V.C.H. Essex*, ii. 130. Gilbert did not, however, grant Leyton church to the abbey; the church of 'Leya' (Dugdale, *Mon.* v. 587–8), identified as Leyton in *V.C.H. Essex*, ii. 130, was the church of 'La Lee' (*Cal. Close*, 1302–7, p. 373) or Lee Chapel, cf. *P.N. Essex* (E.P.N.S.), 163.

[34] Ibid.
[35] *Feud. Aids*, ii. 151, 176.
[36] *Cal. Inq. p.m.* i, p. 203.
[37] Morant, *Essex*, ii. 320.
[38] D.L. 25/1581 (calendar in E.R.O., T/A 8); *Cal. Pat.* 1330–34, 160. This grant was confirmed in 1406 (*Cal. Pat.* 1405–8, 157).
[39] *Cal. Inq. Misc*, iii, p. 307; 'Liston' is printed as 'Lyfton'.
[40] C 137/13; *Feud. Aids*, ii. 225.
[41] S.C. 6/962.
[42] *V.C.H. Essex*, ii. 132; *Feet of F. Essex*, iv. 224.
[43] *L. & P. Hen. VIII*, xx (1), pp. 524–5, 532, 677.
[44] Ibid. xxi (1), p. 351.
[45] *D.N.B.*
[46] C 142/100/30; *Cal. Pat.* 1555–57, 499; *D.N.B.*; W. H. Hutton, *St. John Baptist College*, 23.
[47] C 142/100/30; B.M. Add. Ch. 39412; Kennedy, *Leyton*, 14. Oliver Cromwell was the Protector's uncle.
[48] Kennedy, *Leyton*, 14; B.M. Add. Ch. 39073; C.P. 25(2)/139/1755; E.R.O., Q/RSg 2, 3 (gamekeeper's deputations 1735, 1760).

his estates to his brother, Sir William Ryder (lord mayor of London in 1600), and to Sir Thomas Lake (secretary of state, 1616), husband of Sir William's daughter Mary, in trust to pay off his debts and provide for his children.[49] Later the same year a chancery commission awarded two-thirds of the manor to Sir William Ryder and Sir Thomas Lake, who had bought off Sir Baptist Hicks, to whom it was mortgaged. The remaining third was reserved for Edward Ryder's eldest son, Edward, a royal ward.[50] Sir William Ryder died in 1611, leaving his share to his two daughters, Mary Lake, and Susan, widow of Sir Thomas Caesar, subject to an annuity to their mother.[51] In 1617 Edward Ryder apparently came of age and conveyed his share, including the manor-house, to his cousin Mary, and her husband, Sir Thomas Lake.[52] After Lake died in 1629 the manor appears to have formed part of his widow's jointure; she was described as lady of the manor in 1636.[53]

Lake's son, Sir Thomas Lake, sold the manor in 1650 to Captain George Swanley, Bernard Ozler, and Robert Abbott. Swanley's share is said to have included the site of the manor.[54] John Smith (d. 1655), a London merchant, subsequently purchased Abbott's one-third share, and by his will, dated 1653, devised it, subject to the life interest of his niece, Elizabeth Coker, widow, to the poor of the parishes of St. Swithin and St. Peter Eastgate, Lincoln.[55] Swanley lived in Leyton and took an active part in parish affairs.[56] By his will, proved 1658, he devised his third of the manor to his wife, Barbara (d. 1686) with reversion to his son William (d. 1688).[57] This third subsequently became vested in George Swanley's three daughters, Martha, Lady Clutterbuck, Sarah Limberry, and Mary, wife of John Hanson.[58] In 1696 John Chinnall bought Sarah Limberry's ninth.[59] Lady Clutterbuck's share was purchased by Oliver Martin in 1696 and sold by him the following year to Chinnall, who had by then also acquired Mary Hanson's ninth. In 1703 Chinnall sold Swanley's reconstituted third share to David Gansel.[60] Bernard Ozler's share apparently passed to Robert Ozler, who by his will, proved 1698, left his whole estate to Charles Hopton, his cousin. Hopton sold Ozler's third share of the manor to David Gansel in 1710, probably to raise money for the free school to be provided under

Ozler's will.[61] David Gansel died in 1714[62] and was succeeded by his son, David (d. 1753), and he by his son Col. (later Lt.-Gen.) William Gansel, who died in debt in 1774. General Gansel's affairs passed into Chancery and his heirs did not receive permission to dispose of his property until 1783. Gansel's two-thirds of the manor were then purchased by John Pardoe, a director of the East India Company.[63] In 1794 Pardoe purchased the remaining third from the corporation of Lincoln, less their one-third share in the reversion of the Forest House estate, which they had already sold to Samuel Bosanquet (d. 1806).[64] John Pardoe (d. 1798) was succeeded by his grandson, John Pardoe (d. 1870).[65] By 1843 the demesne comprised only 131 a.[66] John Pardoe was succeeded by his son, the Revd. John Pardoe (d. 1879), vicar of Leyton, 1848–73. His son, the Revd. John Pardoe (d. 1892), rector of Graveley (Herts.), was succeeded by his son, Lt.-Col. Frank Lionel Pardoe (d. 1948). His only surviving son, Lt.-Col. Philip Pardoe, is the present (1966) lord of the manor.[67]

A house called Leyton Grange was occupied by John Hanger, husbandman, in the 1470s.[68] In 1535 Thomas Campion, merchant tailor of London, obtained a 60-year lease of the manor-house of Leyton, in which the parlours, buttery, stable, and hayhouse were mentioned.[69] This lease of the 'grange of Leyton' was bequeathed by him in 1539 to his son, William,[70] subject to his widow's life interest. The manor or grange house was mortgaged to Anthony Holmead by Edward Ryder in 1608.[71] This earliest recorded house probably lay east of Leyton church and may have disappeared about the late 1640s when the site of the grange house and 'the ground on which it stood' is first mentioned, though the gatehouse apparently remained.[72] The house later known as Leyton Grange probably occupied the site of its predecessor; it was built by David Gansel (d. 1753) to his own designs and completed in 1720. The house, although not large, had considerable architectural pretensions. Contemporary engravings show a front elevation of two storeys and five bays, the three central bays being flanked by Corinthian pilasters and crowned by an open scrolled pediment behind which was a small dome; four classical figures stood on the balustraded parapet. The central doorway had a semi-circular porch

[49] P.C.C., 33 Dorset; L.R.L., Deeds (Barns extracts 2, 2a); *D.N.B.* (Ryder and Lake).
[50] L.R.L., Deeds (Barns extracts, 1, 1a, 2, 2a).
[51] Kennedy, *Leyton*, 14; P.C.C., 119 Lawe.
[52] L.R.L., Deeds (Barns extracts, 1, 1a).
[53] C 142/490/97; L.R.L., Deeds (Barns extracts, 3, 3a, and Lee 1).
[54] L.R.L., Deeds (Barns extracts, 12, 12a); Kennedy, *Leyton*, 15; Morant, *Essex*, i. 23; E.R.O., T/P 195/1, no. 5 (Holman MS.).
[55] Kennedy, *Leyton*, 15, 205, 255; *Rep. Char. Com.* (Essex) H.C. 216, p. 159 (1835), xxi (1); E.R.O., D/DBq O3, Q1 (gives date of Smith's death as 5 Apr. 1655); the will, proved 1655 in P.C.C. (349 Aylett), expressed a wish to be buried in Leyton. For the almshouses founded by Smith, see below, p. 239.
[56] L.R.L., L55.6. MS Rate Collection Bk., 1651–1704; his widow was rated for property in Low Leyton Street, 1662.
[57] P.C.C., 539 Wootton (Geo. Swanley), 13 Foot (Barbara Swanley), 156 Exton (Wm. Swanley); L.R.L., L55.6 MS. Rate Collection Bk., 1651–1704 (note of burial of Barbara Swanley, 1686).
[58] P.C.C., 539 Wootton; Burke, *Landed Gentry* (1847), i. 236 (Martha m. Sir Thomas Clutterbuck of Warkworth, d. 1682).
[59] E.R.O., T/P 195/1 (no. 5).
[60] Kennedy, *Leyton*, 15; Strype, *Stow's Survey* (1755, 6th edn.) ii. 777.
[61] Kennedy, *Leyton*, 15, 173–5; E.R.O., T/P 195/1 (no. 5). Robert Ozler's relationship to Bernard is not known. For the free school see below, p. 233.
[62] L.R.L., L97 Q. Transcript of Leyton Bur. Reg.
[63] G. O. Rickword, 'The story of a short-lived County Family' (*E.R.* liii. 81); *E.R.* iv. 50; Kennedy, *Leyton*, 79.
[64] Kennedy, *Leyton*, 15; Act for vesting . . . estates devised by . . . John Smith . . ., 35 Geo. III, c. 54 (priv. act). For the Forest House estate, see below, p. 188.
[65] L.R.L., Deeds (B.R.A. 333/14–16; calendar, E.R.O., T/A 12/2/11); Kennedy, *Leyton*, 15.
[66] E.R.O., D/CT 221.
[67] Burke, *Landed Gentry* (1952 edn.); *Army List* (1966) p. 1472.
[68] *Cal. Close*, 1476–85, 61; *Early Chanc. Proc.* i. 372.
[69] S.C. 6/962.
[70] P.C.C. 31 Dyngeley.
[71] L.R.L., Deeds (Barns extracts 1, 1a; the whereabouts of the originals is unknown; calendar E.R.O., T/A 12/2/8).
[72] E.R.O., T/P 194; L.R.L., Deeds (Barns extracts, 3, 3a, 8, 8a; calendar, E.R.O., T/A 12/2/8).

with a round-headed niche above it. The grounds are shown with an ambitious layout, including converging avenues of trees and a forecourt flanked by out-buildings. The house lay on the line of the present Grange Park Road, north of Church Road.[73] In 1730 Gansel purchased East Donyland Hall.[74] This may explain his sale of Leyton Grange to (Sir) John Strange, later Master of the Rolls,[75] about 1735, thereby separating the house from the manor.[76] Strange (d. 1754) added two wings to the Grange before 1746 and altered the grounds.[77] After his death his son, John, sold the house to Thomas Blayden (d. 1780), governor of Maryland,[78] whose heirs sold it in 1781 to Nathaniel Brassey. Thomas Lane bought it from Brassey in 1796; his son, John, was living there in 1824.[79] William Rhodes, brickmaker, the grandfather of Cecil Rhodes, was John Lane's tenant between 1829 and 1843.[80] John Lane was residing there in 1848.[81] Edward Charrington, the brewer, was the tenant from about 1855 until the Grange was sold in 1860 to the British Land Company, who demolished it in the following year and developed the estate.[82]

When John Pardoe bought part of the manor in 1783 he already owned a red-brick house on the north side of Capworth Street, with grounds stretching back to Lea Bridge Road. He had bought it in 1763 from one of the heirs to Sir Richard Hopkins's estate, which was broken up in 1746. The house, which was square in front with bow-windows at the back, may have been built by Anthony André about 1758 to replace an older one. From 1783 it became Leyton manor-house.[83] Between about 1800 and 1820 it was leased to Thomas Flower Ellis; it was empty between 1826 and 1831, but John Pardoe lived there from 1832 until his death in 1870. The Revd. John Pardoe occupied the house in 1874; it was burnt down in 1884.[84]

The *BARCLAY PARK* estate was built up in the 19th century by the Barclays, the bankers,[85] by the purchase of adjoining properties; the two largest were the house known in the 19th century

as Barclays or Knotts Green House[86] and another house, owned in the 18th century by the Bertie family,[87] known in the late 19th century as Leyton House. The estate was bounded by the present Lea Bridge Road, Leyton Green Road, and James Lane, and adjoined the Forest House estate.

The Knotts Green House property probably originated in the house and 7 a. of land at Diggons Cross, with 7 a. more at Leyton Bridge, for which Thomas Curteys paid rent in 1537–8.[88] In 1631 William Johnson left a house and an old decayed tenement at Diggons Cross, with adjoining closes containing 10 a., and about 21 a. land including an 8 a. close at Leyton Bridge, to his son Thomas. In 1649 Thomas sold this to Thomas Hopkins, whose daughter, Alice, married Sir Thomas Lee. In 1698 the Lees sold it to Peter Cartwright.[89] In 1768 Charles Jackson had a 40-year lease of what appears to be the same property, with its adjoining 10 a., but by then described as on Knotts Green.[90] In 1786 he bought it from the heirs of Richard Burbidge and his wife Mary.[91] In 1787 Gilbert Slater (d. 1793), an East India merchant, replaces Charles Jackson as owner in the land tax assessments.[92] He had married an Elizabeth Jackson (d. 1797) in 1784 and the property may have come to him under some form of settlement.[93] Slater left the house to his wife, who in turn left it to their son, James, a minor. In 1815 James sold it to John McTaggart, whose father John (d. 1810), a Scottish shipping merchant, had acquired the lease of it, with 38 a. land, in 1798.[94] In 1821 John McTaggart sold it to Robert Barclay (d. 1853).[95] In 1843 it amounted to 31 a., with a further 8 a. adjoining, leased from Samuel Bosanquet of Forest House.[96]

The house and grounds owned by the Bertie family in the 18th century were sold in 1788 by Catherine Dorothy, daughter of Peregrine Bertie, with 20 a. of land, to William Masterman (d. 1845).[97] In 1843 Masterman owned about 50 a. in Leyton and the Walthamstow Slip.[98] His son, John, died in 1862, when the house and about 27 a. were sold

73 *Vitruvius Britannicus*, iii (1725), pl. 94 (reproduced in *Essex in Pictures*, E.R.O. Publications No. 15, 1952); 'Leyton Grange . . . the seat of David Gansel . . . who designed and executed it himself', bird's-eye view engraved by T. Schynvoet and printed by Jos. Smith (1729); 'The Grange, Leyton . . . the seat of John Lane esq.', by J. C. Carter (E.R.O., Pictorial Collections); Gough, *Britannia*, ii. 50 (quoted, Walford, *Greater London*, 484); E.R.O., T/P 194; Kennedy, *Leyton*, 317–18.
74 *E.R.* liii. 81; Morant, *Essex*, ii. 186.
75 *D.N.B.*; Lysons, *London*, iv. 168–9.
76 E.R.O., T/P 194; Strype, *Stow's Survey* (1755, 6th edn.), ii. 777.
77 J. Rocque, *Carte topographique des villes de Londres . . . et de leurs environs*, 1746; E.R.O., T/P 194.
78 Lysons, *London*, iv. 162, 172; E.R.O., T/P 194; Strype, *Stow's Survey* (1755, 6th edn.) ii. 777. Blayden first appears in the rate books in 1756: L.R.L., L55.6 MS. Poor Rates, 1755–74.
79 Kennedy, *Leyton*, 76, 316; L.R.L., L55.6 MS. Poor Rates 1755–1825.
80 Kennedy, *Leyton*, 317; L.R.L., L55.6 MS. Poor Rates, 1838–40; *D.N.B.* (Cecil Rhodes); *E.R.* lvi. 19–22.
81 *White's Dir. Essex* (1848).
82 *Kelly's Dir. Essex* (1855); Kennedy, *Leyton*, 317–18; F. Temple, 'Leyton Grange' (*Leytonstone Express and Independent*, 17 Nov. 1950).
83 L.R.L., L55.6 MS., Poor Rates, 1755 f.; Kennedy, *Leyton*, 315; E.R.O., D/DWv T80; L.R.L., Deeds (B.R.A. 333.12; calendar E.R.O., T/A 12/2/11).

84 Kennedy, *Leyton*, 315; *White's Dir. Essex* (1848); L.R.L., L55.6 MS., Poor Rates, 1783–1835; *Kelly's Dir. Essex* (1874); F. Temple, 'Story of some modern street names' (*Leytonstone Expr. and Ind.* 20 Apr. 1951).
85 P. W. Matthews (ed. A. W. Tuke), *Hist. of Barclays Bank*, 30–50.
86 Kennedy, *Leyton*, 332.
87 Ibid. 333; Lysons, *London*, iv. 170.
88 S.C. 6/962 (Stratford Langthorne Accts. 1537–8).
89 E.R.O., T/A 12/2/6, 11, 13. F. Temple's identification of Knotts Green House with the messuage and 12 a. land by Knotts Green owned by the Goldsmith family in the 17th century (cf. *An account of Knotts Green otherwise Barclays*) does not appear to be correct.
90 E.R.O., D/DB T792/5.
91 E.R.O., D/DB T792/3, 5, 6.
92 E.R.O., Q/RPl 59, 60. Slater had been Jackson's tenant in 1786.
93 Elizabeth's relationship to Charles Jackson has not been found; she was the daughter of Philip Jackson, who, with John Jackson, was trustee during her son's minority: E.R.O., D/DB T793/6. On the Slater tomb at Hendon, the arms incorporate those of Jackson: *E. Nat.* xxvi. 167.
94 E.R.O., Q/RPl 59–88, D/DB T793/4; F. Temple, *Account of Knotts Green otherwise Barclays*, 13.
95 E.R.O., Sale Cat. A1023; Temple, *Knotts Green*, 13–14.
96 E.R.O. D/CT 221 (tithe map and award).
97 E.R.O., D/DB T792/7, 8; Kennedy, *Leyton*, 333.
98 E.R.O., D/CT 221, 382.

to Joseph Gurney Barclay, son of Robert.[99] By 1863 the house had come to be known as Leyton House.[1]

The Barclays also bought neighbouring fields and small properties, and by 1898, when J. G. Barclay died,[2] the estate, with park and gardens, covered a compact 100 a. In 1898 the estate was auctioned and, with the exception of the house and 2½ a. grounds, sold for development.[3]

The original house at Diggons Cross, for which Thomas Hopkins was assessed at 11 hearths in 1662, and his widow, Sarah, at 12 in 1670 and 1674,[4] had been pulled down some years before 1786, and replaced by a 'capital modern built house', unnamed but described as 'on Knotts Green', perhaps built by Charles Jackson.[5] The new house was a plain two-storeyed building of yellow brick with a mansard slate roof.[6] From a brick dated 1791 it appears that Gilbert Slater, who occupied it from 1786 to 1793,[7] built bow-windowed extensions on each side. In contrast to the plain exterior the interior was elaborately decorated, possibly by Slater. The entrance hall had plaster moulded panels. Other rooms were enriched by plaques, mouldings, and Adam-style ceilings, and by mahogany and satinwood doors. The first-floor landing had an open-columned screen, and open, oval balustraded gallery. Slater, an ardent gardener, planted the grounds with rare items collected from China, the East Indies, and America.[8] After 1821 Robert Barclay added an east wing to the house, which became known as Barclays or Knotts Green House. In 1854 an observatory was built in the grounds.[9] In 1900 Knotts Green House was bought by Livingstone medical college for missionaries, which had opened in Bow in temporary premises in 1893. During the Second World War the college was occupied by the army. It reopened in 1946 but moved to Reigate (Surr.) soon after 1947.[10] The house remained empty until 1951 when it was acquired by Leyton borough council.[11] In 1952 the Livingstone Court flats were built in the grounds.[12] The house itself, leased as offices for a few years after 1954,[13] was demolished in 1961.[14] A block of flats called Livingstone College Towers was built on the site in 1963.[15]

The Bertie family's house, called Leyton House from the late 19th century, is said to have been built in 1712 and pulled down in 1915.[16] A watercolour dated 1902 shows an 18th-century house of two storeys, the main front of five windows having attics above, and flanked on each side by flat-roofed bays.[17] The site was occupied in 1968 as a bus garage. Further south the former gardener's lodge stands at right angles to the road, backing on Barclay Hall. It was originally a substantial timber-framed house, probably of the 17th century, but the front and side walls have been rebuilt in brick. Only the back wall and the tie-beam roof contain original timbers. The building was attached about 1896 to the Barclay Hall mission[18] as a house for the missioner. It was modernized in 1949.[19]

The *BOURNE* estate in Leytonstone was created by Robert Harrington of Leytonstone, a native of Witham-on-the-Hill (Lincs.), who, by will proved 1657, left all his lands in Leyton to the poor of Bourne (Lincs.).[20] The copyhold lands, in the manor of Ruckholt, had been surrendered to the use of his will in 1650.[21] The Bourne trustees do not appear to have been admitted until 1673.[22] In 1736 the copyhold was described as 5 houses and 47 a. land.[23] In 1843 the estate comprised some 39 a., including the Crown Inn, Leytonstone, the west side of Leytonstone High Road from Church Lane to the present railway line (including 20 a. of land occupied by Protheroe and Morris, nurserymen), and 11 a. of inclosed marshland meadow, part of Tumbling mead and the site later of the Temple Mills sidings waggon works.[24] The nursery ground was developed as a building estate in 1894.[25] The estate, which in 1962 amounted to 28 a.,[26] produced in 1967 an income of £12,334, derived from rents and managed by trustees.[27]

The *FOREST HOUSE* estate, near Whipps Cross, lay between the forest, the Phillebrook, and James Lane, and included part of the Walthamstow Slip.[28] It originated in 1492, when the abbot of Stratford, lord of the manor of Leyton, leased to John More of London, stockfishmonger, three crofts called 'Cristemassebreche', containing about 20 a., for three consecutive terms of 99 years

[99] Kennedy, *Leyton*, 333; E.R.O., *Sale Cat.* A1023; E.R.O., D/CT 221, 382.
[1] O.S. Map 25″, LXXIII.1 (1863 edn.). It should not be confused with the original Leyton House, in Church Road, still known as such in 1863, but known as St. Agnes Orphanage by 1882.
[2] *E.R.* vii. 137.
[3] Temple, *Knotts Green*, 15–17; E.R.O., *Sale Cat.* A1023.
[4] E.R.O., Q/RTh 1, 5; E 179/246/22.
[5] E.R.O., D/DB T792/5, 6.
[6] Pevsner, *Essex* (2nd edn.), 268; L.R.L., L72.2 Prints.
[7] E.R.O., Q/RPl 59–66.
[8] *E.Nat.* xxvi. 162–8, 198–204.
[9] Temple, *Knotts Green*, 15–16; G. F. Bosworth, *Some more Walthamstow houses* (Walthamstow Ant. Soc. xxix), 14. For the house in 1865 see above, plate f.p. 188.
[10] *Livingstone College Year Bk.* 1900–10, pp. 8–9; C. E. Harford, 'Livingstone College: past, present and future' (*Climate*, v. 30–5); L.R.L., L35 Pamph. Letters (1955) from S. Hoyte, on principals of college; F. Temple, *Knotts Green House*, 18.
[11] L.R.L., *Leyton B.C. Mins. and Reps.*, 1950–1, 1951–2.
[12] *Yesterday, today and tomorrow: housing in Leyton.*
[13] Temple, *Knotts Green*, 19.
[14] Pevsner, *Essex* (2nd edn.), 268; photographs of the house and its interior, taken before demolition, are in L.R.L. (L72.2 Prints).

[15] *Yesterday, today and tomorrow.* See also below, p. 213.
[16] L.R.L., 72.2 Prints (pencil drawing of back view of Leyton House by Miss Thomas, with notes).
[17] L.R.L., L72.2 Prints (watercolour of Leyton House by A.G.S. 1902).
[18] See p. 231.
[19] Inf. from Mr. L. Medley.
[20] L.R.L., General deeds (1655); *Bourne, Lincolnshire: the Official Guide* (1963). Morant, *Essex*, i. 23, confuses this bequest with John Smith's bequest by will dated 1653 of a third of the manor of Leyton to the poor of two parishes in Lincoln City (see above, p. 186) and cf. Lysons, *London*, iv. 161, and Hammock, *Leytonstone*, 18–19.
[21] E.R.O., D/DCw M39.
[22] Ibid. M40.
[23] E.R.O., D/DCw Z1.
[24] E.R.O., D/CT 221; the main estate is also named on the 1721 map of Ruckholt manor (Kennedy, *Leyton*, f. p. 18).
[25] *Leyton Local Bd. Cttee. Reps.* 1894–5; Hammock, *Leytonstone*, 18–19.
[26] *Bourne . . . Official Guide* (1963).
[27] Inf. from Clerk to Bourne United Charities Trustees.
[28] An account of this estate is given in F. Temple, *The house and estate known as Forest House* (1957).

WALTHAMSTOW: PALACE THEATRE, BUILT IN 1903

LEYTON: LONDON CITY MISSION GARDEN PARTY AT BARCLAYS IN 1865

WOODFORD: SLATE FACTORY AND RAY HOUSE ABOUT 1776

WEST HAM: HAM HOUSE IN THE LATER 18TH CENTURY
Demolished 1872

(expiring 1789).[29] In 1650, when the manor was divided into three parts,[30] the profits of the lease were similarly divided. In 1750 Samuel Bosanquet (d. 1765) secured from David Gansel renewal of the lease as to two-thirds of the property for 300 years from its expiry in 1789, on the same terms as before.[31] Lincoln corporation were apparently prepared to negotiate a similar renewal as to their one-third share, but instead in 1780 sold to Samuel Bosanquet (d. 1806), the leaseholder, the reversion expectant (in 1789) of their one-third share.[32] In 1858 the trustees of John Pardoe sold to Samuel R. Bosanquet the reversion of the remaining two-thirds.[33]

At an unknown date John More's lease came into the hands of Richard Barnes, whose widow, Agatha, in 1568, granted it to Thomas Powle and others, in trust for herself and her children.[34] In 1579 Powle and the children sold it, with 'the Forest house', to Henry Johnson of Woodford,[35] whose widow, Dorothy, sold it in 1592 to Ralph Colston, skinner.[36] Barnes, Powle, and Colston were all keepers of Leyton walk in Waltham forest.[37] In 1599 Ralph also bought from Oliver Cromwell, lord of the manor, a lease of an orchard, for two consecutive terms of 99 years, backdated to 1591.[38] In 1601 Ralph sold both leases, said to cover 33 a. and the orchard, to Sir Thomas Baker (d. 1625) of Sissinghurst (Kent). Sir Thomas already owned a house and 16 a. freehold land, which he had acquired about 1594 from Edmund Withypoll; these lay in Walthamstow (the Slip) and had hitherto divided the leasehold crofts.[39] Sir Thomas's son, Thomas (d. 1657), was heir to the freehold, and also inherited the leasehold, which had formed his mother Constance's jointure, on her death in 1625.[40] In 1658 his widow, Alice, married Charles, Lord Goring (d. 1671), who became earl of Norwich in 1663. Thomas Baker had died intestate, and it appears that Alice, who administered the estate, retained the leasehold portion, while the freehold portion was inherited by Sir John Hanmer, whose mother, Elizabeth, was Thomas's sister. In 1665 the estate was reunited when Sir John conveyed the freehold to Lord and Lady Norwich.[41] Shortly before her death in 1680 Lady Norwich, in financial difficulties, assigned Forest House and 44 a. of land to Sir Henry Capel and his wife Dorothy, her niece and

next-of-kin.[42] They redeemed mortgages made by Lady Norwich and in 1681 sold the estate to (Sir) James Houblon (d. 1700), a founder of the Bank of England, and friend of Evelyn and Pepys.[43] In 1703 Sir James's sons, Wynne and James, sold it to Sir Gilbert Heathcote (d. 1733), another founder of the Bank and lord mayor of London (1710), reputed to be the richest commoner in England and the meanest.[44] In 1743 Sir Gilbert's son, Sir John, sold it to Samuel Bosanquet (d. 1765), a London merchant of Huguenot descent.[45] The estate as conveyed by Heathcote appears to have extended to Whipps Cross, including the site of the house later known as Forest Lodge.[46] In the next hundred years, during which the estate descended in succession to Samuel Bosanquet (d. 1806), governor of the Bank of England (1792), and his son Samuel (d. 1843), it was consolidated by the purchase of Whitings Grove (1783) and enlarged by acquisitions elsewhere in Leyton.[47] In 1843 Samuel R. Bosanquet (d. 1882) owned some 139 a. in Leyton and the Walthamstow Slip.[48] After 1831 Dingestow Hall (Mon.) became the Bosanquets' permanent home,[49] but until the 1920s the family continued to be one of the two largest landholders in Leyton.[50] In 1889 Samuel C. Bosanquet (d. 1925) sold Forest House and 44 a. grounds to the West Ham board of guardians.[51] Forest Lodge was sold in 1900[52] and 30 Bosanquet properties on the west of Leyton High Road, with a rental value of £1,804 a year, in 1926.[53]

By 1568 the leasehold estate included a dwelling-house.[54] By 1579 there were two, the chief one called the Forest House.[55] It lay at the north-east end of James Lane. Between 1601 and 1625 Sir Thomas Baker enlarged the 'great' house,[56] which was known as Goring House during the occupancy of the earl of Norwich but called Forest House in his will.[57] In 1664 Lord Norwich secured a 99-year lease of an acre of the adjoining forest waste, with licence to inclose it; and in 1681 Sir Henry Capel was licensed to build a brick wall round the garden created there.[58] According to the hearth tax assessments of 1662, 1670, and 1674 it was the largest house in Leyton, with 23 hearths.[59] In 1683 John Evelyn recorded that James Houblon was building a new house.[60] This was the house which, with later alterations, including a stuccoed exterior and perhaps

[29] S.C. 6/962; E.R.O., D/DBq T1/1, D/DBq T1/24A, D/DAc 154. Strype erroneously associated Forest House with the abbot of Waltham, and was copied by Salmon, Morant, Wright, and Kennedy (*Leyton*, 329). The confusion may have arisen from references to Waltham forest in documents associated with the house.
[30] See p. 186.
[31] E.R.O., D/DBq T1/67, 68.
[32] Act for vesting absolutely one third part of three crofts . . , 20 Geo. III, c. 21 (priv. act).
[33] E.R.O., D/DBq E8, f. 26.
[34] E.R.O., D/DBq T1/2, D/DBq T1/24A, D/DAc 154.
[35] E.R.O., D/DBq T1/4, D/DBq T1/24A, D/DAc 154.
[36] E.R.O., D/DBq T1/5. Ralph was the son of Gabriel, and the brother of Elizabeth (see below, p. 195).
[37] See p. 204 and Fisher, *Forest of Essex*, 384.
[38] E.R.O., D/DBq T1/6, D/DBq T1/24A, D/DAc 154.
[39] E.R.O., D/DBq T1/7, 10, 11, D/DAc 154; Temple, *Forest House*, 8.
[40] E.R.O. D/DBq T1/7, 24A, 19.
[41] E.R.O., D/DBq T1/13, 17, 24A; *Diary of John Evelyn*, ed. E. S. de Beer, iii. 538, iv. 306.
[42] E.R.O., D/DBq T1/19-22.
[43] E.R.O., D/DBq T1/24A, 29, 31, T/P 120.

[44] E.R.O., D/DBq T1/33-4; *D.N.B.*
[45] E.R.O., D/DBq T1/50, 52, 55, 58-9. See also below, p. 257. For the Bosanquet family, see G. L. Lee, *Story of the Bosanquets* (1966).
[46] See sketch plan, E.R.O., D/DBq T1/85.
[47] E.R.O., D/Bq E8.
[48] E.R.O., D/CT 221, 382; cf. E.R.O., D/DBq T10/1.
[49] Temple, *Forest House*, 25.
[50] Cf. *Kelly's Dir. Essex* (1922). The other was Earl Cowley.
[51] See p. 214.
[52] E.R.O., D/DBq T4.
[53] E.R.O., D/DBq E7.
[54] E.R.O., D/DBq T1/2.
[55] E.R.O., D/DBq T1/4.
[56] '. . . did newly erect part of . . .', *Proc. Epping Forest Com.*, pp. 1966-7.
[57] E.R.O., D/DBq T1/18, 67, 68.
[58] E.R.O., D/DBq T1/24A, 30.
[59] E.R.O., Q/RTh 1, 5; E 179/246/22.
[60] *Diary of John Evelyn*, ed. E. S. de Beer, iv. 306. Evelyn had visited the earl of Norwich at Forest House in 1669 and admired the pictures there which Thomas Baker had acquired in Spain: ibid. iii. 538.

the addition of the third storey, survived until 1964. It had eleven bays, a capped parapet, and a four-column Tuscan portico.[61] To the north-west stood a red-brick stable range of the original date. The entrance hall of the house and many of the first-floor rooms had late-17th-century panelling, some of it painted. There was a fine well staircase with twisted balusters and moulded panelling. Decorative work in the Adam style was commissioned by the Bosanquets, the initials SB being painted with classical subjects on one of the ceilings. Sir John Soane's workmen were busy at the house in 1786 and the front was altered to his design in 1787, but the bills only amounted to £130.[62] The house was assessed in 1785 for 80 windows, a number only exceeded in Leyton by the Great House.[63] Mary Bosanquet, the Wesleyan preacher, grew up there.[64] The Bosanquet family occupied it until 1831 after which it was let until about 1884. After the West Ham guardians bought it in 1889, it lay empty for several years until it was adapted as an auxiliary workhouse for about 300 old men.[65] Transferred to West Ham borough council in 1930, it became a home for old people.[66] It closed in 1962, when a new hostel, Samuel Boyce Lodge, was opened in the grounds. In 1964 it was demolished and the site sold to the N.E. Metropolitan Hospital Board.[67] A long stretch of the red-brick garden wall, presumably that erected by Sir Henry Capel in 1681, is still standing.

The GREAT HOUSE estate lay in the centre of Leyton, on the east side of the High Road, opposite the sports ground. It adjoined the Moyer House estate on the east, and was mainly copyhold of the manor of Leyton. In 1686 Nathaniel Tench (d. 1710), one of the first directors of the Bank of England, became a ratepayer in Leyton,[68] having apparently united two properties hitherto separately rated. One of these may have been the house known later as Walnut Tree House and now as Essex Hall.[69] In 1697 Nathaniel's son, Fisher Tench (d. 1736, created a baronet 1715) was admitted with his wife Elizabeth to a capital messuage and 29 a. of land on the surrender of his father.[70] In 1713 Fisher Tench also acquired, from the Atlee family, the adjoining copyhold property called Cross House alias Bushes (which had belonged to Thomas Pullison in 1572),[71] with 30 a. of land.[72] Sir Fisher was succeeded by his son, Sir Nathaniel

Tench (d. 1737), and he by his sister Jane, who in 1740 married a widower, Adam Soresby.[73] When she died in 1752 her stepson, William Soresby, was admitted.[74] He surrendered the estate in 1758 to Thomas Oliver (1740–1803), whose father, Richard (d. 1763), a West India merchant, acted for him and may have bought it in his name. Thomas's son, Richard, was admitted in 1803.[75] At that date the estate comprised some 94 a.,[76] including the Great House, Cross House, Walnut Tree House,[77] and Knotts and Brooklands.[78] In 1805 William Fry was admitted, then in 1806 John Theophilus Daubuz (d. 1830).[79] The estate continued in the Daubuz family until the late 1870s.[80] In 1843, with Knotts and Brooklands, it comprised some 133 a.[81] Walnut Tree House and the house on the site of the original Cross House were sold to Jesse Jackson, a builder, about 1878.[82] The Great House was sold to developers with 50 a. of land in 1881 and the estate built over in the 1880s and 1890s,[83] the house itself being demolished in 1905.

Essex Hall, formerly Walnut Tree House, which is thought to be the oldest surviving building in Leyton today (1968), may be the original house acquired by Nathaniel Tench about 1686. It always belonged to the Great House estate, and, though it was said to have been kept as a dower-house, it was usually let after the Great House was built to the north-east of it.[84] It is a structurally timber-framed building of two storeys, probably dating from the 16th century. Later alterations have obscured most of its ancient features but the first-floor jetties have survived at the front, along one side, and at a gable-end at the rear. The house appears to have been remodelled c. 1700 and again in the early 19th century, giving the long front facing Jesse Road and the two sides a largely Georgian appearance. Most of the sash windows and the wide central porch with Doric columns date from the early 19th century. Also in the 19th century sheets of slate were screwed to the framing to give a flush surface externally. The house contains a late-16th-century stone fire-place with a frieze carved with arabesques and an early-18th-century staircase with twisted and turned balusters. A sundial in the garden formerly bore the date 1666.[85] In 1804, when Richard Oliver leased the house to Robert Smith, it was called Walnut Tree House, and in 1813 when J. T. Daubuz leased it to Joseph Cotton,

---

[61] Pevsner, *Essex* (2nd edn.), 269.
[62] Dorothy Stroud, *Architecture of Sir John Soane*, 158; inf. from Miss D. Stroud.
[63] E.R.O., T/P 150.
[64] G. L. Lee, *Story of the Bosanquets*, 57–8.
[65] *Official Record, Visit of ... King and Queen with ... Princess Mary, to Whipps Cross Hospital*, 1917; Wilkinson, *Leyton*, 20; West Ham Corporation Act, 1898, 61 & 62 Vict. c. 259, pt. VIII (local act); L.R.L., L34 Pamphlet, *Souvenir of opening of new infirmary*, 1903; Temple, *Forest House*, 28.
[66] D. McDougall, *Fifty Years a borough*, 193.
[67] W. Ham C.B.C. *Welfare Cttee. Reps.* 1959–64.
[68] L.R.L., L55.6 MS. Rate Collection Bk., 1651–1704.
[69] L.R.L., L72.2 Pamph. (M. L. Savell, 'Walnut Tree House', TS.).
[70] E.R.O., D/DU 101/1 (1737). Fisher Tench also replaces Nathaniel in the rate book in 1697: L.R.L., L55.6 MS.
[71] E.R.O., D/DB T729.
[72] E.R.O., D/DU 101/1 (1713).
[73] Kennedy, *Leyton*, 326; E.R.O., D/DU 101/1 (1737, 1740).

[74] E.R.O., D/DU 101/1 (1752); M. L. Savell, 'Echoes of Old Leyton', No. 14, 'The Great House Estate', *Walthamstow Guardian*, 4 June 1965.
[75] E.R.O., D/DU 101/1 (1758), 101/3 (1803); E. Gunn, *The Great House*, 13.
[76] L.R.L., L72.2 Pamph. (Newscutting, 1803, Sale of estate of Thomas Oliver).
[77] E.R.O., D/DB T1554, 1559.
[78] See p. 192.
[79] E.R.O., D/DU 101/3 (1805, 1806). For the Daubuz family, see M. L. Savell, 'Daubuz Family' (L.R.L., TS.).
[80] Savell, 'The Daubuz Family' (L.R.L., TS.); Savell, 'The Innes Family' (L.R.L., TS).
[81] E.R.O., D/CT 221. The estate still comprised 130 a. in 1867, when a plan was made of it: E.R.O., D/DU 686.
[82] Savell, 'The Innes Family', p. 8 (L.R.L., TS.); L.R.L., L72.2 Pamphlet (Savell, 'Walnut Tree House', TS.).
[83] E.R.O., D/DCy T19; L.R.L., L72.2 F. (Great House Estate Sale Plan, 1881); L72.2 Plan (c. 1895); L72.2 Plan. S. (*post* 1895).
[84] L.R.L., L72.2 Pamph. (Savell, 'Walnut Tree House', TS.).
[85] Kennedy, *Leyton*, 330.

previously an elder brother of Trinity House and father of William Cotton, preservation of the large walnut tree in the garden was stipulated.[86] The 1804 lease provided that the house should not be used for a school, tavern, or factory, but it did indeed become a school about 1870.[87] Since 1890 it has been let to the Leyton Constitutional (now Conservative) Club, and known as Essex Hall.[88]

The Great House was built by Fisher Tench, probably before 1712, when his 'handsome mansion house' is mentioned.[89] It is possible that 'Tench Hall' named on a map of c. 1700, was the new house.[90] It was a large mansion of two storeys, basement, and attics, built in the 'Wren' style of the period.[91] The walls were of dark red brick with dressings of lighter brickwork and stone. The entrance front faced the high road[92] and consisted of a central block flanked by lower and slightly recessed side wings. The main block had full-height Corinthian pilasters and a central pediment, while the wings had rusticated stone quoins. The whole façade, of thirteen bays, was surmounted by a modillion cornice, a panelled parapet, and hipped roofs with dormer-windows; six large stone vases broke the line of the parapet. The garden front was of similar size and character. The cupola now on the tower of St. Mary's church[93] may have been a central feature of the house. Internally there were doorcases, panelling, and a fine staircase, of the original date.[94] Paintings on the ceilings and staircase dome, of gods, goddesses, cupids, and flowers, said to have been executed by Sir James Thornhill, still survived in 1895.[95] A stable range with a pedimented central feature stood at right angles to the house at its south-west end and the grounds were elaborately laid out with canals and vistas.[96] The main floor (including the drawing room and dining room) and first floor were remodelled in the later 18th century according to plans made for Thomas and Richard Oliver by the Adam brothers.[97] Decorative features included a fine plaster ceiling and delicately carved chimney-piece and doors in the drawing room, all of which survived in 1901–2.[98] Sash windows were probably inserted throughout

the house at this time. The central portico with columns on the entrance front may also have dated from this remodelling, though it could have been later.[99] In 1785 the house was assessed for 98 windows, the highest assessment in Leyton.[1] After the death of Lewis Charles Daubuz in 1839 the house was often let. It was occupied for a few years from 1850 by Canon Nathaniel Woodard's military and engineering school, where boys from Lancing College studied science, fortification, map reading, surveying, and Hindustani.[2] In 1855 it was a boarding-house.[3] The last Daubuz to occupy it, in 1858–60, was James, Lewis's son.[4] In 1883 the estate developers sold it to the tenant, who was using it as a private lunatic asylum.[5] In 1895 it was put up for sale again, with the remaining 5 a. of grounds, as a building estate.[6] After remaining on the market for some time[7] it was demolished in 1905[8] and flats built on the site. In 1909 a memorial plaque was put up.

Cross House had been pulled down by 1806 and the house now known as Grove House built on the site, which lies farther south in High Road.[9] It was occupied by Magdalen Daubuz, sister of John Theophilus, who left it to her in 1830. When she died in 1844 she left it to her niece, Mrs. Robert Innes, who let it until 1878, when she sold it to Jesse Jackson, who lived there. Since 1879 it has been known as Grove House.[10] It is a three-storeyed house of yellow brick with a columned porch and bay-windows. For the late-Victorian treatment of the bay-windows Jesse Jackson was probably responsible, and he may also have added the top storey. The house now (1968) belongs to the Leyton and District Trades Hall and Institute.

The *HALIWELL PRIORY* estate originated in the 12th-century gift to the priory of Haliwell in St. Leonard, Shoreditch, by Gunnore de Valognes of the 'vill' of Leyton, and the 40s. rent substituted for this in 1201.[11] The estate lay in Ruckholt manor, mainly between the present Langthorne Road (in 1721 called Hollewel Lane),[12] and Leytonstone High Road, and included Halywell (later Holloway) Down.[13] In the late 15th century the priory demesne

[86] E.R.O., D/DB T1554, 1559; *D.N.B.*
[87] See p. 238.
[88] Wilkinson, *Leyton*, 20; L.R.L., L72.2 Pamph. (Savell, 'Walnut Tree House', TS.).
[89] L.R.L., L55 MS. Chwdns' Accts. 1681–1723 (vestry min. 1712); Gunn, *Great House*, 19.
[90] Robert Morden and Joseph Pask, *Essex, c.* 1700.
[91] Gunn, *Great House*, 17, 21–2. Gunn has suggested that William Dickinson, one of Wren's assistants, may have carried out the design. Dickinson was married at Leyton in 1701 (Kennedy, *Leyton*, 10) but no other evidence has been found to connect him with the Great House. The marriage register describes him as 'bachelor, clerk to Sir Christopher Wren, Kt., for the works at Greenwich'. As the register distinguishes carefully between bachelors and widowers, the entry must relate to William Dickinson junior (d. 1725), not his father, William Dickinson senior (d. 1702); both of the Dickinsons worked under Wren: H. M. Colvin, *Biog. Dict. Eng. Architects*, 173.
[92] Gunn (p. 18) refutes the statement sometimes made (e.g. Kennedy, *Leyton*, 327) that the 19th-century front of the house was originally the back, and that the house was once E shaped.
[93] See p. 218.
[94] Gunn, *Great House, passim*; L.R.L., L72.2 Prints.
[95] E.R.O., *Sage Colln. Sale Cats.* Vol. 1/6; Gunn, *Great House*, 19.
[96] Gunn, *Great House*, 12; Kennedy, *Leyton*, 326; E.R.O., T/A 2/12/13 (1715, agreement with neighbour to preserve a 'fair and clear view').

[97] A. T. Bolton, *Architecture of Robert and James Adam*, 21. Photographs of the drawings are in L.R.L., where they may be compared with photographs of the house (L72.2 Prints). Gunn was not aware of the existence of these plans, which are in the Soane Museum.
[98] Gunn, *Great House*, 20; L.R.L., L72.2 Prints.
[99] Gunn, *Great House*, 22.
[1] E.R.O., T/P 150.
[2] L.R.L., L35 Pamph. M. L. Savell, 'Canon Nathaniel Woodard and the Woodard Military and Engineering School' (TS.).
[3] Kennedy, *Leyton*, 329.
[4] Ibid.
[5] Ibid.; E.R.O., *Sage Colln. Sale Cats.* Vol. 1/6.
[6] E.R.O., *Sage Colln. Sale Cats.* Vol. 1/6; Wilkinson, *Leyton*, 20.
[7] Gunn, *Great House*, 17.
[8] Photographs and drawings of the house, before and during demolition, are in L.R.L., L72.2 Prints. Measured drawings of the house, made in 1901–2 are reproduced in E. Gunn, *The Great House, Leyton*, 1903 (London Survey Monograph No. 4); the originals are in L.R.L.
[9] Kennedy, *Leyton*, 338.
[10] Ibid.; Savell, 'Daubuz Family' (L.R.L., TS.), Savell, 'Innes Family' (L.R.L., TS.)
[11] See p. 194. For Haliwell Priory, see *V.C.H. Middlesex*, i. 174–8.
[12] Kennedy, *Leyton*, f.p. 18. The original of this 1721 map of Ruckholt is in L.R.L.
[13] *E.R.* xiv. 204 f.

lands, listed in a tithe dispute with Stratford Abbey, comprised 87 a.[14] In 1535 the estate was valued at £3 6s. 8d.[15] In 1542 it was granted to Morgan Phillips *alias* Wolfe (d. 1552), the King's goldsmith,[16] who was granted the manor of Rayhouse in Barking in the same year.[17] In 1550 Phillips bought remission from the Crown of yearly rent for the property.[18] The estate descended with Rayhouse until 1570, when it was in the possession of Walter Morgan and his wife Jane,[19] but by 1581 it had become separated from Rayhouse.[20] Its subsequent ownership has not been traced, but it is said to have been broken up.[21]

The estate called *KNOTTS*, later *THE POPLARS*, from which Knotts Green probably took its name, is first mentioned in 1588,[22] and may have originated in the estate in Leyton and Walthamstow inherited by William Knott from his father Thomas before 1451.[23] In 1452 William sold this estate to Henry Benet, goldsmith of London, who sold it in 1456 to John Wardale, clerk.[24] In 1576 Thomas Pullison bought from Walter Fish four pastures, all 'lately parcels of . . . Knotts in Leyton or Walthamstow'; this suggests that the estate had partly broken up.[25] In succeeding centuries the ownership of fields in the Knotts Green area was constantly changing. In 1587 Robert Rowe[26] died seised of the capital messuage called Knotts 'and other tenements there', his son and heir Thomas (later Sir Thomas) being a minor.[27] Thomas, explorer of the Amazon and first English ambassador to India and Turkey,[28] parted with it, for in 1611 Toby Wood died seised of it with over 20 a. of land.[29] In 1630 his son and heir Toby claimed for Knotts common of pasture in the forest, with pannage, estimating the lands at 100 a.[30] In 1670 this claim was repeated on behalf of Mary Bland, widow.[31] In 1671 John Bland was party to a conveyance of the capital messuage called Knotts to Mathias Goodfellow,[32] a merchant who occurs in hearth tax lists of 1670 and 1674, assessed for 14 hearths,[33] and who is rated at £50 from 1669 to 1685. In 1686 Goodfellow is replaced in the rate books by Captain Thomas Pulman (d. 1703), who is rated until 1702.[34] The estate has not been traced further by name, but the location given in 1685 and 1698 of a small croft which abutted westward on the estate held at times by Thomas Rowe, John Bland, and Mathias Goodfellow, shows that it lay north of Wild Street Lane (now Lea Bridge Road).[35] It may, therefore, be identified with the 'capital mansion' and grounds on either side of Hoe Street and opposite the pond in the road, which was owned in the mid 18th century, with 34 a. of land, by Peter Cartwright's heirs.[36] It is shown, with the pond, on Rocque's map, 1741–5. The property was acquired in 1791 by Henry Wildman; it then comprised about 46 a., including adjoining land and Court House in Walthamstow. The whole estate was sold in 1819 to William Copeland (d. 1826), partner of the potter, Josiah Spode. His son, William Taylor Copeland, as lord mayor of London in 1835, entertained Princess Victoria and her mother, the duchess of Kent, to lunch there.[37] In 1843 Copeland held it with about 29 a. in Leyton; the whole estate was sold in 1854 and broken up.[38] The house on the site in 1775, then called the White House, was apparently being rebuilt at that date.[39] The altered or new house, known later as The Poplars, was described as one of the largest and finest in Leyton.[40] In 1892, when it was put on the market with 8 a. as a building estate, it had 17 bedrooms.[41] It was demolished about 1893, when the plans of the layout of the Poplars estate were approved.[42] The only known picture shows part of the front of a brick building having a central three-storeyed block of five bays with an oval window in its pediment; the central windows have stone architraves with a balustrade below that on the first floor. There were lower flanking wings with balustraded parapets.[43]

The *KNOTTS AND BROOKLANDS* estate probably originated as part of the 15th-century Knotts estate described above. In 1537 Robert Elrington[44] was the manorial tenant of land at Phillebrook called Brokeland and also of land at Knotts Green.[45] Forty-five acres called 'Knottes lands' were mortgaged in 1542 by John Elrington and his son Robert[46] and in 1545 John Elrington and his wife, Ursula, sold a messuage and 29 a. to George Baldock.[47] In 1572 an arbitration award against Henry Wolley acknowledged their son,

[14] E.A.T. ii. 191.
[15] Valor Eccl. (Rec. Com.), i. 395.
[16] L. & P. Hen. VIII, xvi. p. 576.
[17] V.C.H. Essex, v. 209.
[18] Cal. Pat. 1549–51, 222.
[19] Morant, Essex, i. 23; V.C.H. Essex, v. 209; Cal. Pat. 1569–72, 65.
[20] C 66/1064 m. 35; C.P. 25(2)/131/1683; C 66/1211 m. 17.
[21] Wright, Essex, ii. 497.
[22] C 142/220/36.
[23] Cal. Close, 1447–54, 333; E.R.O., D/DB T729. In 1415 a Richard Knotte was abbot of Stratford: V.C.H. Essex, ii. 133.
[24] Feet of F. Essex, iv. 45, 51. See also above, p. 184.
[25] L.R.L., L72.2, Pamphlet (Extracts made by F. Temple of deeds at Westminster Abbey, especially W.A.M. 3363).
[26] Son of Sir Thomas Rowe, Lord Mayor of London in 1568.
[27] C 142/220/36; Lysons, London, iv. 280–1.
[28] D.N.B.
[29] C 142/329/175.
[30] Ibid.; Fisher, Forest, 376–7; Proc. Epping Forest Com., p. 1878.
[31] Proc. Epping Forest Com., p. 1879.
[32] L.R.L., General deeds (1671).

[33] E.R.O., Q/RTh 5; E 179/246/22; Kennedy, Leyton, 322–3.
[34] L.R.L., L55.6 MS.
[35] L.R.L., Deeds (Lee 6, 9).
[36] E.R.O., D/DE T184, D/DB T792/3.
[37] G. F. Bosworth, Some Walthamstow Houses (W.A.S. xii), 21–2; Kennedy, Leyton, 337–8; D.N.B., Josiah Spode.
[38] E.R.O., D/CT 221; Bosworth, Some Walthamstow Houses (W.A.S. xii), 22.
[39] L.R.L., L55.6 Rate Bks. There was more than one White House in Leyton (cf. Kennedy, Leyton, 337).
[40] Kennedy, Leyton, 337–8. Cf. Bosworth, Some Walthamstow Houses (W.A.S. xii), 21–2.
[41] E.R.O., Sale Cat., A557; the plan shows a large house of irregular shape, a substantial part of it behind the main front.
[42] Wilkinson, Leyton, 23; Leyton Local Bd. Cttee. Reps. 1893–4.
[43] L.R.L., Prints (photograph, n.d., much obscured by shrubbery).
[44] The alternative form, Elderton (cf. V.C.H. Essex, iv. 255), is sometimes used.
[45] S.C. 6/962.
[46] E.R.O., D/DB T729.
[47] Feet of F. Essex, iv. 280.

Robert's title to 24 a., called Knotts and Brooklands, lying east of the high road leading from the church to Stratford, abutting north on Cross House.[48] This description shows that the estate lay in that part of Leyton High Road known by 1838 as Blue Row,[49] and now backing on Buckland Road, together with the land in Phillebrook to the east and south. In 1645, when the estate contained 28 a. of freehold land with houses, under the will of Edward Martin, weaver, a moiety of it was charged with the provision of bibles for the children of the parishes of Bermondsey and St. Olave, Southwark, (Surr.), and St. George (Lond.).[50] In 1796 this legacy was producing £9 a year, but was said to be capable of improvement on the expiry of a long lease.[51] By 1803 the estate was being held with the Great House.[52] In 1811 John Theophilus Daubuz, who held the lease with three more years to run and who already owned the other half of the estate, bought the freehold of the half charged with the provisions of Martin's will. The estate, which then consisted of 21 dwellings and 26 a. of land,[53] continued in the Daubuz family,[54] held with the Great House estate.[55] The Blue Row houses were sold about 1853 and the land in the 1870s.[56]

The manor of *MARK* in Leyton and Walthamstow is dealt with under Walthamstow.[57]

The *MOYER HOUSE* estate, built up in the 17th century, combined two adjoining properties, Masters and the Brewhouse. Masters, which lay on the south side of Masters (later Wallwood or Moyers) Lane, now Hainault Road, belonged to Richard Hanger, who by his will (proved 1479) left 5 marks to repair the road leading from that house to the church.[58] Thomas Hanger, great-grandson and heir of Richard, sold Masters in 1530 to Morgan Wolfe, the King's goldsmith.[59] It was held of the manor of Leyton, and in 1541 Wolfe was granted the annual 17*d.* rent formerly payable to Stratford Abbey.[60] The estate had descended by 1570 to Morgan Wolfe's son, Walter Morgan, and his wife Jane.[61] Jane, widowed, was holding it in 1585 when Seth Lacy and John Mathew sold the reversion of Masters after her death to Hugh Kayle. Kayle's son Robert sold it in 1617 to Robert Hudson.[62] In 1649 Hudson's executors sold it, with about 19 a. of land, to Captain Lawrence Moyer (d. 1685), warden of Trinity House,[63] an outspoken Parliamentarian.[64]

The Brewhouse estate, also held of the manor of Leyton, lay mainly between Masters and Wallwood.[65] Before 1449 it belonged to John Hanger, and it may have come into Richard Hanger's hands about that date.[66] The land comprised 17 a. in 1537, when it was held by John Hanger.[67] It was copyhold, and in 1562 Francis Hanger surrendered it with the land to John Pragell, after whose death Richard Stoneley was admitted in 1585.[68] In 1590 Stoneley surrendered it to John Fuller, who mortgaged it in 1592 to Thomas More,[69] with an additional 9 a. of pasture by Wallwood. In 1599, the money not having been repaid, More was admitted, but returned the property to Fuller on condition that he should not alienate it for six years to anyone but More, who was then to have it below the market price and be repaid his admission fine. The property finally came into More's hands in 1606 and was immediately sold to Richard Baldock, but reserving to More and his son, Christopher Cresacre, the foot- and cart-way from Wallwood to their dwelling house. As this way[70] led off the high road past Masters and the Brewhouse property, this suggests that the More house was that shown on Rocque's map (1741–5) on the north side of the lane, near the junction with the high road, on the site occupied in the late 19th century by Lea House and Lamb's printing works.[71] The covenant reserving the way was repeated in 1615 in favour of Cresacre More, when Richard Baldock sold the Brewhouse estate to Robert Hudson. In 1649 Hudson's executors sold this estate also, by then apparently freehold, to Lawrence Moyer. It then comprised the house and 26 a. of land.[72]

Lawrence Moyer's estate passed after his widow's death in 1687 to his nephew Lawrence (d. 1721), son of Samuel Moyer. By 1739 the estate stretched from Moyer's Lane to the angle of Grove Green Road beyond the Phillebrook, and amounted to 69 acres.[73] Lawrence's son and heir Benjamin[74] died in 1759. His daughters Lydia (d. 1822), who married John Heathcote,[75] and Catherine Moyer (d. 1831), succeeded to the estate as coheirs. Catherine left it to her nephew, John Heathcote (d. 1838), for life, then to his third son, the Revd. George Heathcote.[76]

The Moyer land was let to farmers after the death of Benjamin Moyer. Twelve acres farmed together in 1843 became known as Cashford's farm.[77] The remaining 48 a., farmed in the 19th century by the

---

[48] E.R.O., D/DB T729. For Cross House, see above, p. 190.

[49] L.R.L., L55.6 MS. Rates 1838.

[50] Act for vesting in J. T. Daubuz . . . moiety of premises in Low Leyton . . . , 51 Geo. III, c. 183 (priv. act).

[51] Lysons, *London*, i. 557.

[52] L.R.L., L72.2 Pamphlet (Newscutting 1803, Sale of estate of late Thomas Oliver). For Great House estate see above, p. 190.

[53] 51 Geo. III, c. 183 (priv. act).

[54] cf. L.R.L., L55.6 Poor Rates, 1840–1, pp. 46 f.

[55] See tithe map, E.R.O., D/CT 221. See also above, p. 190.

[56] L.R.L., L55.6 MS. Rate Bks. 1852–78.

[57] See p. 260.

[58] E.R.O., D/AER 1/11.

[59] E.R.O., D/DLc T28. For Morgan Wolfe, see *V.C.H. Essex*, v. 209.

[60] *L. & P. Hen. VIII*, xvi, p. 277; S.C. 6/962.

[61] *Cal. Pat.* 1569–72, p. 65.

[62] E.R.O., D/DLc T24, 28, D/DQ 53/51.

[63] E.R.O., D/DLc T24, D/DQ 53/51; Kennedy, *Leyton*, 27; E.R.O., T/P 150.

[64] *Cal. S. P. Dom.* 1660–1, 516; E.R.O., Q/SR 406/35.

[65] E.R.O., D/DLc T28, T/M 173, D/CT 221 (tithe map and award).

[66] *Cal. Close*, 1447–54, 165–6.

[67] S.C. 6/962.

[68] E.R.O., D/DLc T28.

[69] See p. 223.

[70] Shown on a map of Wallwood, 1777: E.R.O., T/M 173. Rocque (1741–5) also shows it, without naming it; he incorrectly names Grove Green Road 'Wallwood Lane'.

[71] More's Leyton estate comprised two copyhold tenements. Comparison of the tithe map (E.R.O., D/CT 221, nos. 228, 229) with the Leyton court rolls (E.R.O., D/DU 101/1–3) confirms that the two adjoining sites on the north of Wallwood Lane, near the high road were copyhold.

[72] E.R.O., D/DLc T28, D/DQ 53/52.

[73] Kennedy, *Leyton*, f.p. 18; E.R.O., T/M 173, T/M 403, T/P 150.

[74] See *V.C.H. Essex*, v. 102. [75] Ibid.

[76] E.R.O., T/P 150.

[77] Ibid.; Kennedy, *Leyton*, 338–9; E.R.O., D/CT 221.

Bent family, with a farm-house built after 1843 near the angle of Grove Green Road, were known as Bents or Grove farm.[78] Shortly before his death in 1893 George Heathcote sold the estate for development. By 1894 the Tottenham and Forest Gate railway ran across it and occupied a large area for sidings and goods yards.[79]

Masters became known as Moyer House. Captain Lawrence Moyer mentions in his will that he had enlarged it.[80] It was always occupied by the Moyer family, and in 1783 was described as the oldest house in the parish.[81] It was also one of the largest, being assessed for 12 hearths in 1662, and for 69 windows in 1785.[82] Benjamin's widow, Frances, lived there with her daughter Catherine until her death in 1804, and Catherine, the last occupant, until her own death in 1831. By 1832 the house had been pulled down;[83] but some out-buildings remained, converted to a farm cottage for the tenant of Cashford's farm.[84]

The manor of *RUCKHOLT* lay in the south and south-east of the parish and included the hamlet of Leytonstone.[85] In 1815 it comprised 892 a.[86] 'Leintuna' was held in 1066 by Swein the swarthy as a manor and 3 hides, worth 20s.[87] In 1086 it was held in demesne by Peter de Valognes and was worth 40s.[88] Gunnore de Valognes, great-granddaughter of Peter, gave the 'vill' of Leyton to Haliwell priory; in 1195 the gift was confirmed by Richard I.[89] In 1201, apparently in settlement of a dispute arising out of this gift, Gunnore and her second husband Robert fitz Walter bought from the priory some lands in Leyton, but granted to it 40s. of rent in Leyton.[90] In 1201, too, the wood of 'Rocholt' ('rook wood'), held by Hugh de Marney, is mentioned.[91] Robert outlived both his wife and their daughter and heir Christine, widow of William de Mandeville, earl of Essex. After his death in 1235 the Valognes barony devolved upon three co-heirs, daughters of Gunnore's cousin, William de Valognes (d. 1219).[92] These three, Lora, wife of Henry de Balliol, chamberlain of Scotland, Isabel, wife of David Comyn, and Christine, wife of Peter de Maule,[93] in 1240 granted a carucate in Leyton for ½ knight's fee to William de Marney; William was holding the wood of Ruckholt in 1248.[94] In 1257 Peter de Maule and his wife Christine granted a messuage and a carucate in Leyton to William de

Bumpstead for ½ knight's fee.[95] The connexion between this and the preceding transaction is not clear. In 1275 Robert de Bumpstead gave John de Munchensy £20 for life from his lands in Leyton, 'for his praiseworthy counsel'.[96] In 1284 or 1285 William, son of Robert de Bumpstead, granted his manor called 'Rocholte Hall' to Sir Richard de la Vache.[97] In 1286 it was agreed that William was to hold the manor of Richard in fee tail for ½ knight's fee, but in the event of William dying childless the manor was to revert to Richard, after the death of William's wife, Maud.[98] William de Bumpstead was alive and holding ½ knight's fee in 1303, but dead by 1316, when his widow, Maud, had letters of protection.[99] In 1331–2 his son William vested the manor in trustees, including John de Shordych and his wife Ellen. This was apparently a settlement in advance of his marriage to Joan, daughter of Nicholas de Shordych, about 1341, when the manor was vested for life in Sir John de Shordych with remainder to William, Joan, their heirs, and the heirs of William.[1] In 1345 the manor was forfeited to the Crown, because William had been hanged for killing Sir John de Shordych.[2] The Crown returned it to Joan, William's widow, later in the year, but she died soon after without issue. In 1346 Sir Richard de la Vache, cousin and heir of the other Sir Richard de la Vache, held as ½ knight's fee the manor formerly held by William de Bumpstead,[3] having succeeded to the reversion of the estate. In 1359 Sir Richard's surviving trustee enfeoffed Adam Fraunceys, citizen and mercer of London, and his wife Agnes.[4] Adam Fraunceys died in 1375 and was succeeded by his son, Adam, who, as a knight, was holding the manor in 1412.[5] Sir Adam Fraunceys died in 1417;[6] his wife Margaret (d. 1444 or 1445), held Ruckholt in dower until her death.[7] The manor then passed to their daughter, Agnes, wife of Sir William Porter. Agnes died in 1461; her heir was Sir Thomas Charleton, son of her sister, Elizabeth, who had married Thomas Charleton.[8] Sir Thomas died seised of the manor in 1465 and was succeeded by his son, Sir Richard.[9] Between 1417 and 1465 the manor was regarded as part of the honor of Warenne because Steeple Bumpstead, the chief holding of the Bumpstead family, formed part of that honor in 1086.[10] Sir Richard was killed in 1485 at Bosworth. By a

[78] E.R.O., T/P150, D/CT 221; O.S. Map 6″, Essex, LXXIII (1873–82 edn.).
[79] E.R.O., T/P150; E. Carter, *Hist. Geog. of Railways*, 472.
[80] E.R.O., T/P150. A small perspective view drawing of the house on a map of 1739 shows the wing he added: E.R.O., T/M 403.
[81] Kennedy, *Leyton*, 270.
[82] E.R.O., Q/RTh 1, T/P 150.
[83] E.R.O., T/P 150.
[84] Kennedy, *Leyton*, 338–9; E.R.O., D/CT 221.
[85] Kennedy, *Leyton*, map of manor of Ruckholt, 1721, f.p. 18. The original is in L.R.L.
[86] E.R.O., D/DCy P2B.
[87] *V.C.H. Essex*, i. 536.
[88] Ibid.
[89] *E.R.* xiv. 204; Dugdale, *Mon.* iv. 393.
[90] *Cur. Reg. R.* i. 450, 454; *Feet of F. Essex*, i. 22. For the Haliwell Priory estate, see above, p. 191.
[91] *Cur. Reg. R.* i. 454.
[92] *The Ancestor*, xi. 129–35; Farrer, *Feudal Cambs.* 165; *V.C.H. Essex*, iv. 251; I. J. Sanders, *English Baronies*, 12.
[93] The name is variously spelt (e.g. Maune, Manne, Mamine).
[94] *Feet of F. Essex*, i. 140, 168.

[95] Ibid. i. 217.
[96] *Abbrev. Plac.* (Rec. Com.), 265. See also below, p. 205.
[97] Morant, *Essex*, i. 24; Hatfield House, Cecil MS. 291 (cartulary of Adam Fraunceys), ff. 1v–2v. Cf. J.I. 1/243 m. 12, which identifies Robert as 'of Bumpstead Steeple' and names the manor 'Rochenhall'.
[98] *Feet of F. Essex*, ii. 54; Cecil MS. 291.
[99] *Feud. Aids*, ii. 151; *Cal. Pat. 1313–1327*, 457; Farrer, *Honors and Knights' Fees*, iii. 401.
[1] *Feet of F. Essex*, iii. 59; Farrer, *Honors and Knights' Fees*, iii. 401; Cecil MS. 291.
[2] *Cal. Inq. Misc.* ii, p. 486.
[3] *Cal. Close, 1343–6*, 625–6; *Feud. Aids*, ii. 176; Cecil MS. 291.
[4] *Feet of F. Essex*, iii. 124; Cecil MS. 291.
[5] S. L. Thrupp, *Merchant Class of Medieval London*, 341; *Feud. Aids*, vi. 438.
[6] C 138/29.
[7] E.R.O., T/P 195/1 (no. 5) (Holman, MS. History of Leyton).
[8] C 140/4.
[9] Kennedy, *Leyton*, 18–19; E.R.O., T/P 195/1 (no. 5).
[10] C 138/29; C 140/4; E.R.O., T/P 195/1 (no. 5); *V.C.H. Essex*, i. 475.

subsequent Act of Attainder his lands were for-feited to the Crown, who granted Ruckholt to Sir John Risley.[11] Ruckholt then descended along with King's Place in Chigwell,[12] until 1592, when William, Lord Compton, sold it to Henry Parvishe.[13] Parvishe died in 1593, having settled the manor on his wife, Elizabeth, daughter of Gabriel Colston, for life.[14] The widow married Michael Hicks, secretary to Lord Burleigh; Hicks held courts in right of his wife from 1595 to 1611, and after his death in 1612 she held them in her own name until 1633.[15] In 1635 Gabriel Parvishe, son and heir of Henry Parvishe, sold the manor to his stepbrother, Sir William Hicks, Bt.[16] It descended with the baronetcy until 1720, when Sir Harry Hicks, Bt., grandson of Sir William, sold it to Robert Knight, cashier of the South Sea Company.[17] Later the same year Knight sold it to his brother-in-law, Benjamin Collyer,[18] who mortgaged it in 1727 to Robert Knight the younger, and in 1731 was forced to part with his equity of redemption to Knight. In 1731 Knight sold Ruckholt to the trustees under the will of Frederick Tylney of Tylney Hall, Rotherwick (Hants). Tylney's will, proved in 1725, made provision for his niece, Dorothy Glynne, wife of Richard Tylney, Earl Tylney, and her children. Her eldest son Richard died unmarried in 1736, and the estate passed to his brother John.[19] Ruckholt subsequently descended as part of the Wanstead House estate.[20] In 1843 the demesne comprised 264 a.[21]

A house was in existence by 1257,[22] known by 1284 as Ruckholt Hall.[23] Henry Parvishe, lord of the manor from 1592 to 1593, is said to have built a manor-house,[24] probably the Ruckholte listed in 1594 in Norden's *Description of Essex* among houses of note.[25] Reference in 1719 to the old house 'which stood near the now house' suggests that Parvishe's house was built on a new site.[26] Ancient entrench-ments still visible at Ruckholt in 1803, including a moated circular embankment, may have marked the site of the medieval house.[27] Parvishe's house was described by Evelyn in 1659 as a melancholy old house surrounded by trees and rooks; Pepys in

1665 thought it a 'good seat . . . let run to ruin'. Its condition was probably the result of Sir William's misfortunes during the Civil War and Inter-regnum.[28] Sir William Hicks, 2nd baronet, who succeeded his father in 1680, at great expense encased the house in brick and improved it in other ways.[29] A map of 1721 shows it standing on the south side of Temple Mills Lane (now Ruckholt Road), half-H-shaped in plan, its main axis lying north–south and the wings projecting on the east front. Between 1721 and 1728 Benjamin Collyer altered the grounds, converting the Phillebrook to the north into a canal shaped like a keyhole, with an ornamental island at the west end.[30] The Tylneys did not occupy the house after purchasing the manor in 1731; it was converted into a public breakfasting house by William Barton between 1742 and 1744. For about six years the place was popular with the gentry, who were entertained with music and other gaieties on Monday mornings during the summer.[31] The house was pulled down in 1755–7; the materials sold included a marble hall chimney-piece about 13 feet high with trophies and entablature.[32] A farm-house, in existence by 1777, was built north of Temple Mills Lane with farm buildings lying south of the lane near the site of Ruckholt.[33] It was occupied by Samuel Turner until his death in 1804, when he was succeeded by his son, William,[34] who farmed about 180 a. at Ruckholt.[35] He was succeeded by his son-in-law, John Tyler, who was farming Ruckholt in 1843, and continued to do so until his death in 1880.[36] The house was occupied as a cottage hospital from 1889 to 1891,[37] when it was pulled down and Ruckholt Road board school[38] built on the site.[39]

The *WALLWOOD* estate lay in the north of Leytonstone, most of it in the manor of Leyton, but the south-east portion, including Wallwood house, in Ruckholt manor. It originated in the wood granted to Stratford Abbey by Richard Corbutio before 1200.[40] The abbey was licensed in 1248 to inclose the wood, and in 1253 it was disafforested.[41] In 1291 it was known as Corpychonesfrith, and by

[11] *Cal. Pat.*, 1485–94, 209–10; *Cal. Inq. p.m. Hen. VII*, i, pp. 22–3; ibid. iii, p. 477; *Rot. Parl.* (Rec. Com.), vi. 276.
[12] *V.C.H. Essex*, iv. 29.
[13] *Complete Peerage*, iii. 390–1; C.P. 25(2)/135/1726; B.M. Add. Ch. 24999.
[14] C 142/236/74; Kennedy, *Leyton*, 30.
[15] Morant, *Essex*, i. 24; *D.N.B.*; E.R.O., D/DCw M39; Kennedy, *Leyton*, 349.
[16] E.R.O., D/DCw T9.
[17] Ibid.; Kennedy, *Leyton*, 19.
[18] E.R.O., D/DCw T9; Morant, *Essex*, i. 25. For map of manor drawn up for Collyer, 1721, see Kennedy, *Leyton*, f.p. 18.
[19] E.R.O., D/DCw T9; Kennedy, *Leyton*, 19; E.R.O., Q/RSg 2 (entry, 7 Oct. 1731, gives date of authority by Richard Tylney as 5 Aug. 1731); E.R.O., D/DCw M41 (last court held by Collyer, 26 Jan. 1730/1).
[20] See p. 324.
[21] E.R.O., D/CT 221.
[22] *Feet of F. Essex*, i. 217.
[23] Cecil MS. 291, ff. 1v–2v; Morant, *Essex*, i. 24.
[24] E.R.O., T/P 195/1, no. 5 (Holman MS.).
[25] J. Norden, *Description of Essex* (Camd. Soc. 1st ser. ix), 34, and map.
[26] E.R.O., T/P 195/1, no. 5. Holman must be mistaken in identifying the old house as Parvishe's; there is no evidence of a house being built on a new site after 1593.
[27] E. W. Brayley and J. Britton, *Beauties of England* (1803), iv. 447; *V.C.H. Essex*, i. 285. A map of 1728

shows a circular mound adjoining the manor house on the west: E.R.O., D/DCy P3A.
[28] *Diary of John Evelyn* (Everyman edn.), i. 336; Kennedy, *Leyton*, 31, 319–20; *V.C.H. Essex*, ii. 239; *E.R.* xvii. 195.
[29] B. M. Lansdowne MS. 93, f. 55.
[30] Kennedy, *Leyton*, f.p. 18; E.R.O., D/DCy P3A (Survey of Ruckholt manor, 1728).
[31] Strype, *Stow's Survey* (1755–6, 6th edn.), ii. 776; Lysons, *London*, iv. 163; Kennedy, *Leyton*, 319.
[32] L.R.L., L72.2 Pamphlet (Newspaper cutting, June 1755, announcement of sale of materials of Ruckholt House); Strype, *Stow's Survey*, ii. 776; L.R.L., L47 MS. Ves. Min. Aug. 1757.
[33] Chapman and André, *Map of Essex*, 1777, sheet xxi; E.R.O., D/DCy P3, f. 86 (this map of c. 1815 marks the upper and lower gardens and traces of a canal west of the site of Ruckholt; there is no indication of the canaliza-tion of the Phillebrook). Cf. O.S. Map 6″, Essex, LXXIII (1873–82 edn.).
[34] Kennedy, *Leyton*, 318–19; E.R.O., D/DCy P3, f. 1.
[35] E.R.O., D/DCy P3; L.R.L., L55.6 MS. Rate Bk., 1807–25, e.g. rate assessed June 1812.
[36] Kennedy, *Leyton*, 318–19; E.R.O., D/CT 221; *White's Dir. Essex* (1848), 249.
[37] See p. 213.
[38] See pp. 235, 237.
[39] L.R.L., *San. Cttee. Reps.* 1889–91; L47 MS. Local Bd. mins. Nov. 1889.
[40] See p. 185.
[41] See p. 204.

1323 Wallewood[42] perhaps from the earthworks built to inclose it.[43]

After the Dissolution Wallwood was described as the king's wood in 1538.[44] The grants of the manor of Leyton to Lord Wriothesley in 1544–5 did not mention Wallwood, though his licence in the same year to alienate to Sir Ralph Warren included unnamed woods belonging to the manor. It is clear, however, that Wallwood was regarded as Crown property in the 16th century, with the Crown appointing woodwards.[45] A survey of the king's woods in 1604 included Wallwood,[46] but stated that Edward Ryder, as lord of the manor of Leyton, had challenged the Crown's title in the courts in Elizabeth I's reign.[47] Ryder actually devised Wallwood with the manor of Leyton on his death in 1609.[48] His grandson, Skinner Ryder, also claimed it in 1653,[49] but in 1655 a decree was made confirming the lord protector in possession[50] and in 1660 Ryder finally relinquished his claim.[51]

In 1660 Gobert Sykes was holding, presumably of the Crown, woodgrounds called Wallwood containing, with a small piece of marsh, 173 a. That year he leased them for 21 years to a Leyton grazier, Edmund Osmond, with covenants for the upkeep of the ditches, mounds, walls, and fences which inclosed the grounds, and an agreed allotment of timber for the purpose.[52] In 1693 the Crown leased Wallwood for 99 years to Richard Savage, Lord Colchester, later Earl Rivers.[53] Between 1679 and 1710 the wood was cleared[54] and became a farm. The Crown lease to Lord Colchester was acquired by the Owsley family, perhaps after the death of Lord Colchester in 1712 or of his daughter and heir Elizabeth in 1715,[55] and almost certainly by 1721.[56] The Owsleys also held by 1721 some copyhold property in Ruckholt manor, adjoining the Wallwood estate and farmed with it.[57] In 1778 Dorothea Owsley was granted a new lease from the Crown.[58] A map of 1777[59] shows that the Crown estate then comprised 159 a. lying south-west of the forest and Assembly Row.

From 1778 Wallwood farm descended separately from the dwelling-house which had been built on the estate.[60] The Crown lease of the farm was inherited from Dorothea Owsley by Robert Adams, grazier,

who was being rated for it from 1778.[61] It came later into the possession of Philip Sansom of Leytonstone House (d. 1815), whose daughter Elizabeth bought the farm from the Crown, as 119 a., in 1820.[62] She still held it in 1843, when it comprised 122 a. farmed by Richard Payze.[63] In 1850 Charles Sansom began the development of the farm as the Fillebrook estate; by 1860 the large brick houses in Fillebrook Road, backing on the railway line, had been built. Fairlop Road was laid out next, followed by Colworth, Wallwood, Hainault, Bulwer, and Lytton Roads.[64] The central part of this area was not built on at first, but let for grazing or for nursery-gardens. By 1887, however, there were 1,000 houses on the estate, which was completed by 1890.[65]

The original Wallwood farm-house adjoined Leytonstone High Road; it was built on the Owsleys' copyhold property in Ruckholt manor, and was in existence by 1721.[66] Richard Payze, the farm tenant, occupied it in 1843.[67] When the building of the railway in the 1850s cut off the farm-house from the farm a new farm-house was built at the end of Moyers Lane (now Hainault Road).[68] This disappeared with the development of the estate.[69]

There was no mention of a dwelling-house in the Crown lease of Wallwood to Lord Colchester in 1693,[70] but the evidence of the rate books suggests that by 1697 a house existed, which was occupied by Newdigate Owsley until his death in 1714, except for the years 1703–9, when John Lescalleet was the occupant.[71] By 1721 it was known as Wallwood House.[72] Charles Owsley (d. 1731), son of Newdigate, also lived there, from about 1719 until his death. From 1732 a succession of tenants of the Owsleys occupied the house.[73] In 1778 Dorothea Owsley leased it with about 40 a. of land for 31 years (the term of her own Crown lease) to Thomas Farrer, who had been occupying it since 1764. On Farrer's bankruptcy in 1783 his lease was sold to Robert Williams.[74] Between 1803 and 1812 George Millet occupied the house.[75] Williams died in 1814 just before the execution of a new 99-year Crown lease on his behalf backdated to 1809, the end of the Owsleys' term. The lease, which stipulated that the house was to be rebuilt within the next four years at a cost of at least £4,800, was

[42] *P.N. Essex* (E.P.N.S.), 102–3.

[43] E.R.O., D/DC 41/208. The suggestion in *P.N. Essex*, 102–3, that the name may derive from the wood's proximity to Roman remains found at Leyton Grange, and earthworks near Ruckholt, is unlikely. Wallwood was over ½ mile from Leyton Grange and even farther from Ruckholt; it adjoined neither.

[44] S.C. 6/962.

[45] *L & P. Hen. VIII*, xx (1), pp. 524–5, 532, 677; *E.R.* xv. 66; Fisher, *Forest*, 156, 319; *Cal. Pat. 1555–7*, p. 487, 1557–8, p. 458–9.

[46] *Rep. Sel. Cttee. on Royal Forests* (Essex), *1863*, H.C. 339, p. 88 (1863), vi.

[47] Ibid.

[48] P.C.C., 33 Dorset.

[49] *Cal. S. P. Dom. 1653–4*, 278; *E.A.T.* 3rd ser. i. 118.

[50] Fisher, *Forest*, 319.

[51] *Cal. S.P. Dom. 1660–1*, 294.

[52] E.R.O., D/DC 41/208.

[53] Lysons, *London*, iv. 164; *E.A.T.* 3rd ser. i. 120; E.R.O., D/DK T50.

[54] See p. 197.

[55] *E.A.T.* 3rd ser. i. 120.

[56] Thomas Archer's map of Ruckholt 1721 (Kennedy, *Leyton*, f.p. 18) shows Wallwood House and adjoining fields as 'Ouesley'.

[57] Ibid.

[58] E.R.O., D/DK T50.

[59] Thomas Richardson's map of estate called Wallwood in lease from the Crown, 1777: P.R.O., M.P.E. 441 (photocopy, E.R.O., T/M 173). The copyholds in Ruckholt manor and two freeholds (one Leytonstone House) are shown on a map of 1815–16: E.R.O., D/DCy P3, f. 96.

[60] See below.

[61] Lysons, *London*, iv. 650; *E.A.T.* 3rd ser. i. 123.

[62] E.R.O., T/M 173; *E.A.T.* 3rd ser. i. 123 (this incorrectly quotes the date as 1830).

[63] E.R.O., D/CT 221.

[64] *E.A.T.* 3rd ser. i. 123; O.S. Map 6″, Essex, LXXIII (1873–1882 edn.), marks 'Phillebrook' and Fairlop Roads.

[65] *E.A.T.* 3rd ser. i. 123–4.

[66] Ibid. 121; Kennedy, *Leyton*, f.p. 18.

[67] E.R.O., D/CT 221 (no. 75).

[68] O.S. Map 6″, Essex, LXXIII (1873–82 edn.).

[69] The site adjoined the junction of Leigh Road and Hainault Road, on the east side.

[70] E.R.O., D/DK T50.

[71] *E.A.T.* 3rd ser. i. 120.

[72] Kennedy, *Leyton*, f.p. 18.

[73] *E.A.T.* 3rd ser. i. 120–1.

[74] Ibid. 120–2; E.R.O., D/DPx T1; E.R.O., T/M 173.

[75] *E.A.T.* 3rd ser. i. 122. For Captain George Millett of the Loyal Leyton Volunteers, see Kennedy, *Leyton*, 290–4.

assigned in 1815 to William Cotton, the philanthropist, son of Captain Joseph Cotton of Walnut Tree House.[76] In 1816 the vestry consented to Cotton's inclosure of part of the forest, bringing the Wallwood boundary on the north-east up to the present (1968) Whipps Cross Road.[77] In 1817 Cotton purchased Wallwood House with 39 a. from the Crown.[78] The new house was erected in 1817–18 to the designs of John Walters on a site north-north-east of the old house; the contract with the builder, Thomas Cubitt, specified the use of Ipswich facing bricks and the best Portland stone.[79] It was a severely plain square building of two storeys with a pedimented portico on double columns on the north-west entrance front; the principal rooms faced south-east on the advice of Humphry Repton. A lower L-shaped wing, which may have incorporated older work, adjoined the main block on the south-west. It is known that some out-buildings of the former house and the kitchen garden had been retained.[80] William Cotton died in 1866; his son Sir Henry sold the estate in 1874 to John Griffin, who mortgaged it the following year.[81] Development plans, first laid before the local board in 1883,[82] were delayed by a boundary dispute with the adjoining Fillebrook estate, and by 1890 only six buildings were erected in Colworth Road.[83] By 1893 the Imperial Bank, Ltd., now the mortgagee and itself in liquidation, was in possession of the estate, which was sold in 1894 by the London Joint Stock Bank to Ernest Edward Rayner. In the same year Rayner sold Wallwood house with 5 a. to Thomas Ashbridge Smith. The Wallwood Park estate was then laid out on the remainder of the property.[84] T. A. Smith occupied Wallwood House until about 1921; the house was demolished shortly afterwards.[85]

ECONOMIC HISTORY. Until the 18th century the main occupation of the parish was agriculture. In 1086 six holdings in Leyton comprised 15 hides and 30 a.[86] Seven and a half plough-teams cultivated the arable, but it was noted that two could be added to one of Robert son of Corbutio's holdings. There was woodland for 490 swine (or $19\frac{1}{2}$ to each 100 a.),[87] and 149 a. of meadow. A rouncey, 15 swine, and 60 sheep completed the stock. The recorded population of 22 villeins, 19 bordars, and 2 priests had increased since 1066, when there were 16 villeins, 12 bordars, and 6 serfs. The Domesday details show that Corbutio's two holdings in the centre and north-east

had deteriorated. Since 1066 6 of 7 plough-teams, $7\frac{1}{2}$ fisheries, and a mill had disappeared, and the value had fallen from £7 to £3. But the smaller holding of Peter de Valognes in the south and east had improved. When he received it the only stock was 2 plough-teams, but since then a third had been added, also a rouncey and 11 swine; at 40s. the value of the holding had doubled.[88] De Montfort's holding in the south-east, adjoining Wanstead Flats, carried all the sheep listed.

The Domesday figures suggest that most of the woodland in 1086 lay in the north of the parish, where there was pasture for 310 swine on the Corbutio family's manor.[89] On the de Valognes manor in the south there was only woodland for 30 swine.[90] There is evidence of medieval forest clearance for cultivation taking place in the north-east in the names 'Degonesbraches' (1454), 'Clerks brachis' (1464), and 'Cristmassebreche' (1492).[91] In the 1590s 30 a. of woodland remained in Ruckholt manor in the south,[92] and 40 a. of woodland and 300 a. of heath and furze in Leyton manor in the north.[93] Three woods in the parish paid tithe to the vicar, Wallwood, Whitings Grove, and Ley Spring.[94] In 1604 Wallwood contained 120 a. well set with timber, though lately wasted and spoiled.[95] In 1679 it still carried 1,900 oaks and 4,000 hornbeams.[96] But by 1710 it had been felled and turned to arable and pasture.[97] So had Whitings Grove, 5 a., licensed to be felled in 1682.[98] Ley Spring was still standing in 1710[99] and in 1721 contained 18 a.;[1] but it was gone by 1843, when a 3 a. plantation behind Assembly Row was virtually all the woodland left in the parish.[2]

Field names of about 1480[3] imply open field cultivation in the Middle Ages. Arable fields included Northfield, Eastfield (29 a.), Broadfield (58 a.), and Cobingdowne. Cobingdowne recurs in 1648 as 7 a. called Copie Downe in the Common field, and in 1720 as 2 a. of arable in the Common field, called Copping Down.[4] Tenants' landholdings listed about 1480 included 10 of 5 a., each with 1 r. of meadow, and 4 more which were multiples of similar holdings, 3 of 10 a. with $\frac{1}{2}$ a. of meadow, and 1 of 20 a. with 1 a. of meadow.[5] This uniformity of size also suggests farming in common.[6] At least one of these 5 a. holdings with 1 r. of meadow survived in 1629.[7] Similar 5 a. holdings, each paying 18d. rent, existed in 1185 on the nearby Templars' estate in Leyton and Hackney (Mdx.). There the rent for a 10 a. holding (3s.) was the same as that for

[76] E.R.O., D/DPx T1; D.N.B.,; Hammock, *Leytonstone*, 12–13.
[77] Kennedy, *Leyton*, 302; *E.A.T.* 3rd ser. i. 122.
[78] E.R.O., T/M 173, D/DPx T1, 2, 5.
[79] E.R.O., D/DB T1564.
[80] E.R.O., D/DPx T5 (sale particulars, 1874); J. C. Loudon (ed.), *The landscape gardening . . . of Humphry Repton*, 500–4; L.R.L., L72.2 Prints.
[81] E.R.O., D/DPx T5.
[82] L.R.L., *Housing and Lighting Cttee. Reps.* 12 June 1883.
[83] *E.A.T.* 3rd ser. i. 125; E.R.O., *Sale Cat.* A508.
[84] Ibid.; L.R.L., Deeds (T.C. 104); *Local Bd. Highways Cttee. Rep.* 11 Sept. 1894.
[85] W. H. Weston, *Story of Leyton and Leytonstone*, 190; *Kelly's Dir. Essex* (1906–22); *Kelly's Dir. Leytonstone . . .* (1925).
[86] *V.C.H. Essex*, i. 444, 497, 515, 536, 546.
[87] This ratio includes the Walthamstow and Wanstead Slips.   [88] *V.C.H. Essex*, i. 536–7.
[89] *V.C.H. Essex*, i. 546; see above, p. 185.

[90] *V.C.H. Essex*, i. 536; see above, p. 194.
[91] *Cal. Close*, 1452–61, 353; E.R.O., D/DB T729, D/DBq T1/1; P. H. Reaney, *Walthamstow Place-Names* (Walthamstow Ant. Soc. xxiv), 44.
[92] Morant, *Essex*, i. 24.   [93] Ibid. i. 23.
[94] Newcourt, *Repertorium*, ii. 381.
[95] *Rep. Sel. Cttee. on Royal Forests (Essex), 1863.* H.C. 339, p. 88 (1863), vi.
[96] E.R.O., D/DCv 1 f. 16.
[97] Newcourt, *Repertorium*, ii. 381.
[98] Ibid.; E.R.O., D/DCv 1 f. 17.
[99] Newcourt, *Repertorium*, ii. 381.
[1] Kennedy, *Leyton*, pl. f.p. 18.
[2] E.R.O., D/CT 221.   [3] *E.A.T.* ii. 189–94.
[4] E.R.O., T/A 12/2/8; L.R.L., Deeds (Barns 8, 14, 14a). The original 1720 deed hangs framed on the east gallery staircase in the church. The 2 a. lay on the east side of Church Road, south of Capworth Street.
[5] *E.A.T.* ii. 191–2.
[6] Cf. *V.C.H. Essex*, v. 106.
[7] E.R.O., D/DCw M39 (calendared, D/DCw Z1).

half a virgate, and the rent for a virgate (6s.) was the equivalent of the rent of four 5 a. holdings, which suggests that 5 a. represented a quarter virgate in a hide of 80 a.[8] But by 1480 references to crofts, including one of 5 a., show inclosure taking place; and 19 a. called Prests croft, lying in 5 crofts in Le Brache, show cleared woodland being cultivated in severalty.[9] In 1537–8 seven tenants were paying rents of assize for Leyton manor demesne once held in 67 parcels, but by then alienated and amalgamated.[10]

Leyton's open arable fields did not survive, but some of the marshland continued to be held in common, and common pasture rights on the marsh and on the forest were an integral part of Leyton's farming until conditions changed in the late 19th century. The whole marshland was probably open in the Middle Ages. Haliwell Priory's demesne included an acre in parcels in Ruckholt common mead, later known as Townham or Tumbling mead.[11] In the 17th century Tumbling mead was still held in parcels varying from 1 r. to 6 a.; parcels combined in ownership were described in 1614 as lying together or lying dispersed in the common meadow.[12] All the Ruckholt marsh was, however, inclosed by 1747, when only 184 a. of 451 a. of marshland in the parish remained open, all in Leyton manor.[13]

The strips on the surviving open marsh, or lammas land, are shown on a map reduced in 1818 from the map made in 1747, and on the tithe map of 1843.[14] Wooden posts marked the boundaries of the plots,[15] which were occupied in severalty from April to August, when they were thrown open.[16] Leyton's inhabitants intercommoned with Walthamstow,[17] the northern portion of the Leyton marshes being known as Walthamstow Common mead.[18] In the 17th century the Leyton cattle were usually turned in on Lammas Day (1 August),[19] and probably remained until Lady Day (25 March). After the alteration of the calendar in 1752[20] apparently Leyton continued to turn in the cattle on 1 August (New Lammas Day),[21] not, as in Walthamstow, on Old Lammas Day (13 August).[22] But the marshes were closed, as in Walthamstow, on Old Lady Day (6 April).[23] Grazing rights were considered in 1876 to belong to the inhabitants generally, without regard to tenements.[24]

The value of the marsh to its several owners lay in the hay crop.[25] When, as in 1663, 1709, and 1713, rain flooded the marshes, preventing mowing and gathering the hay by the customary date, a general meeting of parishioners set a later date to open the marsh.[26] The marsh reeve (hayward, bailiff, or marshal) was a manorial officer, often the inhabitants' nominee, and apparently appointed for life. In 1754 the inhabitants forwarded their nomination to the lords of both manors, but later the office was always associated with Leyton manor.[27] In 1876 the reeve occupied the lord's cottage at the marsh gate in Marsh Lane. His main duty was to mark the cattle,[28] and by 1876 he kept the marking fees, formerly the lord's perquisite.[29]

The commoners' rights were jealously guarded. To protect owners living in Hackney (Mdx.), the Lea Bridge Turnpike Act of 1757 exempted from tolls their carts driven across the bridge to collect hay from Leyton, and their horses and cattle driven across to pasture.[30] When the Northern and Eastern railway company acquired part of the marsh in 1838–9, the company had to build a cattle way under the line.[31] Of 28 a. taken at the time about 5 a. comprised lammas land;[32] in 1841 the commoners decided to use the compensation paid for their loss of rights in these acres to pay the parish share of building the union workhouse.[33] In 1854 the Inclosure Commissioners agreed that the compensation negotiated for 15 a. of lammas land taken by the East London Waterworks Co. should be invested on behalf of the Leyton and Leytonstone national schools.[34] The compensation negotiated by a commoners' committee in 1868 for a further 25 a. taken by the waterworks company,[35] and for some 10 a. taken by the Great Eastern Railway Co. in the 1870s[36] was also invested. In 1884 the stock was handed over to the local board, sold, and the James Lane recreation ground bought in 1885 with the proceeds.[37]

In 1890 the waterworks company, assuming that they could, if necessary, take powers to compel the sale of lammas rights over a further 6 a. bought by them, laid rails to their new filter beds, crossing a bridlepath, and put up fences. The commoners, already agitating for the marsh to be preserved as an open space, refused to sell their rights. On

[8] B. A. Lees, *Records of the Templars in England in the twelfth century*, xciii–xcv, 16–17. See also below, p. 201.
[9] *E.A.T.* ii. 191–2. See also above, p. 197.
[10] S.C. 6/962.
[11] *E.A.T.* ii. 191; *Cur. Reg. R.* i. 454; *Feet of F. Essex*, i. 22, 168; *Cal. Pat.* 1549–51, p. 222. Tumbling Mead is shown on maps of 1721 (Kennedy, *Leyton*, f.p. 18) and 1728 (E.R.O., D/DCy P3A).
[12] E.R.O., D/DCw M36, 39 (calendared D/DCw Z1).
[13] E.R.O., D/SH 2, 29; L.R.L., L69 Plan (Map of Leyton level, 1747).
[14] E.R.O., D/SH 29, D/CT 221. See also railway plan, 1838 (E.R.O., Q/RUm 1/65).
[15] E.R.O., D/DBq L2.
[16] Wilkinson, *Leyton*, 51.
[17] See p. 265.
[18] Chapman and André, *Map of Essex*, 1777, sheet xxi.
[19] Kennedy, *Leyton*, 371.
[20] The Act, 24 Geo. II, c. 23, made special provision to continue the opening and closure of commons controlled by fixed feasts on the 'natural days'.
[21] Kennedy, *Leyton*, 389; Wilkinson, *Leyton*, 51.
[22] See p. 265.
[23] Wilkinson, *Leyton*, 51.
[24] E.R.O., D/DBq L2.

[25] Corpn. of Lond. R.O., River Lea: Proceedings in Star Chamber, etc. ff. 17–18.
[26] Kennedy, *Leyton*, 371–2; L.R.L., L55 MS. Chwdns. Accts. 1681–1723 (1709, 1713).
[27] Kennedy, *Leyton*, 372; E.R.O., D/DBq L2; Wilkinson, *Leyton*, 51; E.R.O., D/DU 101/1 (1713); L.R.L., L47 MS. Ves. Mins. 1752–81 (1754).
[28] E.R.O., D/DBq L2, D/DU 101/1 (1720).
[29] E.R.O., D/DBq L2.   [30] 30 Geo. II, c. 59.
[31] Wilkinson, *Leyton*, 52.
[32] E.R.O., D/CT 221, Q/RUm 1/65.
[33] L.U.D.C., *Rep. of Clerk as to Leyton Charities* (1906), 17; L.R.L., L47 MS. Vestry Mins. 1834–74. For the Union workhouse see above and below, pp. 181, 214.
[34] L.U.D.C., *Rep. of Clerk as to Leyton Charities* (1906), 9; E.R.O., Q/RDc 80; L.R.L., L47 MS. Vestry Mins. 1834–74. See also below, p. 234.
[35] L.R.L., L47 MS. Vestry Mins. 1834–74; E.R.O., D/DBq L2.
[36] E.R.O., D/DBq L2; L.R.L., L47 MS. Vestry Mins. 1874–1904; Wilkinson, *Leyton*, 52.
[37] Leyton U.D.C., *Rep. of Clerk as to Leyton Charities* (1906), 17; L.R.L., L47 MS. Vestry Mins. 1874–1904, Local Bd. Mins., 1883–6; *L.U.D.C. Year Bk.* 1919–20; W. H. Weston, *Story of Leyton and Leytonstone*, 195, wrongly identifies the ground bought as the Coronation Gardens.

Lammas Day, 1892, when the company had failed to remove the rails and fence, the people of Leyton, led by a member of the local board, tore them up. The company took proceedings against the commoners, who retaliated by appointing a Lammas Lands Defence Committee to oppose the parliamentary Bill promoted by the company. Compromise was reached in 1893, and confirmed by the East London Waterworks Act, 1894. The company withdrew all claim to inclose any part of the marsh, stayed its proceedings, and paid all costs, with £100 to improve the bridleway. In return the rails were allowed to remain.[38]

By 1893 over 65 a. of lammas land had been bought and dislammased, and only some 111 a. remained.[39] The commoners' committee campaigned tirelessly for their preservation.[40] As Leyton became suburban lammas rights ceased to have economic value and were hardly exercised. Under the Leyton U.D.C. Act, 1904, the council was empowered to acquire the remaining lammas lands as open spaces and recreation grounds, provided the commoners accepted extinguishment of their rights.[41] This was agreed at a thinly attended public meeting early in 1905.[42] The last compensation claims were settled by 1909.[43] In 1920 a small balance of funds held by surviving members of the commoners' committee was handed to the urban district council to endow a prize for schoolchildren.[44]

The right to pasture horses and cattle on all open and commonable places in Waltham Forest was claimed by the lords of the manors of Leyton and Ruckholt for themselves and their tenants in 1630 and 1653.[45] The owner of Temple Mills claimed similar rights.[46] The owner of Knotts claimed them not only in the vill and wastes adjoining but also throughout the 'lawn' or sheep-pasture.[47] The Leyton lawn may have originated in the grant made in 1189 to Stratford Abbey of the right to pasture 960 sheep on the heath between Ham Frith and Walthamstow without interference of the forester.[48] The Upper Walk and Nether Walk, comprising 16 a. by Whitings Grove, were included among parcels of the farm called Knotts sold in 1576.[49] Pannage for swine was claimed for Leyton manor

and Knotts in 1630[50] and for Ruckholt manor in 1653.[51] It was also claimed in the mid 17th century by the leaseholder of the Forest House estate,[52] with pasture and gravel rights.[53]

The beasts put on the forest were marked by the parish reeve with the Leyton mark.[54] Another of the reeve's duties was to see that uncommonable beasts, like goats, were taken off the forest or impounded.[55] In 1871 the Leyton reeve claimed to mark one horse or two cows for every £4 rent, at a fee of 3d. a head, and valued his office at £12 a year.[56]

Like the lammas rights, the forest pasture rights ceased by the late 19th century to have any economic value. In 1871, when the Epping Forest proceedings were launched against the lords of the forest manors[57] about 80 Leyton commoners filed claims to pasture rights, but only 15 of them had ever exercised them,[58] and in 1873 it was stated that for many years not more than a dozen beasts had been turned out by commoners.[59] After the Epping Forest Act, 1878, the parish kept its right to nominate a reeve for appointment by the Conservators,[60] but by 1960 the office was mainly honorary.[61]

In 1599 the manor of Leyton was said to contain 200 a. of arable, 260 a. of meadow, and 420 a. of pasture.[62] This predominance of grass in the centre and north-east of the parish continued, an ideal setting for the planned pleasure grounds and plantations of Leyton's wealthier residents.[63] In 1843, when private gardens occupied 148 a. in the parish, most of the larger householders also owned many acres of meadowland beyond their grounds.[64] In the south and east of the parish, however, arable predominated. In 1592 Ruckholt manor was said to contain 150 a. of arable, 44 a. of meadow, and 24 a. of pasture.[65] On Ruckholt and Warren farms in 1807 there were 142 a. of arable to 90 a. of meadow and pasture;[66] and in 1843, 194 a. of arable to 74 a. of meadow.[67] On Wallwood farm in 1777 there were 98 a. of arable to 56 a. of grass,[68] and in 1843 97 a. of arable to 24 a. of meadow.[69] In the whole parish arable and meadow were said in 1796 to be about equal,[70] but by 1843 there were 912 a. of grass to 605 a. of arable.[71] This increase of grassland may

[38] L.R.L., L47 MS. Vestry Mins. 1874–1904; L47 MS. Local Bd. Mins. 1891–3, 1893–4; Wilkinson, Leyton, 52; G. A. Blakeley, Walthamstow marshes and lammas rights (Walthamstow Ant. Soc. N.S. i), 13–16; East London Waterworks Act, 1894, 57 & 58 Vict. c. 162, s. 22 (local act); Stratford Express, 28 Jan. 1905.
[39] Wilkinson, Leyton, 51; L.R.L., L47 MS. Vestry Mins. 1874–1904; L59.2 MS. Leyton lammas lands rep. by Hen. Ough & Son, 1893–4, with map.
[40] Blakeley, Walthamstow marshes, 15–16.
[41] Leyton U.D.C. Act, 1904, 4 Edw. VII, c. 140 (local act).
[42] Blakeley, Walthamstow marshes, 15–16; Stratford Express, 28 Jan. 1905. For the use of the lammas lands after 1904, see below, p. 212.
[43] L.R.L., L47 Pamph. U.D.C. Chairman's address, 1909.
[44] L.U.D.C. Mins. and Reps. 1919–20, pp. 576, 673–4; L53.5 Pamph. Scheme for Inauguration of Prize Fund for Schools (1926 reprint of Educ. Cttee. Rep. of Mar. 1920).
[45] Proc. Epping Forest Com. pp. 1876–8, 1882–3.
[46] Ibid., p. 1878.
[47] Ibid., pp. 1878–9; Fisher, Forest, 268, 296, 298.
[48] Cal. Chart. R. 1257–1300, 311–12.
[49] L.R.L., L72.2 Pamphlet (F. W. Temple's extracts from Westminster Abbey muniments: W.A.M. 3363).
[50] Proc. Epping Forest Com. pp. 1876–8; Fisher ,Forest, 310.

[51] Fisher, Forest, 310–11.
[52] See p. 188.
[53] E.R.O., D/DBq T1/8.
[54] Proc. Epping Forest Com. pp. 1906–7, 1911; E.R.O., D/DU 403/22, ff. 405, 450–71. For the Leyton mark, see below, p. 204.
[55] Proc. Epping Forest Com. p. 1910.
[56] Final Rep. of Epping Forest Com. H.C. 187 p. 116 (1877), xxvi; E.R.O., D/DW E19, D/DU 403/2, f. 635.
[57] Fisher, Forest, 362.
[58] E.R.O., D/DU 403/1, 2.
[59] Proc. Epping Forest Com. 958.
[60] Fisher, Forest, 370; L.R.L., L47 MS. Vestry Mins. 1878, 1890.
[61] E.R.O., T/P149, p. 3.
[62] Morant, Essex, i. 23.
[63] John Rocque, Survey of London, 1741–5 (1748 edn.), sheet iv.
[64] E.R.O., D/CT 221.
[65] Morant, Essex, i. 24.
[66] E.R.O., D/DCy P17.
[67] E.R.O., D/CT 221.
[68] E.R.O., T/M 173.
[69] E.R.O., D/CT 221.
[70] Lysons, London, iv. 158.
[71] E.R.O., D/CT 221. These figures do not include the common marsh and forest waste.

explain why proportionately fewer families were supported by agriculture in 1831 than in 1811, and why a slight decrease in population in 1831 was attributed to families leaving the parish for want of employment.[72]

Leyton's produce helped to supply London. The parish was assigned, with Hackney (Mdx.), to Thomas Arundel, as chancellor in 1387 and as archbishop of York in 1389, for the livery of his household in the city, because he owned no lordships or towns near by.[73] A similar assignment was made in 1401 for life to the king's son Thomas.[74] In 1612 it was stated that market people travelled across the Leyton marshes four days a week to London, by way of Lockbridge and Hackney.[75] In 1775 there were three nurserymen and eight market-gardeners in Leyton.[76] One of these was Spencer Turner (d. 1776), the gardener-botanist, whose nursery at Holloway Down, between Irish Lane and the Thatched House in Wanstead, was established about 1761.[77] In 1796 nurseries occupied 25 a., and a further 200 a. of arable were usually cropped with potatoes.[78] Potato cropping brought the Irish into the parish. Numbers of them were there by 1766.[79] By 1815 the present Langthorne Road was known as Irish Lane.[80] By 1819 the winter distress of seasonally employed Irish was overburdening the poor rate.[81]

In 1839 potatoes, turnips, green peas, green clover, and tares were being grown for London consumption, while all the marshland and two-thirds of the upland grass were being mown, sometimes twice, for hay.[82] A watercress-grower is mentioned in 1863 and 1882.[83] In 1843 nurseries occupied some 29 a.[84] The Holloway Down nursery was sold to the Victoria Land and Settlement Co. in 1865[85] and built over. Pamplin's nursery at Black Marsh farm, Lea Bridge Road, was given up soon after 1870; Finlay Fraser's nursery, Lea Bridge Road, and the American nursery of Protheroe & Morris in Leytonstone High Road, flourished until the early 1890s.[86]

Graziers are first mentioned in 1660, when Wallwood was leased with 173 a. to a Leyton grazier, at a rent of £100.[87] A Leicestershire grazier occupied Wallwood farm from 1778.[88] The annual market

for Welsh, Scottish, and north of England cattle, held on the forest flats from late February to early May,[89] attracted dealers such as Thomas and Charles Burrell. Settled in Leyton by 1839, in 1843 they occupied 85 a. of meadow, besides a quantity of arable.[90] They bought Scottish cattle, drove them south, and turned them out on the forest to fatten before sale.[91] The Burrells, who ceased business between 1863 and 1870,[92] lived in Leyton, but by 1873 there were said to be more cattle on the forest belonging to strangers than those of the neighbourhood.[93]

In 1843 Ruckholt farm, with Warren, comprised over 200 a., Wallwood farm over 100 a., and seven others between 40 a. and 70 a.[94] As farms were sold for suburban building, cowkeepers replaced farmers, supplying milk to the new population. One was listed in 1870, two in 1872, and by 1882 there were fourteen.[95] But by 1905 only 20 a. of arable and 175 a. of permanent grass remained,[96] and by 1912 only one cowkeeper.[97]

From the 18th century Leyton's wealthy residents, with their fine houses and spacious grounds, employed so many servants and small tradesmen that the church could not hold them all.[98] The gentry's requirements explain the existence, in 1775, of a milliner and dancing-master,[99] and in 1832 of two hairdressers, six milliners, dress- and straw-hat-makers, a portrait painter, a professor of music, and a bird-stuffer.[1] In 1811 the families supported by trade, manufacture, or handicraft exceeded in number those supported by agriculture.[2] In 1831 about 11 per cent of the total population were employed as servants.[3]

Gravel-digging and brick- and tile-making are mentioned from the 17th century.[4] There were brickfields in the Walthamstow Slip and in Ruckholt manor,[5] where brickearth was dug under manorial licence.[6] A brickyard was rated in Leyton in 1775.[7] William Rhodes of Leyton Grange, brickmaker, took out a patent in 1833 for the improved manufacture of bricks.[8] Several brick manufacturers occur in the late 19th century.[9]

A brewhouse with its vessels and utensils is mentioned in 1449.[10] A brewery rated in Leyton in 1775 and 1812[11] may have been the one in Leyton

[72] Census, 1811, 1831.
[73] Cal. Pat. 1385-9, p. 282, 1388-92, p. 30.
[74] Ibid. 1399-1401, p. 403. Thomas was created Duke of Clarence in 1412.
[75] E.R.O., Q/SR 196/116-18, 198/138; Assizes 35/54/T/29.
[76] L.R.L., L55.6 MS. Rate Bk., 1775-83.
[77] E. Nat. xxvii. 45-8.
[78] Lysons, London, iv. 158.
[79] Guildhall MS. 9558, f. 218. See also E.R.O., Q/SBb 263/3 (1770).
[80] E.R.O., D/DCy P3, p. 90.
[81] See p. 207.
[82] R. Allison, 'The changing landscape of south-west Essex from 1600 to 1850' (Lond. Univ. Ph.D. thesis, 1966), 303, 317.
[83] White's Dir. Essex (1863); Kelly's Dir. Essex (1882). There is a water-colour painting in L.R.L., c. 1870, of watercress beds south of the corner of Osborne Road.
[84] E.R.O., D/CT 221.
[85] E. Nat. xxvii. 48; E.R.O., D/DCy T19.
[86] Kelly's Dir. Essex (1855-1906); O.S. Map 6", Essex, LXXIII (1873-82 edn.); Leyton Local Bd. Cttee. Reps. 1894-5. See also p. 266.
[87] E.R.O., D/DC 41/208.
[88] E.A.T. 3rd ser. i. 123.
[89] Lysons, London, iv. 157.

[90] Pigot's Dir. Essex (1839); E.R.O., D/CT 221.
[91] Proc. Epping Forest Com., pp. 967-8.
[92] White's Dir. Essex (1863); Kelly's Dir. Essex (1870).
[93] Proc. Epping Forest Com., pp. 967-8.
[94] E.R.O., D/CT 221.
[95] Kelly's Dir. Essex (1870-82).
[96] Bd. of Agric. Rtns. of Acreages, 1905.
[97] Kelly's Dir. Essex (1912).
[98] Kennedy, Leyton, 51, 56.
[99] L.R.L., L55.6 MS. Rate Bk. 1775-83, Rate Collection Bk. 1774-5.
[1] Pigot's Dir. Essex (1832).   [2] Census, 1811.
[3] Calculated from Census, 1831.
[4] Proc. Epping Forest Com., pp. 1965, 1971. See also below, p. 205.
[5] E.R.O.: T/M 252; D/DCw M36-7, 41 (e.g. 1686, 1716, 1727, 1736, 1763, 1794); D/SH 2, f. 191 (1748). Two Ruckholt fields are shown on maps of 1721 (Kennedy, Leyton, f.p. 18) and 1728 (E.R.O., D/DCy P3A); the latter also shows the gravel pit by the Green Man.
[6] E.R.O., D/DCw M37 (1707).
[7] L.R.L., L55.6 MS. Rate Bk. 1775-83.
[8] E.R. xix. 115, lvi. 82.
[9] Kelly's Dir. Essex (1872); L.R.L., L47 MS. Local Bd. Mins. 1883-6 (1885); E.R.O., D/DCy T27 (1878 lease).
[10] Cal. Close, 1447-54, pp. 165-6. See also above, p. 193.
[11] L.R.L., L55.6 MS. Rate Bks. 1775-83, 1807-26.

High Road[12] listed from 1823 to 1848.[13] Four alehouses were licensed in 1579, 3 of them in Leytonstone.[14] By 1631 there were 5.[15] The vestry tried in 1757 to limit their numbers, but by 1766 8 were rated.[16] By 1863 there were 11 inns and 6 beerhouses.[17] In 1911 Leyton had one public house to every 3,564 of the population.[18]

Leyton had 9½ fisheries on the Lea in 1066, but none in 1086.[19] There was a mill on Harold's manor of Leyton in 1066, but none in 1086.[20] There was also a mill before 1066 on Swein the swarthy's manor (Ruckholt), but in 1086 it was said to have been taken away.[21] This may have been the mill said to have been given by Swein's nephew, Aelfnoth, to Westminster Abbey,[22] and, if so, it was the mill in Leyton held of the abbey by Ralph Baynard in 1086.[23] That mill is treated under West Ham.[24]

Temple Mills, on the West Ham boundary, originated before 1185 in a grant made to the Knights Templars by William of Hastings, steward to Henry II, of a tract of meadow and marsh on or near the river Lea; this was later identified as lying in Hackney (Mdx.) and included some meadow in St. Mary Hope in Leyton. In 1185 the Templars seem to have had no mill in Leyton or Hackney, but by 1278 they had a water-mill in Leyton.[25] In 1308 this mill, held of the king and valued at £1 6s. 8d., adjoined another of the same value in Hackney, both being under one roof.[26] After the dissolution of the Order of Templars the mills passed to the Hospital of St. John of Jerusalem, Clerkenwell, being held of the manor of Hackney.[27] The Order of St. John was dissolved in 1540,[28] and though reconstituted in Mary's reign and its former lands and liberties in Leyton restored in 1558,[29] its possessions were again annexed to the Crown in the following reign. In 1593 the mills were leased to Clement Goldsmith for 40 years. There were still two water-mills under one roof, one each in Leyton and Hackney, called Ruckholt Mills and Temple Mills; with them were held adjoining meadows and a plot where a leather mill had once stood, with the watercourse belonging to it.[30] About this time a powder mill was built near the old mills, apparently on the site of the leather mill.[31] This was one of several early powder mills

in the neighbourhood.[32] When it blew up it was replaced by a 'cutters' mill, which was decayed by 1628.[33] The mills were still held by the Crown in 1608,[34] but at some date thereafter, perhaps when the Crown lease ran out in 1633, they were acquired by Richard Trafford, whose son John leased them in 1637 to Abraham Baker. Baker had already been the tenant for over ten years; he had enlarged and modified the two old mills, and about 1627 built new ones, probably on the leather mill plot, to grind rape seed and smalt. In 1637 he was operating starch, oil, and smalt mills.[35] In 1680 the mills belonged to the Samyne family, who sold them soon after.[36] Some time before 1720 the mills were acquired by a company formed in 1695 to manufacture brass kettles and tin and latten plates.[37] A logwood mill also belonged to the Temple Mills in 1706, perhaps on the leather mill plot.[38] In 1738 a machine was patented by Adrian van Bommenaer, manufacturer of Low Leyton, for twining and twisting yarn into thread for superfine lace and cambrics.[39] This manufacture was to be carried out in part of premises acquired by two of his partners, Conrad de Smith and George Heathcote, 'at or near' Leyton.[40] This was a mill, since Conrad de Smith was ordered to draw his sluices in 1740,[41] and as it appears to have been close to Temple Mills, it was probably the logwood mill. By 1757 the brass works had been superseded by the manufacture of sheet lead[42] which was still in operation in 1814.[43] A reference in 1770, however, implies that the mills also ground corn.[44] From about 1821 to 1826 the mills were unoccupied,[45] but from about 1829 to 1832 were being used for flock-making.[46] In 1834 the mills were again disused and in the following year the Leyton premises were acquired by the East London Waterworks Company.[47] The mills, which were principally of wood, spanned the stream adjoining the White Hart in Hackney.[48] They were pulled down by 1854.[49]

There was a post mill near Phillebrook in 1739,[50] but it is not shown on maps of 1748 or 1777.[51] A windmill was listed at Leytonstone about 1840[52] but does not appear on the tithe map in 1843.[53]

Obnoxious trades never gained a foothold in Leyton. A soap-boiler was rated near Holloway Down, Leytonstone, in 1775,[54] but in 1800, when the

[12] E.R.O., D/CT 221 (no. 516).
[13] Pigot's Dir. Mdx. (1823); Pigot's Dir. Essex (1839); Robson's Gazetteer of Home Counties (c. 1840); E.R.O., D/DB T1157; White's Dir. Essex (1848).
[14] E.R.O., Q/SR 73/7–29.
[15] Fisher, Forest, 87.
[16] Kennedy, Leyton, 281–3.
[17] White's Dir. Essex (1863).
[18] V.C.H. Essex, v. 58.
[19] V.C.H. Essex, i. 380.
[20] V.C.H. Essex, i. 546.
[21] Ibid. 536.   [22] See p. 89.
[23] V.C.H. Essex, i. 444.
[24] See p. 89.
[25] B. M. Lees, Records of the Templars in England in the twelfth century, l, xc, xci, 16–17, 173 (n. 5).
[26] Ibid. 173.
[27] Lysons, London, ii. 454.
[28] J. D. Mackie, The Earlier Tudors, 1485–1558, 399.
[29] Cal. Pat. 1557–8, p. 321; W. J. Pinks, Hist. Clerkenwell, 16.
[30] E.R.O., D/DU 193/23.
[31] E.R.O., T/P 48/1, ff. 181–2.
[32] Cf. p. 77.
[33] E.R.O., T/P 48/1, ff. 181–2.

[34] B.M. Add. MS. 16273, f. 15.
[35] L.R.L., General deeds (1637); E.R.O., T/P 48/1, ff. 178–82.
[36] C 78/1302 (7).
[37] C 78/1700(1); V.C.H. Essex, ii. 469.
[38] E.R.O., D/SH 1, f. 309.
[39] E.R. lvi. 19.
[40] E.R.O., D/DC 27/1051.
[41] E.R.O., D/SH 2, f. 23.
[42] Ibid., f. 363.
[43] V.C.H. Essex, ii. 421.
[44] E.R.O., Q/SBb 263/3.
[45] L.R.L., L55.6 MS. Rate Bks.; Pigot's Dir. Mdx. (s.v. Hackney, 1823, 1826).
[46] L.R.L., L55.6 MS. Rate Bks.; Pigot's Dir. Essex (1832), p. 693; Pigot's Dir. London (1832), p. 364.
[47] L.R.L., L55.6 MS. Rate Bks.; E.R.O., D/CT 221 (no. 474), D/SH 3A, f. 336.
[48] E. Walford, Greater London, i (1894), 488–9.
[49] E.R.O., D/SH 4 (1854).
[50] E.R.O., T/M 403.
[51] John Rocque, Survey of ... London, 1741–5 (1748 edn.), sheet iv; Chapman and André, Map of Essex, 1777, sheet xxi.
[52] Robson's Gazetteer of the Home Counties, c. 1840.
[53] E.R.O., D/CT 221.
[54] L.R.L., L55.6 MS. Rate Bk. 1775–83.

stench from a slaughtering and boiling-house there was considered unwholesome, the vestry ordered the proprietor to move.[55] When the British Land Co. developed the same area in 1871 a covenant banned noxious trades and manufactures.[56] The only offensive trade reported in 1885 was fish-frying.[57]

Modern industry developed mainly in north-west Leyton, notably in Lea Bridge Road and Church Road, and in the neighbourhood of the two High Roads, often occupying disused buildings such as mission halls and schools. It never became so well established in Leytonstone as in Leyton.[58] In 1879 no factory of any size existed.[59] The growing industry then was the building trade, which absorbed over 10 per cent of Leyton's occupied males by 1891.[60] In 1902 only four factories employed more than 40 hands: E. R. Alexander & Sons, printers, A. G. Martin, bootmakers, Shenstone & Co. Ltd., pianoforte manufacturers, and the London Electric Wire Co.[61] A Leyton printer was listed in 1859 and printing has been a well-established local trade since 1872. Martin's boot factory, and two others completed in 1910–11,[62] introduced an industry which took root; modern footwear firms include the large Arcola Shoe Works Ltd. in Leyton High Road. A pianoforte-maker was listed in 1848[63] and ivory cutters or pianoforte key makers in 1872, 1882, and 1905. Shenstone's, established in 1870, and one of three firms making pianos in 1905, ceased manufacture about 1926.[64] An ivory turner's business, G. W. Ellis, in existence by 1905, making billiard balls, survived to the 1950s. The London Electric Wire Co. Ltd., established in 1899, grew rapidly,[65] merging about 1912 with Thomas Smith's Leytonstone wire works as the London Electric Wire Co. & Smith's Ltd. By 1921 the company, manufacturing electric cables, wire, and flex, employed 1,306 workers.[66] In the 1960s it was the largest employer of labour in Leyton, and the largest manufacturer of insulated wire in Europe. One small early firm, which built organs, was founded in 1899 by R. Spurden Rutt, and remained unique.[67] Many well-known churches, including the City Temple and Chapel Royal, Greenwich, and over 50 churches in Essex and Middlesex, had their organs built or rebuilt by Rutt. The business closed about 1960 after the death of the founder.

Leyton was still reported in 1932 to have comparatively few factories,[68] but since 1902 the clothing trade, engineering and tool-making, and the manufacture of packaging materials and soft drinks had all spread. A shirt manufacturer was listed in 1872. By 1905 many small firms made blouses, mantles, and underclothing. About 1927 the Bow Shirt Manufacturing Co. opened new works in Leyton;

hosiery and knitwear firms followed by 1937.[69] Over 20 firms were in production by 1957, the largest being Aquascutum (Manufacturers) Ltd. Specialist firms included John Roberts & Sons (Embroidery) Ltd., established over 30 years before, and M. M. Shire Ltd., fur dressers and dyers. The manufacture of neckties, introduced after 1945, by 1966 was being carried on by eight firms. Horticultural engineers and a manufacturer of flour-making machinery were listed in 1872. Other engineering firms, some electrical, soon followed. Acme Seals Ltd., making lead seals, founded in 1903, were still in production in the 1960s. The machine tool industry, established since the 1920s, is carried on today by such firms as Leytool Ltd. A box-maker and a cardboard-manufacturer existed in 1872. Between the two wars the foundation of D. Smith and Sons, followed by C. H. G. Jourdan, expanded the manufacture of cardboard cartons. Smith's were taken over by British Celylind Ltd. about 1960.[70] One mineral water company existed in 1882; by 1905 there were five. This trade, however, declined. By 1957 only one firm, Biddle & Gingell, established about 1926, survived; they were still in production in the 1960s. Several specialist firms founded before the First World War were still in production in the 1960s: Hedley & Co., manufacturing ethyl chloride, were established by 1905; Drew, Clark & Co. (patent extension ladders), founded in 1901, moved to Leyton in 1907[71] and the Caribonum Co. Ltd. (carbon paper and typewriter ribbons) was founded shortly before 1912.

New industries were established between the two world wars, and the Leyton and Leytonstone Chamber of Commerce was formed in 1930. Glassware was being manufactured by 1927. Ascott's of West Ham opened a branch factory in Leyton High Road about 1927, making billiard tables. A boiled-sweet factory opened in 1930, and Copeland & Jenkins Ltd. in 1933 introduced the manufacture of plastic products. In 1938 Thermos Ltd. (vacuum flasks) moved from Tottenham to a new factory at Leyton; this was enlarged in 1947, but closed in 1961 when the firm moved to Brentwood.[72] The manufacture of furniture, introduced in the mid 1930s, has expanded since 1945, including antique reproductions. In the 1950s factories were opened by Ilford Ltd. for photographic materials[73] and Potter and Moore Ltd. for perfumery. As a result in the increase in local industry in 1921–51, the number of people working in Leyton increased about 40 per cent, even though the occupied resident population declined.[74]

From the mid 19th century many workers found employment in service industries,[75] particularly

[55] L.R.L., L47 MS. Vestry Mins. 1781–1811.
[56] L.R.L., Deeds (T.C. 118. 1).
[57] L.R.L., L47 MS. Local Bd. Mins. 1883–6.
[58] Unless otherwise stated the information on modern industry is based on: *Kelly's Dir. Essex* (1859 and later edns.); *Kelly's Dir. Walthamstow, Leyton, and Leytonstone* (1905); *Leyton Official Guide* (1927, 1934, 1937, 1949, 1952, 1958, c. 1962); *Leyton and Leytonstone Chamber of Commerce Trade Index* (1949) and *Trades Dir.* (1957–8); and *Waltham Forest Trades Dir.* (1966).
[59] L.R.L., L47 MS. Local Bd. Mins. 1877–81.
[60] *V.C.H. Essex*, v. 20.
[61] *Leyton U.D.C. Eng. and Survs. Rep.* 1902–3.
[62] L.R.L., L47 Pamphlet. *Address of Leyton U.D.C. Chairman*, 1911.
[63] *White's Dir. Essex* (1848).

[64] Weston, *Leyton and Leytonstone*, 202.
[65] *Leyton U.D.C. Eng. & Surv. Reps.* 1908, 1912.
[66] Weston, *Leyton and Leytonstone*, 202; *V.C.H. Essex*, v. 17.
[67] R. S. Rutt, 'Fifty years of organ building' (*Jnl. of S. W. Essex Tech. Coll.* ii (4) (1948), 206).
[68] *New Survey of London Life and Labour*, iii, *Survey of Social Conditions* (1) *The Eastern Area* (1932), p. 398.
[69] Ibid.
[70] Inf. from Mr. J. H. Boyes.
[71] *Waltham Forest Off. Guide* (1968), 99.
[72] Inf. from Mr. J. H. Boyes.
[73] *V.C.H. Essex*, v. 254.
[74] Ashworth, 'Types of social and econ. devt. in suburban Essex' (ch. III of *London aspects of change*), 71.
[75] See p. 211.

West Ham: Keir Hardie Estate, Canning Town
Looking north

Leyton: Temple Mills Railway Marshalling Yard
Looking north-west

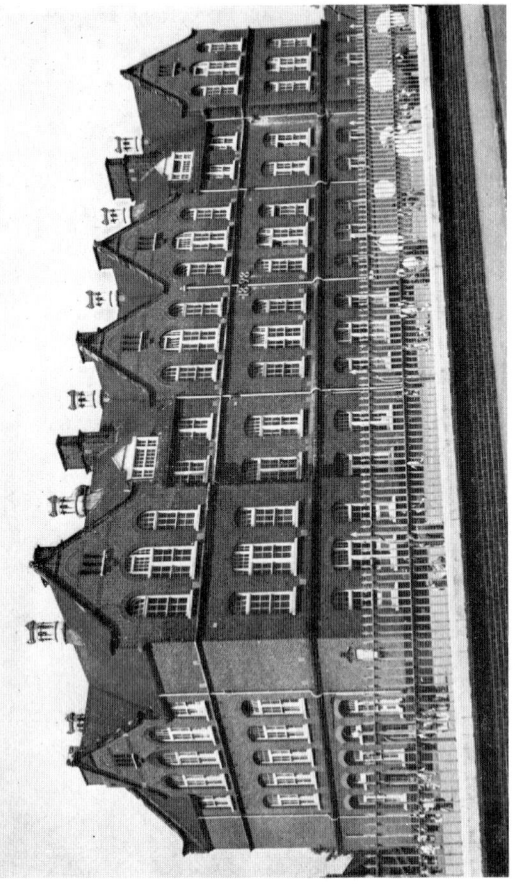

East Ham: Central Park Primary Schools, opened 1899

Leyton: Langthorne Hospital, formerly West Ham Union Workhouse, built 1840

East Ham: Manor Park Methodist Church, built 1964

West Ham: Butcher's Shop, Water Lane, Stratford, built c. 1860

the railways.[76] In 1897 the wagon department of the Great Eastern Railway's works at Stratford was moved to Temple Mills, and by 1912 employed 600 men.[77] The marshalling yard at Temple Mills grew steadily and when a £3½ million modernization scheme was completed in 1958, with electronic automatic controls, became not only the largest in Britain but the most up to date in the world.[78] The wagon works were modernized at the same time.[79] There has been remarkable growth in the present century, too, in the laundry and dry-cleaning business, and in the motor vehicle service industry. By 1961 more workers were employed in service industries than on production.[80]

MARSHES. The original drainage of the Leyton marshes has traditionally been attributed to King Alfred's manœuvres to outwit the Danes in 895.[81] There is no evidence to support this. The agriculture of the marshland is described elsewhere.[82] From 1604 the commissioners of sewers for Thames-side from West Ham to Mucking taxed the Leyton level.[83] This may represent an extension of the commissioners' jurisdiction, as the level is not included in the 1563 survey of their levels and does not appear to have been rated before 1604.

A map was made of the level in 1747, distinguishing open and inclosed marsh, and surveys of 1818 and 1850 were based on it. Stretching from Walthamstow to Temple Mills Lane the level's eastern boundary was virtually the large ditch or common sewer which, as the Dagenham commissioners' sewer, came to be known in the late 19th century as the Dagenham brook. As its western boundary was the river Lea the level included nearly 60 a. of Hackney marsh, between the Waterworks river and the Lea. In Leyton the level comprised some 451 a., of which 184 a. were open in 1747 and 181 a. in 1850.[84] In 1748 it was suggested that the uplands which drained into the common sewer on the east might also be liable to tax, but no enlargement of the level followed.

The level was rated for its own needs and was supervised by its own marsh jury, who made their presentments at the court of sewers.[85] The commissioners appointed a collector and 'expenditor', and a marsh bailiff to see that the court's orders were carried out. The latter appointment was not the same as that of manorial marsh bailiff or reeve.[86] The level's acreage rate in the 17th and 18th centuries was usually only a few pence, compared with the shillings or even pounds paid by the Thames-side levels. This was because the commissioners maintained no walls or banks to protect the level from flooding by the Lea. Their concern was to keep drainage channels flowing, in particular the Dagenham brook. This was often blocked. Of 22 orders made in 1696 20 were to cut, drag, and scour, and the other 2 to repair marsh footbridges, which the commissioners also supervised. The marshes were always liable to flood with excessive rain, as in 1663, when they were under water on Lammas Day,[87] and with spring tides. There were many complaints in the 16th and 17th centuries against the millers at Temple Mills for penning up the water at such times, flooding the marshes, instead of pulling up the flood gates.[88]

In the 19th century the character of the marshland changed. Many acres were bought and built on by railway, water, and gas undertakings. With the spread of domestic building in the Lea Bridge Road and Grange Park districts in the 1860s, and the use of natural watercourses as household drains, pollution of the marshland channels set the commissioners a new problem. With the upland draining to the marsh, the Dagenham brook became foul not only with Leyton's sewage, but with Walthamstow's as well. The commissioners' efforts to clean the brook were supported by the Lee conservancy board, who had statutory powers to prevent sewage draining into the Lea or its tributaries.[89] The Leyton vestry and local board faced repeated remonstrance from both bodies from 1870,[90] with peremptory letters and threats of proceedings. In 1883 the commissioners, satisfied at last with the local board's schemes for sewage disposal,[91] authorized connexion of the board's new works to the Dagenham brook for discharge to the Waterworks river, subject to satisfactory reports on the treated effluent.[92] Complaints that untreated sewage was entering the brook from Walthamstow persisted up to 1895, but pressure from both marsh juries and from the commissioners, the Lee conservancy, and the Leyton local board and district council, eventually ended the nuisance.[93]

Under the Land Drainage Act, 1930, responsibility for the Leyton marshes passed from the commissioners of sewers to the Lee conservancy catchment board.[94] In 1938 the board took powers to alleviate flooding in the Lea valley.[95] The scheme, which included construction of a flood relief channel from Tottenham marsh to Leyton, widening the Lea between Leyton and Hackney, demolishing Temple Mills Road bridge, and filling in the Waterworks river,[96] was delayed by the Second World War. The Waterworks river still flowed

[76] V.C.H. Essex, v. 12, 20; E.R.O., T/Z 25/464; Weston, Leyton and Leytonstone, 202.
[77] Great Eastern Railway Mag. ii (1912), p. 260, iii (1913), pp. 75–6.
[78] Stratford Express, 10 Jan. 1958; C. J. Allen, 'Britain's high speed marshalling yard' (Boy's Own Paper, Aug. 1960). For the marshalling yard in 1965 see plate f.p. 202.
[79] Stratford Express, 9 Jan. 1959.
[80] Census, 1961.
[81] Wilkinson, Leyton, 51; V.C.H. Essex, v. 165.
[82] See p. 198.
[83] The information in this section is based, unless otherwise stated, on the records of the Havering and Dagenham Commissioners of Sewers: E.R.O., D/SH 1–5 (Presentment Bks. 1691–1894), D/SH 3A (Survey, 1850), D/SH 7 (Survey, 1563), D/SH 26 (Rates Analysis Bk., 1736, quoting from 1583), D/SH 29 (Map of Leyton Level, 1818, copied 1864, based on map of 1747 and referred to in 1850 Survey); L.R.L., L69 Plan: J. Noble, Map of Leyton Level, 1747.
[84] For lammas rights on the open marsh, see p. 198.
[85] V.C.H. Essex, v. 33.　　[86] See p. 198.
[87] L.R.L., L55.6 MS. Rate Collection Bk. 1651–1704.
[88] E.R.O., T/P 48/1, ff. 163, 202–3.
[89] L.R.L., L47 MS. Vestry Mins. 1834–74.
[90] V.C.H. Essex, v. 43; L.R.L., L47 MS. Leyton Local Bd. Mins. 1877 f.　　[91] See p. 211.
[92] L.R.L., L47 MS. Local Bd. Mins. 1883–6.
[93] L.R.L., L47 MS. Local Bd. Mins. 1886–9; Local Bd. San. Cttee. Reps. 1885, 1892–4; Walthamstow U.D.C. Chmns'. Ann. Reps. 1895, 1896. See also below, p. 283.
[94] Hilda Grieve, Great Tide, 55.
[95] Lee Conservancy Catchment Board Act, 1938, 1 & 2 Geo. VI. c. 91.
[96] Ibid.; E.R.O., C/DP 396, 403.

alongside Quartermile Lane in 1950, but was filled in by 1952.[97] The Dagenham brook was diverted under the railway to the Lea. Work on the Leyton section of the flood relief channel, diverting the old Shortlands sewer to an outfall at The Friends, was completed in the late 1950s,[98] and the rest soon after.[99]

FOREST. Leyton parish lay wholly in the ancient Forest of Essex.[1] In the Middle Ages it was in the bailiwick of Becontree hundred.[2] When smaller 'walks' replaced bailiwicks in the 16th century, Leyton became part of Leyton and Wanstead walk, with the Romford–Bow road as its southern boundary.[3] Beyond the Bow road lay the Leyton 'purlieu' whose rangers' duty was to drive back into Leyton walk wild beasts straying out of the forest.[4] There was a forest lodge in the walk belonging to the Crown; it was repaired in 1725 at a cost of £151.[5] It stood on the south-west part of the lower forest (Wanstead Flats), in the vicinity of the present Sidney Road, in line with the avenue leading to Lake House, Wanstead.[6]

In 1541 Richard Barnes was granted for life the office of keeper of Leyton walk, which John Holland had held.[7] In 1558 Barnes forfeited the office for killing about 50 deer in three years without warrant, and Thomas Powle was granted the office, also for life.[8] Subsequent chief foresters or keepers are listed by W. R. Fisher.[9]

In the mid 16th century the woodward of Wallwood in Leyton manor was appointed by the Crown for life and was entitled to an annual fee charged on the manor of Leyton; the appointment was probably made by Stratford Abbey before the Dissolution.[10] The lord of Ruckholt manor claimed in the 17th century to appoint his own woodward, though he had to be sworn at the forest court.[11]

The Leyton reeve is first mentioned in 1489 with the 'Fourmen' who assisted him.[12] He was nominated by the vestry, but appointed and sworn by the Forty Day Court, to which he was responsible.[13] He kept the parish marking-iron, the Leyton mark being an 'N' surmounted by a crown.[14]

The deer were preserved for royal sport. Elizabeth I killed a buck in Leyton walk in 1591, as did the French ambassador and the king of Portugal.[15]

The number of deer in the walk at the time varied from 3 fawns to 30 head.[16] Sir William Hicks entertained Charles II at Ruckholt after hunting.[17] By that time the deer were diminishing, and in 1670 Sir William, as lieutenant of the forest, was fined £50 for not enforcing a warrant for restraint in destroying them, and allowing them to be killed, particularly for himself.[18] The deer continued to dwindle. By 1844 the under-keeper was uncertain whether the walk still harboured a brace or not.[19] In 1872 the Leyton manor bailiff remembered no deer on the Leyton waste for 20 years.[20]

Slaughter of the deer, clearance of the woodland that sheltered them,[21] and inclosure of their feeding grounds, all contributed to their extinction. Most early inclosures probably still allowed the deer entry. The original licence granted to Stratford Abbey in 1248 to inclose the wood of Leyton,[22] later known as Wallwood,[23] reserved free passage in and out for the deer. It was the subsequent emparking and disafforestation of 1253 that shut them out.[24] By the late 17th century the gentry were being licensed to replace with brick walls the ditches and pales which had previously inclosed their gardens and orchards without keeping out the deer.[25] Thenceforward the forest waste in Leyton appears to have been gradually whittled away, an acre or rood or two at a time, to build a cottage or house, or enlarge a garden or forecourt.[26] Between 1700 and 1850 31 grants and inclosures of waste in Leyton manor amounted to little more than 10 a., and 12 grants in Ruckholt to under 3 a.[27] But it was enough to rouse anxiety in the inhabitants, and by the mid 18th century the vestry's consent to inclosure was required, as well as licence from the lord of the manor and the forest court. An inclosure made in 1766 against the wishes of the vestry cost the offender £100 in compensation to the poor,[28] and in 1767 the occupant of a recent inclosure was warned to remove his pales and level his ditches if he did not wish 'the proper persons having common right on the forest' to do so for him.[29] In 1805 the vestry resolved that satisfactory payments to provide bread for the poor should in future be a condition of consent.[30]

In 1843 there still remained 237 a. of common or waste in the parish.[31] But in 1856 Viscount Wellesley

[97] L.R.L., L53.5 Prints: photos. 1950 and 1952; Leyton Official Guide (c. 1962), plan.
[98] L.R.L., L53.5, 53.6 Prints: photos. 1950–1, 1954–9; Lee Cons. Catchment Bd., Engineer's Rep. on High (Surge) Tide, 1 Feb. 1953, 8.
[99] Lee Cons. Catchment Bd., Visits of Inspection to works in the Lower Reaches, 1960, 1961; Leyton Official Guide (c. 1962), plan.
[1] W. R. Fisher, Forest of Essex, f.p. 21, p. 395.
[2] Ibid. f.p. 137.
[3] Ibid. 384; L. & P. Hen. VIII, xx, p. 320; Cal. Pat. 1557–8, 458; E.R. xiv. pl. f.p. 192, p. 195.
[4] Fisher, Forest, f.p. 50, pp. 161, 163–4, 170.
[5] Epping Forest Commission: Rolls of Court of Attachments, i. 84.
[6] The Lodge is named on J. Rocque's Survey of London (1741–5), and Chapman and André's Map of Essex, 1777, sheet xxi.
[7] Cal. Pat. 1557–8, 458–9.   [8] Ibid.
[9] Fisher, Forest, 384.
[10] Cal. Pat. 1555–7, 487; E.R.O., D/DBq L2; S.C. 6/962.
[11] Fisher, Forest, 174.
[12] Ibid. 177; Proc. Epping Forest Com., pp. 1898–9.
[13] Proc. Epping Forest Com., pp. 1911, 1921–2; L.R.L. L47 MS. Vestry Mins. 1748, 1805.

[14] Proc. Epping Forest Com. 1911; Fisher, Forest, plate f.p. 299. For the duties of the reeve, see above, p. 199.
[15] E.R. xv. 66.
[16] Ibid.   [17] Fisher, Forest, 120 n.
[18] Ibid. 218.
[19] E.R.O., D/DCy Z3.
[20] E.R.O., D/DW E19.
[21] See p. 197.
[22] Cal. Pat. 1247–58, 9.
[23] See p. 195.
[24] Proc. Epping Forest Com. 959.
[25] E.R.O., D/DCv 1, ff. 20, 21; D/DBq T1/30; see also above, p. 189.
[26] Proc. Epping Forest Com., pp. 1940, 1982–3, 2018–19; L.R.L., L47 MS. Vestry Mins. 1768, 1801, 1804–8; E.R.O., D/DCv 1, ff. 16, 17, 19; Fisher, Forest, 327; E.R.O., D/DC 41/212.
[27] Proc. Epping Forest Com., pp. 2018–19.
[28] L.R.L., L47 MS. Vestry Mins. 1766; Kennedy, Leyton, 299–305; see also below, p. 207.
[29] L.R.L., L47 MS. Vestry Mins. 1767. For common rights on the forest, see above, p. 199.
[30] L.R.L., L47 MS. Vestry Mins. 1805; for the Inhabitants' Charity which grew out of this, see below, p. 240.
[31] E.R.O., D/CT 221.

bought the Crown's forest rights in the manors of Ruckholt, Woodford, and Wanstead for £1,891,[32] and this purchase was followed between 1857 and 1869 by 22 inclosures made in Ruckholt manor containing over 41 a.[33] This compared with 11 grants of waste and inclosures totalling only 2 a. between 1800 and 1850.[34] No inclosures had been made in Leyton manor between 1850 and 1870[35] but the lord, who claimed the right to dig turf and gravel, had exercised the latter right extensively, supplying the parish surveyor and the turnpike trustees;[36] Samuel Bosanquet, as owner of Forest House, had also dug gravel.[37]

By 1870, while 136 a. of waste, still subject to Crown rights, remained open in Leyton manor, only 35 a., released from Crown rights, remained open in Ruckholt.[38] Under the Epping Forest Act, 1878, 212 a. in Leyton were preserved as part of the forest and dedicated to the public.[39] Excursions to the forest were already popular; on one day in 1874 the Leyton surveyor counted as many as 90 pleasure vans driving to the forest along Lea Bridge Road.[40] Two islands of forest waste at Leyton Green and Harrow Green were handed over to the Leyton local board in 1883 to be maintained as ornamental inclosures, the soil remaining vested in the forest conservators.[41]

LOCAL GOVERNMENT AND POOR- RELIEF TO 1836.

The only surviving records for the manor of Leyton are court books, 1713–1880.[42] Courts leet and view of frankpledge, with twelve suitors, were held in 1713, 1715, 1734, and 1736. The last court baron was held in 1842, after which all business was transacted 'out of court'. The Leyton constable is mentioned in 1381.[43] The last constable (chosen by the vestry three weeks before)[44] was sworn in 1715. The lord appointed the marsh hayward, whose duties are described elsewhere.[45] A pound keeper is mentioned in 1796.

John de Munchensy was holding view of frankpledge in Leyton, probably at Ruckholt, in 1272–3.[46] Court records for Ruckholt manor exist for the period 1509 to 1848.[47] Courts leet were usually held once a year between 1509 and 1558, fairly regularly from 1567 to 1618, and at increasing intervals between 1625 and 1658. After 1658 only three were held, in 1686, 1687, and 1705. The distinction between leet and baron business was not always clearly made in Elizabethan times; in 1567 an order against sheltering women was made at the court baron. The courts baron were held at similar intervals to the leets before 1658, usually with them until 1571. No courts were held between 1658 and 1673; between 1673 and 1688 courts baron were held at intervals of one to five years. Between 1705 and 1848 courts were held at irregular intervals of one to four years, but sometimes with two or more courts in a year. The longest interval between courts was the ten years between 1742 and 1752. Between 1509 and 1705 an average of twelve suitors attended courts with leet business or view of frankpledge; the maximum was seventeen (in 1654) and the minimum five (in 1512, 1513, and 1517). Courts described as 'of view of frankpledge' occur between 1509 and 1687. The assize of bread and ale was exercised between 1510 and 1611. Reference is made in 1595, 1609, and 1610 to provision of weights and measures by the lord, and an unlicensed alehouse was presented in 1654. Civil and quasi-criminal jurisdiction continued to be exercised at times up to 1705; at the last court leet a cottage built on the waste was presented. The last highway presentments occur in 1686 and 1687; no bridges were presented after 1611. 'Inmates' are last mentioned in 1653. The last case of assault occurs in 1609; an arrest for theft of cloth was made in 1516. A solitary instance of presentment for failure to wear caps according to the statute is found in 1595. The election of a constable, described in 1578 and 1705 as for Leytonstone, is frequently recorded between 1511 and 1705. The last swearing of a constable was in 1727 at a court baron. Ale-tasters were elected between 1509 and 1705. A headborough was chosen in 1578, 1631, 1686–7, and 1705. A tithingman was elected at irregular intervals between 1584 and 1653. In 1532 the lord was ordered to make a pair of stocks and a pair of gallows on the manor boundary; stocks are last mentioned in 1610, when their lack for seven years was presented, together with that of the pillory and tumbrel. A pound is mentioned by name only in 1567, but the last case of beasts being impounded occurs in 1607. The erection of a pair of butts was ordered in 1567; they are last mentioned in 1610 as in decay.

Leyton has a fine collection of parish records,[48] including vestry minutes from 1618. Before 1681 the only regular vestry meeting was in Easter week, when officers were chosen. Between 1654 and 1657[49] and after 1671 the surveyors were chosen at a separate meeting. From 1681 the vestry held another meeting soon after Easter, to nominate pensioners, inspect accounts, and make the rate; from 1698

[32] *Sewers v. Glasse and others* (1871), Answer of W. B. Glasse and A. Collyer-Bristow, p. 4; E.R.O., D/DCy T76.
[33] Fisher, *Forest*, 356.
[34] *Proc. Epping Forest Com.*, pp. 2018–19.
[35] Ibid.
[36] E.R.O., D/DW E19, D/DXj 1.
[37] E.R.O., D/DU 403/1, ff. 100–2; Fisher, *Forest*, 371; E.R.O., D/DBq L5; *Final Rep. of Epping Forest Com.* H.C. 187, pp. 5, 116 (1877), xxvi.
[38] *Final Rep. of Epping Forest Com.* H.C. 187, pp. 107, 109–11 (1877), xxvi; E.R.O., D/DW E19.
[39] W. H. Weston, *Story of Leyton and Leytonstone*, 197–8; *L.U.D.C. Year Bk.* 1919–20.
[40] L.R.L., L53.4 MS. Local Bd. Highway Cttee. Mins., 1874.
[41] Weston, *Leyton and Leytonstone*, 203; *L.U.D.C. Eng. and surveyor's annual reps.*, 1900, 1901; L.R.L., L53.4 MS. Highway Cttee. Mins. 1882, L47 MS. Local Bd. Mins. 1881–6.

[42] E.R.O., D/DU 101/1, 3, 4 (calendar, T/A 12/2/16, 18–20); D/DU 101/1A (calendar T/A 12/2/17) has a few extracts from 1704.
[43] *Cal. Close*, 1381–5, 74.
[44] L.R.L., L47 MS. Vestry Mins.
[45] E.R.O., D/DBq L2; see also above, p. 198.
[46] *Rot. Hund.* (Rec. Com.), i. 152; see also above, p. 194.
[47] E.R.O., D/DCw M34–42 (calendar, D/DCw Z1). The information on Ruckholt manor court is from these records.
[48] L.R.L., L47 MS. Vestry Mins. 1618 f., L55 MS. Chwdns. Accts. 1681 f., L55.6 MS. Overseers' Rates 1651 f. and Accts. 1775 f., and other items relating to, e.g. apprentices, the workhouse, employment of the poor, relief. For a complete list, see *Cat. Essex Par. Recs.* (2nd edn. 1966), 150–1; many extracts are printed in J. Kennedy, *Hist. Leyton*. The information in this section, unless otherwise stated, is based on these records.
[49] In accordance with the Ordinance of 31 Mar. 1654, *Acts & Ords. of Interr.* ed. Firth and Rait, ii. 862.

these meetings were held twice a year. In 1759 the vestry decided to meet monthly. The Easter meeting was held in the church, but others usually in public houses or, from 1715, a coffee house. From 1742 the vestry met in the workhouse. In 1712 the members limited their refreshment to 40s. twice a year; from 1723 this allowance was halved. Attendances, recorded from 1639, were small, about five to eleven, but most of those present were people of influence and wealth. In the 17th century, judging from the signatures, substantial parishioners took the chair. From 1664 to 1695 the chairman was usually the lord of the manor of Ruckholt, or another magistrate; the vicar only signed first when these were not present. From 1695, when Sir William Hicks ceased to attend, the vicar, John Strype, took the chair. Thenceforward the vicar usually presided, and in his absence a parish officer. From 1668 all vicars except John Dubordieu (1738–54) attended regularly. A select vestry was set up in 1819, but discontinued in 1823.[50]

In 1679 the rateable value of the parish was £2,005. In 1765 it was £3,033, rising to £4,205 in 1776, £6,095 in 1806, and £8,038 in 1826. The vestry took a firm line with rate defaulters. The churchwardens' and poor-rates were usually separate until 1779, when they were combined. They were separated again in 1826. Constables' rates were occasionally made, but their charges were usually included in the churchwarden's or another officer's rate. It is clear from a case in 1761 that the highway 'rate' was made up of fines for not performing statute labour. When the surveyor spent more than he collected, the deficiency was met by a special rate or put into the poor or churchwardens' rate.

Parish offices were customarily served in turn, the order being determined by the antiquity of each house. Experienced substitutes were often employed. There were two churchwardens, each serving one year as junior, then a second as senior warden. In 1760 the vestry ruled that the senior warden should do the business. Between 1847 and 1853 the vicar began to nominate a third warden. In 1852 the vestry objected, and from 1854 to 1873 continued to elect both wardens. From 1874, when E. J. Brewster (1873–80) claimed his right to nominate, the parish had a vicar's (or high) and a people's (or low) warden.

The two overseers of the poor are sometimes described before 1721 as one each for Leyton and Leytonstone, but in 1787 as first and second overseer; the senior overseer is mentioned later. By 1775 it was usual for the beadle, described below, to act as an extra overseer. From 1801 to 1820 these duties fell on the 'out beadle'. From 1821 the office of paid assistant overseer superseded that of out beadle.

There were two surveyors of highways, one each for Leyton and Leytonstone, until the turnpike trustees took over Leytonstone High Road in 1722. Thereafter only one was appointed. A paid sur-

veyor was appointed continuously from 1767.[51] In 1832 Leyton was reported to be the only parish in the neighbourhood with a salaried surveyor.

There were two constables, one each for Leyton and Leytonstone.[52] From 1637 the vestry always chose the Leyton constable. The Leytonstone constable was elected by them from 1651 to 1657, and occasionally after 1657 with the consent of the lord of the manor of Ruckholt, or by his appointment. From 1733 the vestry elected both constables.

The office of beadle, paid on the churchwardens' rate, was created in 1718 to deal with inmates, vagrants, and uncertificated newcomers. The beadle became a trusted servant of the vestry, employed on every kind of parish business. In 1801 the duties were divided between a 'church beadle', who was also sexton, and an 'out beadle', to deal with all 'out business', especially investigation of newcomers. From 1821 the out beadle became the assistant overseer. The office of church beadle survived that of out beadle, and continued to be held with that of sexton.

The parish clerk is first mentioned in 1623.[53] In 1653 he was elected by the vestry, but later clerks were nominated and appointed by the vicar. They were first paid a salary in 1802.

Before 1820 the vestry minutes were usually kept by the vicar. The workhouse master acted as vestry clerk from 1820 to 1836; the former master continued to act after the workhouse closed, and in 1841 a salary was authorized.

It was usual for two or more of the offices of clerk, sexton, beadle, workhouse master, assistant overseer, or substitute churchwarden or constable, to be held by the same man.

Highway defaulters with carts or labour were presented at quarter sessions in 1624, 1642, and 1668.[54] In 1734 the vestry agreed with the Middlesex and Essex turnpike surveyor to settle the £31 10s. composition due from the parish by sending to work on the turnpike the teams of 13 householders, owing between them 70 days' statute labour; a day's work was worth 9s. The Leyton surveyor had to co-operate with the overseers in the employment of parish labourers on the roads.

The parish repaired the Leyton whipping post in 1651, and built a new one in 1756. A brick watchhouse was built near the stocks, by the vicarage, in 1690; it was pulled down in 1740 and not replaced. New stocks were built in 1756; in 1774 they were removed from the vicarage and put beside the newly-built cage. The cage was demolished in 1843.

In Leytonstone a watch-house was built in 1691, and new stocks in 1708, 1735, and 1759.[55] A cage was built in 1812; it was rebuilt at Harrow Green in 1833 and abandoned in 1859.[56]

To discourage housebreakers in this wealthy neighbourhood[57] the vestry paid rewards to informers. In the early 19th century they hired night patrols in winter, armed with rattles and swords,

[50] See also below.
[51] In accordance with 7 Geo. III, c. 42.
[52] E.R.O., Q/SR 11/14. See also above, for the Leytonstone constable.
[53] Kennedy, Leyton, 120.
[54] E.R.O., Q/SR 245/34, 318/48, 418/33.
[55] See above, for responsibility of Ruckholt manor for stocks.

[56] For a painting of the Harrow Green cage, c. 1859, see L.R.L., Kennedy, Hist. Leyton (extra illus.), f.p. 408. It is also shown on the tithe map, E.R.O., D/CT 221B (1843).
[57] For cases, see E.R.O., Cal. Assize Files in P.R.O. (index s.v. Leyton) and E.R.O., T/P 110/45 (newspaper reports).

to protect both residents and churchyard. In 1821 the Hackney watch were rewarded for apprehending a grave-robber.

From 1840 Leyton, as part of the Central criminal court district, was included in the Metropolitan police district.[58]

From 1768, when a fire-engine and buckets were bought by subscription, the vestry provided an engine-house by the church porch and maintained the engine on the churchwardens' account.[59]

To support their poor the vestry had, in addition to the poor-rate, eight endowed alms-houses and accumulating funds for free bread.[60] There was also ample wealth to tap in hard times, as in 1789, when £63 was subscribed. The poor-rate was calculated on the estimated numbers of pensioners, and of children to apprentice, in the months ahead. Thus in 1672, with four pensioners, the rate was 2½d., raising £24; but in 1675, with seven pensioners, and five children to bind at £6 each, with £4 for their clothing, the rate was 8d., raising £72. The overseers were little more than rate collectors, most of the casual relief being ordered by the church-wardens, and paid on their rate. The vestry relieved the victims of bereavement, sickness, accident, disablement, and lunacy. They paid rents, doctors' bills, and the charges of London hospitals. They released debtors from prison, redeemed personal possessions from pawn, and once gave a man a loan to help him to 'traffic in old iron'. After 1697 the regular poor had to wear badges.

From 1698 the poor rate had to be made twice a year. From 1705 to 1732 it was about 8d., raising about £87, but in the 1720s the number of pensioners, hitherto a dozen or so, increased to over twenty. By 1737 there were 31, 13 of them children. That year the poor-rate was 1s. 1d., producing £145. The churchwardens' casual expenses showed the same upward trend, and the vestry therefore decided to build a workhouse, which was opened in 1742. The poor-rate, however, never again fell below 1s. 1d.

In 1766 the vestry protested to the lords of the manors that grants of herbage and waste were causing hardship to the poor.[61] The vestry had tried to abolish pensions, but they were being paid again by 1764 and in 1780 cost £104. That year the combined rate was 3s., producing £612. Whereas in 1709 there were 10 poor families in Leytonstone and 21 in Leyton, by 1789 there were 98 in Leytonstone and 111 in Leyton. With this mounting poverty the vestry sought economy in good management, without relaxing efforts to alleviate genuine distress.

From 1771 a regular apothecary was employed, salaried from 1780. From 1795 there were two, one for each side of the parish. From 1797 the poor were inoculated at parish expense. In 1798 a dispensary was established at the workhouse. From 1798 a parish midwife was employed; by 1826 there were two.

Trouble was taken to find suitable trades for the children, particularly if disabled. They usually went for a trial period to the master, before being bound, and the beadle had to visit all apprentices from time to time, to report on their treatment. From the

1770s a number went to Middlesex silk-weavers, and from 1802 to Barking fishermen.

From 1786 parish expenditure was always over £1,000, and from 1803 over £2,000. The rate rose to 6s. between 1801 and 1804, and only once fell below 5s. thereafter. The cost of pensioners never fell below £400 after 1812, and rose to £725 in 1818. The cost of casual relief, never below £200 after 1807, rose to £444 in 1817, swollen by the effects of seasonal employment.[62] In 1819 the general vestry threatened to review the assessments of farmers if they did not stop turning off each winter Irish immigrants hired in spring and summer. A small scheme launched by the vestry in 1813 to employ the casual poor in carding and spinning coarse wool seems to have proved inadequate, for from 1817 the winter poor were set to digging gravel and carting it without horses. A press report suggests that some parishioners opposed this degrading mode of employment.[63] Of 38 poor carting gravel in one February week in 1819 31 were Irish.

In 1818 the parish expenditure was £3,144, a figure not equalled before or after, and the rate was 7s. The select vestry, set up in 1819, four years later analysed the causes of increasing distress. Though prices had been declining, wages had been reduced proportionately, and the failure of the farmer at Ruckholt in 1822–3 had thrown a number of labourers out of work. There was much sickness, due to overcrowding, not least in lodging-houses full of Irish. But the select vestry could find no evidence of mismanagement contributing to the rising cost, and in 1823 handed back control to the general vestry.

In 1826 resolutions regulating relief included a scaled means test: a married man with four children earning 10s. a week did not qualify. With strict rules, the rate was held at 5s., raising about £2,000, until 1836, when responsibility for Leyton's poor passed to the West Ham guardians.

The workhouse, built in 1742 on ground behind the alms-houses leased for 99 years from David Gansel, was a brick building resembling John Strype's vicarage.[64] It cost £502, borrowed in the parish, to build and equip. The house was enlarged in 1783. In 1800 the house, its ground, and adjoining coach-houses, were bought for £275, of which £200 was borrowed in the parish. In 1811 a workroom was built on the site of the coach-houses. In 1819 the house had 9 bedrooms and 30 beds.

A salaried master and mistress were employed. A small workhouse committee functioned until about 1761, the overseers paying over their rate to one of its members, as treasurer. From 1775 meticulous accounts were kept. Local tradesmen usually served the house in rotation until 1816, when the vestry ordered that all provisions should go to competitive tender. Unsatisfactory suppliers received short shrift. In 1776 the weekly allowance for each man was increased from 4 to 7 lb. of wheaten bread, and to 36 oz. of meat.

Those in the house picked oakum, and from 1797 also stripped feathers and spun flax. They were allowed part of their earnings. A few went out of

[58] V.C.H. Essex, v. 34.
[59] For the later history of the fire service see p. 213.
[60] See p. 239.
[61] For the parish funds for the poor built up from compensation payments for inclosures, see pp. 204, 240.

[62] See p. 200.
[63] L.R.L., L59.2 Pamphlet.
[64] Cf. L.R.L., L72.2 Print and L72.4 Print. For the vicarage, see below, p. 215.

the house to work. Between 1797 and 1836 there were seldom fewer than 30 in the house; in 1801 there were 53.

The workhouse was closed in 1836 and demolished in 1842, the site being thrown into the churchyard. The separate workroom, retained as a vestry room, was demolished in 1938.[65]

From 1709 the parish owned a copyhold property on the west side of Leyton High Road, opposite the William IV public house.[66] In 1685 the lord of the manor of Leyton had granted John Willett, labourer, a 99-year lease of 16 perches of waste, with an ancient cottage, for an annual rent of 1s. 6d.[67] In 1709 the parish, which had paid £14 5s. the year before to release Willett's widow, Sarah, from prison,[68] took over the remainder of the lease 'for the use of the Parish'.[69] After Sarah's death in 1716[70] the parish let the cottage; the rent, applied by the churchwardens to the poor, was usually added to the bread fund. The property was known successively as the parish house, Ballard's houses (after 1758), and High Street cottages. In 1785 the parish bought a renewal of the lease for two lives from the lord of the manor.[71] From 1820 the rent was transferred from the vicar and churchwardens to the overseer. By then there were six cottages on the site, and by 1842, when they were let at £40 a year, seven, insured for £700. When the apportionment of charity income between Leyton and Leytonstone was considered in 1854, doubt was expressed whether it was correct to apply the rent to the poor-rate, or whether it had been given originally for charity. The vestry resolved in 1856 to divide the rent between the Leyton and Leytonstone national schools, in the same proportions as the parish charities.[72] Doubt about the origin of the property persisted. In 1888 the vestry agreed with the local board to hand over the income for the maintenance of the recreation ground.[73] The following year the property was enfranchised, the cottages demolished, their materials sold, and tenders for building leases invited. The site was still vacant in 1904, when the Leyton U.D.C. Act settled all doubts by vesting it in the U.D.C.[74] The land was let for various purposes by the council until 1928, when it was let on a building lease, and is now (1968) occupied by shops.[75]

LOCAL GOVERNMENT AFTER 1836. Under the General Highway Act, 1835,[76] the vestry remained responsible for parish roads not maintained by the turnpike trustees, and continued to employ a paid surveyor.[77] In 1851, following the example of Walthamstow, it appointed a highway board of six members,[78] though not qualified to do so, as the population of the parish was under 5,000. The board employed a surveyor, clerk, and rate collector.[79] From 1857 the vestry was referring to this board complaints of sewage discharged into open ditches from newly-built houses, and from 1859 applications for new roads to be adopted. In 1859 the vestry appointed a nuisances removal committee. In the 1860s, with new building continuing, opinion was divided as to the best machinery of government. In 1864 a movement to set up a local board was defeated as premature. But the highway board's membership was increased to 12 or more and in 1865 it was also constituted the nuisances removal committee. The same year Leytonstone's water supplies and sewerage were reported inadequate. In 1866 the vestry, under government pressure, resolved to constitute it a special drainage district comprising the whole parish east of the Woodford railway line, including the Wanstead ditch. Under the Sanitary Act, 1866, appointment of the nuisances removal committee was taken over by the West Ham guardians,[80] but the vestry's powers were restored by the 1868 Act. The same year a government inspector, looking into complaints against the vestry as sewer authority, urged the formation of a local board. But the vestry continued to rely on the highway board, delegating to it its powers under the sanitary acts, requiring the submission to the board of drainage plans before buildings were begun, and appointing a sanitary committee with strictly limited powers. Attempts to discredit the board by challenging their accounts, and even accusing them of 'chewing up the ratepayers' money in sundry dinners',[81] were rejected by the justices. In 1867 the vestry successfully opposed a proposal to include the parish in a highway district under the Highways Act, 1862. But when the Public Health Act, 1872, threatened to transfer to the unpopular West Ham guardians the powers of the parish for sewerage and sanitary purposes, the vestry at last petitioned for the appointment of a local board.

In 1873 the Leytonstone special drainage district was dissolved and the civil parish of Leyton, together with the Walthamstow Slip, constituted an urban sanitary district.[82] The Wanstead Slip was added to the district in 1875.[83] Minor boundary adjustments with Wanstead were made in 1887 and 1900.[84] The board's membership was 15, increased to 24 in 1893, when the district was divided into 4 wards.[85] In 1888 the board was constituted also

[65] See also pp. 209–10.
[66] E.R.O., D/CT 221, no. 271; D/DU 101/4 (loose plan). The site is now (1968) occupied by nos. 811–17 High Road.
[67] Unless otherwise stated this account is based on Kennedy, *Leyton*, 152, 260, 306–13.
[68] L.R.L., L55 MS. Chwdns. Accts. 1681–1722.
[69] L.R.L., L47 MS. Vestry Mins. 1686–1723.
[70] L.R.L., L55 MS. Chwdns. Accts. 1681–1722.
[71] L.R.L., L47 MS. Vestry Mins. 1781–1811.
[72] Ibid. 1834–74.
[73] L.R.L., L47 MS. Local Bd. Mins. 1886–9.
[74] *Rep. of Clerk as to Leyton Charities*, 1906, p. 17.
[75] *L.U.D.C. Mins. and Reps.* 1918–19, p. 61; *L.B.C. Mins. and Reps.* 1926–7, p. 543, 1927–8, pp. 224, 336, 445, 1928–9, p. 36.
[76] 5 & 6 Wm. IV, c. 50.
[77] L.R.L., L47 MS. Vestry Mins. 1834–74.
[78] Ibid.

[79] L.R.L., L53.4 MS. Highway Cttee. Mins. 1851–61. Apart from the other refs. given, the following information about local government up to the formation of the local board of health is taken from minutes of the vestry, 1834–74 (L.R.L., L47 MS.) and its highway board, 1851–61, 1868–73 (L53.4 MS.).
[80] W.H.L., W. Ham Union Mins. (6 Sept. 1866).
[81] L.R.L., L55.6 Q. Printed poster.
[82] Local Govt. Bd.'s Prov. Orders Confirmation Act, 1873, No. 2, 36 & 37 Vict. c. 82 (local act).
[83] Local Govt. Bd's Prov. Orders Confirmation (Leyton etc.) Act, 1875, 38 & 39 Vict. c. 193 (local act).
[84] Local Govt. Bd's Prov. Orders Confirmation (No. 2) Act, 1887, 50 & 51 Vict. c. 84 (local act); L.R.L., L47 MS. Local Bd. Mins. 14 Sept. 1886; *L.U.D.C. Year Bk.* 1919–20, p. 28.
[85] L.R.L., L47 MS. Local Bd. Mins., 6 Oct. 1891, 6 Apr. 1893.

a burial board,[86] and in 1894 the electric lighting authority under the Electric Lighting Acts, 1882 and 1888.[87]

The board met in the vestry room until 1882 when public offices, designed by J. Knight, were opened in Leyton High Road.[88] These were outgrown by 1892, and in 1894–6 a new town hall was built beside the old one.[89]

The board's staff was headed by the part-time clerk, who was also vestry clerk and had been clerk to the highway board.[90] From 1877 he also became the board's solicitor, on a fee basis. When he resigned in 1879 his successor was required to be resident and attend three hours a day at the board's offices, and his salary included the legal business. By 1882 the clerk's duties required daily and regular attendance during office hours, and from that date he was allowed a small sum on the petty cash account for clerical help. The local board's surveyor had also worked for the highway board. In 1881 a resident full-time road surveyor was appointed to help him. When the surveyor resigned in 1882 the board advertised for a full-time resident engineer and surveyor. The appointment of William Dawson, a civil engineer experienced in municipal work in London, Portsmouth, and Bristol, at this crucial stage of Leyton's growth introduced vigour and confidence to the board's work.[91] The rate collector received a commission until 1885. In 1886 a salary was substituted, and a second collector appointed. The board also appointed, on an annual basis, a sanitary inspector and a medical officer. In 1890 the board stopped paying on commission for assistance with private street improvements. Instead, this work became the responsibility of the clerk's and surveyor's offices. In view of this, the terms of both appointments were altered, to include allowances for the employment of staff. But in 1894 the board invited its finance committee to consider the advantages of all departmental staff being engaged directly by the board.

The press were being admitted to the board's meetings by 1878. In 1887 malpractices in tendering for road contracts, exposed by the press, were investigated, and two contractors who admitted operating a 'knockout' were debarred from tendering. A succession of ratepayers' associations kept watch on the board's proceedings from 1879.

The board held office just before and during the years when Leyton had a bigger proportionate growth rate than any other English town with over 50,000 inhabitants.[92] It took over from the vestry a loan debt of £5,150;[93] by 1893 it had borrowed £197,234. In its first year of office the board's estimated district expenditure was £5,000, requiring a rate of 2s. 6d. on a rateable value of about £50,000.[94] By 1892 the estimated year's expenditure was

£24,319; though with the district's increasing value the poundage was still under 3s.

The cause of this increasing expenditure was the acceleration of building. In 1871 there were 1,768 houses in the parish.[95] Building was steady but not unduly heavy in the 1870s, the number of houses rising to over 3,000 by 1879. But by 1881 about 700 houses were being built each year. The board's first building by-laws came into force in 1877. In 1881 the board's sanitary committee stated that builders were ignoring them. When Dawson became surveyor in 1882 he immediately inspected every house being built. With few exceptions he found the by-laws were indeed being contravened, and he charged 32 builders by name. The board supported him, authorizing the serving of notices and, if necessary, legal proceedings. A deputation of builders to the board was rebuffed, and within a year or two most of them had come into line or left the district. By 1892 the by-laws were being generally observed. In the previous ten years some 7,000 plans had been approved.[96]

Building on this scale created problems. The provision of sewerage and other public services is dealt with below.[97] The streets taken over by the local board from the vestry were in a bad state, but by 1884 the board had borrowed £85,000 for their make-up and improvement, and in 1887–8 a further £21,000 was spent. Between 1874 and 1893 the mileage of maintained streets rose from about 20 to over 45. In 1884 Frog Row was pulled down to widen Leyton High Road, and Moyers Lane (now Hainault Road), Church Lane in Leytonstone, and James Lane were also widened. In 1894 the board took compulsory powers to widen Leyton High Road and Holloway Road.[98]

The health of the district was consistently good, with the exception of the Harrow Green area, where, in the early 1880s, the death rate from infectious diseases was above the national average, owing to the insanitary state of the small shared houses built in the 1860s. The sanitary inspector's visits were concentrated there with noticeable improvement. Milk was often the source of infection. A smallpox epidemic in 1885–6, with 98 cases involving 24 deaths, was mainly at Harrow Green, among families employed over the district boundary in the infected area of West Ham. An isolation hospital was provided from 1889.[99]

Under the Local Government Act, 1894, the local board was replaced by an urban district council[1] of 24 members, representing 4 wards.[2] In 1903 the district was redivided into 9 wards, each with 3 members; in 1920 the number of wards was increased to 10, bringing the membership to 30. In 1910 an extension to the town hall was opened in Ruckholt Road.[3]

[86] Ibid. 5 June 1888.
[87] Elec. Lighting Orders Confirmation (No. 2) Act, 1894, 57 & 58 Vict. c. 50 (local act).
[88] Wilkinson, *Leyton*, 68. Apart from the other refs. given, the following information about the local board is taken from the board's records in L.R.L. The most important are: L47 MS. Local Bd. Mins., 1877 sqq.; *Local Bd. Cttee. Reps.*, 1880–1, 1883 sqq.; L53.4 MS. Highways and Lighting Cttee. Mins., 1873 sqq.
[89] Wilkinson, *Leyton*, 59–60. See also above and below, pp. 182, 237.
[90] L.R.L., L53.4 MS. Highway Cttee. Mins. 1868–73.
[91] Wilkinson, *Leyton*, 71.   [92] *V.C.H. Essex*, v. 6.

[93] Local Govt. Bd.'s Prov. Orders Confirmation Act, 1873, No. 2, 36 & 37 Vict. c. 82 (local act).
[94] L.R.L., L55.6 MS. General District Rate Bk. 1873.
[95] *Census*, 1871.
[96] *L.U.D.C. Engineer and Surveyor's Reps.* 1895–1907.
[97] See p. 211.
[98] 57 & 58 Vict. c. 46 (local act).
[99] See p. 213.   [1] 56 & 57 Vict. c. 73.
[2] Apart from the other refs. given, the information about the U.D.C. is taken from its *Mins. and Cttee. Reps.* 1895–1926 and *Year Bks.* 1895–9, 1919–26, in L.R.L.
[3] E.R.O. T/A 12/2/2; L.R.L., L47 Pamph. *U.D.C. Chairman's address*, 1909.

The council's staff in 1895, taken over from the local board, numbered fewer than 20. As wages were paid by the clerk a small book-keeping section developed in his department. In 1897 the council resolved that all officials, except the clerk and medical officer, should be full-time; that the next clerk should be full-time, and that, while the book-keeping should remain under the control of the clerk, the next vacancy should be filled by a professional accountant.[4]

From 1905, pressed by the Local Government Board, the medical officer gave up his private practice and became a full-time officer. From 1906 an accountant replaced the book-keeper, though a local bank manager continued to act as treasurer until 1926. From 1923, when Ralph Vincent, clerk since 1879, resigned, that appointment, too, became full-time.

After the district council took over from the local board, the rate of building did not slacken until about 1904; 8,602 plans were approved in the council's first eight years of office. By 1907 it had 66 miles of road, including 10 miles of main road.[5] Between 1891 and 1901 the population grew by 56·7 per cent[6] and by 1904 exceeded 100,000.[7] The sanitary and financial powers of the U.D.C. were increased by an Act of 1898 which also authorized it to provide recreational amenities and to take over private tramways.[8] An Act of 1904[9] strengthened its existing powers, including those as electricity authority, and empowered it to extend the tramways and acquire the remaining lammas lands.[10] In 1897 the charity commissioners had appointed the district council trustees of the vestry room and adjoining fire-engine shed; the 1904 Act transferred the premises absolutely to the council.[11] Under the Education Act, 1902, the council became the local education authority.[12]

Most of the services provided or improved by the council are described elsewhere.[13] It adopted the Small Dwellings Acquisition Act, 1899,[14] in 1909. In the next eighteen years 430 applications were dealt with and £143,486 advanced.[15] In 1915–16 about 1,300 houses were damaged or wrecked by bombing[16] and after the war the council took the first steps to provide municipal housing.[17] Road widening and improvement continued.[18]

By 1903 the council's loan indebtedness was £568,009[19] and by 1926 £848,182. The district rate after 1895, still made half-yearly, was usually over 3s. a year, but did not exceed 4s. until 1916.

It had been steadied by the continuing rise in rateable value, from £303,190 in 1899 to £512,614 in 1913. After the war, however, the poundage rose sharply, to 9s. by 1921, though it fell thereafter to 6s. Consistently the separate poor-rate (which included the county and police rates) was higher than the district rate, rising from 1921 to over 16s.

Before the First World War party politics were unknown in the council chamber,[20] and elections were fought not on party lines but on matters of burning local interest.[21] According to the Leyton ratepayers' association, which was active from 1903, it was the Labour party which introduced the 'political virus'. After the 1920 election Labour members virtually controlled the council, which became the target for the protests of the middle classes union and the ratepayers' association against the soaring combined rate (£1 6s. 4d. in 1921), though the council was responsible for less than half of it. As a result of this organized hostility the council's attempt in 1921 to promote a Bill providing for a staff superannuation scheme, improved borrowing facilities, and increased powers for street improvements (all proposals later brought into effect) was defeated. The 1921 election produced stalemate on the council, followed from 1922 by domination by the association's candidates up to the time of incorporation.[22]

Municipal incorporation was being seriously discussed in Leyton as early as 1891, but without result. A formal petition to the Privy Council in 1920, held up by two royal commissions on local government, was granted in 1926. The borough retained the urban district's division into 10 wards, each thenceforward represented by one alderman and three members.[23]

In 1936 part of Kirkdale Road school was adapted as offices for the education department. When classes began at the South-West Essex Technical College in 1938 the old technical institute became an extension to the town hall. In 1948, as part of a general office reorganization, the health department moved out of the town hall to premises in Sidmouth Road. By 1962 the corporation employed 680 officers and staff.[24]

After 1926 local elections were never free of party politics. In the 1920s and 1930s the choice lay between the Labour candidates and those of the ratepayers' association, who denied that they represented a combination of the political enemies of the Labour party or received support from political funds.

[4] L.R.L., L47 Pamph. *U.D.C. Chairman's address,* 1898; for the staff schedule, see *U.D.C. Mins. and Reps.,* 1897–8, pp. 309–15.
[5] *Eng. and Survs. Annual Reps.* 1895–1907.
[6] *V.C.H. Essex,* v. 5.
[7] Leyton U.D.C. Act, 1904, 4 Edw. VII, c. 240 (local act).
[8] Leyton U.D.C. Act, 1898, 61 & 62 Vict. c. 175 (local act).
[9] Leyton U.D.C. Act, 1904.
[10] See p. 199.
[11] Leyton U.D.C. Act, 1904, s. 156; *Rep. of Clerk as to Leyton Charities,* 1906, pp. 16–17.
[12] See p. 233.   [13] See pp. 183, 211.
[14] 62 & 63 Vict. c. 44.
[15] *Leyton B.C. Charter Day, 1926: souvenir programme,* 34.
[16] Weston, *Leyton and Leytonstone,* 215.
[17] See p. 213.
[18] Local Govt. Bd's Prov. Orders Confirmation (No 1) Act, 1897, 60 & 61 Vict. c. 4 (local act); Local Govt. Bd.'s

Prov. Orders Confirmation (No. 13) Act, 1900, 63 & 64 Vict. c. 182 (local act); Min. of Health Prov. Orders Confirmation (No. 2) Act 1924, 14 & 15 Geo. V, c. 14 (local act).
[19] L.R.L., L32.5 Pamph. *Thirty Years: a generation of service 1903–1933,* p. (d).
[20] E. Campfield, *Leyton Official Guide,* 1912, p. 12; L.R.L., L47 Pamph. *U.D.C. Chairman's address,* 1909, 1910.
[21] L.R.L., L32.5 Pamph. *Thirty Years . . . 1903–1933,* p. 4.
[22] Ibid. 14–22.
[23] L.R.L., L47 MS. Local Bd. Mins. 1889–91, 1891–3; E.R. i. 15; Wilkinson, *Leyton,* 75; L.R.L., L47 Pamph. *U.D.C. Chairman's address,* 1898; *Charter Day, 1926: souvenir programme,* 10–13; L.R.L., L32.5 Pamph. *Thirty Years . . . 1903–1933,* p. 7. Apart from the other refs. given, the following information about the borough council is taken from its *Mins. and Cttee. Reps.* 1926–65 and *Year Bks.* 1926–63 in L.R.L.
[24] *Leyton Official Guide* (c. 1962), 13.

Labour members controlled the council from 1924 to 1931, but thereafter, up to the Second World War, control alternated, with two-thirds of the electorate never voting in local elections.[25] After the Second World War the council was always controlled by Labour.[26]

The corporation obtained additional powers in 1928 to widen both High Roads, Cathall Road, Church Lane, and Mount Grove Road;[27] and in 1929 to lay out and develop surplus land bought under this order, and the earlier order of 1894.[28] An Act of 1950 strengthened all the council's existing powers, particularly those concerning defective buildings.[29] In 1961 Leyton's first smoke control order came into force.[30]

During the Second World War Leyton, though part of the administrative county of Essex, came under the operational control of the London civil defence region.[31] After the war the corporation's overriding problem was housing. Bombing had demolished 1,757 houses and damaged 26,181 more.[32] At the same time much outworn property needed replacing: about one-fifth of the land for residential development was occupied by houses built before 1875, and three-fifths more with those built between 1875 and 1914. Of the total estimated capital expenditure of £1,386,000 for 1959–60, £830,000 was for housing and a further £360,000 for advances to house purchasers.[33] The council's schemes are described in another section.[34]

In 1965 Leyton was combined with Walthamstow and Chingford to form the London borough of Waltham Forest.[35]

PUBLIC SERVICES. The Lea Bridge gasworks were built in 1853 by the South Essex Gaslight and Coke Co.[36] They only supplied part of Leyton, and were later sold to the County & General Gas Consumers Co., established in 1856 and incorporated in 1857.[37] In 1864 the company's operation in Leyton was statutorily restricted to the area north of Park Road, Coopers Lane, and James Lane.[38]

The company was bought out in 1868 and the Lea Bridge District Gaslight & Coke Co. formed.[39] In 1878 this was reincorporated with statutory powers as the Lea Bridge District Gas Co.[40] The rest of Leyton was supplied by the West Ham Gas Co., incorporated in 1856.[41] This had laid pipes in Leytonstone by 1857.[42] In 1871 the Park Road, Coopers Lane, James Lane line was agreed as the boundary between the two companies.[43] The West Ham Gas Co. was absorbed by the Gas Light & Coke Co. in 1910.[44] From 1910 to 1949 Leyton was supplied by this and the Lea Bridge company. In 1949, after the Gas Act, 1948, the assets of both companies were transferred to the North Thames gas board.[45]

Under powers obtained by the local board in 1894[46] the urban district council built an electricity generating station in Cathall Road, which supplied the district from 1896.[47] The works were progressively enlarged[48] to supply street lighting[49] and the tramways.[50] By 1924, besides building substations, the council was obtaining a bulk supply from Walthamstow[51] and by 1926 also from the County of London Electric Supply Co.[52] In 1948 the undertaking was vested in the London electricity board.[53]

A main drain was constructed at Leytonstone soon after it was constituted a special drainage district in 1866.[54] By 1878, under pressure from the Lee conservancy and the Havering and Dagenham commissioners,[55] the local board had built filtration tanks, and a sewer connecting to them the private drainage of the Grange Park area; a scheme had also been prepared for a main drain in Leyton High Road.[56] But the commissioners were not satisfied, and West Ham local board, which had been protesting for some ten years,[57] joined its complaints to theirs. In 1878 the West Ham board secured a Chancery order restraining the Leyton board from passing sewage into the Wanstead ditch and polluting the Channelsea river. To meet this crisis, the board in 1879 commissioned a consulting engineer to carry out a sewerage scheme. In 1883 new works

---

[25] L.R.L., L32 Pamph. *Thirty Years . . . 1903–1933,* pp. 23–6; L32.5 *Leyton and Leytonstone Truth-teller,* 1927–37; E.R.O., T/P 181/7.

[26] Local inf.

[27] Min. of Health Prov. Orders Confirmation (No. 4) Act, 1928, 18 & 19 Geo. V, c. 18 (local act), confirming Leyton Order 1928.

[28] Min. of Health Prov. Orders Confirmation (No. 4) Act, 1929, 19 & 20 Geo. V, c. 20 (local act), confirming Leyton Order 1929; for 1894 order, see above, p. 209.

[29] Leyton Corporation Act, 1950, 14 Geo. VI, c. 38 (local act).

[30] *Leyton Quarterly,* no. 3, July 1960, p. 13; no. 4, Nov. 1960, p. 3; no. 5, Summer 1961, p. 7.

[31] *Essex County Council: Rep. of A.R.P. Cttee. 1939–45,* 7–8.

[32] Ibid., Schedule II, p. 27.

[33] *Leyton Quarterly,* no. 1, Oct. 1959, p. 6; no. 2, Apr. 1960, pp. 2–3; *Yesterday, today and tomorrow: housing in Leyton.* The advances were made under powers given under the Housing (Miscellaneous Provisions) Act, 1958, as amended by the House Purchase and Housing Act, 1959.

[34] See p. 213.

[35] London Government Act, 1963, c. 33; *Walthamstow Matters,* iv. 31–2.

[36] L.R.L., L53.4 MS. Highway Cttee. Mins. 1851–61; L47 MS. Vestry Mins. 1834–74; Lea Bridge District Gas Act, 1878, 41 & 42 Vict. c. 49 (local act).

[37] County & General Gas Consumers Co. Ltd. (Lea Bridge District) Act, 1864, 27 & 28 Vict. c. 259 (local act).

[38] Ibid.

[39] E.R.O., D/F 5/10/1; Lea Bridge District Gas Act, 1878, 41 & 42 Vict. c. 49 (local act.)

[40] Lea Bridge District Gas Act, 1878.

[41] *V.C.H. Essex,* v. 45.

[42] L.R.L., L47 MS. Vestry Mins. 1834–74.

[43] Lea Bridge District Gas Act, 1878: 2nd schedule.

[44] *V.C.H. Essex,* v. 45.

[45] Ibid. 75. The minutes of the Lea Bridge District Gas Co. 1868–1949 are in E.R.O., D/F 5/10/1–5.

[46] L.R.L., L47 MS. Local Bd. Mins. 1893–4; Electric Lighting Orders Confirmation (No. 2) Act, 1894, 57 & 58 Vict. c. 50 (local act).

[47] Wilkinson, *Leyton,* 40, 63; *L.U.D.C. Year Bk.* 1919–20, p. 30.

[48] L.R.L., L47 Pamph. *U.D.C. Chairman's address,* 1898; *Eng. and Surveyor's Reps.* 1895–1907.

[49] See below.

[50] See p. 183.

[51] *L.U.D.C. Year Bk.* 1924–5, p. 23.

[52] *L.B.C. Year Bk.* 1926–7, p. 35.

[53] Ibid. 1950–1, p. 45. This was under the Electricity Act, 1947, 10 & 11 Geo. VI, c. 54.

[54] L.R.L., L47 MS. Vestry Mins. 1834–74; E.R.O., T/M 402. See also above, p. 208.

[55] See p. 203.

[56] L.R.L., L47 MS. Vestry Mins. 1834–1904 and Local Bd. Mins. 1877 sqq.; E.R.O., D/SH 4, 5. Unless otherwise stated the information that follows on sewerage is taken from these sources.

[57] V.H.M., P 24/1/10 (8 Feb. 1869).

were opened in Auckland Road to dispose of all the district's sewage by chemical precipitation in tanks. The Rivers Purification Association contracted to run the works, but by the end of 1884 was in financial difficulties and abandoned them at two days' notice. The board's surveyor, Dawson,[58] took them over, and under his management they became among the finest in England.[59] Schemes were soon in hand to separate surface water drainage from the main sewers. By 1892 most roads had separate stormwater drains and the sewage works were being enlarged.[60]

In 1906 Leyton applied for admission to London's main drainage system,[61] but this was not agreed to until 1925.[62] From 1927, when the district's sewage was connected by a new main outfall sewer to the L.C.C. system at Hackney, the Leyton tanks were used for storage of stormwater only.[63] In 1962 a £2 million programme, spread over fifteen years, was in progress to enlarge the sewers laid down in the late 19th century.[64]

The accumulation of residual sludge at the sewage works[65] was dealt with by installing a destructor in 1896, which also burned household refuse.[66] The local board had adopted a regular system of dust collection in 1894,[67] and with the success of its destructor Leyton gained some reputation as a pioneer of sanitary improvement.[68] From 1909 increasing quantities of pressed sludge were sold as manure.[69] In 1962–3 the corporation adopted a scheme for bulk disposal of refuse, after salvage, by tipping outside the borough. The destructor continued to consume material unsuitable for this method.[70]

From 1853 Leyton was included in the area within which the East London Waterworks Co. was empowered to supply water.[71] In 1834 the company had moved its intake works from Old Ford to Lea Bridge,[72] and in 1852 and 1853 was empowered to construct filter beds there.[73] By 1878 its mains served the whole district[74] but with the rapid growth of population both mains and storage proved inadequate, especially in Leyton-

stone. In the 1880s complaints of interrupted supplies were frequent, and in 1884 47 wells were still supplying domestic users.[75] The local board put pressure on the company, which disclaimed in 1891 any liability to furnish a constant supply to districts outside the metropolitan area.[76] The board and, from 1895, district council, persevered, however, and in 1898 the district was brought within the limits in which the company was statutorily bound to maintain a constant supply.[77] In 1904 the company was taken over by the Metropolitan water board.[78] By 1914 every house in Leyton had a piped supply from the board.[79]

The Lighting and Watching Act, 1833, was adopted in Leyton in 1863 and in Leytonstone in 1869.[80] The streets were lit by gas supplied by the two companies[81] in accordance with their boundary arrangement.[82] Conversion to electricity began in 1901, the last gas lamps being discontinued in 1908. From 1909 until nationalization in 1948 the whole district was lit by electricity supplied by the local authority.[83]

The forest land open to the public from 1878 was controlled by the conservators.[84] The James Lane recreation ground was bought in 1885 by the lammas land commoners and local board[85] and enlarged in 1902.[86] In 1901–2 a 4 a. plot near the town hall, bought by the U.D.C. in 1898, was laid out like East Ham's central park and named the Coronation Gardens.[87] The gardens were extended to Oliver Road in 1913. The lammas lands acquired in 1904[88] were at once laid out as playing fields.[89] By 1920 some 125 a. of recreation ground and open space were being maintained by the council.[90] In 1930 the corporation bought the football ground in Brisbane Road,[91] and the recreation ground in Skelton's Lane, which was opened in 1931. The Seymour Road recreation ground was laid out about 1952, partly on land bought in 1931 for allotments.

Public baths were opened in Cathall Road in 1902.[92] In 1931 an adjoining public wash-house was built.[93] More modern baths were opened in Leyton

[58] See p. 209.
[59] Wilkinson, *Leyton*, 39. A plan of the works is in E.R.O., D/DCy T21.
[60] L.R.L., *Local Bd. San. Cttee. Reps.* 1891, 1892; *M.O.'s Reps.*
[61] *V.C.H. Essex*, v. 44.
[62] L.C.C. (General Purposes) Act, 1925: 15 & 16 Geo. V, c. 119, Pt. VI (local act).
[63] *V.C.H. Essex*, v. 77; *L.B.C. Year Bk.* 1927–8, p. 36; J. D. Watson, *Rep. on Sewerage and Sewage Disposal in Lee Valley*, 27, 30.
[64] *Leyton Official Guide* (c. 1962), 15; *Leyton Quarterly*, no. 2, Apr. 1960, p. 12.
[65] L.R.L., *Local Bd. San. Cttee. Reps.* 1892.
[66] L.R.L., L47 MS. Local Bd. Mins. 1891–4; *Eng. and Survs. Reps.* 1895–1907; Wilkinson, *Leyton*, 39, 63.
[67] L.R.L., *Local Bd. San. Cttee. Reps.* 1894; Wilkinson, *Leyton*, 39.
[68] L.R.L., L47 Pamph. U.D.C. *Chairman's address*, 1898.
[69] *Eng. and Survs. Rep.* 1909–10; *L.U.D.C. Year Bk.* (1919–20 and later edns.).
[70] *L.B.C. Year Bk.* (1962–3), 55, and local inf.
[71] E. London Waterworks Act, 1853, 16 & 17 Vict. c. 166 (local act).
[72] *V.C.H. Essex*, v. 38.
[73] Ibid.; L.R.L., L47 MS. Vestry Mins. 1834–74. See also above, p. 198.
[74] L.R.L., L47 MS. Local Bd. Mins. 1877–81.
[75] L.R.L., L53.4 MS. Highways and Lighting Cttee. Mins. 1882: *Local Bd. San. Cttee. Reps.* 1884 sqq.

[76] L.R.L., L47 MS. Local Bd. Mins. 1889–91. For the relations between the company and the Leyton public at this date, see also above, p. 198.
[77] Leyton U.D.C. Act, 1898, 61 & 62 Vict. c. 175, s. 56.
[78] *V.C.H. Essex*, v. 39.
[79] Ibid. 40.
[80] L.R.L., L47 MS. Vestry Mins. 1834–74.
[81] *Eng. and Survs. Reps.* 1895–1907.
[82] See above.
[83] *Eng. and Survs. Reps.* 1901–2, 1908–9.
[84] See p. 205.
[85] See p. 198, and L.R.L., L47 MS. Local Bd. Mins. 1883–6.
[86] Apart from the other refs. given, the inf. on recreation grounds and open spaces is taken from *Leyton U.D.C. and B.C. Year Bk.* (1919 and later edns.); *Eng. and Survs. Reps.* 1895–1907; *U.D.C. Mins. and Reps.* 1897 sqq.; and *B.C. Mins. and Reps.* 1929 sqq. (all in L.R.L.).
[87] L.R.L., L47 Pamph. U.D.C. *Chairman's address*, 1898.
[88] See p. 199.
[89] A. P. Wire, *Guide to Leyton*, 1910, pp. 27–8.
[90] *V.C.H. Essex*, v. 51.
[91] *Leyton and Leytonstone Truth-teller*, no. 2 (4th ser.), Nov. 1931.
[92] Apart from the other refs. given, the inf. on baths is taken from the *Leyton U.D.C.* and *B.C. Year Bks.* 1895–9, 1919 sqq. and *Council Mins. and Reps.* (all in L.R.L.).
[93] *Leyton Official Guide* (1949), 32.

High Road in 1934.[94] In 1923, with the forest conservators' consent, Leyton and Walthamstow councils agreed on improvements to a swimming pool dug by the unemployed at Whipps Cross in 1905.[95] Under this joint management the pond was converted by unemployed labour into a bathing lake opened in 1932,[96] and in 1937 into a modern open air swimming pool, now called the Whipps Cross Lido.[97]

From 1768 the vestry housed and maintained the parish fire equipment[98] and from 1778 paid an engine keeper. For some years after 1809 it was appointing 12 engine men. In 1865 it bought a new manual engine, and a volunteer fire brigade was formed[99] based on the engine house by the vestry room in Church Road. From 1877 the local board paid for horsing the appliances, and in 1878 contributed to the cost of a second engine house, built in St. John's churchyard,[1] Church Lane, Leytonstone, by the churchwardens, who had bought a hose cart. From 1880 the board maintained both stations and paid two engine keepers. In 1881 it bought a manual engine for Leytonstone, so a third station was set up at Harrow Green for the hose cart. In 1893 the board and the volunteers each bought a steam fire-engine.[2] Well equipped, connected by telephone to the police, with electric call bells to its members, the brigade's reputation became international. It won a prize at the Paris Exhibition in 1900.[3] In 1903 the U.D.C. appointed the first paid fireman,[4] and by 1909 was employing a duty man, day and night, at each station.[5] In 1914 the council rebuilt the Harrow Green station, which became the main station,[6] and in 1919 it replaced the horse-drawn engines by three motor engines.[7] By this time it was entirely responsible financially for the brigade,[8] though in 1927 there were still only 12 professional firemen, as defined by the Fire Brigade Pensions Act, 1925,[9] in a brigade of over 30 members. The combination of professional and auxiliary manning continued until 1941,[10] when the brigade became part of the national fire service.[11] In 1948 it became part of the Essex county fire brigade,[12] and in 1965 was absorbed in the Greater London fire brigade.[13]

The district council made advances to ratepayers to buy small houses from 1909.[14] In 1920 work began on its first housing scheme, 142 houses on the Barclay estate.[15] In 1925, of its loan debt of £824,284, £195,199 was attributable to housing, more than any other single service, including education, and excluding £42,297 for house purchase loans.[16] In 1926 146 houses were being built on the Nursery Park estate.[17] By 1938 over 350 municipal dwellings had been built, including 19 under a slum clearance scheme.[18] After the Second World War, to ease the immediate shortage, 418 temporary dwellings were erected, some of them on forest land at Whipps Cross, others scattered on vacant plots and bomb sites. Some were still occupied in 1965.[19] Between 1945 and 1954 161 war-destroyed houses were rebuilt, and of 762 new permanent dwellings 733 were built by the local authority.[20] In 1951 sites available for housing totalled only 13½ a. To overcome this land shortage, the redevelopment of substandard property begun in the 1950s was planned on a 'leap-frog' system, a reserve of housing being created ahead of each clearance. The process began with Villiers Close, completed in 1959, on the site of the council's old works depot at Ive farm; this rehoused Crescent Road families, whose old houses were then demolished, clearing a site for the next stage.[21] Building upward at higher population densities also compensated for lack of land. In 1961 the first eleven-storey tower block was completed on the Leyton Grange estate, followed in 1963 by a second at Leyton Green, and the seventeen-storey Livingstone College Towers block. Between 1948 and 1964 the corporation completed nearly 2,000 dwellings.[22]

Before 1889 the local board sent infectious cases to Plaistow or to London hospitals. When the London hospitals refused to accept any more, a few beds were set up as a temporary arrangement, first in Ruckholt farm-house, then, from 1891, in cottages at the sewage works, while abortive discussions went on with neighbouring authorities for a joint scheme.[23] In 1896 an iron hospital with 48 beds was erected on another part of the sewage works site, in Auckland Road. This, later enlarged to 94 beds, served

[94] Ibid. (1934), 35; *Leyton and Leytonstone Truth-teller*, no. 2 (6th ser.), Nov. 1933; L.R.L., L32.5 Pamph. *Thirty Years: a generation of service*, 26.
[95] *Rep. R. Com., Poor Laws and Relief, 1909* [Cd. 4795], p. 321, H.C. (1909), xliv.
[96] *Leyton Official Guide* (1934), 12.
[97] Ibid. (1949), 37, (c. 1962), 25.
[98] See p. 207.
[99] L.R.L., L47 MS. Vestry Mins. 1752–1874; L37 Pamph. Printed appeal for contribution to funds, 1865. Many of the brigade's records, incl. mins. 1879–1919, are in L.R.L.: L37 MS.
[1] E.R.O., D/CF 17/4.
[2] L.R.L., L53.4 MS. Local Bd. Highway Cttee. Mins. 1873–83; L47 MS. Local Bd. Mins. 1877–81, 1891–3; Wilkinson, *Leyton*, 56.
[3] Wilkinson, *Leyton*, 56; *Eng. and Survs. Reps.* 1895–1907 (these include annual tables from 1897 of all fires attended, with details of the brigade's equipment and personnel); L47 Pamph. *U.D.C. Chairman's Address*, 1909.
[4] L.R.L., L96 Pamph. *Leyton Express and Independent* cutting, 1962, obit. of W. Wilkinson; *L.B.C. Mins. and Reps.* 1927, p. 827.
[5] L.R.L., L47 Pamph. *U.D.C. Chairman's address*, 1909.
[6] *Eng. and Survs. Rep.* 1913–14.
[7] *L.U.D.C. Mins. and Reps.* 1918–19, p. 349, 1919–20, p. 107.
[8] *L.U.D.C. Year Bk.* 1919–20, p. 13; L51.5 MS. Fire

Brigade Wages Bk. 1919–22; *L.U.D.C. Mins. and Reps.* 1919 sqq.; *L.B.C. Mins. and Reps.* 1926 sqq.
[9] 15 & 16 Geo. V, c. 47; *L.B.C. Mins. and Reps.* 1927, p. 827.
[10] e.g. *L.B.C. Mins. and Reps.* 1931–2, p. 1016, 1933–4, p. 347, 1934–5, p. 186, 1937–8, p. 700, 1939–40, p. 650.
[11] Under the Fire Services (Emergency Provisions) Act, 1941, 4 & 5 Geo. VI c. 22.
[12] Under the Fire Services Act, 1947, 10 & 11 Geo. VI, c. 41.
[13] Under the London Government Act, 1963, 11 & 12 Eliz. II, c. 33, s. 48.
[14] See p. 210.
[15] *Leyton Borough Council, Charter Day, 1926: souvenir programme*, 34; *Leyton and Leytonstone Truth-teller*, no. 1, Sept. 1927.
[16] *L.U.D.C. Year Bk.* (1925–6), 43.
[17] *Charter Day, 1926: souvenir programme*, 34; *Leyton and Leytonstone Truth-teller*, no. 1, Sept. 1927; *Yesterday, today and tomorrow: housing in Leyton*, 1964–5.
[18] *Yesterday, today and tomorrow*; *V.C.H. Essex*, v. 66.
[19] *Yesterday, today and tomorrow*; *V.C.H. Essex*, v. 67.
[20] *V.C.H. Essex*, v. 67.
[21] *County of Essex Devt. Plan, 1952: Rep. of Survey*, pt. II, Met. Essex, table 2; *Leyton Quarterly*, no. 1, Oct. 1959, p. 6; no. 2, Apr. 1960, pp. 2–3.
[22] *Leyton Official Guide* (c. 1962), 15; *Yesterday, today and tomorrow*.
[23] L.R.L., L47 MS. Local Bd. Mins. 1877–86; *Local Bd. San. Cttee. Reps.* 1885–91.

until 1939, closing after Leyton bought a half-share in Walthamstow's isolation hospital at Chingford.[24]

Langthorne hospital, built in 1840 as the West Ham union workhouse,[25] was enlarged in 1865, 1883, 1897–8, 1913, and 1930.[26] After the First World War it became known as the central home.[27] Following the Local Government Act, 1929,[28] it was transferred in 1930 to the West Ham borough council, which ran it as a home for the chronic sick, aged, and infirm; in 1936 there were about 1,800 beds.[29] Under the National Health Service Act, 1946,[30] it became part of the Leytonstone group of the N.E. Metropolitan regional hospital board,[31] and was renamed Langthorne hospital in 1948.[32] New wards were opened in 1960.[33] Since 1965 it has become part of the Forest group, and in 1966 had 600 beds for long-stay cases.[34]

In 1889 the West Ham guardians bought Forest House and its 44 a. of grounds at Whipps Cross.[35] An infirmary was built in the grounds and opened in 1903.[36] After the First World War it was known as Whipps Cross hospital.[37] From 1930, like Langthorne hospital, it was managed by the West Ham council.[38] In 1936 it provided 741 beds for acute medical and surgical cases; it was recognized as a training school.[39] It was enlarged in 1938–40.[40] Since 1946 it has belonged to the same hospital groups as Langthorne hospital.[41] It was enlarged again in 1953 and in 1966 had 955 beds for acute cases.[42]

The Leyton, Walthamstow and Wanstead Children's and General voluntary hospital, now known as the Connaught hospital, is described under Walthamstow.[43]

Leyton's public libraries from the adoption of the Public Libraries Acts in 1891 to 1955 have been described elsewhere.[44] The new Harrow Green branch library was opened in 1960.[45] The total bookstock of the Leyton libraries in 1964, shortly before they were combined with the Walthamstow and Chingford libraries to form Waltham Forest public libraries, was 257,008.[46]

PARLIAMENTARY REPRESENTATION. Under the Representation of the People Act, 1918,

Leyton, previously part of the Walthamstow division, became a parliamentary borough with two divisions, east and west.[47] Under the Representation of the People Act, 1948, the two divisions were combined to form a single constituency, the first election under the new arrangement being held in 1950.[48]

The 1918 election and by-election were won by Liberal Coalition and Unionist Coalition candidates; in 1922 two Conservative members were returned. In 1923 one seat fell to Labour, the other being retained by the sitting Conservative. The Conservatives won both seats in 1924, but lost them to Labour in 1929. The Conservatives recovered both seats in 1931, but lost one to Labour in 1935 and both in 1945.[49] From 1950 to 1964 the single constituency was held for Labour by a local non-conformist, the Revd. Reginald Sorensen, first elected in 1929, and its representative without break since 1935. At the 1964 general election he again had a majority of 7,926; but he was persuaded to accept a life peerage, to create a vacancy for the foreign secretary, Mr. Patrick Gordon Walker, who had been defeated at Smethwick in a contest embittered by racial issues. The by-election which followed early in 1965 produced 'the most astonishing election result since the war'. There was a massive abstention of Labour voters, widely interpreted as resentment against the 'disposal' of Lord Sorensen and introduction of a newcomer, and on a low poll, the Conservative was elected by a majority of 205.[50] Leyton returned to its Labour allegiance at the general election in 1966, when Mr. Gordon Walker defeated the same Conservative opponent by a majority of 8,646.[51]

CHURCHES. In 1086 there was a priest on Robert son of Corbutio's manor of Leyton,[52] and another on Hugh de Montfort's manor, later Cann Hall, Wanstead.[53] The church of Leyton was granted to Stratford Abbey with the manor about 1200 by Richard Corbutio[54] and descended with the manor until the partition in 1650. Abbott's third descended with his third of the manor to the corporation of

[24] L.R.L., *M.O.'s Rep.* 1896; *L.U.D.C. Mins. and Reps.*; *L.B.C. Mins. and Reps.*; L 47 Pamph. *U.D.C. Chairman's address*, 1909; *L.U.D.C.* and *L.B.C. Year Bks.*; *Kelly's Dir. Essex*, 1914; *Leyton Official Guide* (1922), 16; *Charter Day, 1926: souvenir programme*, 33. For the isolation hospital at Chingford see below, p. 285, and *V.C.H. Essex*, v. 100.

[25] *White's Dir. Essex* (1848). The date is on the chapel. For the hospital see above, plate f.p. 203.

[26] *Leytonstone Hospital Information Handbook*; West Ham Corpn. Act, 1898, 61 & 62 Vict. c. 259, pt. VIII (local act).

[27] *Kelly's Dir. Essex* (1922 and later edns.).

[28] 19 Geo. V, c. 17.

[29] D. McDougall, *Fifty years a borough*, 112, 192.

[30] 9 & 10 Geo. VI, c. 81.

[31] *Leytonstone Hospital Information Handbook*.

[32] *Leyton Official Guide* (c. 1952), 47.

[33] Ibid. (c. 1962), 9.

[34] *London Borough of Waltham Forest: Health and Welfare Services Handbook*, 1966, pp. 49–50.

[35] *Official Record, Visit of . . . the King and Queen, . . to Whipps Cross War Hospital*, 1917. For Forest House, see above, p. 189.

[36] L.R.L., L32.5 Pamph. *Thirty years: a generation of service*, 6; L34 Pamph. *Souvenir of opening of the new infirmary*, 1903; A. P. Wire, *Guide to Leyton*, 1910, p. 19.

[37] *Kelly's Dir. Leytonstone, Wanstead and Snaresbrook* (1925).

[38] McDougall, *Fifty years a borough*, 112, 192–3.

[39] Ibid.

[40] *Leytonstone Hospital Information Handbook*.

[41] See above. For Forest House itself after 1946 see p. 190.

[42] *London Borough of Waltham Forest Health and Welfare Services Handbook*, 1966, pp. 49–50; *Leytonstone Hospital Information Handbook*.   [43] See p. 285.

[44] *V.C.H. Essex, Bibliography*, 330.

[45] *Official Guide* (c. 1962), 20.

[46] *Leyton Public Libraries Annual Rep.* 1963–4.

[47] Wilkinson, *Leyton*, preface, p. 64; *E.R.* xxvii. 61; W. H. Weston, *Story of Leyton and Leytonstone*, 223.

[48] *L.B.C. Year Bk.* (1950–1).

[49] The Leyton members are listed in the *U.D.C.* and *B.C. Year Bks.* Their political affiliations can be traced in: *Leyton and Leytonstone Express and Independent* 21 Dec. 1918; *Who's Who*, 1927; *E.R.* xxviii. 3, 80; and *Kelly's Dir. Leytonstone, Wanstead and Snaresbrook* (1925), p. A20.

[50] *Illustrated London News*, 30 Jan. 1965, p. 31; *Guardian*, 22 Jan. 1965; *The Times*, 14 Nov. 1964.

[51] *Whitaker's Almanack* (1967).

[52] *V.C.H. Essex*, i. 546.   [53] *V.C.H. Essex*, i. 497.

[54] E.R.O., T/P 195/1, no. 5 (Holman MS.). The church of 'Leya' given to Stratford Abbey by Gilbert de Montfitchet (Newcourt, *Repertorium*, ii. 380) was not Leyton, but Lee Chapel (see above, p. 185 n. 33).

Lincoln, from whom it was purchased in 1794 by John Pardoe, except for the next presentation to the vicarage, which had previously been sold.[55] The other two-thirds of the advowson passed to the Gansels, who presented to the vicarage in 1738 and 1754.[56] The heirs of Gen. William Gansel (d. 1774) sold their two-thirds to Nicholas Corsellis in 1783.[57] Thomas Spurrier of Walsall presented his son, Thomas Hector Spurrier, in 1797, having purchased the next turn of the corporation of Lincoln; but by 1811 the advowson was vested solely in the Pardoes.[58] Between 1870 and 1874 the advowson became vested in Edward Jones Brewster, vicar of Leyton 1873–80.[59] He died in 1898 and his representatives presented in 1899 and the Simeon Trustees in 1900. Since 1907, when his widow died, the living has been in the gift of the Simeon Trustees.[60]

In 1254 the rectory was valued at 10 marks[61] and in 1291 at £5 6s. 8d.[62] By agreements made in 1222 and c. 1480 the tithes of Leyton were apportioned between Stratford Abbey and Haliwell Priory, whose endowment by the de Valognes family had included tithes in the manor of Ruckholt.[63] After the Dissolution the tithes which Haliwell Priory had held appear to have descended with the priory's Leyton estate until 1570, when they were held by Walter Morgan and his wife Jane.[64] In 1598 they were held by Thomas Vaughan,[65] but no later reference to them has been found. The great tithes were partitioned in 1650, but only descended with the advowson in the case of Abbott's third share. Ozler's share descended to Robert Haselar, who sold it in 1773 to Robert James of Leyton, from whom it passed to his son, Richard.[66] Swanley's share was devised by Gen. William Gansel to his nephew, David Jebb, from whom it was purchased by Richard James in 1801.[67] James's two-thirds were in the hands of his executors in 1831[68] and of William Frith of Hackney (Mdx.) by 1840.[69] In 1843 Frith's two-thirds were commuted for £246; the remaining third, the property of John Pardoe, was commuted for £123. An area of 281 a. was exempt from tithe as demesne land of Stratford Abbey.[70]

The vicarage, a poor one, is first mentioned in 1254, when it was said to be scarce worth 40s.[71] It was valued at £1 13s. 4d. in 1291,[72] £7 12s. in 1535,[73] and

£30 in 1604.[74] Its endowments were listed in 1650 as a vicarage house, an acre of glebe, small tithes worth £16 a year, and £3 a year charged on the manor of Leyton; this was being augmented by £50 out of New Barns in West Ham.[75] In 1656 the vestry ordered that the vicar, Philip Anderton, should receive £100 a year, the balance being made up by free contributions.[76] In 1661 the value was again £30,[77] but in 1669 the inhabitants agreed to subscribe £69 a year to support their new incumbent, John Strype. The agreement implies that his predecessor, John Cox, had been assisted in the same way.[78] The augmentation of the living was discussed by Strype with the bishop in 1687, but in 1703 its basic value was apparently still £30.[79] An offer by Ozler in 1697 to sell his share of the great tithes to the bishop, to settle them on the vicarage, came to nothing because the bishop hoped he might be persuaded to devise them.[80] John Dubordieu estimated that in 1738–9, his first year as vicar, he received about £94 from all sources, including contributions.[81] This suggests that the income was still being augmented by subscription. By 1831, however, the gross income was £554.[82] The increase may be explained partly by the multiplication of fees with a growing population, but mainly by the enhanced value of the small tithes, which were commuted in 1843 for £394, plus 1s. per head of cattle turned out on the tithable lammas lands.[83] The small tithes had probably grown at the expense of the great tithes, which they exceeded in 1843. A similar situation is found at East Ham,[84] though there is no evidence of the details of the process in Leyton. In 1685 the vicar's glebe comprised two separate half-acres in the common marsh;[85] in 1843 the total was 3 r. 37 p.[86]

A vicarage house existed in 1537.[87] It was stated in 1650 to be ruinous and not fit to live in; in 1652 the churchwardens were paying rent for part of it occupied by a poor woman.[88] A cobbler was later living there rent free.[89] In 1677–8 a new vicarage designed by Richard Sadleir of Leyton was built on the north side of Church Road, at the junction with Leyton High Road, at a cost of £216 of which £140 was borne by Strype.[90] It was enlarged in 1849.[91] A new vicarage was built in the garden in 1893.[92] The old vicarage continued to be used as a

[55] Kennedy, *Leyton*, 16–17; Act for vesting . . . estates devised by John Smith . . ., 35 Geo. III, c. 54 (priv. act).
[56] Morant, *Essex*, i. 26.
[57] Kennedy, *Leyton*, 16–17.
[58] Ibid. 16–17, 395; E.R.O., D/DB Q3.
[59] Kennedy, *Leyton*, 16–17; *Kelly's Dir. Essex* (1870, 1874).
[60] *Crockford* (1900); *Essex Almanac* (1901), 70; M. L. Savell, *Old Leyton Church*, 19; *Kelly's Dir. Essex* (1906); *Chelmsford Dioc. Year Bk.*, 1968–9; inf. from Miss M. L. Savell.
[61] *E.A.T.*, N.S. xviii. 17.
[62] *Tax. Eccl.* (Rec. Com.) 22.
[63] *E.A.T.* ii. 189–94.
[64] *Cal. Pat.* 1569–72, 65.
[65] C 142/254/70.
[66] Lysons, *London*, iv. 173; Kennedy, *Leyton*, 16–17; C.P. 25(2)/1476 Mich. 14 Geo. III; *Rep. R. Com. Eccl. Rev.* H.C. 54, p. 254 (1835), xxii.
[67] Kennedy, *Leyton*, 16–17; C.P. 25(2)/1478 Hil. 41 Geo. III.
[68] *Rep. R. Com. Eccl. Rev.* H.C. 54, p. 254 (1835), xxii.
[69] E.R.O., D/CT 221.
[70] Ibid.
[71] *E.A.T.* N.S. xviii. 17.
[72] *Tax. Eccl.* (Rec. Com.), 24.

[73] *Valor. Eccl.* (Rec. Com.), 435.
[74] H. Smith, *Eccl. Hist. Essex*, 17.
[75] Ibid. 248. The £3 charge on the manor dated from before the Dissolution (S.C. 6/962) and was expressly reserved in the 1545 grant of the manor and rectory to Wriothesley: E.R.O., D/DW E19. For New Barns, see above, p. 115.
[76] Kennedy, *Leyton*, 367.
[77] *E.A.T.* N.S. xxi. 76.
[78] L.R.L., L147 MS. Vestry Mins. 1658–1722 (Strype).
[79] B.M. Add. 5853, f. 69v.; *E.R.* xxxviii. 66.
[80] B.M. Add. 5853, f. 71.
[81] G.L.C., DL/C/201, f. 96.
[82] *Rep. R. Com. Eccl. Rev.* H.C. 54, p. 654 (1835), xxii.
[83] E.R.O., D/CT 221. For the lammas lands, see above, pp. 198 sqq.
[84] See p. 25.
[85] Newcourt, *Repertorium*, ii. 381.
[86] E.R.O., D/CT 221.
[87] S.C. 6/962.
[88] Smith, *Eccl. Hist. Essex*, 248; Kennedy, *Leyton*, 137.
[89] G.L.C., DL/C/168. f. 260, DL/C/272, f. 65v.
[90] Ibid.; Kennedy, *Leyton*, 322–5; Newcourt, *Repertorium*, ii. 381; Colvin, *English Architects*, 519.
[91] Kennedy, *Leyton*, 321.
[92] *Leyton Quarterly*, no. 4, Nov. 1960, pp. 2–3.

church house until it was destroyed by bombing in 1941.[93] It was a two-storeyed brick building with a symmetrical front, sash windows, and a pedimented doorway. The interior fittings included an original staircase with turned balusters.[94] The vicarage of 1893 was sold to the corporation in 1958 with the whole vicarage site, and was demolished in 1959. In 1961 a block of flats called John Strype Court was completed on the site.[95] A house in Vicarage Road is now occupied as a vicarage.

In the late 16th and early 17th centuries the patronage seems to have been neglected and the cure badly served. Three vacancies between 1561 and 1617 were filled by the bishop by lapse.[96] George Johnson, vicar 1565–75, who was also vicar of Walthamstow and non-resident, provided a curate at Leyton whose preaching was said to be inaudible.[97] Robert Godfrey (1585–1617) was listed in 1604 amongst insufficient or negligent preachers.[98] Robert Domvile (c. 1626–1638) was questioned at the metropolitical visitation of 1636 on unspecified inconformities, though he denied them.[99] Late in 1638 Thomas Lake was instituted on the presentation of Lady (Mary) Lake.[1] Though a mandate for Lake's induction was issued immediately after,[2] Samuel Keme (d. 1670), the Puritan divine, attended the 1639 Easter vestry meeting as vicar.[3] Lake was summoned as vicar to the archdeacon's visitation a week later, on 22 April, but Keme appeared in his place, the record noting that Lake was 'with Master Rich and not yet inducted'.[4] Later the same year Keme was summoned to a synod as curate of Leyton, but the entry was altered to vicar;[5] he continued to be summoned as vicar until the archidiaconal court ceased in 1641, though there is no record of his institution or induction.[6] He was still described as vicar in 1643, though he had been chaplain and captain of a troop of horse since 1641 and was also said to be 'chaplain at sea' to the lord high admiral, Robert Rich, earl of Warwick.[7] Lake's absence, followed by Keme's departure to war, at a time when the advowson was changing hands, and when both the church and vicarage were in disrepair, probably contributed to the confused and unsettled state of the cure in the following years. Keme's military activities can have left little time for serving the cure, though his family were living in Leyton at least until 1647.[8] It is not known when

he relinquished the living, if, indeed, he ever legally held it, but in 1644 Samuel Toxey was described as vicar.[9]

No minister signed among those attending vestry meetings between 1644 and 1652.[10] Hugh Williams, a sequestrated minister from Norfolk who was living in Leyton from 1647, probably held no official position there, though he may sometimes have conducted services.[11] In 1648 no minister for Leyton was named in the published classical scheme, when Sir William Hicks was designated elder.[12] By 1650, however, Jeremiah Levitt, commended as an able and godly minister, was supplying the cure by order of the Committee for Plundered Ministers.[13] On Levitt's death in 1651 Philip Anderton's appointment was approved by the Westminster Assembly; he is described as minister of the parish and the registers note his formal induction. The church was partly rebuilt during his incumbency, one of the few examples of church building under the Commonwealth. Anderton was indicted in 1661, as vicar, for refusing to preach or use the book of common prayer, and he was ejected in 1662.[14] John Cox (1662–9) was apparently elected minister or preacher in his place by the inhabitants, and though he was neither instituted nor inducted styled himself vicar in the vestry minutes.[15]

Cox's successor, John Strype (1669–1737), the historian, was chosen minister by the votes of 62 inhabitants, who undertook to subscribe annually to augment his income provided he continued the usual custom of his predecessor in preaching twice on Sunday. Among the contributors were Sir William Hicks (£8), two well-known Puritans, Lawrence Moyer (£3) and Daniel Andrews (£3), and John Tabraham (4s.), who may have been a Baptist.[16] In a dispute argued in the consistory court in 1738 between Strype's granddaughter and executrix, Susannah Harris, and his successor John Dubordieu (1738–54), concerning liability for repairs to the vicarage and its out-buildings, evidence was given that the three patrons had complimented the parish on their choice of Strype to be their lecturer or curate. Evidence was also given that Strype was licensed in 1674 by the bishop of London, but never instituted or inducted. The judge ruled, however, that Strype had been the lawful vicar from 1669.[17]

[93] *Leyton Quarterly*, no. 4, Nov. 1960, pp. 2–3; W. H. Weston, *Story of Leyton and Leytonstone*, 104–5 (illus.).
[94] R.C.H.M. *Essex*, ii. 167.
[95] *Leyton Quarterly*, no. 4, Nov. 1960 (pp. 2–3), no. 5, Summer 1961 (p. 5); Savell, *Old Leyton Church*, 7; photograph with notes in E. gallery of church.
[96] Newcourt, *Repertorium*, ii. 382; E.R.O., D/AEM 4, f. 28.
[97] E.R.O., D/AEV 7 (14 July 1572); Newcourt, *Repertorium*, ii. 382, 637.
[98] Smith, *Eccl. Hist. Essex*, 17; E.R.O., D/AEM 4, f. 17.
[99] Smith, *Eccl. Hist. Essex*, 50; Kennedy, *Leyton*, 92, 123.
[1] Newcourt, *Repertorium*, ii. 382; E.R.O., D/AEM 4 (Archdeacon's Induction Bk.). Lady Lake was a notable defaulter on ship money payments: *V.C.H. Essex*, ii. 229.
[2] E.R.O., D/AEM 4.
[3] L.R.L., L47 MS. Vestry Mins. 1618–86; *D.N.B.*; Kennedy, *Leyton*, 115, 351–5. Easter Day fell on 14 Apr.
[4] E.R.O., D/AEV 7, f. 20v.
[5] Ibid., f. 38.
[6] Newcourt, *Repertorium*, ii. 382; E.R.O., D/AEM 4; D/AEV 7, ff. 47v., 52v., 61, 76, 80v.

[7] Kennedy, *Leyton*, 352; *D.N.B.*
[8] Kennedy, *Leyton*, 125; *D.N.B.*
[9] Leyton Par. Reg. A (Bap. 1644). He was later nominated minister of Chingford in the classical scheme published in 1648: Davids, *Nonconf. in Essex*, 419, 280. Kennedy wrongly spells his name Foxi: Kennedy, *Leyton*, 115.
[10] L.R.L., L47 MS. Vestry Mins. 1618–86.
[11] A. G. Matthews, *Walker Revised*, 275; Smith, *Eccl. Hist. Essex*, 346–7; Kennedy, *Leyton*, 93–4, 115–16; Leyton Par. Reg. A. (back page).
[12] Davids, *Nonconformity in Essex*, 256.
[13] Smith, *Eccl. Hist. Essex*, 248.
[14] Kennedy, *Leyton*, 116; A. G. Matthews, *Calamy Revised*, 11; Leyton Par. Reg. A, f. 124; R.C.H.M. *Essex*, ii. 167; Ass. 35/102/2 no. 20.
[15] Newcourt, *Repertorium*, ii. 382; L.R.L., L47 MS. Vestry Mins. 1618–86 and 1658–1722 (Strype); E.R.O., D/AEM 5 (Induction Bk.); G.L.C., DL/C/168, f. 260.
[16] L.R.L., L47 MS. Ves. Mins. 1658–1722 (Strype). For Strype's historical works see *D.N.B.*
[17] Kennedy, *Leyton*, 111, 360; G.L.C., DL/C/168 ff. 259–60, 268; DL/C/272, ff. 65v., 69v.; *D.N.B.*; *E.R.* viii. 193–201.

From 1738 vicars were appointed in the normal way. Separate lecturers were chosen by the parishioners until the middle of the 18th century, the lecturer usually serving also as assistant curate, as master of the free school, or both.[18] David Capon, lecturer 1723–51, assisted Strype until about 1728 by reading prayers on Sundays for 1½ guineas a quarter, and after 1728 took the whole duty as Strype's curate, receiving 16 guineas and half the surplice fees.[19] Thomas Keighley, vicar 1754–97, paid as much as £50 to his curates.[20] Keighley secured his own election as lecturer in 1757, as did his successor, Thomas Hector Spurrier, vicar 1797–1800.[21] There was no election of lecturer thereafter. Spurrier resigned the living, alleging persecution by some parishioners, after a complaint against him had led to a serious charge at the assizes.[22] Charles Henry Laprimaudaye (1800–48) was employing two curates in 1831, one being his nephew.[23] John Pardoe (1848–73), son of the patron, inherited the patronage himself in 1870.[24] In the present century a number of former Leyton clergy, among them two vicars, have been preferred to high office in the church, including three diocesan bishops, an assistant bishop, and two suffragans.[25]

Strype claimed in 1718 that he had preached and administered the sacrament every Christmas day for 50 years.[26] In 1738 there were two services each Sunday and one on feast days; communion was celebrated on the first Sunday in the month.[27] In 1766 and 1835 there were two services each Sunday; in 1882 there were three Sunday services, one weekday service, and one morning and one evening celebration a month. In 1827 there was a parochial library in the vestry.[28]

The parish church of ST. MARY THE VIRGIN stands on the north side of Church Road, and consists of chancel, aisled nave, and embattled north-west tower. It is mainly of the early 19th century, but the tower and parts of the north wall of both nave and chancel date from the 17th century.[29]

In the early 17th century the church comprised nave and chancel so small that the foundations of their north and south walls, uncovered in 1962, lay well within the area of the present nave, and a west tower. About 1610 Sir William Ryder (d. 1611) added a chapel or chancel on the north side of the old chancel.[30] In 1638 the churchwardens were ordered to ceil the church, glaze the windows, shingle the steeple, and set up the communion table at the upper end of the chancel and rail it in with convenient kneeling places, but in 1640 they declared their intention instead to rebuild the church.[31] In 1658–9, when the tower had become so dilapidated as to be ready to fall, it was rebuilt of red brick in a north-west position, with a small lean-to vestry on the north side. At the same time a north aisle was built, also of brick, leading from the tower along the full length of the nave and chancel; a drawing of 1799 shows the north aisle with a gabled roof at two levels, the lower where it adjoined the chancel.[32]

The archdeacon's order of 1638 to provide improved access for communicants does not appear to have been carried out, since in 1693 the chancel was reported to be too narrow for communicants to draw near, the minister having to go from pew to pew to deliver the sacrament.[33] In 1693, during the incumbency of John Strype, the chancel was lengthened, the communion table was railed, and the monument to Sir Michael Hicks and his wife Elizabeth,[34] which had previously occupied the east wall, was moved to the south wall.[35] More than half the cost was contributed by the parishioners. The extended chancel was built of red brick and had a circular east window, two oval windows on the south side, and one on the north side, where Sir William Hicks about the same time or not long after erected his monument, the oval window being incorporated in the design.[36] The south wall also had a central doorway with a gabled porch. Part of the north wall of this 1693 chancel extension survives, forming the lower part of the western end of the present chancel wall; built into it is a stone inscribed 1610 RG which may have been preserved from the old east chancel wall, demolished when the 1693 extension was carried out.[37]

An old west gallery was taken down in 1711 and rebuilt larger and projecting farther forward.[38] This was probably the gallery occupied by the choir until 1963 and subsequently by the organ only. In 1794 the church was restored; the architect was Jesse Gibson (d. 1828).[39] Pictures of the church about this date show a small gable-roofed annexe adjoining the tower and nave in the south-west corner of the church; this was the baptistery in 1811, but when it was built is not known.[40] The enlargement of the church was being discussed by 1810; a plan submitted by John Walters (d. 1821), which included adding a south aisle, was accepted in 1811 and a

[18] B.M. Add. 5853, ff. 67v., 73, 89v.–90; L.R.L., L55 MS. Chwdns Accts. 1681–1723 (1709, 1719); L47 MS. Ves. Mins. 1723–52 (1723, 1751, 1757); Kennedy, Leyton, 183–6.
[19] Kennedy, Leyton, 136, 384; G.L.C., DL/C/272, ff. 69, 69v.; DL/C/168, f. 263v; Guildhall MS. 9550.
[20] Guildhall MS. 9553; W. G. Hammock, Leytonstone and its history, 84.
[21] L.R.L., L47 MS. Vestry Mins. 1752–81 (1757), 1781–1811 (1797).
[22] Kennedy, Leyton, 395–6; Clerical Guide (1822), 20; L.R.L. L47 MS. Vestry Mins. 1781–1811 (1799).
[23] Kennedy, Leyton, 94; Rep. R. Com. Eccl. Rev. H.C. 54, p. 654 (1835), xxii; Guildhall MS. 9560; Hammock, Leytonstone, 84.
[24] See p. 186.
[25] J. T. Inskip, A Man's Job, 62–85; Chel. Dioc. Chron. Oct. 1943, p. 80; E.R. lxiii, 57.
[26] W. H. Weston, Story of Leyton and Leytonstone, 112.
[27] Guildhall MS. 9550.
[28] Ibid. 9558, f. 218, and 9560; E.R.O., D/AEM 1/2, T/P 110/45.

[29] Unless otherwise stated the description of the church and its monuments is based on: R.C.H.M. Essex, ii. 167; Pevsner, Essex, 2nd edn. 267–8; Kennedy, Hist. Leyton; M. L. Savell, Old Leyton Ch.; F. H. Smith, Leyton Par. Ch.; R. Gunnis, Dict. Brit. Sculptors. There are many pictures of the church, its furnishings and monuments in L.R.L. (Prints, L72.1, L72.8, L83.1) and in the church itself.
[30] E.R. xlii. 1; P.C.C., 119 Lawe.
[31] E.R.O., D/AEV 7, ff. 11v., 65v.
[32] Guildhall Libr., Lysons, London (extra. illus.), iv, after p. 164.
[33] E.R.O., D/AEV 7, f. 11v.; E.R. xlii. 1.
[34] See p. 219.
[35] E.R. xlii. 1; E.R.O., T/P 195/1, no. 5.
[36] See also p. 219.
[37] E.R.O., T/P 195/1, no. 5; E.R. xli. 194–5, xliii. 2; E.R.O., Pictorial Collections. Robert Godfrey was vicar in 1610.
[38] L.R.L., L47 MS. Vestry Mins. 1658–1722 (Strype).
[39] H. M. Colvin, Biog. Dict. English Architects, 236; L.R.L., L47 MS. Vestry Mins. 1752–1811.
[40] L.R.L., L72.1 Prints and Plan (1811).

faculty obtained in 1814[41] but the proposal was dropped. In 1817 Thomas Lane of Leyton Grange, churchwarden 1800–16, paid for the erection of a gallery over the communion table to hold 100 Sunday school boys; the girls were accommodated by enlarging the west gallery. The late-17th-century windows in the chancel were probably bricked up during these alterations.[42] In 1822 the church was at last enlarged, apparently to the design of John Shaw (d. 1832). The builder was Thomas Cubitt.[43] A south aisle was added, the same length as the north aisle, with a small gallery at its west end.[44] The new aisle was built of brown stock brick in a plain Gothic style. Twelve feet of the chancel, being the older westernmost part of it, were incorporated in the nave, reducing the chancel to the 1693 extension. A chancel arch and clerestories were built of timber framing covered with lath-and-plaster, and the whole church was reroofed, the old part of the chancel being increased in height to take the new hipped roof of the nave.[45] The nave roof and clerestories were supported on slender clustered 'Gothic' piers of cast iron.[46] A vestry was built on the south side of the chancel, with a small gallery over it; the boys' gallery was demolished and the east chancel wall rebuilt.[47] The tower was heightened by the addition of battlements.[48] In 1853 a new east window was inserted in the chancel and the Hicks monuments were removed to the base of the tower,[49] and in 1884 a new baptistery was built in the south-west corner of the church. The church was restored in 1889, when the communion table and stained glass in the east window were given.[50] The oak chancel screen and altar-piece, copied from Leonardo da Vinci's *Last Supper*, were added in 1920 as a war memorial; the screen was placed under the west gallery in 1963.[51] Extensive restoration was begun in 1929 under the supervision of J. Andrew Minty. In 1932 the chancel was lengthened by 16 feet; the foundation stone of the extension was laid with masonic ceremonial, most of the money having been provided from masonic sources.[52] The lath-and-plaster chancel arch was replaced by concrete, and the vestry enlarged. The hipped roof of the nave was replaced by a gable roof and the cast iron piers were encased in concrete of octagonal section; the clerestory was also rebuilt in concrete.[53] Oval windows were inserted on each side of the sanctuary, larger than their 17th-century prototypes, and the 19th-century Gothic east window was made taller.[54] In 1935 the 17th-century vestry in the north-west corner of the church, which had been used as a stokehole since the 19th century, was restored to its original use. In the same year an oriel window was

built over the south-west doorway. The church suffered damage by bombing during the Second World War, and repairs carried out in 1951 included redecorating the interior and rebuilding the parapet walls of the tower. Oak communion rails, designed by J. Stuart Syme, were erected in 1955 in memory of Canon R. B. Bertin, vicar 1940–52. Restoration work begun in 1962 included reflooring the nave.[55] While work was in progress several burial vaults with later infilling were discovered below the floor. They included a very large one under the west end of the nave which had been constructed in 1711 for Sir Gilbert Heathcote of Forest House.

In 1906 there were three bells, one of the 14th century, possibly by William Dawe, one of 1634 by John Clifton, and one of 1694 by Phillip Wightman. Four were added in 1906, two of them being recast from Clifton's bell. Two more were added in 1928. A sanctus bell in the choir listed in 1552 may have been that shown in 18th-century pictures hanging in a small cupola on the tower. In 1806 this cupola was replaced by the present larger cupola and clock, said to have come from the Great House. In the same year the churchwardens sold a church bell; this may have been the old sanctus bell and the present clock bell one which came with the new cupola and clock. The clock was made by William Addis in 1768; the bell is said to be 17th-century.[56]

The church plate consists of a silver-gilt cup dated 1775, a silver-gilt cup, 3 patens, and a flagon of 1794, a silver-gilt alms-dish of 1733, and 4 alms-dishes of 1836.[57]

The font is believed to be of 15th-century origin, but the pedestal was given in 1827 by William Cotton.[58] The organ, which was apparently bought second-hand at Brighton, was installed in the west gallery in 1822, and was described in 1827 as built by Flight & Robson. When it was rebuilt in 1968 evidence was found that some parts of it dated from about 1760.[59]

An ancient bench against the north wall of the chancel may be a 16th-century houselling bench. A poor-box dated 1626, with a carving of a cripple on the front, is in the south-east porch. An hour-glass dated 1693 came from the Augustinian church at Munich. A beadle's staff dated 1824 was presented to the church in 1905 by Robert Holdgate.[60]

The church has a large and fine collection of monuments, reflecting the wealthy residential character of the parish; but many have been moved from the positions they occupied when they were first listed and described in the 18th century.[61] Under the west gallery are brass inscriptions com-

[41] E.R.O., D/DB Q3; Colvin, *Engl. Architects*, 534, 648; Guildhall MS. 9532/10, ff. 200–4.
[42] *E.R.* xlii. 2–3.
[43] E.R.O., D/DB Q4; Colvin, *Engl. Architects*, 536–8, 648; Revd. R. Bren's notes displayed in church.
[44] L.R.L., L72.1 Plan (1822).
[45] *E.R.* xli. 194, xlii. 3.
[46] E.R.O., T/P 196, Eccl. Ess. ii. 159.
[47] *E.R.* xlii. 3.
[48] Revd. R. Bren's notes displayed in church.
[49] *E.R.* xlii. 3; E.R.O., T/P 196, Eccl. Ess. ii. 159–60.
[50] *E.R.* xlii. 3. [51] Ibid. 4.
[52] Foundation stone on east wall of chancel; inscribed board by east gallery staircase; inf. from Revd. L. Denny.
[53] *E.R.* xli. 195, xlii. 4; Inskip, *A Man's Job*, 64; *Chel. Dioc. Chron.* Mar. 1932, p. 47, July 1932, p. 103; E.R.O., T/P 196, Eccl. Ess. ii. 159–60; *Essex Churchman*,

Apr. 1962; C. H. Crouch, *Short account of . . . fragments discovered during . . . restoration . . . in the parish church of Leyton . . . 1932.*
[54] *E.R.* xlii. 4.
[55] *Essex Churchman*, Apr. 1962.
[56] *Ch. Bells Essex*, 25–6, 323–5; Gunn, *Great House*, 18.
[57] *Ch. Plate Essex*, 18–19.
[58] E.R.O., T/P 196, Eccl. Ess. ii. 161.
[59] E.R.O., D/AEM 1/2; *Essex Churchman*, Apr. 1962; Revd. R. Bren's notes displayed in church; inf. from Revd. L. Denny. A restoration appeal in 1933 claimed that the organ came originally from Brighton Royal Zoo; E.R.O., Libr. Folder, s.v. Leyton.
[60] Brass inscription on staff.
[61] Lysons, *London*, iv. 165–72; *East Anglian*, iii. 55–6, 80–1, 138–9; E.R.O., T/P 195/1, no. 5; T/P 196, Eccl. Ess. ii. 159–248.

memorating Ursula, daughter of Luke Gasper (1493),[62] Lady (Mary) Kingston (1548), Sir Edward Holmden (1616), and the benefaction of Robert Rampston (1585).[63] In the so-called Hicks chapel below the tower are the two largest monuments in the church, moved from the chancel in 1853. The earlier carries alabaster effigies of Sir Michael Hicks (1612) and his wife Elizabeth (1635). It was originally in the form of an altar-tomb but the parts were re-arranged later and the monument now extends along the whole south wall of the chapel. Against the north wall is an equally large memorial, possibly by Bartholomew Adye, which was erected by Sir William Hicks (1702) in his own lifetime.[64] It incorporates a recumbent figure of his father, Sir William Hicks Bt. (1680), flanked by standing figures in Roman dress of the second Sir William and his wife, Lady Marthagnes (1723). Above the central effigy and evidently part of the design, is the stone surround of an oval window of 1693, formerly in the north wall of the chancel.[65]

On the west wall of the north aisle is a monument to William Bosanquet (1813) by John Flaxman. On the north wall are monuments to Samuel Bosanquet (1765), signed by Joseph Pasco of Hackney, Thomas Hawes (1685), attributed to John Annis (d. 1740) or his brother James, Sir John Strange (1754), by Sir Henry Cheere,[66] and Sir Richard Hopkins (1735). On the east wall of the north aisle is an impressive monument to Charles Goring, earl of Norwich (1671). Below the floor at the entrance to the chancel is the ledger slab to John Strype (1737), his wife Susanna (1732), and daughter Hester (1711). Strype's grave is marked by a stone on the fourth chancel step.[67] A monument to E. J. Brewster (1898) in the chancel is by Thomas or Edward Gaffin. A tablet to Newdigate Owsley (1714) and his family by Samuel Tufnell is on the east wall of the south aisle, and the brass depicting Elizabeth Wood (1626), her husband Toby, and their twelve children stands against the wall.[68] Monuments on the south wall include those of Sir Robert Beach-croft (1721), John Story (1786) by John Hickey, and John Hillersden (1807) by John Flaxman.

A monument to Samuel Bosanquet (1806) designed by Sir John Soane, which stood in the churchyard west of the church tower, was demolished in 1957–8, after damage by vandals, and replaced by an inscribed grey granite slab.[69] An altar-tomb in the churchyard, surmounted by an oval urn, to Frances Sherburne (1819) is signed by Thomas Mocock of Leyton.

By will made between 1776 and 1778 Henry March left £200, half the income to maintain the tomb of his wife Elizabeth (1726) in Leyton churchyard and half to the minister serving Leytonstone chapel.[70] This fund is administered (1968) by the churchwardens of St. Mary's, half the income being paid to the vicar of St. John's, Leytonstone.[71] Eleanor Bosanquet, by will proved 1820, left £100 to maintain the monument of her husband, Samuel (1806). The income in 1884, when the monument was restored, was about £3 a year.[72] The fund is administered by the family.[73]

St. Mary's was the only place of Anglican worship in Leyton until 1749, when a chapel was opened in Leytonstone; this became the separate parish of St. John the Baptist, Leytonstone, in 1845.[74] The population growth after 1860 was met at first by the foundation of mission churches, but from 1879, when the parish of Holy Trinity was created for the overcrowded Harrow Green district, the process of subdividing the two mother parishes accelerated. The Walthamstow Slip was added to the parish of Leyton in 1885.[75] By 1903 there were 9 parish churches and 12 missions, including a small Y.W.C.A. mission, in the urban district. Even so, there was a smaller proportion of Anglican than nonconformist worshippers in the district.[76] Another parish was created in 1907, after which there was no change for over twenty years. The wealthy families who had encouraged church building had left the district; two parish churches built in 1902 and 1906 remained uncompleted for lack of funds. One mission closed in the 1920s. In the 1930s some reorganization took place, when three old-established mission churches became parishes, another became a conventional district, and one mission church closed. In 1937 the vicar of St. Mary's noted that as families of established churchgoers left the district, they were not being fully replaced by newcomers.[77] Between 1945 and 1968 one church and two more missions closed, and two parishes were amalgamated.

In the following individual accounts, where it is stated that the advowson of the vicarage was vested in the bishop, this means the bishop of the diocese which then or later included Leyton.[78]

Within St. Mary's parish the iron mission church of ST. PHILIP, Brewster Road, Leyton, was opened in 1897[79] and closed in 1954.[80] The Russell mission, Goldsmith Road, Leyton, was opened in 1900 in an iron church presented by a parishioner and named after E. B. Russell, vicar 1899–1900, who bought the site himself, but died before the opening. A London City missioner was in charge for

[62] *E.R.* ix. 85; E.R.O., T/P 195/1, no. 5; Lysons, *London*, iv. 167.
[63] *Trans. Mon. Brass Soc.* vii. 40; Mill Stephenson, *List of Monumental Brasses*, 126, 744; *E.A.T.* N.S. vi. 166, x. 188–9, xx. 279.
[64] *E.R.* xlii. 3; Chancellor, *Sepulchral Monuments of Essex*, pls. cvii, cviii. The date of death on the monument is 22 Apr. 1703 (cf. E.R.O., T/P 195/1, no. 5), but Sir William was buried on 26 Apr. 1702.
[65] Chancellor (*Sepulchral Monuments*, 307) thought the vacant oval panel 'meaningless' unless it had been intended for an inscription; he was not aware that the oval had once framed the window.
[66] L.R.L., L72.8 Print.
[67] *E.R.* xli. 195–7.
[68] *Antiquary*, xxix. 176. Elizabeth Wood was buried in 1626.
[69] D. Stroud, *Architecture of Sir John Soane*, 164,

pl. f.p. 21; E.R.O., D/DBq L3; inf. from Mr. D. N. Frazer-Taylor, High Warden, and personal observation. A photograph of the monument is in L.R.L.
[70] *Rep. Leyton Charities* (1906), 14–15; Lysons, *London*, iv. 170.
[71] Inf. from Revd. L. Denny.
[72] E.R.O., D/DBq L3; see also above.
[73] Inf. from Revd. L. Denny.
[74] See below.
[75] E.R.O., T/P 75, D/CPc 64.
[76] R. Mudie-Smith, *Relig. Life Lond.* 364–6.
[77] 'Changing Leyton', *Leyton Par. Mag.* Mar. 1937.
[78] In the following accounts, when no source is quoted, the information has been obtained by local inquiry. Fuller accounts are in M. L. Savell, 'Church of England in Leyton' (L.R.L., TS).
[79] *Chs. Barking Deaneries*, 35.
[80] *Leyton Par. Mag.* Jan. 1955.

many years.[81] The mission closed about 1952[82] and the site was bought by the corporation for housing in 1957.[83] The Victoria mission room, adjoining St. Mary's church house in Leyton High Road, was in existence by 1901[84] but is not listed in directories after 1914.[85]

The church of *ST. JOHN THE BAPTIST*, High Road, Leytonstone, originated in 1748, when leading Leytonstone residents, including William Dunster, the poet David Lewis, and Samuel Bosanquet, bought a 99-year lease of a site on the west side of Leytonstone High Road from the trustees of the poor of Bourne (Lincs.) to build a chapel.[86] The patron, David Gansel, opposed the scheme, and the vicar, John Dubordieu, was not helpful. Nevertheless, the chapel opened in 1749, Dunster having told Dubordieu that 'neither bishop, patron nor vicar could hinder their building a meeting'. The services were taken by a Mr. Carter, but Gansel secured a citation against him for officiating in an unlicensed chapel. This led to closure of the chapel until 1754, when it reopened as a chapel of ease to the parish church, with a minister licensed by the bishop.[87] The stipend was provided by the pew-rents.[88] In 1819 the chapel was enlarged and licensed for administration of the sacrament, but the site being leasehold it could not be consecrated.[89] In 1833 the permanent church of St. John the Baptist, built by subscription, with a grant from the Church Building Society, was opened on a site farther north given by William Cotton.[90] It was designed by Edward Blore in the Early English style, in yellow brick with stone dressings, and comprised a small sanctuary, nave, and a tall west tower of three stages surmounted by pinnacles.[91] The old chapel was converted to enlarge the national schools.[92] In 1845 the new parish of St. John was formed.[93] The advowson was vested in the Pardoes until 1874, when it was transferred to the bishop.[94] The growing population of Leytonstone, particularly at Harrow Green, led to the foundation of the churches of Holy Trinity (1874), St. Andrew (1882), St. Margaret (1883), St. Augustine (1886), and St. Columba (1888). Separate parishes were soon assigned to all of these except St. Augustine's. St.

John's itself was enlarged in 1893 by the addition of chancel and choir vestry.[95] The south aisle and new vestries were built in 1910.[96] The south aisle was extended at the east end in 1929 to form a side chapel.[97] In 1956 the church was restored.[98]

The church has a set of plate which is said to have been transferred to St. John's from the old Chapel Royal when it was demolished. It consists of 2 cups and 2 patens of 1779 and a flagon and alms-dish of 1778.[99]

The mission church of *ST. AUGUSTINE OF HIPPO*, Lincoln Street, Leytonstone, originated in open-air services held by St. John's clergy opposite the Bell public house.[1] About 1886[2] an iron building was provided in Mayville Road. This was replaced in 1889 by a temporary brick church.[3] In 1902 a permanent church of plain design was opened on an adjoining site in Lincoln Street, the temporary church becoming the hall.[4] An early curate-in-charge, W. Walker (1894–1916), established a ritualistic tradition.[5] In 1915 St. Augustine's was gutted by German incendiary bombs; the hall was used for services until the church was restored in 1920.[6] A conventional district was formed in 1937.[7] In 1952 a new vestry was built and the church was renovated the following year. From 1962 to 1965 the church was served by a curate of St. John's and from 1965 by the vicar of Holy Trinity doubling as priest-in-charge.[8]

The church of *HOLY TRINITY*, Harrow Green, originated as an iron mission church of St. John, built in Birkbeck Road in 1874 for the Harrow Green district.[9] The permanent church, a plain brick building with painted windows, was opened in 1878.[10] A new parish was formed in 1879 from the parishes of Leyton, Leytonstone, Wanstead, West Ham, and St. Paul, Stratford; the advowson was vested in the bishop.[11] The population of the parish was working-class, mainly railway employees.[12] The choir vestry was added soon after 1903 and the south chapel soon after 1905. The church was damaged in the Second World War but restored. St. Margaret's was taken from Holy Trinity in 1893, and St. Columba's (1895) and St. Luke's (1932) were partly taken from it. In the early

81 *Leytonstone Express and Independent*, 20 Oct. 1900; Mudie-Smith, *Relig. Life Lond.* 364; *Kelly's Dirs. Essex* (1908–17).
82 *Leyton Par. Mag.* May, June, 1952.
83 *Leyton B.C. Mins. and Reps.* 1955–7.
84 *Kelly's Dir. Walthamstow, Leyton and Leytonstone* (1901); Mudie-Smith, *Relig. Life Lond.* 364.
85 *Kelly's Dir. Essex* (1914, 1917).
86 E.R.O., D/DB Q4. For David Lewis, see *D.N.B.*, and for the Bourne estate, see above, p. 188. Chapman and André, *Map of Essex*, 1777, sheet xxi, incorrectly places the chapel north of the road leading off the high road towards Grove Green, instead of just to the south of it.
87 Lysons, *London*, iv. 173–4; Morant, *Essex*, i. 26; Hammock, *Leytonstone*, 51–6, 60. Hammock deals fully with St. John's, and apart from the other sources cited in support the following account is based on his.
88 E.R.O., D/DB Q4.
89 E.R.O., D/DB Q3, 4.
90 *White's Dir. Essex* (1848), p. 251.
91 Pevsner, *Essex* (2nd edn.), 269; Wilkinson, *Leyton*, 24.
92 See p. 234.
93 L.R.L., L47 MS. Vestry Min. 10 Aug. 1844; *Retn. Par. Divided . . . 1818–1856*, H.C. 557, p. 7 (1861), xlviii.
94 *Lond. Gaz.* 11 Aug. 1874 (p. 3939); E.R.O., D/CPc 37, D/CP 11/40.

95 *Churches of Barking Deaneries*, 39; E.R.O., D/CF 31/7, D/CC 44/8.
96 R. H. Sutcliffe, *St John the Baptist, Leytonstone, 1845–1945*.
97 Ibid.; *Chel. Dioc. Chron.* Feb. 1929, p. 20.
98 Cecily L. Lake, *St. John's, Leytonstone; 125th Anniversary, 1833–1958*, 28.
99 *Ch. Plate Essex*, 21.
1 *History of the Church of St. Augustine of Hippo: extracts from the Church Magazine*; Wilkinson, *Leyton*, 24. Unless otherwise stated the following account is based on the *History of . . . St. Augustine*.
2 *St. Augustine's Church, Leytonstone, Year Bk. and Directory, 1948–9*.
3 Wilkinson, *Leyton*, 24.
4 *Kelly's Dir. Essex*, (1906).
5 *Rep. R. Com. Eccl. Discip.* [Cd. 3069], p. 465, H.C. (1906), xxxiii.
6 *Chel. Dioc. Chron.* Apr. 1916, p. 74, June 1920, p. 89, July 1916, p. 137, Feb. 1917, p. 30, June 1920, p. 89.
7 *Chel. Dioc. Yr. Bks.* 1936, 1937.
8 Ibid. 1965–8.
9 Kennedy, *Leyton*, 69–70.
10 Ibid. 70; E.R.O., D/CC 29/6, D/CP 11/38A.
11 *Retn. Parishes Divided . . . 1868–80*, H.C. 413, p. 12 (1881), lxxii; E.R.O., D/CPc 50, D/CP 8/30.
12 *Chs. Barking Deaneries*, 47.

1880s Holy Trinity started a mission in Melrose (now Kingston) Road,[13] moving it about 1890 to a room in Crownfield Road,[14] which was still in use in 1903.[15] By then, however, most of the work had been taken over by the iron mission church of *ST. ALBAN*, opened in Leslie Road in 1892.[16] This closed about 1930.[17] The site is now occupied by a small block of flats called St. Alban's Court.

The church of *ALL SAINTS*, Capworth Street, Leyton, was built in 1864 as a chapel of ease to St. Mary's on a site given by Edward Warner.[18] Built of brick, in the 'Decorated' style, it consists of nave, chancel, and transepts.[19] The tall steeply-pitched roof had to be relaid in 1884.[20] The same year a reredos of Caen stone and alabaster (a copy of that at Sandringham) was placed in the chancel in memory of Major G. C. Capper. In 1886 a new parish was formed, including part of St. James, Walthamstow.[21] The advowson was vested in the vicar of Leyton.[22] In 1883 a Sunday school for 600 children was opened beside the church. A new vestry was added in 1903–4.[23] In 1935 the parish of Emmanuel was taken from All Saints. In 1936, among other alterations, a new baptistery was made on the north-west side of the church.[24]

The church of *ST. ANDREW*, Forest Glade, Leytonstone, originated in 1882,[25] when an iron building was erected in Colworth Road, Forest Glade, as a chapel of ease to St. John's, on a site given by Henry Cotton.[26] A new parish was formed in 1887,[27] the advowson of the vicarage being vested in the bishop.[28] In the same year the first part of the permanent church was opened, comprising the chancel and part of the aisled nave, built of Kentish rag with freestone dressings in the Early English style, to the design of Sir Arthur Blomfield.[29] The rest of the nave and the pinnacled west front were added in 1893.[30] St. Andrew's served the Wallwood estate, which in 1898 was being rapidly developed with houses for city workers.[31] In 1903 it was the best attended church of all denominations in the urban district, the only one with total Sunday congregations of over 1,500.[32] A choir vestry was added in 1913.

The church of *ST. MARGARET OF AN-TIOCH*, Woodhouse Road, Leytonstone, originated in 1884, when an iron mission church in connexion with Holy Trinity was opened in Lansdowne Road to serve the working-class district near Wanstead Flats.[33] The permanent church, opened in 1893, comprised chancel, nave, and north and south aisles, designed by J. T. Newman. The vestries were added in 1899 and Lady Chapel in 1910. The flèche and tower included in the original design were never completed. The church has some notable furnishings. The high altar, carved by the people of Oberammergau, was presented in 1893. A picture of the Madonna and Child is attributed to Murillo or one of his pupils. The rood-beam with three carved figures (1921) and statue of the Madonna and Child (1924) were designed by Sir Charles Nicholson. A separate parish was formed in 1893,[34] the advowson of the vicarage being vested in the bishop.[35] Edward Sant (1893–1902) and later vicars, particularly T. H. Gilbert (1909–17) and F. E. Rance (1918–23), established a ritualistic tradition.[36] In 1895 the old iron church was moved from Lansdowne Road to the site adjoining St. Margaret's, for use as a parish room, but it was burned down in 1908. The church institute was built in 1910 and enlarged in 1930. In 1951 the parish of St. Columba was amalgamated with St. Margaret's,[37] which became known as St. Margaret of Antioch with St. Columba. A mission room for St. Margaret's was built in Pevensey Road in 1897. This became the mission church of *ST. ANSELM* in 1906; it closed by 1926.[38] The mission hall of *ST. CHRISTOPHER* in Acacia Road was associated with St. Margaret's from about 1908 to 1910.[39]

The church of *ST. CATHERINE*, Hainault Road, Leyton, originated in 1885, when an iron room in connexion with St. Mary's was opened in Francis Road to serve the Phillebrook area.[40] St. Catherine's itself was built in 1893.[41] It was a brick building, designed by R. Creed in the Perpendicular style, and consisted of chancel, nave, and north and south aisles, with large mullioned windows.[42] A separate parish was formed in 1894,[43] the advowson of the vicarage being vested in the vicar of Leyton.[44] John Kennedy, the historian of Leyton, was the first vicar of St. Catherine's (1894–1917).[45] A church hall was built in 1895.[46] George Hibbert (d. 1894) of Hibbert House[47] gave over £12,000 towards building and endowing the church and hall; in 1907 a

[13] *Leytonstone Express and Independent Almanac*, 1885.
[14] *Leytonstone Express and Independent*, 1 Jan. 1893; *Chs. Barking Deaneries*, 47.
[15] Mudie-Smith, *Relig. Life Lond.* 364.
[16] Wilkinson, *Leyton*, 24; Kennedy, *Leyton*, 72.
[17] *Chel. Dioc. Year Bk.* 1929, 1932; *Kelly's Dir. Leytonstone, Wanstead and Snaresbrook* (1927, 1933).
[18] Kennedy, *Leyton*, 66; L.R.L., L47 MS. Vestry Min. 1864. Unless otherwise stated, the following account is based on Kennedy, *Leyton*, 66–9.
[19] *Kelly's Dir. Essex* (1882, 1886).
[20] E.R.O., D/AEM 1/2.
[21] *Retn. Parishes Divided . . . 1880–90*, H.C. 386, p. 8 (1890–1), lxi; E.R.O., D/CPc 66.
[22] *Crockford* (1896), 1730.
[23] *All Saints, Leyton, Parochial Reps.* 1887–1904.
[24] *Chel. Dioc. Chron.* Oct. 1935, p. 155.
[25] *Chs. Barking Deaneries*, 49; Wilkinson, *Leyton*, 24. Kennedy, *Leyton*, 72, gives 1880, and is followed by Hammock, *Leytonstone*, 92, Sutcliffe, *St. John the Baptist, Leytonstone*, and C. L. Lake, *St. John's, Leytonstone*, 16.
[26] E.R.O., D/DPx T7.
[27] *Retn. Parishes Divided . . . 1880–90*, H.C. 386, p. 24 (1890–1), lxi; E.R.O., D/CPc 72.
[28] *Crockford* (1896), 1730; E.R.O., D/CC 38/6.

[29] *Chs. Barking Deaneries*, 49; *Kelly's Dir. Essex* (1886, 1890); Wilkinson, *Leyton*, 24.
[30] Kennedy, *Leyton*, 72.
[31] *Chs. Barking Deaneries*, 49.
[32] Mudie-Smith, *Relig. Life Lond.* 364.
[33] *Church of St. Margaret of Antioch, Leytonstone: Jubilee Souvenir, 1893–1943*, 4 f. Unless otherwise stated, the following account is based on this jubilee history and on Kennedy, *Leyton*, 71–2, *Chs. Barking Deaneries*, 55, and Wilkinson, *Leyton*, 24.
[34] *Retn. Parishes Divided . . . 1891–6*, H.C. 302, p. 6 (1897), lxvii (6); E.R.O., D/CPc 82.
[35] *Crockford* (1896), 1730; E.R.O., D/CC 44/9.
[36] *Story of St. Margaret with St. Columba, Leytonstone.*
[37] *Chel. Dioc. Year Bks.* 1952 f.
[38] *Kelly's Dir. Essex* (s.v. Forest Gate, 1922, 1926).
[39] *Story of St. Margaret; Kelly's Dir. Essex* (1906–12).
[40] See below, Christ Church.
[41] Kennedy, *Leyton*, 72–3; E.R.O., D/CC 44/7.
[42] *Chs. Barking Deaneries*, 57.
[43] *Retn. Par. Divided . . . 1891–6*, H.C. 302, p. 12 (1897), lxvii (6); E.R.O., D/CPc 84.
[44] *Crockford* (1896), 1730.
[45] J. Kennedy, *How modern parishes are formed: or the story of the first six years of St. Catherine's, Leytonstone.*
[46] Wilkinson, *Leyton*, 27.   [47] See p. 261.

reredos was erected to his memory.[48] The Phillibrook mission remained in St. Catherine's parish until 1904, when it was separated as Christ Church.[49]

The church of *ST. COLUMBA*, Wanstead Slip, in Ravenstone Road, originated as an iron mission church under Holy Trinity, opened in 1888.[50] A permanent church was opened in 1894. It was designed by E. P. Warren in 'Perpendicular' style and at first comprised chancel, nave, south aisle, Lady chapel, and small south-east turret.[51] The north aisle and vestries were completed later in the same year, by the gift of the Misses Nutter of Wanstead. A new parish was formed in 1895, including part of St. James, Forest Gate.[52] The advowson of the vicarage was vested in the bishop.[53] In 1898 a parish hall, also designed by Warren, was built in Janson Road. The church was wrecked by bombing in 1944 and its shell demolished about 1954.[54] In 1951 St. Columba's parish was amalgamated with that of St. Margaret.[55] Its church hall, surrounded by blocks of flats, was still in use in 1965.[56]

CHRIST CHURCH, Francis Road, Leyton, originated as the Phillibrook mission, in connexion with St. Mary's and later with St. Catherine's. The iron room, built in 1885, was enlarged in 1887 and 1892.[57] A permanent brick church, designed by Sir Arthur Blomfield & Sons,[58] was opened in 1902,[59] adjoining the mission. Funds were difficult to raise in this poor district[60] and only the nave and south aisle were built, the easternmost bay of the nave being used as the chancel, with a temporary east wall of iron built in the chancel arch. A separate parish was formed in 1904,[61] the advowson of the vicarage being vested in the trustees of the Church Trust Fund.[62] In 1959 the east wall was permanently bricked and an east window inserted.[63]

The church of *ST. PAUL*, Essex Road, Leyton, originated as a mission church of St. Mary, provided to serve the Barclay estate development.[64] It opened in 1903 in an iron building bought from the Wesleyans.[65] The first part of a permanent church, designed by G. Streatfeild, was built in 1906. This comprised nave, aisles, and western sections of transepts, with temporary chancel and west porch. A separate parish was formed in 1907, the advowson

of the vicarage being vested in the vicar of Leyton.[66] The original iron church served as hall until a new one was built in 1912. The permanent chancel was completed in 1927[67] and the west porch in 1950. A choir vestry was built in 1954.

The church of *ST. LUKE*, Ruckholt Road, Leyton, originated in 1901 when an iron mission under Holy Trinity was opened for the westernmost parts of the parishes of Holy Trinity and St. Catherine.[68] In 1914 a permanent church was built in grey terracotta to the design of E. D. Hoyland. It comprised aisled nave, apsidal chancel, east vestries, and an uncompleted north-west tower. The building is a striking barn-like structure, having low eaves, mullioned windows, dormers, and a very steeply-pitched pantiled roof, supported internally on wooden pillars.[69] In 1932 a new parish was formed from St. Mary's and Holy Trinity,[70] the advowson of the vicarage being vested in the bishop.[71] The church was badly damaged in the Second World War, but was subsequently restored.

The church of *ST. EDWARD*, Morley Road, Leyton, originated in 1901, when a mission in connexion with St. Mary's was opened in Claude Road. In 1902 a small site was acquired in Morley Road and the mission continued in a tent there and in neighbouring cottages until 1905, when a permanent church was built to the design of G. Streatfeild. It is a red-brick building with mullioned windows and embattled parapets, comprising nave, chancel with apse, and small western turret.[72] A separate parish was formed in 1933,[73] the advowson of the vicarage being vested in the vicar of Leyton.[74] The church closed in 1968.[75]

The church of *EMMANUEL*, Lea Bridge Road, Leyton, originated about 1902, with mission services held in Sybourn Street school in connexion with All Saints.[76] In 1906 a temporary brick church, designed by E. C. Frere, was built at the junction of Lea Bridge Road and Hitcham Road, on a site given by Sir Courtenay Warner.[77] Warner also gave a site in Bloxhall Road for the Bloxhall institute, a mission built in 1912 and run by Emmanuel in collaboration with All Saints church.[78] About 1920 Emmanuel became a mission district.[79] In 1934–5 the permanent church was built beside the tem-

[48] *Leytonstone Express and Independent*, 6 May and 2 Dec. 1893, 25 Oct. 1895, 13 Apr. 1907

[49] E.R.O., D/CPc 106, 107.

[50] Unless otherwise stated, the following account is based on: Kennedy, *Leyton*, 71; *Chs. Barking Deaneries*, 59; and *Leytonstone Express and Independent*, 31 Mar. 1888, 16 June and 17 Nov. 1894, 21 May 1898.

[51] Pevsner, *Essex* (2nd edn.), 269.

[52] *Chel. Dioc. Yr. Bk.* 1915, p. 99; *Rtns. Parishes Divided*, H.C. 302, p. 8 (1897), lxvii (6).

[53] *Crockford* (1896), 1730.

[54] Pevsner, *Essex* (2nd edn. 269); *Story of St. Margaret with St. Columba, Leytonstone*. [55] See above.

[56] *Story of St. Margaret with St. Columba, Leytonstone*.

[57] John Kennedy, *How modern parishes are formed: or the story of the first six years of St. Catherine's, Leytonstone* (c. 1900); Kennedy's printed letter appealing for funds for church to replace iron room (E.R.O., Library Folder, s.v. Leyton).

[58] *Chs. Barking Deaneries*, 57; *Proposed new church, Francis Road, Leyton* (E.R.O., Library Folder, s.v. Leyton).

[59] *Leytonstone Express and Independent*, 7 June 1902; E.R.O., D/CC 53/9.

[60] *Chs. Barking Deaneries*, 57; *Proposed new church, Francis Road* (E.R.O., Library Folder, s.v. Leyton).

[61] *Chel. Dioc. Yr. Bk.* 1915, p. 98; *Kelly's Dir. Essex* (1906); E.R.O., D/CPc 107.

[62] *Crockford* (1909), 1865; *Essex Almanac* (1904), 70.

[63] *Christ Church, Leyton, Par. Mag.* Oct. 1959, p. 1; L.R.L., L72.1 Prints: photographs of east end of church, 1953, 1959.

[64] The account of St. Paul's is based on A. Hicks, 'History of St. Paul's Church, Leyton' (*Par. Mag.* 1927–9).

[65] Mary Fletcher Memorial Methodist Church Trustees Mins. 1893–1923. It was one of their old schoolrooms.

[66] E.R.O., D/CPc 115; *E.R.* xvi. 197; J. T. Inskip, *A Man's Job*, 67–8, 79–80.

[67] *Chel. Dioc. Chron.* Apr. 1927, p. 61, Aug. 1927, p. 126.

[68] *Leytonstone Express and Independent*, 29 June 1901; *Diocesan Year Bks.* 1915 f.

[69] *Leytonstone Expr. and Ind.* 19 Dec. 1914.

[70] *Chel. Dioc. Year Bk.* 1934, p. 135.

[71] *Chel. Dioc. Year Bk.* 1932.

[72] J. T. Inskip, *A Man's Job*, 64–7; *Leytonstone Express and Independent*, 18 Feb. and 7 Oct. 1905.

[73] *Chel. Dioc. Chron.* Sept. 1933, pp. 129, 142.

[74] *Chel. Dioc. Year Bk.* 1934.

[75] Inf. from Revd. L. Denny.

[76] *All Saints Church parochial reps. 1887–1904*.

[77] *Leytonstone Express and Independent*, 21 Apr., 2 June, 13 Oct. 1906.

[78] Ibid. 28 Sept. 1912.

[79] *Chel. Dioc. Year Bk.* 1916, 1920; *Kelly's Dir. Essex* (1917, 1922).

porary one, with aid from local masonic lodges.[80] It was designed by M. Travers and T. F. W. Grant, and is of red brick, in a simple Tudor style externally, and comprises chancel, aisled nave, Lady chapel, and vestries. The interior, baroque in character,[81] is plastered cream, with a red plastered reredos. A separate parish was formed in 1935, the advowson being vested in the bishop.[82] The Bloxhall institute closed about 1956 and was sold in 1959.[83]

ROMAN CATHOLICISM

In the late 16th and early 17th centuries Roman Catholicism was upheld in Leyton by the family of Thomas More (1531–1606), grandson of Sir Thomas More.[84] He settled there in 1582[85] and from that date[86] he, his family, and servants, and their connexions also living in Leyton, were repeatedly charged with recusancy at quarter sessions, at assizes, and in the archdeacon's court. Among those charged with them Lady Guldeford and members of the Gage and Povey families were related by marriage, and the Tyas family were tenants of the Mores on their forfeited estates in Yorkshire. Thomas himself was in prison from 1582 to 1586. In 1593, as required, he registered his name with the vicar and constable.[87] The More family lived quietly on their small Leyton estate,[88] which remained free of sequestration. Mary More, wife of Thomas, was reported in 1605 to be 'no seducer of others . . . bringeth up her children and servants in recusancy . . . of peaceable and quiet carriage'. After the death of Thomas in 1606 the indictments at quarter sessions continued against his son, Christopher Cresacre More, and his household. In 1613 Cresacre took the oath of allegiance[89] and was not presented again after 1614.[90] Between 1616 and 1629 he was frequently licensed to leave Leyton, officially his place of confinement,[91] and appears to have left there about 1617 to settle on the family estate in North Mimms (Herts.), though described as 'of Leyton' in licences up to 1629. Cresacre continued to own the Leyton house[92] until his death in 1649, but after his son, Thomas (d. 1660), conformed in 1650, and the More estates were cleared of penalties, it was probably sold.

In 1676 no papists were reported in Leyton.[93] In 1766 many Irish papists were reported in the parish, and again in 1810 many of the lower class were said to be Irish papists.[94]

St. Patrick's Catholic cemetery, provided by London Roman Catholics, was opened in Union (now Langthorne) Road in 1861.[95] Etloe House was leased in 1856 as a country house for the first Roman Catholic archbishop of Westminster (Cardinal Wiseman), who lived there from 1858 to 1864.[96] But there was no Roman Catholic church in Leyton until 1897, when the Revd. F. C. G. Brown was chosen to found a mission.[97] Services were at first held in the chapel of St. Agnes school and orphanage.[98] In 1900 when St. Joseph's Catholic school was opened in Vicarage Road,[99] the upper storey was registered as a temporary church.[1] Total Sunday attendances in 1903 were 507.[2] A temporary iron church was opened in Primrose Road and registered in 1904.[3]

The permanent church of *ST. JOSEPH* in Grange Park Road was opened in 1924,[4] but not consecrated until 1930, when all debt on the building was cleared.[5] It is a simple brick building with stone dressings, consisting of clerestoried nave and chancel, with north and south chapels. The interior is decorated in a 'Byzantine' style.

Since about 1908 Etloe House, which was sold after Cardinal Wiseman's death in 1865 and privately owned for about 40 years, has been occupied as St. Pelagia's Home.[6] This was provided originally for destitute, and later for mentally defective, girls, and is run by the Sisters of the Sacred Hearts of Jesus and Mary.[7]

PROTESTANT NONCONFORMITY

Nonconformity was slow to gain a permanent footing in Leyton. The burial of all John Tabraham's children unbaptized in the 1670s suggests a family of Baptists in the parish.[8] In 1672 Daniel Andrews's house at Leytonstone was licensed for Presbyterian worship;[9] he had been a prominent vestryman from 1651 to 1662.[10] But Bishop Compton's census of 1676 gave only 8 nonconformists for Leyton.[11]

In 1748 the vicar stated that three of the larger houses in Leytonstone were occupied by dissenters

[80] *Leytonstone Express and Independent*, 9 June 1934, 27 Apr. 1935; *Chel. Dioc. Chron.* June 1934, p. 88, Mar. 1935, p. 39, May 1935, p. 71.
[81] Pevsner, *Essex*, 2nd edn. 268.
[82] *Chel. Dioc. Year Bk.* 1936.
[83] Char. Com. File 141236.
[84] Unless otherwise stated details of the More family in Leyton are taken from *Essex Recusant*, i. 62–74, 95–104, iii. 71–80, iv. 1–5, 55–64, 103–6, v. 49–57, vi. 1–12.
[85] E.R.O., Q/SR 125/52.
[86] Ibid. 81/31.
[87] Ibid. 125/52–3.
[88] See p. 193.
[89] E.R.O., Q/SR 203/123.
[90] Ibid. 207/53–4.
[91] *Acts of P.C.* 1615–16, p. 536, 1616–17, p. 197, 1618–19, p. 413, 1619–21, p. 35, 1621–3, p. 78, 1627–8, p. 446, 1629–30, p. 13.
[92] *Hist. MSS. Com. 6th Rep. App. VIII*, 35a.
[93] William Salt Libr. Stafford, S. 2112.
[94] Guildhall MS. 9558, f. 218.
[95] *White's Dir. Essex* (1863); L.R.L., L47 MS. Vestry Mins. 1860, 1861.
[96] Apparently Cardinal Wiseman did not move to Leyton from Walthamstow until 1858 (see p. 294) although Etloe House rates were being paid in the name of Revd. F. Searle from 1856 (L.R.L., L55.6 MS. Highway Rates), and a tithe commutation rent charge was due in Jan.

1857 (Westminster Archives, L. & P. Cdnl. Wiseman (1857), Box W3/31–34, No. 24). For Cardinal Wiseman, see *D.N.B.*
[97] *Leytonstone Express and Independent*, 6 Mar. 1897; *Cath. Dir.* 1943.
[98] See p. 236.
[99] *Express and Independent Almanack*, 1901, p. 52.
[1] Worship Reg. 37957 (canc. 1904). St. Agnes Orphanage moved to Brentwood soon after, Leyton House and grounds being acquired by the London Electric Wire Co. Ltd.
[2] Mudie-Smith, *Relig. Life Lond.* 366.
[3] Worship Reg. 40777 (canc. 1924).
[4] Ibid. 49497; *Cath. Dir.* 1943; *Brentwood Dioc. Year Bk.* 1953.
[5] *Leytonstone Express and Independent*, 1 Nov. 1930.
[6] Wilkinson, *Leyton*, 23; *Kelly's Dir. Walthamstow, Leyton and Leytonstone*, 1905–8; E.R.O., *Sale Cat.* B553.
[7] *Kelly's Dir. Essex* (1908 and later edns.); *Brentwood Dioc. Year Bk.* 1968.
[8] Kennedy, *Leyton*, 127.
[9] *Cal. S.P. Dom.* 18 May–30 Sept. 1672, 14, 43; G. L. Turner, *Orig. Recs. Early Nonconformity*, i. 480. This was the house later occupied by Emblin's Academy, see below, p. 238.
[10] L.R.L., L47 MS. Ves. Mins. 1618–86.
[11] William Salt Libr. Stafford, S.2112.

or 'persons leaning that way', one a 'rigid Presbyterian', and the other two Dutch and French merchants; these were probably the three gentlemen's families of dissenters reported in 1766.[12] In 1763 Mary Bosanquet introduced Wesleyan Methodism to Leytonstone. By 1780 the followers of both Wesley and George Whitefield were active in Leyton and about that date the first permanent congregation was formed when the two connexions joined in a United Brotherhood of Methodists and Independents. This later divided, the Wesleyans establishing themselves in Leyton, and the Independents (later Congregationalists) in Leytonstone.

Primitive Methodists settled in Leyton in the late 1850s. A second Congregational church was founded in 1869. Great Baptist activity marked the early 1870s, four churches being founded by 1875, three of which still (1968) exist. The Brethren and Strict Baptists followed by 1880. In the 1880s and 1890s, alongside new churches of the main denominations, including one Presbyterian Church of England, many mission halls sprang up, most of them evangelistic and non-sectarian. Prominent among these missions were the Salvation Army and London City Mission. Much effort was concentrated on the poor, overcrowded districts of Harrow Green and Cann Hall.

By 1903 there were 20 churches of the main denominations and some 17 missions. The Baptists, though later comers than the Wesleyans and Congregationalists, were attracting larger total Sunday congregations than either, and the three denominations together were equalling the total attendances of all the Anglican churches. In all, nonconformists were accounting for about 57 per cent of the district's total Sunday attendances.[13] Sixteen of these churches still existed in 1968, though with greatly reduced membership, but one was closed that year. Unitarian and Christian Scientist churches were established before the First World War and Christadelphian, Elim Four Square Gospel, and Jehovah's Witnesses between the two wars. Only the Christian Scientists, Elim, and Jehovah's Witnesses survived to the 1960s. With few exceptions Leyton's nonconformist churches faced dwindling membership and financial insecurity in the 1930s. In 1932, in an attempt to maintain membership, the Fetter Lane Congregational church distributed, house by house, invitation letters to 1,954 families; 915 families did not reply, 393 were not interested, 100 were shortly leaving the district, 388 attended other churches and 158 promised to try to attend, but not one in fact did so.[14] The sole Presbyterian Church of England congregation was dissolved in 1939. The only newcomer among the main denominations after the Second World War was the Presbyterian Church of Wales, which moved to Leytonstone from Walthamstow in 1958. Nine of the more important independent missions (including the Salvation Army) founded before the First World War, still existed

after the Second. There were 29 nonconformist churches and missions active in 1968.

The following accounts of individual churches were completed in 1968.[15] Dates in brackets after ministers' names show the period of their pastorate. Attendance statistics for 1903 are taken from the *Daily News* census.[16]

Baptists. Membership figures in this section are taken from the individual church histories quoted or the *Baptist Handbooks.*

In 1866 a meeting place in Leytonstone was registered for worship of Independents and Baptists.[17] This may have been the Leytonstone High Road Congregationalists' Harrow Green mission, which opened that year.

Goldsmith Road, Leyton, described as a Union Church, existed in 1869, when F. Hughes became pastor. It does not appear to have survived his departure in 1879. Hughes was later pastor of Fillebrook, 1903-7.[18]

Fillebrook church, Fairlop Road, Leytonstone, originated in 1874, when drawing-room meetings were held on the initiative of G. A. Hutchison, founder of the *Boy's Own Paper*.[19] These were followed in 1875 by meetings held in the Weavers' Alms-houses, New Wanstead, and in the open Forest, and then in Kirkdale Road. After George Looseley gave a site on the Fillebrook estate, and the London Baptist Association gave £1,000 towards a building fund, a permanent church was opened in 1878. It is a large brick building with Gothic windows and a flèche above the roof. A hall was built in 1882 and the church enlarged in 1888. A mission was started in a room in Ashville Road in 1888, known at first as the Grove Green mission, but later as the Ashville mission. A hall was opened for it in 1892. Church membership rose from 37 in 1878 to over 500 by 1902. In 1903 total Sunday attendances were 1,169, the second highest in the district for all denominations. Fillebrook was associated with every kind of social and philanthropic work, including temperance. Two houses adjoining the church in Fairlop Road were bought in 1893 and 1919. A new additional Ashville Hall was built in 1923. Membership was still over 500 in 1936. Two new halls were built in Fairlop Road in 1939 and the two houses there reconstructed as an institute. After the Second World War, though Fillebrook continued to be the largest Baptist church in Leyton, membership fell, from 468 in 1946 to 212 by 1966. The Ashville mission closed; the newer Ashville Hall was sold to the Brethren in 1947;[20] the old Ashville Hall was also sold by 1949[21] and is now (1968) used as a factory.

Vicarage Road church, Leyton, was opened in 1875. It was built with the support of the London Baptist Association on a site given by a resident Baptist pastor, E. J. Farley, alarmed at the 'spiritual destitution' of the neighbourhood.[22] In 1894 a larger

[12] Hammock, *Leytonstone*, 52; Guildhall MS. 9558, f. 218.
[13] Mudie-Smith, *Relig. Life Lond.* 364-6, 462. Gainsborough Bridge Primitive Methodist church was omitted from the *Daily News* census.
[14] D. C. Wilkins, *Memories for you*, 19.
[15] In the accounts, when no source is quoted, the information has been obtained by local inquiry. Fuller accounts are in M. L. Savell, 'Churches of Leyton other than Church of England' (L.R.L., TS).
[16] Mudie-Smith, *Relig. Life Lond.* 364-6, 462.

[17] Worship Reg. 17385 (canc. 1897 revn.).
[18] W. T. Whitley, *Baptists of London*, 208, 223.
[19] Unless otherwise stated, this account is based on: J. MacBeath, *Fillebrook's fifty years: the jubilee story, 1878-1928*; *Fillebrook Baptist Church, 75th Anniversary, Oct. 1953*; and Wilkinson, *Leyton*, 31-2.
[20] See p. 226.   [21] *Bapt. Handbk.* (1948, 1949).
[22] Unless otherwise stated, this account is based on *Fifty years of sowing: short history of Vicarage Road, Leyton, Baptist Church, 1875-1925*.

schoolroom was built. A mission hall in Lea Bridge Gardens, in existence by 1885, was taken over in 1887 and run until about 1933.[23] Evangelistic services were also being held by 1897 in Etloe Hall, Church Road.[24] Church membership, which in 1926 was 151, was well maintained in the 1930s. The church was damaged by bombing in the Second World War.[25] By 1966 membership had fallen to 54.

Cann Hall Road church, Leytonstone, originated in 1875 in mission services held by 'The Christian band' in a barn at Cann Hall Farm.[26] Robert Thompson was elected their leader in 1876. A church of 32 members was formed in 1878 and the barn converted into a chapel.[27] In 1881 a small chapel (now the lecture hall) was opened in Cann Hall Road. The property was handed over in 1885 to the London Baptist Association, who built the present church designed by G. Barnes and opened in 1887. In 1892 another storey was added to the original chapel. An affiliated mission started in 1892 over the district boundary in Chandos Road, Stratford, was later known as the Edith Road mission; it united with Stratford New Town church, Major Road, in 1907.[28] The house adjoining the church was bought in 1918, and its ground floor registered for worship in 1920.[29] By 1926 the membership of Cann Hall Road was 391; it fell, however, in the 1930s and thereafter. In 1966 it was 89.

Meetings were held at Zion, Ashville Road, in 1883. A church was formed, under H. Hubbard, and moved in 1884, first to Mount Zion, Lindley Road, then to Park Terrace, Church Road, to the premises occupied from 1880 to 1882 by the Strict Baptists.[30] This church does not appear to have survived.

Harrow Green church, Leytonstone, originated in 1895 in a secession from Cann Hall Road of some members with strong evangelistic views, who erected an iron church in High Road, Leytonstone.[31] In 1902 the first part of the permanent building, called Leytonstone Road Baptist church, was opened at Harrow Green. Total Sunday attendances by 1903 exceeded 500. The building, enlarged in 1906, was also known as the People's Hall.[32] The next year the church took over the Montague Road mission,[33] and from 1908 to 1910 also held bible classes at the Temperance mission hall, Lansdowne Road.[34] In 1925 a new hall was opened. Membership began to fall in the 1930s, from 342 in 1926 to 240 in 1936. In 1940 the church was gutted by bombing. Ser-

vices were carried on in the small hall, and then in the Howard Road mission hall, at first borrowed, then, in 1943,[35] bought from the Leytonstone High Road Congregational church. The church was rebuilt in 1959[36] on the original site as a simple brick building with tall windows, a pantile roof, and a plain square tower. Church membership in 1966 was 52. The Montague Road mission was destroyed in the Second World War.

Strict Baptists. Hainault Road church, Leyton, originated in 1880 when Strict Baptists began to meet for worship in Park Terrace, Church Road, moving to Goldsmith Road in 1882.[37] From 1894 services were held in Wilmot Road, in a chapel bought from the Primitive Methodists. In 1895 a church was formed and H. E. Bond appointed pastor; but after he left in 1896 it was without a pastor for over twenty years. In 1903 total Sunday attendances, 53, were among the lowest in the district. A full-time pastor was again appointed in 1920. In 1926, when church membership was 33, a new church was opened in Hainault Road. In 1933 a new Sunday school was built. By 1946 membership was 148; in 1966 it was 75.

Brethren. Leyton Hall, Goldsmith Road, Leyton, originated in meetings of Christian Brethren held in Goldsmith Road from the late 1870s.[38] Leyton Hall was registered in 1885.[39] In 1912 a larger hall was built on the opposite side of the road. This was badly damaged in the Second World War, but was repaired, and was still in use in 1968, though said to have become non-denominational.[40]

In 1903 Brethren were meeting in halls in Acacia Road and Crownfield Road, Leytonstone,[41] and about 1910 to 1912 in Lansdowne Road, Leytonstone, and in the Church of Christ mission hall in Murchison Road, Leyton.[42] Nothing more is known of these groups, but some of their members may have been associated with the foundation of Ashville Hall.

Ashville Hall, Ashville Road, Leytonstone, Open Brethren met from 1912 in Grove Green Hall, Grove Green Road, which they built.[43] A gospel hall in Grove Green Road is listed in directories from 1912.[44] The hall was enlarged in 1925. Membership in 1932 was over 200. The hall was demolished in 1940 after compulsory purchase, to build the railway subway to replace the level crossing.

[23] *Kelly's Dir. Essex* (1886–1926); *Bapt. Handbk.* (1888 and later edns.); *Expr. and Ind. Alm.* (1885); Whitley, *Bapt. Lond.* 219. This may have been the wooden church shown in a newspaper illustration of 'Bungalow Town' or Lea Bridge Gardens, in 1908 (L.R.L., L66.1 Prints).
[24] Wilkinson, *Leyton*, 35; *Expr. and Ind. Alm.* (1897–1915). The hall is listed as Baptist until 1915, but it was being used by the Grange Park Congregationalists in 1899–1901.
[25] Inf. from Revd. J. Johnson.
[26] Unless otherwise stated this account is based on *Leaves from Memory Lane: Cann Hall Road Baptist Church jubilee celebrations* (1937); *Cann Hall Road Baptist Church: Diamond Jubilee* (1947); and Whitley, *Bapt. Lond.* 217.
[27] L.R.L., L72.1 Print, shows the interior of the converted barn.
[28] Wilkinson, *Leyton*, 31; *Expr. and Ind. Alm.* (1897), p. 117. For its later history, see above, West Ham, p. 127.
[29] Worship Reg. 47800.
[30] Whitley, *Bapt. Lond.* 230.
[31] Unless otherwise stated this account is based on MS. notes compiled by Revd. W. Fancutt (minister 1942–5), in possession of church.

[32] *Expr. and Ind. Alm.* (1908), p. 85.
[33] See p. 232.
[34] *Expr. and Ind. Alm.* (1908–10).
[35] Worship Reg. 60470 (canc. 1959).
[36] Worship Reg. 67282.
[37] Unless otherwise stated this account is based on: Whitley, *Bapt. Lond.*, 245; E.R.O., T/Z 8 (Whitley MSS.); Wilkinson, *Leyton*, 35; and *These 50 years: a brief record of triumphant faith and service*.
[38] Unless otherwise stated this account is based on inf. from Mr. George Offord. The group are listed in *Kelly's Dir. Essex* (1882).
[39] Worship Reg. 28787 (canc. 1914).
[40] L.R.L., Local churches index, 1968.
[41] Mudie-Smith, *Relig. Life Lond.* 365.
[42] *Kelly's Dir. Essex* (1910, 1912); *Kelly's Dir. Leytonstone, Wanstead and Snaresbrook* (1911, 1912).
[43] Unless otherwise stated this account is based on J. B. Watson, 'Meetings of Open Brethren in Leytonstone: brief historical notes on the Brethren of Ashville Hall' (L.R.L., L85 Pamphlet, TS), and on inf. from Mr. R. T. Matthews.
[44] *Kelly's Dir. Essex* (1912 and later edns.).

From 1940 to 1946 services were held in a small wooden hall in Fairlop Road, and from 1946 in the Fillebrook Baptists' second Ashville Hall, which the Brethren bought in 1947. They still occupied it in 1968.

Beachcroft Hall, Beachcroft Road, Leytonstone, was registered for worship of Brethren in 1920.[45] This was probably the group from Leyton Hall said to have started a new church in Leytonstone some time after 1912.[46] The hall, also known as Emmanuel,[47] was still used by Brethren in 1968.

Christian Scientists. The First Church of Christ, Scientist, Whipps Cross Road, Leytonstone, originated about 1906, with services held in a house on the corner of Whipps Cross Road and Forest Glade.[48] In 1908 the group combined with another from Woodford to hold services at the Richter school of music in the High Road. The group moved in 1909 to Haydn House (the Metropolitan academy of music), Fairlop Road, where in 1910 the Leytonstone Christian Science Society was formed. In 1913 the Society moved to Salway college, Fillebrook Road.[49] The Society became the First Church of Christ, Scientist, Leytonstone (Leyton) in 1915.[50] In 1922 the original Whipps Cross site was bought and a temporary building opened in 1923. A permanent church was completed in 1937 on the adjoining site. It is a red-brick building in a simple Georgian style with a semi-circular columned portico; it was designed by T. E. Davidson, Son & Sherwood, and is panelled inside with light oak, which matches the furnishings. The temporary building is now (1968) the reading room.

Congregational. Membership figures in this section are taken from the individual church histories quoted or the *Congregational Year Books.*

Leytonstone High Road church originated in meetings of the followers of George Whitefield, whose Tabernacle preachers were visiting Leyton by about 1780. The group may have been associated with the countess of Huntingdon's Connexion. About 1780 they joined for worship with a group of Methodists, as the United Brotherhood of Methodists and Independents.[51] By her will Mrs. Margaret Peat (d. 1785) left the interest on £1,000, after the death of William Shannon (d. 1804), to provide preachers in Leyton, 'either Mr. Wesley, or the Tabernacle ones, which the people may like best'.[52] The Brotherhood worshipped in Meeting or Chapel Yard in Leyton High Street,[53] in the cottage 'now used as a meeting-house' to which John Turner of Walthamstow was admitted in 1793 on the surrender of William Tilt.[54] It is not clear whether this chapel was originally established by the Methodists or the Independents,[55] but as it was Mrs. Tilt who invited Wesley's preachers to Leyton in the 1770s,[56] it may have been the former. The Brotherhood is said to have dissolved in 1812, leaving the chapel to the Methodists.[57] The break was, however, probably earlier, as Independent places of worship were registered in Leyton in 1798, 1799, and 1809 (two),[58] two of them (1798, 1809) by George Collison, minister of Walthamstow Marsh Street new meeting (1797–1837), tutor at Hoxton college from 1797 to 1801, and then president from 1803 to 1847 of the Village Itinerancy Society's new theological college at Hackney.[59] The division may have arisen from the conflicting influence of two strong personalities, Collison, and the Wesleyan, William Pocock.[60] Independent places of worship were also registered in Leytonstone in 1791 and 1817.[61] In 1826 Collison registered an Independent chapel in Leytonstone High Road, opposite Back Lane, built by subscription, and reported in 1829 to seat upwards of 150.[62] The long association with Collison explains why the Leytonstone High Road church was regarded as originating as a preaching station of Hackney college,[63] and why in 1851 the chapel was described as belonging to the Village Itinerancy Society.[64] In 1829 protracted litigation over Mrs. Peat's legacy, which had been in dispute since 1804, was concluded. The congregation fostered by Collison was accepted, under the name of the Tabernacle society of Leyton, as 'originating from . . . the Tabernacle preachers', and awarded one-third of the legacy, the remainder going to the Wesleyans.[65] This endowment in 1851 produced £20 a year.[66] The chapel was enlarged to seat 200 in 1838.[67] In 1839, under the name of Leytonstone Independent chapel, it was being run by a management committee, but without a full-time pastor. This caused difficulties, and in 1840 the committee resigned and handed over the chapel's affairs to Hackney college. When a full-time pastor was appointed in 1844 it became independent again.[68] A larger temporary iron church, to hold 400, was

[45] Worship Reg. 47900.
[46] Inf. from Mr. G. Offord.
[47] *Kelly's Dir. Essex* (1926). See also below, p. 232.
[48] Unless otherwise stated this account is based on *Historical sketch: First Church of Christ, Scientist, Leytonstone (Leyton)* (1946).
[49] Worship Reg. 45563 (canc. 1915). For Salway College, see below, p. 238.
[50] Worship Reg. 46706 (canc. 1923).
[51] Caesar Caine, *Brief Chronicle of Wesleyan Methodism in Leyton, 1750–1895,* 29; Wilkinson, *Leyton,* 27.
[52] Caine, *Brief. Chron. Wes. Meth.* 39–40.
[53] Ibid. 29; Wilkinson, *Leyton,* 27.
[54] E.R.O., D/DU 101/3. Chapel Yard still existed in 1898, on the west side of High Street, between Capworth Street and Lea Bridge Road, between a tobacconist's shop and Plumstead House (*Kelly's Dir. Walthamstow, Leyton and Leytonstone,* 1898). It still belonged to the Turner family in 1878; it is shown on a plan about that date (E.R.O., D/DU 101/4) and on the 1843 tithe map (E.R.O., D/CT 221, no. 267). It was demolished in the late 1930s.
[55] Kennedy, *Leyton,* 73–4; Wilkinson, *Leyton,* 27.

[56] See p. 228.
[57] Kennedy, *Leyton,* 74.
[58] G.R.O., Retns. Noncf. Mtg. Hos. Cert. to Bps. Cts. before 1852. Nos. 453, 512, 716, 730.
[59] *Cong. Year Bk.* (1847), pp. 142–3; biographical index at Dr. Williams's Libr.
[60] See p. 228.
[61] G.R.O., Retns. Noncf. Mtg. Hos. Cert. to Bps. Cts. before 1852, Nos. 313, 1058.
[62] Ibid. No. 1572; H.O. 129/7/194; E.R.O., Q/CR 3/1/72.
[63] Wilkinson, *Leyton,* 27; Kennedy, *Leyton,* 75.
[64] H.O. 129/7/194.
[65] Caine, *Brief. Chron. Wes. Meth.* 39–40, 43–58, gives a full account of the case, with witnesses' depositions, and pays tribute to Collison's part in bringing about a settlement.
[66] H.O. 129/7/4.
[67] Wilkinson, *Leyton,* 27; *White's Dir. Essex* (1848); H.O. 129/7/194; E. Clarke, *Walthamstow, past, present, and future,* 81.
[68] Unidentified newspaper cutting, 1877, in possession of Church, reporting laying of foundation stone of permanent church.

built in Wellesley (now Michael) Road in 1873, on a site given by William Goodman.[69] The permanent church was built near this iron one in 1877, facing the High Road.[70] It was designed by Lewis Banks, in an elaborate 'Lombardic' style, for 773 persons.[71] Galleries were added in 1888, bringing its capacity to 1,000.[72] The iron church was moved to Chigwell in 1880.[73] The old chapel was used as a preaching station until 1879, then as school and hall until 1885; it was sold about 1886 when the Barclay Hall, near the church, was opened for the school.[74] In 1903 Leytonstone High Road was one of the six best-attended churches in the district with total Sunday congregations over 1,000. Church membership, over 500 by 1899, was 656 in 1920; it was still over 600 in 1930, but had fallen to 440 by 1940. In 1944 the church was damaged by bombing; it was reopened, after repairs, in 1946. Membership in 1967 was 100.

A mission station of Leytonstone High Road was established near Harrow Green by 1867; the Howard Road mission hall was built for it by William Goodman about 1880.[75] It was sold to the Harrow Green Baptists in 1943.[76]

Grange Park church, Grange Park Road, Leyton, was founded in 1870 by Morgan Lloyd.[77] He preached in the grammar school, built in Grange Park Road in 1866,[78] later known as Grange Park Hall. A plot was bought and a church opened in 1874 under Stratford church.[79] In 1875 J. D. Davies was appointed pastor, and in 1877 the church became fully independent under the name of the Leyton Congregational church. A hall was built in 1878. Internal differences developed; Davies resigned in 1880 and the church became 'greatly disorganised', its affairs being temporarily delegated to the London Congregational Union. In 1881 it was reconstituted with a membership of 56, but dissension soon broke out again and in 1886 its collapse seemed imminent. Under W. B. Anstey (1887–93), it recovered. By 1891 membership had grown to 179. An iron school was built in 1894, and the church was enlarged in 1896. Missions which were conducted, first in Lower Faraday (now Sidmouth) Road, then at Etloe Hall, Church Road, were closed in 1898 and 1901 respectively.[80] Total Sunday attendances in 1903 were 671. At that date Sunday services were still being held at Grange Park Hall,[81] but whether these were associated with the Congregationalists is not known. Under G. A. Suttle (1904–13) all debts were cleared and membership rose to nearly 400. New Sunday-school buildings were opened in 1927.[82] Membership, main-

tained steadily at about 240 in the 1930s, was 197 in 1950 and 96 in 1967.

Ramsay Road church, Forest Gate, was founded by the Revd. Charles Higgins in 1888, when an iron building was erected. He remained minister until his death in 1915, although he went blind in 1905. His daughters continued to assist the church for many years.[83] The congregation was never large and the original iron building was still in use in 1967, when membership was 29.

Fetter Lane church, Langthorne Road, Leytonstone, originated as a mission of the Grove church, Stratford, established in Crownfield Road in 1885.[84] In 1891 an iron chapel called the People's Hall was opened in Frith Road. The services were led by E. T. Egg until 1894, when the Fetter Lane church (Lond.), founded in 1660, moved to Leyton. The 30 Fetter Lane members received 84 members of the mission into church fellowship, and the Fetter Lane pastor, R. Snowden, took over the ministry at Frith Road. When he died, Egg was again temporary pastor from 1897 to 1900. The Fetter Lane premises were sold in 1897, and in 1900 a permanent church, designed by P. Morley Horder and built partly with the proceeds, was opened in Union (now Langthorne) Road. The style of the building was strikingly original for its period and the architect may have been influenced by the contemporary work of C. R. Mackintosh in Glasgow. Externally there are small mullioned windows, gables, and large areas of plain plastered walling. The whole building debt was not cleared until 1919. In 1901 membership was 90, but under A. T. Hocking (1906–14) it rose to over 200. In the late 1920s serious differences arose between H. H. Gratton (1921–9) and his congregation, and he resigned. Membership fell by two-thirds in the 1930s, and the financial position became precarious. After 1937 the church was without a pastor for eight years and in danger of closing down. Though it revived after the Second World War, membership in 1967 was only 47. Under an endowment of 1912, four weekly pensions of 5s. are paid to poor persons of sound moral conduct.

Methodists. The three Methodist connexions which united in 1932 had 7 churches in Leyton. One was destroyed in the Second World War, and one closed in 1968; the remaining 5 were still in use in 1968, all in the Leytonstone and Forest Gate circuit. The Leyton Mission circuit, created in 1941, ceased to exist in 1946, and the Leyton (P) circuit in 1959.[85]

[69] Wilkinson, *Leyton*, 27; *Cong. Year Bk.* (1874), p. 411, (1877), p. 489; Worship Reg. 21931 (canc. 1878); unidentified newspaper cutting (as in fn. 68).

[70] *Cong. Year Bk.* (1877), p. 489; *Kelly's Dir. Essex* (1882).

[71] *Cong. Year Bk.* (1877), p. 489.

[72] Hammock, *Leytonstone*, 94; *Cong. Year Bk.* (1897), pp. 220–1; Wilkinson, *Leyton*, 27.

[73] *V.C.H. Essex*, iv. 35.

[74] *Cong. Year Bk.* (1875–86).

[75] Ibid. (1867 and later edns.); inf. from granddaughter of William Goodman.   [76] See p. 225.

[77] *Cong. Year Bk.* (1871), pp. 401–2. Unless otherwise stated this account is based on Wilkinson, *Leyton*, 28, and on *Brief History of the Grange Park Congregational Church, Leyton*.

[78] This private school is listed in *Kelly's Dir. Essex* (1866, 1870, 1874). The building is now occupied as the Liberal Club.

[79] *Cong. Year Bk.* (1874), p. 428.

[80] *Kelly's Dir. Walthamstow, Leyton and Leytonstone* (1895–9); *Cong. Year Bk.* (1901–2). A Congregational mission room in Thornhill Road listed in the *Express and Independent Almanack* (1897 and later edns.) may have been associated with Grange Park Road church, but there is no confirmation in the *Cong. Year Bks.*

[81] Mudie-Smith, *Relig. Life Lond.* 366.

[82] *Leytonstone Express and Independent*, 7 May 1927.

[83] B. M. Shore, 'Notes on the history of Ramsay Road Cong. Ch.' (L.R.L., L85 Pamphlet, MS.).

[84] This account is based on: A. Pye-Smith, *Memorials of Fetter Lane Congregational Church* (1900); D. C. Wilkins, *Memories for you, 1900–1950*; Wilkinson, *Leyton*, 32; *Cong. Year Bk.* (1892–1901). For the Grove church, see above, p. 130.

[85] *Mins. Meth. Conf.* (1940 sqq.); L.R.L., Local churches index, 1968.

In the individual accounts below, ex-Wesleyan (W), ex-Primitive (P), and ex-United (U) churches are treated in that order.

Wesleyan Methodism was introduced to Leytonstone by Mary Bosanquet (1739–1815), daughter of Samuel Bosanquet of Forest House.[86] She was said to have been influenced by a servant, and wrote in her diary when only twelve years old, 'If I knew where to find the Methodists I would tear off all my fine things and run through the fire to them.' Soon after she was twenty-one, having money of her own, and her family fearing that she might influence her brothers, by mutual agreement she left home to live in Hoxton (Lond.). In 1763 she returned to Leytonstone to a house of her own at the bottom of Davies Lane,[87] where she held meetings, undeterred by rowdy local hostility. A society of 25 was formed, and an orphanage was established. Wesley, who preached at Leytonstone in 1764, 1766, and 1767, described the community as 'one truly Christian family', commenting in 1767 'O what a house of God is here'.[88] Mary Bosanquet left Leytonstone for Yorkshire in 1768, taking the children with her. In 1781 she married John Fletcher, vicar of Madeley (Salop.). Without her leadership the Leytonstone society dwindled. When Wesley preached there in 1774 he found it 'shrunk to 5 or 6 members, and will probably soon shrink into nothing'.[89] Methodism revived in the parish, however, through the initiative of Mrs. Tilt, who invited Wesley's preachers to Leyton about this time. In 1777 field preachers were attracting large congregations, causing alarm in the parish vestry, which ordered the constables to report them to the magistrates.[90] About 1780 the group joined with followers of George Whitefield, to form the United Brotherhood of Methodists and Independents, which met in Chapel Yard.[91] Wesley preached in Leyton in 1783, in 1790, when the audience was described as small, and in 1791.[92] William Pocock, a builder and cabinet-maker whose wife was a staunch Methodist, had come to live in Leyton in 1786, and he and his family took a leading part in establishing Methodism there.

Knotts Green (W) chapel and its successor, the Mary Fletcher Memorial (W) church, originated in the eventual dissolution of the Brotherhood, after which its Wesleyan members apparently continued to worship in Chapel Yard.[93] In 1817 a Wesleyan Sunday school was started by John Marshall, probably in the house at Phillebrook which he registered for worship in 1818.[94] That year Leyton, previously in the London circuit, became a preaching place in the newly-formed Waltham Abbey and St. Albans circuit. In the same year H. E. Webster registered a house on Epping Forest for worship; though no denomination was then given, the meeting place he registered at Leytonstone in 1819 was Wesleyan.[95] Probably about this time, too, William Pocock built a wooden preaching room, in use by 1820, in Leyton High Street on the opposite side to Chapel Yard; this does not appear to have been registered. The removal from Chapel Yard could have been occasioned by John Turner's death about 1819, when he left his property, including the chapel, to his widow, Pocock being named as one of his tenants.[96] In 1823 a Wesleyan chapel was built on Knotts Green and registered by Pocock.[97] The land had been provided by Pocock himself and his son, William Fuller Pocock, who was an architect. The chapel was registered again in 1827 after enlargement;[98] in 1829 it seated about 150.[99] In 1828 the Waltham Abbey and Leyton circuit was formed. A two-thirds share of Mrs. Peat's legacy,[1] amounting to £1,333, was awarded to the Wesleyan Methodist Society of Leyton in 1829. In 1831 Leyton became the head of an independent circuit with preaching places as far afield as Waltham Abbey and Chigwell. The Leyton society had 80 members in 1841. The chapel was rebuilt in 1843 to the design of William Willmer Pocock, grandson of William. It was a rectangular brick building with tall round-headed windows set in arched recesses and a pedimented front gable. The agitation for Wesleyan reform found support in Leyton, which in 1850 sent five delegates to the reform meeting at Albion Chapel, Moorgate (Lond.).[2] William Burnett, circuit superintendent from 1848, explained in a letter to the press in 1851 that he treated the reformers in his circuit as 'men and brethren', having no disposition to 'scatter the flock', and claimed that the result was a whole circuit and not a ruin.[3] But his liberal attitude was not acceptable to Conference, and he was superseded as superintendent in 1851 and expelled in 1852.[4] Membership of the Leyton society fell to about 20; the circuit was wrecked by discord and ceased to exist. The Leyton society became incorporated successively in the Islington circuit (from 1853), Hackney circuit (from 1857), and Clapton circuit (from 1876). It gradually revived and in 1877 built a new church, the Mary Fletcher Memorial, on a site at the junction of High Street and James Lane (now Fletcher Road) given by Samuel R. Bosanquet. Designed in an elaborate

[86] Unless otherwise stated, the accounts of early Wesleyan Methodism in Leyton, and of the Knotts Green chapel and Mary Fletcher memorial church, are based on: Caesar Caine, *Brief chronicle of Wesleyan Methodism in Leyton, Essex, 1750–1895*.

[87] The house was not the Cedars, on the corner of Davies Lane, as is usually stated (e.g. *E.R.* xlii. 115, and G. L. Lee, *Story of the Bosanquets*, 59). It lay east of the Pastures, which Mary Bosanquet owned also, forming part of the Pastures estate. The house still existed in 1822, when it was conveyed with the Pastures and is shown on a plan (E.R.O., D/DU 322/1–10), but it had been pulled down by 1843 (E.R.O., D/CT 221). See also above and below, pp. 179, 238.

[88] *Journal of John Wesley* (Standard edn.), v. 101, 102, 152, 155, 191, 195, 239.

[89] Ibid. vi. 11.

[90] L.R.L., L47 MS. Vestry Mins. 1752–81.

[91] See p. 226.

[92] *Jnl. of John Wesley*, vi. 431 d, viii. 36, 121 d.

[93] Kennedy, *Leyton*, 74. See above, p. 226 for the possible date of separation.

[94] G.R.O., Retns. Noncf. Mtg. Hos. Cert. to Bps. Cts. before 1852, No. 1077.

[95] Ibid. Nos. 1068, 1216.

[96] E.R.O., D/DU 101/3 (1821, admission of Mary Turner).

[97] *Wes. Meth. Mag.* 1823, p. 822; G.R.O., Retns. Noncf. Mtg. Hos. Cert. to Bps. Cts. before 1852, No. 1361.

[98] G.R.O., Retns. Noncf. Mtg. Hos. Cert. to Bps. Cts. before 1852, No. 1584; *Wes. Meth. Mag.* 1827, p. 833.

[99] E.R.O., Q/CR 3/1/172.

[1] See p. 226.

[2] *Watchman*, 20 Mar. 1850.

[3] *Wesleyan Times*, 2 June 1851.

[4] *Mins. Wesleyan Conf.* (1852). For Burnett's later career, see below, p. 356.

Gothic style by G. Marshall and built of Kentish rag and Bath stone, it consisted of nave, with apse and west gallery, supported by pinnacled buttresses. A turret surmounted the west entrance, formed by four arches on columns.[5] Temporary iron school-rooms were built near by in 1892 and 1894. In 1895 two arched doorways with columns replaced the single door inside the entrance. The Knotts Green chapel continued to be used as a school and mission room and was renovated in 1895.[6] The permanent Sunday school, matching the church in design, was opened in 1902.[7] Total Sunday attendances in 1903 were 797, with a further 66 at Knotts Green. In the 1930s the society was in grave financial difficulty.[8] In 1940 it was taken over by the Methodist Home Mission department, and the following year became a separate Leyton Mission circuit. The Home Mission supplied pastors until 1946, when the society was incorporated in the Leytonstone and Forest Gate circuit.[9] The Knotts Green chapel was closed in 1940.[10] It was later destroyed by bombing, and in 1951 the site was compulsorily purchased by the borough council for housing.[11] The Mary Fletcher Memorial church closed in 1969 and the congregation transferred to Leyton Tabernacle. The site was sold and church and Sunday school demolished in 1971.[12]

High Road (W), Leytonstone, originated in a proposal in 1872 to build a Fletcher Memorial chapel in Leytonstone, attached to the Stratford circuit.[13] In 1875, with financial support from Sir Francis Lycett, J. Telford was appointed to work in Leytonstone,[14] where meetings had been held since about 1874 at The Shrublands,[15] later the site of the Rex Cinema. A small iron church, nicknamed the 'Leytonstone Pint Pot' or 'Little Sardine Box',[16] was registered in 1876,[17] built on the site adjoining the present church. It was linked with the Stratford circuit, though financially dependent on Lycett. When his support ceased in 1878, the help of the Home Mission department was sought. The permanent church, a substantial brick building with stone dressings and two Italianate west towers, was opened in 1880.[18] Membership rose from 56 in 1880 to 131 in 1883. In 1881 a mission was started in Acacia Road; this apparently closed in 1894.[19] In 1889 the church was enlarged by the addition of a schoolroom, later known as Cowley Hall.[20] Further enlargement took place in 1892 and 1902, completing an extensive range of buildings.[21] By

1903 High Road, with total Sunday congregations of over 1,000, was one of the strongest churches in Leyton. In 1928 membership was 468. A memorial hall was built in 1930. In the same year the society was included in the newly-formed Leytonstone and Forest Gate circuit. The church was demolished in 1968.[22]

Cann Hall (W) mission was started in 1887 by a group from the Grove, Stratford (W). Services were held at first in the open, then in a rented hall in Cann Hall Road.[23] A small iron church was opened in 1898. From 1904 until 1914 the church was served by the Wesley Deaconess Order. An additional iron hall was opened in 1927. The church, originally in the Stratford circuit, has been since 1930 in the Leytonstone and Forest Gate circuit.

Primitive Methodism came to Leyton in the 1850s, but it made little progress until the 1880s, when Alfred Ives began a vigorous ministry there.[24] A separate Leyton (P) circuit existed from 1887 to 1958.

Wilmot Road (P) originated in street preaching, followed by cottage services, in which the Primitive Methodists may have merged with a group of Bible Christians registered in 1857.[25] In 1867 they were meeting in Grange Park Road and were attached to the Third London circuit.[26] A small iron building was erected in Wilmot Road in 1868. It was transferred to the Stratford circuit in 1885 and the Leyton circuit in 1887. With the opening of the permanent Leyton Tabernacle, Wilmot Road became redundant, and in 1894 was sold to the Strict Baptists.

Leyton Tabernacle (P), High Road, Leyton, originated in 1883, when a group under Alfred Ives, minister of the Third London circuit, bought an iron church at the corner of Etchingham Road and Leyton (now High) Road, and formed a society. Apparently an undertaking was given by the Wesleyans of the Stratford circuit not to intrude in the neighbourhood. In 1885 Leyton Road, with Wilmot Road, became a branch of the Stratford circuit, but in 1887 became an independent circuit, with Ives as superintendent. F. W. Wilkinson, one of Leyton's historians, became superintendent in 1891. From about 1885 until the early 1890s a mission was conducted under Ives and Wilkinson in Holloway Road, Harrow Green; a mission room in Cecil Road listed from 1885 to 1890 may also have been associated with their work.[27] In 1893 a permanent

[5] E.R.O., D/DBq Z1 (approved plans).
[6] Wilkinson, *Leyton*, 27; Knotts Green Trustees Min. Bk. 1895–1916 kept (1970) at North Chingford Methodist Ch.
[7] *Leytonstone Express and Independent*, 4 Oct. 1902.
[8] Mary Fletcher Memorial Methodist Church Trustees Min. Bk. 1924 f., kept (1968) at the church.
[9] Ibid.; *Mins. Meth. Conf.* (1940–6).
[10] Knotts Green Trustees Min. Bk. 1919–40, kept (1968) at Mary Fletcher Memorial Methodist Church.
[11] *Leyton B.C. Mins. and Cttee. Reps.* 1950–1, p. 757.
[12] Personal observation and local inf.
[13] Unless otherwise stated this account is based on Stratford Wes. Circuit Min. Bk. 1871–87, and Leytonstone Wes. Meth. Ch., Trustees Min. Bk. 1880–1901 and Ch. Leaders Min. Bks. 1879–1903, 1926–45, kept (1968) in Leytonstone and Forest Gate Methodist Circuit safe.
[14] E.R.O., T/A 306.
[15] Hammock, *Leytonstone*, 94.
[16] *East London Advertiser*, 17 Feb. 1900; *Leytonstone Express and Independent*, 13 Apr. 1889.
[17] Worship Reg. 22697 (canc. 1897 revn.).

[18] Worship Reg. 25046. It was registered as the M. Fletcher Memorial (Leytonstone Methodist Church), Leytonstone. This name was not, however, used, but that of Leytonstone Wesleyan Methodist Church. The Mary Fletcher Memorial Church, Leyton, had opened in 1877.
[19] It continued to be listed in *Kelly's Dir. Walthamstow, Leyton and Leytonstone* up to 1898, and in the *Express and Independent Almanack* to 1902.
[20] *Leytonstone Express and Independent*, 13 Apr. 1889.
[21] Hammock, *Leytonstone*, 94.
[22] Inf. from Revd. O. R. Johnson.
[23] This account is based on *March of Time: an historical review of Cann Hall Methodist Mission Church, 1887–1937*.
[24] Unless otherwise stated, the account of the origin of Primitive Methodism and of the Tabernacle is based on: Wilkinson, *Leyton*, 27–8, and Primitive Methodist Connexion, Stratford Circuit, Mins. 1883–1907, formerly (1954) at 68, Vicarage Rd., Leyton.
[25] See p. 230.
[26] *P.M. Mins. Conf.* (1867).
[27] *Expr. and Ind. Alm.* (1885 and later edns.); *Kelly's Dirs. Essex* (1886, 1890).

church, designed by James Steed in the Gothic style, was opened on a new site, the old site being considered unsuitable after a public house had been built opposite. The old site was sold, but the iron church was re-erected on the new site as a lecture hall and school. In 1940 the Leyton circuit was joined by the two surviving churches of the former Leytonstone and Stratford circuit.[28] The Tabernacle was badly damaged in the Second World War, but restored. The Leyton circuit ceased to exist in 1959, when membership had fallen to 143, and the Tabernacle then joined the Leytonstone and Forest Gate circuit.[29]

Gainsborough Bridge (P), Leytonstone, originated in 1901, when C. Hallam, minister of Stepney Green Tabernacle (Lond.), held services in Colworth Road for new residents of the Wallwood estate.[30] A permanent church, designed by Hallam, was opened in 1902. It is a two-storey building in an Italian baroque style, of white brick with terracotta dressings; these were mostly replaced by concrete when the west wall was rebuilt after damage in the Second World War. The original turret over the roof became unsafe, and was removed in 1930. About 1905 the church, previously in the Stepney Green (P) circuit, became a separate Leytonstone (P) circuit. In 1924 it was amalgamated with Henniker Road, Stratford, and Clinton Road, Forest Gate, both in West Ham, as the Leytonstone and Stratford (P) circuit. The organ, which was installed in 1909, with a grant from Andrew Carnegie, was built by the Leyton firm of R. Spurden Rutt. Under A. Lawton (1911–34) all debt on the church was cleared by 1919 and membership rose from 34 in 1911 to 101 by 1934. In 1941, after Henniker Road was closed, Gainsborough Bridge and Clinton Road were transferred to the Leyton (P) circuit. Gainsborough Bridge was damaged five times in the Second World War, so severely in 1945 that it was closed until 1948. Since 1959 it has been in the Leytonstone and Forest Gate circuit.[31]

United Methodism probably originated in Leyton during the 1880s, in the activities of Free Methodists. A group of Bible Christians, meeting in a house at Phillebrook, were registered for worship from 1857 to 1866,[32] but there is no further reference to them, and they may have merged with the Wilmot Road Primitive Methodists.

Grove Green (U), Leytonstone, originated in 1887 with Free Methodist services in a cottage in Pearcroft Road.[33] A society was formed in 1889 and a small brick church built in Grove Green Road with the help of Richard Mallinson. In 1891 arrangements were made to share pulpits with Cambridge Park, Wanstead. The church was enlarged in 1906. It belonged in turn to the Fifth London (Stratford) circuit, Forest Gate (from 1907), Walthamstow

(from 1913), and Leytonstone and Forest Gate (from 1959).[34] In 1954 membership was 40.

Presbyterian Church of England. St. George's church, Hainault Road, Leytonstone, originated in 1888, when the Revd. G. Drysdale, a retired minister living in the district, built an iron church in Wallwood Road.[35] In 1891 the Presbytery of North London recognized this as a sanctioned charge and in 1893 a permanent building designed by William Wallace was opened in Hainault Road.[36] It is a red-brick building with stone dressings, in the Gothic style, consisting of nave and transepts. Under William Kidd (1895–1919) a debt of £6,000 was paid off, a hall built, and membership raised from 36 to nearly 200. During the 1920s, however, the church began to decline rapidly, and in 1939 it was closed and sold to the Essex county council, which used it as a civil defence depot.

Presbyterian Church of Wales (*Calvinistic Methodists*). Moreia, High Road, Leytonstone, is described under Walthamstow, where it originated.[37]

The Salvation Army. The Leyton Citadel corps originated in 1883.[38] The Etloe mission hall, Church Road, was used for meetings[39] until 1886, when a permanent brick citadel was erected in High Road by F. J. Coxhead, a builder who was also corps sergeant-major. The local press, though inclined to ridicule the corps, admitted that the building seemed 'meant for real use and not for ornament',[40] and within ten years all opposition had died down. In 1908 a Young People's Hall in Lindley Road, also built by Coxhead, was presented by him to the corps with the two adjoining cottages. A revival campaign in 1908 led to the formation of the second Leyton corps in Lea Bridge Road. In 1931 Coxhead built and presented another hall, 'Salvation Castle', in Lindley Road. This is a stone-faced building with battlements. The High Road citadel was badly damaged in the Second World War. The corps finally transferred all its activities to Lindley Road in 1959;[41] the old citadel was sold and later demolished. The Leyton citadel corps has recruited more Salvation Army officers for training than any other corps in the British Isles.

The second Leyton corps originated in the revival of 1908, when a wooden hall was erected in Lea Bridge Road; a larger iron hall, with a brick front, was added soon after 1918.[42] These buildings also were badly damaged in the Second World War. About 1959[43] they were replaced by a permanent hall, with shops forming the ground floor, but this was burned down in 1964[44] and the corps was disbanded.

The Salvation Army was working by 1886 in a hall in Cann Hall Road, Leytonstone,[45] which the

[28] *Mins. Meth. Conf.* (1939, 1940).
[29] Ibid. (1958, 1959).
[30] Unless otherwise stated, this account is based on *Gainsborough Bridge Meth. Ch. 1902–1952*.
[31] *Mins. Meth. Conf.* (1959).
[32] Worship Reg. 7867 (canc. 1866).
[33] Unless otherwise stated this account is based on Wilkinson, *Leyton*, 32, and A. Webster, 'Notes on Grove Green Methodist Church' (L.R.L., L85 Pamphlet, TS.).
[34] Mins. Walthamstow Circuit Mtgs. 1913–25; *Mins. Meth. Conf.* (1945–59).
[35] Unless otherwise stated this account is based on

Wilkinson, *Leyton*, 32, 35, and on inf. from the Presbyterian Historical Society of England.
[36] *The Presbyterian*, 21 Apr., 15 Sept., 6 Oct. 1893.
[37] See p. 302.
[38] Unless otherwise stated the account of Leyton Citadel Corps is based on *These fifty years at Leyton 1, 1883–1933*.
[39] Worship Reg. 27456 (canc. 1897 revn.).
[40] *Leytonstone Express and Independent*, 17 July and 4 Sept. 1886. [41] Worship Reg. 67591.
[42] Inf. from Major I. Watson.
[43] Worship Reg. 43285.
[44] L.R.L., Local churches index, 1968.
[45] *Kelly's Dir. Essex* (1886).

Cann Hall Wesleyan Methodists rented from 1887. The army took it over again about 1898, when the Methodists left,[46] were there in 1903, but had left by 1910.[47]

The Leytonstone corps, Southwell Grove Road, originated in 1899 with open-air meetings on Harrow Green.[48] The brick barracks were built by F. J. Coxhead in Southwell Grove Road in 1901–2. A new Sunday school was built in 1954.

Unitarians. Leytonstone church, Lea Bridge Road, originated in 1908, in meetings held by a group interested in the 'New Theology' movement led by R. J. Campbell, then Congregational minister at the City Temple (Lond.), and founder of the League of Progressive Thought and Social Service.[49] A Leytonstone branch of the League was formed, with membership drawn from many denominations. The early meetings, held from 1909 at the League House, High Road, Leytonstone, were led by Campbell's 'pioneer preachers'. Sunday services, started in 1910, were taken over in 1912 by J. A. Pearson, district minister of the London Unitarian Society, who had already given much help to the branch. In 1913 the services were transferred to Haydn House, Fairlop Road, vacated by the Christian Scientists, though members of the League, then called the Liberal Christian League, continued to attend lectures at League House. A self-governing church was formed in 1917, called the Leytonstone Free church until 1926, when it became the Leytonstone Unitarian church. From 1927 services were held at the Liberal Club, High Road, Leytonstone, while church activities continued at Haydn House. In 1931 a temporary church was built in Lea Bridge Road. It was damaged by bombing in 1940 and for some months, while it was being repaired, services were held in the minister's house. The church was closed soon after 1954. The building is now (1968) a furniture store.

Undenominational Missions. The Welcome mission, Cathall Road, Harrow Green, Leytonstone, was opened by H. E. Lester and A. C. Wood in 1883, in a rented disused public house, as a branch of the Ragged School Union (now the Shaftesbury Society).[50] The public house was later bought and renovated, and in 1896 a large hall built at the back.[51] In 1903 total attendances at its Sunday services exceeded 500. It was particularly noted in 1904 for its 'drift work', organized to help the poorest children of the area.[52] In 1907 an evening institute

was built on an adjoining site. The mission is still (1968) affiliated to the Shaftesbury Society.

The London City Mission hall, Aylmer Road, Leytonstone, was built in 1885 at a cost of £3,000 to seat about 400.[53] Though it was said to be doing excellent work in 1897,[54] by 1903 total Sunday attendances were only 91, perhaps because it was sited in a prosperous district, where mission services would have little appeal. It was closed about 1938.[55] The building was sold. It is now (1968) a clothing factory.

The Barclay Hall mission, High Road, Leyton, was founded before 1885[56] by J. G. Barclay (d. 1898) of Knotts Green, in a small hall built on to the gardener's lodge at Leyton Green. It was originally under the direction of the vicar of St. Mary's church. About 1896 a London City missioner, A. Young, was placed in charge, and shortly before the Barclay family left the district about 1898 the hall was given to the L.C.M.[57] In 1907 a new hall was opened, designed by E. Frere. It is a simple but dignified building of yellow brick, the front having four full-height windows which were fitted originally with louvred shutters. The mission was still active in 1968.

A London City Mission room in Cathall Road, Leytonstone, listed from 1893, ceased about 1911.[58] It may have been the workmen's mission in Cathall Road listed in 1908 and 1910 but not later.[59] A City Mission hall is listed in Park Grove Road in the same neighbourhood from 1912 to 1917.[60]

The L.C.M.'s central hall, Ferndale Road, Leytonstone, originated about 1895, when the five children of Henry Borton, a builders' merchant at Wanstead, began holding evangelistic services in the Assembly Rooms. In 1901 their father built for them the present hall in Ferndale Road, designed in brick and stone with baroque features by T. & W. Stone.[61] It became a centre of evangelism in the district; in 1903 Sunday attendances exceeded 500. In 1948 Miss Beatrice Borton, the only member of the family still working there, invited the London City Mission to take charge.[62] The hall is still (1968) in use.

The work of the London City Mission's Goodman memorial hall, Grove Green Road, Leytonstone, began in 1903 in a house in Pearcroft Road.[63] An iron hall, called Bethsaida,[64] was built in 1906 in Grove Green Road. In 1912 the widow and family of Josiah Goodman built a larger permanent hall in his memory, designed by W. Hood.[65] About 1938 the hall was handed over to the L.C.M. which is still (1968) in charge.

[46] *The March of Time: Cann Hall Methodist Mission Church, 1887–1937*, p. 4.

[47] Worship Reg. 39817 (canc. 1910); *Kelly's Dir. Essex* (1906–10); Mudie-Smith, *Relig. Life Lond.* 365.

[48] C. L. Kingston, 'Brief historical notes on Leytonstone Salvation Army Corps, Southwell Grove Road' (L.R.L., L85 Pamphlet, TS.); *Leytonstone Express and Independent*, 23 Nov. 1901.

[49] This account is based on inf. from Mr. J. W. Peterken and Miss D. Wrigley.

[50] Unless otherwise stated this account is based on the record books at the mission.

[51] *Leytonstone Express and Independent*, 26 Sept. 1896; Wilkinson, *Leyton*, 35.

[52] *Sunday Companion*, 2 Jan. 1904.

[53] *Kelly's Dir. Essex* (1886).

[54] Wilkinson, *Leyton*, 35.

[55] *Kelly's Dir. Leytonstone, Wanstead and Snaresbrook* (1937, 1939).

[56] *Expr. and Ind. Alm.* (1885). It may have been the

hall briefly used by the Salvation Army in 1883, before they settled at Etloe hall (*These fifty years, 1883–1933*). Unless otherwise stated this account is based on: Wilkinson, *Leyton*, 35; *Leytonstone Express and Independent*, 19 Oct. 1907; and inf. from Mr. L. Medley, Barclay Hall missioner.

[57] The Barclays had been associated with the London City Mission for many years: see plate f.p. 188.

[58] *Kelly's Dir. Walthamstow, Leyton and Leytonstone* (1893 and later edns.); *Expr. and Ind. Alm.* (1897–1912).

[59] *Kelly's Dir. Essex* (1908, 1910).

[60] *Expr. and Ind. Alm.* (1912–17).

[61] Hammock, *Leytonstone*, 94; *Leytonstone Express and Independent*, 18 May 1901. For the Assembly Rooms, see below, p. 235.

[62] Inf. from Mr. W. L. Saye.

[63] Unless otherwise stated this account is based on inf. from Mr. S. G. Clayton.

[64] *Expr. and Ind. Alm.* (1909 and later edns.); *Kelly's Dir. Leytonstone, Wanstead and Snaresbrook* (1911, 1912).

[65] *Leytonstone Express and Independent*, 5 Oct. 1912.

Other Churches and Missions. Montague Road, Leytonstone, Gospel temperance mission was registered in 1881, and a hall built in 1888.[66] In 1907 the mission became affiliated to Harrow Green Baptist church.[67]

Swedenborgians (New Jerusalem Church) were meeting by 1895 in a shop in Cann Hall Road. Their leader, T. J. Barlow, also ran a New Church mission hall there, for the Willing Workers juvenile temple. The church moved to Woodford Road, Forest Gate, in West Ham in 1900.[68]

Bethel mission, Acacia Road, is listed from 1895.[69] This may have been the hall where the High Road, Leytonstone, Methodists (W) had a mission, 1881–94;[70] where a Mr. Athill ran a mission in connexion with Daniel's Band from about 1899 to 1901;[71] and where the Brethren were meeting in 1903.[72] An Acacia Road mission hall was sold in 1919, its title dating from conveyances of 1882 and 1885; it is not listed after 1922.[73]

The Lifeboat Evangelical church, Newcomen Road, originated about 1896 when a group called Daniel's Band began to hold services on Wanstead Flats, in the streets, and in Acacia Road. In 1900 a small brick hall called the Lifeboat was built in Newcomen Road.[74] By 1908 a second hall called the Lighthouse had been acquired in Harrow Road.[75] When the Lifeboat hall was badly damaged during the Second World War, all activities were transferred to the Lighthouse. In 1959 the restored Lifeboat Evangelical church was registered for worship as a member of the Fellowship of Free and Independent Evangelical Churches.[76] The Lighthouse hall had been demolished by 1954.

An Evangelical Christian mission, with Thomas Fairbard as pastor, was being conducted in Melbourne Road by 1897. It moved to Peterborough Road about 1906, but appears to have ceased by 1907.[77]

A Church of Christ mission room was registered in Eve Road, Leytonstone, in 1899, and listed in 1900, but not thereafter.[78] A Church of Christ gospel hall in Murchison Road, Leyton, was listed from 1908 to 1914, but apparently had been taken over by the Brethren by 1910.[79]

The Beachcroft Road, Leytonstone, evangelistic mission was listed from 1901.[80] In 1903 total Sunday attendances were 44. By 1911 it was known as Emmanuel mission.[81] It closed about 1916,[82] and was apparently demolished, as a new brick Emmanuel was built on the site in 1919.[83] This was occupied by the Brethren.[84]

An evangelistic mission in Lansdowne Road, Leytonstone, existed in 1903.[85] This was probably the Workmen's mission hall and institute listed from 1903 to 1909, which appears to have been taken over by the Brethren by 1910.[86] A separate temperance mission hall was also listed in Lansdowne Road from 1905 to 1922.[87]

Keswick Hall Evangelical free church, Boundary Road, Leyton, originated as a group who had previously worshipped in the Baptist church on the Walthamstow side of Boundary Road.[88] When the Baptist church moved to Orford Road, Walthamstow, in 1914, some of its members, who found the new church too distant, began to meet in an iron hut on the Walthamstow side of Boundary Road.[89] The leader of this group, T. J. Chappell, influenced by the Keswick Convention, decided to organize an independent undenominational church, and in 1920 the hut was registered as Boundary Gospel Hall for Christians.[90] In 1924 he built Keswick Hall on the Leyton side of the road. He continued to act as its pastor, with one short break, until 1942, when a London City missioner was put in charge. In 1952 the church joined the Fellowship of Independent Evangelical Churches.

Christadelphians had a mission hall in Leytonstone High Road from about 1925 to 1932, when it was sold.[91]

Leyton Elim Four Square Gospel church, Vicarage Road, was founded in 1927, after a campaign at the Cathall Road baths.[92] A regular pastor was appointed from 1930. Services were held in the Grange Park Congregational hall until the church was opened in 1934. It consists (1968) of a brick all-purpose hall, which was enlarged in 1953.

A shop in Lea Bridge Road, Leyton, taken in 1937 for north-east London Jehovah's Witnesses, was registered as Kingdom Hall from 1938 to 1963, when they moved to Walthamstow. In 1954 it was the headquarters of the Walthamstow Congregation.[93]

[66] Worship Reg. 25685 (canc. 1897 revn.); Hammock, *Leytonstone*, 95.
[67] See above.
[68] MS. notes on Harrow Green Bap. Ch. compiled by Revd. W. Fancutt (in possession of Harrow Green church); *Expr. and Ind. Alm.* (1897–1900). For its later history, see above, West Ham, p. 140.
[69] *Kelly's Dir. Walthamstow, Leyton and Leytonstone* (1895 and later edns.).
[70] See p. 229.
[71] *Expr. and Ind. Alm.* (1899–1901).
[72] See p. 225.
[73] E.R.O., *Sale Cat.* A98; *Kelly's Dir. Essex* (1922, 1926).
[74] *Leytonstone Express and Independent*, 29 Sept. 1900; *Expr. and Ind. Alm.* (1899–1902). Unless otherwise stated this account is based on inf. from Revd. T. Carpenter and Mr. N. L. Gooden.
[75] *Kelly's Dir. Essex* (1908 and later edns.). This was probably the Woodhouse mission hall, Harrow Road, in existence by 1885 (*Expr. and Ind. Alm.* 1885 and later edns.).
[76] Worship Reg. 67105.
[77] Wilkinson, *Leyton*, 35; *Kelly's Dir. Essex* (1906); *Kelly's Dir. Walthamstow, Leyton and Leytonstone* (1905–7).
[78] Worship Reg. 37261; *Kelly's Dir. Walthamstow, Leyton and Leytonstone* (1900–1).

[79] *Kelly's Dir. Essex* (1908, 1910, 1912); *Expr. and Ind. Alm.* (1910–14).
[80] *Expr. and Ind. Alm.* (1901 and later edns.).
[81] *Kelly's Dir. Leytonstone, Wanstead and Snaresbrook* (1911).
[82] *Expr. and Ind. Alm.* (1913–17).
[83] Inf. from Mr. G. Offord.
[84] See above.
[85] Mudie-Smith, *Relig. Life Lond.* 462.
[86] *Kelly's Dir. Walthamstow, Leyton and Leytonstone* (1903–7); *Kelly's Dir. Essex* (1906–10); *Expr. and Ind. Alm.* (1904–9).
[87] *Expr. and Ind. Alm.* (1905–17); *Kelly's Dir. Essex* (1910–22); *Kelly's Dir. Walthamstow, Leyton and Leytonstone* (1905).
[88] See p. 295.
[89] Unless otherwise stated this account is based on inf. from Pastor P. D. Chevil.
[90] Worship Reg. 47775.
[91] *Kelly's Dir. Essex* (1926); *Kelly's Dir. Leytonstone, Wanstead and Snaresbrook* (1925–33); L.R.L. Deeds, T.C. 87. 2 (E.R.O., T/A 12/2/1).
[92] This account is based on F. E. Croker, 'Notes on the history of Leyton Elim Church' (L.R.L., L85 Pamphlet, TS.).
[93] Inf. from Mr. J. B. Oliver; Worship Reg. 58127, 69071. See also below, p. 304.

JUDAISM. The Leyton and Walthamstow synagogue is described elsewhere.[94] The Leytonstone and Wanstead synagogue, Drayton Road, Leytonstone, was founded in 1929, with services held privately in Preston Road.[95] A converted house in Drayton Road was opened as a synagogue in 1934,[96] with a membership of 10 families. It was seriously damaged by bombing in 1941, but restored. A community centre was opened in 1954,[97] when the membership was about 170 families. The Jews' burial ground, Forest Gate, is dealt with under West Ham.

EDUCATION. A school board was formed for Leyton in 1874. At that time there were two schools in the parish, at Leyton and Leytonstone, but 1,128 more places were needed.[98] Between 1874 and 1903 the board opened 12 schools (including one temporary), took over one National school (the other being closed), and started a pupil teacher centre. In the same period the Roman Catholics opened a school. Cann Hall lay outside the area of the Leyton school board,[99] but its children crowded the board's school at Harrow Green. In 1880, after complaints from Leyton, Wanstead formed a school board,[1] which built four schools in Cann Hall before 1903.

Under the Education Act (1902) Leyton U.D.C. became a 'Part III' authority, responsible for elementary education throughout the whole district, including Cann Hall.[2] It opened three more elementary schools before the First World War. Secondary education, for which the county became responsible, was already being provided at the technical institute, which had been opened by the U.D.C. in 1896 and had been offering mixed day classes since 1898. The county continued both the evening and day departments of the institute, a private school was recognized as a girls secondary day-school (1905), and the pupil teacher centre became a mixed secondary school. A new high school for all the girls opened in 1911. The boys remained in two high schools until these were amalgamated in 1916. In that year also a junior technical day-school was opened.

In 1919 there were 20 elementary schools (including one Roman Catholic school) in Leyton, with 23,557 places; four of them had overflowed into temporary premises.[3] The oldest school was closed in 1923, and in 1925–6 two schools were reorganized as selective central schools. Two special schools were opened in 1927. In 1932 the council's elementary schools were reorganized on the lines of the Hadow report, one new school being built.[4] The technical institute was closed in 1938, when the South-West Essex technical college opened.

During the Second World War Leyton was an evacuation area; schools were dispersed as far as Wales;[5] those which reopened for returning children did so under emergency and often improvised conditions.[6]

Under the Education Act (1944) the borough became an excepted district within the county's system of divisional administration.[7] In 1948 the schools were reorganized to provide 2 secondary (grammar) schools, 6 secondary (modern) schools, and 10 (including 1 non-provided) primary schools.[8] In 1950 a mixed technical school was added, in 1954 a new primary school, and in 1956 a seventh secondary (modern) school. Of the original 6 modern schools, 5 had been built in 1894–1904. Shortage of land precluded rebuilding these on new sites, but between 1956 and 1964 all 6 were enlarged, as were the two high schools.[9] In 1957 most schools were renamed, usually by omitting the word 'Road'.[10] In 1959 an infants school was closed and its buildings taken over for maladjusted children.

In the following chronological sections the school accounts, which are taken up to 1965, are arranged according to the date of original foundation.[11] They do not attempt to detail temporary wartime arrangements, 1939–45; these can sometimes be traced in the education committee's reports to the council, and in records of individual schools.

Elementary schools founded before 1874. Robert Ozler, by will proved 1698, left £300 to build within 7 years a free school for 7 children from Leyton and 7 from Walthamstow, together with £12 a year to pay a master to teach reading and writing.[12] In 1705, no school having been built, Ozler's executor agreed with the vestry to pay the £12 to Mr. Philips, the master of a private school, to whom several free scholars were thenceforward sent.[13] In 1709 a Chancery decree authorized the purchase of a house and land in the High Road for £270 for the school, and £12 a year, charged on Black Marsh farm, to pay the master.[14] The school opened in 1710 in a thatched cottage, with Philips as master. In the same year £10 left to the poor by Nathaniel Tench was used towards the conversion of the building.[15] Rules drawn up by the trustees in 1710 restricted the free places to boys. The master was allowed to take private pupils. In 1726 the Leyton

[94] See p. 304.
[95] Unless otherwise stated this account is based on inf. from Mr. S. Kalms and the Revd. I. M. Braier.
[96] *Leytonstone Express and Independent*, 1 Sept. 1934.
[97] Ibid. 28 May 1954.
[98] *V.C.H. Essex*, v. 56.   [99] See p. 317.
[1] Kennedy, *Leyton*, 199; *Leyton B.C. Year Bk.* 1952–3, p. 82.
[2] *Leyton B.C. Year Bk.* 1952–3, p. 82; *Leyton Official Guide* (c. 1958), 22.
[3] *Leyton U.D.C. Year Bk.* 1919–20, p. 44.
[4] *Leyton B.C. Mins. and Reps.* 1928–9, p. 846, 1929–30, pp. 144, 159, 340, 1931–2, pp. 661, 968; *Leyton Off. Guide* (1934), 26.
[5] E.R.O., E/Z 6.
[6] *L.B.C. Mins. and Reps.* 1940–5.
[7] *Leyton B.C. Year Bk.* 1946–7, pp. 76–7; *Leyton Off. Guide* (1949), 27.
[8] *L.B.C. Mins. and Reps.* 1947–8, pp. 538, 781.
[9] *Leyton Quarterly*, no. 2, Apr. 1960, 4–5; *Education in Essex*, 1956–60, pp. 24–8, 1960–4, pp. 22–4.
[10] *L.B.C. Mins. and Reps.* 1956–7, p. 422.
[11] The London borough of Waltham Forest adopted a system of comprehensive education in 1968: *Walthamstow Guardian*, 20 Mar. 1970. The subsequent reorganization of Leyton's schools is described in: London B. Waltham Forest, *Secondary Schools in the borough* (1970).
[12] Unless otherwise stated, the information on Ozler's school is based on the following sources: *Rep. of Clerk of Leyton U.D.C. as to Leyton charities*, 1906, 2–9; *29th Rep. Char. Com.* H.C. 216, pp. 157–9 (1835), xxi (1); Kennedy, *Leyton*, 172 f.; M. L. Savell, 'Echoes of Old Leyton No. 10: Troubles with Free Schooling' (*Walthamstow Guardian*, 23 Apr. 1965); *Rep. of Town Clerk on non-ecclesiastical charities of Leyton*, 1927, 1–15.
[13] L.R.L., L47 MS. Vestry Min. 1705.
[14] L.R.L., L55.6 MS. Rates 1807–26 (1812).
[15] Ibid. 1710.

vestry ruled that Walthamstow should share the cost of repairs.[16] About 1764 a larger school was built by subscription. This was rebuilt after a fire in 1779, the cost being met mainly from the poor-rates of the two parishes. The master then agreed to take 10 boys from each parish,[17] but in 1800 the number was reduced to the original 7. By 1808 the school had fallen into disrepute. There were only two free scholars, and the master was running a private girls boarding school; he was arrested for debt in 1810. Under his successor the school recovered. In 1813 William Bosanquet left £200 in trust to buy books, pens, and stationery. By 1818 all the free places were occupied.[18] In 1846 the school was demolished and the trustees joined with those of Leyton National school to build a new one, for girls as well as boys, on the same site.[19]

In 1787 churchmen resolved to open a Sunday school[20] and in 1791 a schoolroom was built for it in the yard of the free school.[21] This schoolroom was used also for a girls school of industry opened in 1794 for 30 girls, and supported by subscription.[22] In 1797–1801 the mistress of the girls school was being paid for stockings and linen supplied to the workhouse.[23] A house was built for the mistress in 1815.[24] In 1834 the mistress was paying £5 5s. rent to the free school master for the girls school and house.[25] The school still existed in 1839.[26]

Leyton National school originated in 1816, when Samuel Bosanquet leased to trustees a corner of Lawyer's field in James Lane, to be used for this purpose.[27] The school was established in 1819. In 1820 there were 136 pupils; attendances were maintained until 1833, but fell thereafter, to 81 by 1846–7, when the master and mistress were paid £75 and £55 respectively.[28] In 1847 the school united with the Ozler free school, and a new mixed school was built by subscription on the free school site, with houses for master and mistress; a wooden building near by served for the infants.[29] From 1854 the school had a share of the income from the commoners' compensation from the waterworks

company,[30] but the same year the Ozler income was apportioned between the Leyton and Leytonstone National schools. The apportionment was amended in 1856, when the rents from the parish's high street cottages were also applied to support both schools.[31]

By 1863 there were 140 boys and girls and 90 infants; fees were graded 1d. to 4d. a week.[32] Grant aid was received by 1865.[33] By 1874 there were no free scholars,[34] but attendances were increasing rapidly. In 1877 the infants school was rebuilt and the boys and girls departments enlarged by subscription, with help from the National Society, to provide 425 places. In the 1880s Hibbert family legacies enabled more improvements to be made,[35] but further enlargement in the 1890s left the trustees deep in debt. In 1900 they transferred the school at a nominal rent to the school board, while the charity's income was applied to repayment of the debt.[36] The school, which then became known as High Road school, was closed in 1903, but reopened by the council in 1904 as a temporary mixed school.[37] It finally closed in 1923.[38] In 1925 the land and premises were returned to the trustees, and sold soon after. Ozler's £12 rent-charge was redeemed in 1922. In 1930 the scheme governing the Ozler foundation was amended by Board of Education order. The charity's assets were invested and shared between Leyton and Walthamstow. Thenceforward the Leyton income was applied to religious instruction and educational awards.[39] The school buildings are now (1968) occupied by several small factories.

Leytonstone National schools were founded by 1815.[40] The schools, usually attended by about 100 boys and girls,[41] stood in the yard of the Leytonstone chapel of ease.[42] In 1835 the schools were pulled down, the chapel itself converted into schools, and houses built for the master and mistress.[43] Paid monitors were assisting in 1846–7.[44] The schools received a share of parish educational charity funds from 1854[45] and annual grants by 1872.[46] About 1874 they were attended by Timah and Shumah, the African bearers who accompanied David Livingstone's body back to England after his

[16] L.R.L., L55.6 MS. Rates 1726.
[17] L.R.L., L47 MS. Vestry Min. 1779; Lysons, *London*, iv. 181.
[18] *Digest of Returns to Sel. Cttee. on Education of Poor*, H.C. 224, p. 261 (1819), ix (1).
[19] The old school, by the Three Blackbirds inn in Leyton High Road, is shown on the tithe map, 1843: E.R.O., D/CT 221 (no. 230).
[20] Wilkinson, *Leyton*, 35.
[21] Kennedy, *Leyton*, 191. See also above, p. 218 for alterations to church in 1817 to accommodate Sunday school children.
[22] L.R.L., L47 MS. Vestry Min. 1794; Lysons, *London*, iv. 181.
[23] L.R.L., L47 MS. Vestry Mins. 1797–1801.
[24] Kennedy, *Leyton*, 192.
[25] *29th Rep. Char. Com.* H.C. 216, p. 159 (1835), xxi (1).
[26] *Pigot's Dir. Essex* (1839).
[27] E.R.O., D/DBq T11/76; the lease is endorsed: 'Piece of ground given up, site being no longer used as National School.' The tithe map, 1843 (E.R.O., D/CT 221) shows a small building, not numbered or listed, hatched like the Leytonstone National school, at the corner of field no. 158, which fits the description in the lease.
[28] *Nat. Soc. Reps.* 1820–38; *Nat. Soc. Enquiry into Church Schools, 1846–7*, pp. 12–13.
[29] *White's Dir. Essex* (1848), 249–50.
[30] See p. 198.
[31] Wilkinson, *Leyton*, 55; L.R.L., L47 MS. Vestry Mins. 1854, 1856. For the High Street cottages, see above, p. 208.

[32] *White's Dir. Essex* (1863), p. 643; Kennedy, *Leyton*, 194.
[33] *Rep. Educ. Cttee. of Council, 1865* [3666], H.C. (1866), xxvii.
[34] *Rep. of Clerk of Leyton U.D.C. as to Leyton charities*, 1906, pp. 1, 5.
[35] *Kelly's Dir. Essex* (1878, 1882, 1886); Kennedy, *Leyton*, 194–6; inf. from Nat. Soc.
[36] *Rep. Leyton charities*, 1906, pp. 5–9; *Reps. of Sch. Bd. Cttees.* 1900, p. 262; L.R.L., L58.75 Pamph. Explanatory letter to *Leytonstone Express and Independent*, 7 Nov. 1900.
[37] *Kelly's Dir. Essex* (1906); *Reps. of Sch. Bd. Cttees.* 1903, pp. 151, 204; L.R.L., L58 MS. Reps. L.U.D.C. Organising Inspr. 1904.
[38] *L.U.D.C. Mins. and Reps.* 1923.
[39] *Rep. of Town Clerk on non-ecclesiastical charities of Leyton*, 1927, 9, 13–14; Char. Com. File 79863; *Education in Essex*, 1928–35, p. 96.
[40] *Nat. Soc. Rep.* 1815, p. 40; E.R.O., D/DCy P2B, ff. 122–3.
[41] *Nat. Soc. Reps.* 1815–38.
[42] E.R.O., D/DCy P2B, ff. 122–3. See also above, p. 220.
[43] W. G. Hammock, *Leytonstone and its history*, 58–60; E.R.O., D/DCw M42, ff. 108, 178–9 (incl. plan of old schools); D/DCw Z1 (1839). The converted chapel is shown on the tithe map, 1843, E.R.O. D/CT 221 (no. 120A), and O.S. 6", Essex, LXXIII (1873–82 edn.).
[44] *Nat. Soc. Enquiry into Church Schs.* 1846–7, pp. 12–13.
[45] See above.
[46] *Rep. Educ. Cttee. of Council, 1872* [C.812], p. 408, H.C. (1873), xxiv.

death in 1873.[47] The schools closed soon after 1876, with the opening of Kirkdale Road board school.[48] The building, later known as the Assembly Rooms, was demolished in 1938.[49]

A British school for girls at Leytonstone was listed in directories from 1855 until 1870.[50] It adjoined the Independent chapel.[51]

Elementary schools founded between 1874 and 1903. The schools in this section, unless otherwise stated, were opened by the Leyton school board.[52] When classes started in the calendar year before any formal opening, the earlier date is given.

Kirkdale Road board school was opened in 1876 with places for 500. By 1891 it had been enlarged to twice that capacity. After it was condemned in 1929 the seniors and juniors were moved to temporary buildings in Connaught Road. Part of Kirkdale Road was reconstructed and reopened for infants in 1932; the rest became education offices in 1936. After a rocket severely damaged the buildings in 1945, the school carried on in two classrooms at Connaught Road school until 1948, when it closed.[53] The education offices were restored.

Church Mead junior mixed and infants schools. Church Road board school was opened in 1877[54] for 540 and by 1891 had been enlarged to twice that capacity. In 1913 new buildings were opened for the girls and infants. The school was reorganized in 1932 for senior girls,[55] junior girls and infants, in 1942 for senior girls, junior mixed, and infants, and in 1948 for junior mixed and infants only.

Harrow Green board school was built on 1 a. of Small Gains, the parish's copyhold charity land,[56] granted to the board in 1874 in return for payment of the fees to enfranchise the whole piece.[57] The school, opened in 1877, was enlarged twice by 1882, increasing its capacity from 565 to 1,200. In 1929 it was condemned and remodelled in 1932 as an infants school. It closed in 1935.

Cann Hall junior mixed and infants schools. Cann Hall Road board school was opened by the Wanstead school board in 1882. It was reorganized in 1932 for senior and junior boys and infants, in 1940 for senior boys, junior mixed, and infants, and in 1948 for junior mixed and infants.

Newport junior mixed and infants schools. Newport Road board school was opened in 1883 for 1,040; by 1898, after extension, it was accommodating 1,854.[58] It was reorganized in 1932 for senior and junior boys and infants, in 1942 for senior boys, junior mixed, and infants, and in 1948 for junior mixed and infants only. It was again enlarged in 1952.[59]

Downsell junior mixed and infants schools. Downsell Road board school was opened by the Wanstead school board in 1887. It was reorganized in 1932 for senior and junior boys and infants, but the senior boys were discontinued in 1942.

Mayville junior mixed and infants schools. Mayville Road board school, opened in 1889, was reorganized in 1932 for senior and junior girls and infants, in 1942 for senior girls, junior mixed, and infants, and in 1948 for junior mixed and infants.

Lea Bridge primary school. Lea Bridge Road board school, opened in 1892 as a mixed school, was very small; only 157 children were attending in 1898; in 1919 it had room for 286. From 1932 it became an infants school only. It became an annexe to Sybourn Street school in 1958-9 and was discontinued in 1959.

Ruckholt Road board school was opened in 1892. In 1926-7 the upper departments became a central school. In 1928 the juniors and infants were merged as an infants department, and in 1929 they were dispersed to other schools; their rooms were taken over by the central school.

Trumpington Road board school, opened by the Wanstead school board in 1894, was reorganized in 1932 for senior girls, junior mixed, and infants, and about 1940 for senior mixed and infants. In 1948 it became a mixed secondary (modern) school, renamed Lake House in 1957. An extension was completed in 1959.[60]

Goodall Road board school was opened in 1895 in temporary buildings, with boys only. The permanent school, completed in 1900,[61] was for boys, girls, and infants. It was reorganized in 1932 for senior girls, junior girls, and infants, and in 1940 for senior mixed and infants. In 1948 it became a mixed secondary (modern) school and was enlarged and modernized in 1959-60.[62]

Capworth Street board school was opened in 1896. It was reorganized in 1932 for senior girls, junior mixed, and infants. In 1948 it became a secondary (modern) school for girls, renamed Leyton Manor in 1957. In 1962 building extensions were completed.[63]

Connaught Road (temporary) mixed school, which opened in 1900, was discontinued in 1904.

High Road (temporary) mixed school, formerly Leyton National school, is dealt with under that school.

Farmer Road board school opened as a temporary mixed school in 1900. The permanent school for boys, girls, and infants was completed in 1903.[64] It was reorganized in 1932 for senior boys, junior boys, and infants, and in 1942 for senior boys, junior

[47] *Essex Churchman*, Oct. 1957.
[48] L.R.L., L58 MS. Leyton Sch. Bd. Mins. A, p. 174; *Kelly's Dir. Essex* (1878); Hammock, *Leytonstone*, 96.
[49] Hammock, *Leytonstone*, 59; L.R.L., L72.3 Print; *Kelly's Dir. Leytonstone, Wanstead and Snaresbrook* (Billiard saloon, 781A High Road), 1937, 1939.
[50] *Kelly's Dir. Essex* (1855-74).
[51] E. Clarke, *Walthamstow, past, present, and future*, 81.
[52] Apart from the additional refs. given, the information on individual schools of all kinds is based on the following sources: *Leyton U.D.C.* (1894-1926) and *Leyton B.C.* (1926-65) *Mins. and Reps.*; L.R.L., L58 MS. (Sch. Bd. Mins., Leyton, 1874-97, and Wanstead, 1880-1903); *Reps. of Educ. Cttees.* 1889-1903; L.R.L., L58 MS. (Reps. of Organizing Inspr. 1903-27 and of H.M.I.s, 1910-31); *Leyton U.D.C. and B.C. Year Bks.*; Wilkinson, *Leyton*, 43 f.; Kennedy, *Leyton*, 196 f.; *Kelly's Dir. of*

Essex (1882 and later edns.). There is a fine collection of school log books, 1876-1948, in L.R.L.: L58 MS.
[53] L.R.L., L58.72 MS. Kirkdale Rd. infs. log bk.
[54] The date '1876' inscribed on the school is that of building.
[55] E.R.O., E/Z 6 (Girls' Sch. Chronicle, 1932-48).
[56] See p. 239.
[57] L.R.L., L47 MS. Vestry Min. 1874; Kennedy, *Leyton*, 221.
[58] L.R.L., L58.76 Pamph. Newport Rd. Sch.; *Rep. of M.O.H.* 1898; *The Builder*, liii, 615 (1887).
[59] *Educ. in Essex*, 1952-6, 20.
[60] Ibid. 1956-60, 26.
[61] L.R.L., L58.69 Pamph. Goodall Rd. sch.
[62] *Leyton Quarterly*, no. 2, Apr. 1960; *Educ. in Essex*, 1956-60, 28.   [63] *Educ. in Essex*, 1960-4, 23.
[64] L.R.L., L58.68 Pamph. Farmer Rd. sch.

mixed, and infants. In 1948 it became a secondary (modern) school for boys, and in 1957 was renamed George Mitchell after an old pupil awarded the V.C. in the Second World War.

Cobbold Road board school, opened by the Wanstead school board in 1900, was reorganized in 1925 as the Tom Hood central school. It was built on the site of Wood House, Cann Hall.

Davies junior mixed and infants schools. Davies Lane board school, opened in 1901,[65] was reorganized in 1932 for senior boys, junior mixed, and infants, and in 1948 for junior mixed and infants.

St. Joseph's Roman Catholic junior mixed and infants schools. St. Agnes Roman Catholic 'poor school' was established about 1874 at Leyton House (renamed Park House). In 1882 it was a mixed school combined with an orphanage.[66] St. Joseph's (R.C.) non-provided mixed school in Vicarage Road was opened in 1900, and the orphanage closed soon after.[67] The upper floor of the new school was used as a temporary chapel until 1904.[68] The school was reorganized for juniors and infants in 1948 and became aided in 1950.[69] An extension was opened in 1959.[70]

Elementary schools founded between 1903 and 1945. The Sybourn junior mixed and infants schools. Sybourn Street council school opened as a mixed school in temporary buildings in 1903. The permanent building was completed in 1910[71] for senior mixed, junior mixed, and infants. In 1919 there were still 300 pupils in the temporary building. The school was reorganized for boys, girls, and infants in 1925–6 (when new infants premises were built),[72] for senior boys, junior mixed, and infants in 1932, and for junior mixed and infants in 1948.

Norlington Road council school for boys, girls, and infants opened in 1904. In 1932 it was reorganized for senior girls, junior girls, and infants. In 1940 the school was badly damaged by bombs. The junior department became mixed in 1942. In 1948 the school became a secondary (modern) school for boys. Extensions were completed in 1964.[73]

The Barclay junior mixed and infants schools originated in Canterbury Road council school. This opened in 1908 in temporary premises with infants only; by 1909 junior mixed were also attending; the permanent school for mixed and infants was completed in 1910.[74] It was enlarged and reorganized in 1914–15 for boys, girls, and infants, but the boys remained in temporary accommodation in St. Andrew's and St. Paul's church halls until 1924,

when a new building was opened for them. The school was enlarged in 1929–31,[75] reorganized for senior boys, junior mixed, and infants in 1932, and for junior mixed and infants in 1948. An extension was completed in 1952.[76]

Connaught Road school, opened in 1932, was built for senior girls and junior mixed departments. The junior mixed department closed in 1948.[77]

Secondary and senior schools founded before 1945. Leyton high school originated in 1898, when the U.D.C., assisted by the county council, opened a mixed day-school of science in the technical institute. It became a county secondary school under the 1902 Act and in 1905 had 201 pupils, over 65 per cent of them from public elementary schools.[78] The girls were transferred in 1911 to a new girls high school in Colworth Road[79] and the boys in 1916 to Leytonstone high school.[80]

Leytonstone high school originated as a pupil teacher centre established by Leyton school board in 1900, and based first on Goodall Road school, then on Davies Lane. In 1905, when there were 95 pupils, it was transferred to temporary buildings at Connaught Road, rented by the county council from the Leyton education committee, where it became a mixed secondary school, recognized in 1907. In 1911 the girls were transferred to the new girls high school, and from 1916, when it was joined by the boys from Leyton high school, it became known as Leyton high school for boys.[81]

Elson House girls high school in Wallwood Road, founded in 1884 as a private school, was placed in 1905 under a representative board of management, and recognized by the board of education as a secondary school. County scholarships were tenable at the school. In 1905 there were 180 pupils, 2·8 per cent of them from public elementary schools.[82] In 1909–10 the school was taken over by the county to be amalgamated with the new girls high school which opened in 1911.[83] Elson House preparatory department continued as a private school until 1967, when it was compulsorily closed.[84]

Leyton high school for girls, Colworth Road, opened in 1911, with the girls from the two mixed high schools, and from Elson House. The first headmistress was the founder of Elson House. The red-brick building, in a 17th-century domestic style, was designed by W. Jacques.[85] A new wing was opened in 1932, and in 1933 a swimming bath for which the school itself raised the money. Further extensions were completed in 1957.[86]

[65] L.R.L., L58.66 Pamph. Davies Lane sch.
[66] *Kelly's Dir. Essex* (1874 and later edns.); E. Walford, *Greater London*, i. 485.
[67] *Leyton Express and Independent Almanack*, 1901, pp. 34, 52; *Leytonstone Express and Independent*, 19 May and 1 Dec. 1900; *Leyton Sch. Bd. Cttee. Reps.* 1903, p. 151.
[68] See p. 223.
[69] E.R.O., C/ME 44, p. 410.
[70] L.R.L., L58.78 Pamph. St. Joseph's sch.
[71] L.R.L., L47 Pamph. *U.D.C. Chairman's address*, 1910.
[72] L.R.L., L72.3 MS. Contract, Sybourn St. infs. sch. 1925.
[73] *Educ. in Essex*, 1960–4, 24.
[74] L.R.L., L47 Pamph. *U.D.C. Chairman's address*, 1910.
[75] L.R.L., L72.3 MS. Contract, Canterbury Rd. sch. 1929; L58.62 Pamph. Canterbury Rd. sch. extensions, 1930–1.
[76] *Educ. in Essex*, 1952–6, 20.

[77] E.R.O., E/Z 7; L.R.L., L58.65 MS. Connaught Rd. junior sch. log bk. 1932–48.
[78] *V.C.H. Essex*, v. 57; M. Sadler, *Rep. Educ. Essex* (1906), 17, 130–4.
[79] F. M. Greeves, *Golden Jubilee History: Leyton C.H.S. for Girls, 1911–61*, 5.
[80] E.R.O., C/ME 12, pp. 78–9.
[81] Ibid.; Sadler, *Rep. Educ. Essex*, 140–5; Greeves, *Leyton C.H.S.*, 5; L.R.L., L58 MS. Reps. Org. Inspr. 1904–5.
[82] Greeves, *Leyton C.H.S.*, 5; Sadler, *Rep. Educ. Essex*, 10, 17, 135–40.
[83] E.R.O., C/ME 5, pp. 228, 587, 660, 723; C/ME 6, pp. 78, 240.
[84] *The Guardian*, 26 July 1967.
[85] Pevsner, *Essex*, 2nd edn., 269.
[86] Greeves, *Leyton C.H.S.*; *Leyton Off. Guide* (1922), 22; *Charter Day, 1926: souvenir programme*, 37; *Educ. in Essex*, 1952–6, 32, 1956–60, 24.

Leyton high school for boys, formed in 1916 by amalgamation of Leyton and Leytonstone high schools, occupied temporary premises at Connaught Road until 1929, when it moved to new buildings in Essex Road. It was enlarged in 1934–5 and again in 1957.[87]

Tom Hood secondary technical (commercial) school. Tom Hood mixed selective central school, named after the poet, who lived near by in Wanstead,[88] was opened in 1925 in the former Cobbold Road elementary school. It was enlarged in 1932. It was closed during the Second World War, but reopened in 1950 as a mixed secondary (technical) school with a commercial bias. A major reconstruction of the school was completed in 1954.[89]

Ruckholt selective central school was established in 1926–7 in part of Ruckholt Road elementary school, with separate girls (1926) and boys (1927) departments. From 1929, when the remaining infants were dispersed, it occupied the whole premises. In 1936 the school became mixed. Selective entry was discontinued from 1940, and the school, in an evacuation camp, closed in 1943. In 1940 bombing demolished most of the original building.[90]

Connaught Road senior girls school was the only senior school built in Leyton between the two world wars. Built under the 1929–32 reorganization programme, on the site vacated by the boys high school, it opened in 1932. In 1948 it became a secondary (modern) school for girls, taking over the adjoining premises of the former junior mixed department. Extensions were built in 1960–1 and 1964.[91]

The other 13 senior schools established in 1932, all single-sex, used parts of existing elementary schools: the boys were at Cann Hall Road, Canterbury Road, Davies Lane, Downsell Road, Farmer Road, Newport Road, and Sybourn Street; the girls were at Capworth Street, Church Road, Goodall Road, Mayville Road, Norlington Road, and Trumpington Road.[92]

Primary schools founded between 1945 and 1965. In the 1948 reorganization 8 elementary schools became primary schools for junior mixed and infants: Cann Hall Road, Canterbury Road, Church Road, Davies Lane, Downsell Road, Mayville Road, Newport Road, and Sybourn Street. The George Tomlinson junior mixed and infants school, Harrington Road, named after the Minister of Education, was opened in 1954.[93]

Secondary schools founded between 1945 and 1965. Six secondary (modern) schools were established in 1948 in existing elementary and senior school buildings. Goodall Road and Trumpington Road (Lake House) were mixed; Capworth Street (Leyton Manor) and Connaught Road were for girls; and Farmer Road (George Mitchell) and Norlington Road for boys. In 1950 Tom Hood central school reopened as a mixed technical school. In 1956 Ruckholt Manor (Ruckholt central rebuilt) was opened as a third mixed secondary (modern) school.[94]

Special schools. Harrow Green school for educationally subnormal children originated as the Knotts Green school for mentally defective children opened in 1927.[95] In 1948 the school moved to new buildings on the site of the former Harrow Green infants school.[96]

Knotts Green open air school for physically defective children was opened in 1927.[97] In 1955 it was discontinued when the premises, renamed Leyton Green school in 1957, became an annexe to the Harrow Green school for educationally subnormal children.[98]

Lea Bridge day-school for maladjusted children opened in 1959 for juniors in the former Lea Bridge infants school.[99] Senior children were later admitted.[1]

Technical education. In 1891 the Leyton local board set up a technical instruction committee. Evening classes started the same year in the town hall and schools. Within a year there were 694 students attending. A technical institute, built with the new town hall, was opened in 1896.[2] In 1898 a day-school was established in the institute, recognized after 1902 as a secondary school.[3] By 1914, in addition to evening classes in commercial subjects, day and evening classes were being held in arts and crafts.[4] The secondary school moved out in 1916. In its place, later in the year, a day engineering and trade school opened with 95 pupils.[5] By 1928 this was providing full-time three-year courses for boys over 12.[6] In the 1930s the institute was recognized for national certificate courses in chemistry (1931), building (1931), mechanical engineering (1932), and electrical engineering (1933). By 1934 there were 2,134 students, and 424 full-time pupils in the junior technical and art schools. A survey of technical education in 1929 had found the institute unsuitable for future expansion. Negotiations for a new site in Leyton having proved fruitless, a site was found in Walthamstow.[7] The Leyton institute closed in 1938 when classes started at the new South West Essex technical college. The institute building became an extension to the town hall.

In 1922 E. J. Davis left to the local education authority a freehold house and grounds, called Broomhill, in Vicarage Road, for use as the Davis homecraft institute; he also endowed school prizes and domestic prizes for the best-kept houses in the district. Practical domestic courses for girls from local

[87] E.R.O., C/ME 12, pp. 78–9; *Charter Day, 1926*, 37; *Educ. in Essex*, 1928–35, 68, 117, and 1956–60, 24.
[88] See p. 321.
[89] E.R.O., E/Z 5: Tom Hood school chronicle; *Charter Day 1926*, 36; *Educ. in Essex*, 1945–52, 29, and 1952–6, 31.
[90] *Charter Day 1926*, 36; L.R.L., L58.51 MS. Ruckholt central sch. boys' log bk. 1927–43.
[91] *Educ. in Essex*, 1956–60, 28, and 1960–4, 22, 24.
[92] See above for the subsequent history of these schools.
[93] *Educ. in Essex*, 1952–6, 21; *Essex Education*, Mar. 1955, 104.   [94] *Educ. in Essex*, 1952–6, 31.
[95] *Leyton Off. Guide* (1927), 12; *Leyton B.C. Year Bk.* 1926–7, p. 49.
[96] L.B.C. *Mins. and Reps.* 1939–40, p. 540, 1944–5, p. 465, 1948–9, p. 196.

[97] *Leyton Off. Guide* (1927), 12; *Leyton B.C. Year Bk.* 1926–7, p. 49.
[98] *Educ. in Essex*, 1952–6, p. 101; L.B.C. *Mins. and Reps.* 1956–7, p. 422; E.R.O., C/ME 49, pp. 440–1.
[99] *Educ. in Essex*, 1956–60, p. 118.
[1] Ibid. 1960–4, p. 96; L.B.C. *Mins. and Reps.* 9581–9, p. 709.
[2] Wilkinson, *Leyton*, 39, 60, 63; L.R.L., L47 MS. Local Bd. Mins. 1891 sqq.   [3] See p. 236.
[4] *Kelly's Dir. Leytonstone, Wanstead and Snaresbrook*, 1914.
[5] E.R.O., C/ME 12, pp. 78–9, 192, 342, 381.
[6] Essex Ed. Cttee: *Rep. of Dir. of Educ. for three years ending 31st Mar. 1928*, 54–5.
[7] *Educ. in Essex*, 1928–35, 78–9.

schools started in 1923. Since the 1950s the institute has been known as the Davis housecraft centre.[8]

Industrial schools. Bethnal Green Union industrial school was established at Leytonstone House in 1868 by the Bethnal Green poor-law guardians, and closed about 1932. From about 1910 the children over 8 years attended Leyton council schools.[9]

The Good Shepherd children's industrial home originated as a children's home and laundry founded by Miss Agnes Cotton in 1865 in Forest Place, Leytonstone.[10] In 1876 she bought the estate in Davies Lane once owned by Mary Bosanquet,[11] including the house built by Daniel van Mildert,[12] which she renamed The Pastures. In 1879 she built in the grounds, on the site once occupied by Mary Bosanquet's house, the Home of the Good Shepherd, with a school-house, chapel, laundry and infirmary. By previous arrangement, on her death in 1899, the home was taken over by the Clewer Sisters of the Anglican Community of St. John the Baptist, Clewer (Berks.). It closed about 1940 when the children were evacuated, and was not reopened after the Second World War.[13]

Private schools and colleges. Hugh Williams, a minister sequestered from a Norfolk living, was keeping a school in Capworth Street in 1656.[14] Philip Anderton, vicar of Leyton from 1651, taught a school after his ejection in 1662.[15] In 1702 John Hewit was teaching a Latin boarding school at Leytonstone.[16] In 1705 he asked John Strype's approval for a licence to teach and to serve as curate.[17] He was author of a poem, 'Leightonstone Air', and taught the naturalist George Edwards.[18] The entry of his burial at Leyton in 1728 describes him as 'schoolmaster'.[19] Another private school conducted in the early 18th century, by Mr. Philips, has been mentioned above.[20] Mark Davis, a Methodist, kept a school in Mary Bosanquet's house in Davies Lane for several years, after she left in 1768.[21]

Leytonstone academy, a boys boarding school, was started in 1765 by John Coulthist (d. 1784) in a house called Andrews; he added a schoolroom and playing fields. In 1785 the school was taken over by William Emblin, who transferred to it his own school from Bow (Mdx.). Hebrew, classical, and modern languages, history, geography, navigation, and merchants' accounts, were taught by the 'most lenient methods'. Emblin died in 1802; his successor was a professor from a royal military college in France. In 1812 the boarding fees were 30 guineas a year. Though reinforced in 1819 by the pupils from Bath House academy, Muswell Hill (Mdx.), the school closed in 1821. The building, later known as Royal Lodge, was burned down in 1878.[22]

A boarding school at the Assembly House, Forest Place, Leytonstone, is shown on a map of 1777[23] and also mentioned in 1798.[24] The schools run there by William and Georgiana Morris, listed in directories from 1839 to 1863, followed by the Misses Medlicott and Norris from 1867 to 1874,[25] were probably in the new Assembly House.[26]

Leyton college, claiming foundation in 1827,[27] was conducted at Walnut Tree House (Essex Hall), c. 1870–86. It took about 40 boarders and 100 day boys; George Westfield was principal for 42 years. It closed by 1890.[28]

Salway House college, in Leyton High Road,[29] a boarding school for boys, was founded about 1832.[30] An engraving shows the school in 1840.[31] Under Dr. J. R. Aldom, principal 1851–85,[32] it was described in 1855 as 'commercial and mathematical'.[33] Aldom was a prominent Wesleyan and his pupils were regularly marched to Knotts Green chapel, of which he was a trustee.[34] For some years after 1870 Aldom also ran Cambridge House girls school, in Lea Hall, Capworth Street.[35] Some time after his death in 1886, and by 1905, a successor moved the boys school to Fillebrook Road, renaming it Salway college. It closed in 1912.[36] Cambridge House closed about 1890.[37]

Between 1839 and 1867 the number of private schools in the parish listed in directories rose only from 3 to 5, including a short-lived grammar school built in Grange Park Road in 1866, but by 1870 there were 12.[38] The demand for schooling created by the population growth of the 1870s, is shown by

[8] *L.U.D.C.* and *L.B.C. Mins. and Reps.*; L34 Pamph. Newspaper cutting, Edw. J. Davis, n.d.; Char. Com. File 100946.

[9] *Kelly's Dir. Essex* (1870 and later edns.); *Kelly's Dir. Leytonstone, Wanstead and Snaresbrook*, 1931, 1933; E.R.O., D/DCy E45, f. 391.

[10] Unless otherwise stated the account of the Home is based on: W. G. Hammock, *Leytonstone*, 13–14; E.R.O., D/DU 322/1–10; *Kelly's Dir. Essex* (1870–1926).

[11] See p. 228.   [12] See p. 179.

[13] *Essex Churchman*, Aug. 1966; inf. from Miss M. L. Savell.

[14] H. Smith, *Eccl. Hist. Essex*, 346–7. See also above, p. 216.

[15] Newcourt, *Repertorium*, ii. 382; E.R.O., D/AEV 7 (Apr.–May 1664). See also above, p. 216.

[16] Lysons, *London*, iv. 182. Hewit first appears in the rates in 1701 (L.R.L., L55.6 MS.).

[17] B.M. Add. MS. 5853 f. 39.

[18] Lysons, *London*, iv. 182; W.H.L., Vertical File 920 (Biography): Notes by P. Thompson on Geo. Edwards (1693–1773) the naturalist. For G. Edwards, see above, p. 64 and *D.N.B.*

[19] Kennedy, *Leyton*, 135.   [20] See p. 233.

[21] F. Temple, 'Mary Bosanquet's house in Leytonstone' (E.R.O., TS); E.R.O., D/DU 322/1–10.

[22] M. L. Savell, 'Echoes of Old Leyton No. 17: Royal Lodge', Pt. 2 (*Walthamstow Guardian*, 9 July 1965); L.R.L., L35 Pamph. Leytonstone Academy Prospectuses, 1785, 1812, 1819; *Gent. Mag.* 1784, p. 716, and 1802, p. 1076;

N. Briggs, *Leisure and Pleasure in Essex*, pl. 17, reproduces an engraving of the school; E.R.O., T/P 110/45; L.R.L., L35 Pamph. Leytonstone Academy, Newspaper advt. 1820.

[23] E.R.O., T/M 173 (plan of Wallwood estate).

[24] *Gent. Mag.* 1798, p. 722.

[25] *Pigot's Dir. Essex* (1839); *White's Dir. Essex* (1848, 1863); *Kelly's Dir. Essex* (1855–74). See also tithe map, 1843 (E.R.O., D/CT 221), no. 37, occupied by Miss Morris 'and others'.   [26] See p. 178.

[27] *Kelly's Dir. Essex* (1886), advts. p. 47.

[28] Kennedy, *Leyton*, 331; *Kelly's Dir. Essex* (1870, 1886, 1890); L.R.L., L35 Pamph. Mrs. Eagleton's MS. notes on Leyton college.

[29] The school is named on O.S. Map 6″, Essex, LXXIII (1873–1882 edn.), near Skelton's Lane.

[30] Wilkinson, *Leyton*, 48.   [31] L.R.L., L72.2 Print.

[32] L.R.L., L96 Print.   [33] *Kelly's Dir. Essex* (1855).

[34] Caesar Caine, *Brief Chronicle of Wesleyan Methodism in Leyton*, 64, 94.

[35] Kennedy, *Leyton*, 332; *Kelly's Dir. Essex* (1870). There is an engraving of the school, with master in mortarboard and gown in L.R.L., L72.2 Print.

[36] Wilkinson, *Leyton*, 48; *Kelly's Dir. Walthamstow, Leyton and Leytonstone* (1905); *Kelly's Dir. Essex* (1912). The house was registered for the worship of Christian Scientists in Jan. 1913: see above, p. 226.

[37] *Kelly's Dir. Essex* (1886, 1890).

[38] *Pigot's Dir. Essex* (1839); *White's Dir. Essex* (1848, 1863); *Kelly's Dir. Essex* (1855 and later edns.). The grammar school building became the Liberal Club.

the existence in 1876 of a school in a small cottage attended by 88 children from 3 to 13 years, where there was 'not sitting and barely standing room and the utmost disorder prevailed'.[39]

The heyday of the private schools came with the peak growth of the 1880s; by 1882 there were 23. In 1890 of 21 listed 14 were in Leytonstone.[40] Many were short-lived, though Leytonstone College for boys in Fillebrook Road, founded in 1883, survived until the late 1920s.[41] By 1906, with increasing public provision for education, the number had fallen to 13; in 1914 there were still 15, but by 1926 only 8.[42]

Henry Green Scholarships. In 1935 Henry Green bequeathed £10,000 to the Leyton education authority to maintain 2 scholars from the council's schools at Oxford, Cambridge, or London universities.[43] In 1945 the Ministry of Education ruled that the endowment should not be transferred to the Essex county council under the 1944 Act.[44]

CHARITIES FOR THE POOR. The parish benefited from a number of small dole charities, the earliest dating from 1584, and from Smith's alms-houses, built in 1653–6, which later attracted a number of endowments.[45] In 1818 the average annual income from the charities for the poor was said to be £116.[46] In 1854 the charity income, and the tenancies of the alms-houses, were apportioned between Leyton and Leytonstone according to population. The proportions were revised in 1856.[47] By a scheme of 1929 all the alms-house and dole charities were combined as the Leyton United Charities.[48] Their total income in 1967 was £241.[49]

THE UNITED CHARITIES. *Alms-house Charities.* John Smith, by will dated 1653, devised land in trust to pay annually 50s. each to 8 inmates of alms-houses then being built by him in Leyton; the will was proved in 1655. The houses were completed in 1656[50] west of the church in Church Road. In 1659 the trustees granted to Thomas Haford, one of Smith's executors, part of Hughes farm, Leyton, subject to a rent-charge of £20, which for many years constituted the charity's main endowment.[51] The alms-houses were extensively repaired in 1739 by subscriptions aided from the poor-rate,[52] and again in 1790 at the expense of William Bosanquet.[53] In 1840 £200 was subscribed to endow a repair fund.[54] In 1885 the houses were rebuilt with the aid

of £2,000 from the Hibbert family, who had for long been the owners of Hughes Farm. Before rebuilding the alms-houses consisted of a single-storeyed brick range with lattice casements and a small central gable; the front had been partly obscured by later porches and outhouses. The new single-storey range was of flint with stone dressings, designed in a Tudor style by Richard Creed.[55]

The alms-house rules of 1711 provided for the admission of men or women, but by 1818 all the inmates were women. From the middle of the 18th century the alms-houses received a succession of endowments, mostly to provide stipends or gifts in kind for the alms-women. In 1739 Richard Jefferys left £155 to pay each of the alms-people £1 2s. 6d. a year until the capital was exhausted. The alms-house income was permanently augmented in 1747, when Charles Phillips, Turkey merchant, gave £12 rent, charged on lands in Mayland and Steeple, for the alms-people.[56] By 1927 this had been commuted for £400 stock. Also in 1747 John Phillips gave £6 rent charged on a house in Dover Street, London, to buy 2 chaldrons of coal to be given to the alms-people, any surplus to be distributed to them in cash. William Bosanquet (d. 1813) left £300 stock to the alms-houses. They also received £300 from Thomas Lane in 1817,[57] £200 from Magdalen Daubuz in 1818, £250 from Catherine Moyer in 1827, and £120 from Mary Bertie in 1832. In 1834 each of the alms-women was receiving 3s. 6d. a week, 6 sacks of coal a year, and 2s. 6d. a year from Archer's charity. In 1848 the alms-house income was £86.[58] The alms-houses received further gifts of £500 from Sarah Hibbert in 1884, £500 from Louisa and Emma Graham in 1886, and £500 from George Hibbert in 1887.[59] In 1967 their total income was £98 from £3,265 stock, and £6 from John Phillips's rent charge (Champion's Gift).[60]

Distributive Charities. Henry Archer, by will dated 1584, left 20s. rent charged on his estate at Coopersale, in Theydon Garnon, to be distributed to the poor at Whitsuntide. By 1834 it was being given to the alms-women. By 1927 the rent-charge had been commuted for £40 stock.

Robert Rampston, by will proved 1585, gave 20s. rent charged on Stone Hall, Little Canfield, for weekly bread. It was still being paid in 1967.[61]

In 1702 Sir William Hicks bequeathed £50 to the poor. In 1707 Lady Hicks added £10, and the combined sum was used to buy a 3½-acre copyhold field called Small Gains adjoining Grove Green, the rent to be spent on bread for the poor. The income

[39] L.R.L., L58 MS. Leyton Sch. Bd. Mins. A, pp. 173–4. The school was at no. 3 Maria Cottages.
[40] *Kelly's Dir. Essex* (1882, 1890).
[41] Ibid. (1890 and later edns.): *Kelly's Dir. Leytonstone Wanstead and Snaresbrook* (1893–4, 1925–7 (advts.), 1931); L.R.L., L35 Pamph. Leytonstone College prospectus.
[42] *Kelly's Dir. Essex* (1906, 1914, 1926).
[43] *Leyton B.C. Year Bk.* 1938–9, p. 75.
[44] Ibid. 1946–7, p. 87.
[45] For Ozler's educational charity, and church charities, see pp. 233, 219. Unless otherwise stated the account of Leyton's charities is based on: *Rep. Com. Char. (Essex)*, H.C. 216, pp. 157–64 (1835), xxi (1); *Rep. Leyton Chars.* (1906); *Rep. Non-eccl. Chars. Leyton* (1927); *Scheme for admn. of Almshouse Char. . . . and others (1929)*; Kennedy, *Leyton*; Wilkinson, *Leyton.*
[46] E.R.O., Q/CR 1/10.
[47] L.R.L., L47 MS. Ves. Mins. 1834–74 (1854, 1856).
[48] Char. Com. File 222518/2; *L.B.C. Year Book,* 1934–5, p. 68.

[49] Char. Com. File 222518.
[50] L.R.L., L47 MS. Vestry Mins. 1723–52 (at 1724 schedule of almshouse papers taken 1680); P.C.C. (349 Aylett).
[51] L.R.L., L55.6 MS. Rates 1807–26 (1812).
[52] L.R.L., L47 MS. Vestry Mins. 1723–52 (1734–5, 1738–9).
[53] Ibid. 1781–1811 (1790).
[54] L.R.L., L47 MS. Vestry Mins. 1834–74 (1854).
[55] Exterior tablet on almshouses; L.R.L., L72.4 Print: photograph, c. 1880.
[56] E.R.O., D/DU 177/41–2.
[57] L.R.L., L59.2 MS. W. Ham Union Inventory of funds and securities.
[58] *White's Dir. Essex* (1848), 250.
[59] Inscribed charity board in church.
[60] Char. Com. File 222518. The name 'Champion's Gift' was apparently applied to John Philips's rent-charge from c. 1929: Char. Com. File 222518/1.
[61] Char. Com. File 222518.

was £3 in 1713[62] and £16 in 1834. In 1874 1 a. was sold to the school board to raise £250 to enfranchise the whole field.[63] The remaining land was let in 1877 on a 99-year building lease, at a ground rent of £75, and by 1906 was covered by houses fronting Lascelles, Florence, and Cathall Roads. In 1929 the charity was included in the scheme and the income applied to the benefit of the alms-houses. The estate was sold in 1956 for £4,750, most of which was invested in an accumulating account to provide an endowment.[64]

The Inhabitants' charity was accumulated mainly from money paid to the parish for the poor from 1766 onwards, in return for permission to inclose forest waste.[65] John Ives added £100 to the fund by his will proved 1821.[66] In 1834 the total stood at £550 stock and the income of £16 10s. was given in weekly bread to the poor. In 1887 Thomas Turner by will left £29 stock to be added to the parish bread fund.[67] The total income in 1967 was £14 9s. 4d.[68]

James Holbrook, by deed dated 1805, gave one-third of a rent of £117 charged on property in Marsh Street, Walthamstow, for bread for distribution to aged and infirm poor. The income in 1967 was £22 18s. 3d.[69]

Charles Smith, by will proved 1845, left £100, the income to be divided among the poor at Christmas. The income in 1967 was £2 8s. 4d.[70]

Louisa Hall, by will proved 1868, left £500 stock, the income to maintain the tomb of her father, William Hall, in Leyton churchyard, the surplus being distributed among the poor. The income in 1967 was £12 10s.[71]

The George Westgate and Good Intent Hospital Gifts originated separately. George Westgate, by will proved 1925, left £100 to the Nurses' training home, Beachcroft Road, for the Leytonstone poor. In 1952 the fund was transferred by the county council to the charity trustees to assist the sick poor of Leytonstone or sick alms-persons. In 1957 £134 standing to the credit of the Good Intent Hospital Aid Society, which had been wound up, was transferred by the registrar of friendly societies to the charity trustees. The two funds were combined and invested in 1957. The income in 1967 was £7 18s.[72]

OTHER CHARITIES. George Hibbert, by will proved 1894, gave £1,000 in trust for the poor; this was invested in stock, and is known as the Hibbert benevolent fund. The income in 1927 was £28. The fund is usually distributed in doles at Christmas.[73]

Under the will of Edward Jones (d. 1917) a trust on behalf of Leyton came into effect in 1947, to preserve the fabric and churchyard of St. Mary's parish church, to augment the stipends of the curates of St. Mary's, and for the benefit of the alms-women. The capital, which is held by the diocese, is invested in shares bought at a cost of £4,700. The income of about £255 a year is distributed by the parochial church council in proportions agreed with the diocese.[74]

WALTHAMSTOW

Growth, p. 241. Domestic Buildings before 1840, p. 245. Transport and Postal Services, p. 250. Worthies and Social Life, p. 251. Manors, p. 253. Economic History, p. 263. Marshes, p. 273. Forest, p. 274. Local Government and Poor-Relief to 1836, p. 275. Local Government after 1836, p. 279. Public Services, p. 282. Parliamentary Representation, p. 285. Churches, p. 285. Roman Catholicism, p. 294. Protestant Nonconformity, p. 294. Judaism, p. 304. Education, p. 304. Charities for the Poor, p. 312.

WALTHAMSTOW MUNICIPAL BOROUGH. *Argent, a maunch gules, on a chief azure a seamew volant between two anchors, argent*

WALTHAMSTOW lies 6½ miles north-east of the City of London, between the river Lea and Epping Forest. It is part of the London borough of Waltham Forest.[1] Until the mid 19th century it was a country parish, noted for its woodland and its fine view across the marshes to London.[2] It then became a dormitory town in which industry played an increasing part. The urban landscape is, however, relieved by the forest and by spacious parks, sports grounds, and reservoirs.

The ancient parish, comprising 4,472 a., was 2½ miles long from north to south. Its boundary marched with Chingford to the north[3] and with Woodford and Wanstead to the east. The long straight southern boundary with Leyton is discussed elsewhere.[4] The ancient course of the Lea formed the west boundary with Hackney, Tottenham, and Edmonton (Mdx.), except at Higham Hill ferry where a piece of the west bank lay in Walthamstow.[5] Most of the west boundary now runs through the reservoirs.

The Walthamstow Slip (98 a.), a detached part of the parish locally situated in Leyton, was merged in Leyton sanitary district in 1873 and in Leyton civil parish in 1878.[6] Another detached part (18 a.), in south-west Chingford, was merged in Chingford in 1882.[7]

Walthamstow became an urban sanitary district in 1873 and a municipal borough in 1929. In 1961 the borough comprised 4,342 a.[8] In 1965 it was combined with Chingford and Leyton as the London borough of

[62] B.M. Add. 5853, f. 103.
[63] See also p. 235.
[64] Char. Com. File 110185.
[65] See p. 204.
[66] cf. charity board in church.
[67] Inscribed charity board in church.
[68] Char. Com. File 222518.
[69] Ibid.　[70] Ibid.　[71] Ibid.
[72] Ibid. 222518/2, 222518/5.
[73] Inf. from Revd. L. Denny.
[74] Inf. from Diocesan Offices and Revd. L. Denny.
[1] O.S. Maps 2½″ sheets TQ 38, 39, and 6″ (1952 edn.) sheets TQ 38 NE., 39 SE. See maps above and below, pp. 180, 248.

[2] E. Clarke, *Walthamstow: its past, present, and future* (1861), 15 ; Pevsner, *Essex* (2nd edn.), 406.
[3] Walthamstow B.C., *Proceedings at inquiry into application . . . for an extension of the Borough, 1932*, 29, 37-8; V.H.M., DRM 12 (at end of volume, perambulation, 1780).
[4] See p. 174.
[5] O.S. Map 6″, Essex, LXV (1868–76 edn.); V.H.M., *Vestiges*, no. 20; *Hist. Essex by Gent.* iv. 211.
[6] See pp. 174, 208.
[7] *V.C.H. Essex*, v. 97, 182; V.H.M., DRM 12 (perambulation 1780).
[8] *Census*, 1961.

Waltham Forest. Unless otherwise stated that year is the terminal point of this article.

The land rises from the Lea to over 200 ft. on the east. The steep mound of Higham Hill is 75 ft. high and Church Hill is 125 ft. Gravel terraces border the marshland alluvium, while farther east is mixed gravel and London clay.[9]

The river Ching, called the Bourne in 1332,[10] entered the parish at Chingford Hatch and flowed west via Salisbury Hall to join the Lea at Hanger's Bourne, now under Banbury reservoir. The Fleet river, known at different periods as Papermill, Coppermill, or Waterworks river, branched from the Lea at Fleetmouth,[11] now under Lockwood reservoir, and rejoined it south of Walthamstow mill. Higham Hill sewer flowed from Chapel End across Blackhorse Lane to Dagenham brook.[12] The brook flowed south to Leyton, joined by Moor ditch from Markhouse common. Most of Moor ditch was piped in the 1880s.[13] Parts of the Higham Hill sewer, Dagenham brook, and Blackmarsh sewer west of the brook,[14] were diverted or filled in when the flood relief channel was built in 1950–60.[15] West of Wood Street, flowing south to Leyton, was the watercourse which gave its name to Shernhall ('filth stream') Street,[16] which it used to flood near Tinker's bridge (Raglan Corner). In Leyton it was called the Phillebrook. It now runs underground.[17]

THE GROWTH OF WALTHAMSTOW.
Stone Age, Bronze Age, Iron Age, and Roman remains have been found in Walthamstow.[18] They include Bronze Age or early Iron Age pile dwellings on the site of the reservoirs.[19]

The recorded population in 1086 was 82.[20] In 1523–4 99 persons were assessed to the subsidy.[21] There were 189 dwellings in the parish in 1670,[22] 301 in 1762, and 386 in 1796.[23] In 1801 the population was 3,006.[24] It rose to 4,959 in 1851 and then more rapidly to 11,092 in 1871. After 1871 it doubled in each decade reaching 95,131 in 1901. During the 1890s Walthamstow was growing faster than any other town of its size except East Ham.[25] By 1911,

when the population was 124,580, growth was nearly complete, though the census peak of 132,972 was not reached until 1931. Numbers had begun to decline by 1938,[26] and the trend continued after the Second World War, to 121,135 in 1951 and 108,845 in 1961.

In 1086 most of the population lived south of Higham Hill and Hale End.[27] Later settlement took place in scattered hamlets and along the busier roads.[28] Inhabitants of The Hale (1285) or north-east 'corner' of the parish lived at Hale End (1498) or Woodend (1477).[29] Higham Hill (1501) in the north-west was a hamlet near Higham Bensted manor-house.[30] Chapel End (1528) lay near St. Edward's chapel and Salisbury Hall, while Church End[31] was beside St. Mary's church. King's End (c. 1760, now Leyton Green) was the village part of the Slip. In 1699 most of the buildings south of Chapel End were in Marsh Street, Church End, Shernhall Street, Clay Street (Forest Road), and Hoe Street. At that period settlement seems to have been increasing in Marsh Street.[32] The population of Higham Hill had declined by 1756.[33] In the early 19th century most habitation in the north was at Chapel End, and in the south in Marsh Street, Church End, Shernhall Street, and Wood Street.

Walthamstow's roads evolved on a gridiron plan. Three east–west routes intersected three north–south routes. The chief north–south road ran from Waltham Holy Cross to Stratford, by Salisbury Hall and bridge (1502),[34] Chapel End,[35] Greenleaf Lane (renamed Hoe Street North in 1887),[36] and Hoe Street to Leyton. Hoe ('ridge') Street is recorded in 1513. Nearer the Lea Amberland (Folly) Lane, mentioned in 1274, led from Chingford Hall to Higham Hill,[37] where it joined Blackhouse (1742), later Blackhorse Lane leading south across Marsh Street into Markhouse Lane to Leyton. Blackhorse Lane was a 'coach lane' by 1690,[38] and Markhouse Lane was widened in 1773.[39] But Amberland Lane, which was a horseway in c. 1527, was never improved.[40] In the late 16th century it was the scene of disputes over the Amberland Gate, the common

[9] V.C.H. Essex, i. 261; Walthamstow Off. Guide (c. 1927), 26.
[10] P.N. Essex (E.P.N.S.), 5; cf. 'Bournefeld' and 'Burnemede' adjoining the river on a plan of c. 1527: G. F. Bosworth, George Monoux (W.A.S. xvii), pl. f.p. 9.
[11] V.H.M., DRM 12 (1780 perambulation); V.H.M., Vestiges, no. 20.
[12] E.R.O., D/CT 382.
[13] O.S. Map 6", Essex, LXV (1868–76 edn.); V.H.M., Mins. Walthamstow Local Bd. (1880–2, 1885).
[14] Its continuation in Leyton was known as Shortlands sewer.
[15] See p. 274.
[16] The older form is Shernewell, scearn wielle: P.N. Essex (E.P.N.S.), 107–8.
[17] V.H.M., Local Bd. Mins. (1893); Clarke, Walthamstow, 48; E.R.O., T/M 167, Q/SR 386/13. See also above, p. 175.
[18] V.C.H. Essex, iii. 197–8.
[19] P.N. Essex (E.P.N.S.), 19; A. R. Hatley, Archaeology in the Walthamstow district (W.A.S., Reprint no. 1, 1967), 12–20.
[20] V.C.H. Essex, i. 537, 555.   [21] E 179/108/150.
[22] E.R.O., Q/RTh 5.
[23] Lysons, London, iv. 223.
[24] Unless otherwise stated these and the following details are from the Census Reports.
[25] V.C.H. Essex, v. 6.   [26] Ibid. 64.
[27] Ibid. i. 537, 555.
[28] Lysons, London, iv. 204–5; Clarke, Walthamstow (1861), 15; A. Hatley, Across the years (W.A.S. N.S. ii), 10

(quoting 1865). Unless otherwise stated the account of the distribution of settlement and the evolution of the road system to 1840 is based on P.N. Essex (E.P.N.S.), 105–9, Reaney, Walthamstow place-names (W.A.S. xxiv), and the following maps: c. 1527 (W.A.S. xvii, 9), 1699 (E.R.O., T/M 252), 1725 (E.R.O., D/DW P7), 1739 (E.R.O., T/M 167), 1742–3 (E.R.O., T/M 168), 1746 (J. Rocque, Survey of London), c. 1760 (E.R.O., D/DQs 31), 1777 (Chapman and André, Essex, sheets xvi, xxi), 1822 (W.A.S. N.S. v, va), and 1843 (E.R.O., D/CT 382).
[29] E.R.O., D/DFc 185, ff. 12–13, 30–2.
[30] Cf. V.H.M., Vestiges, nos. 15, 16. Higham Hill may be 'Tummanhille' or 'townsmen's hill' (1277).
[31] The name does not appear to be recorded until the 19th century (cf. Clarke, Walthamstow, 15).
[32] S. J. Barns, Walthamstow Deeds, 1595–1890 (W.A.S. xi), 21–3, and 1584–1855 (W.A.S. xxxiii), 24–31, Walthamstow vestry mins. 1710–40 (W.A.S. xiii), 4.
[33] J. Stow, Survey of London, enlarged J. Strype (6th edn., with revisions by E. Rowe Mores, 1756), 788.
[34] P. H. Reaney, Court rolls of Salisbury Hall (W.A.S. xxxvi), 13; E.R.O., Q/SR 172/54.
[35] V.C.H. Essex, v. 99 and f.p. 154; E.R.O., Q/SR 172/54.
[36] V.H.M., Vestiges, nos. 54–8. The present Greenleaf Road was built in 1880–4.
[37] V.C.H. Essex, v. 99; Rot. Hund. (Rec. Com.), i. 149.
[38] E.R.O., Q/SR 466/102.
[39] S. J. Barns, Walthamstow vestry mins. 1772–94 (W.A.S. xvi), 58.
[40] V.C.H. Essex, v. 99.

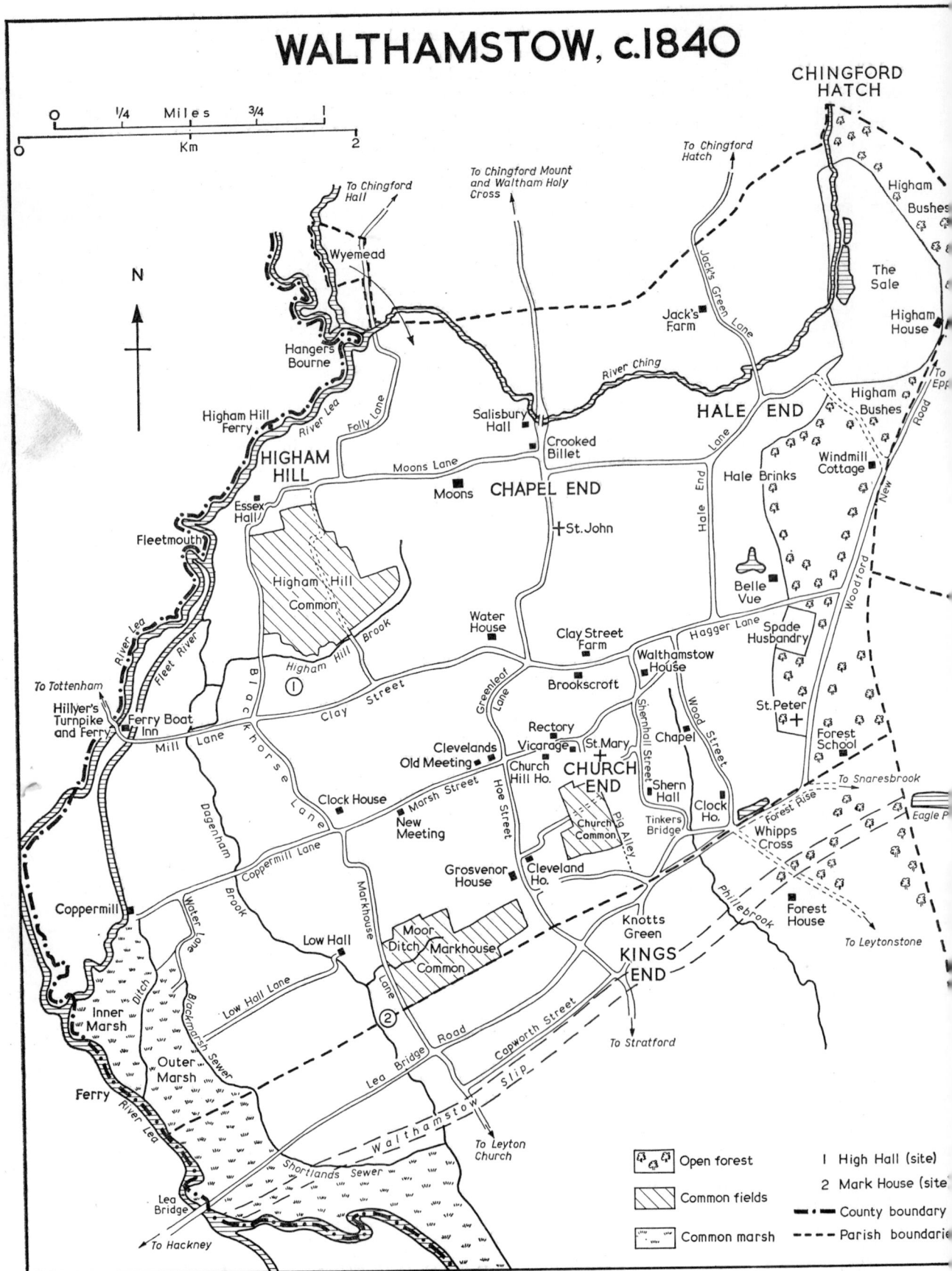

WALTHAMSTOW, c.1840

CHINGFORD HATCH

To Chingford Hall

To Chingford Mount and Waltham Holy Cross

To Chingford Hatch

Wyemead

Higham Bushes

The Sale

Jack's Farm

Jack's Green Lane

Higham House

Hangers Bourne

River Ching

To Epp

Higham Hill Ferry

Salisbury Hall

HALE END

Higham Bushes

HIGHAM HILL

Moons Lane

Crooked Billet

Hale End Lane

Windmill Cottage

Folly Lane

CHAPEL END

Hale Brinks

Essex Hall

Moons

St. John

Belle Vue

Woodford New Road

Fleetmouth

Higham Hill Common

Water House

Clay Street Farm

Hagger Lane

Spade Husbandry

River Lea

Higham Hill Brook

Clay Street

Brookscroft

Walthamstow House

St. Peter

To Tottenham

Blackhorse Lane

Greenleaf Lane

Forest School

Hillyer's Turnpike and Ferry

Ferry Boat Inn

Mill Lane

Clevelands Old Meeting

Rectory Vicarage

St. Mary

Shernhall Street

Chapel

Wood Street

Church Hill Ho.

CHURCH END

To Snaresbrook

Eagle P

Fleet River

Clock House

Marsh Street

Hoe Street

Shern Hall

Clock Ho.

Forest Rise

New Meeting

Church Common

Tinkers Bridge

Whipps Cross

Phillebrook

Coppermill

Coppermill Lane

Grosvenor House

Cleveland Ho.

Pig Alley

Forest House

Dagenham Brook

Water Lane

Low Hall

Moor Ditch

Markhouse Common

Knotts Green

KINGS END

To Leytonstone

Inner Marsh

Blackmarsh Sewer

Low Hall Lane

Markhouse Lane

Lea Bridge Road

Capworth Street

To Stratford

Outer Marsh

Ferry

River Lea

Walthamstow Slip

To Leyton Church

Shortlands Sewer

Lea Bridge

To Hackney

	Open forest	1	High Hall (site)
	Common fields	2	Mark House (site
	Common marsh		County boundary
			Parish boundarie

N

O 1/4 Miles 3/4 1

O Km 2

way or 'folly' which crossed it into Broadmead and gave it the name, Folly Lane.[41] It was still a narrow tree-lined lane in 1971. The third and most easterly north–south route was close to the forest. From Chingford, Green Lane (1368),[42] later Jack's or Inks Green Lane (Larkshall Road and Hale End Road), led past Jack's farm to Hale End, whence the way continued to Wood Street (1513) and Whipps Cross.

The chief east–west route came from Epping and beyond through Walthamstow to Tottenham (Mdx.). It emerged from the forest as Hangerstrete (1519), later Hagger Lane, leading into Clay Street (1437),[43] called in part Priorstrete (1532), and on by Mill Lane to the Lea.[44] Mill Lane was described as a 'continual way' for the parish in 1595, and in 1626 was said to have been much used by King James.[45] Hagger Lane, called a market way in 1647,[46] was no doubt used by Walthamstow traders travelling to Epping market.[47] The journey to Epping was improved in 1828–30 when Woodford New Road was built.[48] Clay Street and Hagger Lane, which led into the new road, were renamed Forest Road in 1886, when Mill Lane became Ferry Lane.[49] North of Clay Street Higham Hill Street or Moons Lane (Billet Road) led from Higham Hill to Chapel End, whence Blind Lane (Wadham Road) went on to Hale End.[50] South of Clay Street Marsh Street (1434) led westward from Hoe Street to the common marsh and Walthamstow mill, and was linked with Wood Street to the east by Church Hill, Back Lane (Prospect Hill), and Wyatts Lane. Marsh Street was renamed High Street in 1882,[51] and continues westwards as Coppermill Lane.

Around Church End a network of lanes, alleys, and footpaths led from Hoe Street, Clay Street, Wood Street, and the south of the parish to the church, rectory, vicarage, and Church common field. It included Parson's or Green Hill Lane, also called Cutthroat Lane (Aubrey Road),[52] the 'church way' across the common (Orford Road), Shernhall (Shornwell, 1433) Street,[53] Hog Lane (1688, probably Pig Alley, now Beulah Path),[54] and Vinegar Alley.[55]

There was apparently a bridge over the Lea at Higham Hill in 1594,[56] but it is not recorded later.

There was a ferry there by 1687, called Boulton's in the 18th century and Games's in the late 19th century. The ferry-house, which belonged to Salisbury Hall manor, stood on the west bank and was rebuilt about 1836. The East London Waterworks Co. bought the ferry about 1870, and it ceased soon after 1897 when Banbury reservoir was built and the channel diverted westward. A footpath and footbridge to Wild marsh, Tottenham (Mdx.), at the south-west corner of the reservoir preserves the crossing.[57]

The most important Lea crossing was to Tottenham (Mdx.) in Mill (Ferry) Lane. It required two bridges in Walthamstow, over the Fleet and the Lea. In 1277 Ralph de Tony was required to make two bridges in Horseholme and Smethemerse,[58] probably for that Tottenham crossing, where several 'holms' or islets were situated. In 1594 'Mill Bridge' was one of the most useful over the Lea.[59] The countess of Rutland was presented at quarter sessions in 1595 for a broken bridge on the way to Tottenham mill.[60] A ferry beside the main bridge, mentioned in 1722,[61] also belonged to Walthamstow Tony manor. The ferry-house, which was probably rebuilt soon after 1738,[62] became the Ferry Boat inn. In 1760 Sir William Maynard rebuilt the main bridge as a private toll-bridge for horses and carriages. Constructed of timber with iron abutments, it was called Ferry Bridge or Hillyer's Turnpike from Sacheverell Hillyer, the ferryman and landlord of the inn.[63] The parishioners, however, claimed the right to ford the river without toll.[64]

Viscount Maynard repaired Ferry Bridge in 1820. Iron trestles replaced the timber ones in 1854.[65] In 1868 the East London Waterworks Co. bought the inn and tolls,[66] and in 1877 the bridge was freed of tolls after the corporation of London bought the rights. The old bridge was demolished in 1915 when the present Ferry Lane bridge was built a little downstream.[67] A new bridge over the Waterworks (Fleet) river in Ferry Lane was built by the district council in 1904.[68] The Ferry Boat inn still survived in 1971.[69]

Water Lane led south from Marsh Street across the marshes to Lockbridge in Leyton. An account

[41] E.R.O., D/DFc 185, ff. 325, 332, D/DQs 31; G. F. Bosworth, *Manors of Low Hall and Salisbury Hall* (W.A.S. vii) 12, 15. For the use of 'folly' in Essex dialect as a hedged pathway or small lane, see E. Gepp, *Essex Dialect Dictionary* (reprint enlarged by J. S. Appleby 1969), 49–50, 174, and H. Cranmer-Byng, *The Magic Mawkin and other tales*, 8.
[42] *Cal. Inq. p.m.* xii, p. 189.
[43] E.R.O., D/DU 36/14.
[44] E.R.O., Q/SR 129/21, 364/25. The lane was named from Tottenham mill.
[45] E.R.O., Q/SR 129/21, 253/54.
[46] Ibid. 332/51.
[47] Ibid. 68/22; cf. 396/9, 397/14, 399/15. See also below, p. 269.
[48] See pp. 277, 342.
[49] V.H.M., *Vestiges*, nos. 54–8.
[50] E.R.O., D/DFc 185 passim, T/P 75.
[51] V.H.M., *Vestiges*, nos. 54–8. Marsh Street is probably 'Werdestrete' (1277): cf. J. L. Fisher, *Medieval farming glossary*, 40 (*werda*, werde = marsh).
[52] G. F. Bosworth, *Some more Walthamstow houses* (W.A.S. xxix), 37.
[53] E.R.O., D/AER 1, f. 170.
[54] E.R.O., Q/SR 457/73–4; Bosworth, *Some more . . . houses*, 33.
[55] S. J. Barns, *Walthamstow vestry mins., 1741–71* (W.A.S. xiv), 37, 39.

[56] J. Norden, *Speculi Britanniae Pars . . . Essex, 1594* (Camden Soc. 1st ser. ix), p. xiv.
[57] E.R.O., D/DQs 31; *Hist. Essex by Gent.* iv. 211; V.H.M., *Vestiges*, no. 20; Hatley, *Across the years*, 28.
[58] Reaney, *Walthamstow Place-names*, 41.
[59] Norden, *Speculi . . . Essex, 1594*, p. xiv.
[60] E.R.O., Q/SR 129/21.
[61] W.A.S., *The Record*, no. 4, pp. 4–5.
[62] S. J. Barns, *Walthamstow deeds, 1595–1890* (W.A.S. xi), 28.
[63] *Hist. Essex by Gent.* iv. 211; G. F. Bosworth, *Manor of Walthamstow Toni* (W.A.S. x), 17; Reaney, *Walthamstow Place-names*, 44; E.R.O., D/DQs 31, Q/RLv 24. From other ferrymen the ferry was variously called Green's, Hughes', Tyler's and Noakes' ferry. For the Ferry Boat inn and the bridge see plate f. p. 250.
[64] V.H.M., P22/1/1 (1868); Bosworth, *Manor of Walthamstow Toni*, 17.
[65] Bosworth, *Manor of Walthamstow Toni*, 17; E.R.O., D/SH 4, f. 21.
[66] V.H.M., P22/1/1.
[67] V.H.M., Walthamstow Local Bd. Mins. (1877); Bosworth, *Manor of Walthamstow Toni*, 17. There had also been tolls to pay on the Middlesex side, at Tottenham mill-house: Hatley, *Across the years*, 28.
[68] *Walthamstow U.D.C. Chmn.'s Ann. Rep.* (1904); Hatley, *Across the years*, 76.
[69] See p. 249.

of that early crossing place from Walthamstow and Leyton to Clapton (Mdx.) is given elsewhere.[70] By 1742 a ferry called Morris's, later High Hill (1868) ferry, was operating from Hackney (Mdx.) across to Walthamstow common marshes. It still existed in 1947.[71]

By the 17th century Walthamstow was an area of large houses mainly occupied by London merchants, bankers, and public officials. Their well-tended gardens and parks were set in a landscape of farmland, forest, and marsh. The village centre developed around St. Mary's church at Church End, where were built in succession the alms-houses (1527 and 1795), workhouse (1730), and schools (1819 and 1828). All those buildings survive and in 1968 Church End was designated a conservation area.[72]

The character of Walthamstow began to change after the railway reached Lea Bridge in 1840[73] and the common fields were broken up in 1850.[74] The inclosure award set out new public carriage roads. At Higham Hill Blackhorse Lane and Common Lane (Higham Hill Road) became public roads, and another (St. Andrew's Road) was made to link them from west to east. In the south of the parish the present Boundary Road and Queens Road were built to link Markhouse Road and Hoe Street. Common Lane between Hoe Street and Church Lane became a carriage road (Orford Road) and the footpath over Church common was diverted, later to become the present Vestry Road.[75] Within this enlarged road framework modern Walthamstow developed, from the south northwards, its old hamlets gradually merging as rows of brick houses covered the intervening farms and private pleasure grounds.[76]

Speculative land societies which laid out the streets and plots determined the pattern of growth. Among them were the National, City of London, Tower Hamlets, and St. Pancras and District societies. Speculative builders who bought the plots in blocks set the styles of domestic building. The house purchasers and tenants were mainly Londoners. Building societies were active in Walthamstow by 1844.[77] Development began before 1850 in South Grove near St. James's chapel, the district closest to Lea Bridge station.[78] After 1850 the development of Markhouse and Church commons began, together with that of the Grosvenor Park estate between Hoe

Street and Church common, which was sold to the National society in 1850.[79] Union and Prospect Roads were laid out on Markhouse common, and the elm avenue in Grosvenor park was replaced by Grosvenor Park Road. The houses between East Avenue and Avenue Road (West Avenue) replaced the avenue of trees leading from Church common to Church Hill, and Beulah, Eden, Pembroke, and other roads were laid out in the vicinity of Church common. Most of the Church common plots cost from £12 to £19; larger plots cost up to £32, and a few corner plots up to £135.[80] Farther north the Tower Hamlets society was developing the area north of Milton Road, between Greenleaf Lane (Hoe Street) and Cutthroat Lane (Aubrey Road). The plots there are said to have cost £7.[81] Between 1851 and 1861 the societies sold 98 a. on which 584 houses were built, most of them in 1855–9.[82] Cottages and middle-class villas which survive from those years in some of the roads named may be distinguished from those built later by the variety of their styles; some of them retain the Regency proportions of the early 19th century.

By 1861 the gentry were moving out.[83] Delays in extending the railway into Walthamstow halted growth in the 1860s, but the opening of the line to Shernhall Street, the introduction of cheap workmen's fares, and completion of the line to Hale End and Chingford in 1870–3 stimulated new building.[84] Development was still most vigorous in the south; of 36 new street names put up in 1878 none was north of Clay Street.[85] By 1876, however, the development of Higham Hill common had begun.[86] In 1877 the Walthamstow Building Society was founded[87] and a branch of the London and Provincial bank was opened in Orford Road in 1880.[88]

In the 1880s T. C. T. Warner, one of the largest landowners in Walthamstow,[89] began to develop the Clock House (Pretoria Avenue) estate. The Warner Estate Co. Ltd. (registered 1891) formed its own building department, the Law Land Building Department Ltd. (1897) now called Courtenay Building Ltd.[90] By 1900 the company had built up most of Blackhorse Lane between Edward Road and Pretoria Avenue and completed a substantial terraced business development of shops and offices at the west end of High Street. In the 1890s many of the Shernhall Street and Wood Street mansions were

[70] See p. 177.
[71] E.R.O., T/M 168, Q/RUm 1/22 (1812); J. Rocque, *Survey of London;* O.S. Map 6″, Essex LXV (1867–73 edn.); O.S. Map 2½″, sheet TQ 38.
[72] W.A.S., *The Record,* no. 10, p. 4, no. 13, p. 1; London Borough of Waltham Forest (St. Mary's Church Area, Walthamstow) Conservation Area Designation Order, 1968. For domestic buildings in the conservation area see below, p. 247, and map, p. 246
[73] See p. 182.
[74] See p. 264.
[75] E.R.O., Q/RDc 38 (award and maps), T/P 75; cf. E.R.O., D/CT 382, and O.S. Map 6″, Essex LXV (1868–76 edn.).
[76] *V.C.H. Essex,* v. 4; *Walthamstow Off. Guide* (1961), 46; *Waltham Forest Off. Guide* (1968), 14; *The Sketch,* 13 July 1898, 484; A. D. Law, *Our Town* (2), 8; Bosworth, *More . . . houses,* 3. James Bird compiled a careful record of the footpaths of his boyhood in the 1850s, in relation to later street development: E.R.O., T/P 75. A useful series of diagram maps showing the stages of Walthamstow's growth, 1842–1961, is in W. G. S. Tonkin, *Anglican ch. in Walthamstow* (W.A.S. N.S. iv), 43–5. There are alphabetical dated lists of Walthamstow's streets, grouped in three

phases, 1850–1900, 1900–30, 1930–65, in V.H.M., *Vestiges,* nos. 54–8, 60–1.
[77] E. Clarke, *Walthamstow, past, present, and future* (1861), 44–5, 48, 60; *London,* vi (1897), 820; E.R.O., D/DB T840/1–3.
[78] H.O. 129/7/194.
[79] Bosworth, *Some . . . houses,* 17; Clarke, *Walthamstow,* 44.
[80] E.R.O., D/DB T840/1–3, T/P 75; V.H.M., *Vestiges,* nos. 54–8.
[81] Clarke, *Walthamstow,* 97; Hatley, *Across the years,* 35.
[82] Clarke, *Walthamstow,* 45; *Kelly's Dir. Essex* (1859).
[83] Clarke, *Walthamstow,* 45.
[84] *V.C.H. Essex,* v. 4, 18–19. See also below, p. 280.
[85] V.H.M., Local Bd. Mins. 1878.
[86] O.S. Map 6″, Essex, LXV (1868–76 edn.).
[87] *Waltham Forest Off. Guide* (1968), 34.
[88] R. Wall, 'Hist. of development of Walthamstow, 1851–1901' (M. Phil. thesis, London, 1968, TS.), 104; *Kelly's Dir. Essex* (1882).
[89] *Kelly's Dir. Essex* (1882).
[90] Wall, 'Development of Walthamstow', pp. 153 f. discusses the early aims and achievements of the Warner Estate Co.

sold for development and also the rectory manor estate (22 a.) between Church Hill and Forest Road.[91] Some 60 a. of Highams Park, 'ripe for building', was offered for sale in 1893.[92] The opening of Blackhorse Road railway station in 1894 began to attract industry to the area north of Ferry Lane. The Warner company bought the Winns estate (86 a.) in 1898 to develop the area west of Lloyd Park; the Belle Vue estate (60 a.) came on the market in 1899 and Salisbury Hall farm in 1904.[93]

The most usual type of domestic building of 1870–1914 was the long terrace of two-storey houses, slate-roofed, of yellow brick sometimes varied with red dressings. Bay-windows and door-ways with plaster ornament were a common feature, seen at its most typical in Lansdowne Road (1894–7). But the terraces built by the Warner company, which often bear the mark 'W', are notable for the quality of their workmanship and are in distinctive styles, often in bold red brick, with gables, recessed porches, and tiled roofs. Terraces of c. 1899–1908 at Highams Park, between Winchester and Chingford Roads, are characterized by fanciful ornament picked out in white plaster on a rough-cast back-ground.

Most houses south of Forest Road, including many designed for two families as flats, were for the working classes, but middle-class terraces were also built, for example on the rectory manor estate between Howard Road and the Drive. In the north-east of the parish near the forest middle-class houses, often semi-detached, predominated. In Montalt Road the Warner company in 1898 com-pleted an impressive row of three-storeyed, six-bedroomed, semi-detached 'Lodges', designed by John Dunn in brown and red brick, overlooking the golf links and Highams Park.[94]

In 1912 the Warner company undertook to co-operate in the urban district council's town planning scheme.[95] That agreement produced in the north and north-east of the town an informal pattern of growth in contrast to the rigid lines of earlier development in the south. The first-fruits of the agreement was an estate of some 300 houses laid out on garden-city lines and built by the company in 1912–14 between Billet Road and Pennant Terrace.[96]

As the houses spread schools and churches fol-lowed. A town hall was established in Orford Road near Church End in 1876, but the town centre was tending to move to High Street, with the growth of its street market, the building there of the new Monoux school (1889), and the opening of the public library (1894) and baths (1900). From c. 1890 industry was competing for sites[97] and after the First World War council housing also, with estates built at Higham Hill (Millfield Avenue), off Forest Road (William Morris Close), and at Hale End (The Hale).[98] The Warner company continued the Billet Road development from Ardleigh Road to Penrhyn Crescent in 1927–8 after purchasing Moons farm (11 a.).[99]

In 1925, 1,689 a. of undeveloped land remained in the district, besides marshland and forest.[1] By 1927 this was reduced to about 987 a., lying mainly in the north where much of it comprised sports grounds owned by London companies.[2] Most of the remaining building land was developed in the 1930s, with middle-class houses like those in The Risings and The Charter Road, and the council's Essex Hall estate at Higham Hill.

In 1927–30 the North Circular Road was extended from Edmonton through Walthamstow to Woodford via the Crooked Billet and the waterworks in Forest Road.[3] It was diverted in 1970–1 north of Waterworks Corner to a roundabout at Grove Road, Woodford.[4]

Walthamstow was severely damaged by bombing in the Second World War,[5] and after the war its appearance was much altered by the scale and variety of municipal housing schemes, such as Priory Court (1946–59), Oak Hill Court (1950), the Drive (1955–64), and Park Court, Grosvenor Park Road (1962).[6] From the late 1960s tower blocks of council flats began to dominate the landscape.[7] Walthamstow's business centres were also transformed. Hoe Street Central Parade, completed in 1958–64, comprises flats, shops, lecture hall, and a clock-tower blazoned with local coats of arms. Opposite the parade were built a tall office block on Church Hill and a shop-ping arcade under maisonettes and offices in High Street.[8] A modern shopping development was in progress in Wood Street also in 1971.

Since the 1930s a new civic centre has been formed in Forest Road by the siting there of the technical college (1938), town hall (1941), assembly hall (1943), and court house (1971). Facing them the tall Y.M.C.A. hostel (1969) designed by Kenneth Lindy completes an impressive group of contem-porary buildings.[9]

Although Walthamstow in 1971 was densely built up, the disposition of the reservoirs on the west[10] and the surviving forest on the east[11] still distinguished it from similar urbanized areas.

DOMESTIC BUILDINGS BEFORE 1840. By the 17th century Walthamstow's popularity as a residential suburb of London was shown by the number of large houses there. In 1670 32 per cent of the houses in the parish had 5 or more hearths and 6 per cent had 10 or more.[12] Few of them survived in 1971,[13] none in private occupation. Unlike similar properties in more remote areas, the Walthamstow houses tended to change hands at

[91] Hatley, *Across the years*, 23, 33; E.R.O., *Sale Cat.* A1066; G. Houghton, *Walthamstow past and present*, 15; G. F. Bosworth, *Rectory manor* (W.A.S. iv), 12–13.
[92] E.R.O., *Sale Cat.* A1050.
[93] Bosworth, *Some . . . houses*, 29, 33.
[94] E.R.O., *Sale Cat.* A824.
[95] *Walthamstow U.D.C. Chmn's. Rep.* (1912).
[96] Ibid. (1914).   [97] See p. 269.
[98] See p. 284.
[99] G. F. Bosworth, *George Monoux* (W.A.S. xvii), 3.
[1] *Walthamstow Off. Guide* (1925), 28.
[2] Ibid. (c. 1927), 28, (1937), 25.
[3] V.H.M., *Vestiges*, no. 53.

[4] W.A.S., *The Record*, no. 7, p. 6, no. 9, p. 6; personal observation.
[5] See p. 282.
[6] Pevsner, *Essex* (2nd edn.), 409–10; S. K. Ruck, *Municipal entertainment and the arts*, 97, pl. 14.
[7] W.A.S., *The Record*, no. 9, pp. 4–5.
[8] Pevsner, *Essex* (2nd edn.), 410.
[9] Inf. from W.R.L. See also above, p. 143. For the town hall see plate f.p. 15.
[10] See p. 283.   [11] See p. 275.
[12] E.R.O., Q/RTh 5.
[13] The survey of surviving buildings was carried out in 1971.

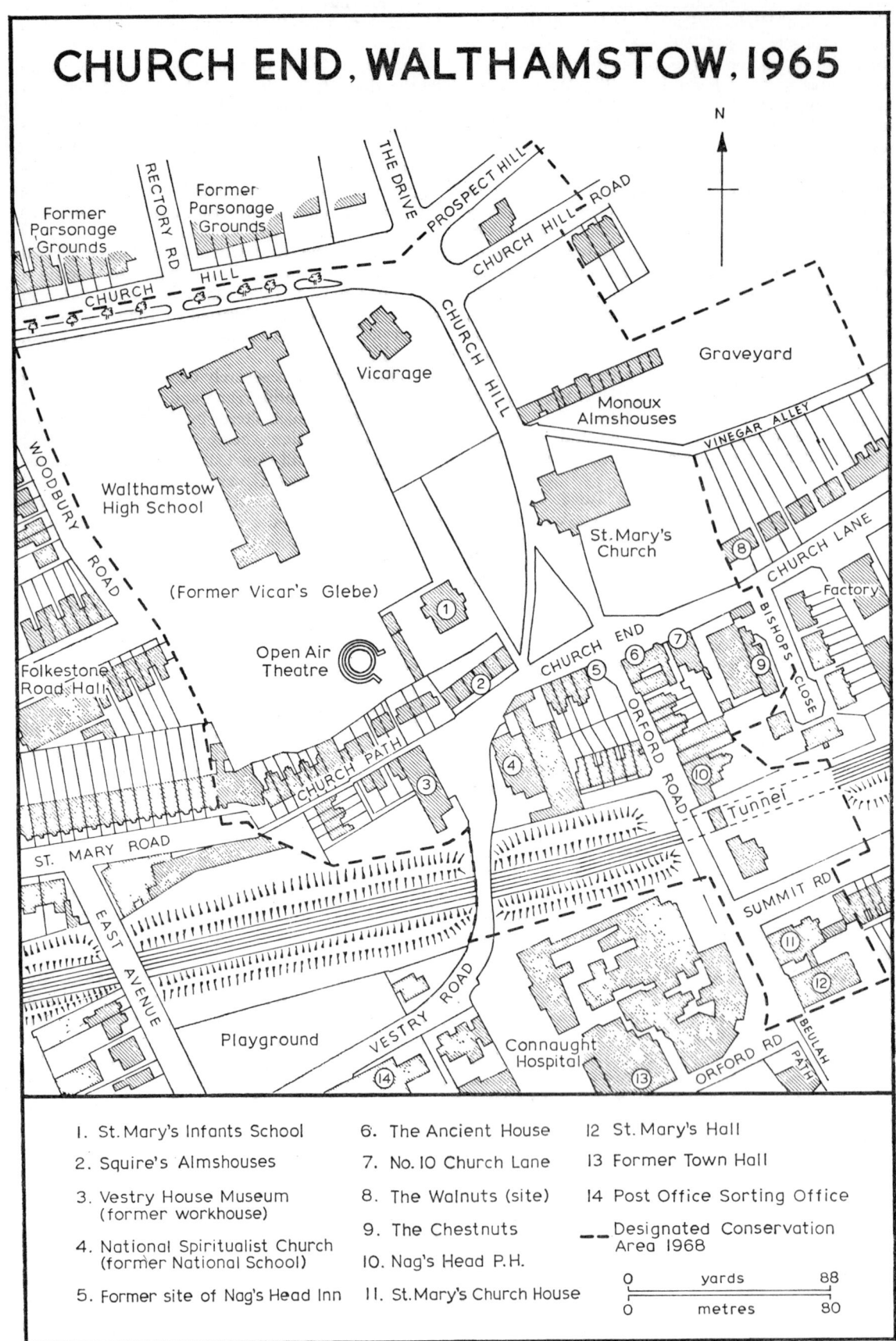

CHURCH END, WALTHAMSTOW, 1965

N

Former Parsonage Grounds

RECTORY RD

Former Parsonage Grounds

THE DRIVE

PROSPECT HILL

CHURCH HILL ROAD

CHURCH HILL

Church Hill

Graveyard

Vicarage

Monoux Almshouses

VINEGAR ALLEY

WOODBURY ROAD

Walthamstow High School

St. Mary's Church

CHURCH LANE

BISHOPS CLOSE

Factory

(Former Vicar's Glebe)

⑧

⑨

Open Air Theatre

①

CHURCH END

⑦

⑥

Folkestone Road Hall

②

⑤

ORFORD ROAD

⑩

Tunnel

CHURCH PATH

③

④

SUMMIT RD

ST. MARY ROAD

⑪

EAST AVENUE

VESTRY ROAD

⑫

Playground

Connaught Hospital

ORFORD RD

BEULAH PATH

⑭

⑬

1. St. Mary's Infants School
2. Squire's Almshouses
3. Vestry House Museum (former workhouse)
4. National Spiritualist Church (former National School)
5. Former site of Nag's Head Inn
6. The Ancient House
7. No. 10 Church Lane
8. The Walnuts (site)
9. The Chestnuts
10. Nag's Head P.H.
11. St. Mary's Church House
12 St. Mary's Hall
13 Former Town Hall
14 Post Office Sorting Office
__ Designated Conservation Area 1968

0 yards 88
0 metres 80

fairly frequent intervals, their successive owners having both the desire and the means to carry out improvements. Thus the tall square houses of the earlier 18th century were often given additional wings, bow-windows, or new fronts. The favourite building materials were then dark red or brown brick with bright red brick dressings, giving way in the late 18th century to lighter brown or yellow stock brick. Stone was not readily available and was seldom used, even for dressings. There are few elegant stucco villas of the early 19th century, although existing houses were sometimes faced with stucco at that period. Even before extensive redevelopment began in the middle of the century, Walthamstow appears to have been losing its appeal as an area for new residences.

At the village centre, Church End, which is now a conservation area, a variety of early buildings survives.[14] The Ancient House (nos. 2–8 Church Lane), once called White House, which faces the churchyard, is the oldest domestic building in the neighbourhood. It has been traced from 1668 when it was held copyhold of the manor of Walthamstow Tony.[15] It is a timber-framed building of late medieval date consisting of a formerly single-storeyed hall, flanked by two-storeyed jettied and gabled cross-wings to the north and south. The arch-braced tie-beam truss with crown-post, which divided the two bays of the open roof to the hall, is still in position. The house was sympathetically restored in 1934 when the close-studded external timbering of the hall and the upper storey of the north wing were exposed, the latter with quadrant braces to the bottom panels.[16] A small double-fronted house (no. 10 Church Lane) of 1830[17] with a Doric porch adjoins the Ancient House on one side. The Nag's Head inn, so named by 1675, stood on the other side until 1859, when the present Nag's Head was built in Orford Road.[18] The Chestnuts,[19] Church Lane, a three-storey building of the earlier 19th century with wings and a projecting ground floor of rusticated stucco, now stands among the modern houses of Bishops Close which were built in its garden. It appears to have been designed as two self-contained units, and may have been built by the Revd. J. F. Roberts, headmaster of the Monoux school 1820–36, to serve both as a boys' boarding-house and a dwelling-house for himself.[20]

Orford House in Orford Road dates from the earlier 19th century.[21] It is a large two-storey stucco building with twin pediments and a recessed central porch with Doric columns. In 1971 it was occupied as a social club. All the other older houses in Orford Road were built after the inclosure of Church common in 1850.

In Shernhall Street, by 1840, there were several mansions,[22] of which only Walthamstow House[23] survived in 1971. It was built c. 1772 and from 1782 to 1842 was the home of the Wigrams.[24] The three-storey entrance front of 9 bays has central steps leading to a Doric porch, flanked by bay-windowed projections rising to the full height of the building. It has enriched ceilings within and an 18th-century staircase. Other 18th century or earlier buildings in Shernhall Street were Winchester House (demolished 1960),[25] Shern Lodge (demolished since 1966), and Brookfield (demolished in the 1890s), the home of the Collards, moneyers of the royal mint.[26]

On Parsonage Hill (Church Hill) the rectory[27] was the only large building until Church Hill House was built on the opposite side of the road in 1784–5.[28] It was a typical gentleman's residence of the period with a three-storey five-bay front and a central pediment. When it was pulled down in 1932 the doorcase was removed to the Vestry House museum.[29]

Many of Walthamstow's oldest and finest buildings were in Marsh (High) Street, where the Old and New meeting-houses[30] and the dwellings of gentry, merchants, physicians, craftsmen, and paupers, shared the street frontage.[31] A group of houses on the north side belonged in 1699 to the merchant, William Coward. They stood on the site of Butler's Place, a large house which existed in 1605.[32] Of those nos. 273 and 275, with carved wood modillioned cornice, were pulled down in 1965,[33] and Clevelands, no. 263, in 1960.[34] Clevelands may have been the house which Sir John Soane altered and enlarged for James Neave in 1781–3. It had a panelled interior and well staircase of c. 1700.[35] Northcott House, no. 115 High Street, was a mid-18th-century house demolished in 1964. It had an elaborate pedimented doorcase with Ionic columns and a radiating fan-light.[36] Clock House (now in Pretoria Avenue) was built in 1813 for Thomas Courtenay Warner. It is said to have occupied the site of the earlier Black House from which Blackhouse (Blackhorse) Lane was named. Clock House, which has been occupied since the 1920s by the London Co-operative Society, is of white Suffolk brick, much altered.[37] At the bottom of Marsh Street

[14] See also p. 244.
[15] A. D. Law, *Walthamstow Village* (W.A.S. N.S. vii), 6.
[16] *Walthamstow Off. Guide* (1961), 47; G. E. Roebuck, *Story of Walthamstow*, 52–3; Law, *Walthamstow Village*, 6. A water-colour by A. B. Bamford (1925) and pencil drawing by Norman Davey (1927) show the house before restoration: V.H.M., Illus. Colln.
[17] Law, *Walthamstow Village*, 12.
[18] Ibid.; V.H.M., *Vestiges*, no. 17.
[19] G. F. Bosworth, *More Walthamstow houses* (W.A.S. xx), 11–14.
[20] See p. 311.   [21] Cf. E.R.O., D/CT 382.
[22] See also p. 256.   [23] See p. 312.
[24] G. F. Bosworth, *Some Walthamstow houses* (W.A.S. xii), 3; Roebuck, *Story of Walthamstow*, 36; W.A.S., *The Record*, no. 8; V.H.M., *Vestiges*, no. 42; E.R.O., Pictorial Colln. (Engr. by J. Hassell, 1804).
[25] E.R.O., T/M 252 (1699); Bosworth, *More . . . houses*, 11, and *Some more . . . houses*, 5; W.A.S., *The Record*, no. 9.
[26] Bosworth, *Some more . . . houses*, 5–13; E.R.O., T/M 252 (1699), T/M 167 (1739, map of Richard Collard's estate).

[27] See p. 262.   [28] V.H.M., Illus. Colln.
[29] Chapman and André, *Map of Essex*, 1777, sheet xvi; Bosworth, *More . . . houses*, 15–17; Hatley, *Across the years*, illus. f.p. 14; *Walthamstow Off. Guide* (1922), 39; *Walthamstow U.D.C. Chmn.'s Reps.* (1917–18). See also below, p. 279.   [30] See pp. 297–8, 300.
[31] Barns, *Walthamstow Deeds, 1595–1900*, 22, and *1584–1855*, 30; S. J. Barns, *Walthamstow vestry mins. 1710–40* (W.A.S. xiii), 23.
[32] E.R.O., T/M 168, 252; Lysons, *London*, iv. 211.
[33] R.C.H.M. *Essex*, ii. 248; W.A.S., *The Record*, no. 9; Bosworth, *Some more . . . houses*, 3.
[34] Bosworth, *Some more . . . houses*, 3; W.A.S., *The Record*, 9. It may have been connected with the Penn family: see below, p. 252.
[35] D. Stroud, *Architecture of Sir John Soane*, 157; S. J. Barns, *Walthamstow Deeds, 1584–1855* (W.A.S. xxxiii), 20–2.
[36] Pevsner, *Essex* (2nd edn.), 408; W.A.S., *The Record*, no. 9.
[37] Bosworth, *More . . . houses*, 21; Roebuck, *Story of Walthamstow*, 46; Hatley, *Across the years*, 29, 96.

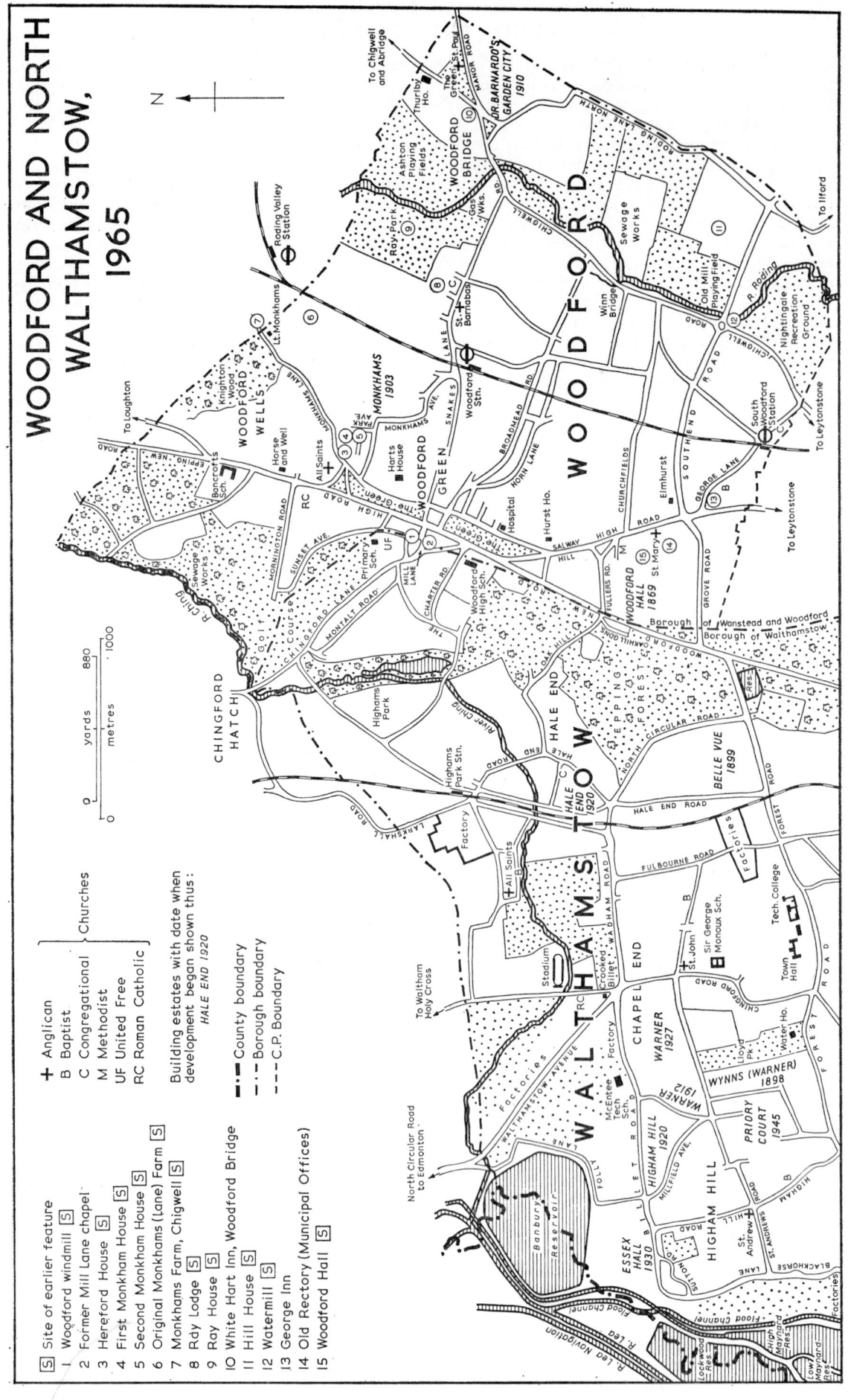

WOODFORD AND NORTH WALTHAMSTOW, 1965

Churches
+ Anglican
B Baptist
C Congregational
M Methodist
UF United Free
RC Roman Catholic

Building estates with date when
development began shown thus :
HALE END 1920

—·—·— County boundary
—··—··— Borough boundary
——— C.P. Boundary

[S] Site of earlier feature
1 Woodford windmill [S]
2 Former Mill Lane chapel
3 Hereford House [S]
4 First Monkham House [S]
5 Second Monkham House [S]
6 Original Monkhams (Lane) Farm [S]
7 Monkhams Farm, Chigwell [S]
8 Rdy Lodge [S]
9 Ray House [S]
10 White Hart Inn, Woodford Bridge
11 Hill House [S]
12 Watermill [S]
13 George Inn
14 Old Rectory (Municipal Offices) [S]
15 Woodford Hall [S]

in Coppermill Lane was the Elms, a 17th-century house demolished in 1968.[38] The Cock and the Chequers inns in Marsh Street existed in the 18th century, if not earlier, as did the Coach and Horses, off Marsh Street in the lane (St. James Street) leading to Markhouse Lane,[39] but all three have been rebuilt. West of Markhouse Lane stood Low Hall and Mark manor-houses.[40]

Much of Hoe Street south of Marsh Street belonged in 1699 to the Conyers family.[41] On the west side, facing east, was the house, later called Grosvenor House, built c. 1600 by Tristram Conyers (d. 1619). An avenue of elms on the opposite side of the street led from the house to Church common. In the later 18th century the house passed to the Grosvenors, who about 1789 rebuilt it in white Suffolk brick.[42] The new house was refronted before 1796 by William Selwyn. It was gutted by fire in 1945 and demolished in 1956.[43] South of Grosvenor House the Chestnuts survives as the finest and least altered of Walthamstow's earlier 18th-century mansions.[44] It is a three-storeyed building of 7 bays with the dates 1745 and 1747 on the rainwater heads, a staircase with twisted balusters, heavily enriched plasterwork to the stair-well, and other contemporary fittings.

On the east side of Hoe Street stands Cleveland House, a tall narrow building of the early 18th century with a full-height staircase and original panelling. Single-storey wings were built on somewhat later and two storeys were added to the south wing in 1871. The whole front appears to have been remodelled at some time. In the 18th century the gardens of Cleveland House were cultivated by the brothers Thomas, Benjamin, and Edward Forster.[45] An improbable tradition associates the house with Barbara Villiers, duchess of Cleveland.[46] It was occupied in 1971 by Waltham Forest health department. Court House, no. 317 Hoe Street, was an elegant five-bay house of c. 1700 damaged by bombing in the Second World War and demolished in 1952.[47]

Clay Street (Forest Road) in 1840 was bordered by mansions set in ample parks. Among them was Water House, previously called Winns, Crickle-wood, or Hawks Capps, and now the William Morris Gallery. That house occupied an ancient moated site. It was the home of Sir Thomas Merry (d. 1654) and of William Pierce, bishop of Bath and Wells (d. 1670). In the middle of the 18th century it was rebuilt as a square three-storeyed house, and has a contemporary staircase and internal fittings. The main façade is of 9 bays with two full-height bows and a Corinthian doorcase.[48] Brookscroft, built between 1554 and 1568, belonged to the Bonnells from 1686 until the mid 18th century. It is said to have been rebuilt c. 1748 as a crenellated mansion,[49] but the house called Brookscroft which survives has no crenellations and appears to be a typical late-18th-century residence of brown brick with a five-bay front and a central pediment. Thorpe Combe, originally a three-storey house of a similar type with lower flanking wings, became a maternity hospital in the 1930s and is now dwarfed by extensions of that period.[50] There were no early inns in Clay Street but beyond it at the end of Mill Lane was the Ferry Boat, now an irregularly-shaped building with stuccoed walls, sash windows, and roofs of old tiles. The core, represented by a central two-storeyed range with dormer-windows, may date from c. 1738.[51]

There were few large houses in north-west Walthamstow. High Hall,[52] Higham Hill,[53] and Salisbury Hall[54] manor-houses have all gone. Moons, near Chapel End, was named from George Monoux, who bought it in 1513. It was described in 1756 as having once been a large moated building, by then greatly reduced in size, and seems to have been rebuilt in the 17th century as a timber-framed farmhouse. It was demolished in 1927.[55] The site is marked by Monoux Grove. Higham Hill Lodge in Blackhorse Lane, now part of the premises of Baird & Tatlock Ltd.,[56] still has its Doric doorcase with semi-circular fan-light and 18th-century iron railings and gates.[57] The Crooked Billet inn at Chapel End, which gave its name to Billet Road, existed in the 18th century, if not earlier,[58] but has since been rebuilt.

Although the attractions of the forest drew residents to the north-east of the parish by the 16th

[38] Bosworth, More . . . houses, 18; W.A.S., The Record, no. 6, pp. 4–5; no. 11, p. 4; Pevsner, Essex (2nd edn.), 409.
[39] E.R.O., Q/RLv 30; T/M 168.
[40] See pp. 257, 261.
[41] E.R.O., T/M 252.
[42] E.R.O., D/DW P7 (map of Edw. Conyers's estate, 1725), Pictorial Colln. (engravings of old Grosvenor House, pubd. 1792 and 1801, the latter with pencil note, 'pulled down 1789'); Beauties of England (3rd edn. 1776), i. 34; J. Stow, London, ed. J. Strype (6th edn. enlarged by E. Rowe Mores 1756), ii. 788; Bosworth, Some . . . houses, 14–17. The 1792 engraving is reproduced in Roebuck, Story of Walthamstow, f.p. 57. For Field Marshal Thomas Grosvenor, 1764–1851, see D.N.B.
[43] Lysons, London, iv. 225; W.A.S., The Record, no. 1, p. 6; Pevsner, Essex (2nd edn.), 408. See also below, p. 311.
[44] W.A.S., The Record, no. 1, p. 6; Bosworth, Some . . . houses, 17. See also below, p. 311.
[45] Bosworth, Some . . . houses, 23, More . . . houses, 33, and Some more . . . houses, 27; Pevsner, Essex (2nd edn.), 408; E.R.O., D/DW P7 (block plan shows shape of house, 1725), and D/CT 382 (1843 block plan); Kelly's Dir. Essex (1917–26). See also below, pp. 251, 312.
[46] It seems more likely that it was associated with Anthony Lowther of Marske in Cleveland (Yorks. N.R.) to whom there is a tablet in the church (1692). He married Sir William Penn's daughter Margaret: see p. 252.
[47] R.C.H.M. Essex, ii. 80 (pl.), 248; Pevsner, Essex (2nd
edn.), 408; Bosworth, Some . . . houses, 19–23; W.A.S., The Record, no. 1, p. 6.
[48] Barns, Walthamstow Deeds, 1595–1890, 4, 19, 30, and 1541–1862, 1, 8; P. H. Reaney, Church of St. Mary (W.A.S. N.S. viii), 42–3, and Walthamstow Place-names, 8–9; 25; R.C.H.M. Essex, ii. 247; Chapman and André, Map of Essex, 1777, sheet xvi; V.C.H. Essex, Bibliography, 331; Bosworth, Some . . . houses, 26; Pevsner, Essex (2nd edn.), 408. See also below, pp. 251–2, 284.
[49] P. H. Reaney, Court rolls of the rectory manor (W.A.S. xxxvii), 22; J. Stow, London, ed. J. Strype (6th edn., enlarged E. Rowe Mores 1756), ii. 788.
[50] Roebuck, Story of Walthamstow, 37; Hatley, Across the years, 45; Bosworth, Some more . . . houses, 5; J. Whittle, '18c. Houses in Forest Road', Jnl. S.W. Essex Tech. Coll., i(1), 17, 19. See also below, p. 285.
[51] See p. 243, and plate f.p. 250.
[52] See p. 255.
[53] See p. 259.
[54] See p. 263.
[55] P. H. Reaney, Court rolls of Salisbury Hall (W.A.S. xxxvi), 14; Stow, London (6th edn.), ii. 788; R.C.H.M. Essex, ii. 248; G. F. Bosworth, George Monoux (W.A.S. xvii), 14; Hatley, Across the years, 47–51.
[56] See p. 270.
[57] Bosworth, More . . . houses, 22; Roebuck, Story of Walthamstow, 40.
[58] E.R.O., Q/RLv 30; Hatley, Across the years, 52.

century, the only early buildings remaining at Wood-ford Side and Hale End are Highams[59] and St. Margaret's. The latter, originally a small double-fronted house of plum-coloured brick dating from the late 17th or early 18th century, has been con-verted by many extensions of various periods into the present substantial house. There were other 18th-century or earlier houses in that part of the parish,[60] but all have disappeared. So has Belle Vue House or Cooke's Folly, built c. 1803 in Hale Brinks Woods for Charles Cooke, to the design of Edward Gyfford. It was an elegant Regency villa with a semi-circular Ionic portico on the west front; the landscaped grounds included an artificial lake. The estate was broken up in 1899, but the house sur-vived to 1937.[61] At Hale End green stood a group of the weatherboarded and often tarred cottages with red pantiled roofs which were typical of the humbler dwellings of the parish.[62] None has survived there.

In 1840 the upper end of Wood Street was crowded with mainly timber cottages and shops. Its insanitary alleys housed some of the parish's poorest inhabi-tants.[63] Only two timber buildings survived in 1971: a single-storeyed butcher's shop and slaughter-house claiming establishment in 1750 and a cottage by the Duke's Head inn. The inn itself existed in 1752[64] but has since been rebuilt. At the lower end of Wood Street were large houses whose rich occupants preferred to use the address 'Whipps Cross'.[65] Clock House on the west side was built by a Dutch merchant, Sir Jacob Jacobson (d. 1735).[66] Its grounds spread over the east side, where he planted an avenue and made a lake, 'Sir Jacob's Water', part of which still exists. Clock House, which was bought by the borough council in 1938 for conversion into flats, is a square three-storey brick building of 5 bays with oak panelling and a fine carved staircase of c. 1700. The front, with its central pediment, was evidently rebuilt in the later 18th century. At the same time a bowed projection was added at the rear, which was embellished in the mid 19th century by an elaborate canopied balcony supported at basement level on stucco-faced arcad-ing. Two Adam-style marble chimneypieces from the house are in Vestry House museum.[67] East of the Clock House lake at Forest Rise stood John Salter's houses, built in 1726.[68] They comprised a single five-bay house with hipped roof and dor-

mers, then called Forest Hall and demolished c. 1935, and a semi-detached pair with wings crowned with shaped gables.[69] Those have also gone.

Farther east on the edge of the forest stands a row of mainly Georgian buildings set back behind early-19th-century cast iron railings with two sets of gateway piers. All form part of Forest School.[70] The oldest building at the centre of the group dates from c. 1760 and was presumably the house owned by Du Boulay in which he started the school in 1834.[71] It is of dark red brick with a two-storey front of 5 bays and a Tuscan porch. There are additions on both sides of various dates from the early 19th century onwards. Other school buildings include the chapel of 1867, which has stained glass of 1875–80 by William Morris. The library contains medieval glass brought from elsewhere.[72] A detached late-18th-century house farther east is also now part of the school.

TRANSPORT AND POSTAL SERVICES.

In 1707 John Gibson of Walthamstow ran a stage-coach service between Walthamstow and Leyton,[73] perhaps the business in Marsh Street sold in 1758 by Joseph Schooling.[74] Schooling's business was probably bought by Francis Wragg, who was rated in Marsh Street from 1759 and was certainly operating coaches by 1761. By 1826 Wragg's coaches ran seven times daily to London. After 1840 the Wraggs also ran a horse bus service to the railway station at Lea Bridge. Wragg's coaches still ran five times daily to Leyton, Lea Bridge, Stratford, and London in 1863, but ceased operating soon after 1870.[75]

A branch railway line from Lea Bridge to Shern-hall Street was opened by the Great Eastern in 1870, with other stations at St. James Street and Hoe Street.[76] In 1872 the Great Eastern line from Bethnal Green through Hackney Downs and Clap-ton was linked to the Walthamstow line at Hall Farm junction. It was continued to Chingford in 1873, when Wood Street replaced Shernhall Street station and Hale End station (Highams Park from 1894) was opened. In 1885 a northern spur linked Hall Farm junction with Coppermill junction on the Broxbourne line. The Chingford line was electrified in 1960, when the northern spur was removed; the Lea Bridge spur was removed in 1967. The Midland

[59] See p. 260.
[60] W.A.S., *The Record*, nos. 9, 11; Bosworth, *More . . . houses*, 30–8; Pevsner, *Essex* (2nd edn.), 409; Roebuck, *Story of Walthamstow*, 64.
[61] E. W. Brayley and J. Britton, *Beauties of England* (1803), v. 445; *E.R.* lxiv. 149–52; Roebuck, *Story of Walthamstow*, 63; G. A. Cooke, *Topog. . . . Essex*, 130–1; Colvin, *Dict. Eng. Archs.*, 256; E.R.O., D/CT 382.
[62] Chapman and André, *Map of Essex*, 1777, sheet xvi; E.R.O., Pictorial Colln. (picture postcards); V.H.M., Illus. Colln. (see also e.g. Blue Cottages in Blackhorse Lane, Budd's Alley in Wood Street, and cottages in Church Lane and Forest Road).
[63] E.R.O., Pictorial Colln. (picture postcards and en-gravings); V.H.M., Illus. Colln.; Bosworth, *Some more . . . houses*, 16.
[64] V.H.M., *Vestiges*, nos. 91–2.
[65] Bosworth, *Some . . . houses*, 34–7, and *Some more . . . houses*, 16.
[66] *Gent. Mag.* v. 387.
[67] V.H.M., *Vestiges*, no. 11; Bosworth, *Some . . . houses*, 33–4; Roebuck, *Story of Walthamstow*, 61; E.R.O., D/CT 382.
[68] See plate.

[69] E.R.O., D/DU 417/8 (elevations and plan of 'south prospect of messuages and buildings of John Salter Esq. near Whipps Cross 1726'); Rocque, *Survey of London*, 1741–5; V.H.M., *Vestiges*, no. 13, and Illus. Colln. (Forest Rise); Bosworth, *Some more . . . houses*, 21; *Kelly's Dir. Essex* (1926). The name 'Forest Rise' is now given to the road linking Upper Walthamstow Road and Whipps Cross. See also below, p. 273.
[70] See p. 311.
[71] *V.C.H. Essex*, ii. 549–50.
[72] Pevsner, *Essex* (2nd edn.), 409; R.C.H.M., *Essex*, ii. 248.
[73] E.R.O., Q/SR 530/34.
[74] V.H.M., *Vestiges*, no. 28.
[75] C. H. Crouch, *Walthamstow monumental inscriptions* (W.A.S. xxiii), Appendix III; S. J. Barns, *Vestry mins. 1741–71* (W.A.S. xiv), 53; *White's Dir. Essex* (1848, 1863); *Robson's Gazetteer* (1840); *V.C.H. Essex*, v. 27; *Kelly's Dir. Essex* (1859, 1870, 1874); Hatley, *Across the years*, 44.
[76] There is a detailed account of Walthamstow's railways in Line 112 Group's *The Railway to Walthamstow & Chingford* (W.A.S. N.S. ix), on which this paragraph is based.

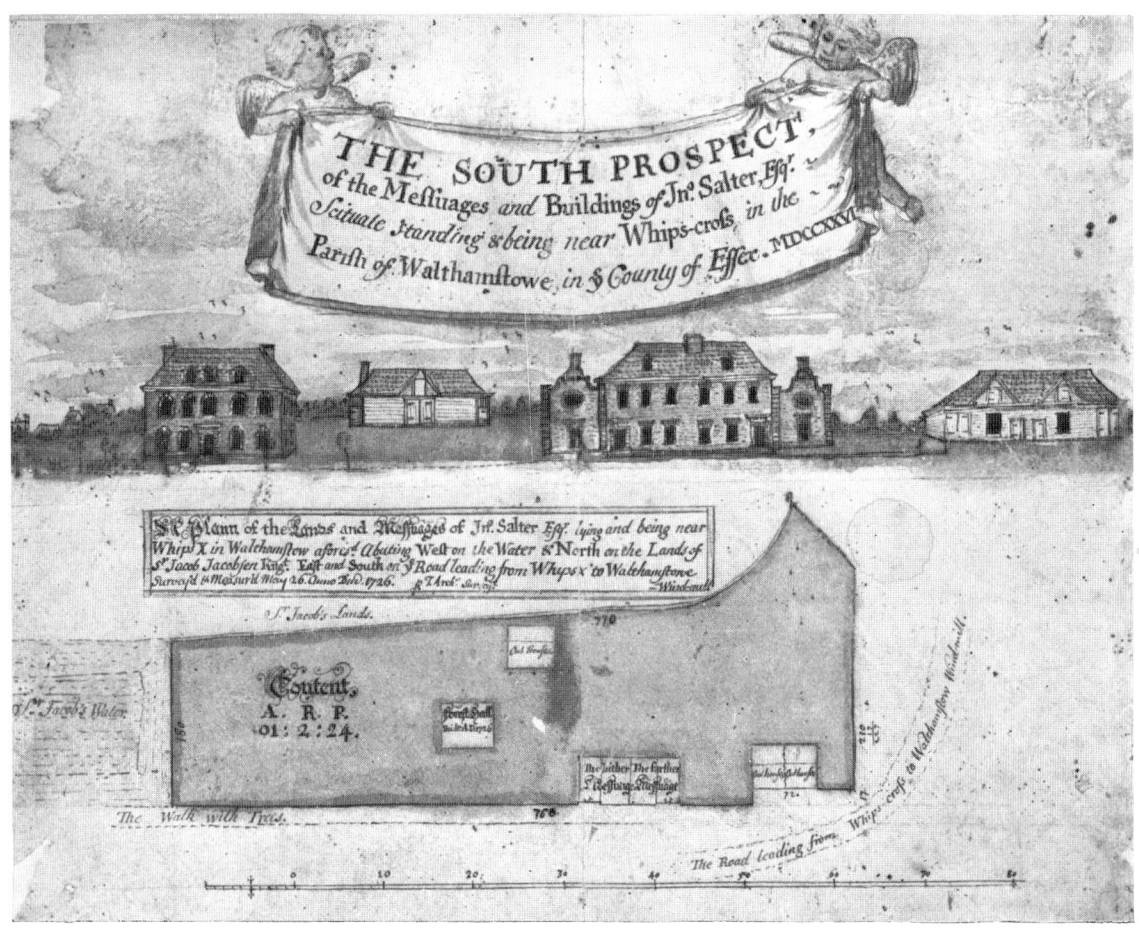

Sir John Salter's Houses, Forest Rise, built 1726, demolished *c.* 1935

Ferry Boat Inn and River Lea in the earlier 19th century, from the south-west

WALTHAMSTOW

LEYTON: DWELLINGS IN LEA BRIDGE GARDENS ABOUT 1930

WALTHAMSTOW: OLD WATERWORKS (FORMER COPPER MILL) ON RIVER LEA
Mill built *c.* 1800, tower 1864

railway's Tottenham and Forest Gate line, completed in 1894, had stations at Blackhorse Road and Walthamstow (Edinburgh Road). It became diesel-operated in 1960. London Transport opened the Victoria underground line between Warren Street and Walthamstow in 1968, with stations at Hoe Street, renamed Walthamstow Central, and Blackhorse Road. The line was completed to Victoria in 1969.

Horse trams were operated in Lea Bridge Road in the 1880s by the Lea Bridge, Leyton and Walthamstow Tramways Co.[77] From 1889 they continued beyond the Bakers Arms to the Rising Sun in Woodford New Road.[78] That route was taken over by Leyton U.D.C. in 1905.[79] The Walthamstow district council opened an electric tramway system in 1905 on four routes: Forest Road; Lea Bridge Road to Higham Hill; Hoe Street to Chingford; and Woodford New Road to Woodford. An agreement made with Leyton and West Ham in 1909 for interrunning from Chingford to Stratford ceased in 1917. In 1924–32 the council modernized the system and renewed interrunning with the Leyton tramways.[80]

The Great Eastern London Suburban Tramways & Omnibus Co. (later the Great Eastern London Motor Omnibus Co.) was formed in 1900, to take over the operation of a horse bus service which the tramways company had instituted between Hoe Street station and Stratford in 1889.[81] The Great Eastern company began running motor buses from Stratford to Walthamstow in 1905 via Hoe Street and High Street to St. James Street. In 1911 the company was merged in the London General Omnibus Co., which extended the service within the district and also provided a through route from Walthamstow to Elephant and Castle.[82] In 1933 Walthamstow's trams and buses were taken over by the London Passenger Transport board.[83] In 1936–7 trolley buses replaced trams,[84] and in their turn were replaced by diesel buses in 1959–60.[85]

There was a postal receiving office in Walthamstow in 1684–5, where the London Penny Post delivered and collected letters once a day.[86] By 1799 there were three daily deliveries. The receiving house, which was in Marsh Street by 1803, was called the Western office in 1820, when there was also an Eastern office in Wood Street. An office listed in 1823 at Thomas Godfrey's[87] may have been at Whipps Cross, where a third office is listed from 1839 to 1866.[88] In 1856 Walthamstow became part of the north-eastern (later eastern) London postal district. In 1869 the Marsh Street office was moved to Markhouse Lane (St. James Street) and a new one was set up in Orford Road, where a telegraph office was opened in 1870.[89] In 1914 a branch office was opened at no. 244 Hoe Street. It moved to its present premises at no. 197 Hoe Street in 1933. Additional branch offices were later opened in St. James Street (1950) and Wood Street (1951). Since 1917 most of Walthamstow has been in the postal district of E. 17, with small parts in E. 4, N. 17, and Woodford Green.

The National Telephone Co. opened a Walthamstow exchange in Priory Avenue and call rooms in 1897.[90] The exchange was moved to Hoe Street in 1909 and taken over by the G.P.O. in 1912. In 1934 many subscribers in the north were transferred to Larkswood exchange, Chingford. Walthamstow exchange closed in 1940 when the balance of subscribers was transferred to the Keystone exchange, Leytonstone. That exchange closed in 1958 when the Coppermill exchange, which opened in 1954 in temporary premises in Jesse Road, Leyton, moved, to a new building in Hoe Street.[91]

WORTHIES AND SOCIAL LIFE. Notable persons who held Walthamstow manors are mentioned elsewhere.[92] Many prominent City merchants were associated with Walthamstow. George Monoux (d. 1544) of Moons, draper and lord mayor, was one of the parish's greatest benefactors.[93] William Coward (1648–1738), merchant planter, lived in Marsh Street, where he built the first nonconformist chapel.[94] The West Ham distiller Peter Lefevre (d. 1751) lived at Winns.[95] Edward Forster the elder (1730–1812), governor of the Royal Exchange, lived at Cleveland House, where his three sons, Thomas (1761–1825), botanist, Benjamin (1764–1829), scientist and naturalist, and Edward the younger (1765–1849), botanist and philanthropist, were brought up. His grandson, Thomas I. M. Forster (1789–1860), naturalist and astronomer, also grew up in Walthamstow.[96] Sir Robert Wigram (1744–1830), chairman of the East India Docks, lived at Walthamstow House. Among his sons were (Sir) James (1793–1866), vice-chancellor of England, and Joseph (1798–1867), bishop of Rochester.[97] Sir William Mallinson (1854–1936), timber-merchant and philanthropist, lived at the Limes.[98]

[77] See p. 183.
[78] V.C.H. Essex, v. 27; Hatley, Across the years, 75–6; L. A. Thomson, By bus, tram, and coach (W.A.S. N.S. xi), 7.
[79] V.C.H. Essex, v. 28.
[80] Walthamstow U.D.C.: Chmns.' Ann. Reps. (1899–1905); Hatley, Across the years, 76–81; W.A.S., The Record, no. 3, p. 5; V.H.M., Vestiges, no. 21; P. G. Gibbins, Walthamstow Tramways, 6, 8.
[81] Thomson, By bus, tram, and coach, 7, 8, 22.
[82] W. G. S. Tonkin, Public transport in Walthamstow before the council tramways (W.A.S. Occ. Pub. iii), 10–11; Walthamstow Off. Guide (1922), 11; Walthamstow U.D.C.: Chmns.' Ann. Reps. (1912–13); V.C.H. Essex, v. 29.
[83] London Passenger Transport Act, 1933.
[84] Hatley, Across the years, 82; V.C.H. Essex, v. 73.
[85] W.A.S., The Record, no. 12, p. 6; Walthamstow Off. Guide (1963), 67.
[86] The following account of the postal service is based, unless otherwise stated, on V.H.M., Vestiges, nos. 93–4.
[87] Pigot's Dir. Essex (1823).
[88] Ibid. (1839); White's Dir. Essex (1848, 1863); Kelly's Dir. Essex (1859, 1866).

[89] V.H.M., P22/1/1–2 (1870).
[90] This paragraph is based on V.H.M., Vestiges, nos. 95–6.
[91] Although not opened until 1958 the building, on the site of Court House, is dated 1956.   [92] See pp. 253 sqq.
[93] G. F. Bosworth, Walthamstow charities (W.A.S. viii), 8–13, 51, George Monoux, the man and his work (W.A.S. xvii), and Original documents relating to the Monoux family (W.A.S. xix, compiled jointly with C. D. Saunders).
[94] D.N.B.; E.R.O., T/M 252; Gent. Mag. viii. 221. His portrait at New College, Hampstead, is reproduced in H. D. Budden, Marsh Street Cong. ch. f.p. 16.
[95] E.R.O., D/DU 257; Bosworth, More . . . houses, 29; Barns, Walthamstow Deeds, 1595–1890, 30. See also above, p. 93.
[96] Essex Journal, iii. 119–42; Bosworth, Some . . . houses, 23, More . . . houses, 33–4, Some more . . . houses, 25–8. There are articles on all the Forsters in D.N.B.
[97] Bosworth, Some . . . houses, 3 sqq., More . . . houses, 5–8. There are articles on James and Joseph Wigram in D.N.B.
[98] Sir W. Mallinson, A sketch of my life; Bosworth, Some more . . . houses, 15–16.

Among eminent Walthamstow churchmen and divines were its vicars, Thomas Cartwright (1634–89), later bishop of Chester, and the antiquary, Edmund Chishull (1671–1733).[99] Nonconformist divines who ministered in Walthamstow included Samuel Slater (d. 1704), Hugh Farmer (1714–87), the biblical critic John Simpson (1746–1812), and Eliezer Cogan (1762–1855).[1]

Public servants who had country houses in Walthamstow included Sir Martin Frobisher (1535?–94), the navigator,[2] Anthony Todd (d. 1798), secretary to the Post Office,[3] and Sir William Batten (d. 1667), surveyor of the Navy, and Admiral Sir William Penn (1621–70), commissioner of the Navy, who both often entertained Pepys there, probably in Marsh Street.[4]

Men distinguished in the professions and the arts who were connected with the parish included the poet George Gascoigne (1525?–77), whose house in Walthamstow was probably Thorpe Hall.[5] John Guillim (1565–1621), writer on heraldry, is said to have lived in Walthamstow,[6] and the composer Martin Peerson (1590–1651?) owned property there.[7] The physician and writer Daniel Whistler (1619–84) was born in Walthamstow.[8] The blind musician and composer John Stanley (1714–86) lived in Salter's Buildings at Forest Rise.[9] The philosophical writer Thomas Solly (1816–75) and the physician Sir Richard Powell (1842–1925) were both born in Walthamstow.[10] William Morris (1834–96) was born in Clay Street at Elm House, and lived at Water House from 1848 to 1856.[11] The newspaper publisher Edward Lloyd (1815–90) bought Water House in 1857.[12]

Benjamin Disraeli (1804–81) attended Dr. Cogan's academy at Essex Hall,[13] as did Samuel Sharpe (1799–1881), the Egyptologist and translator of the Bible, Russell Gurney (1804–78), Recorder of London, and the surgeon Samuel Solly (1805–71).[14] Julian Marshall (1836–1903), art collector and author, attended Forest school[15] and Admiral Sir Cyprian Bridge (1839–1924), naval author, attended Dr. Greig's school at Walthamstow House.[16]

An entertainment hall was built in Orford Road in 1866 by the Walthamstow Public Hall Co. Ltd.[17]

After it was sold to the local board in 1876 as a town hall[18] it was still let for social activities. The Victoria hall, Hoe Street, was built in 1887 by J. F. H. Read, founder in 1867 of the Walthamstow musical society, and John Cropley, a local builder.[19] In 1896 it became a theatre, renamed King's theatre from 1901 to 1907 when, as Victoria hall, it became the town's first cinema. It was pulled down in 1930 to build the Granada cinema. The twin-towered Palace theatre of varieties was built in High Street in 1903.[20] It closed in 1954 and was demolished in 1960. The first purpose-built cinema, the Princes Pavilion, opened in 1910 in High Street; by 1914 there were nine cinemas. Six remained in 1951,[21] but only two in 1965, the Granada and the Regal, Highams Park; two others were still open as bingo halls.[22] Walthamstow greyhound stadium, Chingford Road, opened in 1931.[23]

The district council's High Street baths (1900) were adaptable as a public hall in winter.[24] The public library (1909), High Street, included a lecture hall, used for that purpose until 1920, when the hall became the reference library.[25] Lloyd Park Pavilion, built by the borough in 1937 and modernized in 1965, includes a small theatre. The Assembly hall, Forest Road, was opened by the borough council in 1943.[26] In 1947 the first of an annual series of borough musical festivals was organized.[27] Municipal encouragement of the arts includes maintenance of the William Morris gallery (1950) at Water House, where the Morris collection, the Brangwyn Gift of pictures and sculptures, and the Mackmurdo Gift of furniture and textiles, are housed.[28]

An association for self-improvement which was founded in 1840 to form a circulating library and provide lectures[29] had 1,000 books in 1855 and 80 members in 1865; it seems to have ceased by 1870.[30] Walthamstow working men's club and institute, originally called St. James's club, was founded in 1862 in Marsh Street, moving in 1872 to its present (1971) site, nos. 82 and 84 High Street, where a hall was built and in 1890 additional club premises with two shops for letting in front.[31] The literary institute founded in 1882 is described elsewhere.[32] A co-

[99] D.N.B.
[1] Ibid.; Budden, Marsh St. Cong. ch., 13–16, 22–36.
[2] D.N.B.; G. E. Roebuck, Walthamstow armorial (W.A.S. xxvi), 13; Moore Smith, Fam. of Withypoll, 55.
[3] Bosworth, More . . . houses, 18.
[4] Diary of Samuel Pepys (ed. H. B. Wheatley), passim; E.R.O., Q/RTh 1; D.N.B. Batten's widow married in 1671 the Swedish envoy, Sir James Barkman Leyenberg, who was rated in Marsh Street in 1676, where Lady Penn was also rated. As Sir William Penn's daughter Margaret married Anthony Lowther of Marske in Cleveland (Yorks. N.R.), Clevelands in Marsh Street may have been a Penn family house: Barns, Walthamstow Deeds, 1584–1855, 30; E.R.O., T/P 75, Q/RTh 9; tablet in St. Mary's parish ch.; Diary of Samuel Pepys, i. 266 n., vi. 130 n.
[5] D.N.B.; Roebuck, Walthamstow armorial, 10; Moore Smith, Withypoll family, 56–8; Reaney, Walthamstow Place-names, 39; Bosworth, Some . . . houses, 30; Roebuck, Story of Walthamstow, 63.
[6] Lysons, London, iv. 228; D.N.B.
[7] D.N.B.
[8] Ibid.
[9] Ibid.; V.H.M., Illus. Colln., Vestiges, no. 13.
[10] D.N.B.
[11] Ibid.; J. W. Mackail, Life of Wm. Morris (1922 edn.), 2, 4, 12, 19, 26; Bosworth, Some . . . houses, 25.
[12] D.N.B.
[13] See p. 311.
[14] D.N.B. (s.v. B. Disraeli, R. Gurney, S. Sharpe, S.

Solly); G. F. Bosworth, Essex Hall, Walthamstow, and the Cogan associations (W.A.S. v).
[15] D.N.B.
[16] Ibid.
[17] This paragraph is based unless otherwise stated on W. G. S. Tonkin, Showtime in Walthamstow (W.A.S. Occ. Pub. ix). There is a picture of the public hall in V.H.M., Illus. Colln.
[18] See p. 280.
[19] Bosworth, Some . . . houses, 18; Hatley, Across the years, 39.
[20] See plate f.p. 188.
[21] Walthamstow Off. Guide (1951), 48.
[22] W.A.S., The Record, no. 2, p. 6.
[23] V.C.H. Essex, v. 88; Walthamstow Off. Guide (1951), 46; Waltham Forest Off. Guide (1968), 119; Walthamstow Guardian, 29 May 1931 (correspondence).
[24] Tonkin, Showtime, 6, 23–4.
[25] Ibid. 23–4. The voluntary town lectures committee's minute book, 1915–22, is in W.R.L.
[26] Tonkin, Showtime, 23–4.
[27] Walthamstow Forward, i (2), p. 6; A. D. Law, Our town (2) (W.A.S. Occ. Pub. vii), 34.
[28] S. K. Ruck, Municipal entertainment and the arts in Greater London, 66, 80; V.C.H. Essex, Bibliography, 331.
[29] Its minutes 1840–3 are in W.R.L.
[30] V.C.H. Essex, Bibliography, 321.
[31] Hatley, Across the years, 93; A. G. Barker, Seventy years a club (1933).
[32] V.C.H. Essex, Bibliography, 321.

operative society formed before 1898 was taken over in that year by the Stratford Co-operative and Industrial society.[33] The Walthamstow antiquarian society, founded in 1914, had published 48 monographs by 1970, besides other publications.[34]

A Walthamstow cricket club existed in 1816.[35] The Walthamstow cricket and lawn tennis club, founded in 1862 as an activity of the Walthamstow volunteer rifle corps (formed in 1860), was virtually independent of the corps by 1884; it still existed in 1971.[36] In 1907 there were about 20 cricket clubs.[37] The Rectory Manor tennis and bowling club, which was founded in 1897, was an enlargement of the Walthamstow lawn tennis club which existed in 1895. The club ceased in 1971.[38] Walthamstow Rugby football club, formed c. 1865, was among the leading London clubs in the late 19th century. Clubs formed later included the Walthamstow Alberts and the Saracens.[39] Walthamstow Avenue Association football club, founded in 1901 by former pupils of Pretoria Avenue school as Avenue United and renamed in 1903, won the F.A. Amateur Cup in 1952 and 1961.[40]

MANORS. There were two manors in Walthamstow in 1066, Wilcumestou (Walthamstow) and Hecham (Higham).[41] Both were later subdivided, the manors of Low Hall and the Rectory being formed out of Walthamstow, and Salisbury Hall out of Higham. The origin of the later manor of Mark in Walthamstow and Leyton is obscure.

The manor of *WALTHAMSTOW*, later called *WALTHAMSTOW TONY* or *HIGH HALL*,[42] the largest in the parish, may originally have comprised most of the area south of Chapel End. Its eventual extent is shown on a map of High Hall manor prepared in 1699.[43] Then and later the manor included the detached Walthamstow Slip in Leyton.[44]

Walthamstow was held in 1066 by Waltheof, earl of Huntingdon, as a manor and 10½ hides.[45] He married Judith, niece of William I, in 1070,[46] giving her as dower all his lands east of the Trent.[47] After his execution for conspiracy in 1076 she succeeded him at Walthamstow, which she held in 1086.[48] She was later deprived of the honor of Huntingdon for refusing to marry Simon de Saint Liz,[49] who

acquired it on his marriage, perhaps as early as 1090, to Maud, Judith's elder daughter by Waltheof.[50] Simon had the custody of his wife's younger sister, Alice, Waltheof's coheir. On her marriage to Ralph de Tony II in 1103 Simon gave with her 100 librates of land of the honor of Huntingdon, including Walthamstow.[51]

Ralph de Tony II (d. 1126) was the son of Ralph de Tony I (d. 1102), Domesday lord of the barony of Flamstead (Herts.), with which Walthamstow descended until 1449.[52] After 1126 it was held in turn by Roger de Tony I (d. between 1157 and 1162), Ralph de Tony III (d. 1162), and Roger de Tony II (d. 1209).[53] Ralph de Tony IV, who held Walthamstow in 1212 by serjeanty of personally accompanying the king on his expeditions,[54] died in 1239 on the way to the Holy Land,[55] after leasing the manor with the king's consent to John de Gisors.[56] Ralph's widow, Parnel, in 1240 claimed one-third of it from John de Gisors as dower, but the king, who had the wardship of her son, Roger de Tony III, a minor, warranted the full term of the lease and made other provision for her.[57] After Roger de Tony came of age in 1256 he leased the manor in 1261 for four years to Austin of Hadstock,[58] a London citizen who was a prominent opponent of Simon de Montfort.[59] Roger de Tony and Austin both died in 1264, and in the same year the guardian of Roger's heir, Ralph de Tony V, restored the manor to Austin's son, William of Hadstock, for the full term of the lease.[60] There is some confusion over the custody of the manor in 1265, about the time when the lease ran out and the disturbances of the Barons' War reached their climax at Evesham.[61] William of Hadstock, however, at some date secured a renewal of the lease, for in 1281 he granted to Adam de Bedyk, the king's tailor, and his wife, Joan, William's daughter, an annuity of £100, of which one-third was paid out of his manor of Walthamstow.[62] He still held the manor of Ralph de Tony in 1285, when Adam the tailor, who was clearly identical with Adam de Bedyk, held two carucates as his under-tenant. Those two carucates became the separate manor of Walthamstow Bedyk, later called Walthamstow Frounceys or Low Hall.[63]

Ralph de Tony V died in France in 1295, whereupon the king ordered the manor to be delivered to

[33] *V.C.H. Essex*, v. 60.
[34] W. G. S. Tonkin, *Our Town* (1) (W.A.S. Occ. Pub. vi); Hatley, *Across the years*, 97–8; W.A.S., *The Record*, no. 9, p. 2.
[35] R. G. C. Desmond, *Our Local Press* (W.A.S. N.S. iii), 51.
[36] S. A. Couzens, *Walthamstow Cricket and Lawn Tennis Club: the first hundred years* (1962); inf. from W.R.L.
[37] *V.C.H. Essex*, ii. 611.
[38] W.R.L., File of reports, rules, fixtures, etc., of the Rectory Manor Tennis and Bowling Club (1896–1919); inf. from W.R.L.
[39] *V.C.H. Essex*, ii. 613; W.A.S., *The Record*, no. 5, p. 3; Hatley, *Across the years*, 90; S. A. Couzens, *Walthamstow Cricket and Lawn Tennis Club: the first hundred years*, 4–5.
[40] *Walthamstow Off. Guide* (1963), 57; *Walthamstow*
[41] *V.C.H. Essex*, i. 537, 555. The meaning of 'Wilcumestou' is in dispute: *P.N. Essex* (E.P.N.S.), 103–5; P. H. Reaney, *Walthamstow Place-names* (W.A.S. xxiv), 17–23.
[42] The form 'Manors of Walthamstow Tony and High Hall' does not appear until 1733: see below.
[43] E.R.O., T/M 252; G. F. Bosworth, *Manor of Walthamstow Toni or High Hall* (W.A.S. i). The original map, by Alexander Forbes, hangs in Walthamstow Central Library.

[44] See p. 174.
[45] *V.C.H. Essex*, i. 555.
[46] *Complete Peerage*, vi. 639.
[47] *Chroniques Anglo-Normandes*, ed. F. Michel (1836), ii. 112.
[48] *V.C.H. Essex*, i. 555; *D.N.B.*
[49] *Chroniques Anglo-Normandes*, ii. 123–5.
[50] *Complete Peerage*, vi. 641.
[51] Ibid. xii (1), 761; Ordericus Vitalis, *Ecclesiasticae Historiae Libri Tredecim*, ed. A. Le Prevost, iv. 198; *Chron. Angl.-Norm.* ii. 126; I. J. Sanders, *English Baronies*, 117.
[52] Sanders, *English Baronies*, 117; *Complete Peerage*, xii (1), 757 sqq.; *V.C.H. Herts.* ii. 194.
[53] Ibid.
[54] *Bk. of Fees*, i. 345.
[55] *Complete Peerage*, xii (1), 771.
[56] *Abbrev. Plac.* (Rec. Com.), 110.
[57] Ibid.; *Ex. e Rot. Fin.* (Rec. Com.), i. 344–5; *Bk. of Fees*, ii. 1426; *Complete Peerage*, xii (1), 771.
[58] *Complete Peerage*, xii (1), 772; *Cal. Pat.* 1258–66, 252.
[59] W. H. Blaaw, *The Barons' War*, 174.
[60] Sanders, *English Baronies*, 118; *Cal. Inq. p.m.* ii, p. 54; *Cal. Pat.* 1258–66, 316; *Close R.* 1261–4, 344.
[61] *Cal. Pat.* 1258–66, 316; *Cal. Inq. Misc.* i, p. 201.
[62] *Abbrev. Plac.* (Rec. Com.), 201.
[63] J.I. 1/242 m. 70. For Low Hall manor, see below.

an unnamed man to whom Ralph had leased it without licence before going abroad.[64] Ralph de Tony's heir, Robert de Tony, died childless in 1309, his heir being his sister, Alice.[65]

Alice's second husband, Guy de Beauchamp, earl of Warwick,[66] one of the lords ordainers, died in 1315 holding the manor of her inheritance, their son and heir, Thomas de Beauchamp, being one year year old.[67] Alice's third husband, William de la Zouche of Mortimer,[68] held the manor for life by the courtesy of England after her death in 1324 until he died in 1337, when the manor reverted to his stepson, Thomas de Beauchamp (d. 1369), earl of Warwick.[69]

In 1361 the earl of Warwick acquired the reversion of Walthamstow Bedyk.[70] He was succeeded in 1369 by his son, Thomas de Beauchamp, earl of Warwick,[71] upon whose forfeiture for treason in 1397 the manors of Walthamstow and Low Hall were granted to William le Scrope, earl of Wiltshire. In 1399, however, on the accession of Henry IV, Warwick was restored to his honours and estates. Low Hall was settled on him and his wife Margaret in 1399, and Walthamstow Tony in 1400.[72] He died in 1401, holding both manors.[73] His widow died in 1407. Their son, Richard de Beauchamp, earl of Warwick (d. 1439) succeeded to both manors.[74] They passed to his son, Henry de Beauchamp, duke of Warwick, who died in 1446, leaving Anne, a minor, his daughter and heir.[75] In 1447 Anne's mother, Cecily, duchess of Warwick, was granted the manor of Walthamstow Tony in dower.[76] Anne died in 1449, when her two aunts, the half-sisters Anne and Eleanor, daughters of Richard de Beauchamp, earl of Warwick (d. 1439), became coheirs. Low Hall passed, with Flamstead (Herts.), to the share of Anne, wife of Richard Neville, earl of Warwick. The elder half-sister, Eleanor, inherited Walthamstow Tony in 1450 on the death of Cecily, formerly duchess of Warwick.[77]

Eleanor, who married Thomas de Ros, Lord Ros (d. 1431), and later Edmund Beaufort, earl (later duke) of Somerset (d. 1455), died holding Walthamstow Tony in 1467.[78] Her heir was her grandson, Edmund de Ros, but he was debarred from the

succession by the attainder (1461) and execution (1464) of his father, Thomas de Ros, Lord Ros, so Walthamstow Tony was taken into the king's hands.[79] By 1483 it was known as the 'lordship of Hye Hall'.[80]

On the accession of Henry VII the attainder of Thomas, Lord Ros, was reversed, but his heir, Edmund de Ros, Lord Ros, was abroad at the time, and his lands were reserved to the king during his pleasure.[81] In 1487, when Anne, countess of Warwick, surrendered all her estates to the Crown,[82] Walthamstow Tony was included with Low Hall[83] although it was not part of Anne's inheritance. The terms of this grant almost certainly created the doubts about the Walthamstow Tony title which arose later. In 1492 Edmund, Lord Ros, was judged of insufficient discretion 'to guide himself and his livelihood'; his custody, and the farm of his lands for life, were granted to his brother-in-law, Sir Thomas Lovell (d. 1524), with reversion to the Crown.[84]

Edmund, Lord Ros, died childless in 1508.[85] The manor was not then restored to his heirs, but, wrongly it seems, was retained by the Crown, which from 1520 leased it. Under such leases it was held successively by Sir John Heron (d. 1521), lord of Aldersbrook in Little Ilford, by Margaret his widow, who seems also to have leased Low Hall, by their son Giles, until his execution for treason in 1540, and by Sir Ralph Sadler.[86] In 1544 the Crown granted the manor in fee, subject presumably to the lease, to Paul Withypoll and his son Edmund, lords of the manor of Mark.[87] They alienated it in 1546 to Sadler, who in 1547 surrendered it to the Crown in exchange for other lands.[88]

The manor was once again kept in hand until 1554 when it was granted to Thomas, son of Giles Heron.[89] This grant probably never took effect, for in 1555 the manor was restored to the descendant of the Ros family in the person of Henry Manners, earl of Rutland and Lord Ros, who was the grandson of Eleanor, Lady Manners, sister of Edmund, Lord Ros (d. 1508).[90] Rutland (d. 1563) was succeeded by his son Edward, earl of Rutland.[91] The Rutlands' title was apparently challenged in 1571[92] and in 1583 the Crown actually granted the manor to Theophilus

[64] *Cal. Close, 1288–96*, 432; *Complete Peerage*, xii (1), 773.
[65] *Feud. Aids*, ii. 151; *Cal. Inq. p.m.* v, p. 101.
[66] *Complete Peerage*, xii (1), 774, xii (2), 370–2.
[67] *Cal. Inq. p.m.* v, p. 397.
[68] *Complete Peerage*, xii (1), 774.
[69] Sanders, *English Baronies*, 118; *Cal. Inq. p.m.* viii, p. 65; *Feud. Aids*, ii. 175.
[70] *Feet of F. Essex*, iii. 132.
[71] *Cal. Inq. p.m.* xii, p. 308; *Cal. Close, 1369–74*, 128.
[72] *D.N.B.*; *Cal. Pat. 1396–9*, 207; *Cal. Close, 1399–1402*, 92, 113; *Feet of F. Essex*, iii. 233.
[73] C 137/27/58.
[74] C 137/61/68; C 139/94/37; *Cal. Close, 1405–9*, 180, 184; *Feud. Aids*, ii. 225, vi. 434.
[75] C 139/123/43; *Cal. Pat. 1441–6*, 436–7.
[76] *Cal. Pat. 1446–52*, 37.
[77] *Complete Peerage*, viii. 54–5, 60, xii (2), 378–84; Morant, *Essex*, i. 33; *V.C.H. Herts.* ii. 194; *D.N.B.* The duchess of Warwick remarried, to John Tiptoft, earl of Worcester: *Feet of F. Essex*, iv. 63.
[78] *Complete Peerage*, xii (1), 53; *Cal. Inq. p.m. Hen. VII*, ii, pp. 563–4; C 140/24/4.
[79] *V.C.H. Essex*, v. 101; *Cal. Pat. 1554–5*, 177–9; *Cal. Inq. p.m. Hen. VII*, ii, pp. 563–4; C 140/24/4.
[80] G. S. Fry, *Walthamstow Wills, 1335–1559* (W.A.S. ix), 8.
[81] *Cal. Pat. 1554–5*, 178; *Complete Peerage*, xi. 106–7.

[82] See p. 256.
[83] *Cat. Anct. D.* v, A 11056; *Feet of F. Essex*, iv. 90; C.P. 25(1)/72/292. On the Close Roll only 'Walkhamstowe Frauceys' is mentioned: *Cal. Close, 1485–1500*, 90.
[84] *V.C.H. Essex*, v. 101; *Complete Peerage*, xi. 106–7.
[85] *Cal. Inq. p.m. Hen. VII*, ii, p. 564; *Complete Peerage*, xi. 107.
[86] *L. & P. Hen. VIII*, iii (1), p. 298, iv (3), p. 2664, v, p. 217, ix, p. 382, x, p. 238, xv, p. 380, xvi, p. 331; Morant, *Essex*, i. 33; *Misc. Gen. Her.* N.S. i (1874), 67. For Sir Ralph Sadler, see *D.N.B.* For Aldersbrook, see above, p. 166, and for Low Hall, see below, p. 256.
[87] *L. & P. Hen. VIII*, xxi (1), p. 622; E 318/1240.
[88] *L. & P. Hen. VIII*, xxi (1), p. 152; *Cal. Pat. 1547–8*, 258.
[89] *Cal. Pat. 1553–4*, 472. It was granted as the manor of 'High Hall or Walthamstow Tony or Walthamstow Francis or Low Hall', a multiple title adopted until 1639, although Thomas Heron and his successors never had or claimed Low Hall, which had descended independently since 1449: see below, p. 256.
[90] *Cal. Pat. 1554–5*, 179; cf. *V.C.H. Essex*, v. 101. Eleanor married Sir Robert Manners (d. 1508): Morant, *Essex*, i. 56.
[91] Barns, *Walthamstow Deeds, 1541–1862*, 3; *Complete Peerage*, xi. 257.
[92] Hist. MSS. Com. 24, *12th Rep. IV, Rutland*, i, pp. 95–6 (letters to the earl of Rutland).

Adams, a 'concealer', from whom, and from Robert Adams, Rutland had to purchase it in the same year.[93] This was described in 1612 as a purchase on a defective title.[94]

Edward, earl of Rutland (d. 1587) was succeeded by his daughter Elizabeth, who married William Cecil, son of Thomas Cecil, Lord Burleigh, later earl of Exeter.[95] She died in 1591 leaving a son, William Cecil, Lord Ros, who came of age in 1611.[96] He immediately cut the entail on the Walthamstow portion of the Ros inheritance, apparently in order to mortgage it.[97] In 1616 he married Anne, daughter of Sir Thomas Lake, secretary of state.[98] In the same year he conveyed Walthamstow Tony to his father-in-law for £800,[99] and in 1617, for a further £500, to Arthur Lake, bishop of Bath and Wells, his wife's uncle, Arthur Lake, his brother-in-law, and Nicholas Fortescue.[1] Lady Ros later successfully claimed that the latter conveyance was a settlement in trust for her,[2] but Ros regarded it as a mortgage, and his grandfather, the earl of Exeter, refused his consent to the alienation of the manor.[3]

The marriage soon broke up. Lady Ros accused the countess of Exeter, the young wife of her husband's grandfather, of incest with her husband, and of attempting to poison her father and herself, and forged letters to support her charges. Her brother, (Sir) Arthur Lake, assaulted Ros, who fled abroad and died in 1618.[4] In the same year Lady Ros, her parents, and her brother, were charged with defamation by the countess of Exeter, found guilty in 1619, sentenced to life imprisonment, and heavily fined, while the countess was awarded substantial damages and costs.[5] Lady Ros was released after confessing her guilt, but by judicial decree the earl and countess of Exeter took possession of the manor in satisfaction of the damages she owed. Their interest was subsequently transferred to Thomas, Lord Wentworth and others.[6]

In 1623 the manor was restored to Lady Ros when George Rodney, whom she had married, paid the balance of the debt.[7] In the same year Lady Ros sought to convey to Rodney all her interest in the estate; when the trustees refused to agree, she and her husband sued them.[8] In 1626 the court ruled that the manor be settled on Lady Ros and her husband for life and then on any children of Anne, with reversion to Anne to dispose of at will, should

she die childless.[9] In 1626 the trustees authorized Rodney to sell demesne lands to the value of £2,400 to settle his wife's debts.[10] In the following year Lady Ros settled the reversion of the manor on her husband in fee.[11] When she died in 1630[12] her brother, Sir Thomas Lake, claimed it as her heir,[13] but George Rodney secured possession and in 1639 sold the manor to Charles Maynard(d. 1665), auditor of the Exchequer.[14]

Charles Maynard's son, William, who was created a baronet in 1682, died in 1685. The manor subsequently descended with the baronetcy, and later viscounty, of Maynard until the death in 1865 of Henry Maynard, Viscount Maynard, when the male line became extinct. The manor then passed to Frances Maynard, granddaughter of the last viscount. In 1881 she married Francis Greville, Lord Brooke, later earl of Warwick.[15] Lady Warwick died in 1938.

In 1843 Lord Maynard owned 560 a. in Walthamstow, of which 262 a. were forest waste, most of which became part of Epping Forest.[16] The estate was breaking up in the 1890s, when the site of Shern Hall was developed.[17]

The manor included a capital house and garden in 1264 and 1309.[18] High Hall is mentioned in 1483.[19] In 1612 the manor house of High Hall was let to Robert Hammond.[20] It appears to have been sold later separately from the manor, probably by George Rodney in c. 1626–39, either after his wife's trustees in 1626 authorized him to sell some of the demesne, or when he inherited the manor after her death in 1630.[21] In 1653 Thomas Brooks claimed common of pasture in the forest in respect of High Hall and 40 a. of land.[22] High Hall, in the angle of Clay Street and Blackhorse Lane, its avenue leading westward to the lane, is shown on a map of 1699 and named on maps of 1742, c. 1760, and 1777.[23] It was described in 1768 as a handsome brick farm-house.[24] About that time it was occupied by the Quaker Lewis Weston, whose daughter and heir, Susan, married William Dilwyn, also a Quaker, of Higham Hill Lodge. The two small estates, which adjoined, came to be combined, and High Hall was pulled down between 1822 and 1836. Blackhorse Road board school was later built on the site.[25]

High Hall was replaced as the manor-house by an unnamed 'chief mansion house' which Charles

[93] Morant, *Essex*, i. 33; C 142/218/52; C 142/217/128.
[94] Hist. MSS. Com. 24, *12th Rep. IV, Rutland*, i, p. 438.
[95] C 142/217/28; C 142/218/52; *Complete Peerage*, xi. 109.
[96] *Complete Peerage*, xi. 109; C 142/257/43.
[97] E.R.O., D/DB T1102; Barns, *Walthamstow Deeds, 1595–1890*, 7; Hist. MSS. Com. 24, *12th Rep. IV, Rutland*, i, p. 438.
[98] *Complete Peerage*, xi. 110; *D.N.B.*
[99] C.P. 25(2)/295 Trin. 14 Jas. I.
[1] Ibid. Eas. 15 Jas. I.
[2] Barns, *Walthamstow Deeds, 1595–1890*, 8.
[3] S. R. Gardiner, *Hist. England*, iii. 189–90.
[4] *Complete Peerage*, xi. 110; *Cal. S.P. Dom. 1619–23*, 15, 19, 21.
[5] *Cal. S.P. Dom. 1619–23*, 15, 21.
[6] Barns, *Walthamstow Deeds, 1595–1890*, 9–10. For details of the Star Chamber case, see Gardiner, *Hist. England*, iii. 189–94; *D.N.B.* (s.v. Sir Thomas Lake), and *Cal. S.P. Dom. 1611–18, 1619–23, passim.*
[7] Barns, *Walthamstow Deeds, 1595–1890*, 9–10.
[8] Ibid. 10; E.R.O., D/DB L14.
[9] V.H.M., DTT 11 (previously W.R.L. 5089); printed in Barns, *Walthamstow Deeds, 1595–1890*, 8, but the date of the Chancery decision incorrectly transcribed as 24 Jan. 5 Chas. (*recte* 1 Chas.).
[10] Barns, *Walthamstow Deeds, 1595–1890*, 10–11.
[11] V.H.M., DTT 11 (previously W.R.L. 5089), incorrectly dated 1617 in Barns, *Walthamstow Deeds, 1595–1890*, 8–9.
[12] *Complete Peerage*, xi. 110.
[13] E.R.O., D/DB L14.
[14] Barns, *Walthamstow Deeds, 1595–1890*, 11–13.
[15] *Complete Peerage*, viii. 603–4; Barns, *Walthamstow Deeds, 1595–1890*, 28.
[16] E.R.O., D/CT 382. See also below, p. 275.
[17] V.H.M., *Vestiges*, nos. 84–5.
[18] C 132/31/3; C 134/15/3.
[19] Fry, *Walthamstow Wills, 1335–1559*, 8.
[20] E.R.O., D/DB T1102.
[21] Morant, *Essex*, i. 34; *Hist. Essex by Gent.* iv. 209; Barns, *Walthamstow Deeds, 1595–1890*, 10–11.
[22] *Proc. Epping Forest Com.*, pp. 1876–7.
[23] E.R.O., T/M 168, 252, D/DQs 31; Chapman and André, *Map of Essex 1777*, sheet xvi.
[24] Morant, *Essex*, i. 34.
[25] G. F. Bosworth, *More Walthamstow houses* (W.A.S. xx), 22, 24, *Some more Walthamstow houses* (W.A.S. xxix), 13, and *Manor of Walthamstow Toni* (W.A.S. x), 14; *John Coe's Map of Walthamstow, 1822* and *Index* (W.A.S. n.s. v. va), nos. 447–50.

Maynard bought from George Rodney with other parcels of the demesne in 1636.[26] From the associated field-names it is clear that it was the house in Shernhall Street called Toni Hall in the 18th century and later Shern Hall, which dated from the 17th century.[27] It may be the house which features as decoration on the map of 1699, a two-storey house of 10 bays, with an attic story with 8 dormers divided by a central gable with a large oval window.[28] In the late 19th century it was a brick house of irregular shape and complicated roof pattern, suggesting piecemeal alterations; by then it had been reduced in size and stuccoed.[29] Dr. (later Cardinal) Wiseman was the tenant for several years from 1849.[30] After a fire in 1879 which destroyed the original panelling the house was restored, but demolished in 1896.[31]

The manor of *WALTHAMSTOW BEDYK* or *WALTHAMSTOW FRAUNCEYS*, later called *LOW HALL*, lay in the south-west of the parish, mainly south of Ferry Lane and west of Blackhorse and Markhouse Lanes.[32] It originated as 2 carucates which Adam de Bedyk (d. 1302), the king's tailor, held in 1285 of William of Hadstock, lessee under the Tonys of the manor of Walthamstow Tony, whose daughter he married.[33] In 1303 the manor was defined as $\frac{1}{40}$ of a knight's fee held of Robert de Tony.[34] In 1319 Henry de Bedyk (will proved 1335), probably Adam's son, is included in a Walthamstow tax list second to William de la Zouche who held Walthamstow Tony,[35] and he was lord in 1330.[36] In 1352 his son, Sir Thomas de Bedyk,[37] appears to have conveyed all his lands in Essex to Simon Fraunceys, a city merchant who was twice lord mayor.[38] Fraunceys died in 1358 holding the manor of Bedyks jointly with his wife Maud of the earl of Warwick.[39] Maud still held the manor in 1361.[40] She was still living in 1376,[41] but appears to have died before 1397 when Low Hall was in the hands of Thomas de Beauchamp (d. 1401), earl of Warwick.[42] After this time there appear to have been no more under-tenants and Low Hall descended with Walthamstow Tony until the partition of 1449, when it passed to Richard Neville, earl of Warwick (d. 1471), 'the kingmaker', in right of his wife Anne.[43]

After Warwick had been killed at Barnet Anne's lands were seized by Edward IV and divided between her two daughters. The former Beauchamp estates fell to the share of Isabel (d. 1476), wife of George Plantaganet, duke of Clarence (d. 1478).[44] After Clarence's death Low Hall was administered by the Crown during the minority of his son, Edward, earl of Warwick.[45] In 1485 John Hugford is said to have died seised of the manor[46] but the assertion is dubious. In 1487 the possessions of Anne Neville, countess of Warwick, were restored to her, but only so that she might surrender them to the Crown.[47]

The manor remained with the Crown from 1487 until 1550. In 1488 Sir Thomas Lovell was granted custody for 5 years.[48] In 1520 Low Hall was leased for 21 years to John Jenyns,[49] and in 1528 in reversion to John Lynsey,[50] but about that time the lease appears to have been acquired by Margaret, Lady Heron, who held the lease of Walthamstow Tony.[51] Both leases subsequently passed to Giles Heron (d. 1540), and then, in 1541, to Ralph Sadler.[52] In 1550, having previously disposed of his interest in Walthamstow Tony, Sadler was granted Low Hall at a rent of £10,[53] converted into a fee simple tenure nine years later.[54] Sadler sold the manor in 1560 to Thomas Argall and his wife Margaret.[55]

Thomas Argall (d. 1562) settled Low Hall on his wife Margaret and his son Richard (d. 1589) successively.[56] Margaret married Sir Giles Allington after Argall's death, and they were deemed joint lords in 1582.[57] Margaret Allington, by then widowed again, made her will in 1592.[58] Richard's heir, his second son Richard,[59] probably died between 1593 and 1599, and the manor descended successively to his brothers Thomas (d. 1605) and Sir Reginald (d. 1611).[60] While Sir Reginald's widow, Anne, Lady Argall (d. 1638), held Low Hall for life in dower,[61] his heir, a third brother John, of Great Baddow, sold the manor (presumably the reversion) in 1623 to a fourth brother, the adventurer, Sir Samuel Argall (d. 1626), who devised it to his nephew Samuel, then a minor.[62]

The last-named Samuel was probably identical with Dr. Samuel Argall, physician, who by his will proved 1684 devised Low Hall to his wife Elizabeth for life,[63] who was still living in 1699.[64] She was succeeded by her daughter Elizabeth who married Nathaniel Green. They were joint lords from 1701

26 Barns, *Walthamstow Deeds, 1595-1890*, 12.
27 Morant, *Essex*, i. 34; V.H.M., *Vestiges*, nos. 84-5.
28 E.R.O., T/M 252.
29 Bosworth, *Walthamstow Toni*, pls. f.pp. 3 and 5; Hatley, *Across the years*, 64; V.H.M., *Vestiges*, nos. 84-5.
30 See p. 294.
31 V.H.M., *Vestiges*, nos. 84-5; Hatley, *Across the years*, 64.
32 The bounds of the manor are shown on maps of 1699 (E.R.O., T/M 252) and 1742 (E.R.O., T/M 168).
33 *Cal. Close, 1296-1302*, 609; R. R. Sharpe, *Cal. Hustings Wills*, i. 123-4. See also above, p. 253.
34 *Feud. Aids*, ii. 151.
35 E 179/107/3; *Cal. Inq. p.m.* xii, p. 245. See also above, p. 254.
36 *Cal. Anct. D.* iv. A 9808.
37 *Cal. Close, 1346-9*, 498.
38 Ibid. 1349-54, 467; P. H. Reaney, *Walthamstow Place-names* (W.A.S. xxiv), 4-6.
39 *Cal. Inq. p.m.* x, p. 348.
40 *Feet of F. Essex*, iii. 132.
41 *Cal. Close, 1374-7*, 357.
42 See p. 254.   43 See p. 254.
44 Morant, *Essex*, i. 33; D.N.B.
45 *V.C.H. Essex*, iv. 287.
46 *Cal. Inq. p.m. Hen. VII*, iii, p. 397.
47 *Cal. Close, 1485-1500*, 90; Morant, *Essex*, i. 33; *Cat. Anct. D.* v, A 11056.
48 C 60/300/18; *Cal. Fine R. 1485-1509*, 129.
49 *L. & P. Hen. VIII*, iii (1), p. 298.
50 Ibid. iv (2), p. 1772.
51 *Misc. Gen. Her.* N.S. i. 67.
52 See p. 254.
53 *Cal. Pat. 1549-51*, 267; E 318/1921.
54 *Cal. Pat. 1558-60*, 296; B.M. Add. Ch. 26024.
55 C.P. 25(2)/126/1613.
56 C 142/138/30; C 142/223/77.
57 Notes by Edm. Chishull in Par. Reg.; *Visit. Essex*, i. (Harl. Soc. xiii), 137, 293.
58 P.C.C. *Wills*, iv. 7. In 1592 the Crown granted Low Hall to William Tipper and Robert Dawe; they were 'concealers', and there is no evidence that the grant ever took effect: Morant, *Essex*, i. 33.
59 C 142/223/77; *Visit. Essex*, i. 137.
60 C 142/288/131.
61 Barns, *Walthamstow Deeds, 1584-1855*, 6. For Lady Argall, see also Higham manor.
62 C 142/327/125; C.P. 25(2)/296 Eas. 20 Jas. I; D.N.B.; H. F. Waters, *Gen. Gleanings in England*, ii. 920; *Visit. Essex*, i. 137, 335.
63 P.C.C. 109 Hare. Cf. V.H.M., DLM 1.
64 E.R.O., D/DZg 25.

to 1708, but from 1711 to 1727 courts were held in Nathaniel's name alone.[65]

In 1735 Raphael Courteville and his wife Lucy, daughter of Elizabeth and Nathaniel Green, were joint lords and in 1739 and 1740 Raphael alone.[66] In 1741 Raphael Courteville and his wife Jane, and Elizabeth and Katharine, daughters of Elizabeth and Nathaniel Green, sold Low Hall to Samuel Bosanquet (d. 1765).[67] In 1742 the manor comprised 219 a. demesne, 63 a. copyhold, and about ½ a. of small leaseholds.[68] It subsequently descended in the Bosanquet family.[69] In 1830 Samuel Bosanquet (d. 1843) settled it on his son and heir, Samuel Richard Bosanquet (d. 1882) on his marriage.[70] In 1843 the manor-house and demesne farm comprised 225 a., let to Charles Burrell.[71] They were sold to the local board in 1877.[72] The manor, however, remained vested in the Bosanquet family, who still held it in 1926.[73]

Low Hall manor-house was mentioned in 1397.[74] In 1611 its occupant was Richard Garnett, a moneyer.[75] The house, which was moated,[76] stood between Markhouse Lane and the Dagenham brook. It was a 17th-century two-storey timber-framed building, brick-fronted, with a tiled roof, with later additions on the south-east side.[77] It was destroyed by a flying bomb in 1944.[78]

The manor of *HIGHAM BENSTED* lay in the north of the parish. Its south boundary with High Hall or Walthamstow Tony near Chapel End and Hale End was defined in 1699,[79] but was still disputed in the early 19th century.[80] Higham's boundaries with Salisbury Hall, which had been taken out of it in the 14th century, were not settled until the 19th century. Their fields intermingled and their tenants held copyholds in both manors, which caused much friction, particularly in the 16th century.[81] In 1817 their respective lords accepted that neither manor had any jurisdiction over the other, and agreed to abide by a map defining their boundaries, and that irregular transfers of copyholds be rectified and their record transposed to the correct rolls.[82] Even so, a substantial amendment had to be negotiated in 1825.[83]

Higham ('high home or inclosure')[84] was held in 1066 by Haldan, a free man, as a manor and 5 hides; in 1086 it was held in demesne by Peter de Valognes. One of the 5 hides, held before 1066 by 2 free men, was added to the manor after the Conquest and in 1086 was held of Peter by William.[85] This hide may be identified with the hide of land, 8 a. of meadow, and some woodland in the neighbouring manor of Chingford (St. Paul's) which Peter took away from the chapter of St. Paul's between 1066 and 1086.[86] It was probably the origin of the detached part of Walthamstow in Chingford, south of Chingford Hall.[87] The manor descended with the Valognes barony of Benington (Herts.) until the partition of 1235,[88] when three sisters, Lora (d. between 1265 and 1272), wife of Henry de Balliol, chamberlain of Scotland, Isabel (d. 1253), wife of David Comyn, and Christine (d. between 1291 and 1294), wife of Peter de Maule,[89] apparently shared it.

Lora and Henry de Balliol (d. *c.* 1246) were holding a third of the manor of Higham in 1240.[90] In 1240–1 all three sisters and their husbands were parties to a conveyance of land in Higham to be held of Lora and Henry.[91] Isabel was holding 'Higham' when she died in 1253, leaving William Comyn, a minor, her son and heir.[92] The court of Christine and Peter de Maule at Higham is mentioned in 1257.[93] When Lora's eldest son, Guy de Balliol, Simon de Montfort's standard bearer, was killed at Evesham in 1265,[94] 'Heyham Baillol' was seized by the King.[95] As 'Heyham Comyn' was seized too, it seems likely that William Comyn also supported the rebels.[96] Both estates, however, were restored, for in 1274 Guy de Balliol's younger brother and heir, Alexander, and (Sir) William Comyn (d. 1283) were holding courts at Higham.[97] Two years earlier, in 1272, the third sister, Christine de Maule, had given Alexander de Balliol all her lands in Higham in exchange for his lands in Dersingham (Norf.).[98] She appears, however, to have retained some interest in Higham, for in 1274 she too was holding view of frankpledge at Higham,[99] a right she and Alexander de Balliol still claimed in 1285, when their partner, Sir William Comyn's

[65] P.C.C. Hare 109 (marginal note); C.P. 25(2)/829/Hil. 6 Wm. III; V.H.M., DLM 1.

[66] V.H.M., DLM 1; E.R.O., D/DZg 25.

[67] C.P. 25(2)/1122/Hil. 15 Geo. II; C.P. 43/635/43; E.R.O., D/DZg 25.

[68] D/DBq M1.

[69] V.H.M., DLM 2–4; E.R.O., D/DBq M6; Lysons, *London*, iv. 208. For the Bosanquet succession, see Forest House estate, Leyton.

[70] V.H.M., DLM 4 ff. 135–40.

[71] E.R.O., D/CT 382; see also below, p. 266.

[72] See p. 283.

[73] E.R.O., D/DBq M6.

[74] *Cal. Pat.* 1396–9, 207. See also above, p. 254.

[75] Assizes 35/53A/T (No. 14); Barns, *Walthamstow Deeds, 1595–1890*, 7. For Walthamstow's moneyers, see below, p. 269.

[76] J. Rocque, *Survey of London*, 1746; E.R.O., D/CT 382.

[77] R.C.H.M. *Essex*, ii. 248; Bosworth, *Manor of Low Hall* (W.A.S. vii), f.p. 5 (illus.)

[78] Inf. from V.H.M.

[79] E.R.O., D/DXj 10, ff. 301 sqq.; T/M 252.

[80] E.R.O., D/DXj 11, f. 107; 14, f. 13; and D/DXj 15, 16.

[81] E.R.O., D/DFc 185, ff. 325–40; D/DXj 11, ff. 106–16; 14, ff. 13, 202–5; D/DXj 15, 16; V.H.M., *Vestiges*, nos. 25–6.

[82] V.H.M., DSM 2 ff. 196 sqq. (with map); the agreement is printed in S. J. Barns, *Walthamstow Deeds, 1584–*

1855 (W.A.S. xxxiii), 26–7. John Long of Christ's Hospital, surveyor to the South Sea Co., carried out extensive researches in public and local records in *c.* 1800–17 on behalf of John Harman, into the history and topography of the two manors, as a preliminary to this agreement: E.R.O., D/DXj 10–18. The mass of material he assembled is not always reliably handled; he admits that his observations may be 'more grounded on circumstances than facts': E.R.O., D/DXj 14 f. 3. He also tried to prove that Walthamstow Tony had usurped a large part of Higham Bensted: cf. D/DXj 15 ff. 52, 54.

[83] Barns, *Walthamstow Deeds, 1584–1855*, 28.

[84] P. H. Reaney, *Walthamstow Place-names* (W.A.S. xxiv), 23.

[85] *V.C.H. Essex*, i. 537.

[86] Ibid. v. 103.   [87] See p. 240.

[88] I. J. Sanders, *English Baronies*, 12; *Rot. Dom.* (P.R.S. xxxv), 77; *Feet of F. Essex*, i. 36. See also above, p. 194.

[89] Sanders, *Eng. Baronies*, 12.

[90] *Close R.* 1237–42, 251; *Cal. Close*, 1242–7, 467.

[91] *Feet of F. Essex*, i. 139.

[92] *Cal. Inq. p.m.*, i, p. 72, ii, pp. 411–12.

[93] *Feet of F. Essex*, i. 217.

[94] *Complete Peerage*, i. 387.

[95] *Cal. Inq. Misc.* i, p. 201.

[96] Ibid.

[97] *Cal. Pat.* 1266–72, 9; *Rot. Hund.* (Rec. Com.), i. 152

[98] H. C. Andrews, *Benstede family* (W.A.S. xxxv), 14.

[99] *Rot. Hund.* (Rec. Com.), i. 152; Sanders, *Eng. Baronies*, 13.

heir, John Comyn (d. 1290), was a minor holding in chief 40s. rent in Walthamstow.[1]

In 1303 Alexander de Balliol and William le Plomer held ⅛ knight's fee in Higham,[2] which was later acquired by Adam of Salisbury and descended as the manor of Salisbury Hall.[3] It probably included Christine de Maule's share of the Valognes inheritance. In 1305 Alexander de Balliol sold to John de Benstede, clerk, the reversion of a messuage and a carucate of land at Higham held for life by Robert de Graveleye and his wife Beatrice.[4] That purchase, held in 1339 as ⅙ knight's fee[5] and later called Waterhall or Higham, probably comprised Higham Balliol, Lora's share, as John de Benstede had already in 1303 bought Lora's manor of Benington.[6] Beatrice, later the wife of John de Blounville, held the estate until her death in 1337.[7]

John de Benstede I, who was chancellor of the exchequer in 1305–7,[8] also bought, in 1306, from Richard, son of William de Betuyne of London, a messuage, 180 a. of land, 8 a. of meadow, 4 a. of wood, and 7s. 5d. rent in Higham, Walthamstow, Chingford, and Sewardstone.[9] The purchase probably included 140 a. of land and 8 a. of meadow at Higham which were granted to William de Bettyne and his son William by Hugh Oyledebuf and his wife Emme in 1286.[10] The property was later called Benstedes; its content, and the reference to Chingford, suggest that it included the land which Peter de Valognes took from St. Paul's.[11] Parcels of meadow and pasture called Wydemade (later Wyemead), which belonged to Benstedes in 1368, still lay detached in Chingford in the 19th century.[12] As William Comyn in 1274 held the road called 'Amerland' (later Folly Lane),[13] which led to Wyemead, Benstedes was probably Higham Comyn.

The two estates, Benstedes and Waterhall or Higham, became the manor of Higham Bensted, so called from 1429.[14] Benstedes comprised land held variously of the abbot of Waltham, the rector of Chingford, and the manor of Walthamstow, while Higham or Waterhall was held in chief as part of the manor of Benington.[15]

John de Benstede I died in 1323 holding the estate later called Benstedes.[16] His son Edmund (d. 1333)[17] left John de Benstede II his son and heir,

a minor.[18] Edmund had conveyed his 'manor' in Walthamstow to trustees,[19] who on his death settled it for life on his widow Maud, later wife of John de Caly.[20] In 1339, however, Maud seems to have been dispossessed by Walter de Mauny, guardian of the heir.[21] John de Benstede II, who came of age in 1353,[22] died in 1358 holding Higham and Benstedes.[23] His son and heir, John de Benstede III (d. 1359 or 1360) was succeeded by his brother (Sir) Edward, who came of age in 1376.[24]

Sir Edward de Benstede died in 1432, having previously settled Higham Bensted manor on his wife Joan for life.[25] On her death in 1448,[26] it passed to Sir Edward's great-grandson, (Sir) John de Benstede IV (d. 1466).[27] Sir John's son William, who died childless in 1485, had granted the manor for life to his mother Margery.[28] When Margery de Benstede died in 1488[29] the manor passed to Helen de Benstede, sister of Sir John de Benstede IV.[30]

Helen de Benstede's right was disputed by Henry VII on the grounds of a sale by William de Benstede to Edward IV of the reversion of his manors.[31] The confusion of the years following[32] was no doubt aggravated by the vicissitudes in the descents of the other Walthamstow manors, the uncertainty of their physical boundaries, and the loose use of 'Walthamstow' and 'Higham' as manor names.

In 1493 Helen de Benstede conveyed Higham Bensted manor in Walthamstow, Chingford, and Waltham Holy Cross to John Rysshe (or Russhe) and others.[33] Rysshe apparently took possession of the manor and after his death his widow, Isabel, married Thomas Gray, and together they took the profits and refused to give up possession to the king.[34] Nevertheless, in 1494 a court was held at Higham by Thomas Lovell, to whom Henry VII had committed the custody of Walthamstow Tony and Low Hall in 1488 and 1492,[35] and in 1498 and 1499 the courts were held by the Crown.[36] In 1503, however, Thomas Gray and Isabel conveyed the manor to William Heron, John Heron the elder, and his son John.[37] Sir John Heron (d. 1521) devised it, as the manor of Higham Hill, to his wife Margaret for life, with reversion to his son Giles.[38] When Giles was executed in 1540 the manor was forfeit to the Crown.

---

[1] *Plac. de Quo Warr.* (Rec. Com.), 239; J.I. 1/242 m. 69.
[2] *Feud. Aids,* ii. 151.
[3] See p. 262.
[4] *Feet of F. Essex,* ii. 104; *Cal. Chart. R.* 1300–26, 38.
[5] H. C. Andrews, *Benstede family* (W.A.S. xxxv), 17–18.
[6] Sanders, *Eng. Baronies,* 13 n. 2; Andrews, *Benstede family,* 13, 15.
[7] *Cal. Pat.* 1334–8, 24; *Cal. Close,* 1337–9, 18; *Cal. Inq. p.m.* viii, pp. 62, 175; Andrews, *Benstede family,* 17.
[8] *D.N.B.*
[9] *Feet of F. Essex,* ii. 115. William de Bettone's will, enrolled in 1305, mentions his eldest son, Richard: R. R. Sharpe, *Hustings Wills,* i. 170–1.
[10] *Feet of F. Essex,* ii. 58.
[11] See above.
[12] *Cal. Inq. p.m.* xii, p. 189; S. J. Barns, *Walthamstow Deeds, 1584–1855* (W.A.S. xxxiii), 27; V.H.M., DRM 12 (1780 perambulation at end). See also above, p. 240.
[13] *Rot. Hund.* (Rec. Com.), i. 149b.
[14] *Cal. Pat.* 1422–9, 539; E 210/11278.
[15] *Cal. Inq. p.m.* vi, p. 284, x, p. 373, xii, p. 189, xiv, p. 254; C 139/59/38. The abbot of Waltham held the lordship of Waltham hundred: *V.C.H. Essex,* v. 94.
[16] *Cal. Inq. p.m.* vi, p. 284.
[17] *Cal. Fine R.* 1319–27, 277, 1327–37, 385; *Cal. Inq. p.m.* vi, p. 284, vii, pp. 382, 398.
[18] *Cal. Inq. p.m.* viii, p. 175.

[19] Ibid. vii, p. 398, viii, p. 62; *Cal. Pat.* 1334–8, 24, 26.
[20] *Cal. Pat.* 1334–8, 24, 26; *Cal. Close,* 1337–9, 18, 1339–41, 296; *Cal. Inq. p.m.* viii, pp. 62, 175.
[21] *Cal. Pat.* 1334–8, 557, 1338–40, 243, 1340–3, 7; *Cal. Close,* 1339–41, 296; *Feet of F. Essex,* iii. 76, 82.
[22] *Cal. Inq. p.m.* x, p. 121; *Cal. Close,* 1349–54, 551, 556.
[23] *Cal. Inq. p.m.* x, p. 373; *Cal. Fine R.* 1356–68, 85.
[24] *Cal. Inq. p.m.* x, p. 373, xii, p. 189, xiv, p. 254; *Cal. Close,* 1374–7, 302; *Cal. Fine R.* 1356–68, 96, 330.
[25] C 139/59/38; E 210/11278; *Cal. Pat.* 1422–9, 539; *Feud. Aids,* vi. 439.
[26] *Cal. Close,* 1429–35, 201, 257–8; *Cal. Fine R.* 1445–52, 96; C 139/134/27.
[27] *Cal. Fine R.* 1445–52; C 139/134/27; C 140/38/57; Andrews, *Benstede family,* 35–6; *Cal. Pat.* 1446–52, 452, 1452–61, 487.
[28] *Cal. Inq. p.m. Hen. VII,* i, pp. 27–8.
[29] Andrews, *Benstede family,* 37.
[30] *Cal. Inq. p.m. Hen. VII,* i, pp. 27–8.
[31] C 1/208/22; C 1/207/69.
[32] Cf. E.R.O., D/DXj 14, f. 13.
[33] *Cal. Pat.* 1485–94, 465; *Cal. Close,* 1485–1500, 221.
[34] C 1/207/69, 70.
[35] E.R.O., D/DFc 185, f. 24; see also above, pp. 254, 256.
[36] E.R.O., D/DFc 185, ff. 28, 31.
[37] E.R.O., D/DXj 10, ff. 62, 285–314; C 142/40/72.
[38] Morant, *Essex,* i. 26; *Misc. Gen. Her.* N.S. i (1874), 51.

In 1546 Henry VIII granted Cuthbert Hutton a lease of Higham Bensted for 21 years from the expiration of a lease made by Giles Heron to Sir William Hollys in 1537.[39] Hutton, who held a court in 1550,[40] apparently sub-let parts of the manor to Sir Ralph Sadler and others who already held Walthamstow Tony, Low Hall, and Salisbury Hall. The lack of information on the true boundaries of the four manors confused their tenants, and it is possible that about that time the other manors usurped some of Higham Bensted's holdings.[41]

In 1554 the Crown granted Thomas Heron, son of Giles, the reversion of the manor on the termination of Hutton's lease, together with the annual rent.[42] Thomas Heron held courts from 1554 to 1564,[43] and in 1556 he sold Higham Bushes, which formed part of the demesne, to Roger Capstock.[44]

The Heron family sold the manor in 1566 to (Sir) Thomas Rowe (d. 1570).[45] It descended in the Rowe family for nearly two hundred years. Thomas was succeeded by his third son William[46] who settled Higham Bensted on Anne Cheney for life when he married her in 1580.[47] In 1583 he reunited Higham Bushes with the manor, buying it from Gabriel Colston, who had bought it two years before from Sir Anthony Cooke to whom Roger Capstock sold it in 1560.[48] Those transactions gave rise later to the claim that Higham Bushes was an independent freehold estate, over which copyholders and forest officers had no rights.[49]

William Rowe died in 1596.[50] In 1603 his son and heir, Sir John Rowe, sold the reversion of the manor to (Sir) Reginald Argall, who had married William Rowe's widow, Anne.[51] After Argall died in 1611 his heir, his brother John Argall, in 1612 sold the reversion of the manor to Sir William Rowe, brother of Sir John.[52] After Lady Argall died in 1638 the manor descended in the Rowe family until 1758, when William, son of William Rowe (d. 1744), sold it to Richard Newman.[53]

In 1764 Richard Newman sold the manor to Anthony Bacon,[54] who in 1782 sold it to John Biggin, one of his principal creditors.[55] In 1785 Eleanor Biggin, widow, sold it to William Hornby,

governor of Bombay, who sold it in 1790 to John Harman (d. 1817), a banker.[56]

John Harman's son Jeremiah held the manor in 1843, when the Harman estate comprised some 477 a. of which 157 a. were open forest waste and 89 a. inclosed forest.[57] In 1848 Joseph Sands of Liverpool was said to be lord of the manor, and owner of Higham House, which was unoccupied.[58] In 1849 Edward Warner (d. 1875) bought the manor and Higham House.[59] The manor descended in turn to Sir Courtenay Warner (d. 1934), Sir Edward Warner (d. 1955), and Sir Henry Warner, lord of the manor in 1970.[60] From the late 19th century the Warner family progressively sold off or developed the estate.[61]

Benstedes included a house in 1306.[62] It was described as a chief messuage in 1368, and may have been near Jack's Farm, where a field was still called Bensteads in the 19th century.[63]

The Balliol share of Higham included a house in 1305.[64] By 1368 it was known as Waterhall.[65] It has been suggested that Waterhall was the moated house later called Moons,[66] or it may have been the house which was occupied as the manor-house in the late 16th century, which William Rowe 'almost wholly rebuilt' between 1570 and 1596.[67] Rowe's house, which was called Higham Hill or Higham Hall, stood on the north side of the old junction of Billet Road and Blackhorse Lane (now Sutton Road).[68] There was a chapel in it, described by Edward Rowe Mores in 1756 as having been large and handsome, with the arms of William Rowe and his wife in the wainscot.[69] The size of the house was reduced about 1683, and again c. 1730, when the whole east side of it, including the great hall and chapel, was demolished. The east side was refronted, and by 1768 the house had been converted into two dwellings.[70] It had not been sold with the manor in 1758[71] and had ceased to be the manor-house. It was called Essex Hall from the early 19th century, when the Rowe family let it to Revd. Eliezer Cogan, who kept a school there.[72] In 1861 it was let to the Cooper family, who later bought it from the Rowes; the Misses Cooper used the old schoolrooms as a Sunday

[39] L. & P. Hen. VIII, xxi (1), p. 481.
[40] E.R.O., D/DFc 185, f. 43.
[41] E.R.O., D/DXj 10, ff. 73, 77, 301 sqq., D/DXj 15, 16.
[42] Cal. Pat. 1553–4, 472.
[43] E.R.O., D/DFc 185, ff. 45–65.
[44] E.R.O., D/DXj 10 f. 91.
[45] Cal. Pat. 1563–6, 417; C.P. 25(2)/259 Trin. 8 Eliz.; Morant, Essex, i. 35. Cf. E.R.O., D/DFc 185, f. 67.
[46] Morant, Essex, i. 35.
[47] C 142/246/117; E.R.O., D/DXj 10, f. 120.
[48] E.R.O., D/DXj 10, ff. 91, 100, 112.
[49] E.R.O., D/DXj 15, f. 50; see also below, p. 274.
[50] C 142/327/125.
[51] Ibid.; Allegs. Marr. Lic. Bp. Lond. 1520–1610, i. (Harl. Soc. xxv), 261; E.R.O., D/DFc 185, f. 181. For the Argalls in Walthamstow, see also above and below, pp. 256, 261, 286.
[52] C 142/327/125; Morant, Essex, i. 35.
[53] Visitns. Essex, i (Harl. Soc. xiii), 479; Morant, Essex, i. 35; Lysons, London, iv. 209; G. F. Bosworth, Manor of Higham Bensted (W.A.S. vi), 7, 9; Barns, Walthamstow Deeds, 1584–1855, 6; E.R.O., D/DXj 10, f. 18, D/DFc 185, f. 262. The 1758 sale particulars are in E.R.O., D/DXj 10, ff. 280–3 and 18, f. 88.
[54] Lysons, London, iv. 209.
[55] E.R.O., D/DXj 10, f. 375; Lysons, London, iv. 209; Wright, Essex, ii. 507.
[56] Lysons, London, iv. 209; G. F. Bosworth, Walthamstow Charities (W.A.S. viii), 42.
[57] E.R.O., D/CT 382.
[58] White's Dir. Essex (1848).
[59] E.R.O., Sale Cat. A 1050 (see conditions of sale); M. M. Smith, Highams (W.A.S. Occ. Pub. viii), 9; L. Lewis, 'Architects of the Chapel at Greenwich Hospital', Art Bulletin, xxix (1947), 266; G. F. Bosworth, P. H. Reaney, and G. E. Roebuck, Book of the Walthamstow Museum (W.A.S. xxiib), 25. For the Warner family, see G. F. Bosworth, More Walthamstow Houses (W.A.S. xx), 21–2, C. H. Crouch, Monumental Inscriptions (W.A.S. xxiii), 26, and Smith, Highams, 17.
[60] Smith, Highams 17; inf. from V.H.M.
[61] See pp. 244, 275.
[62] Feet of F. Essex, ii. 115.
[63] Cal. Inq. p.m. xii, p. 189; E.R.O., D/DXj 11, ff. 31–4; John Coe's map of Walthamstow, 1822 (W.A.S. n.s. v, va), no. 85.
[64] Feet of F. Essex, ii. 104.
[65] Cal. Inq. p.m. xii, p. 189.   [66] See p. 249.
[67] Guildhall Libr., Lysons, London (extra illus.) iv. f.p. 209 (engraving from drawing by Edward Rowe Mores, 1756; cf. MS. drawing in E.R.O., D/DFc 185).
[68] Chapman and André, Map of Essex, 1777, sheet xvi. The junction was diverted westward when the Essex Hall estate was laid out in the 1930s.
[69] Stow, Survey of London (6th edn.), ii. 792.
[70] Ibid.; Guildhall Libr., Lysons, London (extra illus.) iv. f.p. 209; Morant, Essex, i. 34; Bosworth, Higham Bensted, 12; R.C.H.M. Essex, ii. 247.
[71] See the particulars of sale: E.R.O., D/DXj 18, f. 88.
[72] Bosworth, Higham Bensted, 12. See also below, p. 311.

school for over fifty years.[73] After the First World War the house and grounds were acquired by the council for housing, and in 1934 Essex Hall was pulled down.[74] An old people's home called Essex Hall, completed in 1970, stands on the site.

Essex Hall was a three-storey brick house with tiled and slated roof. All the windows except those on the east had the solid frames, mullions, and transoms of the Elizabethan period.[75] The reconstructed east front had six sash windows and a Tuscan porch.[76] Original panelling and a 17th-century panelled fire-place and overmantel with fluted Ionic pilasters are preserved, built into the old armoury room in the Vestry House museum.[77]

In 1768 Anthony Bacon built a new brick and stone manor-house designed by William Newton (1735–90) at Higham Bushes on the Woodford boundary.[78] It was at first called Higham Hill,[79] but later Higham House, Higham Hall, or Highams. The five-bay central block had two storeys and a semi-basement, fully exposed by the falling ground on the west side, and was flanked by single-storey wings, each terminating in a pedimented feature. The three central bays on the east front were divided by giant pilasters and surmounted by a pediment; the entrance doorway was approached by a double flight of steps.[80] In 1785–90 William Hornby removed the pediment to add a balustraded third storey and a central cupola.[81] Thus Humphry Repton, commissioned by John Harman in 1793–4 to improve the property, criticized the house as 'extravagantly lofty'.[82] To reduce the apparent height of the west front he designed the present continuous iron balcony to the ground floor rooms, supported on stucco arches forming an arcade in front of the basement windows. The lake created by Repton is now part of Highams Park.[83]

In the 19th century, perhaps when Edward Warner acquired the property in 1849, two extra bays were added at the south end of the west front with a matching extension of Repton's balcony.[84] The addition contained a new drawing room and had full-height bow windows facing south.[85] Probably at the same time the ground level at the centre of the east front was raised, the entrance steps were

removed, a porch was added, and the basement windows in the flanking wings were altered.[86] At an earlier period the roof cupola had been replaced by a wider lantern.[87]

Highams was usually occupied by the lords of the manor until 1902, when it was let.[88] In 1919 it became Woodford county high school for girls. The building is now stuccoed and has been much extended to the north and south, mainly between 1928 and 1938.[89]

The manor of *MARK* in Leyton and Walthamstow lay on both sides of the parish boundary (*mearc*), between the common marsh and Hoe Street.[90] One of the boundary posts was at Mark House, by which name the manor was known in the 15th century.[91] The name survives in Markhouse Road.

It seems possible that the manor originated in two ½ virgates in Leyton held by Herbert of the Mark and Benet of the Mark in 1224, when half-shares in them were claimed by Hugh the tailor and John of Chelmsford in right of their wives.[92] In 1225 Benet granted them and their wives' heirs 8 a. there in return for a life grant of six loads of corn yearly.[93] In 1226 the same parties sued Thomas, son of Herbert, and Maud of the Mark his mother for 36 a. in Leyton which they had given at the request of the defendants to Thomas de Muleton together with the 8 a. which they had acquired from Benet.[94] In 1248 the widow of Thomas at the Mark was concerned in two suits against the prioress of St. Helen's, Bishopsgate, relating to Leyton and Walthamstow.[95]

St. Helen's priory owned the manor by the late 15th century,[96] but whether they already owned it in 1248, or acquired it later, perhaps from the Fraunceys family, is not known. Simon Fraunceys died in 1358 holding the adjoining lands of Low Hall,[97] and his partner in business, Adam Fraunceys, who acquired the manor of Ruckholt in Leyton in 1359,[98] was a benefactor of St. Helen's.[99]

In 1523 the priory, which usually farmed the manor, took it into its own hands from the previous farmer, Ralph Furnival.[1] In 1538 they granted John Rollesley a 99-year lease, but after the priory's dissolution in the same year he exchanged it in 1539 for one of 21 years.[2]

---

[73] G. F. Bosworth, *Essex Hall* (W.A.S. v), 13.
[74] A. D. Law, *Our Town* (2) (W.A.S. Occ. Pub. vii), 30; *Walthamstow Off. Guide* (1935), 14; Smith, *Highams*, 16.
[75] R.C.H.M. *Essex*, ii. 247.
[76] Bosworth, *Essex Hall*, illus. following appendices.
[77] R.C.H.M. *Essex*, ii. 247 (illus.); Bosworth, *Higham Bensted*, 12; G. E. Roebuck, *The Old Armoury* (W.A.S. xxxii).
[78] *Art Bulletin*, xxix, 265–6 (illus.).
[79] Chapman and André, *Map of Essex*, 1777, sheet xvi, shows old and new manor-houses, both called Higham Hill.
[80] *Art Bulletin*, xxix, 265–6.
[81] E. W. Brayley and J. Britton, *Beauties of England*, v. 443; V.H.M., DHE 24 (Humphry Repton's 'Red Book').
[82] V.H.M., DHE 24.
[83] Ibid.; E. Ogborne, *Essex*, 89.
[84] See photograph, c. 1893: E.R.O., *Sale Cat.* A1050.
[85] The addition was certainly later than 1820, when a plan of the Higham House estate (E.R.O., T/M 324) shows in block plan a square house with wings, as designed by Newton, and as described by E. W. Brayley and J. Britton, *Beauties of England* (1803), v. 443 and T. K. Cromwell, *Excursions in Essex* (1819), 50. It was probably after 1842, when a water-colour apparently of that date by John Cawthorn also shows a west front still of 5 bays: Passmore Edwards Museum, Lysons, *London* (extra-illus.), f.p. 702, and inf. from Curator.

[86] Comparison of 1800 view (E.R.O., Pictorial Colln., engraving by S. Rawle) with present front.
[87] Passmore Edwards Mus., Lysons, *London* (extra-illus.), f.p. 702.
[88] Bosworth, *Higham Bensted*, 13; Smith, *Highams*, 10; *Kelly's Dir. Essex* (1906).
[89] Smith, *Highams*, 10 sqq. See also below, p. 359.
[90] *P.N. Essex* (E.P.N.S.), 107.
[91] J. Kennedy, *Hist. Leyton*, 392; G.L.C., DL/C/207 28 Jan. 1523/4.
[92] *Cur. Reg. R.* xi. 568.
[93] Ibid.; *Feet of F. Essex*, i. 70.
[94] *Rot. Litt. Claus.* (Rec. Com.), ii. 204; *Feet of F. Essex*, i. 73; *Cur. Reg. R.* xii. 493 (which gives 'Henry' instead of 'Thomas').
[95] P. H. Reaney, *Walthamstow Place-names* (W.A.S. xxiv), 27.
[96] G.L.C., DL/C/207 28 Jan. 1523/4.
[97] See p. 256.
[98] See p. 194.
[99] J. E. Cox, *Annals of St. Helen's, Bishopsgate*, 27; R. R. Sharpe, *Cal. Hustings Wills*, ii. 171 (printed in full in Cox, op. cit. 362–76). Adam's relationship to Simon is not known: Reaney, *Walthamstow Place-names*, 4–6.
[1] G.L.C., DL/C/207 28 Jan. 1523/4.
[2] *L. & P. Hen. VIII*, xv. 557–8; E 315/211, f. 73; *V.C.H. London*, i. 460.

In 1544 the manor was granted to Paul Withypoll (d. 1547), merchant tailor and M.P. for the City in 1545, and his son (Sir) Edmund (d. 1582).[3] It passed successively to Edmund's grandsons Paul (d. 1585) and (Sir) Edmund Withypoll,[4] the second of whom sold it in 1601 to Sir James Altham (d. 1617), later a baron of the exchequer.[5] From him it passed successively to his son Sir James (d. 1623), to his grandson Sutton Altham (d. 1630), and, as coheirs, to his granddaughters, Elizabeth and Frances Altham.[6] Elizabeth married Arthur Annesley, son of Francis, Lord Mountnorris, in 1638, and Frances married Richard Vaughan, earl of Carberry, in 1637.[7] Soon afterwards the estate appears to have been broken up and sold. In 1649 the Mountnorrises and Carberrys sold the reversion of the manor-house to Thomas Rose, a London draper.[8] The sale included some 60 a. of land, about half the demesne.[9] Other parcels of land were sold to Nathaniel Sturton, a butcher.[10] The manor later came into the hands of either David Gansel (d. 1714) or his son David (d. 1753) and was united with the manor of Leyton.[11] It was purchased by John Pardoe in 1783 from General William Gansel's heirs with the Leyton estate,[12] with which it descended thereafter.[13]

The manor-house, often called Mark House, existed in 1524.[14] Elizabeth Altham, Sir James's widow, had a life interest in it after her husband's death and thus it began to be parted from the manor. As has been said it was separately sold to Thomas Rose in 1649.[15] In the early 18th century it belonged to Samuel Winder.[16] It stood astride the boundary on the west side of Markhouse Road, near Markmanor Avenue,[17] on a field which adjoined the grounds of Hibbert House, Leyton, built in 1803.[18] In the early 18th century it was a brick farm-house, old and dilapidated.[19] By 1775 the half of it which stood in Leyton had fallen down.[20]

The *RECTORY* manor[21] originated in ½ virgate and an acre of meadow given to the priory of Holy Trinity, Aldgate, with the church and its tithes by Alice, daughter of Waltheof, early in the 12th century.[22] It was taken out of the manor of Walthamstow Tony and occupied the highest part of the parish between the present Church Hill and Forest Road, with outlying fields at Chapel End, on Markhouse common, and in the marshes.[23] Courts are known to have been held for the manor between 1509 and 1855.[24] The whole estate was estimated at 72 a. in 1690; 22 a. of this were known as the 'parsonage grounds', which included the site of the manor-house and gardens.[25]

The manor and great tithes descended with the advowson until the death of Lady Argall in 1638.[26] In 1613, however, John Argall sold the reversion of the manor to James Darell and his wife Catherine.[27] The subsequent title to the manor derived from the Darells, although the sequence of descent is obscure.[28] In 1615 the Darells conveyed their interest in the manor to Lionel Wright,[29] who leased it in 1620 for 80 years to Matthias Otten (d. c. 1625), brewer.[30] Otten seems to have bought the reversion of the freehold, which descended to his daughter and coheir Elizabeth, wife of Richard Cooper (d. c. 1688).[31] Cooper was lord of the manor in 1647 and compounded for the sequestration of the rectory in 1651.[32] After he died Elizabeth held the manor until her death in 1669, when she was succeeded in turn by her son Richard (d. 1690) and her daughter Elizabeth (d. 1708).[33] The rectory passed in 1708 to Thomas Fanshawe (d. 1758) of Parsloes in Dagenham, cousin of Richard Cooper the younger.[34] Fanshawe sold it in 1730 to John Fell, wine merchant,[35] in whose family it descended until 1783 when John Fell, and Elizabeth his wife conveyed it to William Cooke (d. 1792).[36] Under Cooke's will it was sold in 1794, and apparently broken up. Stephen Wilson bought the manor, house, and gardens, while John Jackson bought the remaining parsonage grounds. In 1797, after Wilson had become bankrupt,

[3] *L. & P. Hen. VIII*, xix (1), 622; E 318/1921; E.R.O., D/DW E3; C 142/84/52; C 142/197/78; G. C. Moore Smith (rev. P. H. Reaney), *Family of Withypoll* (W.A.S. xxxiv), 13–23.
[4] C 142/197/78; C 142/207/105; Wards 7/21/102; Moore Smith and Reaney, *Withypoll Family*, 49–51.
[5] Moore Smith and Reaney, *Withypoll Family*, 70; C.P. 25(2)/140/1761. For Sir James Altham, see *D.N.B.*
[6] C 142/402/134; C 142/466/51.
[7] *Complete Peerage*, i. 133–4, iii. 7.
[8] E.R.O., T/A 12/2/8 (Misc. copies 1).
[9] Cf. lease of manor in 1601 (E.R.O., D/DGn 364) and sale of manor-house and land in 1649 (E.R.O., T/A 12/2/8).
[10] E.R.O., D/DGn 364 (extracts from deed of 1690).
[11] Morant, *Essex*, i. 24; *E.R.* liii. 81; Kennedy, *Leyton*, 18. See also above, p. 186.
[12] Lysons, *London*, iv. 161 n. 16, 162.
[13] For the Leyton descent, see p. 186.
[14] G.L.C., DL/C/207 28 Jan. 1523/4.
[15] E.R.O., T/A 12/2/8 (Misc. copies 1). The conveyance refers to Lady Ashfield's interest in the house; Elizabeth Altham married Sir John Ashfield as her second husband: *Visits. Essex*, ii (Harl. Soc. xiv), 538–9.
[16] Kennedy, *Leyton*, 18; E.R.O., T/A 12/2/11.
[17] Lysons, *London*, iv. 162. It is named on maps of c. 1635 (E.R.O., T/M 5), and 1742–6 (E.R.O., T/M 168 and John Rocque's *Survey of London*).
[18] Kennedy, *Leyton*, 320–1.
[19] Ibid. 18; E.R.O., T/P 195/1 no. 5 (Holman MSS.).
[20] L.R.L., L55–6 MS. Rate Bk. 1775–83 (1775).
[21] See also p. 276.
[22] E 40 A13850(1).
[23] E.R.O., T/M 252; G. F. Bosworth, *Rectory manor* (W.A.S. iv), 5 and f.p. 12 (plan); P. H. Reaney, *Court rolls of Rectory manor* (W.A.S. xxxvii), 7, 10–12.

[24] Reaney, *Court rolls of Rectory manor*, 13.
[25] E.R.O., D/DW E3, D/DB E64. There are two copies of this 'Particular of Mr. Cowper's estate', both undated, but almost certainly associated with the death of Richard Cooper in 1690.
[26] See p. 286.
[27] Notes by Edm. Chishull in Par. Reg. 1692–1733; E.R.O., D/DB L16. The name is given as John Darell in Lysons, *London*, iv. 219.
[28] A note made in the early 1730s states that no title deeds existed because the 'writings' of the rectory manor had been burned in a fire at the Temple: V.H.M., DRM 12, ff. 11–12.
[29] C.P. 25(2)/294/Trin. 12 Jas. I.
[30] C.P. 25(2)/295/Hil. 17 Jas. I. For the Otten family, see H. C. Fanshawe, *Hist. of Fanshawe Family*, 128, 233, 236–8, and Reaney, *Court rolls of Rectory manor*, 22.
[31] Fanshawe, *Fanshawe Fam.* 128, 237–8.
[32] Bosworth, *Rectory manor*, 16; *Cal. Cttee. for Compounding*, 2862. Edmund Chishull (vicar 1708–33) incorrectly supposed that Elizabeth, wife of Richard Cooper, was the daughter of James and Catherine Darell: Lysons, *London*, iv. 219; E.R.O., D/DB L16.
[33] E.R.O., D/DB L16, E59; Bosworth, *Rectory manor*, 16; G. F. Bosworth, *Walthamstow charities* (W.A.S. viii), 32.
[34] Fanshawe, *Fanshawe Fam.* 236, 324.
[35] Ibid. 324; Bosworth, *Rectory manor*, 16; E.R.O., D/DB L16.
[36] Bosworth, *Rectory manor*, 16; C.P. 25(2)/1309/Trin. 23 Geo. III; E.R.O., Q/RSg 4 (1785); S. J. Barns, *Monumental Inscriptions* (W.A.S. xxvii), 17; Act to enable Joseph Fell Esq. to make a lease . . ., 2 Geo. II, c. 59 (Priv. Act); *Misc. Gen. Her.* 5th ser. iv. 37–8, N.S. iv. 368.

Jackson also bought the manor and parsonage house.[37]

Jackson sold the manor and parsonage in 1813,[38] probably to T. W. Hetherington, who held the manor in 1818.[39] After Hetherington's death in 1825[40] it passed to Captain Thomas Haviside of the East India Company,[41] who held it in 1843[42] and died in 1862.[43] Sir James Vallentin (d. 1870) bought the manor in 1863.[44] The estate was sold to the British Land Co. in 1897 by his trustees,[45] in whom the manor was still vested in 1916.[46]

In the early 18th century the manor was said to represent a fifth of the impropriate estate and the great tithes four-fifths.[47] John Argall did not sell the great tithes with the manor, and died holding them in 1643.[48] They were settled on Thomas, son of Thomas and Alice Argall, on his marriage in 1662.[49] In 1663 he sold them to Robert Shipman, who devised them in 1665 to his wife Dorothy. From her they passed in 1667 to John Mascall, the elder, and descended in his family[50] until they passed to Arthur Asgyll from his sister Anne who had married one of Mascall's descendants in 1733. Asgyll's only daughter, Margaret, who married Alexander Master, devised them about 1785 to Revd. Joseph Cuthbert, their owner in 1796.[51] Under Cuthbert's will, proved 1799, they passed successively to his grandsons Edward Cuthbert (d. 1803) and Richard Orlebar (d. 1833).[52] In 1819 Orlebar sold the tithes on 207 a., mostly to the landowners.[53] He and his son Richard, the main impropriator in 1843, probably sold more, for by then the great tithes on 595 a. were merged with the lands, and those on a further 807 a. were owned by 13 small impropriators. Orlebar's tithes on the remaining 3,034 a. were commuted in 1843 for £402 and those of the small impropriators for a total of £150.[54] The Orlebar family still owned most of the great tithes in 1916.[55]

The rectory house, which is mentioned in 1530,[56] stood on the part of the demesne called Parsonage Hill, not far from the vicarage. It had been pulled down by 1690, though it was still remembered.[57] A new house was built about 1762 by the tenant, John Watson, as a condition of his lease.[58] It was a plain two-storey building with angular corner bays at the west end. It was enlarged in 1783 by William Cooke to the design of (Sir) John Soane, who carried out some further work in 1791.[59] The house was demolished soon after 1897.[60]

The manor of *SALISBURY HALL* originated as ⅛ knight's fee in Higham held in 1303 by Alexander de Balliol and William le Plomer.[61] It lay mainly between Billet Road and the Chingford boundary and its fields on either side of Folly Lane and Chingford Road adjoined those of Higham Bensted.[62] Alexander died in 1310–11[63] and William about 1318.[64] In 1321 William's widow, Agnes, was granted by Alexander le Plomer, for life, extensive lands in Walthamstow, Woolston (Chigwell), and Barking.[65] In 1323 the same lands were conveyed by Alexander to a London pepperer, Adam of Salisbury (d. c. 1330),[66] and from him descended to his son Sir Thomas (d. 1370) and his grandson Paul Salisbury.[67] By his will (proved 1400) Paul directed his feoffees of the manor of 'Higham' to give an entailed estate in it to his daughter Elizabeth.[68] Her lands however, were, for unknown reasons, taken into the king's hands.[69] What became of Elizabeth is not known.

By unascertained stages the manor passed to the Tyrwhitts. Sir William Tyrwhitt, who built Higham chapel in 1442,[70] is said to have received it from Thomas Ketelby in 1450.[71] It seems likely that the Tyrwhitts held the manor continuously to 1541.[72] Sir William Tyrwhitt (d. 1521) was lord in 1509.[73] His son, Sir Robert, sold the manor to the Crown in 1541.[74]

The manor remained in the hands of the Crown until 1590, leased from 1543 to 1564 to Richard Johnson,[75] and from 1564 to Roger Ascham, author

[37] Lysons, *London*, iv. 220; E.R.O., Q/RSg 4 (1792), D/DQ 55/112; C.P. 25(2)/1311/Hil. 37 Geo. III.
[38] E.R.O., D/DQ 55/112.
[39] Bosworth, *Rectory manor*, 12.
[40] Barns, *Mon. Inscriptions*, 21.
[41] Bosworth, *Rectory manor*, 10.
[42] E.R.O., D/CT 382 (nos. 587–90).
[43] C. H. Crouch, *Mon. Inscriptions* (W.A.S. xxiii), 12.
[44] G. F. Bosworth, *Some more Walthamstow houses* (W.A.S. xxix), 8.
[45] Ibid.; Bosworth, *Rectory manor*, 12–13; A. Hatley, *Across the years*, 23.
[46] G. F. Bosworth, *St. Mary's church* (W.A.S. ii), 5.
[47] E.R.O., D/DB L16.   [48] C 142/744/28.
[49] C.P. 25(2)/652/Mich. 14 Chas. II; *Marr. Lic. Archbp. Cant.* (Harl. Soc. xxiv), 65.
[50] E.R.O., D/DQ 55/130, D/DB L16; Lysons, *London*, iv. 220.
[51] E.R.O., D/DQ 55/97; Lysons, *London*, iv. 220.
[52] Bosworth, *St. Mary's church*, 5; S. J. Barns, *Walthamstow Deeds, 1595–1890* (W.A.S. xi), 36–7; E.R.O., D/DQ 55/97.
[53] E.R.O., D/DQ 55/97, D/DC 27/123.
[54] E.R.O., D/CT 382.
[55] Bosworth, *St. Mary's Ch.* 5.
[56] Reaney, *Court rolls of Rectory manor*, 8.
[57] V.H.M., DRM 7; cf. E.R.O., D/DW E3 and D/DB E64 (c. 1690) which list the parsonage grounds but do not mention a house.
[58] Act to enable Joseph Fell Esq. to make a lease . . ., 2 Geo. III, c. 59 (Priv. Act); Morant, *Essex*, i. 37; V.H.M., *Vestiges*, no. 46.
[59] D. Stroud, *Architecture of Sir John Soane* (1961), 157, 159; V.H.M., *Vestiges*, no. 46; Bosworth, *Rectory manor*, illus. f.pp. 1, 4.

[60] Bosworth, *Rectory manor*, 13.
[61] See p. 258.
[62] Cf. E.R.O., T/M 169, D/DQ 55/13; V.H.M., DSM 2 (map, 1817).
[63] I. J. Sanders, *English Baronies*, 13.
[64] *Cal. Close, 1313–18*, 578; E 179/107/10.
[65] *Feet of F. Essex*, ii. 198. William was holding Woolston in 1296: *V.C.H. Essex*, iv. 31.
[66] *Feet of F. Essex*, ii. 206; R. R. Sharpe, *Hustings Wills*, i. 361–2. For the Salisbury family, see P. H. Reaney, *Walthamstowe Place-names* (W.A.S. xxiv), 12–13.
[67] *Feud. Aids*, ii. 176; R. R. Sharpe, *Cal. Letter Bks.*, London H., 170.
[68] G. S. Fry, *Walthamstow Wills* (W.A.S. ix), 1.
[69] *Cal. Fine R. 1399–1405*, 81.
[70] See p. 291.
[71] R. P. Tyrwhitt, *Family of Tyrwhitt*, 103.
[72] It has been suggested that the manor was in the hands of the Crown from 1499 to 1507: P. H. Reaney, *Court rolls of Salisbury Hall* (W.A.S. xxxvi), 5.
[73] C 142/39/104; E 150/307/10; B.M. Add. MS. 18783 ff. 102, 104, 107, 109. Between 1498 and 1505 the manor was known by such variants as Salisburye Powles and Powle or Powels Salesbury, from Paul Salisbury: Reaney, *Walthamstow Place-names*, 34. This probably explains the jurors' statement, otherwise unsupported, after Sir William Tyrwhitt's death, that the manor was held of Margaret (Pole), countess of Salisbury. Their unfounded guess in turn misled Morant into believing that Salisbury Hall derived its name from the countess: Morant, *Essex*, i. 35.
[74] *L. & P. Hen. VIII*, xvi, p. 505; C 54/414/13–15; *Feet of F. Essex*, iv. 257.
[75] *L. & P. Hen. VIII*, xviii, p. 557; *Cal. Pat. 1555–7*, 259.

of the *Scholemaster*, by a grant of 1557.[76] On Ascham's death in 1568[77] the remainder of his 40-year lease came to his widow, Margaret,[78] who married in 1569 Thomas Rampston (d. 1599).[79] Margaret, whose lease was renewed in advance in 1586,[80] probably died between 1590 and 1594.[81] In 1590 Robert Symonds the younger of Whittlesford (Cambs.), who had married Anne, Rampston's daughter, was granted the manor.[82] He raised mortgages on it in 1593, 1597, and 1601,[83] perhaps to rebuild the manor-house. A mortgage of 1619 to Edward Atkyns[84] was still outstanding when Robert Symonds died in 1623.[85] His son, Thomas Symonds, redeemed it in 1626,[86] but mortgaged the manor again in 1647 to Thomas Marsh the elder of Hackney (Mdx.).[87] In 1649 Marsh foreclosed and, with Symonds's consent, sold the manor to Richard Westley of Hempstead.[88]

Westley's administrator sold the manor in 1657 to Richard Edge of Stoke Newington (Mdx.)[89] who was succeeded by his sons Thomas, and James (d. 1715 or 1716).[90] James devised the manor to his kinsman, Richard Sheldon,[91] who died childless in 1736. Sheldon's property was apparently entailed on James and Rice Fellow. Judging from the evidence of court rolls Rice Fellow was sole lord from 1737 to 1761 and was succeeded by his cousin George Dickerdine, who assumed the name of Rice Fellow and sold the manor in 1778 to William Cooke (d. 1787).[92] The manor passed to Cooke's brother Richard (d. 1787), who devised it to John Relph. Relph, believing that he received it only in trust, assigned it to Hannah Cooke, William Cooke's sister, who was lady until 1807.[93] She is said to have devised the manor to Mrs. Rebecca Relph[94] who was lady until 1817, when she conveyed the manor for life to William Vale,[95] who was still living in 1826. The manor continued in the Vale family until 1856. In 1843 it comprised 228 a.[96] From 1856 to 1870 Thomas Oliver was lord. The manor continued in the Oliver family, Edmund Ward Oliver, the last lord, dying in 1917. The estate was broken up in 1904 when Salisbury Hall was sold with 141 a. of land for development.[97]

Salisbury Hall is mentioned in 1499.[98] It stood south of the Ching on the west side of Chingford Road.[99] A new manor-house was built on the same site in the late 16th century, perhaps by Robert Symonds. It was timber-framed and of two storeys, with two-storey projecting gabled porches and tiled roof in two ridges.[1] In 1768 it was described as old and mean,[2] in 1817 as a commodious farm-house, and in 1904 as a comfortable residence.[3] After its demolition in 1952 excavation revealed the medieval foundations.[4]

ECONOMIC HISTORY. Walthamstow remained an agricultural parish until the open arable fields were inclosed and the railway was built in the mid 19th century. In 1086 the two manors contained 15½ hides.[5] The arable was being cultivated by 30 ploughs (4 on the demesne and 26 belonging to the tenants), compared with 23 in 1066 (4 demesne and 19 tenants). There were 98 a. of meadow, woodland for 600 swine, pasture worth 8s., a mill, and a single fishery remaining from the 9½ which existed in 1066. Earl Waltheof's livestock comprised a rouncey, 8 beasts, 35 swine, 60 sheep, and 20 goats. The stock of Peter de Valognes had increased from a single ox to a rouncey, 15 beasts, 37 swine, and 2 hives of bees. The value of both manors had risen, Walthamstow from £15 in 1066 to £28 and 2 oz. of gold in 1086, Higham from £3 to £4 10s. The recorded population had increased from 44 (33 villeins, 3 bordars, 8 serfs) to 82 (46, 28, 8).

The increased value of Higham manor, where Peter de Valognes found only an ox and 1 a. sown when he received it, may be attributed to the live-stock acquired afterwards. The Walthamstow manor figures suggest improvement arising from extension of both the area settled and the acreage cultivated. The recorded population on this manor had grown disproportionately, the number of villeins increasing from 25 to 36, and, more significantly, the number of bordars from one to 25. At the same time the number of ploughs owned by the tenants had increased by seven. The most likely explanation of these developments, as at West Ham,[6] is forest clearance.

The woodland in 1086 was equally divided between the two manors. In 1323–4 17 presentments were made at the forest court for sowing corn land

76 *Cal. Pat.* 1555–7, 259, 406; S.P.12/231/61.
77 *D.N.B.*
78 S.P. 12/231/61; *Cal. Pat.* 1566–9, 385.
79 *Allegs. Marr. Lic. Bp. Lond.* 1520–1610 (Harl. Soc. xxv), 43; G. F. Bosworth, *Manors of Low Hall and Salisbury Hall* (W.A.S. vii), 13; E.R.O., D/DFc 185, ff. 181, 328; V.H.M., *Vestiges*, nos. 25–6.
80 S.P. 12/231/61.
81 *Proc. Cambs. Antiq. Soc.* xxxii. 50.
82 S.P. 12/231/61; E.R.O., D/DFc 185, f. 181.
83 C.P. 25(2)/136/1729; C.P. 25(2)137/1744; Wards 7/69/124.
84 S. J. Barns, *Walthamstow Deeds, 1541–1862* (W.A.S. xxi), 19.
85 C 142/398/130.
86 C.P. 25(2)/415/41.
87 Barns, *Walthamstow Deeds, 1541–1862*, 4.
88 Ibid. 4–5.   89 Ibid.
90 The names of the lords of the manor from 1667, unless otherwise stated, are taken from the manor court books 1667–1908 (V.H.M., DSM 2, 3), extracted in V.H.M., *Vestiges*, no. 45. The relationships of the Edge family and their kinsmen are apparent from the descent of a property they held in Higham Bensted: V.H.M., DHM 6.
91 Lysons, *London*, iv. 210.   92 Ibid.
93 Ibid.; E.R.O., Q/RSg 4 (1787, 1795, 1805), D/DXj 15, ff. 144–5, 147. John Long's notes suggest that

Hannah was William's widow, but Lysons says she was his sister. She is described as 'spinster' in 1790: V.H.M., Buildings File (Salisbury Hall).
94 E.R.O., D/DXj 14, f. 213; 15, f. 147. The relationship between the Cookes and the Relphs is not known.
95 S. J. Barns, *Walthamstow Deeds, 1584–1855* (W.A.S. xxxiii), 28.
96 E.R.O., D/CT 382; Bosworth, *Manors of Low Hall and Salisbury Hall*, 20.
97 Bosworth, *Manors of Low Hall and Salisbury Hall*, 15, 20.
98 Reaney, *Walthamstow Place-names*, 34.
99 E.R.O., Pictorial Colln. (photograph c. 1930 with notes); Chapman and André, *Map of Essex* 1777, sheet xvi. The site is now part of the car park for the greyhound stadium.
1 R.C.H.M. *Essex*, ii, 248; E.R.O., Pictorial Colln.
2 Morant, *Essex*, i. 34.
3 Bosworth, *Manors of Low Hall and Salisbury Hall*, 15, 20, frontispiece (illus. c. 1920).
4 E.R.O., Pict. Colln.; V.H.M., *Vestiges*, no. 45, and 'Report on Salisbury Hall excavations 1953–5' (TS.) by L. J. Carter, director. The timber-framing of the house was carefully photographed during demolition: V.H.M., Illus. Colln.
5 *V.C.H. Essex*, i. 537, 555.
6 See p. 74.

in small inclosures:[7] no doubt those were assarts. From the late 14th century the recurrence of the element 'braec'[8] in local field-names, particularly those bordering the forest, show the spread of cultivation eastward in both manors as woodland was cleared and fresh ground broken for tillage. In 1368 in Higham Bensted 'Brache' contained 62 a. and 'Shepecote Brache' 12 a. These clearances lay north of the Ching, between Jack's farm and Ching-ford Hatch.[9] Farther south, in Tony manor, 2 fields called 'the breaches' (12 a.) east of Hale End Lane, and 5 more side by side south of Hagger Lane, also called 'the breaches' (20 a.) are identified on a map of 1699.[10] Similar clearings in the Rectory manor, including 'Prioures Braches', lay between Hoe Street and Parsonage Hill, and others occur else-where in the parish.[11] Walthamstow was one of the forest parishes from whose landowners Charles I exacted payment in 1621 in return for a general grant of forest land assarted for cultivation in the past and inclosed, and by then usually unidenti-fiable.[12]

Westward of the remaining forest isolated groves survived among the fields, notably Rowden (11 a.), Thorncroft (6 a.), Twelve-acre, and Longdown (8 a.) groves, Salters woods (10 a.), and Great and Little Halebrains or Hale Brinks with 40 a. and 4 a. respectively. Those were progressively reduced in the 17th and 18th centuries by licences to fell timber of full growth.[13] By 1843, apart from the forest, Highams Park,[14] the Hale Brinks woods, and the pleasure grounds of Belle Vue House,[15] only 13 a. of woodland remained.[16]

Newly-cleared land appears to have been farmed in severalty: for example, 'a close called Brache' (1491)[17] and '6 closes called Brauches containing 50 a.' (1622).[18] But elsewhere in the parish a common agriculture was practised, and three open arable fields, which in 1699 contained some 215 a.,[19] sur-vived to the mid 19th century. Mill field or Higham Hill common (104 a.), mentioned in 1478,[20] lay in the north-west of the parish. Buryfield (1369) or Church common (27 a.) lay south of the church, and Markdown (1369), later known as Broomfield or Markhouse common (84 a.), lay east of Markhouse Lane on the Leyton boundary.[21]

In 1765-7 it was customary for each of the three common arable fields to lie fallow in turn.[22] They were divided into individually owned strips: an estate sold in 1795 included 27 a. of arable land in 16 parcels in the three common fields.[23] But the whole parish had the right to pasture horses, cows, and sheep all the year round on the fallow field.[24] In 1800 all three fields were cropped by parish resolu-tion because of the scarcity of corn.[25] In later years the Higham Hill and Church commons were usually thrown open together, alternating with Markhouse common.[26] In 1837 the view was expressed that the value of the common field strips belonging to Low Hall farm would be increased by inclosure, but that they were useful for growing turnips and other green crops.[27] The three common fields comprised in 1843 some 111 strips, two-thirds of them about 1 a. in size.[28] When they were finally inclosed by an award of 1850 they were estimated as 198 a.[29]

Common rights were also enjoyed on the marshes and in the forest. In the north of the parish the tenants of Higham Bensted claimed in 1586 to have customary rights of after-pasture in Great Broad-mead, west of Amberland or Folly Lane, and now under Banbury reservoir.[30] The holdings in Great Broadmead lay in both Higham Bensted and Salis-bury Hall manors. In 1587-91 there were violent disputes between the two manors, when Thomas Rampston of Salisbury Hall tried to close the Amberland or Broadmead gate against William Rowe of Higham Bensted and his tenants, denying them passage either to bring out the hay from their holdings or to drive their cattle in to the after-pasture.[31] No evidence has been found of common rights surviving in Broadmead after the 16th century, but the tenants of both manors still intercommoned on some of the roadside wastes in the early 19th century.[32]

In the south-west of the parish, however, lammas rights survived to the 1930s. The 'great meadow' or common marsh, divided by a ditch into the Inner and Outer meads, comprised in 1699 some 143 a.; it lay south of the mill-stream or Fleet, bounded on the west by the river Lea and on the east by the common sewer which flowed southward from the mill to Leyton.[33] In 1747 it was assessed by the com-missioners of sewers as 149 a. held in 133 plots, of which 122 were of one acre or less.[34] One of the plots in the Outer mead was the Longgrass acre which formed part of the vicarial glebe.[35] Another was the Churchwardens' or Vicar's acre in the Inner mead, held of Low Hall manor, and devised to the churchwardens by the vicar, William Hyll, in 1487 for an anniversary.[36] The hay crop belonged to

[7] Proc. Epping Forest Com. pp. 1932-3.
[8] P. H. Reaney, Walthamstow Place-names (W.A.S. xxiv), 44; P.N. Essex (E.P.N.S.), 575.
[9] Cal. Inq. p.m. xii, p. 189; V.H.M., DSM 2 f. 196v (map, 1822).
[10] E.R.O., T/M 252 (photograph of A. Forbes's map of 1699); G. F. Bosworth, Manor of Walthamstow Toni (W.A.S. i). The original map is displayed in the entrance hall of Walthamstow Library.
[11] E.R.O. T/M 252; P. H. Reaney, Court rolls of Rectory manor (W.A.S. xxxvii), 11, and Walthamstow Place-names, 8, 42-4; G. F. Bosworth, Rectory Manor (W.A.S. iv), f.p. 12.
[12] E.R.O., D/DU 99/14-15; Fisher, Forest, 326.
[13] A. J. Hatley, Hale End (W.A.S. Occ. Pubn. iv), 3-4; E.R.O., D/DCv 1, f. 18 v; T/M 169.
[14] See p. 275.   [15] See p. 250.
[16] E.R.O., D/CT 382.
[17] G. S. Fry, Walthamstow Wills (W.A.S. ix), 12.
[18] E.R.O., D/DFc 185, f. 205.
[19] E.R.O., T/M 252.
[20] E.R.O., D/DFc 185, f. 10.

[21] Reaney, Court rolls of Rectory manor, 11; E.R.O., T/M 252.
[22] E.R.O., D/DB E64.
[23] E.R.O., Sale Cat. B1052.
[24] White's Dir. Essex (1848); E. Clarke, Hist. Waltham-stow (1861), 13.
[25] See p. 278.   [26] Clarke, Walthamstow, 13.
[27] E.R.O., D/DOp B26.
[28] E.R.O., D/CT 382.
[29] E.R.O., Q/RDc 38.
[30] E.R.O., D/DFc 185, ff. 124 sqq., 325, 332; V.H.M., Vestiges, no. 26.
[31] Ibid.   [32] E.R.O., D/DXj 13.
[33] V.H.M., Commissioners of Sewers map of Waltham-stow Level, by John Noble, 1747 (cf. 19th-century copy: E.R.O., D/SH 29); Reaney, Court rolls of Rectory manor 14, and Walthamstow Place-names, 26; E.R.O., T/M 252, 168, D/CT 382.
[34] V.H.M., Map of Walthamstow, 1747.
[35] See p. 286.
[36] G. S. Fry, Walthamstow Wills (W.A.S. ix), 11; E.R.O., D/DBq M6, T/M 168. See also below, p. 315.

the several occupiers of the plots, but once it was gathered, from Lammas Day to Lady Day the marsh was thrown open to pasture horses and cows but not sheep, without limit. After 1752 the commoners continued to observe the old seasonal Lammas and Lady days, turning out the cattle from 13 August to 6 April.[37] In the 19th century there was some doubt whether all the inhabitants of the parish, or ratepayers only, were entitled to turn out their beasts.[38] The marsh bailiff or hayward[39] marked the beasts, and manorial by-laws regulated the marsh. One by-law promulgated between 1677 and 1684 forbade the pasturing of all 'dry' Welsh beasts except those which had wintered in the preceding winter.[40] This may have been intended to preserve the meads from use as a temporary pasture for beasts being driven to the London market from other places. In 1869 the manorial jury protested at a growing practice of putting bullocks on the lammas lands.[41] The Walthamstow and Leyton marshes were originally regarded as common to both parishes.[42] This was still the position in 1861, but by 1873 a fence had apparently been erected on the parish boundary.[43]

In 1841 the lammas rights were extinguished over 25 a. in the common marsh because the land was needed by the Northern and Eastern Railway Co.,[44] and in 1854 over a further 17 a. needed by the East London Waterworks Co.[45] The lammas lands were thus reduced to 100 a.[46] which were bought by the borough council in 1938 and preserved as an open space. The lammas rights which by then none claimed were extinguished.[47]

Common of pasture in the forest was claimed in the 17th century and later for every manor in Walthamstow except apparently Salisbury Hall.[48] Claims were also widely made to estovers, pollards, gravel, turf, and pannage.[49] The forest was commonable for eleven months of the year.[50] The beasts turned out were marked by the parish reeve.[51] In 1790 he was ordered to mark two cows or a horse for every £4 of annual rent, with special provision for the poor.[52] This was still the practice in 1871.[53] The forest pasture rights, which were highly prized, were increasingly threatened by late-18th-century

and 19th-century inclosures.[54] In 1817 a meeting of commoners, convened to protest against inclosure proposals, declared that the benefit they derived from the right of commonage more than compensated for any injury they might sustain from the free range of the deer.[55] But by 1865 the influx of people from London was said to harass the cattle and make many commoners neglect their rights.[56] Complaint was made, too, in the early 1870s, that inclosures and gravel-digging had ruined the grazing.[57] Another cause of bitterness was the inclosure of the cattle drinking ponds at Whipps Cross.[58] Further deterioration was prevented by the Epping Forest Act of 1878, which preserved both the forest and the commoners' right to pasture on it.[59]

Copyhold tenements in Walthamstow descended by the custom of Borough English.[60] Labour services are mentioned on the manor of Higham Comyn in 1253 and 1265,[61] of Higham Balliol in 1265,[62] and of Walthamstow Tony in 1264-5, 1309, and 1337.[63] On the last-named manor in 1437 there were four classes of customary tenant: 25 tenants held 8-acrelands, 25 16-acrelands, four 20-acrelands, and three 24-acrelands.[64] Those tenures suggest local adherence to a 16-acre virgate.[65] In general twice as many works were required of the 16-acreland as of the 8-acreland and so in proportion for all tenants. By 1437 1,325 out of 1,687 labour services had been commuted, harrowing, weeding, hay-making, and works at the mill at $\frac{1}{2}d.$ each, harvesting, carrying, mowing, and binding corn at 1d., reaping at 4d., and ploughing at 8d.[66]

In 1253 an acre of meadow at Higham was worth 18d., compared with 12d. for pasture and 4d. for arable.[67] In 1337 in Walthamstow Tony 100 a. of meadow was nearly twice as valuable as 240 a. of arable.[68] Other evidence of 1264, 1265, and 1315 emphasizes the importance of meadow land.[69] In 1437 in Walthamstow Tony manor a third of the year's income was derived from the sale of hay which realized more than any other single item of receipt and almost as much as the farm of land and pastures and rents of assize combined.[70] In Walthamstow Tony in 1264-5 more than half the demesne arable lay in the marsh.[71] This suggests that cultivation

[37] W. Wilson, *Manual of useful information* (1840), 39-40; Clarke, *Hist. Walthamstow* (1861), 13. For the alteration of the calendar see also above, p. 198.

[38] Ibid.; G. A. Blakeley, *Walthamstow marshes and lammas rights* (W.A.S. N.S. i), 8-9.

[39] See also p. 275.

[40] V.H.M., DTM 1 (1677-1704).

[41] V.H.M., DTM 9.

[42] Barns, *Vestry Mins. 1741-71*, 49; Wilson, *Manual of useful information*, 38.

[43] Clarke, *Hist. Walthamstow*, 13; V.H.M., DTM 9 (1873).

[44] V.H.M., P8/3/6; E.R.O., D/SH 3A f. 349; G. F. Bosworth, *George Monoux* (W.A.S. iii), 10. See also below, p. 313.

[45] Blakeley, *Walthamstow marshes*, 16-18.

[46] Bosworth, *Manor of Walthamstow Toni* (W.A.S. x), 16; V.H.M., P22/1/1; *Walthamstow Off. Guide* (1925), 18.

[47] Blakeley, *Walthamstow marshes*, 22-3; Walthamstow Corporation Act, 1934, 24 & 25 Geo. V, c. 53; *Walthamstow Corporation Bill: Mins. of Evidence: House of Lords (1956)*, 2, 17.

[48] *Proc. Epping Forest Com.* pp. 1876-7, 1886-9; E.R.O., D/DU 403/1-2, ff. 100, 113-15, 310, 454, 676, 797; D/DU 403/22, ff. 216, 233, 259, 269, 272.

[49] Fisher, *Forest*, 244, 310; V.H.M., DTM 6, 7; E.R.O., D/DU 403/1, f. 36.

[50] Lysons, *London*, iv. 204.

[51] W. Wilson, *Manual of useful information*, 41-2; E.R.O., D/DU 403/1, f. 400; *Epping Forest Com.: Rolls of Court of Attachments*, iii. 91, 131; *Proc. Epping Forest Com.* pp. 1906, 1911. See also below, p. 274.

[52] *Epping Forest Com.: Rolls of Court of Attachments*, ii. 142.

[53] E.R.O., D/DU 403/1, f. 400.

[54] See pp. 259, 274-5.

[55] E.R.O., D/DMg E12.

[56] V.H.M., DTM 6, 7.

[57] W.R.L., Septimus Morris's Epping Forest Fund scrapbook.

[58] E.R.O., D/DU 403/1-2 passim.

[59] E. N. Buxton, *Epping Forest*, 20, 169.

[60] G. F. Bosworth, *Manor of Walthamstow Toni* (W.A.S. x), 4; P. H. Reaney, *Court rolls of Rectory manor* (W.A.S. xxxvii), 9.

[61] C 132/14/15; C 145/26 (2).

[62] C 145/26 (2).

[63] C 132/31/3; C 145/26 (2); C 134/15/3; C 135/50/23.

[64] E.R.O., D/DU 36/14 (manorial *compotus*, 1437-8).

[65] Cf. Drayton (Mdx.): *Domesday of St. Paul's* (Camden Soc. 1st ser. lxix), 99.

[66] E.R.O., D/DU 36/14.

[67] C 132/14/15.   [68] C 135/50/23.

[69] C 132/31/3; C 145/26 (2); C 134/49/4.

[70] E.R.O., D/DU 36/14.

[71] C 132/31/3; C 145/26 (2).

was more concentrated on the west side of the manor, near the river Lea, much of it of inclosed marsh, until forest clearance, as already described, spread it eastward.

From the 16th century grassland appears generally to have predominated in the parish, and to have been carefully preserved.[72] A lease of Salisbury Hall in 1658 provided for payment of an additional £3 rent for every acre of meadow broken up for tillage, and also for every acre over 60 a. in any one year ploughed or kept in tillage.[73] There were estimated to be only 425 a. of arable in the parish in 1794.[74] Under pressure of wartime scarcity the acreage under cultivation was increased to 602 a. in 1795, and was 829 a. in 1801, though the average sown was then said to be 700 a.[75] The main crops in 1801 were wheat and oats (585 a.), with small crops of peas (80 a.), barley (63 a.), potatoes (61 a.), rye (24 a.), beans (14 a.), and turnips or rape (2 a.).[76] In 1815 the highest rated land was still inclosed meadow, assessed at 50s. an acre, compared with the best arable at 35s. an acre.[77]

In 1843 there were 2,628 a. of meadow and pasture and 915 a. of arable.[78] Robert Wragg, the coach-master,[79] was farming the largest area, some 312 a., including Clay Street and the Elms farms. Salisbury Hall farm comprised 224 a., and Low Hall, farmed by Charles Burrell, the cattle-dealer,[80] 228 a. About a dozen other farms varied from 45 a. to 130 a.[81] The local board, which bought Low Hall in 1875–7 for sewage disposal,[82] and later the district council, farmed it profitably for many years, mainly with cash crops. But as the area required for filtration grew, by 1907 only 36 a. remained for cropping.[83] The last 141 a. of Salisbury Hall were sold for building in 1904.[84] Building development and reservoir construction reduced agricultural land by 1905 to 853 a. of permanent grass and 265¾ a. of arable.[85] Two of the last of the larger farms to be broken up were Chestnuts (previously Clay Street) farm (67 a.) and Wadham Lodge farm (66 a.). Chestnuts farm was sold to the district council in 1919.[86] Wadham Lodge, devised to Wadham College, Oxford, by John Goodridge in 1652, and sold by the college in 1894 and 1898 to John Hitchman,

was sold as a sports ground and for building in 1919 and the years following.[87]

Hops were being grown at Moons in the late 16th century.[88] Two hopgrounds formed part of the Rectory manor estate in 1686, 1705, and 1732.[89] There were hopfields near Boundary Road up to the late 19th century.[90] An account of the osier grounds near Great Broadmead belonging to Salisbury Hall is given with that of its fishery below.[91] There were also osier grounds farther south in Walthamstow Tony.[92] Grapevines were grown in Sir William Batten's garden in the late 17th century, and according to Samuel Pepys the wine he bottled was acclaimed by his guests as good as any foreign wine.[93] Watercress beds were cultivated at Low Hall and in Higham Street in the late 19th century.[94]

Market- and nursery-gardening developed in the 19th century to meet the needs of London. In 1839 three nurserymen and gardeners were listed.[95] The acreage cultivated as nursery ground in 1843 was, however, probably under 10 a.[96] In 1863 there were 13 gardeners and 5 nurserymen and florists in business, but by 1906 only 1 market-gardener and 2 nurserymen were listed.[97] James Pamplin of Whipps Cross, who also had a nursery in Leyton,[98] was in business by 1839.[99] He appears to have taken over John Gollop's nursery on the east side of Wood Street about 1860.[1] Orange trees were grown at the nursery, which closed about 1893.[2]

Much of Walthamstow's grass supported stock for the London meat market. In 1437 William Honte, a London butcher, paid 26s. 8d. a year to lease the pasture called Oxleas,[3] which lay between the mill-stream and the Lea and is now under Maynard and Lockwood reservoirs.[4] The number of cases of sheep-stealing adjudicated in the late 16th and 17th centuries, some of them involving butchers, suggest that ample flocks of sheep, as well as beef cattle, were being reared.[5] Low Hall, then a farm of 220 a., was tenanted from at least 1837 until 1863 by Charles Burrell, a cattle and sheep salesman supplying Smithfield market, who equipped it with bullock house, cattle yards, pounds for sorting sheep and stock, and a slaughterhouse. The agent of Samuel Bosanquet, the landlord, considered that the farm's

[72] G. F. Bosworth, *Manor of Walthamstow Toni* (W.A.S. x),5; S. J. Barns, *Walthamstow Deeds, 1595–1890* (W.A.S. xi), 7; G. F. Bosworth, *Manor of Higham Bensted* (W.A.S. vi), 5; C.P. 25 (2)/12/65 Trin. 27 Hen. VIII; C.P. 25 (2)/653 Hil. 19 & 20 Chas. II; C.P. 25 (2)/294 Trin. 12 Jas. I; C.P. 25 (2)/295 Hil. 17 Jas. I; C.P. 25 (2)/1309 Trin. 23 Geo. III.

[73] S. J. Barns, *Walthamstow Deeds, 1541–1862* (W.A.S. xxi), 4.

[74] Lysons, *London*, iv. 204.

[75] Ibid.; H.O. 67/16. See also account of open fields given above.

[76] H.O. 67/16.

[77] V.H.M., PV 5 ff. 354–5.

[78] E.R.O., D/CT 382.

[79] See p. 250.   [80] See below.

[81] E.R.O., D/CT 382.

[82] See p. 283.

[83] V.H.M., Mins. Walthamstow Local Bd. 1885, 1891; *Walthamstow U.D.C. Chmns'. Ann. Reps.* 1899, 1906, 1907.

[84] G. F. Bosworth, *Manors of Salisbury Hall and Low Hall* (W.A.S. vii), 15.

[85] Bd. of Agric. Retn. of Acreages, 1905.

[86] E.R.O., *Sale Cat.* A300; G. F. Bosworth, *More Walthamstow houses* (W.A.S. xx), 28–9. The present town hall occupies the site.

[87] Bosworth, *More Walthamstow houses*, 32–3; P. H.

Reaney, *Walthamstow Place-names* (W.A.S. xxiv), 37; *Kelly's Dir. Essex* (1922, 1926); *Shernhall Methodist Ch. Jubilee Souvenir*, 6. See also below, p. 302.

[88] E.R.O., D/DFc 185 (1588, 1593 rentals of Higham Bensted).

[89] Reaney, *Walthamstow Place-names*, 43.

[90] A. Hatley, *Across the years* (W.A.S. N.S. ii), 72.

[91] See p. 267.

[92] S. J. Barns, *Walthamstow Deeds, 1595–1890* (W.A.S. xi), 12, 14.

[93] *Diary of Samuel Pepys* (ed. H. B. Wheatley), vii. 25–6.

[94] V.H.M., Local Bd. Mins. (lease of watercress beds, 1885, 1892); Hatley, *Across the years*, 26.

[95] *Pigot's Dir. Essex* (1839).

[96] E.R.O., D/CT 382 (s.v. John Gollop, James Pamplin, John Humphreys).

[97] *White's Dir. Essex* (1863); *Kelly's Dir. Essex* (1906).

[98] See p. 200.

[99] *Pigot's Dir. Essex* (1839); *White's Dir. Essex* (1848).

[1] *Kelly's Dir. Essex* (1859); E. Clarke, *Walthamstow* (1861), 101–5; Hatley, *Across the years*, 33, 44; G. Houghton, *Walthamstow, past and present*, 7, 24.

[2] *Kelly's Dir. Walthamstow, Leyton and Leytonstone* (1886–94); Hatley, *Across the years*, 33.

[3] E.R.O., D/DU 36/14.

[4] E.R.O., T/M 252.

[5] E.R.O., Calendar of Q/SR *passim*; Assizes 35, e.g. 35/35/H/63, 35/36/H/65, 35/56/H/55.

proximity to London increased its value to Burrell by 50 per cent, and that his rent of £2 10s. an acre could not possibly have been met from common farm produce.[6]

Only one cowkeeper was listed in Walthamstow from 1839 to 1859.[7] A dairyman was first listed in 1866.[8] By 1906 some 46 dairymen were listed, three of them being cowkeepers.[9] One of the three was John Hitchman, who came to Chapel End in 1867. He leased and later bought Wadham Lodge farm, and from 1886 also leased Clay Street or Chestnuts farm.[10] Hitchman began retailing milk in the 1880s. In 1918 the firm of John Hitchman and Sons, dairymen and cowkeepers, was bought out by D. A. Davies, a partner in the firm of Davies and Williams, dairymen in Walthamstow since the early years of the century. The firms were amalgamated as Hitchman's Dairies Ltd., based on Green Pond farm, Higham Hill Road, where cows were still being kept in 1926. In 1938 a large modern dairy for processing milk was opened on Walthamstow Avenue.[11] In 1968 Hitchman's, a member of the Unigate group, had branch dairies in South Chingford, Walthamstow, and Leytonstone.[12]

There were six fisheries in Walthamstow manor in 1066, reduced to one by 1086.[13] A fishery is mentioned in 1264,[14] and is called 'Pappiswer' in 1355.[15] In 1437 two fisheries are mentioned, 'Le Milhouse' and 'Pappeswere'.[16] The manor's free fishery in the Lea is described in 1636 and 1719 as extending from France meadow (Fleetmouth) to Smithy marsh.[17] In the 19th century it was known as the Walthamstow Ferry fishery or Day's Water, its headquarters being at the Ferry Boat inn. A 15-lb. salmon killed there in 1833 may have been the last to be recorded in the river Lea.[18] At Higham there was no fishery in 1086 although there had been 3½ in 1066.[19] In 1355 and 1557 Salisbury Hall held a weir or fishery on the Lea.[20] When the manor was granted to Robert Symonds in 1590 it included the fishery and the profits of osiers from Longers Lane (Hangers Bourne) to Fleetmouth.[21] When the fishery was sold with the manor in 1778 it extended to more than two miles and included a weir and 9 osier

grounds.[22] It was known as the Blue House fishery in 1848, when it was let to subscribers,[23] and as Game's Water in the 1890s. Shortly afterwards it disappeared with the building of the Banbury reservoir.[24]

Walthamstow mill in Coppermill Lane has been used for a variety of industries. A mill existed in Walthamstow manor in 1066 and 1086,[25] and is mentioned again in 1264,[26] 1265,[27] 1355,[28] and 1437.[29] In 1611 four mills are mentioned in association with the manor.[30] That and later references probably imply that at times the mill-stream powered more than one wheel on the same site.[31] The name Powder Mill marsh given to the marsh adjoining the mill in 1699[32] may be a survival from the years before the Civil War, when a number of gunpowder mills were established on the Lea.[33] In 1659 the mill was separated from the manor when Charles Maynard conveyed it to John Samyne of Bromley near Bow (Mdx.).[34] It is mentioned as a paper mill from 1653 to 1703, and the mill-stream was called the Paper Mill river to 1703.[35] In 1703 Pierre Montier a skin-dresser, is first named as the miller; leather mills are recorded on the site in 1710, 1712, and 1718.[36] Montier was followed in turn by Peter Lefevre (Lefebure) in 1711, and Daniel Lefevre in 1713, who was still the operator in 1723.[37] By the early 1740s, when a Mr. Kemp was the operator, linseed was being crushed to produce oil.[38] That business continued until 1806, when the oil mills, recently rebuilt, were put up for sale. The British Copper Co. bought them in 1808 to roll copper. From c. 1809–10 to 1814 the company issued 1d. and ½d. copper tokens, which were probably struck at the mill, as the buildings included a mint. The business was sold in 1824 to Henry Bath & Co. and in 1832 to Williams, Foster & Co., but the name British Copper Co. was retained.[39] The mill, which employed 30 hands in 1848, ceased rolling copper in 1857.[40] In 1860 it was bought by the East London Waterworks company for a pumping station. The Metropolitan water board was still using the mill in 1970, as a store and workshop. It is of stock brick with pantiled roof.[41] An Italianate tower with an

[6] E.R.O., D/DOp B26, D/DBq T12/1. For the Burrell family see also above, p. 200.
[7] Pigot's Dir. Essex (1839); Kelly's Dir. Essex (1855, 1859).
[8] Kelly's Dir. Essex (1866).
[9] Ibid. (1906).
[10] Hatley, Across the years, 54–5; Kelly's Dir. Essex (1870–86); Bosworth, More Walthamstow houses, 28–9, 32–3; V.H.M., Misc. Docs. No. 7(d).
[11] Kelly's Dir. Essex (1870–1926); Walthamstow Guardian, 7 Oct. 1949.
[12] G.P.O. Tel. Dir. (1968); Waltham Forest Off. Guide (1968), 54.
[13] V.C.H. Essex, i. 555.
[14] C 132/31/3.
[15] Cal. Inq. Misc. iii, p. 72.
[16] E.R.O., D/DU 36/14.
[17] S. J. Barns, Walthamstow Deeds, 1595–1890 (W.A.S. xi), 7, 12, 26.
[18] Bosworth, Manor of Walthamstow Toni, 18; V.C.H. Essex, ii. 590; Hatley, Across the years, 90–1.
[19] V.C.H. Essex, i. 537.
[20] Cal. Inq. Misc. iii, p. 72; S.P. 12/231/61.
[21] Morant, Essex, i. 36.
[22] V.H.M., Vestiges, no. 20.
[23] White's Dir. Essex (1848).
[24] Hatley, Across the years, 91.
[25] V.C.H. Essex, i. 555.
[26] C 132/31/3.
[27] C 134/15/3.
[28] Cal. Inq. Misc. iii, p. 72.
[29] E.R.O., D/DU 36/14.
[30] S. J. Barns, Walthamstow Deeds, 1595–1890 (W.A.S. xi), 7.
[31] Cf. accounts of West Ham and Leyton mills, pp. 89, 201.
[32] E.R.O., T/M 252. The name persisted to the 19th century: e.g. E.R.O., D/SH 1, f. 381; D/SH 3A, f. 349.
[33] V.C.H. Essex, ii. 452. See also above, pp. 77, 201.
[34] D. Smith, 'Industrial Archaeology of the Lower Lea Valley', East London Papers, xii (no. 2), 99; J. Coxall, Walthamstow Tokens (W.A.S. xviii), 10–11.
[35] R. S. Smith, Walthamstow in the early nineteenth century (W.A.S., Occ. Pubn. ii), 7; E.R.O., D/SH 1, ff. 24, 80, 102, 126, 171, 247.
[36] E.R.O., D/SH 1, f. 247, 528; V.H.M., Vestiges, no. 82.
[37] E.R.O., D/SH 1, ff. 422–596 passim. Daniel Lefevre cannot be traced further as there are no sewers presentments for some 15 years after 1723. For Peter Lefevre, see above, p. 93.
[38] J. Coxall, Walthamstow Tokens (W.A.S. xviii), 11; E.R.O. T/M 168, D/SH 2 f. 23.
[39] W.A.S., The Record, no. 8, pp. 5, 6; East Lond. Papers, xii (no. 2), 99; Coxall, Walthamstow Tokens, 8–9 and Supplement; V.H.M., Vestiges, no. 82.
[40] White's Dir. Essex (1848); Coxall, Walthamstow Tokens, 11.
[41] See plate f.p. 251.

open arcade to the upper storey was added on the west side by the water company in 1864.[42] The mill-house was demolished in 1941.[43]

Walthamstow windmill and cottage stood on the site of the present Oakhill Gardens and were built by John Hawkes, a Whitechapel millwright, about 1676.[44] The mill, which was a post mill, is shown on maps of 1699 and c. 1700. The latter map distinguishes it from Woodford manor windmill, with which it has often been confused.[45] It stood close to the boundary with Woodford, from which it was approached by Windmill Lane (now Fullers Road).[46] The miller, who was illegally selling beer at the mill in 1745–7, was licensed to do so in 1750.[47] The mill was blown down in 1800[48] and not rebuilt. The thatched mill cottage was demolished c. 1890.[49] The name Mill field at Higham Hill (1478 and later) suggests the existence of a mill there, but there is no direct record of one.[50]

Bricks and tiles were being made in the 17th century, mainly on the manorial forest waste at Higham Bushes, near the Bridle Path.[51] John Russell built a cottage and brick-kiln there about 1607, and was said in 1621 to be licensed to dig clay on 3 a. adjoining.[52] His son, George, who carried on his father's trade,[53] obtained a long lease from William Rowe in 1654/5 extending his rights over a further 36 a. The lease required that a brick and tile house of at least six rooms should be built on the site.[54] George Russell was still making tiles in 1684,[55] but how long his family continued to exploit the concession, which is said to have expired in 1796, is not known.[56] About 1814 the site lay waste, and the ancient brick house called Tile Kiln House was untenanted.[57] The house was pulled down by 1820.[58] In 1768 and 1772 Anthony Bacon granted Andrew Leverton, bricklayer, of Woodford, brother of Thomas Leverton,[59] long-term leases of brick- and tile-making rights over some 11 a. near the Russell workings. But William Hornby bought back the remainder of the leases in 1787, with the stock of bricks and all kilns and equipment,[60] probably to

remove a nuisance from the neighbourhood of Higham House and park. The pits formed by those early diggings, now overgrown, are a feature of the forest on either side of the Bridle Path.

Brickmaking revived in the late 19th century. One brickmaker was listed in 1861 and two in 1878,[61] and in the 1880s several new brickworks were established to meet an increasing local demand. Most of the new brickfields were in the north-west of the parish, notably Wilson's in Billet Road, Stotter's in Folly Lane, and Barltrop's at Chapel End near the Avelings.[62] All those brickworks had apparently closed by 1910.[63]

The local gravel was dug for profit as well as for road repair. In 1702 tenants of Walthamstow Tony were digging gravel and turf on the forest for sale outside the manor.[64] Excessive gravel-digging in the 19th century was an almost universal complaint of the forest commoners.[65] In 1812 the manorial bailiff was publicly selling gravel dug from a 6-acre pit[66] and from 1851 to 1872 increasingly large quantities of gravel, with sand, turf, and loam, were sold by the lord of the manor's agent from the Walthamstow Tony forest waste.[67]

Potteries were set up in Folly Lane, Higham Hill, in 1868 by William Pettit & Son, who produced unglazed pots, saucers, and chimney pots. When the tomato industry developed in the Lea valley production was switched to flower pots. The business closed about 1944.[68]

There were said to be 7 alehousekeepers and victuallers in 1631[69] and in 1670 8 licensed alehousekeepers and 4 unlicensed.[70] In 1769 there were 11 licensed houses; three of those had closed by 1801, and 8 were regularly licensed in 1801–28.[71] In 1848 there were 8 inns and 7 beerhouses, but by 1863 17 inns and taverns and 12 beerhouses,[72] or one public house to 246 persons in the parish. In 1911 there was one public house to 3,114 persons.[73]

A brewer was listed in 1848.[74] In 1859 there were two, one of them being William Hawes, who built the steam-powered Walthamstow Brewery in St.

[42] East London Papers, xii (no. 2), 100.
[43] W.A.S., The Record, no. 5, pp. 5–6.
[44] E.R.O., D/DMg T35.
[45] E.R.O., T/M 252 (photograph of A. Forbes's map of manor of High Hall, 1699) and D/DCw P1 (Map of Woodford manor demesne, c. 1700). For Woodford windmill, see below, p. 349.
[46] E.R.O., D/DCy P2A, D/DCy P3, ff. 185B and 187, D/CT 382 (no. 150); John Coe's map of Walthamstow, 1822 (W.A.S. N.S. v).
[47] V.H.M., DTM 2; Epping Forest Com.: Rolls of Court of Attachments, ii. 24.
[48] E.R.O., D/P 292/8/9 (12 Jan. 1801); W.A.S., The Record, no. 7; V.H.M., Vestiges, no. 24. The mill is actually shown on O.S. Map 1″ Essex (1805 edn.), but on the preliminary drawing for the map, 1799–1800, the windmill symbol has been struck through.
[49] V.H.M., Vestiges, no. 24; Essex Jnl. iii. 137–8; Bosworth, Some more . . . houses, 25–6; E.R.O., D/DMe T3/3, F1/10.
[50] E.R.O., D/DFc 185, f. 10, D/DB E64; P. H. Reaney, Place-Names of Walthamstow (W.A.S. xxiv), 38. Windmills shown on sketch maps prepared by John Long c. 1809 in an attempt to reconstruct the topography of Higham manor are not confirmed by other sources and may be conjectural: E.R.O., D/DXj 11, ff. 47, 99.
[51] For other scattered brickfields, see Forbes's map, 1699: E.R.O., T/M 252.
[52] Proc. Epping Forest Com. p. 1965; E.R.O., D/DU 99/14.
[53] E.R.O., Q/SR 366/47, 376/9, 376/37, 379/48, 422/118.
[54] E.R.O., D/DXj 10, ff. 162, 348, and 13, f. 2.

[55] G.L.C., DL/C/241, f. 179v.
[56] E.R.O., D/DXj 13, f. 2 and no. 173.
[57] E.R.O., D/DXj 10, f. 348; D/DXj 13 nos. 172–3.
[58] E.R.O., T/M 324; John Coe's Map of Walthamstow, 1822 (W.A.S. N.S. v.), no. 179.
[59] See p. 346. Thomas and Andrew were the sons of a Woodford builder, Lancelot Leverton; Andrew's son, William, was an architect, his daughter Jane married an architect, James Donaldson, and his grandson, Thomas Leverton Donaldson (1795–1885) was one of the founders of the R.I.B.A.: E.R.O., D/DXj 10, f. 225; D.N.B. (s.v. Thomas Leverton and Thomas Leverton Donaldson); Colvin, Biog. Dict. of Eng. Architects ,182, 364–5.
[60] E.R.O., D/DXj 10, ff. 214, 224, 233.
[61] E. Clarke, Walthamstow, 101–5; Kelly's Dir. Essex (1878).
[62] Kelly's Dir. Essex (1882–90); Hatley, Across the years, 13, 48; V.H.M., Local Bd. Mins. 1888, 1891.
[63] Kelly's Dir. Essex (1910).
[64] V.H.M., DTM 1.
[65] E.R.O., D/DU 403/1–2.
[66] E.R.O., D/DCy Z2 f. 189.
[67] E.R.O., D/DU 403/3, ff. 821–3.
[68] Hatley, Across the years, 26–7, 48; Kelly's Dir. Essex (1882–1926).
[69] Fisher, Forest, 87.
[70] Assizes, 35/111/3 no. 46.
[71] E.R.O., Q/RLv 24–82.
[72] White's Dir. Essex (1848, 1863).
[73] V.C.H. Essex, v. 58.
[74] White's Dir. Essex (1848

James Street.[75] The Essex Brewery Co. Ltd. was formed in 1871 to buy Hawes's brewery,[76] but apparently failed to attract subscribers, for the brewery was acquired by Collier Bros., who operated it as the Essex Brewery, until 1922. It was then sold to Tollemache's Breweries Ltd., to whom it still belonged in 1968.[77]

In the late 16th and 17th centuries Walthamstow traders were buying butter, cheese, eggs, and poultry, at Brentwood, Romford, Epping, and Waltham Abbey markets, to sell later by retail.[78] There was no market in Walthamstow until the early 1880s, when costermongers began to set up stalls in Marsh (now High) Street. The local board was at first unfriendly to them,[79] but by 1891 they had gained the support of local shopkeepers, and in 1892 the board tacitly accepted their presence by adopting regulations for stallholders.[80] Statutory powers to regulate street trading were first obtained by the borough council in 1932.[81]

An unusual early industry in Walthamstow was the minting of coins by contract for the royal mint. There are repeated references to moneyers from the late 16th century.[82] In 1664 30 hearths in moneyers' houses were exempted from tax.[83] Four consecutive members of the Collard family were appointed master moneyers between 1684 and 1791 when the last of them, James Collard, died.[84]

A weaver is mentioned in 1574.[85] In 1772 a workshop set up by Samuel Tull of London to spin pack thread, employing vagrant and workhouse labour, was closed by the parish vestry.[86]

Many of the inhabitants found employment with the gentry. In 1831 no less than 10·7 per cent of the population was in domestic service.[87] The families of the well-to-do supported a variety of luxury trades. Directories issued between 1823 and 1863 included lace-menders, hairdressers and perfumers, straw hat-, stay-, and umbrella-makers, china and toy dealers, and music teachers and piano tuners.[88]

Between the 1860s and 1890s the most important industrial growth was in the building trade. The number of builders listed in directories increased from 5 in 1866 to 37 in 1890.[89] Many small handicrafts were also springing up, most noticeably from c. 1874, such as the manufacture of fancy boxes,

venetian blinds, 'toy paper cap fireworks',[90] picture frames, umbrellas, baskets, looking glasses, and organs. Small firms making mechanical toys, furniture, surgical instruments, and ginger beer, were the forerunners of important industries which became established later.

In the 1890s manufacturing industry on a larger scale began to move into Walthamstow. The new population provided plenty of labour, and the opening of the Tottenham & Forest Gate railway in 1894 improved communications.[91] The most striking growth before 1918 was in electrical engineering, and in the manufacture of motor vehicles, scientific and photographic instruments and apparatus, and celluloid and casein compositions.[92] At the same time the variety of craft industries continued to grow, and included by 1905 such products as pattern cards, tinware, brushes, dolls' houses, billiard tables, pianos, lamps, scales, and baby carriages. Clothing firms, many of them employing outworkers, were mainly engaged in the collar, shirt, blouse, and neckwear trades. In 1910 23 cycle manufacturers were listed, representing about 16 per cent of those in Essex, though doubtless many of them were small works merely assembling components.[93] A pioneer but precarious venture launched before the First World War was the production of motion pictures. Glass and rubber goods, typewriter equipment, briar pipes, false teeth, and screws, all became significant local products before 1918.

The present large factory sites at Hale End and in Fulbourne Road, and the broad factory complex in Blackhorse Lane, originated in this early stage of Walthamstow's industrial growth. Other firms were dispersed mainly in Forest Road, High Street, Hoe Street, and Shernhall Street. In 1897 96 factories and workshops were registered for inspection. By 1912 the figure was 110 factories, 138 workshops, 458 workplaces, and 1,069 outworkers.[94] About a dozen firms were by then employing from 300 to 1,000 persons.[95]

In 1921, although Walthamstow, after West Ham, had the most highly developed industry in southwest Essex, over 58 per cent of the occupied population still depended on employment outside the

[75] E.R.O., D/DU 533/2; *Kelly's Dir. Essex* (1859–70); *White's Dir. Essex* (1863); E. Clarke, *Walthamstow*, 101–5.
[76] E.R.O., D/DU 533/2.
[77] *Kelly's Dir. Essex* (1874 and later edns.); G. F. Bosworth, *Some Walthamstow houses* (W.A.S. xii), 23; *Walthamstow Guardian*, 12 Aug. 1949; G.P.O. *Tel. Dir. London* (1968).
[78] E.R.O., Q/SR 55/49, 61/46, 68/22, 392/16, 393/11, 396/9, 397/14, 399/15, 493/63. Cf. *V.C.H. Essex*, v. 129, 165.
[79] W.A.S., *The Record*, no. 5, p. 3; V.H.M., Local Bd. Mins. 1886.
[80] V.H.M., Local Bd. Mins. 1891, 1892.
[81] Walthamstow Corporation Act, 22 & 23 Geo. V, c. 13 (Local Act).
[82] e.g. S. J. Barns, *Walthamstow Deeds, 1595–1890* (W.A.S. xi), 7, 14; E.R.O., Q/SR 460/4, D/AER 24, f. 198; and throughout the Essex quarter sessions rolls (E.R.O., Q/SR).
[83] E.R.O., D/DCv 1, f. 5v; cf. Act for establishing additional revenue . . . 13 & 14 Chas. II, c. 10, s. 20.
[84] G. F. Bosworth, *Some more Walthamstow houses* (W.A.S. xxix), 10.
[85] E.R.O., Q/SR 48/8.
[86] S. J. Barns, *Walthamstow Vestry Mins. . . . 1772–94* (W.A.S. xvi), 57.
[87] *Census*, 1831.

[88] *Pigot's Dir. Essex* (1823, 1839); *White's Dir. Essex* (1848, 1863); *Kelly's Dir. Essex* (1855, 1859).
[89] Unless otherwise stated this paragraph is based on *Kelly's Dir. Essex* (1866–1890) and *White's Dir. Essex* (1863).
[90] V.H.M., Local Bd. Mins. (1879).
[91] J. E. Martin, *Greater London and Industrial Geography*, 21, 49, 51–2. Unless otherwise stated general information on the distribution, date, and variety of industries established in Walthamstow from the 1890s to 1970 has been based on: *Kelly's Dir. Walthamstow, Leyton & Leytonstone* (1886–1908); *Kelly's Dir. Essex* (1890–1926); *Walthamstow Trades Dir.* (1953); Walthamstow Chamber of Commerce, *Year Book* (1953–4) and *Classified Dir.* (1955–6, 1965–6); *Kelly's Dir. London* (1956 and later edns.); G.P.O. *Lond. Postal Area Tel. Dir.* (1968). These sources have also been used to check and supplement those quoted in the notes on individual firms; for a few firms they are the sole evidence.
[92] *V.C.H. Essex*, v. 117; *Asea Electric Ltd.* (1949); *Sixty years of progress: a pictorial history of Fuller Electric Ltd.* (1898–1958).
[93] *Essex Jnl.* iii. 57.
[94] *Walthamstow U.D.C.: Chmns'. Ann. Reps.* (1897, 1912).
[95] A. T. Fryer, 'Walthamstow' (*The Home Missionary Field*, June 1913).

district.[96] Between the two world wars, however, industrial growth accelerated, particularly in the north-west of the town, where communications were further improved by the opening of the new Ferry Lane bridge in 1915, and completion of the North Circular Road in 1925–30.[97] After 1934 industrial settlement was encouraged in the south-west of the borough also by the council's promotion of the Lea Bridge factory estate at Low Hall.[98] New industries introduced in 1918–39 included the manufacture of security systems, luggage, paper and paper products, batteries, and ice cream.

During the Second World War the premises of several firms were damaged by bombing, but there were also firms which moved to Walthamstow when their premises were destroyed elsewhere, and after the war industry recovered rapidly. In 1951 it was estimated that although 53·6 per cent of the working population still travelled daily to work outside the borough, probably more workers than at any time found employment in local industries.[99] In 1954 the approximate numbers employed in the main productive industries were: general, electrical, and constructional engineering, 4,800; clothing, including footwear, 4,100; plastics goods, 3,000; furniture, including radio cabinets, 3,400; rubber goods, 2,100; mica goods, 1,600; metal goods, 1,500; scientific instruments and photographic equipment, 1,400; batteries, 1,100.[1]

Engineering, and the manufacture of plastic, rubber, and mica goods, and of furniture, continued to expand, but by 1961 there was a reduction in the numbers employed in the clothing trade.[2] Walthamstow was still, however, an important centre of the specialized trade of necktie-making. Outworking played a significant part in the impressive output achieved by small necktie firms.[3] In 1969 out of 79 necktie manufacturers listed in the London area 14 were settled in Walthamstow. Although several factories ceased in the 1950s and 1960s, new industries took their place, and in 1964–5 the Walthamstow council built a second factory estate at Brunner Road.[4] In 1967 the Waltham Forest council planned to enlarge the Lea Bridge factory estate alongside Staffa Road and Argall Avenue. The factory estates were designed to resite firms displaced by redevelopment.[5] In 1969 the main concentrations of industry were at Hale End, in Fulbourne Road, in Walthamstow Avenue and Billet Road, in Blackhorse Lane, and on the two council-owned industrial estates.

Most of the firms described below have been included for their long life, their size, or their unusual nature. They have been grouped according to the Standard Industrial Classification. Unless otherwise stated they were all still in production in 1968–9.

Food and drink manufacturers were among the earliest firms to become established. A. H. Simpkins, Ltd., mineral waters, was founded in 1887 at Forest Gate, moved to Grosvenor Park Road in 1889, and later to Hoe Street. The business ceased at some date after 1939.[6] Gillard & Co. Ltd., pickles and other foods, was founded by 1892 in High Street at the Chestnuts, which was renamed the Vintry Works. The present factory in Westbury Road was built in 1931.[7] Shales & Co. Ltd., ice cream, moved from Southend to Shernhall Street in 1934. Its premises were damaged by bombing during the Second World War.[8] The business ceased about 1959.

The manufacture of chemicals gained little foothold in Walthamstow. A branch plant of A. Boake, Roberts & Co. Ltd. of West Ham, since 1966 Bush, Boake, Allen Ltd., perfumery and flavour chemicals, was established in Blackhorse Lane about 1956.[9] Pharmaceutical preparations, however, have been represented for many years by Leslie's Ltd., medical dressings. Originally druggists' sundrymen of Leicester and Warwick, Leslie's, which moved to High Street in 1900, was one of the first two firms in Britain to develop self-adhesive plasters. The present factory in Higham Hill Road was built in 1937. It was damaged by bombing in the Second World War, and by fire in 1967.[10]

Engineering and the manufacture of electrical goods have dominated Walthamstow's industry. Peter Hooker Ltd., printers' engineers, commemorated in Hookers Road, was one of the earlier firms to settle in Blackhorse Lane, c. 1901. It ceased c. 1921. H.T.B. Ltd., engineers of printers' sheet-feeding machines, was founded in 1923 in Blackhorse Lane. About 400 workers were employed in 1949. In 1968 the company was a member of the Baird & Tatlock group.[11] W. B. Bawn & Co. Ltd., agricultural tractors, boilers, and road waggon tanks, moved to Blackhorse Lane in 1940 after being bombed out of Poplar. In 1945 its new premises were also damaged by bombing. The firm moved to Bury St. Edmund's (Suff.) in 1970, taking with them a conspicuous local feature: the life-size figure of a 17th-century naval helmsman, salvaged from the old premises at Poplar and re-erected over the Blackhorse Lane entrance.[12]

Two important firms specialized in scientific instruments and apparatus. Baird & Tatlock (London) Ltd., originally a Glasgow firm, then of Hatton Garden (Lond.), moved to Blackhorse Lane in 1902, taking over Higham Hill Lodge. In 1959 the company became a division of the Derbyshire Stone group, which came in turn to be associated with Tarmac Derby Ltd. In 1969 Tarmac Derby sold its interest in Baird & Tatlock, which became an associate of G. D. Searle & Co. Ltd. of U.S.A.

[96] *V.C.H. Essex*, v. 17, 19.
[97] W.A.S., *The Record*, no. 9, p. 6; V.H.M., *Vestiges*, no. 53; *Walthamstow Guardian*, 20 Mar. 1970 (Supplement); *Walthamstow Off. Guide* (1922), 11, (1925), 11, 13, (1929), 9, (1961), 73; G. F. Bosworth, *More Walthamstow houses* (W.A.S. xx), 22.
[98] A. D. Law, *Our Town*, ii (W.A.S. Occ. Pub. vii), 36; *Walthamstow Off. Guide* (c. 1939), 30.
[99] *Walthamstow Off. Guide* (1951), 21; V.H.M., *Vestiges*, no. 11; *Census*, 1951.
[1] *Walthamstow Off. Guide* (1954), 30–1.
[2] Ibid. (1961), 74.
[3] Martin, *Greater London*, 51–2, 172–4.
[4] *Walthamstow Independent*, 18 Oct. 1963, 24 Jan. 1964; *Walthamstow Guardian*, 20 Mar. 1970.

[5] *Walthamstow Guardian*, 16 June 1967.
[6] *Walthamstow Off. Guide* (1939), 14.
[7] Hatley, *Across the years*, 68, 73; Bosworth, *Some more Walthamstow houses*, 3; R.C.H.M. *Essex*, ii. 248; date on building. There were several houses called the Chestnuts in Walthamstow.
[8] *Walthamstow Guardian*, 27 May 1949.
[9] Martin, *Greater London*, 143. See also above, p. 82.
[10] *Walthamstow Guardian*, 6 May 1949; *Waltham Forest Off. Guide* (1968), 58, 107.
[11] *Walthamstow Guardian*, 24 July 1949; *Waltham Forest Off. Guide* (1968), 31.
[12] *Walthamstow Guardian*, 11 Feb. 1949, 10 July 1970.

There were some 600 employees in 1970.[13] Short & Mason Ltd., also previously of Hatton Garden (Lond.), moved to Macdonald Road in 1910. The firm supplied scientific instruments for the Scott and Shackleton polar expeditions and for Everest climbers. The business moved to Wood Street about 1958, and left Walthamstow about 1969 after merger in Taylor Instrument Companies (Europe) Ltd., Leighton Buzzard (Beds.), a subsidiary of Sybron Corp., U.S.A.[14]

Barnet Ensign Ross Ltd., photographic apparatus, originated in 1908, when Spratt Bros. of Hackney (Mdx.), a branch of Houghtons Ltd., established the Ensign Works in Fulbourne Road. Known later successively as the Houghton-Butcher Manufacturing Co. Ltd., Ensign Ltd., and, after union with Elliott & Sons Ltd. of Barnet, as Barnet Ensign Ltd., in 1948 the company amalgamated with Ross Ltd. as Barnet Ensign Ross Ltd. In 1949 the company had about 800 employees. In 1954 the business moved to a sister works at Clapham and its premises were acquired in the following year by Fuller Electric.[15]

Sainsbury Bros. Ltd., the Clock Factory, Blackhorse Road, specialized in church and turret clocks. The firm was in business c. 1882–1908.[16]

Asea (Great Britain) Ltd. and Fuller Electric Ltd. manufacture electric motors and transformers. The joint business originated in 1905, when the Fuller-Wenstrom Electrical Manufacturing Co., which assembled and distributed electric motors manufactured in Sweden, moved from West London to Blackhorse Lane. In 1906 the name of the company was changed to Fuller Electrical and Manufacturing Co., and in 1910 a second company was formed, Allmänna Svenska Electric Co. Ltd. The English and Swedish interests remained associated through all subsequent reorganizations. A new factory was built in Fulbourne Road in 1915, where the manufacture of transformers began in 1919. The factory, which was enlarged in 1923 and 1935–9, was damaged by bombing in 1944. The empty factory of Barnet Ensign Ross on the opposite side of Fulbourne Road was bought in 1955 and renamed the West Works. Branch factories at Poplar, Birmingham, and Leyton were then closed and their work transferred to Walthamstow, where some 1,000 workers were employed. In 1957 Fuller Electric was acquired by the Brush group, which in turn merged with the Hawker Siddeley group. By agreement with Asea (Great Britain) Ltd., a subsidiary of Allmänna Svenska Elektriska Atkiebolaget of Sweden, the company continued under licence to manufacture the Swedish type of motor and transformer.[17]

The Micanite & Insulators Co. Ltd., insulating materials, originated as the Mica Insulator Co. Ltd. formed in 1901 at Stansted Mountfitchet, and removed to Blackhorse Lane in 1902. The firm, which employed large numbers of women and girls, built a larger factory in 1907. It was extended again in 1928–9, when associations were formed with Associated Electrical Industries Ltd. and English Electric Co. Ltd. In 1939 a subsidiary, British Tego Gluefilm Ltd., went into production. The number of employees rose from about 600 during the First World War to about 1,700 in 1955. In 1958 the company became an associate of the A.E.I. group, which was a subsidiary in 1969 of the General Electric and English Electric Companies Ltd.[18]

Philips Records Ltd. bought a factory in Walthamstow Avenue in 1958, which became one of the most modern pressing plants in Europe.[19] The Ever Ready Co. (Great Britain) Ltd., batteries, built a factory in Forest Road in 1931–2, which replaced a number of smaller plants.[20] Associated Fire Alarms Ltd., originally a Bethnal Green firm, took over premises in Sutherland Road in 1920. In the 1950s the works were moved to Claremont Road. In 1960 the company became associated with a burglar alarm group, Auto-Call, and in 1961 the Billet Road premises of King's Laundries were bought. There were over 300 employees at the two factories in 1965.[21]

The vehicle industry was one of the earliest to develop in Walthamstow, mainly in Blackhorse Lane. The Central Cycle & Motor Works and the Relyante Motor Works Ltd. were established there by 1905, the Vanguard Motor Omnibus Co. in 1906, and the Motor Omnibus Construction Co. by 1907. In 1908 the London General Omnibus Co. took over Vanguard, and in 1911 formed the Associated Equipment Co. Ltd. (A.E.C.), which manufactured omnibuses in Walthamstow until 1926–7, when the firm moved to Southall (Mdx.).[22] An employee at one of the motor vehicle works near the Standard public house in Blackhorse Lane in 1910 later published an account of working conditions there.[23]

The Bremer Engineering Co., Grosvenor Park Road, listed 1912–26, was apparently a motor cycle business. But its founder, Frederick Bremer (1872–1941), had built in 1892–4 the first British car with an internal combustion engine. The Bremer car was run by its designer on the Woodford New Road, preceded by a red flag, but was never put into production. The prototype, however, survived. It was given by Bremer to the Vestry House museum in 1933, was restored in 1962–3, and completed the veteran car run to Brighton in 1965.[24] In 1947 the Ford Motor Co. established a subsidiary

[13] Ibid. 3 June 1949; G. F. Bosworth, *More Walthamstow houses* (W.A.S. xx), 24; *Waltham Forest Off. Guide* (1968), 93; *Who owns whom* (1969); inf. from Baird & Tatlock (London) Ltd., Blackhorse Lane. For Higham Hill Lodge, see also above, p. 249.
[14] *Walthamstow Guardian*, 14 Jan. 1949; *Who owns whom* (1969).
[15] *Barnet Ensign Ross Ltd.: a significant alliance* (c. 1948); *Walthamstow Guardian*, 1 July 1949, 20 Aug. 1954.
[16] V.H.M., *Vestiges*, no. 18.
[17] Asea Electric Ltd., *Hist. of Asea Electric Ltd. and Fuller Electrical and Manufacturing Co. Ltd., of London, during fifty years' development* (1949); Fuller Electric Ltd., *Sixty years of progress: a pictorial history of Fuller Electric Ltd.* (1898–1958); Martin, *Greater London*, 22, 103; *Walthamstow Guardian*, 7 Oct. 1955; *Walthamstow Mercury & Post*, 16 Oct. 1958.

[18] *Electrical Times*, 4 Feb. 1935; Micanite and Insulators Co. Ltd., *M. and I.: 50 years folio* (1951), and *The first 60 years, 1901–1961*; Martin, *Greater London*, 22, 122; *Who owns whom* (1969).
[19] *Waltham Forest Off. Guide* (1968), 113.
[20] *Ever Ready Co. (Great Britain) Ltd. 1901–1951* (1953); Martin, *Greater London*, 123.
[21] *Walthamstow Guardian*, 4 Feb. 1949, 27 Oct. 1961, 21 Feb. 1964, 3 Sept. 1965; *Walthamstow Post*, 2 Apr. 1953.
[22] W.A.S., *The Record*, no. 1, pp. 3–4; Martin, *Greater London*, 44. See also *V.C.H. Middlesex*, iv. 48.
[23] R. M. Fox, *Smoky Crusade* (1938), 58–82.
[24] *The East Briton*, iii (1), 1–3; Hatley, *Across the years*, 46; *Waltham Forest Off. Guide* (1968), 17–18; V.H.M., *The Bremer Car—its history and restoration*, and biographical inf. (TS.)

engineering plant in Blackhorse Lane, which ceased about 1967.[25]

The aircraft pioneer, A. V. Roe (1877–1958), in 1909 achieved on the marshes the first powered flight of a British aircraft, the Triplane, built under the railway arches.[26]

Metal goods manufactured in Walthamstow varied widely. H. C. Jones & Sons (Walthamstow) Ltd., Tower Hamlets Road, were established as sheet metalworkers in Walthamstow before 1901.[27] By 1957 the firm was specializing in dustbins. About 1964–5 it moved to Barking. Collinson's Precision Screw Co. Ltd. was founded in 1916 in Macdonald Road. The present factory in Forest Road was built in 1933 and enlarged in 1939.[28] Hobbs, Hart & Co. Ltd., strong-room doors, locks, and safes, was one of the first firms to settle on the Lea Bridge factory estate, where extensive works built in Staffa Road were in production by 1935. About 1965 the company became a subsidiary of Chubb & Son Ltd.[29]

The outstanding business in leather goods is S. Noton, Ltd., manufacturer of 'Crown' luggage. The company, founded in 1928, went into production in Blackhorse Lane in 1929. In 1949 there were 450 employees. In 1968 the company was the largest manufacturer in Europe of moulded luggage for air travel.[30]

Among clothing manufacturers probably the oldest is Hookways Ltd., previously Hookway, Sons & Cook. Founded in Aldersgate Street (Lond.), Hookways moved to Hoe Street in 1899 and built its present factory in Forest Road in 1899–1900. The firm, which originally made collars, braces, and umbrellas, by 1949 was specializing in high-grade poplin shirts.[31] E. Garner Ltd., dresses and suits, originated in 1904 as a small private dressmaking business in Elmsdale Road. In 1911 a factory, mainly for blouses, was opened in High Street, where a larger factory was built in 1929, soon after the firm started to make dresses.[32] L. S. & J. Sussman Ltd., shirt-makers, settled in Forest Road in 1940 after being bombed out of Bishopsgate (Lond.),[33] and remained until c. 1955, when the firm moved to Leyton. Rael-Brook Ltd., shirts, moved its head office to Forest Road, where it already had one of its factories, in 1964. The firm was owned in 1969 by English Calico Ltd.[34]

Among manufacturers of weatherproof clothing, the Express Rubber Co. Ltd., makers of Telemac and Mattamac, moved to Forest Road from Leyton about 1935[35] and remained until about 1956. Aquascutum rainwear was manufactured in Forest Road for a few years in the 1950s.[36]

Duroglass Ltd., laboratory glassware, built a factory in Blackhorse Lane during the First World War. It closed in 1926, but reopened in 1932 to produce lighting glassware and, later, television components.[37] The firm ceased about 1965, when the premises were taken over by Industrial Glass Co. Ltd., which itself ceased by 1968.

Furniture of all kinds has always featured among Walthamstow's products. Libraco Ltd., library furniture, is listed in directories from 1912 to 1926. F. Wrighton & Sons Ltd., high-class domestic furniture, previously at Brampton Road, Hackney (Mdx.) and briefly, 1929–32, in Leyton, built the Brampton Works on a six-acre site in Billet Road in 1933. In 1949 the firm had two subsidiaries, Globe-Wernicke Ltd., bookcases, and Wrighton Aircraft Ltd. The former was discontinued about 1967.[38]

Several important firms manufactured paper and paper and board products. T. J. Wright & Sons, Ltd., pattern card makers, were established in Blackhorse Lane by 1902. The business appears to have ceased about 1954. A. E. Bangham & Co. Ltd., paper hats and novelties, was founded in 1925 in Grove Road, with six workers. The firm moved to Borwick Avenue in 1936. Its premises were damaged by bombing in 1940 and 1944 but were rebuilt in 1945. In 1949 100 workers and 100 outworkers were employed. Later the firm moved to the old motion picture studio in Wood Street. A new factory was built on the site when the studio was burned down in 1959.[39] St. Andrew Mills Ltd., makers of paper and paper goods such as tissues, opened in 1932 in St. Andrew Road. A factory was built near the mills in 1949. In 1955, when the mills were taken over by Bowater-Scott Corporation Ltd., there were 400 employees.[40]

Printing, and publishing of newspapers, are two of Walthamstow's oldest industries. The printing firm of James Phelp, Beulah Road, was founded in 1862. In 1870 Phelp assisted in printing Walthamstow's first weekly newspaper, the *Walthamstow Chronicle and Leyton Intelligence*, owned and edited by another printer, Joseph Shillinglaw. Phelp also produced a paper of his own, the *Gazette*, in 1870 and 1880. As J. C. Phelp & Son his firm continued until c. 1955.[41] The Walthamstow Press Ltd. was formed about 1923 to print the *Walthamstow Guardian*, founded in 1876 and previously printed in London. It bought the premises and plant of W. H. Everett, a High Street printer then recently deceased. In 1935 it moved to Guardian House in Forest Road, where a new foundry and rotary plant were installed. In 1937 the Press took over another local firm of printers, Buck Brothers & Harding Ltd., a partnership formed in 1912 by two older firms.[42]

[25] Martin, *Greater London*, 96; *Waltham Forest Off. Guide* (1968), 107.
[26] *Essex Jnl.* vi. 13; W.A.S. *The Record*, no. 2, pp. 4–5; V.H.M., Illus. Colln.
[27] *Walthamstow Off. Guide* (1951), 64.
[28] *Walthamstow Guardian*, 10 June 1949.
[29] *Walthamstow Off. Guide* (1935), 1, 31, 33; *Who owns whom* (1969).
[30] *Walthamstow Guardian*, 28 Jan. 1949; *Walthamstow Forest Off. Guide* (1968), 111.
[31] *Walthamstow Guardian*, 28 Oct. 1949; Martin, *Greater London*, 51–2.
[32] *Walthamstow Guardian*, 11 Mar. 1949; *Walthamstow Post*, 15 Mar. 1951.
[33] *Walthamstow Guardian*, 20 May 1949; *Walthamstow Post*, 1 Mar. 1951.
[34] *Waltham Forest Off. Guide* (1968), 113; *Who owns whom* (1969).

[35] *Walthamstow Guardian*, 25 Mar. 1949; *Leyton Off. Guide* (1934, 1937).
[36] *Walthamstow Off. Guide* (1951, 1954). See also above, p. 202.
[37] *Walthamstow Post*, 22 Mar. 1951.
[38] Ibid. 11 Dec. 1958; *Walthamstow Guardian*, 14 Oct. 1949; *Essex Jnl.* iii, 56–7; inf. from F. Wrighton & Sons Ltd., Billet Road, E.17; *Who owns whom* (1969).
[39] *Walthamstow Guardian*, 8 July 1949; Martin, *Greater London*, 200; W. Tonkin, *Showtime in Walthamstow* (W.A.S., Occ. Pub. ix), 29. For the motion picture studio, see below, under motion picture industry.
[40] *Walthamstow Guardian*, 1 Apr. 1949, 4 Feb. 1955.
[41] R. G. C. Desmond, *Our local press* (W.A.S. n.s. iii), 14, 18.
[42] Ibid. 16–17, 40–1. The Walthamstow Press should not be confused with another of the same name founded in 1905 and ceased 1908: ibid. 27.

Among other miscellaneous industries the Stepney Tyre & Rubber Co. Ltd., established in Blackhorse Lane by 1919,[43] ceased about 1958. R. A. Rooney & Sons Ltd., brush manufacturer, moved from London to its present premises in Higham Hill Road in 1901 and enlarged them in 1920. Many outworkers were employed in this trade.[44] The Crusader Manufacturing Co. Ltd., typewriter supplies, was founded about 1914 in Berwick Road. It moved in 1968 to the new Brunner Road industrial estate. Hollebrand Brothers, Farnborough Avenue, makers of briar pipes, was founded about 1914. Another briar pipe manufacturer, Hardcastle Pipes Ltd., moved in 1936 from Camden Town to Coronation Works in Forest Road.[45] The business ceased about 1968.

Toys have been manufactured on a large scale in Walthamstow for many years. A. Wells & Co. Ltd., later known as Wells-Brimtoy Distributors Ltd., mechanical toys, was established about 1920 in Somers Road. Between the World Wars it captured a large part of the German trade. The factory was moved some time after 1938 to Stirling Road, where there were about 700 employees in 1949. The works closed about 1965.[46] Britains Ltd., metal toys including authentically designed model soldiers, built a factory in Sutherland Road in 1951. In 1966 the firm adopted plastic in place of metal. The factory was transferred in 1968 to a new four-acre site in Blackhorse Lane.[47]

The plastics industry developed very early in Walthamstow. In 1896 British Xylonite, the first large outside company to move into Walthamstow, bought Jack's Farm (50 a.) at Hale End and opened a factory built there in 1897. The company pioneered the manufacture of celluloid in Britain and in 1921 began to produce lactoid, a non-inflammable substitute for it. In 1939 the Xylonite group was formed in association with the Distillers Co. Ltd. The Hale End works, under the name of Halex Ltd., became the centre of production of the group's plastics goods, such as combs and toothbrushes, with virtually a monopoly of table-tennis balls. In 1949 there were some 1,000 employees. A new factory was opened in 1960. In 1969 Halex Ltd. and British Xylonite Co. Ltd. were owned by Bakelite Xylonite Ltd.[48] National Plastics Ltd., plastics building components, moved to Walthamstow Avenue from Birmingham about 1953. In 1963 Celanese Building Components Ltd., a member of the Courtauld's group, joined them there to market their products.[49]

An unusual industry at Walthamstow was the production of motion pictures.[50] The Precision Film Co. built a studio at Whipps Cross in 1910. It ceased production in 1915. The British & Colonial Kinematograph Co. took over a roller skating rink in Hoe Street as studios in 1913. The company employed such actors as Jack Buchanan and Lilian Braithwaite, and produced *When London Sleeps* (1914) and *The Battle of the Somme* (1916). It was dissolved in 1924. The Cunard Film Co. Ltd. built a studio in Wood Street in 1913–14. Among its 'stars' were Gladys Cooper and Owen Nares. The company, which ceased in 1915, included *The Call of the Drum* (1914) among its productions. The Broadwest Film Co. took over the Wood Street studio in 1916 and specialized in filming novels and stage plays. Among its actors were Matheson Lang and Ronald Colman. The company went bankrupt in 1924 and its studio was taken over by British Filmcraft Ltd. in 1926. Its productions included a series on Dick Turpin filmed on location in Epping Forest. The industry was, however, struggling unsuccessfully against competition from Hollywood. The Wood Street studio was still in use in 1931–2 by Metropolitan Films Ltd., and in 1932 by Audible Filmcraft Ltd., but after 1933 it was occupied as a factory. It was burned down in 1959. The factory of A. E. Bangham & Co. Ltd.[51] occupies the site.

MARSHES. Walthamstow was one of the levels under the jurisdiction of the Havering and Dagenham commissioners of sewers.[52] It was not included in a survey of their levels in 1563,[53] but was rated in 1604 and 1613, and regularly from 1633.[54] The level extended from Fleetmouth to the Leyton boundary, and comprised the marshland lying between the river Lea and Dagenham brook, together with the meadows bordering the east bank of the brook. In 1747 it was measured as 809 a., of which 149 a. were open and 660 a. inclosed. There was little change for over 100 years; in 1850 144 a. were still open.

A marsh bailiff and a treasurer were appointed for the level, responsible to the commissioners, and a marsh jury to present defects. The bailiff saw that the orders of the court of sewers were carried out; he had no connexion with the manorial marsh bailiff, whose duties were associated with the agricultural use of the marshland and common rights of the inhabitants, which are described elsewhere.[55] The commissioners' concern was to maintain the drainage system of the level. To this end they levied an acreage rate on the owners and occupiers of lands in the level. Walthamstow was usually the lowest rated level under the commissioners' jurisdiction, assessed at a few pence only, having no problem from tidal flooding like the Thames-side levels, and no walls against the Lea to maintain. The court's orders related mainly to dragging and scouring ditches and sewers, cutting back willows, maintaining the banks of the Fleet or mill-stream, and pre-

[43] *Petition for Incorporation*, 1919, 6; *Walthamstow Guardian*, 18 Nov. 1949.
[44] *Walthamstow Guardian*, 15 July 1949.
[45] Ibid. 25 Feb. 1949.
[46] Ibid. 21 Jan. 1949; *Walthamstow Post*, 26 Dec. 1957; *Walthamstow Off. Guide* (1951), 69; inf. from Walthamstow Ref. Library.
[47] *The Builder*, 1 June 1951; *Walthamstow Post*, 1 May 1958; *Walthamstow Guardian*, 24 Dec. 1967.
[48] *British Xylonite Co. Ltd.: Fifty years, 1877–1927*; *The Xylonite Group: Seventy-five years, 1877–1952*; *Walthamstow U.D.C. Chmn.'s Ann. Rep.* (1896); *Walthamstow Guardian* 15 Apr. 1949, 23 Sept. 1960, *Walthamstow Post*, 22 Feb. 1921; *Who owns whom* (1969).

[49] *Walthamstow Guardian*, 20 Aug. 1954; *Waltham Forest Off. Guide* (1968), 95.
[50] The account of the motion picture industry is based on W. Tonkin, *Showtime in Walthamstow* (W.A.S., Occ. Pub. ix), 9, 24–5.
[51] See p. 272.
[52] *V.C.H. Essex*, v. 33.
[53] E.R.O., D/SH 7.
[54] E.R.O., D/SH 26, ff. 57–8. The following account is based, unless otherwise stated, on records of the Havering and Dagenham commissioners of sewers: E.R.O., D/SH 1–3, 3A, 4, 5, 26, 29; V.H.M., Map of Walthamstow Level by John Noble 1747.
[55] See p. 264.

venting the occupant of the mill from penning up so much water that it overflowed them. The court also supervised foot-bridges laid across the common sewers.

From the mid 19th century the commissioners' responsibilities were increased by the construction of the railway and water companies' works on the marshland, requiring modification from time to time of the elaborate marsh drainage system. From the 1870s the commissioners waged an unremitting and successful campaign against a new threat, pollution of the watercourses by domestic sewage.[56] The recurring flood risk, however, remained their chief preoccupation.[57]

In 1934, under the Land Drainage Act, 1930, the Lee conservancy catchment board took over responsibility for the Walthamstow marshes from the commissioners of sewers.[58] Parliamentary sanction was given in 1938 to the construction of a flood relief channel from Tottenham through Walthamstow, eastward of the reservoirs, to an outfall in Leyton. Work on the channel, delayed by the Second World War, began in 1950.[59] The scheme involved building bridges to carry both railway lines and Forest Road over the new channel, and the diversion and filling in of parts of the Dagenham brook, Higham Hill sewer, and Blackmarsh sewer. The work was completed in 1960.[60]

FOREST. Walthamstow lay wholly in the royal forest of Waltham.[61] In the Middle Ages it was in the bailiwick of Becontree hundred.[62] When the forest was reorganized in smaller 'walks' in the 16th century, a Walthamstow walk was formed.[63]

The chief forester or master keeper of the Walthamstow walk was appointed by the lord warden, usually for life, with a yearly fee of £12 paid by the exchequer and an allowance of 20 loads of dead logwood and a buck and doe annually.[64] The salary seems to have ceased by 1711.[65] W. T. Copeland, master keeper in 1857, stated in 1863 that his office was then virtually in abeyance. There were two underforesters for the walk in 1630, but only one by 1711, paid £20 a year by the Crown.[66] The lords of the manors of Walthamstow Tony and Higham Bensted both claimed in the 17th century to appoint their own

woodwards.[67] The Walthamstow forest reeve, first mentioned in 1489,[68] was appointed by the vestry and sworn at the court of attachments.[69] He had charge of the key of the pound and the parish marking iron, the Walthamstow mark being the letter 'O' surmounted by a crown.[70] After 1878 the reeve was appointed by the forest conservators.[71]

By 1721 the stock of deer in the forest was diminishing, and to conserve them a ban on killing them in the walk, including fee deer, was imposed for 3 years.[72] Further restraints were imposed in 1744, 1748, 1754, and 1770.[73] By 1844 there were said to be only 3 or 4 brace in the walk and in 1848 3 brace.[74] In 1863 Copeland stated that he had only had a buck as fee deer once in his life.[75]

The numbers of deer went on dwindling in spite of official restraint because the depredations of poachers,[76] in particular the theft of fawns,[77] and the progressive destruction of their feeding grounds and cover,[78] continued. The widespread clearance of woodland and its inclosure for cultivation which took place in the Middle Ages has been described elsewhere.[79] By the 17th century the deer depended for survival mainly on the belt of open forest which remained on the east side of the parish between Whipps Cross and Chingford Hatch, then estimated as 442 a. in Walthamstow Tony manor[80] and 400 a. in Higham Bushes *alias* The Sale in Higham Bensted manor.[81]

During the next two hundred years the exploitation of Higham Bushes by the lords of the manor of Higham progressively shut out the deer or reduced their means of support in the north-east of the parish. The commoners' rights, described elsewhere,[82] were also eroded. The break-up of Higham Bushes was apparently begun in the mid 17th century by Sir William Rowe, who is said to have sold the timber on the inner 150 a. and fenced it,[83] and to have granted to the Russell family extensive long-term rights to dig gravel and brickearth, and to lop timber, outside the fence.[84] The fenced area was usually known as The Sale and the area outside it as Higham Bushes or Allens Lops. When Higham House was built in 1768 on The Sale's boundary with Woodford[85] Anthony Bacon, followed by his successors, William Hornby and John Harman, sought to convert The Sale into a private park.[86]

[56] See p. 283.
[57] E. Walford, *Greater London* (1898), i. 456; G. A. Blakeley, *Walthamstow Marshes* (W.A.S. N.S. i), 8.
[58] *V.C.H. Essex*, v. 79.
[59] Ibid. 80.
[60] Lee Conservancy Catchment Board Act, 1938, 1 & 2 Geo. VI. c. 91; *V.C.H. Essex*, v. 79; *Lee Cons. Catchment Bd., Visits of Inspection to works in the Lower Reaches*, 1960, 1961. See also above, p. 203.
[61] W. R. Fisher, *Forest of Essex*, 31, 395.
[62] Ibid. 137.
[63] Ibid. 382–3; *E.R.* xiv. 193–5.
[64] Fisher, *Forest*, 146–8; *Epping Forest Commission: Rolls of Court of Attachments*, i. 136. Rep. Sel. Cttee. on Royal Forests (Essex), *1863*. H.C. 339, pp. 34–5, 100 (1863) vi. For grants of the office, 1661–1831, usually for life, see E.R.O., D/DCw T1, D/DB T1132; there is an incomplete list of keepers, 1590–1857, in Fisher, *Forest*, 382–3.
[65] *Cal. Treas. Bks.* xxv. 120.
[66] *Rep. Sel. Cttee. on Royal Forests* (Essex), *1863* . . . 35, 101; Fisher, *Forest*, 145–6, 383; *Cal. Treasury Bks.* xxv. 120, xxvi. 547, et seq.; *Epping Forest Com.: Rolls* . . . ii. 40 (1754), iii. 93 (1809).
[67] Fisher, *Forest*, 174; E.R.O., D/DXj 10, f. 344.
[68] Fisher, *Forest*, 177–8.

[69] E.R.O., D/DU 403/1, f. 400.
[70] Fisher, *Forest*, 270, pl. f.p. 299; W. Wilson, *Manual of Useful Information*, 41–2; *Proc. Epping Forest Com.* p. 1911. For the reeve's duties, see also above, p. 265.
[71] W.R.L., Epping Forest Fund Scrapbook.
[72] *Epping Forest Com.: Rolls* . . . i. 54.
[73] Ibid. i. 171, ii. 7, 24, 30, 41, 103.
[74] E.R.O., D/DCy Z3, ff. 81, 100.
[75] *Rep. Sel. Cttee. on Royal Forests* (Essex), *1863* . . . 34.
[76] For cases see throughout *Epping Forest Com.: Rolls of Court of Attachments*, i–iv.
[77] e.g. E.R.O., Q/SBb 417/19.
[78] Cf. E.R.O., D/DXj 10, f. 398.
[79] See p. 264.
[80] E.R.O., T/M 252 (photograph of map of Walthamstow by A. Forbes, 1699: original framed in W.R.L.).
[81] E.R.O., D/DXj 18, f. 17 (cf. ff. 7, 14, 15, 18). See also above, p. 259.
[82] See p. 265.
[83] E.R.O., D/DXj 10, ff. 340, 347.
[84] E.R.O., D/DXj 10, ff. 348–9; D/DXj 13, f. 2; D/DXj 18, f. 20. For the Russell family's brick- and tile-making operations, see above, p. 268.
[85] See p. 260.
[86] E.R.O., D/DXj 10, ff. 394–7; *Epping Forest Com.: Rolls* . . ., ii. 85, 91, 96, 130.

After the forest verderers had declared in 1787 that Hornby's inclosure plans, if carried out, would ruin the deer and virtually disafforest that part of the walk, much recently erected paling was taken down, and customary roads and ridings through The Sale were reopened.[87] But when John Harman called in Humphry Repton to replan the grounds in 1793, Repton's plans included a sunk pale to exclude the deer from part of the park.[88] Development of Repton's plans led to further objections from the court of attachments in 1794–5. The court accepted the creation of the lake formed by widening the brook, because the water would benefit the deer, but only licensed the inclosure of Great and Little Sale Woods on the flanks of the park on condition that the deer were still free to pass in and out.[89] In 1820 the deer still had pasturage over 250 a. of the 323 a. which comprised the Higham House estate.[90] But in the following year Jeremiah Harman bought the Crown's forest rights in the manor wastes of Higham Hills, estimated at some 300 a., for £1,232, paying the lord warden £352 as compensation for the loss of his rights.[91] From 1821, therefore, the deer could be excluded from the Higham manor wastes at will.

Inclosure in Walthamstow Tony manor was by contrast negligible: 76 grants of waste made between 1700 and 1877 totalled only 10 a.[92] One of these grants, made in 1725, gave John Salter the 1 a. site at Forest Rise on which 'Salter's Buildings', including Forest Hall, were erected.[93]

By 1843 there was some 262 a. of open forest left in Walthamstow Tony manor (including Gilberts Slade and part of the Slip), but only about 157 a. to the north in Higham manor.[94] Between 1851 and 1866 a further 96 a. was inclosed in Higham Bushes, by then usually known as Higham Hills.[95] In 1877 about 240 a. of open forest remained in Walthamstow Tony, still subject to Crown rights, but the open manor waste of Higham Hills, between Chingford Hatch and Oak Hill, was reduced to 13 a.[96]

The forest in Walthamstow was by then a popular resort, visited by thousands in the summer months.[97] The movement to preserve the forest for the public was supported by the Epping Forest Fund Com-

mittee, formed in 1871, of which Septimus Morris of Walthamstow was an active member.[98] In 1876 the corporation of London bought from the Warner trustees some 122 a. of the manor waste of Higham Hills, with the forest rights. This purchase lay partly north-east of Highams Park, where the golf course was later laid out, and partly south of the park, as far as Oak Hill, and was to be held as open space for ever.[99] Following this, under the Epping Forest Act, 1878, about 300 a. of forest in Walthamstow was dedicated to the public. In 1891 a further 30 a. on the west of Highams Park, comprising a long narrow slip which was the last remnant of The Sale, and included the lake, was bought by the corporation of London as forest conservators from (Sir) Courtenay Warner; contributions towards the purchase were made by the local boards of Walthamstow and Woodford, and public subscription.[1] This addition linked the isolated portion of the forest bordering Chingford Lane with the rest of the forest to the south, at Hale End, so that once more Walthamstow's forest formed a continuous belt from Chingford Hatch to Whipps Cross, comprising in 1963 some 360 a.[2]

LOCAL GOVERNMENT AND POOR-RELIEF

TO 1836. Ralph de Tony was holding view of frankpledge in Walthamstow *c.* 1278.[3] In 1592 quarter sessions ordered the countess of Rutland to provide ducking stool and pillory, and in 1645 required the constable to set up stocks and whipping post at the charge of the inhabitants, while the lord of the manor was to provide the pillory.[4] The stocks stood in front of the Vestry House until *c.* 1850.[5]

Court books of the manor of Walthamstow Tony survive from 1677 to 1930.[6] Courts leet and baron were held up to 1895, at Tony (Shern) Hall until 1848 or later,[7] in *c.* 1863–8 at the Ferry Boat inn,[8] and in 1880 at the town hall.[9] The leet met annually on Whit Tuesday,[10] attended by 12–15 jurors. It elected constables and aleconners, normally 2 of each, up to 1881. The election of marsh bailiff or haywarden is first recorded in 1759 and annually from 1767; after 1895, however, the bailiff was

[87] *Epping Forest Com.: Rolls . . .*, ii. 122, 127–8.
[88] M. M. Smith, *Highams* (W.A.S., Occ. Pubn. viii), 6 and plan f.p. 6.
[89] *Epping Forest Com.: Rolls . . .* iii. 7, 12, 22–3.
[90] E.R.O., T/M 324. This map of 1820 distinguishes precisely where the deer could roam freely between Chingford Hatch and Oak Hill. They were totally excluded from 44 a. of the park, from the immediate gardens of Higham House, and from several small built-up inclosures such as Canister House, Selby's, and the Russell family's Tile Kiln House.
[91] E.R.O., D/DU 403/2, ff. 676–7; Fisher, *Forest*, 351–2.
[92] *Proc. Epping Forest Com.* pp. 2018–19.
[93] Ibid., p. 1982; E.R.O., D/DU 417/8 (South prospect and plan of John Salter's messuages and buildings, 1726) and T/A 464/1; G. F. Bosworth, *Some more Walthamstow houses* (W.A.S. xxix), 20. This 'Forest Hall' should not be confused with Forest Hall, Hale End (cf. Bosworth, *More Walthamstow houses*, W.A.S. xx. 31). 'Salter's Buildings' are correctly named on Rocque's *Survey*, 1741–5, but on later maps, e.g. Chapman and André's *Essex*, 1777, sheet xvi, and O.S. Map 6″, Essex, LXV (1868–76 edn.), the name has been incorrectly attached to the group of houses lying to the north. See also above, p. 250.
[94] E.R.O., D/CT 382 (nos. 128, 151–2, 1129); cf. E.R.O., T/M 252.
[95] Fisher, *Forest*, 356–7; E.R.O., D/DU 403/1, f. 36; V.H.M., DTM 6, 7.

[96] *Final Rep. Epping Forest Com.* H.C. 187, pp. 90–5, 112 (1877), xxvi.
[97] *Guide to Epping Forest* (pub. J. Shillinglaw, 1872), price 2d. (pasted in Epping Forest Fund Scrapbook in W.R.L.); V.H.M., DTM 10 (1876).
[98] W.R.L., Scrapbook of the committee's campaign, 1871–82, compiled by Septimus Morris, with reports, letters, subscription lists, and newscuttings. Morris lived in Pembroke Road.
[99] *Final Rep. Epping Forest Com.*, 14–15, 50.
[1] V.H.M., Mins. Walthamstow Local Bd. (1890–1); Bosworth, *Manor of Higham Bensted* (W.A.S. vi), 15; *Walthamstow Off. Guide* (1922), 28; E. N. Buxton, *Epping Forest*, 27 and plan f.p. 26; A. Hatley, *Across the years* (W.A.S. n.s. ii), 95.
[2] *Walthamstow Off. Guide* (1963), 31–2.
[3] J.I. 3/35B m. 53 *d.*
[4] E.R.O., Q/SR 119/31, Q/SBa 2/57.
[5] *Walthamstow Off. Guide* (*c.* 1911), 25.
[6] V.H.M., DTM 1–12; duplicate rolls, 1677–1798, are in E.R.O. (D/DQ 14/194–210). Unless otherwise stated the account of the courts is based on those records.
[7] Morant, *Essex*, i. 34; *White's Dir. Essex* (1848).
[8] *White's Dir. Essex* (1863); G. F. Bosworth, *Manor of Walthamstow Toni* (W.A.S. x), 18; V.H.M., P22/1/1.
[9] V.H.M., Walthamstow Local Bd. Mins. 1880.
[10] Morant, *Essex*, i. 34.

appointed by the steward out of court.[11] The leet was still actively involved in parish life in the late 17th century: it regulated the lammas lands and cattle pounds, and apparently exercised some authority over the parish officers, closely supervising the work of the parish surveyors, and in 1736 presenting the churchwardens for failing to keep the stocks in repair. But its influence gradually diminished after the parish reverted to an open vestry.[12] After *c.* 1730 it did little more than elect the officers, only occasionally asserting itself, as in 1745–7, when several tenants were presented for selling beer without licence. From 1895 to 1930 all manorial business was transacted out of court, mainly conveyances of copyholds, enfranchisements, and from 1922 extinguishment of manorial incidents.

The two small manors which broke away from Walthamstow Tony played little part in parish government. Low Hall had a copyholders' customary court, for which court books exist from 1693 to 1883.[13] The Rectory manor held a court baron at irregular intervals, rolls surviving for the years 1535 and 1554–1706, with copies to 1764.[14] Although courts leet, view of frankpledge, and the assize of bread and ale were included in the grant of the Rectory manor to the Withypolls in 1544,[15] there is no record of a leet being held.

Peter de Maule and his wife Christine had a court at Higham in 1257, with the right to try pleas moved by the King's writ and judge thieves.[16] In 1274 and 1285 William Comyn, Alexander de Balliol, and Christine de Maule were said to hold view of frankpledge and the assize of bread and ale at Higham.[17] Extracts from Higham Bensted court rolls exist from 1353[18] and original rolls from 1559 to 1793.[19] The manor held both courts leet, until 1664, and courts baron. In 1796 the courts formerly held for Higham Bensted were said to be about to be renewed,[20] but although that possibility was still being explored in 1809[21] there is no record of any later courts being held.[22] The number of jurors attending the leet varied from 11 to 18.[23] They elected one constable. In 1588 it was said to be customary for the same constable to serve both Higham and Salisbury Hall, chosen by each manor in turn; this was confirmed in 1593. One aletaster was usually chosen,

though two were chosen in 1640 and 1650. The last recorded election of officers was in 1664. The leet reported in 1588 that the stocks were broken and in 1640 that both stocks and whipping post were lacking. In 1590 the court was enforcing the statute for wearing caps. Pound breaking was presented in 1657 and keeping 'inmates' in 1664.

Court rolls for Salisbury Hall survive from 1499 to 1507 and court books from 1667 to 1908.[24] The manor held both court leet and baron. The last leet was held in 1730. A lease of the manor-house in 1658 reserved the right to hold courts there twice a year.[25] In 1499–1507 the number of leet jurors varied from 11 to 15. In those years apparently a constable was elected annually, but by 1588 in alternate years to serve both Salisbury Hall and Higham.[26] The last recorded election of constable was in 1730. An aleconner was chosen in 1502 and in 1504–7. In 1501 the lord was presented for allowing his gallows at Rodon (Rowden) Ende and his pillory to fall into ruin.

Walthamstow vestry minutes are only preserved from 1710 to 1820; churchwarden's and overseers' records in broken series date from the mid 18th century.[27] In 1624 the vicar, a churchwarden, and the inhabitants successfully petitioned the bishop of London to establish a select vestry, to avoid disorder at church meetings. The select vestry, comprising the vicar or curate, the churchwardens, and 17 parishioners, was co-optative, and dealt with the whole business of the church and parish. Meetings were called by the vicar or curate; a quorum of 10 including the minister and churchwardens was required for a full vestry.[28] The select vestry, no record of whose work survives, still existed in 1706, but by 1710 the parish had reverted to an open vestry.[29]

The open vestry met regularly in Easter week and in December, or September after 1767, with frequent but irregular meetings at other times as business required. Sometimes it met in the church, but after 1730 usually in the vestry room in the workhouse, with adjournments to the Chequers or Nag's Head. The vicar normally took the chair. Attendances before 1725 varied from 2 to 18, but were usually below 10. After 1782 they were sometimes as high

[11] Bosworth, *Manor of Walthamstow Toni*, 8; G. F. Blakeley, *Walthamstow marshes and lammas rights* (W.A.S. N.S. i), 11.
[12] See below.
[13] V.H.M., DLM 1–4; G. F. Bosworth, *Manors of Low Hall and Salisbury Hall* (W.A.S. vii), 9. See also E.R.O., D/DBq M1–6, for abstracts, stewards' papers, rentals, and survey, 1742–1926.
[14] V.H.M., DRM 1–6, 11; G. F. Bosworth, *Rectory manor* (W.A.S. iv), 9 and app. II; P. H. Reaney, *Court rolls of the Rectory manor* (W.A.S. xxxvii).
[15] See p. 286.
[16] *Feet of F. Essex*, i. 217.
[17] *Rot. Hund.* (Rec. Com.), i. 152; *Plac. de Quo Warr.* (Rec. Com.), 239*b*.; J.I. 1/242 m. 70.
[18] E.R.O., D/DFc 185. The original court rolls before 1558 are said to have been accidentally destroyed while in the possession of the family of Edward Rowe Mores (d. 1778), who made the extracts. Rowe Mores lived at Etloe House, Leyton (see above, pp. 178–9) and his library, including the volume of extracts, was sold in 1779: E.R.O., D/DXj 10, f. 375; V.H.M., Misc. file (Higham Bensted).
[19] V.H.M., DHM 1–6.
[20] Lysons, *London*, iv. 205.
[21] E.R.O., D/DXj 11, ff. 83–103.
[22] Inf. from Sir Henry Warner.

[23] E.R.O., D/DFc 185. Unless otherwise stated the account of the Higham leet is taken from this source and from V.H.M., DHM 6.
[24] Reaney, *Court Rolls of Salisbury Hall* (W.A.S. xxxvi); V.H.M., DSM 2–3; cf. V.H.M., *Vestiges*, no. 45. Unless otherwise stated the account of the Salisbury Hall leet is based on these sources.
[25] Barns, *Walthamstow Deeds, 1541–1862* (W.A.S. xxi), 4.
[26] See above.
[27] For a list of Walthamstow parish records, see *Cat. Essex Par. Recs.* (2nd edn., 1966), 222–4. Unless otherwise stated the following information on parish government and poor-law is based on: V.H.M., PV 1–5 (vestry mins.), P8/3/2–5 (workhouse management cttee. mins. and parish notes), and P12/1 (overseers' accts.). The resolutions and rules of the parish reorganization of 1779–80 were printed in 1785: E.R.O., D/DB O1. Extracts from the parish records are printed in S. J. Barns, *Walthamstow in the 18th century* (W.A.S. xiii, xiv, xvi).
[28] Newcourt, *Repertorium*, ii. 636; Transcripts in Par. Reg. (1692–1733) by Edmund Chishull, vicar 1708 f., who supplied Newcourt with particulars of the parish, and in V.H.M., 'Particulars relating to parish of Walthamstow extracted . . . by William Pamplin' (MS. 1789), f. 104.
[29] Possibly when Edmund Chishull became vicar in 1708.

as 36; in 1805 116 were present to elect a beadle. The average in 1800–20 was 16.[30] The parish did not appoint a select vestry after 1819, continuing, as had been its practice for many years, to appoint committees from time to time.[31]

Churchwardens and overseers were elected regularly at Easter. The surveyors were nominated separately, later in the year. The vestry did not, except on rare occasions, appoint a constable.[32] Parishioners were often loath to serve as officers.[33] Some paid fines, rising from £10 in 1711 to £45 in 1820, for exemption for life. Fines were paid by 5 out of 8 nominated in 1777. In 1780 the vestry complained that some of those elected employed unsuitable substitutes.

Two churchwardens were chosen, both by the parishioners. One was usually re-elected the following year, becoming 'head' or 'senior' warden.[34] Two overseers were appointed, dividing the year between them. In 1809 the vestry complained that people in office for only six months could not become competent in their duties. The workhouse master, or beadle, often acted as assistant or extra overseer, but from 1820 a full-time paid assistant overseer was employed.[35]

Up to 1766 two surveyors were appointed in December, one for the marsh side or lower division, and one for the forest side or upper division. From 1767 a paid surveyor, nominated in September, was appointed,[36] but after 1825 the parish reverted to the annual election of two substantial householders as unpaid surveyors.[37]

A beadle was first appointed in 1739, to deal with strangers, vagrants, and beggars. He soon became the messenger and servant of the vestry and its officers, dignified from 1742 by uniform. The duties of the post were detailed in 1779.

The parish clerk, entitled to an annual pension under the will of George Monoux (d. 1544),[38] by 1724 also received a salary from the vestry. From 1749 a salaried vestry clerk was also employed. This new office soon exceeded in importance that of parish clerk. The duties of Richard Banks, appointed vestry clerk in the parish reorganization of 1779–80, included making the rate books and collecting the parish rates and rents. Two or more of the offices of vestry clerk, parish clerk, workhouse master, beadle, constable, and assistant overseer were sometimes combined.

The rateable value of the parish in 1713 was £4,362. In 1781 it was £8,290, rising to £11,846 in 1808 and £17,568 in 1830.[39] In the early 18th century the churchwarden was reimbursed by an annual rate for his expenditure on both church and poor, while each overseer had a separate poor-rate,

assessed half-yearly, to pay pensioners. After about 1743 the overseers' half-yearly rates usually met the cost of workhouse, pensioners, medical attendance, and casual poor. From 1779 a combined half-yearly rate was levied and apportioned between church and poor. A 1d. constable's rate is mentioned in 1717 but the constable's expenses were normally paid from the church or, later, the poor-rate. Occasional surveyors' rates were raised, but by 1806 regular annual compositions for statute duty, assessed on rental values, were being levied.[40]

Digging, carting, and spreading gravel formed the main element in Walthamstow's highway maintenance until the late 19th century. From the late 16th century the work was done by statute labour.[41] Defaulters were frequently presented at quarter sessions between 1601 and 1662; in 1647 no fewer than 46 cart days and 231 days' labour were lost through default.[42] In 1760 the vestry advised the new surveyors to insist on local dignitaries paying their full due for their carriages, and to prosecute those who refused to pay their share for the highways. This suggests that by then money compositions were replacing statute labour, though this was still the basis of Walthamstow's highway maintenance in 1796.[43] In 1780 the assistant surveyor was ordered to employ the poor on the roads whenever possible. Exceptionally large payments for pauper labour were made in 1828–30, during the construction of Woodford New Road.

In 1765 a watch-house or cage was built against the workhouse east wall. It was pulled down in 1912.[44] From 1819 to 1831 a police committee supported by subscription employed armed night patrols in winter. They were augmented by day patrols during the unrest of 1830–1.[45] The vestry adopted the Lighting and Watching Act (1830) in 1831, appointing inspectors who levied a rate and employed a sergeant and squad of constables.[46] When this arrangement ceased in 1833, the police committee was revived, raised a voluntary rate, and hired patrols until 1835, when the vestry adopted the Lighting and Watching Act (1833) for watching only, in the parish south of Clay Street and Hagger Lane. The small police force then employed was disbanded in 1840.[47]

In 1771 Ralph Fresselicque gave the parish a fire-engine. The vestry bought a better one in 1791. Repairs carried out in 1815 were paid on the churchwardens' rate.[48] In 1831 the vestry's lighting and watching committee became responsible for its maintenance, the police sergeant acting as engine keeper.[49] Fire arrangements after 1836 are described below.[50]

---

[30] *Walthamstow Matters*, iii. 33.

[31] Before 1819 important committees were appointed in 1760, 1780, 1809, 1814.

[32] e.g. 1764, when a replacement constable was elected, and 1779 when the beadle was recommended to the magistrates. For the regular appointment of constables, see above.

[33] e.g. E.R.O., Q/SR 455/39, 40, 527/6.

[34] *Walthamstow Matters*, i. 7; V.H.M., *Vestiges*, nos. 67–8.

[35] This was in accordance with the Vestries Act, 1819, 59 Geo. III, c. 12.

[36] In accordance with the Highway Acts of 1766 (7 Geo. III, c. 42) and 1772–3 (13 Geo. III, c. 78).

[37] V.H.M., P21/1/2.

[38] Bosworth, *Hist. of Walthamstow Charities, 1487–1920* (W.A.S. viii), 10–11; V.H.M., *Vestiges*, nos. 67–8.

[39] Bosworth, *Chaps. in hist. Walthamstow* (W.A.S. xxii), 24.

[40] V.H.M., P21/1/1–2.

[41] E.R.O., Q/SR 200/39, Q/SBa 1/33.

[42] E.R.O., Q/SR 152/3, 200/39, 221/34, 294/33, 334/9, 393/23.

[43] Lysons, *London*, iv. 204.

[44] There is a commemorative plaque on the wall of the vestry house museum. The position of the cage is marked on the wall.

[45] V.H.M., P8/3/27–8, P8/3/5. There are no committee minutes extant for 1822–6, but it is clear from internal evidence in the surviving volumes that the patrols were continuous.

[46] V.H.M., P8/3/29. The Act was 11 Geo. IV c. 27.

[47] V.H.M., P8/3/28–9; the Act was 3 & 4 Wm. IV, c. 90.

[48] V.H.M., *Vestiges*, no. 67.

[49] V.H.M., P8/3/29.

[50] See p. 284.

Walthamstow's poor benefited from many endowments, including alms-houses.[51] In the early 18th century the parish supported regular pensioners including children; in 1710 there were 20 of them. In 1711 spinning-wheels and reels were to be provided to employ them; some were also to twine silk. The children were later apprenticed, usually to Londoners. In 1764 the beadle was ordered twice a year to visit all children put out. Casual relief included payments for rent, house repairs, medical care, midwifery, London hospital charges, and clothing; also provision of the tools and materials of trade, and money to redeem articles from pawn.

In 1725, besides 13 alms-people, Walthamstow's poor comprised 94 widows, single poor, and labourers with families. In the next year, to remedy the increasing cost of the poor and save paying pensions and rents, the vestry rented a house in Hoe Street for 3 years as a workhouse. Some pensions, however, continued to be paid. A workhouse was built at Church End in 1730–1. In 1741 the vestry required all those receiving relief, with their families, to be badged; this order appears to have lapsed, for it was renewed in 1760. The cost of poor-relief continued to rise and pensions to be paid. When the workhouse was enlarged in 1756 pensions were intended to cease, but by 1759 they were costing £112 a year. In 1742 a shilling rate for the year was sufficient for both church and poor; by 1763 the rate for the poor alone was 1s. 8d., by 1798 3s., and by 1818 4s. The total cost of the poor in 1763–4 was £584; in 1815 it was £1,725. In 1779, when pensions were costing over £6 a week, the increase in the number of poor was attributed to the departure of so many men for military service. A determined attempt that year to discontinue pensions and bring all those capable of work into the house still left a pension list of 36.

When exceptional distress followed a bad harvest in 1800 and corn was scarce, a general meeting of inhabitants decided to cultivate Markhouse common field (68 a.).[52] The owners and occupiers undertook to pay the overseers 10s. an acre for bread for the poor as soon as the corn was carried. The inhabitants also resolved to supply the poor with potatoes and cured herrings at a reduced price.

The annual cost of the poor was £2,807 in 1819 and never thereafter fell below £2,000. The average weekly cost per head in the workhouse, about 3s. in the late 1770s, was 6s. in 1821. The annual poor-rate was 5s. 3d. in 1829. The cost of the outdoor poor soared in 1830–1, £782 being paid out to those incapable of work, and £690 to those who worked. Stringent means of economy, including discontinuing payment of rents, reduced the rate from 5s. in 1834 to 3s. 6d. in 1835. That year the poor-rate met a total cost of £2,436, which included, besides the county rate (£262) and the management of the workhouse, £513 for pensions, £109 for illegitimate children, and £85 for lunatics. In 1836 the parish's responsibility for the poor was taken over by the West Ham poor law union.

The workhouse, later called the Vestry House and Armoury, now the museum, was built in 1730–1

on an acre of land in Buryfield. The cost was met by a loan and by the sale of the capital of the Turner and Compton charities.[53] Sir Henry Maynard in his will, proved 1738, left £50 to make the workhouse more comfortable;[54] this was spent on a brewhouse built soon after 1743. A large workroom with a loft room over it was added to the workhouse in 1756. The vestry room by the main south entrance was extended into the front yard in 1779.[55]

From 1726 to 1754 the vestry employed a salaried master and mistress. From 1755 to 1780 the poor were usually farmed to contractors at weekly rates varying from 2s. to 3s. a head. In 1762 an agreement to farm the poor on the product of two 7d. rates was short-lived, the contractor surrendering the agreement after 3 months and being reappointed at 2s. 4d. a head. From 1780 the vestry employed a qualified salaried master and mistress, supervised by the parish officers and a regular visiting committee. The 1780 rules required the men and boys to garden, pick oakum, and spin hemp or flax; the women and girls to do the domestic work, and spin flax for sheeting, hemp for sacks, and yarn for stockings to be knitted for the house. The master appointed in 1785 proposed to employ the poor in winding cotton for the tallow-chandler. The problem of employment was, however, never solved. In 1828 a visiting committee found the inmates with no occupation but household and garden tasks. When they were again found idle in 1831 the able-bodied men were sent to work in West Ham workhouse[56] and the women and children were given materials to knit and sew. In 1834 oakum was ordered. The diet laid down in 1780 was second bread, beer, and meat 3 times a week, with no stint of other things, but no waste. Some teaching was provided for the children in the house.[57] A parish doctor was being elected annually by 1739; from 1804 two were sometimes appointed.[58] A dispensary was established in 1828.

From 1747 to 1753 the number of inmates averaged 31, mainly women and children; men below 60 were rare unless sick or incapacitated. In 1779 there were 37 occupants, though there were beds for 50 and, since the enlargement of 1756 room for 80 if more beds were provided. In 1828, when there were 48 in the house, it was described as much too small, in bad condition, and incapable of holding more, but by 1834 there were 80 inmates. In 1836 the house was taken over by the West Ham guardians, who kept it open, with those of Woodford and West Ham, to serve the union until the new union house at Leytonstone was completed. In 1841 there were 77 inmates awaiting transfer.[59]

After their transfer the workhouse building was divided. The vestry and parish officers, and later the local board, occupied the older part of it until the town hall was built,[60] while the 1756 extension became the Metropolitan police station. The building became vested in the Walthamstow charity trustees, who let the Vestry House from 1882 to 1892 to the Literary and Scientific Institute and then to private tenants. In 1930 Miss C. Demain

[51] See p. 312.
[52] For the common fields, see p. 264.
[53] See p. 315.
[54] Barns, *Walthamstow Deeds, 1595–1890* (W.A.S. xi), 28.
[55] *Walthamstow Matters*, ii. 4, 6.
[56] See p. 98.
[57] See p. 305.
[58] *Walthamstow Matters*, iii. 31.
[59] *Census*, 1841; E.R.O., T/P 75; White's *Dir. Essex*, 1848; L.R.L., L59. 2 MS. (house list of poor, 16 Aug. 1836).
[60] *Walthamstow Matters*, iii. 33; *Kelly's Dir. Essex* (1878).

Saunders gave the remainder of her lease, which the trustees extended, to the corporation, so that the Vestry House might become a museum of local history and antiquities, which was opened in 1931.[61] The police continued to occupy the extension until 1870; after 1870 it was let for a time as the headquarters or armoury of the Walthamstow volunteers and later as a builder's workshop. The corporation acquired the lease of the armoury also in 1933, and opened it as an extension to the museum in 1934.[62] In 1944 the charity trustees sold the whole building to the corporation.[63]

The museum is a dignified two-storey building of brown stock brick with hipped tile roofs. Its plan is irregular as a result of the extensions of 1756 and 1779. The south front was originally symmetrical and of five bays, with segmental-headed sash windows and a central doorway. The vestry room extension of 1779 destroyed the western end of the façade. The doorway survives with, above it, a stone tablet inscribed 'This house erected An. Dom. MDCCXXX if any would not work neither should he eat'; it was executed by Samuel Chandler of Wanstead (fl. 1721–41), a statuary of contemporary note.[64] The site of the former cage against the east wall of the building is marked by an inscription. Some original 18th-century panelling and staircases remain, but the Tudor and Jacobean panelling and chimneypiece in the former armoury came from Essex Hall after its demolition in 1934. The late-18th-century doorcase with half-round pilasters, flat hood, and copper-framed fan-light now in the east wall of the armoury came from Church Hill House, demolished in 1932.[65]

In 1565 the parish owned a house adjoining the churchyard. Waste on either side of it was granted to the parish and churchwardens in 1568, and by 1670 the churchwardens held in trust for the poor buildings on both sides of the south gate of the church,[66] shown on a map of 1699.[67] By the early 18th century they comprised 5 cottages, which were encroaching on the churchyard. In 1713 the vestry ordered their back doors, opening upon the churchyard, to be stopped up, and decided that when the cottages became vacant or the occupants could be moved to the Monoux alms-houses, they should be demolished and the south side of the churchyard fenced. These conditions were satisfied in 1721, when the cottages were pulled down.[68]

LOCAL GOVERNMENT AFTER 1836. The vestry's most important civil responsibility after 1836 was the care of parish roads.[69] At first the

vestry continued to choose two surveyors each year, but by 1845 it was delegating its responsibility to a committee, described by 1851 as a highway board.[70] This mode of management so impressed the Leyton vestry that in 1851 they followed Walthamstow's example.[71] The board met in the old workhouse, as did the vestry, and employed the vestry clerk as its clerk, also an assistant surveyor, a rate collector paid on commission, and an engine keeper. One of its members acted as treasurer.

The spread of speculative building in the 1850s soon presented the vestry with sanitary problems, and a nuisances removal committee was appointed some time before 1857, comprising the members of the parish highway board with additional members elected by the vestry. This committee appointed an inspector and was attended, unpaid, by the clerk to the highway board. In 1862 the vestry combined the two authorities by forming an enlarged highway board at whose monthly meetings the nuisances and highway business was dealt with in turn. In 1866 the clerk advised the board that in view of the Sanitary Act, 1866, he considered their powers as nuisance authority to be at an end, since they had become vested in the West Ham guardians. For two years the guardians appointed a small nuisance removal committee,[72] which continued the inspector's appointment, employed a rate collector on commission, and was attended unpaid by the highway board clerk. In 1868 the vestry constituted the south-east corner of the parish, roughly eastward of Church End and Pig Alley (now Beulah Path), a special drainage district. Later in the same year, following the Sanitary Act, 1868, the vestry resumed its powers as sanitary authority, annually thereafter electing a committee composed of the members of the highway board to exercise them in the whole parish outside the special drainage district. The committee might not, however, borrow money without the vestry's consent. The highway board maintained some 21 miles of road on an average rate of 6d. The cost of sewers laid by the board was met by special rates levied on the roads served. During an outbreak of cholera in 1866 the board met weekly, and appointed a temporary highways assistant to enable the assistant surveyor, who was also the nuisances inspector, to concentrate on his sanitary duties.

In 1873 the special drainage district was dissolved and the civil parish constituted as an urban sanitary district, excluding the Walthamstow Slip, which became incorporated in the Leyton urban sanitary district.[73] The small detached portion of Walthamstow

[61] V.C.H. Essex Bibliography, 331; Book of the Walthamstow Museum, 1931 (W.A.S. xxiiB), 8–9.
[62] Bosworth, Some Walthamstow houses (W.A.S. xii), 10–11; G. E. Roebuck, The old armoury (W.A.S. xxxii); E.R.O., T/P 75; Vestry House Museum (1968), 3.
[63] Char. Com. File G 25/50; inf. from Town Clerk's Dept., Waltham Forest.
[64] R. Gunnis, Dict. Brit. Sculptors, 91.
[65] Bosworth, Some . . . houses, 10–11; Roebuck, The old armoury; Vestry House Museum.
[66] V.H.M., Vestiges, no. 14.
[67] W.R.L., Map of manor of High Hall by A. Forbes, 1699; photograph of map in E.R.O., T/M 252; also reproduced in Bosworth and Roebuck, Manor of Walthamstow Toni (W.A.S. i).
[68] V.H.M., Vestiges, no. 14; Barns, Walthamstow Vestry Minutes . . . 1710–1740 (W.A.S. xiii), 6–7.
[69] Under the General Highway Act, 1835, 5 & 6 Wm. IV, c. 50.
[70] See s. 18 of the Act. No vestry minutes survive for this period after 1836 and unless otherwise stated the following account of Walthamstow's parish highway board is based on other parish records preserved in the Waltham Forest Vestry House Museum: P21/1/4–9 (Highway Cttee. Accts. 1836–51); P24/1/1 (Nuisances Cttee. Draft Mins. 1857–61); P22/1/1 (Highway Bd. Mins. 1862–73); P24/1/3 (Nuisances Cttee. Mins. 1866–72); P24/1/10 (Walthamstow S.E. Sp. Drainage Dist. Mins. 1868–72). See also E. Clarke, Hist. Walthamstow: its past, present and future (1861).
[71] L.R.L., L47 MS. Vestry Mins. 1834–74 (1851).
[72] The W. Ham guardians appointed their first committee on 6 Sept. 1866 (W.H.L., W. Ham P.L. Guardians Mins.), not 1861, as recorded in V.H.M., P24/1/3.
[73] V.H.M., P24/1/3 (22 Aug. 1872); Local Govt. Bd.'s Prov. Orders Confirmation Act, 1873, no. 2, 36 & 37 Vict. c. 82 (local act). See also above, p. 208.

in Chingford, south of Chingford Hall, was merged in Chingford in 1882.[74]

The district was governed by a local board of health of 12 members, increased to 18 in 1891, when the district was divided into 4 wards.[75] A well-balanced board was elected in 1873, comprising three each of farmers and builders and the rest businessmen and gentry; among them were four experienced members of the parish highway board, one of whom, Ebenezer Clarke, became the first chairman.[76] The board met in the Vestry House until 1876, when the public hall in Orford Road, built in 1866,[77] was bought and enlarged as a town hall. Another wing was added in 1890–1. The ornate mid-Victorian front of the town hall still survives as part of Connaught Hospital.[78]

The vestry and highway board clerk, William Houghton, became the local board's part-time clerk.[79] His son, Gilbert, succeeded him in 1879, on the same terms, after a proposal to appoint a full-time clerk had been defeated. Some clerical help was authorized in 1885, and in 1887, when the clerk became also solicitor to the board, a full-time assistant clerk and accountant was appointed. But the clerk continued to act part-time and to be entitled to various fees and costs. A majority on the board consistently opposed a full-time appointment. W. G. Cluff, its chief advocate, in 1893 mustered only 3 supporters. The resistance may have been influenced by regard for the Houghton family and their long professional association with local affairs.[80]

A part-time professional surveyor was appointed in 1874; but the parish surveyor employed full-time by the vestry and parish highway board since before 1845[81] continued with the local board as inspector of nuisances until 1880 and as assistant and road surveyor until 1891. When the part-time surveyor resigned in 1879 the board, urged by Cluff, appointed in 1880 a resident, full-time surveyor, who also took over the post of inspector of nuisances. Responsibility for the district's sewerage schemes led to redesignation of the appointment as engineer, surveyor, and inspector in 1884, when a full-time assistant inspector was authorized and office staff provided. From 1886 the engineer was relieved of the inspector's duties entirely, and a separate appointment made. The engineer's office was re-organized in 1891, to administer the growing direct labour force.

The board's rate collector was paid on commission. A second collector was appointed from 1889, and in 1894 fixed salaries replaced payment by commission. A part-time medical officer was appointed from 1874. A bank manager acted as treasurer to the board.

The press were admitted to the board's meetings

from the first. For five years the board's minutes record nothing but harmony among its members. But after the election of W. G. Cluff[82] in 1879 its meetings were seldom without controversy. Cluff proposed publication of the board's accounts, proper custody of its records, and admission of ratepayers as spectators at board meetings. He pressed for legal action against builders contravening the by-laws, and for the use of direct labour on the board's own work. As returning officer in 1883 he criticized malpractices at a local election. Cluff had a considerable following outside the board. In 1879 a public meeting of ratepayers endorsed the course adopted by him and his two most constant supporters; yet in 1883 the board's chairman, W. B. Whittingham, condemned them as a minority aiming to 'usurp the authority which must repose in the majority'. Nevertheless, by 1894 Cluff's persistence had secured acceptance of all the most important matters raised by him, except the appointment of a full-time clerk.

The board inherited from the parish highway board the unmade roads and poor drainage of earlier unrestricted developments, notably in the Church common area, and on the Tower Hamlets estate. At the same time speculative building was accelerating. The product of 1d. rate, £190 in 1877, rose to £425 by 1887. The number of houses in the district rose from 2,079 in 1871 to 7,970 in 1891.[83] The population doubled in two successive decades, 1871–81 and 1881–91.[84] The board's first by-laws, adopted in 1874, required approval of building plans. By 1894 the board had considered some 2,500 applications, the largest one for 108 houses in Leucha Road in 1892. Over 500 houses a year were being built by 1886, falling to about 300 a year by 1892.[85] Some builders ignored the by-laws, and in 1880 the board ordered that no new house be occupied until certified by the surveyor. Differences between the board and builders came to a head in 1887–8, when the surveyor reported persistent breaches of the regulations. Notices were served on 31 builders; discussions with them followed, minor adjustments of the by-laws were agreed, and from 1890 the surveyor reported improved standards.

The board's schemes for sewage disposal are described below.[86] They accounted for about three-quarters of the money borrowed by the board. The £2,000 debt taken over by the board from the South-Eastern special drainage district in 1873 had risen to £116,008 by 1895.[87] Apart from loans for sewerage and public buildings the rest of the debt was mainly attributable to road works. By 1890 the board was responsible for over 50 miles of roads. Between 1881 and 1891 20 miles of gravel paths were replaced by asphalt or flagged pavements.[88]

[74] *V.C.H. Essex,* v. 97.

[75] A. D. Law, *Our Town,* pt. 2 (W.A.S., Occ. Pubn. vii), 4, 6. Unless otherwise stated the account of the work of the local board is based on Law, *Our Town* (2), on the board's MS. and printed Mins. and Reps. 1873–94 deposited in Walthamstow Vestry House Museum, and on the *Chairman's Annual Reps.,* 1891–3.

[76] *Walthamstow Matters,* iv. 21. E. Clarke was the author of *Walthamstow: its past, present and future* (1861).

[77] See p. 252.

[78] See p. 285.

[79] G. Houghton, *Walthamstow Past and Present,* 11.

[80] William Houghton was in practice in Walthamstow by 1848, and vestry clerk by 1857; his son Gilbert joined the practice in 1868: *White's Dir. Essex* (1848), V.H.M.

P24/1/1, G. Houghton, *Walthamstow Past and Present,* 11.

[81] V.H.M., P21/1/6.

[82] Son of William Cluff of Grosvenor House: Bosworth, *Walthamstow Charities, 1487–1920* (W.A.S. viii), 47.

[83] *V.C.H. Essex,* v. 3.

[84] Ibid.; *Incorporation of Walthamstow, 1921: Statistics of district,* 5.

[85] *Kelly's Dirs. Essex,* (1886, 1890); *Walthamstow Local Bd., Survs. Reps.* 1890–2.   [86] See p. 283.

[87] Walthamstow B.C., *Official Souvenir . . . of . . . charter of incorporation, 1929,* 38.

[88] *Walthamstow's advance, 1881–1891: address by W. B. Whittingham on retirement after 10 years as chairman of the local board.*

The board bought a site for an isolation hospital, provided a public library, reorganized the fire service, increased recreation space, and took the first steps towards providing baths, technical education, and a local electricity supply. It initiated the use of direct labour in refuse collection and other municipal works, and by attacking the use of polluted wells and pressing for their replacement by mains supplies reduced the incidence of typhoid.[89]

The district's rateable value rose from £61,000 in 1873 to £177,000 in 1895; but with the mounting cost of public services in the same time the poundage of the general district rate doubled, from 1s. 6d. to 3s. 1d. The board's estimated expenditure in 1873 was £3,138; its expenditure in 1894–5 was £58,185, including £16,810 for loan charges.[90]

Under the Local Government Act, 1894, the local board was replaced in 1895 by an urban district council of 18 members representing 4 wards. The membership was increased to 22 in 1897 when a fifth ward was created, to 27 in 1905, and to 33 in 1913, when the number of wards was increased to 6.[91] The council was constituted the electric lighting authority in 1895.[92] In 1903 it became the local authority for elementary education[93] and in the same year was empowered to construct and operate municipal tramways.[94]

By the 1890s local elections were being fought on party lines. From 1894 to 1921 the U.D.C. was controlled in turn by the Ratepayers' Association, later called the Moderates (1894–7, 1901–4, 1913–21) and the Radical and Progressive Association (1897–1901, 1904–13).[95] The Progressives were led to victory in 1897 by J. J. McSheedy (councillor 1894–1904), a fiery young Irishman who was editor of the *Walthamstow Reporter*, and who was the storm centre of local politics at that period.[96] Socialist or Labour candidates contested U.D.C. elections occasionally from 1894 and regularly from 1905, but without success before 1919. The *Walthamstow Guardian*, supporting the Moderates, exploited the fear of Socialism engendered by contemporary events in West Ham. Lack of local support for Labour before the First World War is shown by the Osborne case of 1908.[97] In 1919 the Socialists won 4 seats. They increased their representation in 1920, and in 1921 gained control of the council. They never lost it, though their majority was sometimes very small. They were assisted by the failure of shifting opposition groups to maintain a common front against them.

The council continued to meet in the Orford Road town hall, which was again enlarged in 1900. The education committee took over Clevelands in High Street from the school board.[98] In 1911 offices were provided for the public health and school

attendance departments at the Water House in Lloyd Park.

When Gilbert Houghton retired in 1895 the post of clerk became full-time; but Houghton remained solicitor to the council until 1902 when C. S. Watson was appointed clerk and solicitor.[99] An accountant's department was created in 1899, but a bank manager continued to act as treasurer until 1927, when the accountant became treasurer. The engineer's and surveyor's functions were separated in 1899, and two departments created. These were reunited in 1923. The medical officer's appointment became full-time in 1906.

The rate of building increased sharply in 1896, to reach its peak in 1898–1902; in those five years some 8,800 plans were passed. Between 1891 and 1901 the number of houses rose from 7,970 to 16,083 and the population from 46,346 to 95,131.[1] In 1899 Walthamstow was described as one of the largest municipal areas in the country, expected to achieve a population equal to West Ham.[2] The chairman reported in 1898 that council business was becoming very heavy, but it is clear from his successors' reports that the council, like the local board, welcomed the growth of the district and worked hard to keep pace with it. By 1905 the council had built public baths, an isolation hospital, an electricity generating station, and a refuse destructor;[3] it had inaugurated municipal tramways,[4] established a technical institute[5] and a professional fire brigade, and laid out a public park.[6] Direct labour was increasingly employed on every kind of municipal work. The district's death-rate was consistently below the national average, and infant mortality, which averaged 151·5 per 1,000 live births in 1896–1900, was halved by 1916–19. By 1909 the medical officer reported that typhoid had been practically banished. In 1910 among the country's 77 'great towns' only five had a better health record than Walthamstow. The problem of sewage disposal,[7] one of the council's most pressing anxieties in its early years, was finally resolved in 1928 when Walthamstow's sewage was diverted into the London system. In 1912 the council prepared a town planning scheme and secured the co-operation of the Warner and Salisbury Hall estate companies in laying out their developments on town planning lines.

Between 1895 and 1929 the council spent nearly £17 million to provide the spreading district with all necessary services.[8] Consistently from 1900 to 1920 the heaviest expenditure was required for road works.[9] By 1929 the council was responsible for 82 miles of highway and 16 miles of tramway.[10] From 1918, however, the council regarded the postwar house famine as its most urgent problem.

[89] See also p. 283.
[90] Walthamstow B.C., *Official Souvenir . . . 1929*, 38.
[91] Law, *Our Town* (2), 9. Unless otherwise stated the account of the work of the urban district council is based on the *Chairman of the U.D.C.'s Annual Reports, 1895–1919*, *Walthamstow U.D.C. Mins. and Reps.*, and Law, *Our Town* (2).
[92] *V.C.H. Essex*, v. 46.
[93] See p. 304.   [94] See p. 251.
[95] Unless otherwise stated this paragraph is based on the *Walthamstow Guardian*'s accounts of local elections 1894–1929, reported in late March or early April.
[96] *London*, vi. 820, vii. 190; R. G. C. Desmond, *Our local press* (W.A.S. n.s. iii), 21–7; *The Municipal Jnl. and London*, viii. 363.

[97] *V.C.H. Essex*, v. 62.
[98] *Hist. Walthamstow Sch. Bd. 1880–1903*, 69, 103; *Kelly's Dir. Essex* (1912); *Incorporation of Walthamstow, 1921: Statistics . . .*, 20.
[99] G. Houghton, *Walthamstow past and present*, 11.
[1] *V.C.H. Essex*, v. 5.
[2] *The Mun. Jnl. and London*, viii. 363.
[3] See pp. 283–5.
[4] See p. 251.   [5] See p. 311.
[6] See p. 284.   [7] See p. 283.
[8] Walthamstow B.C. *Official souvenir . . . 1929*, 38.
[9] *Incorporation of Walthamstow, 1921: Statistics . . .* 40.
[10] Walthamstow B.C. *Official souvenir . . . of . . . incorporation . . . 1929*, 42.

Advances under the Small Dwellings Acquisition Act, 1899, had been made since 1902, but from 1920 council house building became the largest item of municipal expenditure. In 1920–4 the council bought 154 a. of land for housing.[11] By 1929 more than 800 houses had been built, over half of them by direct labour, and nearly £900,000 of the district's debt of over £2 million was attributable to housing.[12]

Municipal incorporation was publicly discussed as early as 1892. In 1907–8 the council considered transfer to the county of London, as a metropolitan borough.[13] After the First World War the *Walthamstow Guardian* led the movement in favour of incorporation which preceded a petition to the Privy Council in 1920. The decision, delayed by a succession of royal commissions on local government, was again postponed in 1926, when the council, under pressure from its employees, to ensure the maintenance of essential services agreed to cut off the supply of electricity to local factories during the General Strike. The fine subsequently imposed at Stratford Court for this 'neglect of duty' was negligible, but the government's displeasure delayed the grant of borough status until 1929.[14]

The borough council comprised 36 councillors, representing 6 wards, and 12 aldermen. The charter mayor was the lord of the manor of Higham, Col. Sir Courtenay Warner. The Socialists retained control, usually with a large majority, throughout the life of the borough council.[15] During the 1930s the opposition was again weakened by its own divisions. In 1947–51 the Conservatives reduced the Socialist majority to 4, but it rose again thereafter.

The Orford Road town hall, with additional offices at the Water House in Lloyd Park,[16] was used until 1941. In that year a new town hall was completed on a site to the north of Forest Road, next to the recently built South-West Essex technical college. The architect was P. D. Hepworth and the town hall formed the central block of what was planned as an impressive civic centre. Faced with white stone, it has a central portico rising through all three storeys. The front is dominated by a tall square clock turret, sheathed in copper and surmounted by an octagonal lantern. In style the building, with its wrought iron balconies and decorative sculpture, reflects the Swedish influence of the inter-war years. The forecourt is laid out on formal lines with a central circular pool and fountain. An assembly hall flanking the forecourt to the east was completed to the original design in 1943. A court house on the opposite side was in course of construction in 1971. Its design by K. Krumins breaks away from that of the earlier buildings, the architectural emphasis being horizontal rather than vertical.[17]

A separate cleansing department was inaugurated in 1933 and a building works department in 1938. In 1945 a borough architect's department was created. The engineer and surveyor's department was merged in this in 1952, as were the cleansing and building works departments in 1959. In 1960 all these functions were divided between two departments, a borough architect's, with building works, and a borough engineer and surveyor's, with cleansing.

Walthamstow Corporation Acts were obtained in 1931, 1932, and 1934[18] enabling the council, *inter alia*, to control street trading by licences and by-laws (1932) and to acquire the remaining lammas lands (1934). The Walthamstow Savings Bank, Ltd., was incorporating in 1932, its trading activities restricted to lending money to the corporation.[19]

In 1932 Walthamstow was the highest populated non-county borough in the country; most of its houses were small artisan dwellings built before the First World War, 83 per cent of them with a rateable value under £20.[20] Though part of the administrative county of Essex, Walthamstow came under the operational control of the London civil defence region in the Second World War, during which 1,288 out of 32,000 houses were destroyed, 3,707 badly damaged, and 25,152 slightly damaged.[21] The council's predominant task after the war was to replace destroyed, damaged, and outdated houses. Between 1945 and 1960 the council bought 158 a. of land for housing. The Walthamstow Corporation Act, 1956,[22] strengthened the council's powers to control building and improve defective premises. The council's own schemes are described below. By 1964 the council was responsible for 106 miles of road maintenance.[23]

In 1965, under the London Government Act, 1963, Walthamstow was combined with Chingford and Leyton as the London borough of Waltham Forest.[24] The town hall in Forest Road became the administrative centre of the new borough.

PUBLIC SERVICES. The development of gas, electricity, and water supplies, and of sewerage, has been outlined elsewhere.[25] The South Essex Gaslight and Coke Co.'s works at Lea Bridge supplied part of Walthamstow with gas from 1854.[26] The company's successors[27] continued to supply Walthamstow, the whole parish being included in their limits from 1864. By 1900 their mains had reached Hale End. A small portion of north-east

[11] *Walthamstow B.C. Year Bk.* 1959–60, 46–7.
[12] *Walthamstow Official Guide* (1929), 24; Walthamstow B.C. *Official souvenir . . . 1929*, 38, 43.
[13] *V.C.H. Essex*, v. 36.
[14] Law, *Our Town* (2), 26–8; *Official souvenir . . . 1929*, 5–7; *Walthamstow Guardian*, 14, 21 May, 9, 16, 23 July 1926. Unless otherwise stated the account of the borough council is based on Law, *Our Town* (2), and on the *B.C. Mins. and Reps.*, *Year Bks.* 1948–64, and *Official Guides*, 1951–63.
[15] *Walthamstow Guardian*, accounts of local elections 1929–63, reported early in Nov. to 1947, and in mid May 1948–63.
[16] *Walthamstow Off. Guide* (c. 1939), 20.
[17] Inf. from W.R.L. For the Forest Road town hall see plate f. p. 15.
[18] Walthamstow Corpn. Act, 1931, 21 & 22 Geo. V,

c. 12 (local act); Walthamstow Corpn. Act, 1932, 22 & 23 Geo. V, c. 13 (local act); Walthamstow Corpn. Act, 1934, 24 & 25 Geo. V, c. 53 (local act).
[19] *Walthamstow Public Services, 1935*, 37.
[20] Walthamstow B.C. *Proceedings at an inquiry . . . into the application . . . for an extension to the borough, 1932*, 12, 33.
[21] *Essex County Council: Rep. of A.R.P. Cttee. 1939–1945*, 27.
[22] Walthamstow Corpn. Act, 1956, 4 & 5 Eliz. II, c. 84 (local act).
[23] *Year Bk.* (1964–5); *Official souvenir . . . 1929*, 42.
[24] *Walthamstow Matters*, No. 4, pp. 31–2; *V.C.H. Essex*, v. 81 n. 24.
[25] *V.C.H. Essex*, v. 37–47, 75–81.
[26] Ibid. 45.
[27] See under Leyton, p. 211.

Walthamstow was supplied by the Gas Light and Coke Co.[28]

An electricity generating station in Exeter Road built by the urban district council opened in 1901. It closed in 1968 and was demolished in 1969.[29]

Walthamstow was included in the area of supply of the East London Waterworks Co., one of the predecessors of the Metropolitan water board, from 1853.[30] The company's intake was moved from Lea Bridge to the Copper Mills in 1854 when an aqueduct was completed. Between 1853 and 1904 the company built one reservoir at the junction of Hagger Lane and Woodford New Road, and twelve covering over 360 a. of the Walthamstow marshes. The Racecourse reservoir was converted to filter beds in 1968–9.[31] In 1874 the company's mains had not reached Higham Hill or Chapel End, and even where mains were laid many households still depended on unsatisfactory pumps and wells. In 1876 only 5 of 70 houses in the St. James Street area, with mains near by, had water laid on. Cases of typhoid in the 1870s were usually traced to polluted water supplies. The local board unremittingly urged on owners to connect their properties to the mains, and on the company to extend its mains, improve pressure in the higher parts of the district, and provide a constant supply.[32] The mains supply was constant by 1911[33] and by 1914 every house was connected to it.[34]

In the mid 19th century Walthamstow's sewage drained into ditches and watercourses which flowed either into the Phillebrook at Tinkers Bridge or into the Dagenham brook on the marsh, and so through Leyton to the Lea. As building spread after 1850 lengths of ditch which caused local offence were bricked over or piped. In 1859 Leyton's first complaint of fouling of the Phillebrook was dismissed on the grounds that the drainage was 'following the ancient course'.[35] In 1868 the south-east corner of the parish was constituted a special drainage district.[36] In 1875–7 under pressure from the Dagenham commissioners of sewers, the Lee conservancy, and the Leyton local board, which in 1875 secured an injunction restraining Walthamstow from passing sewage into the Dagenham brook,

Walthamstow local board bought Low Hall farm and built outfall works. These treated the sewage by chemical precipitation and broad irrigation. In 1876 a small scheme was completed to drain north-east Walthamstow's sewage into tanks at Hale End. The sewage from the south-east was diverted westwards from Tinkers Bridge to Low Hall in 1880, and the works were enlarged in 1885 to take the north-eastern sewage from Hale End.[37] For some years the Low Hall works were not entirely successful and in 1895 Leyton threatened to reopen legal proceedings. That year the urban district council applied for permission to drain into the L.C.C.'s northern outfall sewer, but were refused because the sewer had insufficient capacity. The Low Hall works were satisfactorily modified, but the application to join the L.C.C. system was renewed in 1904 and subsequently.[38] Agreement was reached in 1925 and in 1928 all Walthamstow sewage except storm water was turned into the L.C.C. system.[39]

The local board inaugurated domestic refuse collection in 1874 under contract. The work was taken over by the surveyor's department in 1891,[40] and a refuse and sludge destructor built at Low Hall farm in 1904.[41] Refuse disposal extensions were opened in 1937.[42]

Selbourne Road recreation ground (4 a.) originated in 1850, when 2 a. on Church common were allotted for public recreation under an inclosure award. This land was sold in 1869 to the Great Eastern railway company and the Selborne Road site bought with the proceeds. The vestry handed over the ground to the local board in 1876. After excavating the cutting the railway company conveyed what was left of the 2 a. as a playground for the Orford Road National school; it survives as the Vestry Road children's playground.[43] The Higham Hill (12 a.) and Queen's Road (2 a.) recreation grounds originated as the gravel pits on Higham Hill (4 a.) and Mark House (2 a.) commons allotted to the parish surveyors for road maintenance under the inclosure award of 1850. When the pits were exhausted in the 1890s the local board fenced and levelled them for recreation. In 1906 the Selborne Road, Higham Hill, and Queen's Road grounds

[28] V.C.H. Essex, v. 45; County and General Gas Consumers Co. Ltd. (Lea Bridge District) Act, 1864, 27 & 28 Vict. c. 259 (local act); Lea Bridge District Gas Act, 1878, 41 & 42 Vict. c. 49 (local act); U.D.C. Chmn.'s Ann. Rep. 1900; Incorporation of Walthamstow, 1921: Statistics . . . 33.
[29] Electric Lighting Orders Confirmation (No. 3) Act, 1895, 58 & 59 Vict. c. 68 (local act); Walthamstow B.C. Official Guide (1937), 20–1; A. D. Law, Our Town (2), 29; W.A.S., The Record, no. 12, p. 2, no. 13, p. 2.
[30] East London Waterworks Act, 1853, 16 & 17 Vict. c. 166 (local act).
[31] V.C.H. Essex, v. 38; O.S. Map 2½", sheets TQ 38 and 39; Walthamstow U.D.C. Chmns.' Ann. Reps. 1896, 1899; Incorporation of Walthamstow, 1921: statistics of district, 5; E.R.O., T/P 75 (letter from E. London Waterworks Co. 1904); A. R. H. Hatley, Archaeology in the Walthamstow District (W.A.S. Reprint No. 1), 24; W.A.S. The Record, no. 11, p. 4; East London Papers, xii (no. 2), 110.
[32] V.H.M., Walthamstow Local Bd. Mins. 1874 f.
[33] Walthamstow Official Guide (c. 1911), 22.
[34] V.C.H. Essex, v. 40.
[35] V.H.M., P22/1/1, 2, P24/1/1, 3; W. Tyler and G. W. Holmes, Hist. of sewage question of Walthamstow (1909), 3–4; V.H.M., Vestiges, nos. 54–8. For the nuisances removal committee and parish highway board see above, p. 279.

[36] V.H.M., P24/1/3, 10; G. Houghton, Walthamstow past and present, 12–13.
[37] E.R.O., D/SH 4; V.H.M., P24/1/3; V.C.H. Essex, v. 43; V.H.M., Walthamstow Local Bd. Mins. 1874 f.; Tyler and Holmes, Hist. sewage question, 4–5; E.R. xxxvii. 31; L.R.L., L47 MS. Leyton Local Bd. Mins. (1880, 1884); Walthamstow U.D.C. Chmn.'s Ann. Rep. 1895.
[38] E.R.O., D/SH 4, 5; V.H.M., Walthamstow Local Bd. Mins. 1877 f.; Walthamstow U.D.C. Surveyor's Rep. 1887–8 and Chmns.' Reps. 1895–1914; L.C.C. Ann. Rep. 1895–6, p. 63; V.C.H. Essex, v. 44; Tyler and Holmes, Hist. sewage question, 5.
[39] London County Council (General Purposes) Act, 1925, 15 & 16 Geo. V, c. 119, Pt. VI (local act); Walthamstow U.D.C. Mins. and Reps. 1927–8; Walthamstow Official Guide (1933), 12.
[40] V.H.M., Walthamstow Local Bd. Mins. and Cttee. Reps.; Walthamstow Matters, No. 4, p. 28.
[41] Walthamstow U.D.C. Chmns.' Ann. Reps. 1904, 1905; Walthamstow B.C. Official souvenir . . . of . . . incorporation . . . 1929, 43.
[42] Law, Our Town (2), 34.
[43] E.R.O., Q/RDc 38; V.H.M., Walthamstow Local Bd. Mins. 1876; G. F. Bosworth, Hist. of Walthamstow Chars. (W.A.S. viii), 46–7; W. Houghton, Walthamstow: its highways and byways, 20. There is a commemorative plaque on the old Vestry Road Post Office sorting office opposite the playground.

were laid out by the unemployed, under local distress relief schemes. They also laid out 8½ a. adjoining Low Hall farm, opened in 1910 as St. James's Park.[44] The Higham Hill common (Green Pond Road) and Markhouse common (Queen's Road) allotments also date from 1850 when the inclosure award set aside 10 a. at Higham Hill and 6 a. on Markhouse common for the labouring poor.[45]

In 1898 the family of Edward Lloyd (1815–90)[46] gave the urban district council Winns or the Water House, once the home of William Morris, with 9½ a. of grounds, on condition that the council bought the adjoining 9¾ a. Lloyd Park was opened in 1900. About 16 a. of the adjoining Aveling Park estate were bought in 1912 as an addition to the park, and laid out in 1921.[47] The small Stoneydown gardens were opened in 1920.[48]

In 1920 Walthamstow was estimated to have 40·5 a. of parks maintained by the council.[49] In addition, there were 358 a. of open forest within the urban district and some 30 a. more in Highams Park controlled by the forest conservators; the local board had contributed towards the purchase of Highams Park by the conservators in 1891.[50] Under the Walthamstow Corporation Act, 1934, the corporation bought about 100 a. of the remaining lammas lands for recreation.[51]

A disused sewage tank at Low Hall farm was opened as a swimming bath in the summer of 1889 and 1890.[52] The High Street baths adjoining the library opened in 1900. They were enlarged in 1923 and demolished in 1968. In 1966 new baths were opened in Chingford Road. The Whipps Cross Lido, managed jointly by Walthamstow and Leyton, is treated under Leyton.

The parish highway board appointed the keeper of the fire-engine, and in 1863 had the hand-drawn manual engine adapted to a horse. In 1871 a second-hand manual engine, bought out of the poor-rate, replaced the old one.[53] After 1873 the local board ran the fire service. In 1883 the engine keeper was authorized to enlist six regular firemen, paid for each fire attended provided they arrived within half an hour of the engine. In 1887 a small curricle engine was bought, a second station established in St. James Street, another engine keeper appointed, and two more men enlisted on the same terms as the other six. In 1892 the curricle engine was moved to a new station in Willow Walk, to be known as the High Street station; the old engine remained at Church End. In 1893–4 the local board initiated a voluntary fire brigade, supported by subscribers and run by a voluntary committee. The board, however, appointed the officers, approved the rules, paid the engineer, and owned stations and equipment. When the volunteer brigade took over in 1894, the firemen previously employed were discharged. A steam engine was bought in the same year and a new High Street station opposite Storey Road was completed in 1895.[54] The local board had reserved the right to resume control, which the urban district council did in 1897–8. The volunteers were gradually replaced by full-time firemen, until by 1906 the whole brigade was professional. In 1912 two motor combinations replaced the horsed appliances. In 1924 the High Street station was replaced by a new one at the junction of Countess and Forest Roads.[55]

The urban district council completed over 520 houses at Hale End, Higham Hill, and Forest Road in 1920–2.[56] By 1938 1,627 municipal dwellings were built including 176 under slum clearance schemes; this was more than in any other borough in metropolitan Essex. The largest schemes were at Higham Hill and in Forest Road.[57] To relieve the housing shortage after the Second World War 535 temporary bungalows were provided in 1945–8.[58] The first permanent scheme, Priory Court, off Countess Road, was begun in 1946 and comprised 414 flats mainly in six-storey blocks. This was a departure from traditional municipal housing, for, with little undeveloped land left, in Walthamstow's post-war schemes flats and maisonettes predominated.[59] In 1954 the council began to clear sites for redevelopment in the Prospect Hill area, and near St. James Street station.[60] Between 1945 and 1964 5,151 new dwellings were built within the borough and a further 645 on Canvey Island and at Billericay.[61] In 1964–5 large areas of terrace houses built before 1900 in the vicinity of South Grove and off Boundary Road were demolished for redevelopment.[62]

A public dispensary supported by subscription was opened in Orford Road in 1873. It moved in 1913 to no. 105 Hoe Street, where it remained until it closed in 1942.[63]

[44] E.R.O., Q/RDc 38; V.H.M., Walthamstow Local Bd. Mins.; *Walthamstow U.D.C. Chmns.' Ann. Reps.* 1895, 1905–6, 1908–10. A smaller gravel pit (1 a.) on Church common was also awarded to the surveyors in 1850 was sold when it was exhausted and the money invested to relieve the rates: Bosworth, *Walthamstow Charities*, 46; W. Houghton, *Acct. of benefactions in Walthamstow*, 14.
[45] E.R.O., Q/RDc 38; Clarke, *Walthamstow*, 14. The allotments were still in use in 1971.
[46] He was the founder of *Lloyd's Weekly News*: D.N.B.
[47] *Walthamstow U.D.C. Chmns.' Ann. Reps.* 1898, 1900, 1912; R. G. C. Desmond, *Our local press* (W.A.S. N.S. iii), 9–10; *Incorporation of Walthamstow, 1921: statistics . . . 22.
[48] A. D. Law, *Our Town* (2), 26; *Walthamstow B.C. Year Bk.* 1964–5, p. 27.   [49] *V.C.H. Essex*, v. 51.
[50] *Incorporation of Walthamstow, 1921: statistics . . . 22; G. F. Bosworth, *Chapters in hist. of Walthamstow* (W.A.S. xxii), 21–2; V.H.M., Walthamstow Local Bd. Mins. 1890–1; *Walthamstow Official Guide*, 1922, p. 28.
[51] Walthamstow Corporation Act, 1934, 24 & 25 Geo. V, c. 53.
[52] This paragraph is based on: V.H.M., Walthamstow Local Bd. Mins. 1889–90; *Walthamstow U.D.C. Chmn.'s Ann. Rep.* 1900; Law, *Our Town* (2), 26; *Walthamstow Off. Guide* (1925), 47; *Waltham Forest Off. Guide* (1968), 75; W.A.S., *The Record*, no. 13, p. 4.

[53] V.H.M., P22/1/1, P24/1/3. For earlier fire arrangements see above, p. 277.
[54] V.H.M., Walthamstow Local Bd. Mins. and Reps. 1873–94; A. Hatley, *Across the years*, 19–20; *Walthamstow U.D.C. Chmn.'s Ann. Rep.* 1895.
[55] *Walthamstow U.D.C. Chmns.' Ann. Reps.* 1897–1906; Law, *Our Town* (2), 7, 10–12; *Walthamstow B.C. Official souvenir . . . of . . . incorporation . . . 1929*, 44; *Incorporation of Walthamstow, 1921: statistics . . .*, 26.
[56] Law, *Our Town* (2), 25; *Walthamstow Public Services, 1935*, 36; *Incorporation of Walthamstow, 1921: statistics . . .*, 57–8; *Walthamstow Off. Guide* (1925), 28.
[57] *Walthamstow Off. Guide* (c. 1927), 28, (1929), 24, (1931), 16, (1933), 12, (1935), 12; *V.C.H. Essex*, v. 66; *Walthamstow B.C. Year Bk.* (1964–5), 29–30; Law, *Our Town* (2), 30.   [58] *V.C.H. Essex*, v. 66.
[59] *Walthamstow Forward*, i (3), 11–12; Law, *Our Town* (2), 30; *Your Walthamstow, 1947*, 8; *Walthamstow Off. Guide* (1954), 25.   [60] Law, *Our Town* (2), 30.
[61] *Walthamstow B.C. Year Bk.* (1959–60), 46–7, (1964–5), 29–30; *Walthamstow Off. Guide* (1961), 60, 64.
[62] W.A.S., *The Record*, no. 2, pp. 3–4.
[63] *Kelly's Dir. Essex* (1874–1926); *Walthamstow Off. Guide* (1922), 25, (c. 1939), 18; W. G. S. Tonkin, *Anglican Church in Walthamstow* (W.A.S. N.S. iv), 25. See also below, p. 317.

Connaught Hospital, Orford Road, previously known as the Leyton, Walthamstow, and Wanstead hospital, originated as a voluntary cottage hospital for children founded in 1877–8 in Brandon Road off Wood Street.[64] In 1880 it moved to Salisbury Road, where it remained until 1894, when the gift of Holmcroft, Orford Road, made its expansion as a children's and general hospital possible. It was enlarged in 1897 and 1903 and by 1925 had 50 beds. Additions made in 1926–7 included completion of the Leyton and Leytonstone war memorial ward in 1927. The hospital was renamed Connaught in 1928, the duchess of Connaught having been patron since 1894. Comely Bank, Orford Road, was bought as a clinic in 1930. The hospital, which was enlarged again in 1934, had 118 beds in 1939. After the Second World War the Orford Road National school building was acquired as a pathology department. In 1958–9 the old Orford Road town hall was also acquired and now forms the main entrance to the hospital.

In 1893, after Plaistow and Highgate hospitals refused to accept any more Walthamstow smallpox patients, temporary isolation arrangements were made at Low Hall farm. An isolation hospital, built by the urban district council in the grounds of Larkswood Lodge, Chingford, opened in 1901. This was enlarged in 1905 and a pavilion for tuberculosis patients opened in 1914. A half-share in the hospital was bought by Leyton in 1938, when it became known as the Leyton and Walthamstow joint hospital. It ceased to deal with infectious diseases in 1953 and is now known as Chingford hospital.[65] Thorpe Coombe maternity hospital, Forest Road, was opened by the borough council in 1934.[66] The above three hospitals were all taken over by the N.E. Metropolitan regional hospital board in 1948.

A municipal smallpox hospital was established at Low Hall farm in 1929; it was closed in 1940 after being damaged by incendiary bombs.[67]

Brookfield voluntary orthopaedic hospital, established at Hale End in 1923, and governed by a council of representatives of Essex local authorities, closed in 1939.[68] There was a hospital for Jewish incurables at The Berthons, Whipps Cross, in 1899–1900.[69]

A burial board was constituted in 1870[70] and opened a cemetery in Queen's Road in 1872.[71] The board was dissolved in 1896 when its functions were taken over by the urban district council.[72]

Walthamstow public libraries and museums to 1955 have been described elsewhere.[73] The central library in High Street (1909) occupies a 'Wren'-style building of red brick with stone dressings designed by J. W. Dunford.[74] In 1963 the rebuilding of Hale End branch library at Highams Park was completed, and shops in Coppermill Lane were converted as a temporary St. James Street branch.[75]

Grosvenor House junior training centre for handicapped children opened in 1970 on the site of Grosvenor House.[76]

PARLIAMENTARY REPRESENTATION. Under the Representation of the People Act, 1918, Walthamstow, previously part of the Walthamstow county division, became a parliamentary borough with two divisions, east and west.[77]

At the 1918 election Walthamstow East was won by a Conservative and the West by a Coalition Labour candidate. The Conservatives held the East until 1929. The West was won by Labour in 1922, but lost to the Liberals in 1924. In 1929 both seats were won by Labour: Walthamstow West was regained by Valentine (later Baron) McEntee, first mayor of Walthamstow, who had previously held it in 1922–4. He retained it until 1950. The Conservatives won back the East in 1931 and held it until 1945. From 1945 to 1951 both seats were held by Labour. Clement R. (later Earl) Attlee, prime minister 1945–51, represented Walthamstow West from 1950 to 1955. The Conservatives won back Walthamstow East in 1955, held it in 1959 and 1964, but lost it again in 1966. Walthamstow West was consistently held by Labour until the by-election of 1967, when a Conservative won it for the first time in its history. Walthamstow East was regained by the Conservatives at the by-election of 1969. In 1970 Labour regained Walthamstow West, while the Conservatives held the East.[78]

CHURCHES. At a date between 1103 and 1130 a member of the Tony family gave Walthamstow church with all its tithe to St. Peter of Châtillon by Conches (Eure, France).[79] This gift in its full form was not in fact perpetual for after the death of Ralph de Tony c. 1126, but probably not before 1141, his widow Alice gave the church with its tithes and a little land to Holy Trinity priory, Aldgate. This was done at the request of 'Orderic the priest', apparently

[64] The account of Connaught hospital is based on: G. F. Bosworth, *Some more Walthamstow houses* (W.A.S. xxix), 32–3; *Kelly's Dir. Essex* (1882–1926); A. Hatley, *Across the years*, 91; *Walthamstow Off. Guide* (1925–c. 1939, 1961); A. D. Law, *Walthamstow Topics*, 11; Leyton B.C. *Charter Day, 1926: souvenir programme*, 37–8; *Connaught Hosp. Reps.*
[65] V.H.M., Walthamstow Local Bd. Mins. 1877 f.; *Walthamstow U.D.C. Chmns.' Ann. Reps.* 1898–1905; *V.C.H. Essex*, v. 100; *Walthamstow Off. Guide* (1925), p. 28, (c. 1939), 17; Walthamstow B.C. *Official souvenir . . . of . . . incorporation*, 1929, 39; Law, *Our Town* (2), 32.
[66] Law, *Our Town* (2), 10, 31–2. For Thorpe Coombe, see G. F. Bosworth, *More Walthamstow houses* (W.A.S. xx), 5.
[67] *Walthamstow Off. Guide* (c. 1939), 17; *Walthamstow B.C. Mins. and Reps.* 1929–30, p. 88, 1938–9, pp. 1050, 1057, 1939–40, p. 1058.
[68] *Walthamstow pub. services, 1935*, 47; *Walthamstow Off. Guide* (c. 1927), 30; Law, *Our Town* (2), 10, 31.

[69] *Kelly's Dir. Walthamstow etc.* (1899–1900); *Kelly's Dir. Essex* (1906), 561.
[70] *Incorporation of Walthamstow, 1921: Statistics*, 23.
[71] *Kelly's Dir. Essex* (1874).
[72] *Chmn. of U.D.C.'s Ann. Rep.* 1896.
[73] *V.C.H. Essex Bibliography*, 331. For the Vestry House museum, see also above, p. 279 and for the Water House, see above, p. 252.
[74] Pevsner, *Essex* (2nd edn.), 407.
[75] Law, *Our Town* (2), 34; *Waltham Forest Off. Guide* (1968), 68.
[76] *Walthamstow Guardian*, 12 June 1970.
[77] This section is based unless otherwise stated on: *E.J.* iii. 179–85, iv. 9–26; A. D. Law, *Our Town* (2) (W.A.S. Occ. Pub. vii), 38.
[78] Inf. from W.R.L.
[79] *Gallia Christiana* (ed. D. de Sainte-Marthe), xi. Instr., cols. 128–33 and p. 552. The gift cannot have been earlier than 1103, when Ralph de Tony (d. c. 1126) acquired Walthamstow on his marriage with Alice, daughter of Waltheof and Judith: see above, p. 253.

the rector, who had become a monk of Holy Trinity.[80] When Alice's son Roger confirmed the gift *c.* 1147 he reserved ⅔ of the tithes from the manorial demesne, to which Châtillon was still entitled.[81] Châtillon leased its share of the tithes to Holy Trinity in 1174 for a rent of 25s.[82] and sold that share outright in 1243.[83] In 1206 Roger de Tony still held the tithes of certain ancient meadows and mills, of which the prior of Holy Trinity 'claimed nothing as yet',[84] but when a vicarage was ordained about 1219 and a vicar instituted on the presentation of Holy Trinity the great tithes were confirmed to the priory.[85] The right to the advowson was disputed later in the 13th century. In 1254 the patron was said to be the heir of Ralph de Tony (d. 1239)[86] but in 1264 the priory.[87] In 1285 the priory purchased the Tony claim for 7 marks.[88] It retained both rectory and advowson until its dissolution in 1532.[89] In 1544 the Crown granted both to Paul Withypoll (d. 1547) and his son Edmund (d. 1582)[90] and they descended in that family until 1600 when Sir Edmund Withypoll (d. 1619), Paul's great-grandson, sold them to (Sir) Reginald Argall (d. 1611).[91] After Reginald's death his widow held them in dower[92] until her own death in 1638, when the impropriate estate was dismembered.[93]

Sir Reginald Argall's heir was his brother John of Great Baddow.[94] In 1617 John (d. 1643) sold the reversion expectant of the advowson to Dr. Henry King, archdeacon of Colchester, later bishop of Chichester.[95] King's right to the patronage was challenged after Lady Argall's death by her son by a former marriage, William Rowe.[96] It was still in dispute in 1650[97] and the Argall family appear to have contested it in the late 1650s.[98] John Millington presented in 1657, by what right is not known,[99] but King had won his case by 1660, when he presented.[1]

Elizabeth and Mary, daughters and coheirs of King's son Henry, married Isaac Houblon and Edmund Wyndham respectively; in 1689 the Houblons and Mary Wyndham, widow, presented,[2] then sold the advowson in the same year to John Conyers (d. 1724).[3] It remained in the Conyers family[4] until 1821 when it was sold to William Wilson (vicar 1822–48),[5] passing to his second son, Alfred W. Wilson (vicar 1848–50) about 1850, when he presented Thomas Parry (1850–92).[6] By 1856 it was in the hands of Edward Warner[7] who held it until 1878 when it was transferred to the Simeon Trustees, who still hold it.[8]

The church land and great tithes of Walthamstow formed the rectory manor, the descent of which is treated elsewhere.[9] The tithes of Higham also belonged from 1147 to Holy Trinity,[10] and were probably those given to Walthamstow church at its consecration by Ralph Round (fl. 1130).[11] The value of the rectory during the Middle Ages was said to be 40s. in 1254,[12] a figure which seems improbably low. It was £16 13s. 4d. in 1291,[13] and £10 in 1515.[14]

At its ordination the vicarage was endowed with the small tithes and the altar dues, subject to a quit-rent to Holy Trinity.[15] In 1254 it was valued at 100s.[16] and in 1535 at £13 6s. 8d.[17] By 1526 the vicars held as glebe, copyhold of the rectory manor, an acre of meadow in Out mead, called Longgrass acre, and two crofts (5 a.), one called Wastells, near the vicarage. Gabriel Grant (vicar 1612–38), who resented the impropriation, described them in 1615 as a 'poor handful of fields' and tried unsuccessfully to establish that they were freehold.[18] From about 1626 Lady Argall was paying him an allowance of £20 a year.[19] In 1649 an augmentation of £40 a year was ordered from the tithes sequestered from Thomas Argall, but there is no evidence that it

[80] *V.C.H. London*, i. 473; E.R.O., D/DB L16; E 40 A13850 (1); Cartulary of Holy Trinity, Aldgate (Lond. Rec. Soc. vii), pp. 3, 229; B.M. Cott. Ch. xiii. 18 (15). For discussion of the date of the grant, see P. H. Reaney, *Church of St. Mary, Walthamstow* (W.A.S. N.S. viii), 8–9. The year 1108 often quoted probably arises from the ambiguity of R. Newcourt, *Repertorium*, ii. 634, which refers to the year of the foundation of Holy Trinity priory. The gift was confirmed by Pope Eugenius III in 1147: Dugdale, *Mon.* vi. 154.
[81] E 40 A13850 (3).
[82] E 40 A13850 (6). For discussion of the date, see Reaney, *Church of St. Mary*, 9.
[83] E 40 A13850 (7).
[84] *Cur. Reg. R.* iv. 69–70, 172.
[85] E 40 A13850 (4, 5); B.M. Cott. Ch. xiii. 18; E.R.O., D/DB L16.
[86] *E.A.T.* N.S. xviii. 17.
[87] C 132/31/3.
[88] *Feet of F. Essex*, ii. 46; J.I. 1/242 m. 25.
[89] Newcourt, *Repertorium*, ii. 636–7.
[90] L. & P. Hen. VIII, xix, p. 622; C 142/84/52.
[91] C 142/197/78; C 142/207/105; G. C. Moore Smith and P. H. Reaney, *Family of Withypoll* (W.A.S. xxxiv), 67–77; C.P. 25(2)/139/1759; Lysons, *London*, iv. 219; E.R.O., D/DB L16.
[92] S. J. Barns, *Walthamstow deeds, 1584–1855* (W.A.S. xxxiii), 6.
[93] E.R.O., D/DB L16; Lysons, *London*, iv. 219–20.
[94] *Visitations of Essex* (Harl. Soc.) i. 137; *Visitations of Essex, 1664*, ed. J. J. Howard, 8; *E.A.T.* N.S. x. 309.
[95] E.R.O., D/DB L16.
[96] Ibid.; Davids, *Evang. Nonconf. in Essex*, 206; B. W. Quintrell, 'The Southern Divisional Cttee. for Southern Essex during the Civil Wars' (M.A. thesis, Manchester, 1962), 126–7.
[97] Lambeth MS. 910(8), pp. 154–7.

[98] E.R.O., D/DB E59 (letter from Isaac Houblon to John Conyers, 1688).
[99] Lambeth MS. 998, p. 175.
[1] Newcourt, *Repertorium*, ii. 637.
[2] Ibid. 635, 637; E.R.O., D/DW E1/9.
[3] E.R.O., D/DB T1111; C.P. 25(2)/827/Eas. 1 Wm. & Mary.
[4] For the Conyers family, see G. F. Bosworth, *Some Walthamstow houses* (W.A.S. xii), 14–16 and *V.C.H. Essex*, v. 119.
[5] E.R.O., D/AEM 2/6; Guildhall MS. 9560; *Rep. R. Com. on Ch. Revenues*, H.C. 54, p. 676 (1835), xxii.
[6] Guildhall MS. 9531/32, p. (II) 10, 47.
[7] *Clergy List* (1856).
[8] G. F. Bosworth, *St. Mary's Ch.* (W.A.S .ii), 5; *Kelly's Dir. Essex* (1874, 1878); *Chelmsford Diocesan Yr. Bk.* (1968).
[9] See p. 261.
[10] Dugdale, *Mon.* vi. 154.
[11] *Johannis Saresberiensis Opera*, ed. J. A. Giles, i. 115–16. A dispute over those tithes between Holy Trinity and the church of Waltham (Holy Cross) in the mid 12th century does not appear sufficient to justify the suggestion (*E.A.T.* N.S. vii. 330–1) that Walthamstow may have been a daughter church of Waltham Holy Cross. The dispute probably arose because a small part of Higham Bensted was held of Waltham Abbey: see above, p. 258.
[12] *E.A.T.* N.S. xviii. 17.
[13] *Tax. Eccl.* (Rec. Com.), 22.
[14] Reaney, *Court rolls of Rectory Manor*, 8; Bosworth, *Rectory Manor*, 14.
[15] E 40 A13850 (5).
[16] *E.A.T.* N.S. xviii. 17.
[17] *Valor Eccl.* (Rec. Com.), i. 435.
[18] Bosworth, *Rectory Manor*, 9; Reaney, *Court rolls of Rectory Manor*, 14–15, 18–19; cf. E.R.O., D/DB E60.
[19] E.R.O., D/DB L16.

ever was paid.[20] In 1650 the vicarage was worth £40, comprising small tithes (£32) and 5 a. of glebe (£8).[21] The vicar's income was increased in the 18th century by bequests under the wills of Henry Maynard (d. 1686) and Elizabeth Cooper (d. 1708).[22] In 1796 they produced £34 8s. 10d. and £6 6s. respectively.[23] Four more acres of glebe, called Wildgods, had been bought with the Cooper bequest.[24] In the mid 18th century the vicarage was assessed at £150.[25] Its gross annual income in 1831 was £811.[26] The small tithes were commuted in 1843 for £601 and the vicar had in addition 11½ a. of glebe.[27] The glebe was enfranchised in 1912 and the greater part of the two crofts near the vicarage sold to Essex county council, which built the girls high school there. Wildgods was sold about the same time, and by 1928 the Longgrass acre also.[28]

The chancel belonged to the rector in the Middle Ages,[29] but from the early 17th century it was apparently claimed by the vicars. In 1615 Grant insisted that Lady Argall's pew in 'my chancel', built in 1611 with his predecessor's approval, was occupied by favour of the vicar and not of right, and that his consent was required before her son, William Rowe, could build another. In 1628 Grant signed a letter authorizing Rowe's pew, and the letter was endorsed by four of Grant's successors.[30] The rector's rights were reasserted in 1669, when the Coopers began to lease pews in the chancel and charge for burial in it.[31] Edmund Chishull (vicar 1708–33) revived the vicar's claim, perhaps as a source of additional income, and apparently won its recognition in 1724. In 1730, however, the new rector reasserted his rights and was finally confirmed in them by decision of the diocesan chancellor in 1734.[32] The parish had not acquired the chancel by 1818 but had done so by 1917.[33]

A vicarage house existed in 1487.[34] It was in poor condition in 1565.[35] About 1620 it was described, perhaps on information supplied by the aggrieved Gabriel Grant, as 'an old, rotten house . . . in times past an alehouse', with 5 or 6 chambers,

kitchen, milkhouse, and buttery, and 6 a. of barren ground adjoining; the vicar himself had built a cowhouse, stable, and hayhouse at his own cost, worth more than all the rest.[36] Although orders were given by the sequestrators in 1643 for the house to be repaired, in 1650 it was reported partly pulled down and unfit for habitation.[37] In 1683, however, it was in good repair,[38] and was said in 1690 to have been pulled down and rebuilt by public subscription several times in the last 60 years.[39] It was blown down in the great storm of 1703, half rebuilt in 1704 as a house of '4 small rooms on a floor', and later completed.[40] A drawing dated 1790 shows a substantial house, the centre block having 2 storeys of 5 bays, with a porch, 3 dormer-windows in the roof, and small wings on either side.[41] The vicarage was very much out of repair by 1803, but was rebuilt by 1810.[42] A new one was built in 1903 on the same site, north-west of the church.[43]

George Monoux (d. 1544) endowed a chantry in Walthamstow church by his will dated 1541. The alms-priest, in addition to his prayers, was to sing in the choir and to teach. At its suppression in 1548 the chantry was valued at £6 13s. 4d.[44] Seven lights were maintained in the church before the Reformation; between 1426 and 1537 some 140 bequests were made for their upkeep by 52 testators, the most popular being Our Lady light. The others were the Rood or Holy Cross light, and the Trinity, St. Katherine, Hocking, Sepulchre, and Plough lights.[45]

From the late 16th to the early 18th centuries parish life suffered as a result of a succession of disputes and unsatisfactory appointments to the living. Henry Siddall (1557–63), previously deprived of Woodford for marriage,[46] was collated to Walthamstow by the bishop by lapse. He complained that he could not serve the cure properly because he had been forcibly evicted from the vicarage house and glebe lands by the patron who did not recognize him as vicar.[47] Siddall's successor, Richard Pattenson (1563–5), prosecuted several of his parishioners in

[20] *Cal. Cttee. for Compounding*, iii. 1947.
[21] H. Smith, *Eccl. Hist. Essex*, 248–9.
[22] Bosworth, *Walthamstow Charities* (W.A.S. viii), 24, 32, 49. See also below, p. 315.
[23] Lysons, *London*, iv. 221.
[24] Bosworth, *Walthamstow Chars.* 32; E.R.O., D/DB L16.
[25] Guildhall MSS. 9550 and 9556, f. 62.
[26] *Rep. R. Com. on Ch. Revenues*, H.C. 54, p. 676 (1835), xxii.   [27] E.R.O., D/CT 382.
[28] Bosworth, *Rectory Manor*, 10, and *More Walthamstow houses* (W.A.S. xx), 14; *Kelly's Dir. Essex* (1917); inf. from V.H.M. Wildgods was on the south side of Billet Road where the present Guildsway leads off it.
[29] Reaney, *Court rolls of Rectory Manor*, 8; Bosworth, *Rectory Manor*, 14.
[30] E.R.O., D/DW C1; Reaney, *Court rolls of Rectory Manor*, 19–20; Reaney, *Ch. of St. Mary*, 31–8. Some of the original documents in the case, including the 1628 letter with its endorsements, which Dr. Reaney believed not to have survived (*Ch. of St. Mary*, 37), are in E.R.O., D/DB L16. Dr. Grant was related to the Argalls by marriage, his sister Sarah being the wife of John Argall, heir expectant of the rectory: *E.A.T.* N.S. x. 309.
[31] E.R.O., D/DB E64, D/DW E3, D/DB L16; Barns, *Walthamstow deeds, 1584–1855*, 17–19; *E.A.T.* N.S. xix. 276.
[32] E.R.O., D/DB L16; V.H.M., DRM 12, ff. 19–23. DRM 12 contains the arguments presented on both sides, ff. 11–12, 14–19. Another account of the arguments on the vicar's side is in V.H.M., 'Particulars . . . extracted by William Pamplin in 1789' (MS.), ff. 85–102.
[33] Barns, *Walthamstow Vestry Mins. 1772–94*, 77; V.H.M., DPV 4, f. 284; E.R.O., D/DQ 55/112; Bosworth, *Rectory Manor*, 12. The chancel may have been acquired between 1820 and 1896, the period covered by the missing vestry minutes.
[34] Fry, *Walthamstow Wills*, 11.
[35] E.R.O., D/AEV 1, f. 4; C1/1467/52.
[36] E.R.O., D/DB L16. This undated extract, taken from an unidentified bishop's register, has been attributed to *c.* 1612–24 by checking the names of the two churchwardens making the return, in the E.R.O. indexes.
[37] *C.J.* iii. 401; Lambeth MS. 910(8), pp. 154–7.
[38] *E.A.T.* N.S. xix. 276.
[39] V.H.M., DRM 7.
[40] V.H.M., *Vestiges*, nos. 43, 46; Newcourt, *Repertorium*, ii. 636.
[41] V.H.M., 'Particulars relating to parish of Walthamstow extracted . . . by William Pamplin in 1789' (MS.).
[42] E.R.O., D/AEV 29; Guildhall MS. 9558, f. 373.
[43] The date is inscribed on the north side of the house.
[44] *V.C.H. Essex*, ii. 527–8; Bosworth, *St. Mary's Ch.* 6, *George Monoux* (W.A.S. xvii), 17–18, and *Walthamstow Charities*, 10, 51; Bosworth and C. D. Saunders, *Original docs. relating to Monoux family* (W.A.S. xix), 8. See also below, pp. 289, 309, 313.
[45] Fry, *Walthamstow Wills*, passim.
[46] See p. 353. Unless otherwise stated the dates of incumbents are taken from Newcourt, *Repertorium*, ii. 637.
[47] Newcourt, *Repertorium*, ii. 637; C 1/1467/52–7.

1563 for withholding tithes[48] and appears later to have abandoned the living.[49] John Reynolds (1583–1611) was listed in 1604 among insufficient or negligent ministers.[50] After his death the contentious Gabriel Grant was at odds with his patron, as described above, and in 1635 was charged with adultery.[51] As a result of the dispute over the advowson after Grant's death in 1638, the living was for many years void and supplied by curates.[52] The income of the vicarage was sequestrated by the bishop until 1644, when the House of Commons, on the petition of the inhabitants, ordered that it be paid to Richard Lee, an active covenanter who had been officiating since 1643.[53] About 1649 the Committee for Plundered Ministers appointed John Wood to supply the cure.[54] His unpopularity provoked a riotous demonstration in the church and most of the inhabitants refused to attend his services. In 1650 the parish was in 'great distraction' and Wood's ability in question.[55] By 1651 he had been replaced by John Pigot.[56] The admission to the vicarage in 1658 of Thomas Cartwright, later bishop of Chester, was apparently the first normal appointment of a vicar for twenty years.[57] But parish life was again disrupted in 1669 when Andrew Casse (1666–79), 'an unhappy and obnoxious person', suddenly abandoned the parish one Sunday morning and never returned. For ten years the cure was sequestrated, until eventually Casse resigned and the bishop collated Isaac Wright (1679–89) by lapse.[58] The chancel dispute, renewed during the incumbency of Edmund Chishull, the antiquary, brought fresh discord to the parish, culminating in a brawl in 1730 when the rector with his servants tried forcibly to occupy the patron's pew in the chancel.[59]

In 1733 two services were being held on Sundays and by the late 18th century three, with two sermons, and mid-week services as well.[60] Edmund Chishull employed a curate,[61] as did Thomas Wetenhall (1759–76).[62] During the incumbency of Edward Conyers (1779–1822), who was also vicar of Epping and lived there, William Sparrow served as curate for 39 years.[63] William Wilson (1822–48), who established three chapels of ease between 1829 and 1842, was employing two curates in 1831 and four by 1837.[64]

The church of ST. MARY, which bore that dedication by c. 1147,[65] stands at the top of Church

Hill, between Church Hill Road and Church Lane, at the heart of Church End or 'the village'. It comprises a nave of five bays, small chancel with low vestries on each side, embattled west tower, north and south aisles with chapels, and north and south porches. The walls are partly of flint and stone and partly of brick. The whole building is rendered in mustard-coloured cement. The church was partly rebuilt in the 16th century and extensively altered, restored, and enlarged from the 18th century onwards.[66] When the external rendering was renewed after the Second World War important details of the earlier structure were exposed and recorded.[67] The church has a fine group of monuments.

Although a church was in existence early in the 12th century, the oldest surviving work in the present building appears to date from the 13th century.[68] It consists of the remains of circular piers and responds at the base of the three westernmost bays of the nave arcades and suggests that the Norman church was then either rebuilt or enlarged by the addition of aisles.[69] The walls of the north aisle were originally of squared stone blocks and faced flints. A tower built of Kentish ragstone existed by 1431.[70] A round stone panel on the northwest buttress of the tower with a carved *Agnus Dei* is probably of the 15th century.[71]

About 1535 the church was extensively restored and altered, partly at the expense of George Monoux (d. 1544) of Moons, and partly from a legacy from Robert Thorne (d. 1532). Thorne, like Monoux, was a London merchant who came originally from Bristol. He had no known connexion with Walthamstow except family and business relationships with the Withypoll family. By his will he left £1,000 to be spent at the discretion of his executors for the good of his soul. The executors were Paul Withypoll, whose brother Richard became vicar of Walthamstow in 1534, and Emanuel Lucar, Paul's son-in-law. The money, a huge sum in the 16th century, was spent on rebuilding the south aisle and porch of Walthamstow church, and an inscription recording the fact, dated 1535, was placed in the east window of the aisle.[72] The new aisle extended the length of the nave and chancel, forming the Thorne chapel at the east end. Both aisle and porch were built of brick, on stone and flint foundations which may have been partly those of the original structure.[73] The aisle was flat-roofed, and the clerestory win-

---

[48] E.R.O., D/AEA 2.
[49] G.L.C., DL/C/332, f. 113v; E.R.O., D/AEV 1, f. 4.
[50] H. Smith, *Eccl. Hist. Essex*, 17; Newcourt, *Repertorium*, ii. 637; E.R.O., D/AEV 4, f. 178.
[51] Smith, *Eccl. Hist. Essex*, 48; *E.A.T.* N.S. xviii 27.
[52] H. Smith, 'Sequence of the parochial clergy in Essex 1640–1664' (TS. in E.R.O. Libr.), 13.
[53] *E.A.T.* N.S. vii. 283 n. (quoting *C.J.* iii. 401); Lambeth MS. 910 (8), pp. 154–7; Newcourt, *Repertorium*, ii. 637 n.; E.R.O., D/DB L16; Smith. *Eccl. Hist. Essex*, 99, 193.
[54] E.R.O., D/DB L16; Lambeth MS. 910 (8), pp. 154–7. Though Wood called himself 'vicar' he was not appointed as such.
[55] *Cal. S.P. Dom.* 1649–50, 331–2, 344, 361–2, 371; E.R.O., Q/SR 343/61; Lambeth MS. 910 (8), pp. 154–7.
[56] E.R.O., D/DB L16.
[57] Lambeth MS. 998, p. 175; *E.A.T.* N.S. vii. 283. For Thomas Cartwright, see *D.N.B.*
[58] E.R.O., D/DB L16; V.H.M., 'Particulars of the parish . . . extracted . . . by William Pamplin in 1789' (MS.), ff. 93, 100.   [59] Ibid.; *D.N.B.*
[60] Guildhall MSS. 9550, 9558, f. 373.
[61] Guildhall MS. 9550.

[62] Ibid. 9555, 9556, p. 62, 9531/21, f. (2) 69.
[63] Ibid. 9558, f. 373; E.R.O., D/AEM 2/3, D/AEV 29; Reaney, *Church of St. Mary*, 59; *V.C.H. Essex*, v. 133.
[64] Guildhall MS. 9560; *Rep. R. Com. on Ch. Revenues*, H.C. 54, p. 676 (1835), xxii; W. G. S. Tonkin, *Anglican Church in Walthamstow* (W.A.S. N.S. iv), 10.
[65] E 40 A13850 (3).
[66] For plans of the church in 1916 and 1969, see Bosworth, *St. Mary's Ch.* (W.A.S. ii), f.p. 16, and Reaney, *Ch. of St. Mary*, pl. iv.
[67] V.H.M., *Vestiges*, nos. 32–4, 64–5, 69–70; Tonkin, *Anglican Ch. in Walthamstow*, 30–1; Reaney, *Ch. of St. Mary*, 7. Unless otherwise stated all references to the medieval stone and flint structure are taken from the reports in *Vestiges*.
[68] R.C.H.M. *Essex*, ii. 246.
[69] Reaney, *Ch. of St. Mary*, 12–13.
[70] Fry, *Walthamstow Wills*, 2.
[71] R.C.H.M. *Essex* ii. 247.
[72] G. C. M. Smith, revised P. H. Reaney, *Family of Withypoll* (W. A. S. xxxiv), 24–30, 36–8; Lysons, *London*, iv. 211.
[73] V.H.M., *Vestiges*, nos. 32–4.

dows above it which are shown in later pictures were probably inserted at this time. Above the Thorne inscription in the east window were depicted the Four Evangelists, and in the other windows of the aisle the arms of the Merchant Taylors' company, of which Thorne was a member, and of the City of London, of which he was lord mayor.[74] The extension of the south aisle eastwards of the chancel arch did away with the original south door to the chancel. It was replaced by a small stone doorway in the south wall of the Thorne chapel, which was bricked up in 1720,[75] and revealed when the external rendering was renewed in 1960.

The upper parts of the north aisle and tower were rebuilt in red brick about the same time as the south aisle was reconstructed, the medieval masonry being retained to about 14 feet above ground level in the north aisle, and about 20 feet in the outer walls of the tower. The tower arch was almost entirely rebuilt in brick, but the stone bases of its jambs, apparently dating from the 15th century, survive.[76] An inscription recorded that George Monoux paid for the aisle and his arms were depicted in the windows.[77] At the same time he built a chapel at the east end of the north aisle, divided from the chancel by an arch. The roof of the chapel, in which there was a loft,[78] was higher than that of the aisle, and gabled. No evidence was found in the 1960s of any earlier building on the chapel site. The ownership of the seats in the restored north aisle was apparently granted by the parish to Monoux and his heirs. By 1635 the repair of the north aisle and chapel was regarded as the responsibility of the Monoux trustees, although the right to the pews had in fact been several times conveyed as appurtenant to the property of Moons.[79]

The restoration of the tower is also usually attributed to Monoux.[80] Since bequests for rebuilding were made in 1517–19,[81] it is possible that its rebuilding was begun before that of the north aisle,

with Monoux perhaps contributing most towards completion of the work.

In the 17th century, through the negligence of the Monoux trustees, the Monoux chapel and north aisle were often in disrepair.[82] A great deal of restoration was carried out in the 18th century. In 1748 the vestry decided to repair the battlements, walls, and gutter, of the south side of the church, if necessary from one end of it to the other. The battlements of the whole church were repaired in 1752, and in 1764 the church was closed while the roof, gutters, and parapet were repaired.[83] In 1768 the nave and north and south aisles had leaded roofs, while the chancel and Monoux chapel roofs were tiled.[84] Alterations in the 18th century included the erection of a cupola on the tower about 1715, by the bequest of Susan Samms,[85] and the blocking up, probably before 1719, of the east window of the Thorne chapel.[86] In 1784 unspecified work costing £1,250 was carried out at the church by (Sir) John Soane.[87] It was probably in the chancel, as Soane was already employed by the rector, William Cooke, on the alterations to the rectory house already described.

Throughout the 18th century the need grew for more seating in the church. In 1710–11 a west gallery was built,[88] and in 1774 a gallery over the south aisle, designed by Joel Johnson[89] and lit by skylights in the flat roof.[90] The part of the Monoux estate charged with the repair of the north aisle and chapel had been in the ownership of the Marshall family since before 1710,[91] and in 1782, by agreement with the Revd. Edmund Marshall and Joshua Marshall, the parish assumed responsibility for the north aisle and chapel as well as the Monoux school and alms-houses.[92] A gallery over the north aisle was built in 1806–7 and the south gallery altered to correspond with it. The clerestory windows were removed, the aisles were heightened, and three small windows were inserted below their new embattled parapets to light the galleries.[93] The work

[74] Smith, Family of Withypoll, 30.
[75] S. J. Barns, Vestry Mins. 1710–40 (W.A.S. xiii), 9. It may have been the original medieval door removed to a new position.
[76] Cf. R.C.H.M. Essex, ii. 246.
[77] E.R.O., T/P 195/1 (Holman MSS.); Reaney, Ch. of St. Mary, 20, 23; cf. V.H.M. Vestiges, nos. 64–5. George Monoux acquired the lease of the rectory manor in 1533.
[78] E.A.T. N.S. xix. 276. It is shown on late-18th-century NW. views of the church.
[79] Lysons, London, iv. 211, 213; Bosworth, Walthamstow Charities, 51; Edmund Chishull's notes in the parish register, 1692–1733; V.H.M., Vestiges, nos. 64–5; Bosworth and Saunders, Docs. relating to Monoux family, 15; Bosworth, Manor of Higham Bensted (W.A.S. vi), 13; V.H.M., PV 4, f. 286 and 'Particulars of the parish . . . extracted . . . by William Pamplin in 1789' (MS.), ff. 107–9.
[80] e.g. J. Weever, Ancient Funeral Monuments (1631), 598.
[81] Fry, Walthamstow Wills, 16–17.
[82] Bosworth and Saunders, Docs. relating to Monoux Family, 12, 15; E.R.O., D/AEV 7, f. 11; E.A.T. N.S. xix. 276; Chishull's notes in parish register; Rep. Com. Char. Essex, H.C. 216, p. 28 (1835), xxi(1).
[83] S. J. Barns, Vestry Mins. 1741–71 (W.A.S. xiv), 32, 34, 43–5. It has been suggested that the extensive restoration apparent in the fabric of the upper part of the south aisle throughout its length and in the parapet of the north aisle followed damage by the great storm of 1703: V.H.M., Vestiges, nos. 32–4, 64–5, 69–70. But there is no evidence that the church was damaged in 1703, or of any work being done before 1748.

[84] Morant, Essex, i. 37. In 1661 150 lb. of lead was stolen from the church: Assizes 35/102/2(21).
[85] Bosworth, Walthamstow Chars. 33; S. J. Barns, Memorials in the Ch. (W.A.S. xxvii), 27.
[86] It still existed when Chishull became vicar in 1708 (cf. Chishull's notes in parish register) but is not shown in late-18th-century NE. views of the church, and the Thorne glass is not mentioned by Holman who visited the church in 1719 and noted the Monoux glass: E.R.O., T/P 195/1.
[87] D. Stroud, Architecture of Sir John Soane (1961), 157; Pevsner, Essex (2nd edn.), 406 n. Owing to the extensive later alterations to the chancel, no evidence remains of any work which may have been done in 1784.
[88] Barns, Vestry Mins. 1710–40, 6.
[89] Barns, Vestry Mins. 1741–71, 39–40, 46, and Vestry Mins. 1772–94 (W.A.S. xvi), 58; Colvin, Biog. Dict. Eng. Architects, 322–3.
[90] Shown, for example, on a drawing of 1794 (Guildhall Libr. Lysons, London (extra illus.), iv. following p. 210) and on the engraving (1805) for D. Hughson's Description of London.
[91] Barns, Vestry Mins. 1741–71, 39–40, 45; E.R.O., D/DB E62. In 1710 Edward Marshall stated that his father Joshua had bought the part of the Monoux estate charged with the alms-house and school charities and repair of the chapel.
[92] Barns, Vestry Mins. 1772–94, 58, 76–7; Bosworth, Walthamstow Charities, 51. See also below, pp. 309, 313. For the church and alms-houses in 1785 see plate f.p. 307.
[93] V.H.M., PV 5, ff. 190, 197; E.R.O., Pictorial Coll. (St. Mary's Ch. leaflet, c. 1886, and unidentified engraver's preliminary pencil sketch of SW. view, 1813).

was carried out by William Pocock.[94] By 1813 the exterior of the south aisle was rendered.[95]

In 1817–18 the church was restored and enlarged to the design of Charles Bacon (d. 1818).[96] The alterations were structurally of yellow brick. The chancel, already occupied since the 17th century by a number of pews, was heightened to unite its 2 bays with the 3 bays of the nave, leaving only a small sanctuary, in which the previous large pointed east window of five lights with tracery was replaced by a wheel window. The pulpit was moved into the centre of the chancel. The Monoux and Thorne chapels were raised higher than the aisles, and the north and south galleries continued to the east end of the church. Two tall lancet windows on each side replaced the original north and south chapel windows, and the present trefoil windows were inserted in their east walls. As Bacon mentions 'rough cast Derby lime' he probably continued the process of rendering the exterior to give it a uniform appearance.

In 1830 a small vestry was built on at the east end.[97] The cupola was taken down in 1836.[98] A north porch existed by 1843,[99] built some time after 1799.[1] In 1843 the three original bays of the nave arcades were raised with the aisles to the same height as the two chapel bays. Two of the medieval circular piers supporting the arcades were heightened in an octagonal form, while two others were apparently rebuilt. The earlier aisle windows were replaced by uniform lancet windows.[2] In 1876 the interior of the church was made more open; the box-pews were removed, and the gallery fronts were set back. At the same time the low plaster ceiling was replaced by a high wooden one. A few years later stone mullions and new glass were inserted in the lancet windows.[3]

A chancel extension was built in 1938, flanked by 2 vestries; a five-light lancet window replaced the wheel window in the east wall.[4] The north side of the tower parapet and the south aisle were damaged by bombing in 1940 and during restoration in 1942 the south gallery was removed. The church was extensively restored between 1949 and 1968.[5]

The church had at least one bell in 1431. Richard Blakgrave in 1525 left a share of his goods to buy a bell.[6] In 1552 there were 5 bells, and a hand bell which was sold.[7] The largest bell was recast in 1727 by John Waylett.[8] There were 6 bells in 1768, which were replaced in 1778 by a complete new peal of eight bells cast by Thomas Pack and William Chapman.[9] In 1852 the tenor bell was replaced by one cast by C. & G. Mears.[10] The old bell-frame was replaced in 1896, the eight bells were rehung, no. 3 being recast, and two treble bells were added, all by John Warner and Sons.[11] There were 10 bells in 1969.[12]

The church had one silver-gilt communion cup in 1552.[13] In 1674 all the silver plate, comprising 2 flagons, 2 cups with covers, and a basin, was stolen and apparently never recovered.[14] This incident probably gave rise to the later tradition that Dick Turpin took the Walthamstow church plate and held it to ransom.[15] The lost plate was replaced by a cup and paten of 1680,[16] a cup and paten of 1685–6, and two flagons and two alms-dishes of 1685.[17] The church also has alms-dishes dated 1843 and 1906, a cup of 1904, and a paten of 1901.[18]

There is a stoup on the north wall of the south porch.[19] The white veined marble font, a fluted bowl on a baluster stem, was given in 1714.[20] The Royal Arms, of carved and painted wood, dates from 1742. The beadle's staff is dated 1779[21] and the clock 1807.[22]

The inscriptions on 100 memorials in the church were recorded in 1910.[23] Other memorials, no longer extant, were recorded by Strype in 1720, and Daniel Lysons in 1796, including a brass to William Hyll (1487), vicar,[24] which had gone by 1756. In the north aisle is a marble monument to Lady Lucy Stanley (d. 1601),[25] whose effigy kneels

[94] Probably William Pocock of Leyton, see above, p. 228.

[95] E.R.O., Pictorial Coll. (1813 engraver's sketch, distinguishing areas of brick, stone, plaster, etc.).

[96] Bosworth, *Rectory Manor*, 12; *White's Dir. Essex* (1848); E.R.O., D/DQ 14/42 (Charles Bacon's diary, 1816–17); V.H.M., PV 5, ff. 424–5, 455, 472. For discussion of the implications of the alterations, see Reaney, *Ch. of St. Mary*, 60–1, V.H.M., *Vestiges*, nos. 32–4, 64–5, 69–70, and Tonkin, *Anglican Ch. in Walthamstow*, 29–30. The immediate effect of Bacon's work is best shown by comparing the 1813 engraver's sketch from SW. (E.R.O., Pictorial Coll.) with an engraved SE. view by M.S. dated 1819 (reproduced Bosworth, *St. Mary's Ch.*, f.p. 8).

[97] Reaney, *Ch. of St. Mary*, 61.

[98] Bosworth, *St. Mary's Ch.*, 8.

[99] See plan of church on tithe map: E.R.O., D/CT 382.

[1] E.R.O., Pictorial Coll. (engraving of N. door, 1786); Guildhall Libr., Lysons, *London* (extra illus.), iv, following p. 210 (colour-wash drawing of church from NE.).

[2] E.R.O., Pictorial Coll. (St. Mary's Ch. leaflet, *c.* 1886); *White's Dir. Essex* (1848); Walford, *Greater London*, i. 467.

[3] *Kelly's Dir. Essex* (1878); E.R.O., Pictorial Coll. (St. Mary's Ch. leaflet, *c.* 1886); Bosworth, *St. Mary's Ch.* 7; Walford, *Greater London*, i. 467.

[4] *Chelmsford Dioc. Chron.* Nov. 1937, p. 165; Reaney, *Ch. of St. Mary*, 71.

[5] Reaney, *Ch. of St. Mary*, 72–6; V.H.M., *Vestiges*, nos. 32–4, 64–5, 69–70.

[6] Fry, *Walthamstow Wills*, 2, 18.

[7] *E.A.T.* N.S. ii. 246.

[8] V.H.M., PV 1, f. 161. For John Waylett see *Ch. Bells Essex*, 119–21. He is described in the vestry minutes as 'bell-founder at Windmill Hill'.

[9] *Ch. Bells Essex*, 136–7, 435–6; Barns, *Vestry Mins. 1772–94*, 65–7, 72, 76.

[10] Bosworth, *St. Mary's Ch.* 8; *Ch. Bells Essex*, 435.

[11] *E.R.* vi. 5; *Ch. Bells Essex*, 141, 434–5.

[12] Reaney, *Ch. of St. Mary*, 58.

[13] *E.A.T.* N.S. ii. 246.

[14] Assizes 35/115/1 (15).

[15] *Ch. Plate Essex*, 37.

[16] Ibid. 36; E.R.O., D/AEV 12, f. 21. They were using a pewter flagon in 1683.

[17] *Ch. Plate Essex*, 36–7; Bosworth, *St. Mary's Ch.* 11, and *Walthamstow Chars.* 49.

[18] *Ch. Plate Essex*, 36–7.

[19] R.C.H.M. *Essex*, ii. 247.

[20] Ibid. pl. xxxii, 247; Barns. *Vestry Mins. 1710–40*, 7–8; Pevsner, *Essex* (2nd edn.), 406.

[21] Pevsner, *Essex*, 406; Bosworth, *St. Mary's Ch.* 11.

[22] Inscription on tower.

[23] S. J. Barns, *Monumental Inscriptions, Walthamstow* (W.A.S. xxvii).

[24] Ibid. 29–31. Unless otherwise stated the account of the monuments is based on: R.C.H.M. *Essex*, ii. 246–7; Pevsner, *Essex* (2nd edn.) 43, 406; Tonkin, *Ang. Ch. in Walthamstow*, 31–2; F. Chancellor, *Ancient Sepulchral Monuments of Essex*; Reaney, *Ch. of St. Mary*; Bosworth, *St. Mary's Ch.* 14–16; John Stow, *Survey of London*, enlarged by John Strype, 1720 (6th edn. 1754–5), ii. 782–7. In this edition Strype's accounts of Chingford, Leyton, Walthamstow, and West Ham, were brought up to date to 1756 (*sic*) by Edward Rowe Mores (see index, vol. ii, under Chingford, etc.).

[25] V.H.M., Biographical files (Stanley). There is an identical inscription on the Stanley monument in Tong church (Salop.), see Mrs. Esdaile, 'Shakespeare's verses in Tong Ch. Salop', *Shropshire Arch. Soc. Trans.* 1938.

under an arch before a prayer desk with four smaller kneeling figures representing her daughters. On the floor is a mutilated brass of Thomas Hale and his wife (1588), both figures being palimpsest, with parts of figures, c. 1450, on the reverse. Among a number of memorials to members of the Bonnell family, including Sarah (d. 1766), founder of the charity school at West Ham,[26] is the monument at the east end of the Monoux chapel to the family of Captain John Bonnell (d. 1703). It comprises a stone sarcophagus and a large inscribed banner and achievement which once surmounted it but is now displayed apart. Also in the Monoux chapel are brass inscriptions to the vicar Henry Crane (1436) and William Rowe (1596), and on the north arcade are inlaid the kneeling brass figures of George Monoux (d. 1544) and his wife Anne, all that remains of the tomb originally built under the arch dividing the Monoux chapel from the chancel.[27] On the north wall of the chancel is a fine monument designed by Nicholas Stone and erected by Sir Thomas Merry of Winns (later Water House) to his wife Mary (d. 1632), with demi-figures of them both in oval niches and busts of their four children in relief below. On the south wall of the chancel is the monument to Henry Maynard (1686), one of Walthamstow's greatest benefactors,[28] whose family owned the manor of Walthamstow Tony. It is an inscribed marble tablet surmounted by urns and attended by cherubs. At the west end of the south aisle is the tomb of Sigismund Trafford (d. 1723), who was born in 1643 in Capworth Street in the Walthamstow Slip.[29] It was erected between 1689 and 1719[30] with life-size figures of Trafford and his wife Susannah (d. 1689) in Roman dress with a child between them. A tablet to William Raikes (d. 1824) is by Sir Richard Westmacott and one to Elizabeth Morley (d. 1837) is by W. G. Nicholl.

An early chapel at Higham gave its name to Chapel End.[31] In 1441–2 Sir William Tyrwhitt founded a chantry of one chaplain in a chapel of St. Edward lately built by him at Higham; he granted to the chaplain the chapel, a house, and 4 a. of land at Higham.[32] Various sites near Chapel End have been suggested for the chapel.[33] The most likely may be the holding on the south-west corner of the Chapel End cross-roads, which comprised in 1817 and 1822 a small house and garden, and a 4-acre meadow called Chapel field.[34] Although the chapel's builder was later, if not at the time, lord of the manor of Salisbury Hall, the chapel was regarded as belonging to the lord of the manor of Higham.[35] It

was described in 1519 as a free chapel.[36] Nothing more is known of the chantry. The chapel is not mentioned after 1563 until 1648 when the sequestrators granted £50 for the minister of the chapel in the hamlet of Higham, two miles from the parish church. This may have been an attempt to restore it, for in 1650 the chapel was reported in ruin and the Higham court leet vainly suggested that it be rebuilt since the neighbourhood was so far from the parish church.[37]

The private chapels or oratories of the Rowe family in the manor-house of Higham and of George Monoux in his house, Moons, near Chapel End, are described elsewhere.[38]

Apart from the early chapel at Higham, St. Mary's parish church was the only Anglican place of worship until 1829. In that year a chapel of ease, St. John's, was built at Chapel End on the initiative of the vicar, William Wilson, who later established two more chapels of ease, St. Peter's-in-the-Forest (1840), and St. James's (1842) at the lower end of Marsh Street. In 1844 parishes were formed for all three chapels of ease. After 1870 more churches were built to serve the rapidly increasing population, and by 1903 there were 12 churches and 7 missions in Walthamstow. But although in 1903 St. Mary's was the best attended church in Walthamstow of any denomination, the proportion of Anglicans among total church attendances was only some 40 per cent.[39] One more church and another mission church were founded before the First World War. In the 1930s the numbers of regular church-goers decreased. Two mission churches closed at the outbreak of the Second World War and during the war two churches were destroyed by bombing. In 1970 11 churches and 1 chapel remained.

The following accounts of individual churches and missions are arranged under parishes, listed in order of their formation. Where it is stated that the advowson was vested in the bishop, this means the bishop of the diocese which then or later included Walthamstow.[40]

St. Mary's conducted several missions which did not become independent churches. In 1894 St. Mary's clergy were holding evening services in the Victoria hall, Hoe Street, which had been registered in the previous year.[41] *CHRIST CHURCH* mission, Shrubland Road, probably originated about 1895 as St. Mary's mission on Hoe Street bridge. In 1904 the mission moved to Shrubland Road where an iron building acquired from the Post Office was put up and altered by the addition of a chancel

26 See p. 146.
27 Newcourt, *Repertorium*, ii. 635; Bosworth, *George Monoux* (W.A.S. xvii), 16 (illus.); E.R.O., T/P 195/1 (Holman MSS.) describes the original tomb.
28 See p. 315.
29 Morant, *Essex*, i. 36; cf. E.R.O., D/DAc 153.
30 The faculty for the monument was obtained in 1689 (E.R.O., T/A 366) and Holman described it in 1719 (E.R.O., T/P 195/1).
31 Stow, *Survey* (6th edn.), ii. 792; Lysons, *London*, iv. 210.
32 *Cal. Pat.* 1441–6, 41–2; Hist. MSS. Com. *9th Rep.* I, 40a. Lysons (*London*, iv. 210) suggests that the dedication was to Edward the Confessor.
33 Lysons, *London*, iv. 210; Stow, *Survey* (6th edn.), ii. 792; E.R.O., D/DXj 10, f. 328; 11, ff. 37–8; Reaney, *Walthamstow Place-Names*, 29.
34 V.H.M., DSM 2, f. 196v; *John Coe's Map of Walthamstow, 1822* (W.A.S., N.S. v. vA), nos. 320, 321; V.H.M., Extracts from Joel Johnson's 'Anecdotes': John-

son (d. 1799) thought it was George Monoux's private chapel which had stood in Chapel field.
35 E.R.O., D/DFc 185, f. 237.
36 V.H.M., Translation of Monoux Ledger Book (TS.; original B.M. Add. MS. 18783), p. 189.
37 H. Smith, 'Sequence of parochial clergy in Essex, 1640–64' (TS. in E.R.O. Libr. citing MSS. Bodl. 325/91, 326/111), 14; E.R.O., D/DFc 185, ff. 70, 237. 38 See pp. 259, 294.
39 R. Mudie-Smith, *Relig. Life Lond.* 367, 369, 462; *V.C.H. Essex*, v. 59. Christ Church and St. Alban's missions were omitted from the 1903 survey; St. Andrew's mission church, Chingford Lane, listed in the survey under Walthamstow, was a mission of a Woodford parish church, All Saints (see below, p. 355).
40 Unless otherwise stated the accounts are based on W. G. S. Tonkin, *Anglican Church in Walthamstow* (W.A.S. N.S. iv, pubd. 1963).
41 W.R. 34017. The registration of the Victoria hall (see also above, p. 252) was not on behalf of any particular denomination. The hall became a theatre in 1896.

and vestry.[42] The mission closed about 1939 and was later demolished. In 1910 a mission was opened in the Pioneer café, Hoe Street, with evening services for the residents of High Street. Before 1889 a mission cottage was built in Vestry Road by Alfred Janson as a centre for the social work of his two sisters.[43]

The church of *ST. JOHN*, Chingford Road, was built in 1829-30 as a chapel of ease to St. Mary's. A separate parish was formed in 1844, the advowson of the vicarage being vested in the vicar of St. Mary's. In 1923 the original church, which had for some years been structurally weak, was demolished. A new one on the same site, designed in a Gothic style by H. P. Burke Downing and built of brown brick with stone dressings, was consecrated in 1924. Because of lack of funds only three bays of the nave were built at that time. A fourth bay and a permanent west wall were added in 1961. Parts of St. John's parish were transferred to those of St. Luke (1903), St. Andrew (1911), All Saints (1912), and St. Edmund, South Chingford (1922).

The church of *ST. PETER*, Woodford New Road, commonly called 'St. Peter's-in-the-Forest', was built in 1840 as a chapel of ease to St. Mary's to the design of John Shaw (1803-70). It was a small square building of yellow brick in a Romanesque style with an eastern apse and south-west tower. A separate parish was formed in 1844. The advowson of the vicarage, originally vested in the vicar of St. Mary's, was transferred in 1859 to Edward Warner who had given £1,000 for a vicarage house, and it has continued in the Warner family.[44] In 1887 the church was extended westwards so that the tower stood at the centre of the south side; the east end was reorganized as a chancel. The interior was renovated in 1936-7 by Martin Travers. In 1945 the church was badly damaged by a rocket bomb. Repairs and alterations completed in 1951 included a further western extension containing vestries and entrance lobby. The sanctuary, chancel, and west windows were altered in 1958. The cemetery, consecrated in 1845, is the only one attached to a modern Anglican church in Walthamstow. Parts of the parish of St. Peter have been transferred to All Saints, Woodford Wells (1875), All Saints, Highams Park (1912), and St. Anne, Chingford Hatch (1956).

The church of *ST. JAMES*, St. James Street, was built in 1842 on a site given by the vicar of St. Mary's and S. R. Bosanquet. A separate parish was formed in 1844. The advowson of the vicarage was transferred in 1873 by the vicar of St. Mary's to the bishop. In 1875 St. Saviour's became the parish church of St. James's parish with St. James's as its chapel of ease. From 1882 to 1885, while the new church of St. Michael and All Angels was being built, St. James's was the centre of work for a mission district.[45] The church was demolished and rebuilt in 1902-3. The new building, designed by J. E. K. and J. P. Cutts, contained the altar, east

window, and many of the bricks from the old church. It was dedicated to *ST. JAMES THE GREATER*. The parish of St. James the Greater, formed in 1904, was taken out of the old parish of St. James (alias St. Saviour). In 1941 its vicar became responsible for the parish of St. Oswald after that church had been bombed. Part of St. Oswald's parish was united with St. James the Greater in 1949. In 1957 St. James the Greater was placed temporarily under the vicar of St. Barnabas. It was closed in 1960 and was later demolished. The parish was merged in that of St. Barnabas in 1961. Some furnishings from St. James the Greater went to a mission church at Widford; others, including an altar from the first church of St. James, were used for a chapel of St. James in St. Barnabas' church.

The church of *ST. ANDREW*, St. Andrew's Road, originated in 1871, when an iron mission church was erected to serve this part of St. John's parish. A brick hall was built in Higham Hill Road in 1890. A conventional district was formed for St. Andrew in 1908, which became a separate parish in 1911 when a permanent church designed by Hoare & Wheeler was built on the site of the old iron one. The advowson of the vicarage was vested in the vicar of St. Mary's. The church, a large aisled building of dark brown brick with simple Gothic windows, was left incomplete at the east end owing to lack of funds.[46] It was badly damaged by bombs in 1940 and 1944 and was closed in 1969, when a new church was planned. Until completion of the new church, services were transferred to the new church hall in Church Road,[47] built in 1962, when the original hall was sold to the borough council and demolished to make way for redevelopment.

The church of *ST. SAVIOUR*, Markhouse Road, which in 1875 became the parish church of St. James's parish, was erected in 1874 from designs by T. F. Dolman.[48] It is the only church left in Walthamstow which dates from the great days of the Gothic Revival. Built of stone in a correct 13th-century style, it consists of aisled nave, apsidal chancel, and tall north-west tower with broach-spire. The church and vicarage house and an endowment of £100 a year were given by Richard Foster and John Knowles. The mission hall of *ST. ALBAN*, Ashford Road, was built in 1889 as a mission of St. Saviour's. A mission room in Gosport Road listed in 1903-5 may have been connected with it.[49] St. Alban's closed in 1939. It was later used as a factory until 1966, when it was bought by Walthamstow borough council for demolition.[50] The 'Navvy Mission', an iron building in Station Road, was in use from 1896 to 1908. In 1945 the church was badly damaged by fire. Repairs were started three years later and the church was rededicated in 1950. Parts of the parish of St. James were transferred to those of St. Barnabas (1901) and St. James the Greater (1904). Since 1963 the name of the parish has been changed to St. Saviour.[51]

[42] The iron building was the original Post Office sorting office erected in 1885 near Hoe Street railway station, and replaced in 1903 by a brick building in Vestry Road: V.H.M., *Vestiges*, nos. 93-4.
[43] Bosworth, *More Walthamstow houses* (W.A.S. xx), 13; *Kelly's Dir. Walthamstow, Leyton and Leytonstone* (1889, 1890, 1902); *Walthamstow Town Almanack* (1895).
[44] *Chelmsford Dioc. Yr. Bk.* (1968-9).
[45] See p. 293.
[46] *Essex Churchman*, Aug. 1962.
[47] Church notice board, 13 Jan. 1970.
[48] Pevsner, *Essex* (2nd edn.), 407.
[49] *Kelly's Dir. Walthamstow, Leyton and Leytonstone* (1903-5); Mudie-Smith, *Relig. Life Lond.* 369.
[50] W.A.S., *The Record*, no. 7, p. 6.
[51] Inf. from Chelmsford Diocesan Secretary, Apr. 1970.

The church of *ST. STEPHEN*, Grove Road, originated in 1874 when a temporary church was built in Copeland Road on a site given by Alfred Janson and Henry Ford Barclay to serve that part of St. Mary's parish.[52] A conventional district was assigned to St. Stephen in 1874, which became a separate parish in 1881, formed partly from St. Mary's, Walthamstow and partly from St. Mary's, Leyton. The advowson of the vicarage was vested in the Church Patronage Society. A permanent church, designed by W. G. Habershon and adjoining the temporary one, was consecrated in 1878. About 1891 a mission of St. Stephen's was opened in Western Road in the hall previously occupied by Miss Barclay's school[53] and the Forest mission.[54] The hall, which was given to St. Stephen's by the Barclays, was sold after the mission ceased during the First World War.[55] Another mission in West Street, known as St. Stephen's schools, was opened between 1894 and 1898.[56] It was demolished in 1961. The church of St. Stephen was demolished in 1969 because it was structurally weak. The church hall, built in Copeland Road in 1880, was altered for use as a church.[57] In 1969 the parish was placed in the care of the vicar of St. Mary's.[58]

The church of *ST. MICHAEL AND ALL ANGELS*, Palmerston Road, the largest in Walthamstow, was built in 1885, to the design of J. M. Bignall, to serve the area of St. James's parish north of the Great Eastern railway. The cost was met by public subscription assisted by the bishop of St. Albans' fund. The building, of brown and red brick with stone dressings, is in the Early English style, and has a very lofty nave and chancel with lower side aisles. A separate parish was formed in 1887, the advowson being vested in the bishop. The church of *ST. PAUL*, Courtenay Road, was built in 1900 as a mission church of St. Michael's, on a site given by T. Courtenay Warner. It was closed in 1917, but reopened in 1919 as the centre of a mission district. The church was damaged by bombing during the Second World War and completely restored after the war. From 1954 the vicar of St. Michael's exercised pastoral care. The church of St. Paul was closed in 1964.[59]

The church of *ALL SAINTS*, Selwyn Avenue, originated in 1898 when All Saints, Castle Avenue, a red brick structure with stone dressings in the Perpendicular style, was built as a mission of St. Peter's. Elizabeth Ainslie (d. 1901) of Rolls in Chingford contributed to the cost of the building, and by her will gave £1,000, the income from which was to be used towards the stipend of the mission curate until a separate parish of All Saints should be formed, and then to become part of the endowment of the benefice. A conventional district was formed for All Saints in 1907. A new parish, taken from those of St. Peter and St. John, was formed in 1912, the advowson of the vicarage being vested in the bishop. In the same year a new and larger parish church, designed by Hoare & Wheeler, was built

in Selwyn Avenue, where there had been an iron mission room, known as St. Matthew's, since 1908.[60] The building, of brown brick with Decorated windows, is incomplete at the east end. The original church in Castle Avenue, subsequently known as *ALL-SAINTS-ON-THE-HILL*, became a chapel of ease to the new church. Part of All Saints parish was transferred in 1956 to that of St. Anne, Chingford.

The church of *ST. BARNABAS*, St. Barnabas Road, originated in 1900 when an iron mission church was erected within the parish of St. Saviour. A separate parish was formed in 1901, the advowson of the vicarage being vested in the bishop. In 1903 a permanent church was built at the expense of Richard Foster, who also gave the sites for the church, church hall, and vicarage house.[61] The church, of red brick with stone dressings, was designed by W. D. Caröe and has a small spired turret at the north-west angle and late-Gothic windows. In 1961 the parish of St. Barnabas was united with that of St. James the Greater; St. Barnabas became the parish church. After the demolition of St. James the Greater a chapel of St. James was formed in the south aisle of St. Barnabas.

The church of *ST. GABRIEL*, Havant Road, originated in 1881 as a mission of St. Mary's. Services were held in a shop in Wood Street and in the grounds of a house in Forest Rise. After two years the name of St. Gabriel was adopted. In 1884 a mission room was built on land given by Sir F. W. J. FitzWygram, Bt. A permanent church, planned to adjoin the mission room, was never built for lack of funds. A separate parish of St. Gabriel was formed in 1919, the advowson of the vicarage being vested in the Simeon Trustees. The church of *ST. MARK*, Shernhall Street, was founded in 1900 as a mission, originally called St. Bride's, in the parish of St. Mary. Services were held in a laundry in Raglan Road until an iron building was erected in 1901. A permanent church was built in 1908 to the design of W. A. Lewis. In 1919 St. Mark was included in the new parish of St. Gabriel. In 1937 a conventional district was formed for St. Mark, but in 1940 this was again merged in St. Gabriel's parish. St. Mark's church was badly damaged by a land mine in 1941 and finally wrecked by a flying bomb in 1944. One of the blocks of council flats built on the site is named St. Mark's House.

The church of *ST. LUKE*, Greenleaf Road, originated in 1900–1 as a mission of St. Mary's. Services were conducted in Greenleaf Road board school until a church room was built in 1901–2, and later in 1902 a church, both to the design of Bottle and Olley of Yarmouth. A separate parish was formed in 1903, taken from St. Mary's and St. John's parishes, the advowson of the vicarage being vested in the Simeon Trustees. The church is of brown and red brick with wood traceried windows and a small south tower. In 1923 the chancel was widened and new furnishings installed.[62]

[52] *Chs. Barking Deaneries*, 50.
[53] See p. 307.   [54] See p. 298.
[55] *Kelly's Dir. Essex* (1912, 1917); *Walthamstow, Leyton and Dist. Alm.* (1913).
[56] *Chs. Barking Deaneries*, 50; Mudie-Smith, *Relig. Life Lond.* 462.
[57] Inf. from Waltham Forest Libraries.
[58] Inf. from Chelmsford Diocesan Secretary, and Waltham Forest Libraries.

[59] W.A.S., *The Record*, no. 2, p. 2. The building was demolished in 1971.
[60] The new parish church was dedicated to All Saints, and not to St. Matthew as originally intended, in order to take advantage of the provisions of Miss Ainslie's will.
[61] *Essex Churchman*, Oct. 1963.
[62] *Walthamstow and District Times*, 1 Nov. 1901, 18 Apr. 1902; *Walthamstow Guardian*, 18 Apr., 10 Oct. 1902, 12 Apr. 1935.

The church of *ST. OSWALD*, York Road, was originally a mission of St. Michael's. It was built in 1909–10 to the design of Olley and Haward. The site was partly the gift of Richard Foster, who stipulated that the church was to be 'a nursery of advanced catholic teaching'. The church was closed in 1917 after a dispute with the bishop over ritualistic practices.[63] In December 1918, however, the conventional district of St. Oswald was formed and the church reopened a month later. A separate parish of St. Oswald, taken from that of St. Michael, was formed in 1924. St. Oswald's church was destroyed by a bomb in 1940. The altar was placed in the church of St. James, and, when that was demolished, was sent to the mission at Hastingwood in North Weald. In 1955 the parish of St. Oswald was divided between those of St. Michael and All Angels and St. James. The benefice was united with that of St. James. The site of St. Oswald's was sold in 1957 to the borough council, which built flats there.

ROMAN CATHOLICISM. Between 1574 and 1597 the Hale family of Moons were repeatedly prosecuted for recusancy. A private chapel had been licensed at Moons in 1536 and this may well have been used for secret Roman Catholic worship in the later 16th century.[64] In 1598 William Humphrey was cited for harbouring a 'papistical woman' thought to be a common messenger between recusants,[65] but he was never indicted as a recusant himself. Indictments of a few Walthamstow recusants continued to 1629,[66] but in 1676 no papists were enumerated in the parish.[67] In 1766 one Roman Catholic family was reported.[68] This was the Bradshaw family, who may have given hospitality to the Jesuit mission conducted in Walthamstow from 1769 to 1772 by John Talbot, a priest who remained there until 1779. By 1780 there were 32 papists in the parish.[69] In the 1840s mass was being said in private houses, with the support of Captain George Collard (d. 1853) and his wife. In 1847 Captain Collard conveyed some land to his wife for her disposal for charitable purposes and in the same year she gave by deed a 2-acre site in Shernhall Street to build the mission chapel of *ST. GEORGE*. This small building of Kentish ragstone was opened in 1849 by Dr. (later Cardinal) Nicholas Wiseman, who was then living at Shern Hall and was one of the trustees.[70] Differences had arisen by 1851[71] and in 1853 Mrs. Collard abandoned the faith, quarrelled with the priest, revoked all gifts she had

made, and locked up the chapel. Wiseman built a small temporary chapel until the other was re-opened in 1854, and in 1855 the trustees' title to the land conveyed to them by Mrs. Collard in 1847 was confirmed by a Chancery decree.[72]

The Walthamstow mission also served Woodford, Leyton, Wanstead, and Chingford, until their own missions opened. The present church, dedicated to *OUR LADY AND ST. GEORGE*, was opened in 1901, a massive brick building in the Early English style with circular apse and domed roof and a Lady chapel on the north side.[73] Six other chapels were added later. In 1903 Sunday attendances totalled 746.[74] The church of *OUR LADY OF THE ROSARY AND ST. PATRICK*, Blackhorse Road, was opened in 1908[75] and the church of *CHRIST THE KING*, Chingford Road, in 1932.[76]

PROTESTANT NONCONFORMITY. A Presbyterian meeting was licensed in Walthamstow in 1672, and not long afterwards a permanent congregation of Presbyterians existed in Marsh Street.[77] Their numbers and prestige grew in the 18th century; by 1778 there were said to be many dissenters in the parish, all Presbyterians except one family of Quakers and one of Baptists.[78] In 1786 some members of the Marsh Street congregation broke away to form a new meeting, which later became a Congregational church. Independent meetings were registered in private houses in 1798 and 1799,[79] and a permanent Independent congregation was formed in Wood Street in 1807.[80] Other meetings of unknown denomination were registered in private houses in 1818, 1822, and 1833.[81] Baptists were worshipping in Marsh Street in 1849, and from the 1850s the Wood Street Independent church became a Union church. Congregationalists, who formed another church in 1861,[82] remained the leading nonconformist group until the 1870s, when permanent congregations were formed by Wesleyan and Primitive Methodists, Baptists, and Strict Baptists. Intensive missionary activity followed among Walthamstow's new population, including much social work in the poorer districts and among young people. The denominations already established spread, and were joined by the Free Methodists, Brethren, and Salvation Army in the 1880s, Unitarians and Presbyterian Church of England in the late 1890s, and Presbyterian Church of Wales and Friends by 1903.

[63] *Strange doctrines, being an interview between the Bishop of Chelmsford and a deputation from St. Oswald's mission church, Walthamstow* (1917).
[64] E.R.O., Q/SR 47/73 and *passim* to 138/23; Assizes 35/30/T (44), 35/32/T (61, 63), 35/36/T (32, 34, 43); G. F. Bosworth, *Manor of Higham Bensted* (W.A.S. vi), 13–14; *Essex Recusant*, i. 17–24.
[65] E.R.O., D/AEA 19, f. 48v.
[66] E.R.O., Q/SR 151/16 and *passim* to 266/42–3; Assizes 35/42/H (46), 35/43/T(95), 35/57/H(8), 35/62/H(3).
[67] William Salt Libr. Stafford, S. 2112.
[68] Guildhall MS. 9558, f. 373; *Essex Recusant*, ii. 94.
[69] *Cath. Rec. Soc.* xiii. 162; *Essex Recusant*, iii. 99, iv. 116, v. 34; W. O'Grady, *Centenary souvenir of St. George's, Walthamstow, 1849–1949*, 19.
[70] E.R.O., T/P 114/13; *White's Dir. Essex* (1848); H.O. 129/7/194; and W. O'Grady, *Centenary souvenir of St. George's*, on which the rest of this account, unless otherwise stated, is based. Cardinal Wiseman lived at Shern Hall

from 1849 to 1858, when he moved to Etloe House, Leyton: O'Grady, op. cit. 55.
[71] West. Arch. L. & P. Bp. Wiseman 1851 (Box 29), no. 46.
[72] A second deed of 1848 by which Mrs. Collard gave more land to the mission was declared void in 1855 after the suit at law, and the land was reconveyed to Mrs. Collard; see also below, p. 314.
[73] *Walthamstow Guardian*, 13 Dec. 1901.
[74] R. Mudie-Smith, *Relig. Life Lond.* 369.
[75] *Walthamstow Guardian*, 9 Oct. 1908.
[76] *Cath. Dir.* 1969.   [77] See p. 297.
[78] Guildhall MS. 9558, f. 373.
[79] Rtns. Nonconf. Mtg. Hs. cert. to Bps. Cts. bef. 1852, nos. 464, 490.
[80] See p. 298.
[81] Rtns. Nonconf. Mtg. Hs. cert. to Bps. Cts. bef. 1852, nos. 1078, 1285, 1788.
[82] Trinity Congregational church, see p. 299.

In 1903 there were some 46 nonconformist churches and missions in Walthamstow, with Sunday congregations totalling over 13,827[83] or about 56·5 per cent of worshippers of all denominations in the district. In terms of Sunday attendances the Congregationalists still had the largest nonconformist following, but the Free Methodists were close behind, the Lighthouse in Markhouse Road attracting congregations only exceeded in Walthamstow by those of the parish church of St. Mary.

The three main denominations founded no new churches after 1913, but between the two World Wars Spiritualists and small fundamentalist and pentecostal groups became established. In the 1930s membership generally fell and many churches were burdened by debt. During the Second World War dispersal of members and bomb damage increased the difficulties of many churches and compelled reorganization and retrenchment when it ended. The only newcomers after 1945 were small sects such as the Church of the Nazarene. In 1963 37 places of nonconformist worship were listed.[84] Two of these had closed by 1970.

The accounts of individual churches were completed in 1970. Dates in brackets after ministers' names show the years of their pastorate. Attendance statistics for 1903 are from the *Daily News* census.[85]

Baptists. A room in Marsh Street was registered for Baptist worship by John Glaskin of Hackney, minister, in 1849.[86] A permanent congregation was established in the 1850s, when Wood Street Independent chapel, under a Baptist pastor, became a Union church.[87] Between 1874 and 1906 6 Baptist churches were formed; 5 of them were still active in 1970, with another founded in 1913. Membership figures quoted below are from the *Baptist Handbooks*.

Central church, Orford Road, originated in 1874 in services held for the Markhouse common district.[88] An iron hall was erected on the corner of Boundary and Boston Roads in 1875 and a permanent church was built in 1880.[89] A mission was opened at Higham Hill in 1886, and during the pastorate of W. Murray (1892–1914) a mission was begun in High Street. By 1907 there were 358 members. In 1914 the present church was built in Orford Road. It is a large red-brick building in the Gothic style with a south-west tower. Membership fell from 318 in 1915 to 296 in 1916 when some of the original Boundary Road members, finding their new church too distant, seceded and opened a small iron hut in Boundary Road.[90] In 1939 Central church had 349 members, and in 1967 269. The Boundary Road church, closed in 1914, was later taken over by the Walthamstow and Leyton Synagogue.[91]

Higham Hill church, Higham Hill Road, originated in 1885 when services began in a shop in that road.[92] The following year Boundary Road Baptist church opened a Higham Hill mission in St. Andrew's Road. From 1888, if not before, this was conducted in the old British schools building, previously occupied by the Friends.[93] A church was formed in 1896. The present church was opened in 1904. In 1921 there were 300 members, in 1939 205, and in 1967 66.

Erskine Road Spurgeon Memorial church, which originated in High Street in 1898, may have begun as a mission of Boundary Road.[94] About 1901 an iron hall was erected in Erskine Road, registered in 1902 as the Spurgeon Memorial church.[95] The church appears to have ceased about 1911–12, when there were 32 members.[96] The earlier date is the more likely if a tradition that the church furnishings went to Spruce Hill Baptist church is correct.[97] The Erskine Road site, on the corner of Melville Road, was occupied in 1970 as a school meals centre.

Blackhorse Road church was founded in 1898, with the help of the Pioneer Mission.[98] There were 120 members in 1903. The present church was opened in 1932.[99] There were 129 members in 1939 and 24 in 1967.

The Tabernacle, Greenleaf Road, originated in 1902 in a tent mission sponsored by the Pioneer Mission on Church Hill, on the site later occupied by the Strict Baptists.[1] Under the leadership of E. E. Welton, then a student pastor, a group met in Hoe Street until 1903, when Forest Road board school, Greenleaf Road, was hired. A church was formed in 1905 and a school-chapel opened and registered in 1906 as the Central Baptist Hall, Greenleaf Road.[2] Welton was pastor from 1905 to 1915. The chapel was enlarged in 1915 and re-registered as the Tabernacle.[3] In 1921 there were 281 members and by 1922 the church was clear of debt, with the help of a gift from (Sir) William Mallinson. In 1939 there were 306 members. The Tabernacle was destroyed by bombing in 1944, but services continued in a hall. The rebuilt Tabernacle, a contemporary compact building, opened in 1949. In 1967 church membership was 212.

Spruce Hill church, Brookscroft Road, originated about 1904, when J. S. Rideout, caretaker of Livingstone College,[4] at the suggestion of R. H. Eastty,

[83] R. Mudie-Smith, *Relig. Life London*, 367–9, 462. The Welsh Presbyterian church was omitted by the Walthamstow enumerators.

[84] *Walthamstow Off. Guide* (1963), 65–6.

[85] Mudie-Smith, *Relig. Life Lond.* 367–9, 462.

[86] Rtns. Noncf. Mtg. Hs. cert. to Bps. Cts. bef. 1852, no. 2312.

[87] See p. 298, Wood Street Congregational church, Vallentin Road.

[88] Unless otherwise stated, the account of Central church is based on: W. T. Whitley, *Baptists of London*, 219; *Walthamstow and District Times*, 17, 27 Oct. 1913; *Walthamstow Guardian*, 11 June 1926; *Bapt. Handbks.*

[89] *Kelly's Dir. Essex* (1886). In 1882 it was known as Markhouse Common Baptist chapel: *Shillinglaw's Walthamstow Dir. and Alm. for 1882*.

[90] For the later history of this group, see under Leyton, Keswick Hall, p. 232.

[91] Inf. from Pastor P. D. Chevil.

[92] Unless otherwise stated the account of Higham Hill is based on: Whitley, *Bapt. Lond.* 219, 234; *Walthamstow Guardian*, 2 Dec. 1904, 5 Oct. 1934; E.R.O., T/Z 8; and *Bapt. Handbks.*

[93] *Kelly's Dir. Walthamstow, Leyton and Leytonstone* (1886–8).

[94] Whitley, *Bapt. Lond.*, 247; *Walthamstow Leyton and Dist. Almanack* (1909–11); E.R.O., T/Z 8.

[95] *Bapt. Handbks.*; Worship Reg. 39158; local inf.

[96] *Bapt. Handbk.* (1912); *Kelly's Dir. Essex* (1910, 1912, s.v. Revd. R. H. Eastty).

[97] See p. 296.

[98] Whitley, *Bapt. Lond.* 247; Worship Reg. 37093.

[99] *Walthamstow Guardian*, 28 Oct. 1932; Worship Reg. 54227.

[1] Unless otherwise stated this account is based on P. E. Bennett and P. E. Chant, *The trumpet call obeyed*.

[2] Worship Reg. 42112.

[3] Ibid. 46515.

[4] See p. 188.

minister of Erskine Road, started services in a disused shop at the junction of Thorpe and St. John's Roads.[5] In 1905 an iron church was erected in Brookscroft Road and registered as Spruce Hill Baptist church.[6] The present church was opened in 1911.[7] The original furniture, including the pulpit, is said to have come from the Erskine Road church, but was replaced in 1937, when the interior was reconstructed, with a pulpit and gallery over 200 years old from a church in north London.[8] Membership was 71 in 1939, and 37 in 1967.

Highams Park, Cavendish Road, originated in 1913 when Greenleaf Road members started a mission in Selwyn Avenue school.[9] A church was formed in 1915[10] and a building erected on the present site about 1917.[11] The present church was opened in 1932.[12] Membership, which was 82 in 1939, rose after the Second World War from 189 in 1949 to 293 in 1956, when a Fellowship hall was opened.[13] In 1967 there were 279 members. In 1969 pre-school playgroups were organized in the hall.[14]

Forest Road Hall, Hervey Park Road, was built and registered in 1892.[15] It is said to have originated earlier as the Forest mission of Wood Street Union Church,[16] but was regarded as a Baptist place of worship by 1903, when Sunday attendances totalled 210. It was listed as a mission of the Erskine Road church in 1908 and until that church closed; it continued to be listed until 1926, but was included in 1928 among extinct or amalgamated Baptist missions.[17] The building was, however, listed as a mission in 1951,[18] was registered as unsectarian in 1961,[19] and was in regular use in 1970.[20]

Old Union Baptists. Wood Street church originated in 1894 when two groups meeting in Hoe Street under J. Hamilton and T. A. Tucker united. The combined congregation moved to the old Independent church in Wood Street in 1895. This was occupied until 1907, when the present brick church, with steep roof and broad entrance porch flanked by round windows, was built farther down Wood Street.[21]

Highams Park Tabernacle, Fulbourne Road, was founded in 1904 by T. A. Tucker as a mission in Station Parade, moving to Hale End Road in 1905 and Cavendish Road in 1906. When the present church in Fulbourne Road was built in 1910 the pastor was T. H. Squire.[22]

Strict Baptists. Church Hill (Commercial Street Memorial) church, sometimes called Cairo Road church, was formed by the union of Zion, Maynard Road, and Commercial Street church (Lond.).[23] Zion church originated in 1874 in Orford Road; services were held in the public hall there in 1875 and in Maynard Road from 1876. In 1890 Zion was joined by a congregation which since 1886 had been meeting in the Grammar school, East Avenue.[24] The Particular Baptists of Commercial Street, whose church was formed in 1633 in Wapping, sold their premises in 1909 and in 1911 invited Zion to join them in building a new church at Walthamstow. The union was effected in 1913, and the Commercial Street Memorial church was opened in 1914.[25] A branch church was opened at King's Road, Chingford, in 1929.[26] There were 87 members in 1939 and 21 in 1967.

Selborne Road Tabernacle originated in 1882 when J. Copeland, pastor of Zion, Maynard Road, held meetings in St. James Street. A church was formed in Marsh (High) Street in 1883, with H. Dunkley as minister, and moved to Selborne Road on the east corner of Vernon Road in 1886, probably on completion of plans to build a church there. The Tabernacle was sold to the Midland Railway about 1891–2.[27]

Brethren. The Brethren had an unusually strong following in Walthamstow. In 1903 there were 8 separate meetings, with Sunday attendances totalling 1,511, higher than those of Brethren in any other district in south-west Essex, and exceeded only by Croydon and Greenwich in the whole of London.

Folkestone Road hall may have originated in missions held at the town hall in 1884 on the application of Mr. Morris, whose plans for an iron hall in Queens Road were approved the same year.[28] The Brethren were certainly worshipping in the Queens Road hall by 1886.[29] The hall was enlarged in 1887.[30] A new hall in Folkestone Road was opened in 1889.[31] It was rebuilt in 1963 in a contemporary style.[32]

Higham Hill gospel hall, St. Andrew's Road, originated in 1887 when workers from the parent assembly in Queens Road held meetings in an iron room in Oatland Rise.[33] The present hall was built in 1897 and opened in the following year. After

[5] Inf. from Mr. S. J. Smith.
[6] Whitley, *Bapt. Lond.* 253; Worship Reg. 41390.
[7] *Walthamstow Guardian*, 15 Sept. 1911; Worship Reg. 45291.
[8] Inf. from Mr. C. T. Thorne and Mr. S. J. Smith.
[9] Bennett and Chant, *The trumpet call obeyed*, 12–13.
[10] Whitley, *Bapt. Lond.* 256.
[11] *Walthamstow Off. Guide* (1963), 65.
[12] *Walthamstow Guardian*, 26 Feb. 1932.
[13] Ibid. 14 Sept. 1956.
[14] Personal observation.
[15] *Cong. Yr. Bk.* (1892), 454; Worship Reg. 33395. Plans for a meeting-room in 'Hervey Road' were passed in 1888: V.H.M., Mins. Walthamstow Local Bd.
[16] See below under Congregationalists.
[17] *Kelly's Dir. Essex* (1906–26); *Kelly's Dir. Walthamstow etc.* (1905, 1908); *Bapt. Handbk.* (1908–12); Whitley, *Bapt. Lond.* 298.
[18] *Walthamstow Off. Guide* (1951), 49.
[19] Worship Reg. 68205.
[20] Local inf. and personal observation.
[21] Whitley, *Bapt. Lond.* 243; *Kelly's Dir. Walthamstow etc.* (1895–1908); Worship Reg. 37461, 43020; personal observation.

[22] Whitley, *Bapt. Lond.* 252; *Walthamstow Guardian*, 18 Nov. 1910; Worship Reg. 44756.
[23] Unless otherwise stated this account is based on: E. F. Kevan, *London's oldest Baptist Church: Wapping 1633–Walthamstow 1933*; Whitley, *Bapt. Lond.* 103–4, 216, 235; *Kelly's Dir. Essex* (1914–26).
[24] The Grammar school was a private school run by John Spry and David Davis in East Avenue c. 1882–6: *Kelly's Dirs. Essex* (1882–6).
[25] Worship Reg. 46054.
[26] Cf. *V.C.H. Essex*, v. 112.
[27] Whitley, *Bapt. Lond.*, 230; V.H.M., Mins. Walthamstow Local Bd. 1885; *Kelly's Dir. Essex* (1886); V.H.M., *Vestiges*, no. 38; Worship Reg. 32067 (1890); *Kelly's Dir. Walthamstow etc.* (1891–2).
[28] V.H.M., Mins. Walthamstow Local Bd. 1884.
[29] V.H.M., *Vestiges*, no. 38.
[30] V.H.M., Mins. Walthamstow Local Bd. 1887; Worship Reg. 30889 (canc. 1890).
[31] Notice board outside Folkestone Road hall; Worship Reg. 32177.
[32] Personal observation.
[33] Unless otherwise stated this account is based on *Higham Hill Gospel Hall: Jubilee, 1887–1937* (1937).

the First World War the hall was enlarged and a baptistery built, but by 1937 membership was declining. In 1963 the hall was still associated with the Brethren, but no Sunday services were being held.[34] In 1970 the hall was occupied by the Church of God.[35]

Wadham hall, Wadham Road, originated in 1903 in children's services held in Chapel End school.[36] These continued to 1938 when the former Primitive Methodist church in Wadham Road was taken over by the Brethren.[37] This church was demolished in 1953 and rebuilt as Wadham hall.[38]

The Christian Mission, Collingwood Road, was being conducted by the Brethren in 1903.[39] Previously leased to the Primitive Methodists,[40] the hall was listed as unsectarian from 1905 to 1922, when it apparently closed.[41] In 1903 the Brethren were also worshipping in the Clarendon hall,[42] in a gospel hall in Selborne Road, and in the 'New Room', Maude Road, and were holding children's services in Maynard Road schools and the Workmen's hall.[43] The Selborne Road gospel mission closed about 1912.[44] The Maude Road room may be identified with the Clockhouse gospel preaching room listed in directories.[45] Services ceased there about the late 1950s and in 1970 the small brick building was in use as a store.[46]

South Grove gospel hall, Markhouse Road, originated as a mission of Trinity Congregational church.[47] It was taken over in 1925 by Brethren from Folkestone Road, who bought the building in 1933. Brethren still worshipped there in 1970.[48]

In 1953 a former brick surface air-raid shelter in Highams Park behind Tamworth Avenue was registered by Brethren as a community centre.[49] It ceased a few years later and in 1969 the shelter was used as a council storage hut.[50]

Congregationalists. Membership figures given below are from the *Congregational Year Books.*

Marsh Street church, High Street, is usually said to have originated in 1672, when the house of Samuel Slater, a minister removed in 1661 from the lectureship of St. James, Bury St. Edmunds (Suff.), was licensed for Presbyterian meetings.[51] At first the congregation does not seem to have thriven, for

Slater was assessed to the Walthamstow hearth tax in 1672 but not in 1673,[52] and there were no nonconformists in Walthamstow in 1676.[53] In 1690–2 a meeting at Walthamstow was being supplied by preachers from London, at the expense of 'some Gent'.[54] This was no doubt William Coward, a wealthy London merchant and Jamaica planter who settled in Walthamstow some time after 1673 but before 1693.[55] Coward built a meeting-house in 1695 on land he owned on the north side of Marsh Street. He registered his own house for Presbyterian worship in 1716, and in 1718 he also registered the Marsh Street meeting-house for Independent worship.[56] There was apparently no settled minister, but visiting preachers included Philip Doddridge and probably Isaac Watts also, both friends of Coward. By his will, dated 1735,[57] Coward devised the meeting-house to trustees for use by Protestant dissenters. He pulled it down not long after, intending to rebuild it, but died in 1738 before doing so. His executors, however, conveyed the site in trust for the congregation and contributed towards erecting another meeting-house, which was registered for Presbyterian worship in 1739.[58] During the ministry of Hugh Farmer (1737–80) congregations increased, and in 1759 the meeting-house was extended on the west side and a vestry room built on the north side.[59] The Unitarian views of Joseph Fawcett (minister 1780–7) aroused controversy at Marsh Street, and in 1786 the evangelical members seceded to form a New Meeting.

The Old Meeting in Marsh Street survived to the 1830s, with the support of the Solly family of Leyton House in the Walthamstow Slip; trustees appointed in 1795 included three members of the family.[60] Though the meeting was reported in 1810 to be diminished,[61] its most distinguished pastor, Dr. Eliezer Cogan (1801–16),[62] is said to have attracted large congregations. Three brief pastorates followed, but after 1823 there was no settled ministry. A student pastor was appointed by Isaac Solly in 1829, and in that year a 'Socinian' congregation was still reported in Walthamstow.[63] But in 1837 it was stated that no service had been held for 3 years.[64] The chapel, listed as Unitarian, still

[34] *Walthamstow Off. Guide* (1963), 65.
[35] Personal observation and local inf.
[36] *Walthamstow Off. Guide* (1963), 65 and inf. from Walthamstow Ref. Libr.
[37] Worship Reg. 58090.
[38] *Walthamstow Off. Guide* (1963), 65; V.H.M., *Vestiges*, no. 39.
[39] Mudie-Smith, *Relig. Life Lond.* 368.
[40] See p. 301.
[41] *Kelly's Dir. Walthamstow etc.* (1905 f.); *Kelly's Dir. Essex* (1906–22).
[42] This hall has not been identified.
[43] This cannot be certainly identified. In 1882 there was a Working Men's hall in St. James's Path near Willow Walk (*Shillinglaw's Dir. 1882*). *Kelly's Dir. Essex* (1902, s.v. Woodford) lists a Workmen's hall, Mill Lane, under places of worship; this was the old Congregational chapel, see R. L. Galey, *Woodford Green United Free Ch.* 116. There was also a Workmen's hall at 82/4 High Street: see above, p. 252.
[44] *Walthamstow, Leyton and Dist. Almanack* (1909–13).
[45] Ibid.; *Kelly's Dir. Essex* (1906–26).
[46] Local inf. and personal observation.
[47] See p. 299.
[48] *Trinity Cong. Ch. Hist.* (1961), 20; Worship Reg. 51419; personal observation.
[49] Worship Reg. 64006.
[50] Local inf. and personal observation.

[51] A. G. Matthews, *Calamy Revised*, 444–5; Davids, *Annals Evang. Nonconf.* 627–8; *D.N.B.* (s.v. Samuel Slater and Hugh Farmer); H. D. Budden, *Marsh Street Cong. Ch.* 13. Unless otherwise stated this account is based on Budden's book. Slater should not be confused with his father (also Samuel, d. 1670), who was removed by 1661 from St. Katherine's by the Tower (Lond.).
[52] E.R.O., Q/RTh 5, 7, 9/1.
[53] William Salt Libr. Stafford, S. 2112 (Bp. Compton's Census).
[54] A. Gordon, *Freedom after ejection*, 40–1.
[55] *D.N.B.*; E.R.O., Q/RTh 5, 7, 9/1; Assizes 35/134/229.
[56] Rtns. Nonconf. Mtg. Hs. cert. to Bps. Cts. bef. 1852, no. 258, 282.
[57] *D.N.B.*
[58] S. J. Barns, *Walthamstow deeds, 1584–1855* (W.A.S. xxxiii), 20.
[59] Ibid. 21; *D.N.B.*
[60] Barns, *Walthamstow deeds, 1584–1855* (W.A.S. xxxiii), 23.
[61] Guildhall MS. 9558, f. 373.
[62] See also p. 311. Dr. Cogan and his wife were both buried in the New Gravel Pit (Unitarian) churchyard, Paradise Place, Hackney (Mdx.): *Misc. Gen. Her.* N.S. iv. 437.
[63] E.R.O., Q/CR 3/1.
[64] *Rep. Com. on Non-Parochial Registers* [148], p. 17, H.C. (1837–8), xxviii.

existed in 1839[65] and 1843,[66] but it had been pulled down by 1861.

The Marsh Street New Meeting opened in 1787 on a site given by William Couldery on the south side of Marsh Street. Part of the site became a burial ground. In 1792 Thomas Fletcher bequeathed £1,000 in trust for the minister's benefit. Under the vigorous ministry of George Collison (1797–1837)[67] the New Meeting was increasing by 1810.[68] Collison began another meeting in Wood Street in 1807, and by 1829 had under his ministerial direction Marsh Street New Meeting, 2 licensed rooms elsewhere in the parish, and a small chapel at Leytonstone, with an average of 500 worshippers.[69] The Marsh Street numbers continued to increase under J. J. Freeman (1837–46) and in 1838 side galleries were added to the church. By 1851 average Sunday attendances totalled 630.[70] In 1868 the Charity Commissioners agreed that the site of the Old Meeting, then in the hands of Isaac Solly, son of the last of its trustees to die, should be transferred to the New Meeting trustees to build a larger church. This new church, on the Old Meeting site, was opened in 1871. It was built of stone in the Gothic style, to the design of John Tarring & Son. The Conway hall, built in memory of Samuel Conway (minister 1871–95), was added in 1899. By 1903 the church had 369 members and total Sunday attendances of 770, besides attendances totalling 713 at the Conway hall and 2 other associated missions. Church membership at Marsh Street was 257 in 1939 but had fallen to 171 by 1949. As a result of bomb damage in 1944 the steeple became unsafe and was taken down in 1954.[71] The church closed in 1965, its congregation joining Trinity church. The church and Conway hall were demolished in the same year and replaced by shops.[72] The original New Meeting in Marsh Street was retained as a mission from 1871 to 1875, when it was let to the Primitive Methodists.[73] In 1899 the building was sold to them, but the graveyard, including the grave of George Collison, was retained by the Congregationalists until soon after 1962, when it was sold to the borough council.[74] The Primitive Methodists faced the front of the church with decorative stucco, inserted tracery in the windows, and added a porch, but the original structure of 1787 can still be recognized. It is a large rectangular building of brown brick with a rear gallery internally. The tall round-headed side windows are set in arched recesses below a dentil cornice. The altered two-storeyed front has similar windows with a central Venetian window above the entrance, the whole being crowned by a low-pitched gable. After the original New Meeting was taken over in 1875, the Marsh Street mission was transferred to the Marsh Street British schools built opposite Buxton Road in 1872.[75] When the schools were conveyed to the school board in 1881 the church reserved the right to their evening and week-end use, and the mission was conducted there until the buildings were sold in 1938. The following year a new Marsh Street mission, built by the Shaftesbury Society, was opened in Truro Road on the site of the previous Unitarian church; it is conducted jointly by the Congregationalists and the Society.[76] Marsh Street's Coppermill Lane mission, begun in 1896 and reorganized in 1898 as a branch church, ceased during the First World War.

Wood Street church, Vallentin Road, originated in 1807, when George Collison, minister of Marsh Street New Meeting, registered a 'new house' in Wood Street for Independent worship.[77] It was a small low-ceilinged hall opposite the Duke's Head, and was probably the meeting 'not of long date' described as 'Methodist' in 1810.[78] A small leasehold church was built on a different site in 1811,[79] and was under Collison's oversight in 1829.[80] When the lease expired, the landlord, Richard Jones, accepted a nominal rent for the church, but in 1843, after his bankruptcy, it was put up for sale with his other property.[81] It was bought in 1844 by Ebenezer Clarke,[82] who demolished it and in 1845 built another church on the site. Wood Street Independent church[83] was formally constituted in 1848 with 8 members, including 5 from the Clarke family. W. H. Hooper (minister 1851–80) was a Baptist. During his pastorate Wood Street grew rapidly to a peak of 292 members in 1880. In 1854 a new church, which became known as Wood Street Union, was built in Vallentin Road.[84] The old church survived as no. 160, Wood Street, with a shop-front, until 1969, when it was derelict.[85] In 1860 a gallery was added to the new church and the building was widened a few years later. In 1861 the church, with the help of Marsh Street, was supporting a mission near Markhouse Lane, and another at Hale End, perhaps in the building registered in that year for 'Protestants'.[86] Forest mission work at Whipps Cross, begun in the open by a missioner employed by the Barclay family in the 1860s, was later developed by Wood Street members. It was being conducted by 1886 in Miss Barclay's school hall[87] in Western Road, until 1891, when the hall was taken over by St. Stephen's church.[88] The mission was

[65] Pigot's Dir. Essex (1839).
[66] E.R.O., D/CT 382 (no. 573).
[67] See p. 226.
[68] Guildhall MS. 9558, f. 373.
[69] E.R.O., Q/CR 3/2.
[70] H.O. 129/7/194.
[71] Walthamstow Guardian, 19 Feb. 1954.
[72] S. Hanson, A. D. Law, and W. G. S. Tonkin, Marsh Street Congregations (W.A.S. Occ. Pubns. xi), 6; inf. from Miss S. Hanson.
[73] Cong. Yr. Bk. (1874–6).
[74] The inscriptions in the burial ground are recorded in Hanson, Law, and Tonkin, Marsh Street Congregations (W.A.S. Occ. Pubns. xi).
[75] See p. 306.
[76] Walthamstow Guardian, 28 Apr., 22 Sept. 1939.
[77] Rtns. Nonconf. Mtg. Hs. cert. to Bps. Cts. bef. 1852, no. 672.
[78] Guildhall MS. 9558, f. 373; E. Clarke, Walthamstow, past, present, and future (1861), 23.

[79] Clarke, Walthamstow, 23–4. Unless otherwise stated the account of Wood Street is based on Clarke and on E. Timberlake, Hist. Wood St. Cong. Ch.
[80] E.R.O., Q/CR 3/2.
[81] S. J. Barns, Walthamstow deeds, 1584–1855 (W.A.S. xxxiii), 29; E.R.O., D/CT 382 (no. 721).
[82] Author of Walthamstow, past, present, and future (1861).
[83] White's Dir. Essex (1848).
[84] Whitley, Bapt. Lond. 177; Cong. Yr. Bk. (1877 and later edns.); Worship Reg. 5923.
[85] Personal observation. The old church was later occupied by the London City Mission, Salvation Army, and Old Baptist Union, see pp. 296, 303.
[86] Worship Reg. 11408.
[87] See p. 307.
[88] Kelly's Dir. Walthamstow etc. (1886–91); W. G. S. Tonkin, Anglican Ch. in Walthamstow, 60. Western Road is included in the earlier directories, 1886–90, as Weston Road.

known as the Forest, Whipps Cross, or Chestnut Walk mission. It is said to have moved to Forest Road Hall, Hervey Park Road, but does not appear to have been associated with Wood Street after 1893.[89] In 1880 Wood Street was affiliated to both the Congregational Union and the Baptist Association. The Baptist affiliation ceased in 1930 when the church became Wood Street Congregational church.[90] In 1903 there were 203 members, but during the pastorate of W. E. Bickerstaff (1909–16) some members left, suspecting his interest in the New Theology; in the First World War the issue of pacifism further divided the congregation. There were only 85 members in 1921, but 118 by 1939. In 1940 the church was wrecked by bombing, but services continued in the adjoining halls. The church was demolished in 1952 and a smaller one was opened in 1956.[91] In 1968 there were 36 members.

Trinity, Orford Road, originated in 1861, when some Marsh Street members seceded, and after holding private services built a small wooden hall called the Ark, where student-pastors officiated.[92] A brick church was opened in 1864. The present church was built adjoining it in 1870, and enlarged in 1900. The earlier church became the lecture hall. Under J. W. Ellis (1878–90) the church grew. The South Grove mission was started in 1881 in an iron hall in South Grove (later Brunner) Road; a permanent mission and schoolroom were built in 1889 fronting Arkley and Markhouse Roads.[93] In 1882 Trinity also built a large Sunday school in West Avenue.[94] Under D. H. Cooper (1893–1903) membership rose to 370 by 1903, when Sunday attendances totalled 632, besides 266 at two missions. The second mission, in Church Hill Road, had been built by Mrs. Carter of the Limes, Shernhall Street, some time before 1882,[95] and was taken over by Trinity in 1898. From 1901 to 1915 Trinity also superintended a third mission, Spruce Hill.[96] During the pastorate of S. B. James (1906–16), who favoured the New Theology and later became a Socialist, many members left. In 1921 membership was 136. To ease growing financial difficulties the church reduced its responsibilities. In 1925 the South Grove mission was handed over to the Brethren[97] and the Church Hill Road mission to the London City Mission.[98] In 1935 the West Avenue Sunday school was let for storage; it was sold in 1952 and in 1970 was occupied by a pet-food firm.[99]

Membership in 1939 was 109. In 1944–5 the church was severely damaged by bombing. It was restored in 1959 and in 1965 was joined by the Marsh Street congregation. The combined membership in 1968 was 93. In 1969–70 the church building was much altered.[1]

Highams Park church, Malvern Avenue, originated as a mission of Woodford Union church.[2] Services were started in a cottage at Hale End in 1875 by both Baptist and Congregational members in the early months of their secession from Woodford Congregational church. A small iron hall was built in 1881[3] and enlarged in 1887. In 1893 a church of 23 members was formed in fellowship with Woodford Union church. A new church was built in 1897 and registered the following year as Congregational and United Free Methodist.[4] It was also known as Hale End Free church. In 1905 it became independent of the Woodford Union church, and in 1915 it was reregistered for Congregational worship.[5] From about 1912 the church was known as Highams Park church.[6] In 1927 a hall was built, where services were held after the church was damaged by bombing during the Second World War.[7] The church was reopened after restoration in 1949. There were 79 members in 1968.

Spruce Hill church, Brookscroft Road, originated in 1893 as a mission begun independently by some members of Trinity church.[8] A mission church was built in 1900.[9] In 1901 Trinity accepted its oversight and about this time A. A. Mathews became superintendent.[10] A men's Brotherhood founded by this mission later became the Mathews Memorial United Methodist church.[11] The mission appears to have become independent of Trinity in 1915.[12] Membership was always small. The church was temporarily closed in 1942 but reopened with a lay pastor in 1943. It closed about 1946. The building, which was opposite Woodend Road, was sold about 1952 and demolished; in 1969 the site was occupied by shops.[13]

Friends. Several Quakers lived in the parish in the late 17th century,[14] and one family in 1778,[15] that of Lewis Weston of High Hall, who refused to pay his rates in 1779.[16] Though such wealthy 19th-century residents as John Harman of Highams, John Gurney Fry of Hale End House, and Joseph Gurney Barclay of the Limes were Quakers,[17]

[89] Whitley, *Bapt. Lond.* 177; *Cong. Yr. Bk.* (1886–93); *Bapt. Handbk.* (1886–93). For Forest Road hall, see Baptists.

[90] *Cong. Yr. Bk.* (1931–2); *Bapt. Handbk.* (1931–2).

[91] Worship Reg. 65732.

[92] Unless otherwise stated the account of Trinity church is based on: *Hist. of Trinity Cong. Ch.* (1961); *Cong. Yr. Bks.*; *Trinity Mag.* Mar. 1926.

[93] J. Shillinglaw, *Walthamstow Dir. and Almanac for 1882*; *Kelly's Dir. Essex* (1890, 1906–22). Plans for an iron mission room in South Grove Road were passed in 1876: V.H.M., Local Bd. Mins.

[94] Shillinglaw, *Walthamstow Dir. . . . 1882*.

[95] G. F. Bosworth, *Some more Walthamstow houses* (W.A.S. xxix), 15; Shillinglaw, *Walthamstow Dir. . . . 1882*.

[96] See below.   [97] See p. 297.

[98] See p. 303.

[99] Personal observation.

[1] Local inf. and personal observation.

[2] Unless otherwise stated this account is based on R. L. Galey, *Hist. Woodford Green United Free Church*, 57, 100–2.

[3] Cf. A. Hatley, *Across the years*, 56, 60. The plans for the hall were approved in 1880: V.H.M., Mins. Walthamstow Local Bd.

[4] Worship Reg. 36890.

[5] Ibid. 46496.

[6] *Cong. Yr. Bk.* (1912 and later edns.).

[7] A. G. Kidd, 'The Pioneers' (TS., among records of Woodford Green United Free Church); foundation stone.

[8] *Trinity Mag.* Mar. 1926.

[9] *Cong. Yr. Bk.* (1901), 514, (1902 and later edns.).

[10] *Walthamstow Guardian*, 21 June 1935; *Hist. Trinity Cong. Ch.*, 9.

[11] See p. 302.

[12] *Cong. Yr. Bk.* (1915 and later edns.).

[13] Ibid. (1941–7); *Hist. Trinity Cong. Ch.*; local inf. and personal observation.

[14] *E.R.* lvii. 62, 71; Assizes 35/102/2(15), 35/124/2(12).

[15] Guildhall MS. 9558, f. 373.

[16] S. J. Barns, *Walthamstow Vestry Mins. . . . 1772–1794* (W.A.S. xvi), 68, 71.

[17] John Harman was described as a Quaker in 1810 when he was a witness in a court case: G.L.C., DL/C/293.

there was no meeting-house in the parish until about 1870, when the Friends had a small place of worship at Higham Hill, which was also a day-school.[18] This meeting-house was taken over by the Baptists about 1888.[19] In 1903 a mission hall opened in Greenleaf Road as a branch of the Bedford Institute Association. Friends' hall, adjoining the mission hall, was opened in 1906.[20] In 1921 the Walthamstow Educational settlement was established at the hall, which became a centre of educational and social work among adults and young people.[21] An extension was opened in 1964.[22] The settlement is maintained jointly by the Friends and the borough council.

Methodists. The three Methodist connexions which united in 1932 had 11 churches in Walthamstow in 5 different circuits. One church closed in 1937. In the same year the ex-United and ex-Primitive Methodist Walthamstow circuits combined to form a Walthamstow (Amalgamated) circuit, which was joined at the same time by the ex-Wesleyan church previously in the Wanstead and Woodford circuit. The ex-United church previously in the Hackney circuit joined the Walthamstow circuit in 1941. By then every church in the circuit faced financial problems, some very serious.[23] One church was destroyed in the Second World War and two were so severely damaged that eventually they closed. The remaining 7 churches were still in use in 1970, all of them in the Walthamstow and Chingford circuit[24] which had been formed in 1968.

In the individual accounts below ex-Wesleyan (W), ex-Primitive (P), and ex-United (U) churches are treated in that order. Membership figures for 1969 are taken from the circuit plan.[25]

In 1810 a Methodist meeting-house 'not of long date' was reported,[26] but this was probably the Independent meeting-house registered in Wood Street in 1807.[27] In 1816 H. E. Webster registered a building at Chapel End; no denomination was given, but in 1819 he registered premises at Leytonstone as 'Wesleyan'.[28] In 1821 George Lawrence registered premises in Wood Street for Wesleyan worship.[29] Methodist services were held in Mr. Penn's house in Union Road for a short time in 1858. In the 1860s there was a Methodist Sunday

school at Higham Hill and services were also held at the public hall in Orford Road.[30]

Church Hill (W) originated as a church built on Prospect Hill in 1872.[31] It was at first in the Hackney circuit and from 1876 in the Clapton circuit. In 1898 a new church was opened on Church Hill and Prospect Hill was taken over by the Presbyterians.[32] In 1941, when the church transferred to the new Chingford circuit, it was in debt, its manse, still mortgaged, had been demolished by bombing, and total Sunday attendances had fallen to 50.[33] In 1944 the church itself was destroyed by bombing; it was not rebuilt, and the site was later sold for offices.[34]

Blackhorse Road (W) originated about 1881 when a building near the Clock House was used as a mission for the St. James Street district. An iron church in the Clapton circuit was opened in 1883, and a larger red-brick church in 1899.[35] The church was damaged by bombing in 1940.[36] When it was transferred to the Chingford circuit in 1941 it was being used as a furniture store, while sparsely attended services were held in the iron building.[37] The society dispersed not long afterwards. The church was occupied in 1970 by a basketware firm.[38]

Handsworth Avenue, formerly Highams Park (W), originated in 1906–7 as a society in the Wanstead and Woodford circuit.[39] The church was opened in 1909. In 1937 it was transferred to the new amalgamated Walthamstow circuit[40] and assumed its present name. In 1969 there were 49 members.

Primitive Methodism was brought to Walthamstow in 1875 by R. S. Blair and other preachers of the Eighth London (Poplar) circuit. It was spread from 1876 by an intensive campaign led by Thomas Jackson, a missionary from Sheffield.[41] Four churches were established in eight years. The Walthamstow churches were attached to the Home Mission department until 1890, when they were transferred to the London Mission. In 1916 they were formed into the Walthamstow (P) circuit, which in 1937 amalgamated with the Walthamstow (U) circuit to form the Walthamstow (A) circuit.[42]

High Street (P) originated in 1875 when Blair took a lease of the old Marsh Street New Meeting Independent chapel.[43] This, once 'considered to have the most aristocratic congregation in the neighbourhood', became a centre for work among

[18] *Kelly's Dir. Essex* (1870). See also below, p. 307.
[19] *Kelly's Dir. Walthamstow etc.* (1886–8).
[20] *Walthamstow Guardian*, 7 Dec. 1906.
[21] *Walthamstow Off. Guides* (1929), 16, (1937), 11; *Friends' Hall: programme of Jubilee Celebrations, 1903–1953.*
[22] Inf. from Friends' Hall.
[23] Walthamstow Circuit Mtg. Mins. 1925–44, f. 312.
[24] Walthamstow Methodist church records in the charge of the circuit superintendent in 1969 were listed in the course of preparation of the following account, and a copy has been lodged with the National Register of Archives. These records were examined by courtesy of the superintendent, Revd. J. Morgan.
[25] *Walthamstow and Chingford Circuit Plan*, Oct. 1969–Jan. 1970.
[26] Guildhall MS. 9558, f. 373.
[27] See above.
[28] Rtns. Nonconf. Mtg. Hs. cert. to Bps. Cts. bef. 1852, nos. 973, 1216.
[29] Ibid., no. 1234.
[30] V.H.M., *Vestiges*, no. 38.
[31] *Wesleyan Chapel Cttee. Reps.* 1872–3; *Rtns. Wes. Chapels and Preaching Places*, 1873; Worship Reg. 20594.
[32] *Walthamstow Guardian*, 24 Sept. 1897, 8 Apr. 1898; *Methodist Recorder*, 16 Mar. 1898.

[33] Walthamstow Circuit Quarterly Mtg. Mins. 1925–44, ff. 310–12 (and attached Report).
[34] V.H.M., *Vestiges*, no. 39; *Hist. Trinity Cong. Ch.* (1961); personal observation.
[35] Worship Reg. 26793, 37031 (canc. 1946); *Walthamstow Guardian*, 3 Feb. 1883, 15 July 1898, 6 July 1934. An unidentified mission hall in Blackhorse Lane listed in 1882 may have been the original Wesleyan Methodist mission: *Shillinglaw's Walthamstow Dir.... 1882.*
[36] *Methodist Census*, 1940.
[37] Walthamstow Circuit Qu. Mtg. Mins. 1925–44, ff. 310–12 (and attached Report).
[38] Personal observation and inf. from Revd. H. G. Powell.
[39] This account is based on *Handsworth Av. Methodist Ch. Golden Jubilee, 1909–1959: souvenir booklet*, and on the Wanstead and Woodford Circuit Quarterly Mtg. Mins. (inf. extracted by Mr. G. Harrington).
[40] Walthamstow Circuit Mtg. Mins. 1925–44 and *Circuit Plans.*
[41] H. B. Kendall, *Origin and Hist. of Prim. Methodism*, ii. 507–8.
[42] *P.M. Mins. Conf.*, 1886 f.; Walthamstow Circuit Qu. Mtg. Mins., 1925–44, ff. 194–200.
[43] See p. 298.

the poor.[44] After conducting a nine-month mission, Blair offered the chapel to the General Missionary Committee, which appointed Thomas Jackson in 1876 to open a Walthamstow mission and also temporarily to superintend the existing Bethnal Green mission.[45] The latter closed in 1879, but the new mission flourished.[46] By 1880 the Walthamstow society had 61 members, and missions had been opened in Wood Street, on Markhouse common, at Chapel End and Higham Hill, and on the Tower Hamlets estate.[47] In 1899 the freehold of the church was bought from the Congregationalists and the building was altered with financial aid from (Sir) William Mallinson and Sir W. P. Hartley.[48] The church was enlarged in 1926 by a first-floor extension at the back, built on stilts over the old Congregational burial ground.[49] Although the building had been altered High Street survived in 1969 as the oldest nonconformist place of worship still in use in Waltham Forest. There were then 76 members.

Wadham Road (P), Chapel End, originated in 1878 as a mission of Marsh (later High) Street. Services were held in the open and in a disused skittle-alley until a mission hall and site were given in 1880 by John Hitchman of Wadham Farm.[50] In 1903 it was the smallest of the Primitive Methodist churches. A new hall was built in 1923,[51] but closed in 1937 when its members transferred to the Mathews Memorial church.[52] The hall was later used by the Brethren.[53]

Higham Hill (P), Gloucester Road, originated as a mission of Marsh Street (later High Street). A school-chapel was opened in 1879 on a site given by John Hitchman; there were 10 members in 1880. A second schoolroom opened in 1904 and a third in 1908. Membership, however, remained small, and the projected church on the corner of Gloucester Road was never built.[54] In 1969 there were 20 members.

Hawthorne Road (P) originated in 1880, when missionaries from Marsh Street held open-air services on the Tower Hamlets estate. A church was built in 1882 with financial aid from John Hitchman. It had closed by 1917, and was bought in 1924 by St. Luke's church as a parish hall.[55] In 1964 the building was bought by the borough council for demolition,[56] but it still existed in 1970 in use as a

store. It is a well-proportioned yellow-brick building designed in a 'classical' nonconformist style, with stone dressings and brick pilasters.[57]

A mission hall in Colchester Road was leased for a year by the Walthamstow (P) mission in 1886. In the following year a newly-built mission room in Collingwood Road was leased instead and retained until 1897, when it closed for lack of workers.[58]

Of Walthamstow's United Methodist churches four had originally been Free Methodist, two in the Hackney circuit and two in the Fifth London (later Forest Gate) circuit. The earliest was founded in 1888 and the other three by 1903, when their total congregations almost equalled those of the long-established Congregationalists. They were all included in the Walthamstow circuit formed in 1913, to which one other church was later added. In 1937 Walthamstow (U) circuit amalgamated with the Walthamstow (P) circuit.[59]

The Lighthouse (U), Markhouse Road, originated in 1887, when members of Pembury Grove in the Hackney circuit opened a Walthamstow mission in Myrtle Road. A church was formed in 1888.[60] In 1889 Captain King of the Bullard King line of steamers, who was already associated with Free Methodist churches in West Ham,[61] helped to provide the present site and gave an iron hall. The permanent church was opened in 1893; its unusual design, with a lighthouse angle turret and revolving beam, was perhaps influenced by Captain King's seafaring connexions. A Young People's institute was opened in 1902. This was the best-attended nonconformist church in Walthamstow in 1903, with total Sunday congregations of 1,523; there were 361 members by 1904.[62] The members were drawn from the working classes of the district and became noted for their missionary and social activities.[63] In 1941 the Lighthouse transferred from the Hackney to the Walthamstow circuit.[64] There were 82 members in 1969.

Shern Hall (U), Shernhall Street, originated in 1896, mainly through the efforts of (Sir) William Mallinson. A temporary iron church, in the Fifth London (Stratford), later Forest Gate, circuit, was opened in 1897, and by 1898 there were 88 members.[65] The permanent church, designed by

[44] R. S. Blair, *Reaching the masses*, 23.
[45] Kendall, *Hist. Prim. Meth. Ch.* ii. 507–8.
[46] Jackson's combined appointment in 1876 explains why the minutes of the Bethnal Green mission, 1874–9, and of the new Walthamstow mission, 1877–98, are entered in the same volume.
[47] *Walthamstow Guardian*, 13 Nov. 1880; Mins. Qu. Mtgs. Bethnal Green and Walthamstow Missions, 1874–98.
[48] *Walthamstow Guardian*, 10 Sept. 1926.
[49] Ibid.; Hanson, Law, and Tonkin, *Marsh Street Congregations* (W.A.S., Occ. pub., xi), 6.
[50] *Walthamstow Gdn.* 13 Nov. 1880, 10 Sept. 1926; Mins. Quarterly Mtgs. Walthamstow Mission, 1877–98; Blair, *Reaching the masses*, 27; Worship Reg. 25613 (canc. 1924). For John Hitchman, see A. Hatley, *Across the Years*, 14, 54–5.
[51] *Walthamstow Gdn.* 10 Sept. 1926; Worship Reg. 49505 (canc. 1938).
[52] Walthamstow Circuit Quarterly Mtg. Mins. 1925–44, f. 209.
[53] See p. 297.
[54] Blair, *Reaching the masses*, 26; *Walthamstow Guardian*, 3 Jan., 13 Nov. 1880, 12 Feb. 1904, 18 Oct. 1907, 21 May 1909, 10 Sept. 1926. In *Kelly's Dirs. Essex* this church is listed as Norfolk Road, Higham Hill.
[55] Blair, *Reaching the masses*, 27; Mins. Quarterly Mtgs. Walthamstow Mission, 1877–98; W. G. S. Tonkin,

Anglican Church in Walthamstow (W.A.S., N.S. iv), 74; *Kelly's Dir. Essex* (1914, 1917).
[56] W.A.S., *The Record*, no. 2, p. 2.
[57] Personal observation.
[58] Worship Reg. 30849; Mins. Quarterly Mtgs. Walthamstow Mission, 1877–98; V.H.M., Mins. Walthamstow Local Bd. 1887.
[59] Walthamstow Circuit Qu. Mtg. Mins. 1913–25, and 1925–44, ff. 194–200.
[60] Unless otherwise stated this account is based on *The Lighthouse Methodist Church: a short history (Jubilee booklet 1887–1937)*.
[61] Inf. from Mr. G. Atwell; Album *penes* Mr. P. A. Payne.
[62] *Church extension in London and its suburbs, 1874–1904*, 24–6; V.H.M., *Vestiges*, no. 38.
[63] *Walthamstow Guardian*, 19 Jan. 1934.
[64] Walthamstow Circuit Qu. Mtg. Mins. 1925–44, ff. 303–4.
[65] The account of Shern hall is based on: Shern Hall Trustees' Mins. 1896–1956; Schedule of Deeds, 1934; *Sir William Mallinson, Bart., J.P.: a sketch of my life*, 92–7, 111–12; *Shern Hall Methodist Church Jubilee Souvenir, 1948*; *Church Extension . . . 1874–1904*, 31–3. Some early local directories list the church as Oliver Road U.M.F. Church, or include it under Roland Road (e.g. *Kelly's Dir. Walthamstow etc.*, 1899–1900).

G. Baines & Son, opened in 1901. It is of red brick with stone dressings, in the Gothic style, with a clock-tower. The land required to enlarge the original site was given by Mallinson. By 1904 the society had 252 members. An institute, designed by Sir A. Gilder, was built in 1907–9 in Oliver Road, adjoining the church. It replaced the old iron church, which was sold.[66] In 1913 Shern Hall, with 339 members, became the head of the new Walthamstow circuit.[67] As Mallinson intended at its foundation the church became a lively centre of social Christian work. He was treasurer of the church from 1896 until his death in 1936 and contributed lavishly to its funds. Among his larger benefactions were the Wadham Lodge sports ground in Kitchener Road, vested in trustees in 1920, houses in Oliver Road given to provide Shern Hall with income, and the remodelling and furnishing of a side room as a chapel in 1934 in memory of his wife. In 1925 he vested in trustees £10,000 deposited in his name in the Shern Hall (Methodist) Building Society, founded in 1922,[68] the interest to help to maintain churches in the circuit and support their ministers and the capital to form a reserve fund for the building society. Shern Hall was severely damaged by bombing in 1940 and in 1944–5, but was later restored. In 1969 there were 170 members. In 1965 the Equity and Atlas Building Societies were merged in the Shern Hall (Methodist) Building Society, which in 1967 merged with the Magnet and North West Building Society and became known as the Magnet Building Society.[69]

Lloyd Park (U), Forest Road, originated in 1902, when missionaries from the Lighthouse held services in the Empire cinema.[70] An iron building, called the Lloyd Park hall, was opened in 1903, in the Hackney circuit. In 1911 the society transferred from the Hackney to the Forest Gate circuit, and in 1913 to the new Walthamstow circuit.[71] A permanent church, Lloyd Park Central hall, was completed in 1914. This incorporated shops for letting. An institute was added in 1923. The church was severely damaged by bombing in 1940 and 1944. Services continued in the Institute until the church closed in 1956. The premises, which had been burdened with debt, were sold to the Salvation Army in 1958.

Winchester Road (U), Highams Park, opened in 1903 in an iron building on a site given by John Hitchman.[72] The permanent church was opened in 1904. It was in the London Fifth (Stratford), later

Forest Gate, circuit until 1913 when it was transferred to the new Walthamstow circuit; there were then 133 members.[73] The society in its early years received much help from Shern Hall members. The church was damaged in 1940[74] but was later repaired. After the Second World War a community centre was built beside the church, comprising the Sunday school (1956) and the Memorial and Hodgson halls (1960).[75] These new buildings are of greyish-pink brick in a contemporary style. In 1969 the church had 179 members.

Mathews Memorial (U), Penrhyn Crescent, originated as a men's meeting connected with the Spruce Hill Congregational mission and led for many years by A. A. Mathews (d. 1921).[76] In 1908 the old iron church from Shern Hall was bought for the meetings and erected in Brettenham Road. It became known as the Men's Own Brotherhood hall, Chapel End.[77] In 1924 the hall was reconstituted as the Mathews Memorial United Methodist church, in the Walthamstow circuit. A permanent church, in Penrhyn Crescent, was opened in 1930, and buildings for youth work were added in 1962. The church had 128 members in 1969.

Presbyterian Church of England. St. Columba's church, Prospect Hill, originated in 1898 when Presbyterians took over the former Wesleyan church there.[78] A new church was built on the site in 1906.[79] It was almost destroyed by bombing in 1941, but services continued in improvised premises until it was rebuilt in 1957.[80] It was closed in 1968 and demolished by 1971.[81]

Presbyterian Church of Wales (Calvinistic Methodists). Moreia, Church Hill, later in High Road, Leytonstone, originated in 1901, when Welsh residents began to meet for worship under the supervision of the Stratford Welsh church.[82] From 1901 to 1927 services were held in the Modern school, Grove Road, whose owner, J. O. Davies, was one of the church's first deacons. The church joined the London Welsh Methodist Presbytery in 1903. When the school closed in 1927 a Congregational church hall in Pembroke Road was hired, then the Y.M.C.A. hall on Church Hill until it was sold in 1932. D. A. Davies then bought Church Hill House, demolished it,[83] and converted the stable in 1933 into the Moreia church.[84] In 1958 the Walthamstow congregation, with help from members of the former Welsh church at Stratford in West Ham,[85] built a

---

[66] See below.
[67] Walthamstow Circuit Qu. Mtg. Mins. 1913–25 (21 July 1913).
[68] *Walthamstow Independent*, 10 Jan. 1969.
[69] Ibid.; *Walthamstow Guardian*, 2 Apr. 1965.
[70] Unless otherwise stated the following account is based on: Lloyd Park Meth. Ch. records, including Trustees' Mins. 1902–58, Church Leaders' Mtgs. Mins. 1923–9, Church Members Mtgs. Mins. 1902–34, General Files of Correspondence etc., and MS. and TS. notes on the history of the church; *Church Extension . . .* 53; *Methodist Times*, 30 Aug. 1923.
[71] Walthamstow Circuit Qu. Mtg. Mins. 1913–25 (21 July 1913).
[72] Unless otherwise stated the following account is based on *Church Extension . . .* 55–6 and on inf. from Mr. G. R. Easton.
[73] Walthamstow Circuit Qu. Mtg. Mins. 1913–25 (21 July 1913).
[74] *Methodist Census*, 1940.
[75] *Walthamstow Guardian*, 27 May 1960; *Walthamstow Post*, 5 May 1960.

[76] This account is based on *Walthamstow Guardian*, 21 June 1935; Shern Hall Trustees' Mtgs. Mins., 1896–1930; Walthamstow Circuit Qu. Mtg. Mins. 1922 f.
[77] *Walthamstow, etc. . . . Almanack* (1913).
[78] *Mins. of Presbytery of London North*, Apr. 1897–Mar. 1902; *Walthamstow Guardian*, 8 Apr. 1898; Worship Reg. 36936. See also R. S. Robson, 'Presbyterianism in Walthamstow' (*Walthamstow Guardian*, 29 Aug., 5, 12, 19 Sept. 1919).
[79] *Walthamstow Guardian*, 22 June 1906; Worship Reg. 42770.
[80] *Jnl. of Presb. Hist. Soc.* ix. 15; *Walthamstow Off. Guide* (1963), 67; *St. Columba's Presb. Ch. Jubilee: 1898–1958* (1958).
[81] W.A.S., *The Record*, no. 12, p. 3; inf. from V.H.M.
[82] Unless otherwise stated this account is based on inf. from Mr. E. R. Langdon.
[83] See also pp. 247, 279.
[84] The date '1933' is inscribed on the building.
[85] See p. 138.

new church in High Road, Leytonstone.[86] It is a brick building in a contemporary style, designed by T. & H. Llewelyn Daniel. The Walthamstow Moreia was taken over by the Church of the Nazarene.[87]

The Salvation Army. The Walthamstow Citadel, Forest Road, originated in a tent mission after which, in 1888, the Army registered for worship premises at a school in High Street.[88] A Citadel, with shops below, designed by W. Gilbee Scott, was built about 1891–2 on the site of Ball's boxing booths.[89] By 1903 its Sunday congregations totalling 932 were second only to the Lighthouse among nonconformist places of worship. In 1958 the Army bought the former Lloyd Park Methodist church, which was registered as the Citadel in 1961.[90] In 1970 the old Citadel was occupied as shops and storage.

A hall at the corner of Oatland Rise and St. Andrew's Road, Higham Hill, was registered in 1901.[91] A Young People's hall was added about 1929.[92] The buildings were destroyed by bombing about 1941–2 and in 1970 St. Andrew's Court flats stood on the site.[93]

In Wood Street the Army was using the old Independent church in 1894, and from c. 1899 to the 1920s ran a Women's Social Work home at the Clock House, Whipps Cross.[94] A hall which was registered in 1908 was closed in 1922.[95]

At Highams Park a hall registered in the Avenue in 1909 may have been associated with the work of an Eventide home being run there about 1912.[96] A hall was registered in Hoe Street in 1910.[97]

Spiritualists. The National Spiritualist church, Vestry Road, originated in 1920, when services were started in a hall adjoining the Post Office sorting office.[98] In 1924 the congregation took over the present premises, the old National school, opposite the museum.[99] Walthamstow Spiritualist Lyceum church was meeting in the Workmen's hall, High Street, in 1929.[1] Its present church in Coleridge Road was opened in 1933.[2] Walthamstow First Christian Spiritualist Church, Prospect Hill, was registered in 1953 but ceased by 1954.[3]

Unitarians and Free Christians. The Free Christian church, no. 60 Orford Road, originated in

1897 when a Unitarian iron church was erected in Truro Road.[4] R. W. Sorensen, who became honorary pastor of the church in 1916, still held that office in 1970. He was Labour M.P. for Leyton, 1929–31, and without break from 1935 to 1964, when he was created a life peer.[5] Under his leadership the church was notable for the courage of its convictions. During the First World War the members held pacifist meetings in the open, and in 1919, during the blockade of Germany, put up posters with the text, 'If thine enemy hunger feed him'. In 1938 the church was sold,[6] but the congregation continued to meet in borrowed halls[7] until bombing and evacuation scattered them in the Second World War. In 1945 services were resumed in a house in Orford Road. In 1970 the church had 30 members.

Undenominational Missions. Brandon Road railway mission was founded about 1883 and an iron hall built beside the railway in 1886. The hall was damaged by bombing in the Second World War, but rebuilt, and another prefabricated hall was bought in 1949.[8] The mission was still in use in 1969 in spite of the redevelopment of this area.[9]

The London City Mission conducted a mission in Wood Street in the old Independent church from 1886 to 1893.[10] In 1925 the L.C.M. took over the Church Hill Road mission hall from Trinity Congregational church and rebuilt it in 1951.[11] The mission closed in 1970.[12]

Other Churches and Missions. Bethesda mission hall, Wood Street, was registered in 1892 but had ceased by 1899.[13] Seventh Day Adventists formed a church in 1922 on the site previously occupied by the Walthamstow and Leyton synagogue on the corner of Boundary and Devonshire Roads. The present red-brick church was built in 1928.[14] The Pentecostal Hall, Wood Street, was registered in 1926; its members moved the same year to Emmanuel Hall, Erskine Road, where services of the Pentecostal Church of the Assemblies of God were still being held in 1970.[15] The Assembly hall, Maynard Road, was registered by Christians in 1937, but this had ceased by 1954.[16] Bethany hall, no. 69 Grove Road, was registered in 1940.[17] Christian Tulipeans registered Tulip hall, no. 18

[86] Worship Reg. 66719.
[87] See p. 304.
[88] Worship Reg. 30737 (canc. 1897 revision); inf. from Capt. J. Cottell. The school may have been Miss E. Leakey's Young Ladies' Middle Class schools, High Street: *Kelly's Dir. Essex* (1886).
[89] V.H.M., Walthamstow Local Bd. Mins. 1891–2; Worship Reg. 33931 (canc. 1960); A. Hatley, *Across the Years*, 71–2.
[90] Worship Reg. 68054; V.H.M., *Vestiges*, no. 39.
[91] Worship Reg. 38564.
[92] Ibid. 51892.
[93] Local inf. and personal observation.
[94] *Kelly's Dir. Walthamstow etc.* (1894, 1899–1908); G. F. Bosworth, *Some Walthamstow Houses* (W.A.S. xii), 34; *Kelly's Dir. Essex* (1906–26).
[95] Worship Reg. 43368 (canc. 1922).
[96] Ibid. 43573; *Kelly's Dir. Essex* (1912).
[97] Worship Reg. 44434.
[98] *Walthamstow Guardian*, 9 July 1920; inf. from Miss S. Hanson.
[99] Ibid. 26 Sept. 1924.
[1] Ibid. 18 Jan. 1929.
[2] *Walthamstow Off. Guide* (1963), 67.

[3] Worship Reg. 63757 (canc. 1954).
[4] Unless otherwise stated this account is based on: *Walthamstow Guardian*, 14 Oct. 1938; *The Inquirer*, 13 Sept. 1969, p. 5; *Kelly's Dir. Walthamstow etc.* (1898 and later edns.); *Gen. Assembly of Unitarian and Free Christian Chs. Dir.* (1968–9); and inf. from Lord Sorensen.
[5] See p. 214.
[6] It was demolished to build the new Marsh Street mission, see p. 298.
[7] *Walthamstow Guardian*, 22 Mar. 1940.
[8] Ibid. 10 June 1949; *Walthamstow Post*, 26 May 1955; V.H.M., Local Bd. Mins., 1886 (plans approved); *Kelly's Dir. Essex* (1890 and later edns.).
[9] Personal observation.
[10] *Kelly's Dir. Walthamstow etc.* (1886–93).
[11] *Walthamstow Off. Guide* (1963), 66.
[12] *Walthamstow Guardian*, 20 Feb. 1970.
[13] Worship Reg. 33509.
[14] *Walthamstow Off. Guide* (1963), 67.
[15] Worship Reg. 50277, 50546; *Walthamstow Off. Guide* (1963), 66; personal observation.
[16] Worship Reg. 57639. It may have been the old Baptist Zion.
[17] Ibid. 59536.

Montalt Road, in 1942; this had ceased by 1954.[18] Christadelphians were meeting in Roberts hall, Wadham Road, in 1958.[19] The Church of the Nazarene took over the Welsh Presbyterian church on Church Hill in 1958;[20] it still existed in 1970. Jehovah's Witnesses bought the Fiesta Co-operative hall (originally a Salvation Army hall) in Hoe Street in 1962 and registered it as Kingdom hall in 1963; they were still worshipping there in 1970.[21] In 1970 members of the Church of God were meeting in Higham Hill gospel hall, previously occupied by the Brethren.[22]

JUDAISM. Walthamstow and Leyton synagogue, Boundary Road, was founded in 1902, on the corner of Devonshire Road.[23] Sabbath attendances totalled 72 in 1903.[24] Between 1914 and 1922 the synagogue took over the former Boundary Road Baptist church.[25] The Samuel Goldman Memorial hall adjoining was built in 1956.[26] The New Federated synagogue, Queens Road, was established in 1923, and rebuilt in red and yellow brick in 1928.[27] In 1968 the Boundary Road and Queens Road congregations amalgamated to form the Waltham Forest Hebrew Congregation, worshipping mainly at the Boundary Road synagogue, but still holding high festival services at the Queens Road synagogue.[28] Highams Park and Chingford Affiliated Synagogue, Marlborough Road, was founded in 1932, in hired premises. A yellow-brick single-storey synagogue opened in 1937. Membership rose from 274 in 1949 to 400 in 1964. In 1968 the Marc and Adele Blair hall for youth work was built on to the synagogue, in matching style, completing a symmetrical front.[29]

EDUCATION. A school board for Walthamstow was formed compulsorily in 1880[30] and was ordered by the Education Department to provide accommodation for an additional 950 children. A census taken in 1877 had shown that there were 2,665 children aged 5–13 in the parish; of those 2,175 were on the books of elementary schools and 370 at private schools.[31] In 1880 there were 5 Anglican schools, 5 run by Protestant nonconformists, and 3, including an orphanage and an industrial school, by Roman Catholics. The Ozler school in Leyton, opened 1710, provided places for children from Walthamstow although by 1877 Walthamstow was not using the school.[32] Woodford Green National schools in Sunset Avenue probably provided places for Walthamstow children too.[33] The school board offered to take over existing schools but only the

nonconformist schools accepted. By 1903 the board had built 13 permanent and 2 temporary schools, providing 16,150 places. It had established two special schools, a part-time pupil teacher centre, and six evening continuation centres. Three more schools planned by the board were completed by the Walthamstow education committee in 1904–6. Two of the National schools had closed by 1903.[34] The Monoux school, founded as a charity school in 1527, had been reorganized in new premises[35] and was providing secondary education for boys. An Art school had been founded by Walthamstow Literary Institute, a technical institute and secondary day-school by Walthamstow urban district council, and a girls high school by private subscription.

Under the Education Act, 1902, Essex county council became responsible for secondary education, and Walthamstow U.D.C., as a 'Part III Authority', for elementary education. In addition to the schools planned by the school board, the U.D.C. built between 1907 and 1929 a higher elementary school, four other elementary schools, and a nursery school, one of the earliest in the country. Reorganization based on the Hadow Report was completed in 1929. Between 1930 and 1940 the borough council built two infants schools, a special school, and a senior school. Two new Roman Catholic schools for juniors and infants had been built in 1930–1. At that time three Anglican schools remained.

A report in 1906 showed the weakness of public secondary education in Walthamstow.[36] It recommended amalgamation of the Monoux school and the boys secondary school at the technical institute, adoption by the county of the girls high school and the art school, the continuance of the pupil teacher centre, and establishment of a higher elementary school. By 1916 the recommendations had been adopted, except those on the art school, which closed in 1915, and the pupil teacher centre, which was not recognized by the Board of Education in 1906 and closed in 1909.[37] A trade and engineering school for boys (1917) and a girls commercial school (1919), both founded by the county council, were absorbed by the South-West Essex technical college opened in Forest Road in 1938.[38] An adult education settlement was founded by the Society of Friends in 1921.[39]

The wartime evacuation of school children, 1939–44, closed some schools temporarily.[40] Under the Education Act, 1944, the borough became an Excepted District within the county's system of divisional administration. Reorganization in 1945–6 removed many senior departments, as secondary modern schools, from buildings they had shared with

[18] Worship Reg. 60009.
[19] Christadelphian Auxiliary Lecturing Soc., Pocket Diary (1958), 177.
[20] Walthamstow Off. Guide (1963), 66.
[21] Worship Reg. 69071; local inf. and inf. from Walthamstow Ref. Libr. This congregation worshipped before 1963 in Leyton, see above, p. 232.
[22] Personal observation and local inf.
[23] V.C.H. Essex, v. 59; Worship Reg. 39190; Kelly's Dir. Walthamstow, Leyton and Leytonstone (1903).
[24] Mudie-Smith, Relig. Life Lond. 265.
[25] Inf. from Pastor P. D. Chevil. For Boundary Road Baptist church, see p. 295.
[26] Personal observation.
[27] Walthamstow Off. Guide (1963), 66; personal observation.
[28] Walthamstow Guardian, 21 June 1968.

[29] Inf. from Sec. of United Synagogue; Worship Reg. 57614; personal observation.
[30] Lond. Gaz. 6 May 1880, p. 2916.
[31] History of Walthamstow School Board, 9–10.
[32] Char. Com. File 230700 A/6. See above, p. 233.
[33] See p. 358.
[34] Hist. Walthamstow Sch. Bd. 11; Kelly's Dir. Essex (1890, 1906).
[35] V.C.H. Essex, ii. 528, 550–1.
[36] M. E. Sadler, Rep. Sec. and Higher Educ. in Essex (1906), 183.
[37] V.C.H. Essex, v. 57; E.R.O., C/ME 2, sect. 41, p. 10 (1906), C/ME 4, p. 467.
[38] Walthamstow Off. Guide (1939), 11.
[39] See p. 300.
[40] A. D. Law, Our Town (2) (W.A.S. Occ. Pub. vii), 35.

juniors and infants. In 1957 many of the schools were renamed, usually by dropping words such as 'street' from original names. Three new secondary schools, an infants school, and a junior school were built in 1957–64.[41]

Elementary schools founded before 1880. St. Mary's National school, Church End, was built in 1819 to replace the girls Blue school, which since 1782 had been conducted by the vestry in association with the Monoux school foundations. The new school appears also to have absorbed the children from a Church Sunday school, a workhouse school, and a Church infants school,[42] and probably also Miss Russell's school. These, and one other earlier school, are described in the following paragraphs before the main account of St. Mary's school.

The Blue school originated as the school maintained by the Monoux and Maynard foundations.[43] When the parish took over the Monoux charity in 1782 the school was reorganized; the number of boys was increased to 30 and 20 girls were admitted. The parish augmented the endowments and also employed the girls' mistress. By 1807 the name Blue school had been adopted from the uniforms originally provided by Joel Johnson.[44] In 1815 the number of girls was increased to 30. The room used by the Sunday school was enlarged to accommodate them, and the monitorial system of teaching was adopted. In 1818 30 boys and 30 girls were being taught and clothed.[45] After the girls school was absorbed by St. Mary's National school in 1819, the boys school continued separately as the Monoux school.[46] It seems likely that a good many of the boys transferred to the National school.

A Church Sunday school, supported by subscription and called the Brown school, was founded in 1789.[47] By 1807 the average attendance was 66.[48] In 1818, when the school received its first payment of £5 from Mary Newell's charity, over 100 children were taught and clothed. The poorer classes were invited to attend and were admitted to day schools when vacancies occurred.[49] Some children were awarded places at the Blue school and Miss Russell's school.[50]

The workhouse school is first recorded in 1741, when the parish was employing an 80-year-old widow to teach sewing and reading.[51] A schoolmistress was paid weekly in 1776. In 1777 the workhouse rules provided for regular instruction.[52] In 1807 there were ten children in the school.[53]

A Church infants school, with 30 children, existed in 1796.[54] This was probably the school conducted for many years by William Sparrow, curate of St. Mary's 1777–1816, and supported by collections at the sacrament with occasional aid from the vestry. It still existed in 1818.[55]

Lady Wigram was maintaining a charity school in 1807 for 12 children, but it seems to have closed by 1818.[56]

From 1815 or earlier 50 girls were clothed and educated in the principles of the Established Church by Miss Russell. Her school still existed in 1818.[57]

St. Mary's National school, for 200 boys and girls, with teachers' houses attached, was built in 1819 in Vestry Road opposite the present Vestry House museum.[58] It was enlarged in 1825,[59] and by 1830 attendance was over 460.[60] A rapid decline in the following years was probably due in part to the foundation of other church schools in Walthamstow. In 1847 there were only 143 children in the school,[61] but attendance later increased and educational standards improved.[62] The school was again enlarged in 1855.[63] In 1866 the boys were transferred to a new building in Orford Road. The girls remained in the Vestry Road building, which was further enlarged in 1880.[64] In 1890 the two departments provided places for 1,062 and the average attendance was 633. From 1866–7 the school received a government grant.[65] In 1904 the boys returned to Vestry Road and the girls took their place in Orford Road. The boys school was closed in 1906 and the Vestry Road building was sold in 1920,[66] but still survived in 1970 as the National Spiritualist church.[67] It is a structure of yellow brick with sash windows, probably owing much of its present form to the enlargement of 1825. A single-storeyed central block, perhaps the original school, is flanked by two-storeyed side wings. In the centre, at eaves level, is an inscribed stone of 1819 with a raked top; it was probably reset in this position in 1825 when a second inscription was added. The girls school in Orford Road was closed in 1949. In 1970 its buildings, of brown brick with red and blue dressings and Gothic features, were part of Connaught hospital.[68]

Marsh Street British school. In 1789 dissenters established a school in Marsh Street New Meeting

[41] The London borough of Waltham Forest adopted a system of comprehensive education in 1968: *Walthamstow Guardian*, 20 Mar. 1970. The reorganization is described in: Lond. B. Waltham Forest, *Secondary schools in the Borough* (1970).
[42] V.H.M., PV 5, ff. 469–78, 492.
[43] Ibid., ff. 458–9, 460–1.
[44] E.R.O., D/AEM 2/4; V.H.M., G. F. Bosworth's extracts from Joel Johnson's anecdotes; V.H.M., *Vestiges*, no. 68.
[45] V.H.M., PV 5, ff. 340, 346, 458–9.
[46] R. S. Smith, *Walthamstow in the early 19th century*, (W.A.S. Occ. Pub. ii), 29.
[47] V.H.M., P 25/14; V.H.M., P 25/16.
[48] E.R.O., D/AEM 2/4.
[49] V.H.M., PV 5, ff. 460–5.
[50] V.H.M., P 25/11–12.
[51] S. J. Barns, *Walthamstow vestry minutes . . . 1741–71* (W.A.S. xiv), 50.
[52] S. J. Barns, *Walthamstow vestry minutes . . . 1772–94* (W.A.S. xvi), 63, 65.
[53] E.R.O., D/AEM 2/4.
[54] Lysons, *London*, iv. 229.

[55] V.H.M., PV 5, ff. 23, 462–3.
[56] E.R.O., D/AEM 2/4; V.H.M., PV 5, ff. 458–9.
[57] V.H.M., P 25/11–12, PV 5, ff. 462–3.
[58] V.H.M., PV 5, f. 492.
[59] Nat. Soc., *Rep. Essex Soc.* (1825), 20.
[60] Nat. Soc., *Ann. Rep.* (1830), 81.
[61] Nat. Soc. *Enquiry into Ch. Schs.* 1846–7, 20–1.
[62] *Mins. of Educ. Cttee. of Council, 1849–50* [1215], p. 376, H.C. (1850), xliii; ibid. *1850–1* [1357], pp. 298, 307, 309, H.C. (1851), xliv; ibid. *1851–2* [1479], p. 176, H.C. (1852), xxxix; ibid. *1855–6* [2058], p. 87, H.C. (1856), xlvii.
[63] Inscription on building.
[64] G. F. Bosworth, *Some Walthamstow houses* (W.A.S. xii), 13, 18; *Kelly's Dir. Essex* (1882, 1890).
[65] *Rep. of Educ. Cttee. of Council, 1866–7* [3882], p. 571, H.C. (1867), xxii; ibid. *1890–1* [C. 6438–1], p. 591, H.C. (1890–1), xxvii.
[66] G. F. Bosworth, *Hist. Walthamstow charities* (W.A.S. viii), 33.
[67] See p. 303.
[68] W. G. S. Tonkin, *Anglican church in Walthamstow* (W.A.S. n.s. iv), 23.

chapel yard, after the master of the Monoux school had spoken abusively of them when chastising a pupil who attended the chapel.[69] It was planned for both sexes, but in 1807 there were twelve girls and in 1818 twenty girls only in the school.[70] From their green dresses it was known as the Green school.[71] In 1839 a new British school for boys and girls was built behind the chapel at a cost of about £400.[72] This school absorbed the Green school and also a small British school which had previously been meeting at Wood Street Independent church.[73] It was at first supported chiefly by subscriptions and chapel collections, but by 1877 it was receiving an annual government grant.[74] In 1863 there were 180 pupils.[75] In 1872 a new building providing 173 additional places was opened in Marsh Street, opposite Buxton Road. Miss Hall contributed £1,000 towards the cost.[76] In 1881 the school was transferred to the school board. In 1884 a new building was erected for 540 boys in Marsh Street near Willow Walk.[77] The girls and infants remained in the older buildings until they were closed in 1908. The boys school was closed in 1932.[78]

The Grey school of industry was listed in 1807 as a dissenting school with 19 children. It was said to have been founded and to be supported by Mrs. Solly,[79] and thus seems likely to have been associated with the Marsh Street Old Meeting.[80] It still existed in 1818.[81]

St. Mary's infants school, Church End, was founded in 1824 in a barn by the vicar, William Wilson.[82] He was encouraged by Samuel Wilderspin (1792?–1866), who conducted his brother Joseph Wilson's school at Spitalfields on the principles of Robert Owen. William Wilson became an advocate of infant education and his school quickly won a reputation at least equal to that of Wilderspin's.[83] In 1828 a school was built in the churchyard for 150 children between 2 and 7 years of age.[84] Wilson followed closely Wilderspin's methods, stressing the value of 'instruction by amusement' and exhorting teachers to have an affectionate regard for the children. The school was a preparatory school for poor children, who went on to St. Mary's National school.[85] The foundation of other infants

schools in the parish may have contributed to the decline in attendance, to 76 in 1847, but by 1882 140 children attended and the school was known as the Central infants chool.[86] It became a voluntary Controlled school in 1951.[87] The building of 1828, standing west of the church, has a dignified 5-bay front of yellow brick. The three central bays, which contain the entrance porch and tall round-headed windows, project slightly under a raked parapet. The flanking bays, of which one has been altered, were both originally two-storeyed, the lower windows being set in arched recesses.[88] In 1928 the building was restored and later extended.[89]

St. Peter's National school, Woodford New Road, existed by 1846–7 when there were 50 pupils.[90] By 1872 it was receiving an annual government grant.[91] In 1889 the octagonal school building in the churchyard was enlarged for 190 children, but it had closed by 1903 and was demolished in 1958.[92]

Hale End National infants school existed in 1840, and may have been the infants school established in 1835.[93] In 1846–7 there were 44 pupils.[94] The school still existed in 1863, but seems to have closed by 1867.[95]

St. John's National school, Chapel End, was built in 1835, on the south side of the new St. John's church, with the aid of a government grant and local subscriptions. It was intended as a Sunday school but by 1838, if not before, it seems to have become a day-school for boys and girls who paid a penny a week.[96] In 1847 there were 50 children.[97] The school was receiving an annual government grant by 1866.[98] It was closed about 1884, but from 1886 to 1903 the buildings were rented by the school board for use as a temporary infants school.[99]

St. Saviour's junior and infants school, Markhouse Road, originated in 1842 when St. James's National school was built on the north side of St. James's church.[1] In 1847 there were 27 boys and 34 girls at the school. Junior boys were transferred to St. Mary's National school at about 9 years of age.[2] A new school was built in 1874 in Markhouse Lane (later Road) by public subscription; by the end of that year the attendance was 250. The old building in St. James Street was used as a church hall until

---

[69] V.H.M., Bosworth's extracts from Joel Johnson's anecdotes; Char. Com. File 230700 A/6; see also above, p. 298.

[70] H. D. Budden, *Marsh St. Congregational Church*, 39; E.R.O., D/AEM 2/4; V.H.M., PV 5, ff. 462–3.

[71] E. Clarke, *Walthamstow, past, present and future* (1861), 23; E.R.O., D/AEM 2/4.

[72] Budden, *Marsh St. Cong. Ch.* 45.

[73] E. Timberlake, *Hist. Wood St. Cong. Ch.* 3.

[74] *Rep. of Educ. Cttee. of Council, 1877–8* [C. 2048–I], p. 709, H.C. (1878), xxviii; V.H.M., File of cuttings compiled by G. F. Bosworth.

[75] *White's Dir. Essex* (1863), 649.

[76] *Rep. of Educ. Cttee. of Council, 1878–9* [C. 2342–I], p. 890, H.C. (1878–9), xxiii; Budden, *Marsh St. Cong. Ch.* 55.

[77] *Hist. Walthamstow Sch. Bd.* 16, 99.

[78] Walthamstow U.D.C., *Ed. Cttee. Mins.* xviii. 166, xlii. 38, 67.

[79] E.R.O., D/AEM 2/4.   [80] See p. 297.

[81] V.H.M., PV 5, ff. 462–3.

[82] G. F. Bosworth, *Chapters in hist. of Walthamstow* (W.A.S. xxii), 29. For this school see plate f.p. 306.

[83] S. Wilderspin, *Early discipline illus.* 19–21; C. Birchenough, *Hist. Elem. Educ.* 47–8; H. C. Barnard, *Short Hist. English Educ.* 71.

[84] *Kelly's Dir. Essex* (1882); W. Wilson, *Manual of useful information . . . Walthamstow*, 34.

[85] W. Wilson, *Manual of Instruction for Infants Schools* (1829 edn.); Wilson, *National Education as a means to the Improvement of National Morals: a sermon . . .* (1829); Wilson, *Infant education: a sermon . . .* (1826).

[86] *Nat. Soc. Enquiry into Ch. Schs.*, 1846–7, pp. 20–1; *Kelly's Dir. Essex* (1882).

[87] Inf. from Essex Educ. Cttee.

[88] V.H.M., Illus. Colln. (drawing by Helmore, 1845).

[89] A. D. Law, *Walthamstow Village* (W.A.S. n.s. vii), 11.

[90] *Nat. Soc. Enquiry into Ch. Schs.* 1846–7.

[91] *Rep. of Educ. Cttee. of Council, 1872–3*, [C. 812] p. 410, (1873), xxiv.

[92] E.R.O., D/CF 27/10; Tonkin, *Anglican Ch. in Walthamstow*, 22; *Hist. Walthamstow Sch. Bd.* 11.

[93] Wilson, *Manual of Information*, 42; *Nat. Soc. Ann. Rep.* (1835), 52.

[94] *Nat. Soc. Enquiry into Ch. Schs.* 1846–7.

[95] *White's Dir. Essex* (1863), 649; *Kelly's Dir. Essex* (1867).

[96] Nat. Soc. files; *Nat. Soc. Ann. Rep.* (1838), 30; Wilson, *Manual of information*, 42.

[97] *Nat. Soc. Enquiry into Ch. Schs.* 1846–7.

[98] *Rep. of Educ. Cttee. of Council, 1866–7* [3882], p. 571, H.C. (1867), xxii.

[99] V.H.M., Walthamstow Sch. Bd. Mins. 1885–1903.

[1] *White's Dir. Essex* (1848), 256.

[2] *Nat. Soc. Enquiry into Ch. Schs.* 1846–7.

WALTHAMSTOW: INFANTS SCHOOL, CHURCH END, ABOUT 1825

LITTLE ILFORD: MANOR HOUSE IN 1865
Demolished about 1900

WALTHAMSTOW: ST. MARY'S CHURCH AND MONOUX SCHOOL AND ALMS-HOUSES IN 1785

it was demolished in 1902. In 1889 a school for 250 boys was built next to St. Saviour's church; the girls and infants remained in the school built in 1874. In 1875 St. Saviour's became the parish church of St. James's parish, and from that time the school in the two buildings in Markhouse Lane was known as St. Saviour's school.[3] Average attendance rose from 452 in 1890–1 to 769 in 1908, but fell to 615 in 1914.[4] The school, temporarily closed during the Second World War, was reorganized in 1945 for infants (in the 1874 building) and mixed juniors.[5] In 1954 it was granted Aided status.[6] In 1962 the 1874 building was closed; the infants and junior departments were combined in the building next to St. Saviour's church, which was modernized for the purpose.[7]

Shernhall Street British school was connected with Wood Street Congregational chapel. An earlier school attached to that chapel had been merged in the Marsh Street British school.[8] The lecture room which replaced the first chapel in 1845 may have been used as a day school in the 1860s when the building of a new school was being planned.[9] By 1868 Wood Street British school was receiving an annual government grant.[10] In 1872 a new building for 72 infants and 108 boys and girls was erected in Shernhall Street; it was still called Wood Street school in 1880.[11] The boys were dismissed at the end of 1876, and the school reopened for girls only.[12] In 1880 it was transferred to the school board which enlarged it.[13] It seems to have closed by 1906 when the building was in use as a special school.[14]

St. George's Roman Catholic school was founded in 1850,[15] with aid from the Catholic Poor School Committee,[16] in Raglan Road, formerly Shernhall Place. In 1887 the attendance was 51.[17] From 1898 until 1904 the school was run by the Poor Handmaids of Jesus Christ. In 1903 there were 160 children aged 4 to 14 in one undivided building. In 1908 the school was modernized and enlarged. In 1921 two rooms for 70 infants were built next to St. George's church hall. After St. Mary's junior and infants school opened in 1931,[18] the elder children from St. Mary's orphanage and Wiseman House hostel[19] attended St. George's which became

a senior school. In 1938 St. George's moved to Wiseman House.[20]

Miss Barclay's school. In 1858 Miss Barclay of Leyton built and maintained a school for girls off Chestnut Walk in the present Western Road. It was a brick building with a small gabled porch.[21] In 1861 it was described as a British school for boys and girls.[22] It was taken over by the school board, which leased the building 1882–4. During that time it became known as Whipps Cross school.[23] By 1886 the building was a mission.[24] It still existed in 1970 as a factory.

Higham Hill junior and infants school, St. Andrew's Road. A British school existed at Higham Hill in 1870 in a building belonging to the Society of Friends.[25] It was already overcrowded when the school was taken over by the school board in 1880.[26] A new school, the first to be built by the board, was opened in St. Andrew's Road for 1,102 children in 1883, and enlarged in 1902.[27] The boys department was closed and a junior mixed department opened in 1911.[28] In 1946 the school was reorganized for junior mixed and infants.[29]

Boundary Road infants school. There was an infants school in Boundary Road in 1878; it may have been connected with the Baptist congregation who built an iron hall in Boundary Road in 1875.[30] The school was taken over by the school board in 1880[31] and seems to have closed by 1886.[32]

Elementary schools founded between 1880 and 1903. All schools in this section, unless otherwise stated, were opened by the Walthamstow school board.

Thomas Gamuel junior mixed and infants school. Gamuel Road board school was opened in 1883 for girls and infants. A boys department was added in 1887.[33] In 1946 the school was reorganized for juniors and infants.[34]

Henry Maynard junior mixed and infants school, Maynard Road. Maynard Road board school opened in 1884; an infants department was added in 1885.[35] By 1903 the school had been enlarged and in 1912 had places for 1,494.[36] It was reorganized in 1929 for juniors and infants.[37]

[3] *Kelly's Dir. Essex* (1890); Tonkin, *Anglican Ch. in Walthamstow*, 22–3, 49.
[4] *Rep. of Educ. Cttee. of Council, 1890–1* [C..6438–I], p. 591, H.C. 1890–1, xxvii; *Kelly's Dir. Essex* (1908, 1914).
[5] Nat. Soc. files.
[6] Inf. from Essex Ed. Cttee.
[7] Tonkin, *Anglican Ch. in Walthamstow*, 23. The school moved to new buildings behind St. Saviour's church (Verulam Avenue) in 1971: inf. from Walthamstow Ref. Libr.; see also below, p. 312.
[8] See p. 306.
[9] Clarke, *Walthamstow*, 24.
[10] *Rep. of Educ. Cttee. of Council, 1868–9* [4139], p. 529, H.C. (1868–9), xx.
[11] E.R.O., E/P 131; *Kelly's Dir. Essex* (1886); *Hist. Walthamstow Sch. Bd.*, 98. It should not be confused with Wood Street temporary boys school in Wood Street chapel, which was leased by the school board 1881–4 and 1893–9: V.H.M., Walthamstow Sch. Bd. Mins. 1881–4, 1893–9.
[12] Char. Com. File 230700 A/6.
[13] *Hist. Walthamstow Sch. Bd.* 17, 98.
[14] See p. 310.
[15] G. F. Bosworth, *Chapters in the Hist. of Walthamstow* (W.A.S. xxii), 29; there seems to have been a separate school held in St. George's church in 1851–4, run by the Ursuline sisters: W. O'Grady, *Cent. souvenir of St. George's*, 19.

[16] *Ann. Reps. Cath. Poor Sch. Cttee.* 1864, xxxviii.
[17] *Rep. of Educ. Cttee. of Council, 1887–8* [C. 5467–I], p. 571, H.C. (1888), xxxviii.
[18] See p. 309.
[19] See p. 312.
[20] W. O'Grady, *Centenary souvenir of St. George's, Walthamstow*, 29–30, 49; *Kelly's Dir. Essex* (1910). St. George's original building in Raglan Road, with its two inscribed dates, 1850 and 1908, still existed in 1971, as the Angel Printing Press.
[21] *Essex Standard*, 12 Nov. 1858.
[22] Clarke, *Walthamstow*, 25.
[23] V.H.M., Walthamstow Sch. Bd. Mins. 1882–4.
[24] See p. 298.
[25] *Kelly's Dir. Essex* (1870), 230.
[26] V.H.M., Walthamstow Sch. Bd. Mins. 1880.
[27] *Hist. Walthamstow Sch. Bd.*, 16, 17.
[28] *Kelly's Dir. Essex* (1910, 1912).
[29] Inf. from Essex Educ. Dept. and Min. of Educ.
[30] *Kelly's Dir. Essex* (1878); see also above, p. 295.
[31] *Hist. Walthamstow Sch. Bd.* 11.
[32] Cf. *Kelly's Dir. Essex* (1882, 1886).
[33] *Kelly's Dir. Essex* (1912).
[34] Inf. from Essex Educ. Dept.
[35] *Kelly's Dir. Essex* (1912).
[36] *Hist. Walthamstow Sch. Bd.* 17; *Kelly's Dir. Essex* (1912).
[37] Inf. from Min. of Educ.

Pretoria Avenue board school opened in 1888 and had been enlarged by 1903.[38] It was reorganized for junior boys, junior girls, and infants in 1928, and for junior mixed and infants in 1935.[39] The infants department closed in 1936 and the rest of the school in 1938.[40] In 1955 two special schools were moved into the building,[41] which had been used as a store by the education department.[42]

Mark House infants school, Markhouse Road. Markhouse Road board school opened in 1891.[43] The boys and girls departments, burnt down in 1906 and reopened in 1908, were reorganized as a secondary school in 1946.[44] The infants school closed in 1966.[45]

Greenleaf infants school, Forest Road. Forest Road board school opened in 1894 and had been enlarged by 1903.[46] It was reorganized for juniors and infants in 1946.[47] In 1963 the junior school was closed and its buildings demolished. A new infants building was opened on the site in 1965.[48]

Coppermill infants school, Edward Road. Coppermill Road board school was opened in 1897.[49] A junior mixed department was opened in 1910.[50] The school was reorganized in 1946 for mixed juniors and infants and for infants only in 1963.[51]

Woodside junior mixed and infants school, Wood Street. Wood Street board school was opened in 1899 with places for 1,466.[52] A junior mixed department opened in 1901.[53] The school was reorganized for mixed juniors and infants in 1945.[54]

Queens Road board school opened in 1900 with accommodation for 1,434.[55] In 1920 a central school, later George Gascoigne school, was formed from the boys and girls departments.[56] The infants department closed in 1936.[57]

Blackhorse infants school, Clifton Avenue and Tavistock Avenue. Blackhorse Road board school was built in 1901.[58] It was reorganized in 1945 for juniors and infants[59] and in 1963 for infants only.[60]

William Morris school, Gainsford Road. Gainsford Road board school, opened in 1902, was renamed William Morris in 1903 because it was built on land adjoining Elm House, where he lived.[61] In 1906 part of it became a higher elementary school, which was transferred in 1910 to Greenleaf Road.[62] The remainder was reorganized in 1928 for

senior boys, senior girls, and mixed juniors[63] and closed in 1932.[64]

Chapel End junior and infants school, Roberts Road and Brookscroft Road. Chapel End board school was built in 1903.[65] It was reorganized for juniors and infants in 1945. New buildings for 240 infants were completed by 1960.[66]

Elementary schools founded between 1903 and 1945. Unless otherwise stated, all schools in this section were built by Walthamstow urban district council. The first three were planned by the school board.[67]

Selwyn junior and infants school, Selwyn Avenue. Selwyn Avenue council school was opened in 1904. It was enlarged in 1912 and a girls department added.[68] In 1946 it was reorganized for juniors and infants.[69]

Joseph Barrett junior and infants school, Warwick Road. Joseph Barrett council school was opened in 1905.[70] Between 1924 and 1936 it also contained a centre for physically defective children.[71] In 1946 it was reorganized as a secondary modern school, later renamed Warwick.[72]

Mission Grove junior and infants school. Mission Grove council school was opened in 1906 for girls and infants.[73] In 1932 the girls department was reorganized for mixed juniors.[74] The junior department was taken over by the Ministry of Food in 1939, and reopened in 1946.[75]

The Winns junior and infants school, Fleeming Road. Winns Avenue council school was opened in 1907 with departments for infants, mixed juniors, and senior girls and boys.[76] In 1945 it was reorganized for juniors and infants.[77] Some of the school buildings were occupied in 1945–57 by the younger pupils of the technical school,[78] and in 1958–62 by William Fitt secondary school.[79]

Edinburgh junior school, Edinburgh Road, was opened in 1907 as a junior council school.[80] It was reorganized in 1929 for senior girls, and in 1946 for mixed juniors.[81]

William Elliott Whittingham[82] boys council school, Higham Hill Road, opened in 1911. It was reorganized for senior boys in 1929 and closed in 1959.[83]

[38] *Hist. Walthamstow Sch. Bd.* 16, 17.
[39] Inf. from Min. of Educ.
[40] *Walthamstow Ed. Cttee. Mins.* xlviii. 20, 61.
[41] See p. 310.
[42] *Walthamstow B.C. Yr. Bk.* (1954).
[43] *Kelly's Dir. Essex* (1906).
[44] A. R. Hatley, *Across the years* (W.A.S. N.S. ii), 19; see also below, p. 310.
[45] W.A.S., *The Record*, no. 7, p. 6.
[46] *Hist. Walthamstow Sch. Bd.* 16, 17.
[47] Inf. from Min. of Educ. and Essex Educ. Dept.
[48] *Walthamstow Topics* (W.A.S. Occ. Pub. x), 22; Law, *Our Town* (2), 34.
[49] *Hist. Walthamstow Sch. Bd.* 16.
[50] *Kelly's Dir. Essex* (1912).
[51] Inf. from Essex Educ. Dept.
[52] *Hist. Walthamstow Sch. Bd.* 16.
[53] *Kelly's Dir. Essex* (1906).
[45] Inf. from Essex Educ. Dept.
[55] *Hist. Walthamstow Sch. Bd.* 16.
[56] Inf. from Min. of Educ.; *Kelly's Dir. Essex* (1922).
[57] *Walthamstow Ed. Cttee. Mins.* xlv. 279, xlvi. 26.
[58] *Hist. Walthamstow Sch. Bd.* 16.
[59] Inf. from Min. of Educ. and Essex Educ. Dept.
[60] Law, *Our Town* (2), 34; *Walthamstow Off. Guide* (1963), 53.
[61] *Hist. Walthamstow Sch. Bd.* 16, 18.

[62] See p. 309.
[63] *Kelly's Dir. Essex* (1906–10); inf. from Min. of Educ.
[64] *Walthamstow Ed. Cttee. Mins.* xlii. 38, 67.
[65] *Hist. Walthamstow Sch. Bd.* 16.
[66] Inf. from Min. of Educ.; *Education in Essex* (1956–60), 23.
[67] *Hist. Walthamstow Sch. Bd.* 17.
[68] *Kelly's Dir. Essex* (1906, 1922).
[69] Inf. from Min. of Educ. and Essex Educ. Dept.
[70] *Kelly's Dir. Essex* (1906).
[71] See p. 310.
[72] See p. 310.
[73] *Kelly's Dir. Essex* (1906).
[74] *Walthamstow Ed. Cttee. Mins.* xlii. 38, 67.
[75] E.R.O., C/ME 41, p. 362.
[76] *Kelly's Dir. Essex* (1912).
[77] Inf. from Essex Educ. Dept.
[78] See p. 311.
[79] E.R.O., C/ME 52, p. 392; inf. from Essex Educ. Dept. See also below, p. 310.
[80] *Kelly's Dir. Essex* (1912).
[81] Inf. from Essex Educ. Dept.
[82] Chairman, Walthamstow Sch. Bd., 1891–6: *Hist. Walthamstow Sch. Bd.* f.p. 20.
[83] *Kelly's Dir. Essex* (1912); inf. from Min. of Educ. and Essex Educ. Dept.; E.R.O., C/ME 52.

Roger Ascham junior and infants school, Billet Road. The junior school was opened in 1929; an infants department was added in 1932.[84]

St. Patrick's Roman Catholic junior and infants school, Longfield Avenue, was opened in 1930. By 1952 a nursery class was attached to it.[85] It was granted Aided status in 1952.[86]

St. Mary's Roman Catholic junior and infants school, Shernhall Street, opened in 1931 in the grounds of St. Mary's orphanage, as a maintained school for resident and parish children.[87] It was given Aided status in 1951.[88]

Thorpe Hall infants school, Hale End Road, opened in 1935,[89] and Sidney Burnell[90] infants school, Handsworth Avenue, opened in 1940 and enlarged in 1953,[91] were built by the borough council.

Secondary and senior schools founded before 1945.[92] Sir George Monoux[93] grammar school for boys, Chingford Road. The foundation of this school in 1527 in the Monoux alms-house building next to St. Mary's church and much of its earlier history have been described elsewhere.[94] The school was reorganized in 1782 as the school which became known as the Blue school.[95] When the Blue school ceased in 1819 the Monoux school continued to provide free instruction in classical languages, but pupils had to pay for instruction in English subjects.[96] In 1832 there were only 5 pupils.[97] In 1866 there were 17, and the school was virtually a private school subsidized by a small endowment.[98] It closed in 1878, was reorganized under a new scheme in 1884, reopened in 1886 in the Trinity schoolrooms in West Avenue, and moved to new buildings in High Street in 1889.[99] An inquiry made in 1906 found that, because of lack of funds, some teaching was ineffective, the curriculum was on the wrong lines, and the supply of books and equipment was poor.[1] In 1916 the school was taken over by the county council and amalgamated with the boys day-school from Grosvenor House technical institute.[2] Extensive new buildings, of red brick with stone dressings in a simple Tudor style, were opened in Chingford Road in 1927 and enlarged in 1932 and 1961.[3] The High Street building of 1889 is used by departments of the borough council.[4]

The Monoux school was established as a separate foundation from the Monoux alms-house charity by a scheme of 1893, amended in 1896.[5] A succession of schemes from 1895 made financial adjustments between the Walthamstow Parochial Charities trustees and the grammar school foundation. The scheme of 1907 required the trustees to pay to the foundation annually the alms-priest's £6 13s. 4d., £10 in lieu of the old schoolroom and master's house in the churchyard, £21 7s. 3d. from the Inhabitants' Donation, £50 from the surplus of Wise's charity, and $\frac{4}{19}$ of the Maynard charity. These contributions were continued by the scheme of 1957.[6] In addition a scheme of 1920 allowed the sale of the High Street school premises to Essex county council subject to a rent-charge of £150 payable to the foundation. The income provides scholarships and educational grants.[7]

Walthamstow county high school for girls, Church Hill, was opened as a private school in 1890 by a committee of subscribers.[8] It met at first in Trinity schoolroom, West Avenue, but moved to Church Hill House a few months later.[9] In 1906 there were 108 girls and 4 boys at the school; the teaching was 'excellent and cultivated'.[10] The school was taken over by the county council in 1911, and in 1913 moved to new buildings on the old vicarage glebe. It was enlarged in 1918, 1928–9, and 1962.[11]

William McGuffie secondary modern school. Greenleaf Road higher elementary school was opened by the urban district council in 1910. It was known as North West central school by 1922.[12] It was reorganized in 1932 as a senior school for 360 boys and 360 girls[13] and renamed McGuffie.[14]

George Gascoigne secondary modern school, Queen's Road. In 1920 the senior departments of Queen's Road elementary school[15] were reorganized to form a central school, later known as South Walthamstow central school. It was renamed Gascoigne in 1933,[16] took over the Queen's Road infants building in 1937,[17] became a mixed school by 1948, and was closed in 1966.[18]

St. George's Roman Catholic secondary modern school, Shernhall Street, originated in 1921 when a selective central class was provided at St. George's school, Raglan Road.[19] In 1938 Wiseman House,

---

[84] *Walthamstow Official Guide* (1963), 53.
[85] Ibid.; *Education in Essex* (1945–52), 18.
[86] Inf. from Min. of Educ.
[87] W. O'Grady, *Centenary souvenir of St. George's*, 30; W.A.S., *The Record*, no. 8, p. 1.
[88] E.R.O., C/ME 45, p. 20.
[89] *Walthamstow Official Guide* (1963), 53.
[90] Walthamstow Director of Education, 1920–40: inf. from W.R.L.
[91] *Walthamstow Official Guide* (1963), 53; *Education in Essex* (1952–6), 21.
[92] For technical schools see p. 310.
[93] There is no evidence that George Monoux was knighted. He is not described as 'Knight' in his wills or inquisition *post mortem*, and the inscription on his brass in the parish church is a late version of the original: cf. P. H. Reaney, *Church of St. Mary* (W.A.S. N.S. viii), 24.
[94] *V.C.H. Essex*, ii. 527. [95] See p. 305.
[96] M. E. Sadler, *Rep. Sec. and Higher Educ. in Essex* (1906), 155.
[97] *Rep. Com. Char.* H.C. 60, p. 141 (1833), xviii.
[98] Sadler, op. cit. 155.
[99] G. F. Bosworth, *Walthamstow Charities* (W.A.S. viii), 12. For the Trinity schoolrooms, see above, p. 299.
[1] Sadler, op. cit. 158–62.
[2] *Walthamstow Off. Guide* (1922), 18; E.R.O., C/ME 12 (1916), 117–18.

[3] Essex C.C., *Rep. Dir. Educ.* (1928), 37, 70; *Educ. in Essex* (1928–35), 117, (1960–4), 22. The school was enlarged again in 1970–2: inf. from V.H.M.
[4] *Walthamstow Official Guide* (1963), 60; *Waltham Forest Official Guide* (1968), 73.
[5] G. F. Bosworth, *Walthamstow charities* (W.A.S. viii), 12; Sadler, *Rep. Sec. and Higher Educ. Essex*, 155–6.
[6] Char. Com Files. See also below, pp. 315–16.
[7] Bosworth, *Walthamstow charities*, 13.
[8] *V.C.H. Essex*, ii. 551; *Kelly's Dir. Essex* (1890); *Walthamstow Topics* (W.A.S. Occ. Pub. x), 22.
[9] V.H.M., *Vestiges*, no. 40.
[10] M. E. Sadler, *Rep. Sec. and Higher Educ. Essex*, 170, 171.
[11] G. E. Roebuck, *Story of Walthamstow*, 50; *Walthamstow Official Guide* (1922), 20; *Educ. in Essex* (1928–35), 116, (1960–4), 23.
[12] *Kelly's Dir. Essex* (1912, 1922).
[13] Law, *Our Town* (2), 33.
[14] *Walthamstow Topics*, p. 21. It was named after William McGuffie (d. 1930), chairman of the U.D.C. in 1929, in recognition of his work for education in the district.
[15] Inf. from Min. of Educ.; see also p. 308.
[16] *Walthamstow Educ. Cttee. Mins.* xlii. 96.
[17] Ibid. xlv. 279, xlvi. 26.
[18] *W.B.C. Yr. Bk.* (1948); W.A.S., *The Record*, no. 7, p. 6.
[19] W. O'Grady, *Centenary Souvenir of St. George's*, 29.

Shernhall Street, was opened as St. George's senior school for boys and girls.[20] After the Second World War the managers acquired the adjoining premises of the old Shernhall Street special school[21] and senior pupils from Wanstead, Woodford, and Leyton were transferred to St. George's.[22] The school was given Aided status in 1950.[23] It was enlarged in 1963.[24]

Sidney Burnell[25] secondary modern school, Handsworth Avenue, opened as a senior school in 1940[26] and was enlarged in 1960.[27]

Primary schools founded after 1945. Stoneydown Park junior school, Blackhorse Road, opened in 1963.[28] St. Helen's Roman Catholic infants school, built behind St. George's church, Shernhall Street, opened in 1968.[29]

Secondary schools founded after 1945. Five secondary modern schools were established in 1945–6, in existing elementary school buildings. Chapel End, enlarged in 1961,[30] Mark House,[31] and Coppermill (Beaconsfield)[32] were mixed. Blackhorse Road (Willowfield, Tavistock Avenue) for girls became mixed in 1961; new buildings were completed in 1962.[33] Joseph Barrett (Warwick) for boys and girls was enlarged in the 1950s.[34] Mark House was closed in 1966.[35]

William Fitt[36] secondary (modern) school, Cazenove Road, opened in 1957 at Winns Avenue. In 1962 it moved to its present site.[37]

Sidney Chaplin[38] secondary (modern) school, Folly Lane, opened in 1959.[39]

Special and nursery schools. Walthamstow school board was quick to give effect to legislation requiring special education for handicapped children. In 1893 it took a census of blind and deaf children and arranged to send the blind to an institution.[40] In 1900 it opened a deaf school and in 1903 one for the mentally handicapped. Walthamstow U.D.C. opened a school for the blind in 1918 and one for the physically handicapped in 1924.

William Morris school for the deaf, Hale End Road, opened in 1900 at Queen's Road school. In 1902 it moved to a new building for 20 children

at William Morris school, Gainsford Road.[41] It was combined with Hale End open air school in 1949 and moved to Hale End in 1952.[42] It was closed in 1969, when Hawkswood school opened at Chingford.[43]

Margaret Brearley[44] school for the educationally subnormal, Pretoria Avenue, opened in 1903 in the former Marsh Street schools.[45] A special centre in Shernhall Street opened for girls in 1906 and for boys in 1909.[46] The school moved to Hale End open air school in 1940, then in 1955 to Pretoria Avenue, where it was given its present name.[47]

Joseph Clarke[48] school for the partially sighted, Pretoria Avenue, was opened in 1918 in Gainsford Road for blind and partially sighted children. In 1940 it moved first to Shernhall Street and then to Hale End open air school.[49] It moved in 1948 to Wood Street schools[50] and to Pretoria Avenue in 1954.[51] The school takes children from outside the borough.[52]

Brookfield House school for the physically handicapped, Oak Hill, originated in 1924 when a centre at Joseph Barrett school and a residential hospital school at Brookfield orthopaedic hospital were opened.[53] In 1936 the school moved to new premises at Hale End, and became known as Hale End open air school.[54] It was renamed Wingfield House in 1957.[55] In 1964 it was moved to new buildings in the former Brookfield hospital grounds and renamed Brookfield House.[56]

Low Hall Lane nursery school, opened by the U.D.C. in 1929, is said to have been one of the first in the country.[57]

Technical education. In 1891 Walthamstow appointed a technical instruction committee which received grants from the county council and allotted money to the school board and the art school.[58] By 1906 there were classes at an art school and a technical institute and manual instruction centres at four elementary schools.[59]

Walthamstow science and art technical school. In 1883 Walthamstow Literary Institute founded a school of art in Trinity schoolroom, West Avenue, which was united to the Science and Art Depart-

[20] *Walthamstow Topics*, p. 21.
[21] E.R.O., C/ME 39B, pp. 142, 206–7; C/ME 41, pp. 184, 563.
[22] E.R.O., C/ME 40, pp. 509, 531; C/ME 42, p. 558.
[23] E.R.O., C/ME 45, p. 20.
[24] *Educ. in Essex* (1960–4), 23. Since 1970 the school has been called Cardinal Wiseman senior high school.
[25] Director of Educ., Walthamstow, 1920–40: inf. from W.R.L.
[26] *Walthamstow Official Guide* (1963), 53.
[27] *Educ. in Essex* (1956–60), 26.
[28] Ibid. (1960–4), 20.
[29] *Walthamstow Guardian*, 29 Nov. 1968.
[30] Inf. from Min. of Educ.; *Educ. in Essex* (1960–4), 22.
[31] Inf. from Min. of Educ.; W.A.S., *The Record*, no. 7, p. 6.   [32] E.R.O., C/ME 40, p. 618.
[33] Inf. from Min. of Educ.; E.R.O., C/ME 40, p. 367; Lond. B. Waltham Forest, *Secondary Schools . . .* (1970), 9; *Educ. in Essex* (1960–4), 22.
[34] Inf. from Essex Educ. Dept.; *Educ. in Essex* (1952–6), 32, (1956–60), 25.
[35] W.A.S., *The Record*, no. 7, p. 6.
[36] 'Father' of the council: *Walthamstow Guardian*, 6 Sept. 1957.
[37] Inf. from Essex Educ. Dept.; E.R.O., C/ME 51, p. 287; C/ME 52, p. 392; *Educ. in Essex* (1960–4), 23.
[38] Vice-chairman, Walthamstow Educ. Cttee. (d. 1967): inf. from W.R.L.

[39] Lond. B. Waltham Forest, *Secondary schools* (1970), 9.
[40] *Hist. Walthamstow Sch. Bd.* 16.
[41] *Walthamstow Topics*, p. 20; *Hist. Walthamstow Sch. Bd.* 16, f.p. 64; *Kelly's Dir. Essex* (1912).
[42] *Walthamstow Topics*, p. 22; E.R.O., C/ME 43, p. 65.
[43] Inf. from V.H.M.
[44] Head teacher, Marsh St. special centre 1903–23: *Walthamstow Guardian*, 8 Feb. 1957.
[45] Law, *Our Town* (2), 10.
[46] *Kelly's Dir. Essex* (1910).
[47] *Educ. in Essex* (1952–6), 101; *Walthamstow Topics*, pp. 21–2.
[48] M.O.H., Walthamstow L. Bd. and U.D.C. 1890–1930: inf. from W.R.L.
[49] *Walthamstow Topics*, pp. 21, 22.
[50] Ibid., p. 22.
[51] E.R.O., C/ME 48, p. 564; *Educ. in Essex* (1952–6), 101.
[52] *Educ. in Essex* (1960–4), 100.
[53] Law, *Our Town* (2), 10.
[54] *Walthamstow Topics*, p. 22.
[55] Walthamstow B.C. Ed. Cttee. *Renaming of schools . . . 1957.*
[56] *Educ. in Essex* (1960–4), 99.
[57] Walthamstow Corporation, *Official Souvenir . . . 1929*, 39; Law, *Our Town* (2), 10.
[58] V.H.M., Local Bd. Mins. 1891, 1892.
[59] *Kelly's Dir. Essex* (1906).

ment, South Kensington.[60] It moved to Grosvenor House, Hoe Street, in 1892, and to Court House, Hoe Street, in 1900.[61] In 1906 it had 'vigorous life, a strong artistic tradition, and an excellent record', and was receiving a government grant.[62] It was taken over by Walthamstow education committee in 1906[63] and closed in 1915.[64]

South West Essex technical college[65] and McEntee technical school. A technical institute and day-school was founded at Grosvenor House, Hoe Street, in 1897. By 1906 700 students were attending evening classes.[66] The day-school, which was said in 1906 to be used as a compromise between a higher elementary school and a technical school,[67] was closed in 1916, the pupils being transferred to the Monoux school and the girls county high school.[68] The county council opened a junior trade and engineering school for boys at Grosvenor House in 1917, and a commercial and trade school for girls in 1919 at the Chestnuts, also in Hoe Street.[69] In 1938 the two trade schools became part of the South West Essex technical college which replaced the technical colleges of Walthamstow and Leyton and Leyton school of art. The new college was officially opened in a new building on the north side of Forest Road in 1939. It had been designed in the neo-Georgian style by J. Stuart and at that time was the largest and most monumental public building in Walthamstow. The very long three-storeyed red-brick front has stone dressings and is interrupted at the centre by a Corinthian portico with figure sculpture in the pediment. Classes started in the building in 1938, but because of large enrolments Grosvenor House and the Chestnuts in Hoe Street were reopened by the college in 1939 for evening classes and later housed the overflow from the county technical school as well. After Grosvenor House was burnt down in 1945, the younger pupils of the technical school were moved temporarily to part of Winns Avenue school.[70] In 1957 the whole technical school moved to new buildings in Billet Road[71] and was renamed McEntee county technical school.[72]

William Morris technical school, Gainsford Road, opened in 1933 as a senior school, in the previous elementary school buildings. It was reorganized as a mixed technical school in 1948.[73]

Private schools. In 1820 there were about 5 private schools in Walthamstow. The narrow curriculum at the Monoux school at that time led some tradesmen, farmers, and artisans to send their children to private schools.[74] By 1840 the number of private schools had doubled.[75] In 1880 370 pupils were attending them.[76] At their peak, about 1886, 31 schools were listed, including 2 orphanages, but by 1906 about a third of them had closed or left Walthamstow.[77] The number declined after the First World War. In 1963 there were 4 private schools and a day nursery.[78]

Robert MacFarlane ran a successful boarding school at Shern Lodge, also called Shernhall House, from c. 1770 until he left Walthamstow c. 1795. Dr. J. W. Niblock ran a private school at Shern Lodge in 1830 which in 1833 moved to the Priory, then called Clay Hill House, in Clay Street (Forest Road),[79] where it still existed in 1843.[80] It seems to have closed by 1848.[81] In 1801 Dr. Eliezer Cogan[82] founded his academy at Essex Hall where it flourished until his retirement in 1828.[83] It provided a classical education for the sons of the rich of varied denominations, and several of its pupils became distinguished.[84] Paradise House academy, Whipps Cross, belonging to Stephen Eardley, had 94 pupils, mostly boys, in 1811.[85] Fanny Keats attended two schools in Marsh Street, Miss Caley's and Miss Tuckey's, probably from about 1815.[86] In 1820 John Coe built a school in Wyatt's Lane.[87] The Revd. J. F. Roberts, headmaster of the Monoux school 1820–36, boarded boys at the Walnuts, Church Lane, and later at the Chestnuts opposite, who attended the Monoux school as his private fee-paying pupils.[88] Mrs. Milford's ladies school, Marsh Street, mentioned in 1822, existed for more than 20 years.[89]

The early history of the Forest school, founded in 1834 in a house on the edge of the forest in the extreme south-east corner of the parish, is described elsewhere.[90] It has been much enlarged since 1950. It now has 143 boarders and 331 day pupils between the ages of 8 and 19.[91]

An undenominational school and home for daughters of missionaries was founded in 1838 by Mrs. Foulger and her friends in Marsh Street.[92]

[60] *Walthamstow Topics*, p. 19; *Kelly's Dir. Essex* (1886).
[61] *Walthamstow Topics*, p. 19; G. F. Bosworth, *Some Walthamstow houses* (W.A.S. xii), 23.
[62] Sadler, *Rep. Sec. and Higher Educ. in Essex*, 179.
[63] E.R.O., C/ME 12, section 41, pp. 14–15.
[64] E.R.O., C/ME 10, p. 851.
[65] The technical college became part of the North-East London Polytechnic (Waltham Forest Precinct) in 1970: *Walthamstow Guardian*, 20 Mar. 1970.
[66] *V.C.H. Essex*, ii. 550, v. 57. Classes started in Sept. 1896: *Jnl. S.W. Essex Tech. Coll.* ii (2), 111.
[67] Sadler, *Rep. Sec. Educ.* 163.
[68] E.R.O., C/ME 12, pp. 117–18; V.H.M., *Vestiges*, no. 40.
[69] *Walthamstow Official Guide* (1922), 20; E.R.O., C/ME 14, pp. 305, 405.
[70] *Walthamstow Official Guide* (1939), 11; E.R.O., C/ME. 35, p. 8; C/ME 34, pp. 766–7; C/ME 40, pp. 37–8; W.A.S., *The Record*, no. 1, pp. 5–6; Pevsner, *Essex* (2nd edn.), 407.
[71] *Educ. in Essex* (1956–60), 25.
[72] E.R.O., C/ME 51 p. 287. It was named after Lord and Lady McEntee jointly: inf. from V.H.M.
[73] Inf. from Min. of Educ.; *Educ. in Essex* (1945–52), 28.
[74] *Rep. Comm. Char.*, H.C. 60, p. 141 (1833), xviii.
[75] *Robson's Gazetteer of the Home Counties* (c. 1840).
[76] *Hist. Walthamstow Sch. Bd.* 9.
[77] *Kelly's Dir. Essex* (1878–1906).
[78] *Walthamstow Off. Guide* (1963), 54.

[79] G. E. Roebuck, *Story of Walthamstow*, 61; G. F. Bosworth, *Some more Walthamstow houses* (W.A.S. xxix), 5–7.
[80] E.R.O., D/CT 382.   [81] *White's Dir. Essex* (1848).
[82] Pastor (1801–16) of the Old Meeting, see p. 297.
[83] G. F. Bosworth, *Essex Hall, Walthamstow, and the Cogan Associations* (W.A.S. v), 6–7.   [84] See p. 252.
[85] Smith, *Walthamstow in the early 19th cent.* (W.A.S. Occ. Pub. ii), 9–10.
[86] Bosworth, *Some more Walthamstow houses* (W.A.S. xxix), 4; E. M. Forster, *Abinger Harvest*; *Pigot's Dir. Essex and Mdx.* (1823–4); *D.N.B.* (s.v. John Keats).
[87] G. F. Bosworth, *Walthamstow Charities* (W.A.S. viii), 22; *John Coe's Map of Walthamstow in 1822*, and Index (W.A.S. n.s. v, va), no. 815b. Coe's wife was the former mistress of the girls' Blue school: V.H.M., PV 5, f. 347.
[88] Roebuck, *Walthamstow*, 52; *Rep. Com. Char. Essex*, pp. 104–1; G. F. Bosworth, *More Walthamstow houses* (W.A.S. xx), 11–13; inf. from V.H.M.
[89] *Coe's Map of Walthamstow*, 1822; *Robson's Gazetteer* (c. 1840); *White's Dir. Essex* (1848).
[90] *V.C.H. Essex*, ii. 549–50. For the early buildings see above, p. 250. See also G. F. Bosworth, *Some Walthamstow houses* (W.A.S. xii), 39–43.
[91] *Public and Preparatory Sch. Year Bk.* (1970), 211.
[92] E. Pike and C. E. Curryer, *Story of Walthamstow Hall*, 17.

It was supported by subscription and provided for about 45 pupils.[93] A school for missionaries' sons, which was added in 1842, moved to Blackheath in 1857 and later to Mottingham (Kent).[94] The girls school was enlarged in 1866[95] and in 1882 moved to Sevenoaks (Kent) as Walthamstow Hall.[96]

Between 1842 and 1860 Dr. Glennie Greig conducted a preparatory school for 70–80 boys at Walthamstow House, Shernhall Street.[97] There was a Roman Catholic poor-law school for girls at Walthamstow House in 1882;[98] it may have been opened as early as 1867.[99] In 1901 it housed 170 girls and was called St. Mary's Orphanage.[1] In 1926 it was described as a convent school.[2] It probably ceased to be a school in 1931,[3] but is still a convent and children's home.[4]

Mrs. Sarah Thomas had a preparatory school for girls in Beulah Road in 1870; it had moved by 1890 to Carisbrooke Terrace, Hoe Street, where her husband, the Revd. T. Thomas, had a gentlemen's school, Carisbrooke college, from 1884.[5] By 1905 he had given up the boys school.[6] His wife kept the girls school until she retired in 1911.[7] There was a school at the same address until at least 1926.[8]

In 1904 the Poor Handmaids of Jesus Christ[9] opened a Roman Catholic private school in the Drive. It was destroyed by bombs during the Second World War.[10]

Walthamstow Modern school, Grove Road, which existed in 1901,[11] prepared many boys for the secondary school at the technical institute, for the Monoux school, and for other London schools.[12] It closed in 1927.[13]

Eastfield school, established in 1886, was a girls school with kindergarten, transition, and collegiate sections; little boys were prepared for the Monoux school.[14] It still existed in 1926.[15]

The Jewish independent infants day-school, which opened in 1960 in Boundary Road, moved in 1971 to the premises in Markhouse Road occupied until 1970 by St. Saviour's junior and infants school.[16]

Walthamstow school of shorthand and typewriting, founded in 1895 and known from 1933 as Walthamstow business college, closed in 1957. A branch of Clark's college opened at Cleveland House, Hoe Street, in 1913 and closed in 1966.[17]

Palmerston commercial college and Grosvenor school of shorthand existed in the 1920s.[18]

Industrial schools. St. Nicholas' Roman Catholic industrial school was founded in 1855 by Cardinal Wiseman, in a house on the corner of Shernhall Street and Church Lane.[19] It was transferred to Manor Park in 1868,[20] but by 1870 the Walthamstow buildings had been reopened as St. John's home industrial school.[21] In 1873 a new school was built.[22] Grave irregularities at the school were exposed at an inquiry in 1895.[23] It closed in 1928, and in 1930 became a hostel for boys called Wiseman House. The building was sold in 1937 to become, in 1938, St. George's Roman Catholic senior school.[24]

The North London industrial truant school, founded in 1883 jointly by Hornsey, Tottenham, and Edmonton school boards, opened at Northcott House, no. 115 Marsh Street, in 1884.[25] It seems to have closed between 1937 and 1940.[26]

William Mallinson Scholarship Trust. In 1927 (Sir) William Mallinson gave £10,700 to the borough of Walthamstow to provide scholarships for Walthamstow students at English universities.[27]

CHARITIES FOR THE POOR.[28] In 1786 the parish poor were benefiting from 16 dole charities, the earliest dating from 1541, and from the Monoux school[29] and alms-houses founded in 1527; the total income was £258. From 1816 to 1827 the charity account always showed a balance which was misapplied in aid of the churchwarden's general account. In 1825–6 the loss to the charities was increased when the parish collector embezzled £150. The total income in 1831 was £850. In 1861 most of the charities were administered by the churchwardens alone or with the vicar or overseers. The annual income in 1877 was £1,166.

Following a local inquiry held by the charity commissioners in 1876 a report in 1878 recommended the formation of a governing body for all the charities. The vestry accepted the recommendation, but some existing trustees rejected it, so all the important charities except Monoux were excluded from the scheme adopted in 1880. Under

93 Clarke, *Walthamstow*, 26; *White's Dir. Essex* (1848).
94 H. D. Budden, *Story of Marsh St. Congregational Church*, 45.
95 Pike and Curryer, op. cit. 29–30.
96 Budden, op. cit. 45.
97 Bosworth, *Some Walthamstow houses*, 6–8.
98 J. Shillinglaw, *Walthamstow Dir. and Almanac* (1882).
99 O'Grady, *Cent. Souvenir of St. George's*, 48.
1 *Walthamstow Guardian*, 13 Dec. 1901.
2 *Kelly's Dir. Essex* (1926).
3 See also p. 309.
4 Inf. from St. Mary's Convent; *Catholic Dir.* (1943).
5 *Kelly's Dir. Essex* (1870–1910); *Walthamstow Court Guide . . .* (1884).
6 *Kelly's Dir. Walthamstow* (1905).
7 A. R. Hatley, *Across the years*, 66–7.
8 *Kelly's Dir. Essex* (1912–26).
9 See p. 307.
10 O'Grady, *Cent. Souv. of St. George's*, 49.
11 Inf. from Mr. E. R. Langdon. See p. 302.
12 M. E. Sadler, *Rep. on Sec. and Higher Educ.* 181.
13 Inf. from Mr. E. R. Langdon.
14 M. E. Sadler, op. cit. 181.
15 *Kelly's Dir. Essex* (1926).
16 *Walthamstow Off. Guide* (1963), 53; inf. from the principal, Rabbi E. Salasnik.

17 *Walthamstow Topics*, pp. 20, 22; for Cleveland House see above, p. 249.
18 *Kelly's Dir. Essex* (1922, 1926).
19 O'Grady, *Centenary Souvenir of St. George's*, 45; W.H.L., Canon B. Foley, 'The Origin of Manor Park Parish' (TS. notes); Clarke, *Walthamstow*, 94.
20 W. O'Grady, *Centenary Souvenir of St. George's*, 45; see above, p. 42.
21 *Kelly's Dir. Essex* (1870); *Lond. Gaz.* 21 Feb. 1871, p. 641.
22 *Kelly's Dir. Essex* (1882).
23 H.C. 107 (1895), lxxx. The inquiry provides a great deal of information on conditions in the school in 1895.
24 See p. 309.
25 *Kelly's Dir. Essex* (1906).
26 V.H.M., W.B.C. General Rate Bks. (1937), and File C.D. 20 (Northcott House).
27 G. F. Bosworth, *Some more Walthamstow houses* (W.A.S. xxix), 15; inf. from Mr. F. A. Wright, Trust Secretary; W. Mallinson, *A sketch of my life*, 112.
28 Unless otherwise stated this section is based on: G. F. Bosworth, *Walthamstow charities* (W.A.S. viii); *Rep. Com. Char.* H.C. 60, pp. 129–74 (1833), xviii; Char. Com. Files (esp. files 230700 and G25/50); W. Houghton, *Account of benefactions in parish of St. Mary, Walthamstow . . . 1877*.
29 See p. 309.

that scheme, which was amended in 1891, 13 charities came to be administered by 15 governors. The income was to be applied according to the donors' wills pending further schemes. The confusion caused by this division of administration, and by the diverse objects of the Monoux and Maynard bequests, was resolved by schemes of 1893, by which the Monoux school became a separate foundation with its own board of governors, and 1895, by which the charities regulated by the 1880 and 1891 schemes and most of the remaining charities were combined as Walthamstow Parochial Charities, managed by a board of trustees. The 1895 scheme provided for the appropriate sums to be allotted to the Monoux school foundation, and to carrying out the special provisions in the Compton, Turner, Maynard, and Corbett charities for sermons, reading prayers, and attendance at services, and in the Trafford and Morley charities for care of memorials. The Cluff charity was to be applied according to the donor's wish. The rest of the income was to maintain the alms-people, to support institutions and organizations providing care and nursing for the sick, and to provide temporary financial relief to those in need of it, including emigrants and young persons entering trade or employment.

By a scheme of 1957 the Parochial Charities of 1895 and the later charities of Worton and Cossar were reorganized as Walthamstow Alms-house and General Charities, having a total income in 1957 of £5,503. The purposes to which the income, including that of the Cluff charity, has been applied since 1957 are substantially those of the 1895 scheme, but aid to emigrants is no longer among them. The scheme allows in addition a wide range of gifts of necessities such as fuel, food, clothing, and furniture, and grants for holidays and domestic help. In 1958 the Alms-house and General Charities were allotted a quarter of the Mallinson Fund in Aid of Connaught hospital.[30]

A few charities not included in the 1957 scheme are also administered by the trustees. These are described separately below, with others outside the scheme. Educational charities are described elsewhere.[31]

ALMS-HOUSE AND GENERAL CHARITIES. *Alms-house Charities.* In 1527 George Monoux (d. 1544) acquired land on the north side of St. Mary's churchyard for the erection of 14 rooms for a schoolmaster, 8 poor men, and 5 poor women.[32] The building was completed before his death. By his will dated 1541 he settled on 5 trustees £42 17s. 4d. from the profits of an estate of about 40 houses in Star Alley, All Hallows, Staining (Lond.) to enable them to pay £6 13s. 4d. annually to the alms-priest for keeping the free school, £1 6s. 8d. to the parish clerk for singing in the parish church and helping to teach the children, £5 for coal for the alms-houses, 7s. 7d. weekly to the 13 alms-people (1d. a day each), and

£5 13s. 4d. for an obit in the parish church. The trustees were also to repair the alms-houses and the Monoux chapel in the parish church. The estate, which the trustees were forbidden to alienate, was worth about £50 a year when Monoux died. It was shown in 1635 that Edward Alford, grandson of one of the original trustees, and his son John had abused their trust and withheld payments, and that the alms-houses, which needed rebuilding, and the alms-people had become a burden on the parish.[33] In 1655 a report made following a petition from the inhabitants stated that by 1599 all but 14 of the houses comprised in Monoux's will had been sold, the obit had been discontinued since 1548, and only £32 15s. 5d. had been paid yearly for charitable purposes until 1599, when Elizabeth Alford's gift[34] increased the charity to £41 15s. 5d. An order of the Commissioners for Charitable Uses in 1658 to pay £115 from the London rents was not obeyed. Work seems to have been done to the building c. 1700, perhaps following Henry Maynard's bequest (1686) of £50 to repair the free school.

In 1782 the Monoux trustees assigned to the parish the north aisle and Monoux chapel,[35] the school, and alms-houses, in return for reduction of the yearly rent-charge from £41 14s. 4d.[36] to £21. The balance of the endowment was to be raised from pew rents and burials in the north aisle. Some receipts for burials were paid to the charity account up to 1793 but none subsequently; pew rents were received until 1820. After 1782 no further repairs were carried out by the Monoux trustees. Extensive repairs to the alms-houses costing £275 which were found necessary soon after 1782 were paid for by subscription and the poor-rate. Further extensive repairs in 1823 were paid for by loans charged on the parish rates.[37] The alms-house charity was augmented in the 19th century by the gifts of Banks, Harman, Bedford, Collard, and Cossar,[38] but the recommendation by the Charity Commission in 1832 that the parish should raise funds to buy a rent-charge of £20 14s. 4d. to compensate for the improper alienation of part of the endowment in 1782 was not adopted. In 1842 £429, the residue after expenses of compensation received from the railway company for extinction of marsh lammas rights,[39] was spent on restoring the alms-houses. The £21 rent charge was redeemed in 1874 for £700. The Monoux school became a separate foundation in 1893.[40] Under the 1957 scheme the number of alms-people was varied to not less than 4 men and 4 women.

The alms-house building is a long two-storeyed brick range, partly cement-rendered, with a steeply pitched tile roof. At the centre is a timber-framed and gabled cross-wing with a jettied upper storey. As originally planned the wing contained the schoolmaster's rooms with 7 single-room dwellings to the east of it and 6 to the west.[41] Above the latter was the schoolroom, partly open to the roof. The east end

---

[30] See p. 317.   [31] See pp. 309, 312.
[32] Cf. *V.C.H. Essex,* ii. 527. See also above, p. 309.
[33] G. F. Bosworth and C. D. Saunders, *Original documents relating to the Monoux family* (W.A.S. xix), 7–16.
[34] See below, p. 314.
[35] See p. 289.
[36] The sum is variously quoted as £41 15s. 5d. and £41 14s. 4d. depending on calculation of the pensions as 365 days at 1d. each a day or 52 weeks at 7d. each weekly.
[37] P. H. Reaney, *Church of St. Mary* (W.A.S. n.s. viii), 55.
[38] See below, p. 314.
[39] See p. 265.
[40] See p. 309.
[41] A crude elevational drawing of the alms-houses, 1527, from George Monoux's Ledger Book (B.M. Add. MS. 18783) is reproduced in G. F. Bosworth, *George Monoux* (W.A.S. xvii), f.p. 5.

appears to have been largely rebuilt, probably in the late 18th or early 19th century.[42] The western half, of 16th-century red brick, survived in something approaching its original form until it was destroyed by bombing in 1940. It had retained a corbelled brick chimney at the gable-end, flanked by windows with 4-centred heads.[43] At an earlier date there was a small staircase projection at the front, giving access to the schoolroom.[44] In 1955 the whole western half of the range was rebuilt in red brick[45] and given a stone entrance in the Tudor style, surmounted by a carved and inscribed tablet.

Elizabeth Alford, daughter-in-law of one of the original trustees of Monoux's will, vested in her executors by deed of 1589 a rent-charge of £9 for the alms-house poor. As executor of her will her son Edward, the Monoux trustee in 1599, conveyed to trustees a rent-charge out of property in All Hallows, Staining (Lond.), providing £5 yearly to be distributed in clothing, £2 on St. Thomas's day, and £2 on herrings on Ash Wednesday. In 1635 the inhabitants also complained of the unsatisfactory distribution of this charity, which came to be combined with the original Monoux rent-charge.[46]

Richard Banks by his will dated 1812 left £800 stock after the death of his wife, who held it for life, to the Monoux alms-house poor. The income was received from 1825. It was converted in 1890 to an annuity of £22 15s. 6d.

John Harman by his will proved 1817 gave £400 to his son Jeremiah for distribution to the poor. Jeremiah, who added £100, gave £150 to the poor of Woodford and Chingford, distributed £65 in Walthamstow in 1817, and gave the remaining £285 to the churchwardens to apply at their discretion. The sum was invested on behalf of the Monoux alms-house poor. It was converted in 1890 to an annuity of £8 11s. 11d.

William Bedford by his will dated 1822 left £500 stock in trust for the poor in Monoux's alms-houses. Each of the 13 alms-people were to receive 30s. a year in half-yearly instalments; the residue of the income was to maintain his vault in the churchyard. In 1890 it was converted into an annuity of £15.

Elizabeth Collard by will proved 1842 left £500 in trust for the inmates of the Monoux and Squire alms-houses. The capital was invested. In 1957 the income was £4 5s. 4d.

In 1795 Mary Squire erected 6 alms-houses on the west side of St. Mary's churchyard for the widows of tradesmen, members of the Established Church. She transferred to trustees £1,100 stock, £3 of the annual income to be spent on maintenance of the alms-houses, the balance to provide pensions of £5 a year for the alms-women. John Conyers gave the land on which the houses were built. By her will

proved 1797 Mary Squire also left £1,800 stock to pay a further £8 a year to each widow, the balance to be spent on coal for 12 poor householders. In 1798 Robert Barker added £200 stock to the endowment. The income in 1831 from £3,100 was £87. By the scheme of 1895 preference was given to applicants who had been reduced by misfortune from better circumstances. A scheme of 1924 allowed the appointment of widows, otherwise qualified but not the widows of tradesmen, when there were no fully qualified applicants. The income in 1957 was £77 10s. The alms-houses comprise a single-storey yellow-brick range with a low-pitched slate roof. There are 6 one-room dwellings, the two in the centre being surmounted by a pediment and an inscribed tablet dated 1795. The building has been extended at the rear and restored.

Mary Cox by her will proved 1889 gave £150 in trust, the income to be distributed among 6 aged women in Squire's alms-houses. The legacy was invested in £154 stock. The income in 1957 was £3 17s.

John Cossar, carpenter, by his will proved 1892 left the reversion of his freehold house in Forest Road after the death of his wife Susanna to the trustees of Squire's alms-houses for their repair. In 1894, when Susanna was still alive, the commissioners ordered that the house be sold within 6 months of her death. She died before 1919 and the proceeds of the sale was invested in £116 stock. The income in 1957 was £4 2s. 4d.

Mrs. Jane Sabina Collard by deed of 1859 gave in trust land in Maynard Road and in Pound Field, south of Shernhall Street.[47] The rents were to accumulate for 21 years and were then to be used to build alms-houses on the Maynard Road site for men over 60 years of age who had not been domestic servants nor received poor-relief. By 1876 the trustees had bought more land in Maynard Road and invested the accumulating rents in £333 stock. The income from rents and stock was then £37.[48] Mrs. Collard, who remarried after Captain Collard's death, died in 1865.[49] She left much property personally to the three trustees of her alms-house charity, who received these bequests between 1876 and 1881.[50] Two of the trustees, William Houghton and Arthur Foulger, apparently believed that Mrs. Collard intended the gifts to supplement her alms-house endowment and in 1881 or earlier gave £5,000 to the Collard trust.[51]

In 1881 brick alms-houses for ten men were completed on the north side of Maynard Road.[52] They form a single-storey range with central gabled porch. A scheme for their management was approved in 1885. Much of the charity's income, derived from rents and £3,360 stock, was provided

[42] It has been suggested (R.C.H.M. *Essex*, ii. 247–8) that rebuilding took place *c.* 1700, but in view of the large sums spent in 1782, 1823, and 1842 a later date is more probable, perhaps an archaic style being deliberately adopted.

[43] R.C.H.M. *Essex*, ii. 247–8.

[44] V.H.M., Illus. Colln. (water-colour by Dillon, 1785); see plate f.p. 307.

[45] V.H.M., *Vestiges*, no. 1.

[46] Bosworth and Saunders, *Orig. docs. relating to Monoux family*, 15.

[47] The date of the deed is sometimes quoted as 1851, but the evidence supports the later date. Some, if not all, of the land conveyed in 1859 had been given by Mrs. Collard in 1848 to St. George's Roman Catholic mission, and was not recovered by her until 1855: *Walthamstow*

Guardian, 23 Dec. 1876 (evidence given by W. Houghton at inquiry into Walthamstow's charities); W. O'Grady, *Centenary souvenir of St. George's*, 25–7; see also above, p. 294.

[48] W. Houghton told the inquiry in 1876 that the charity would come into operation in 1880: *Walthamstow Guardian*, 23 Dec. 1876.

[49] St. Mary's Burial Register; inscription on tombstone in churchyard. Her second husband was Thomas Jones Burton.

[50] Correspondence in *Walthamstow Guardian*, 10, 17, 31 Dec. 1881. The lapse of time since her death may have been due to the fact that her second husband survived her.

[51] *Walthamstow Guardian*, 31 Dec. 1881 (letter from W. E. Whittingham).

[52] Ibid. 23 July, 19 Nov. 1881.

by the auxiliary endowment of Houghton and Foulger, including most of the stock and ground rents bought in 1883–5 for £853. More ground rents were bought in 1889. In 1895 the alms-houses were included in the combined scheme for Waltham-stow Parochial Charities, the alms-men to be chosen according to the terms of Mrs. Collard's gift. In 1920 the income from rents was £102 and from stock £67. The Shernhall Street field, occupied partly as allotments, was sold in 1947. The income of the charity in 1957 was £132 from rents and £283 from £9,175 stock.

General Charities. William Hyll, vicar 1470–87, by will dated 1487 left an acre of meadow to the church on condition that the church-wardens kept his anniversary and those of his parents. In 1826 the rent, then £2 5s., was being paid into the general charities account. The land was sold in 1938. The income in 1957 was £12.

Robert Rampston (d. 1585) left £2 a year to the Walthamstow poor charged on Stone Hall, Little Canfield. In 1796 it was being distributed in bread, although the donor did not specify this use. Since 1895 it has been applied to the purposes of the general charities.

Thomas Colby, alms-priest (d. 1609), by his will left all his estate in trust for the poor of the parish and alms-houses. In 1633 an inquisition revealed breach of trust and ordered restitution of about £120 to the parish. With that money in 1636 the church-wardens bought 12 a. of land called Hellbrinkes (Hale Brinks) in Hale End Lane, which was let and the rent distributed to fulfil Colby's will. The value of the land rose from £7 a year in 1636 to £17 in 1786 and £50 in 1817. By 1895 it was let as allotments at £43. Part of the land sold in 1924 and 1957, and a small part exchanged for part of the Belle Vue estate in 1938. In 1957 income from the land, still let as allotments, and stock was £142.

William Conyers by deed of 1623 conveyed a rent-charge of £7 10s. from lands at Hale End to the churchwardens to provide bread for 12 poor persons every Sunday in memory of his uncle, Tristram Conyers. The rent-charge was redeemed in 1926 for £400 stock which in 1957 produced an income of £10.

Richard Garnett by his will proved 1643 left a rent-charge of £3 from land in Marsh Street to provide bread and one or two pence for the poor on Sundays. In 1893 the rent-charge was transferred from the property in Marsh Street to the ground on which no. 33 York Terrace, Selborne Road, was built. The income was £4 in 1957.

Thomas Gamuel by his will dated 1643 left about 6 a. of copyhold land in trust to provide 12 penny loaves weekly for the poor, the balance to be distributed yearly in money. In 1786 the income from the land, Prior's croft or Honeybone field in Mark-house Road, and part of Markhouse common, was £4 15s. The property was enfranchised in 1855. A small piece was sold in 1873 to build St. Saviour's school, and in 1883 Walthamstow school board leased land to build Gamuel Road school.[53] Honey-bone field was let as allotments. More land was sold in 1925 and 1956. In 1957 the proceeds of sales

represented £885 stock and the income from rents and interest amounted to £237.

The Inhabitants Donation was established in 1650 when several unnamed parishioners gave £95 in trust to buy land for the relief of the poor. The Breaches or Winsbeach field (16 a.) south of Hagger Lane was bought. The vestry seems to have replaced the original trustees and to have let the land. Apparently one acre of the land which was copyhold may have been lost to the parish by failure to declare the trust in the court rolls. In 1832 the land was found to be about 13 a. let at £49. A small piece of land was sold in 1877 to the railway company. The rest was let soon after on building leases and developed as Hempstead, Fyfield, and Forest Roads, and 'Fernhill' (later Fernhill Court).[54] Much of the land was sold in 1953–7. The income in 1957 from stock and ground rents was £587.

Edward Corbett by will proved 1676 left land let at £7 a year to the poor of Walthamstow, and land let at £3 to provide annually on his birthday £1 to the minister for a sermon, 5s. to the clerk, and £1 10s. to the churchwardens for a supper. It was stated in 1832 that the last mentioned payment was never so applied. The income on the land in Wyatts Lane and Wood Street was £85 in 1832, when part of it was let on a building lease at a nominal rent of 1s. Most of the income was applied to coal and monthly pensions of 10s. to 10 poor widows. In 1918 the rents produced £172. Part of the land in Wyatt's Lane was sold in 1949. The income in 1957 from stock and rents was £583.

Henry Maynard (d. 1686) by his will dated 1686 left £950 in trust to buy land to provide income for the minister (£400), the schoolmaster (£200), and the poor (£300), and small annual gifts to the parish clerk, churchwardens, and overseers (£50). In 1690 his executor bought Higham Hill farm (52 a.) for £1,000, but although a Chancery order in 1691 apportioned the estate the charity had not been settled by 1706, when the court ordered that trustees be appointed to whom it should be conveyed. Lengthy Chancery proceedings over the arrears[55] and their distribution were concluded soon after 1714. In 1719 a copyhold farm called Stretman's (30 a.) at Hale End was bought with £450 of the arrears. From 1758 the income from the two farms was divided into nineteen parts allotted proportionately to the purposes of the will. In 1809 the vestry ordered the parish officers to distribute the share of the poor as coal or food instead of money.[56] By 1832 it had for many years been distributed in coal. Stretman's farm was enfranchised in 1890. Small pieces of land at Higham Hill were sold to the railway company in 1871, the water company in 1900, and Metropolitan water board in 1905. In 1921 the urban district council compulsorily purchased 16 a. at Higham Hill and by 1957 most of the land had been sold, and the income from the remaining land, let as allotments, and stock was £1,456. The income in 1969 was £1,836.

Anthony and Dinah Compton by wills dated 1703 and 1706 left £20 and £5 respectively in trust to buy bread for the poor on New Year's day. Thomas Turner of Aldersgate by will dated 1711 left £130

[53] See pp. 306–7.
[54] G. F. Bosworth, *Some more Walthamstow houses* (W.A.S. xxix), 23–4.
[55] Cf. Newcourt, *Repertorium*, ii. 636.
[56] V.H.M., PV 5, ff. 262–3.

to Walthamstow, where he was buried, in trust for the upkeep of his tomb and to pay 15s. to the churchwardens of St. Botolph's, Aldersgate (Lond.), if they attended St. Mary's church once a year. Any remaining income was to be spent on bread for the poor of Walthamstow every Sunday. In 1729 the vestry sold for £187 the stock (£175) which represented the capital of the Compton and Turner gifts[57] in order to buy land on Church common and build a workhouse, and agreed that an annual sum representing 5 per cent interest on £180 be provided from the parish rate to buy bread, maintain Turner's tomb, and pay the churchwardens of St. Botolph's, according to the donors' wills. An account of the workhouse is given elsewhere.[58] A piece of the garden was sold to the railway company in 1873. The workhouse land and buildings were sold in 1944. The scheme of 1957 permits continued payment to the churchwardens of St. Botolph's as directed by Turner's will. The income in 1957 was £84.

Sigismund Trafford by will dated 1723 left £10 rent-charge to pay the sexton 10s. a year to clean his monument in the parish church and to raise £50 stock for the repair of the monument and vault, the surplus to be distributed as the minister and churchwardens saw fit. The balance was added to the general charity account. The income in 1957 was £10.

Edmund Wise by will dated 1732 or 1734 left to the churchwardens 6 a. freehold land at Holloway Down in Leyton let at £5 yearly on condition that they maintained his and his mother's tombs. In 1832 the land was leased at £21 yearly and the balance paid to the general charity account. In 1827-8 £15 10s. had been paid in 10s. pensions monthly to poor widows. In 1828-9 £20 19s. was distributed in potatoes. In 1869-77 the land was let on building leases. In 1957 the income was £124. Much of the land was sold in 1959-65.

Jeremiah Wakelin (d. March 1736/7) by his will dated 1735 gave the rents of 1½ a. of copyhold land in Pound field, Shernhall Street, to the churchwardens to be distributed in bread or meat on New Year's day as long as his heirs retained his pew in the parish church, the use of his grave under the gallery, and the privilege of erecting a family monument. The land was let in 1786 at £3 and in 1832 at £12 10s. It was enfranchised in 1862. In 1873 the church-wardens bought a strip of land to gain a right of way from Pound field to Maynard Road. In 1885 the land was leased for £44 to the school board, which built Maynard Road schools on the site.[59] The income in 1957 was £44.

Thomas Legendre, draper, by his will proved 1753 left £600 in trust to buy land to provide coal for the poor, preferably widows, and the residue of his estate to his executor John Fisher. The charitable bequest was void under the Mortmain Act, 1736, but John Fisher gave for the purposes of the will £564 stock to be transferred to the trustees of Katherine Woolball's charity.

Katherine Woolball by her will proved 1756 left £400 in trust for the benefit of the poor at Christ-

mas. Stock to the value of £445 was purchased which, with the addition of Fisher's gift, provided £1,009 stock vested in the same trustees. In 1832 the joint income of £30 5s. 4d. was usually distributed in coal. In 1890 and 1895 the stocks of Woolball's and Legendre's charities were converted into annuities of £13 7s. 3d. and £16 18s. 1d. respectively.

Thomas Sims by will proved 1782 left £100 in trust to repair his family monument. It was so applied in 1827-8. In 1832 the surplus was being paid to the general charity account. The annuity was transferred to the Official Trustees of Charitable Funds in 1879 and under the schemes of 1895 and 1957 applied to the purposes of the general charities. The income in 1957 was £2 10s.

James Holbrook,[60] brewer, of St. Botolph's, Aldgate (Lond.), was providing in 1786-88 10 sixpenny loaves weekly for the poor of Walthamstow. By deed dated 1805 he gave £39 charged on land at the bottom of Marsh Street for a weekly gift of bread. The earlier gift seems to have led to the belief that only 10 loaves were to be bought weekly and the residue was applied to other gifts. In 1832 the charity commissioners stressed that the whole sum was to be spent on bread. The land became part of the reservoir in Coppermill Lane[61] and the rent-charge of £39 was being paid in 1957 by the Metropolitan water board.

John Rigge by will dated 1806 left £100 in trust to repair his family vault. In 1832 the surplus was being paid to the general charity account; this use was permitted under the schemes of 1895 and 1957. The income in 1957 was £2 10s.

John Morley by his will proved 1845 left £300 stock to the vicar and churchwardens in trust for the maintenance of his family monuments in the parish church, the surplus to buy bread for the poor. The income in 1957 was about £8.

William Cluff by his will proved 1874 gave £1,000 in trust to be invested to buy 5 sacks of coal each for 30 poor people at Christmas and as much bread as the balance would buy. Since 1957, when the income on £471 stock was £14 it has been applied to the purposes of the general charities.

Daniel Maclaurin by will proved 1877 left £150 in trust for the poor. The income in 1895 was £4 5s. In 1902 most of the stock was sold to buy land in Havant Road which was let on a building lease. The income in 1957 was £27 11s.

Thomas Worton of the Cock, High Street, by will proved 1922 left over £45,000 to the poor of Walthamstow.[62] Under a scheme of 1924 £7,812 stock was transferred to the Connaught hospital to build and equip the Thomas Worton ward of 10 beds for the exclusive use, so far as possible, of the poor of Walthamstow.[63] The income from the remaining £30,208 stock was to be administered by the Walthamstow Parochial Charities trustees and applied to the general purposes of those charities, including the alms-houses. The income in 1957 was £1,128.

The Walthamstow Ecclesiastical Charity was formed under the 1957 scheme. £70 stock belonging to the Walthamstow charities was allotted to carrying out the provisions in Trafford's and Corbett's

[57] The 1729 vestry minute inadvertently omitted A. Compton's name from the resolution: S. J. Barns, *Vestry mins. 1710-40* (W.A.S. xiii), 16-17.   [58] See p. 278.
[59] *Hist. Walthamstow Sch. Bd.* 100; see also above, p. 307.
[60] See also p. 240.
[61] Bosworth, *Some more . . . houses*, 13.
[62] *Pub. Services of Walthamstow, 1935.*
[63] Before 1928 the hospital was called Leyton, Walthamstow, and Wanstead hospital.

charities for cleaning Trafford's tomb and for paying the vicar for a sermon and the parish clerk for attendance on Corbett's birthday.[64]

OTHER CHARITIES. The following charities were not included in the 1895 and 1957 schemes.

Elizabeth Cooper's bequest under her will dated 1708 is described elsewhere.[65]

Mary Newell by will dated 1810 gave two-thirds of the income from £500 to apprentice one boy each year, the son of members of the Established Church. She left the remaining third to the Sunday school.[66] The income, which was received in 1818,[67] was £15. A scheme of 1942 permitted the charity to be used, in so far as it could not be usefully applied in apprenticing, to assist poor boys, sons of Walthamstow parents of the Established Church, preparing for or engaged in any trade, occupation, or service.

The Spade Husbandry charity was founded in 1834 when Lord Maynard granted about 11 a. of copyhold land in Hagger Lane to be let in ¼ a. plots at 8s. each a year and cultivated with the spade as allotments. The rents were to be used to reduce the poor rate. The land, popularly called 'Canada', was enfranchised in 1924. In 1939 3½ a. was sold to the Metropolitan water board. A scheme of 1941, which appointed the trustees of Walthamstow Parochial Charities managers of the allotments, allowed them to apply any income which could not be used to rent land to buy necessities for the poor, but not to relieve the rates. The income in 1969 was £160.[68]

Elizabeth Cass by will dated 1838 left £4,000 stock, reduced by expenses to £3,547 stock, to pay £30 annually to the vicar and churchwardens, who were to distribute the rest of the income to poor people of the Established Church not receiving parochial aid. In 1965–6 the capital was £3,547 and £60 was distributed to 58 people, many of them in alms-houses.

Sarah Hibbert by will proved 1884 left £200 for the poor of St. Saviour's parish. The legacy was augmented by public subscription and applied to buy land and erect an iron building for a soup kitchen. The property was sold in 1896 for £200 which was invested in £176 4s. stock. The income in 1965 was £4 8s.

Walthamstow Sick Poor fund was established by a scheme of 1955 by which the assets of the Walthamstow dispensary[69] were to be administered under that title, for the benefit of the sick poor, by the trustees of the Alms-house and General Charities. The income in 1969 was £322 8s.

Hale End District Association Sick Children's fund originated in the Hale End District Association Hospital charity founded by a declaration of trust in 1925. By a scheme of 1952 under the new title the income was to be applied to sick children of the deserving poor in the parish of All Saints, Highams Park, and, subject thereto, to sick adults. It is administered by the Walthamstow Alms-house and General Charities trustees. The income in 1969 from £1,754 stock was £43.

Sir William Mallinson (d. 1936) by deed of gift dated 1935 set up an endowment in aid of Connaught hospital.[70] It was represented by £8,740 stock in 1958, when a scheme divided it into four Mallinson Funds, in aid of the Walthamstow Alms-house and General Charities, the William Mallinson Scholarship Trust,[71] the Walthamstow Child Welfare society,[72] and the Connaught hospital amenities fund.

LOST CHARITIES Matthew Humberstone by will dated 1708 gave £500 to erect alms-houses and a school. He also provided for an endowment of £14 yearly, pensions to the alms-people, and £10 for the poor. His widow paid £10 in 1710 but the rest of the will was not executed.[73] A lying-in charity either existed or was planned in 1797[74] but nothing further is known of it.

WANSTEAD

WANSTEAD lies about 7 miles north-east of the City of London.[1] It is a dormitory suburb straddling the arterial road to Southend and Colchester and forming part of the London borough of Redbridge. The ancient parish extended from Wanstead Flats north for about 4 miles to the boundary with Woodford. The western boundary marched with Leyton and Walthamstow, and the river Roding formed the eastern boundary. The south-west of the parish comprised a spur called the Wanstead Slip which ran south of Leyton down to the marshes near Temple Mills, and included a small detached part

locally situated in West Ham. This was more or less coterminous with the manor of Cann Hall, which was originally in Leyton but appears to have become part of Wanstead by the early 13th century.[2] The main body of the Wanstead Slip (207 a.) was merged in Leyton sanitary district in 1875 and was constituted a separate civil parish (Cann Hall) in 1894.[3] The detached part of the Slip (38 a.) was merged in West Ham local government district in 1875.[4] In the same area a small adjustment of the boundary between Wanstead and West Ham had been made in 1790.[5] In the south-east corner of the

[64] See above, pp. 315–16.
[65] See p. 287.   [66] See p. 305.
[67] V.H.M., PV 5, ff. 411–12.
[68] In 1967 the corporation of London was seeking to obtain powers to acquire compulsorily the Spade Husbandry land to replace the forest land taken away by the construction of the Waterworks Corner diversion of the North Circular Road: Walthamstow Independent, 26 May 1967.
[69] The dispensary owned no. 105 Hoe Street, £793 stock, and £1,935 cash. See also above, p. 284.
[70] W. Mallinson, A sketch of my life, 111.
[71] See p. 312.

[72] Founded in 1915: G. F. Bosworth, More Walthamstow houses (W.A.S. xx), 7.
[73] W. Houghton, Account of benefactions in the parish of St. Mary, 1876, p. 7.
[74] V.C.H. Essex, Bibliography, 296.
[1] O.S. Map 2½" TQ 38, 39, 48, 49. See map above, p. 180.
[2] See p. 326.
[3] See p. 174. Developments in Cann Hall after 1875 are treated under Leyton.
[4] See p. 43.
[5] W.H.L., W. Ham Vestry Mins. 25 Feb. 1790.

parish Aldersbrook appears to have been transferred from Wanstead to Little Ilford early in the 16th century.[6] That substantial change evidently took place without legal formalities and caused boundary disputes at later periods.[7] Later boundary changes included the transfer of 96 a. of Wanstead Flats to East Ham in 1901.[8]

In the mid 19th century Wanstead parish comprised 2,002 a.[9] A local board of health was formed for the parish in 1854. In 1931 Wanstead urban district contained 1,679 a.[10] In 1934 it was united with that of Woodford and in 1937 the combined district became a municipal borough. Wanstead and Woodford became part of Redbridge in 1965. In general that year has been taken as the terminal point of this article.

The land, which is mainly gravel, rises from the Roding to a height of about 100 ft. in the west.[11] Seventeenth-century maps show two streams flowing across the south of the parish into the Roding.[12] These, and the Roding itself, were altered and diverted in the late 17th and early 18th centuries, when the owners of Wanstead House constructed elaborate artificial lakes and watercourses, some of which still survive.[13] The Snaresbrook (formerly Sayesbrook), another tributary of the Roding, rose in the north-west of the parish, to which area it gave its name.[14] The river Holt, or Wanstead ditch, entered the parish from Leyton, where the Woodford road crosses the boundary, running south-east through Voluntary Place into the Basin in Wanstead Park. Immediately north of Blake Hall a branch of it forked west: that was probably the stream, also called the Holt, which re-emerged below the Green Man in Leyton, running south to Cann Hall.[15] Neither the Snaresbrook stream nor the Holt is now visible above ground.[16] The Eagle pond, Snaresbrook Road, was called Snares pond in 1746.[17] It is a prominent feature, favoured by anglers. About 1619 a mineral spring was discovered at Wanstead, which for a short period became a fashionable spa. The spring may have been at Bushwood.[18]

Until the 19th century Wanstead retained much woodland, part of Epping Forest, small patches of which still survive at Bushwood and Snaresbrook. Wanstead Flats form a wide expanse of ancient heath. North of them are Wanstead Park and Wanstead golf course, which together form a remnant of a larger park formerly attached to Wanstead House, demolished in the 19th century.

Roman remains found in and around Wanstead Park indicate a substantial settlement.[19] In the Middle Ages Wanstead was a small, sparsely populated rural parish on the southern fringe of Epping Forest. In 1086 the total recorded population of the two manors which later comprised the parish was only 18.[20] In 1327 there were 10 persons assessed for taxation in Wanstead and Little Ilford, taken together.[21] As late as 1670 there were no more than 40 houses in Wanstead.[22] In 1762, however, there were 112, and by 1796 some 150.[23] In 1801 the population was 918.[24] It rose slowly to 2,742 in 1861, and then faster to 5,119 in 1871. By 1891 the population of the parish was 26,292, but that of the local board district (excluding Cann Hall) was only 7,092. In 1931, the last census before the union with Woodford, Wanstead urban district numbered 19,183 inhabitants. In 1961 the four wards of the borough lying in Wanstead had a total population of some 28,000.[25]

Little is known of the medieval pattern of settlement and no buildings survive from that period. The original parish church of St. Mary was a few yards from the present building, which replaced it in 1790. In the Middle Ages Wanstead House, the manor-house, probably stood near the church, as it certainly did in later centuries. Before the 16th century it was of no great size. The manorial buildings of Cann Hall seem to have been even more modest. No other medieval buildings are known by name except Naked Hall, later Aldersbrook.

From the 16th century Wanstead House, under a succession of royal and titled owners, was greatly enlarged. In the 18th century it was rebuilt as a Palladian mansion dominating the parish.[26] By then, however, the village also was growing. Most of the houses lay north of the park, in the present High Street and in Wanstead (later George) Lane (now Eastern Avenue and Nutter Lane). There were some large houses at Snaresbrook, and cottages at Mobs Hole, a forest-side hamlet later called Nightingale Green.[27] Wanstead's communications with the outside world then depended mainly on the Leytonstone, Woodford, and Chigwell roads, which were controlled by the newly-formed Middlesex and Essex turnpike trust.[28] Leytonstone, leading to London, was approached by an unnamed avenue, now Cambridge Park. North of Leytonstone the main road (now Hollybush Hill and Woodford Road) led to Woodford and Epping, with a branch (now New Wanstead and Hermon Hill) to Chigwell and Ongar. Running south from Wanstead, across the park and the Lower Forest (Wanstead Flats), were several paths or tracks. Access to the east was by South (or Parsons, later Redbridge) Lane over Red Bridge to Ilford.

Red (formerly Hockley's) Bridge over the Roding existed in the 16th century and was probably older.[29]

---

[6] See p. 167. Cf. H. Smith, *Eccl. Hist. Essex*, 247.
[7] e.g. in 1613 (E.R.O., D/DQs 17) and 1723 (E.R.O., D/P 292/8/7).
[8] *Census*, 1901, 1911.
[9] O.S. Map 6″, Essex, LXV and LXXIII (surv. 1863–73).
[10] Census, 1931.
[11] The topography favours the interpretation of Wanstead as meaning 'hill place': *P.N. Essex* (E.P.N.S.), 109.
[12] e.g. J. Speed, *Map of Essex* (1610).
[13] See p. 325.
[14] J. Rocque, *Environs of London* (1744–6), sheet iv; E.R.O., D/CT 384 (Tithe Map, 1841); J. E. Tuffs, *Story of Wanstead and Woodford*, 28. For the tenement called Sayes see below p. 323.
[15] E.R.O., D/CT 384; D/DCw P47; D/DCy P3, pp. 115, 119, 154, 160. See also above, p. 175.

[16] Cf. W. Eastment, *Wanstead through the Ages* (1969 edn.), 113–14; Tuffs, *Wanstead and Woodford*, 94.
[17] Rocque, *Environs London* (1744–6), sheet iv.
[18] M. Christy and M. Thresh, *Mineral Waters and Medicinal Springs of Essex*, 11–12.
[19] *V.C.H. Essex*, iii. 198.   [20] Ibid. i. 438, 497.
[21] E 179/107/13 m. 23d. Most of those assessed were probably in Wanstead.
[22] E.R.O., Q/RTh 5.   [23] Lysons, *London*, iv. 241.
[24] *Census Reps.* 1801 sqq.: cf. *V.C.H. Essex*, v. 5, 64.
[25] Some of the ward boundaries cut across the parish boundaries.
[26] J. Rocque, *Environs Lond.* (1744–6) sheet iv; Chapman and André, *Map of Essex* (1777), sheets xvi, xxi.
[27] Cf. Eastment, *Wanstead*, 110–11.
[28] See p. 342.
[29] *E. Nat.* vii. 104; E.R.O., Q/CP 1, f. 32; *P.N. Essex*, 99.

From the 17th century to the 19th its repair was the subject of disputes between the parishes of Wanstead and Barking and the riparian landowners.[30] It appears to have been rebuilt about 1642 and again in 1840–1.[31] The present bridge, which carries Eastern Avenue, was built by the Ministry of Transport in 1923–6.[32]

Many of the larger houses shown on 18th-century maps were probably new. Wanstead was beginning to attract wealthy residents, especially those with interests in London,[33] and in 1762 70 of the 112 houses in the parish were said to be 'mansions'.[34] After Wanstead House the largest residence in 1700 was probably that later called the Grove, or Wanstead Grove, which lay in spacious grounds east of High Street. It is said to have been built about 1690 by Sir Francis Dashwood, Bt., son of a Turkey merchant.[35] Matthew Wymondesold, owner in the mid 18th century, was a successful financier.[36] The estate was bought in 1759 by Humphrey Bowles, in whose family it remained for a century.[37] The house, at the junction of the Avenue and Grove Park, was rebuilt c. 1822 but demolished in 1889.[38] Two early-18th-century features from its grounds still survive behind small modern houses in the Avenue: a red-brick gazebo (at no. 20) and a 'temple' with an Ionic portico (at no. 14). Bleak (later Blake) Hall, a large house at the west end of South Lane, was built c. 1690, and evidently much extended later; it was demolished in 1909.[39] Smaller 17th-century houses included Grove Cottage, Nutter Lane, a timber-framed building demolished c. 1957.[40]

Among early-18th-century houses was an impressive group of five in the Mall (the east side of High Street).[41] Of those the Manor House (West Essex Conservative Club) survives, as a red-brick building of seven bays with an original shell-hood to the doorway.[42] The adjoining Sheridan House is of slightly later date. The other three houses had by 1971 been wholly or partly demolished, and shops had been built over their front gardens. West of High Street was Spratt Hall, which existed by 1746 but was demolished in the later 19th century.[43] Reydon Hall and Elm Hall, which stand together in Eastern Avenue, are large early-18th-century houses, similar in style to those in the Mall, but much altered.[44] In 1971 they were occupied as flats. Near them, in Nutter Lane, is the Applegarth, which is said by a plaque on the front to have been built c. 1710, but has later features. For many years,

up to 1926, it was the home of the Nutter family, benefactors to the parish.[45] Several late-18th-century buildings also survive at Snaresbrook. Nos. 23 and 25 Woodford Road are an attached pair of tall brown-brick houses with Doric doorcases. Snaresbrook House, in the same road, is a large stucco building, probably of c. 1800, with later additions. Willow Holme, Snaresbrook Road, is a three-storey house, originally one of a pair. In 1971 it was being extended in matching style. The Eagle hotel, Woodford Road, is Wanstead's oldest inn. As the Spread Eagle it is said to have existed in the 17th century,[46] but the present building dates from the 18th century. The George (formerly George and Dragon), High Street, is recorded from 1716, but was rebuilt c. 1902.[47] It bears a tablet, dated 1752, with a cryptic inscription commemorating a cherry pie.[48] The Thatched House inn, Leytonstone High Road, mentioned in 1791, was rebuilt about 1875 100 yd. farther south.[49] The growth and wealth of the parish in the 18th century was also reflected in its public buildings. The church, extended in 1709–10, was replaced in 1790 by a much larger building. The first parish school, which still survives, was built in High Street in 1796. The Assembly rooms, built c. 1725, have disappeared, and their site is unknown.[50]

Nearly all the new building in the 19th century was in the centre and north of the parish. The demolition of Wanstead House (1823–4) did not immediately stimulate growth. The manorial demesne could not be broken up,[51] and this restricted development in the south of the parish where most of the demesne lay. It did not, however, prevent the inclosure by the manor court of the woodland and waste in and north of the old village. In the 1830s the court began to make frequent 'voluntary grants' of small pieces of waste for building purposes.[52] Some were in Voluntary Place, which may have been named from them. The pace of inclosure quickened after 1840.[53]

During the earlier 19th century cottages, some of them built on new inclosures, increased in number, in spite of opposition from the vestry, which feared that such building would attract poor to the parish.[54] By 1841 more than half Wanstead's dwellings were cottages.[55] One or two of the cottages built c. 1800–50 still survived in 1971 on the west side of High Street. Many of the larger houses built during that period, as before, were at Snaresbrook.[56] The most notable new building was the Royal Wanstead

[30] E.R.O., Q/CP 3, ff. 4, 140; J. E. Oxley, *Barking Vestry Mins.* 161; E.R.O., D/P 292/8/7, 19 May 1755 sqq.; ibid. 292/8/10, 24 Nov. 1811 sqq.
[31] Eastment, *Wanstead*, 99; cf. E.R.O., Q/SR 331/28: refs. to the 'newbuilt bridge'; E.R.O., T/P 94/1.
[32] *Ilford Official Handbk.* (1958), 22; Tuffs, *Wanstead and Woodford*, 110.
[33] D. Defoe, *Tour through Great Britain*, ed. G. D. H. Cole, i. 5–6.
[34] Lysons, *London*, iv. 241.
[35] Morant, *Essex*, i. 31; *D.N.B.* s.v. Dashwood, F., baron le Despenser.
[36] Named on Rocque's map (1744–6); cf. *D.N.B.* s.v. Pound, Jas.
[37] Eastment, *Wanstead*, 49, 55, 83–90; E.R.O., Library Vert. Folder, 'Wanstead Grove, the seat of the Hon. Anne Rushout'.
[38] E.R.O., T/P 94/7; *Architectural History*, xiv. 27.
[39] Tuffs, *Wanstead and Woodford*, 39, 81; J. Oliver, *Map of Essex* (1696).
[40] R.C.H.M., *Essex*, ii. 250; Tuffs, op. cit. 122.
[41] Eastment, op. cit. 100; R.C.H.M., *Essex*, ii. 249.

[42] R.C.H.M., *Essex*, ii. 249.
[43] Named on Rocque's Map (1744–6); Eastment, *Wanstead*, 96.
[44] Pevsner, *Bdgs. of Essex* (1965 edn.), 413; R.C.H.M. *Essex*, ii. 249. (Elm House, i.e. Hall.)
[45] Eastment, *Wanstead*, 98; *Kelly's Dir. Essex* (1926 and earlier edns.); Char. Com. files.
[46] Tuffs, *Wanstead and Woodford*, 40, 99.
[47] E.R.O., D/DB T545; Eastment, op. cit. 106.
[48] E.R.O., Vert. Folder, Newscutting signed W.H.B.
[49] E.R.O., D/P 292/8/9, 14 Aug. 1791; *Kelly's Dir. Essex* (1870, cf. 1878); O.S. Map 6", Essex, LXV (surv. 1863–9).
[50] *Gents. Mag.* Feb. 1806, 188. Their reopening was recorded in 1755: E.R.O., D/DU 546/2.
[51] See p. 326.
[52] E.R.O., D/DCw M10 and 11.
[53] See p. 329.
[54] E.R.O., D/P 292/8/10, 14 Nov. 1821.
[55] As distinct from 'houses', 'residences', or 'mansions': E.R.O., D/CT 384.
[56] E.R.O., D/DCy P3 (map 1815–16); O.S. Map 6", Essex, LXV and LXXIII (surv. 1863–73).

school, Hollybush Hill (1843). The Merchant Seamen's orphan asylum, Hermon Hill, now Wanstead Hospital, was erected in 1861.[57] The Weavers' alms-houses, New Wanstead, were built in 1859.[58]

Wanstead was still a village in 1856, when the railway arrived. During the next twenty-five years there was building near Snaresbrook station: in Hermon Hill[59] and the new roads east of it, and at New Wanstead, a name now used only for the road, but originally applied to the whole area between that road and Cambridge Park.[60] Between c. 1880 and 1900 building went on steadily on old and new sites. The rapid development of Cann Hall is described under Leyton.[61] The Spratt Hall estate was cut up for building in 1885–7.[62] Part of the Oak Hall estate, in Redbridge Lane West, was cut up at the same time, and the remainder about 1892.[63] The Grove estate was gradually developed after 1889, with houses in Grove Park and the Avenue.[64] The Drive estate at Snaresbrook was laid out in 1895–6.[65] Between 1900 and 1914 new building took place mainly in the south of the parish. The large Aldersbrook estate (c. 1900–10) formed a distinct and isolated township in the triangle between the park, the flats, and the City of London cemetery.[66] The Lake House estate (c. 1908–14) lay west of Blake Hall Road, between Bushwood and Lake House Road.[67] The Blake Hall estate, south of Cambridge Park, was cut up c. 1909.[68]

Most building since 1914 has been on the eastern side of the parish. The opening of Eastern Avenue in the 1920s was followed by development north and south of it. In north-east Wanstead Nightingale farm was sold for building shortly before 1939.[69] By then there was little building-land left, and later building has consisted mainly of in-filling. During the Second World War most of Wanstead's houses were damaged and several hundred were destroyed. The Lake House estate suffered most.[70]

The houses built in Wanstead between 1860 and 1918 were larger on average than those in neighbouring suburbs,[71] and included a large proportion of detached and semi-detached types. Since 1918 the shortage of land and increasing urbanization have restricted house sizes, and have stimulated the building of flats, including a tall block at the corner of New Wanstead and High Street, and others in Eastern Avenue. In 1971 High Street was in process of redevelopment as the main shopping centre of Wanstead. The older buildings, many of them damaged by bombing, were gradually being replaced by modern blocks.

Modern development has preserved the lines of most of the old roads, though some of their names have been changed. During the early 19th century Long-Wellesley, the lord of the manor, made several attempts to close public paths across his park, but he was only partly successful.[72] An Act of 1816 authorized the construction of Blake Hall Road in place of a former track, and gave protection to certain paths in the park, including three which later became Overton Drive, St. Mary's Avenue, and Langley Drive.[73] The most important modern road is Eastern Avenue (1925), the arterial road to Southend and Colchester.[74] Its western end, at Wanstead, was formed by widening George Lane as far as Elm Hall and building an extension down to Red Bridge. Eastern Avenue, and its feeder Cambridge Park, cuts through the centre of Wanstead, and its heavy traffic has changed the character of the town.

In 1681 Wanstead was served by a daily coach from Aldgate.[75] There were five daily services in 1791: three from Aldgate and two from Whitechapel.[76] In the early 19th century services to the village did not improve much, but Snaresbrook was served by frequent coaches along the Woodford Road, and others running to London via Walthamstow.[77] Early in the present century there was a horse bus service between Wanstead and Leytonstone and another between Wanstead and Forest Gate.[78] By 1911 the motor bus route from Elephant and Castle ended at Wanstead.[79]

The Loughton branch of the Eastern Counties railway, opened in 1856, ran through Wanstead, and Snaresbrook station was built in High Street.[80] The branch was electrified in 1947 when it was taken over by London Transport as part of the Central (underground) line.[81] The Central line extension from Leytonstone to Newbury Park, opened at the same time, included Wanstead station, Eastern Avenue, built in 1937–8 to the design of Charles Holden.[82]

From 1692 Wanstead was within the London penny post area, with a daily collection and delivery.[83] There was a receiving house there in 1794.[84] When the London postal area was divided in 1856 Wanstead became a sub-office of Leytonstone in the north-eastern (later in the eastern) district.[85] At the reorganization of 1917 it was placed along with Leytonstone in the E. 11 sub-district.[86] A

[57] Pevsner, *Bdgs. of Essex*, 413.
[58] This charity is associated with the Weavers' Company, who under a Scheme of 1968 may admit any poor person.
[59] Probably named from the family of Jeremiah Harman (fl. 1813): E.R.O., D/P 292/8/10, 8 Mar. 1813. The Harmans also held land in Walthamstow: see above, p. 259.
[60] O.S. Map 6″, Essex, LXV and LXXIII (surv. 1863–73); *Kelly's Dir. Essex* (1878 and 1882).
[61] See p. 181.
[62] E.R.O., T/P 94/7.
[63] Ibid.; E.R.O., *Sale Cat.* A 494.
[64] E.R.O., T/P 94/7.
[65] Ibid.
[66] E.R.O., T/P 94/9; ibid. *Sale Cat.* A 1076. It had been part of the manor of Aldersbrook: see above, p. 167.
[67] E.R.O., T/P 94/7; A. N. Harrisson, *Hist. Park Ward, Wanstead*, 13.
[68] Eastment, *Wanstead*, 90.
[69] Tuffs, *Wanstead and Woodford*, 110.
[70] S. Tiquet, *It happened here*, passim. In the whole borough of Wanstead and Woodford 509 houses were destroyed.

[71] *V.C.H. Essex*, v. 50.
[72] W.H.L., Hiram Stead, 'Materials for the Hist. of Wanstead House etc.', ff. 64, 129; E.R.O., T/B 39.
[73] Woodford and Ilford Roads Act, 56 Geo. III, c. 8 (local and personal); *Proc. Woodford Antiq. Soc.* ii. 16.
[74] *Redbridge Official Guide* (1969), 47.
[75] T. de Laune, *Present state of London*, 435.
[76] *Universal Brit. Dir.* (1791), i. 605.
[77] *Johnstone's Lond. Dir.* (1822–3), 22, 38; *Robson's Lond. Dir.* (1833), 29; *Robson's Dir. Essex* (1840); *White's Dir. Essex* (1848), 265; *V.C.H. Essex*, v. 23; *Proc. Woodford Antiq. Soc.* ii. 16–17; Eastment, *Wanstead*, 123–4.
[78] Eastment, *Wanstead*, 127.
[79] *V.C.H. Essex*, v. 29.
[80] Ibid. 24.
[81] Ibid. 72; Tuffs, *Wanstead and Woodford*, 121.
[82] *V.C.H. Essex*, v. 72; Pevsner, *Essex*, 413.
[83] T. de Laune, *Present state of London* (1692).
[84] G. Brummell, *Local Posts of London, 1680–1840*, 81.
[85] *Brit. Postal Guide* (1856).
[86] *Post Office Guide* (1917).

branch office was opened in Hermon Hill in 1948, replacing a previous sub-office in High Street.[87] The telegraph was available at Wanstead from 1871.[88] The National Telephone Co. had a call office in High Street by 1893.[89] The company's exchange, opened in Wellesley Road by 1902, had passed to the G.P.O. by 1912.[90]

Gas was first supplied to Wanstead by the West Ham Gas Co. in 1864.[91] Electricity was supplied to the Aldersbrook area by East Ham borough council from c. 1914.[92] The rest of Wanstead was first supplied in 1926 by the County of London Electricity Supply Co.[93] Before the 19th century water supply came from wells and pumps. A common well on the heath (presumably Wanstead Flats) existed c. 1532.[94] In 1713 the parish vestry resolved to set up a street pump for the poor.[95] The East London Waterworks Co. extended its mains to Wanstead in 1857, but as late as 1874 its supply there was very inadequate.[96] Wanstead sewage works originated in 1883–5, when the local board bought a site beside the Roding in the south-eastern corner of the parish.[97]

A fire-engine, given to the parish vestry by Daniel Waldo in 1729,[98] remained in service at least until 1778.[99] A later engine, bought in 1874, was housed at the George and then at the local board offices in Church Path.[1] A new fire station was opened in Wanstead Place in 1913, and in 1919 the first motor fire-engine went into service. The fire station was closed in 1957.[2] An isolation hospital was built by the local board in Empress Avenue, Aldersbrook, in 1893.[3] It was bombed and closed in the Second World War.[4] Wanstead hospital, Hermon Hill, was opened by Essex county council in 1938, in the former Merchant Seamen's orphan asylum.[5] Spratt Hall (later Christ Church) Green, High Street, was bought by the local board as a public park about 1860.[6] Wanstead Park, Wanstead Flats, Bushwood, and several smaller public open spaces are administered by the corporation of London as conservators of Epping Forest.[7]

There was a circulating library in Wanstead in 1845.[8] A parish library for the poor, opened about 1873, offered a selection of 400 volumes on payment of a penny a year; it still existed in 1893.[9] Essex county council opened a small branch library in High Street in 1944 and another in Park Road, Aldersbrook, in 1950.[10] The former was in 1969 transferred to a new building in Spratt Hall Road, erected by Redbridge borough council.[11]

The Becontree assembly rooms and archery ground, Bushwood, are said to have originated in the 1850s.[12] The premises became a Quaker meeting-house in 1870.[13] A cricket match in Wanstead Park was recorded in 1834.[14] The present Wanstead cricket club was founded c. 1880, but traces its descent from an earlier club at Woodford.[15] It has supplied several first-class players, including J. W. H. T. Douglas (1882–1930), captain of Essex and England. Wanstead golf club, founded 1893, claims to be the second oldest in Essex.[16] Its club house was once part of the out-buildings of Wanstead House. The cricket ground and the golf course adjoin Wanstead Park. They belong to Wanstead Sports Ground Ltd., which was formed in 1920 to buy them from the Cowley estate, and to protect the site from building. The Linkside lawn tennis club, founded 1913, was an offshoot of the cricket club.[17] Cultural societies have included the Wanstead industrial and art association, founded c. 1894, and surviving in 1913,[18] and the Aldersbrook local parliament (fl. 1913).[19] The Wanstead young men's association, founded in 1877, merged in 1935 with the Wanstead literary society to form the Wanstead literary and debating society (1935–60).[20]

Among notable residents of Wanstead was James Bradley (1693–1762), astronomer royal, who was trained at Wanstead by his uncle James Pound (rector 1707–24), himself a distinguished astronomer and friend of Sir Isaac Newton. In 1717 Pound and Bradley set up in Wanstead Park one of the largest telescopes in Europe, mounted on a maypole taken from the Strand.[21] William Penn (1644–1718), Quaker leader and founder of Pennsylvania, was brought up at Wanstead.[22] Richard Brinsley Sheridan (1751–1816), dramatist and parliamentary orator, lived there c. 1795, probably in the house in High Street later called Sheridan House.[23] Thomas Hood (1799–1845), poet, lived at Lake House c. 1832–5.[24] Among several lord mayors of London living at Wanstead were Sir William Plomer (d. 1801)[25] and Sir William Curtis, Bt. (1752–1829).[26] Wanstead House had several eminent

---

[87] Inf. from Regional Director, London Postal Region; *London Post Offices and Streets* (1950).

[88] P.M.G. Mins. (1871–4).

[89] *Kelly's Leytonstone, Wanstead etc. Dir.* (1893).

[90] *Kelly's Dir. Essex* (1902, 1912).

[91] E.R.O., D/P 292/8/11, May 1864; inf. from N. Thames Gas Board.

[92] Tuffs, *Wanstead and Woodford*, 112; *East Ham B.C. Mins.* (1912–13), 742.

[93] *V.C.H. Essex*, v. 75; Tuffs, op. cit. 112.

[94] E.R.O., D/DCw M1.

[95] E.R.O., D/P 292/8/6, 29 June 1713.

[96] Inf. from Metropolitan Water Board.

[97] E.R.O., T/P 94/7; see also *Wanstead and Woodford Official Guides* (1954, 1964).

[98] E.R.O., D/P 292/8/6, 19 May 1729.

[99] E.R.O., D/P 292/8/7, 3 Apr. 1758; 292/8/9, 22 Dec. 1777, 7 Dec. 1778.

[1] *Wanstead Par. Mag.* Jan. 1874; Eastment, *Wanstead*, 169–70; E.R.O., T/P 94/15; *Express and Independent Almanack* (1893), 88.

[2] Inf. from Essex County Fire Brigade.

[3] *E. Nat.* vi. 105; *Wanstead Par. Mag.* (1910). The site was then in Wanstead, but boundary changes later took it into East Ham.

[4] Tuffs, *Wanstead and Woodford*, 111.

[5] Inf. from the Secretary, Wanstead Hosp.

[6] Tuffs, op. cit. 90.

[7] See p. 330.

[8] *Kelly's Dir. Essex* (1845): Julia Scales.

[9] Eastment, *Wanstead*, 167.

[10] Inf. from Essex Co. Library.

[11] *The opening of Wanstead Library* (pamph. 1969).

[12] A. Hadley, *Wanstead Friends' Mag.*, 26; Tuffs, op. cit. 96.

[13] See p. 335.

[14] W.H.L., Hiram Stead, 'Materials for the Hist. of Wanstead Ho. etc.', f. 129.

[15] G. Berridge, *The First Century* (1966).

[16] Ibid. 39; Eastment, *Wanstead*, 143.

[17] Berridge, op. cit. 42; Eastment, op. cit. 146.

[18] W.H.L., H. Stead, 'Materials', ff. 150, 163.

[19] Ibid., f. 161. For other cultural bodies and activities see Eastment, *Wanstead*, 148–51.

[20] E.R.O., D/Z 39.

[21] *D.N.B.* Bradley, J., Pound, J.; Eastment, *Wanstead*, 130–7. For other notable rectors see below, p. 333.

[22] *D.N.B.*

[23] Tuffs, *Wanstead and Woodford*, 61–2.

[24] *D.N.B.*

[25] *Topographer and Genealogist*, ii. 279.

[26] *D.N.B.*; Eastment, *Wanstead*, 142.

residents, including the earl of Leicester in the 16th century and Sir Josiah Child in the 17th, and many distinguished visitors.[27]

Three orphanages were established in Wanstead in the mid 19th century. The Royal Wanstead school was founded at Hackney in 1827 as the Infant Orphan asylum, and was transferred to new buildings, south of the Eagle pond at Snaresbrook, in 1843.[28] The charity, maintained by public subscription, and conducted on Anglican lines, was originally intended for children from respectable families under the age of 8, but in 1852 it was decided to keep boys up to 14 and girls up to 15.[29] The number of children was about 500–600 during the later 19th century, after which it declined.[30] It was closed in 1971. The school buildings form an impressive range, especially when seen across the pond from Snaresbrook Road.[31] They were designed by (Sir) George Gilbert Scott in Jacobean style, of grey stone with buff stone dressings.[32]

The Commercial Travellers' school originated in 1845, when Robert Cuffley, himself a traveller, took the lead in raising funds to provide a school for the children of deceased or necessitous commercial travellers.[33] A house was bought in George Lane and the school opened there in 1847. By 1854 there were 135 children, and in 1855 the school was moved to Pinner (Mdx.), where it survived until 1967.

The Merchant Seamen's orphan asylum, established in 1827 at St. George's in the East (Lond.), was transferred in 1862 to a new building in Hermon Hill, Wanstead, which provided places for 300 orphans of British merchant seamen.[34] The building was taken over in 1921 by the convent of the Good Shepherd, as a refuge for women and girls,[35] and later became Wanstead hospital.[36] It stands in a commanding position on high ground, and was designed by G. C. Clarke as a fine example of the 'Venetian Gothic' style.[37]

MANORS. The statement that land at Wanstead was given to Westminster Abbey by Alfric in 1065 comes from a spurious charter, not supported by other evidence.[38] In 1086 the manor of *WANSTEAD*, comprising one hide, was held of the bishop of London by Ralph son of Brian.[39] It was said to have belonged formerly to the canons of St. Paul's, but that statement has been questioned.[40] The overlordship of the manor subsequently descended with the see of London.[41] After the death of Ralph son of Brian the tenancy in demesne appears to have been split between his two sons, Brian FitzRalph and Jordan de Briset (or Jordan Fitz-Ralph), the founder of Clerkenwell Priory.[42] The grandson of Brian FitzRalph, also called Brian FitzRalph, was holding ½ hide at Wanstead in 1210–12.[43] The other half of the manor seems to have been divided on the death of Jordan de Briset between his daughters, Lettice, wife of Henry Foliot, Emme, wife of Reynold de Ginges, and Maud.[44] Maud's share passed to Robert Brito, who before 1176 subinfeudated it to Hugh of Hesdin (or Hosdeng).[45] Before 1182 Brito conveyed his rights in the property, including a capital messuage and a mark's rent, to Clerkenwell Priory, which thus became the intermediate tenant between the bishop and Hugh of Hesdin.[46] Hugh of Hesdin or his heirs probably secured the demesne tenancy of the whole of the manor. His son held the advowson of Wanstead in 1208,[47] and in 1242 his grandson owed service to Sir Ralph de Ginges, presumably in respect of Emme de Ginges's share of the manor.[48]

Hugh of Hesdin was succeeded by his son Ralph of Hesdin, who in 1197 acknowledged his service due to the nuns of Clerkenwell for ⅙ knight's fee in Wanstead.[49] Ralph (d. 1222) was succeeded by his son Hugh of Hesdin.[50] Hugh (d. 1242) held at the time of his death extensive lands in Wanstead and (East?) Ham, including 169 a. in demesne and 20 a. meadow.[51] His widow Alice was granted custody of his lands in Essex and Buckinghamshire.[52] His son and heir Ralph of Hesdin died in 1247 leaving Joan his daughter and heir.[53]

Joan of Hesdin, who was still alive in 1259, was later succeeded by her father's sister Alice, wife of William Huntercombe (d. 1271).[54] Alice's son Thomas Huntercombe, also known as Thomas Hesdin, succeeded to Wanstead, which he was holding in 1303 for ½ knight's fee.[55] He died in 1327 leaving the manor to his son John Huntercombe.[56] In 1345 the manor was settled jointly on John Huntercombe (d. 1349) and his wife Christine (d. 1361).[57] On Christine's death Wanstead passed to their son (Sir) John Huntercombe, who died in 1368, holding the manor jointly with his wife Margaret, of the Bishop of London, Waltham Abbey, and the priories of Clerkenwell and Holy Trinity, Aldgate.[58] Holy Trinity, lord of Cann Hall, had in 1275 acquired from Reynold, son of Sir Ralph de Ginges, the annual quit-rent due to him from Wanstead manor.[59]

[27] See pp. 324–6.
[28] *White's Dir. Essex* (1848).
[29] W.H.L., Hiram Stead, 'Materials for Hist. Wanstead House', f. 142.
[30] *White's Dir. Essex* (1863); *Kelly's Dir. Essex* (1862 sqq.).
[31] See plate f.p. 325.
[32] Pevsner, *Essex*, 413.
[33] Paragraph based on: inf. from the Secretary, Royal Pinner Sch. Foundation; E.R.O., *Excursions in Essex* (extra-illus.), ii. 196 (newscutting, n.d.). Some records of this school have been deposited with the Greater London Council Record Dept.
[34] *Kelly's Dir. Essex* (1882).
[35] *Kelly's Dir. Leytonstone etc.* (1926), A25.
[36] See p. 321.
[37] Pevsner, *Essex*, 413.
[38] C. Hart, *Early Charts. Essex* (Saxon), 30.
[39] *V.C.H. Essex*, i. 438.
[40] Ibid. 340 n.
[41] As recorded in inquisitions *post mortem* down to 1447: see C 139/126/20.

[42] For the pedigree of this family see *Gen. Mag.* ix. 585.
[43] *Red Bk. Exch.* (Rolls Ser.), ii. 541.
[44] *Cart. St. Mary Clerkenwell*, ed. W. O. Hassall (Camden Soc. 3rd ser. lxxi), 65.
[45] Ibid. 63.
[46] Ibid. 62.
[47] B.M. Cott Ch. XIII. 20.
[48] *Cal. Inq. p.m.* i. 287–8.
[49] *Genealogist*, N.S. xx. 228; *Feet of F. Essex*, i. 11.
[50] I. J. Sanders, *English Baronies*, 117.
[51] *Cal. Inq. p.m.* i. 287–8.
[52] *Excerpta e Rot. Fin.* (Rec. Com.), i. 389.
[53] Sanders, *Baronies*, 117.
[54] Ibid.
[55] Ibid.; *Feud. Aids*, ii. 151. See also *Knights of Edw. I* (Harl. Soc.), 251.
[56] Sanders, *Baronies*, 117.
[57] *Feet of F. Essex*, iii. 75; *Cal. Inq. p.m.* ix. 324 and xi. 64.
[58] *Cal. Inq. p.m.* xii. 204.
[59] *Cat. Anct. D.* i, A 757.

Margaret Huntercombe held the manor until her death in 1377.[60] Her son and heir John Huntercombe was then aged 15, but while the wardship of two-thirds of his land was granted to William Hanley and John James, Huntercombe himself was granted a share, with John James, in the remaining third.[61] In 1381, though still under age, John Huntercombe was granted freedom of the other two-thirds as he was about to go overseas.[62] At his death in 1383 he and his wife Margaret jointly held the manor of the bishop of London, and two other tenements, Naget Hall and Sayes.[63] Naget (later Naked) Hall, which they held of Barking Abbey, appears to have descended with Wanstead until the early 16th century, when it became the manor of Aldersbrook in Little Ilford.[64] Sayes, held of Waltham Abbey, was in the north of Wanstead parish, extending into Woodford. It passed with the manor of Wanstead down to the 19th century, when it comprised two fields called Great and Little Seas, totalling some 50 a.[65]

Margaret Huntercombe's life interest in the manor was confirmed in 1383.[66] Her son John Huntercombe died without issue in 1391.[67] Henry Popham was holding the manor in 1412, presumably as a lessee.[68] Margaret Huntercombe was still alive in 1427, when the reversion of the manor was bought by Robert Tatersal, draper and alderman of London, and his wife Amy from William Rous, who traced his title from Sir John Huntercombe (d. 1368).[69] The conveyance was, however, defective in law, since the manor was entailed on Rous and his heirs and not on him alone.[70] Robert Tatersal knew this, and on his death-bed, overcome with remorse, directed that after the deaths of Margaret Huntercombe and William Rous the manor should be conveyed to Rous's heirs.[71] Tatersal, and presumably Margaret Huntercombe also, were dead by October 1429, when Tatersal's widow Amy presented to the rectory of Wanstead.[72] In 1436 John, son of Robert Tatersal, swore an oath to carry out his father's instructions or to satisfy William Rous's heirs, as his faith and conscience required.[73] The exact requirements of his conscience are not revealed, but in 1437 he made some kind of settlement which secured the manor to himself in fee.[74]

John Tatersal died in 1447, leaving John, aged 6, his son and heir.[75] His widow Agnes later married William Kene, who presented to the rectory as

late as 1457.[76] John Tatersal the son appears to have died without issue, and to have been succeeded by his sister Amy (or Anne), who with her husband (Sir) Ralph Hastings presented to the rectory in 1471.[77] Ralph (d. 1495) directed in his will that Amy might dispose of the manor as she wished.[78] She appears to have sold it to Henry VII in 1499. In that year the King paid £360 for Sir Ralph Hastings's land at Wanstead, and presented to the rectory.[79]

Both Henry VII and Henry VIII took a personal interest in the manor and sometimes hunted there.[80] Wanstead park was inclosed,[81] and from the beginning of his reign Henry VIII placed manor and park under a succession of keepers chosen from his close associates.[82] His last keeper was Sir Richard (later Lord) Rich, appointed in 1543.[83] In 1549 Edward VI granted Rich the lordship of the manor, the park, and the advowson of Wanstead.[84] In 1567 Rich leased most of the estate to James Lord, of Danbury, a baron of the Exchequer.[85] The lease later passed to Joan Lord, widow of James, who conveyed it to Thomas Lord and Lawrence Bingham.[86] Richard, Lord Rich, died in 1567, leaving Wanstead to his son Robert, Lord Rich, on condition that it was retained by his executors for seven years to the uses of his will.[87] In 1578 the freehold of the manor and the residue of the lease were bought by Robert Dudley, earl of Leicester.[88] At the same time Leicester bought the neighbouring manor of Stonehall in Ilford, which subsequently descended with Wanstead.[89]

Leicester mortgaged Wanstead and Stonehall in 1580 to Thomas Skinner for £4,000.[90] Skinner later threatened foreclosure, but Leicester appears to have redeemed the mortgage and held the manors to his death in 1588.[91] He often visited Wanstead and he bought land to enlarge the park.[92] The manor was confirmed in 1588 to his widow Lettice.[93] In 1590 she and her third husband, Sir Christopher Blount, were granted licence to convey the estate to Sir George Cary and Philip Butler, probably for the purpose of mortgaging it to repay some of Leicester's debts.[94] They failed, however, to repay his debt to the queen, and she seized the manor of Wanstead, retaining it until 1593, when she released it to Robert Devereux, earl of Essex, in exchange for other manors.[95] Essex was the son of the countess of Leicester by her first husband,

[60] Cal. Close 1364–8, 433; Cal. Inq. p.m. xv, p. 15.
[61] Cal. Fine R. 1369–77, 403; ibid. 1377–83, 16.
[62] Cal. Close 1377–81, 452.
[63] C 136/32/4.   [64] See p. 166.
[65] E.R.O., D/CT 384 and 408 (tithe maps of Wanstead and Woodford); E.R.O., D/DCw P9 (map of pt. of Wanstead, c. 1775).
[66] Cal. Close 1381–5, 321.
[67] C 136/32/4.
[68] Feud. Aids, vi. 442.
[69] Feet of F. Essex, iv. 12; V.C.H. Bucks. iii. 265.
[70] Cal. Plea and Mem. R. London (1413–37), ed. A. H. Thomas, 291, 298–9.
[71] Ibid.
[72] Newcourt, Repertorium, ii. 639.
[73] Cal. Plea and Mem. R. London (1413–37), 291, 298–9.
[74] C 139/126/20.
[75] Ibid.
[76] Cal. Pat. 1494–1509, 163; Newcourt, Repertorium, ii. 639. Kene and others had presented to the rectory in 1446, possibly as trustees.
[77] Newcourt, Repertorium, ii. 639; Lysons, London, iv. 232.

[78] P.C.C. 27 Vox.
[79] Excerpta Historica, ed. S. Bentley, 121; Newcourt, Repertorium, ii. 639.
[80] See below, p. 324.
[81] See p. 328.
[82] e.g. L. & P. Hen. VIII, i. pp. 340, 537; iii, p. 479; iv, pp. 196, 2034; xvi, p. 174; xviii, p. 526.
[83] Ibid. xviii, p. 526. Rich was also keeper of the new royal park at Chingford: V.C.H. Essex, v. 108.
[84] Cal. Pat. 1548–9, 390; E.R.O., D/DCw T3 A/53.
[85] E.R.O., D/DCw T3C/5.   [86] Ibid.
[87] C 142/147/41; E.R.O., D/DP O40/1.
[88] E.R.O., D/DCw T3C/5 and 7.
[89] V.C.H. Essex, v. 210.
[90] E.R.O., D/DCw T3C/19 and 26.
[91] Ibid. T3C/27, 28, 32, 33; B.M. Harl. Roll D. 35/24.
[92] W.H.L., Hiram Stead, 'Materials for the History of Wanstead House', 43. See also p. 324 below.
[93] C 66/1316, m. 20.
[94] C 66/1350, m. 28; C.P. 25(2)/134/178; E.R.O., D/DCw T3C/30. His debts totalled £53,000: B.M. Harl. Roll D. 35, ff. 56–63.
[95] Cal. S.P. Dom. 1591–4, 386.

and in 1590 she and Blount had entailed Wanstead and Stonehall upon him.[96] After his disgrace at court Essex spent much of his time at Wanstead.[97] In 1598, however, he sold the two manors to Charles Blount, Lord Mountjoy, elder brother of Sir Christopher Blount, for £4,300.[98] Lord Mountjoy, who was created earl of Devonshire in 1603, died in 1606, having settled the manors on Mountjoy Blount (later Lord Mountjoy and earl of Newport) his bastard son by Penelope, Lady Rich (d. 1607), whom Devonshire had married after her divorce in 1605.[99]

Mountjoy Blount sold Wanstead and Stonehall in 1617 to George Villiers, earl (later duke) of Buckingham, in order to secure a peerage.[1] In 1618–19 Buckingham's estate at Wanstead was valued at £362 a year.[2] He sold both manors in 1619 to Sir Henry Mildmay, for £7,300.[3] Mildmay, who later became master of the king's jewel-house but joined the Parliamentary side in the Civil War, suffered forfeiture at the Restoration.[4] In 1661 the king granted Wanstead and Stonehall to the duke of York, who sold them to Sir Robert Brooke.[5] Since Brooke was Mildmay's son-in-law,[6] this may have been an arrangement to mitigate the effects of the forfeiture, and Pepys states that Mildmay was at Wanstead House when he died.[7] Brooke (d. 1669) left the manors in trust to pay his debts.[8] In 1673–4 they were sold by the trustees and Brooke's heirs (his sister Mary Brooke and his nephew Nathaniel Bacon), to (Sir) Josiah Child (Bt.) for £11,500.[9] William Mildmay, son of Sir Henry, was a party to the sale, and seems to have had an interest in the manors up to that time.

Child (d. 1699) amassed a large fortune as an East India merchant.[10] He was succeeded by his son Sir Josiah Child, Bt. (d. 1704), who in 1699 leased Wanstead and Stonehall for 90 years to his half-brother Richard Child.[11] On Sir Josiah's death without issue Richard Child succeeded to his title and estates.[12] He built the great Wanstead House and was created Viscount Castlemaine (1718) and Earl Tylney (1733). In 1734 he took the surname of Tylney in consequence of his wife inheriting the large estates of that family. He was succeeded on his death in 1750 by his son John Tylney, Earl Tylney (d. 1784), who in 1734 had acquired a long lease of part of West Ham manor.[13] Having no

descendants Tylney devised his estates to his sister's son, Sir James Long, Bt., of Draycot Cerne (Wilts.), who was already a rich landowner.[14] From Sir James (d. 1794) the Wanstead estate passed in succession to his infant son Sir James Long, Bt., who died without issue in 1805, and his eldest daughter Catherine Tylney Long. Catherine (d. 1825) married in 1812 William Wellesley-Pole (d. 1857), later earl of Mornington, nephew of the duke of Wellington, who took the surname of Pole-Tylney-Long-Wellesley.[15] A financial crisis led to the demolition in 1823–4 of Wanstead House,[16] but the estate was not then broken up. In the 1840s William Pole-Tylney-Long-Wellesley still owned some 1,400 a. in the parishes of Wanstead (436 a.), Woodford, Leyton, Little Ilford, and Barking.[17] He was still holding manor courts at Wanstead in 1856.[18] The manor passed to his son William, earl of Mornington (d. 1863), who left it in trust to his father's cousin Henry Wellesley, Earl Cowley (d. 1884).[19] In 1880 Cowley sold part of Wanstead Park (184 a.) to the corporation of London for preservation as part of Epping Forest.[20] His family sold the rest of the park in 1920 to Wanstead Sports Ground Ltd., but still held some land in Wanstead in the 1930s.[21]

Wanstead House, originally called Wanstead Hall, lay about 300 yd. south-east of St. Mary's church.[22] Up to the 14th century it was probably small but by 1499 it was of sufficient size to serve as a royal hunting-lodge, and it seems to have been rebuilt or considerably enlarged in the later 16th century. Between 1715 and 1722 it was completely rebuilt as a Palladian mansion. It was demolished in 1823–4.

The manor-house was valued at only 1s. a year in 1271 and 6s. in 1350.[23] Henry VII visited Wanstead occasionally, as did Henry VIII during the early years of his reign.[24] Repairs were carried out in 1510–11 and 1542 but in 1549 the house was 'in great ruin'.[25] Richard, Lord Rich, owner 1549–67, is said to have rebuilt it.[26] Princess (later Queen) Mary stayed there in 1550–51 and 1553, and Elizabeth I in 1561 and on several later occasions.[27] Leicester is supposed to have improved and enlarged the building.[28] His probate inventory (1588)[29] mentions the great gallery, which contained, *inter alia*, a billiard table, an organ virginal, portraits of Henry VIII, Mary, and Elizabeth, and a few books.

[96] E.R.O., D/DCw T3A/87.
[97] *Cal. S.P. Dom.* 1598–1601, 84, 92.
[98] E.R.O., D/DCw T3C/41.
[99] *D.N.B.*; C 142/306/146.
[1] *Cal. S.P. Dom.* 1611–18, 504; C.P. 43/139. Blount later alleged that Wanstead had been 'conveyed away' during his minority: *Cal. S.P. Dom.* 1629–31, 459.
[2] Hist. MSS. Com. 23, *12th Rep. I, Cowper*, p. 103.
[3] E.R.O., D/DGn 180.
[4] H. St. J. Mildmay, *Brief Memoir of Mildmay family*, 135.
[5] E.R.O., D/DGn 181; D/DCw T3A/59.
[6] E.R.O., D/DCw T3A/78.
[7] *Pepys's Diary*, ed. H. B. Wheatley, iv. 386.
[8] E.R.O., D/DCw T3A/67–70, 78; D/DGn 158 and 194.
[9] Ibid. Child had been living at Wanstead at least since 1668: E.R.O., D/P 292/1/1, f. 33.
[10] G.E.C. *Complete Baronetage*, iv. 106.
[11] Ibid. 107; E.R.O., D/DCw T3C/128.
[12] *Complete Baronetage*, iv. 107; *Complete Peerage*, iii. 92.
[13] Ibid.; *E. Nat.* xxii. 205. See above, p. 68.
[14] E.R.O., D/DQs 12; *Complete Baronetage*, iii. 92.
[15] *Complete Peerage*, ix. 240.
[16] See below.

[17] E.R.O., D/CT 384, 408, 221, 191, 18. [Tithe awards, with dates ranging from 1838 to 1853.]
[18] E.R.O., D/DCw M6–11.
[19] E.R.O., D/DCy F2.
[20] *Kelly's Dir. Essex* (1886); *E.R.* vii. 229; *Epping Forest Map* (1882).
[21] G. Berridge, *The First Century*, 39; E.R.O., D/DCy T56.
[22] For the earlier name see e.g. *Feud. Aids*, vi. 442. The later name was used from the 16th century onwards.
[23] C 132/39/8; C 135/104/26.
[24] *Excerpta Historica*, ed. S. Bentley, 132; *Letters etc. Ric. III and Hen. VII*, ed. J. Gairdner, i. 233, 239; *Mems. Hen. VII*, ed. J. Gairdner, (Rolls Ser.), 102, 126, 128; *L. & P. Hen. VIII*, ii (2), pp. 1444, 1340; iii (2), pp. 1537, 1544.
[25] Ibid. ii (2), pp. 4445–6, 1450; Ibid. Addenda, i (1), p. 532; *Cal. Pat.* 1548–9, 390.
[26] Nichols, *Progresses of Queen Elizabeth*, ii. 94 n.
[27] Nichols, *Progresses*, i. 92–4, 222; J. Stowe, *Annals of England* (1631 edn.), 613; *Cal. S.P. Dom.* 1581–90, 11; *Acts of P.C.* 1578–80, 254; Hist. MSS. Com. 24, *12th Rep. IV, Rutland*, p. 127; ibid. 9, *Salisbury (Cecil)*, ii. p. 403.
[28] *E.R.* vii. 215.
[29] B.M. Harl. Roll D. 35, ff. 24–36 (and see *Arch.* lxiii. 1).

East (Garden) Front in 1823

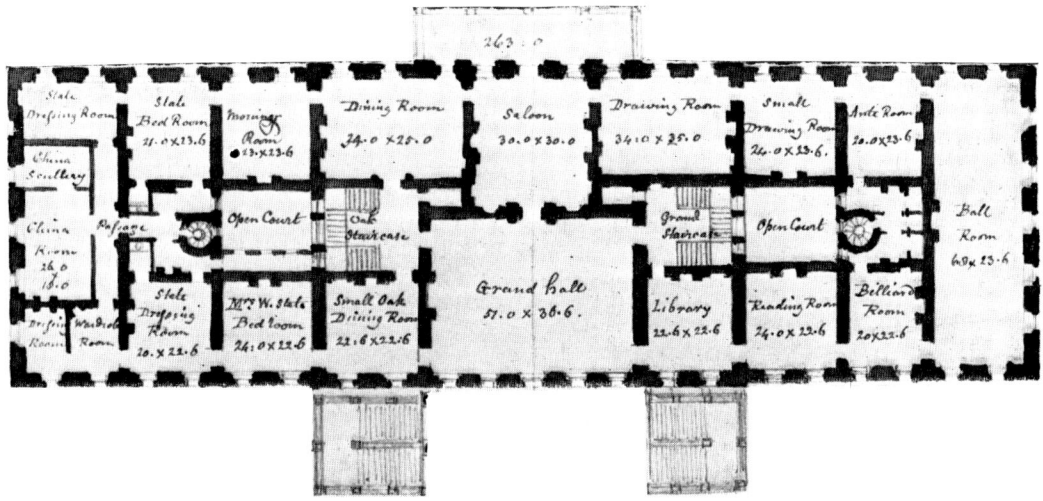

Principal Ground Floor in 1823

View from the north-west in 1781

WANSTEAD HOUSE

WANSTEAD: ROYAL WANSTEAD SCHOOL, BUILT IN 1843

LEYTON: RED LION INN, LEYTONSTONE, BUILT IN 1890

There were also a chapel, little gallery, great chamber, and some 20 bedrooms, one of which was kept ready for the queen. The furnishing included several tapestries. Among out-buildings were a stillhouse, brewhouse, dairy, forge, and stables. Leicester had kept 58 horses.

James I often visited Wanstead House and Charles I did so both as prince of Wales and as king.[30] When bought by (Sir) Josiah Child in 1673–4 the house, with 40 hearths, was one of the largest in Essex.[31] At that period it was a quadrangular two-storey building with many gables.[32] The symmetrical west (entrance) front of nine bays was approached across a forecourt flanked on each side by a three-storey gatehouse. The irregular east front was probably the oldest part of the building. Pepys thought the house 'a fine seat, but old-fashioned'.[33] Child made no important alterations to the building, but spent much money on laying out the grounds.[34] Evelyn in 1683 commented especially on the new fishponds and walnut plantations.[35] According to Defoe Sir Josiah added 'innumerable rows of trees . . . avenues and vistos, to the house, all leading up to the place where the old house stood, as to a centre'.[36] Further work on the park was carried out by Sir Richard Child soon after he succeeded to the estate. According to one statement this was started in 1706 and was one of the last designs of George London.[37] Drawings of c. 1715 show, running eastwards from the house, a short canal with a bowling green at the far end, flanking which was a formal parterre.[38] Farther east was the Roding, regimented into canals. North-east of the house was an orangery and west of it a lake across which ran the main drive leading to Leytonstone, flanked by avenues of trees in quincunx formation. Towards the end of his life, after rebuilding the house, the first Earl Tylney appears to have carried out further alterations to the park on slightly less formal lines.[39] The short canal and parterre were replaced by a terrace and a lawn. Farther east the diversion of the river into canals was elaborated, while to the south new serpentine ponds were made. The lake west of the house was enlarged to form an octagon called the Basin and the drive deflected round both sides of it.[40] By 1746 the park covered most of the parish between Wanstead Flats and South (Redbridge) Lane, with radiating avenues extending as far as Leytonstone and Snaresbrook.[41]

Wanstead House was completely rebuilt by Sir Richard Child to the design of Colen Campbell between 1715 and 1722. It was 'the archetype of the Palladian great house'.[42] The exterior, rectangular and cased in Portland stone, was some 260 ft. long and 75 ft. deep. On the west (entrance) front the principal storey of 21 bays was set above a rusticated ground floor and had as its central feature a grand Corinthian prostyle portico, from which a perron staircase descended on each side to the forecourt. Above the principal floor, centrally placed, was another storey of nine bays, containing two mezzanine floors. There was also a basement floor.[43] The east (garden) front was similar to the west front except that the central feature, not salient, comprised only a pediment and Corinthian pilasters; the perron staircase leading down from a balcony on the principal floor appears to have been removed between 1781 and 1823. No view of the completed house shows the great central cupola which dominates the roof in Campbell's drawings, and that feature was probably never built. In the 1720s and 1730s there were plans to extend the house to the west by adding quadrant colonnades and wings,[44] enclosing a spacious forecourt. They were apparently not carried out, but instead of the wings low walls were built, decorated with urns and obelisks.[45]

The grand entrance hall was 51 ft. long, 36 ft. wide, and 36 ft. high.[46] Behind it, looking across the gardens, was the saloon, forming a 30-ft. cube. At the south end of the house, running the whole depth, was the ballroom. That was the room depicted in William Hogarth's 'Assembly at Wanstead House' (1729), which shows an interior in the style of Inigo Jones, with a tall marble chimney piece surmounted by consoles and a scroll pediment. The woodwork was painted green, with gilded ornaments and mouldings. An inventory of the contents in 1822, together with earlier descriptions, provide details of the rich furnishing and ornaments brought together by successive owners of the house.[47] The hall contained two statues from the ruins of

[30] *Cal. S.P. Dom.* 1611–18, 73, 135–6, 199, 381, 568; 1619–23, 54, 62, 75, 178, 424, 616; 1623–5, 18, 278, 296, 299; 1627–8, 250; 1629–31, 388–9; 1635–6, 569; Lysons, *Lond.* iv. 235; *Acts of P.C.* 1623–5, 268; Hist. MSS. Com. 58, *Bath (Harley),* ii, p. 68.

[31] E 179/246/22.

[32] *Supplement du Nouveau Théâtre de la Grande Bretagne* (1728), pls. v, vi, vii (engravings by J. Kip from drawings by L. Knyff, after the enlargement of the church (1710) but before the rebuilding of the house.)

[33] *Pepys's Diary,* ed. H. B. Wheatley, iv. 386.

[34] *Arch.* xii. 186.

[35] *Jn. Evelyn's Diary,* ed. E. S. de Beer, iv. 305–6.

[36] D. Defoe, *Tour through Great Britain,* ed. G. D. H. Cole, i. 89–90.

[37] W.H.L., Hiram Stead, 'Materials for Hist. Wanstead House', 28. In 1713 Adam Holt, gardener at Wanstead, noted that his field had been made into a canal and kitchen garden, and his house demolished: E.R.O., D/DK F1. Tree-planting was in progress in 1715: *V.C.H. Essex,* iii. 198.

[38] *Suppl. du Nouveau Théâtre de la Grande Bretagne,* pls. v–vii; *E.R.* vi. 59 (John Macky's description, 1724). Cf. I. Dunlop and F. Kimball, 'Gardens of Wanstead House', *Country Life,* cviii (1950), 294–8: these writers maintain that Sir Josiah Child was responsible for the formal gardens as well as the ponds and plantations.

[39] I. Dunlop and F. Kimball, op. cit. 297–8.

[40] These features, shown on Rocque's drawings of 1735, can be seen in later maps or pictures. Certain other features on Rocque's drawings were apparently projected but never executed.

[41] J. Rocque, *Environs of London* (1744–6), sheet iv.

[42] H. E. Stutchbury, *The Architecture of Colen Campbell,* 27–30, 147; *Vetruvius Britannicus* (1715), pls. 21–7. For views and descriptions see also: E.R.O. Pictorial Coll; Redbridge L.B. Ref. Libr., engravings (1781) by G. Robertson and J. Fittler; B.M. Add. MS. 36362, ff. 114–17 (drawings and plans by J. Buckler, 1823); *Hist. Essex by Gent.* iv. 228; *Country Life,* cviii. 294.

[43] For the floors see W.H.L., *Wanstead House Sale Cat.* (1822).

[44] Cf. *E.R.* vi. 58.

[45] In 1965–6 Mr. J. R. Smith excavated these walls: see his thesis 'William Wellesley Pole and the Essex estates of the Tylney Long family' (Lond. Univ. Hist. Diploma, 1969), ch. ii.

[46] For the interior see: F. Kimball, 'Wanstead House', *Country Life,* lxxiv (1933), 605–7; Stutchbury, op. cit. 27–30, 147; B.M. Add. MS. 36362, ff. 115, 116; *E.R.* vi. 58; *E.R.* vii. 222–3; *Hist. Essex by Gent.* iv. 228; E. W. Brayley and J. Britton, *Beauties of England and Wales* (1803), v. 466–7; W.H.L., *Wanstead Ho. Sale Cat.* (1822).

[47] Ibid.

Herculanaeum, and paintings by Andrea Casali. Its ceiling was painted by William Kent, with figures representing Morning, Noon, and Night. The ball-room was hung with tapestries said to have come from the old house and to have dated from Leicester's time. Among many other treasures were paintings by Holbein, Raphael, Rembrandt, and Van Dyck.

Wanstead House ranked with the greatest mansions of the time and was much admired.[48] Even Horace Walpole, who was inclined to ridicule the taste of its parvenu owners, admitted the grandeur of the scene.[49] Many distinguished guests went there, to enjoy a hospitality reputed to be unprecedented since the days of Wolsey.[50] Few changes seem to have been made to the house or the park in the later 18th century. Many of the art treasures already mentioned were bought by the second Earl Tylney during his residence in Italy.[51] He built the grotto (c. 1762) and probably also the temple, both on the eastern side of the park.[52] The orangery was demolished in 1799.[53] By the early 19th century the landscaping of the park had been softened, especially on the east side, by the natural growth of trees.[54] During the minorities following Sir James Long's death in 1794 the house was sometimes let. Louis Joseph, Prince de Condé, was living there in 1807.[55] William Pole-Tylney-Long-Wellesley, who became master of Wanstead House on his marriage to Catherine Long in 1812, lived there and for a few years entertained in grand style. In 1814 it was said that he was setting up Wanstead House to surpass Carlton House and that the interior was being transformed into a 'uniform blaze of burnished gold'.[56] At the same time he was altering the park in preparation for a fête to celebrate his son's baptism and the return from the war of his uncle the duke of Wellington.[57] By 1820, however, Long-Wellesley was in desperate financial straits resulting mainly though not entirely from his extravagance and bad management.[58] Under the marriage settlement he and Catherine had only limited power to mortgage the estate and could not sell any land. Their most valuable disposable assets were the fabric and contents of Wanstead House. The contents were sold in 1822.[59] The building was sold for demolition in 1823 to Stannard and Athow of Norwich.[60] As a result of these sales the possessions of the Tylney Longs were widely scattered.[61]

The site of Wanstead House is marked by a depression on the first hole of Wanstead golf course. North of it part of the 18th-century stable court, of brick and weather-boarded timber, survives as the golf club house. The stone piers of the main entrance gates, bearing Sir Richard Child's monogram, still stand in Overton Drive, and the temple, now keepers' cottages, in the centre of Wanstead Park. East of the temple are the ruins of the grotto, which was gutted by fire in 1884.[62] Some of the ornamental waters survive, including the Basin, and Perch, Heronry, and Shoulder of Mutton ponds. Two other ponds, at the south end of Blake Hall Road, have disappeared.[63] The westernmost contained an island on which was Lake House, an early-18th-century building said to have been a banqueting hall or summer-house. It was later a residence. Thomas Hood (1799–1845), the poet, lived there 1832–5.[64] It was demolished in 1908.[65]

The manor of CANN HALL or CANONS HALL comprised most of the Wanstead Slip, together with a few fields in West Ham.[66] The manor originated in Hugh de Montfort's Domesday holding of 3 hides and 30 a. in Leyton.[67] Two hides of that holding were given by Montfort's daughter Adela and her first husband Simon de Moulins to the canons of Holy Trinity, Aldgate, and the grant was confirmed by the king about 1121.[68] Adela's second husband, Robert de Vere, later confirmed the gift, as did King Stephen.[69] A tithe composition relating to Cann Hall was made in 1208 between Holy Trinity and the rector of Wanstead.[70] It suggests that the manor was by then in Wanstead, though the priory's tenants were still being described as 'of Leyton' as late as 1369.[71]

Holy Trinity retained Cann Hall until the priory's dissolution in 1532. In 1533 several petitions were made to the Crown for possession of the manor, though the poverty of its buildings made it no great prize.[72] It was granted in 1534 for life to Nicholas Sympson, a groom of the Privy Chamber, who in the following year was given licence to hold it jointly with his wife Joan in survivorship.[73] Nicholas died in 1552 or 1553 and Joan in 1562.[74] Cann Hall then passed to Nicholas Strelley, whose father John Strelley (d. 1559), vintner of London, had obtained the reversion in 1554; in 1559 the manor had been valued at £10 a year.[75]

[48] e.g. D. Defoe, Tour through Great Britain, ed. Cole, i. 89–90; Arthur Young, Six Weeks Tour through Southern Counties (3rd edn.), 233, 368–70; Kalm's Visit to England, 1748, ed. J. Lucas, 175–6.
[49] Letters of Horace Walpole, iii. 322; iv. 396.
[50] W.H.L., Hiram Stead, 'Materials for the history of Wanstead House', 71, cf. 18, 19, 30, 34, 41, 44.
[51] Ibid. 19.
[52] Ibid. 19; E. W. Brayley and J. Britton, Beauties of England and Wales (1803), v. 467. A gift of rock for the grotto is mentioned in 1761–2: E.R.O., D/DU 546/2.
[53] E.R.O., Sale Cat. B 284.
[54] E.R.O., Map of Wanstead Park Estate, 1815–16.
[55] E.R. xlix. 192; lxiii. 73.
[56] H. Stead, 'Materials for the History of Wanstead House', 71.
[57] Ibid. 71–2. About that time he commissioned a design from Humphry Repton: D. Stroud, Humphry Repton, 173.
[58] J. R. Smith, 'William Wellesley Pole and the Essex estates of the Tylney Long family' (Lond. Univ. Hist. Dipl. 1969).
[59] Ibid. ch. v; W.H.L., Wanstead Ho. Sale Cat. (1822): the contents, in over 5,000 lots, realized £41,000.
[60] It realized £10,000: Annual Reg. (1823), 65. Demoli-

tion took about a year: W.H.L., H. Stead, 'Materials' (small bound vol.), 9 v (sale 1824, after demolition).
[61] See e.g.: E.R.O., Vert. File, Sale Cat. 6 Aug. 1839; H. E. Stutchbury, Architecture of Colen Campbell, 30; E. Nat. i. 79; V.C.H. Essex, iv. 111; E.R. lii. 70; H. Stead, 'Materials', 73. R.C.H.M., City of Cambridge, i, pls. 47, 50; ii. p. 371. And, see above, p. 132.
[62] E.R. vii. 224. For the grotto before the fire see O. Dawson, Story of Wanstead Pk. illus. f.p. 24.
[63] Cf. Chapman and André, Map of Essex (1777), sheet xxi.
[64] Ibid.; Essex Times, 2 Nov. 1907; E.R. xvi. 176; E.R.O., Pictorial Coll. (Mint O/S): plans, elevations and sections.
[65] Wanstead U.D.C., Med. Off. Rep. (1908), 3.
[66] For Wanstead Slip see p. 317.
[67] See p. 185.
[68] Regesta Reg. Angl. Norm. ii. 158, cf. xv.
[69] Cal. Chart. R. 1341–1417, 267.
[70] See p. 332.
[71] P. H. Reaney, Court Rolls of Rectory Manor of Walthamstow (W.A.S. xxxvii), 12.
[72] L. & P. Hen. VIII, vi, p. 322.
[73] Ibid. vi, p. 56; vii, p. 119; C 66/664 m. 30.
[74] E.A.T. N.S. xi. 153.
[75] Cal. Pat. 1553–4, 80–1; C 142/125/44.

Nicholas Strelley (d. 1611) left as heir his daughter Cecily, wife of Humphrey Cardinall of Great Humby (Lincs.),[76] but Cann Hall was claimed by Robert Woolhouse, Cecily's cousin, under an entail created in John Strelley's will.[77] The claimants evidently compromised. Woolhouse took two-thirds of Cann Hall, while the other third was retained by Cecily and Humphrey Cardinall, who appear, in fact, to have been holding it by 1603.[78]

The Cardinalls' third of the manor was bought in 1619 by Thomas Boothby, who transferred it soon after to his son Richard.[79] The other two-thirds descended from Robert Woolhouse (d. 1634) to his son Thomas,[80] who appears to have sold it to Richard Boothby in or soon after 1639.[81] Richard Boothby was certainly holding the whole manor from 1652.[82] He sold it in 1662 to James Flesher (d. 1671), stationer of London.[83] Under Flesher's will Cann Hall was sold in 1671 to William Colegrave for £2,750.[84]

The manor remained in the Colegrave family until the 19th century, being usually let to tenants. William Colegrave the purchaser appears to have been identical with the man of that name who died in 1721.[85] In 1715 he was listed among Roman Catholics refusing oaths of loyalty.[86] The estate was then on lease to John Hewitt and Richard St. Pierre.[87] At that period the perquisites of the manor were worth about £65 a year, and the farm about £105.[88] Cann Hall passed in succession to William Colegrave's sons Henry (d. 1722) and William (d. 1749).[89] William (d. 1793), son of the last-named William Colegrave, was succeeded by his brother Robert (d. 1801).[90] In 1799 the manor comprised 230 a. let to three tenants.[91]

Robert Colegrave was succeeded by his sister's son John Manby (d. 1819).[92] William Manby (d. 1868), nephew and heir of John Manby, took the name of Colegrave.[93] In 1840 he sold 3 a. to the Northern and Eastern Railway Co. for £1,000.[94] In 1841 his estate comprised 205 a. in Wanstead and 17 a. in West Ham.[95] Most of it was occupied by Richard Plaxton, who was still there in 1855.[96] In 1862 the tenant was John Robinson.[97] John Manby Colegrave, who succeeded his father as lord of the manor in 1868, died in 1879.[98] Most of the estate was developed for building c. 1880–95,[99] but the Colegraves retained part of it until 1900.[1] Among local street names commemorating them and their connexions are Colegrave, Downsell, Ellingham, and Worsley Roads.[2]

In 1533 the only buildings attached to the manor were two old barns and a little cottage.[3] By 1746 Cann Hall included buildings on both sides of Cann Hall Lane.[4] In 1841 the main farm buildings lay north of the lane, and there was a cottage to the south of it.[5] By the 1860s the cottage, enlarged, had become a residence with ornamental gardens called Cann Hall; the buildings north of the lane were called Cann Hall farm.[6] None of the buildings has survived.

ECONOMIC HISTORY. In 1086 the manor of Wanstead, comprising one hide, contained 2 tenants' ploughs and 1½ on the demesne (1 in 1066). There was woodland for 300 swine, while a mill and a saltpan had been added since 1066. There were 3 villeins, 8 bordars (7 in 1066), but no serfs (2 in 1066).[7] Hugh de Montfort's manor, later Cann Hall, comprised 3 hides, with 1¼ tenants' plough (1 in 1066) and 1 on the demesne (2 in 1066). There was woodland for 150 swine and 30 a. meadow. The livestock comprised 60 sheep, while 4 swine had been added since 1066. There were a priest, a villein, and three bordars (6 villeins, 4 bordars, and 2 serfs in 1066).[8]

It is clear from these details that both manors were only small forest hamlets. Wanstead manor, which was the more densely wooded, had no livestock, except for the plough-teams. The mill and the saltpan were both probably at Aldersbrook, which until the 16th century was part of Wanstead manor. Millfield, at Aldersbrook, is mentioned in 1535.[9] The Roding is tidal up to Aldersbrook, but not normally above it.[10] The mill was acquired by Clerkenwell priory in or before 1176.[11]

The wealth of woodland and the restrictions imposed by the forest laws largely determined the economic life of the parish down to the 19th century.[12] As late as 1796 some 70 per cent of the parish was still woodland or forest waste,[13] and even in

[76] C 142/322/153.
[77] Ibid. Woolhouse was son of John Strelley's eldest daughter.
[78] Ibid.; C.P. 25(2)/294 Mich. 9 Jas. I; C 66/463; C.P. 25(2)/385 Eas. 1 Jas. I.
[79] Lysons, London, iv. 236; Misc. Gen. Her. 5th ser. i. 182, 191.
[80] C 142/559/135.
[81] Lysons, London, iv. 236; Misc. Gen. Her. 5th ser. i. 191.
[82] E.R.O., D/DHf T9 and M57.
[83] Misc. Gen. Her. 5th ser. i. 191; E.R.O., D/DB T994; Lysons, London, iv. 236; P.C.C. 4 Duke.
[84] E.R.O., D/DB T994.
[85] Ibid. T995.
[86] J. Cosin, Rom. Cath. Nonjurors of 1715, 28; J. O. Payne, Recs. of Eng. Caths. of 1715, 14.
[87] Cf. E.R.O., Q/RRo 1/8; D/P 292/8/6.
[88] Morant, Essex, i. 31.
[89] E.R.O., D/DB T994–5.
[90] Ibid.; E.R.O., D/DB F133.
[91] E.R.O., D/DB T994. In 1820 Cann Hall farm (112 a.) and Cann Hall Cottage farm (103 a.) were advertised to let as separate lots: E.R.O., T/P 110/45.
[92] Burke's Landed Gentry (1871), 261.
[93] Ibid.; E.R.O., D/DB T995.
[94] E.R.O., D/DB T995.

[95] E.R.O., D/CT 384 and 160.
[96] Kelly's Dir. Essex (1855).
[97] Ibid. (1862).
[98] E.R.O., D/DB T993.
[99] L.R.L., Leyton Loc. Bd. Mins. 3 Aug. 1880 (Downsell, Leyton, Manby and Stewart Rds.); L.R.L., L53.4.MS. Leyton L.B. Highway and Lighting Ctee. Mins. 12 Sept. 1882 (extension of Cann Hall estate); Leyton U.D.C. Engineer and Surveyor's Rep. (1895) stated that the Wanstead Slip was then practically built over.
[1] E.R.O., D/DB F133.
[2] Downsell, in South Weald, and Little Ellingham (Norf.) were other estates held by the Colegraves. Worsley was a family connexion: Burke's L.G. (1871), 261; E.R.O., D/DB T995 and F133.
[3] L. & P. Hen. VIII, vi, p. 322.
[4] J. Rocque, Environs of London (1744–6), sheet iv.
[5] E.R.O., D/CT 384.
[6] O.S. Map 25″, London, XI (surv. 1863–7).
[7] V.C.H. Essex, i. 438.
[8] Ibid. 497.
[9] See p. 166.
[10] Cf. V.C.H. Essex, v. 184. Ilford golf course lies opposite Aldersbrook.
[11] E.A.T. N.S. xxiii. 42.
[12] For the forest see also p. 329.
[13] Lysons, London, iv. 231

1841 the figure was over 40 per cent.[14] From early times the Lower forest (Wanstead Flats) contained much open heath, which by ancient and unusual custom was used to pasture sheep as well as other cattle.[15] The Domesday sheep of Cann Hall probably grazed there. In 1189 Richard I granted to Stratford Abbey in West Ham the right to pasture sheep on the heath.[16] That was probably in confirmation of a grant by Ralph of Hesdin, lord of Wanstead manor.[17] In 1230, during a dispute, Ralph's son Hugh of Hesdin seized some of the abbey's sheep on the heath.[18] Wanstead Flats continued to afford valuable pasture and to be the subject of disputes in later centuries.[19]

In 1271 the manor of Wanstead contained 180 a. arable, 6½ a. pasture, and 27 a. meadow.[20] Eight customary tenants performed an annual total of 439 labour services, and owed the rents of 19 hens and 122 eggs, as well as money rents. By 1361 the arable on the manor had increased to 200 a., and the pasture to 20 a., but there were only 22 a. meadow, and only 300 labour services were being performed.[21] Little is known of Cann Hall during the Middle Ages. A custumal (1331) and a rental (1369), both concerning an estate at 'Leyton' held by the priory of Holy Trinity, Aldgate, probably relate to Cann Hall.[22] In 1331 there were ten tenants, whose holdings varied in size from 10 a. to 1 a. They all owed haymaking, hoeing, and sheep-dipping services, and the six smallest tenants also owed regular weekly services. Ten tenants were listed in 1369, but only seven owed labour services. Only one had a surname occurring also in the 1331 custumal, which suggests that Wanstead had suffered much in the Black Death.

Wanstead Park appears to have been inclosed shortly before 1512.[23] This probably increased the cultivable area of the manor, and compensated at least partly for the loss of Aldersbrook, which became a separate manor about that time. In 1535 the manor of Wanstead included 128 a. arable and 24 a. meadow in the park, and 40 a. meadow in North mead and Sayes, in the north of the parish.[24]

After the 16th century the proportion of grassland to arable tended to increase. In 1670 Cann Hall manor contained 86 a. arable, 59 a. pasture, 36 a. marsh, and 8 a. woodland.[25] That marsh, lying near the river Lea, was the only such land in the parish. At the same period part of Wanstead manor, held by a tenant-farmer, contained 110 a. arable and 70 a. meadow.[26] The enlargement and landscaping of

Wanstead Park in the late 17th and early 18th centuries[27] greatly altered the face of the parish, reducing still further the amount of arable.[28] In 1796 Wanstead contained some 450 a. grassland but only 150 a. arable.[29] Here, as in neighbouring parishes, there was great demand for grazing land, and much of the park was being used for that purpose.[30]

It was estimated in 1796 that the arable in Wanstead comprised 100 a. corn and 50 a. potatoes.[31] During the following decades market-gardening increased, especially at Cann Hall. In 1811 there were some 200 a. potatoes in the parish.[32] When Cann Hall manor farm was advertised as to let in 1820 it was described as capital arable land, suitable for cabbages, turnips, and potatoes, and well suited for supplying the London markets.[33] In 1841 the parish contained some 290 a. arable, 610 a. meadow and pasture, 200 a. inclosed woodland, and 670 a. forest waste, including Wanstead Flats.[34] Much of the grassland lay beside the Roding, in the northeast of the parish. More than half the arable (158 a.) was at Cann Hall. The total area of Cann Hall farm was 201 a. Wanstead manor farm comprised 436 a., and Nightingale farm 91 a.

By the end of the 19th century Cann Hall had been built up, while Wanstead Park and Flats had become places of public recreation.[35] A directory of 1906 lists only two farms, both in the east of the parish, and three nurseries.[36] Nightingale farm, Hermon Hill, and two nurseries are listed in 1926.[37] Nightingale farm was developed for building in the late 1930s.[38]

At the end of the 18th century an annual cattle market was held on Wanstead Flats in March and April.[39] An Easter pleasure fair was held on the flats in the late 19th century, and continued until 1913 or later.[40]

Industry has never been important in Wanstead. Until the 19th century the villagers worked mainly in agriculture or in the service of the city merchants residing in the parish. A glover was mentioned in 1643, a goldsmith in 1644, and a brickmaker in 1685–6.[41] Gravel-pit field at Cann Hall, recorded in 1841, recalls a former industry in that area.[42] A few years earlier gravel-digging had been carried on in the parish by paupers under the supervision of the overseer of the poor.[43] Whether it was exploited commercially is not known. A brick field, on the northern edge of Wanstead Flats, was in operation c. 1830–90.[44] Stone-masons, for whom there was

[14] E.R.O., D/CT 384.
[15] See p. 330.
[16] Cal. Chart. 1257–1300, 311–13.
[17] Cur. Reg. R. xiv, p. 79. [18] Ibid.
[19] e.g. Fisher, Forest, 287–8.
[20] C 132/39/8.
[21] C 135/158/32.
[22] P. H. Reaney, Court Rolls of Rectory Manor of Walthamstow (W.A.S. xxxvii), 12.
[23] L. & P. Hen. VIII, i, p. 340, cf. iii, p. 479: appointment of Charles Brandon, later duke of Suffolk, as keeper, in succession to Hugh Denys.
[24] E.R.O., D/DCw M15. For Sayes (Seas) see above, p. 323.
[25] E.R.O., D/DB T994.
[26] E.R.O., D/DCw T3A/76.
[27] See p. 325.
[28] See Chapman and André, Map of Essex, 1777, sheet xxi.
[29] Lysons, Lond. iv. 231.
[30] E.R.O., D/DQs 113/4; R. Allison, 'Changing Landscape of S.W. Essex, 1600–1850' (Ph.D. Lond. 1966), 324 n.
[31] Lysons, op. cit. 231.
[32] Ibid. (Suppl.), 359.
[33] E.R.O., T /P 110/45.
[34] E.R.O., D/CT 384: the figures estimated in 1839 were slightly different from those in the final schedule.
[35] See pp. 320, 330.
[36] Kelly's Dir. Essex (1906). [37] Ibid. (1926).
[38] J. E. Tuffs, Wanstead and Woodford, 110.
[39] See p. 169.
[40] W.H.L., H. Stead, 'Materials for the history of Wanstead House etc.', 153. The fair is mentioned in Arthur Morrison's Tales of Mean Streets.
[41] E.R.O., Q/SR 319/34, 322/21, 449/53.
[42] E.R.O., D/CT 384.
[43] E.R.O., D/P 292/8/10, 2 May 1833.
[44] R. Allison, 'Changing Landscape of S.W. Essex, 1600–1850', 250 and n.; White's Dir. Essex (1848), 264; Jones's Woodford, Wanstead etc. Dir. (1883, 1887); O.S. Map 6", Essex LXV (surv. 1863–9).

much work in the large cemeteries south of the flats, are occasionally listed in directories from the 1860s.[45] A few small manufacturing industries have arisen during the present century.[46] Among those existing in 1968 were the Essex Engineering Co., Nelson Road (tool makers) and W. H. Collings & Son, Nightingale Lane (reinforced concrete).

FOREST. Wanstead lay within the Forest of Essex.[47] It was part of the forest bailiwick of Becontree during the Middle Ages, and later of the Leyton 'walk'.[48] In 1086 it was densely wooded.[49] Much of the woodland had disappeared by the early 17th century, but there are few contemporary records of the process. Ralph of Hesdin (d. 1222) claimed freedom to assart 30 a. in the manor under a charter of Richard I.[50] In 1293 it was stated that Wanstead wood had some time previously been taken into the king's hand for waste committed there during the minority of Thomas Hesdin (or Huntercombe).[51] The inclosure of Wanstead Park in the early 16th century[52] probably involved some disafforestation. In 1563 Lord Rich, who was lieutenant of the forest as well as lord of Wanstead, sought the government's permission to inclose and fell a considerable area of woodland in the north-west of the parish called Great and Little Shrubbage.[53] Although most of it was the lord's wood, it included some common land, and Rich complained that his deer were continually disturbed by people and cattle. He claimed that he himself, as lieutenant, had never refused anyone permission to fell or inclose wood on a freehold. His appeal failed, but it shows that the forest was sometimes attacked even by those officially charged to defend it.

A sketch map of the forest c. 1640 includes Great Shrubbage with Parsons Grove (another name for Little Shrubbage) beside it to the east.[54] Farther south were two small adjoining woods called Cann Hall Grove and Grittens, east of which was Wanstead Heath, stretching across to the pale of Wanstead Park. The heath, also called the lower forest and later Wanstead Flats, extended into several parishes but was mainly in Wanstead. It is recorded as early as the 12th century.[55] In the 17th century, as before, small-scale inclosures of the forest were not infrequent,[56] but in 1673–4, when Sir Josiah Child bought the manor, Great Shrubbage still comprised 160 a. and Little Shrubbage 60 a. while there was another 100 a. common woodland within the parish.[57]

Some woodland also remained in Wanstead Park, and Child increased it by new plantations.[58] By 1746 Cann Hall Grove and Grittens had disappeared, but Great and Little Shrubbage remained, as well as the lower forest, part of which then extended as far south as the present Romford Road, Manor Park.[59] The position was much the same 60 years later,[60] but then followed a period in which Wanstead was the centre of the battle for the preservation of the whole forest.

The forest was threatened by the Crown, by lords of the forest manors and other large landowners, and by the forest officers themselves.[61] The lord of the manor of Wanstead at that time was also the hereditary lord warden of the forest. Sir Richard Child, later Earl Tylney, had bought the office in 1709.[62] He and his son the second earl probably prized it mainly as a post of dignity[63] and of leadership in the social and sporting life of the district.[64] William Pole-Tylney-Long-Wellesley, who became lord warden on his marriage in 1812, was at first zealous in defence of the forest, but by 1831 was openly supporting inclosures.[65] In 1831 he appointed the steward of his manor of Wanstead as steward also of the court of attachments. The steward's loyalty, as he later confessed, was mainly to his manor, and inclosures through the manor court became frequent in the following years.[66] In the 1850s, after destroying Hainault Forest, the Crown resumed the sale of its forestal rights to the lords of manors: those of Cann Hall were sold in 1856 and those of Wanstead manor in 1856.[67]

In 1841 there were still some 650 a. forest waste in the parish,[68] but by 1871 more than half of it had been inclosed in small parcels by Wanstead manor court.[69] In most parts of the parish inclosures do not seem to have provoked resistance, but public opinion was sensitive to encroachments on Wanstead Flats. In 1822 the vestry resolved to resist such encroachments by every legal means,[70] and in 1851–2 Long-Wellesley, now Lord Mornington, succeeded in inclosing 34 a. of the flats only after a legal battle with the tenant of Cann Hall and other commoners.[71] Earl Cowley's attempt in 1871 to inclose another piece of the flats precipitated the last phase of the Epping Forest controversy.[72] The Epping Forest Commission, in its final report (1877) stated that 250 a. open waste remained in the manor of Wanstead, most of it on Wanstead Flats, and 73 a. in Cann Hall manor, all on the flats.[73] In 1876 the City of London had bought the soil of the Cann

[45] *White's Dir. Essex* (1863), 658; *Kelly's Dir. Essex* (1870 sqq.).
[46] *Kelly's Dir. Essex* (1922 sqq.).
[47] W. R. Fisher, *Forest of Essex*, 21 sqq., 395, 403.
[48] Ibid. 137; *E.R.* xiv, map f.p. 193. Leyton 'walk' was sometimes called Leyton and Wanstead 'walk', or Wanstead 'walk': Fisher, op. cit. 146, 219.
[49] See p. 327.
[50] Corporation of London Rec. Off. MS. 2.5 (Documents re Sewers v. Glasse.).
[51] *Chanc. Inq. p.m.* ii, p. 471.
[52] See p. 323.
[53] B.M. Lansd. MSS. 6 (47). The forms 'Shrubbett' and 'Shrubbush' also occur.
[54] *E.R.* xiv, map f.p. 193.   [55] See p. 95.
[56] Fisher, *Forest*, 326–7.
[57] E.R.O., D/DGn 194, cf. D/DCw T3A/73, where Little Shrubbage is estimated at 100 a. and the common woodland at 60 a.
[58] See p. 325.
[59] J. Rocque, *Environs of London* (1744–6), sheet iv.

[60] O.S. Map 1″, sheet I (1805 edn.).
[61] See also *V.C.H. Essex*, iv. 114; v. 290.
[62] Fisher, *Forest*, 120 sqq.
[63] E.R.O., Pictorial Coll. (Mint Binder): Wanstead House . . . Seat of Earl Tylney: 'as Earl Tylney is hereditary ranger of Epping Forest, the whole of that . . . may be regarded as his park.'
[64] *V.C.H. Essex*, ii. 583.
[65] Fisher, *Forest*, 123 sqq., 336 sqq.
[66] Fisher, *Forest*, 341 sqq., 356; R. Allison, 'Changing Landscape of S.W. Essex, 1600–1850' (Lond. Ph.D. 1966), 117 n., 121, and Table 'H'; E.R.O., D/DCw M14; *E.R.* l. 164.
[67] Fisher, *Forest*, 351–2 E.R.O., D/DCY T76.
[68] E.R.O., D/CT 384.
[69] *Final Rep. Epping Forest Com.* H.C. 187, pp. 95–106 (1877), xxvi; Fisher, *Forest*, 356.
[70] E.R.O., D/P 292/8/10: 14 Nov. 1821, 16 Apr. 1822.
[71] *E.R.* l. 164–5.   [72] See p. 169.
[73] *Final Rep. Epping For. Com.* H.C. 187, pp. 95–106 (1877), xxvi.

Hall waste.[74] In 1880 it bought 184 a. of Wanstead Park from Earl Cowley.[75] Under the Epping Forest Act, 1878, and the subsequent arbitration award Wanstead Flats and Wanstead Park were preserved as part of the forest, along with a few smaller areas, including Bushwood, near Leytonstone, George Green, at Cambridge Park, and Eagle Pond, Snaresbrook.[76] Wanstead Flats has occasionally been threatened with development even since 1878. In 1907 it was proposed that a concert hall should be built on the Forest Gate side of the flats.[77] After the Second World War both West Ham and East Ham attempted to secure part of the flats for building, but they met determined and successful resistance from Wanstead.[78]

The lords and tenants of the manors in Wanstead, like those elsewhere in the forest, enjoyed rights of common pasture. Those of Wanstead manor had the special right of sheep pasture on the flats.[79] The parish cattle mark was a 'Q' surmounted by a cross.[80] In the 19th century, and probably earlier, it was used also to mark beasts from Aldersbrook.[81] The commoners of both Wanstead and Cann Hall manors had the right of turbary in the forest.[82] The lord of Wanstead manor claimed the right to take honey and beeswax.[83] He also claimed estovers and sometimes even the right to fell mature trees or to license their felling by his tenants. The wider claims were rejected by the court of justice seat in 1673, as they had been by the government in Lord Rich's time,[84] but until the 19th century there was rarely any opposition to small-scale felling licensed by the manor courts.

LOCAL GOVERNMENT. Court rolls survive for the manor of Wanstead from 1523 to 1856, with considerable gaps in the 16th and 17th centuries.[85] Courts leet and baron were being held up to 1643, after which only courts baron are recorded. The leet appointed a constable (to 1629), an aleconner (to 1585), and a woodward (to 1536). In the 16th century it frequently presented breaches of the assizes of bread and ale. Scolds were presented in 1532 and 1535 and a barrator also in 1535. In 1575 the court noted that there were no stocks in the manor and ordered a pair to be provided. Litigation between tenants of the manor is occasionally recorded in the rolls. A manorial pound existed in 1637. On the manor of Cann Hall courts were apparently still being held in 1731,[86] but no court rolls are known to exist.

The parish records of Wanstead form a large collection including vestry minutes 1688–1883, select vestry minutes 1819–36, and overseers' rates and accounts for various dates between 1718 and

1836.[87] Before 1777 the minutes rarely state where vestry meetings were held. From 1777 to 1786 the meeting-place was usually a public house or sometimes the church. From 1786 to 1832 meetings were usually at the church. The village school was used occasionally from 1814, and from 1833 was the usual meeting-place. The vestry met about four times a year between 1688 and 1750, and about six times a year between 1750 and 1836. Until 1810 the attendance was usually between 5 and 10. After 1810 it was usually between 10 and 20. At important meetings it was sometimes over 30. The rector seems always to have taken the chair when present. In his absence it was usually taken by a churchwarden. Each successive rector attended regularly except Richard Goodere (1750–69). Samuel Glasse (1786–1812) seems to have been the strongest chairman. The lords of the manor of Wanstead rarely attended except on special occasions. William Pole-Tylney-Long-Wellesley appeared once only (July 1812), when he took the chair. The lords of Cann Hall, who were non-resident, hardly ever attended. Up to 1714 the vestry appointed annually a small number of auditors of the parish officers' accounts. In 1800 it set up a standing committee of audit, meeting monthly. In 1768 an *ad hoc* committee on 'the state of the poor' was appointed. In 1819 the parish set up a select vestry which functioned until 1836. This comprised 20 members elected annually. It met every fortnight in the school under the chairmanship of the rector and later of a churchwarden or overseer.

Until the later 18th century there were only one churchwarden, one overseer of the poor, one parish constable, and one surveyor of highways. A second overseer was appointed from 1761, a second churchwarden (nominated by the rector) from 1787, and a second constable from 1791 or 1792. About 1787 the vestry also abandoned its peculiar recent custom of sending each churchwarden to be sworn in at quarter sessions. These changes were no doubt inspired by Samuel Glasse. No additional surveyor was appointed. The officers often employed deputies, some of whom served for years at a stretch. A deputy might act for more than one officer at the same time. It was not unusual for deputies to receive small payments from the vestry as well as from their principals, though such use of parish funds sometimes aroused opposition in the vestry. From the later 18th century, as the parish grew, the employment of paid officers became more frequent. From 1808 to 1822 the vestry employed a salaried assistant surveyor, part-time. An assistant overseer, appointed from 1820, also acted as rate-collector, and in 1833 he was directed to serve full-time, without other employment. Both constables

[74] *Final Rep. Epping For. Com.* H.C. 187, p. 51, (1877).
[75] See p. 324.
[76] *Epping Forest Arbitration Map* 1882). Bushwood had been inclosed between 1851 and 1871, but under the Act was thrown open again.
[77] *Stratford Expr.* 13 Apr. 1907: art. by E. J. Dixon.
[78] A. N. Harrisson, *Hist. Park Ward, Wanstead,* 19; W.H.L. Pamphs., File re Wanstead Flats defence ctee. 1946.
[79] Fisher, *Forest,* 287, 291; *Cur. Reg. R.* xiv. 79; *Cal. Inq. p.m.* i, pp. 287–8; E.R.O., D/DCw M4.
[80] Fisher, *Forest,* f.p. 299. [81] *E.R.* l. 172.
[82] R. Allison, 'Changing Landscape of S.W. Essex, 1600–1850', f. 92 n.
[83] Corporation of London Rec. Off. MS. 2.5 (Sewers v. Glasse); Fisher, *Forest,* 58.

[84] R. Allison, op. cit., f. 86 n. For Rich's attempt see above, p. 329
[85] E.R.O., D/DCw M1–10; D/DM M168; D/DU 182/16.
[86] E.R.O., D/DHf M57, and T9.
[87] When this section was originally drafted some of the records were missing. They have since been found, and the whole collection has been deposited in the Essex Record Office. All the records are listed in *Essex Parish Records* (2nd edn.), 225–6. In its final form the following account of parish government, up to 1836, is based mainly on: the vestry minutes (E.R.O., D/P 292/8/6–10); select vestry mins. (D/P 292/8/16–17); overseers' rates (D/P 292/11/19–29, 45–58); and overseers' accounts (D/P 292/12/4–16). Use has also been made of notes from some of these records supplied by Mr. D. Haley.

received a small salary from 1804. From 1825 there was only one constable, salaried and full-time.

The work of vestry clerk appears to have been performed by the rector, Thomas Juson, throughout his incumbency (1724–49), and in 1731 it was agreed that he should receive an honorarium for this service. After his time a separate vestry clerk was employed, being paid fees or a small salary. The vestry employed various minor officials. There are references to the parish (or church) clerk throughout the period covered by the vestry minutes. For some years in the mid 18th century the post was held in conjunction with that of assistant overseer. A beadle appointed in 1770 was also vestry clerk. In 1825 the beadle was also organ-blower and bell-ringer.

Information concerning the finances of the parish is incomplete, and is especially deficient for the years c. 1790–1810, when it would be most valuable.[88] In Wanstead, as elsewhere, the parish income came mainly from the poor-rates, but church-rates, which before the 19th century were used partly for civil purposes, seem to have provided a larger proportion of the income than was usual in south-west Essex. In the 1690s a separate constable's rate was sometimes levied, but later the constable's bills were charged to the poor-rate or to the church-rate. In the 18th century the surveyor's expenses were met mainly from a levy (not a rate) in commutation of statute labour, with occasional help from the poor-rates or church-rates. The main and recurrent costs of poor-relief were charged on the poor-rates, but casual relief was often provided from the church-rate. In the 19th century, and especially after the appointment of the select vestry, a clearer distinction was made in the use of poor-rates and church-rates, and it also became customary to levy a highway rate. The rateable value of the parish rose from £1,021 in 1688 to £6,178 in 1836.

There is no reference to a parish poorhouse until 1727, when the vestry leased a house from Lord Castlemaine for that purpose and repaired it with the aid of some small legacies recently made to the parish. In 1737 this house accommodated 17 people, mostly old but including 5 children in one family. They occupied tenements of one, two, or three rooms, for which they paid rent. At that period the inmates seem to have given little trouble except by falling behind with the rent. As poverty increased, the poorhouse came to be used for 'problem' families rather than for the aged. In 1761 the vestry resolved to ask the help of the magistrates in enforcing discipline there, and ordered the inmates to 'attend strictly to the service of the church' on pain of forfeiting their allowances. In 1785, after further difficulties, the lease of the house was given up, and the vestry began to farm out paupers to Overton's workhouse at Mile End (Lond.).

The Mile End workhouse appears to have been the only lodging provided by the parish for any of its poor between 1786 and 1801. Those sent there were neither kindly nor efficiently treated and the vestry gradually became reluctant to subject parishioners to such conditions. After 1801, when the parish again provided some poorhouse accommodation, it continued to send its most difficult paupers to London workhouses. The Mile End workhouse continued to be used to a small extent until 1825–6,

but after 1820 places were usually sought in the workhouses at Stepney Green, Bethnal Green, Hoxton, or the Borough. Lunatics were usually sent to an asylum at Bethnal Green.

In 1801 the vestry leased a house at Holloway Down to accommodate paupers. It was given up in 1814, but from 1821 two cottages were being rented from the lord of Wanstead manor; they were probably the two parish houses described in the select vestry's report of November 1831 as being in Poor House Alley. The parish also rented a ten-room house and three cottages at Holloway Down (1831–6) and two cottages in George Row (1834–6). In 1834 the select vestry reported that the parish held only four houses, in which were placed the aged and infirm poor, then numbering 13 adults and 5 children. This return seems to ignore the houses on Holloway Down, possibly because their inmates paid rent.

Before 1727 poor-relief consisted mainly of pensions or doles to a few of the aged. Between 1693 and 1699 there was only one regular pensioner. The original poorhouse, leased in 1727, was at first used as a form of cheap accommodation rather than an alternative to out-relief. In 1729 there were 7 parish pensioners, drawing 2s.–3s. a week each. During the next thirty years the number was usually between 5 and 12. In 1749 the vestry resolved to provide relief in kind instead of weekly pensions, which the poor were thought to misspend. This had no lasting effect. Pensions continued, along with doles of food, clothing, and fuel, which the vestry had always provided. These forms of out-relief, along with medical aid, accounted for most of the poor-rate. Payments for medical treatment figure occasionally in the parish records from 1688. From 1759 the vestry was paying a regular retainer to a doctor (between 1794 and 1808 two doctors) who received additional payments for vaccinations and midwifery. Occasional use was made of specialist doctors from outside the parish, as in 1823 when the vestry paid the large sum of 12 gns. for treating the deformed feet of a child. Many payments were made to those nursing the sick poor and to the London hospitals which received the worst cases.

The vestry did its best to prevent the able-bodied from becoming a burden on the rates. In apprenticing pauper children care was usually taken to find suitable masters and even to consult the wishes of the children themselves. Since there was little or no industry in Wanstead most apprentices had to be bound outside the parish, to Barking fishermen, or to such craftsmen as weavers, tailors, shoemakers, or barbers, in east London or West Ham. During the Napoleonic wars any boy who wished to go to sea could depend on the immediate help of the vestry, even if, like one apprentice in 1802, he had lost his settlement in Wanstead. Apart from those going to sea, few children were sent far from home; but in 1788 four went to a woollen factory at Cuckney (Notts.). Able-bodied adults were encouraged to follow their own trades, for which they were often given tools or materials. Under the select vestry the poor were put to work in the parish gravel-pits, on the roads, in the forest, or on local farms. From 1831 onwards more money was paid to the casual poor for work than for relief.

[88] Some of the parish records seem to have been lost about 1813: D/P 292/8/10, Mar. and June 1813.

Despite its numerous wealthy residents Wanstead was finding the burden of poor-relief uncomfortably heavy by the end of the 18th century. Before 1750 the rates levied for all purposes had rarely been more than 2s. in the pound, which produced £110 in 1718, and £142 in 1740. After 1750 they began to rise, and by the 1780s 4s. was not unusual, producing about £360, of which about £300 was spent on relief.[89] During the later years of the Napoleonic wars they reached 6s. or more, and in 1816 the poor-rates alone amounted to 7s., producing over £1,900. The vestry tried various expedients to keep down the costs of relief. A proposal in 1800 to build a parish mill came to nothing. In 1801 the vestry built a communal bakehouse, but the baker who had agreed to manage it withdrew and that project also seems to have been abandoned. Also in 1801 a scheme was launched to provide cheap food for the poor. The necessary funds were drawn from the rates, public subscriptions, or private charity, and the scheme continued at least until 1810.

After 1816 the cost of relief fell. The lavish expenditure by William Pole-Tylney-Long-Wellesley at Wanstead House during that period probably eased the burden of poverty in the parish. The select vestry, soon after formation in 1819, introduced a stricter scale of relief, and ordered that paupers who were dissatisfied with it should be farmed out to London workhouses. The gross expenditure of the overseers had dropped from £1,865 in 1817 to to £1,573 in 1819; in 1820 it was further reduced to £1,128.[90] Economy was maintained after 1820. This policy culminated in a new code of regulations drawn up in 1833. The overseers were to apply rigid scales of relief. No unmarried man was to be relieved or employed between April and October. Work in the parish gravel-pits was to be more strictly controlled. The wages of parish labourers was to be prohibitively low. The code was so effective that in September 1834 the select vestry claimed to have cut the rates by nearly a quarter, and to have checked 'the spirit of pauperism'. The overseers' expenditure, which had been £1,265 in 1828, fell to £1,202 in 1833, and £1,083 in 1835. In the year ending Lady Day 1834 29 able-bodied men were being employed; 33 infirm men and 6 women were being employed part-time; 14 totally disabled men and 28 women were receiving relief. The parish was also supporting 24 children. How far the select vestry's economies caused hardship to the poor is not clear. The select vestry certainly did not fail to keep the workhouses and the poorhouses under constant surveillance.

The Wanstead vestry never had to deal with any serious problems of law and order. A parish watch-house was repaired in 1693, and in 1711 the vestry ordered two sentry-boxes to be made. Stocks were also set up in 1711, and a cage was built beside them in 1714. A new cage was completed in 1818. About 1830 the parish instituted an armed watch against body snatchers. The watchmen used the vestry room in the church until 1831, when a sentry-box was erected in the churchyard.[91] This was presumably the stone box, given in memory of the Wilton family, which still stood there in 1971.[92]

Wanstead became part of West Ham poor law union in 1836, and of the Metropolitan police district in 1840. A local board of 9 members was set up for the parish in 1854.[93] From 1894 Wanstead was governed by an urban district council of 9 members.[94] In 1934 the urban district was united with that of Woodford, and in 1937 the combined urban district was incorporated as a municipal borough.[95] In 1965 Wanstead and Woodford was amalgamated with Ilford and parts of Chigwell and Dagenham as the London borough of Redbridge.[96]

WANSTEAD AND WOODFORD MUNICIPAL BOROUGH. *Azure, a cross flory argent between, in the first and fourth quarters, a leopard's face, and in the second and third quarters, a martlet, or.*

CHURCHES. There was a church at Wanstead by 1208.[97] The rector was then John of St. Lawrence, a canon of St. Paul's, and there was also a vicar, probably provided by the canon to serve the cure. No later reference has been found to a vicar. The advowson of the rectory descended with the manor of Wanstead until the 19th century, except for occasional turns.[98] About 1825 the next presentation was sold.[99] The advowson appears to have been finally alienated from the manor during the 1890s. By 1898 it had been acquired by the Misses Mary, Jessie, and Gertrude Nutter of Wanstead, who in that year conveyed the reversion, after their deaths, to the bishop of the diocese.[1] The bishop of Chelmsford became patron in 1926.[2]

In 1208, after a dispute between the rector and the priory of Holy Trinity, Aldgate, it was agreed that the priory should retain the tithes of Cann Hall, paying to the rector 4 qr. grain.[3] The payment continued to be made by the owners of Cann Hall down to the 19th century, in spite of occasional attempts by rectors to overthrow the agreement.[4] The rectory was valued at only £4 in 1254,[5] and in 1291 it was among the poorest Essex livings, being valued at only £2.[6] In 1535 it was assessed at £6 13s. 4d.[7] It was valued at £70 in 1604 and at £72 in 1650.[8] In 1650 an augmentation of £28 was granted by

89 Cf. E.R.O., Q/CR 1/1.
90 Ibid. Q/CR 1/12.
91 E.R.O., D/P 292/8/10, 22 Sept. 1831.
92 W. Eastment, *Wanstead*, 35.
93 *Kelly's Dir. Essex* (1890).
94 Ibid. (1894).
95 Wanstead and Woodford Official Guide (1964–5).
96 London Govt. Act, 1963, c. 33.
97 B.M. Cott. Ch. XIII, 18, 20.
98 *E.A.T.* N.S. xviii. 17; Newcourt, *Repertorium*, ii. 639; Guildhall MS. 9558, f. 374; *Crockford's Cler. Dir.* passim. John Torrell, who presented in 1450, had probably bought that turn. Elizabeth I presented by lapse in 1586 when Leicester was abroad.

99 E.R.O., D/AEM 2/6.
1 *Handbk. Chs. Barking Deaneries*, 33–4; E.R.O., D/CPc 94; *Crockford's Cler. Dir.* (1899 sqq.); *Kelly's Dir. Essex* (1898 sqq.); for the Nutters see *Ch. Pl. Essex*, 42.
2 *Chel. Dioc. Yr. Bk.* (1927). Miss G. Nutter died in 1926: Char. Com. files.
3 B.M. Cott. Ch. XIII, 18, 20; cf. Newcourt, *Repertorium*, ii. 639.
4 As in 1276: *Cat. Anct. D.* v. A 13660; and in the early 16th century: G.L.C. DL/C/206, f. 91v.
5 *E.A.T.* N.S. xviii. 17.
6 *Tax. Eccl.* (Rec. Com.), 24.
7 *Valor Eccl.* (Rec. Com.), i. 435.
8 H. Smith, *Eccl. Hist. Essex*, 18, 247.

Parliament, but it had been withdrawn by 1655.[9] In the earlier 18th century the rectory was valued at £140.[10] The tithes were commuted in 1841 for £404, of which £2 was due from the owners of Cann Hall.[11] There were then 80 a. glebe situated in the north-east and north-west of the parish. Of that 32 a. were sold in 1867[12] and most of the remainder by 1902.[13]

The ancient rectory house stood in South (or Parsons, later Redbridge) Lane, north of Wanstead Park.[14] In 1732 Earl Tylney granted the rector free use of water piped from the supply at Wanstead House.[15] About 1830 the rectory was rebuilt on or near the same site.[16] It was sold in 1924 to Essex county council, which demolished it and built Wanstead county high school there.[17] A new rectory was later built in Wanstead Place, opposite Christ Church.

William Smith, rector from 1542, was deprived in 1554 as a married priest.[18] Humphrey Maddison, who was rector when the Civil War began, signed the Protestation of 1641 along with his leading parishioners, headed by Sir Henry Mildmay.[19] Maddison also signed the Essex Testimony (1648), and in 1650 was described as 'an able godly preaching minister'.[20] He died in 1653, and the rectory was held by Paul Amiraut (1654–6) and Leonard Hoar (1656–60), each of whom was presented by Sir Henry Mildmay.[21] The presentation of Hoar was repeated later in 1656 by the Lord Protector.[22] With a title derived from a regicide and Cromwell himself it is not surprising that Hoar was ejected in 1660.[23] Thomas Harrison, who replaced him (1660–7), was deemed to have succeeded Maddison, Amiraut also being ignored.[24] In the 18th century, as far as is known, the rectors were usually resident and there are occasional references to assistant curates.[25] James Pound, rector 1707–24, is mentioned above.[26] Samuel Glasse (1786–1812) was a theologian, an advocate of Sunday schools, and a chaplain to the king.[27]

The ancient parish church, demolished in 1790, stood about 70 ft. south of the present one. Its site is still traceable in the churchyard by a line of gravestones marking the central aisle and memorial slabs marking the chancel. It was enlarged and renovated in 1709–10 by Richard Allison, a Wanstead builder, at a cost of £300, provided by subscription.[28] The walls were raised throughout to the same height as those of the chancel, involving the removal of the arcade between the nave and north aisle. The timber west tower was replaced by one of brick 54 ft. high, and a west gallery was erected. The south porch was removed and a west porch

formed under the tower. Allison's work was faulty, and in 1714 the parish vestry compelled him to repair some of it. A drawing of the church from the south made c. 1715 shows a north aisle, a tower of three stages, and a box-like projecting sanctuary with roundheaded east window and roof pediment.[29] The tower seen from the west is well shown in a water-colour (1788) by J. M. W. Turner.[30] By 1786, when Samuel Glasse became rector, the church had become too small for its growing parish. Having rebuilt the church in his previous parish of Hanwell (Mdx.), he immediately launched a rebuilding scheme at Wanstead, for which statutory powers were obtained.[31]

WANSTEAD, ST. MARY'S CHURCH, PULPIT

The site of the present church of *ST. MARY* was given by Sir James Long, Bt., out of his park.[32] The building cost £9,150 of which £3,500 was raised by subscription and most of the balance by tontine. The foundation stone was laid in 1787 and the building completed in 1790 in a classical style to the design of Thomas Hardwick. The church has not been substantially altered since it was built. It is of brick cased in Portland stone, comprising nave, chancel, north and south aisles, west porch,

[9] Ibid. 209, 211.
[10] Guildhall MSS. 9550 and 9556, f. 62.
[11] E.R.O., D/CT 384.
[12] Wanstead Par. Ch., Docs. in Black Folder.
[13] *Kelly's Dir. Essex*, 1902, cf. 1898.
[14] Chapman and André, *Map of Essex*, 1777, sheet xxi.
[15] E.R.O., D/DCw T6.
[16] E.R.O., D/AEM 2/6; Guildhall MS. 9531/24, f. 571.
[17] See p. 336.
[18] Newcourt, *Repertorium*, ii. 639; cf. H. E. P. Grieve, 'The deprived married clergy of Essex, 1553–61' (*Trans. R. Hist. S.* 4th ser. xxii. 141).
[19] Wanstead Par. Ch., Parish Register (photo: E.R.O., T/P 88).
[20] H. Smith, *Eccl. Hist. Essex*, 108, 247.
[21] Ibid. 350–1; Lambeth MS. 997(1), f. 70.
[22] H. Smith, *Eccl. Hist. Essex*, 351.

[23] Ibid. 379; *D.N.B.* He returned to America and became president of Harvard.
[24] Newcourt, *Repertorium*, ii. 639.
[25] E.R.O., D/P 292/8/6 sqq.; Guildhall MS. 9550.
[26] See p. 321.   [27] *D.N.B.*
[28] D/P 292/8/6; *Stow's Survey of Lond.* ed. J. Strype, ii(6), 121; E.R.O., D/DB T545/15; E.R.O., T/A 366.
[29] *Supplement du Nouveau Théâtre de la Grande Bretagne* (1728), pls. v, vi, vii.   [30] *E.R.* x. 131.
[31] *E.R.* x. 130; Act for rebuilding the church of . . . Wanstead, 27 Geo. III, c. 63; Act for amending an Act . . . for rebuilding the church of . . . Wanstead, 29 Geo. III, c. 14; E.R.O., D/P 292/8/9.
[32] Paragraph based on: *E.R.* x. 130–5; E.R.O., D/P 292/8/9; Guildhall MS. 9531/22, f. 32v–36; Ogborne, *Essex*, 65–7; Pevsner, *Essex*, 412; E.R.O., D/P 292/28/2–10 (papers on the building of the church).

and bell-turret. The nave arcades of five bays have tall Corinthian columns. There are north, south, and west galleries, and a vestry at the east end of the south aisle. The Tuscan porch is supported by two pairs of columns, and above it the west front has a central pediment surmounted by a clock turret crowned by a domed bell cupola with paired Ionic columns. There are box pews and a fine pulpit with sounding-board. Much of the stained glass was destroyed in the Second World War and has not been replaced, but two small circular windows depicting the royal arms of George III and those of Sir James Long remain at the east end of the north and south aisles respectively. The original east window, said to have been copied from Murillo's painting of Christ bearing the Cross, at Magdalen College, Oxford, was replaced in 1890 by a memorial window to the Revd. W. Pitt Wigram, rector 1837–64. An organ was bought for the church about 1802, a new one in 1847, and the present one, in the west gallery, in 1923.[33] The fine brass chandelier in the chancel was given in 1899.[34]

The present church has five bells, dated 1789, 1843, and 1899 (three). The old church is said to have had three bells. In the church of Thorington (Suff.) is a bell inscribed 'Samuel Owen made me for Wanstead 1596'. It was given to Thorington in 1598 by (Sir) Edward Coke.[35] Whether it was ever in fact at Wanstead is not known. Perhaps it was a cancelled order.[36] The church plate includes two cups with paten covers, a flagon, two alms-dishes, a spoon, and an oval dish, all of silver dated 1790.[37] It was recast from earlier plate given in 1705 and 1707, the cost, including some additional silver, being met by Samuel Glasse.

The church contains several monuments from the earlier building, the most notable of which is a large marble monument to Sir Josiah Child, Bt. (1699) and his son Barnard (1698) against the south wall of the chancel. Sir Josiah's figure, in Roman costume and Stuart wig, stands between Corinthian columns under a segmental pediment on which recline two angels with trumpets.[38] There are tablets to Capt. John Morice (1638) and Mary Williamson (1683) on the walls of the north and south gallery stairs respectively. On the east wall of the north gallery is a monument to George Bowles (1817) by (Sir) Francis Chantrey. Floor slabs in the church-yard, on the site of the old church, include the indent of a lost brass, said to have been that of Sir John Huntercombe (1368).[39] A sentry-box in the church-yard probably dates from 1831.[40]

St. Mary's was the only Anglican church in Wanstead until 1861 when a chapel of ease, *CHRIST CHURCH*, Wanstead Place, was built of stone in the Early English style to the design of (Sir) George Gilbert Scott.[41] The south aisle was added in 1867 and the north tower and spire in 1868–9. The building was set back from High Street beyond a public park. Christ Church has remained a chapel of ease, but missions elsewhere within the ancient parish resulted in the formation of the new parishes of Holy Trinity, South Woodford, and St. Gabriel, Aldersbrook. The parish of Holy Trinity, Harrow Green (1879), also included part of Wanstead.[42] In 1898 St. Mary's had a mission room in George Lane.[43] The mission church of *ST. JOHN*, Nightingale Green (later Cowley Road), which existed in 1903 and later,[44] was probably also attached to St. Mary's.

The church of *HOLY TRINITY*, South Woodford, Hermon Hill, originated in 1882, when an iron building was erected.[45] A separate parish was formed in 1888, out of Wanstead and Woodford, the advowson of the vicarage being vested in the bishop of the diocese. A permanent church designed by J. Fowler in a correct late Norman style was completed in 1890. Most of its cost was met by the Misses Nutter, who also endowed the living.

The church of *ST. GABRIEL*, Aldersbrook, Aldersbrook Road, originated in 1903, when an iron building was erected.[46] A separate parish was formed in 1914 out of Wanstead and Little Ilford, the advowson of the vicarage being vested in the rector of Wanstead. A permanent church, designed by Charles Spooner in Perpendicular style, was completed in the same year, with the aid of contributions from the Misses Nutter.

ROMAN CATHOLICISM.[47] A mass centre was opened in Wanstead in 1910 by the parish priest of Walthamstow. In 1918 it was transferred to the hall of the newly-opened St. Joseph's convent school, Cambridge Park. Wanstead became a separate parish in 1919; the church of *OUR LADY OF LOURDES* was opened in 1928, and completed in 1934–9.

PROTESTANT NONCONFORMITY. Quakers were assembling at Wanstead at least as early as 1671, and by 1673 they had bought a building in George Lane for use as a meeting-house.[48] William Penn belonged to the meeting in the 1670s.[49] Wanstead was at first part of Ham and Waltham monthly meeting and from 1691 of Barking monthly meeting. By 1692 most of the Wanstead members had died or

[33] E.R.O., D/P 292/8/9; *White's Dir. Essex* (1848), 263; W. Eastment, *Wanstead through the Ages*, 34.
[34] Eastment, op. cit. 33.
[35] *Ch. Bells Essex*, 437–8, cf. 65.
[36] The bell was cast during the Earl of Essex's brief tenure of the manor of Wanstead.
[37] *Ch. Plate Essex*, 42–4.
[38] R.C.H.M., *Essex*, ii. 249, and illus. f.p. 250; E.R.O., *Stuart Essex* (1966), cover illus.; Pevsner, *Essex*, 412.
[39] For church and churchyard monuments, including some which have disappeared, see: Lysons, *Lond.* iv. 238; Eastment, *Wanstead*, 35; *E.R.* x. 133.
[40] See p. 332.
[41] For Christ Church see: E.R.O., T/P 94/11; *Christ Church, Wanstead, 1881–1961*; *Essex Churchman*, May 1955.
[42] See p 220.
[43] *Chs. Barking Deaneries*, 33–4.
[44] R. Mudie-Smith, *Relig. Life Lond.* 363; *Kelly's Dir. Essex* (1917, 1926).
[45] Paragraph based on: *Chs. Barking Deaneries*, 51; *Kelly's Dir. Essex* (1886, 1890, 1894); E.R.O., D/AEM 1/9.
[46] Paragraph based on: *St. Mary's and Christ Church, Wanstead . . . our daughter church of St. Gabriel's* (1913); *Kelly's Dir. Essex* (1917); Pevsner, *Essex*, 413.
[47] Paragraph based on inf. from Revd. J. V. Hemming.
[48] Unless otherwise stated this account, up to 1716, is based on the following records in Friends' Ho. Libr.: Waltham M.M. Minutes; Barking M.M. Minutes and Accounts; Essex Q.M. Mins. See also Beck and Ball, *London Friends' Meetings*, 274. For the site, identified by Mr. J. Smith, cf. E.R.O., D/DB P32, D/DGn 231, D/DCy P3, f. 150.
[49] *Hist. MSS. Com. 11th Rep. App. VII*, 16.

moved away, and the meeting-house was put up for sale. No buyer could be found, however, and it apparently remained in use until 1716, when it was sold to Joseph Wright, himself a Quaker, who demolished it and used the site to enlarge his own house.[50]

The present Quaker meeting at Wanstead originated in a shift of population during the later 19th century. Many of the wealthy Friends who had attended the Plaistow meeting-house[51] were moving farther from London, and about 1868 some of them began to meet for worship at Wanstead.[52] In 1870 the Becontree assembly rooms and archery ground at Bushwood were bought for a meeting-house,[53] mainly at the expense of J. Gurney Barclay. Substantial alterations were made to the building, and some of the furnishings, including oak panelling, were brought from Plaistow. In its early years the new meeting-house was attended by such prominent families as the Smith Harrisons, Godlees, Barclays, and Fowlers. Between 1870 and 1900 the total membership was about 85. From 1900 it rose steadily to a peak of 234 in 1930, after which it declined. The meeting-house was rebuilt in 1968 as a polygonal structure of white brick.[54]

Wanstead Congregational church, Grosvenor Road, originated in 1864.[55] At that time there was no nonconformist church at Wanstead, though shortlived meeting-houses had been registered in 1821 and 1844.[56] The first Congregational services were held in the court room of the Weavers' alms-houses, New Wanstead, and in 1865 the church was formally constituted with Benjamin Beddow as minister. Of the 24 original members 5 were inmates of the alms-houses. The building committee bought the Anglican church of St. Luke, King's Cross, which was being demolished to make way for St. Pancras railway station, and re-erected it on a site in the centre of Wanstead given by G. H. Wilkinson. It is of stone rubble with freestone dressings. A few alterations were made. The nave was shortened by one bay, only part of the chancel was rebuilt, and the nave clerestory and the north door were omitted. The church was opened in 1867. The cost was higher than expected, and the small congregation, heavily in debt, was preoccupied with money matters. Beddow found this situation intolerable and resigned in 1869. The debt was finally cleared in 1876, and for the next forty years the church flourished and grew, reaching a peak membership of about 200 in 1910. In 1903 it was the strongest free church in Wanstead.[57] During the pastorate of Nicholas

Hurry (1873–82) a mission, founded in 1870 in George Lane, Woodford, became an independent church.[58] Hurry favoured the revivalism of Moody and Sankey, and for a time the church used Sankey's hymns. In 1897 the Grove Hall was built behind the church to accommodate a growing Sunday school. The church was badly damaged by bombing in 1940 and was re-dedicated after repairs in 1949. In 1951 the original schoolroom, now called the Cromwell Hall, was repaired.

Hermon Hill (ex-Wesleyan) Methodist church originated in 1869, when a small building was erected.[59] It was in the Hackney and later in the Clapton circuit. The present church was built in 1877 and in 1879 was included in the new Wanstead and Woodford circuit.[60] It was enlarged in 1882 and 1886. In the early years Hermon Hill's membership was small and after 1900 it was outstripped by that of Woodford, but after the Second World War it increased to over 250.

Cambridge Park (ex-United) Methodist church was founded about 1865 by Free Methodists from Forest Gate.[61] The church, and the old hall behind it, were built in 1875.[62] The Cambridge Park hall was added in 1900, but most of it was burnt down in 1962, and the Warren Hall was built on the site in 1964.[63] Like the Free Methodist churches in West Ham[64] Cambridge Park was originally in the Third London circuit, from which it passed to the Fifth London (or Forest Gate) circuit. It was later transferred successively to the Walthamstow circuit and the Leytonstone and Forest Gate circuit.[65]

Wanstead Baptist church, Wellington Road, originated in 1889,[66] when William Coverley held services in the open air in Cowley Road, and later in a dilapidated carpenter's shop.[67] With the help of friends at Spurgeon's College he raised money to buy a site in Wellington Road and to erect an iron hall there. A church of 16 members was formed in 1894, with Coverley and Edward Scoones as co-pastors. In 1904 a schoolroom, vestry, baptistery, and kitchen were added, and further extensions were made in 1930. The membership has always been very small, and the church has depended mainly on lay pastors.

Aldersbrook Baptist church, Dover Road,[68] grew out of a small undenominational mission which existed in 1898.[69] A hall was built in Dover Road in 1902 and in 1906 the church was formally constituted. The present church building, adjoining the hall, was erected in 1909. During the 1930s the membership rose to a peak of about 100, from

[50] E.R.O., D/DA T488, 490.
[51] See p. 132.
[52] Beck and Ball, *London Friends' Meetings* (1869), 275, states that the meetings had been started 'just recently'.
[53] The remainder of this paragraph is based on: Friends' Ho., Ratcliff and Barking M.M. Mins.; Hadley, *Wanstead Friends' Mtg.*; Reminiscences of Theodore Godlee and Edith Lister (notes collected by Dorothy Pollard); *E.R.* lx. 194–5.
[54] Eastment, *Wanstead*, 40.
[55] Account based on: Wanstead Cong. Ch. Deacons' Min. Bk. and Church Min. Bk.; *Cong. Year Bks.*; D. Speedyman, *Wanstead Cong. Ch. 1865–1965*.
[56] G.R.O., Rtns. Noncf. Mtg. Ho. cert. to Bps. Cts. before 1852, nos. 1213 and 2202.
[57] R. Mudie-Smith, *Relig. Life Lond.* 363.
[58] See p. 357.
[59] The information in this paragraph, which was supplied by Mr. G. Harrington, is based on: Wanstead Wesleyan

Ch. Bdg. Committee Mins. 1896 sqq.; Wanstead and Woodford Circuit Schedules and Trust Deeds.
[60] *Hall's Circuits and Ministers*, 316. Presumably Wanstead had been in the Clapton circuit 1876–9.
[61] *Meth. Free Ch. Mag.* 1865; Eastment, *Wanstead*, 40.
[62] Foundation stone; Worship Reg. 22609; inf. from Mr. Pitney.
[63] Cambridge Pk. Meth. Ch., *Opening of Warren Hall* (1964).
[64] See p. 136.
[65] *U.M. Mins. Conf.* passim; *Methodist Census*, 1940; local inf.
[66] Paragraph based on the following sources, all in the keeping of the church secretary: Church Min. Bks.; Reminiscences of William Coverley (MS.); 'These Sixty Years' (TS.); *Wanstead Baptist Ch.* (jubilee pamph.).
[67] Probably in Nightingale Lane: Worship Reg. 31848.
[68] Paragraph based on inf. from Revd. L. B. Crowe.
[69] Cf. *Kelly's Dir. Essex* (1898).

which it later declined. The church was bombed during the Second World War but was completely renovated thereafter.

JUDAISM. Woodford and District Liberal synagogue, Marlborough Road, South Woodford, was built in 1965.[70]

EDUCATION. A school board was formed for Wanstead in 1880, after complaints from Leyton that Wanstead children were crowding Harrow Green school.[71] At that time Wanstead's only public elementary school was the Church school. Between 1882 and 1900 the school board built four schools with nearly 5,000 places, all at Cann Hall. Under the Education Act (1902) those four schools were all placed under the Leyton 'Part III' authority.[72] The rest of Wanstead then became the direct responsibility of the Essex county council which in 1908–11 built an elementary school with manual instruction centre attached and an infants school, all at Aldersbrook. A county technical school built in central Wanstead in 1912 was closed in 1930. Before the First World War secondary education was thought to be adequately provided by the local private schools,[73] and Wanstead county high school was not opened until 1924. In 1930–4 Aldersbrook school was reorganized, and in 1937 a Roman Catholic infants school was opened. Since the Second World War the county council has built a new primary and a new secondary (modern) school, and the Roman Catholic school has been provided with permanent buildings, as a primary school.

Primary schools. Wanstead Church of England primary school, High Street, is said to have been established in 1786 by the rector, Samuel Glasse.[74] In 1795 he and his leading parishioners petitioned Sir James Long, Bt., for leave to build a school on the forest waste of the manor.[75] Presumably the school was then in temporary premises. The foundation stone of the permanent building was laid in 1796.[76] In 1807 there were 28 boys and 37 girls in the school, of whom 12 boys and 15 girls were being clothed.[77] The school was supported by subscriptions. Some permanent endowments were also received, which by 1834 were producing £20 yearly.[78] The main endowment of £470 had been given by George Bowles, partly in his lifetime and partly by his will dated 1813. The girls department was described in 1807 as a school of industry, and the school accounts for 1839–55 show that the sale

of the girls' work raised a few pounds each year.[79] Shortly after 1818 the school went into union with the National Society.[80] After 1832 attendance rose steadily, and by 1846–7 there were 105 boys and girls, and 50 infants in a separate department.[81] In 1861 the boys department began to receive an annual government grant.[82] The school was enlarged in 1865, and from that time a grant was also received for the girls.[83] In 1875 the Education Department reported that the Wanstead boys department was among the best in Essex in writing and arithmetic.[84] The school was reorganized in 1934 for junior boys, junior girls, and infants, and in 1953 for mixed juniors and infants; it was granted Aided status in 1950.[85] The buildings, several times enlarged, include the original schoolroom of 1796.[86]

Aldersbrook county junior mixed and infants school, Harpenden Road, originated in 1908, when the county council opened an elementary school in Ingatestone Road.[87] A separate infants school was opened in 1911 on an adjoining site in Harpenden Road. In 1930 the Ingatestone Road school was reorganized for mixed seniors and mixed juniors, and in 1934 the juniors were combined with the Harpenden Road infants. The buildings were enlarged in 1934–5. During the Second World War the school was temporarily reorganized in one department. In 1948 it was again divided into a senior mixed (secondary modern) school and a junior mixed and infants school.

Nightingale county junior and infants schools, Ashbourne Avenue, South Woodford, were built on land formerly part of Nightingale farm.[88] The junior school was opened in 1954 and the infants school in 1956.

Our Lady of Lourdes Roman Catholic primary school, Chestnut Drive, originated in 1937, when a parochial infants school was opened in the church in Cambridge Park.[89] In 1961 the present buildings were completed for mixed juniors and infants and the school was granted Aided status.

Technical and secondary schools. Wanstead technical school, Woodbine Place, was built by the county council in 1912.[90] It was closed in 1930. A cookery and handicraft centre was attached to the county council's school at Aldersbrook (1908).

Wanstead mixed county high school was opened in 1924 in the old rectory, Redbridge Lane.[91] Permanent new buildings in the rectory grounds were completed in 1927. During the Second World War the school was evacuated to Newent (Glos.). The buildings were extended in 1964.

Nightingale mixed county secondary modern school, Elmcroft Avenue, was opened in 1957,

[70] Foundation stone.
[71] J. Kennedy, *History of the Parish of Leyton*, 199; *Leyton B.C. Year Bk.* (1952–3), 82.
[72] For those schools see pp. 235–6.
[73] M. E. Sadler, *Rep. Secondary and Higher Educ. in Essex* (1906), 150–1.
[74] Lysons, *London* (1796), iv. 244.
[75] E.R.O., D/DCy Z2.
[76] E.R.O., D/P 292/28/7.
[77] E.R.O., D/AEM 2/4.
[78] *Rep. Com. Char. (Essex)*, H.C. 216, p. 267 (1835), xxi (1); cf. Ogborne, *Essex*, 70.
[79] E.R.O., D/P 292/25/2.
[80] *Nat. Soc. Reps.* 1820 sqq.
[81] *Nat. Soc. Enquiry into Church Schs.* 1846–7, pp. 20–1.
[82] W. Eastment, *Wanstead*, 77.

[83] Ibid.
[84] *Essex County Standard*, 18 Aug. 1875.
[85] Inf. from Essex Educ. Dept.
[86] The foundation stone still survived in 1971.
[87] Paragraph based on: *Essex Educ. Ctee. Mins.*; inf. from Essex Educ. Dept.
[88] Paragraph based on: *Educ. in Essex* (1952–6), 20; ibid. (1956–60), 21; E.R.O., Cat. Title Deeds of E.C.C. Schs.; inf. from Essex Educ. Dept.
[89] Paragraph based on: Inf. from Revd. J. V. Hemming and Essex Educ. Dept.; *Educ. in Essex* (1960–64), 20.
[90] Paragraph based on: *Essex Educ. Ctee. Mins.*; E.R.O., Cat. Title Deeds of E.C.C. Schs.; *Kelly's Dir. Leytonstone, Wanstead, etc.* (1911 sqq.).
[91] Paragraph based on: *Essex Educ. Ctee. Mins.*; Wanstead Co. H.S., *Programme of Opening* (1927).

adjoining the junior and infants schools of the same name; it was enlarged in 1969.[92]

The origin of Aldersbrook mixed county secondary school has been described above.

Private schools. In 1807 there were three small private schools in Wanstead.[93] During the 19th century the number of private schools listed in directories slowly increased to a peak of 11 in 1898.[94] Among the few which survived for more than a short time were those of Ann Jenkins (c. 1848–70) and Mary Easton (c. 1863–1902). A report of 1906 mentions three private schools recognized by the Board of Education: Wanstead high school, Wanstead college, and Gowan Lea.[95] Wanstead high school, in Wellesley Road and later in High Street, was kept by Emily Walker (c. 1890–1908). Wanstead college, Woodford Road (c. 1892–1933), kept by Mr. and Mrs. Beecham Martin, was merged after Mrs. Martin's death with the neighbouring Gowan Lea.[96] Gowan Lea, Woodford Road, was founded by 1902 and closed in 1970. Its name was a rebus of the names of Miss Gowlett and Miss Freeman, joint principals c. 1902–8.[97] St. Joseph's Roman Catholic convent school, Cambridge Park, was opened in 1918 by the Sisters of Mercy, who came from Commercial Road, London.[98]

CHARITIES FOR THE POOR.[99] Wanstead Parochial Charities,[1] registered with the Charity Commission in 1962, include the following charities for the poor which together are administered by the rector and churchwardens of St. Mary's: Tylney, Plomer, Waldo, Bowles and Rushout, Rushout (for blankets), the Lying-in charity, Plampin, Hill, Spering, and Searle. In 1970 the income from these charities was distributed to the poor in the form of Christmas gifts. The Scott charity was separately administered, also by the rector and churchwardens. In 1928 the Charity Commission ruled that beneficiaries of Wanstead's charities might come from any part of the ancient parish, irrespective of modern boundary changes.

Robert Rampston (d. 1585) left a rent of £1 for the poor, charged on Stone Hall in Little Canfield. In 1834 it was spent along with the income from Tylney's, Waldo's, and Plomer's charities, on gifts of food, clothing, and cash. It was still being received in 1865,[2] but payment seems to have lapsed by c. 1880.

Frances Harrison, by her will dated 1689, with codicil 1690, devised for the benefit of the poor, a reversionary interest in her house in Wanstead. It seems unlikely that the reversion ever took effect, though the parish sought a legal opinion on the matter as late as 1838.[3]

John Tylney, Earl Tylney (d. 1784), bequeathed £100 stock in trust for the poor. In 1962 the income was £2 10s.

Robert Mangles in 1791 gave £69 stock in trust for the poor. It was stated in 1820 that the income of £2 had not been received since 1811, and there is no evidence of any later payments.

Thomas Lyttleton, assistant curate of Wanstead, in 1799 gave £50 for the poor, secured on a cottage in Cann Hall Lane, the occupier of which was to pay an annual rent-charge of £1 10s. In 1834 the occupier stated that £50 had been given to his father towards the building of the cottage on condition that he paid £1 10s. a year to the poor for the duration of his 21-year lease, starting in 1802. The rent was actually paid only until 1821.

William Plomer in 1803 gave £166 stock in trust for the poor. In 1962 the income was £4.

Mrs. Rebecca Waldo in 1810 gave £37 10s. stock in trust for the poor. In 1962 the income was £4 10s.

George Bowles of the Grove, by will proved 1817, gave £500 stock in trust to provide a donation of £1 each to 20 poor families on New Year's day. The income proved insufficient, and Anne Rushout, Bowles's niece and his successor at the Grove, during her lifetime made a voluntary gift of £2 10s. a year to enable the donations to be fully made. By her will proved 1849 she added £166 to the trust fund. In 1962 the total income was £16 13s. 4d.

Anne Rushout, by her will proved 1849, also gave £180 stock in trust to provide blankets for the poor. In 1962 the income was £4 10s.

The Lying-in charity was founded in 1864 by public subscription to provide maternity benefits for poor women.[4] The trust fund, which in 1865 totalled £166, was increased to £266 by further subscriptions in 1914. In 1962 the income was £6 13s. 4d.

Mrs. Fanny Plampin, by her will proved 1864, gave £100 stock in trust to maintain a family vault in the parish church, the residue for poor widows not receiving poor-relief. The trustees maintained the vault until 1928, when the Charity Commission pointed out that they had been contravening the rule against perpetuities. In 1962 the income was £2 10s.

Margaret Hill, by will proved 1878, gave £500 stock in trust to provide blankets, clothing, or bread for the poor at Christmas. In 1962 the income was £12 10s.

Mrs. Mary Spering, by will proved 1884, gave £403 stock in trust for poor widows aged 60 years and over. In 1962 the income was £10.

Mary Ann Tickell Scott, by will proved 1922, gave £1,000 in trust for gifts at Christmas to 25 poor women, aged over 60 years and communicants of the Church of England. In 1953 the income was £35, which was distributed in cash to 18 persons. By 1971 the income was being used for the maintenance of the graves in the churchyard of St. Mary's.

Mrs. Emma Florence Jane Searle, by will proved 1958, gave ⅑ of her residuary estate, amounting to £1,833, in trust to Wanstead Parochial Charities. In 1962 the income was £94.

[92] *Educ. in Essex* (1952–6), 20; ibid. (1956–60), 21; inf. from Essex Educ. Dept.

[93] E.R.O., D/AEM 2/4.

[94] *White's Dir. Essex* (1848 and 1863); *Kelly's Dir. Essex* (1870 sqq.).

[95] M. E. Sadler, *Rep. Sec. Educ. Essex* (1906), 150.

[96] Eastment, *Wanstead*, 80.

[97] *Kelly's Dir. Essex* (1902 sqq.); M. E. Sadler, *Rep. Sec. Educ. Essex* (1906), 150; inf. from Mrs. H. G. Powell. Gowan Lea claimed to have been founded in 1855: *Wanstead and Woodford Official Guide* (1954), 7.

[98] Inf. from Revd. J. V. Hemming.

[99] Unless otherwise stated this section is based on: *Rep. Com. Char. (Essex)*, H.C. 216, pp. 265–8 (1835), xxi (1); Char. Com. files; E.R.O., D/P 292/8/16 (Report on parochial funds 10 Jan. 1820); inf. from Mr. E. T. Collyer, secretary to Wanstead charity trustees.

[1] This is a prescriptive title, used for many years before 1962. No scheme has been made to regulate this group of charities.

[2] E.R.O., D/P 292/25/3.

[3] Ibid. 292/25/6.　　　　[4] Ibid. 292/25/3.

WOODFORD

WOODFORD was an ancient parish of 2,146 a.,[1] lying about 8 miles north-east of the City of London, at the northern end of Becontree hundred. Its western and northern boundaries ran through Epping Forest, part of which still survives in this area. A local board was formed for the parish in 1873. In 1934 the urban district was amalgamated with that of Wanstead, to the south, and in 1937 the borough of Wanstead and Woodford was formed. In 1965 Wanstead and Woodford, together with Ilford, became the London borough of Redbridge. That year has been taken as the terminal point of the present article, though a little later information has been included.

Along much of the western side of Woodford is a ridge about 200 ft. high, now marked by the High Road. From this the parish slopes gently eastwards down to the river Roding. The soil is mainly London clay, with patches of gravel on the higher parts, and originally supported forest over much of the area.

Woodford was never a compact village; separate hamlets, only tenuously linked together, grew up along the High Road and at Woodford Bridge in the north-east corner of the parish. The wooded surroundings made the parish attractive to wealthy Londoners from at least the 15th century, and their mansions became a feature of Woodford. During the 19th century improved roads and the railway brought Woodford within the range of middle class city workers. Streets of houses built for them, and later ribbon development, joined up the scattered settlements, and 20th-century estates have since filled in most of the remaining space. Yet Woodford remains a green and leafy place. Many of the estates are of the garden-suburb type. There are recreation grounds along the Roding and greens at Woodford Bridge. Patches of woodland and large greens fringe the High Road and Woodford New Road. Knighton wood in the north covers 37 a., and the north-western corner of the parish, bounded by the river Ching, is largely cleared and open forest land, of which Woodford golf course forms part.

In 1801 the population was 1,745. This indicates the residential character of the place, since inhabitants of purely agricultural villages of similar area in Essex numbered only about 300.[2] Many of the inhabitants of Woodford must have been domestic servants;[3] they would have replaced some of the negroes recorded in the parish in 1679–1766.[4] During the earlier 19th century the population grew slowly to 2,774, but after the coming of the railway it increased more rapidly to 4,609 in 1871, and 7,154 in 1881.[5] This rate of growth was maintained during the earlier 20th century. In 1961 the population was well over 32,000 but it had increased only slightly during the previous decade.[6]

The oldest road through the parish entered the village from the north-east. Coming from Abridge, it crossed the Roding by a ford, from which the village derived its name, and continued along the western bank, eventually veering south-west towards London. Around the ford, in the area now known as Woodford Bridge, a medieval village grew up. The earliest list of Woodford residents, drawn up about 1235,[7] shows most of the tenants living in this neighbourhood: Thomas de Muscegros almost certainly held land on the border next to Chigwell, where a branch of his family owned land; William ad aquam, or atte Ree, was one of a family from which Ray House derived its name; Richard Gal gave his name to Gales Farm; Thomas and Robert de ponte took their name from the bridge, as did Alexander and Goscelin atte bridge mentioned in 1239.[8] Alan de la Burgate belonged to an extensive family which held lands in both Woodford and Chigwell, and his name indicates that the bury or manor-house was at one time in this corner of the village, as Burgate-strete,[9] possibly the present Manor Road, certainly was. Near by was a pasture called Eldbury and a coppice called Eldburyshrubs;[10] their names suggest that the original manor-house had been abandoned long before 1235. The principal tenant in the list was John de monte, who probably held Hill House. A lane, following more or less the line of the present Roding Lane North, linked Hill House with the community at Woodford Bridge and gave access to the meadows; it is mentioned in 1271 as forming part of the boundary with Barking parish.[11] Rowdon Lane is mentioned in 1517 to the south of Gales Farm;[12] this seems to correspond with the present Roding Lane North. Its straighter southern section was in 1403 called Long Lane.[13]

From the ford a way known as 'the Lane' struck westwards for about a mile before turning north towards Chingford. Maud in the Lane (1235) gave her name to a tenement called Lanes, later Sakes. From the Sake family the lane became known as Sakes Lane, later corrupted as Snakes Lane.[14] The way now followed by the High Road, along the western border of the parish, was then only a track. It seems to have been the highway in the forest from London to Epping Heath mentioned in 1341.[15] Because of the need to preserve the forest it remained little more than a track until the 17th century,[16] but settlements were made beside it. William de fonte (1285) probably lived at Woodford Wells.[17] Benet Mascall (1235) was associated with Marshalls, a tenement on the green near the end of Snakes Lane. Adjoining it was Harts, named from the family of Richard Hert who was living in 1270.[18] The later site of the manor-house, in the extreme south-west corner of the parish, was certainly established in the

---

[1] V.C.H. Essex, ii. 348. See map above, p. 248.
[2] V.C.H. Essex, ii. 345, cf. 344–54.
[3] E. J. Erith, Woodford, Essex, 1600–1836 (Woodford Hist. Soc. x), 36. In 1908 Mrs. Masters kept a servants' registry office: Kelly's Dir. Essex, 1908, p. 628.
[4] E.R. xxvii. 151.   [5] V.C.H. Essex, ii. 345.
[6] Census, 1901–61. The wards of the borough in 1961 did not coincide exactly with the parish bounds.
[7] B.M. Cott. MS. Tib. c. ix, f. 205.
[8] Select Pleas of the Forest (Selden Soc. xiii), 69.

[9] Cf. S.C. 2/173/31.
[10] Cf. Eldebury (1468): S.C. 2/173/38; Yelberysshrubs (1512): E.R.O., D/DCw M16.
[11] S.C. 2/173/30. A Roman origin has been suggested: E.A.T. N.S. xvii, 189.
[12] S.C. 2/174/43.   [13] S.C. 2/174/42A.
[14] P.N. Essex, 110.
[15] Cat. Anct. D. i. B 777 (Edw. I should read Edw. III).
[16] V.C.H. Essex, v. 116; E.R. lvi. 182–5.
[17] P.N. Essex, 111.   [18] S.C. 2/173/30.

12th century and possibly before the Conquest. Robert *de aula* evidently lived near the manor house in 1235. Beside it the church was built, and below it the demesne lands ran down the southern portion of the village towards the river. The rector's glebe was also at this end of Woodford. The church and manor-house were thus built at some distance from the main area of settlement, and the hamlet which later grew up near them had become known as Church End by the 18th century.

Woodford grew slowly until the later 15th century when London citizens began to buy houses in the parish, some possibly as investments but others for residence during at least part of the year. From the later 16th century onwards they began to build their own larger, more elaborate houses. One result of this was that by 1622 the village had grown sufficiently to warrant enlarging the church. By 1670 about 70 families were living in the parish,[19] some of them quite humble, such as those who had erected cottages on the manorial waste or who were living as 'inmates' in others' households.[20] More than half the parishioners were then living in houses with 3 or fewer hearths. At the same time Woodford showed a much greater proportion of larger houses, with 8 or more hearths, than neighbouring parishes: in Woodford 18 out of 72 houses came into this category, compared with 8 out of 92 in Chingford, 7 out of 40 in Wanstead, and 23 out of 189 in Walthamstow.[21]

This development continued into the 18th century. In 1748 the houses in Woodford were said to be scattered and 'of brick, several storeys high, well built, and some of them handsome. The inhabitants are partly farmers, but still more gentlemen.' Londoners who did not own houses there often rented them for the summer; rooms in Woodford were often more expensive than in London itself.[22] In 1762 there were said to be 178 houses in the parish, of which 156 were 'mansions', and 22 cottages, and by 1796 the total number of houses was about 250.[23]

In the late 18th and early 19th centuries most of the houses were clustered along the High Road from Woodford Wells in the north, through Woodford Row (or Green), to Salway Hill, Church End, and along George Lane in the south; Woodford Bridge was a separate hamlet. A few farms filled the intervening area.[24] After the opening of the new road through the forest from Walthamstow in 1828 some 50 extra houses were built in its neighbourhood.[25] Many of these were on land inclosed from the waste; in 1838 nine were said to be new inclosures, but development was confined to the existing areas of settlement.[26] With the coming of the railway in 1856

houses began to be built in various parts of the parish.[27] The Crown sold its rights in the forest and many more small inclosures were made from the waste.[28]

As late as 1876 Woodford still comprised widely separated hamlets.[29] At Church End the British Land Co., which had bought the Woodford Hall estate in 1869, had already laid out roads west of the church, and houses were being built on some of the plots. Along the High Road there were a few large 18th-century houses.[30] At Woodford Green were the best shops, overlooking the green, and a number of mansions.[31] The growing population of Woodford Green was attested by its fine Congregational church, built in 1874, its Methodist Free church, and by the church of All Saints, near by at Woodford Wells, also built in 1874.

Woodford Wells was connected with Woodford Green by a row of small, roadside cottages.[32] The north-western section of the parish comprised a large piece of forest land. In spite of attempts by Bernard Whetstone and other lords of the manors to reclaim some of this area, it remained woodland until the middle of the 19th century. Apart from a few scattered cottages the house called Manor House, built on the site of the workhouse, was the only building there until it, in turn, was replaced by Bancroft's school in 1889.[33] After the break-up of the Wanstead House estate in 1882, the great wood at Woodford was felled and the land brought under cultivation or developed for housing. The site of the spring, first mentioned in 1285, from which the area took its name,[34] is uncertain. It was described in 1766 as being near the Three Wells public house (also known as the Old Wells), which stood on the west side of High Road, to the north of the New Wells public house, which was farther from the spring. The site was also described in 1796 as being near the nine-mile-stone.[35] In the early 18th century the spring was reputed to have medicinal properties, but had fallen into neglect before 1768.[36]

Woodford Bridge was the most detached of the hamlets. The houses clustered along the road and round the Green and since 1854 it had had its own church. It was still in 1965 known locally as 'the village'. Near Woodford station, also about 1876 or before, a small estate consisting of Prospect Road, West Grove, and Avenue Road, was being developed,[37] and Snakes Lane was becoming built up.[38]

During the late 19th and early 20th centuries the settled areas were expanded, and by 1922 few fields in the parish were still being cultivated.[39] As the families of the gentry moved out, their homes were pulled down and the grounds laid out for housing estates.[40] Some building took place in the extreme

[19] *E.R.O.*, Q/RTh 5. Cf. Wm. Salt Lib. Stafford, Bp. Compton's Census, 1676.
[20] E.R.O., D/DCw M23, 26; Fisher, *Forest of Essex*, 327.
[21] E.R.O., Q/RTh 5. Cf. *V.C.H. Essex*, iv. 306.
[22] *Kalm's Account of his Visit to England*, trans. J. Lucas, 166, 168.
[23] Lysons, *London*, iv. 280; cf. Guildhall MS. 9558, p. 400.
[24] Chapman and André, *Map of Essex* (1777), sheet xvi; Erith, *Woodford*, map f.p. 125.
[25] *White's Dir. Essex* (1848). For this road see below.
[26] E.R.O., D/CT 408.
[27] *Kelly's Dir. Essex* (1870).
[28] See below, p. 351.
[29] S. Thorne, *Handbk Environs London*, 736.
[30] Ibid.; E. Walford, *Greater London*, 459.
[31] Thorne, *Environs*, 736.

[32] Walford, *Greater Lond.* 464.
[33] O.S. Map 6″, Essex LXV (1863–76 edn.). Cf. pp. 352, 359.
[34] *P.N. Essex*, 110–11.
[35] B.M. Add. MS. 34650, f. 206; Lysons, *London*, iv. 287; Chapman and André, *Map of Essex*, 1777, sheet xvi; E.R.O., D/DCw P8, D/DCy P2B, f. 96. For discussion of possible sites, see M. Christy and Miss M. Thresh, *Hist. Mineral Waters and Medicinal Springs of Essex*, 31–4.
[36] Morant, *Essex*, i. 39; Christie and Thresh, *Hist. Mineral Waters . . .*, 31–4; *Ambulator*, 1796, p. 319.
[37] O.S. Map 6″, Essex LXV (1863–76 edn.).
[38] E. Poultney, *Twenty-five years ago*, 18.
[39] See below, p. 349.
[40] Cf. P. Willmott and M. Young, *Family and Class in a London Suburb*, 6–7, 10.

north of the parish, more at the southern end. On Monkhams estate the southern part had been developed by 1914 and the remaining part was completed in garden-suburb style during the 1930s.[41] A similar development in the north-western sector of the parish, begun about this time, was still continuing in 1965, but south of Snakes Lane virtually all the available open space was built over by 1939.[42] During the 1920s an average of 660 new houses were built each year; this figure rose to 1,600 in the 1930s.[43] Much of this building was under the control of operative and provisional planning schemes.[44]

Modern houses in Woodford are mostly detached or semi-detached, set in their own gardens, and have three or four bedrooms. Some council houses were built in the 1920s and many more were built after the Second World War,[45] but in 1961 62 per cent of the houses in Wanstead and Woodford were still owner-occupied.[46] Broadmead, the largest of the post-war council estates[47] was completed in 1968. The scheme includes six tower blocks of flats, maisonettes, a community centre, shops, and a raised central concourse above an extensive car park. Many new residents moved from places nearer London. Woodford is now a dormitory suburb for middle-class city workers, with only a few working-class enclaves.[48] Dwellings being built in the late 1960s were mainly in the form of flats.

There were 5 inns in Woodford in 1753: the George, White Hart, Ship and Castle, New Wells, and Old Wells.[49] The number licensed rose to 9 by 1770, but fell again to 5 by 1828.[50] Two White Hart inns existed by 1776.[51] The George at Church End, which existed as Horns Inn in 1657,[52] is now a two-storey red-brick building dating from the early 18th century, with sash windows, a coved cornice, a porch with Tuscan columns, and an addition in the same style at the south end. The White Hart at Church End, which was a posting house in 1848,[53] has an early-19th-century yellow-brick front of three storeys with a central porch. The Castle at Woodford Green, which was also a posting house,[54] is a stucco-faced building of similar size and date. The present Horse and Well at Woodford Wells existed as the Horse and Groom by the early 1770s,[55] and became licensed as the Horse and Wells about 1784, when the Old Wells ceased; the New Wells had ceased before 1776.[56] The Horse and Well, also known as the Woodford Wells in 1838,[57] stands back from the east side of High Road; it is an early-19th-century brick building with a whitewashed front. The well-known huntsman, Tom Rounding,[58] was the landlord for nearly fifty years from 1792.[59] At Woodford Bridge the White Hart and the Crown and Crooked Billet both existed in the late 18th century;[60] the

former was rebuilt c. 1900 with an ornate front, but the latter is a late-18th-century structure, though much altered. The Three Jolly Wheelers at Woodford Bridge was established later, between 1828 and 1848.[61]

Of the many houses built in Woodford in the 18th century only a few survived in 1969, though as late as 1954 there was still 'a quite uncommonly complete stretch' of them near St. Mary's church in South Woodford, 'some in generous gardens'.[62] At least six of these on the east side of High Road were demolished in the late 1950s and 1960s. Those that remained in 1969 included Elmhurst, West Lodge (nos. 114–18), and Holmleigh (no. 140). Elmhurst is a three-storey late-18th-century mansion of brown brick with a later south wing. The front has a central pediment, balustrades to the first-floor windows and a round-headed doorway with vermiculated quoins and a fanlight. By 1969 three tower blocks had been built in the grounds as halls of residence for Queen Mary College and the old house had been converted as a library and offices. The former West Lodge, a mid-18th-century house, later extended and faced with stucco, was standing empty in 1969 on a site designated for a new building for South Woodford library.[63] Holmleigh, a square three-storey house of dark red brick dating from the later 18th century, was also empty in 1969.

On the west side of High Road are the former rectory[64] and the White Hart Hotel.[65] The Grove, or Grove Hall, which stood at the junction of High Road and the Southend Road, was demolished to make way for an office block in 1958.[66] It was a large building with mainly Georgian external features, but with earlier brickwork at the rear and traces of 16th- or 17th-century work internally. The road frontage, of nine bays, was of the early 18th century and had a central doorway with Corinthian pilasters and a segmental pediment. Impressive gate-piers with stone urns flanked the drive entrance and the stable block was of late-17th-century date. The house belonged to the Eaton family from at least 1701, to the Monins family between 1769 and 1854, and to the Squire family during the early 20th century.[67]

The George inn faces High Road at its junction with George Lane.[68] Near by, concealed by later buildings on the road frontage, is Grove Lodge, an elaborate Tudor-style villa dated 1835. Further south in High Road several more humble 18th- and early-19th-century houses are surrounded by modern commercial development. In Grove Crescent some of the earliest middle-class semi-detached houses, built before 1864,[69] were still standing in 1969.

At Salway Hill (now part of High Road) there were several large residences in the 18th and 19th

[41] See below, p. 347.
[42] O.S. Map 2½″, TQ 49 (1949 edn.); J. E. Tuffs, *Wanstead and Woodford*, 113–14.
[43] Willmott and Young, op. cit. 2.
[44] *Official Guide* (1964–5).   [45] Ibid.
[46] *Census*, 1961, p. 207.
[47] *Redbridge Official Guide* (1969), 49.
[48] Willmott and Young, op. cit., 3, 88, 98, 120, 137.
[49] E.R.O., Q/SBb 195/12.
[50] E.R.O., Q/RLv 25, 82.
[51] Ibid. 30.
[52] See p. 360.
[53] *White's Dir. Essex* (1848), 268.
[54] Ibid.
[55] E.R.O., Q/RLv 25–30.

[56] Ibid. 30–45.
[57] E.R.O., D/CT 408 (no. 240).
[58] *V.C.H. Essex*, ii. 567, 583; *E.R.* vi. 77–9, vii. 226.
[59] E.R.O., Q/RLv 46–82, D/CT 408.
[60] E.R.O., Q/RLv 30.
[61] Ibid. 82; *White's Dir. Essex* (1848), 268.
[62] N. Pevsner, *Essex* (1st edn.), 397–8.
[63] Inf. from South Woodford Library.
[64] See p. 353.
[65] See above.
[66] *Wanstead and Woodford Official Guide* (1964–5).
[67] Inf. from Ministry of Housing and Local Govt., based on a MS. account by C. H. Crouch.
[68] See above.
[69] O.S. Map 1/2,500, Essex LXV. 11 (1864).

centuries. The most important survivor is Hurst House, or the Naked Beauty, of which the central block was apparently built between 1711 and 1735.[70] Later in the 18th century lower side wings were added, which terminated in stables and out-buildings, surmounted on both sides by tall domed cupolas.[71] The greater part of these wings had disappeared by the early 1930s when the house was restored. Not long after this work was completed in 1935, the house was gutted by fire, and in 1937 the central block was reconstructed to the original design, the present small wings being added.[72] The two-storey front of the central block is stucco-faced and divided into bays by full-height Corinthian pilasters supporting an entablature; the parapet is crowned by stone vases. The central doorway has Corinthian pilasters, a segmental pediment, and an enriched tympanum. The garden front is of dark red brick, and its bay-windows of brown brick are probably later 18th-century additions. Internally a fine staircase of the original date survived the fire.

At Woodford Green there are considerable remains of the hamlet of Woodford Row. On the west side, south of the Castle Hotel, is a small and comparatively unaltered double-fronted house of the later 18th century (nos. 383–5). The adjoining pair may be of similar date with early-19th-century alterations, including a cast-iron veranda. Set back at an angle to the north of the Castle is Lanehurst, a two-storey early-18th-century red brick house with a weatherboarded rear and a five-bay front. Further north several early-19th-century buildings along High Road have been altered by the insertion of large shop fronts. Mill Lane and the Square, the latter containing brick and weatherboarded cottages, still preserve their 19th-century character. Over-looking the Green in High Elms stands a stucco house of c. 1800, formerly called Higham Villa, and in Links Road are several cottage pairs of the earlier 19th century. The Terrace, at the west end of Broadmead Road, consists of mid-Victorian semi-detached houses of brown brick.

On the east side of Woodford Green, where the two medieval tenements of Harts and Marshalls had stood, Sir Humphrey Handforth, Master of the Wardrobe to James I, built a mansion called Harts in 1617. It was a gabled building which, before it was demolished, had acquired some Georgian features. Its principal resident in the 18th century was Richard Warner (d. 1775), who established a botanical garden there; his studies were printed in 1771 as *Plantae Woodfordiensis*.[73] Warner may have built the sham 'chapel' or 'abbey' ruin in the garden, a structure of flint and brick of which scanty remains,

incorporating some reset medieval fragments, survive. Warner's name is perpetuated in Warner's Path, between Harts and the Green, and in Warner's Pond, on the west side of High Road. Harts House was rebuilt in 1816 as a three-storey stucco-faced mansion with an entrance front of seven bays, the three central bays being recessed with an Ionic colonnade on the ground floor. In 1920 the property was acquired for a hospital and the mansion was occupied in 1969 as a nurses' home.[74]

Among houses at Woodford Green which no longer exist was Hereford House, an early timber-framed building, described as 'ancient' in 1815. This stood at the north-west corner of (old) Snakes Lane.[75] Its name derived from Price Devereux, 10th Viscount Hereford, who was admitted tenant in 1739, after the death, several years earlier, of Leicester Martin, whose daughter and heir, Elizabeth, Devereux's wife, died before admission. Devereux died in 1748, when the property passed under his will to Robert Moxon whose son John let it as the poorhouse; after John's death his father's trustees sold it to Nicholas Pearse.[76] There was a tradition that it was once a hunting-seat of the earl of Essex.[77] The house was pulled down by Brice Pearse between 1820 and 1838,[78] after the diversion of Snakes Lane. The many-gabled Grove House stood on the Green near the present entrance to Snakes Lane. It was built by John Lambert, a London grocer: arms of the Grocers' Company figured in the internal decorations and a stone escutcheon outside bore Lambert's initials and those of his third wife with the date 1580. One room had wall-paintings of rural scenes dated 1617. The house was demolished in 1832, but some relics of it were preserved in Essex House, which was built on the site; these were destroyed when Essex House was bombed in 1944.[79] Prospect House, a large Georgian building erected by Robert Moxon and occupied by him in 1777,[80] has also disappeared.

There was little residential development at Woodford Wells until the 19th century. A group of detached and semi-detached houses, mostly dating from the first half of the century, were still standing at the corner of Inmans Row and along the east side of High Road in 1969 (even nos. 488–514). Adjoining them a stucco terrace of three-storey houses was empty and derelict. Further north the Horse and Well was almost the only survivor of a slightly earlier row of buildings. On the opposite side of the road, to the south of Bancroft's school, some generously spaced mid-19th-century houses were fast disappearing in 1969, but surviving older buildings included Ivy House dating from the early

[70] C. S. Jones, *Fifty Pictures* (1st edn.), 64.
[71] *Woodford Antiq. Soc.* v. 9 (late 18th cent. print).
[72] Ibid. 1–24 and note of Sept. 1937; E.R.O., Sale Cat. A18; J. E. Tuffs, *Wanstead and Woodford*, 114; Pevsner, *Essex* (2nd edn.). 434 n.; *Wanstead and Woodford Official Guide* (1964–5), 47.
[73] Lysons, *London*, iv. 283–4; *Gent. Mag.* 1789, 583 (illus.); cf. *V.C.H. Essex, Bibliography*, 137.
[74] Pevsner, *Essex* (2nd edn.), 434; *Wanstead and Woodford Official Guide* (1964–5), 59. For Harts Hospital, see below, p. 343, and for Warner's Pond c. 1770 see plate f.p. 354.
[75] E.R.O., D/DCy P2B, ff. 194–5, 253 (plan); B. Page, *Fifty Pictures* (2nd edn.), 29 (illus.); Tuffs, *Wanstead and Woodford*, 29.
[76] E.R.O., D/DCw M27 (ff. 31–4, 42, 99, 108), M28 (ff. 245–8), M32/1–2; Erith, *Woodford*, 29–30, 37–8;

E.R.O., D/DB T657. Its use as the poorhouse (1792–1820) later led to the misconception that Hereford House was on the site of the later Manor House and Bancroft's School: Page, *Fifty Pictures*, 29; Tuffs, *Wanstead and Woodford*, 29.
[77] *Woodford Antiq. Soc.* viii. 2 n. It is curious that Elizabeth's father was called 'Leicester', a name also held by the 6th and 7th Viscounts Hereford. A John Devereux was living in Woodford in c. 1623–32 (E.R.O., D/DCw M19, 20) and if there was some connexion between the Martin and Devereux families in Woodford before the marriage of Elizabeth to Price Devereux, there may be substance in the tradition.
[78] E.R.O., Q/RHi 4/28 (plan), D/CT 408 (tithe map).
[79] *Gent. Mag.* 1828 (1), 208, and 1833 (2), 393; *Woodford Antiq. Soc.* viii. (illus.); R.C.H.M. *Essex*, ii. 269.
[80] *Hist. Essex by Gent.* iv. 204 (illus.); Chapman and André, *Map of Essex* (1777), sheet xvi.

19th century, where Edward Forster the younger lived from 1834 until his death in 1849, and the late-18th-century mansion, formerly called the Oaks, which became the Convent of the Poor Clares in 1920.[81] To the east of the junction of High Road and Epping New Road such houses as Knighton House and Nottingham Villas[82] had given way by 1969 to modern residential development, but Knighton Villas, four large three-storey pairs of *c.* 1850, were still standing. Scattered houses and cottages built in the first half of the 19th century in Whitehall Road also remained.

At Woodford Bridge, where most of the development has taken place in the 20th century, a few cottages have survived from the former hamlet. A row in Chigwell Road, opposite the White Hart, dates from the 18th and early 19th centuries, but two of the cottages and an 18th-century house called the Chestnuts were demolished in 1969. The older buildings on the opposite side of the road have mostly been replaced. Three of the larger residences in the area are still standing. Gwynne House in Manor Road, on the site of the medieval tenement of Guynes, was rebuilt or remodelled in 1816 by Henry Burmester, his architect being J. B. Papworth.[83] It is a two-storey mansion of brown brick with a frontage of seven bays and a central Doric porch. The property, comprising 64 a., was acquired by Dr. Barnardo's Homes in 1910 and during the next twenty years detached houses for boys were erected in the grounds. The chapel, a large building of brown brick dating from 1932 and designed in a free Perpendicular style by W. H. Godfrey, ceased to be used for services in 1968.[84] The former Roding House in Roding Lane North is also part of the Homes. It is a tall three-storey building of the later 18th century with a central porch supported on fluted Doric columns. Thurlby House in Chigwell Road, occupied as a branch library, is a late-18th-century building with a two-storey front, originally of five bays; later additions include an early-19th-century Tuscan porch and a bay-window. The house was occupied by Dr. Barnardo's Homes before the Second World War, and in 1927 a small graveyard was consecrated in its then extensive grounds. Although surrounded by a council housing estate in 1969, the graveyard was still in use.[85]

Woodford's residential nature was emphasized by its roads: in the early 18th century it was comparatively easy to reach the place from London, more difficult to pass beyond it.[86] Of the two present main roads from London the 'lower road', now called Chigwell Road, was subject to flooding by the river and by the mill stream.[87] It was often presented as being in need of repair, not least when King

James I wished to pass along it.[88] Additional hazards were the bridges. In 1404 attention was drawn to the condition of Woodford Bridge, 'Mellebregge', and 'Herryesbregge'. The last-named, for which the lessees of Woodford Hall and Hill House were jointly responsible, must have crossed the Roding between those two estates.[89] Woodford bridge was a horse bridge until 1573, when the lord of the manor agreed to replace it with a cart bridge, he paying one-fifth costs and the county four-fifths. The same proportions were to be observed in paying for repairs.[90] The new bridge was still incomplete in 1605 and there were frequent complaints about its inadequacy and disputes as to who should pay for its repair.[91] By 1680 there was an adjoining foot bridge.[92] In 1768 a stone bridge, planned in 1752, was built. This was destroyed by floods and rebuilt in 1771.[93] It consisted of three semicircular arches of brown brick with stone rustications; the approach walls were splayed. Responsibility for its upkeep passed in 1785 to the Middlesex and Essex turnpike trust, which was reimbursed by quarter sessions,[94] and ultimately to the county council.[95] It was replaced in 1962 by a new and wider bridge. Further south along the lower road, at the point where a stream joins the Roding near the present Wansford Road, was Winn bridge. It was frequently in need of repair since, like Woodford bridge before 1573, responsibility for its upkeep rested with the lord of the manor.[96] It also passed into the care of the Middlesex and Essex turnpike trust,[97] and was adopted as a county bridge in 1872.[98]

The 'upper road', being neither the main highway from London nor an important parish thoroughfare, suffered even more neglect than the lower road. Only towards the end of the 17th century, after the road had been opened up as far as Harlow, did traffic increase. In 1721 the Middlesex and Essex turnpike trust was created to develop the road from Whitechapel to the end of Woodford and was so successful that in 1736 it was given control over the lower road as well.[99] The trust built Woodford New Road, from Walthamstow to Woodford Wells, in 1828,[1] and this, joined with the Epping New Road, begun by the Epping and Ongar highway trust in 1834, provided a high-class turnpike road running along the western boundary of Woodford and avoiding the awkward gradients through Buckhurst Hill.[2]

Snakes Lane, which joined the upper and lower roads, was often flooded by the Roding. In 1820 its course west of a pond, on a site now marked by the Broadway next to Woodford station, was diverted in a more southerly direction to reach the Green by way of Foules Lane. Previously it had turned sharply north for about 150 yards before bearing

[81] For Edward Forster see p. 251, and for the Poor Clares see p. 355.
[82] O.S. Map 1/2,500, Essex LXV. 3 (1864).
[83] Colvin, *Biog. Dict. Eng. Architects*, 440.
[84] Inf. from Superintendent, Dr. Barnardo's Homes, Woodford Bridge.
[85] Ibid.
[86] For a parallel modern illustration cf. *Official Guide*, 49: trolley buses were allowed to come only as far as the borough border.
[87] E.R.O., Q/SR 43/119, 111/41; see also below, p. 349.
[88] Erith, *Woodford*, 94–5; *E.R.* xvii. 167.
[89] S.C. 2/174/42A. The mill bridge was a foot bridge.
[90] E.R.O., Q/SR 169/71.

[91] E.R.O., Q/SR 170/67, and Q/SR *passim*, and Q/CP 2, 3 *passim*.
[92] E.R.O., Q/CP 3, f. 470.
[93] Erith, *Woodford*, 98; *E.A.T.* N.S. xxi, f.p. 152.
[94] E.R.O., Q/ABp 1.
[95] E.R.O., Q/ABz 1 sqq.
[96] C 47/58/300; E.R.O., Q/SR 19/27 and 42, 74/33, 93/19; E.R.O., Q/CP 2 and 3.
[97] Erith, *Woodford*, 100.
[98] E.R.O., Q/ABp 55, Q/ABz 2/4, Q/ABz 3.
[99] Erith, *Woodford*, 94, 100–1.
[1] *Official Guide* (1964–5).
[2] Erith, *Woodford*, 102; B. Winstone, *Epping and Ongar Highway Trust*, 205.

westwards to the Green, which it met just north of the present Monkhams Avenue. At the same time Warner's Path was diverted farther to the west, narrowing the Green and extending the boundaries of the estates on the east side of it; and a new road was made across the Green from the turnpike road (High Road) to Monkhams Lane, replacing the old entry to the lane by Hereford House. Brice Pearse of Monkhams, who gained most from these diversions, had agreed with the vestry to rebuild Snakes Lane on the present shorter course, and also paid £1,000 towards a new workhouse.[3]

In the late 18th and early 19th centuries the upper and lower roads, together with Snakes Lane and George Lane, the latter connecting South Woodford with the lower road, were the only thoroughfares through the parish. Two lanes led westwards through the forest to Chingford Hatch, and another branched southwards from the High Road to Wanstead; a bequest for this purpose had been made in 1625.[4] In the north of the parish Monkhams Lane led from Woodford Wells to a farm. There were also a few turnings off the High Road and paths across the Green.

In 1856 the Eastern Counties railway extended its line to Woodford,[5] bisecting the parish. Stations were built at Snakes Lane and George Lane, where the railway crossed the existing connecting roads of the parish. A loop line to Ilford, with a halt at Roding Valley, Chigwell, was opened in 1903.[6] The railway was electrified in 1947, when it was taken over by London Transport.[7] This had the effect of closing the level crossings at Snakes Lane and George Lane, a pedestrian subway being provided at the first and a flyover bridge at the second. After the closure of Snakes Lane to through traffic, Broadmead Road, with a new bridge over the line, became the main connecting link between the upper and lower roads. During the development of building estates in the late 19th and 20th centuries many new local roads came into being to serve them. In 1932 the Southend arterial road, crossing the south of the parish from west to east, was built as an extension of the North Circular Road.[8] By the 1960s both this and the High Road, the latter one of the principal north-eastern routes out of London, were carrying continuous streams of heavy traffic through Woodford.

Public road transport was slow to serve Woodford. In 1823 25 coaches a day passed between London and Epping.[9] In the 1860s coaches ran through Woodford from Chigwell to London, and some started in the village; a horse bus ran along the upper road from Buckhurst Hill until about 1870.[10] But in 1891 the horse tramway from Clapton was taken only as far as the Walthamstow section of Woodford New Road, and in 1911 the motor bus route from

Elephant and Castle ended at Wanstead. The first motor bus service to Woodford Bridge started in 1914.[11]

The roads had been used to carry mails from a much earlier date. From 1692 Woodford was within the area covered by the London penny post.[12] There was a receiving house there in 1794.[13] Woodford became a head office, in the north-eastern district of London, in 1856.[14] Further sub-division in 1917 put the southern third of Woodford in the E. 18 district, the rest of the parish remaining as the Woodford Green district, which had been constituted in 1880.[15] It was possible to telegraph from Woodford post office in 1870.[16] A telephone exchange was opened by the National Telephone Co. in 1904.[17] Since 1927 subscribers have been served by the Buckhurst exchange.[18]

In 1864 the West Ham Gas Co., which since 1856 had been empowered to supply gas to Woodford, relinquished its interest in all except the south-west corner of the parish to the Chigwell and Woodford Bridge Gas Co., formed in 1863. The works of the latter were situated between Snakes Lane and the Roding, near Woodford Bridge.[19] Both companies were later absorbed by the Gas Light and Coke Co., which was in turn transferred to the North Thames gas board in 1949.[20] In 1924 the County of London Electric Supply Co. was authorized to supply Woodford,[21] which it did two years later.[22]

Water was drawn from wells and pumps, some of which still survive; the iron pump at Woodford Bridge, erected in 1834,[23] lasted until 1962. After 1859 some water was piped to Woodford by the East London Waterworks Co., and by 1914 its successor, the Metropolitan water board, was supplying every house in the parish.[24]

A committee was appointed in 1831, during a cholera scare, to remove minor nuisances, but it was left to the local board to introduce substantial sanitary reforms.[25] In 1882 they were empowered to purchase land for sewage works on the river Ching to serve the north-east district, and on the river Roding, by Winn Bridge, to serve the rest.[26] The former now drains into the Chingford system and the latter, recently modernized, serves the greater part of Woodford.[27]

A fire-engine was purchased about 1820 and kept at the workhouse.[28] By 1882 there was a fire station, which soon moved to Horn Lane, and by 1898 a fire brigade at Maybank Road had been started on a voluntary basis.[29]

The Jubilee hospital, Woodford Green, was opened in 1899, having been financed by (Sir) John Roberts (Bt.). It has been extended to provide 54 beds.[30] Harts House was bought by East Ham council in 1920 and used as a hospital for some years

[3] E.R.O., Q/RHi 4/28; Erith, *Woodford*, 44, 102–4.
[4] *E.A.T.* N.S. xiii. 114; cf. *V.C.H. Essex*, v. 99.
[5] *V.C.H. Essex*, v. 24.   [6] *E.R.* lix. 60.
[7] *V.C.H. Essex*, v. 72
[8] Tuffs, *Wanstead and Woodford*, 115.
[9] *Woodford Antiq. Soc. Proc.* ii. 16–17.
[10] J. E. Tuffs, *Wanstead and Woodford*, 87; E. Poultney, *Twenty-five Years Ago*, 1.
[11] *V.C.H. Essex*, v. 27, 29.
[12] T. De Laune, *Present State of London* (1692).
[13] G. Brumell, *Local Posts of London 1680–1840*, 90.
[14] *Brit. Postal Guide*, 1856.
[15] *Post Office Guide*, 1917, 1880.
[16] *Kelly's Dir. Essex*, 1870.

[17] *Nat. Telephone Jnl.* Oct. 1907, p. 135.
[18] *G.P.O. List of Telephone Exchanges*, 1927 f.
[19] E.R.O., D/DLc T47.
[20] *V.C.H. Essex*, v. 45, 75.   [21] Ibid. 75.
[22] J. E. Tuffs, *Wanstead and Woodford*, 116.
[23] Erith, *Woodford*, 79.
[24] Tuffs, op. cit. 71, 106; *V.C.H. Essex*, v. 38, 40.
[25] Erith, op. cit. 57, 79.
[26] 45 & 46 Vict. c. 64 (local act).
[27] *Official Guide* (1964–5).
[28] Erith, op. cit. 79.
[29] *Kelly's Dirs. Essex*, 1882, 1890, 1898. Cf. E. Poultney, *Twenty-five Years Ago*, 12.
[30] *Official Guide* (1964–5); *Kelly's Dir. Essex*, 1906.

until ward blocks were built. These now provide 100 beds. The hospital specializes in chest complaints.[31]

Much land has been set aside for recreational purposes. The Ashton playing fields at Woodford Bridge cover 50 a.; the facilities for athletics, cricket, football, and tennis are administered by a trust. A council sports ground of 32 a. lies to the west of Roding Lane North, Ray Park of 30 a. is north of Snakes Lane, and Old Mill playing field (26 a.) and Nightingale recreation ground (40 a.) adjoin the Roding in the south-east. There are several private sports grounds, a golf course, opened in 1890,[32] which extends into Walthamstow, and a number of smaller pleasure gardens. Indoor recreations may be found in the Sir James Hawkey Hall, opened by the council in 1955.[33] The Wilfred Lawson temperance hotel, founded by Andrew Johnston and erected in a commanding position on Woodford Green in 1883, was similarly used. For some years the urban district council had offices there.[34] It is now (1965) used as a nurses' training centre. The Plaza cinema, George Lane, was built in 1932 and the Majestic cinema, High Road, in 1935.[35]

A parish library was begun in 1828,[36] and by 1863 there was a literary institute, which seems to have closed by 1870.[37] Woodford Art and Industrial society was established in 1877 to encourage amateur skill; it had ceased to exist by 1926.[38] Until 1965 library services in Woodford were provided by the Essex county council, which opened three branches, at South Woodford, Woodford Bridge, and Woodford Green. The last of these, at the Broadway, was opened in 1961.[39] A wide variety of social, cultural, and sporting activities is available,[40] some organizations, such as the Women's Institute, being particularly strong.[41]

Many of Woodford's more distinguished residents have been wealthy landowners. Among them were at least three lord mayors: Sir John Lyon and Benjamin Thorowgood, who were lords of the manor,[42] and Sir Thomas White (lord mayor in 1877).[43] Michael Godfrey (d. 1695), son of a London merchant who lived at the Rookery, George Lane, became deputy governor of the Bank of England, which he had helped to establish.[44] Job Matthew, governor of the Bank, was buried at Woodford in 1802.[45] Sir Thomas Rowe, the explorer and diplomatist, was lord of Woodford manor, and was buried in the church.[46] Another man who travelled widely and wrote about his experiences was Godfrey T. Vigne (1801–63) whose home, the Oaks in the High Road, was perhaps more widely known for the pack of harriers kept there.[47]

Sydney Smith (1771–1845), wit, and preacher, was born at Woodford,[48] as was Arthur W. Haddan (1816–73), historian and biblical scholar.[49] Few rectors distinguished themselves,[50] but of the curates, Thomas Maurice (1754–1824), who left the curacy in 1785, is remembered for his *Indian Antiquities*[51] and J. M. Rodwell (1808–1900) was another orientalist.[52] Among architects Thomas Leverton (1743–1824) returned to the village of his birth to design Woodford Hall in 1771[53] and J. B. Papworth (1775–1847) directed the building of Ray Lodge as the first stage of his distinguished career as an architect and draughtsman.[54] G. Street (1824–81), one of the leading architects of the Gothic revival, was a native.[55] Literary figures include Coventry Patmore, the poet, who was born at Woodford in 1823,[56] and William Morris, writer, artist, and craftsman, who spent his childhood at Woodford Hall 1840–8.[57] E. Sylvia Pankhurst (d. 1960), suffragette leader and writer, lived at Woodford for many years.[58]

Sir Winston Churchill (1874–1965) represented Woodford in Parliament from 1924 to 1964. In 1959 a bronze statue of him was erected on Woodford Green.

MANORS. The manor of *WOODFORD HALL*, which comprised the greater part of the parish, is first mentioned in the charter of doubtful authenticity by which Edward the Confessor confirmed Harold's grant of lands to the canons of Waltham Holy Cross.[59] The boundaries of the manor then stretched westwards from *Angrices burne* (the river Roding) to *ealdermannes hæcce* and *cynges hæcce*. If the last was Chingford Hatch, the alderman's hatch must have been in the south-west corner of Woodford;[60] a gate called Grovehacche, near Hall Grove, close to the point where the vills of Walthamstow, Wanstead, and Woodford met, was mentioned in 1414.[61] The manor granted to Waltham provided the prebend of one canon, and from it he had to furnish the community with rations for two weeks in the year.[62] The northern portion of Woodford, known as Monkhams, did not belong to Waltham Abbey but to Stratford Langthorne Abbey.[63] Most of the parish east of the river belonged to Hill House. This messuage may originally have been copyhold of Woodford Hall, later enfranchised.[64] From the 15th century it was regarded as a demesne tenement of the manor,[65] and in grants after the Dissolution the manor and Hill House are always mentioned as distinct properties.

[31] *Official Guide* (1964–5); see also above, p. 24.
[32] *V.C.H. Essex*, ii. 594.
[33] *Official Guide* (1964–5); inf. from Branch Librarian, Woodford Green.
[34] *Kelly's Dirs. Essex*, 1886, 1898, 1906; *E.R.* xxxi. 114.
[35] J. E. Tuffs, *Wanstead and Woodford*, 113–14.
[36] *Official Guide* (1964–5).
[37] *V.C.H. Essex, Bibliography*, 321.
[38] *Kelly's Dir. Essex*, 1882, 1922, 1926.
[39] *Official Guide* (1964–5).
[40] Ibid.
[41] Willmott and Young, *Family and Class in a London Suburb*, 88, 98.
[42] See below, p. 345.
[43] *Official Guide* (1964–5).
[44] *D.N.B.*; *E.R.* xxx. 240.
[45] Ogborne, *Essex*, 72.
[46] *D.N.B.*; *E.R.* xx. 135.
[47] *D.N.B.*; *V.C.H. Essex*, ii. 579.

[48] *E.R.* vi. 137.
[49] *D.N.B.*
[50] See below, p. 353.
[51] *D.N.B.*; *E.R.* xlvi. 49.
[52] *D.N.B.*
[53] Ibid.
[54] Ibid.
[55] Ibid.
[56] Ibid.; *E.R.* vi. 23.
[57] J. W. Mackail, *Life of Wm. Morris*, 5–6, 19.
[58] *Who's Who*, 1927 f.; *Who Was Who 1951–60*.
[59] Morant, *Essex*, i. 38; C. Hart, *Early Charters o Essex, Saxon Period*, p. 30.
[60] *P.N. Essex*, 110.
[61] S.C. 2/173/34.
[62] W. Winters, *Hist. Waltham Abbey*, 150.
[63] See below.
[64] Cf. *Bracton's Note Bk.*, ed. Maitland, iii. 527.
[65] S.C. 2/174/42A.

The canons of Waltham retained Woodford after the Conquest. In 1086 the manor comprised 5 hides and was valued at 100s.[66] When Waltham was reconstituted by Henry II in 1177, he confirmed its possessions, including the manor and church of Woodford.[67] The abbey acquired more lands in Woodford during the 13th century, including a messuage and 60 a. of land worth 100s. a year, which about 1258 were appropriated by the abbot, claiming the convent's foundation charter as his authority: the land had been forfeited when Margaret, wife of John atte Mille of Woodford, was executed for murdering her husband.[68] This holding can be traced in 1468,[69] and 1536, when the fields of which it was composed included Rowdone and Mellemede.[70]

In 1267 William de Luketon, a lay-brother of Waltham Abbey, was entrusted with the keeping of the manor.[71] During the last two centuries of the abbey's existence, the abbots leased the Woodford demesnes to a succession of tenants. William Sandre was the lessee in 1404[72] and William Tynge in 1465.[73] In the later 15th and early 16th centuries the Hickman family lived there.[74] In 1538, just before the Dissolution, the manor, together with Hill House, was let to William Waverley for £30 p.a.[75] At that date the fixed rents accruing to the manor amounted to £4 7s. 10d., out of which 3s. 4d. was paid to the woodward, and 4s. was paid for a pasture of 10 a. called Eldbury.[76]

In 1541, after the Dissolution, Robert Fuller, the last abbot of Waltham, obtained a grant for life of the manor of Woodford with many other estates.[77] These he enjoyed for little more than a year. In 1545 Henry VIII granted to (Sir) John Lyon, alderman and grocer of London, and Alice his wife, the manor of Woodford, with Hill House, Eldbury, and the advowson of the rectory.[78] In 1547 the Crown recovered the manor from Lyon,[79] in exchange for other land, mostly in Berkshire but including Monkhams in Woodford, and granted it to Sir Anthony Browne, master of the horse, and his (second) wife, Elizabeth. None of Browne's children by Elizabeth survived and, after his death in 1548,[80] the reversion of the manor was granted in 1552 to Elizabeth's second husband, Edward Fiennes, Lord Clinton and Say,[81] whom she married in that year.[82]

In 1553 Fiennes was licensed to alienate the manor to Robert Whetstone, citizen and haberdasher of London,[83] which he did early in 1554.[84] Whetstone was a rich man, with estates in several counties. He died in 1557 or 1558,[85] having devised the manor of Woodford to Bernard, his eldest son by his second wife Margaret.[86] Bernard was still alive in 1601,[87] but by 1603 he had been succeeded by his son, Sir Bernard Whetstone,[88] who lived outside the county.[89] Sir Bernard (d. 1624) was succeeded by his son, also called Bernard.[90] The last-named Bernard sold the manor in 1639 to his mortgagee, Sir William Acton,[91] having previously sold 'most of the copyholds and almost all the demesnes', leaving rents of only £140 out of an original £600.[92] Acton conveyed the manor in 1640 to Sir Thomas Rowe (d. 1644), the traveller and diplomatist.[93] Rowe's widow Eleanor held the manor until her death in 1675,[94] after which her trustee and executor Sir Thomas St. George sold it in 1678 to (Sir) Benjamin Thorowgood, alderman of London, who became lord mayor in 1685.[95] Thorowgood (d. 1694) was followed by his son Richard,[96] who in 1710 sold the estate to Sir Richard Child, lord of the manor of Wanstead.[97] Woodford manor was then incorporated in the Wanstead estate with which it subsequently descended.[98]

Although Sir Richard Child retained the manor of Woodford, he sold the hall and most of the remaining demesne lands to Christopher Crow, so that by 1838 only about 80 a. in Woodford remained as part of the Wanstead estate.[99] Crow sold the hall to William Hunt in 1727, after obtaining a private Act of Parliament.[1] The hall remained in that family until about 1801 when it was bought by John Maitland.[2] In 1777 the hall, with 56 a. lying behind and a further 92 a., was leased to John Goddard, a Rotterdam merchant,[3] whose widow died there in 1814.[4] By 1820 Maitland himself had taken up residence.[5] He inherited the manor of Loughton in 1825[6] and died at Woodford Hall in 1831.[7] His son William Whitaker Maitland succeeded him and leased the hall first to William Cox,[8] then, in 1840, to William Morris, father of William Morris the poet and craftsman. The Morris family remained there until 1848.[9] In 1869 the Woodford Hall estate was sold to the British Land Co. for building development.

[66] V.C.H. Essex, i. 446.
[67] J. Farmer, Hist. Waltham Abbey, 40.
[68] B.M. Add. MS. 37665, f. 240. The document is dated 43rd year of the reign (presumably Henry III). The holding is not mentioned in an extent of the manor of c. 1235.
[69] S.C. 2/173/38.
[70] E.R.O., D/DCw M16.
[71] Cal. Pat. 1266–72, 62.
[72] S.C. 2/174/42A.
[73] B.M. Add. MS. 37665, f. 258.
[74] Misc. Gen. Her., 5th ser., v. 193; Genealogist, N.S. xvii, 279.
[75] S.C. 6/964, m. 110.   [76] Ibid. m. 111.
[77] L. & P. Hen. VIII, xvi, p. 715.
[78] Ibid. xx(2), p. 223.
[79] Ibid. xxi(2), p. 409; Cal. Pat. 1547, 39–41.
[80] D.N.B.
[81] Cal. Pat. 1550–53, 366; ibid. 1553, 168.
[82] D.N.B.
[83] Cal. Pat. 1553–4, 350. The name is variously spelt Whetstons, Whitestones, Whetstone.
[84] C.P. 25(2)/70/577.
[85] In 1558 his widow presented to the rectory: Newcourt, Repertorium, ii. 680.
[86] E.A.T. N.S. xiv. 42.
[87] E.R.O., Q/SR 155/24.

[88] W. R. Fisher, Forest of Essex, 59.
[89] E.R.O., Q/SR 169/85.
[90] Visits. of Essex (Harl. Soc.), i. 520; C 142/430/167; Morant, Essex, i. 38.
[91] E.R.O., D/DCy T2; D/DCw T4 (deed of 1637).
[92] E. J. Erith, Woodford, Essex, 1600–1836, 98: possibly an exaggeration.
[93] Lysons, London (1796 edn.), iv. 274; E.R.O., D/DCw T4 (deed of 1640); E.R. xx. 135–143.
[94] Morant, Essex, i. 38.
[95] E.R.O., D/DCw M26, D/DMe T1/5, 7–11.
[96] Morant, Essex, i. 38.
[97] E.R.O., D/DMe T1/15, 16, 19, 20.
[98] See p. 324.
[99] E.R.O., D/CT 408, D/DMe T1/38–54; Morant, Essex, i. 38.
[1] Morant, Essex, i. 38; 1 Geo. II, c. 8 (priv. act).
[2] Lysons, London, Suppl. (1811), 364; E.R.O., Q/RPl 74, 75.
[3] E.R.O., D/DMe T5/1; D.N.B.: Sir Ch. M. Pole.
[4] Gent. Mag. 1814 (i), 96.
[5] Ibid. 1820 (ii), 563.
[6] V.C.H. Essex, iv. 119.
[7] Gent. Mag. 1831 (i), 380.
[8] E.R.O., D/CT 408.
[9] J. W. Mackail, Life of William Morris, 5–6, 19.

The house was used until 1900 as Mrs. Gladstone's convalescent home.[10] It was then demolished and the parish church memorial hall was built in front of the site in 1902.[11] The chapel of the convalescent home survives as part of a house in Buckingham Road.[12]

The original manor-house was probably at Woodford Bridge, where the field name Eldbury, mentioned above, survived until the 16th century. Before 1235, however, another house was in use, on the 'upper' road.[13] A map of about 1700 shows the demesne lands, including Hall Grove at the southwest corner of the parish.[14] It is crudely drawn but gives a fairly detailed elevation of the old hall, which was a gabled three-storey building, apparently of the early 17th century. By 1771, William Hunt, nephew of the purchaser of 1727, had pulled down the hall and was in process of rebuilding it,[15] to the design of Thomas Leverton.[16] Expensive improvements to this property, especially to the garden in front of the house, were carried out in 1804[17] in accordance with designs by Humphry Repton; but his plan for a large portico with Ionic columns does not seem to have been carried out,[18] for Victorian prints show short, curving flights of steps leading up, over a semi-basement, to the front door. The hall was a three-storey building with a frontage of five bays, the middle three of which were slightly advanced and surmounted by a pediment. The main block was flanked by single-storey wings with hipped roofs.[19] This house was set in about 50 a. of park.[20] In 1810 Charles Bacon designed an entrance gateway and a ruin in the park.[21]

The custom of Borough English prevailed in this manor.[22] Several examples of succession to a copyhold by the youngest son are known for the period 1488 to 1536.[23] The custom was still in being at the beginning of the 20th century.[24]

The manor of MONKHAMS alias BUCKHURST alias MUNCKENHILL was a small estate extending into Chigwell.[25] William de Montfitchet endowed the abbey of Stratford Langthorne with his wood of Buckhurst in 1135,[26] and this became known as Monkenbuckhurst to distinguish it from other beech hursts in the area.[27] The estate was augmented by grants of land in Chigwell, but part of it was always in Woodford. In 1253 the abbot of Stratford was granted free warren on his demesnes at Woodford and elsewhere,[28] and in 1291 he was taxed for temporalities in Woodford worth £1 a year.[29] Early-16th-century references in the Woodford court rolls indicate that the land lay to the north of the old Sakes (now Snakes) Lane.[30] By 1640 the name 'Monkham' was used for some of the woodland between Sakes Lane and the parish boundary, but the original estate probably extended eastwards towards Rayhouse as well as including land in Buckhurst Hill to the north.[31] It was never called a manor in medieval times, and the abbot of Waltham, probably as lord of the manor of Woodford Hall, claimed jurisdiction over it in 1525,[32] but in 1630 royalties there were claimed on behalf of the owner of Buckhurst,[33] and in 1646 it was described as a manor or farm.[34]

In 1547, after the Dissolution, Edward VI granted the tenement called Buckhurst alias Monkhill and the wood called Monkgrove to Alderman Sir John Lyon of London and Alice his wife in part-exchange for the manor of Woodford Hall; Buckhurst was to be held in chief by $\frac{1}{40}$ knight's fee and Monkgrove was to be held in free socage.[35] For the remainder of the 16th century the estate descended as described under Chigwell parish.[36] During the 17th century it consisted of 3 or 4 tenements and about 300 a., and was generally leased in two parts. In 1612 George and John Lyon sold the property to James Holden,[37] who then granted John a 99-year lease of the larger part.[38] In 1616 John Lyon granted the residue of his term to Thomas Hill,[39] who acquired the freehold a few days later.[40] Hill acquired both the freehold and leasehold interests of the remaining part of the estate in 1631–2.[41] In 1646 the whole property was again on a 99-year lease and this passed to[42] William and George Nutt in 1649.[43] In that year the property was split up afresh when the freehold reversion of the larger moiety, lying almost entirely in Chigwell, was conveyed to the Nutts.[44] It was this portion which descended with the Nutt family and was eventually merged with the Luxborough estate in Chigwell. It included Little Monkhams in Woodford, which in 1838 was owned by Christopher Mills and let to Jonas Death.[45]

Possession of the other moiety, lying entirely in Woodford and including Monkham Grove, remained with the Hill family: there are various references to its members living at Monkhams in the later 17th and early 18th centuries.[46] John Hill of Enfield (Mdx.) felled wood there from at least 1718 until

[10] E. Walford, *Greater London*, i. 459–61; 'Scrutator Diaconalis' [A. Fuller], *The Church at George Lane* (1909), 15.
[11] Date on building.
[12] J. E. Tuffs, *Wanstead and Woodford*, 103.
[13] See above, p. 338.
[14] E.R.O., D/DCw P1.
[15] *Hist. Essex by Gent.* iv. 203.
[16] *D.N.B.*
[17] *E.R.* xxxvii. 102.
[18] E.R.O., T/B 92; O.S. Map 6″, Essex, LXV (1863–76 edn.).
[19] E.R.O., Pictorial Coll.; print formerly in the possession of the late Canon J. L. Fisher.
[20] J. W. Mackail, *Life of William Morris*, 5.
[21] H. M. Colvin, *Biog. Dict. Eng. Architects*, 51.
[22] Morant, *Essex*, i. 39.
[23] E.R.O., D/DCw M16 (admissions to copyholds enrolled by cellarer of Waltham Abbey).
[24] *V.C.H. Essex*, ii. 319 n.
[25] It has been described in so far as it relates to Chigwell in *V.C.H. Essex*, iv. 28.
[26] B.M. Harl. Ch. 53, E 15.

[27] A. R. J. Ramsey, *Monkhams* (Woodford Hist. Soc. pt. xi), 2–3.
[28] *Cal. Chart. R.* 1226–57, 433.
[29] *Tax. Eccl.* (Rec. Com.), 26.
[30] S.C. 2/174/42B; see also S.C. 12/Port. 7/54.
[31] Ramsey, *Monkhams*, 6–7; map of foresters' walks in Waltham Forest reproduced in *E.R.* xiv. pl. bef. p. 193.
[32] *E.R.* xiv. 169.
[33] *Cal. S.P. Dom.* 1629–31, 345.
[34] E.R.O., D/DB T346.
[35] *Cal. Pat.* 1547–8, 39, 41; *Cal. S.P. Dom.* 1547–80, 4.
[36] *V.C.H. Essex*, iv. 28, to which this paragraph is supplementary.
[37] E.R.O., D/DB T346.   [38] E.R.O., D/DDa T32.
[39] E.R.O., D/DDa T40.
[40] E.R.O., D/DDa T41.
[41] E.R.O., D/DDa T39 and T32.
[42] E.R.O., D/DB T346.
[43] E.R.O., D/DDa T39.
[44] E.R.O., D/DDa T39 and T42.
[45] E.R.O., D/DDa T43, D/CT 408 (no. 377).
[46] E.R.O., D/DB T346; D/DCw M 23, 26; Erith, *Woodford*, 69; *Woodford Antiq. Soc. Proc.* i. 9–10.

1733[47] when he mortgaged his freehold.[48] By 1735 Thomas North had an interest in the premises.[49] He and his wife Mary, who were rated as of 'Muncomegrove' in 1738, built a new house.[50] Their son Thomas Cox North sold the property in 1760 to Eliab Harvey (d. 1769).[51] In 1775 Harvey's executors obtained statutory power to sell it,[52] and they did so soon after to Sir James Wright of Rayhouse.[53] Wright auctioned part of his Woodford estates in 1803: Monkham Farm was bought by George Brown and Monkham House, leased since 1795 to Mrs. Pearse,[54] by Nicholas Pearse,[55] who conveyed it to Brice Pearse in 1809.[56] The Pearse family had already acquired Hereford House, the adjoining property.[57] Brice Pearse died in 1812 but his son, also Brice,[58] continued to build up the estate. In 1814 he acquired Monkham Farm from George Brown and, during the next few years, various fields near Snakes Lane.[59] About 1820 he bought from John Hall a large mansion and other property on the south side of Snakes Lane.[60] Approval given by the justices in 1820 to divert Snakes Lane to the south-west[61] enabled him to consolidate the enlarged estate, which by 1838 comprised the mansion, renamed Monkham House, Monkham farm-house, the 'old farm-house', and 233 a., mainly pasture.[62] Pearse called part of his estate the manor of Hill House. The original Hill House had been in the opposite, south-east corner of the parish, but its name had later been used for the part of Woodford Hall manor north-west of Monkhams Lane, in which area Pearse had bought land.[63] He died in 1842,[64] and in 1844 Elliot Macnaughton bought the estate.[65] He sold it in 1864 to Henry Ford Barclay.[66] By that time the fields around the house had been turned into a park of some 70 a., 30 a. of which were copyhold of Woodford manor.[67] Before his death in 1891 Barclay extended his holding to include a large part of the original Monkhams wood west of the railway line.[68] In 1892, when Arnold F. Hills purchased the estate for £36,350,[69] it consisted largely of woodland, divided into Knighton wood, Bristow's wood, and Pea Field wood.[70] James Robert Twentyman bought the estate in 1903,[71] and began to sell

building plots. Before 1914 the southern part of the estate had been laid out and, after Twentyman's death in 1928, his trustees disposed of the remainder for development.[72] The name Monkhams has been given to an avenue, a drive, and a lane in the area.

There was a husbandman's dwelling-house at Monkham Grove by 1527.[73] When the estate was divided, the 'capital' house called Buckhurst or Buckhouse, Munckenhill or Monkhams, so distinguished by 1631,[74] remained attached to the Woodford moiety.[75] There were two separate sites of 'Munkom Houses' in c. 1640.[76] One corresponded with the site, astride the Woodford-Chigwell boundary, occupied by Monkham Farm (Chigwell) and the house now known as Little Monkhams, the other with the site to the south-east, near the present railway line, known as Monkham or Lane farm.[77] Monkham farm-house in Chigwell, which was rebuilt in brick by Thomas Hill in c. 1649,[78] was demolished in 1936;[79] but Little Monkhams, a much-altered timber-framed house, probably of the late 16th or early 17th century, was still standing in 1969. Lane farm appears to have occupied the site of the original 'capital' house,[80] which was probably never more than a farm-house. Between 1735 and 1758 Thomas and Mary North built a modest new gentleman's house,[81] about half a mile to the south-west of the farm, on the north side of Snakes Lane, adjoining Hereford House.[82] Their extensive felling and stubbing in Monkham Grove and fencing off of it from the forest between 1737 and 1752 was probably associated with building this house and laying out of its grounds.[83] The house, which was known by 1803 as Monkham House,[84] was pulled down after Brice Pearse bought John Hall's house on the south side of Snakes Lane and transferred the name to it.[85] The second Monkham House was a large two-storey stucco building with a plain parapet. The east front had 5 windows and a Tuscan porch, and the south front had 3 full-height bows, each of 3 windows. It was apparently built in the early 19th century, but if so, it replaced an earlier house, shown on the site in 1777.[86] At the end of the 19th century elaborate fountains and

[47] Ramsey, *Monkhams*, 7.
[48] E.R.O., D/DB T687 (deed of 1733).
[49] E.R.O., D/DB T657 (deed of 1804; schedule).
[50] Ramsey, *Monkhams*, 7–8; E.R.O., D/DB T711.
[51] E.R.O., D/DB T657 (deed of 1760); *Gent. Mag.* 1769, 511.
[52] 15 Geo. III, c. 50 (priv. act).
[53] E.R.O., D/DB T657 (deed of 1804; schedule); D/DB T1322, f. 21.
[54] E.R.O., D/DU 357/14.
[55] E.R.O., D/DB T657 (2 deeds of 1804).
[56] Ibid. (deed of 1829); E.R.O., D/DCy P2A (no. 947) and P2B, f. 39. The Nicholas Pearse of Woodford (d. 1792) and his wife Sarah (d. 1812), the parents of Brice Pearse, must be distinguished from the Nicholas and Sarah Pearse of Loughton, who died in 1825 and 1846 respectively: *Woodford Antiq. Soc. Proc.* i. 8–9; *V.C.H. Essex*, iv. 128.
[57] E.R.O., D/DB T657, D/DCy P2A (no. 944) and P2B, f. 39. For Hereford House, see above, p. 341.
[58] *Woodford Antiq. Soc. Proc.* i. 8–9.
[59] E.R.O., D/DB T657 (deed of 1829), D/DCy P2A (no. 960) and P2B, f. 39.
[60] E.R.O., D/DCy P2B, ff. 37, 196–7, 253, Q/RHi 4/28 (plan).
[61] E.R.O., Q/RHi 4/28.   [62] E.R.O., D/CT 408.
[63] E.R.O., D/DCy P3; *E.R.* xiv. 169.
[64] Plaque in church.   [65] E.R.O., D/DB T1068.
[66] Ibid.   [67] B.M., Maps 136. a. 8 (34).
[68] Ramsey, *Monkhams*, 11.

[69] E.R.O., D/DB T1068; *Sale Cats.* A 325, 1068 (plan).
[70] E.R.O., D/DCy 72, P28.
[71] E.R.O., D/DB T1068 (plan).
[72] Ramsey, *Monkhams*, 11.
[73] *Woodford Antiq. Soc. Proc.* i. 7; *V.C.H. Essex*, iv. 28; *E.R.* xiv. 168.
[74] E.R.O., D/DDa T32, 39.
[75] Cf. E.R.O., D/DDa T32 and D/DB T711.
[76] E.R.O., T/M 5, 147.
[77] Chapman and André, *Map of Essex*, 1777, sheet xvi; O.S. Map 6", Essex, LXV (1868–76 edn.); E.R.O., D/CT 78, 408.
[78] E.R.O., D/DDa T39 (deed of 1649); cf. E.R.O., D/DB T345 (deed of 1669).
[79] *V.C.H. Essex*, iv. 28.
[80] A field called 'The Ridges', always associated with the 'capital' house (e.g. in 1632: E.R.O., D/DDa T32), was close to the 'old farmhouse' in 1838 (E.R.O., D/CT 408).
[81] E.R.O., D/DB T657 (deed of 1804, schedule), D/DB T711.
[82] E.R.O., Q/RHi 4/28, D/DCy P2B, ff. 37, 196–7, 253; Ramsey, *Monkhams*, 8.
[83] Ramsey, *Monkhams*, 7–8.
[84] E.R.O., D/DU 357/14. This sale particular details the rooms in the house.
[85] Cf. E.R.O., D/DU 357/14, D/DCy P2A (no. 947) and P2B, f. 39, and D/CT 408 (no. 286).
[86] *E.R.* xiv. photo, p. 165; E.R.O., Q/RHi 4/28, D/CT 408; Chapman and André, *Map of Essex*, 1777, sheet xvi; Ramsey, *Monkhams*, 10.

illuminations were installed.[87] The house was demolished in 1930 when Park Avenue was built.[88] A new Monkhams farmstead was built between 1825 and 1838, nearer Monkham House and fronting Monkhams Lane to the south-west of the old Lane farm.[89] The old farm-house was still standing in 1892, but when the railway was built in 1856 the line cut though its farm buildings.[90]

The principal estate at Woodford Bridge was *RAYHOUSE*. It was never a manor, though sometimes described as such by confusion with Rayhouse in Barking; until the 19th century it was a copyhold tenement held of the manor of Woodford Hall.[91] Until the 15th century it was held by the family of atte Ree as a messuage and 30 a. of land. William *ad aquam* or atte Ree was holding a virgate at Woodford about 1235–70,[92] Richard is mentioned in 1271,[93] John and William in 1404,[94] and Thomas in 1414.[95] In 1451 John atte Ree, a hereditary bondsman (*nativus de sanguine*) held a heriotable messuage called Rayhouse and 30 a. of land as well as 10 a. of molland,[96] which he surrendered to the use of his wife Joan, with reversion to William Ripton.[97] Ripton's heir, also William, was probably a minor when his father died, because the holding was granted to a London citizen, William Stondon. In 1498 Stondon surrendered Rayhouse to the use of his wife Maud, and on her death in 1514 her brother, John Hykman, succeeded to the property after a dispute. Hykman surrendered Rayhouse to John Hatfield, a London vintner, and Eleanor his wife, to whom William Ripton also released his claim. John Hatfield alias Pylbarough (d. 1518) was followed by his son John Pylbarough, who greatly enlarged the holding, acquiring the copyhold of Old Counsedews, another virgate at Woodford Bridge, the half-virgate of Gales and Netherhouse in Woodford Row, besides several small crofts and pieces of meadow.[98]

John Pylbarough remained as tenant after the Dissolution[99] but his successors cannot be traced until 1663 when William Stone, M.D., and his wife Dorothy, together with Anne, widow of Josiah Clerke, surrendered Rayhouse to the use of John Norman, a London cooper.[1] At the beginning of the 18th century the Cleland family gained possession of the estate[2] but in 1732 William Cleland surrendered it to the use of Alvar Lopez Suasso.[3] In 1736 Suasso conveyed it to James Hannot,[4] who in 1760 leased part of the farm.[5] His heir, Bennet Hannot, sold Rayhouse about 1770 to Sir James Wright, some-

time British minister at Venice, who took up residence in the two-storey five-bay brick mansion.[6] Sir James also acquired several adjacent estates, including Monkhams house and farm.[7] In 1793 he started to build Ray Lodge, near Ray House, for his son George, employing as architect John (later John Buonarotti) Papworth, then aged only 18.[8] Sir James died in 1804 and was succeeded by his son, Sir George Wright, Bt., who in 1807 sold his Rayhouse estate to Benjamin Hanson Inglish.[9] Inglish was admitted to the two houses and 133 a. land.[10] Ray House was then on lease to J. V. Purrier, and Ray Lodge to Sir William Fraser.[11] After Inglish's death in 1834 the lands were split up and auctioned, John Cutts being the largest purchaser.[12] In 1840 the owner of Ray House was Thomas Lewis[13] and in 1876 G. T. Benton.[14] Ray House was rebuilt after a fire at the turn of the century and was sold in 1924 to Bryant & May Ltd. as a country club and sports ground.[15] In 1958 it was sold to the borough council and became a public park.[16]

The name of the early tenants shows that the estate was by the river and a 16th-century reference[17] shows that it covered both banks by 'Reyhouse-brygge'. In a map of 1777 the estate is shown astride the Roding by Woodford Bridge.[18] Ray Lodge has disappeared and all that survives of the 18th-century Ray House is its octagonal walled garden at the north end of Ray Park, still used as a plant nursery. The name of Ray Lodge is preserved in Ray Lodge Road and Ray Lodge Close. Ray Park, the gas works, and the Ashton playing fields now cover most of the rest of the area.

ECONOMIC HISTORY. The wealth of woodland in Woodford long determined the economic life of the village, providing timber and some pasture, while restricting the amount of arable land. The Domesday survey with its estimate that 500 swine could be pastured there indicates that Woodford was densely wooded.[19] Monkhams was originally all wood, and there also pannage was important.[20]

Some clearances had been made in the woodland at an early date. In 1066 there was arable for 2 ploughs on the demesne and for the relatively large number of 13 on the rest of the vill. There were then 13 villeins, 4 bordars, and 4 serfs; by 1086 there were still 13 villeins but 7 bordars, and no serfs; the number of ploughs owned by manorial tenants had fallen to seven. The 26 a. of meadow by the river

---

[87] *E.R.* l. 105. [88] Ramsey, *Monkhams*, 11.
[89] Chapman and André, *Map of Essex*, 1777, sheet xvi; O.S. Map 1″, Essex (1805) and preliminary drawings (1799–1800); E.R.O., D/DCy P2A (no. 960) and P2B, f. 39; C. and J. Greenwood, *Map of Essex*, 1825; E.R.O., D/CT 408 (nos. 325 and 314).
[90] O.S. Map 6″, Essex, LXV (1868–76 edn.); E.R.O., *Sale Cat.* A1068 (plan).
[91] E.R.O., D/DCy P3.
[92] B.M. Cott. MS. Tib. c. ix, f. 205; S.C. 2/173/30.
[93] Ibid. [94] S.C. 2/174/42A.
[95] S.C. 2/173/34.
[96] Land held in villeinage by a money rent: cf. *P.N. Essex*, 127.
[97] E.R.O., D/DCw M16. [98] Ibid.
[99] S.C. 2/174/43. In 1542 he sold a messuage and 7 a. to Ralph Johnson, tenant of Woodford Hall: *Feet of F. Essex*, iv. 256.
[1] E.R.O., D/DCw M24.
[2] E.R.O., D/DCw, map of *c*. 1700. The map shows fields marked 'sold to Cleland'.

[3] E.R.O., D/DCw M25.
[4] E.R.O., D/DB T657 (deed of 1804; schedule).
[5] E.R.O., D/DC 23/760.
[6] E.R.O., D/DB T657 (deed of 1804; schedule); D/DU 357/14; Q/RPl 66. For Ray House *c*. 1776 see plate f.p. 189.
[7] E.R.O., D/DU 357/14.
[8] Ibid.; H. M. Colvin, *Biog. Dict. Eng. Architects*, 437, 439.
[9] E.R.O., D/DLc T47, ff. 7–21.
[10] Ibid. ff. 1–6. See also E.R.O., D/DCy P3 (Wanstead Park records).
[11] E.R.O., D/DLc T47, ff. 1–6.
[12] Ibid. ff. 32–6.
[13] E.R.O., D/CT 408.
[14] J. Thorne, *Environs London*, 737.
[15] J. E. Tuffs, *Wanstead and Woodford*, 120.
[16] *Wanstead and Woodford Off. Guide* (1964–5), 21.
[17] E.R.O., D/DCw M16.
[18] Chapman and André. *Map of Essex*, 1777, sheet xvi.
[19] *V.C.H. Essex*, i. 375. For the Forest see below, p. 350.
[20] *V.C.H. Essex*, ii. 130.

accounts for the large number of 100 sheep. There were also 6 'beasts', 50 swine, and 40 goats in 1086.[21]

The amount of arable land gradually increased. Richard I acquitted the canons of Waltham of various assarts made in the forest, including 32 a. at Woodford,[22] and in 1200 the abbot accounted for 4 a. of pasture at Woodford which had been converted to tillage.[23] By the 17th century the demesne was largely arable.[24]

The demesne at Woodford was never extensive, but about 1235 the men of the vill held between them some 15 virgates.[25] They held either one virgate (the standard 30 a.) or a fraction of a virgate, for which they did service in proportion. Some paid a money rent[26] and sent one man to work in the lord's meadow at hay-time and two or three men to the boon works, but more paid no rent, working on the demesne two days a week and three days in August and September.

There is some evidence of open fields. Names such as Brodfeld and Suthfeld, which occur in 1517,[27] may indicate them. Common fields and meadows are mentioned in the 17th century[28] and in 1653 two cows or one horse were allowed in the common meadow for every acre held.[29] As late as 1700 the demesne included 5 parcels containing 5 a. in the common field.[30] The tithe map shows strips only in the common meadow (now Old Mill playing field).[31]

By the mid 18th century the fields had been inclosed with hedges. Wheat, oats, and peas were being grown for the London market, but pasture farming was more profitable. Londoners paid weekly rates to graze their horses or cattle on Woodford fields. Local farmers also kept many cows and bought animals to fatten for city butchers.[32] In 1801 206 persons were engaged in agriculture compared with 148 in trade and handicrafts.[33] A market-gardener is mentioned in 1812.[34]

By 1814 the greater part of Woodford was pasture.[35] Larger residences with their gardens and paddocks took up so much space that by 1838 only six farms were left: the home farms of Woodford Hall, Ray House, and Monkhams, together with Hill House and Gales east of the Roding, and Milkwell farm. There were then 339 a. of arable land compared with 1,120 a. of pasture or meadow.[36] Pasture remained important; about 1900 the district round Woodford and Chingford was known as the 'Hay Country',[37] and in 1905 there were still 523 a. of permanent grass compared with 317 a. of arable and 216 a. of woodland.[38] But by 1922 only three farms—Monkhams, Milkwell, and one at Woodford Bridge—were being worked[39] and in the following years these too were cut up for building. Some nursery-gardens were cultivated in the early 20th century[40] and a few cattle are still (1965) grazed at Woodford.

There was a water-mill in Woodford in 1066, though it had ceased to work 20 years later.[41] In 1605 and 1610 there were complaints that the water pent up for Sir Bernard Whetstone's mill flooded the highway.[42] By 1635 the mill had been taken down and in 1641 the mill-house was deserted.[43] It was still standing in the late 19th century approximately where the Southend road now crosses the river.[44]

Woodford windmill existed by 1628.[45] It belonged to the demesne of Woodford manor, with which it descended until 1710.[46] The mill, which was a post-mill, stood on a piece of waste on the southern edge of Woodford Wood, with a house adjoining, just on the Woodford side of the boundary with the manor of Higham Bensted in Walthamstow, in the vicinity of the present Mill Road.[47] There are several references in the 17th century to cottages built near it on the Higham Bensted waste.[48] In 1677 the justices ordered the mill to be fenced because it was danger-ous to cattle and passers-by.[49] An attempt by a Walthamstow miller, perhaps the operator of the newly-erected Walthamstow windmill,[50] to burn it down in 1699 was apparently unsuccessful.[51] The mill probably ceased working by 1723, when Christopher Crow, after buying the demesne lands of Woodford manor, leased the 'millhouse at Wood-ford Row' to the churchwardens and overseers from 1724 to 1745 as the Woodford poorhouse. When the lease expired it was not renewed, and the mill and adjoining house had disappeared by 1757.[52]

The making of bricks and tiles is mentioned at Woodford in 1506,[53] and a few years later the tenant of Ray House was licensed to dig clay from his land for this purpose.[54] A field in this corner of Woodford was called Long Tyle Killin from at least 1609.[55] Soon after buying Ray House, about 1776, Sir James Wright established a factory there for making artificial slates. The business was discontinued soon after his death in 1804, and the factory, built of artificial slate, was demolished before 1811.[56] Sir

[21] Ibid. i. 446.
[22] W. R. Fisher, *Forest of Essex*, 321; *Cal. Chart. R.* 1226–57, 305.
[23] *Pipe R. 1200* (P.R.S. N.S. xii), 45.
[24] Fisher, op. cit. 59. See also below, p. 350.
[25] B.M. Cott. MS. Tib. c. ix, f. 205.
[26] Cf. later references to molland in: E.R.O., D/DCw M16; S.C. 2/174/43.
[27] E.R.O., D/DCy M4.
[28] Fisher, *Forest of Essex*, 271.
[29] E. J. Erith, *Woodford*, 80.
[30] E.R.O., D/DCw P1.
[31] E.R.O., D/CT 408.
[32] J. Lucas (trans.), *Kalm's account of his visit to England* [1748], 166–7.
[33] Erith, *Woodford*, 36.
[34] G.L.C., DL/C/298.
[35] Ogborne, *Essex*, 73.
[36] E.R.O., D/CT 408.
[37] *E.R.* lx. 22.
[38] Bd. of Agric. and Fish., Acreage Rtns. 1905.
[39] *Kelly's Dir. Essex*, 1922, 694.
[40] *V.C.H. Essex*, ii. 480.
[41] Ibid. i. 446.
[42] E.R.O., Q/SR 171/65, 189/84.

[43] E.R.O., Q/SR 287/10; C 142/497/41.
[44] O.S. Map 6″, Essex, LXV (1868–76 edn.); Erith, *Woodford*, plan f.p. 125.
[45] E.R.O., D/DFc 185, f. 214.
[46] E.R.O., D/DCw T4 (1637, 1640), D/DMe T1/5 (1658), D/DMe T1/7–11 (1678), D/DMe T1/15–16, 19–20 (1710–11).
[47] E.R.O., D/DCw P1 (map of Woodford manor and estate c. 1700); cf. D/DCw P8 (Map of Woodford Wood, 1757). It is also shown on a map of c. 1640 reproduced in *E.R.* xiv. 193; there is an 18th-century enlarged copy of this: E.R.O., T/M 147.
[48] e.g. E.R.O., D/DFc 185, ff. 214, 233, 236.
[49] E.R.O., Q/SR 436/15.
[50] See p. 268.
[51] E.R.O., Q/SR 500/2, 5, 6.
[52] Morant, *Essex*, i. 38; E.R.O., D/DMe T1/40, D/DMe E1/2, D/DCw P8; Erith, *Woodford*, 16–20.
[53] E.R.O., D/DCy M1.
[54] E.R.O., D/DCw M16.
[55] *E.R.* lix. 2.
[56] Lysons, *London*, iv. 287; ibid. Supplement (1811), 365; *V.C.H. Essex*, ii. 417; *Patent artificial slate-manu-factory at Woodford Bridge, Essex . . .*, 17. For the slate factory c. 1776 see plate f.p. 189.

James's son Sir George invented a method of cutting stone pipes, chimney pots, and other objects from solid stone, leaving the core available for use as columns. He patented this process in 1805 and formed a company, but left Ray House before the inadequacy of his weak, porous pipes was revealed in Manchester, where he had been authorized to supply water.[57] Later in the 19th century bricks and tiles were still being made in this part of the parish.[58] A few are still made there now (1965).

Before the coming of the railway road transport provided much occupation in the village. In 1686 there were beds for 19 guests and stabling for 31 horses.[59] In 1848, besides the inns and posting-houses, there were 5 blacksmiths, 4 horse-hirers, 2 saddlers, 3 wheelwrights, 2 omnibus proprietors, and 2 carriers.[60] During the past forty years a small amount of light industry has grown up in what is essentially a dormitory town. The industries include the making of plate-glass, refrigerators, furniture, and sports equipment.

FOREST. The whole of Woodford was within the ancient Forest of Essex. In the Middle Ages it was part of the forest bailiwick of Becontree.[61] In the 16th century, when the bailiwicks were replaced by smaller 'walks', the parish comprised Woodford walk.[62]

In 1203 King John licensed the inclosure of Monkhams wood.[63] In 1225 an agreement was made between the abbot of Waltham and the king about the great wood attached to the demesne at Woodford. This wood, a rectangular projection at the north-west extremity of the parish, was to remain within the royal forest until Henry III came of age, when the canons were to be allowed to fence it and render it extra-forestal; in exchange Epping and Nazeing were then to be thrown back into the forest.[64] These grants were no doubt rendered void by Henry III's revocation of the Charter of the Forest in 1228,[65] but the great wood was nevertheless a valuable asset to the canons. In 1292 they obtained a royal licence to sell timber at Woodford to the value of £15.[66] Another licence was obtained in 1327,[67] and in 1342, when the canons were in financial straits, they were licensed to cut timber to the value of £200 in their woods at Epping, Theydon (Bois), Loughton, and Woodford.[68] On both these occasions the wood was described as being within the bounds of the forest of Waltham. At Monkhams the lessee was licensed to fell and fence the grove in 1631, providing that ridings were left so that the king could continue to hunt,[69] and during the early 18th century timber was frequently felled there, sometimes without licence.[70]

The main disadvantage of the forest to farmers in the area was the immunity enjoyed by deer. Sir Bernard Whetstone complained in 1603 that although the greater part of his demesne was arable land he had been unable to plough any of it during the previous ten years because of the depredations of deer. In spite of this, he was still obliged to pay composition wheat and oats for the king's household.[71] After the Restoration John Hayes was allowed to retain fences round Knighton wood only on condition that he left open the customary deer leaps.[72] At Monkhams, in the earlier 18th century, the Norths were several times in trouble with the courts of attachments for illegally erecting high fences which prevented the passage of deer.[73]

As some compensation for the ravages of deer the wood also provided pasturage. In early days swine were herded in the forest; hence the importance of pannage and agreements made between the lords of the adjoining manors about inter-commoning, such as that of 1240 between the abbot of Waltham and William le Breton, lord of Chigwell.[74] Pannage dues on Woodford manor amounted to 12s. 10½d. in 1367.[75] In the 17th century no pigs were allowed to root in the forest unless they had been properly ringed.[76] There are several references at this time to occupiers of land in Woodford claiming common of pasture as well as estovers.[77] At the close of the 18th century the occupiers of lands within the bounds of the forest had the right to pasture horses and cows during the whole year except the fence month. The general rule was to admit one horse or two cows for every £4 annual rent. The parish reeve branded cattle with the mark for Woodford parish:[78] 'M' surmounted by a crown in the shape of a recumbent 'E'.[79] Nevertheless, according to local farmers, this privilege of common-age was not equal to a tenth of the losses they continually sustained from deer breaking down fences and destroying crops. Against them no fences, however laboriously contrived, availed. In addition, the farmers complained that the forest was well known as the resort of idle, profligate men whose careers began with deer-stealing, as also of hardened fugitives from justice.[80] In 1960 there were still 100 branded cattle loose in the forest.[81]

The problem of deer and other depredators lessened as more woodland was cleared. This was a gradual process. In 1572 Bernard Whetstone was licensed to fence in a quarter of the woodland of his manor,[82] an action that led to riots.[83] At Monkhams c. 1640 woodland extended as far south as Snakes Lane, but the wooded area had shrunk considerably by 1777 and still more by the early 19th century.[84] Knighton wood was originally part of

[57] *E.R.* xix. 113–14.
[58] *Kelly's Dir. Essex,* 1878f; O.S. Map 6″, Essex, LXV (1897 edn.).
[59] *E.R.* liii. 11.
[60] *White's Dir. Essex* (1848), 268.
[61] W. R. Fisher, *Forest of Essex,* f.pp. 21, 29, 137, p. 395.
[62] Ibid. 382; *E.R.* xiv, map f.p. 192.
[63] *V.C.H. Essex,* ii. 130.
[64] *Cal. Pat.* 1225–32, 2.
[65] Fisher, *Forest,* 24–9.
[66] *Cal. Pat.* 1281–92, 505.
[67] *Cal. Inq. p.m.* ii. 108.
[68] *Cal. Pat.* 1340–43, 566.
[69] B.M. Add. MS. 24781, f. 113 (transcript of Forest Court proceedings). In 1514 the lessee was obliged to inclose the wood: *E.R.* xiv. 168.

[70] *Woodford Antiq. Soc. Proc.* i. 9–10.
[71] Fisher, *Forest,* 59.
[72] *Cal. S.P. Dom.* 1660–70, 617–18; cf. Fisher, *Forest,* 328.
[73] *Woodford Antiq. Soc. Proc.* i. 10.
[74] *Feet of F. Essex,* i. 127.
[75] E.R.O., D/DCy M1.
[76] E.R.O., D/DCw M19.
[77] B.M. Add. MS. 24781, ff. 116–21; Fisher, *Forest,* 244.
[78] A. Young, *Agric. of Essex,* 162.
[79] Fisher, *Forest,* 299.
[80] Young, *Agric. of Essex,* 162.
[81] P. Willmott and M. Young, *Family and Class in a London Suburb,* 9.
[82] E.R.O., Q/SR 40/33.   [83] Ibid. 44/28.
[84] *E.R.* xiv, map f.p. 192; Chapman and André, *Map of Essex,* sheet xvi; Ramsey, *Monkhams,* 8.

Woodford Hall manor but had been alienated before 1642.[85] Attempts were made to inclose and clear it in 1670 and again a hundred years later. Neither attempt was wholly successful, in spite of the fact that the owner had obtained a lease from the Crown in 1773,[86] and Knighton wood still survives. Nevertheless, during the 17th and 18th centuries many encroachments on woodland waste were allowed by the lord of the manor and sanctioned by the justices of the forest,[87] so that by 1843 396 a. of common land at Woodford had been inclosed.[88]

In 1856 and 1862 the Commissioners of Woods and Forests sold the Crown's forest rights in Woodford, and the process of inclosure was accelerated. Between 1851 and 1871 a total of 182 a. was inclosed, leaving only 69 a. of open forest within the manor of Woodford.[89] Under the Epping Forest Act (1878) and the subsequent arbitration, however, 209 a. in the manor and parish of Woodford were preserved as part of the forest. This consisted mainly of Woodford Green, strips on either side of the High Road, and along the bank of the Roding, and a large part of the north-west corner of the parish over which the golf course is laid out.[90] Possibly the last private inclosure of land in the forest occurred in 1910, when the tenant of the Roses inclosed a pond outside his house.[91] Knighton wood (37 a.) was added to Epping Forest in 1930, when it was bought by the corporation of the City of London from the trustees of the estate of E. N. Buxton.[92]

LOCAL GOVERNMENT. During the Middle Ages the abbot of Waltham, as lord of the manor, held courts for Woodford. He took the profits of justice[93] and, from the 13th century at least, held a view of frankpledge there.[94] In 1465 the abbot rebutted the demand of the abbess of Barking that the farmer of Woodford manor should make suit at her hundred court. He claimed that, because of the annual payment of 4s. to the exchequer, and references in the great roll of 1287 and 1344, Woodford manor was quit of that service. He maintained also that the manor was provided with the necessary instruments for correction and punishment, such as tumbrel and gallows, while such offenders as could not be dealt with at Woodford could be carried to Waltham gaol.[95]

Court rolls exist for 1270-1, 1581, 1606, 1615-68, and 1727-32,[96] and court books for 1670-1732 and 1735-1848.[97] A court leet was held most years after Easter, but occasionally in October and for a few years at both times. A jury of between 12 and 18 made presentments for the usual petty offences, including encroachments on the waste, the unlicensed sale of ale, sheltering strangers, and the failure to scour ditches or repair roads. The court also regulated grazing on the common. As well as constables one or two bread- and ale-tasters were usually elected. The number of presentments increased during the Interregnum but tended to lessen afterwards, and no court leet was held after 1718. Monkhams was not included in the jurisdiction of Woodford Hall manor court.[98] A court baron was always combined with the court leet but as many as three more courts baron might be held during the year.

The surviving parish records of Woodford are very numerous.[99] They include a parish book 1641-79, vestry minutes 1679-1851, churchwardens' accounts from 1737, and overseers' accounts from 1765. They have been fully analysed in a book, upon which the following paragraphs are based.[1]

The monthly vestry meetings, held usually in church, sometimes in a public house, were attended by 10 or more residents of the parish who paid scot and lot. From at least 1657 the more wealthy residents carried out an annual audit. In 1776 the vestry clerk, who had previously served unpaid, was granted £10 10s. a year.

Two overseers were appointed each year. Each overseer served for 2 consecutive years; the first year the appointment was nominal, as the duties were carried out by the overseer in his second year. Two or three years later he would expect to be appointed junior churchwarden and, the next year, 'upper' warden. Occasionally, in the early 18th century, the rector appointed his own warden. From 1786 a salaried assistant to the overseers was appointed. Two constables were usually elected in the court leet, having been nominated at the preceding Easter vestry. In the absence of courts leet the appointment of constables was confirmed by justices. Substantial inhabitants were often elected constables. After 1746 paid beadles were infrequently appointed. In 1788 the parish was divided and one constable was appointed for the 'town' and one for Woodford Bridge.

Fining to avoid parish office was allowed from at least 1641.[2] In 1781 service by deputy was prohibited and during 1782-6 and from 1809 onwards a scale of fines was established for those who did not wish to serve.

The money raised by churchwardens' rates was not always used for church repairs; payments for poor-relief, vestry dinners, or killing vermin are found in their accounts.[3] Until 1700 overseers and constables levied separate rates; thereafter the former reimbursed the latter for their expenses. The rate was 4d. an acre in 1647 but after 1659 rates were assessed on property values: 1s. in the pound in 1707, rising in the late 18th century to 9s. in 1801, and the equivalent of 16s. in 1817 and 1834.[4]

From the 17th century there was a parish poorhouse (often called the alms-house) comprising

[85] E.R.O., Q/SR 44/28; Cal. S.P. Dom. 1660-70, 617.
[86] Fisher, Forest, 328, 331; G. A. Selwyn, Manors held by lease from the Crown (1787), 13.
[87] B.M. Add. MS. 24781, ff. 9, 23, 204-13; E.A.T. N.S. xi. 170.
[88] Fisher, Forest, 271.
[89] Final Rep. Epping Forest Com., H.C. 187, map, and schedule pp. 83-90 (1877), xxvi.
[90] Ibid.; Epping Forest Arbitration Map, 1882; Wanstead & Woodford Off. Guide (1964-5), 25.
[91] E.R. lv. 175.
[92] A. Qvist, Epping Forest, 36; J. A. Brimble, London's Epping Forest, 148; E.R.O., Sale Cat. A 273.
[93] Pipe R. 1199 (P.R.S. N.S. x), 91.
[94] Rot. Hund. (Rec. Com.), i. 152.
[95] B.M. Add. MS. 37665, f. 258.
[96] S.C. 2/173/30, 31, 33-8, and 174/42, 43; E.R.O., D/DCw M17-25.
[97] E.R.O., D/DCw M26-30.
[98] E.R.O., D/DCw M19.
[99] Cat. Essex Par. Recs. 2nd edn., 237-9.
[1] E. J. Erith, Woodford, Essex, 1600-1836.
[2] E.R.O., D/DCw M21.
[3] F. G. Emler, Hist. of Woodford Parish Church, 121-5.
[4] Erith, Woodford, 11-12. The actual rate in 1817 was 7s. following a revaluation in 1804. Erith analyses the overseers' expenditure in a graph at the end of the book.

3 cottages by the turnpike at Woodford Bridge.[5] Because it was too small to accommodate all in need of relief paupers were boarded out, often with other paupers, or were paid pensions, until 1724, when the millhouse at Woodford Row was leased for 21 years as a workhouse[6] and all pensioners were ordered into it. But most of the inmates were incapable of heavy work, and outdoor relief had to be continued. On the expiration of the lease in 1745 Woodford paupers were farmed out to a succession of London contractors. Outdoor relief continued only for those who could be supported on less than the cost of sending them to the contractor.

In 1783 the vestry again opened a workhouse within the parish, leasing a building in Monkhams Lane. This was replaced in 1792 by Hereford House in Snakes Lane,[7] also leased. Oakum picking was the chief occupation, but it became increasingly difficult to find materials for the poor to work on. Outdoor relief largely ceased between 1786 and 1794, but under the pressures of war and bad harvests it became necessary to subsidize food and fuel for the poor, in 1796 by means of voluntary subscriptions and in 1801 by a special rate; and justices of the peace were occasionally persuaded to grant orders for the payment of pensions. In 1818 between 6 and 7 per cent of the population of Woodford were receiving some relief.

In 1820 a new workhouse was built on waste land in the north of the parish leased from the lord of the manor. Brice Pearse of Monkhams gave £1,000 towards this. At first there was little work for the inmates, but by 1827 land around the house was being cultivated, and in 1829 adjoining land was inclosed and made copyhold after the parish had agreed to surrender to the lord of the manor the lease of the poorhouse at Woodford Bridge. In 1836 the workhouse was taken over by West Ham union.[8] It was sold a few years before 1848 and converted into a residence called Manor House.[9] The site is now (1965) occupied by Bancroft's school.

The overseers sometimes paid for nurses to attend the sick or assisted the latter to enter one of the London hospitals. Grants were also made for the maintenance of lunatics, the more violent ones being sent to private asylums. In 1775, following outbreaks of smallpox, a doctor was appointed to attend poor parishioners at an annual salary. In 1778 a pesthouse was built on a site adjoining that on which the workhouse of 1820 was built.[10] When not required for the sick this was used to house the ordinary poor.

Quarter sessions records indicate that crime was less prevalent in Woodford than in most Essex parishes, though the forest provided cover for thieves. In 1771 an association of inhabitants was formed to provide rewards for the capture of felons. A police horse patrol, who received an allowance from quarter sessions, was stationed in the parish by 1826. In 1839 Woodford was brought into the area of the Metropolitan police.[11]

The lord of the manor was presented in 1584 and 1653 for failing to maintain the stocks.[12] A cage is mentioned in 1694 and in the early 19th century one was standing, together with stocks, on the green by the High Road opposite the White Hart. This cage, a small brick building, was demolished in 1930.[13]

Responsibility for the repair of Woodford and Winn bridges was frequently debated in quarter sessions, and individual landowners were occasionally presented in courts leet for failing to repair sections of highway, but the main responsibility for the upkeep of roads rested with the vestry. Highway rates rarely seem to have been levied until the later 18th century. Six days each year were set aside for the performance of statute labour but in 1733 labourers paid 5s. as composition. In 1721 the Middlesex and Essex turnpike trust became responsible for the upper road and in 1736 for the lower road. The vestry compounded with the trustees for repairs to sections of the roads within the parish, the money being paid from the overseers' or churchwardens' accounts, not the surveyors'. Road work was sometimes found for unemployed labourers in the early 19th century.

No select vestry was introduced under the Sturges Bourne Act (1818), probably because the vestry was already appointing committees to deal with particular problems, such as the workhouse. The Local Government Act (1858) was adopted in 1873 when a local board of 9 members was set up. From 1894 Woodford was governed by an urban district council of 12 members. Four wards were created in 1914.[14] The urban district was united with that of Wanstead in 1934 and in 1937 the combined urban district was incorporated as a municipal borough.[15] In 1965 Wanstead and Woodford was amalgamated with Ilford and parts of Chigwell and Dagenham as the London borough of Redbridge.[16]

CHURCHES. A church was evidently in existence by 1177 when it was confirmed among the possessions of the canons of Waltham Holy Cross.[17] In 1191 the Pope assigned this church, among others, to the use of the sacristy at Waltham.[18] What exactly was effected by this measure is uncertain. The benefice does not seem to have been appropriated, even temporarily, and its incumbent has always been styled a rector. But part of the income may have been reserved for the sacristy: a composition was made in 1224 between the abbot of Waltham and the rector of Woodford to settle certain divisions of tithe and other matters, although no mention was then made of the sacristy.[19]

The advowson descended with the lordship of the manor until 1898,[20] except for occasional turns. Thus, for example, Sir Thomas More presented *pro hac vice* in 1526, Robert Browne, by what right

[5] E.R.O., D/DCy P2B, f. 103, D/DCy P3, ff. 25, 191 (plan).　[6] See p. 349.

[7] Tuffs, *Wanstead and Woodford*, 29; E.R.O., D/DCy P2B, ff. 194–5, 253 (plan). For Hereford House, see above, p. 341.

[8] For the site see E.R.O., D/CT 408.

[9] *White's Dir. Essex*, 1848; O.S. Map 6″, Essex LXV (1876 edn.).

[10] E.R.O., D/CT 408.

[11] *V.C.H. Essex*, v. 34.

[12] E.R.O., Q/SR 90/36; D/DCw M23.

[13] J. W. Mackail, *Life of Wm. Morris*, 6; *E.R.* xxix. 138 and xxxix, 196.

[14] E.R.O., C/M 2/20, p. 1057.

[15] *Wanstead and Woodford Official Guide* (1964–5).

[16] London Govt. Act, 1963, c. 33.

[17] J. Farmer, *History of Waltham Abbey*, 40.

[18] B.M. Harl. MS. 391, f. 133.

[19] B.M. Harl. MS. 4809, f. 21.

[20] *Crockford* (1898), 683, 1931.

is unknown, in 1558, and Henry Fanshawe for one turn in 1561.[21] The theologian Henry Isaacson acquired two turns, presenting in succession his younger brother William (1619) and William's son Richard (1645).[22] In 1824 the next presentation was bought by William, Lord Maryborough, for £4,200.[23] In 1898 the Revd. J. B. Brearley bought the advowson.[24] In 1904 his mortgagee sold it to Lady Henry Somerset.[25] Lady Henry conveyed it in 1914 to her sister, Adeline Russell, duchess of Bedford (d. 1920).[26] In 1930 the duchess's executors sold it to the diocese, for vesting in the bishop.[27]

In 1224 the rector was allowed to claim pasture for 8 cows, 6 horses, 40 sheep, and 20 pigs over a year old, with their offspring.[28] This considerable number of animals suggests that the rector was a man of substance, but in 1254 the benefice was valued at only 100s.,[29] and in 1291 it was among the poorest livings, being valued at £2.[30] In 1535 it was assessed at £11 12s.[31] In 1604 it was reckoned to be worth £66 13s. 4d. a year, in 1650 £79 (of which tithe produced £72, glebe £7),[32] and in the mid 18th century £170,[33] while in 1829-31 the value of the rectory averaged £788.[34] The tithes were commuted for £676 in 1840.[35] A terrier of 1610 includes a rectory house, barn, and stable, with a close of 3 a. beside the barn. There were 3 a. of meadow in the common mead, 'the Parson's Grove', and another acre of wood on the north side of Jack of Lea's Grove.[36] In 1840 there were 16 a. of glebe.[37] The large rectory house was purchased in 1934 for use as council offices, having been in lay ownership since before 1928.[38] Although the house may incorporate part of an earlier 18th-century building, the main structure dates from c. 1800. It is a square three-storeyed house of dark red brick with yellow brick window-heads, having an entrance front of seven bays and a central doorway flanked by glazed lights and surmounted by a fanlight. A Regency bow window on the south side formerly had a canopied balcony above it. A house north of the churchyard, in Buckingham Road, now (1965) serves as the rectory.

Henry Siddall, rector from 1530, was deprived in 1555 as a married priest; he was later reconciled and became vicar of Walthamstow in 1557.[39] Richard Wood (1561-89) was listed in 1585 among Essex's

non-preaching clergy.[40] Robert Wright (1589-1619), later bishop successively of Bristol and of Lichfield and Coventry, was non-resident; Woodford was the first of many country livings he acquired and seldom visited.[41] William Isaacson (1619-45), a pluralist, was deprived of a London living after 1642, but kept Woodford.[42] He was succeeded by his son Richard (1645-53), who was commended in 1650 as an able and good minister.[43] Zachariah Cawdrey (1654-60) was presented to Woodford after being ejected from Barthomley (Ches.) as a royalist. At the restoration he recovered Barthomley and resigned Woodford, where he was succeeded by William Master (1661-84).[44] Master was another pluralist, as was James Altham (1729-66).[45]

With many of its rectors holding other livings, Woodford was often served by curates. The names of many of these curates survive.[46] By 1779 the incumbent was paying the curate £50 a year.[47] In the middle of the 17th century communion was celebrated only quarterly[48] and in 1682 there were complaints that the reader, not being in full orders, was unable to give absolution, and that the rector read the services perfunctorily.[49] By the early 18th century two services were being held on Sundays, with communion celebrated monthly; by the 1760s there were three Sunday services and also mid-week services.[50]

Woodford parish church has been dedicated to *ST. MARY* since at least the 14th century, though it has sometimes been known as St. Margaret's.[51] Nothing survives of the medieval building. It consisted of a nave, 2 aisles, a chancel with a vestry on its north side, and a tower.[52] Late-18th- and early-19th-century views show a chancel with 2 lancet east windows divided by 3 buttresses, in each of which is an empty niche; on the south wall of the chancel a dormer and a 'Tudor' window had been inserted.[53] By 1621 more accommodation was needed; the north wall of the old church was pulled down and an aisle erected at the expense of Elizabeth Elwes (d. 1625).[54] The new north wall had to be rebuilt in 1719.[55] This aisle had 2 dormers and 2 round-headed 2-light windows in the north wall, and 3 lancet windows in each of the east and west walls. By 1638 further accommodation was being provided

[21] Newcourt, *Repertorium*, ii. 679-80.
[22] *D.N.B.* (Henry Isaacson); Emler, *Hist. Woodford Par. Ch.* 63-4.
[23] C.P. 25(2)/1530 Trin. 5 Geo. IV; E.R.O., D/AEM 2/6.
[24] *Crockford* (1898), 683, 1931.
[25] E.R.O., D/CP 20/68.
[26] E.R.O., D/CP 20/68; *Burke's Peerage* (1963), p. 2264; *Chelmsford Dioc. Yr. Bk.* 1915, p. 79.
[27] *Dioc. Yr. Bk.* 1922 f; *Chel. Dioc. Chron.* June 1930, p. 92; E.R.O., D/CP 20/68; *Lond. Gaz.* 1931, pp. 1627-8.
[28] B.M. Harl. MS. 4809, f. 21.
[29] *E.A.T.* n.s. xviii. 17.
[30] *Tax. Eccl.* (Rec. Com.), 24.
[31] *Valor Eccl.* (Rec. Com.), i. 435.
[32] H. Smith, *Eccl. Hist. Essex*, 18, 248.
[33] Guildhall MS. 9556, p. 63.
[34] *Rep. Com. Eccl. Revenues*, H.C. 54, p. 680 (1835), xxii.
[35] E.R.O., D/CT 408.
[36] Newcourt, *Repertorium*, ii. 679.
[37] E.R.O., D/CT 408.
[38] J. E. Tuffs, *Wanstead and Woodford*, 85, 112-13; A. H. Gander, *Woodford and its church*, 15. By 1969 it had been renamed The Courthouse and was used by the North-East London Area for quarter sessions and various offices.
[39] H. Grieve, 'The deprived married clergy in Essex, 1553-1561' (*Trans. R. Hist. Soc.*, 4th ser., xxii. 152).

Unless otherwise stated, details of the Woodford clergy are taken from Newcourt, *Repertorium*, ii. 679-80, F. G. Emler, *Hist. Woodford Par. Ch.* 60-9, Venn, *Alumni Cantab.* and Foster, *Alumni Oxon.*
[40] T. W. Davids, *Nonconformity in Essex*, 95.
[41] *D.N.B.*; H. Smith, *Eccl. Hist. Essex*, 18.
[42] *D.N.B.* (Henry Isaacson); Smith, *Eccl. Hist. Essex*, 122.
[43] Lambeth MS. 910(8), ff. 149-50.
[44] *D.N.B.*; Davids, *Nonconf. in Essex*, 257.
[45] W. Master was rector of St. Vedast (Lond.) 1671-84, and J. Altham was vicar of Latton, 1730-58.
[46] Cf. E.R.O., D/AEV 4, ff. 2a, 61b, 76a, D/AEV 29; Guildhall MSS. 9550, 9553, 9555, 9560 *passim*; G.L.C., DL/C/298; F. G. Emler, *Woodford Parish Ch.* 70.
[47] Guildhall MS. 9553.
[48] H. Smith, *Eccl. Hist. Essex*, 73.
[49] E.R.O., D/AEV 11, f. 107a.
[50] Guildhall MSS. 9550, 9558 *passim*; F. G. Emler, op. cit. 19; *V.C.H. Essex*, ii. 76.
[51] *E.A.T.* n.s. vii. 364. Newcourt, followed by Morant, *Essex*, i. 39, and Ogborne, *Essex*, 71, give St. Margaret.
[52] Morant, *Essex*, i. 39.
[53] F. G. Emler, op. cit., pls. f.pp. 8, 15; cf. also Ogborne, *Essex*, 71.
[54] G.L.C., DL/C/228, ff. 233-8; Emler, op. cit. 7.
[55] Emler, op. cit. 15.

by a west gallery.[56] In 1644 Sir Thomas Rowe left £80 towards building a second aisle but nothing was done until 1691, when the south wall was in danger of falling, and it was decided to enlarge the church by building a south aisle. This was completed by 1694, with the aid of a church rate and voluntary contributions.[57] The new aisle had round-headed windows of 2 lights in the south wall and of 3 lights in the east wall, all with 'Gothic' glazing-bars, and a square-headed south doorway.

By 1705 the church was again decayed and the spire was so dangerous that it had to be removed. The tower, which was of timber on a base of flint, chalk, and ragstone, was demolished and a new brick tower, incorporating some of the old materials, was built in 1708. The remainder of the church was repaired at the same time. The work was met out of church-rates during the next 20 years.[58] The new tower was topped by 4 angle turrets and a lantern. These were removed in 1817, a plain battlement substituted, and the whole cemented over, but in 1899 the cement was stripped off and the top was restored to the original design.[59]

The need for more accommodation prompted sporadic discussion in the 18th century, but nothing was done, and in 1811 many parishioners still lacked seats.[60] By then the fabric of the building was ruinous and rebuilding the only solution. The vestry therefore decided to take down the side walls of the chancel and extend the aisles to the length of the chancel, thus forming an approximate square. At the same time the walls were to be raised, the north and south windows enlarged, the roofs renewed, and new galleries made inside. The work was completed in 1817. The cost was met by subscriptions, fines from inhabitants refusing to serve parish offices, and the sale of annuities payable out of parish rates.[61] The church, designed by Charles Bacon,[62] consisted of a nave with 2 aisles divided by thin arcades on slender pillars, lit by lancet windows and a small central lantern. A small area at the east end was arranged as a sanctuary. In 1889 a chancel was added, together with a vestry on its south side and an organ chamber on the north. At the same time the west gallery was removed and the tower arch opened into the nave. These alterations were carried out in the Perpendicular style by W. O. Milne.[63] The organ was moved to the south side in 1912 and the space vacated used as a chapel.[64] After the Second World War the north and south galleries, which excluded much light, were removed.[65]

In 1708 there were 4 bells[66] but after the tower was rebuilt a ring of 6 bells, cast by Richard Phelps and dated 1721, was hung. There is also a sanctus bell dated 1708.[67] A silver flagon and 2 silver bowls were in use in the 1680s,[68] but all the communion plate was stolen in 1773[69] and the present plate is modern. A silver christening bowl, dated 1777, was presented by Henry Burmester of Gwynne House in 1817.[70]

Several monuments from the old church were preserved[71] including a painted and gilded alabaster monument to Rowland Elrington, haberdasher and merchant adventurer of London (d. 1595) in the south aisle, a tablet to Robert Wynch (d. 1595) and a relief to Elizabeth Elwes (d. 1625), both in the chancel, and several large 18th-century marble cartouches. Among many memorials in the church-yard are a marble column with entablature to Peter Godfrey (1742) and the heavy Raikes mausoleum (1797). A large altar-tomb in the Greek Revival style commemorates William Morris of Woodford Hall (d. 1847) and prominently displays his newly-granted arms. The remnant of a giant yew tree still shades the south entrance to the church. Sir John Roberts, Bt., who financed the building of the parish church Memorial Hall in 1902, bequeathed £4,000 to it in 1917.[72]

As the population of Woodford increased, St. Mary's church became inadequate. Its position on the High Road in the south-western corner of the parish was always inconvenient for parishioners at Woodford Bridge and Woodford Wells. In 1851 a large room, used as an infant school, was being rented at Woodford Bridge for services[73] and it was there that the first new district chapelry was created, when the church of *ST. PAUL*, Manor Road, was built in 1854.[74] C. B. Waller, who as an assistant curate at Woodford had been mainly responsible for raising the money for St. Paul's, became the first vicar. He was succeeded by his son, who served there until 1919. After a fire in 1886 the church was rebuilt in stone in the Decorated style, consisting of nave and aisles, chancel, and north-west tower with spire, the base of which forms a porch.[75] The advowson of the vicarage is held by the rector of Woodford.

The church of *ALL SAINTS*, Inmans Row, Woodford Wells, was built in 1874, on a site, facing the Green, given by H. F. Barclay of Monkhams. In the following year a consolidated chapelry was formed from parts of the parishes of St. Mary, Woodford, and St. Peter-in-the-Forest, Waltham-stow.[76] A separate ecclesiastical parish was formed in 1906.[77] Originally there were no endowments and the incumbent was dependent on pew rents of £283 a year. The church, a stone building designed by F. E. C. Streatfeild in the Early English style, has a chancel, nave, south aisle, north transept, and a north-east tower with a shingled broach-spire. In 1876 a north aisle was added and in 1885 a choir vestry. The advowson of the vicarage is held by trustees.[78]

[56] E.R.O., D/AEV 7.
[57] Emler, *Woodford Par. Ch.*, 7–8.
[58] E.R.O., D/AEV 17, f. 67v; G.L.C., DL/C/250, ff. 377–96; Emler, op. cit. 9–14.
[59] A. Hughes, *Ch. of Woodford in Essex*, 10.
[60] Emler, op. cit. 17, 20, 21, 24. For the church in 1809 see plate.
[61] Emler, op. cit. 28, 30, 36, 44; Woodford Parish Church Act, 56 Geo. III, c. 9 (local and personal).
[62] Emler, op. cit. 33.
[63] H. M. Colvin, *Biog. Dic. of Eng. Architects, 1660–1804* under Ch. Bacon.
[64] Emler, *Woodford Par. Ch.*, 44, 52–4.
[65] After this article was completed, the church was gutted in Jan. 1969 by a fire started by vandals, which left only the tower and external walls intact.

[66] G.L.C., DL/C/250, f. 377v. There had been 3 bells and a sanctus bell in 1552: *E.A.T.* N.S. ii. 247.
[67] *Ch. Bells Essex*, 455.
[68] *E.A.T.* N.S. xviii. 201, xix. 275.
[69] Emler, *Woodford Par. Ch.* 91.
[70] *Ch. Plate Essex*, 45; Emler, op. cit. 88–92.
[71] R.C.H.M. *Essex*, ii. 269.
[72] Char. Com. file 96481; *Kelly's Dir. Essex*, 1906.
[73] H.O. 129/7/194.
[74] *Parishes divided etc.*, H.C. 557, p. 41 (1861), xlviii.
[75] *Chel. Dioc. Chron.* Nov. 1919, p. 141; *Essex Churchman*, Jan. 1959.
[76] H. H. Stevens, *All Saints Ch., 1874–1936*, 4–5.
[77] A. Hughes, *Ch. of Woodford in Essex*, 15.
[78] H. H. Stevens, op. cit. 5–6, 12; *Jones's Woodford Dir.* 1883, p. 26.

Woodford Row and Warner's Pond about 1770

St. Mary's Church in 1809

WOODFORD

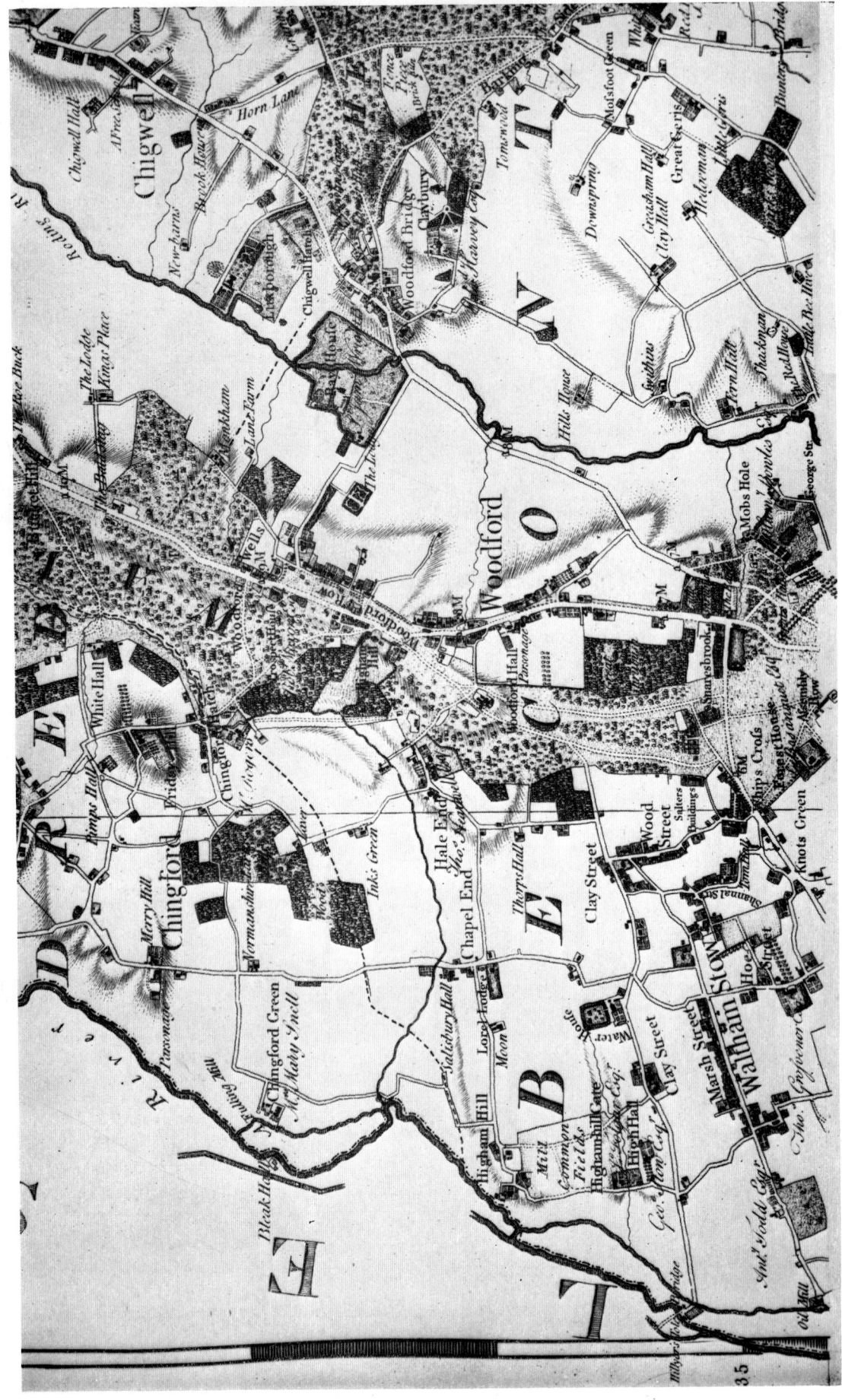

WALTHAMSTOW, WOODFORD, AND WANSTEAD (NORTH) IN 1777

Scale c. 1·5 in. to 1 mile

The mission church of *ST. ANDREW*, Ching-ford Lane, in All Saints parish, originated about 1880 with services held in the Working Men's hall (the old Congregational chapel) and, by 1882, in a rented room in the Square near by.[79] An iron church was erected in 1888. In 1923 the decayed iron was stripped off the wooden frame and replaced with cement-rendered expanded metal after the frame had been moved a few yards northwards to make room for a hall, vestry, and kitchen. At the same time the original wooden bell-tower was removed and the roof was slated.[80]

CHRIST CHURCH mission, Burlington Place, also in All Saints parish, was an iron building opened about 1889 after services had been held for some years at Knighton Lodge. It was closed in 1904 and the building was sold.[81]

The mission church of *ST. GEORGE*, Horn Lane, was promoted before 1903 by Andrew Johnston as an undenominational hall. It was staffed by Church Army captains and became attached to All Saints. In 1911 it was transferred to the new parish of St. Barnabas. Services were discontinued in 1956 and the building was adapted for use as a youth club. It appears that it was never consecrated and that the name St. George's is modern. Another mission chapel attached to All Saints was begun in Horn Lane in 1903 but was never completed; it was known as St. Bartholomew's.[82]

In 1882 a chapel of ease to St. Mary's was erected in Grove Hill and dedicated to *ST. PHILIP AND ST. JAMES*. Its seating capacity was later doubled. A hall was built in 1905[83] and a men's club in 1910.[84] The chapel is a low building of red brick with dormer-windows. In 1951 a conventional district was formed, the living of which was in the gift of the bishop.[85] This became an ecclesiastical district in 1962.[86]

The church of *ST. BARNABAS*, Snake's Lane, originated as an iron mission church attached to St. Paul's, erected in 1904.[87] A new church of brick and stone in Early Perpendicular style was built 1910–11, consisting of aisled nave, chancel, Lady chapel, and organ chamber.[88] The nave, originally of only 2 bays, was completed in 1964[89] by extending the arcades in the form of blank walls, each pierced by 2 arched openings, and by closing the west front with a chequer-board effect of window and wall. In 1911 a new parish was formed from parts of the parishes of St. Paul, All Saints, and Holy Trinity, South Woodford. The vicarage is in the gift of the bishop.[90]

The parish of Holy Trinity extends into South Woodford but the church itself is in Hermon Hill, Wanstead.[91]

ROMAN CATHOLICISM. The Roman Catholic parish of Woodford was formed in 1894.[92] The church of *ST. THOMAS OF CANTERBURY*, High Road, Woodford Green, and the Franciscan friary adjoining it to the south, were built in 1895 at the expense of Henrietta Pelham-Clinton (d. 1913) dowager duchess of Newcastle.[93] The church is built of red brick with stone dressings in the Early English style. The duchess occupied a house called the Oaks, immediately north of the church, which in 1920 became the convent of the Poor Clares (Colettines).[94] It is a late-18th-century building of brown brick having a two-storeyed front of five bays and a central doorway with a Tuscan porch; there are large additions in a similar style at both ends. The duchess also gave a site for the convent of the Holy Family of Bordeaux, Mornington Road, Woodford Green, which was built in 1898.[95]

PROTESTANT NONCONFORMITY. There is little early evidence of nonconformity in Woodford. Thomas Doolittle, who had been ejected from his London living in 1660, came to Woodford to escape the plague in 1665, when 'many resorted to his house for worship', but before 1672 he had returned to London.[96] Nicholas Lockyer, a Puritan divine, settled at Woodford some time after 1670 but there is no evidence that he was a proselytizer;[97] in 1676 no nonconformists were recorded.[98] By 1766 there were only two or three families of Presbyterians and some of those attended the parish church.[99]

John Wesley visited Woodford in 1787.[1] His preaching may have stimulated the formation, during the next few years, of Woodford Congregational chapel, which two early references describe as Methodist.[2] Another group described as Methodist in 1810, 'meeting in a different quarter of the parish', can probably be identified with the 'Independents, Calvinists', who registered private houses in 1804 and 1805, and with the Woodford Bridge mission of the Zion Itinerant Society which existed in 1812, when it was transferred to the London Itinerant Society. In the following year Woodford Bridge chapel was built for the mission. In 1816 it was visited by Wesleyan preachers of the Waltham Abbey circuit, and soon after the first Wesleyan society was formed. Its success at Woodford Bridge so undermined the position of the Independents that their chapel closed in 1822.[3] In 1829 the Wesleyan society, meeting in the house of Robert Johnson, was in the Waltham Abbey and Leyton (later the Leyton) circuit.[4] It still existed in 1851,[5] but there is no later trace of it. It probably disappeared during the Reform agitation of 1851–2.

[79] Ibid. 26; *Kelly's Dir. Essex*, 1886.
[80] *1888–1963: St. Andrew's, Chingford Lane* (pamphlet in church).
[81] H. H. Stevens, op. cit. 27.
[82] Ibid. 28; R. Mudie-Smith, *Relig. Life London*, 371; inf. from Mr. A. W. Bass.
[83] Date on building.
[84] *Kelly's Dir. Essex*, 1886, 1908, 1926.
[85] E.R.O., D/CP 20/69.
[86] E.R.O., D/CPc 401.
[87] *E.R.* xiii. 183.
[88] *E.R.* xx. 45, 153.
[89] Plaque in church.
[90] *Kelly's Dir. Essex*, 1937.
[91] See above, p. 334.
[92] *Cath. Dir.* 1965.

[93] *Kelly's Dir. Essex*, 1898.
[94] Tuffs, *Wanstead and Woodford*, 105; inf. from Abbess of Poor Clare Convent.
[95] Inf. from Superior of Convent of Holy Family.
[96] T. W. Davids, *Nonconformity in Essex*, 606.
[97] *D.N.B.*
[98] Wm. Salt Libr., Stafford, Bp. Compton's census, 1676.
[99] Guildhall Lib. MS. 9558, f. 400.
[1] *Jnl. of J. Wesley* (standard edn.), vii. 235d.
[2] Guildhall MS. 9558, f. 400.
[3] R. L. Galey, *Hist. Woodford Green United Free Ch.* 47, 106–9, 112–15.
[4] E.R.O., Q/CR 3/2; *Hall's Circuits and Ministers* (1897 edn.), 319.
[5] H.O. 129/7/194.

At Woodford Green the first Wesleyan society seems to have been founded in the 1830s. In or soon after 1837 this took over the old Congregational chapel in Mill Lane.[6] It was in the Leyton circuit, and by 1842 the residence of the circuit minister.[7] The Reform movement was strong in that circuit,[8] and William Burnett, who had been its superintendent since 1848, was replaced in 1851 and expelled from the Wesleyan Connexion in 1852.[9] He remained at Woodford and became the minister of the independent Wesleyan (later United Methodist Free) church described below.[10] The members from Mill Lane evidently went with him, for there is no trace of that society after 1852.

When Burnett retired in 1874 most of his congregation wished to reunite with the Wesleyan Connexion. Having failed to persuade the U.M.F.C. Assembly to agree to this, they seceded and began to hold services in the old Mill Lane chapel.[11] The Wesleyan Conference sent a missionary minister there in 1875, and in 1876–7 the present church was built in Derby Road.[12] It was at first in the Clapton circuit, but in 1879 a separate Wanstead and Woodford circuit was formed.[13] In 1888 that circuit was extended to Woodford Bridge, where services were held in a hired room, and later in a hall. A site for a church was given in 1889, but none was erected and in 1902 the work there was discontinued. The site was sold in 1932.[14]

The independent Wesleyans led by William Burnett registered a chapel at Woodford (Green) in 1857.[15] This was replaced in 1869 by a new one on the same prominent site, at the junction of Links Road and High Road.[16] The society remained independent until 1871, when it joined the U.M.F.C.[17] In 1862 a daughter church was founded at Chingford Hatch.[18] The secession that followed Burnett's retirement left his Woodford church almost empty, but it was joined in 1875 by a group of seceders from the Woodford Congregational church. The combined congregation formed itself in 1876 into the Woodford Union church, with 84 members, of whom 60 were Congregational, 14 Baptist, and 10 Methodist, under the leadership of Burnett's successor, George Atchison.[19] The new church adopted a Congregational form of government and organization, while retaining links, for certain purposes, with the U.M.F.C.

By 1900, when Atchison retired from the pastorate, the church was flourishing, with over 300 members, and a daughter church had been built at Highams Park, Walthamstow.[20] Atchison was succeeded by Joseph Hocking, a well-known novelist,[21] who promoted the building of a new church on a near-by site in High Elms. This was completed in 1904. The old building was bought by (Sir) J. R. Roberts (Bt.), who presented it for public use; it is now (1965) Woodford Green men's club. It is a brick building of 2 storeys, an attic and a semi-basement, with windows of various shapes. At the south-east corner is a bell-tower, capped with lead. The initials WM (for Wesleyan Methodists) are worked over the east doorway. Some features of the present building date from its conversion after 1904.[22] In 1941 the possibility of amalgamation between the Union church and Woodford Congregational church was discussed, and in the following years the two churches co-operated in various ways. In 1944, when the Congregational church was bombed, its congregation joined that of the Union church and in 1947 the two bodies were formally amalgamated as the Woodford Green United Free church, with 400 members. The building is of red brick with yellow terracotta dressings, and consists of an aisled nave with transepts, characterized by semi-circular windows and flying-buttresses.

In 1875 the Union church opened a Sunday school in Churchfields Board school for children of the Woodford Hall estate. This was moved to a new hall in Fullers Road, built in 1909. In 1946 it became a branch of the United Free church; it closed in 1968. The Wilfred Lawson mission of the Union church, opened in 1907, closed in 1940.[23]

The Primitive Methodists were represented in Woodford for a few years, but were never strong. They registered a church in Snakes Lane in 1888, but it had ceased by 1913.[24] A Primitive Methodist mission in Granville Road, South Woodford, appears to have closed between 1906 and 1908.[25]

Woodford Congregational church was founded about 1790. As Providence chapel, for Independents, it was registered in 1795 by William Whitefoot, who was a minister of the countess of Huntingdon's Connexion at Enfield (Mdx.).[26] This was clearly identical with, or a precursor of Woodford New Chapel, Mill Lane, which according to a much later statement was built in 1798 after missionaries of the London Itinerant Society, and students from the countess's college at Cheshunt, had preached on the Green, and later in a room in Horn Lane.[27] The new chapel was sponsored by the trustees of Cheshunt College. Additional evidence concerning its origin is provided by a statement made in 1790, that there was a Methodist meeting, lately established, at

[6] *White's Dir. Essex*, 1848, p. 266; E.R.O., D/CT 408.
[7] *Mins. Wesleyan Conference*, 1844 f.; Galey, *Hist. Woodford Green U. F. Ch.* 47–8. [8] See p. 228.
[9] *Hall's Circuits and Ministers*, 164; *Mins. Wesleyan Conf.* 1852.
[10] Much help has been received from Mr. R. Galey in tracing Burnett's career and the history of the churches with which he was connected. See also his *Hist. Woodford Green United Free Ch.* published in 1968.
[11] *Wesleyan Times*, 19 and 26 Dec. 1874, 2 Jan. 1875, 22 July 1876.
[12] Wanstead and Woodford Meth. Circuit, Quarterly Meeting Recs. (examined by Mr. G. Harrington); *Wesleyan Chapel Ctee. Rep.*, 1876.
[13] *Hall's Circuits and Ministers*, 316.
[14] Wanstead and Woodford Meth. Circuit, Q.M. Recs.
[15] Worship Reg., 7864 (14 Mar. 1857).
[16] A. G. Kidd, 'The Pioneers' (TS. Hist. Woodford Green United Free Ch.), chap. iii.

[17] *U.M.F.C. Mins. Conf.* 1900: obit. of W. Burnett.
[18] Meth. Arch. Dept., Pamph. Box 'London': *Meth. Ch., Chingford Hatch, Centenary 1962*; *V.C.H. Essex*, v. 112; Galey, *Hist. Woodford Green U. F. Ch.* 94–5.
[19] A. G. Kidd, 'The Pioneers', chap. iii, for this and the following 2 paragraphs; the 1876 figures, from the Union Church Bk., have been supplied by Mr. R. Galey.
[20] See p. 299.
[21] 1860–1937: see *D.N.B.*
[22] Galey, *Hist. Woodford Green U. F. Ch.* 51.
[23] Ibid. 95–100, 105–6.
[24] Worship Reg., 30794 (1 May 1888).
[25] *Kelly's Dir. Essex*, 1906, 1908.
[26] G.R.O., Rtns. Mtg. Houses before 1852, no. 375; *Life and Times of Selina, Countess of Huntingdon* (1840), ii, 113.
[27] Unless otherwise stated, this account of Congregationalism in Woodford is taken from A. G. Kidd, 'The Pioneers'. See also Galey, *Hist. Woodford Green U. F. Ch.*

Woodford, and by another made in 1810, that the
Methodists had a 'regular meeting-house erected
in 1794'.[28] The context of these statements, and
other evidence, makes it unlikely that they refer
to Wesleyan Methodists, but at this period followers
of the countess of Huntingdon were sometimes
described as Methodists, and indeed even used the
title themselves,[29] and it is to their chapel that the
statements almost certainly refer. In 1815 a church
was formed, at a meeting presided over by the Revd.
George Collison of Walthamstow. The chapel was
used until 1837, when a larger building was erected
in Horn Lane, and was called Providence. That
name is said to have been chosen by a benefactor
of the church; this does not exclude the possibility
that he was recalling the name used in 1795. The
old chapel, which stands in Savill Row, just off
Mill Lane, is a small brick building evidently refronted in 1890.[30] It became after 1837 in succession
a Wesleyan chapel, a British school, a Workmen's
hall, and an Anglican mission hall. After 1910 it was
used solely for secular purposes; in 1965 it was a
store for glass.

Services in the new Congregational church continued to be conducted by supply preachers[31] until
1840, after which there was usually a resident
minister. Additions, including a new schoolroom,
were made in 1861. The building was a rectangular
stucco-faced building in the neo-classical style with
a Corinthian portico of three bays.[32] It was demolished in 1873 and a third church, built on the same
site, was opened in 1874. This was designed by
Rowland Plumbe,[33] and built of stone in the Early
English style with a tall spire, 'the high water mark
of Congregational Church building in Essex'.[34]
Much of the cost was borne by the Spicer family of
Harts.

During the vigorous ministry of Edward T. Egg
(1859–82) missionary work was carried on at Buckhurst Hill, Ray Lodge, Sewardstone Green, Chingford, Hermon Hill, South Woodford, and Chigwell
Road; a new Sunday school was opened, and in
1861 the church joined the Essex Congregational
Union.[35] But there were internal dissensions and in
1875, as described above, about a third of the
congregation, including all the Baptist members,
seceded, joined the Free Methodists, and formed
the Union Church. Under Egg's successor, W. E.
Anderton (1884–1905) the Congregational church
prospered, and by 1901 its membership (including
that of the daughter churches at Ray Lodge and
Woodford Bridge) was over 300.[36] The church was
wrecked by flying bombs in 1944, and, instead of
rebuilding, the congregation joined Woodford Union
church to form, in 1947, Woodford Green United
Free church.

As a result of missionary activity from Woodford
Congregational church, a chapel was erected in
Globe Road, near Ray Lodge, in 1865. From 1886
onwards a resident minister was appointed who, in
1890, was given the supervision of two associated
missions at Woodford Bridge (established in 1868)
and Chigwell (begun about 1866), which then combined to erect an iron building in Smeaton Road,
Chigwell.[37] In 1900 a new, Gothic church, designed
by F. Boreham, and costing £3,500, was built in
Snakes Lane,[38] near the chapel, which remained in
use as a mission-room until its purchase by the New
Apostolic church. An institute was added in 1920.
In 1930 Ray Lodge Congregational church became
independent of the parent church at Woodford
Green.

A Congregational mission was established in 1870
in a cottage in Victoria Road, near George Lane,
and two years later a temporary iron church was
erected at the corner of Daisy Road, on the site now
(1965) occupied by the Salvation Army citadel. The
first pastor was appointed in 1876.[39] Though the
building was twice enlarged, a bigger one was soon
needed.[40] In 1879 land in George Lane was purchased, and in 1886 a new church was completed to
the design of Thomas Arnold in the Early English
style.[41]

Congregational mission-rooms were opened in
Crescent Road in 1887, Granville Road in 1901,[42] and
Beechcroft Road in 1907.[43] The last is still in use.

A Baptist school-chapel was opened in George
Lane in 1883, and three years later a minister was
settled there.[44] In 1895–6 the present stone church
in the 13th-century style was built in front of the
school-chapel.[45] It was registered in 1896,[46] just
before about half the congregation seceded to form
a separate church in Eastwood Road.[47] In 1900 the
seceders were joined by the minister from George
Lane.[48] The Eastwood Road building had been
given up by 1903[49] and its congregation moved to an
iron building in Maybank Road, known in 1906 as
South Woodford Free church and in 1911 as South
Woodford Union church.[50] This congregation ceased
to exist in 1920. Baptists then used the building in
Maybank Road as a church hall until 1933 when
they sold it to the Christian Brethren.[51]

Baptist missions were opened in Avenue Road in
1947 and in a pavilion off Broadmead Road in 1948.[52]
As numbers at the latter increased, members built
their own temporary church of wood in Chigwell
Road in 1957. This was constituted Broadmead
Baptist church in 1963.[53]

The Salvation Army used the Congregationalists'
iron building in Daisy Road from 1886. After buying
the site in 1906,[54] they built the present brick citadel,
opened in 1907.[55]

[28] Guildhall MS. 9558, f. 400.
[29] *Life and Times of Selina, Countess of Huntingdon* (1840),
pp. iv, v.
[30] Date on keystone.
[31] Cf. E.R.O., Q/CR 3/2.
[32] *E.R.* liii. 117; cf. C. S. Jones, *Fifty Pictures of Old
Woodford*.
[33] *Cong. Yr. Bk.* 1874.   [34] *E.R.* liii. 117.
[35] *Cong. Yr. Bk.* 1861.   [36] Ibid. 1901.
[37] Cf. *V.C.H. Essex*, iv. 35.
[38] *Cong. Yr. Bk.* 1901.
[39] 'Scrutator Diaconalis' [Albert Fuller], *The Church at
George Lane*, 20, 25.
[40] Ibid. 23.   [41] Ibid. 34, 49, 73.
[42] *Cong. Yr. Bks.* 1887, 1904.

[43] A. Fuller, op. cit., 75.
[44] *Baptist Handbk.* 1889.
[45] Ibid. 1896, p. 319.
[46] Worship Reg. 35679 (7 Oct. 1896).
[47] *Bapt. Handbk.* 1898, 1899.
[48] Ibid. 1901.
[49] R. Mudie-Smith. *Relig. Life of London*, 370.
[50] *Kelly's Dir. Essex*, 1906; Worship Reg., 40841 (24
Jan. 1905), 44843 (20 June 1911).
[51] *Kelly's Dir. Essex*, 1926; inf. from Church Secretary,
Latchett Evangelical Church.
[52] *Bapt. Handbk.* 1947, 1948.
[53] Ibid. 1965; local inf.
[54] A. Fuller, op. cit. 23–4.
[55] Date on building.

Grove Road Evangelical church is the outcome of work begun by Edward Hobbs (1825–1907) in 1877 amongst the gipsies encamped on Mill Plain, west of Chelmsford Road, where the evangelist 'Gipsy' Smith was born. To satisfy their spiritual as well as material needs, a mission was opened in a stable in Grove Road. In 1883 the present hall was built, and in 1894 the adjoining building, which is used for departmental activities, was added. The mission was formed into a church in 1949, when an ordained minister was appointed. It is affiliated to the Fellowship of Independent Evangelical churches.[56]

The Christian Brethren purchased the Baptists' iron chapel at the corner of Maybank and Latchett Roads in 1933. They replaced this with a brick building, called Maybank Hall, in 1952, and in 1962 added a new, adjoining, building, called Latchett Evangelical church. Maybank Hall is now used mainly for youth work.[57] Since 1944 the Brethren have also used a hall in Canfield Road.[58] Salway Hall Evangelical church was opened in 1933. In 1966 it had an active membership of nearly 200, including two missionaries in India and one in Argentina.[59] Meetings of the National Spiritualist church have been held at Ellerslie Hall, Washington Road, since 1953.[60] The New Apostolic church opened in the former Ray Lodge Congregational chapel in 1954.[61] A Moravian church, built in 1906, had closed by 1922.[62] A gospel mission was being held in a room in Barclay House, High Road, in 1914.[63]

JUDAISM. A congregation was formed and affiliated to the United Synagogue in 1947. Services were held in a large room attached to a member's house. In 1951 a house and land in Churchfields were purchased, and in 1952 the Wanstead and Woodford Affiliated Synagogue was erected on the site. The house is used for religious classes and by a youth club. There were 492 members in 1964.[64]

EDUCATION. In 1796 there was a Sunday school at Woodford, apparently Anglican, where most of the children of the poor were taught and clothed charitably.[65] By 1807, if not before, the only Sunday school was being held by Dissenters, but in 1801 two day schools of industry were founded, one attended by 20 boys and the other by 20 girls, and both supported by voluntary contributions.[66] The boys were accommodated in the workhouse from 1810 and the girls from 1815.[67]

Woodford Green county primary school, Sunset Avenue, originated as a National school for boys, opened in 1814.[68] This soon absorbed the boys school of industry. By 1818 attendance had fallen from 90 to 69 and some supporters withdrew their subscriptions on the ground that the school encouraged delinquency and impeded juvenile employment. It was thereupon agreed that no boy should be kept after the age of 14, that part-time schooling should be arranged for those obtaining employment before that age, and that the curriculum should be confined to reading, writing, and only a little arithemetic.[69] The girls school of industry was probably absorbed a year or two before 1820,[70] when a building for the National school was erected on a site west of the present Links Road, just over the boundary in Walthamstow.[71] In 1846–7 the total expenses of the school were some £130, of which £60 was paid to the master and £30 to the mistress. There was a clothing club attached to the girls department.[72] By 1865 the school was receiving an annual grant.[73] During the early 19th century the number of pupils was often less than 120[74] but in 1872 it rose to 186.[75] In 1880 the school was taken over on lease by the school board, which enlarged it in 1889.[76] A scheme of 1898 provided that various small bequests to the National school should provide exhibitions for higher education.[77] In 1907 the boys department was rebuilt and other departments were enlarged.[78] In 1937 the school was reorganized for mixed juniors and infants, and in 1953 the Essex education committee bought the freehold of the premises.[79]

St. Paul's Church of England school, Woodford Bridge, was opened in 1859, in association with the National Society. In the following year it was moved from temporary premises to a new building near the church, erected with the aid of a government grant. It was receiving an annual grant by 1865.[80] The attendance rose from 59 in 1865 to 154 in 1872.[81] Between 1886 and 1890 the school was taken over by the school board, but it seems to have been closed by 1906.[82] The building, which stands in a prominent position on the green, is of red brick with stone dressings; it was in use in 1965 as the church hall. In 1851 a room at Woodford Bridge, rented by the clergy for church services, was also being used for an endowed infants school.[83] This may have survived until the 1890s when there was a National infants school at Woodford Bridge.[84]

From 1806 until at least 1861, when a new schoolroom in Horn Lane was built, the Congregationalists held a Sunday school in their Mill Lane

56 Inf. from Mr. E. E. Mead, Trustee and Elder.
57 Inf. from Church Secretary.
58 Worship Reg. 60747 (20 Mar. 1944).
59 Ibid. 54637 (18 Aug. 1933); inf. from Mr. W. S. Loynes.
60 Worship Reg. 63981 (23 June 1953).
61 Inf. from Church Secretary.
62 Kelly's Dir. Essex, 1908, 1922.
63 Worship Reg. 46133 (30 Apr. 1914).
64 Inf. from Sec. United Synagogue; foundation stone.
65 Lysons, London, iv. 286.
66 E.R.O., D/AEM 2/4; Lysons, London, Supplement (1811), 365.
67 E. J. Erith, Woodford, Essex, 1600–1836, 80.
68 Nat. Soc. Rep. 1814, p. 21.
69 Ibid. 1818, pp. 240–1.
70 Ibid. 1818, 1820; Erith, Woodford, 80.
71 Kelly's Dir. Essex, 1886; E.R.O., D/CT 408.

72 Nat. Soc. Enquiry into Ch. Schs. 1846–7, pp. 22–3.
73 Rep. Educ. Cttee. of Council, 1865 [3666], p. 519, H.C. (1866), xxvii.
74 Nat. Soc. Reps., 1820–38; White's Dir. Essex, 1848, 1863.
75 Rep. Educ. Cttee. of Council, 1872 [C. 812], p. 410, H.C. (1873), xxiv.
76 Ibid. 1880; Kelly's Dir. Essex (1890).
77 Char. Com. Files 62132, 79890.
78 Kelly's Dir. Essex (1908).
79 Inf. from Min. of Educ. and Essex Educ. Cttee.
80 Educ. Cttee. of Council, Tabulated Reps. on Schs. in Essex, Norfolk and Suffolk, 1859–60, p. 13; Rep. Educ. Cttee. of Council, 1865.
81 Rep. Educ. Cttee. of Council, 1872.
82 Kelly's Dir. Essex, 1886, 1890, 1906.
83 H.O. 129/7/194.
84 Kelly's Dir. Essex, 1894, 1898.

chapel. This building was also used for a British school formed in 1854,[85] which in 1859 had 85 pupils under a master and two pupil-teachers.[86] There were 100 pupils when it was closed in 1871.[87]

In 1871 a school board was formed for Woodford.[88] Besides taking over the two church schools already described, the board built two new schools, both of which survive as county primary schools. The first of these was Churchfields, opened in 1873 with 273 places. An infants department was added in 1885. The school was enlarged in 1891 and substantially rebuilt in 1908. The average attendance was 223 in 1878 and 788 in 1899.[89] The school was reorganized in 1937 for juniors and infants.[90]

Oakdale county junior and infants schools. Cowslip Road board school, for girls and infants, was opened in 1897. By 1922 this was being used for girls and boys, the infants being accommodated in a temporary building erected in the previous year on a neighbouring site in Oakdale Road.[91] The school was reorganized for juniors and infants in 1937. In 1953 separate new buildings for juniors and infants were opened in Oakdale and Woodville Roads, and renamed Oakdale.[92]

Ray Lodge county junior and infants schools originated as Snakes Lane council elementary school, opened in 1904, with accommodation for about 1,000 children.[93] In 1937 the girls department was reorganized for junior girls, the boys department remaining unchanged. In 1950 the school was divided into mixed juniors and infants.[94]

Woodford Bridge Garden City council elementary school was opened in 1913 for boys from the local Dr. Barnardo's Home. In 1946 the boys were transferred to other Woodford schools but the building was later used as a temporary primary school for the Hainault L.C.C. estate (1948–54), as an annexe of Roding junior school (1954–5), and an annexe of St. Barnabas secondary boys school (1956–65).[95]

Roding junior mixed and infants schools. North Woodford primary school, Roding Lane, was built in 1939 and used by the fire service during the Second World War. It was opened as a county junior school in 1946, when single-storey buildings were added. It was reorganized in 1952 for mixed juniors and infants, and renamed Roding.[96]

St. Anthony's Roman Catholic school, Mornington Road, was opened in 1900 as an elementary school. It was reorganized for juniors and infants in 1946. A new block was opened in 1965.[97] The school has Aided status.

Madeira Grove special school for mentally defective children was opened in 1913 and closed in 1939.[98] The building is now (1965) used as a clinic.

Woodford's oldest secondary school is Bancroft's, founded in 1727 and moved to High Road, Woodford Wells, in 1889. Its earlier history has been described in a previous volume.[99] It became a Direct Grant school in 1919. Science laboratories were opened in 1910, an art and handicraft block, an assembly hall, and a science block in 1937, and a boarders' recreation block in 1964. In 1965 the school contained 430 boys, of whom 30 were foundation scholars, 250 held local authority free places, and the remainder were fee-paying. There were 90 boarders.[1] The original buildings, of red brick with stone dressings, stand round a quadrangle and were designed in the Tudor style by Sir Arthur Blomfield.[2] The central feature of the impressive three-storey front range is an embattled gatehouse tower with an oriel window and angle turrets.

Woodford county high school, High Road, Woodford Green, was opened for 100 girls in 1919 in Highams, an 18th-century house, which lies mainly in Walthamstow. In 1928 a north wing was added, in 1929 an assembly hall, and in 1938 a south wing. In 1965 there were 630 girls.[3]

St. Barnabas county secondary (modern) schools for boys and girls were opened as senior schools under the same roof in 1937. In 1965 the first part of a new boys school was opened on the playing-field. The girls school took over the whole of the original building in 1968 when the boys school was completed.[4]

St. Paul's Roman Catholic secondary (modern) school was opened in 1960 in temporary accommodation at the Dominican convent, Chingford, and at Debden and Woodford primary schools. In 1964 a permanent building was opened at the corner of High Road and Sydney Road. The school has Aided status.[5]

Among early private schools at Woodford was a boarding school at which James Greenwood (d. 1737), grammarian, taught.[6] By 1807 there were 5 private day-schools for about 50 young boys and girls, the teachers being paid 'partly by the more opulent parishioners, partly by the parents themselves'.[7] In 1848 there were at least 7 private boarding- and 2 day-schools, in 1863 4 boarding- and 7 day-schools.[8] During the rest of the 19th century directories usually list 11 private schools of various kinds, and by 1926 the number had risen to fifteen.[9] There were still in 1965 some 7 private schools, including a nursery school for deaf children and a Roman Catholic school for girls.[10]

St. Aubyn's preparatory school for boys, Woodford Green, was founded in 1884 by Rhoda and Fanny Crump assisted by other members of their family.[11] It was originally accommodated in two

[85] A. G. Kidd, 'The Pioneers' (TS. Hist. Woodford Green United Free Ch.); R. L. Galey, *Woodford Green United Free Ch.* 115.
[86] Educ. Cttee. of Council, *Tabulated Reps.* 1859–60.
[87] Galey, *Woodford Green United Free Ch.* 115–16.
[88] *Kelly's Dir. Essex*, 1890.
[89] *Rep. Educ. Cttee. of Council, 1878*; *Kelly's Dir. Essex* (1899, 1910).
[90] Inf. from Essex Educ. Cttee.
[91] *Kelly's Dir. Essex* (1906, 1922).
[92] Inf. from Essex Educ. Cttee. and Min. of Educ.
[93] *Kelly's Dir. Essex* (1906).
[94] Inf. from Essex Educ. Cttee. and Min. of Educ.
[95] Ibid.; inf. from London Borough of Redbridge.
[96] Ibid. and inf. from Headmaster.
[97] *Kelly's Dir. Essex* (1926); inf. from Essex Educ. Cttee. and Headmistress.

[98] *Kelly's Dir. Essex* (1922, 1926); inf. from L.B. of Redbridge.
[99] *V.C.H. Essex*, ii. 548–9.
[1] *Kelly's Dir. Essex* (1922); inf. from Headmaster.
[2] N. Pevsner, *Essex* (2nd edn.), 432.
[3] Inf. from Headmistress; cf. p. 260, and M. M. Smith, *Highams* (Walthamstow Antiq. Soc. Occ. Pubn. viii).
[4] Inf. from school secretary.
[5] *St. Paul's, Woodford Green* (pamphlet for official opening); inf. from Headmaster.
[6] *E.R.* xlvi. 49.
[7] E.R.O., D/AEM 2/4.
[8] *White's Dir. Essex* (1848, 1863).
[9] *Kelly's Dir. Essex* (1878 f.).
[10] *Wanstead and Woodford Official Guide* (1964–5).
[11] This account of the school is based on: *St. Aubyn's School Magazine, 75th Anniversary Number* (1961).

houses, which still survive, opposite Bancroft's school in High Road. In 1893 the school moved to Woodford Green, occupying premises on the site of the present Hawkey Hall. By 1906 it was recognized by the Board of Education.[12] A second move, to Pyrmont House, Woodford Green, took place at the end of the First World War. In 1922 the school, with about 100 day boys and 15 boarders, was bought from the Crumps by Lt.-Col. W. H. Colley, who was still headmaster in 1969. New buildings and a swimming bath were added in 1927–35. The school was evacuated to Cumberland in 1939, but returned to Woodford in 1946. In 1954 Mr. H. H. Colley, son of Lt.-Col. Colley, became joint headmaster. By 1969 it had been decided to accept no more boarders, in order to provide additional accommodation for day boys. The school then included a newly-built junior department. St. Aubyn's now takes boys between the ages of 5 and 13½.[13] Since 1922 many have proceeded to public schools on scholarships or through the common entrance examination.

Archbishop Harsnett provided for 4 Woodford boys to attend his schools at Chigwell, founded in 1629, 2 at the English school and 2 at the Latin,[14] though in 1835 there was none at the latter.[15] John Fowke (d. 1691) of Claybury, Ilford, by his will endowed places at Christ's Hospital (Lond., now Horsham, Suss.) for 8 boys, of whom 2 were to be from Woodford.[16] This charity was regulated by a scheme of 1899.[17]

CHARITIES FOR THE POOR.[18] Under a scheme of 1899 all the following charities for the poor were combined under the name of the Woodford Parochial Charities. In 1961 the total income from these charities was £116, most of which was spent on gifts of coal, food, and clothing.

Robert Rampston (d. 1585) left rent-charges for the poor of various Essex parishes. That for Woodford was £1 a year, charged on Stone Hall in Little Canfield.[19] It was still being paid in 1961.

Elizabeth Elwes, by will dated 1625, left £40 to buy land, the rent from which was to be given to the poor. In or before 1645 this money, with another £100 belonging to the parish, was lent to John Hayes at 5 per cent interest. In 1657 he repaid £40 of it, and for the remaining £100, which included Mrs. Elwes's legacy, undertook to pay £5 a year as a permanent rent-charge on his estate of Horns Inn (later the George) and land adjoining Parsons Grove in Wanstead. This rent, known as Poor's Stock, was by the end of the 17th century being used to provide premiums for apprenticing poor children. In 1857 it was stated that 'the charity will now revert to its

original application of general relief to the poor'. The rent was still being paid by the owner of the George Inn in 1899, but was subsequently redeemed for £200 stock.[20]

Sir Henry Lee, some time before 1658, gave for the poor an annual rent of £2 charged on his land at Woodford.[21] In 1835 and 1899 this was being paid from the Naked Beauty (later Hurst House) estate. It was later redeemed for £80 stock.

A number of small sums bequeathed for the poor in the 18th and earlier 19th centuries came to be administered together. William Prescott, by will proved 1731, Richard Warner (d. 1775) and Robert Moxon, by will proved 1786, each left £50. Hannah Cooke, by will dated 1809, left £20, and John Godfrey, by will dated 1810, left £10 10s.[22] In 1829 the total capital of these charities was £260 stock, the income from which was spent on bread for the poor.

Another group of charities consisted of £500 left by Jonathan Rogers about 1811, £100 left by John Harman (d. 1817), and sums totalling £85 given at unknown dates by three other persons. In 1834 the combined capital of these charities was £731, and the income was spent on clothing for the poor in October.

Ellen Hawkes, daughter of the above Jonathan Rogers, by her will proved 1818, left £300 stock for the poor. In 1834 the income was spent along with that from the previous group of charities.

Ellen Dod (d. 1814) directed that stock should be bought to provide an income of £10. From this £1 1s. was to be paid to a preacher on New Year's Day, Epiphany, Good Friday, and Ascension Day, and 10s. to a priest for saying prayers on Easter Eve. The remaining income was to be spent on bread for the poor on the sermon days: £1 6s. on Good Friday and £1 on the other four days. In 1899 the capital fund was £334.

Henry Burmester, by will proved 1823, left £100 in trust to provide bread for the poor.

John Popplewell, by deed poll of 1820, which took effect on his death, gave £500 stock, in trust to maintain a tomb in the church, and to provide coal for the poor, 10s. being given to the parish clerk for administering the charity. In 1831, shortly after his death, his sisters Ann and Rebecca Popplewell added £300 to the capital of this charity. The clause relating to the tomb seems to have been ineffective.

J. Strudwicke Bunce, by will proved 1875, left £693 in trust to provide coal at Christmas for 25 aged poor.[23]

Thomas Reed, by will proved 1885, left £1,000 in trust to provide clothing for the poor in October.

Educational charities are described in another section.[24]

[12] M. Sadler, *Rep. Sec. and Higher Educ. in Essex* (1906), 150.
[13] *Redbridge Official Guide* (1966–7 and 1969 edns.).
[14] *V.C.H. Essex*, ii. 544.
[15] *Rep. Com. Char.* (*Essex*), H.C. 216, p. 164 (1835), xxi (1).
[16] *Rep. Com. Char.* H.C. 312, p. 100 (1820), v; *V.C.H. Essex*, v. 194, 248.
[17] Char. Com. File 62132.
[18] Unless otherwise stated this section is based on: *Rep. Com. Char.* (*Essex*), H.C. 216, p. 164 (1835), xxi(1); Char.

Com. File 62132 and Woodford G File; E.R.O., D/P 167/1/1, 167/8/2, 167/25/1–17.
[19] *Rep. Com. Char.* (*Essex*), H.C. 60, p. 157 (1833), xxviii.
[20] Char. Com. File 68877.
[21] E.R.O., D/P 167/1/1, f. 63. This was probably Sir Henry Lee who died in 1620: *Genealogist*, N.S. xii. 155; *E.A.T.* N.S. vii. 364.
[22] Morton Rockliffe's gift of £10, by his will dated 1777, was spent and not invested: E.R.O., D/P 167/8/2.
[23] Char. Com. File 28835.　　　　[24] See above.

INDEX

CORRIGENDA TO PREVIOUSLY PUBLISHED VOLUMES

NOTE. For earlier Corrigenda to volumes I and II see volume III, pages 256–8. In the preparation of the present list much help was received from the staff of the Essex Record Office and the students who have worked there.

Vol. I,　page 375, lines 27–8, *for* 'drops to 18' *read* 'is about 36'
"　　　"　407, line 15, *for* 'Sandford' *read* 'Sampford'
"　　　"　407, line 7 from end, *for* 'Reydon' *read* 'Roydon'
"　　　"　444*a*, line 15 from end, *for* 'Fauton' *read* 'Fanton'
"　　　"　457*b*, line 17, *for* '(Ivo)' *read* '(Hugh)'
"　　　"　457, note 5, *for* 'Ivo' *read* 'Hugh'
"　　　"　472*b*, *s.v.* CANEFELDA, *for* '1½ ploughs' *read* '1 plough'
"　　　"　501, note 8, lines 2 and 3, *delete* 'Barnwalden (now Barn Hall) in', *and for* 'Knights' *read* '(Knights)'; line 7, *for* 'Barnwalden' *read* 'Tolleshunt (Knights)'
"　　　"　515, note 2, *after* 'Temple Mills' *insert* 'in Leyton'
"　　　"　582*c*, *before* 'Hugh de St. Quintin' *insert new entry* 'Hugh the nephew of Herbert, 457*b*'
"　　　"　582*c*, *s.v.* 'Ivo', *delete the whole entry*
"　　　"　590*a*, *s.v.* 'Estoleia', *after* '395,' *insert* '430*a*,'
"　　　"　595*a*, *s.v.* Roxwell, *after* 'note 433*b*' *insert* ', note 468*a*'
"　　　"　596*b*, *s.v.* Temple Mills, *for* 'West Ham' *read* 'Leyton'

Vol. II,　page 10, *for* 'Thundersley' *read* 'Thunderley'
"　　　"　22, line 17, *for* 'on 14 February, 1545–6' *read* 'since 14 February 1536'
"　　　"　22, line 19, *for* '£12 5*s*. 3*d*.' *read* '£12 5*s*. 4*d*.'
"　　　"　72, line 24, *for* 'rector' *read* 'vicar'
"　　　"　129, note 41, *for* 'Round' *read* 'Fry'
"　　　"　220, line 6, *for* 'Soken' *read* 'Sokens'
"　　　"　228, line 6, *for* 'Nettleswell' *read* 'Netteswell'
"　　　"　248, line 2, *after* '1685' *insert footnote number* '1a' *and at foot of page insert before note 1 new footnote* '1a D.N.B.'
"　　　"　293, note 8, *for* 'cvi' *read* 'cvii'
"　　　"　337, note 1, *for* 'Osborne' *read* 'Ogborne'
"　　　"　340, line 1, *for* 'in 1836' *read* 'under the Act of 1836'
"　　　"　379*b*, line 21, *for* '1848' *read* '1864'
"　　　"　528, line 3 from end, *for* '1557' *read* '1558'
"　　　"　546, last 4 lines, *for* 'Bonnell's School, . . . Stratford and Plaistow.' *read* 'Bonnell's School.'

Vol. III, page 63, line 6 from end, *for* 'Wid' *read* 'Chelmer'
"　　　"　214*a*, *s.v.* Chelmer, riv., *after* 'iii. 13, 29' *insert* ', 63'
"　　　"　217*c*, *s.v.* Dagenham, ind., *for* '474' *read* '475'
"　　　"　217*c*, *s.v.* Dagenham, marsh, *for* '474' *read* '475'
"　　　"　225*a*, *s.v.* Ham, West, ch., *delete* '475'
"　　　"　225*c*, *s.v.* Harwich, *before* 'quays' *insert* 'pop., 354;'
"　　　"　236*b*, *s.v.* Netteswell, *before* 'man.' *insert* 'land in, ii. 228;'
"　　　"　243*a*, *s.v.* Romford, geol., *for* 'i. 337' *read* 'ii. 337'
"　　　"　247*b*, *s.v.* Stratford, in West Ham, inds., *delete* '375' *and* '406*n*'
"　　　"　249*b*, *s.v.* Thunderley, in Wimbish, *before* '107' *insert* '10,'
"　　　"　249*b*, *s.v.* Thundersley, ch., *delete* '10,'
"　　　"　252*c*, *s.v.* Waytemore Castle, *for* '391' *read* '291'
"　　　"　253*b*, *s.v.* Wid, riv., *delete* 'iii. 63'
"　　　"　257, line 29, *for* 'clergyman' *read* 'clergymen'

Vol. IV, page 3, line 2 from end and last line, *for* '1226–7' *read* '1227–8'
  ,,   ,, 55, note 90, *for* '19' *read* '20'
  ,,   ,, 60, note 61, *for* 'Budford' *read* 'Budworth'
  ,,   ,, 65*b*, line 24, *for* 'Ivo' *read* 'Hugh'
  ,,   ,, 75*b*, line 10 from end, *for* '£2,830' *read* '£21,830'
  ,,   ,, 115, note 18, *for* 'T.' *read* 'J.'
  ,,   ,, 151*a*, lines 9 and 10 from end, *before* 'his brother' *insert* 'Maud, daughter of'; *after* 'Fitz Hamon, *for* 'whose daughter . . . married' *read* 'and wife of'
  ,,   ,, 153*a*, line 2, *for* 'sack' *read* 'shock' in two places
  ,,   ,, 158, note 22, *for* 'D/P 128/8/3' *read* 'D/P 124/8/3'
  ,,   ,, 159, note 27, *for* 'D/P 128/8/3' *read* 'D/P 124/8/3'
  ,,   ,, 162, notes, *for* '27' *read* '37'
  ,,   ,, 192*b*, lines 26–7, *for* 'Thomas Browne died in 1488' *read* 'Robert Browne died in 1488'
  ,,   ,, 194*a*, lines 19–20, *read* 'at £14 10*s*. in 1535.[56] Tithes were commuted in 1843'
  ,,   ,, 219, note 93, *for* 'references below are to' *read* 'the following account is based on'
  ,,   ,, 221, note 6, *for* 'D/P 140/8/8' *read* 'D/P 140/18/8'
  ,,   ,, 227*a*, lines 28 and 34, *for* '1438' *read* '1437'
  ,,   ,, 228, note 12, *for* 'D/DM 175' *read* 'D/DM M175'
  ,,   ,, 249, note 7, *for* 'xvi' *read* 'xxxvi'
  ,,   ,, 258*b*, line 7 from end, *after* 'churches' *insert* ', schools,'
  ,,   ,, 275*a*, line 11, *for* '1647' *read* '1648'
  ,,   ,, 275*a*, line 17, *for* '1861' *read* '1865'
  ,,   ,, 277*a*, lines 15–17, *for* 'what they owed . . . to the Jews' *read* 'their debts to the King, to the executors of the will of Hubert de Burgh, and to the Jews'
  ,,   ,, 277*a*, line 5 from end, *for* 'Terays' *read* 'Theydon'
  ,,   ,, 291, notes 10 and 13, *for* '150' *read* '50'
  ,,   ,, 296, note 6, *for* 'E 179/107/110–11' *read* 'E 179/107/10–11'
  ,,   ,, 316*b*, *s.v.* Brown, *after* '('Capability'), 245;' *insert* 'Rob., 192;'
  ,,   ,, 323*a*, *s.v.* Herbert, Ivo nephew of, *for* 'Ivo' *read* 'Hugh'
  ,,   ,, 323*c*, *before* entry Hughes, Adml. Sir Edw. *insert new entry* 'Hugh nephew of Herbert, 65'
  ,,   ,, 323*c*, *s.v.* Ivo, *delete whole entry*
  ,,   ,, 325*a*, *s.v.* Lewis, Revd. Morgan, *for* '85' *read* '84'
  ,,   ,, 326*a*, *s.v.* Maitland, Revd. John Whitaker (d. 1909), *delete* '121,'
  ,,   ,, 326*a*, *s.v.* Maitland, Cmdr. J. W., *after* '116*n*' *insert* ', 119, 121'
  ,,   ,, 330, *s.v.* Robert, earl of Gloucester, *for* '(Mabel)' *read* '(Maud)'
  ,,   ,, 330, *s.v.* Robert Fitz Hamon, *after* 'Hamon' *insert* 'and his dau. Maud,'
  ,,   ,, 334*b*, *s.v.* Terays, *delete whole entry*
  ,,   ,, 334*b*, *s.v.* Theydon, *after* 'Hen. de, 276' *insert* ', 277'
  ,,   ,, 337*c*, *for* 'Wynter' *read* 'Wyther'

Vol. V, page 19, line 3, *for* 'pedestrains' *read* 'pedestrians'
  ,,   ,, 119*a*, line 7 from end, *for* 'son' *read* 'grandson'
  ,,   ,, 123, note 9, *for* 'D/DW E27/11, 2' *read* 'D/DW E27/11, 12'
  ,,   ,, 206, note 87, *for* 'A1077' *read* 'A1007'
  ,,   ,, 252b, lines 22–3 from end, *for* '. The latter was' *read* ', both of which were'
  ,,   ,, 256*b*, line 18 from end, *for* 'Seven Kings Park . . . 34a.' *read* 'Westwood recreation ground (9a.)'
  ,,   ,, 256*b*, lines 15 and 16 from end, *for* 'The original . . . two parks' *read* 'The Westwood ground and the original portion of Goodmayes Park'
  ,,   ,, 261*a*, line 8, *for* 'Hutton' *read* 'Britton'
  ,,   ,, 276*a*, line 5, *for* '1461' *read* '1460'
  ,,   ,, 297*b*, line 20, *delete* 'a wheelwright'
  ,,   ,, 304*a*, *s.v.* Barking, inf. mort., *before* '84' *insert* '55,'
  ,,   ,, 304*b*, *s.v.* Beckton, rly., *before* '25' *insert* '24,'
  ,,   ,, 304*c*, *s.v.* Borough English, *before* '142' *insert* '104,'
  ,,   ,, 305, *before* entry Brixham *insert* 'Britton, Mrs. E. F., 261'
  ,,   ,, 306*a*, *s.v.* Chingford, inf. mort., *before* '84' *insert* '55,'
  ,,   ,, 309*c*, *s.v.* Ham, East, inf. mort., *before* '84' *insert* '55,'
  ,,   ,, 309*c*, *s.v.* Ham, West, inf. mort., *before* '84' *insert* '55,'

CORRIGENDA

Vol. V, page 310*b*, *s.v.* Herts. and Essex Aeroplane Club, *before* '146' *insert* '141,'
,, ,, 310*c*, *s.v.* Hutton, *delete* 'Mrs. E. F. 261;'
,, ,, 311*a*, *s.v.* Ilford, inf. mort., *before* '84' *insert* '55,'
,, ,, 311*b*, *s.v.* Johnson, Jn., County Surveyor, *for* '214' *read* '244'
,, ,, 312*a*, *s.v.* Leyton, inf. mort., *before* '84' *insert* '55,'
,, ,, 318*a*, *s.v.* Walthamstow, housing, *before* '100' *insert* 'hosp.,'
,, ,, 318*a*, *s.v.* Walthamstow, inf. mort., *before* '84' *insert* '55,'
,, ,, 318*a*, *s.v.* Wanstead, inf. mort., *before* '84' *insert* '55,'
,, ,, 318*c*, *s.v.* Woodford, inf. mort., *before* '84' *insert* '55,'

Bibliography
,, page 13*a*, item 2 from end, *for* '1863' *read* '1563'
,, ,, 18*a*, item 8, *for* 'E.R. xlii' *read* 'E.R. xxii'
,, ,, 48*b*, *s.v.* POPULATION, last item, *for* 'ii. 105' *read* 'i. 80'
,, ,, 79*b*, *s.v.* **De Horne** family, *for* 'Jocamnica' *read* 'Jocaminca'
,, ,, 91*b*, *s.v.* **Griggs**, Sir William, *for* '1910' *read* '1905–6'
,, ,, 92*a*, *s.v.* **Gurney**, Joseph J., 6th line, *for* '1854' *read* '1855'
,, ,, 92*a*, *s.v.* **Gurney**, Samuel, *for* 'Geldart, T. [H. R.]' *read* 'Geldart, H. R.'
,, ,, 96*a*, *s.v.* **Heron**, Sir John, *for* '[d. 1525?]' *read* '[d. 1521]'
,, ,, 114*b*, *s.v.* **Palavicino**, Sir Horatio, *for* 'Woodford' *read* 'Ilford'
,, ,, 136*b*, *s.v.* **Waldegrave** (formerly Wentworth), *for* 'Smallridge' *read* 'Smallbridge'
,, ,, 140*b*, *s.v.* **Wiseman**, Thomas, *for* 'Catholic Rec. Soc. ix' *read* 'Catholic Rec. Soc. vii'
,, ,, 141*a*, *s.v.* **Woodstock**, Thomas of, *delete* 'bur. at Saffron Walden'
,, ,, 147*a*, item 5 from end, *for* 'Soc.' *read* 'Assoc.'
,, ,, 147*b* item 12, *delete* 'Eastbury Hall'
,, ,, 149*b*, *s.v.* **Biography**, *delete* 'Tudor, J.'
,, ,, 163*b*, *s.v.* Kimball, D., *for* 'Soc.' *read* 'Assoc.'
,, ,, 171, note 1, *for* 'p.' *read* 'pp. 29,'
,, ,, 172*b*, item 4, *for* '[c. 1895.]' *read* '[1896.]'
,, ,, 173*b*, *s.v.* CHINGFORD, item 1, *for* 'MORGAN, J. H.' *read* 'MORGAN, J. M.'
,, ,, 177*a*, item 11, *for* '1812' *read* '1815'
,, ,, 178*a*, item 11, *for* '[19—?]' *read* '[c. 1960]'
,, ,, 182*b*, last item, *before* 'Two sallies forth . . .' *insert one line space*
,, ,, 184*a*, item 3, *for* '201' *read* '203'
,, ,, 193*a*, *s.v.* COLNE, EARLS, *after* 'DODDS, J. A.' *insert* '(pub.)'
,, ,, 197*a*, line 16, *for* 'Fuzze House' *read* 'Furze House'
,, ,, 199*b*, item 7, *before* 'List of persons entitled . . .' *insert one line space*
,, ,, 201*b*, line 4, *for* '1804' *read* '1904'
,, ,, 215*a*, item 2, *after* 'Arch. xxvii (1838), 77' *insert* '; xxix (1842),'
,, ,, 224*a*, item 10, *after* '84' *insert* ', 94–5'
,, ,, 241*a*, item 7 from end, *for* 'xv.' *read* 'xxv.'
,, ,, 253*b*, *s.v.* NETTESWELL, item 2, *for* 'xxv.' *read* 'xxxv.'
,, ,, 256, note 1, *for* '917' *read* '9, 17'
,, ,, 260*b*, note 4, *add* 'For the honor of Rayleigh see p. 262'
,, ,, 264*a*, *s.v.* RODING, MARGARET, Sale Catalogues:, *for* 'Marks Hall' *read* 'Garnish Hall'
,, ,, 278*a*, *s.v.* TENDRING RURAL DISTRICT, *for* '1889', *read* '1890'
,, ,, 281*b*, item 3, *for* '1935' *read* '1936'
,, ,, 281*b*, *delete* item 4, 'The Grays . . . 1936.'
,, ,, 294*a*, item 3, *for* 'N.D.' *read* '[c. 1881]'
,, ,, 295*b*, *s.v.* **Biography**, *for* 'Sheridan, R. C.' *read* 'Sheridan, R. B.'
,, ,, 308*a*, item 7 from end, *for* 'N.D.' *read* '[c. 1900]'
,, ,, 308*b*, *s.v.* **Biography**, *delete* 'Palavicino, Sir H.'
,, ,, 328*a*, line 15 from end, *after* '£27,000' *insert* ', and opened in 1935'
,, ,, 334*c*, *for* 'Buckely' *read* 'Buckley'
,, ,, 347*a*, *s.v.* Strype, J., *for* '127' *read* '129'

14 12